COLLINS GEM

ITALIAN DICTIONARY

ITALIAN·ENGLISH
ENGLISH·ITALIAN

HarperCollinsPublishers

Arnoldo Mondadori Editore

first published in this edition 1982
third edition 1993

© William Collins Sons & Co. Ltd. 1982, 1989
© HarperCollins Publishers 1993

ISBN 0 00 470047-3

Catherine E. Love
Paolo L. Rossi, Davina M. Chaplin,
Fernando Villa, Ennio Bilucaglia,
Michela Clari

editorial staff / segreteria di redazione
Elspeth Anderson, Anne Bradley, Angela
Campbell, Susan Dunsmore, Joyce
Littlejohn, Vivian Marr

The first edition of this book was prepared for
Collins Publishers by

LEXUS

Typeset by Morton Word Processing Ltd, Scarborough

Printed in Great Britain by
HarperCollins Manufacturing, Glasgow

INDICE

CONTENTS

INTRODUZIONE

Vi ringraziamo di aver scelto il Dizionario inglese Collins Gem e ci auguriamo che esso si riveli uno strumento utile e piacevole da usare nello studio, in vacanza e sul lavoro.

In questa introduzione troverete alcuni suggerimenti per aiutarvi a trarre il massimo beneficio dal vostro nuovo dizionario, ricco non solo per il suo ampio lemmario ma anche per il gran numero di informazioni contenute in ciascuna voce. Ciò vi consentirà di imparare a capire ed esprimervi correttamente in un inglese attuale.

All'inizio del dizionario troverete l'elenco delle abbreviazioni usate nel testo e l'illustrazione della pronuncia espressa con i simboli fonetici. In fondo troverete un utile elenco delle forme dei verbi irregolari italiani e inglesi, seguito da una sezione finale con i numeri e le ore.

COME USARE IL DIZIONARIO COLLINS GEM

Per imparare ad usare in modo efficace il dizionario è importante comprendere la funzione delle differenziazioni tipografiche, dei simboli e delle abbreviazioni usati nel testo. Vi forniamo pertanto qui di seguito alcuni chiarimenti in merito a tali convenzioni.

I lemmi

Sono le parole in **neretto** elencate in ordine alfabetico. Il primo e l'ultimo lemma di ciascuna pagina appaiono al margine superiore.

Dove opportuno, informazioni sull'ambito d'uso o il livello di formalità di certe parole vengono fornite tra parentesi in corsivo e spesso in forma abbreviata dopo la trascrizione fonetica (es. (*COMM*), (*col*)).

In certi casi più parole con radice comune sono raggruppate sotto lo stesso lemma. Tali parole appaiono in neretto ma in un carattere leggermente ridotto (es. **acceptance**).

Esempi d'uso del lemma sono a loro volta in neretto ma in un carattere diverso dal lemma (es. **to be cold**).

La trascrizione fonetica

La trascrizione fonetica che illustra la corretta pronuncia del lemma è in parentesi quadra e segue immediatamente il lemma (es. **knead** [niːd]). L'elenco dei simboli fonetici è alle pagine xi-xii.

Le traduzioni

Le traduzioni sono in carattere tondo e se si riferiscono a diversi significati del lemma sono separate da un punto e virgola. Spesso diverse traduzioni di un lemma sono introdotte da una o più parole in corsivo in parentesi tonda: la loro funzione è di chiarire a quale significato del lemma si riferisce la traduzione. Possono essere sinonimi, indicazioni di ambito d'uso o di registro del lemma (es. **party** *(POL)* *(team)* *(celebration)*, **laid back** *(col)* etc.).

Le "parole chiave"

Un trattamento particolare è stato riservato a quelle parole che, per frequenza d'uso o complessità, necessitano una strutturazione più chiara ed esauriente (es. **da, di, avere** in italiano, **at, to be, this** in inglese). Il simbolo ♦ e dei numeri sono usati per guidarvi attraverso le varie distinzioni grammaticali e di significato e, dove necessario, ulteriori informazioni sono fornite in corsivo tra parentesi.

Informazioni grammaticali

Le parti del discorso (noun, adjective ecc.) sono espresse da abbreviazioni convenzionali in corsivo *(n, a* ecc) e seguono la trascrizione fonetica del lemma.

Eventuali ulteriori informazioni grammaticali, come ad esempio le forme di un verbo irregolare o il plurale irregolare di un sostantivo, seguono tra parentesi la parte del discorso (es. **fall** *vi* (*pt* **fell,** *pp* **fallen, man** *n* (*pl* **men**)).

INTRODUCTION

We are delighted you have decided to buy the Collins Gem Italian Dictionary and hope you will enjoy and benefit from using it at school, at home, on holiday or at work.

This introduction gives you a few tips on how to get the most out of your dictionary — not simply from its comprehensive wordlist but also from the information provided in each entry. This will help you to read and understand modern Italian, as well as communicate and express yourself in the language.

The Collins Gem Italian Dictionary begins by listing the abbreviations used in the text and illustrating the sounds shown by the phonetic symbols. You will find Italian verb tables and English irregular verbs at the back, followed by a final section on numbers and time expressions.

USING YOUR COLLINS GEM DICTIONARY

A wealth of information is presented in the dictionary, using various typefaces, sizes of type, symbols, abbreviations and brackets. The conventions and symbols used are explained in the following sections.

Headwords

The words you look up in a dictionary — "headwords" — are listed alphabetically. They are printed in **bold type** for rapid identification. The two headwords appearing at the top of each page indicate the first and last word dealt with on the page in question.

Information about the usage or form of certain headwords is given in brackets after the phonetic spelling. This usually appears in abbreviated form and in italics (e.g. (*fam*), (*COMM*)).

Where appropriate, words related to headwords are grouped in the same entry (**illustrare, illustrazione**) in a slightly smaller bold type than the headword.

Common expressions in which the headword appears are shown in a different bold roman type (e.g. **aver freddo**).

Phonetic spellings

Where the phonetic spelling of headwords (indicating their pronunciation) is given, it will appear in square brackets immediately after the headword (e.g. **calza** ['kaltsa]). A list of these symbols is given on pages xi-xii

Translations

Headword translations are given in ordinary type and, where more than one meaning or usage exists, these are separated by a semi-colon. You will often find other words in italics in brackets before the translations. These offer suggested contexts in which the headword might appear (e.g. **dura** (*pietra*) or (*lavoro*)) or provide synonyms (e.g. **duro** (*ostinato*)).

"Key" words

Special status is given to certain Italian and English words which are considered as "key" words in each language. They may, for example, occur very frequently or have several types of usage (e.g. **da, di, avere**). A combination of lozenges and numbers helps you to distinguish different parts of speech and different meanings. Further helpful information is provided in brackets and in italics in the relevant language for the user.

Grammatical information

Parts of speech are given in abbreviated form in italics after the phonetic spellings of headwords (e.g. *vt, av, cong*).

Genders of Italian nouns are indicated as follows: *sm* for a masculine and *sf* for a feminine noun. Feminine and irregular plural forms of nouns are also shown (**dottore, essa; droga, ghe**).

Feminine adjective endings are given as are plural forms (**dito, a**).

ABBREVIAZIONI

ABBREVIATIONS

aggettivo	**adj**	adjective
abbreviazione	**abbr**	abbreviation
avverbio	**adv**	adverb
amministrazione	**ADMIN**	administration
aeronautica, viaggi aerei	**AER**	flying, air travel
aggettivo	**ag**	adjective
agricoltura	**AGR**	agriculture
amministrazione	**AMM**	administration
anatomia	**ANAT**	anatomy
architettura	**ARCHIT**	architecture
astronomia, astrologia	**ASTR**	astronomy, astrology
l'automobile	**AUT**	the motor car and motoring
avverbio	**av**	adverb
aeronautica, viaggi aerei	**AVIAT**	flying, air travel
biologia	**BIOL**	biology
botanica	**BOT**	botany
inglese della Gran Bretagna	**BRIT**	British English
consonante	**C**	consonant
chimica	**CHIM, CHEM**	chemistry
congiunzione	**conj**	conjunction
familiare (! da evitare)	**inf(!)**	colloquial usage (! particularly offensive)
commercio, finanza, banca	**COMM**	commerce, finance, banking
informatica	**COMPUT**	computers
congiunzione	**cong**	conjunction
edilizia	**CONSTR**	building
sostantivo usato come aggettivo, non può essere usato né come attributo, né dopo il sostantivo qualificato	**cpd**	compound element: noun used as adjective and which cannot follow the noun it qualifies
cucina	**CUC, CULIN**	cookery
davanti a	**dav**	before
determinativo: articolo, aggettivo dimostrativo o indefinito etc	**det**	determiner: article, demonstrative etc
diritto	**DIR**	law
economia	**ECON**	economics
edilizia	**EDIL**	building
elettricità, elettronica	**ELETTR, ELEC**	electricity, electronics

ABBREVIAZIONI

ABBREVIATIONS

esclamazione	**escl, excl**	exclamation
femminile	**f**	feminine
familiare (! da evitare)	**fam(!)**	colloquial usage (! particularly offensive)
ferrovia	**FERR**	railways
figurato	**fig**	figurative use
fisiologia	**FISIOL**	physiology
fotografia	**FOT**	photography
(verbo inglese) la cui particella è inseparabile dal verbo	**fus**	(phrasal verb) where the particle cannot be separated from main verb
nella maggior parte dei sensi; generalmente	**gen**	in most or all senses; generally
geografia, geologia	**GEO**	geography, geology
geometria	**GEOM**	geometry
impersonale	**impers**	impersonal
informatica	**INFORM**	computers
insegnamento, sistema scolastico e universitario	**INS**	schooling, schools and universities
invariabile	**inv**	invariable
irregolare	**irg**	irregular
grammatica, linguistica	**LING**	grammar, linguistics
maschile	**m**	masculine
matematica	**MAT(H)**	mathematics
termine medico, medicina	**MED**	medical term, medicine
il tempo, meteorologia	**METEOR**	the weather, meteorology
maschile o femminile, secondo il sesso	**m/f**	either masculine or feminine depending on sex
esercito, lingua militare	**MIL**	military matters
musica	**MUS**	music
sostantivo	**n**	noun
nautica	**NAUT**	sailing, navigation
numerale (aggettivo, sostantivo)	**num**	numeral adjective or noun
	o.s.	oneself
peggiorativo	**peg, pej**	derogatory, pejorative
fotografia	**PHOT**	photography
fisiologia	**PHYSIOL**	physiology
plurale	**pl**	plural
politica	**POL**	politics
participio passato	**pp**	past participle
preposizione	**prep**	preposition

ABBREVIAZIONI

ABBREVIATIONS

psicologia, psichiatria	**PSIC, PSYCH**	psychology, psychiatry
tempo passato	**pt**	past tense
sostantivo che non si usa al plurale	**q**	uncountable noun: not used in the plural
qualcosa	**qc**	
qualcuno	**qn**	
religione, liturgia	**REL**	religions, church service
sostantivo	**s**	noun
	sb	somebody
insegnamento, sistema scolastico e universitario	**SCOL**	schooling, schools and universities
singolare	**sg**	singular
soggetto (grammaticale)	**sog**	(grammatical) subject
	sth	something
congiuntivo	**sub**	subjunctive
soggetto (grammaticale)	**subj**	(grammatical) subject
termine tecnico, tecnologia	**TECN, TECH**	technical term, technology
telecomunicazioni	**TEL**	telecommunications
tipografia	**TIP**	typography, printing
televisione	**TV**	television
tipografia	**TYP**	typography, printing
inglese degli Stati Uniti	**US**	American English
vocale	**V**	vowel
verbo	**vb**	verb
verbo o gruppo verbale con funzione intransitiva	**vi**	verb or phrasal verb used intransitively
verbo riflessivo	**vr**	reflexive verb
verbo o gruppo verbale con funzione transitiva	**vt**	verb or phrasal verb used transitively
zoologia	**ZOOL**	zoology
marchio registrato	**®**	registered trademark
introduce un'equivalenza culturale	**≈**	introduces a cultural equivalent

TRASCRIZIONE FONETICA
PHONETIC TRANSCRIPTION

CONSONANTS CONSONANTI

VOWELS VOCALI

NB The pairing of some vowel sounds only indicates approximate equivalence/La messa in equivalenza di certi suoni indica solo una rassomiglianza approssimativa.

NB **p, b, t, d, k, g** are not aspirated in Italian/sono seguiti da un'aspirazione in inglese.

puppy	p	*padre*	
baby	b	*bambino*	
tent	t	*tutto*	
daddy	d	*dado*	
cork kiss chord	k	*cane che*	
gag guess	g	*gola ghiro*	
so rice kiss	s	*sano*	
cousin buzz	z	*svago esame*	
sheep sugar	ʃ	*scena*	
pleasure beige	ʒ		
church	tʃ	*pece lanciare*	
judge general	dʒ	*giro gioco*	
farm raffle	f	*afa faro*	
very rev	v	*vero bravo*	
thin maths	θ		
that other	ð		
little ball	l	*letto ala*	
	ʎ	*gli*	
rat brat	r	*rete arco*	
mummy comb	m	*ramo madre*	
no ran	n	*no fumante*	
	ɲ	*gnomo*	
singing bank	ŋ		
hat reheat	h		
yet	j	*buio piacere*	
wall bewail	w	*uomo guaio*	
loch	x		

heel bead	iː i	*vino idea*	
hit pity	ɪ		
set tent	e	*stella edera*	
apple bat	æ a	*epoca eccetto*	
after car calm	ɑː	*mamma amore*	
fun cousin	ʌ		
over above	ə		
urn fern work	ɜː		
wash pot	ɔ	*rosa occhio*	
born cork	ɔː		
	o	*ponte ognuno*	
	ø	*föhn*	
full soot	ʊ	*utile zucca*	
boon lewd	uː		

DIPHTHONGS DITTONGHI

ɪə	*beer tier*	
ɛə	*tear fair there*	
eɪ	*date plaice day*	
aɪ	*life buy cry*	
au	*owl foul now*	
əu	*low no*	
ɔɪ	*boil boy oily*	
uə	*poor tour*	

MISCELLANEOUS

VARIE

* per l'inglese: la "r" finale viene pronunciata se seguita da una vocale.

' precede the stressed syllable/precede la sillaba accentata.

ITALIAN PRONUNCIATION

VOWELS

Where the vowel **e** or the vowel **o** appears in a stressed syllable it can be either open [ɛ], [ɔ] or closed [e], [o]. As the open or closed pronunciation of these vowels is subject to regional variation, the distinction is of little importance to the user of this dictionary. Phonetic transcription for headwords containing these vowels will therefore only appear where other pronunciation difficulties are present.

CONSONANTS

c before "e" or "i" is pronounced *tch*.

ch is pronounced like the "k" in "kit".

g before "e" or "i" is pronounced like the "j" in "jet".

gh is pronounced like the "g" in "get".

gl before "e" or "i" is normally pronounced like the "lli" in "million", and in a few cases only like the "gl" in "glove".

gn is pronounced like the "ny" in "canyon".

sc before "e" or "i" is pronounced *sh*.

z is pronounced like the "ts" in "stetson", or like the "d's" in "bird's-eye".

Headwords containing the above consonants and consonantal groups have been given full phonetic transcription in this dictionary.

NB All double written consonants in Italian are fully sounded: eg. the *tt* in "tutto" is pronounced as in "ha*t t*rick".

ITALIANO - INGLESE
ITALIAN - ENGLISH
A

a (*a+il* = **al**, *a+lo* = **allo**, *a+l'* = **all'**, *a+la* = **alla**, *a+i* = **ai**, *a+gli* = **agli**, *a+le* = **alle**) *prep* **1** (*stato in luogo*) at; (: *in*) in; **essere alla stazione** to be at the station; **essere ~ casa/~ scuola/~ Roma** to be at home/at school/in Rome; **è ~ 10 km da qui** it's 10 km from here, it's 10 km away **2** (*moto a luogo*) to; **andare ~ casa/~ scuola** to go home/to school **3** (*tempo*) at; (*epoca, stagione*) in; **alle cinque a five** (o'clock); ~ **mezzanotte/Natale** at midnight/ Christmas; **al mattino in the morning**; ~ **maggio/primavera in May/ spring**; ~ **cinquant'anni at fifty** (years of age); ~ **domani** see you tomorrow!

4 (*complemento di termine*) to; **dare qc ~ qn** to give sth to sb

5 (*mezzo, modo*) with, by; ~ **piedi/ cavallo** on foot/horseback; **fatto ~ mano** made by hand, handmade; **una barca ~ motore** a motorboat; ~ **uno ~ uno** one by one; **all'italiana** the Italian way, in the Italian fashion

6 (*rapporto*) a, per; (: *con prezzi*) at; **prendo 500.000 lire al mese** I get 500,000 lire a *o* per month; **pagato ~ ore** paid by the hour; **vendere qc ~ 500 lire il chilo** to sell sth at 500 lire a *o* per kilo

abbacchi'ato, a [abbak'kjato] *ag* downhearted, in low spirits

abbagli'ante [abbaʎ'ʎante] *ag* dazzling; ~**i** *smpl* (*AUT*): **accendere gli ~i** to put one's headlights on full (*BRIT*) *o* high (*US*) beam

abbagli'are [abbaʎ'ʎare] *vt* to dazzle; (*illudere*) to delude; **ab'baglio**

sm blunder; **prendere un abbaglio** to blunder, make a blunder

abbai'are *vi* to bark

abba'ino *sm* dormer window; (*soffitta*) attic room

abbando'nare *vt* to leave, abandon, desert; (*trascurare*) to neglect; (*rinunciare a*) to abandon, give up; ~**rsi** *vr* to let o.s. go; (*lasciarsi andare*) to give o.s. up to; **ab-ban'dono** *sm* abandonment; neglect; (*SPORT*) withdrawal; (*fig*) abandon; **in abbandono** (*edificio, giardino*) neglected

abbas'sare *vt* to lower; (*radio*) to turn down; ~**rsi** *vr* (*chinarsi*) to stoop; (*livello, sole*) to go down; (*fig: umiliarsi*) to demean o.s.; ~ **i fari** (*AUT*) to dip *o* dim (*US*) one's lights

ab'basso *escl*: ~ **il re!** down with the king!

abbas'tanza [abbas'tantsa] *av* (*a sufficienza*) enough; (*alquanto*) quite, rather, fairly; **non è ~ furbo** he's not shrewd enough; **un vino ~ dolce** quite a sweet wine, a fairly sweet wine; **averne ~ di qn/qc** to have had enough of sb/sth

ab'battere *vt* (*muro, casa*) to pull down; (*ostacolo*) to knock down; (*albero*) to fell; (: *sog: vento*) to bring down; (*bestie da macello*) to slaughter; (*cane, cavallo*) to destroy, put down; (*selvaggina, aereo*) to shoot down; (*fig: sog: malattia, disgrazia*) to lay low; ~**rsi** *vr* (*avvilirsi*) to lose heart; **abbat'tuto, a** *ag* (*fig*) depressed

abba'zia [abbat'tsia] *sf* abbey

abbece'dario [abbetʃe'darjo] *sm* primer

abbel'lire *vt* to make beautiful; (*ornare*) to embellish

abbeve'rare *vt* to water; ~**rsi** *vr* to

drink

'**abbia** etc vb vedi avere

abbicci [abbit'tʃi] sm inv alphabet; (sillabario) primer; (fig) rudiments pl

abbi'ente ag well-to-do, well-off ♦ smpl: **gli ~i** the well-to-do

abbi'etto, a ag = abietto

abbiglia'mento [abbiʎʎa'mento] sm dress no pl; (indumenti) clothes pl; (industria) clothing industry

abbigli'are [abbiʎ'ʎare] vt to dress up

abbi'nare vt: ~ (a) to combine (with)

abbindo'lare vt (fig) to cheat, trick

abbocca'mento sm talks pl, meeting

abboc'care vt (tubi, canali) to connect, join up ♦ vi (pesce) to bite; (tubi) to join; ~ (all'amo) (fig) to swallow the bait

abboc'cato, a ag (vino) sweetish

abbona'mento sm subscription; (alle ferrovie etc) season ticket; **fare l'~** to take out a subscription (o season ticket)

abbo'narsi vr: ~ **a un giornale** to take out a subscription to a newspaper; ~ **al teatro/alle ferrovie** to take out a season ticket for the theatre/the train; **abbo'nato, a** smf subscriber; season-ticket holder

abbon'dante ag abundant, plentiful; (giacca) roomy

abbon'danza [abbon'dantsa] sf abundance; plenty

abbon'dare vi to abound, be plentiful; ~ **in** o **di** to be full of, abound in

abbor'dabile ag (persona) approachable; (prezzo) reasonable

abbor'dare vt (nave) to board; (persona) to approach; (argomento) to tackle; ~ **una curva** to take a bend

abbotto'nare vt to button up, do up

abboz'zare [abbot'tsare] vt to sketch, outline; (SCULTURA) to rough-hew; ~ **un sorriso** to give a hint of a smile; **ab'bozzo** sm

sketch, outline; (DIR) draft

abbracci'are [abbrat'tʃare] vt to embrace; (persona) to hug, embrace; (professione) to take up; (contenere) to include; ~**rsi** vr to hug o embrace (one another); **ab'braccio** sm hug, embrace

abbrevi'are vt to shorten; (parola) to abbreviate

abbreviazi'one [abbrevjat'tsjone] sf abbreviation

abbron'zante [abbron'dzante] ag tanning, sun cpd

abbron'zare [abbron'dzare] vt (pelle) to tan; (metalli) to bronze; ~**rsi** vr to tan, get a tan; **abbronza'tura** sf tan, suntan

abbrusto'lire vt (pane) to toast; (caffè) to roast

abbru'tire vt to exhaust; to degrade

abbu'ono sm (COMM) allowance, discount; (SPORT) handicap

abdi'care vi to abdicate; ~ **a** to give up, renounce

aberrazi'one [aberrat'tsjone] sf aberration

a'bete sm fir (tree); ~ **rosso** spruce

abi'etto, a ag despicable, abject

'abile ag (idoneo): ~ **(a qc/a fare qc)** fit (for/to do sth); (capace) able; (astuto) clever; (accorto) skilful; ~ **al servizio militare** fit for military service; **abilità** sf inv ability; cleverness; skill

abili'tato, a ag qualified; (TEL) which has an outside line; **abilitazi'one** sf qualification

a'bisso sm abyss, gulf

abi'tacolo sm (AER) cockpit; (AUT) inside; (: di camion) cab

abi'tante smf inhabitant

abi'tare vt to live in, dwell in ♦ vi: ~ **in campagna/a Roma** to live in the country/in Rome; **abi'tato, a** ag inhabited; lived in ♦ sm (anche: centro abitato) built-up area; **abitazi'one** sf residence; house

'**abito** sm dress no pl; (da uomo) suit; (da donna) dress; (abitudine, disposizione, REL) habit; ~**i** smpl (*vestiti*) clothes; **in ~ da sera in** evening dress

abitu'ale *ag* usual, habitual; (*cliente*) regular

abitu'are *vt:* ~ **qn a** to get sb used o accustomed to; **~rsi a** to get used to, accustom o.s. to

abitudi'nario, a *ag* of fixed habits ♦ *smf* regular customer

abi'tudine *sf* habit; **aver l'~ di fare qc** to be in the habit of doing sth; **d'~** usually; **per ~** from o out of habit

abo'lire *vt* to abolish; (*DIR*) to repeal

abomi'nevole *ag* abominable

abo'rigeno [abo'ridʒeno] *sm* aborigine

abor'rire *vt* to abhor, detest

abor'tire *vi* (*MED: accidentalmente*) to miscarry, have a miscarriage; (*: deliberatamente*) to have an abortion; (*fig*) to miscarry, fail; **a'borto** *sm* miscarriage; abortion; (*fig*) freak

abrasi'one *sf* abrasion; **abra'sivo, a** *ag, sm* abrasive

abro'gare *vt* to repeal, abrogate

A'bruzzo *sm:* **l'~, gli ~i the** Abruzzi

'abside *sf* apse

a'bulico, a, ci, che *ag* lacking in will power

abu'sare *vi:* ~ **di** to abuse, misuse; (*alcool*) to take to excess; (*approfittare, violare*) to take advantage of; **a'buso** *sm* abuse, misuse; excessive use

a.C. *av abbr* (= *avanti Cristo*) B.C.

a'cacia, cie [a'katʃa] *sf* (*BOT*) acacia

'acca *sf* letter H; **non capire un'~** not to understand a thing

acca'demia *sf* (*società*) learned society; (*scuola: d'arte, militare*) academy; **acca'demico, a, ci, che** *ag* academic ♦ *sm* academician

acca'dere *vb impers* to happen, occur; **acca'duto** *sm:* **raccontare l'accaduto** to describe what has hap-

pened

accalappi'are *vt* to catch; (*fig*) to trick, dupe

accal'care *vt* to crowd, throng; **~si** *vr:* **~si (in)** to crowd (into)

accal'darsi *vr* to grow hot

accalo'rarsi *vr* (*fig*) to get excited

accampa'mento *sm* camp

accam'pare *vt* to encamp; (*fig*) to put forward, advance; **~rsi** *vr* to camp

accani'mento *sm* fury; (*tenacia*) tenacity, perseverance

acca'nirsi *vr* (*infierire*) to rage; (*ostinarsi*) to persist; **acca'nito, a** *ag* (*odio, gelosia*) fierce, bitter; (*lavoratore*) assiduous, dogged; (*fumatore*) inveterate

ac'canto *av* near, nearby; ~ **a** *prep* near, beside, close to

accanto'nare *vt* (*problema*) to shelve; (*somma*) to set aside

accapar'rare *vt* (*COMM*) to corner, buy up; (*versare una caparra*) to pay a deposit on; **~si qc** (*fig: simpatia, voti*) to secure sth (for o.s.)

accapigli'arsi [akkapiʎ'ʎarsi] *vr* to come to blows; (*fig*) to quarrel

accappa'toio *sm* bathrobe

accappo'nare *vi:* **far ~ la pelle a qn** (*fig*) to bring sb out in goose pimples

accarez'zare [akkaret'tsare] *vt* to caress, stroke, fondle; (*fig*) to toy with

acca'sarsi *vr* to set up house; to get married

accasci'arsi [akkaʃ'ʃarsi] *vr* to collapse; (*fig*) to lose heart

accat'tone, a *smf* beggar

accaval'lare *vt* (*gambe*) to cross; **~rsi** *vr* (*sovrapporsi*) to overlap; (*addensarsi*) to gather

acce'care [attʃe'kare] *vt* to blind ♦ *vi* to go blind

ac'cedere [at'tʃedere] *vi:* ~ **a** to enter; (*richiesta*) to grant, accede to

accele'rare [attʃele'rare] *vt* to speed up ♦ *vi* (*AUT*) to accelerate; ~ **il passo** to quicken one's pace; **acce-**

le'rato sm (FERR) slow train; **ac-celera'tore** sm (AUT) accelerator; **accelerazi'one** sf acceleration

ac'cendere [at'tʃɛndere] vt (fuoco, sigaretta) to light; (luce, televisione) to put o switch o turn on; (AUT: motore) to switch on; (COMM: conto) to open; (fig: suscitare) to in-flame, stir up; **~rsi** vr (luce) to come o go on; (legna) to catch fire, ignite; **accen'dino** sm, **accen-di'sigaro** sm (cigarette) lighter

accen'nare [attʃen'nare] vt to indi-cate, point out; (MUS) to pick out the notes of; to hum ♦ vi: **~ a** (fig: allu-dere a) to hint at; (: far atto di) to make as if; (: fig: allu-dere a) to hint at; (: far atto di) to make as if; **~ un saluto** (con la mano) to make as if to wave; (col capo) to half nod; **accenna a piove-re** it looks as if it's going to rain

ac'cenno [at'tʃenno] sm (cenno) sign; nod; (allusione) hint

accensi'one [attʃen'sjone] sf (vedi accendere) lighting; switching on; opening; (AUT) ignition

accen'tare [attʃen'tare] vt (parlan-do) to stress; (scrivendo) to accent

ac'cento [at'tʃɛnto] sm accent; (FO-NETICA, fig) stress; (inflessione) tone (of voice)

accen'trare [attʃen'trare] vt to cen-tralize

accentu'are [attʃentu'are] vt to stress, emphasize; **~rsi** vr to be-come more noticeable

accerchi'are [attʃer'kjare] vt to sur-round, encircle

accerta'mento [attʃerta'mento] sm check; assessment

accer'tare [attʃer'tare] vt to ascer-tain; (verificare) to check; (reddito) to assess; **~rsi** vr: **~rsi (di)** to make sure (of)

ac'ceso, a [at'tʃeso] pp di accende-re ♦ ag lit; on; open; (colore) bright

acces'sibile [attʃes'sibile] ag (luogo) accessible; (persona) approachable; (prezzo) reasonable; (idea): **~ a qn** within the reach of sb

ac'cesso [at'tʃɛsso] sm (anche IN-FORM) access; (MED) attack, fit; (impulso violento) fit, outburst

acces'sorio, a [attʃes'sɔrjo] ag sec-ondary, of secondary importance; **~i** smpl accessories

ac'cetta [at'tʃetta] sf hatchet

accet'tabile [attʃet'tabile] ag accept-able

accet'tare [attʃet'tare] vt to accept; **~ di fare qc** to agree to do sth; **ac-cettazi'one** sf acceptance; (locale di servizio pubblico) reception; (ac-cettazione bagagli (AER) check-in (desk)

ac'cetto, a [at'tʃetto] ag: (ben) **~** welcome; (persona) well-liked

accezi'one [attʃet'tsjone] sf meaning

acchiap'pare [akkjap'pare] vt to catch

acci'acco, chi [at'tʃakko] sm ail-ment

acciaie'ria [attʃaje'ria] sf steelworks sg

acci'aio [at'tʃajo] sm steel

acciden'tale [attʃiden'tale] ag acci-dental

acciden'tato, a [attʃiden'tato] ag (terreno etc) uneven

acci'dente [at'tʃidɛnte] sm (caso im-previsto) accident; (disgrazia) mis-hap; **non si capisce un ~** it's as clear as mud; **~i!** (fam: per rabbia) damn (it)!; (: per meraviglia) good heavens!

accigli'ato, a [attʃiʎ'ʎato] ag frown-ing

ac'cingersi [at'tʃindʒersi] vr: **~ a fare** to be about to do

acciuf'fare [attʃuf'fare] vt to seize, catch

acci'uga, ghe [at'tʃuga] sf anchovy

accla'mare vt (applaudire) to ap-plaud; (eleggere) to acclaim; **accla-mazi'one** sf applause; acclamation

acclima'tare vt to acclimatize; **~rsi** vr to become acclimatized

ac'cludere vt to enclose; **ac'cluso, a** pp di accludere ♦ ag enclosed

accocco'larsi vr to crouch

accogli'ente [akkoʎ'ʎɛnte] ag welcoming, friendly; **accogli'enza** sf reception; welcome

ac'cogliere [ak'kɔʎʎere] vt (ricevere) to receive; (dare il benvenuto) to welcome; (approvare) to agree to, accept; (contenere) to hold, accommodate

accol'lato, a ag (vestito) high-necked

accoltel'lare vt to knife, stab

ac'colto, a pp di **accogliere**

accoman'dita sf (DIR) limited partnership

accomia'tare vt to dismiss; ~**rsi** vr: ~**rsi (da)** to take one's leave (of)

accomoda'mento sm agreement, settlement

accomo'dante ag accommodating

accomo'dare vt (aggiustare) to repair, mend; (riordinare) to tidy; (conciliare) to settle; ~**rsi** vr (sedersi) to sit down; **s'accomodi!** (venga avanti) come in!; (si sieda) take a seat!

accompagna'mento [akkompaɲa'mento] sm (MUS) accompaniment

accompa'gnare [akkompaɲ'nare] vt to accompany, come o go with; (MUS) to accompany; (unire) to couple; ~ **la porta** to close the door gently

accomu'nare vt to pool, share; (avvicinare) to unite

acconcia'tura [akkontʃa'tura] sf hairstyle

accondi'scendere [akkondiʃ'ʃendere] vi: ~ **a** to agree o consent to; **accondi'sceso, a** pp di **accondiscendere**

acconsen'tire vi: ~ **(a)** to agree o consent (to)

acconten'tare vt to satisfy; ~**rsi di** to be satisfied with, content o.s. with

ac'conto sm part payment; **pagare una somma in** ~ to pay a sum of money as a deposit

accoppia'mento sm coupling, pairing off; (TECN) coupling

accoppi'are vt to couple, pair off; (BIOL) to mate; ~**rsi** vr to pair off; to mate

acco'rato, a ag heartfelt

accorci'are [akkor'tʃare] vt to shorten; ~**rsi** vr to become shorter

accor'dare vt to reconcile; (colori) to match; (MUS) to tune; (LING) to accord; ~ **qc con qc** to make sth agree with sth; (DIR) to grant; ~**rsi** vr to agree, come to an agreement; (colori) to match

ac'cordo sm agreement; (armonia) harmony; (MUS) chord; **essere d'~** to agree; **andare d'~** to get on well together; **d'~!** all right!, agreed!

ac'corgersi [ak'kɔrdʒersi] vr: ~ **di** to notice; (fig) to realize; **accorgi'mento** sm shrewdness no pl; (espediente) trick, device

ac'correre vi to run up

ac'corso, a pp di **accorrere**

ac'corto, a pp di **accorgersi** ♦ ag shrewd; **stare** ~ to be on one's guard

accos'tare vt (avvicinare): ~ **qc a** to bring sth near to, put sth near to; (avvicinarsi a) to approach; (socchiudere: imposte) to half-close; (: porta) to leave ajar ♦ vi (NAUT) to come alongside; ~**rsi a** to draw near, approach; (fig) to support

accovacci'arsi [akkovat'tʃarsi] vr to crouch

accoz'zaglia [akkot'tsaʎʎa] (peg) sf (di idee, oggetti) jumble, hotchpotch; (di persone) odd assortment

accredi'tare vt (notizia) to confirm the truth of; (COMM) to credit; (diplomatico) to accredit; ~**rsi** vr (fig) to gain credit

ac'crescere [ak'kreʃʃere] vt to increase; ~**rsi** vr to increase, grow; **accresci'tivo, a** ag, sm (LING) augmentative; **accresci'uto, a** pp di **accrescere**

accucci'arsi [akkut'tʃarsi] vr (cane) to lie down

accu'dire vt (anche: vi: ~ **a**) to attend to

accumu'lare vt to accumulate

accumula'tore sm (ELETTR) accumulator

accura'tezza [akkura'tettsa] sf care; accuracy

accu'rato, a ag (diligente) careful; (preciso) accurate

ac'cusa sf accusation; (DIR) charge; **la pubblica ~** the prosecution

accu'sare vt: **~ qn di qc** to accuse sb of sth; (DIR) to charge sb with sth; **~ ricevuta di** (COMM) to acknowledge receipt of

accu'sato, a sm/f accused; defendant

accusa'tore, 'trice sm/f accuser ♦ sm (DIR) prosecutor

a'cerbo, a [a'tʃerbo] ag bitter; (frutta) sour, unripe; (persona) immature

'acero [a'tʃero] sm maple

a'cerrimo, a [a'tʃerrimo] ag very fierce

a'ceto [a'tʃeto] sm vinegar

ace'tone [atʃe'tone] sm nail varnish remover

A.C.I. ['atʃi] sigla m (= Automobile Club d'Italia) ≈ A.A.

'acido, a ['atʃido] ag (sapore) acid, sour; (CHIM) acid ♦ sm (CHIM) acid

'acino ['atʃino] sm berry; **~ d'uva** grape

'acne sf acne

'acqua sf water; (pioggia) rain; **~e** sfpl (di mare, fiume etc) waters; **fare ~** (NAUT) to leak, take in water; **~ in bocca!** mum's the word!; **~ corrente** running water; **~ dolce** fresh water; **~ minerale** mineral water; **~ potabile** drinking water; **~ salata** salt water; **~ tonica** tonic water

acqua'forte (pl **acque'forti**) sf etching

ac'quaio sm sink

acqua'ragia [akkwa'radʒa] sf turpentine

a'cquario sm aquarium; (dello zodiaco): **A~** Aquarius

acqua'santa sf holy water

ac'quatico, a, ci, che ag aquatic; (SPORT, SCIENZA) water cpd

acqua'vite sf brandy

acquaz'zone [akkwat'tsone] sm cloudburst, heavy shower

acque'dotto sm aqueduct; waterworks pl, water supply

'acqueo, a ag: **vapore ~** water vapour

acque'rello sm watercolour

acqui'rente sm/f purchaser, buyer

acqui'sire vt to acquire

acqui'stare vt to purchase, buy; (fig) to gain; **a'cquisto** sm purchase; **fare acquisti** to go shopping

acqui'trino sm bog, marsh

acquo'lina sf: **far venire l'~ in bocca a qn** to make sb's mouth water

ac'quoso, a ag watery

'acre ag acrid, pungent; (fig) harsh, biting

a'crobata, i, e sm/f acrobat

acu'ire vt to sharpen

a'culeo sm (ZOOL) sting; (BOT) prickle

a'cume sm acumen, perspicacity

a'custica sf (scienza) acoustics sg; (di una sala) acoustics pl

a'cuto, a ag (appuntito) sharp, pointed; (suono, voce) shrill, piercing; (MAT, LING, MED) acute; (MUS) high-pitched; (fig: dolore, desiderio) intense; (: perspicace) acute, keen

ad (dav V) prep = **a**

adagi'are [ada'dʒare] vt to lay o set down carefully; **~rsi** vr to lie down, stretch out

a'dagio [a'dadʒo] av slowly ♦ sm (MUS) adagio; (proverbio) adage, saying

adatta'mento sm adaptation

adat'tare vt to adapt; (sistemare) to fit; **~rsi** (a) (ambiente, tempi) to adapt (to); (essere adatto) to be suitable (for)

a'datto, a ag: **~ (a)** suitable (for),

right (for)

addebi'tare vt: ~ qc a qn to debit sb with sth; (fig: incolpare) to blame sb for sth

ad'debito sm (COMM) debit

adden'sare vt to thicken; ~rsi vr to thicken; (nuvole) to gather

adden'tare vt to bite into

adden'trarsi vr: ~ in to penetrate, go into

ad'dentro av (fig): essere molto ~ in qc to be well-versed in sth

addestra'mento sm training

addes'trare vt to train; ~rsi vr to train; ~rsi in qc to practise (BRIT) o practice (US) sth

ad'detto, a ag: ~ a (persona) assigned to; (oggetto) intended for ♦ sm employee; (funzionario) attaché; ~ commerciale/stampa commercial/press attaché; gli ~i ai lavori authorized personnel; (fig) those in the know

addì av (AMM): ~ 3 luglio 1978 on the 3rd of July 1978 (BRIT), on July 3rd 1978 (US)

addi'accio [ad'djattʃo] sm (MIL) bivouac; dormire all'~ to sleep in the open

addi'etro av (indietro) behind; (nel passato, prima) before, ago

ad'dio sm, escl goodbye, farewell

addirit'tura av (veramente) really, absolutely; (perfino) even; (direttamente) directly, right away

ad'dirsi vr: ~ a to suit, be suitable for

addi'tare vt to point out; (fig) to expose

addi'tivo sm additive

addizio'nare [addittsjo'nare] vt (MAT) to add (up); **addizio'ne** sf addition

addob'bare vt to decorate; **ad'dobbo** sm decoration

addol'cire [addol'tʃire] vt (caffè etc) to sweeten; (acqua, fig: carattere) to soften; ~rsi vr (fig) to mellow, soften

addolo'rare vt to pain, grieve; ~rsi

(per) to be distressed (by)

ad'dome sm abdomen

addomesti'care vt to tame

addormen'tare vt to put to sleep; ~rsi vr to fall asleep, go to sleep

addos'sare vt (appoggiare): ~ qc a qc to lean sth against sth; (fig): ~ la colpa a qn to lay the blame on sb; ~rsi qc (responsabilità etc) to shoulder sth

ad'dosso av (sulla persona) on; mettersi ~ il cappotto to put one's coat on; non ho soldi ~ I don't have any money on me; ~ a (sopra) on; (molto vicino) right next to; stare ~ a qn (fig) to breathe down sb's neck; dare ~ a qn (fig) to attack sb

ad'dotto, a pp di addurre

ad'durre vt (DIR) to produce; (citare) to cite

adegu'are vt: ~ qc a to adjust o relate sth to; ~rsi vr to adapt; **adegu'ato, a** ag adequate; (conveniente) suitable; (equo) fair

a'dempiere vt to fulfil, carry out

adem'pire vt = adempiere

ade'rente ag adhesive; (vestito) close-fitting ♦ smf follower; **ade'renza** sf adhesion; **aderenze** sfpl (fig) connections, contacts

ade'rire vi (stare attaccato) to adhere, stick; ~ a to adhere to, stick to; (fig: società, partito) to join; (: opinione) to support; (: richiesta) to agree to

ades'care vt to lure, entice

adesi'one sf adhesion; (fig) agreement, acceptance; **ade'sivo, a** ag, sm adhesive

a'desso av (ora) now; (or ora, poco fa) just now; (tra poco) any moment now

adia'cente [adja'tʃɛnte] ag adjacent

adi'bire vt (usare): ~ qc a to turn sth into

adi'rarsi vr: ~ (con o contro qn per qc) to get angry (with sb over sth)

a'dire vt (DIR): ~ le vie legali to take legal proceedings '**adito** *sm*: dare ~ a to give rise to

adocchi'are [adok'kjare] *vt* (*scorgere*) to catch sight of; (*occhieggiare*) to eye

adole'scente [adole'ʃɛnte] *ag, smf* adolescent; **adole'scenza** *sf* adolescence

adope'rare *vt* to use; ~rsi *vr* to strive; ~rsi per qn/qc to do one's best for sb/sth

ado'rare *vt* to adore; (*REL*) to adore, worship

adot'tare *vt* (*figlio*) (*decisione, provvedimenti*) to pass; **adot'tivo, a** *ag* (*genitori*) adoptive; (*figlio, patria*) adopted; **adozi'one** *sf* adoption

adri'atico, a, ci, che *ag* Adriatic ♦ *sm*: l'A~, il mare A~ the Adriatic, the Adriatic Sea

adu'lare *vt* to adulate, flatter

adulte'rare *vt* to adulterate

adul'terio *sm* adultery

a'dulto, a *ag* adult; (*fig*) mature ♦ *sm* adult, grown-up

adu'nanza [adu'nantsa] *sf* assembly, meeting

adu'nare *vt* to assemble, gather; ~rsi *vr* to assemble, gather; **adu'nata** *sf* (*MIL*) parade, muster

a'dunco, a, chi, che *ag* hooked

a'ereo, a *ag* air *cpd*; (*radice*) aerial ♦ *sm* aerial; (*aeroplano*) plane; ~ a reazione jet (plane); ~ da caccia fighter (plane); ~ di linea airliner; **ae'robica** *sf* aerobics *sg*; **aerodi'namica** *sf* aerodynamics *sg*; **aero'dinamico, a, ci, che** *ag* aerodynamic; (*affusolato*) streamlined; **aero'nautica** *sf* (*scienza*) aeronautics *sg*; **aeronautica militare** air force; **aero'plano** *sm* (aero)plane (*BRIT*), (air)plane (*US*); **aero'porto** *sm* airport; **aero'sol** *sm inv* aerosol

'**afa** *sf* sultriness

af'fabile *ag* affable

affacen'dato, a [affatʃen'dato] *ag* (*persona*) busy

affacci'arsi [affat'tʃarsi] *vr*: ~ (a) to appear (at)

affa'mato, a *ag* starving; (*fig*): ~ (di) eager (for)

affan'nare *vt* to leave breathless; (*fig*) to worry; ~rsi *vr*: ~rsi per qn/qc to worry about sb/sth; **af'fanno** *sm* breathlessness; (*fig*) anxiety, worry; **affan'noso, a** *ag* (*respiro*) difficult; (*fig*) troubled, anxious

af'fare *sm* (*faccenda*) matter, affair; (*COMM*) piece of business, (business) deal; (*occasione*) bargain; (*DIR*) case; (*fam: cosa*) thing; ~i *smpl* (*COMM*) business *sg*; **Ministro degli A~i esteri** Foreign Secretary (*BRIT*), Secretary of State (*US*); **affa'rista, i** *sm* profiteer, unscrupulous businessman

affasci'nante [affaʃʃi'nante] *ag* fascinating

affasci'nare [affaʃʃi'nare] *vt* to bewitch; (*fig*) to charm, fascinate

affati'care *vt* to tire; ~rsi *vr* (*durar fatica*) to tire o.s. out

af'fatto *av* completely; **non** ... ~ not ... at all; **niente** ~ not at all

affer'mare *vt* (*dichiarare*) to maintain, affirm; ~rsi *vr* to assert o.s., make one's name known; **afferma-zi'one** *sf* affirmation, assertion; (*successo*) achievement

affer'rare *vt* to seize, grasp; (*fig: idea*) to grasp; ~rsi *vr*: ~rsi a to cling to

affet'tare *vt* (*tagliare a fette*) to slice; (*ostentare*) to affect; **af-fet'tato, a** *ag* sliced; affected ♦ *sm* sliced cold meat

affet'tivo, a *ag* emotional, affective

af'fetto *sm* affection; **affettu'oso, a** *ag* affectionate

affezio'narsi [affettsjo'narsi] *vr*: ~ a to grow fond of

affian'care *vt* to place side by side; (*MIL*) to flank; (*fig*): ~ qc a qc to place sth next to o beside sth; ~rsi a qn to stand beside sb

affia'tato, a *ag*: essere molto ~i (*coppia*) to get on very well; (*gruppo, amici*) to make a good team

affibbia're vt (fig: dare) to give

affi'dabile ag reliable

affida'mento sm (DIR: di bambino) custody; (fiducia): **fare ~ su** qn to rely on sb; **non dà nessun ~** he's not to be trusted

affi'dare vt: ~ qc o qn a qn to entrust sth o sb to sb; ~**rsi** vr: ~**rsi a** to place one's trust in

affievo'lirsi vr to grow weak

affig'gere [affid͡ʒere] vt to stick up, post up

affi'lare vt to sharpen

affili'are vt to affiliate; ~**rsi** vr: ~**rsi a** to become affiliated to

affi'nare vt to sharpen

affinché [affin'ke] cong in order that, so that

af'fine ag similar; **affinità** sf inv affinity

affio'rare vi to emerge

affissi'one sf billposting

af'fisso, a pp di **affiggere** ♦ sm bill, poster; (LING) affix

affit'tare vt (dare in affitto) to let, rent (out); (prendere in affitto) to rent; **af'fitto** sm rent; (contratto) lease

af'fliggere [af'flidd͡ʒere] vt to torment; ~**rsi** vr to grieve; **af'flitto, a** pp di **affliggere**; **afflizi'one** sf distress, torment

afflosci'arsi [afflof'farsi] vr to go limp; (frutta) to go soft

afflu'ente sm tributary; **afflu'enza** sf flow; (di persone) crowd

afflu'ire vi to flow; (fig: merci, persone) to pour in; **af'flusso** sm influx

affo'gare vt, vi to drown; ~**rsi** vr to drown; (deliberatamente) to drown o.s.

affol'lare vt to crowd; ~**rsi** vr to crowd; **affol'lato, a** ag crowded

affon'dare vt to sink

affran'care vt to free, liberate; (AMM) to redeem; (lettera) to stamp; (: meccanicamente) to frank (BRIT); meter (US); ~**rsi** vr to free o.s.; **affranca'tura** sf (di francobollo) stamping; franking (BRIT);

me-tering (US); (tassa di spedizione) postage

af'franto, a ag (esausto) worn out; (abbattuto) overcome

af'fresco, schi sm fresco

affret'tare vt to quicken, speed up; ~**rsi** vr to hurry; ~**rsi a fare** qc to hurry o hasten to do sth

affron'tare vt (pericolo etc) to face; (assalire: nemico) to confront; ~**rsi** vr (reciproco) to come to blows

af'fronto sm affront, insult

affumi'care vt to fill with smoke; to blacken with smoke; (alimenti) to smoke

affuso'lato, a ag tapering

a'foso, a ag sultry, close

'**Africa** sf: l'~ Africa; **afri'cano, a** ag, smf African

afrodi'siaco, a, ci, che ag, sm aphrodisiac

a'genda [a'd͡ʒɛnda] sf diary

a'gente [a'd͡ʒɛnte] sm agent; ~ **di cambio** stockbroker; ~ **di polizia** police officer; **agen'zia** sf agency; (succursale) branch; **agenzia di collocamento** employment agency; **agenzia immobiliare** estate agent's (office) (BRIT), real estate office (US); **agenzia pubblicitaria/viaggi** advertising/travel agency

agevo'lare [ad͡ʒevo'lare] vt to facilitate, make easy

a'gevole [a'd͡ʒevole] ag easy; (strada) smooth

aggan'ciare [aggan't͡ʃare] vt to hook up; (FERR) to couple

ag'geggio [ad'd͡ʒedd͡ʒo] sm gadget, contraption

agget'tivo [add͡ʒet'tivo] sm adjective

agghiacci'ante [aggjat'tʃante] ag (fig) chilling

agghin'darsi [aggin'darsi] vr to deck o.s. out

aggior'nare [add͡ʒor'nare] vt (opera, manuale) to bring up-to-date; (seduta etc) to postpone; ~**rsi** vr (tenersi al corrente) o (keep) o.s. up-to-date; **aggior'nato, a** ag up-to-date

aggi'rare [add͡ʒi'rare] vt to go round;

(fig: ingannare) to trick; ~**rsi** vr to wander about; **il prezzo s'aggira sul milione** the price is around the million mark

aggiudi'care [addʒudi'kare] vt to award; (all'asta) to knock down; ~**rsi qc** to win sth

ag'giungere [ad'dʒundʒere] vt to add; **aggi'unta** sf addition; **aggi'unto, a** pp di **aggiungere** ♦ ag assistant cpd ♦ sm assistant; **sindaco aggiunto** deputy mayor

aggius'tare [addʒus'tare] vt (accomodare) to mend, repair; (riassettare) to adjust; (fig: lite) to settle; ~**rsi** vr (arrangiarsi) to make do; (con senso reciproco) to come to an agreement

agglome'rato sm (di rocce) conglomerate; (di legno) chipboard; ~ **urbano** built-up area

aggrap'parsi vr: ~ **a** to cling to

aggra'vare vt (aumentare) to increase; (appesantire: anche fig) to weigh down, make heavy; (fig: pena) to make worse; ~**rsi** vr (fig) to worsen, become worse

aggrazi'ato, a [aggrat'tsjato] ag graceful

aggre'dire vt to attack, assault

aggre'gare vt: ~ **qn a qc** to admit sb to sth; ~**rsi** vr to join; ~**rsi a** to join, become a member of

aggressi'one sf aggression; (atto) attack, assault

aggres'sivo, a ag aggressive

aggrot'tare vt: ~ **le sopracciglia** to frown

aggrovigli'are [aggroviʎ'ʎare] vt to tangle; ~**rsi** vr (fig) to become complicated

agguan'tare vt to catch, seize

aggu'ato sm trap; (imboscata) ambush; **tendere un ~ a qn** to set a trap for sb

agguer'rito, a ag fierce

agi'ato, a [a'dʒato] ag (vita) easy; (persona) well-off, well-to-do

'agile ['adʒile] ag agile, nimble; **agilità** sf agility, nimbleness

'agio ['adʒo] sm ease, comfort; **vivere negli ~i** to live in comfort; **mettersi a proprio ~** to make o.s. at home o comfortable

a'gire [a'dʒire] vi to act; (esercitare un'azione) to take effect; (TECN) to work, function; ~ **contro qn** (DIR) to take action against sb

agi'tare [adʒi'tare] vt (bottiglia) to shake; (mano, fazzoletto) to wave; (fig: turbare) to disturb; (: incitare) to stir (up); (: dibattere) to discuss; ~**rsi** vr (mare) to be rough; (malato, dormitore) to toss and turn; (bambino) to fidget; (emozionarsi) to get upset; (POL) to agitate; **agi'tato, a** ag rough; restless; fidgety; upset, perturbed; **agitazi'one** sf agitation; (POL) unrest, agitation; **mettere in agitazione qn** to upset o distress sb

'agli ['aʎʎi] prep + det vedi **a**

'aglio ['aʎʎo] sm garlic

a'gnello [aɲ'ɲɛllo] sm lamb

'ago (pl aghi) sm needle

ago'nia sf agony

ago'nistico, a, ci, che ag athletic; (fig) competitive

agoniz'zare [agonid'dzare] vi to be dying

agopun'tura sf acupuncture

a'gosto sm August

a'graria sf agriculture

a'grario, a ag agrarian, agricultural; (riforma) land cpd

a'gricolo, a ag agricultural, farm cpd; **agricol'tore** sm farmer; **agricol'tura** sf agriculture, farming

agri'foglio [agri'fɔʎʎo] sm holly

agrimen'sore sm land surveyor

agritu'rismo sm farm holidays pl

'agro, a ag sour, sharp; ~**dolce** ag bittersweet; (salsa) sweet and sour

a'grume sm (spesso al pl: pianta) citrus; (: frutto) citrus fruit

aguz'zare [agut'tsare] vt to sharpen; ~ **gli orecchi** to prick up one's ears

a'guzzo, a [a'guttso] ag sharp

'ai ['ai] prep + det vedi **a**

'Aia sf: **l'~** the Hague

'aia *sf* threshing-floor

ai'rone *sm* heron

aiu'ola *sf* flower bed

aiu'tante *smf* assistant ♦ *sm* (MIL) adjutant; (NAUT) master-at-arms; ~ di campo aide-de-camp

aiu'tare *vt* to help; ~ qn (a fare) to help sb (to do)

ai'uto *sm* help, assistance, aid; (aiutante) assistant; venire in ~ di qn to come to sb's aid; ~ chirurgo assistant surgeon

aiz'zare [ait'tsare] *vt* to incite; ~ i cani contro qn to set the dogs on sb

al *prep* + *det vedi* **a**

'ala (pl 'ali) *sf* wing; fare ~ to fall back, make way; ~ destra/sinistra (SPORT) right/left wing

'alacre *ag* quick, brisk

a'lano *sm* Great Dane

a'lare *ag* wing cpd

'alba *sf* dawn

Alba'nia *sf*: l'~ Albania

al'batro *sm* albatross

albeggi'are [albed'dʒare] *vi*, *vb impers* to dawn

alberghi'ero, a [alber'gjero] *ag* hotel cpd

al'bergo, ghi *sm* hotel; ~ della gioventù youth hostel

'albero *sm* tree; (NAUT) mast; (TECN) shaft; ~ genealogico family tree; ~ a gomiti crankshaft; ~ di Natale Christmas tree; ~ maestro mainmast; ~ di trasmissione transmission shaft

albi'cocca, che *sf* apricot; **albi'cocco, chi** *sm* apricot tree

'albo *sm* (registro) register, roll; (AMM) notice board

'album *sm* album; ~ da disegno sketch book

al'bume *sm* albumen

'alce [alt∫e] *sm* elk

al'colico, a, ci, che *ag* alcoholic ♦ *sm* alcoholic drink

alcoliz'zato, a [alkolid'dzato] *smf/ag* alcoholic

'alcool *sm* alcohol; **alco'olico** *etc* = **alcolico** *etc*

al'cuno, a (det: dav sm: alcun +C, V, alcuno +s impura, gn, pn, ps, x, z; dav sf: alcuna +C, alcun' +V) det (nessuno): non ... ~ no, not any; ~i, e det pl, some, a few; non c'è ~a fretta there's no hurry, there isn't any hurry; senza alcun riguardo without any consideration ♦ pron pl: ~i, e some, a few

aldilà *sm*: l'~ the after-life

alfa'beto *sm* alphabet

alfi'ere *sm* standard-bearer; (MIL) ensign; (SCACCHI) bishop

'alga, ghe *sf* seaweed no pl, alga

'algebra ['aldʒebra] *sf* algebra

Alge'ria [aldʒe'ria] *sf*: l'~ Algeria

ali'ante *sm* (AER) glider

'alibi *sm inv* alibi

a'lice [a'lit∫e] *sf* anchovy

alie'nare *vt* (DIR) to alienate, transfer; (rendere ostile) to alienate; ~rsi qn to alienate sb; **alie'nato, a** *ag* alienated; transferred; (fuor di senno) insane ♦ *sm* lunatic, insane person; **alienazi'one** *sf* alienation; transfer; insanity

ali'eno, a *ag* (avverso): ~ (da) opposed (to), averse (to) ♦ *sm/f* alien

alimen'tare *vt* to feed; (TECN) to feed; to supply; (fig) to sustain ♦ *ag* food cpd; ~i *smpl* foodstuffs; (anche: negozio di ~i) grocer's shop; **alimentazi'one** *sf* feeding; supplying; sustaining; (gli alimenti) food

ali'mento *sm* food; ~i *smpl* (cibo) food sg; (DIR) alimony

a'liquota *sf* share; (d'imposta) rate

alis'cafo *sm* hydrofoil

'alito *sm* breath

all. *abbr* (= allegato) encl

'alla *prep* + *det vedi* **a**

allacci'are [allat't∫are] *vt* (scarpe) to tie, lace up; (cintura) to do up, fasten; (due località) to link; (luce, gas) to connect; (amicizia) to form

alla'gare *vt* to flood; ~rsi *vr* to flood

allar'gare *vt* to widen; (vestito) to let out; (aprire) to open; (fig: dilatare) to extend

allar'mare *vt* to alarm

al'larme sm alarm; ~ aereo air-raid warning

allar'mismo sm scaremongering

allat'tare vt to feed

'alle prep + det vedi **a**

alle'anza [alle'antsa] sf alliance

alle'arsi vr to form an alliance; **alle'ato, a** ag allied ♦ sm/f ally

alle'gare vt (accludere) to enclose; (DIR: citare) to cite, adduce; (denti) to set on edge; **alle'gato, a** ag enclosed ♦ sm enclosure; **in allegato** enclosed

allegge'rire [alleddʒe'rire] vt to lighten, make lighter; (fig: soffe-renza) to alleviate, lessen; (: lavoro, tasse) to reduce

alle'gria sf gaiety, cheerfulness

al'legro, a ag cheerful, merry; (un po' brillo) merry, tipsy; (vivace: colore) bright ♦ sm (MUS) allegro

allena'mento sm training

alle'nare vt to train; ~**rsi** vr to train; **allena'tore** sm (SPORT) train-er, coach

allen'tare vt to slacken; (disciplina) to relax; ~**rsi** vr to become slack; (ingranaggio) to work loose

aller'gia, 'gie [aller'dʒia] sf allergy; **al'lergico, a, ci, che** ag allergic

alles'tire vt (cena) to prepare; (esercito, nave) to equip, fit out; (spettacolo) to stage

allet'tare vt to lure, entice

alleva'mento sm breeding, rearing; (luogo) stock farm

alle'vare vt (animale) to breed, rear; (bambino) to bring up

allevi'are vt to alleviate

alli'bire vi to be astounded

allibra'tore sm bookmaker

allie'tare vt to cheer up, gladden

alli'evo sm pupil; (apprendista) ap-prentice; (MIL) cadet

alliga'tore sm alligator

alline'are vt (persone, cose) to line up; (TIP) to align; (fig: economia, salari) to adjust, align; ~**rsi** vr to line up; (fig: a idee): ~**rsi a** to come into line with

'allo prep + det vedi **a**

al'iocco, a, chi, che sm tawny owl ♦ sm/f oaf

allocuzi'one [allokut'tsjone] sf ad-dress, solemn speech

al'lodola sf (sky)lark

alloggi'are [allod'dʒare] vt to ac-commodate ♦ vi to live; **al'loggio** sm lodging, accommodation (BRIT), accommodations (US); (appartamen-to) flat (BRIT), apartment (US)

allontana'mento sm removal; dis-missal

allonta'nare vt to send away, send off; (impiegato) to dismiss; (perico-lo) to avert, remove; (estraniare) to alienate; ~**rsi** vr: ~**rsi (da)** to go away (from); (estraniarsi) to be-come estranged (from)

al'lora av (in quel momento) then ♦ cong (in questo caso) well then; (dunque) well then, so; **la gente d'~** people then o in those days; **da ~ in poi** from then on

allor'ché [allor'ke] cong (formale) when, as soon as

al'loro sm laurel

'alluce [allutʃe] sm big toe

alluci'nante [allutʃi'nante] ag awful; (fam) incredible

allucinazi'one [allutʃinat'tsjone] sf hallucination

al'ludere vi: ~ **a** to allude to, hint at

allu'minio sm aluminium (BRIT), aluminum (US)

allun'gare vt to lengthen; (disten-dere) to prolong, extend; (diluire) to water down; ~**rsi** vr to lengthen; (ragazzo) to stretch, grow taller; (sdraiarsi) to lie down, stretch out

allusi'one sf hint, allusion

al'luso pp di **alludere**

alluvi'one sf flood

al'meno av at least ♦ cong: (se) ~ if only; (se) ~ **piovesse!** if only it would rain!

a'logeno, a [a'lɔdʒeno] ag: **lampa-da ~a** halogen lamp

a'lone sm halo

'**Alpi** *sfpl*: **le** ~ the Alps
alpi'nismo *sm* mountaineering, climbing; **alpi'nista, i, e** *smif* mountaineer, climber
al'pino, a *ag* Alpine; mountain *cpd*
al'quanto *av* rather, a little; ~, a *det* a certain amount of, some ♦ *pron* a certain amount, some; ~i, e *det pl*, *pron pl* several, quite a few
alt *escl* halt!, stop! ♦ *sm*: **dare l'**~ to call a halt
alta'lena *sf (a funi)* swing; *(in bilico, anche fig)* seesaw
al'tare *sm* altar
alte'rare *vt* to alter, change; *(cibo)* to adulterate; *(registro)* to falsify; *(persona)* to irritate; ~**rsi** *vr* to alter; *(cibo)* to go bad; *(persona)* to lose one's temper
al'terco, chi *sm* altercation, wrangle
alter'nare *vt* to alternate; ~**rsi** *vr* to alternate; **alterna'tiva** *sf* alternative; **alterna'tivo, a** *ag* alternative; **alter'nato, a** *ag* alternate; *(ELETTR)* alternating; **alterna'tore** *sm* alternator
al'terno, a *ag* alternate; **a giorni** ~**i** on alternate days, every other day
al'tezza [al'tettsa] *sf* height; width, breadth; depth; pitch; *(GEO)* latitude; *(titolo)* highness; *(fig: nobiltà)* greatness; **essere all'**~ **di** to be on a level with; *(fig)* to be up to o equal to; **altez'zoso, a** *ag* haughty
al'ticcio, a, ci, ce [al'tittʃo] *ag* tipsy
altipi'ano *sm* = altopiano
alti'tudine *sf* altitude
'**alto, a** *ag* high; *(persona)* tall; *(tessuto)* wide, broad; *(sonno, acque)* deep; *(suono)* high(-pitched); *(GEO)* upper; *(: settentrionale)* northern ♦ *sm* top (part) ♦ *av* high; *(parlare)* aloud; **il palazzo è ~ 20 metri** the building is 20 metres high; **ad** ~**a voce** aloud; **a notte** ~**a** in the dead of night; **in** ~ up, upwards; at the top; **dall'**~ **in** o **al basso** up and

down; **degli** ~**i e bassi** *(fig)* ups and downs; ~**a fedeltà** high fidelity, hi-fi; ~**a finanza** high finance; ~**a moda** haute couture; ~**a società** high society
alto'forno *sm* blast furnace
altolo'cato, a *ag* of high rank
altopar'lante *sm* loudspeaker
altopi'ano *(pl* **altipiani***) sm* plateau, upland plain
altret'tanto *a ag*, *pron* as much; *(pl)* as many ♦ *av* equally; **tanti auguri!** — **grazie,** ~ all the best! — thank you, the same to you
'altri *pron inv (qualcuno)* somebody; *(: in espressioni negative)* anybody; *(un'altra persona)* another (person)
altri'menti *av* otherwise

'**altro, a** *det* **1** *(diverso)* other, different; **questa è un'**~**a cosa** that's another o a different thing
2 *(supplementare)* other; **prendi un** ~ **cioccolatino** have another chocolate; **hai avuto** ~**e notizie?** have you had any more o any other news?
3 *(nel tempo)*: **l'**~ **giorno** the other day; **l'altr'anno** last year; **l'**~ **ieri** the day before yesterday; **domani l'**~ the day after tomorrow; **quest'**~ **mese** next month
4: **d'**~**a parte** on the other hand
♦ *pron* **1** *(persona, cosa diversa o supplementare)*: ~, **un'**~, **un'**~**a** another (one); **lo farà un** ~ someone else will do it; ~**i, e** others; **gli** ~**i** *(la gente)* others, other people; **l'uno e l'**~ both (of them); **aiutarsi l'un l'**~ to help one another; **da un giorno all'**~ from day to day; *(nel giro di 24 ore)* from one day to the next; *(da un momento all'altro)* any day now
2 *(sostantivato: solo maschile)* something else; *(: in espressioni interrogative)* anything else; **non ho** ~ **da dire** I have nothing else o I don't have anything else to say; **più che** ~ above all; **se non** ~ at least; **tra l'**~

among other things; **ci manchereb-be** ~! that's all we need!; **non faccio** ~ **che lavorare** I do nothing but work; **contento?** — ~ **che!** are you pleased? — and how!; *vedi* **senza; noialtri; voialtri; tutto**

---

al'tronde *av:* **d'**~ on the other hand
al'trove *av* elsewhere, somewhere else
al'trui *ag inv* other people's ♦ *sm:* **l'**~ other people's belongings *pl*
altru'ista, i, e *ag* altruistic
al'tura *sf* (*rialto*) height, high ground; (*alto mare*) open sea; **pesca d'**~ deep-sea fishing
a'lunno, a *smf* pupil
alve'are *sm* hive
'alveo *sm* riverbed
al'zare [al'tsare] *vt* to raise, lift; (*issare*) to hoist; (*costruire*) to build, erect; ~**rsi** *vr* to rise; (*dal letto*) to get up; (*crescere*) to grow tall (o taller); ~ **le spalle** to shrug one's shoulders; ~**rsi in piedi** to stand up, get to one's feet; **al'zata di spalle** lifting, raising; **un'alzata di spalle** a shrug
a'mabile *ag* lovable; (*vino*) sweet
a'maca, che *sf* hammock
amal'gamare *vt* to amalgamate
a'mante *ag:* ~ **di** (*musica etc*) fond of ♦ *smf* lover/mistress
a'mare *vt* to love; (*amico, musica, sport*) to like
amareggi'ato, a [amared'dʒato] *ag* upset, saddened
ama'rena *sf* sour black cherry
ama'rezza [ama'rettsa] *sf* bitterness
a'maro, a *ag* bitter ♦ *sm* bitterness; (*liquore*) bitters *pl*
ambasci'ata [ambaʃ'ʃata] *sf* embassy; (*messaggio*) message; **ambascia'tore, 'trice** *smf* ambassador/ambassadress
ambe'due *ag inv:* ~ **i ragazzi** both boys ♦ *pron inv* both
ambien'tare *vt* to acclimatize; (*romanzo, film*) to set; ~**rsi** *vr* to get used to one's surroundings

ambi'ente *sm* environment; (*fig: insieme di persone*) milieu; (*stanza*) room
am'biguo, a *ag* ambiguous; (*persona*) shady
am'bire *vt* (*anche: vi:* ~ *a*) to aspire to
'ambito *sm* sphere, field
ambizi'one [ambit'tsjone] *sf* ambition; **ambizi'oso, a** *ag* ambitious
'ambo *ag inv* both
'ambra *sf* amber; ~ **grigia** ambergris
ambu'lante *ag* travelling, itinerant
ambu'lanza [ambu'lantsa] *sf* ambulance
ambula'torio *sm* (*studio medico*) surgery
a'meno, a *ag* pleasant; (*strano*) funny, strange; (*spiritoso*) amusing
A'merica *sf:* **l'**~ America; **l'**~ **latina** Latin America; **ameri'cano, a** *ag, smf* American
ami'anto *sm* asbestos
a'mica *sf vedi* **amico**
ami'chevole [ami'kevole] *ag* friendly
ami'cizia [ami'tʃittsja] *sf* friendship; ~**e** *sfpl* (*amici*) friends
a'mico, ci, che *smf* friend; (*amante*) boyfriend/girlfriend; ~ **del cuore** *o* **intimo** bosom friend
'amido *sm* starch
ammac'care *vt* (*pentola*) to dent; (*persona*) to bruise; ~**rsi** *vr* to bruise
ammaes'trare *vt* (*animale*) to train; (*persona*) to teach
ammai'nare *vt* to lower, haul down
amma'larsi *vr* to fall ill; **amma'lato, a** *ag* ill, sick ♦ *smf* sick person; (*paziente*) patient
ammali'are *vt* (*fig*) to enchant, charm
am'manco, chi *sm* (*ECON*) deficit
ammanet'tare *vt* to handcuff
ammas'sare *vt* (*ammucchiare*) to amass; (*raccogliere*) to gather together; ~**rsi** *vr* to pile up; to gather; **am'masso** *sm* mass; (*mucchio*) mass, heap; (*ECON*) stockpile

ammat'tire *vi* to go mad

ammaz'zare [ammat'tsare] *vt* to kill; **~rsi** *vr* (*uccidersi*) to kill o.s.; (*rimanere ucciso*) to be killed; **~rsi di lavoro** to work o.s. to death

am'menda *sf* amends *pl*; (*DIR, SPORT*) fine; **fare ~ di qc** to make amends for sth

am'messo, a *pp di* ammettere ♦ *cong*: ~ **che** supposing that

am'mettere *vt* to admit; (*riconoscere: fatto*) to acknowledge, admit; (*permettere*) to allow, accept; (*supporre*) to suppose

ammez'zato [ammed'dzato] *sm* (*anche: piano ~*) mezzanine, entresol

ammic'care *vi*: ~ **(a)** to wink (at)

amminis'trare *vt* to run, manage; (*REL, DIR*) to administer; **amministra'tivo, a** *ag* administrative; **amministra'tore, a** *ag* administrator; (*di condominio*) flats manager; **amministratore delegato** managing director; **amministrazi'one** *sf* management; administration

ammiragli'ato [ammira'ʎʎato] *sm* admiralty

ammi'raglio [ammi'raʎʎo] *sm* admiral

ammi'rare *vt* to admire; **ammira'tore, 'trice** *sm/f* admirer; **ammirazi'one** *sf* admiration

ammissi'one *sf* admission; (*approvazione*) acknowledgment

ammobili'ato, a *ag* furnished

am'modo *av* properly ♦ *ag inv* respectable, nice

am'mollo *sm*: **lasciare in ~ to leave to soak

ammo'niaca *sf* ammonia

ammoni'mento *sm* warning; admonishment

ammo'nire *vt* (*avvertire*) to warn; (*rimproverare*) to admonish; (*DIR*) to caution

ammon'tare *vi*: ~ **a** to amount to ♦ *sm* (*total*) amount

ammorbi'dente *sm* fabric conditioner

ammorbi'dire *vt* to soften

ammortiz'zare [ammortid'dzare] *vt* (*ECON*) to pay off, amortize; (*: spese d'impianto*) to write off; (*AUT, TECN*) to absorb, deaden; **ammortizza'tore** *sm* (*AUT, TECN*) shock-absorber

ammucchi'are [ammuk'kjare] *vt* to pile up, accumulate

ammuf'fire *vi* to go mouldy (*BRIT*) *o* moldy (*US*)

ammutina'mento *sm* mutiny

ammuti'narsi *vr* to mutiny

ammuto'lire *vi* to be struck dumb

amnis'tia *sf* amnesty

'amo *sm* (*PESCA*) hook; (*fig*) bait

a'modo *av* = ammodo

a'more *sm* love; **~i** *smpl* love affairs; **il tuo bambino è un ~** your baby's a darling; **fare l'~ o all'~** to make love; **per ~ o per forza** by hook or by crook; **amor proprio** self-esteem, pride; **amo'revole** *ag* loving, affectionate

a'morfo, a *ag* amorphous; (*fig: persona*) lifeless

amo'roso, a *ag* (*affettuoso*) loving, affectionate; (*d'amore: sguardo*) amorous; (*: poesia, relazione*) love *cpd*

am'piezza [am'pjettsa] *sf* width, breadth; spaciousness; (*fig: importanza*) scale, size

'ampio, a *ag* wide, broad; (*spazioso*) spacious; (*abbondante: vestito*) loose; (*: gonna*) full; (*: spiegazione*) ample, full

am'plesso *sm* (*eufemismo*) embrace

ampli'are *vt* (*ingrandire*) to enlarge; (*allargare*) to widen

amplifi'care *vt* to amplify; (*magnificare*) to extol; **amplifica'tore** *sm* (*TECN, MUS*) amplifier

am'polla *sf* (*vasetto*) cruet

ampu'tare *vt* (*MED*) to amputate

a'muleto *sm* lucky charm

anabbagli'ante [anabbaʎ'ʎante] *ag* (*AUT*) dipped (*BRIT*), dimmed (*US*); **~i** *smpl* dipped (*BRIT*) *o* dimmed (*US*) headlights

a'nagrafe sf (registro) register of births, marriages and deaths; (ufficio) registration office

analfa'beta, i, e ag, smf illiterate

anal'gesico, a, ci, che [anal'dʒɛziko] ag, sm analgesic

a'nalisi sf inv analysis; (MED: esame) test; ~ **grammaticale** parsing; **ana'lista, i, e** smf analyst; (PSIC) (psycho)analyst

analiz'zare [analid'dzare] vt to analyse; (MED) to test

analo'gia, 'gie [analo'dʒia] sf analogy

a'nalogo, a, ghi, ghe ag analogous

'ananas sm inv pineapple

anar'chia [anar'kia] sf anarchy; **a'narchico, a, ci, che** ag anarchic(al) ♦ sm/f anarchist

'ANAS sigla f (= Azienda Nazionale Autonoma delle Strade) national roads department

anato'mia sf anatomy; **ana'tomico, a, ci, che** ag anatomical; (sedile) contoured

'anatra sf duck

'anca, che [anka] (ANAT) hip; (ZOOL) haunch

an'dazzo [an'dattso] (peg) sm: **prendere un brutto ~** to take a turn for the worse

andiri'vieni sm inv coming and going

'andito sm corridor, passage

an'drone sm entrance hall

a'neddoto sm anecdote

ane'lare vi: ~ **a** (fig) to long for, yearn for

a'nelito sm (fig): ~ **di** longing o yearning for

a'nello sm ring; (di catena) link

a'nemico, a, ci, che ag anaemic

a'nemone sm anemone

aneste'sia sf anaesthesia; **anes'tetico, a, ci, che** ag, sm anaesthetic

anfite'atro sm amphitheatre

an'fratto sm ravine

an'gelico, a, ci, che [an'dʒɛliko] ag angelic(al)

'angelo [andʒelo] sm angel; ~ **cus-tode** guardian angel

run ♦ vi to go; (essere adatto): ~ **a** to suit; (piacere): **il suo comporta-mento non mi va** I don't like the way he behaves; **ti va di andare al cinema?** do you feel like going to the cinema?; **andarsene** to go away; **questa camicia va lavata** this shirt needs a wash o should be washed; ~ **a cavallo** to ride; **in macchina/aereo** to go by car/plane; ~ **a fare** qc to go and do sth; ~ **a pescare/sciare** to go fishing/skiing; ~ **a male** to go bad; **come va?** (lavoro, progetto) how are things?; **come va? — bene, grazie!** how are you? — fine, thanks!; **va fatto entro oggi** it's got to be done today; **ne va della nostra vita** our lives are at stake; **an'data** sf going; (viaggio) outward journey; **biglietto di sola andata** single (BRIT) o one-way ticket; **biglietto di andata e ritorno** return (BRIT) o round-trip (US) ticket; **andra'tura** sf (modo di andare) walk, gait; (SPORT) pace; (NAUT) tack

an'cora[1] av still; (di nuovo) again; (di più) some more; (persino): ~ **più forte** even stronger; **non** ~ not yet; ~ **una volta** once more, once again; ~ **un po'** a little more; (di tempo) a little longer

'ancora[2] sf anchor; **gettare/levare l'**~ to cast/weigh anchor; **anco'raggio** sm anchorage; **anco'rare** vt to anchor; **ancorarsi** vr to anchor

anda'mento sm progress, movement; course; state

an'dante ag (corrente) current; (di poco pregio) cheap, second-rate ♦ sm (MUS) andante

an'dare sm: **a lungo** ~ in the long

anghe'ria [ange'ria] sf vexation

an'gina [an'dʒina] sf tonsillitis; ~ **pectoris** angina

angli'cano, a ag Anglican

angli'cismo [angli'tʃizmo] sm anglicism

anglo'sassone ag Anglo-Saxon

ango'lare ag angular

angolazi'one [angolat'tsjone] sf (FOT etc, fig) angle

'angolo sm corner; (MAT) angle

an'goscia, sce [an'goʃʃa] sf deep anxiety, anguish no pl; **angosci'oso, a** ag (d'angoscia) anguished; (che dà angoscia) distressing, painful

angu'illa sf eel

an'guria sf watermelon

an'gustia sf (ansia) anguish, distress; (povertà) poverty, want

angusti'are vt to distress; ~**rsi** vr: ~**rsi (per)** to worry (about)

an'gusto, a ag (stretto) narrow; (fig) mean, petty

'anice ['anitʃe] sm (CUC) aniseed; (BOT) anise

a'nidride sf (CHIM): ~ **carbonica/solforosa** carbon/sulphur dioxide

'anima sf soul; (abitante) inhabitant; **non c'era ~ viva** there wasn't a living soul

ani'male sm, ag animal; ~ **domestico** pet

ani'mare vt to give life to, liven up; (incoraggiare) to encourage; ~**rsi** vr to become animated, come to life; **ani'mato, a** ag animate; (vivace) lively, animated; (: strada) busy; **anima'tore, 'trice** sm/f guiding spirit; (CINEMA) animator; (di festa) life and soul; **animazi'one** sf liveliness; (di strada) bustle; (CINEMA) animation; **animazione teatrale** amateur dramatics

'animo sm (mente) mind; (cuore) heart; (coraggio) courage; (disposizione) character, disposition; **avere in ~ di fare qc** to intend o have a mind to do sth; **perdersi d'~** to lose heart

'anitra sf = anatra

anna'cquare vt to water down, dilute

annaffi'are vt to water; **annaffia'toio** sm watering can

an'nali smpl annals

annas'pare vi to flounder

an'nata sf year; (importo annuo) annual amount; **vino d'~** vintage wine

annebbi'are vt (fig) to cloud; ~**rsi** vr to become foggy; (vista) to become dim

annega'mento sm drowning

anne'gare vt, vi to drown; ~**rsi** vr (accidentalmente) to drown; (deliberatamente) to drown o.s.

anne'rire vt to blacken ♦ vi to become black

an'nesso, a pp di **annettere** ♦ ag attached; (POL) annexed; ... **e tutti gli ~i e connessi** and so on and so forth

an'nettere vt (POL) to annex; (accludere) to attach

annichi'lire [anniki'lire] vt = **annichilare**

anni'darsi vr to nest

annien'tare vt to annihilate, destroy

anniver'sario sm anniversary

'anno sm year

anno'dare vt to knot, tie; (fig: rapporto) to form

annoi'are vt to bore; (seccare) to annoy; ~**rsi** vr to be bored; to be annoyed

an'noso, a ag (problema etc) ageold

anno'tare vt (registrare) to note, note down; (commentare) to annotate; **annotazi'one** sf note; annotation

annove'rare vt to number

annu'ale ag annual

annu'ario sm yearbook

annu'ire vi to nod; (acconsentire) to agree

annul'lare vt to annihilate, destroy; (contratto, francobollo) to cancel; (matrimonio) to annul; (sentenza) to quash; (risultati) to declare void

annunci'are [annun'tʃare] vt to announce; (dar segni rivelatori) to herald; **annuncia'tore, 'trice** smlf (RADIO, TV) announcer; **l'Annunciazi'one** sf the Annunciation

an'nuncio [an'nuntʃo] sm announcement; (fig) sign; ~ **pubblicitario** advertisement; ~**i economici** classified advertisements, small ads

'annuo, a ag annual, yearly

annu'sare vt to sniff, smell; ~ **tabacco** to take snuff

'ano sm anus

anoma'lia sf anomaly

a'nomalo, a ag anomalous

a'nonimo, a ag anonymous ♦ sm (autore) anonymous writer (o painter etc); **società** ~**a** (COMM) joint stock company

anores'sia sf (MED) anorexia

anor'male ag abnormal ♦ smlf subnormal person; (eufemismo) homosexual

ANSA sigla f (= Agenzia Nazionale Stampa Associata) press agency

'ansa sf (manico) handle; (di fiume) bend, loop

'ansia sf anxiety

ansietà sf = **ansia**

ansi'mare vi to pant

ansi'oso, a ag anxious

'anta sf (di finestra) shutter; (di armadio) door

antago'nismo sm antagonism

an'tartico, a, ci, che ag Antarctic ♦ sm: **l'A~** the Antarctic

An'tartide sf: l'~ Antarctica

ante'dente [ante'tʃe'dɛnte] ag preceding, previous

ante'fatto sm previous events pl; previous history

antegu'erra sm pre-war period

ante'nato sm ancestor, forefather

an'tenna sf (RADIO, TV) aerial; (ZOOL) antenna, feeler; (NAUT) yard; ~ **parabolica** satellite dish

ante'prima sf preview

anteri'ore ag (ruota, zampa) front; (fatti) previous, preceding

antia'ereo, a ag anti-aircraft

antia'tomico, a, ci, che ag antinuclear; **rifugio** ~ fallout shelter

antibi'otico, a, ci, che ag, sm antibiotic

anti'camera sf anteroom; **fare** ~ to wait (for an audience)

antichità [antiki'ta] sf inv antiquity; (oggetto) antique

antici'pare [antitʃi'pare] vt (consegna, visita) to bring forward, anticipate; (somma di denaro) to pay in advance; (notizia) to disclose ♦ vi to be ahead of time; **anticipazi'one** sf anticipation; (di notizia) advance information; (somma di denaro) advance; **an'ticipo** sm anticipation; (di denaro) advance; **in anticipo** early, in advance

an'tico, a, chi, che ag (quadro, mobili) antique; (dell'antichità) ancient; **all'~a** old-fashioned

anticoncezio'nale [antikontʃettsjo'nale] sm contraceptive

anticonfor'mista, i, e ag, smlf nonconformist

anti'corpo sm antibody

an'tidoto sm antidote

anti'furto sm (anche: **sistema** ~) anti-theft device

anti'gelo [anti'dʒɛlo] ag (liquido) ~ (per motore) antifreeze; (per cristalli) de-icer

An'tille sfpl: **le** ~ the West Indies

antin'cendio [antin'tʃendjo] ag inv fire cpd

antio'rario [antio'rarjo] ag: **in senso** ~ anticlockwise

anti'pasto sm hors d'œuvre

antipa'tia sf antipathy, dislike; **anti'patico, a, ci, che** ag unpleasant, disagreeable

antiquari'ato sm antique trade; **un oggetto d'~** an antique

anti'quario sm antique dealer

anti'quato, a ag antiquated, old-fashioned

antise'mita, i, e ag anti-Semitic

anti'settico, a, ci, che ag, sm antiseptic

antista'minico, a, ci, che ag, sm

antihistamine

antolo'gia, 'gie [antolo'dʒia] *sf* anthology

anu'lare *ag* ring *cpd* ♦ *sm* third finger

'anzi ['antsi] *av* (*invece*) on the contrary; (*o meglio*) or rather, or better still

anzianità [antsjani'ta] *sf* old age; (*AMM*) seniority

anzi'ano, a [an'tsjano] *ag* old; (*AMM*) senior ♦ *sm/f* old person; senior member

anziché [antsi'ke] *cong* rather than

anzi'tutto [antsi'tutto] *av* first of all

apa'tia *sf* apathy, indifference

a'patico, a, ci, che *ag* apathetic

'ape *sf* bee

aperi'tivo *sm* apéritif

a'perto, a *pp di* **aprire** ♦ *ag* open; all'~ in the open (air)

aper'tura *sf* opening; (*ampiezza*) width, spread; (*POL*) approach; (*FOT*) aperture; ~ **alare** wing span

'apice ['apitʃe] *sm* apex; (*fig*) height

ap'nea *sf*: **immergersi in ~** to dive without breathing apparatus

a'postolo *sm* apostle

a'postrofo *sm* apostrophe

appa'gare *vt* to satisfy; ~rsi *vr*: ~rsi di to be satisfied with

ap'palto *sm* (*COMM*) contract; dare/prendere in ~ **un lavoro** to let out/undertake a job on contract

appan'nare *vt* (*vetro*) to mist; (*metallo*) to tarnish; (*vista*) to dim; ~rsi *vr* to mist over; to tarnish; to grow dim

appa'rato *sm* equipment, machinery; (*ANAT*) apparatus; ~ **scenico** (*TEATRO*) props *pl*

apparecchi'are [apparek'kjare] *vt* to prepare; (*tavola*) to set ♦ *vi* to set the table; **apparecchia'tura** *sf* equipment; (*macchina*) machine, device

appa'recchio [appa'rekkjo] *sm* piece of apparatus, device; (*aeroplano*) aircraft *inv*; ~ **televisivo/telefonico** television set/telephone

appa'rente *ag* apparent; **appa'renza** *sf* appearance; **in** *o* **all'apparenza** apparently, to all appearances

appa'rire *vi* to appear; (*sembrare*) to seem, appear; **appari'scente** *ag* (*colore*) garish, gaudy; (*bellezza*) striking

ap'parso, a *pp di* **apparire**

apparta'mento *sm* flat (*BRIT*), apartment (*US*)

appar'tarsi *vr* to withdraw; **appar'tato, a** *ag* (*luogo*) secluded

apparte'nere *vi*: ~ **a** to belong to

appassio'nare *vt* to thrill; (*commuovere*) to move; ~rsi **a qc** to take a great interest in sth; to be deeply moved by sth; **appassio'nato, a** *ag* passionate; (*entusiasta*): **appassionato (di)** keen (on)

appas'sire *vi* to wither

appel'larsi *vr* (*ricorrere*): ~ **a** to appeal to; (*DIR*): ~ **contro** to appeal against; **ap'pello** *sm* roll-call; (*implorazione*, *DIR*) appeal; **fare appello a** to appeal to

ap'pena *av* (*a stento*) hardly, scarcely; (*solamente*, *da poco*) just ♦ *cong* as soon as; (*non*) ~ **furono arrivati ... as** soon as they had arrived ...; ~ ... **che** *o* **quando** no sooner ... than

ap'pendere *vt* to hang (up)

appen'dice [appen'ditʃe] *sf* appendix; **romanzo d'~** popular serial

appendi'cite [appendi'tʃite] *sf* appendicitis

Appen'nini *smpl*: **gli ~** the Apennines

appesan'tire *vt* to make heavy; ~rsi *vr* to grow stout

ap'peso, a *pp di* **appendere**

appe'tito *sm* appetite; **appeti'toso, a** *ag* appetising; (*fig*) attractive, desirable

appia'nare *vt* to level; (*fig*) to smooth away, iron out

appiat'tire *vt* to flatten; ~rsi *vr* to become flatter; (*farsi piatto*) to flatten o.s.; ~**rsi al suolo** to lie flat on the ground

appic'care vt: ~ **il fuoco a** to set fire to, set on fire

appicci'care [appittʃiˈkare] vt to stick; (fig): ~ **qc a qn** to palm sth off on sb; ~**rsi** vr to stick; (fig: persona) to cling

appi'eno av fully

appigli'arsi [appiʎˈʎarsi] vr: ~ **a** (afferrarsi) to take hold of; (fig) to cling to; **ap'piglio** sm hold; (fig) pretext

appiso'larsi vr to doze off

applau'dire vt, vi to applaud; **ap'plauso** sm applause

appli'care vt to apply; (regolamento) to enforce; ~**rsi** vr to apply o.s.; **applicazi'one** sf application; enforcement

appoggi'are [appodˈdʒare] vt (mettere contro): ~ **qc a qc** to lean o rest sth against sth; (fig: sostenere) to support; ~**rsi** vr: ~**rsi a** to lean against; (fig) to rely upon; **ap'poggio** sm support

appollai'arsi vr (anche fig) to perch

ap'porre vt to affix

appor'tare vt to bring

apposita'mente av specially; (apposta) on purpose

ap'posito, a ag appropriate

ap'posta av on purpose, deliberately

appos'tarsi vr to lie in wait

ap'prendere vt (imparare) to learn; (comprendere) to grasp

appren'dista, i, e smf apprentice

apprensi'one sf apprehension; **appren'sivo, a** ag apprehensive

ap'presso av (accanto, vicino) close by, near; (dietro) behind; (dopo, più tardi) after, later ♦ ag inv (dopo): **il giorno ~** the next day; ~ **a** (vicino a) near, close to

appres'tare vt to prepare, get ready; ~**rsi** vr: ~**rsi a fare qc** to prepare o get ready to do sth

ap'pretto sm starch

apprez'zabile [appretˈtsabile] ag

noteworthy, significant

apprezza'mento [apprettsaˈmento] sm appreciation; (giudizio) opinion

apprez'zare [appretˈtsare] vt to appreciate

ap'proccio [apˈprɔttʃo] sm approach

appro'dare vi (NAUT) to land; (fig): **non ~ a nulla** to come to nothing; **ap'prodo** sm landing; (luogo) landing-place

approfit'tare vi: ~ **di** to make the most of, profit by

approfon'dire vt to deepen; (fig) to study in depth

appropri'arsi vr: ~ **di qc** to appropriate sth

appropri'ato, a ag appropriate

approssi'marsi vr: ~ **a** to approach

approssima'tivo, a ag approximate, rough; (impreciso) inexact, imprecise

appro'vare vt (condotta, azione) to approve of; (candidato) to pass; (progetto di legge) to approve; **approvazi'one** sf approval

approvvigio'nare [approvvidʒoˈnare] vt to supply; ~ **qn di qc** to supply sb with sth

appunta'mento sm appointment; (amoroso) date; **darsi** ~ to arrange to meet (one another)

appun'tato sm (CARABINIERI) corporal

ap'punto sm note; (rimprovero) reproach ♦ av (proprio) exactly, just; **per l'~!, ~!** exactly!

appu'rare vt to check, verify

apribot'tiglie [apribotˈtiʎʎe] sm inv bottleopener

a'prile sm April

a'prire vt to open; (via, cadavere) to open up; (gas, luce, acqua) to turn on ♦ vi to open; ~**rsi** vr to open; ~**rsi a qn** to confide in sb, open one's heart to sb

apris'catole sm inv tin (BRIT) o can opener

a'quario sm = **acquario**

'aquila sf (ZOOL) eagle; (fig) genius

aqui'lone *sm (giocattolo)* kite; *(vento)* North wind

A'rabia 'Saudita *sf:* **l'~** Saudi Arabia

'arabo, a *ag, sm/f* Arab ♦ *sm (LING)* Arabic

a'rachide [a'rakide] *sf* peanut

ara'gosta [a'rakide] *sf* crayfish; lobster

a'rancia, ce [a'rantʃa] *sf* orange; **aranci'ata** *sf* orangeade; **a'rancio** *sm (BOT)* orange tree; *(colore)* orange ♦ *ag inv (colore)* orange; **aranci'one** *ag inv:* (*color*) arancione bright orange

a'rare *vt* to plough *(BRIT)*, plow *(US)*

a'ratro *sm* plough *(BRIT)*, plow *(US)*

a'razzo [a'rattso] *sm* tapestry

arbi'trare *vt (SPORT)* to referee; to umpire; *(DIR)* to arbitrate

arbi'trario, a *ag* arbitrary

ar'bitrio *sm* will; *(abuso, sopruso)* arbitrary act

'arbitro *sm* arbiter, judge; *(DIR)* arbitrator; *(SPORT)* referee; *(: TENNIS, CRICKET)* umpire

ar'busto *sm* shrub

'arca, che *sf (sarcofago)* sarcophagus; **l'~ di Noè** Noah's ark

ar'cangelo [ar'kandʒelo] *sm* archangel

ar'cata *sf (ARCHIT, ANAT)* arch; *(ordine di archi)* arcade

archeolo'gia [arkeolo'dʒia] *sf* arch(a)eology; **arche'ologo, a, gi, ghe** *sm/f* arch(a)eologist

ar'chetto [ar'ketto] *sm (MUS)* bow

archi'tettare [arkitet'tare] *vt (fig: ideare)* to devise; *(: macchinare)* to plan, concoct

archi'tetto [arki'tetto] *sm* architect; **architet'tura** *sf* architecture

ar'chivio [ar'kivjo] *sm* archives *pl*; *(INFORM)* file

arci'ere [ar'tʃere] *sm* archer

ar'cigno, a [ar'tʃiɲɲo] *ag* grim, severe

arci'vescovo [artʃi'veskovo] *sm* archbishop

'arco *sm (arma, MUS)* bow; *(ARCHIT)* arch; *(MAT)* arc

arcoba'leno *sm* rainbow

arcu'ato, a *ag* curved, bent; **dalle gambe ~e** bow-legged

ar'dente *ag* burning; *(fig)* burning, ardent

'ardere *vt, vi* to burn

ar'desia *sf* slate

ar'dire *vi* to dare ♦ *sm* daring; **ar'dito, a** *ag* brave, daring, bold; *(sfacciato)* bold

ar'dore *sm* blazing heat; *(fig)* ardour, fervour

'arduo, a *ag* arduous, difficult

'area *sf* area; *(EDIL)* land, ground

a'rena *sf* arena; *(per corride)* bullring; *(sabbia)* sand

are'narsi *vr* to run aground

areo'plano *sm* = **aeroplano**

'argano *sm* winch

argente'ria [ardʒente'ria] *sf* silverware, silver

Argen'tina [ardʒen'tina] *sf:* **l'~** Argentina; **argen'tino, a** *ag, sm/f* Argentinian

ar'gento [ar'dʒento] *sm* silver; **~ vivo** quicksilver

ar'gilla [ar'dʒilla] *sf* clay

'argine [ar'dʒine] *sm* embankment, bank; *(diga)* dyke, dike

argo'mento *sm* argument; *(motivo)* motive; *(materia, tema)* subject

argu'ire *vt* to deduce

ar'guto, a *ag* sharp, quick-witted; **ar'guzia** *sf* wit; *(battuta)* witty remark

'aria *sf* air; *(espressione, aspetto)* air, look; *(MUS: melodia)* tune; *(: di opera)* aria; **mandare all'~ qc** to ruin o upset sth; **all'~ aperta** in the open (air)

'arido, a *ag* arid

arieggi'are [arjed'dʒare] *vt (cambiare aria)* to air; *(imitare)* to imitate

ari'ete *sm* ram; *(MIL)* battering ram; *(dello zodiaco)*: **A~** Aries

a'ringa, ghe [a'ringa] *sf* herring *inv*

'arista *sf (CUC)* chine of pork

aristo'cratico, a, ci, che ag aristocratic

arit'metica sf arithmetic

arlec'chino [arlek'kino] sm harlequin

'arma, i sf weapon, arm; (parte dell'esercito) arm; chiamare alle ~i to call up (BRIT), draft (US); sotto le ~i in the army (o forces); alle ~i! to arms!; ~ **da fuoco** firearm

ar'madio sm cupboard; (per abiti) wardrobe; ~ **a muro** built-in cupboard

armamen'tario sm equipment, instruments pl

arma'mento sm (MIL) armament; (: materiale) arms pl, weapons pl; (NAUT) fitting out; manning

ar'mare vt to arm; (arma da fuoco) to cock; (NAUT: nave) to rig, fit out; to man; (EDIL: volta, galleria) to prop up, shore up; ~**rsi** vr to arm o.s.; (MIL) to take up arms; **ar'mata** sf (MIL) army; (NAUT) fleet; **arma'tore** sm shipowner; **arma'tura** sf (struttura di sostegno) framework; (impalcatura) scaffolding; (STORIA) armour no pl, suit of armour

armeggi'are [armed'dʒare] vi: ~ (intorno a qc) to mess about (with sth)

armis'tizio [armis'tittsjo] sm armistice

armo'nia sf harmony; **armonico, che** ag (MUS) harmonica; ~ **a bocca** mouth organ; **ar'monico, a, ci, che** ag harmonic; (fig) harmonious; **armoni'oso, a** ag harmonious

armoniz'zare [armonid'dzare] vt to harmonize; (colori, abiti) to match ♦ vi to be in harmony; to match

ar'nese sm tool, implement; (oggetto indeterminato) thing, contraption; **male in** ~ (malvestito) badly dressed; (di salute malferma) in poor health; (di condizioni economiche) down-at heel

'arnia sf hive

a'roma, i sm aroma; fragrance; ~**i** smpl (CUC) herbs and spices; **aro'matico, a, ci, che** ag aromatic; (cibo) spicy

'arpa sf (MUS) harp

ar'peggio [ar'pedd ʒo] sm (MUS) arpeggio

ar'pia sf (anche fig) harpy

arpi'one sm (gancio) hook; (cardine) hinge; (PESCA) harpoon

arrabat'tarsi vr to do all one can, strive

arrabbi'are vi (cane) to be affected with rabies; ~**rsi** vr (essere preso dall'ira) to get angry, fly into a rage; **arrabbi'ato, a** ag rabid, with rabies; furious, angry

arraf'fare vt to snatch, seize; (sottrarre) to pinch

arrampi'carsi vr to climb (up)

arran'care vi to limp, hobble

arran'giare [arran'dʒare] vt to arrange; ~**rsi** vr to manage, do the best one can

arre'care vt to bring; (causare) to cause

arreda'mento sm (studio) interior design; (mobili etc) furnishings pl

arre'dare vt to furnish; **arreda'tore, 'trice** sm/f interior designer; **ar'redo** sm fittings pl, furnishings pl

ar'rendersi vr to surrender

arres'tare vt (fermare) to stop, halt; (catturare) to arrest; ~**rsi** vr (fermarsi) to stop; **ar'resto** sm (cessazione) stopping; (fermata) stop; (cattura, MED) arrest; **subire un arresto** to come to a stop o standstill; **mettere agli arresti** to place under arrest; **arresti domiciliari** house arrest sg

arre'trare vt, vi to withdraw; **arre'trato, a** ag (lavoro) behind schedule; (paese, bambino) backward; (numero di giornale) back cpd; **arretrati** smpl arrears pl

arric'chire [arrik'kire] vt to enrich; ~**rsi** vr to become rich

arricci'are [arrit'tʃare] vt to curl;

il naso to turn up one's nose

ar'ringa, ghe *sf* harangue; (*DIR*) address by counsel

arrischi'are [arris'kjare] *vt* to risk; ~rsi *vr* to venture, dare; arri'schi'ato, a *ag* risky; (*temerario*) reckless, rash

arri'vare *vi* to arrive; (*accadere*) to happen, occur; ~ a (*livello, grado etc*) to reach; lui arriva a Roma alle 7 he gets to *o* arrives at Rome at 7; non ci arrivo I can't reach it; (*fig: non capisco*) I can't understand it

arrive'derci [arrive'dertʃi] *escl* goodbye!

arrive'derla *escl* (*forma di cortesia*) goodbye!

arri'vista, i, e *smf* go-getter

ar'rivo *sm* arrival; (*SPORT*) finish, finishing line

arro'gante *ag* arrogant

arro'lare *vb* = arruolare

arros'sire *vi* (*per vergogna, timidezza*) to blush, flush; (*per gioia, rabbia*) to flush

arros'tire *vt* to roast; (*pane*) to toast; (*ai ferri*) to grill

ar'rosto *sm, ag inv* roast

arro'tare *vt* to sharpen; (*investire con un veicolo*) to run over

arroto'lare *vt* to roll up

arroton'dare *vt* (*forma, oggetto*) to round; (*stipendio*) to add to; (*somma*) to round off

arrovel'larsi *vr*: ~ (il cervello) to rack one's brains

arruf'fare *vt* to ruffle; (*fili*) to tangle; (*fig: questione*) to confuse

arruggi'nire [arruddʒi'nire] *vt* to rust; ~rsi *vr* to rust; (*fig*) to become rusty

arruo'lare (*MIL*) *vt* to enlist; ~rsi *vr* to enlist, join up

arse'nale *sm* (*MIL*) arsenal; (*cantiere navale*) dockyard

'arso, a *pp di* ardere ♦ (*bruciato*) burnt; (*arido*) dry; ar'sura *sf* (*calore opprimente*) burning heat; (*siccità*) drought

'arte *sf* art; (*abilità*) skill

arte'fatto, a *ag* (*cibo*) adulterated; (*fig: modi*) artificial

ar'tefice [ar'tefitʃe] *smf* craftsman/woman; (*autore*) author

ar'teria *sf* artery

'artico, a, ci, che *ag* Arctic

artico'lare (*ANAT*) *ag* of the joints, articular ♦ *vt* to articulate; (*suddividere*) to divide, split up; articola'zi'one *sf* articulation; (*ANAT, TECN*) joint

ar'ticolo *sm* article; ~ di fondo (*STAMPA*) leader, leading article

'Artide *sm*: l'~ the Arctic

artifici'ale [artifi'tʃale] *ag* artificial

arti'ficio [arti'fitʃo] *sm* (*espediente*) trick, artifice; (*ricerca di effetto*) artificiality

artigia'nato *sm* (*attività*) craftsmanship; craftsmen *pl*

artigi'ano, a [arti'dʒano] *sm* craftsman/woman

artiglie'ria [artiʎʎe'ria] *sf* artillery

ar'tiglio [ar'tiʎʎo] *sm* claw; (*di rapaci*) talon

ar'tista, i, e *smf* artist; ar'tistico, a, ci, che *ag* artistic

'arto *sm* (*ANAT*) limb

ar'trite *sf* (*MED*) arthritis

ar'trosi *sf* osteoarthritis

ar'zillo, a [ar'dzillo] *ag* lively, sprightly

a'scella [aʃ'ʃella] *sf* (*ANAT*) armpit

ascen'dente [aʃʃen'dente] *sm* ancestor; (*fig*) ascendancy; (*ASTR*) ascendant

ascensi'one [aʃʃen'sjone] *sf* (*ALPINISMO*) ascent; (*REL*): l'A~ the Ascension

ascen'sore [aʃʃen'sore] *sm* lift

a'scesa [aʃ'ʃesa] *sf* ascent; (*al trono*) accession

a'scesso [aʃ'ʃesso] *sm* (*MED*) abscess

'ascia ['aʃʃa] (*pl* 'asce) *sf* axe

asciugaca'pelli [aʃʃugaka'pelli] *sm* hair-drier

asciuga'mano [aʃʃuga'mano] *sm* towel

asciu'gare [aʃʃu'gare] vt to dry; ~rsi vr to dry o.s.; (diventare asciutto) to dry

asci'utto, a [aʃ'ʃutto] ag dry; (fig: magro) lean; (: burbero) curt; restare a bocca ~a (fig) to be disappointed

ascol'tare vt to listen to; **ascol'ta'tore, 'trice** smf listener; **as'colto** sm: essere o stare in ascolto to be listening; dare o prestare ascolto (a) to pay attention (to)

as'falto sm asphalt

asfissi'are vt to suffocate, asphyxiate; (fig) to bore to tears

'Asia sf: l'~ Asia; **asi'atico, a, ci, che** ag, smf Asiatic, Asian

a'silo sm refuge, sanctuary; ~ (d'infanzia) nursery(-school); ~ nido crèche; ~ politico political asylum

'asino sm donkey, ass

'asma sf asthma

'asola sf buttonhole

as'parago, gi sm asparagus no pl

aspet'tare vt to wait for; (anche COMM) to await; (aspettarsi) to expect ♦ vi to wait; ~rsi vr to expect; ~ un bambino to be expecting (a baby); questo non me l'aspettavo I wasn't expecting this; **aspetta'tiva** sf wait; expectation; **inferiore all'aspettativa** worse than expected; **essere in aspettativa** (AMM) to be on leave of absence

as'petto sm (apparenza) aspect, appearance, look; (punto di vista) point of view; di bell'~ good-looking

aspi'rante ag (attore etc) aspiring ♦ smf/c candidate, applicant

aspira'polvere sm inv vacuum cleaner

aspi'rare vt (respirare) to breathe in, inhale; (sog: apparecchi) to suck (up) ♦ vi: ~ a to aspire to; **aspi'ratore** sm extractor fan

aspi'rina sf aspirin

aspor'tare vt (anche MED) to remove, take away

'aspro, a ag (sapore) sour, tart; (odore) acrid, pungent; (voce, clima, fig) harsh; (superficie) rough; (paesaggio) rugged

assaggi'are [assad'dʒare] vt to taste

assag'gini [assad'dʒini] smpl (CUC) selection of first courses

as'sai av (molto) a lot, much; (: con ag) very; (a sufficienza) enough ♦ ag inv (quantità) a lot of, much; (numero) a lot of, many; ~ contento very pleased

assa'lire vt to attack, assail

as'salto sm attack, assault

assapo'rare vt to savour

assassi'nare vt to murder; to assassinate; (fig) to ruin; **assas'sinio** sm murder; assassination; **assas'sino, a** ag murderous ♦ sm murderer; assassin

'asse sm (TECN) axle; (MAT) axis ♦ sf board; ~ sf da stiro ironing board

assedi'are vt to besiege; **as'sedio** sm siege

asse'gnare [assen'nare] vt to assign, allot; (premio) to award

as'segno [as'senno] sm allowance; (anche: ~ bancario) cheque (BRIT), check (US); **contro** ~ cash on delivery; ~ **circolare** bank draft; ~ **sbarrato** crossed cheque; ~ **di viaggio** traveller's cheque; ~ **a vuoto** dud cheque; ~i **familiari** ≈ child benefit no pl

assem'blea sf assembly

assen'nato, a ag sensible

as'senso sm assent, consent

as'sente ag absent; (fig) faraway, vacant; **as'senza** sf absence

asses'sore sm (POL) councillor

asses'tare vt (mettere in ordine) to put in order, arrange; ~rsi vr to settle in; ~ **un colpo a qn** to deal sb a blow

asse'tato, a ag thirsty, parched

as'setto sm order, arrangement; (NAUT, AER) trim; **in** ~ **di guerra** on a war footing

assicu'rare vt (accertare) to ensure; (infondere certezza) to assure;

(fermare, legare) to make fast, secure; *(fare un contratto di assicurazione)* to insure; ~rsi vr *(accertarsi)*: ~rsi **(di)** to make sure (of); *(contro il furto etc)*: ~rsi **(contro)** to insure o.s. (against); **assicu'rata** sf *(anche: lettera assicurata)* registered letter; **assicu'rato, a** ag insured; **assicurazi'one** sf assurance; insurance

assidera'mento sm exposure

as'siduo, a ag *(costante)* assiduous; *(frequentatore etc)* regular

assi'eme av *(insieme)* together; ~ a (together) with

assil'lare vt to pester, torment

as'sillo sm *(fig)* worrying thought

as'sise sfpl *(DIR)* assizes; **Corte d'A~** Court of Assizes; ≈ Crown Court *(BRIT)*

assis'tente smf assistant; ~ **sociale** social worker; ~ **di volo** *(AER)* steward/stewardess

assis'tenza [assis'tentsa] sf assistance; ~ **ospedaliera** free hospital treatment; ~ **sanitaria** health service; ~ **sociale** welfare services pl

as'sistere vt *(aiutare)* to assist, help; *(curare)* to treat ♦ vi: ~ **a** *(qc)* *(essere presente)* to be present (at sth), to attend (sth)

'asso sm ace; **piantare qn in** ~ **to** leave sb in the lurch

associ'are [asso't∫are] vt to associate; *(rendere partecipe)*: ~ **qn a** *(affari)* to take sb into partnership in; *(partito)* to make sb a member of; ~rsi vr to enter into partnership; ~rsi **a** to become a member of, join; *(dolori, gioie)* to share in; ~ **qn alle carceri** to take sb to prison

associazi'one [assot∫at'tsjone] sf association; *(COMM)* association, society; ~ **a delinquere** *(DIR)* criminal association

asso'dato, a ag well-founded

assog'gettare [assoddʒet'tare] vt to subject, subjugate

asso'lato, a ag sunny

assol'dare vt to recruit

as'solto, a pp di **assolvere**

assoluta'mente av absolutely

asso'luto, a ag absolute

assoluzi'one [assolut'tsjone] sf *(DIR)* acquittal; *(REL)* absolution

as'solvere vt *(DIR)* to acquit; *(REL)* to absolve; *(adempiere)* to carry out, perform

assomigli'are [assomi∆'∆are] vi: ~ **a** to resemble, look like

asson'nato, a ag sleepy

asso'pirsi vr to doze off

assor'bente ag absorbent ♦ sm: ~ **igienico** sanitary towel; ~ **interno** tampon

assor'bire vt to absorb; *(fig: far proprio)* to assimilate

assor'dare vt to deafen

assorti'mento sm assortment

assor'tito, a ag assorted; matched, matching

as'sorto, a ag absorbed, engrossed

assottigli'are [assotti∆'∆are] vt to make thin, to thin; *(aguzzare)* to sharpen; *(ridurre)* to reduce; ~rsi vr to grow thin; *(fig: ridursi)* to be reduced

assue'fare vt to accustom; ~rsi **a** to get used to, accustom o.s. to

as'sumere vt *(impiegato)* to take on, engage; *(responsabilità)* to assume, take upon o.s.: *(contegno, espressione)* to assume, put on; *(droga)* to consume; **as'sunto, a** pp di **assumere** ♦ sm *(tesi)* proposition

assurdità sf inv absurdity; **dire delle** ~ to talk nonsense

as'surdo, a ag absurd

'asta sf pole; *(modo di vendita)* auction

astan'teria sf casualty department

as'temio, a ag teetotal ♦ smif teetotaller

aste'nersi vr: ~ **(da)** to abstain (from), refrain (from); *(POL)* to abstain (from)

aste'risco, schi sm asterisk

'astice ['astit∫e] sm lobster

asti'nenza [asti'nentsa] sf abstinence; **essere in crisi di** ~ to suffer from withdrawal symptoms

'**astio** sm rancour, resentment

as'**tratto, a** ag abstract

'**astro** sm star

'**astro...** prefisso: **astrolo'gia** [astrolo'dʒia] sf astrology; **as'trologo, a, ghi, ghe** smf astrologer; **astro'nauta, i, e** smf astronaut; **astro'nave** sf space ship; **astro-no'mia** sf astronomy; **astro-'nomico, a, ci, che** ag astronomic(al)

as'**tuccio** [as'tuttʃo] sm case, box, holder

as'**tuto, a** ag astute, cunning, shrewd; **as'tuzia** sf astuteness, shrewdness; (azione) trick

A'**tene** sf Athens

ate'**neo** sm university

'**ateo, a** ag, smf atheist

at'**lante** sm atlas

at'**lantico, a, ci, che** ag Atlantic ♦ sm: l'A~, l'Oceano A~ the Atlantic, the Atlantic Ocean

at'**leta, i, e** smf athlete; **at'letica** sf athletics sg; **atletica leggera** track and field events pl; **atletica pesante** weightlifting and wrestling

atmos'**fera** sf atmosphere

a'**tomico, a, ci, che** ag atomic; (nucleare) atomic, atom cpd; **nuclear**

'**atomo** sm atom

'**atrio** sm entrance hall, lobby

a'**troce** [a'trotʃe] ag (che provoca orrore) dreadful; (terribile) atrocious

attacca'**mento** sm (fig) attachment, affection

attacca'**panni** sm hook, peg; (mobile) hall stand

attac'**care** vt (unire) to attach; (cucendo) to sew on; (far aderire) to stick (on); (appendere) to hang (up); (assalire: anche fig) to attack; (iniziare) to begin, start; (fig: contagiare) to pass on ♦ vi to stick, adhere; ~**rsi** vr to stick, adhere, here; ~**rsi** vr to stick, adhere; (trasmettersi per contagio) to be contagious; (afferrarsi): ~**rsi (a)** to cling (to); (fig: affezionarsi): ~**rsi (a)** to become attached (to); ~ **discorso** to

start a conversation; **at'tacco, chi** sm (azione offensiva: anche fig) attack; (MED) attack, fit; (SCI) binding; (ELETTR) socket

atteggia'**mento** [atteddʒa'mento] sm attitude

atteggi'**arsi** [atted'dʒarsi] vr: ~ **a** to pose as

attem'**pato, a** ag elderly

at'**tendere** vt to wait for, await ♦ vi: ~ **a** to attend to

atten'**dibile** ag (storia) credible; (testimone) reliable

atte'**nersi** vr: ~ **a** to keep o stick to

atten'**tare** vi: ~ **a** to make an attempt on; **atten'tato** sm attack; attentato alla vita di qn attempt on sb's life

at'**tento, a** ag attentive; (accurato) careful, thorough; **stare a qc** to pay attention to sth ♦ escl be careful!

attenu'**ante** sf (DIR) extenuating circumstance

attenu'**are** vt to attenuate; (dolore, rumore) to lessen, deaden; (pena, tasse) to alleviate; ~**rsi** vr to ease, abate

attenzi'**one** [atten'tsjone] sf attention ♦ escl watch out!, be careful!

atter'**raggio** [atter'raddʒo] sm landing

atter'**rare** vt to bring down ♦ vi to land

atter'**rire** vt to terrify

at'**tesa** sf waiting; (tempo trascorso aspettando) wait; **essere in attesa di qc** to be waiting for sth

at'**teso, a** pp di attendere

attes'**tato** sm certificate

'**attico, ci** sm attic

at'**tiguo, a** ag adjacent, adjoining

attil'**lato, a** ag (vestito) close-fitting, tight; (persona) dressed up

'**attimo** sm moment; **in un ~ in a** moment

atti'**nente** ag: ~ **a** relating to, concerning

atti'**rare** vt to attract

atti'**tudine** sf (disposizione) aptitude; (*atteggiamento*) attitude

atti'vare *vt* to activate; (*far funzionare*) to set going, start

attività *sf inv* activity; (*COMM*) assets *pl*

at'tivo, a *ag* active; (*COMM*) profit-making, credit *cpd* ♦ *sm* (*COMM*) assets *pl*; **in ~** in credit

attiz'zare [attit'tsare] *vt* (*fuoco*) to poke

'atto *sm* act; (*azione, gesto*) action, act, deed; (*DIR: documento*) deed, document; **~i** *smpl* (*di congressi etc*) proceedings; **mettere in ~** to put into action; **fare ~ di fare qc** to make as if to do sth

at'tonito, a *ag* dumbfounded, astonished

attorcigli'are [attortʃiʎ'ʎare] *vt* to twist; **~rsi** *vr* to twist

at'tore, 'trice *smf* actor/actress

at'torno *av* round, around, about; **~ a** round, around, about

at'tracco, chi *sm* (*NAUT*) docking *no pl*; berth

attra'ente *ag* attractive

at'trarre *vt* to attract; **attrat'tiva** *sf* (*fig: fascino*) attraction, charm; **at'tratto, a** *pp di* **attrarre**

attraversa'mento *sm*: **~ pedonale** pedestrian crossing

attraver'sare *vt* to cross; (*città, bosco, fig: periodo*) to go through; (*sog: fiume*) to run through

attra'verso *prep* through; (*da una parte all'altra*) across

attrazi'one [attrat'tsjone] *sf* attraction

attrez'zare [attret'tsare] *vt* to equip; (*NAUT*) to rig; **attrezza'tura** *sf* equipment *no pl*; rigging; **attrezzo** *sm* tool, instrument; (*SPORT*) piece of equipment

attribu'ire *vt*: **~ qc a qn** (*assegnare*) to give o award sth to sb; (*quadro etc*) to attribute sth to sb; **attri'buto** *sm* attribute

at'trice [at'tritʃe] *sf vedi* **attore**

at'trito *sm* (*anche fig*) friction

attu'ale *ag* (*presente*) present; (*di*

attualità) topical; (*che è in atto*) actual; **attualità** *sf inv* topicality; (*avvenimento*) current event; **attual'mente** *av* at the moment, at present

attu'are *vt* to carry out; **~rsi** *vr* to be realized

attu'tire *vt* to deaden, reduce

au'dace [au'datʃe] *ag* audacious, daring, bold; (*provocante*) provocative; (*sfacciato*) impudent, bold; **au'dacia** *sf* audacity, daring; boldness; provocativeness; impudence

audiovi'sivo, a *ag* audiovisual

audizi'one [audit'tsjone] *sf* hearing; (*MUS*) audition

'auge ['audʒe] *sf*: **in ~** popular

augu'rare *vt* to wish; **~rsi qc** to hope for sth

au'gurio *sm* (*presagio*) omen; (*voto di benessere etc*) (good) wish; **essere di buon/cattivo ~** to be of good omen/be ominous; **fare gli ~i a qn** to give sb one's best wishes; **tanti ~i!** all the best!

'aula (*scolastica*) classroom; (*universitaria*) lecture theatre; (*di edificio pubblico*) hall

aumen'tare *vt, vi* to increase; **au'mento** *sm* increase

au'reola *sf* halo

au'rora *sf* dawn

ausili'are *ag, sm, smf* auxiliary

aus'picio [aus'pitʃo] *sm* omen; (*protezione*) patronage; **sotto gli ~i di** under the auspices of

aus'tero, a *ag* austere

Aus'tralia *sf*: **l'~** Australia; **australi'ano, a** *ag, sm/f* Australian

'Austria *sf*: **l'~** Austria; **aus'triaco, a, ci, che** *ag, sm/f* Austrian

au'tentico, a, ci, che *ag* (*quadro, firma*) authentic, genuine; (*fatto*) true, genuine

au'tista, i *sm* driver

'auto *sf inv* car

autoade'sivo, a *ag* self-adhesive ♦ *sm* sticker

autobiogra'fia *sf* autobiography

auto'botte *sf* tanker

'autobus *sm inv* bus

auto'carro *sm* lorry (BRIT), truck

autocorri'era *sf* coach, bus

au'tografo, a *ag, sm* autograph

auto'linea *sf* bus company

au'toma, i *sm* automaton

auto'matico, a, ci, che *ag* automatic ♦ *sm* (bottone) snap fastener; (fucile) automatic

automazi'one [automat'tsjone] *sf* automation

auto'mezzo [auto'mɛddzo] *sm* motor vehicle

auto'mobile *sf* (motor) car

autono'mia *sf* autonomy; (di volo) range

au'tonomo, a *ag* autonomous, independent

autop'sia *sf* post-mortem (examination), autopsy

auto'radio *sf inv* (apparecchio) car radio; (autoveicolo) radio car

au'tore, 'trice *smf* author

auto'revole *ag* authoritative; (persona) influential

autori'messa *sf* garage

autorità *sf inv* authority

autoriz'zare [autorid'dzare] *vt* (permettere) to authorize; (giustificare) to allow, sanction; **autorizzazi'one** *sf* authorization

autoscu'ola *sf* driving school

autos'top *sm* hitchhiking; **autostop'pista, i, e** *smf* hitchhiker

autos'trada *sf* motorway (BRIT), highway (US)

auto'treno *sm* articulated lorry (BRIT), semi (trailer) (US)

autovei'colo *sm* motor vehicle

autovet'tura *sf* (motor) car

au'tunno *sm* autumn

avam'braccio [avam'brattʃo] (pl (f) -cia) *sm* forearm

avangu'ardia *sf* vanguard

a'vanti *av* (stato in luogo) in front; (moto: andare, venire) forward; (tempo: prima) before ♦ *prep* (luogo): ~ a before, in front of; (tempo): ~ **Cristo** before Christ ♦ *escl*

(entrate) come (o go) in!; (MIL) forward!; (coraggio) come on! ♦ *sm inv* (SPORT) forward; ~ **e indietro** backwards and forwards; **andare** ~ to go forward; (continuare) to go on; (precedere) to go (on) ahead; (orologio) to be fast; **essere** ~ **negli studi** to be well advanced with one's studies

avanza'mento [avantsa'mento] *sm* progress; promotion

avan'zare [avan'tsare] *vt* (spostare in avanti) to move forward, advance; (domanda) to put forward; (promuovere) to promote; (essere creditore): ~ **qc da qn** to be owed sth by sb ♦ *vi* (andare avanti) to move forward, advance; (fig: progredire) to make progress; (essere d'avanzo) to be left, remain; **avan'zata** *sf* (MIL) advance; **a'vanzo** *sm* (residuo) remains *pl*, left-overs *pl*; (MAT) remainder; (COMM) surplus; **averne d'avanzo di qc** to have more than enough of sth; **avanzo di galera** (fig) jailbird

ava'ria *sf* (guasto) damage; (: meccanico) breakdown

a'varo, a *ag* avaricious, miserly ♦ *sm* miser

a'vena *sf* oats *pl*

PAROLA CHIAVE

a'vere *sm* (COMM) credit; **gli ~i** (ricchezze) wealth *sg*

♦ *vt* **1** (possedere) to have; **ha due bambini/una bella casa** she has (got) two children/a lovely house; **ha i capelli lunghi** he has (got) long hair; **non ho da mangiare/bere** I've (got) nothing to eat/drink, I don't have anything to eat/drink

2 (indossare) to wear, have on; **aveva una maglietta rossa** he was wearing *o* he had on a red tee-shirt; **ha gli occhiali** he wears *o* has glasses

3 (ricevere) to get; **hai avuto l'assegno?** did you get *o* have you had the cheque?

4 (*età, dimensione*) to be; **ha 9 anni** he is 9 (years old); **la stanza ha 3 metri di lunghezza** the room is 3 metres in length; *vedi* **fame; paura** etc

5 (*tempo*): **quanti ne abbiamo oggi?** what's the date today?; **ne hai per molto?** will you be long?

6 (*fraseologia*): **avercela con qn** to be angry with sb; **cos'hai?** what's wrong o what's the matter (with you)?; **non ha niente a che vedere** o **fare con me** it's got nothing to do with me

♦ *vb aus* **1** to have; **aver bevuto/mangiato** to have drunk/eaten

2 (+*da* +*infinito*): ~ **da fare qc** to have to do sth; **non hai che da chiederlo** you only have to ask him

'**avi** *smpl* ancestors, forefathers

aviazi'one [avjat'tsjone] *sf* aviation; (*MIL*) air force

avidità *sf* eagerness; greed

'**avido, a** *ag* eager; (*peg*) greedy

avo'cado *sm* avocado

a'vorio *sm* ivory

Avv. *abbr* = avvocato

avvalla'mento *sm* sinking *no pl*; (*effetto*) depression

avvalo'rare *vt* to confirm

avvam'pare *vi* (*incendio*) to flare up

avvantaggi'are [avvantad'dʒare] *vt* to favour; ~**rsi** *vr*: ~**rsi negli affari/sui concorrenti** to get ahead in business/of one's competitors

avvele'nare *vt* to poison

avve'nente *ag* attractive, charming

avveni'mento *sm* event

avve'nire *vi*, *vb impers* to happen, occur ♦ *sm* future

avven'tarsi *vr*: ~ **su** o **contro qn/qc** to hurl o.s. o rush at sb/sth

avven'tato, a *ag* rash, reckless

avven'tizio [avven'tittsjo] *ag* (*impiegato*) temporary; (*guadagno*) casual

av'vento *sm* advent, coming; (*REL*): **l'A~** Advent

avven'tore *sm* (*regular*) customer

avven'tura *sf* adventure; (*amorosa*) affair

avventu'rarsi *vr* to venture

avventu'roso, a *ag* adventurous

avve'rarsi *vr* to come true

av'verbio *sm* adverb

avver'sario, a *ag* opposing ♦ *sm* opponent, adversary

av'verso, a *ag* (*contrario*) contrary; (*sfavorevole*) unfavourable

avver'tenza [avver'tɛntsa] *sf* (*ammonimento*) warning; (*cautela*) care; (*premessa*) foreword; ~**e** *sfpl* (*istruzioni per l'uso*) instructions

avverti'mento *sm* warning

avver'tire *vt* (*avvisare*) to warn; (*rendere consapevole*) to inform, notify; (*percepire*) to feel

av'vezzo, a [av'vettso] *ag*: ~ **a** used to

avvia'mento *sm* (*atto*) starting; (*effetto*) start; (*AUT*) starting; (*: dispositivo*) starter; (*COMM*) goodwill

avvi'are *vt* (*mettere sul cammino*) to direct; (*impresa, trattative*) to begin, start; (*motore*) to start; ~**rsi** *vr* to set off, set out

avvicen'darsi [avvitʃen'darsi] *vr* to alternate

avvici'nare [avvitʃi'nare] *vt* to bring near; (*trattare con: persona*) to approach; ~**rsi** *vr*: ~**rsi (a qn/qc)** to approach (sb/sth), draw near (to sb/sth)

avvi'lire *vt* (*umiliare*) to humiliate; (*degradare*) to disgrace; (*scoraggiare*) to dishearten, discourage; ~**rsi** *vr* (*abbattersi*) to lose heart

avvilup'pare *vt* (*avvolgere*) to wrap up; (*ingarbugliare*) to entangle

avvi'nazzato, a [avvinat'tsato] *ag* drunk

av'vincere [av'vintʃere] *vt* to charm, enthral; **avvin'cente** *ag* captivating

avvinghi'are [avvin'gjare] *vt* to clasp; ~**rsi** *vr*: ~**rsi a** to cling to

avvi'sare *vt* (*far sapere*) to inform; (*mettere in guardia*) to warn; **av'viso** *sm* warning; (*annuncio*) announcement; (: *affisso*) notice; (*inserzione pubblicitaria*) advertisement; a mio avviso in my opinion

avvis'tare *vt* to sight

avvi'tare *vt* to screw down (*o* in)

avviz'zire [avvit'tsire] *vi* to wither

avvo'cato, 'essa *smf* (DIR) barrister (BRIT), lawyer; (*fig*) defender, advocate

av'volgere [av'voldʒere] *vt* to roll up; (*avviluppare*) to wrap up; **~rsi** *vr* (*avvilupparsi*) to wrap o.s. up;

avvol'gibile *sm* roller blind (BRIT), blind

avvol'toio *sm* vulture

azi'enda [ad'dzjɛnda] *sf* business, firm, concern; **~ agricola** farm

azio'nare [attsjo'nare] *vt* to activate

azi'one [at'tsjone] *sf* action; (COMM) share; **azio'nista, i, e** *smf* (COMM) shareholder

a'zoto [ad'dzɔto] *sm* nitrogen

azzan'nare [attsan'nare] *vt* to sink one's teeth into

azzar'darsi [addzar'darsi] *vr*: **~ a fare** to dare (to) do; **azzar'dato, a** *ag* (*impresa*) risky; (*risposta*) rash

az'zardo [ad'dzardo] *sm* risk

azzec'care [attsek'kare] *vt* (*risposta etc*) to get right

azzuf'farsi [attsuf'farsi] *vr* to come to blows

az'zurro, a [ad'dzurro] *ag* blue ♦ *sm* (*colore*) blue; **gli ~i** (SPORT) the Italian national team

B

bab'beo *sm* simpleton

'babbo *sm* (*fam*) dad, daddy; **B~ natale** Father Christmas

bab'buccia, ce [bab'buttʃa] *sf* slipper; (*per neonati*) bootee

ba'bordo *sm* (NAUT) port side

ba'cato, a *ag* worm-eaten, rotten

'bacca, che *sf* berry

baccalà *sm* dried salted cod; (*fig*: *peg*) dummy

bac'cano *sm* din, clamour

bac'cello [bat'tʃɛllo] *sm* pod

bac'chetta [bak'ketta] *sf* (*verga*) stick, rod; (*di direttore d'orchestra*) baton; (*di tamburo*) drumstick; **~ magica** magic wand

baci'are [ba'tʃare] *vt* to kiss; **~rsi** *vr* to kiss (one another)

baci'nella [batʃi'nɛlla] *sf* basin

ba'cino [ba'tʃino] *sm* basin; (MINERALOGIA) field, bed; (ANAT) pelvis; (NAUT) dock

'bacio [′batʃo] *sm* kiss

'baco, chi *sm* worm; **~ da seta** silkworm

ba'dare *vi* (*fare attenzione*) to take care, be careful; (*occuparsi di*): **~ a** to look after, take care of; (*dar ascolto*): **~ a** to pay attention to; **bada ai fatti tuoi!** mind your own business!

ba'dia *sf* abbey

ba'dile *sm* shovel

'baffi *smpl* moustache *sg*; (*di animale*) whiskers; **ridere sotto i ~** to laugh up one's sleeve; **leccarsi i ~** to lick one's lips

ba'gagli [ba'gaʎʎi] *smpl* luggage *sg*

bagagli'aio [bagaʎ'ʎajo] *sm* luggage van (BRIT) *o* car (US); (AUT) boot (BRIT), trunk (US)

bagli'ore [baʎ'ʎore] *sm* flash, dazzling light; **un ~ di speranza** a ray of hope

ba'gnante [baɲ'ɲante] *smf* bather

ba'gnare [baɲ'ɲare] *vt* to wet; (*inzuppare*) to soak; (*innaffiare*) to water; (*sog*: *fiume*) to flow through; (: *mare*) to wash, bathe; **~rsi** *vr* (*al mare*) to go swimming *o* bathing; (*in vasca*) to have a bath

ba'gnato, a [baɲ'ɲato] *ag* wet

ba'gnino [baɲ'ɲino] *sm* lifeguard

'bagno [′baɲɲo] *sm* bath; (*locale*) bathroom; **~i** *smpl* (*stabilimento*) baths; **fare il ~** to have a bath; (*nel mare*) to go swimming *o* bathing; **fare il ~ a qn** to give sb a bath; **mettere a ~** to soak; **~ schiuma** bubble bath

bagnoma'ria [baɲɲoma'ria] *sm*:

cuocere a ~ to cook in a double saucepan

'baia sf bay

baio'netta sf bayonet

balbet'tare vi to stutter, stammer; (bimbo) to babble ♦ vt to stammer out

balbuzi'ente [balbut'tsjɛnte] ag stuttering, stammering

bal'cone sm balcony

baldac'chino [baldak'kino] sm canopy

bal'danza [bal'dantsa] sf self-confidence, boldness

'baldo, a ag bold, daring

bal'doria sf: fare ~ to have a riotous time

ba'lena sf whale

bale'nare vb impers: **balena** there's lightning ♦ vi to flash; **mi balenò un'idea** an idea flashed through my mind; **ba'leno** sm flash of lightning; **in un baleno** in a flash

ba'lestra sf crossbow

ba'lìa sf: in ~ di at the mercy of

'balla sf (di merci) bale; (fandonia) (tall) story

bal'lare vt, vi to dance; **bal'lata** sf ballad

balle'rina sf dancer; ballet dancer; (scarpa) ballet shoe

balle'rino sm dancer; ballet dancer

bal'letto sm ballet

'ballo sm dance; (azione) dancing no pl; **essere in ~** (fig: persona) to be involved; (: cosa) to be at stake

ballot'taggio [ballot'taddʒo] sm (POL) second ballot

balne'are ag seaside cpd; (stagione) bathing

ba'locco, chi sm toy

ba'lordo, a ag stupid, senseless

'balsamo sm (aroma) balsam; (lenimento, fig) balm

balu'ardo sm bulwark

'balza ['baltsa] sf (dirupo) crag; (di stoffa) frill

bal'zare [bal'tsare] vi to bounce; (lanciarsi) to jump, leap; **'balzo** sm bounce; jump, leap; (del terreno)

crag

bam'bagia [bam'badʒa] sf (ovatta) cotton wool (BRIT), absorbent cotton (US); (cascame) cotton waste

bam'bina ag, sf vedi **bambino**

bambi'naia sf nanny, nurse(maid)

bam'bino, a sm/f child

bam'boccio [bam'bɔttʃo] sm plump child; (pupazzo) rag doll

'bambola sf doll

bambù sm bamboo

ba'nale ag banal, commonplace

ba'nana sf banana; **ba'nano** sm banana tree

'banca, che sf bank; ~ **dei dati** data bank

banca'rella sf stall

ban'cario, a ag banking, bank cpd ♦ sm bank clerk

banca'rotta sf bankruptcy; **fare** ~ to go bankrupt

ban'chetto [ban'ketto] sm banquet

banchi'ere [ban'kjere] sm banker

ban'china [ban'kina] sf (di porto) quay; (per pedoni, ciclisti) path; (di stazione) platform; ~ **cedevole** (AUT) soft verge (BRIT) o shoulder (US)

'banco, chi sm bench; (di negozio) counter; (di mercato) stall; (di officina) (work-)bench; (GEO, banca) bank; ~ **di corallo** coral reef; ~ **degli imputati** dock; ~ **dei pegni** pawnshop; ~ **di nebbia** bank of fog; ~ **di prova** (fig) testing ground; ~ **dei testimoni** witness box

Bancomat ® sm inv automated banking; (tessera) cash card

banco'nota sf banknote

'banda sf band; (di stoffa) band, stripe; (lato, parte) side; ~ **perforata** punch tape

banderu'ola sf (METEOR) weathercock, weathervane

bandi'era sf flag, banner

ban'dire vt to proclaim; (esiliare) to exile; (fig) to dispense with

ban'dito sm outlaw, bandit

bandi'tore sm (di aste) auctioneer

'bando sm proclamation; (esilio) ex-

ile, banishment; ~ **alle chiacchie-**
re! that's enough talk!
'**bandolo** sm: **il** ~ **della matassa**
(*fig*) the key to the problem
bar sm *inv* bar
'**bara** sf coffin
ba'**racca, che** sf shed, hut; (*peg*)
hovel; **mandare avanti la** ~ to
keep things going
bara'**onda** sf hubbub, bustle
ba'**rare** vi to cheat
ba'**ratro** sm abyss
barat'**tare** vt: ~ **qc con** o to barter
sth for, swap sth for; **ba'ratto** sm
barter
ba'**rattolo** sm (*di latta*) tin; (*di ve-*
tro) jar; (*di coccio*) pot
'**barba** sf beard; **farsi la** ~ to
shave; **farla a** ~ **a qn** (*fig*) to do
sth to sb's face; **che** ~! what a
bore!
barbabi'**etola** sf beetroot (BRIT),
beet (US); ~ **da zucchero** sugar
beet
bar'**barico, a, ci, che** ag barbar-
ian; barbaric
'**barbaro, a** ag barbarous; ~**i** smpl
barbarians
barbi'**ere** sm barber
bar'**bone** sm (*cane*) poodle; (*vaga-*
bondo) tramp
bar'**buto, a** ag bearded
'**barca, che** sf boat; ~ **a remi** rowing boat; ~ **a vela** sail(ing) boat;
barcai'olo sm boatman
barcol'**lare** vi to stagger
bar'**cone** sm (*per ponti di barche*)
pontoon
ba'**rella** sf (*lettiga*) stretcher
ba'**rile** sm barrel; cask
ba'**rista, i, e** sm/f barman/maid;
bar owner
ba'**ritono** sm baritone
ba'**rlume** sm glimmer, gleam
ba'**rocco, a, chi, che** ag, sm ba-
roque
ba'**rometro** sm barometer
ba'**rone** sm baron; **baro'nessa** sf
baroness
'**barra** sf bar; (*NAUT*) helm; (*linea*

grafica) line, stroke
barri'**care** vt to barricade; **bar-**
ri'cata sf barricade
barri'**era** sf barrier; (*GEO*) reef
ba'**ruffa** sf scuffle
barzel'**letta** [bardzel'letta] sf joke,
funny story
ba'**sare** vt to base, found; ~**rsi** *vr*:
~**rsi su** (*sog: fatti, prove*) to be
based o founded on; (: *persona*) to
base one's arguments on
'**basco, a, schi, sche** ag Basque ♦
sm (*copricapo*) beret
'**base** sf base; (*fig: fondamento*) basis; (*POL*) rank and file; **di** ~ basic;
in ~ **a** on the basis of, according to;
a ~ **di caffè** coffee-based
ba'**setta** sf sideburn
ba'**silica, che** sf basilica
ba'**silico** sm basil
bassi'**fondi** smpl (*fig*) dregs; **i** ~
(*della città*) the slums
'**basso, a** ag low; (*di statura*) short;
(*meridionale*) southern ♦ sm bottom,
lower part; (*MUS*) bass; **la** ~**a** Italia southern Italy
bassorili'**evo** sm bas-relief
'**basta** *escl* (that's) enough!, that will
do!
bas'**tardo, a** ag (*animale, pianta*)
hybrid, crossbreed; (*persona*) illegitimate, bastard (*peg*) ♦ sm/f illegitimate child, bastard (*peg*)
bas'**tare** vi, *vb impers* to be enough,
be sufficient; ~ **a qn** to be enough
for sb; **basta chiedere** o **che chie-**
da a un vigile you have only to o
need only ask a policeman
basti'**mento** sm ship, vessel
basto'**nare** vt to beat, thrash
baston'**cino** [baston'tʃino] sm (*SCI*)
ski pole
bas'**tone** sm stick; ~ **da passeggio**
walking stick
bat'**taglia** [bat'taʎʎa] sf battle; fight
bat'**taglio** [bat'taʎʎo] sm (*di campa-*
na) clapper; (*di porta*) knocker
battagli'**one** [battaʎ'ʎone] sm bat-
talion
bat'**tello** sm boat

bat'tente sm (imposta: di porta) wing, flap; (: di finestra) shutter; (batacchio: di porta) knocker; (: di orologio) hammer; **chiudere i ~i** (fig) to shut up shop

'**battere** vt to beat; (grano) to thresh; (percorrere) to scour ♦ vi (bussare) to knock; (urtare): ~ **contro** to hit o strike against; (pioggia, sole) to beat down; (cuore) to beat; (TENNIS) to serve; ~**rsi** vr to fight; ~ **le mani** to clap; ~ **i piedi** to stamp one's feet; **~ su un argomento** to hammer home an argument; **~ a macchina** to type; **~ bandiera italiana** to fly the Italian flag; **~ in testa** (AUT) to knock; **in un batter d'occhio** in the twinkling of an eye

bat'teri smpl bacteria

batte'ria sf battery; (MUS) drums pl

bat'tesimo sm baptism; christening

battez'zare [batted'dzare] vt to baptize; to christen

batticu'ore sm palpitations pl

batti'mano sm applause

batti'panni sm inv carpet-beater

battis'tero sm baptistry

battis'trada sm inv (di pneumatico) tread; (di gara) pacemaker

battitap'peto sm vacuum cleaner

'**battito** sm beat, throb; ~ **cardiaco** heartbeat; ~ **della pioggia/dell'orologio** beating of the rain/ ticking of the clock

bat'tuta sf blow; (di macchina da scrivere) stroke; (MUS) bar; beat; (TEATRO) cue; (frase spiritosa) witty remark; (di caccia) beating; (PO-LIZIA) combing, scouring; (TEN-NIS) service

ba'ule sm trunk; (AUT) boot (BRIT), trunk (US)

'**bava** sf (di animale) slaver, slobber; (di lumaca) slime; (di vento) breath

bava'glino [bavaʎ'ʎino] sm bib

ba'vaglio [ba'vaʎʎo] sm gag

'**bavero** sm collar

ba'zar [bad'dzar] sm inv bazaar

baz'zecola [bad'dzekola] sf trifle

bazzi'care [battsi'kare] vt to frequent ♦ vi: ~ **in/con** to frequent

be'ato, a ag blessed; (fig) happy; ~ **te!** lucky you!

bec'caccia, ce [bek'kattʃa] sf woodcock

bec'care vt to peck; (fig: raffreddore) to pick up, catch; ~**rsi** vr (fig) to squabble

beccheggi'are [bekked'dʒare] vi to pitch

bec'chino [bek'kino] sm gravedigger

'**becco, chi** sm beak, bill; (di caffettiera etc) spout; lip

Be'fana sf old woman who, according to legend, brings children their presents on the Epiphany; (Epifania) Epiphany; (donna brutta): **b~** hag, witch

'**beffa** sf practical joke; **farsi ~e di qn** to make a fool of sb; **bef'fardo, a** ag scornful, mocking; **bef'fare** vt (anche: beffarsi di) to make a fool of, mock

'**bega, ghe** sf quarrel

'**begli** ['beʎʎi] ag vedi **bello**

'**bei** ag vedi **bello**

bel ag vedi **bello**

be'lare vi to bleat

'**belga, gi, ghe** ag, sm/f Belgian

'**Belgio** ['beldʒo] sm: **il ~** Belgium

bel'lezza [bel'lettsa] sf beauty

'bella ag (SPORT) decider; vedi anche **bello**

PAROLA CHIAVE

'**bello, a** (ag: dav sm **bel** +C, **bell'** +V, **bello** +s impura, gn, pn, ps, x, z, pl **bei** +C, **begli** +s impura etc o V) ag 1 (oggetto, donna, paesaggio) beautiful, lovely; (uomo) handsome; (tempo) beautiful, fine, lovely; **le belle arti** fine arts

2 (quantità): **una ~a cifra** a considerable sum of money; **un bel niente** absolutely nothing

3 (rafforzativo): **è una truffa ~a e buona!** it's a real fraud!; **è bell'e finito** it's already finished

♦ sm 1 (bellezza) beauty; (tempo)

fine weather
2: adesso viene il ~ now comes the best bit; **sul più ~** at the crucial point; **cosa fai di ~?** are you doing anything interesting?
♦ *av:* **fa ~** the weather is fine, it's fine

'belva *sf* wild animal
belve'dere *sm inv* panoramic viewpoint
benché [ben'ke] *cong* although
'benda *sf* bandage; *(per gli occhi)* blindfold; **bendare** *vt* to bandage; to blindfold
'bene *av* well; *(completamente, affatto)*: **è ben difficile** it's very difficult ♦ *ag inv:* **gente ~ well-to-do people** ♦ *sm* good; **~i** *smpl (averi)* property *sg*, estate *sg*; **io sto ~/poco ~** I'm well/not very well; **va ~** all right; **volere un ~ dell'anima a qn** to love sb very much; **un uomo per ~** a respectable man; **fare ~ a** to do the right thing; **fare ~ a** *(salute)* to be good for; **fare del ~ a qn** to do sb a good turn; **~i di consumo** consumer goods
bene'detto, a *pp di* **benedire** ♦ *ag* blessed, holy
bene'dire *vt* to bless; to consecrate; **benedizi'one** *sf* blessing
benedu'cato, a *ag* well-mannered
benefi'cenza [benefi'tʃɛntsa] *sf* charity
bene'ficio [bene'fitʃo] *sm* benefit; **con ~ d'inventario** *(fig)* with reservations
be'nefico, a, ci, che *ag* beneficial; charitable
beneme'renza [beneme'rɛntsa] *sf* merit
bene'merito, a *ag* meritorious
be'nessere *sm* well-being
benes'tante *ag* well-to-do
benes'tare *sm* consent, approval
be'nevolo, a *ag* benevolent
be'nigno, a [be'ninɲo] *ag* kind, kindly; *(critica etc)* favourable; *(MED)* benign

benin'teso *av* of course
bensì *cong* but (rather)
benve'nuto, a *ag, sm* welcome; **dare il ~ a qn** to welcome sb
ben'zina [ben'dzina] *sf* petrol *(BRIT)*, gas *(US)*; **fare ~** to get petrol *(BRIT)* o **dare** *(US)*; **benzi'naio** *sm* petrol *(BRIT)* o gas *(US)* pump attendant
'bere *vt* to drink; **darla a ~ a qn** *(fig)* to fool sb
ber'lina *sf* *(AUT)* saloon (car) *(BRIT)*, sedan *(US)*
Ber'lino *sf* Berlin
ber'noccolo *sm* bump; *(inclinazione)* flair
ber'retto *sm* cap
bersagli'are [bersaʎ'ʎare] *vt* to shoot at; *(colpire ripetutamente, fig)* to bombard; **bersagliato dalla sfortuna** dogged by ill fortune
ber'saglio [ber'saʎʎo] *sm* target
bes'temmia *sf* curse; *(REL)* blasphemy
bestemmi'are *vi* to curse, swear; to blaspheme ♦ *vt* to curse, swear at; to blaspheme
'bestia *sf* animal; **andare in ~** *(fig)* to fly into a rage; **besti'ale** *ag* beastly; animal *cpd*; *(fam)*: **fa un freddo bestiale** it's bitterly cold; **besti'ame** *sm* livestock; *(bovino)* cattle *pl*
be'ttola *(peg)* dive
be'tulla *sf* birch
be'vanda *sf* drink, beverage
bevi'tore, 'trice *sm/f* drinker
be'vuta *sf* drink
be'vuto, a *pp di* **bere**
bi'ada *sf* fodder
bianche'ria [bjanke'ria] *sf* linen; **~ intima** underwear; **~ da donna** ladies' underwear, lingerie
bi'anco, a, chi, che *ag* white; *(non scritto)* blank ♦ *sm* white; *(intonaco)* whitewash ♦ *sm/f* white, white man/woman; **in ~** *(foglio, assegno)* blank; *(notte)* sleepless; **in ~ e nero** *(TV, FOT)* black and white; **mangiare in ~** to follow a bland

diet; **pesce in ~** boiled fish; **andare in ~** (*non riuscire*) to fail; **~ dell'uovo** egg-white

biasi'mare *vt* to disapprove of, censure; **bi'asimo** *sm* disapproval, censure

'**bibbia** *sf* bible

bibe'ron *sm inv* feeding bottle

'**bibita** *sf* (soft) drink

biblio'teca, che *sf* library; (*mobile*) bookcase; **bibliote'cario, a** *smf* librarian

bicarbo'nato *sm:* **~ (di sodio)** bicarbonate (of soda)

bicchi'ere [bik'kjɛre] *sm* glass

bici'cletta [bitʃi'kletta] *sf* bicycle; **andare in ~** to cycle

bidé *sm inv* bidet

bi'dello, a *smf* (*INS*) janitor

bi'done *sm* drum, can; (*anche: ~ dell'immondizia*) (dust)bin; (*fam: truffa*) swindle; **fare un ~ a qn** (*fam*) to let sb down; to cheat sb

bien'nale *ag* biennial

bi'ennio *sm* period of two years

bi'etola *sf* beet

bifor'carsi *vr* to fork; **biforca-zi'one** *sf* fork

bighello'nare [bigello'nare] *vi* to loaf (about)

bigiotte'ria [bidʒotte'ria] *sf* costume jewellery; (*negozio*) jeweller's (*selling only costume jewellery*)

bigli'ardo [biʎ'ʎardo] *sm* = **biliardo**

bigliette'ria [biʎʎette'ria] *sf* (*di stazione*) ticket office; booking office; (*di teatro*) box office

bigli'etto [biʎ'ʎetto] *sm* (*per viaggi, spettacoli etc*) ticket; (*cartoncino*) card; (*anche: ~ di banca*) (bank)note; **~ d'auguri/da visita** greetings/visiting card; **~ d'andata e ritorno** return (ticket), round-trip ticket (*US*)

bignè [biɲ'ɲe] *sm inv* cream puff

bigo'dino *sm* roller, curler

bi'gotto, a *ag* over-pious ♦ *smf* church fiend

bi'lancia, ce [bi'lantʃa] *sf* (*pesa*) scales *pl*; (*: di precisione*) balance;

(*dello zodiaco*): **B~** Libra; **~ commerciale/dei pagamenti** balance of trade/payments; **bilanci'are** *vt* (*pesare*) to weigh; (*: fig*) to weigh up; (*pareggiare*) to balance

bi'lancio [bi'lantʃo] *sm* (*COMM*) balance(-sheet); (*statale*) budget; **fare il ~ di** (*fig*) to assess; **~ consuntivo** (final) balance; **~ preventivo** budget

'**bile** *sf* bile; (*fig*) rage, anger

bili'ardo *sm* billiards *sg*; billiard table

bi'lico, chi *sm:* **essere in ~** to be balanced; (*fig*) to be undecided; **tenere qn in ~** to keep sb in suspense

bi'lingue *ag* bilingual

bili'one *sm* (*mille milioni*) thousand million; (*milione di milioni*) billion (*BRIT*), trillion (*US*)

'**bimbo, a** *smf* little boy/girl

bimen'sile *ag* fortnightly

bimes'trale *ag* two-monthly, bimonthly

bi'nario, a *ag* (*sistema*) binary ♦ *sm* (*railway*) track o line; (*piattaforma*) platform; **~ morto** dead-end track

bi'nocolo *sm* binoculars *pl*

bio... *prefisso:* **bio'chimica** [bio'kimika] *sf* biochemistry; **biode-gra'dabile** *ag* biodegradable; **bio-gra'fia** *sf* biography; **biolo'gia** *sf* biology; **bio'logico, a, ci, che** *ag* biological

bi'ondo, a *ag* blond, fair

bir'bante *sm* rogue, rascal

biri'chino, a [biri'kino] *ag* mischievous ♦ *smf* scamp, little rascal

bi'rillo *sm* skittle (*BRIT*), pin (*US*); **~i** *smpl* (*gioco*) skittles *sg* (*BRIT*), bowling (*US*)

'**biro** ® *sf inv* biro ®

'**birra** *sf* beer; **a tutta ~** (*fig*) at top speed; **birra chiara** = lager; **birra scura** = stout; **birre'ria** *sf* = bierkeller

bis *escl, sm inv* encore

bis'betico, a, ci, che *ag* illtempered, crabby

bisbigli'are [bisbiλ'λare] *vt, vi* to whisper

'bisca *sf* gambling-house

'biscia, sce ['biʃʃa] *sf* snake; ~ **d'acqua** grass snake

bis'cotto *sm* biscuit

bises'tile *ag*: **anno** ~ leap year

bis'lungo, a, ghi, ghe *ag* oblong

bis'nonno, a *smf* great grandfather/grandmother

biso'gnare [bizoɲ'ɲare] *vb impers*: **bisogna che tu parta/lo faccia** you'll have to go/do it; **bisogna parlargli** we'll (*o* I'll) have to talk to him

bi'sogno [bi'zoɲɲo] *sm* need; ~ **i** *smpl*: **fare i propri** ~**i** to relieve o.s.; **avere** ~ **di qc/di fare qc** to need sth/to do sth; **al** ~, **in caso di** ~ if need be; **biso'gnoso, a** *ag* needy, poor; **bisognoso di** in need of, needing

bis'tecca, che *sf* steak, beefsteak

bisticci'are [bistit'tʃare] *vi* to quarrel, bicker; ~**rsi** *vr* to quarrel, bicker; **bis'ticcio** *sm* quarrel, squabble; (*gioco di parole*) pun

'bisturi *sm* scalpel

bi'sunto, a *ag* very greasy

'bitter *sm inv* bitters *pl*

bi'vacco, chi *sm* bivouac

'bivio *sm* fork; (*fig*) dilemma

'bizza ['biddza] *sf* tantrum; **fare le** ~**e** (*bambino*) to be naughty

biz'zarro, a [bid'dzarro] *ag* bizarre, strange

biz'zeffe [bid'dzeffe]: **a** ~ *av* in plenty, galore

blan'dire *vt* to soothe; to flatter

'blando, a *ag* mild, gentle

bla'sone *sm* coat of arms

blate'rare *vi* to chatter, blether

blin'dato, a *ag* armoured

bloc'care *vt* to block; (*isolare*) to isolate, cut off; (*porto*) to blockade; (*prezzi, beni*) to freeze; (*meccanismo*) to jam; ~**rsi** *vr* (*motore*) to stall; (*freni, porta*) to jam, stick; (*ascensore*) to stop, get stuck

'blocco, chi *sm* block; (*MIL*) block-

ade; (*dei fitti*) restriction; (*quadernetto*) pad; (*fig: unione*) coalition; (*il bloccare*) blocking; isolating; cutting-off; blockading; freezing; jamming; **in** ~ (*nell'insieme*) as a whole; (*COMM*) in bulk; ~ **cardiaco** cardiac arrest

blu *ag inv, sm* dark blue

'blusa *sf* (*camiciotto*) smock; (*camicetta*) blouse

'boa *sm inv* (*ZOOL*) boa constrictor; (*sciarpa*) feather boa ♦ *sf* buoy

bo'ato *sm* rumble, roar

bo'bina *sf* reel, spool; (*di pellicola*) spool; (*di film*) reel; (*ELETTR*) coil

'bocca, che *sf* mouth; **in** ~ **al lupo!** good luck!

boc'caccia, ce *sf* (*malalingua*) gossip; **fare le** ~**ce** to pull faces

boc'cale *sm* jug; ~ **da birra** tankard

boc'cetta [bot'tʃetta] *sf* small bottle

boccheggi'are [bokked'dʒare] *vi* to gasp

boc'chino [bok'kino] *sm* (*di sigaretta, sigaro: cannella*) cigarette-holder; cigar-holder; (*di pipa, strumenti musicali*) mouthpiece

'boccia, ce ['bɔttʃa] *sf* (*da vino*) decanter, carafe; (*palla*) bowl; **gioco delle** ~**ce** bowls *sg*

bocci'are [bot'tʃare] *vt* (*proposta, progetto*) to reject; (*INS*) to fail; (*BOCCE*) to hit; **boccia'tura** *sf* failure

bocci'olo [bot'tʃɔlo] *sm* bud

boc'cone *sm* mouthful, morsel

boc'coni *av* face downwards

'boia *sm inv* executioner; hangman

boi'ata *sf* botch

boicot'tare *vt* to boycott

'bolide *sm* meteor; **come un** ~ like a flash, at top speed

'bolla *sf* (*MED*) blister; (~ **papale**) papal bull; ~ **di consegna** (*COMM*) delivery note

bol'lare *vt* to stamp; (*fig*) to brand

bol'lente *ag* boiling; boiling hot

bol'letta *sf* bill; (*ricevuta*) receipt;

essere in ~ to be hard up

bollet'tino sm bulletin; (COMM) note; ~ **di spedizione** consignment note

bol'lire vt, vi to boil; **bol'lito** sm (CUC) boiled meat

bolli'tore sm (CUC) kettle; (per riscaldamento) boiler

'bollo sm stamp; **bollo per patente** driving licence tax

'bomba sf bomb; **tornare a ~** (fig) to get back to the point; ~ **atomica** atom bomb

bombarda'mento sm bombardment; bombing

bombar'dare vt to bombard; (da aereo) to bomb

bombardi'ere sm bomber

bom'betta sf bowler (hat)

'bombola sf cylinder

bo'naccia, ce [bo'nattʃa] sf dead calm

bo'nario, a ag good-natured, kind

bo'nifica, che sf reclamation; reclaimed land

bo'nifico, ci sm (riduzione, abbuono) discount; (versamento a terzi) credit transfer

bontà sf goodness; (cortesia) kindness; **aver la ~ di fare qc** to be good o kind enough to do sth

borbot'tare vi to mumble; (stomaco) to rumble

'borchia ['borkja] sf stud

borda'tura sf (SARTORIA) border, trim

'bordo sm (NAUT) ship's side; (orlo) edge; (striscia di guarnizione) border, trim; **a ~ di** (nave, aereo) aboard, on board; (macchina) in

bor'gata sf hamlet

bor'ghese [bor'geze] ag (spesso peg) middle-class; bourgeois; **abito** ~ civilian dress; **borghe'sia** sf middle classes pl; bourgeoisie

'borgo, **ghi** sm (paesino) village; (quartiere) district; (sobborgo) suburb

'boria sf self-conceit, arrogance

boro'talco sm talcum powder

bor'raccia, ce [bor'rattʃa] sf canteen, water-bottle

'borsa sf bag; (anche: ~ **da signora**) handbag; (ECON): **la B~** (valori) the Stock Exchange; ~ **nera** black market; ~ **della spesa** shopping bag; ~ **di studio** grant; **borsai'olo** sm pickpocket; **borsel'lino** sm purse; **bor'setta** sf handbag; **bor'sista**, **i**, **e** sm/f (ECON) speculator; (INS) grant-holder

bos'caglia [bos'kaλλa] sf woodlands pl

boscai'olo sm woodcutter; forester

'bosco, **schi** sm wood; **bos'coso**, **a** ag wooded

'bossolo sm cartridge-case

bo'tanica sf botany

bo'tanico, **a**, **ci**, **che** ag botanical ♦ sm botanist

'botola sf trap door

'botta sf blow; (rumore) bang

'botte sf barrel, cask

bot'tega, **ghe** sf shop; (officina) workshop; **botte'gaio**, **a** sm/f shopkeeper; **botte'ghino** sm ticket office; (del lotto) public lottery office

bot'tiglia [bot'tiλλa] sf bottle; **bottiglie'ria** sf wine shop

bot'tino sm (di guerra) booty; (di rapina, furto) loot

'botto sm bang; crash; **di ~** suddenly

bot'tone sm button; **attaccare ~ a qn** (fig) to buttonhole sb

bo'vino, **a** ag bovine; **~i** smpl cattle

boxe [bɔks] sf boxing

'bozza ['bɔttsa] sf draft; sketch; (TIP) proof; **boz'zetto** sm sketch

'bozzolo ['bɔttsolo] sm cocoon

BR sigla fpl = **Brigate Rosse**

brac'care vt to hunt

brac'cetto [brat'tʃetto] sm: **a ~** arm in arm

bracci'ale [brat'tʃale] sm bracelet; (distintivo) armband; **braccia'letto** sm bracelet, bangle

bracci'ante [brat'tʃante] sm (AGR) day labourer

bracci'ata [brat'tʃata] *sf* (*nel nuoto*)
stroke

'**braccio** ['brattʃo] (*pl(f)* **braccia**)
sm (*ANAT*) arm; (*pl(m)* **bracci**: *di
gru, fiume*) arm; (: *di edificio*) wing;
~ **di mare** sound; **bracci'olo** *sm*
(*appoggio*) arm

'**bracco, chi** *sm* hound

bracconi'ere *sm* poacher

'**brace** ['bratʃe] *sf* embers *pl*; **braci'ere** *sm* brazier

braci'ola [bra'tʃɔla] *sf* (*CUC*) chop

bra'mare *vt*: ~ **qc/di** fare to long
for sth/to do

'**branca, che** *sf* branch

branchia ['brankja] *sf* (*ZOOL*) gill

'**branco, chi** *sm* (*di cani, lupi*)
pack; (*di uccelli, pecore*) flock; (*peg:
di persone*) gang, pack

branco'lare *vi* to grope, feel one's
way

'**branda** *sf* camp bed

bran'dello *sm* scrap, shred; **a ~i** in
tatters, in rags

bran'dire *vt* to brandish

'**brano** *sm* (*di libro*) passage

bra'sato *sm* braised beef

Bra'sile *sm*: **il ~** Brazil; **brasi-
li'ano, a** *ag*, *sm/f* Brazilian

'**bravo, a** *ag* (*abile*) clever, capable,
skilful; (*buono*) good, honest; (:
bambino) good; (*coraggioso*) brave;
~! well done!; (*al teatro*) bravo!

bra'vura *sf* cleverness, skill

'**breccia, ce** ['brettʃa] *sf* breach

bre'tella *sf* (*AUT*) link; **~e** *sfpl* (*di
calzoni*) braces

'**breve** *ag* brief, short; **in ~** in short

brevet'tare *vt* to patent

bre'vetto *sm* patent; **~ di pilotag-
gio** pilot's licence (*BRIT*) o license
(*US*)

'**brezza** ['breddza] *sf* breeze

'**bricco, chi** *sm* jug; **~ del caffè**
coffeepot

bric'cone, a *sm/f* rogue, rascal

briciola ['britʃola] *sf* crumb

briciolo ['britʃolo] *sm* (*specie fig*)
bit

'**briga, ghe** *sf* (*fastidio*) trouble,

bother; **pigliarsi la ~ di fare** qc to
take the trouble to do sth

brigadi'ere *sm* (*dei carabinieri etc*)
≈ sergeant

bri'gante *sm* bandit

bri'gata *sf* (*MIL*) brigade; (*gruppo*)
group, party

'**briglia** ['briʎʎa] *sf* rein; **a ~ sciolta**
at full gallop; (*fig*) at full speed

bril'lante *ag* bright; (*anche fig*) brilliant; (*che luccica*) shining ♦ *sm* diamond

bril'lare *vi* to shine; (*mina*) to blow
up ♦ *vt* (*mina*) to set off

'**brillo, a** *ag* merry, tipsy

'**brina** *sf* hoarfrost

brin'dare *vi*: ~ **a qn/qc** to drink to
o toast sb/sth

'**brindisi** *sm inv* toast

'**brio** *sm* liveliness, go; **bri'oso, a** *ag*
lively

bri'tannico, a, ci, che *ag* British

'**brivido** *sm* shiver; (*di ribrezzo*)
shudder; (*fig*) thrill

brizzo'lato, a [brittso'lato] *ag* (*persona*) going grey; (*barba, capelli*)
greying

'**brocca, che** *sf* jug

broc'cato *sm* brocade

broccolo *sm* broccoli *sg*

'**brodo** *sm* broth; (*per cucinare*)
stock; ~ **ristretto** consommé

brogli'accio [broʎ'ʎattʃo] *sm* scrib-
bling pad

'**broglio** ['brɔʎʎo] *sm*: ~ **elettorale**
gerrymandering

bron'chite [bron'kite] *sf* (*MED*)
bronchitis

'**broncio** ['brontʃo] *sm* sulky expression; **tenere il ~** to sulk

'**bronco, chi** *sm* bronchial tube

bronto'lare *vi* to grumble; (*tuono,
stomaco*) to rumble

'**bronzo** [brondzo] *sm* bronze

bru'care *vt* to browse on, nibble at

brucia'pelo [brutʃa'pelo]: **a ~** *av*
point-blank

bruci'are [bru'tʃare] *vt* to burn;
(*scottare*) to scald ♦ *vi* to burn; **brucia'tore** *sm* burner; **brucia'tura** *sf*

'bruco, **chi** *sm* caterpillar; grub

brughi'era [bru'gjɛra] *sf* heath, moor

bruli'care *vi* to swarm

'brullo, **a** *ag* bare, bleak

'bruma *sf* mist

'bruno, **a** *ag* brown, dark; *(persona)* dark(-haired)

'brusco, **a**, **schi**, **sche** *ag (sapore)* sharp; *(modi, persona)* brusque, abrupt; *(movimento)* abrupt, sudden

bru'sio *sm* buzz, buzzing

bru'tale *ag* brutal

'bruto, **a** *ag (forza)* brute *cpd* ♦ *sm* brute

brut'tezza [brut'tettsa] *sf* ugliness

'brutto, **a** *ag* ugly; *(cattivo)* bad; *(malattia, strada, affare)* nasty, bad; ~ **tempo** bad weather; **brut'tura** *sf (cosa brutta)* ugly thing; *(sudiciume)* filth; *(azione meschina)* mean action

Bru'xelles [bry'sɛl] *sf* Brussels

bub'bone *sm* swelling

'buca, **che** *sf* hole; *(avvallamento)* hollow; ~ **delle lettere** letterbox

buca'neve *sm inv* snowdrop

bu'care *vt (forare)* to make a hole (o holes) in; *(pungere)* to pierce; *(biglietto)* to punch; ~**rsi** *vr (con eroina)* to mainline; ~ **una gomma** to have a puncture

bu'cato *sm (operazione)* washing; *(panni)* wash, washing

'buccia, **ce** ['buttʃa] *sf* skin, peel; *(corteccia)* bark

bucherel'lare [bukerel'lare] *vt* to riddle with holes

'buco, **chi** *sm* hole

bu'dello *sm (ANAT: pl(f) ~a)* bowel, gut; *(fig: tubo)* tube; *(vicolo)* alley

bu'dino *sm* pudding

'bue *sm* ox; *(anche: carne di ~)* beef

'bufalo *sm* buffalo

bu'fera *sf* storm

buf'fetto *sm*: **fare un ~ sulla guancia a qn** to give sb an affectionate pinch on the cheek

'buffo, **a** *ag* funny; *(TEATRO)* comic

buf'fone *sm* buffoon; *(peg)* clown

bu'gia, **'gie** [bu'dʒia] *sf* lie; *(candeliere)* candleholder; **bugi'ardo**, **a** *ag* lying, deceitful ♦ *sm/f* liar

bugi'gattolo [budʒi'gattolo] *sm* poky little room

'buio, **a** *ag* dark ♦ *sm* dark, darkness; **fa** ~ **pesto** it's pitch-dark

'bulbo *sm (BOT)* bulb; ~ **oculare** eyeball

Bulga'ria *sf*: **la** ~ Bulgaria

bul'lone *sm* bolt

buona'notte *escl* good night! ♦ *sf*: **dare la** ~ **a** to say good night to

buona'sera *escl* good evening!

buon gi'orno [bwon'dʒorno] *escl* good morning (o afternoon)!

buongu'staio, **a** *sm/f* gourmet

buon'gusto *sm* good taste

PAROLA CHIAVE

bu'ono, **a** *(ag: dav sm* **buon** *+C o V,* **buono** *+s impura, gn, pn, ps, x, z; dav sf* **buon'** *+V) ag* **1** *(gen)* good; **un buon pranzo/ristorante** a good lunch/restaurant; **(stai)** ~! behave!

2 *(benevolo)*: ~ **(con)** good (to), kind (to)

3 *(giusto, valido)* right; **al momento** ~ at the right moment

4 *(adatto)*: ~ **a/da** fit for/to; **essere** **a nulla** to be no good o use at anything

5 *(auguri)*: **buon compleanno!** happy birthday!; **buon divertimento!** have a nice time!; ~**a fortuna!** good luck!; **buon riposo!** sleep well!; **buon viaggio!** bon voyage!, have a good trip!

6: **a buon mercato** cheap; **di buon'ora** early; **buon senso** common sense; **alla** ~**a** *ag* simple ♦ *av* in a simple way, without any fuss

♦ *sm* **1** *(bontà)* goodness, good

2 *(COMM)* voucher, coupon; ~ **di cassa** cash voucher; ~ **di consegna** delivery note; ~ **del Tesoro** Treasury bill

buontem'pone, a *sm/f* jovial person

burat'tino *sm* puppet

'**burbero, a** *ag* surly, gruff

'**burla** *sf* prank, trick; **bur'lare** *vt*: burlare qc/qn, burlarsi di qc/qn to make fun of sth/sb

burocra'zia [burokrat'tsia] *sf* bureaucracy

bur'rasca, sche *sf* storm

'**burro** *sm* butter

bur'rone *sm* ravine

bus'care *vt* (*anche*: ~rsi: *raffreddore*) to get, catch; **buscarle** (*fam*) to get a hiding

bus'sare *vi* to knock

'**bussola** *sf* compass; **perdere la** ~ (*fig*) to lose one's bearings

'**busta** *sf* (*da lettera*) envelope; (*astuccio*) case; **in** ~ **aperta/chiusa** in an unsealed/sealed envelope; ~ **paga** pay packet

busta'rella *sf* bribe, backhander

'**busto** *sm* bust; (*indumento*) corset, girdle; **a mezzo** ~ (*foto*) half-length

but'tare *vt* to throw; (*anche*: ~ *via*) to throw away; ~ **giù** (*scritto*) to scribble down; (*edificio*) to pull down, demolish; (*cibo*) to gulp down; (*pasta, verdura*) to put into boiling water

C

ca'bina *sf* (*di nave*) cabin; (*da spiaggia*) beach hut; (*di autocarro, treno*) cab; (*di aereo*) cockpit; (*di ascensore*) cage; ~ **telefonica** call *o* (*tele*)phone box

ca'cao *sm* cocoa

'**caccia** ['kattʃa] *sf* hunting; (*con fucile*) shooting; (*inseguimento*) chase; (*cacciagione*) game ♦ *sm inv* (*aereo*) fighter; (*nave*) destroyer; ~ **grossa** big-game hunting; ~ **all'uomo** manhunt

cacciabombardi'ere [kattʃabom-

bar'djɛre] *sm* fighter-bomber

cacciagi'one [kattʃa'dʒone] *sf* game

cacci'are [kat'tʃare] *vt* to hunt; (*mandar via*) to chase away; (*ficcare*) to shove, stick ♦ *vi* to hunt; ~**rsi** *vr* (*fam*: *mettersi*): ~**rsi tra la folla** to plunge into the crowd; **dove s'è cacciata la mia borsa?** where has my bag got to?; ~**rsi nei guai** to get into trouble; ~ **fuori** qc to whip *o* pull sth out; ~ **un urlo** to let out a yell; **caccia'tore** *sm* hunter; **cacciatore di frodo** poacher

caccia'vite [kattʃa'vite] *sm inv* screwdriver

'**cactus** *sm inv* cactus

ca'davere *sm* (dead) body, corpse

ca'dente *ag* falling; (*casa*) tumble-down

ca'denza [ka'dɛntsa] *sf* cadence; (*andamento ritmico*) rhythm; (*MUS*) cadenza

ca'dere *vi* to fall; (*denti, capelli*) to fall out; (*tetto*) to fall in; **questa gonna cade bene** this skirt hangs well; **lasciar** ~ (*anche fig*) to drop; ~ **dal sonno** to be falling asleep on one's feet; ~ **dalle nuvole** (*fig*) to be taken aback

ca'detto, a *ag* younger; (*squadra*) junior *cpd* ♦ *sm* cadet

ca'duta *sf* fall; **la** ~ **dei capelli** hair loss

caffè *sm inv* coffee; (*locale*) café; ~ **macchiato** coffee with a dash of milk; ~ **macinato** ground coffee

caffel'latte *sm inv* white coffee

caffetti'era *sf* coffeepot

cagio'nare [kadʒo'nare] *vt* to cause, be the cause of

cagio'nevole [kadʒo'nevole] *ag* delicate, weak

cagli'are [kaʎ'ʎare] *vi* to curdle

'**cagna** ['kaɲɲa] *sf* (*ZOOL, peg*) bitch

ca'gnesco, a, schi, sche [kaɲ'nesko] *ag* (*fig*): **guardare qn in** ~ to scowl at sb

cala'brone *sm* hornet

cala'maio *sm* inkpot; inkwell

cala'maro *sm* squid

cala'mita *sf* magnet

calamità *sf inv* calamity, disaster

ca'lare *vt (far discendere)* to lower; *(MAGLIA)* to decrease ♦ *vi (discendere)* to go (o come) down; *(tramontare)* to set, go down; ~ **di peso** to lose weight

'calca *sf* throng, press

cal'cagno [kal'kaɲɲo] *sm* heel

cal'care *sm* limestone ♦ *vt (premere coi piedi)* to tread, press down; *(premere con forza)* to press down; *(mettere in rilievo)* to stress; ~ **la mano** to overdo it, exaggerate

'calce ['kaltʃe] *sm*: **in ~ at** the foot of the page ♦ *sf* lime; *(EDIL)* ~ **viva** quicklime

calces'truzzo [kaltʃes'truttso] *sm* concrete

calci'are [kal'tʃare] *vt, vi* to kick; **calcia'tore** *sm* footballer

'calcio ['kaltʃo] *sm (pedata)* kick; *(sport)* football, soccer; *(di pistola, fucile)* butt; *(CHIM)* calcium; ~ **d'angolo** *(SPORT)* corner (kick); ~ **di punizione** *(SPORT)* free kick

'calco, chi *sm (ARTE)* casting, moulding; cast, mould

calco'lare *vt* to calculate, work out, reckon; *(ponderare)* to weigh (up); **calcola'tore, 'trice** *ag* calculating ♦ *sm* calculator; *(fig)* calculating person; **calcolatore elettronico** computer; **calcola'trice** *sf (anche: macchina calcolatrice)* calculator

'calcolo *sm (anche MAT)* calculation; *(infinitesimale etc)* calculus; *(MED)* stone; **fare i propri ~i** *(fig)* to weigh the pros and cons; **per ~** out of self-interest

cal'daia *sf* boiler

caldeggi'are [kalded'dʒare] *vt* to support

'caldo, a *ag* warm; *(molto ~)* hot; *(fig: appassionato)* keen; hearty ♦ *sm* heat; **ho ~** I'm warm; I'm hot; **fa ~** it's warm; it's hot

calen'dario *sm* calendar

'calibro *sm (di arma)* calibre, bore; *(TECN)* callipers *pl*; *(fig)* calibre; **di**

grosso ~ *(fig)* prominent

'calice ['kalitʃe] *sm* goblet; *(REL)* chalice

ca'ligine [ka'lidʒine] *sf* fog; *(mista con fumo)* smog

'callo *sm* callus; *(ai piedi)* corn

'calma *sf* calm

cal'mante *sm* sedative, tranquillizer

cal'mare *vt* to calm; *(lenire)* to soothe; ~**rsi** *vr* to grow calm, calm down; *(vento)* to abate; *(dolori)* to ease

calmi'ere *sm* controlled price

'calmo, a *ag* calm, quiet

'calo *sm (COMM: di prezzi)* fall; *(: di volume)* shrinkage; *(: di peso)* loss

ca'lore *sm* warmth; heat; **in ~** *(ZOOL)* on heat

calo'ria *sf* calorie

calo'roso, a *ag* warm

calpes'tare *vt* to tread on, trample on; **"è vietato ~ l'erba"** "keep off the grass"

ca'lunnia *sf* slander; *(scritta)* libel

cal'vario *sm (fig)* affliction, cross

cal'vizie [kal'vittsje] *sf* baldness

'calvo, a *ag* bald

'calza ['kaltsa] *sf (da donna)* stocking; *(da uomo)* sock; **fare la ~** to knit; ~**e di nailon** nylons, (nylon) stockings

cal'zare [kal'tsare] *vt (scarpe, guanti: mettersi)* to put on; *(: portare)* to wear ♦ *vi* to fit; **calza'tura** *sf* footwear

calzet'tone [kaltset'tone] *sm* heavy knee-length sock

cal'zino [kal'tsino] *sm* sock

calzo'laio [kaltso'lajo] *sm* shoemaker; *(che ripara scarpe)* cobbler; **calzole'ria** *sf (negozio)* shoe shop

calzon'cini [kaltson'tʃini] *smpl* shorts

cal'zone [kal'tsone] *sm* trouser leg; *(CUC) savoury turnover made with pizza dough*; ~**i** *smpl (pantaloni)* trousers *(BRIT)*, pants *(US)*

cambi'ale *sf* bill (of exchange); *(pagherò cambiario)* promissory note

cambia'mento *sm* change

cambi'are *vt* to change; *(modificare)* to alter, change; *(barattare)*; ~ (qc con qn/qc) to exchange (sth with sb/for sth) ♦ *vi* to change, alter; ~rsi *vr (variare abito)* to change; ~ **casa** to move (house); ~ **idea** to change one's mind; ~ **treno** to change trains

'cambio *sm* change; *(modifica)* alteration, change; *(scambio, COMM)* exchange; *(corso dei cambi)* rate (of exchange); *(TECN, AUT)* gears *pl*; **in ~ di** in exchange for; **dare il ~ a qn** to take over from sb

'camera *sf* room; *(anche: ~ da letto)* bedroom; *(POL)* chamber, house; ~ **ardente** mortuary chapel; ~ **d'aria** inner tube; *(di pallone)* bladder; **C~ di Commercio** Chamber of Commerce; **C~ dei Deputati** Chamber of Deputies, ≈ House of Commons *(BRIT)*, ≈ House of Representatives *(US)*; ~ **a gas** gas chamber; ~ **a un letto/a due letti/matrimoniale** single/twin-bedded/double room; ~ **oscura** *(FOT)* dark room

came'rata, i, e *smf* companion, mate ♦ *sf* dormitory

cameri'era *sf (domestica)* maid; *(che serve a tavola)* waitress; *(che fa le camere)* chambermaid

cameri'ere *sm* (man)servant; *(di ristorante)* waiter

came'rino *sm (TEATRO)* dressing room

'camice ['kamitʃe] *sm (REL)* alb; *(per medici etc)* white coat

cami'cetta [kami'tʃetta] *sf* blouse

ca'micia, cie ['kamitʃa] *sf (da uomo)* shirt; *(da donna)* blouse; ~ **di forza** straitjacket; **camici'otto** *sm* casual shirt; *(per operai)* smock

cami'netto *sm* hearth, fireplace

ca'mino *sm* chimney; *(focolare)* fireplace, hearth

'camion *sm inv* lorry *(BRIT)*, truck *(US)*; **camion'cino** *sm* van

cam'mello *sm (ZOOL)* camel; *(tessuto)* camel hair

cammi'nare *vi* to walk; *(funzionare)* to work, go

cam'mino *sm* walk; *(sentiero)* path; *(itinerario, direzione, tragitto)* way; **mettersi in ~** to set o start off

camo'milla *sf* camomile; *(infuso)* camomile tea

ca'morra *sf* camorra; racket

ca'moscio [ka'mɔʃʃo] *sm* chamois

cam'pagna [kam'paɲɲa] *sf* country, countryside; *(POL, COMM, MIL)* campaign; **in ~** in the country; **andare in ~** to go to the country; **fare una ~** to campaign; **campa'gnola** *sf (AUT)* cross-country vehicle; **campa'gnolo, a** *ag* country *cpd*

cam'pale *ag* field *cpd*; *(fig)*: **una giornata ~** a hard day

cam'pana *sf* bell; *(anche: ~ di vetro)* bell jar; **campa'nella** *sf* small bell; *(di tenda)* curtain ring; **campa'nello** *sm (all'uscio, da tavola)* bell

campa'nile *sm* bell tower, belfry; **campani'lismo** *sm* parochialism

cam'pare *vi* to live; *(tirare avanti)* to get by, manage

cam'pato, a *ag*: ~ **in aria** unsound, unfounded

campeggi'are [kamped'dʒare] *vi* to camp; *(risaltare)* to stand out; **campeggia'tore, 'trice** *smf* camper; **cam'peggio** *sm* camping; *(terreno)* camp site; **fare (del) campeggio** to go camping

cam'pestre *ag* country *cpd*, rural

campio'nario, a *ag*: **fiera ~a** trade fair ♦ *sm* collection of samples

campio'nato *sm* championship

campi'one, 'essa *smf (SPORT)* champion ♦ *sm (COMM)* sample

'campo *sm* field; *(MIL)* field; *(: accampamento)* camp; *(spazio delimitato: sportivo etc)* ground; field; *(di quadro)* background; **i ~i** *(campagna)* the countryside; ~ **da aviazione** airfield; ~ **di battaglia** *(MIL, fig)* battlefield; ~ **di concentramento** concentration camp; ~ **di**

golf golf course; ~ **da tennis** tennis court; ~ **visivo** field of vision

campo'santo (pl **campisanti**) sm cemetery

camuf'fare vt to disguise

'Canada sm: **il** ~ Canada; **cana'dese** ag, smf Canadian ♦ sf (anche: **tenda canadese**) ridge tent

ca'naglia [ka'naʎʎa] sf rabble, mob; (persona) scoundrel, rogue

ca'nale sm (anche fig) channel; (artificiale) canal

'canapa sf hemp

cana'rino sm canary

cancel'lare [kantʃel'lare] vt (con la gomma) to rub out, erase; (con la penna) to strike out; (annullare) to annul, cancel; (disdire) to cancel

cancelle'ria [kantʃelle'ria] sf chancery; (quanto necessario per scrivere) stationery

cancelli'ere [kantʃel'ljere] sm chancellor; (di tribunale) clerk of the court

can'cello [kan'tʃello] sm gate

can'crena sf gangrene

'cancro sm (MED) cancer; (dello zodiaco): C~ Cancer

candeg'gina [kanded'dʒina] sf bleach

can'dela sf candle; ~ **(di accensione)** (AUT) spark(ing) plug

cande'labro sm candelabra

candeli'ere sm candlestick

candi'dato, a smf candidate; (aspirante a una carica) applicant

'candido, a ag white as snow; (puro) pure; (sincero) sincere, candid

can'dito, a ag candied

can'dore sm brilliant white; purity; sincerity, candour

'cane sm dog; (di pistola, fucile) cock; **fa un freddo** ~ it's bitterly cold; **non c'era un** ~ there wasn't a soul; ~ **da caccia/guardia** hunting/guard dog; ~ **lupo** alsatian

ca'nestro sm basket

'canfora sf camphor

cangi'ante [kan'dʒante] ag iridescent

can'guro sm kangaroo

ca'nile sm kennel; (di allevamento) kennels pl; ~ **municipale** dog pound

ca'nino, a ag, sm canine

'canna sf (pianta) reed; (: indica, da zucchero) cane; (bastone) stick, cane; (di fucile) barrel; (di organo) pipe; ~ **fumaria** chimney flue; ~ **da pesca** (fishing) rod; ~ **da zucchero** sugar cane

can'nella sf (CUC) cinnamon

cannel'loni smpl pasta tubes stuffed with sauce and baked

cannocchi'ale [kannok'kjale] sm telescope

can'none sm (MIL) gun; (: STORIA) cannon; (tubo) pipe, tube; (piega) box pleat; (fig) ace

can'nuccia, ce [kan'nuttʃa] sf (drinking) straw

ca'noa sf canoe

ca'none sm canon, criterion; (mensile, annuo) rent; fee

ca'nonico, ci sm (REL) canon

ca'noro, a ag (uccello) singing, song cpd

canot'taggio [kanot'taddʒo] sm rowing

canot'tiera sf vest

ca'notto sm small boat, dinghy; canoe

cano'vaccio [kano'vattʃo] sm (tela) canvas; (strofinaccio) duster; (trama) plot

can'tante smf singer

can'tare vt, vi to sing; **cantau'tore, 'trice** smf singer-composer

canti'ere sm (EDIL) (building) site; (anche: ~ **navale**) shipyard

canti'lena sf (filastrocca) lullaby; (fig) sing-song voice

can'tina sf (locale) cellar; (bottega) wine shop

'canto sm song; (arte) singing; (REL) chant; chanting; (poesia) poem, lyric; (parte di una poesia) canto; (parte, lato): **da un** ~ on the one hand; **d'altro** ~ on the other hand

canto'nata *sf* corner; **prendere una ~** (*fig*) to blunder

can'tone *sm* (*in Svizzera*) canton

can'tuccio [kan'tuttʃo] *sm* corner, nook

canzo'nare [kantso'nare] *vt* to tease

can'zone [kan'tsone] *sf* song; (*POESIA*) canzone; **canzoni'ere** *sm* (*MUS*) songbook; (*LETTERATURA*) collection of poems

'caos *sm inv* chaos; **ca'otico, a, ci, che** *ag* chaotic

C.A.P. *sigla m* = **codice di avviamento postale**

ca'pace [ka'patʃe] *ag* able, capable; (*ampio, vasto*) large, capacious; **sei ~ di farlo?** can you o are you able to do it?; **capacità** *sf inv* ability; (*DIR, di recipiente*) capacity; **capaci'tarsi** *vr*: **capacitarsi di** to make out, understand

ca'panna *sf* hut

capan'none *sm* (*AGR*) barn; (*fabbricato industriale*) (factory) shed

ca'parbio, a *ag* stubborn

ca'parra *sf* deposit, down payment

ca'pello *sm* hair; **~i** *smpl* (*capigliatura*) hair *sg*

capez'zale [kapet'tsale] *sm* bolster; (*fig*) bedside

ca'pezzolo [ka'pettsolo] *sm* nipple

capi'enza [ka'pjentsa] *sf* capacity

capiglia'tura [kapiʎʎa'tura] *sf* hair

ca'pire *vt* to understand

capi'tale *ag* (*mortale*) capital; (*fondamentale*) main, chief ♦ *sf* (*città*) capital ♦ *sm* (*ECON*) capital; **capi'talismo** *sm* capitalism; **capi'talista, i, e** *ag, smf* capitalist

capi'tano *sm* captain

capi'tare *vi* (*giungere casualmente*) to happen to go, find o.s.; (*accadere*) to happen; (*presentarsi: cosa*) to turn up, present itself ♦ *vb impers* to happen; **mi è capitato un guaio** I've had a spot of trouble

capi'tello *sm* (*ARCHIT*) capital

ca'pitolo *sm* chapter

capi'tombolo *sm* headlong fall, tumble

'capo *sm* head; (*persona*) head, leader; (*: in ufficio*) head, boss; (*: in tribù*) chief; (*di oggetti*) head; top; end; (*GEO*) cape; **andare a ~** to start a new paragraph; **da ~** over again; **~ di bestiame** head *inv* of cattle; **~ di vestiario** item of clothing

'capo... *prefisso*: **capocu'oco, chi** *sm* head cook; **Capo'danno** *sm* New Year; **capo'fitto: a capofitto** *av* headfirst, headlong; **capo'giro** *sm* dizziness *no pl*; **capola'voro, i** *sm* masterpiece; **capo'linea** (*pl* **capi'linea**) *sm* terminus; **capo'lino** *sm*: **fare capolino** to peep out (*o in etc*); **capolu'ogo** (*pl* **-ghi** o **capilu'oghi**) *sm* chief town, administrative centre

capo'rale *sm* (*MIL*) lance corporal (*BRIT*), private first class (*US*)

'capo... *prefisso*: **capostazi'one** (*pl* **capistazi'oni**) *sm* station master; **capo'treno** (*pl* **capi'treno** o **capo'treni**) *sm* guard

capo'volgere [kapo'voldʒere] *vt* to overturn; (*fig*) to reverse; **~rsi** *vr* to overturn; (*barca*) to capsize; (*fig*) to be reversed; **capo'volto, a** *pp di* **capovolgere**

'cappa *sf* (*mantello*) cape, cloak; (*del camino*) hood

cap'pella *sf* (*REL*) chapel; **cap-pel'lano** *sm* chaplain

cap'pello *sm* hat

'cappero *sm* caper

cap'pone *sm* capon

cap'potto *sm* (over)coat

cappuc'cino [kapput'tʃino] *sm* (*frate*) Capuchin monk; (*bevanda*) frothy white coffee

cap'puccio [kap'puttʃo] *sm* (*copricapo*) hood; (*della biro*) cap

'capra *sf* (she-)goat; **ca'pretto** *sm* kid

ca'priccio [ka'prittʃo] *sm* caprice, whim; (*bizza*) tantrum; **fare i ~i** to be very naughty; **capricci'oso, a** *ag* capricious, whimsical; naughty

Capri'corno *sm* Capricorn

capri'ola *sf* somersault

capri'olo *sm* roe deer

'capro *sm* billy-goat; ~ **espiatorio** *(fig)* scapegoat

'capsula *sf* capsule; *(di arma, per bottiglie)* cap

cap'tare *vt (RADIO, TV)* to pick up; *(cattivarsi)* to gain, win

cara'bina *sf* rifle

carabini'ere *sm member of Italian military police force*

ca'raffa *sf* carafe

cara'mella *sf* sweet

ca'rattere *sm* character; *(caratteristica)* characteristic, trait; **avere un buon** ~ to be good-natured; **carat-te'ristica, che** *sf* characteristic, trait, peculiarity; **caratte'ristico, a, ci, che** *ag* characteristic; **caratte-riz'zare** *vt* to characterize, distinguish

car'bone *sm* coal

carbu'rante *sm (motor)* fuel

carbura'tore *sm* carburettor

car'cassa *sf* carcass; *(fig: peg: macchina etc)* (old) wreck

carce'rato, a [kartʃe'rato] *sm/f* prisoner

'carcere ['kartʃere] *sm* prison; *(pena)* imprisonment

carci'ofo [kar'tʃɔfo] *sm* artichoke

car'diaco, a, ci, che *ag* cardiac, heart *cpd*

cardi'nale *ag, sm* cardinal

'cardine *sm* hinge

'cardo *sm* thistle

ca'renza [ka'rɛntsa] *sf* lack, scarcity; *(vitaminica)* deficiency

cares'tia *sf* famine; *(penuria)* scarcity, dearth

ca'rezza [ka'rettsa] *sf* caress; **care'z'zare** *vt* to caress, stroke, fondle

'carica, che *sf (mansione ufficiale)* office, position; *(MIL, TECN, ELETTR)* charge: **ha una forte** ~ **di simpatia** he's very likeable; *vedi anche* **carico**

cari'care *vt* to load; *(aggravare: anche fig)* to weigh down; *(orologio)* to wind up; *(batteria, MIL)* to charge

'carico, a, chi, che *ag (che porta un peso)*: ~ **di** loaded o laden with; *(fucile)* loaded; *(orologio)* wound up; *(batteria)* charged; *(colore)* deep; *(caffè, tè)* strong ♦ *sm (il caricare)* loading; *(ciò che si carica)* load; *(fig: peso)* burden, weight; **persona a** ~ dependent; **essere a** ~ **di qn** *(spese etc)* to be charged to sb

'carie *sf (dentaria)* decay

ca'rino, a *ag* lovely, pretty, nice; *(simpatico)* nice

carità *sf* charity; **per** ~! *(escl di rifiuto)* good heavens, no!

carnagi'one [karna'dʒone] *sf* complexion

car'nale *ag (amore)* carnal; *(fratello)* blood *cpd*

'carne *sf* flesh; *(bovina, ovina etc)* meat; ~ **di manzo/maiale/pecora** beef/pork/mutton; ~ **tritata** mince *(BRIT)*, hamburger meat *(US)*, minced *(BRIT)* o ground *(US)* meat

car'nefice [kar'nefitʃe] *sm* executioner; hangman

carne'vale *sm* carnival

car'noso, a *ag* fleshy

'caro, a *ag (amato)* dear; *(costoso)* dear, expensive

ca'rogna [ka'roɲɲa] *sf* carrion; *(fig: fam)* swine

ca'rota *sf* carrot

caro'vana *sf* caravan

caro'vita *sm* high cost of living

carpenti'ere *sm* carpenter

car'pire *vt*: ~ **qc a qn** *(segreto etc)* to get sth out of sb

car'poni *av* on all fours

car'rabile *ag* suitable for vehicles; **"passo ~"** "keep clear"

car'raio, a *ag*: **passo** ~ vehicle entrance

carreggi'ata [karred'dʒata] *sf* carriageway *(BRIT)*, (road)way

car'rello *sm* trolley; *(AER)* undercarriage; *(CINEMA)* dolly; *(di macchina da scrivere)* carriage

carri'era *sf* career; **fare** ~ to get on; **a gran** ~ at full speed

carri'ola *sf* wheelbarrow

'carro sm cart, wagon; ~ **armato** tank; ~ **attrezzi** breakdown van

car'rozza [kar'rɔttsa] sf carriage, coach

carrozze'ria [karrottse'ria] sf body, coachwork (BRIT); (officina) coach-builder's workshop (BRIT), body shop

carroz'zina [karrot'tsina] sf pram (BRIT), baby carriage (US)

'carta sf paper; (al ristorante) menu; (GEO) map; plan; (documento, da gioco) card; (costituzione) charter; ~e sfpl (documenti) papers, documents; **alla** ~ (al ristorante) à la carte; ~ **assegni** bank card; ~ **assorbente** blotting paper; ~ **bollata** o **da bollo** official stamped paper; ~ **di credito** credit card; ~ (geografica) map; ~ **d'identità** identity card; ~ **igienica** toilet paper; ~ **d'imbarco** (AER, NAUT) boarding card; ~ **da lettere** writing paper; ~ **libera** (AMM) unstamped paper; ~ **da parati** wallpaper; ~ **verde** (AUT) green card; ~ **vetrata** sandpaper; ~ **da visita** visiting card

cartacar'bone (pl **cartacar'bone**) sf carbon paper

car'taccia, ce [kar'tattʃa] sf waste paper

cartamo'neta sf paper money

carta'pecora sf parchment

carta'pesta sf papier-mâché

car'teggio [kar'teddʒo] sm correspondence

car'tella sf (scheda) card; (custodia: di cartone) folder; (: di uomo d'affari etc) briefcase; (: di scolaro) schoolbag, satchel; ~ **clinica** (MED) case sheet

car'tello sm sign; (pubblicitario) poster; (stradale) sign, signpost; (ECON) cartel; (in dimostrazioni) placard; **cartel'lone** sm (pubblicitario) advertising poster; (della tombola) scoring frame; (TEATRO) playbill; **tenere il cartellone** (spettacolo) to have a long run

carti'era sf paper mill

car'tina sf (AUT, GEO) map

car'toccio [kar'tɔttʃo] sm paper bag

carto'le'ria sf stationer's (shop)

carto'lina sf postcard; ~ **postale** ready-stamped postcard

car'tone sm cardboard; (ARTE) cartoon; ~**i animati** smpl (CINEMA) cartoons

car'tuccia, ce [kar'tuttʃa] sf cartridge

'casa sf house; (specialmente la propria casa) home; (COMM) firm, house; **essere a** ~ to be at home; **vado a** ~ **mia/tua** I'm going home/ to your house; ~ **di cura** nursing home; ~ **dello studente** student house; ~e **popolari** ≈ council houses (o flats) (BRIT), ≈ public housing units (US)

ca'sacca, che sf military coat; (di fantino) blouse

casa'linga, ghe sf housewife

casa'lingo, a, ghi, ghe ag household, domestic; (fatto a casa) homemade; (semplice) homely; (amante della casa) home-loving; ~**ghi** smpl household articles; **cucina** ~**a** plain home cooking

cas'care vi to fall; **cas'cata** sf fall; (d'acqua) cascade, waterfall

ca'scina [kaʃ'ʃina] sf farmstead

'casco, schi sm helmet; (del parrucchiere) hair-drier; (di banane) bunch

casei'ficio [kazei'fitʃo] sm creamery

ca'sella sf pigeon-hole; ~ **postale** post office box

casel'lario sm filing cabinet; ~ **giudiziale** court records pl

ca'sello sm (di autostrada) tollhouse

ca'serma sf barracks pl

ca'sino sm (confusione) row, racket; (casa di prostituzione) brothel

casinò sm inv casino

'caso sm chance; (fatto, vicenda) event, incident; (possibilità) possibility; (MED, LING) case; **a** ~ at random; **per** ~ by chance, by accident; **in ogni** ~, **in tutti i** ~ in any case, at any rate; **al ~** should the opportunity arise; **nel ~ che** in case; **~ mai** if by chance; **~ limite** borderline case

caso'lare sm cottage

'cassa sf case, crate, box; (bara) coffin; (mobile) chest; (involucro: di orologio etc) case; (macchina) cash register; (luogo di pagamento) checkout (counter); (fondo) fund; (istituto bancario) bank; **~ automatica prelievi** automatic telling machine, cash dispenser; **~ continua** night safe; **~ integrazione:** mettere in **~ integrazione** ≈ to lay off; **~ mutua** o **malattia** health insurance scheme; **~ di risparmio** savings bank; **~ toracica** (ANAT) chest

cassa'forte (pl **casseforti**) sf safe

cassa'panca (pl **cassapanche** o **cassepanche**) sf settle

casse'rola sf = **casseruola**

casseru'ola sf saucepan

cas'setta sf box; (per registratore) cassette; (CINEMA, TEATRO) box-office takings pl; **film di ~** box-office draw; **~ di sicurezza** strongbox; **~ delle lettere** letterbox

cas'setto sm drawer; **casset'tone** sm chest of drawers

cassi'ere, a sm/f cashier; (di banca) teller

'casta sf caste

cas'tagna [kas'taɲɲa] sf chestnut

cas'tagno [kas'taɲɲo] sm chestnut (tree)

cas'tano, a ag chestnut (brown)

cas'tello sm castle; (TECN) scaffolding

casti'gare vt to punish; **cas'tigo, ghi** sm punishment

castità sf chastity

cas'toro sm beaver

cas'trare vt to castrate; to geld; to doctor (BRIT), fix (US)

casu'ale ag chance cpd

cata'comba sf catacomb

ca'talogo, ghi sm catalogue

catarifran'gente [catarifran'dʒɛnte]

sm (AUT) reflector

ca'tarro sm catarrh

ca'tasta sf stack, pile

ca'tasto sm land register; land registry office

ca'tastrofe sf catastrophe, disaster

catego'ria sf category

ca'tena sf chain; **~ di montaggio** assembly line; **~e da neve** (AUT) snow chains; **cate'naccio** sm bolt

cate'ratta sf cataract; (chiusa) sluice-gate

cati'nella sf: **piovere a ~e** to pour, rain cats and dogs

ca'tino sm basin

ca'trame sm tar

'cattedra sf teacher's desk; (di università) chair

catte'drale sf cathedral

catti'veria sf malice, spite; naughtiness; (atto) spiteful act; (parole) malicious o spiteful remark

cattività sf captivity

cat'tivo, a ag bad; (malvagio) bad, wicked; (turbolento: bambino) bad, naughty; (: mare) rough; (odore, sapore) nasty, bad

cat'tolico, a, ci, che ag, sm/f (Roman) Catholic

cat'tura sf capture

cattu'rare vt to capture

cauccíù [kaut'tʃu] sm rubber

'causa sf cause; (DIR) lawsuit, case, action; **a ~ di, per ~ di** because of; **fare o muovere ~ a qn** to take legal action against sb

cau'sare vt to cause

cau'tela sf caution, prudence

caute'lare vt to protect; **~rsi** vr: **~rsi (da)** to take precautions (against)

'cauto, a ag cautious, prudent

cauzi'one [kaut'tsjone] sf security; (DIR) bail

cav. abbr = **cavaliere**

'cava sf quarry

caval'care vt (cavallo) to ride; (muro) to sit astride; (sog: ponte) to span; **caval'cata** sf ride; (gruppo di persone) riding party

cavalca'via *sm inv* flyover

cavalci'oni [kaval'tʃoni]: **a ~ di** *prep* astride

cavali'ere *sm* rider; (*feudale, titolo*) knight; (*soldato*) cavalryman; (*al ballo*) partner; **cavalle'resco, a, schi, sche** *ag* chivalrous; **caval-le'ria** *sf* chivalry; (*milizia a cavallo*) cavalry

cavalle'rizzo, a [kavalle'rittso] *sm/f* riding instructor; circus rider

caval'letta *sf* grasshopper

caval'letto *sm* (*FOT*) tripod; (*da pittore*) easel

ca'vallo *sm* horse; (*SCACCHI*) knight; (*AUT*: *anche*: ~ *vapore*) horsepower; (*dei pantaloni*) crotch; **a ~ on** horseback; **a ~ di** astride, straddling; **~ di battaglia** (*fig*) hobby-horse; **~ da corsa** racehorse

ca'vare *vt* (*togliere*) to draw out, extract, take out; (: *giacca, scarpe*) to take off; (: *fame, sete, voglia*) to satisfy; **cavarsela** to get away with it; to manage, get on all right

cava'tappi *sm inv* corkscrew

ca'verna *sf* cave

'cavia *sf* guinea pig

cavi'ale *sm* caviar

ca'viglia [ka'viʎʎa] *sf* ankle

ca'villo *sm* quibble

'cavo, a *ag* hollow ♦ *sm* (*ANAT*) cavity; (*grossa corda*) rope, cable; (*ELETTR, TEL*) cable

cavolfi'ore *sm* cauliflower

'cavolo *sm* cabbage; (*fam*): **non m'importa un ~** I don't give a damn; **~ di Bruxelles** Brussels sprout

cazzu'ola [kat'tswɔla] *sf* trowel

c/c *abbr* = **conto corrente**

CD *sm inv* CD

CD-ROM [tʃidi'rom] *sm inv* CD-ROM

ce [tʃe] *pron, av* vedi **ci**

cece [tʃe] *sm* chickpea

cecità [tʃetʃi'ta] *sf* blindness

Cecoslo'vacchia [tʃekoslo'vakkja] *sf*: **la ~** Czechoslovakia

'cedere [tʃedere] *vt* (*concedere: posto*) to give up; (*DIR*) to transfer,

make over ♦ *vi* (*cadere*) to give way, subside; **~ (a)** to surrender (to), yield (to), give in (to); **ce'devole** *ag* (*terreno*) soft; (*fig*) yielding

cedola [tʃedola] *sf* (*COMM*) coupon; voucher

cedro [tʃedro] *sm* cedar; (*albero da frutto, frutto*) citron

C.E.E. [tʃe] *sigla f* (= *Comunità Economica Europea*) EEC

ceffo [tʃeffo] (*peg*) *sm* ugly mug

cef'fone [tʃef'fone] *sm* slap, smack

ce'lare [tʃe'lare] *vt* to conceal; **~rsi** to hide

cele'brare [tʃele'brare] *vt* to celebrate; **celebrazi'one** *sf* celebration

'celebre [tʃelebre] *ag* famous, celebrated; **celebrità** *sf inv* fame; (*persona*) celebrity

'celere [tʃelere] *ag* fast, swift; (*corso*) crash course

ce'leste [tʃe'leste] *ag* celestial; heavenly; (*colore*) sky-blue

'celibe [tʃelibe] *ag* single, unmarried ♦ *sm* bachelor

'cella [tʃella] *sf* cell

'cellula [tʃellula] *sf* (*BIOL, ELETTR, POL*) cell; **cellu'lare** *sm* cellphone

cellu'lite [tʃellu'lite] *sf* cellulite

cemen'tare [tʃemen'tare] *vt* (*anche fig*) to cement

ce'mento [tʃe'mento] *sm* cement; **~ armato** reinforced concrete

'cena [tʃena] *sf* dinner; (*leggera*) supper

ce'nare [tʃe'nare] *vi* to dine, have supper

'cencio [tʃentʃo] *sm* piece of cloth, rag; (*per spolverare*) duster

'cenere [tʃenere] *sf* ash

'cenno [tʃenno] *sm* (*segno*) sign, signal; (*gesto*) gesture; (*col capo*) nod; (*con la mano*) wave; (*allusione*) hint, mention; (*breve esposizione*) short account; **far ~ di sì/no** to nod (one's head)/shake one's head

censi'mento [tʃensi'mento] *sm* census

cen'sore [tʃen'sore] sm censor

cen'sura [tʃen'sura] sf censorship; censor's office; (fig) censure

cente'nario, a [tʃente'narjo] ag (che ha cento anni) hundred-year-old; (che ricorre ogni cento anni) centennial, centenary cpd ♦ sm/f centenarian ♦ sm centenary

cen'tesimo, a [tʃen'tezimo] ag, sm hundredth

cen'tigrado, a [tʃen'tigrado] ag centigrade; **20 gradi ~i** 20 degrees centigrade

cen'timetro [tʃen'timetro] sm centimetre

centi'naio [tʃenti'najo] (pl(f) -aia) sm: **un ~ (di)** a hundred; about a hundred

'cento ['tʃento] num a hundred, one hundred

cen'trale [tʃen'trale] ag central ♦ sf: **~ telefonica** (telephone) exchange; **~ elettrica** electric power station; **centra'lista** sm/f operator; **cen-tra'lino** sm (telephone) exchange; (di albergo etc) switchboard

cen'trare [tʃen'trare] vt to hit the centre of; (TECN) to centre

cen'trifuga [tʃen'trifuga] sf spin-drier

'centro ['tʃentro] sm centre; **~ civico** civic centre; **~ commerciale** shopping centre; (città) commercial centre

'ceppo ['tʃeppo] sm (di albero) stump; (pezzo di legno) block

'cera ['tʃera] sf wax; (aspetto) appearance, look

ce'ramica, che [tʃe'ramika] sf ceramic; (ARTE) ceramics sg

cerbi'atto [tʃer'bjatto] sm (ZOOL) fawn

'cerca ['tʃerka] sf: **in o alla ~ di** in search of

cer'care [tʃer'kare] vt to look for, search for ♦ vi: **~ di fare qc** to try to do sth

cerchia ['tʃerkja] sf circle

'cerchio ['tʃerkjo] sm circle; (giocat-tolo, di botte) hoop

cere'ale [tʃere'ale] sm cereal

ceri'monia [tʃeri'monja] sf ceremony

ce'rino [tʃe'rino] sm wax match

'cernia [tʃernja] sf (ZOOL) stone bass

cerni'era [tʃer'njera] sf hinge; **~ lampo** zip (fastener) (BRIT), zipper (US)

'cernita ['tʃernita] sf selection

'cero ['tʃero] sm (church) candle

ce'rotto [tʃe'rɔtto] sm sticking plaster

certa'mente [tʃerta'mente] av certainly

cer'tezza [tʃer'tettsa] sf certainty

certifi'cato sm certificate; **~ medico/di nascita** medical/birth certificate

---

PAROLA CHIAVE

'certo, a ['tʃerto] ag (sicuro): **~ (di/che)** certain o sure (of/that)
♦ det 1 (tale) certain; **un ~ signor Smith** a (certain) Mr Smith
2 (qualche; con valore intensivo) some; **dopo un ~ tempo** after some time; **un fatto di una ~a importanza** a matter of some importance; **di una ~a età** past one's prime, not so young
♦ pron: **~i, e** pl some
♦ av (certamente) certainly; (senz'altro) of course; **di ~** certainly; **no (di) ~!, ~ che no!** certainly not!; **sì ~** yes indeed, certainly

---

cer'vello, i [tʃer'vello] (ANAT: pl(f) -a) sm brain

'cervo, a ['tʃervo] sm/f stag/doe ♦ sm deer; **~ volante** stag beetle

ce'sello [tʃe'zɛllo] sm chisel

ce'soie [tʃe'zoje] sfpl shears

ces'puglio [tʃes'puʎʎo] sm bush

ces'sare [tʃes'sare] vi, vt to stop, cease; **~ di fare qc** to stop doing sth

'cesso ['tʃesso] sm (fam) (gabinetto) bog

'cesta ['tʃesta] sf (large) basket

ces'tino *sm* basket; (*per la carta straccia*) wastepaper basket; ~ **da viaggio** (*FERR*) packed lunch (o dinner)

'cesto ['tʃɛsto] *sm* basket

'ceto ['tʃɛto] *sm* (social) class

cetrio'lino [tʃetrio'lino] *sm* gherkin

cetri'olo [tʃetri'ɔlo] *sm* cucumber

CFC *sm inv* (= *clorofluorocarburo*) CFC

cfr. *abbr* (= *confronta*) cf

CGIL *sigla f* (= *Confederazione Generale Italiana del Lavoro*) *trades union organization*

PAROLA CHIAVE

che [ke] *pron* 1 (*relativo: persona: soggetto*) who; (: *oggetto*) whom, that; (: *cosa, animale*) which, that; **il ragazzo** ~ **è venuto** the boy who came; **l'uomo** ~ **io vedo** the man (whom) I see; **il libro** ~ **è sul tavolo** the book which *o* that is on the table; **il libro** ~ **vedi** the book (which *o* that) you see; **la sera** ~ **ti ho visto** the evening I saw you

2 (*interrogativo, esclamativo*) what; ~ (**cosa**) **fai?** what are you doing?; **a** ~ (**cosa**) **pensi?** what are you thinking about?; **non sa** ~ (**cosa**) **fare** he doesn't know what to do; **ma** ~ **dici!** what are you saying!

3 (*indefinito*): **quell'uomo ha un** ~ **di losco** there's something suspicious about that man; **un certo non so** ~ an indefinable something

♦ *det* 1 (*interrogativo: tra tanti*) what; (: *tra pochi*) which; ~ **tipo di film preferisci?** what sort of film do you prefer?; ~ **vestito ti vuoi mettere?** what (o which) dress do you want to put on?

2 (*esclamativo: seguito da aggettivo*) how; (: *seguito da sostantivo*) what; ~ **buono!** how delicious!; ~ **bel vestito!** what a lovely dress!

♦ *cong* 1 (*con proposizioni subordinate*) that; **credo** ~ **verrà** I think he'll come; **voglio** ~ **tu studi** I want you to study; **so** ~ **c'eri** I

know (that) you were there; **non** ~: **non** ~ **sia sbagliato, ma** ... not that it's wrong, but ...

2 (*finale*) so that; **vieni qua,** ~ **ti veda** come here, so (that) I can see you

3 (*temporale*): **arrivai** ~ **eri già partito** you had already left when I arrived; **sono anni** ~ **non lo vedo** I haven't seen him for years

4 (*in frasi imperative, concessive*): ~ **venga pure!** let him come by all means!; ~ **tu sia benedetto!** may God bless you!

5 (*comparativo: con più, meno*) than; *vedi anche* **più; meno; così** *etc*

---

cheti'chella [keti'kella]: **alla** ~ *av* stealthily, unobtrusively

---

PAROLA CHIAVE

chi [ki] *pron* 1 (*interrogativo: soggetto*) who; (: *oggetto*) who, whom; ~ **è?** who is it?; **di** ~ **è questo libro?** whose book is this?, whose is this book?; **con** ~ **parli?** who are you talking to?; **a** ~ **pensi?** who are you thinking about?; **di voi?** which of you?; **non so a** ~ ~ **rivolgermi** I don't know who to ask

2 (*relativo*) whoever, anyone who; **dillo a** ~ **vuoi** tell whoever you like

3 (*indefinito*): ~ ... ~ ... some ... others ...; ~ **dice una cosa,** ~ **dice un'altra** some say one thing, others say another

---

chiacchie'rare [kjakkje'rare] *vi* to chat; (*discorrere futilmente*) to chatter; (*far pettegolezzi*) to gossip; **chiacchie'rata** *sf* chat; **chi'acchiere** ['tʃakkjere] *sfpl*: **fare due** *o* **quattro chiacchiere** to have a chat; **chiacchie'rone, a** *ag* talkative, chatty; gossipy ♦ *sm/f* chatterbox; gossip

chia'mare [kja'mare] *vt* to call; (*rivolgersi a qn*) to call (in), send for; ~**rsi** *vr* (*aver nome*) to be called; **mi chiamo Paolo** my name is Paolo, I'm called Paolo; ~ **alle armi** to call up; ~ **in giudizio** to summon; **chia'mata** *sf* (TEL) call; (MIL) call-up

chia'rezza [kja'rettsa] *sf* clearness, clarity

chia'rire [kja'rire] *vt* to make clear; (*fig: spiegare*) to clear up, explain; ~**rsi** *vr* to become clear

chi'aro, a [kjaro] *ag* clear; (*luminoso*) clear, bright; (*colore*) pale, light

chiaroveg'gente [kjaroved'dʒɛnte] *smf* clairvoyant

chi'asso [kjasso] *sm* uproar, row; **chias'soso, a** *ag* noisy, rowdy; (*vistoso*) showy, gaudy

chi'ave [kjave] *sf* key ♦ *ag inv* key *cpd*; ~ **d'accensione** (AUT) ignition key; ~ **inglese** monkey wrench; ~ **di volta** keystone; **chiavis'tello** *sm* bolt

chi'azza [kjattsa] *sf* stain; splash

'chicco, chi [kikko] *sm* grain; (*di caffè*) bean; ~ **d'uva** grape

chi'edere [kjɛdere] *vt* (*per sapere*) to ask; (*per avere*) to ask for ♦ *vi*: ~ **di qn** to ask after sb; (*al telefono*) to ask for o want sb; ~ **qc a qn** to ask sb sth; to ask sb for sth

chi'erico, a [kjɛriko] *sm* cleric; altar boy

chi'esa [kjɛza] *sf* church

chi'esto, a *pp di* **chiedere**

'chiglia [kiʎʎa] *sf* keel

'chilo [kilo] *sm* kilo; **chilo'grammo** *sm* kilogram(me); **chi'lometro** *sm* kilometre

'chimica [kimika] *sf* chemistry

'chimico, a, ci, che [kimiko] *ag* chemical ♦ *smf* chemist

'china [kina] *sf* (*pendìo*) slope, descent; (BOT) cinchona

chi'nare [ki'nare] *vt* to lower, bend; ~**rsi** *vr* to stoop, bend

chi'nino [ki'nino] *sm* quinine

chi'occiola [kjɔttʃola] *sf* snail; **scala a** ~ spiral staircase

chi'odo [kjɔdo] *sm* nail; (*fig*) obsession

chi'oma [kjɔma] *sf* (*capelli*) head of

hair; (*di albero*) foliage

chi'osco, schi [kjɔsko] *sm* kiosk, stall

chi'ostro [kjɔstro] *sm* cloister

chiro'mante [kiro'mante] *smf* palmist

chirur'gia [kirur'dʒia] *sf* surgery; ~ **estetica** cosmetic surgery; **chi'rurgo, ghi** o **gi** *sm* surgeon

chissà [kis'sa] *av* who knows, I wonder

chi'tarra [ki'tarra] *sf* guitar

chi'udere [kjudere] *vt* to close, shut; (*luce, acqua*) to put off, turn off; (*definitivamente: fabbrica*) to close down, shut down; (*strada*) to close; (*recingere*) to enclose; (*porre termine*) to end ♦ *vi* to close, shut; to close down, shut down; to end; ~**rsi** *vr* to shut, close; (*ritirarsi: anche fig*) to shut o.s. away; (*ferita*) to close up

chi'unque [ki'unkwe] *pron* (*relativo*) whoever; (*indefinito*) anyone, anybody; ~ **sia** whoever it is

chi'uso, a [kjuso] *pp di* **chiudere** ♦ *sm* (*di corso d'acqua*) sluice, lock; (*recinto*) enclosure; (*di discorso etc*) conclusion, ending; **chiu'sura** *sf* closing; shutting; closing o shutting down; enclosing; putting o turning off; ending; (*dispositivo*) catch; fastening; fastener

---

ci [tʃi] (*dav lo, la, li, le, ne diventa ce*) *pron* **1** (*personale: complemento oggetto*) us; (: *a noi: complemento di termine*) (to) us; (: *riflessivo*) ourselves; (: *reciproco*) each other, one another; (*impersonale*): ~ **si veste** we get dressed; ~ **ha visti** he's seen us; **non** ~ **ha dato niente** he gave us nothing; ~ **vestiamo** we get dressed; ~ **amiamo** we love one another o each other

2 (*dimostrativo: di ciò, su ciò, in ciò etc*) about (o on o of) it; **non so cosa far**~ I don't know what to do about it; **che c'entro io?** what have

I got to do with it?

◆ av (qui) here; (lì) there; (moto attraverso luogo): ~ passa sopra un ponte a bridge passes over it; non ~ passa più nessuno nobody comes this way any more; esser~ vedi essere

C.ia abbr (= compagnia) Co.

cia'batta [tʃa'batta] sf mule, slipper

ci'alda ['tʃalda] sf (CUC) wafer

ciam'bella [tʃam'bella] sf (CUC) ring-shaped cake; (salvagente) rubber ring

ci'ao ['tʃao] escl (all'arrivo) hello!; (alla partenza) cheerio! (BRIT), bye!

ciarla'tano [tʃarla'tano] sm charlatan

cias'cuno, a [tʃas'kuno] (det: dav sm: ciascun +C, V, ciascuno +s impura, gn, pn, ps, x, z; dav sf: ciascuna +C, ciascun' +V) det every, each; (ogni) every ◆ pron each (one); (tutti) everyone, everybody

ci'barie [tʃi'barje] sfpl foodstuffs

cibo ['tʃibo] sm food

ci'cala [tʃi'kala] sf cicada

cica'trice [tʃika'tritʃe] sf scar

cicca ['tʃikka] sf cigarette end

ciccia ['tʃittʃa] sf (fam) (carne) meat; (grasso umano) fat, flesh

cice'rone [tʃitʃe'rone] sm guide

ci'clismo [tʃi'klizmo] sm cycling;

ci'clista, i, e sm/f cyclist

ciclo ['tʃiklo] sm cycle; (di malattia) course

ciclomo'tore [tʃiklomo'tore] sm moped

ci'clone [tʃi'klone] sm cyclone

ci'cogna [tʃi'koɲɲa] sf stork

ci'coria [tʃi'korja] sf chicory

ci'eco, a, chi, che ['tʃɛko] ag blind ◆ sm/f blind man/woman

ci'elo ['tʃɛlo] sm sky; (REL) heaven

'cifra ['tʃifra] sf (numero) figure; numeral; (somma di denaro) sum, figure; (monogramma) monogram, initials pl; (codice) code, cipher

'ciglio [ˈtʃiʎʎo] (delle palpebre:

pl(f) **ciglia**) sm (margine) edge, verge; (eye)lash; (eye)lid; (sopracciglio) eyebrow

'cigno ['tʃiɲɲo] sm swan

cigo'lare [tʃigo'lare] vi to squeak, creak

'Cile ['tʃile] sm: il ~ Chile

ci'lecca [tʃi'lekka] sf: far ~ to fail

cili'egia [tʃi'ljɛdʒa] sf cherry; **cili'egio** sm cherry tree

cilin'drata [tʃilin'drata] sf (AUT) (cubic) capacity; **una macchina di grossa** ~ a big-engined car

ci'lindro [tʃi'lindro] sm cylinder; (cappello) top hat

'cima ['tʃima] sf (sommità) top; (di monte) top, summit; (estremità) end; in ~ a at the top of; da ~ a fondo from top to bottom; (fig) from beginning to end

'cimice ['tʃimitʃe] sf (ZOOL) bug; (puntina) drawing pin (BRIT), thumbtack (US)

cimini'era [tʃimi'njɛra] sf chimney; (di nave) funnel

cimi'tero [tʃimi'tɛro] sm cemetery

ci'murro [tʃi'murro] sm (di cani) distemper

'Cina ['tʃina] sf: la ~ China

cin'cin [tʃin'tʃin] escl cheers!

cin cin [tʃin'tʃin] escl = cincin

'cinema ['tʃinema] sm inv cinema; **cine'presa** sf cine-camera

ci'nese [tʃi'nese] ag, sm/f, sm Chinese inv

'cingere ['tʃindʒere] vt (attorniare) to surround, encircle; ~ **la vita con una cintura** to put a belt round one's waist

cinghia ['tʃingja] sf strap; (cintura, TECN) belt

cinghi'ale [tʃingj'ale] sm wild boar

cinguet'tare [tʃingwet'tare] vi to twitter

'cinico, a, ci, che ['tʃiniko] ag cynical ◆ sm/f cynic; **ci'nismo** sm cynicism

cin'quanta [tʃin'kwanta] num fifty; **cinquan'tesimo, a** num fiftieth

cinquan'tina [tʃinkwan'tina] sf (se-

rie): **una ~ (di)** about fifty; (*età*): **essere sulla ~ di** to be about fifty

'cinque [ˈtʃiŋkwe] *num* five; **avere ~ anni** to be five (years old); **il ~ dicembre 1988** the fifth of December 1988; **alle ~** (*ora*) at five (o'clock)

cinque'cento [tʃinkweˈtʃɛnto] *num* five hundred ♦ *sm*: **il C~** the sixteenth century

'cinto, a [ˈtʃinto] *pp di* **cingere**

cin'tura [tʃinˈtura] *sf* belt; **~ di salvataggio** lifebelt (*BRIT*), life preserver (*US*); **~ di sicurezza** (*AUT, AER*) safety ♦ seat belt

ciò [tʃɔ] *pron* this; that; **~ che** what; **~ nonostante** *o* **nondimeno** nevertheless, in spite of that

ci'occa, che [ˈtʃɔkka] *sf* (*di capelli*) lock

ciocco'lata [tʃokkoˈlata] *sf* chocolate; (*bevanda*) (hot) chocolate; **cioccola'tino** *sm* chocolate; **cioc'co'lato** *sm* chocolate

cioè [tʃoˈɛ] *av* that is (to say)

ciondo'lare [tʃondoˈlare] *vi* to dangle; (*fig*) to loaf (about); **ci'ondolo** *sm* pendant

ci'otola [ˈtʃɔtola] *sf* bowl

ci'ottolo [ˈtʃɔttolo] *sm* pebble; (*di strada*) cobble(stone)

ci'polla [tʃiˈpolla] *sf* onion; (*di tulipano etc*) bulb

ci'presso [tʃiˈprɛsso] *sm* cypress (tree)

'cipria [ˈtʃiprja] *sf* (face) powder

'Cipro [ˈtʃipro] *sm* Cyprus

'circa [ˈtʃirka] *av* about, roughly ♦ *prep* about, concerning; **a mezzogiorno ~** about midday

'circo, chi [ˈtʃirko] *sm* circus

circo'lare [tʃirkoˈlare] *vi* to circulate; (*AUT*) to drive (along), move (along) ♦ *ag* circular ♦ *sf* (*AMM*) circular; (*di autobus*) circle (line); **circolazi'one** *sf* circulation; (*AUT*): **la circolazione** (the) traffic

'circolo [ˈtʃirkolo] *sm* circle

circon'dare [tʃirkonˈdare] *vt* to surround

circonfe'renza [tʃirkonfeˈrɛntsa] *sf* circumference

circonvallazi'one [tʃirkonvallatˈtsjone] *sf* ring road (*BRIT*), beltway (*US*); (*per evitare una città*) by-pass

circos'critto, a [tʃirkosˈkritto] *pp di* **circoscrivere**

circos'crivere [tʃirkosˈkrivere] *vt* to circumscribe; (*fig*) to limit, restrict; **circoscrizi'one** *sf* (*AMM*) district, area; **circoscrizione elettorale** constituency

circos'petto, a [tʃirkosˈpetto] *ag* circumspect, cautious

circos'tante [tʃirkosˈtante] *ag* surrounding, neighbouring

circos'tanza [tʃirkosˈtantsa] *sf* circumstance; (*occasione*) occasion

cir'cuito [tʃirˈkuito] *sm* circuit

CISL [tʃizl] *sigla f* = **Confederazione Italiana Sindacati Lavoratori**) *trades union organization*

'ciste [ˈtʃiste] *sf* = **cisti**

cis'terna [tʃisˈtɛrna] *sf* tank, cistern

'cisti [ˈtʃisti] *sf* cyst

C.I.T. [tʃit] *sigla f* = **Compagnia Italiana Turismo**

ci'tare [tʃiˈtare] *vt* (*DIR*) to summon; (*autore*) to quote; (*a esempio, modello*) to cite; **citazi'one** *sf* summons *sg*; quotation; (*di persona*) mention

ci'tofono [tʃiˈtɔfono] *sm* entry phone; (*in uffici*) intercom

città [tʃitˈta] *sf inv* town; (*importante*) city; **~ universitaria** university campus

cittadi'nanza [tʃittadiˈnantsa] *sf* citizens *pl*, inhabitants *pl* of a town or city; (*DIR*) citizenship

citta'dino, a [tʃittaˈdino] *ag* town *cpd*; city *cpd* ♦ *sm/f* (*di uno Stato*) citizen; (*abitante di città*) townsman, city dweller

ci'uco, a, chi, che [ˈtʃuko] *sm/f* ass, donkey

ci'uffo [ˈtʃuffo] *sm* tuft

ci'vetta [tʃiˈvetta] *sf* (*ZOOL*) owl; (*fig: donna*) coquette, flirt ♦ *ag inv*: **auto/nave ~** decoy car/ship

'civico, a, ci, che [ˈtʃiviko] *ag* civic; (*museo*) municipal, town *cpd*;

municipal, city *cpd*

ci'vile [tʃi'vile] *ag* civil; (*non militare*) civilian; (*nazione*) civilized ♦ *sm* civilian

civilizzazi'one [tʃiviliddzat'tsjone] *sf* civilization

civiltà [tʃivil'ta] *sf* civilization; (*cortesia*) civility

'clacson *sm inv* (*AUT*) horn

cla'more *sm* (*frastuono*) din, uproar, clamour; (*fig*) outcry; **clamo'roso,** **a** *ag* noisy; (*fig*) sensational

clandes'tino, **a** *ag* clandestine; (*POL*) underground, clandestine ♦ *sm/f* stowaway

clari'netto *sm* clarinet

'classe *sf* class; **di ~** (*fig*) with class; of excellent quality

'classico, **a, ci, che** *ag* classical; (*tradizionale: moda*) classic(al) ♦ *sm* classic; classical author

clas'sifica *sf* classification; (*SPORT*) placings *pl*

classifi'care *vt* to classify; (*candidato, compito*) to grade; **~rsi** *vr* to be placed

'clausola *sf* (*DIR*) clause

'clava *sf* club

clavi'cembalo [klavi'tʃembalo] *sm* harpsichord

cla'vicola *sf* (*ANAT*) collar bone

cle'mente *ag* merciful; (*clima*) mild; **cle'menza** *sf* mercy, clemency; mildness

'clero *sm* clergy

cli'ente *sm/f* customer, client; **clien'tela** *sf* customers *pl*, clientele

'clima, i *sm* climate; **cli'matico,** **a,** **ci, che** *ag* climatic; **stazione climatica** health resort; **climatizzazi'one** *sf* (*TECN*) air conditioning

'clinica, a *sf* (*scienza*) clinical medicine; (*casa di cura*) clinic, nursing home; (*settore d'ospedale*) clinic

'clinico, **a, ci, che** *ag* clinical ♦ *sm* (*medico*) clinician

clo'aca, che *sf* sewer

'cloro *sm* chlorine

cloro'formio *sm* chloroform

club *sm inv* club

c.m. *abbr* = **corrente mese**

coabi'tare *vi* to live together, live under the same roof

coagu'lare *vt* to coagulate ♦ *vi* to coagulate; (*latte*) to curdle; **~rsi** *vr* to coagulate; to curdle

coalizi'one [koalit'tsjone] *sf* coalition

co'atto, a *ag* (*DIR*) compulsory, forced

'COBAS *sigla mpl* (= *Comitati di base*) independent trades unions

coca'ina *sf* cocaine

cocci'nella [kottʃi'nella] *sf* ladybird (*BRIT*), ladybug (*US*)

'coccio ['kottʃo] *sm* earthenware; (*vaso*) earthenware pot; **~i** *smpl* (*frammenti*) fragments (of pottery)

cocci'uto, a [kot'tʃuto] *ag* stubborn, pigheaded

'cocco, chi *sm* (*pianta*) coconut palm; (*frutto*): **noce di ~** coconut ♦ *sm/f* (*fam*) darling

cocco'drillo *sm* crocodile

cocco'lare *vt* to cuddle, fondle

co'cente [ko'tʃente] *ag* (*anche fig*) burning

co'comero *sm* watermelon

co'cuzzolo [ko'kuttsolo] *sm* top; (*di capo, cappello*) crown

'coda *sf* tail; (*fila di persone, auto*) queue (*BRIT*), line (*US*); (*di abiti*) train; **con la ~ dell'occhio** out of the corner of one's eye; **mettersi in ~** to queue up (*BRIT*), line up (*US*); to join the queue (*BRIT*) o line (*US*); **~ di cavallo** (*acconciatura*) ponytail

co'dardo, a *ag* cowardly ♦ *sm/f* coward

'codice ['koditʃe] *sm* code; **~ di avviamento postale** postcode (*BRIT*), zip code (*US*); **~ fiscale** tax code; **~ della strada** highway code

coe'rente *ag* coherent; **coe'renza** *sf* coherence

coe'taneo, a *ag*, *sm/f* contemporary

'cofano *sm* (*AUT*) bonnet (*BRIT*), hood (*US*); (*forziere*) chest

'cogli ['koʎʎi] *prep* + *det* = **con** + **gli**; *vedi* **con**

'cogliere [ˈkɔʎʎere] vt (fiore, frutto) to pick, gather; (sorprendere) to catch, surprise; (bersaglio) to hit; (fig: momento opportuno etc) to grasp, seize, take; (: capire) to grasp; ~ qn in flagrante o in fallo to catch sb red-handed

co'gnato, a [koɲˈɲato] smf brother/sister-in-law

cognizi'one [koɲɲitˈtsjone] sf knowledge

co'gnome [koɲˈɲome] sm surname

'coi prep + det = con + i; vedi con

coinci'denza [kointʃiˈdɛntsa] sf coincidence; (FERR, AER, di autobus) connection

coin'cidere [koinˈtʃidere] vi to coincide; **coin'ciso, a** pp di coincidere

coin'volgere [koinˈvɔldʒere] vt: ~ in to involve in; **coin'volto, a** pp di coinvolgere

col prep + det = con + il; vedi con

cola'brodo sm inv strainer

cola'pasta sm inv colander

co'lare (liquido) to strain; (pasta) to drain; (oro fuso) to pour ♦ vi (sudore) to drip; (botte) to leak; (cera) to melt; ~ a picco vt, vi (nave) to sink

co'lata sf (di lava) flow; (FONDERIA) casting

colazi'one [kolatˈtsjone] sf (anche: prima ~) breakfast; (anche: seconda ~) lunch; fare ~ to have breakfast (o lunch)

co'lei pron vedi colui

co'lera sm (MED) cholera

'colica, sf (MED) colic

'colla sf glue; (di farina) paste

collabo'rare vi to collaborate; ~ a to collaborate on; (giornale) to contribute to; **collabora'tore, 'trice** smf collaborator; contributor

col'lana sf necklace; (collezione) collection, series

col'lant sm inv tights pl

col'lare sm collar

col'lasso sm (MED) collapse

collau'dare vt to test, try out; **col'laudo** sm testing no pl; test

'colle sm hill

col'lega, ghi, ghe smf colleague

collega'mento sm connection; (MIL) liaison

colle'gare vt to connect, join, link; ~rsi vr (RADIO, TV) to link up; ~rsi con (TEL) to get through to

col'legio [kolˈlɛdʒo] sm college; (convitto) boarding school; ~ elettorale (POL) constituency

'collera sf anger

col'lerico, a, ci, che ag quick-tempered, irascible

col'letta sf collection

collettività sf community

collet'tivo, a ag collective; (interesse) general, everybody's; (biglietto, visita etc) group cpd ♦ sm (POL) (political) group

col'letto sm collar

collezio'nare [kollettsjoˈnare] vt to collect

collezi'one [kolletˈtsjone] sf collection

colli'mare vi to correspond, coincide

col'lina sf hill

col'lirio sm eyewash

collisi'one sf collision

'collo sm neck; (di abito) neck, collar; (pacco) parcel; ~ del piede instep

colloca'mento sm (impiego) employment; (disposizione) placing, arrangement

collo'care vt (libri, mobili) to place; (persona: trovare un lavoro per) to find a job for, place; (COMM: merce) to find a market for

col'loquio sm conversation, talk; (ufficiale, per un lavoro) interview; (INS) preliminary oral exam

col'mare vt: ~ di (anche fig) to fill with; (dare in abbondanza) to load o overwhelm with; **'colmo, a** ag: colmo (di) full (of) ♦ sm summit, top; (fig) height; al colmo della disperazione in the depths of despair; è il colmo! it's the last straw!

co'lombo, a smf dove; pigeon

co'lonia sf colony; (per bambini)

holiday camp; **(acqua di)** ~ (eau de) cologne; **coloni'ale** ag colonial ♦ sm/f colonist, settler

co'lonna sf column; ~ **vertebrale** spine, spinal column

colon'nello sm colonel

co'lono sm (coltivatore) tenant farmer

colo'rante sm colouring

colo'rare vt to colour; (disegno) to colour in

co'lore sm colour; a ~i in colour, colour cpd; **farne di tutti i** ~i to get up to all sorts of mischief

colo'rito, a ag coloured; (viso) rosy, pink; (linguaggio) colourful ♦ sm (tinta) colour; (carnagione) complexion

co'loro pron pl vedi **colui**

co'losso sm colossus

'colpa sf fault; (biasimo) blame; (colpevolezza) guilt; (azione colpevole) offence; (peccato) sin; **di chi è la** ~? whose fault is it?; è ~ **sua** it's his fault; **per** ~ **di** through, owing to; **col'pevole** ag guilty

col'pire vt to hit, strike; (fig) to strike; **rimanere colpito da qc** to be amazed o struck by sth

'colpo sm (urto) knock; (: affettivo) blow, shock; (: aggressivo) blow; (di pistola) shot; (MED) stroke; (rapina) raid; **di** ~ suddenly; **fare** ~ to make a strong impression; ~ **di grazia** coup de grâce; ~ **di scena** (TEATRO) coup de théâtre; (fig) dramatic turn of events; ~ **di sole** sunstroke; ~ **di Stato** coup d'état; ~ **di telefono** phone call; ~ **di testa** (sudden) impulse o whim; ~ **di vento** to gust (of wind)

coltel'lata sf stab

col'tello sm knife; ~ **a serramanico** clasp knife

colti'vare vt to cultivate; (verdura) to grow, cultivate; **coltiva'tore** sm farmer; **coltivazi'one** sf cultivation; growing

'colto, a pp di **cogliere** ♦ ag (istruito) cultured, educated

'coltre sf blanket

col'tura sf cultivation

co'lui (f **co'lei**, pl **co'loro**) pron the one; ~ **che parla** the one o the man o the person who is speaking; **colei che amo** the one o the woman o the person (whom) I love

'coma sm inv coma

comanda'mento sm (REL) commandment

coman'dante sm (MIL) commander, commandant; (di reggimento) commanding officer; (NAUT, AER) captain

coman'dare vi to be in command ♦ vt to command; (imporre) to order, command; ~ **a qn di fare** to order sb to do; **co'mando** sm (ingiunzione) order, command; (autorità) command; (TECN) control

co'mare sf (madrina) godmother

combaci'are [komba'tʃare] vi to meet; (fig: coincidere) to coincide

com'battere vt, vi to fight; **combatti'mento** sm fight; fighting no pl; (di pugilato) match

combi'nare vt to combine; (organizzare) to arrange; (fam: fare) to make, cause; **combinazi'one** sf combination; (caso fortuito) coincidence; **per combinazione** by chance

combus'tibile ag combustible ♦ sm fuel

com'butta (peg) sf: **in** ~ in league

'come av 1 (alla maniera di) like; ti comporti ~ lui you behave like him o like he does; bianco ~ la neve (as) white as snow; ~ se as if, as though

2 (in qualità di) as a; lavora ~ autista he works as a driver

3 (interrogativo) how; ~ ti chiami? what's your name?; ~ sta? how are you?; com'è il tuo amico? what is your friend like?; ~? (prego?) pardon?, sorry?; ~ mai? how come?; ~ mai non ci hai avvertiti? why on earth didn't you warn us?

4 (*esclamativo*): ~ **sei bravo!** how clever you are!; ~ **mi dispiace!** I'm terribly sorry!

◆ *cong* **1** (*in che modo*) how; **mi ha spiegato** ~ **l'ha conosciuto** he told me how he met him

2 (*correlativo*) as; (*con comparativi di maggioranza*) than; **non è bravo** ~ **pensavo** he isn't as clever as I thought; **è meglio di** ~ **pensassi** it's better than I thought

3 (*appena che, quando*) as soon as; ~ **arrivò, iniziò a lavorare** as soon as he arrived, he set to work; *vedi* **così; tanto**

'**comico, a, ci, che** *ag* (*TEATRO*) comic; (*buffo*) comical ◆ *sm* (*attore*) comedian, comic actor; (*comicità*) comic spirit, comedy

co'mignolo [ko'miɲɲolo] *sm* chimney top

cominci'are [komin'tʃare] *vt, vi* to begin, start; ~ **a fare/col fare** to begin to do/by doing

comi'tato *sm* committee

comi'tiva *sf* party, group

co'mizio [ko'mittsjo] *sm* (*POL*) meeting, assembly

com'mando *sm inv* commando (squad)

com'media *sf* comedy; (*opera teatrale*) play; (: *che fa ridere*) comedy; (*fig*) playacting *no pl*; **commedi'ante** (*peg*) *smf* third-rate actor/actress; (*fig*) sham

commemo'rare *vt* to commemorate

commenda'tore *sm* official title awarded for services to one's country

commen'tare *vt* to comment on; (*testo*) to annotate; (*RADIO, TV*) to give a commentary on; **commenta'tore, 'trice** *smf* commentator; **com'mento** *sm* comment; (*a un testo, RADIO, TV*) commentary

commerci'ale [kommer'tʃale] *ag* commercial, trading; (*peg*) commercial

commerci'ante [kommer'tʃante]

smf trader, dealer; (*negoziante*) shopkeeper

commerci'are [kommer'tʃare] *vt, vi*: ~ **in** to deal *o* trade in

com'mercio [kom'mertʃo] *sm* trade, commerce; **essere in** ~ (*prodotto*) to be on the market *o* on sale; **essere nel** ~ (*persona*) to be in business; ~ **all'ingrosso/al minuto** wholesale/retail trade

com'messa *sf* (*COMM*) order

com'messo, a *pp di* **commettere** ◆ *smf* shop assistant (*BRIT*), sales clerk (*US*) ◆ *sm* (*impiegato*) clerk; ~ **viaggiatore** commercial traveller

commes'tibile *ag* edible; ~**i** *smpl* foodstuffs

com'mettere *vt* to commit

commi'ato *sm* leave-taking

commi'nare *vt* (*DIR*) to threaten; to inflict

commissari'ato *sm* (*AMM*) commissionership; (: *sede*) commissioner's office; (: *di polizia*) police station

commis'sario *sm* commissioner; (*di pubblica sicurezza*) ≈ (police) superintendent (*BRIT*), (police) captain (*US*); (*SPORT*) steward; (*membro di commissione*) member of a committee *o* board

commissio'nario *sm* (*COMM*) agent, broker

commissio'ne *sf* (*incarico*) errand; (*comitato, percentuale*) commission; (*COMM: ordinazione*) order; ~**i** *sfpl* (*acquisti*) shopping *sg*

commit'tente *smf* (*COMM*) purchaser, customer

com'mosso, a *pp di* **commuovere**

commo'vente *ag* moving

commozi'one [kommot'tsjone] *sf* emotion, deep feeling; ~ **cerebrale** (*MED*) concussion

commu'overe *vt* to move, affect; ~**rsi** *vr* to be moved

commu'tare *vt* (*pena*) to commute; (*ELETTR*) to change *o* switch over

comò *sm inv* chest of drawers

como'dino *sm* bedside table

comodità *sf inv* comfort; convenience

'comodo, a *ag* comfortable; (*facile*) easy; (*conveniente*) convenient; (*utile*) useful, handy ♦ *sm* comfort; convenience; **con ~** at one's convenience *o* leisure; **fare il proprio ~** to do as one pleases; **far ~** to be useful *o* handy

compae'sano, a *sm/f* fellow countryman; person from the same town

com'pagine [kom'padʒine] *sf* (*squadra*) team

compa'gnia [kompa'ɲia] *sf* company; (*gruppo*) gathering

com'pagno, a [kom'paɲɲo] *sm/f* (*di classe, gioco*) companion; (*POL*) comrade

compa'rare *vt* to compare

compara'tivo, a *ag, sm* comparative

compa'rire *vi* to appear; **com'parsa** *sf* appearance; (*TEATRO*) walk-on; (*CINEMA*) extra; **comparso, a** *pp di* **comparire**

compartecipazi'one [kompartetʃi pat'tsjone] *sf* sharing; (*quota*) share; **~ agli utili** profit-sharing

comparti'mento *sm* compartment; (*AMM*) district

compas'sato, a (*persona*) composed

compassi'one *sf* compassion, pity; **avere ~ di qn** to feel sorry for sb, to pity sb

com'passo *sm* (pair of) compasses *pl*; callipers *pl*

compa'tibile *ag* (*scusabile*) excusable; (*conciliabile, INFORM*) compatible

compa'tire *vt* (*aver compassione di*) to sympathize with, feel sorry for; (*scusare*) to make allowances for

com'patto, a *ag* compact; (*roccia*) solid; (*folla*) dense; (*fig: gruppo, partito*) united, close-knit

com'pendio *sm* summary; (*libro*) compendium

compen'sare *vt* (*equilibrare*) to

compensate for, make up for; **~ qn di** (*rimunerare*) to pay *o* remunerate sb for; (*risarcire*) to pay compensation to sb for; (*fig: fatiche, dolori*) to reward sb for; **com'penso** *sm* compensation; payment, remuneration; reward; **in compenso** (*d'altra parte*) on the other hand

'compera *sf* (*acquisto*) purchase; **fare le ~e** to do the shopping

compe'rare *vt* = **comprare**

compe'tente *ag* competent; (*mancia*) apt, suitable; **compe'tenza** *sf* competence; (*mancia*) fees

com'petere *vi* to compete, vie; (*DIR: spettare*): **~ a** to lie within the competence of; **competizi'one** *sf* competition

compia'cente [kompja'tʃente] *ag* courteous, obliging; **compia'cenza** *sf* courtesy

compia'cere [kompja'tʃere] *vi*: **~ a** to gratify, please ♦ *vt* to please; **~rsi** *vr* (*provare soddisfazione*): **~rsi di** *o* **per qc** to be delighted at sth; (*rallegrarsi*): **~rsi con qn** to congratulate sb; (*degnarsi*): **~rsi di fare** to be so good as to do; **compiaci'uto, a** *pp di* **compiacere**

compi'angere [kom'pjandʒere] *vt* to sympathize with, feel sorry for; **compi'anto, a** *pp di* **compiangere**

'compiere *vt* (*concludere*) to finish, complete; (*adempiere*) to carry out, fulfil; **~rsi** *vr* (*avverarsi*) to be fulfilled, come true; **~ gli anni** to have one's birthday

compi'lare *vt* (*modulo*) to fill in; (*dizionario, elenco*) to compile

com'pire *vt* = **compiere**

compi'tare *vt* to spell out

com'pito *sm* (*incarico*) task, duty; (*dovere*) duty; (*INS*) exercise; (*: a casa*) piece of homework; **fare i ~i** to do one's homework

com'pito, a *ag* well-mannered, polite

comple'anno *sm* birthday

complemen'tare *ag* complementary; (INS: materia) subsidiary

comple'mento sm complement; (MIL) reserve (troops); ~ **oggetto** (LING) direct object

complessità sf complexity

comples'sivo, a ag (globale) comprehensive, overall; (totale: cifra) total

com'plesso, a ag complex ♦ sm (PSIC, EDIL) complex; (MUS: corale) ensemble; (: orchestrina) band; (: di musica pop) group; in o nel ~ on the whole

comple'tare vt to complete

com'pleto, a ag complete; (teatro, autobus) full ♦ sm suit; al ~ full; (tutti presenti) all present

compli'care vt to complicate; ~**rsi** vr to become complicated; **complicazi'one** sf complication

'complice ['komplitʃe] smf accomplice

complimen'tarsi vr: ~ **con** to congratulate

compli'mento sm compliment; ~**i** smpl (cortesia eccessiva) ceremony sg; (ossequi) regards, compliments; ~**i!** congratulations!; **senza** ~**i!** don't stand on ceremony!; make yourself at home!; help yourself!

complot'tare vt to plot, conspire

com'plotto sm plot, conspiracy

compo'nente smf member ♦ sm component

componi'mento sm (DIR) settlement; (INS) composition; (poetico, teatrale) work

com'porre vt (musica, testo) to compose; (mettere in ordine) to arrange; (DIR: lite) to settle; (TIP) to set; (TEL) to dial

comporta'mento sm behaviour

compor'tare vt (implicare) to involve; (consentire) to permit, allow (of); ~**rsi** vr (condursi) to behave

composi'tore, 'trice smf compositor; (TIP) compositor, typesetter

composizi'one [kompozit'tsjone] sf composition; (DIR) settlement

com'posta sf (CUC) stewed fruit no

pl; (AGR) compost; vedi anche **composto**

compos'tezza [kompos'tettsa] sf composure; decorum

com'posto, a pp di **comporre** ♦ ag (persona) composed, self-possessed; (: decoroso) dignified; (formato da più elementi) compound cpd ♦ sm compound

com'prare vt to buy; **compra'tore, 'trice** smf buyer, purchaser

com'prendere vt (contenere) to comprise, consist of; (capire) to understand

comprensi'one sf understanding

compren'sivo, a ag (prezzo): ~ **di** inclusive of; (indulgente) understanding

com'preso, a pp di **comprendere** ♦ ag (incluso) included

com'pressa sf (MED: garza) compress; (: pastiglia) tablet; vedi anche **compresso**

compressi'one sf compression

com'presso, a pp di **comprimere** ♦ ag (vedi comprimere) pressed; compressed; repressed

com'primere vt (premere) to press; (FISICA) to compress; (fig) to repress

compro'messo, a pp di **compromettere** ♦ sm compromise

compro'mettere vt to compromise

compro'vare vt to confirm

com'punto, a ag contrite

compu'tare vt to calculate; (addebitare): ~ **qc a qn** to debit sb with sth

com'puter sm inv computer

computiste'ria sf accounting, book-keeping

'computo sm calculation

comu'nale ag municipal, town cpd, ≈ borough cpd

co'mune ag common; (consueto) common, everyday; (di livello medio) average; (ordinario) ordinary ♦ sm (AMM) town council; (: sede) town hall ♦ sf (di persone) commune; **fuori del** ~ out of the ordinary; **avere in** ~ to have in common, share; **mettere in** ~ to share

comuni'care vt (notizia) to pass on, convey; (malattia) to pass on; (ansia etc) to communicate; (trasmettere: calore etc) to transmit, communicate; (REL) to administer communion to ♦ vi to communicate; to ~vi (propagarsi): ~rsi a to spread to; (REL) to receive communion

comuni'cato sm communiqué; ~ **stampa** press release

comunicazi'one [komunikat'tsjone] sf communication; (annuncio) announcement; (TEL): ~ (telefonica) (telephone) call; **dare la** ~ **a qn** to put sb through; **ottenere la** ~ to get through

comuni'one sf communion; ~ **di beni** (DIR) joint ownership of property

comu'nismo sm communism; **comu'nista, i, e** ag, sm/f communist

comunità sf inv community; **C~ Economica Europea** European Economic Community

co'munque cong however, no matter how ♦ av (in ogni modo) in any case; (tuttavia) however, nevertheless

con prep with; **partire col treno** to leave by train; ~ **mio grande stupore** to my great astonishment; ~ **tutto ciò** for all that

co'nato sm: ~ **di vomito** retching

'conca, che sf (GEO) valley

con'cedere [kon't∫edere] vt (accordare) to grant; (ammettere) to admit, concede; ~**rsi qc** to treat o.s. to sth, to allow o.s. sth

concentra'mento [kont∫entra'mento] sm concentration

concen'trare [kont∫en'trare] vt to concentrate; ~**rsi** vr to concentrate; **concentrazi'one** sf concentration

conce'pire [kont∫e'pire] vt (bambino) to conceive; (progetto, idea) to conceive (of); (metodo, piano) to devise

con'cernere [kon't∫ernere] vt to concern

concer'tare [kont∫er'tare] vt (MUS) to harmonize; (ordire) to devise, plan; ~**rsi** vr to agree

con'certo [kon't∫erto] sm (MUS) concert; (: componimento) concerto

concessio'nario [kont∫essjo'narjo] sm (COMM) agent, dealer

con'cesso, a [kon't∫esso] pp di **concedere**

con'cetto [kon't∫etto] sm (pensiero, idea) concept; (opinione) opinion

concezi'one [kont∫et'tsjone] sf conception

con'chiglia [kon'kiʎʎa] sf shell

'concia ['kont∫a] sf (di pelle) tanning; (di tabacco) curing; (sostanza) tannin

conci'are [kon't∫are] vt (pelli) to tan; (tabacco) to cure; (fig: ridurre in cattivo stato) to beat up; ~**rsi** vr (sporcarsi) to get in a mess; (vestirsi male) to dress badly

concili'are [kont∫i'ljare] vt to reconcile; (contravvenzione) to pay on the spot; (favorire: sonno) to be conducive to, induce; (procurare: simpatia) to gain; ~**rsi qc** to gain o win sth (for o.s.); ~**rsi qn** to win sb over; ~**rsi con** to be reconciled with; **conciliazi'one** sf reconciliation; (DIR) settlement

con'cilio [kon't∫iljo] sm (REL) council

con'cime [kon't∫ime] sm manure; (chimico) fertilizer

con'ciso, a [kon't∫izo] ag concise, succinct

conci'tato, a [kont∫i'tato] ag excited, emotional

concitta'dino, a [kont∫itta'dino] sm/f fellow citizen

con'cludere vt to conclude; (portare a compimento) to conclude, finish, bring to an end; (operare positivamente) to achieve ♦ vi (essere convincente) to be conclusive; ~**rsi** vr to come to an end, close; **conclusi'one** sf conclusion; (risultato) result; **conclu'sivo, a** *ag* conclusive; (*finale*) final; **con'cluso, a** *pp di* **concludere**

concor'danza [konkor'dantsa] *sf* (*anche* LING) agreement

concor'dare *vt* (*tregua, prezzo*) to agree on; (LING) to make agree ♦ *vi* to agree; **concor'dato** *sm* agreement; (REL) concordat

con'corde *ag* (*d'accordo*) in agreement; (*simultaneo*) simultaneous

concor'rente *sm/f* competitor; (INS) candidate; **concor'renza** *sf* competition

con'correre *vi*: ~ (**in**) (MAT) to converge *o* meet (in); ~ (**a**) (*competere*) to compete (for); (: INS: *a una cattedra*) to apply (for); (*partecipare: a un'impresa*) to take part (in), contribute (to); **con'corso, a** *pp di* **concorrere** ♦ *sm* competition; (INS) competitive examination; **concorso di colpa** (DIR) contributory negligence

con'creto, a *ag* concrete

concussi'one [konkus'sjone] *sf* (DIR) extortion

con'danna *sf* sentence; conviction; condemnation

condan'nare *vt* (DIR): ~ **a** to sentence to; ~ **per** to convict of; (*disapprovare*) to condemn; **condan'nato, a** *sm/f* convict

conden'sare *vt* to condense; ~**rsi** *vr* to condense; **condensazi'one** *sf* condensation

condi'mento *sm* seasoning; dressing

con'dire *vt* to season; (*insalata*) to dress

condi'videre *vt* to share; **con-di'viso, a** *pp di* **condividere**

condizio'nale [kondittsjo'nale] *ag* conditional ♦ *sm* (LING) conditional ♦ *sf* (DIR) suspended sentence

condizio'nare [kondittsjo'nare] *vt* to condition; **ad aria condizionata** air-conditioned

condizi'one [kondit'tsjone] *sf* condition; ~**i** *sfpl* (*di pagamento etc*) terms, conditions; **a** ~ **che** on condi-

tion that, provided that

condogli'anze [kondoʎ'ʎantse] *sfpl* condolences

condo'minio *sm* joint ownership; (*edificio*) jointly-owned building

condo'nare *vt* (DIR) to remit; **con'dono** *sm* remission; **condono fiscale** conditional amnesty for people evading tax

con'dotta *sf* (*modo di comportarsi*) conduct, behaviour; (*di un affare etc*) handling; (*di acqua*) piping; (*incarico sanitario*) country medical practice controlled by a local authority

con'dotto, a *pp di* **condurre** ♦ *ag*: **medico** ~ local authority doctor (*in country district*) ♦ *sm* (*canale, tubo*) pipe, conduit; (ANAT) duct

condu'cente [kondu'tʃente] *sm* driver

con'durre *vt* to conduct; (*azienda*) to manage; (*accompagnare: bambino*) to take; (*automobile*) to drive; (*trasportare: acqua, gas*) to convey, conduct; (*fig*) to lead ♦ *vi* to lead; **condursi** *vr* to behave, conduct o.s.

condut'tore *ag*: **filo** ~ (*fig*) thread ♦ *sm* (*di mezzi pubblici*) driver; (FISICA) conductor

con'farsi *vr*: ~ **a** to suit, agree with

confederazi'one [konfederat'tsjone] *sf* confederation

confe'renza [konfe'rentsa] *sf* (*discorso*) lecture; (*riunione*) conference; ~ **stampa** press conference; **conferenzi'ere, a** *sm/f* lecturer

confe'rire *vt*: ~ **qc a qn** to give sth to sb, bestow sth on sb ♦ *vi* to confer

con'ferma *sf* confirmation

confer'mare *vt* to confirm

confes'sare *vt* to confess; ~**rsi** *vr* to confess; **andare a** ~**rsi** (REL) to go to confession; **confessio'nale** *ag*, *sm* confessional; **confessi'one** *sf* confession; (*setta religiosa*) denomination; **confes'sore** *sm* confessor

con'fetto *sm* sugared almond; (MED) pill

confezio'nare [konfettsjo'nare] *vt*

(vestito) to make (up); (merci, pacchi) to package

confezio'ne [konfet'tsjone] sf (di abiti: da uomo) tailoring; (: da donna) dressmaking; (imballaggio) packaging; ~ regalo gift pack; ~i per signora ladies' wear; ~i da uomo menswear

confic'care vt: ~ qc in to hammer o drive sth into; ~rsi vr to stick

confi'dare vi: ~ in to confide in, rely on ♦ vt to confide; ~rsi con qn to confide in sb; **confi'dente** smf (persona amica) confidant/confidante; (informatore) informer; **confi'den-za** sf (familiarità) intimacy, familiarity; (fiducia) trust, confidence; (rivelazione) confidence; **confidenzi'a-le** ag familiar, friendly; (segreto) confidential

configu'rarsi vr: ~ a to assume the shape o form of

confi'nare vi: ~ con to border on ♦ vt (POL) to intern; (fig) to confine; ~rsi vr (isolarsi): ~rsi in to shut o.s. up in

Confin'dustria sigla f (= Confederazione Generale dell'Industria Italiana) employers' association, ≈ CBI (BRIT)

con'fine sm boundary; (di paese) border, frontier

con'fino sm internment

confis'care vt to confiscate

con'flitto sm conflict

conflu'enza [konflu'entsa] sf (di fiumi) confluence; (di strade) junction

conflu'ire vi (fiumi) to flow into each other, meet; (strade) to meet

con'fondere vt to mix up, confuse; (imbarazzare) to embarrass; ~rsi vr (mescolarsi) to mingle; (turbarsi) to be confused; (sbagliare) to get mixed up; ~ le idee a qn to mix sb up, confuse sb

confor'mare vt (adeguare): ~ a to adapt o conform to; ~rsi vr: ~rsi (a) to conform to

confor'tare vt to comfort, console;

confor'tevole ag (consolante) comforting; (comodo) comfortable

con'forto sm comfort, consolation; comfort

confron'tare vt to compare

con'fronto sm comparison; **in** o **a** ~ **di** in comparison with, compared to; **nei miei** (o tuoi etc) ~i towards me (o you etc)

confusi'one sf confusion; (chiasso) racket, noise; (imbarazzo) embarrassment

con'fuso, a pp di **confondere** ♦ ag (vedi confondere) confused; (imbarazzato) embarrassed

confu'tare vt to refute

conge'dare [kondʒe'dare] vt to dismiss; (MIL) to demobilize; ~rsi vr to take one's leave; **con'gedo** sm (anche MIL) leave; **prendere congedo da qn** to take one's leave of sb; **congedo assoluto** (MIL) discharge

conge'gnare [kondʒeɲ'nare] vt to construct, put together; **con'gegno** sm device, mechanism

conge'lare [kondʒe'lare] vt to freeze; ~rsi vr to freeze; **congela'tore** sm freezer

congestio'nare [kondʒestjo'nare] vt to congest

congesti'one [kondʒes'tjone] sf congestion

conget'tura [kondʒet'tura] sf conjecture, supposition

con'giungere [kon'dʒundʒere] vt to join (together); ~rsi vr to join (together)

congiunti'vite [kondʒunti'vite] sf conjunctivitis

congiun'tivo [kondʒun'tivo] sm (LING) subjunctive

congi'unto, a pp di **congiungere** ♦ ag (unito) joined ♦ smf relative

congiun'tura [kondʒun'tura] sf (giuntura) junction, join; (ANAT) joint; (circostanza) juncture; (ECON) economic situation

congiunzi'one [kondʒun'tsjone]

(LING) conjunction
congi'ura [kon'dʒura] sf conspiracy; **congiu'rare** vi to conspire
conglome'rato sm (GEO) conglomerate; (fig) conglomeration; (EDIL) concrete
congratu'larsi vr: ~ con qn per qc to congratulate sb on sth
congratulazi'oni [kongratulat'tsjoni] sfpl congratulations
con'grega, ghe sf band, bunch
con'gresso sm congress
congu'aglio [kon'gwaʎʎo] sm balancing, adjusting; (somma di denaro) balance
coni'are vt to mint, coin; (fig) to coin
co'niglio [ko'niʎʎo] sm rabbit
coniu'gare vt (LING) to conjugate; ~rsi vr to get married; **coniu'gato, a** ag (sposato) married; **coniugazi'one** sf (LING) conjugation
'coniuge ['kɔnjudʒe] sm/f spouse
connazio'nale [konnattsjo'nale] sm/f fellow-countryman/woman
connessi'one sf connection
con'nesso, a pp di connettere
con'nettere vt to connect, join ♦ vi (fig) to think straight
conni'vente ag conniving
conno'tati smpl distinguishing marks
'cono sm cone; ~ gelato ice-cream cone
cono'scente [konoʃ'ʃɛnte] sm/f acquaintance
cono'scenza [konoʃ'ʃɛntsa] sf (il sapere) knowledge no pl; (persona) acquaintance; (facoltà sensoriale) consciousness no pl; **perdere** ~ to lose consciousness
co'noscere [ko'noʃʃere] vt to know; ci siamo conosciuti a Firenze we (first) met in Florence; **conosci'tore, 'trice** sm/f connoisseur; **conosci'uto, a** pp di conoscere ♦ ag well-known
con'quista sf conquest
conqui'stare vt to conquer; (fig) to gain, win

consa'crare vt (REL) to consecrate; (: sacerdote) to ordain; (dedicare) to dedicate; (fig: uso etc) to sanction; ~rsi a to dedicate o.s. to
consangu'ineo, a sm/f blood relation
consa'pevole ag: ~ di aware o conscious of; **consapevo'lezza** sf awareness, consciousness
'conscio, a, sci, sce ['kɔnʃo] ag: ~ di aware o conscious of
consecu'tivo, a ag consecutive; (successivo: giorno) following, next
con'segna [kon'seɲɲa] sf delivery; (merce consegnata) consignment; (custodia) care, custody; (MIL: ordine) orders pl; (: punizione) confinement to barracks; **pagamento alla** ~ cash on delivery; **dare qc in** ~ a qn to entrust sth to sb
conse'gnare [konseɲ'ɲare] vt to deliver; (affidare) to entrust, hand over; (MIL) to confine to barracks
consegu'enza [konse'gwɛntsa] sf consequence; **per** o **di** ~ consequently
consegu'ire vt to achieve ♦ vi to follow, result
con'senso sm approval, consent
consen'tire vi: ~ a to consent o agree to ♦ vt to allow, permit
con'serva sf (CUC) preserve; ~ **di frutta** jam; ~ **di pomodoro** tomato purée
conser'vare vt (CUC) to preserve; (custodire) to keep; (: dalla distruzione etc) to preserve, conserve; ~rsi vr to keep
conserva'tore, 'trice sm/f (POL) conservative
conservazi'one [konservat'tsjone] sf preservation; conservation
conside'rare vt to consider; (reputare) to consider, regard; ~ **molto** qn to think highly of sb; **considerazi'one** sf consideration; (stima) regard, esteem; **prendere in considerazione** to take into consideration; **conside'revole** ag considerable
consigli'are [konsiʎ'ʎare] vt (perso-

na) to advise; (*metodo, azione*) to recommend, advise, suggest; **~rsi** *vr*: **~rsi con qn** to ask sb for advice; **consigli'ere, a** *smf* adviser ♦ *sm*: **consigliere d'amministrazione** board member; **consigliere comunale** town councillor; **con'siglio** *sm* (*suggerimento*) advice *no pl*, piece of advice; (*assemblea*) council; **consiglio d'amministrazione** board; **il Consiglio dei Ministri** (*POL*) ≈ the Cabinet

consis'tente *ag* thick; solid; (*fig*) sound, valid; **consis'tenza** *sf* consistency, thickness; solidity; validity

con'sistere *vi*: **~ in** to consist of; **consis'tito, a** *pp di* **consistere**

conso'lare *ag* consular ♦ *vt* (*confortare*) to console, comfort; (*rallegrare*) to cheer up; **~rsi** *vr* to be comforted; to cheer up

conso'lato *sm* consulate

consolazi'one [konsolat'tsjone] *sf* consolation, comfort

'console[1] *sm* consul

con'sole[2] [kon'sɔl] *sf* (*quadro di comando*) console

conso'nante *sf* consonant

'consono, a *ag*: **~ a** consistent with, consonant with

con'sorte *smf* consort

con'sorzio [kon'sɔrtsjo] *sm* consortium

con'stare *vi*: **~ di** to consist of ♦ *vb impers*: **mi consta che** it has come to my knowledge that, it appears that

consta'tare *vt* to establish, verify; **constatazi'one** *sf* observation; **constatazione amichevole** *jointly-agreed statement for insurance purposes*

consu'eto, a *ag* habitual, usual; **consue'tudine** *sf* habit, custom; (*usanza*) custom

consu'lente *smf* consultant; **consu'lenza** *sf* consultancy

consul'tare *vt* to consult; **~rsi** *vr*: **~rsi con qn** to seek the advice of sb; **consultazi'one** *sf* consultation;

consultazioni *sfpl* (*POL*) talks, consultations

consul'torio *sm*: **~ familiare** family planning clinic

consu'mare *vt* (*logorare: abiti, scarpe*) to wear out; (*usare*) to consume, use up; (*mangiare, bere*) to consume; (*DIR*) to consummate; **~rsi** *vr* to wear out; to be used up; (*anche fig*) to be consumed; (*combustibile*) to burn out; **consuma'tore** *sm* consumer; **consumazi'one** *sf* (*bibita*) drink; (*spuntino*) snack; (*DIR*) consummation; **con-su'mismo** *sm* consumerism; **con'sumo** *sm* consumption; wear; use

consun'tivo *sm* (*ECON*) final balance

con'tabile *ag* accounts *cpd*, accounting ♦ *smf* accountant; **contabilità** *sf* (*attività, tecnica*) accounting, accountancy; (*insieme dei libri etc*) books *pl*, accounts *pl*; (*ufficio*) accounts department

conta'dino, a *smf* countryman/woman; farm worker; (*peg*) peasant

contagi'are [konta'dʒare] *vt* to infect

con'tagio [kon'tadʒo] *sm* infection; (*per contatto diretto*) contagion; (*epidemia*) epidemic; **contagi'oso, a** *ag* infectious; contagious

conta'gocce [konta'gottʃe] *sm inv* (*MED*) dropper

contami'nare *vt* to contaminate

con'tante *sm* cash; **pagare in ~i** to pay cash

con'tare *vt* to count; (*considerare*) to consider ♦ *vi* to count, be of importance; **~ su qn** to count *o* rely on sb; **~ di fare qc** to intend to do sth; **conta'tore** *sm* meter

contat'tare *vt* to contact

con'tatto *sm* contact

'conte *sm* count

conteggi'are [konted'dʒare] *vt* to charge, put on the bill; **con'teggio** *sm* calculation

con'tegno [kon'teɲɲo] *sm* (*compor-*

tamento) behaviour; (*atteggiamento*)
attitude; **darsi un ~** to act nonchalant; to pull o.s. together

contem'plare *vt* to contemplate,
gaze at; (*DIR*) to make provision for

contemporanea'mente *av*
simultaneously; at the same time

contempo'raneo, a *ag*, *smf* contemporary

conten'dente *smf* opponent, adversary

con'tendere *vi* (*competere*) to compete; (*litigare*) to quarrel ♦ *vt*: **~ qc
a qn** to contend with *o* be in competition with sb for sth

conte'nere *vt* to contain; **conteni'tore** *sm* container

conten'tare *vt* to please, satisfy;
~rsi di to be satisfied with, content
o.s. with

conten'tezza [konten'tettsa] *sf* contentment

con'tento, a *ag* pleased, glad; **~ di**
pleased with

conte'nuto *sm* contents *pl*; (*argomento*) content

con'tesa *sf* dispute, argument

con'teso, a *pp di* **contendere**

con'tessa *sf* countess

contes'tare *vt* (*DIR*) to notify; (*fig*)
to dispute; **contestazi'one** *sf* (*DIR*)
notification; dispute; (*protesta*) protest

con'testo *sm* context

con'tiguo, a *ag*: **~ (a)** adjacent
(to)

continen'tale *ag*, *smf* continental

conti'nente *ag* continent ♦ *sm*
(*GEO*) continent; (: *terra ferma*)
mainland; **conti'nenza** *sf* continence

contin'gente [kontin'dʒɛnte] *ag*
contingent ♦ *sm* (*COMM*) quota;
(*MIL*) contingent; **contin'genza** *sf*
circumstance; (*ECON*): (**indennità**
di) **~** cost-of-living allowance

continu'are *vt* to continue (with),
go on with ♦ *vi* to continue, go on; **~**
a fare qc to go on *o* continue doing

sth; **continuazi'one** *sf* continuation

continuità *sf* continuity

con'tinuo, a *ag* (*numerazione*)
continuous; (*pioggia*) continual, constant; (*ELETTR*): **corrente ~a** direct current; **di ~** continually

'conto *sm* (*calcolo*) calculation;
(*COMM*, *ECON*) account; (*di ristorante*, *albergo*) bill; (*fig: stima*) consideration, esteem; **fare i ~i con qn**
to settle one's account with sb; **fare**
~ su qn/qc to count *o* rely on sb;
rendere ~ a qn di qc to be accountable to sb for sth; **tener ~ di qn/qc**
to take sb/sth into account; **per ~ di**
on behalf of; **per ~ mio** as far as
I'm concerned; **a ~i fatti, in fin dei**
~i all things considered; **~ corrente**
current account; **~ alla rovescia**
countdown

con'torcere [kon'tortʃere] *vt* to
twist; (*panni*) to wring (out); **~rsi**
vr to twist, writhe

contor'nare *vt* to surround

con'torno *sm* (*linea*) outline, contour; (*ornamento*) border; (*CUC*)
vegetables *pl*

con'torto, a *pp di* **contorcere**

contrabbandi'ere *smf* smuggler

contrab'bando *sm* smuggling, contraband; **merce di ~** contraband,
smuggled goods *pl*

contrab'basso *sm* (*MUS*) (double)
bass

contraccambi'are *vt* (*favore etc*)
to return

contraccet'tivo, a [kontratt'ʃet'tivo]
ag, *sm* contraceptive

contrac'colpo *sm* rebound; (*di
arma da fuoco*) recoil; (*fig*) repercussion

con'trada *sf* street; district

contrad'detto, a *pp di* **contraddire**

contrad'dire *vt* to contradict; **contraddit'torio, a** *ag* contradictory;
(*sentimenti*) conflicting ♦ *sm* (*DIR*)
cross-examination; **contraddizi'r**
sf contradiction

contraf'fare vt (persona) to mimic; (alterare: voce) to disguise; (firma) to forge, counterfeit; **contraf'fatto, a** pp di **contraffare** ♦ ag counterfeit; **contraffazi'one** sf mimicking no pl; disguising no pl; forging no pl; (cosa contraffatta) forgery

contrap'peso sm counterbalance, counterweight

contrap'porre vt: ~ qc a qc to counter sth with sth; (paragonare) to compare sth with sth; **contrap'posto, a** pp di **contrapporre**

contraria'mente av: ~ a contrary to

contrari'are vt (contrastare) to thwart, oppose; (irritare) to annoy, bother; **~rsi** vr to get annoyed

contrarietà sf adversity; (fig) aversion

con'trario, a ag opposite; (sfavorevole) unfavourable ♦ sm opposite; essere ~ a qc (persona) to be against sth; in caso ~ otherwise; avere qc in ~ to have some objection; al ~ on the contrary

con'trarre vt to contract; **contrarsi** vr to contract

contrasse'gnare [kontrasseɲ'ɲare] vt to mark; **contras'segno** sm (distintivo) distinguishing mark; spedire in contrassegno to send C.O.D.

contras'tare vt (avversare) to oppose; (impedire) to bar; (negare: diritto) to contest, dispute ♦ vi: ~ (con) (essere in disaccordo) to contrast (with); (lottare) to struggle (with); **con'trasto** sm contrast; (conflitto) conflict; (litigio) dispute

contrat'tacco sm counterattack

contrat'tare vt, vi to negotiate

contrat'tempo sm hitch

con'tratto, a pp di **contrarre** ♦ sm contract; **contrattu'ale** ag contractual

contravvenzi'one [kontravven'tsjone] sf contravention; (ammenda) fine

contrazi'one [kontrat'tsjone] sf contraction; (di prezzi etc) reduction

contribu'ente smf taxpayer; ratepayer (BRIT), property tax payer (US)

contribu'ire vi to contribute; **contri'buto** sm contribution; (tassa) tax

'contro prep against; ~ **di me/lui** against me/him; **pastiglie ~ la** tosse throat lozenges; ~ **pagamento** (COMM) on payment ♦ prefisso:

contro'battere vt (fig: a parole) to answer back; (: confutare) to refute; **controfi'gura** sf (CINEMA) double; **controfir'mare** vt to countersign

control'lare vt (accertare) to check; (sorvegliare) to watch, control; (tenere nel proprio potere, fig: dominare) to control; **con'trollo** sm check; watch; control; **controllo delle nascite** birth control; **control'lore** sm (FERR, AUTOBUS) (ticket) inspector

controprodu'cente [kontroprodu'tʃɛnte] ag counterproductive

contro'senso sm (contraddizione) contradiction in terms; (assurdità) nonsense

controspio'naggio [kontrospio'nadd͡ʒo] sm counterespionage

contro'versia sf controversy; (DIR) dispute

contro'verso, a ag controversial

contro'voglia [kontro'vɔʎʎa] av unwillingly

contu'macia [kontu'matʃa] sf (DIR) default

contusi'one sf (MED) bruise

convale'scente [konvaleʃ'ʃɛnte] ag, smf convalescent; **convale'scenza** sf convalescence

convali'dare vt (AMM) to validate; (fig: sospetto, dubbio) to confirm

con'vegno [kon'veɲɲo] sm (incontro) meeting; (congresso) convention, congress; (luogo) meeting place

conve'nevoli smpl civilities

conveni'ente ag suitable; (vantaggioso) profitable; (: prezzo) cheap; **conveni'enza** sf suitability; advantage; cheapness; **le convenienze** sfpl social conventions

conve'nire vi (riunirsi) to gather, assemble; (concordare) to agree; (tornare utile) to be worthwhile ♦ vb impers: **conviene fare questo** it is advisable to do this; **conviene andarsene** we should go; **ne convengo** I agree

con'vento sm (di frati) monastery; (di suore) convent

convenzio'nale [konventsjo'nale] ag conventional

convenzi'one [konven'tsjone] sf (DIR) agreement; (nella società) convention; **le ~i** sfpl social conventions

conver'sare vi to have a conversation, converse

conversazi'one [konversat'tsjone] sf conversation; **fare ~** to chat, have a chat

conversi'one sf conversion; **~ ad U** (AUT) U-turn

conver'tire vt (trasformare) to change; (POL, REL) to convert; **~rsi** vr: **~rsi (a)** to be converted (to); **conver'tito, a** sm/f convert

con'vesso, a ag convex

con'vincere [kon'vintʃere] vt to convince; **~ qn di qc** to convince sb of sth; **~ qn a fare qc** to persuade sb to do sth; **con'vinto, a** pp di convincere; **convinzi'one** sf conviction, firm belief

convis'suto, a pp di convivere

con'vitto sm (INS) boarding school

con'vivere vi to live together

convo'care vt to call, convene; (DIR) to summon; **convocazi'one** sf meeting; summons sg

convogli'are [konvoʎ'ʎare] vt to convey; (dirigere) to direct, send; **con'voglio** sm (di veicoli) convoy; (FERR) train

convulsi'one sf convulsion; **~ di riso** fits of laughter

con'vulso, a ag (pianto) violent, convulsive; (attività) feverish

coope'rare vi: **~ (a)** to cooperate (in); **coopera'tiva** sf cooperative; **cooperazi'one** sf cooperation

coordi'nare vt to coordinate; **coordi'nate** sfpl (MAT, GEO) coordinates; **coordi'nati** smpl (MODA) coordinates

co'perchio [ko'pɛrkjo] sm cover; (di pentola) lid

co'perta sf cover; (di lana) blanket; (da viaggio) rug; (NAUT) deck

coper'tina sf (STAMPA) cover, jacket

co'perto, a pp di coprire ♦ ag covered; (cielo) overcast ♦ sm place setting; (posto a tavola) place; (al ristorante) cover charge; **~ di** covered in o with

coper'tone sm (telo impermeabile) tarpaulin; (AUT) rubber tyre

coper'tura sf (anche ECON, MIL) cover; (di edificio) roofing

'copia sf copy; **brutta/bella ~** rough/final copy

copi'are vt to copy; **copia'trice** sf copier, copying machine

copi'one sm (CINEMA, TEATRO) script

'coppa sf (bicchiere) goblet; (per frutta, gelato) dish; (trofeo) cup, trophy; **~ dell'olio** oil sump (BRIT) o pan (US)

'coppia sf (di persone) couple; (di animali, SPORT) pair

coprifu'oco, chi sm curfew

copri'letto sm bedspread

co'prire vt to cover; (occupare: carica, posto) to hold; (suono, odore) to cover; **~rsi** vr (cielo) to cloud over; (vestirsi) to wrap up, cover up; (ECON) to cover o.s.; **~rsi di** (macchie, muffa) to become covered in

co'raggio [ko'raddʒo] sm courage, bravery; **~!** (forza!) come on!; (animo!) cheer up!; **coraggi'oso, a** ag courageous, brave

co'rallo sm coral

co'rano sm (REL) Koran

co'razza [ko'rattsa] sf armour; (di animali) carapace, shell; (MIL) armour(-plating); **coraz'zata** sf battleship

corbelle'ria sf stupid remark; **~e**

sfpl nonsense *no pl*

'**corda** *sf* cord; (*fune*) rope; (*spago, MUS*) string; **dare ~ a qn** to let sb have his (*o* her) way; **tenere sulla ~ qn** to keep sb on tenterhooks; **tagliare la ~** to slip away, sneak off; **~e vocali** vocal cords

cordi'ale *ag* cordial, warm ♦ *sm* (*bevanda*) cordial

cor'doglio [kor'dɔʎʎo] *sm* grief; (*lutto*) mourning

cor'done *sm* cord, string; (*linea: di polizia*) cordon; **~ ombelicale** umbilical cord

Co'rea *sf:* **la ~** Korea

coreogra'fia *sf* choreography

cori'andolo *sm* (*BOT*) coriander; **~i** *smpl* confetti *sg*

cori'care *vt* to put to bed; **~rsi** *vr* to go to bed

'**corna** *sfpl vedi* corno

cor'nacchia [kor'nakkja] *sf* crow

corna'musa *sf* bagpipes *pl*

cor'netta *sf* (*MUS*) cornet; (*TEL*) receiver

cor'netto *sm* (*CUC*) croissant; **~ acustico** ear trumpet

cor'nice [kor'nitʃe] *sf* frame; (*fig*) setting, background

cornici'one [korni'tʃone] *sm* (*di edificio*) ledge; (*ARCHIT*) cornice

'**corno** (*pl(f)* **-a**) *sm* (*ZOOL*) horn; (*pl(m)* **-i**: *MUS*) horn; **fare le ~ a qn** to be unfaithful to sb; **cor'nuto,** **a** *ag* (*con corna*) horned; (*fam!: marito*) cuckolded ♦ *sm* (*fam!*) cuckold; (*: insulto*) bastard (*!*)

Corno'vaglia [korno'vaʎʎa] *sf:* **la ~** Cornwall

'**coro** *sm* chorus; (*REL*) choir

co'rona *sf* crown; (*di fiori*) wreath; **coro'nare** *vt* to crown

'**corpo** *sm* body; (*cadavere*) (dead) body; (*militare, diplomatico*) corps *inv*; (*di opere*) corpus; **prendere ~** to take shape; **a ~ a ~** hand-to-hand; **~ di ballo** corps de ballet; **~ di guardia** guardroom; **~ insegnante** teaching staff

corpo'rale *ag* bodily; (*punizione*) corporal

corpora'tura *sf* build, physique

corporazi'one [korporat'tsjone] *sf* corporation

corpu'lento, **a** *ag* stout

corre'dare *vt:* **~ di** to provide *o* furnish with; **cor'redo** *sm* equipment; (*di sposa*) trousseau

cor'reggere [kor'rɛddʒere] *vt* to correct; (*compiti*) to correct, mark

cor'rente *ag* (*fiume*) flowing; (*acqua del rubinetto*) running; (*moneta, prezzo*) current; (*comune*) everyday ♦ *sm:* **essere al ~ (di)** to be well-informed (about); **mettere al ~ (di)** to inform (of) ♦ *sf* (*movimento di liquido*) current, stream; (*spiffero*) draught; (*ELETTR, METEOR*) current; (*fig*) trend, tendency; **la vostra lettera del 5 ~ mese** (*COMM*) your letter of the 5th of this month; **cor'rente'mente** *av* commonly; **parlare una lingua correntemente** to speak a language fluently

'**correre** *vi* to run; (*precipitarsi*) to rush; (*partecipare a una gara*) to race, run; (*fig: diffondersi*) to go round ♦ *vt* (*SPORT: gara*) to compete in; (*rischio*) to run; (*pericolo*) to face; **~ dietro a qn** to run after sb; **corre voce che ... it is rumoured that ...**

cor'retto, **a** *pp di* **correggere** ♦ *ag* (*comportamento*) correct, proper; **caffè ~ al cognac** coffee laced with brandy

correzi'one [korret'tsjone] *sf* correction; marking; **~ di bozze** proofreading

cor'ridoio *sm* corridor

corri'dore *sm* (*SPORT*) runner; (*: su veicolo*) racer

corri'era *sf* coach (*BRIT*), bus

corri'ere *sm* (*diplomatico, di guerra*) courier; (*posta*) mail, post; (*COMM*) carrier

corrispet'tivo *sm* (*somma*) amount due

corrispon'dente *ag* corresponding ♦ *smf* correspondent

corrispon'denza [korrispon'dentsa] *sf* correspondence

corris'pondere *vi* (*equivalere*): ~ **(a)** to correspond (to); (*per lettera*): ~ **con** to correspond with ♦ *vt* (*stipendio*) to pay; (*fig: amore*) to return; **corris'posto, a** *pp di* **corrispondere**

corrobo'rare *vt* to strengthen, fortify; (*fig*) to corroborate, bear out

cor'rodere *vt* to corrode; ~**rsi** *vr* to corrode

cor'rompere *vt* to corrupt; (*comprare*) to bribe

corrosi'one *sf* corrosion

cor'roso, a *pp di* **corrodere**

cor'rotto, a *pp di* **corrompere** ♦ *ag* corrupt

corrucci'arsi [korrut'tʃarsi] *vr* to grow angry *o* vexed

corru'gare *vt* to wrinkle; ~ **la fronte** to knit one's brows

corruzi'one [korrut'tsjone] *sf* corruption; bribery

'corsa *sf* running *no pl*; (*gara*) race; (*di autobus, taxi*) journey, trip; **fare una** ~ to run, dash; (*SPORT*) to run a race

cor'sia *sf* (*AUT, SPORT*) lane; (*di ospedale*) ward

cor'sivo *sm* cursive (writing); (*TIP*) italics *pl*

'corso, a *pp di* **correre** ♦ *sm* course; (*strada cittadina*) main street; (*di unità monetaria*) circulation; (*di titoli, valori*) rate, price; **dar libero** ~ **a** to give free expression to; **in** ~ in progress, under way; (*annata*) current; ~ **d'acqua** river, stream; (*artificiale*) waterway; ~ **serale** evening class

'corte *sf* (*cortile*) yard; (*DIR, regale*) court; **fare la** ~ **a qn** to court sb; ~ **marziale** court-martial

cor'teccia, ce [kor'tettʃa] *sf* bark

corteggi'are [korted'dʒare] *vt* to court

cor'teo *sm* procession

cor'tese *ag* courteous; **corte'sia** *sf* courtesy; **per cortesia ...** excuse

me, please ...

cortigi'ana [korti'dʒana] *sf* courtesan

cortigi'ano, a [korti'dʒano] *sm/f* courtier

cor'tile *sm* (court)yard

cor'tina *sf* curtain; (*anche fig*) screen

'corto, a *ag* short; **essere a** ~ **di qc** to be short of sth; ~ **circuito** short-circuit

'corvo *sm* raven

'cosa *sf* thing; (*faccenda*) affair, matter, business *no pl*; (*che*) ~? what?; (*che*) **cos'è?** what is it?; **a** ~ **pensi?** what are you thinking about?

'coscia, sce ['kɔʃʃa] *sf* thigh; ~ **di pollo** (*CUC*) chicken leg

cosci'ente [koʃ'ʃɛnte] *ag* conscious; ~ **di** conscious *o* aware of; **cosci'enza** *sf* conscience; (*consapevolezza*) consciousness; **coscienzi'oso, a** *ag* conscientious

cosci'otto [koʃ'ʃɔtto] *sm* (*CUC*) leg

cos'critto *sm* (*MIL*) conscript

PAROLA CHIAVE

così *av* **1** (*in questo modo*) like this, (in) this way; (*in tal modo*) so; **le cose stanno** ~ this is the way things stand; **non ho detto** ~! I didn't say that!; **come stai?** — (e) ~ **così** — how are you? — so-so; **e** ~ **via** and so on; **per** ~ **dire** so to speak

2 (*tanto*) so; ~ **lontano** so far away; **un ragazzo** ~ **intelligente** such an intelligent boy

♦ *ag inv* (*tale*): **non ho mai visto un film** ~ I've never seen such a film

♦ *cong* **1** (*perciò*) so, therefore

2: ~ **... come** as ... as; **non è** ~ **bravo come** he's not as good as you; ~ **... che** so ... that

---

cosid'detto, a *ag* so-called

cos'metico, a, ci, che *ag, sm* cosmetic

cos'pargere [kos'pardʒere] *vt*: ~ **di**

to sprinkle with; **cos'parso, a** pp di cospargere

cos'petto sm: **al ~ di** in front of; in the presence of

cos'picuo, a ag considerable, large

cospi'rare vi to conspire; **cospirazi'one** sf conspiracy

'costa sf (tra terra e mare) coast(line); (litorale) shore; (ANAT) rib; **la C~ Azzurra** the French Riviera

costà av there

cos'tante ag constant; (persona) steadfast ♦ sf constant

cos'tare vi, vt to cost; **~ caro** to be expensive, cost a lot

cos'tata sf (CUC) large chop

cos'tato sm (ANAT) ribs pl

costeggi'are [kosted'dʒare] vt to be close to; to run alongside

cos'tei pron vedi costui

costi'era sf stretch of coast

costi'ero, a ag coastal, coast cpd

costitu'ire vt (comitato, gruppo) to set up, form; (collezione) to put together, build up; (sog: elementi, parti: comporre) to make up, constitute; (rappresentare) to constitute; (DIR) to appoint; **~rsi alla polizia** to give o.s. up to the police

costituzio'nale [kostituttsjo'nale] ag constitutional

costituzi'one [kostitu'tsjone] sf setting up; building up; constitution

'costo sm cost; **a ogni o qualunque ~, a tutti i ~i** at all costs

'costola sf (ANAT) rib

cos'toro pron vedi costui

cos'toso, a ag expensive, costly

cos'tretto, a pp di costringere

cos'tringere [kos'trindʒere] vt: **~ qn a fare qc** to force sb to do sth; **costrizi'one** sf coercion

costru'ire vt to construct, build; **costruzi'one** sf construction, building

cos'tui (f cos'tei, pl cos'toro) pron (soggetto) he/she; pl they; (complemento) him/her; pl them; **si può sapere chi è ~?** (peg) just who is that

fellow?

cos'tume sm (uso) custom; (foggia di vestire, indumento) costume; **~i** smpl (condotta morale) morals, morality sg; **il buon ~** public morality; **~ da bagno** bathing o swimming costume (BRIT), swimsuit; (da uomo) bathing o swimming trunks pl

co'tenna sf bacon rind

co'togna [ko'toɲɲa] sf quince

coto'letta sf (di maiale, montone) chop; (di vitello, agnello) cutlet

co'tone sm cotton; **~ idrofilo** cotton wool (BRIT), absorbent cotton (US)

'cotta sf (fam: innamoramento) crush

'cottimo sm: **lavorare a ~** to do piecework

'cotto, a pp di cuocere ♦ ag cooked; (fam: innamorato) head-over-heels in love

cot'tura sf cooking; (in forno) baking; (in umido) stewing

co'vare vt to hatch; (fig: malattia) to be sickening for; (: odio, rancore) to nurse ♦ vi (fuoco, fig) to smoulder

'covo sm den

co'vone sm sheaf

'cozza ['kɔttsa] sf mussel

coz'zare [kot'tsare] vi: **~ contro** to bang into, collide with

C.P. abbr (= casella postale) P.O. Box

crack [kræk] sm inv (droga) crack

'crampo sm cramp

'cranio sm skull

cra'tere sm crater

cra'vatta sf tie

cre'anza [kre'antsa] sf manners pl

cre'are vt to create; **cre'ato** sm creation; **crea'tore, 'trice** ag creative ♦ sm creator; **crea'tura** sf creature; (bimbo) baby, infant; **creazi'one** sf creation; (fondazione) foundation, establishment

cre'dente sm/f (REL) believer

cre'denza [kre'dentsa] sf belief; (armadio) sideboard

credenzi'ali [kreden'tsjali] sfpl credentials

'credere *vt* to believe ♦ *vi*: ~ **in,** ~ **a** to believe in; ~ **qn onesto** to believe sb (to be) honest; ~ **che** to believe *o* think that; ~**rsi furbo** to think one is clever

'credito *sm (anche COMM)* credit; *(reputazione)* esteem, repute; **comprare a** ~ to buy on credit

'credo *sm inv* creed

'crema *sf* cream; *(con uova, zucchero etc)* custard; ~ **solare** sun cream

cre'mare *vt* to cremate

Crem'lino *sm*: **il** ~ the Kremlin

'crepa *sf* crack

'crepaccio [kre'pattʃo] *sm* large crack, fissure; *(di ghiacciaio)* crevasse

crepacu'ore *sm* broken heart

cre'pare *vi (fam: morire)* to snuff it, kick the bucket; ~ **dalle risa** to split one's sides laughing

crepi'tare *vi (fuoco)* to crackle; *(pioggia)* to patter

cre'puscolo *sm* twilight, dusk

'crescere ['kreʃʃere] *vi* to grow ♦ *vt (figli)* to raise; **'crescita** *sf* growth; **cresci'uto, a** *pp di* **crescere**

'cresima *sf (REL)* confirmation

'crespo, a *ag (capelli)* frizzy; *(tessuto)* puckered ♦ *sm* crêpe

'cresta *sf* crest; *(di polli, uccelli)* crest, comb

'creta *sf* chalk; clay

cre'tino, a *ag* stupid ♦ *smf* idiot, fool

cric *sm inv (TECN)* jack

'cricca, che *sf* clique

'cricco, chi *sm* = **cric**

crimi'nale *ag, smf* criminal

'crimine *sm (DIR)* crime

'crine *sm* horsehair; **crini'era** *sf* mane

crisan'temo *sm* chrysanthemum

'crisi *sf inv* crisis; *(MED)* attack, fit; ~ **di nervi** attack *o* fit of nerves

cristalliz'zare [kristalid'dzare] *vi* to crystallize; ~ **rsi** *vr* to crystallize; *(fig)* to become fossilized

cris'tallo *sm* crystal

cristia'nesimo *sm* Christianity

cristi'ano, a *ag, smf* Christian

'Cristo *sm* Christ

cri'terio *sm* criterion; *(buon senso)* (common) sense

'critica, che *sf* criticism; **la** ~ *(attività)* criticism; *(persone)* the critics *pl; vedi anche* **critico**

criti'care *vt* to criticize

'critico, a, ci, che *ag* critical ♦ *sm* critic

Croa'zia [kroa'ttsja] *sf* Croatia

cri'vello *sm* riddle

'croce ['krotʃe] *sf* cross; **in** ~ *(di traverso)* crosswise; *(fig)* on tenterhooks; **la C~** **Rossa** the Red Cross

croce'figgere *etc* [krotʃe'fiddʒere] = **crocifiggere** *etc*

croce'via [krotʃe'via] *sm inv* crossroads *sg*

croci'ata [kro'tʃata] *sf* crusade

cro'cicchio [kro'tʃikkjo] *sm* crossroads *sg*

croci'era [kro'tʃɛra] *sf (viaggio)* cruise; *(ARCHIT)* transept

croci'figgere [krotʃi'fiddʒere] *vt* to crucify; **crocifissi'one** *sf* crucifixion; **croci'fisso, a** *pp di* **crocifiggere**

crogi'olo [kro'dʒɔlo] *sm (fig)* melting pot

crol'lare *vi* to collapse; **'crollo** *sm* collapse; *(di prezzi)* slump, sudden fall

cro'mato, a *ag* chromium-plated

'cromo *sm* chrome, chromium

cromo'soma, i *sm* chromosome

'cronaca, che *sf* chronicle; *(STAMPA)* news *sg*; *(: rubrica)* column; *(TV, RADIO)* commentary; **fatto** *o* **episodio di** ~ news item; ~ **nera** crime news *sg*; crime column

'cronico, a, ci, che *ag* chronic

cro'nista, i *sm (STAMPA)* reporter

crono'logia [kronolo'dʒia] *sf* chronology

cro'nometro *sm* chronometer; *(a scatto)* stopwatch

'crosta *sf* crust

cros'tacei [kros'tatʃei] *smpl* shell-fish

cros'tata *sf* (CUC) tart

cros'tino *sm* (CUC) croûton; (*: da antipasto*) canapé

'cruccio ['kruttʃo] *sm* worry, torment

cruci'verba *sm inv* crossword (puzzle)

cru'dele *ag* cruel; **crudeltà** *sf* cruelty

'crudo, a *ag* (*non cotto*) raw; (*aspro*) harsh, severe

cru'miro (*peg*) *sm* blackleg (BRIT), scab

'crusca *sf* bran

crus'cotto *sm* (AUT) dashboard

CSI *sigle f inv* (Comunità Stati Indipendenti) CIS

'Cuba *sf* Cuba

'cubico, a, ci, che *ag* cubic

'cubo, a *ag* cubic ♦ *sm* cube; **elevare al ~** (MAT) to cube

cuc'cagna [kuk'kaɲɲa] *sf:* **paese della ~** land of plenty; **albero della ~** greasy pole (*fig*)

cuc'cetta [kut'tʃetta] *sf* (FERR) couchette; (NAUT) berth

cucchiai'ata [kukkja'jata] *sf* spoonful

cucchia'ino [kukkja'ino] *sm* teaspoon; coffee spoon

cucchi'aio [kuk'kjajo] *sm* spoon

'cuccia, ce ['kuttʃa] *sf* dog's bed; **a ~!** down!

'cucciolo ['kuttʃolo] *sm* cub; (*di cane*) puppy

cu'cina [ku'tʃina] *sf* (*locale*) kitchen; (*arte culinaria*) cooking, cookery; (*le vivande*) food, cooking; (*apparecchio*) cooker; **~ componibile** fitted kitchen; **cuci'nare** *vt* to cook

cu'cire [ku'tʃire] *vt* to sew, stitch; **cuci'trice** *sf* stapler; **cuci'tura** *sf* sewing, stitching; (*costura*) seam

cucù *sm inv* = **cuculo**

cu'culo *sm* cuckoo

'cuffia *sf* bonnet, cap; (*da infermiera*) cap; (*da bagno*) (bathing) cap; (*per ascoltare*) headphones *pl*, headset

cu'gino, a [ku'dʒino] *sm/f* cousin

'cui *pron* **1** (*nei complementi indiretti: persona*) whom; (*: oggetto, animale*) which; **la persona/le persone a ~ accennavi** the person/people you were referring to *o* to whom you were referring; **i libri di ~ parlavo** the books I was talking about *o* about which I was talking; **il quartiere in ~ abito** the district where I live; **la ragione per ~** the reason why **2** (*inserito tra articolo e sostantivo*) whose; **la donna i ~ figli sono scomparsi** the woman whose children have disappeared; **il signore, dal ~ figlio ho avuto il libro** the man from whose son I got the book

culi'naria *sf* cookery

'culla *sf* cradle

cul'lare *vt* to rock

culmi'nare *vi:* **~ con** *o* **in** to culminate in

'culmine *sm* top, summit

'culo (*fam!*) *sm* arse (Brit!), ass (US!); (*fig: fortuna*): **aver ~** to have the luck of the devil

'culto *sm* (*religione*) religion; (*adorazione*) worship, adoration; (*venerazione: anche fig*) cult

cul'tura *sf* culture; education, learning; **cultu'rale** *ag* cultural

cumula'tivo, a *ag* cumulative; (*prezzo*) inclusive; (*biglietto*) group *cpd*

'cumulo *sm* (*mucchio*) pile, heap; (METEOR) cumulus

'cuneo *sm* wedge

cu'oca *sf vedi* **cuoco**

cu'ocere ['kwɔtʃere] *vt* (*alimenti*) to cook; (*mattoni etc*) to fire ♦ *vi* to cook; **~ al forno** (*pane*) to bake; (*arrosto*) to roast; **cu'oco, a, chi, che** *sm/f* cook; (*di ristorante*) chef

cu'oio *sm* leather; **~ capelluto** scalp

cu'ore *sm* heart; **~i** *smpl* (CARTE) hearts; **avere buon ~** to be kind-hearted; **stare a ~ a qn** to be

portant to sb

cupi'digia [kupi'didʒa] *sf* greed, covetousness

'cupo, a *ag* dark; *(suono)* dull; *(fig)* gloomy, dismal

'cupola *sf* dome; cupola

'cura *sf* care; *(MED: trattamento)* (course of) treatment; **aver ~ di** *(occuparsi di)* to look after; **a ~ di** *(libro)* edited by; **~ dimagrante** diet

cu'rare *vt (malato, malattia)* to treat; *(: guarire)* to cure; *(aver cura di)* to take care of; *(testo)* to edit; **~rsi** *vr* to take care of o.s.; *(MED)* to follow a course of treatment; **~rsi di** to pay attention to

cu'rato *sm* parish priest; *(protestante)* vicar, minister

cura'tore, 'trice *sm/f (DIR)* trustee; *(di antologia etc)* editor

curio'sare *vi* to look round, wander round; *(tra libri)* to browse; **~ nei negozi** to look o wander round the shops

curiosità *sf inv* curiosity; *(cosa rara)* curio, curiosity

curi'oso, a *ag* curious; **essere ~ di** to be curious about

cur'sore *sm (INFORM)* cursor

'curva *sf* curve; *(stradale)* bend, curve

cur'vare *vt* to bend ♦ *vi (veicolo)* to take a bend; *(strada)* to bend, curve; **~rsi** *vr* to bend; *(legno)* to warp

'curvo, a *ag* curved; *(piegato)* bent

cusci'netto [kuʃʃi'netto] *sm* pad; *(TECN)* bearing ♦ *ag inv:* **stato ~** buffer state; **~ a sfere** ball bearing

cu'scino [kuʃ'ʃino] *sm* cushion; *(guanciale)* pillow

'cuspide *sf (ARCHIT)* spire

cus'tode *sm/f* keeper, custodian

cus'todia *sf* care; *(DIR)* custody; *(astuccio)* case, holder

custo'dire *vt (conservare)* to keep; *(assistere)* to look after, take care of; *(fare la guardia)* to guard

'cute *sf (ANAT)* skin

C.V. *abbr (= cavallo vapore)* h.p.

D

da *(da+il* = **dal**, *da+lo* = **dallo**, *da+l'* = **dall'**, *da+la* = **dalla**, *da+i* = **dai**, *da+gli* = **dagli**, *da+le* = **dalle**) *prep* **1** *(agente)* by; **dipinto ~ un grande artista** painted by a great artist

2 *(causa)* with; **tremare dalla paura** to tremble with fear

3 *(stato in luogo)* at; **abito ~ lui** I'm living at his house *o* with him; **sono dal giornalaio/~ Francesco** I'm at the newsagent's/Francesco's (house)

4 *(moto a luogo)* to; *(moto per luogo)* through; **vado ~ Pietro/dal giornalaio** I'm going to Pietro's (house)/to the newsagent's; **sono passati dalla finestra** they came in through the window

5 *(provenienza, allontanamento)* from; **arrivare/partire ~ Milano** to arrive/depart from Milan; **scendere dal treno/dalla macchina** to get off the train/out of the car; **si trova a 5 km ~ qui** it's 5 km from here

6 *(tempo: durata)* for; *(: a partire da: nel passato)* since; *(: nel futuro)* from; **vivo qui ~ un anno** I've been living here for a year; **è dalle 3 che ti aspetto** I've been waiting for you since 3 (o'clock); **~ oggi in poi** from today onwards; **~ bambino** as a child, when I *(o* he *etc)* was a child

7 *(modo, maniera)* like; **comportarsi ~ uomo** to behave like a man; **l'ho fatto ~ me** I did it (by) myself

8 *(descrittivo):* **una macchina ~ corsa** a racing car; **una ragazza dai capelli biondi** a girl with blonde hair; **un vestito ~ 100.000 lire** a 100,000 lire dress

dab'bene *ag inv* honest, decent

da 'capo *av* = **daccapo**

daccapo 74 decantare

dac'capo av (di nuovo) (once) again; (dal principio) all over again, from the beginning

dacché [dak'ke] cong since

'dado sm (da gioco) dice o die; (CUC) stock (BRIT) o bouillon (US) cube; (TECN) (screw)nut; **giocare a ~i** to play dice

da 'fare sm = daffare

daf'fare sm work, toil

'dagli ['daʎʎi] prep + det vedi da

'dai prep + det vedi da

'daino sm (fallow) deer inv; (pelle) buckskin

dal prep + det vedi da

dall' prep + det vedi da

'dalla prep + det vedi da

'dalle prep + det vedi da

'dallo prep + det vedi da

dal'tonico, a, ci, che ag colour-blind

'dama sf lady; (nei balli) partner; (gioco) draughts sg (BRIT), checkers sg (US)

damigi'ana [dami'dʒana] sf demijohn

da'naro sm = denaro

da'nese ag Danish ♦ sm/f Dane ♦ sm (LING) Danish

Dani'marca sf: **la ~** Denmark

dan'nare vt (REL) to damn; **~rsi** vr (fig: tormentarsi) to be worried to death; **far ~ qn** to drive sb mad; **dannazi'one** sf damnation

danneggi'are [danned'dʒare] vt to damage; (rovinare) to spoil; (nuocere) to harm

'danno sm damage; (a persona) harm, injury; **~i** smpl (DIR) damages; **dan'noso, a** ag: dannoso (a, per) harmful (to), bad (for)

Da'nubio sm: **il ~** the Danube

'danza ['dantsa] sf: **la ~** dancing; **una ~** a dance

dan'zare [dan'tsare] vt, vi to dance

dapper'tutto av everywhere

dap'poco ag inv inept, worthless

dap'prima av at first

'dardo sm dart

'dare sm (COMM) debit ♦ vt to give;

(produrre: frutti, suono) to produce ♦ vi (guardare): **~ su** to look (out) onto; **~rsi** vr: **~rsi a** to dedicate o.s. to; **~rsi al commercio** to go into business; **~rsi al bere** to take to drink; **~ da mangiare a qn** to give sb sth to eat; **~ per certo qc** to consider sth certain; **~ per morto qn** to give sb up for dead; **~rsi per vinto** to give in

'darsena sf dock; dockyard

'data sf date; **~ di nascita** date of birth

da'tare vt to date ♦ vi: **~ da** to date from

'dato, a ag (stabilito) given ♦ sm datum; **~i** smpl data pl; **~ che** given that; **un ~ di fatto** a fact

'dattero sm date

dattilogra'fare vt to type; **dattilogra'fia** sf typing; **datti'lografo, a** sm/f typist

da'vanti av in front; (dirimpetto) opposite ♦ ag inv front ♦ sm front; **~ a** in front of; facing, opposite; (in presenza di) before, in front of

davan'zale [davan'tsale] sm windowsill

d'a'vanzo [da'vantso] av = davanzo

da'vanzo [da'vantso] av more than enough

dav'vero av really, indeed

'dazio ['dattsjo] sm (somma) duty; (luogo) customs pl

DC sigla f = Democrazia Cristiana

d. C. ad abbr (= dopo Cristo) A.D.

'dea sf goddess

'debito, a ag due, proper ♦ sm debt; (COMM: dare) debit; **a tempo ~** at the right time; **debi'tore, 'trice** sm/f debtor

'debole ag weak, feeble; (suono) faint; (luce) dim ♦ sm weakness; **debo'lezza** sf weakness

debut'tare vi to make one's debut; **de'butto** sm debut

deca'denza [deka'dɛntsa] sf decline; (DIR) loss, forfeiture

decaffei'nato, a ag decaffeinated

decan'tare vt to praise, sing the

praises of

decapi'tare *vt* to decapitate

decappot'tabile *ag, sf* convertible

dece'duto, a [detʃe'duto] *ag* deceased

de'cennio [de'tʃennjo] *sm* decade

de'cente [de'tʃɛnte] *ag* decent, respectable, proper; (*accettabile*) satisfactory, decent

de'cesso [de'tʃɛsso] *sm* death; **atto di** ~ **death** certificate

de'cidere [de'tʃidere] *vt*: ~ **qc** to decide on sth; (*questione, lite*) to settle sth; ~ **di fare/che** to decide to do/that; ~ **di qc** (*sog: cosa*) to determine sth; ~**rsi (a fare)** to decide (to do), make up one's mind (to do)

deci'frare [detʃi'frare] *vt* to decode; (*fig*) to decipher, make out

deci'male [detʃi'male] *ag* decimal

'decimo, a ['detʃimo] *num* tenth

de'cina [de'tʃina] *sf* ten; (*circa dieci*): **una** ~ **(di)** about ten

decisi'one [detʃi'zjone] *sf* decision; **prendere una** ~ to make a decision

de'ciso, a [de'tʃizo] *pp di* **decidere**

declas'sare *vt* to downgrade; to lower in status

decli'nare (*pendio*) to slope down; (*fig: diminuire*) to decline; (*tramontare*) to set, go down ♦ *vt* to decline; **declinazi'one** *sf* (*LING*) declension; **de'clino** *sm* decline

decodifica'tore *sm* (*TEL*) decoder

decol'lare *vi* (*AER*) to take off; **de'collo** *sm* take-off

decolo'rare *vt* to bleach

decom'porre *vt* to decompose; **decomporsi** *vr* to decompose; **decom'posto, a** *pp di* **decomporre**

deconge'lare [dekondʒe'lare] *vt* to defrost

deco'rare *vt* to decorate; **decora'tore, 'trice** *sm/f* (*interior*) decorator; **decorazi'one** *sf* decoration

de'coro *sm* decorum; **deco'roso, a** *ag* decorous, dignified

de'correre *vi* to pass, elapse; (*avere effetto*) to run, have effect; **de'corso, a** *pp di* **decorrere** ♦ *sm*

(*evoluzione: anche MED*) course

de'crepito, a *ag* decrepit

de'crescere [de'kreʃʃere] *vi* (*diminuire*) to decrease, diminish; (*acque*) to subside, go down; (*prezzi*) to go down; **decresci'uto, a** *pp di* **decrescere**

de'creto *sm* decree; ~ **legge** decree with the force of law

'dedalo *sm* maze, labyrinth

'dedica, ch~ *sf* dedication

dedi'care *vt* ... dicate

de'dito, a *ag*: ~ **a** (*studio etc*) dedicated *o* devoted to; (*vizio*) addicted to

de'dotto, a *pp di* **dedurre**

de'durre *vt* (*concludere*) to deduce; (*defalcare*) to deduct; **deduzi'one** *sf* deduction

defal'care *vt* to deduct

defe'rente *ag* respectful, deferential

defe'rire *vt*: ~ **a** (*DIR*) to refer to

defezi'one [defet'tsjone] *sf* defection, desertion

defici'ente [defi'tʃɛnte] *ag* (*mancante*): ~ **di** deficient in; (*insufficiente*) insufficient ♦ *sm/f* mental defective; (*peg: cretino*) idiot

'deficit ['dɛfitʃit] *sm inv* (*ECON*) deficit

defi'nire *vt* to define; (*risolvere*) to settle; **defini'tivo, a** *ag* definitive, final; **definizi'one** *sf* definition; settlement

deflet'tore *sm* (*AUT*) quarter-light

de'flusso *sm* (*della marea*) ebb

defor'mare *vt* (*alterare*) to put out of shape; (*corpo*) to deform; (*pensiero, fatto*) to distort; ~**rsi** *vr* to lose its shape

de'forme *ag* deformed; disfigured; **deformità** *sf inv* deformity

defrau'dare *vt*: ~ **qn di qc** to defraud sb of sth, cheat sb out of sth

de'funto, a *ag* late *cpd* ♦ *sm/f* deceased

degene'rare [dedʒene'rare] *vi* to degenerate; **de'genere** *ag* degenerate

de'gente [de'dʒɛnte] *sm/f* bedridden person; (*ricoverato in ospedale*) in-patient

'degli ['deʎʎi] prep + det vedi **di**

de'gnarsi [deɲ'narsi] vr: ~ **di fare** to deign o condescend to do

'degno, a ag dignified; ~ **di** worthy of; ~ **di lode** praiseworthy

degra'dare vt (MIL) to demote; (privare della dignità) to degrade; ~**rsi** vr to demean o.s.

degustazi'one [degustat'tsjone] sf sampling, tasting

'dei prep + det vedi **di**

del prep + det vedi **di**

dela'tore, 'trice sm/f police informer

'delega, ghe sf (procura) proxy

dele'gare vt to delegate; **dele'gato** sm delegate

dele'terio, a ag damaging; (per salute etc) harmful

del'fino sm (ZOOL) dolphin; (STORIA) dauphin; (fig) probable successor

delibe'rare vt to come to a decision on ♦ vi (DIR): ~ **(su qc)** to rule (on sth)

delica'tezza [delika'tettsa] sf (anche CUC) delicacy; frailty; thoughtfulness; tactfulness

deli'cato, a ag delicate; (salute) delicate, frail; (fig: gentile) thoughtful, considerate; (: che dimostra tatto) tactful

deline'are vt to outline; ~**rsi** vr to be outlined; (fig) to emerge

delin'quente sm/f criminal, delinquent; **delin'quenza** sf criminality, delinquency; **delinquenza minorile** juvenile delinquency

deli'rare vi to be delirious, rave; (fig) to rave

de'lirio sm delirium; (ragionamento insensato) raving; (fig): **andare/ mandare in ~** to go/send into a frenzy

de'litto sm crime

de'lizia [de'littsja] sf delight; **deli-zi'oso, a** ag delightful; (cibi) delicious

dell' prep + det vedi **di**

'della prep + det vedi **di**

'delle prep + det vedi **di**

'dello prep + det vedi **di**

delta'plano sm hang-glider; **volo col ~** hang-gliding

de'ludere vt to disappoint; **delusi'one** sf disappointment; **de'luso, a** pp di **deludere**

de'manio sm state property

de'menza [de'mɛntsa] sf dementia; (stupidità) foolishness

demo'cratico, a, ci, che ag democratic

democra'zia [demokrat'tsia] sf democracy

democristi'ano, a ag, sm/f Christian Democrat

demo'lire vt to demolish

'demone sm demon

de'monio sm demon, devil; **il D~** the Devil

de'naro sm money

denomi'nare vt to name; ~**rsi** vr to be named o called; **denominazi'one** sf name; denomination; **denominazione d'origine controllata** label guaranteeing the quality and origin of a wine

densità sf inv density

'denso, a ag thick, dense

den'tale ag dental

'dente sm tooth; (di forchetta) prong; (GEO: cima) jagged peak; **al ~** (CUC: pasta) cooked so as to be firm when eaten; **~i del giudizio** wisdom teeth; **denti'era** sf (set of) false teeth pl

denti'fricio [denti'fritʃo] sm toothpaste

den'tista, i, e sm/f dentist

'dentro av inside; (in casa) indoors; (fig: nell'intimo) inwardly ♦ prep: ~ **(a)** in; piegato in ~ folded over; **qui/là ~** in here/there; ~ **di sé** (pensare, brontolare) to oneself

de'nuncia, ce o **cie** [de'nuntʃa] sf denunciation; declaration; ~ **dei redditi** (income) tax return

denunci'are [denun'tʃare] vt to denounce; (dichiarare) to declare

de'nunzia etc [de'nuntsja] = **denuncia** etc

denutrizi'one [denutrit'tsjone] sf malnutrition

deodo'rante sm deodorant

depe'rire vi to waste away

depila'torio, a ag hair-removing cpd, depilatory

dépli'ant [depli'ã] sm inv leaflet; (opuscolo) brochure

deplo'revole ag deplorable

de'porre vt (depositare) to put down; (rimuovere: da una carica) to remove; (: re) to depose; (DIR) to testify

depor'tare vt to deport

deposi'tare vt (gen, GEO, ECON) to deposit; (lasciare) to leave; (merci) to store

de'posito sm deposit; (luogo) warehouse; depot; (: MIL) depot; ~ bagagli left-luggage office

deposizi'one [depozit'tsjone] sf deposition; (da una carica) removal

de'posto, a pp di **deporre**

depra'vato, a ag depraved ♦ sm/f degenerate

depre'dare vt to rob, plunder

depressi'one sf depression

de'presso, a pp di **deprimere** ♦ ag depressed

deprez'zare [depret'tsare] vt (ECON) to depreciate

de'primere vt to depress

depu'rare vt to purify

depu'tato, a o ''essa sm/f (POL) deputy, ≈ Member of Parliament (BRIT), ≈ Member of Congress (US); **deputazi'one** sf deputation; (POL) position of deputy, ≈ parliamentary seat (BRIT), ≈ seat in Congress (US)

deragli'are [dera/'/are] vi to be derailed; **far** ~ to derail

dere'litto, a ag derelict

dere'tano (fam) sm bottom, buttocks pl

de'ridere vt to mock, deride; **de'riso, a** pp di **deridere**

de'riva sf (NAUT, AER) drift; **anda-**

re alla ~ (anche fig) to drift

deri'vare vi: ~ **da** to derive from ♦ vt to derive; (corso d'acqua) to divert; **derivazi'one** sf derivation; diversion

derma'tologo, a, gi, ghe sm/f dermatologist

der'rate sfpl commodities; ~ **alimentari** foodstuffs

deru'bare vt to rob

des'critto, a pp di **descrivere**

des'crivere vt to describe; **descrizi'one** sf description

de'serto, a ag deserted ♦ sm (GEO) desert; **isola** ~a desert island

deside'rare vt to want, wish for; (sessualmente) to desire; ~ **fare/che qn faccia** to want o wish to do/sb to do; **desidera fare una passeggia-ta?** would you like to go for a walk?

desi'derio sm wish; (più intenso, carnale) desire

deside'roso, a ag: ~ **di** longing o eager for

desi'nenza [dezi'nentsa] sf (LING) ending, inflexion

de'sistere vi: ~ **da** to give up, desist from; **desis'tito, a** pp di **desistere**

deso'lato, a ag (paesaggio) desolate; (persona: spiacente) sorry

des'tare vt to wake (up); (fig) to awaken, arouse; ~**rsi** vr to wake (up)

desti'nare vt to destine; (assegnare) to appoint, assign; (indirizzare) to address; ~ **qc a qn** to intend to give sth to sb, intend sb to have sth; **destina'tario, a** sm/f (di lettera) addressee

destinazi'one [destinat'tsjone] sf destination; (uso) purpose

des'tino sm destiny, fate

destitu'ire vt to dismiss, remove

'desto, a ag (wide) awake

'destra sf (mano) right hand; (parte) right (side); (POL): **la** ~ the Right; **a** ~ (essere) on the right; (andare) to the right

destreggi'arsi [destred'dʒarsi] *vr* to manoeuvre (*BRIT*), maneuver (*US*)

des'trezza [des'trettsa] *sf* skill, dexterity

'destro, a *ag* right, right-hand; (*abile*) skilful, adroit

dete'nere *vt* (*incarico, primato*) to hold; (*proprietà*) to have, possess; (*in prigione*) to detain, hold; **dete'nuto, a** *sm/f* prisoner; **detenzi'one** *sf* holding; possession; detention

deter'gente [deter'dʒɛnte] *ag* detergent; (*crema, latte*) cleansing ♦ *sm* detergent

deterio'rare *vt* to damage; **~rsi** *vr* to deteriorate

determi'nare *vt* to determine; **determinazi'one** *sf* determination; (*decisione*) decision

deter'sivo *sm* detergent

detes'tare *vt* to detest, hate

de'trarre *vt*: ~ (**da**) to deduct (from), take away (from); **de'tratto, a** *pp di* detrarre; **detrazi'one** *sf* deduction; **detrazione d'imposta** tax allowance

de'trito *sm* (*GEO*) detritus

'detta *sf*: **a** ~ **di** according to

dettagli'are [dettaʎ'ʎare] *vt* to detail, give full details of

det'taglio [det'taʎʎo] *sm* detail; (*COMM*): **il** ~ retail; **al** ~ (*COMM*) retail; separately

det'tare *vt* to dictate; **~ legge** (*fig*) to lay down the law; **det'tato** *sm* dictation; **detta'tura** *sf* dictation

'detto, a *pp di* dire ♦ *ag* (*soprannominato*) called, known as; (*già nominato*) above-mentioned ♦ *sm* saying; ~ **fatto** no sooner said than done

detur'pare *vt* to disfigure; (*moralmente*) to sully

devas'tare *vt* to devastate; (*fig*) to ravage

devi'are *vi*: ~ (**da**) to turn off (from) ♦ *vt* to divert; **deviazi'one** *sf* (*anche AUT*) diversion

devo'luto, a *pp di* devolvere

devoluzi'one [devolut'tsjone] *sf* (*DIR*) devolution, transfer

de'volvere *vt* (*DIR*) to transfer, devolve

de'voto, a *ag* (*REL*) devout, pious; (*affezionato*) devoted

devozi'one [devot'tsjone] *sf* devoutness; (*anche REL*) devotion

---

PAROLA CHIAVE

di (*di+il* = **del**, *di+lo* = **dello**, *di+l'* = **dell'**, *di+la* = **della**, *di+i* = **dei**, *di+gli* = **degli**, *di+le* = **delle**) *prep* **1** (*possesso, specificazione*) of; (*composto da, scritto da*) by; **la macchina ~ Paolo/mio fratello** Paolo's/my brother's car; **un amico ~ mio fratello** a friend of my brother's, one of my brother's friends; **un quadro ~ Botticelli** a painting by Botticelli

2 (*caratterizzazione, misura*) of; **una casa ~ mattoni** a brick house, a house made of bricks; **un orologio d'oro** a gold watch; **un bimbo ~ 3 anni** a child of 3, a 3-year-old child

3 (*causa, mezzo, modo*) with; **tremare ~ paura** to tremble with fear; **morire ~ cancro** to die of cancer; **spalmare ~ burro** to spread with butter

4 (*argomento*) about, of; **discutere ~ sport** to talk about sport

5 (*luogo: provenienza*) from; out of; **essere ~ Roma** to be from Rome; **uscire ~ casa** to come out of *o* leave the house

6 (*tempo*) in; **d'estate/d'inverno** in (the) summer/winter; ~ **notte** by night, at night; ~ **mattina/sera** in the morning/evening; ~ **lunedì** on Mondays

♦ *det* (*una certa quantità di*) some; (*: negativo*) any; (*: interrogativo*) any, some; **del pane** (some) bread; **delle caramelle** (some) sweets; **degli amici miei** some friends of mine; **vuoi del vino?** do you want some *o* any wine?

---

dia'bete *sm* diabetes *sg*

di'acono *sm* (*REL*) deacon

dia'dema, i sm diadem; (di donna) tiara

dia'framma, i sm (divisione) screen; (ANAT, FOT, contraccettivo) diaphragm

di'agnosi [di'aɲɲozi] sf diagnosis sg

diago'nale ag, sf diagonal

dia'gramma, i sm diagram

dia'letto sm dialect

di'alogo, ghi sm dialogue

dia'mante sm diamond

di'ametro sm diameter

di'amine escl: **che ~ ...?** what on earth ...?

diaposi'tiva sf transparency, slide

di'ario sm diary; **~ degli esami** (SCOL) exam timetable

diar'rea sf diarrhoea

di'avolo sm devil

di'battere vt to debate, discuss; **~rsi** vr to struggle; **di'battito** sm debate, discussion

dicas'tero sm ministry

di'cembre [di'tʃɛmbre] sm December

dice'ria [ditʃe'ria] sf rumour, piece of gossip

dichia'rare [dikja'rare] vt to declare; **dichiarazi'one** sf declaration

dician'nove [ditʃan'nɔve] num nineteen

dicias'sette [ditʃas'sɛtte] num seventeen

dici'otto [di'tʃɔtto] num eighteen

dici'tura [ditʃi'tura] sf words pl, wording

di'eci ['djɛtʃi] num ten; **die'cina** sf = **decina**

'diesel ['dizəl] sm inv diesel engine

di'eta sf diet; **essere a ~** to be on a diet

di'etro av behind; (in fondo) at the back ♦ prep behind; (tempo: dopo) after ♦ sm back, rear ♦ ag inv back cpd: **le zampe di ~** the hind legs; **~ richiesta** on demand; (scritta) on application

di'fatti cong in fact, as a matter of fact

di'fendere vt to defend; **difen'sivo,**

a ag defensive ♦ sf: **stare sulla difensiva** (anche fig) to be on the defensive; **difen'sore, a** sm/f defender; **avvocato difensore** counsel for the defence; **di'fesa** sf defence; **di'feso, a** pp di **difendere**

difet'tare vi to be defective; **~ di** to be lacking in, lack; **difet'tivo, a** ag defective

di'fetto sm (mancanza): **~ di** lack of; shortage of; (di fabbricazione) fault, flaw, defect; (morale) fault, failing, defect; (fisico) defect; **far ~** to be lacking; **in ~ at fault; in the wrong; difet'toso, a** ag defective, faulty

diffa'mare vt to slander; to libel

diffe'rente ag different

diffe'renza [diffe'rɛntsa] sf difference; **a ~ di** unlike

differenzi'are [differentsjare] vt to differentiate; **~rsi da** to differentiate o.s. from; to differ from

diffe'rire vt to postpone, defer ♦ vi to be different

dif'ficile [diffitʃile] ag difficult; (persona) hard to please, difficult (to please); (poco probabile): **è ~ che sia libero** it is unlikely that he'll be free ♦ sm difficult part; difficulty; **difficoltà** sf difficulty

dif'fida sf (DIR) warning, notice

diffi'dare vi: **~ di** to be suspicious o distrustful of ♦ vt (DIR) to warn; **~ qn dal fare qc** to warn sb not to do sth, caution sb against doing sth; **diffi'dente** ag suspicious, distrustful; **diffi'denza** sf suspicion, distrust

dif'fondere vt (luce, calore) to diffuse; (notizie) to spread, circulate; **~rsi** vr to spread; **diffusi'one** sf diffusion; spread; (anche di giornale) circulation; (FISICA) scattering; **dif'fuso, a** pp di **diffondere** ♦ ag (malattia, fenomeno) widespread

diffi'lato av (direttamente) straight, directly; (subito) straight away

difte'rite sf (MED) diphtheria

'diga, ghe sf dam; (portuale) breakwater

dige'rente [didʒe'rɛnte] *ag* (appa-rato) digestive

dige'rire [didʒe'rire] *vt* to digest; **digesti'one** *sf* digestion; **diges'tivo**, **a** *ag* digestive ♦ *sm* (after-dinner) liqueur

digi'tale [didʒi'tale] *ag* digital; (delle dita) finger *cpd*, digital ♦ *sf* (BOT) foxglove

digi'tare [didʒi'tare] *vt, vi* (IN-FORM) to key (in)

digiu'nare [didʒu'nare] *vi* to starve o.s.; (REL) to fast; **digi'uno, a** *ag*: essere digiuno not to have eaten ♦ *sm* fast; **a digiuno** on an empty stomach

dignità [diɲɲi'ta] *sf inv* dignity; **dig-ni'toso, a** *ag* dignified

'DIGOS ['digɔs] *sigla f* (= Divisione Investigazioni Generali e Operazioni Speciali) police department dealing with political security

digri'gnare [digriɲ'ɲare] *vt*: ~ **i denti** to grind one's teeth

dila'gare *vi* to flood; (fig) to spread

dilani'are *vt* (preda) to tear to pieces

dilapi'dare *vt* to squander, waste

dila'tare *vt* to dilate; (gas) to cause to expand; (passaggio, cavità) to open (up); ~**rsi** *vr* to dilate; (FISICA) to expand

dilazio'nare [dilattsjo'nare] *vt* to delay, defer; **dilazi'one** *sf* delay; (COMM: di pagamento etc) extension; (rinvio) postponement

dileggi'are [diled'dʒare] *vt* to mock, deride

dilegu'are *vi* to vanish, disappear; ~**rsi** *vr* to vanish, disappear

di'lemma, i *sm* dilemma

dilet'tante *smf* dilettante; (anche SPORT) amateur

dilet'tare *vt* to give pleasure to, delight; ~**rsi** *vr*: ~**rsi di** to take pleasure in, enjoy

di'letto, a *ag* dear, beloved ♦ *sm* pleasure, delight

dili'gente [dili'dʒɛnte] *ag* (scrupolo-so) diligent; (accurato) accurate, ac-

curate; **dili'genza** *sf* diligence; care; (carrozza) stagecoach

dilu'ire *vt* to dilute

dilun'garsi *vr* (fig): ~ **su** to talk at length on o about

dilu'viare *vb impers* to pour (down)

di'luvio *sm* downpour; (inondazione, fig) flood

dima'grire *vi* to get thinner, lose weight

dime'nare *vt* to wave, shake; ~**rsi** *vr* to toss and turn; (fig) to struggle; ~ **la coda** (sog: cane) to wag its tail

dimensi'one *sf* dimension; (gran-dezza) size

dimenti'canza [dimenti'kantsa] *sf* forgetfulness; (errore) oversight, slip; **per** ~ inadvertently

dimenti'care *vt* to forget; ~**rsi di qc** to forget sth

di'messo, a *pp di* **dimettere** ♦ *ag* (voce) subdued; (uomo, abito) modest, humble

dimesti'chezza [dimesti'kettsa] *sf* familiarity

di'mettere *vt*: ~ **qn da** to dismiss sb from; (dall'ospedale) to discharge sb from; ~**rsi** (**da**) to resign (from)

dimez'zare [dimed'dzare] *vt* to halve

diminu'ire *vt* to reduce, diminish; (prezzi) to bring down, reduce ♦ *vi* to decrease, diminish; (rumore) to die down, die away; (prezzi) to fall, go down; **diminuzi'one** *sf* decreas-ing, diminishing

dimissi'oni *sfpl* resignation *sg*; **dare** *o* **presentare le** ~ to resign, hand in one's resignation

di'mora *sf* residence

dimo'rare *vi* to reside

dimos'trare *vt* to demonstrate, show; (provare) to prove, demon-strate; ~**rsi** *vr*: ~**rsi molto abile** to show o.s. *o* prove to be very clever; **dimostra 30 anni** he looks about 30 (years old); **dimostrazi'one** *sf* demonstration; proof

di'namica *sf* dynamics *sg*

di'namico, a, ci, che *ag* dynamic

dina'mite *sf* dynamite

'dinamo *sf inv* dynamo

di'nanzi [di'nantsi]: ~ a *prep* in front of

dini'ego, ghi *sm* refusal; denial

dinocco'lato, a *ag* lanky; **cammi-nare** ~ to walk with a slouch

din'torno *av* round, (round) about; ~i *smpl* outskirts; **nei** ~i **di** in the vicinity o neighbourhood of

'dio (*pl* **'dei**) *sm* god; **D~** God; **gli dei** the gods; **D~ mio!** my goodness!, my God!

di'ocesi [di'ɔtʃezi] *sf inv* diocese

dipa'nare *vt* (*lana*) to wind into a ball; (*fig*) to disentangle, sort out

diparti'mento *sm* department

dipen'dente *ag* dependent ♦ *sm/f* employee; **dipen'denza** *sf* dependence; **essere alle dipendenze di** qn to be employed by sb o in sb's employ

di'pendere *vi*: ~ **da** to depend on; (*finanziariamente*) to be dependent on; (*derivare*) to come from, be due to; **di'peso, a** *pp di* **dipendere**

di'pingere [di'pindʒere] *vt* to paint; **di'pinto, a** *pp di* **dipingere** ♦ *sm* painting

di'ploma, i *sm* diploma

diplo'mare *vt* to award a diploma to, graduate (*US*) ♦ *vi* to obtain a diploma, graduate (*US*)

diplo'matico, a, ci, che *ag* diplomatic ♦ *sm* diplomat

diploma'zia [diplomat'tsia] *sf* diplomacy

di'porto: imbarcazione da ~ *sf* pleasure craft

dira'dare *vt* to thin (out); (*visite*) to reduce, make less frequent; **~rsi** *vr* to disperse; (*nebbia*) to clear (up)

dira'mare *vt* to issue ♦ *vi* (*strade*) to branch; **~rsi** *vr* to branch

'dire *vt* to say; (*segreto, fatto*) to tell; ~ **qc a** qn to tell sb sth; ~ **a** qn **di fare** qc to tell sb to do sth; **di sì/no** to say yes/no; **si dice che** ... they say that ...; **si direbbe che** ... it looks (o sounds) as though ...; **dica, signora?** (*in un negozio*) yes,

Madam, can I help you?

diret'tissimo *sm* (*FERR*) fast (through) train

di'retto, a *pp di* **dirigere** ♦ *ag* direct ♦ *sm* (*FERR*) through train

diret'tore, 'trice *sm/f* (*di azienda*) director; manager/ess; (*di scuola elementare*) head (teacher) (*BRIT*), principal (*US*); ~ **d'orchestra** conductor; ~ **vendite** sales director o manager

direzi'one [diret'tsjone] *sf* board of directors; management; (*senso di movimento*) direction; **in** ~ **di** in the direction of, towards

diri'gente [diri'dʒɛnte] *sm/f* executive; (*POL*) leader ♦ *ag*: **classe** ~ ruling class

di'rigere [di'ridʒere] *vt* to direct; (*impresa*) to run, manage; (*MUS*) to conduct; **~rsi** *vr*: **~rsi verso** o **a** to make o head for

dirim'petto *av* opposite; ~ **a** opposite, facing

di'ritto, a *ag* straight; (*onesto*) straight, upright ♦ *av* straight, directly; **andare** ~ to go straight on ♦ *sm* right side; (*TENNIS*) forehand; (*MAGLIA*) plain stitch; (*prerogativa*) right; (*leggi, scienza*): **il** ~ law; ~i *smpl* (*tasse*) duty *sg*; **stare** ~ to stand up straight; **aver** ~ **a** qc to be entitled to sth; ~i **d'autore** royalties

dirit'tura *sf* (*SPORT*) straight; (*fig*) rectitude

diroc'cato, a *ag* tumbledown, in ruins

dirot'tare *vt* (*nave, aereo*) to change the course of; (*aereo: sotto minaccia*) to hijack; (*traffico*) to divert ♦ *vi* (*nave, aereo*) to change course; **dirotta'tore, 'trice** *sm/f* hijacker

di'rotto, a *ag* (*pioggia*) torrential; (*pianto*) unrestrained; **piovere a** ~ to pour, rain cats and dogs; **piangere a** ~ to cry one's heart out

di'rupo *sm* crag, precipice

disabi'tato, a *ag* uninhabited

disabitu'arsi *vr*: ~ **a** to get out of the habit of

disac'cordo *sm* disagreement

disadat'tato, a *ag* (*PSIC*) maladjusted

disa'dorno, a *ag* plain, unadorned

disagi'ato, a [diza'dʒato] *ag* poor, needy; (*vita*) hard

di'sagio [di'zadʒo] *sm* discomfort; (*disturbo*) inconvenience; (*fig: imbarazzo*) embarrassment; **essere a ~** to be ill at ease

disappro'vare *vt* to disapprove of; **disapprovazi'one** *sf* disapproval

disap'punto *sm* disappointment

disar'mare *vt*, *vi* to disarm; **di'sarmo, sm** (*MIL*) disarmament

di'sastro *sm* disaster

disat'tento, a *ag* inattentive; **disattenzi'one** *sf* carelessness, lack of attention

disa'vanzo [diza'vantso] *sm* (*ECON*) deficit

disavven'tura *sf* misadventure, mishap

dis'brigo, ghi *sm* (prompt) clearing up *o* settlement

dis'capito *sm*: **a ~ di** to the detriment of

dis'carica, che *sf* (*di rifiuti*) rubbish tip *o* dump

discen'dente [diʃʃen'dɛnte] *ag* descending ♦ *smf* descendant

di'scendere [di'ʃʃendere] *vt* to go (*o* come) down ♦ *vi* to go (*o* come) down; (*strada*) to go down; (*smontare*) to get off; **~ da** (*famiglia*) to be descended from; **~ dalla macchina/dal treno** to get out of the car/out *o* off the train; **~ da cavallo** to dismount, get off one's horse

di'scepolo, a [diʃ'ʃepolo] *smf* disciple

di'scernere [diʃ'ʃernere] *vt* to discern

di'scesa [diʃ'ʃesa] *sf* descent; (*pendio*) slope; **in ~** (*strada*) downhill *cpd*, sloping; **~ libera** (*SCI*) downhill (race)

di'sceso, a [diʃ'ʃeso] *pp di* discendere

disci'ogliere [diʃ'ʃɔʎʎere] *vt* to dissolve; (*fondere*) to melt; **~rsi** *vr* to dissolve; to melt; **disci'olto, a** *pp di* disciogliere

disci'plina [diʃʃi'plina] *sf* discipline; **discipli'nare** *ag* disciplinary ♦ *vt* to discipline

'disco, schi *sm* disc; (*SPORT*) discus; (*fonografico*) record; (*INFORM*) disk; **~ orario** (*AUT*) parking disc; **~ rigido** (*INFORM*) hard disk; **~ volante** flying saucer

discol'pare *vt* to clear of blame

disco'noscere [disko'noʃʃere] *vt* (*figlio*) to disown; (*meriti*) to ignore, disregard; **disconosci'uto, a** *pp di* disconoscere

dis'corde *ag* conflicting, clashing; **dis'cordia** *sf* discord; (*dissidio*) disagreement, clash

dis'correre *vi*: **~ (di)** to talk (about)

dis'corso, a *pp di* discorrere ♦ *sm* speech; (*conversazione*) conversation, talk

dis'costo, a *ag* faraway, distant ♦ *av* far away; **~ da** far from

disco'teca, che *sf* (*raccolta*) record library; (*luogo di ballo*) disco(thèque)

discre'panza [diskre'pantsa] *sf* disagreement

dis'creto, a *ag* discreet; (*abbastanza buono*) reasonable, fair; **discrezi'one** *sf* discretion; (*giudizio*) judgment, discernment; **a discrezione di** at the discretion of

discriminazi'one [diskriminat'tsjone] *sf* discrimination

discussi'one *sf* discussion; (*litigio*) argument

dis'cusso, a *pp di* discutere

dis'cutere *vt* to discuss, debate; (*contestare*) to question ♦ *vi* (*conversare*): **~ (di)** to discuss; (*litigare*) to argue

disde'gnare [disdeɲ'ɲare] *vt* to scorn

dis'detta *sf* (*di prenotazione etc*) cancellation; (*sfortuna*) bad luck

dis'detto, a pp di disdire

dis'dire vt (prenotazione) to cancel; (DIR): ~ **un contratto d'affitto** to give notice (to quit)

dise'gnare [disen'nare] vt to draw; (progettare) to design; (fig) to outline; **disegna'tore, 'trice** smf designer

di'segno [di'senno] sm drawing; design; outline; ~ **di legge** (DIR) bill

diser'bante sm weed-killer

diser'tare vt, vi to desert; **diser'tore** sm (MIL) deserter

dis'fare vt to undo; (valigie) to unpack; (meccanismo) to take to pieces; (lavoro, paese) to destroy; (neve) to melt; ~**rsi** vr to come undone; (neve) to melt; ~ **il letto** to strip the bed; ~**rsi di qn** (liberarsi) to get rid of sb; **dis'fatta** sf (sconfitta) rout; **dis'fatto, a** pp di disfare

dis'gelo [diz'dʒelo] sm thaw

dis'grazia [diz'grattsja] sf (sventura) misfortune; (incidente) accident, mishap; **disgrazi'ato, a** ag unfortunate ♦ smf wretch

disgre'gare vt to break up; ~**rsi** vr to break up

disgu'ido sm: ~ **postale** error in postal delivery

disgus'tare vt to disgust; ~**rsi** vr: ~**rsi di** to be disgusted by

dis'gusto sm disgust; **disgus'toso, a** ag disgusting

disidra'tare vt to dehydrate

disil'ludere vt to disillusion, disenchant

disimpa'rare vt to forget

disimpe'gnare [dizimpen'nare] vt (persona: da obblighi): ~ **da** to release from; (oggetto dato in pegno) to redeem, get out of pawn; ~**rsi** vr: ~**rsi da** (obblighi) to release o.s. from, free o.s. from

disinfet'tante ag, sm disinfectant

disinfet'tare vt to disinfect

disini'bito, a ag uninhibited

disinte'grare vt, vi to disintegrate

disinteres'sarsi vr: ~ **di** to take no interest in

disinte'resse sm indifference; (generosità) unselfishness

disintossi'care vt (alcolizzato, drogato) to treat for alcoholism (o drug addiction); ~ **l'organismo** to clear out one's system

disin'volto, a ag casual, free and easy; **disinvol'tura** sf casualness, ease

disles'sia sf dyslexia

dislo'care vt to station, position

dismi'sura sf excess; **a** ~ to excess, excessively

disobbe'dire etc = **disubbidire** etc

disoccu'pato, a ag unemployed ♦ smf unemployed person; **disoccupazi'one** sf unemployment

diso'nesto, a ag dishonest

diso'nore sm dishonour, disgrace

di'sopra av (con contatto) on top; (senza contatto) above; (al piano superiore) upstairs ♦ ag inv (superiore) upper ♦ sm inv top, upper part

disordi'nato, a ag untidy; (privo di misura) irregular, wild

di'sordine sm (confusione) disorder, confusion; (sregolatezza) debauchery

disorien'tare vt to disorientate; ~**rsi** vr (fig) to get confused, lose one's bearings

di'sotto av below, underneath; (in fondo) at the bottom; (al piano inferiore) downstairs ♦ ag inv (inferiore) lower; bottom cpd ♦ sm inv (parte inferiore) lower part; bottom

dis'paccio [dis'pattʃo] sm dispatch

'dispari ag inv odd, uneven

dis'parte: in ~ av (da lato) aside, apart; **tenersi** o **starsene in** ~ to keep to o.s., hold aloof

dispendi'oso, a ag expensive

dis'pensa sf pantry, larder; (mobile) sideboard; (DIR) exemption; (REL) dispensation; (fascicolo) number, issue

dispen'sare vt (elemosine, favori) to distribute; (esonerare) to exempt

dispe'rare vi: ~ (**di**) to despair (of); ~**rsi** vr to despair; **dispe'rato,**

a *ag* (*persona*) in despair; (*caso, tentativo*) desperate; **disperazi'one** *sf* despair

dis'perdere *vt* (*disseminare*) to disperse; (*MIL*) to scatter, rout; (*fig: consumare*) to waste, squander; ~**rsi** *vr* to disperse; to scatter; **dis'perso, a** *pp di* **disperdere** ♦ *smf* missing person

dis'petto *sm* spite *no pl*, spitefulness *no pl*; **fare un ~ a** qn to play a (nasty) trick on sb; **a ~ di** in spite of; **dispet'toso, a** *ag* spiteful

dispia'cere [dispja'tʃere] *sm* (*rammarico*) regret, sorrow; (*dolore*) grief; ~**i** *smpl* (*preoccupazioni*) troubles, worries ♦ *vi*: ~ **a** to displease ♦ *vb impers*: **mi dispiace** (**che**) I am sorry (that); **se non le dispiace, me ne vado adesso** if you don't mind, I'll go now; **dispiaci'uto, a** *pp di* **dispiacere** ♦ *ag* sorry

dispo'nibile *ag* available

dis'porre *vt* (*sistemare*) to arrange; (*preparare*) to prepare; (*DIR*) to order; (*persuadere*): ~ qn a to incline *o* dispose sb towards ♦ *vi* (*decidere*) to decide; (*usufruire*): ~ **di** to use, have at one's disposal; (*essere dotato*): ~ **di** to have; **disporsi** *vr* (*ordinarsi*) to place o.s., arrange o.s.; **disporsi a fare** to get ready to do

disposi'tivo *sm* (*meccanismo*) device

disposizi'one [dispozit'tsjone] *sf* arrangement, layout; (*stato d'animo*) mood; (*tendenza*) bent, inclination; (*comando*) order; (*DIR*) provision, regulation; **a ~ di** qn at sb's disposal

dis'posto, a *pp di* **disporre**

disprez'zare [dispret'tsare] *vt* to despise

dis'prezzo [dis'prettso] *sm* contempt

'disputa *sf* dispute, quarrel

dispu'tare *vt* (*contendere*) to dispute, contest; (*gara*) to take part in ♦ *vi* to quarrel; ~ **di** to discuss; ~**rsi** qc to fight for sth

dissan'guare *vt* (*fig: persona*) to

bleed white; (: *patrimonio*) to suck dry; ~**rsi** *vr* (*MED*) to lose blood; (*fig: rovinarsi*) to ruin o.s.

dissec'care *vt* to dry up; ~**rsi** *vr* to dry up

dissemi'nare *vt* to scatter; (*fig: notizie*) to spread

dis'senso *sm* dissent; (*disapprovazione*) disapproval

dissente'ria *sf* dysentery

dissen'tire *vi*: ~ (**da**) to disagree (with)

dissertazi'one [dissertat'tsjone] *sf* dissertation

disser'vizio [disser'vittsjo] *sm* inefficiency

disses'tare *vt* (*ECON*) to ruin; **dis'sesto** *sm* (financial) ruin

disse'tante *ag* refreshing

dis'sidio *sm* disagreement

dis'simile *ag* different, dissimilar

dissimu'lare *vt* (*fingere*) to dissemble; (*nascondere*) to conceal

dissi'pare *vt* to dissipate; (*scialacquare*) to squander, waste

dis'solto, a *pp di* **dissolvere**

disso'lubile *ag* soluble

disso'luto, a *pp di* **dissolvere** ♦ *ag* dissolute, licentious

dis'solvere *vt* to dissolve; (*neve*) to melt; (*fumo*) to disperse; ~**rsi** *vr* to dissolve; to melt; to disperse

dissua'dere *vt*: ~ qn **da** to dissuade sb from; **dissu'aso, a** *pp di* **dissuadere**

distac'care *vt* to detach, separate; (*SPORT*) to leave behind; ~**rsi** *vr* to be detached; (*fig*) to stand out; ~**rsi da** (*fig: allontanarsi*) to grow away from

dis'tacco, chi *sm* (*separazione*) separation; (*fig: indifferenza*) detachment; (*SPORT*): **vincere con un ~ di** ... to win by a distance of ...

dis'tante *av* far away ♦ *ag*: ~ (**da**) distant (from), far away (from)

dis'tanza *sf* distance

distanzi'are [distan'tsjare] *vt* to space out, place at intervals; (*SPORT*) to outdistance; (*fig: supe-*

rare) to outstrip, surpass

dis'tare *vi*: **distiamo pochi chilometri da Roma** we are only a few kilometres (away) from Rome

dis'tendere *vt* (*coperta*) to spread out; (*gambe*) to stretch (out); (*mettere a giacere*) to lay; (*rilassare: muscoli, nervi*) to relax; **~rsi** *vr* (*rilassarsi*) to relax; (*sdraiarsi*) to lie down; **distensi'one** *sf* stretching; relaxation; (*POL*) détente

dis'tesa *sf* expanse, stretch

dis'teso, a *pp di* **distendere**

distil'lare *vt* to distil

distille'ria *sf* distillery

dis'tinguere *vt* to distinguish

dis'tinta *sf* (*nota*) note; (*elenco*) list

distin'tivo, a *ag* distinctive; distinguishing ♦ *sm* badge

dis'tinto, a *pp di* **distinguere** ♦ *ag* (*dignitoso ed elegante*) distinguished; **~i saluti** (*in lettera*) yours faithfully

distinzi'one [distin'tsjone] *sf* distinction

dis'togliere [dis'tɔʎʎere] *vt*: **~ da** to take away from; (*fig*) to dissuade from; **dis'tolto, a** *pp di* **distogliere**

distorsi'one *sf* (*MED*) sprain; (*FISICA, OTTICA*) distortion

dis'trarre *vt* to distract; (*divertire*) to entertain, amuse; **distrarsi** *vr* (*non fare attenzione*) to be distracted, let one's mind wander; (*svagarsi*) to amuse o enjoy o.s.; **dis'tratto, a** *pp di* **distrarre** ♦ *ag* absent-minded; (*disattento*) inattentive; **distrazi'one** *sf* absent-mindedness; inattention; (*svago*) distraction, entertainment

dis'tretto *sm* district

distribu'ire *vt* to distribute; (*CARTE*) to deal (out); (*consegnare: posta*) to deliver; (*lavoro*) to allocate, assign; (*ripartire*) to share out; **distribu'tore** *sm* (*di benzina*) petrol (*BRIT*) o gas (*US*) pump; (*AUT, ELETTR*) distributor; (*automatico*) vending machine; **distribuzi'one** *sf* distribution; delivery

distri'care *vt* to disentangle, unravel

dis'truggere [dis'truddʒere] *vt* to destroy; **dis'trutto, a** *pp di* **distruggere**; **distruzi'one** *sf* destruction

distur'bare *vt* to disturb, trouble; (*sonno, lezioni*) to disturb; **~rsi** *vr* to put o.s. out

dis'turbo *sm* trouble, bother, inconvenience; (*indisposizione*) (slight) disorder, ailment; **~i** *smpl* (*RADIO, TV*) static *sg*

disubbidi'ente *ag* disobedient; **disubbidi'enza** *sf* disobedience

disubbidi'dire *vi*: **~ (a qn)** to disobey (sb)

disugu'ale *ag* unequal; (*diverso*) different; (*irregolare*) uneven

disu'mano, a *ag* inhuman

di'suso *sm*: **andare** o **cadere in ~** to fall into disuse

'dita *fpl di* **dito**

di'tale *sm* thimble

'dito (*pl(f)* **'dita**) *sm* finger; (*misura*) finger, finger's breadth; **~ (del piede)** toe

'ditta *sf* firm, business

ditta'tore *sm* dictator

ditta'tura *sf* dictatorship

dit'tongo, ghi *sm* diphthong

di'urno, a *ag* day *cpd*, daytime *cpd* ♦ *sm* (*anche: albergo ~*) public toilets with washing and shaving facilities *etc*

'diva *sf vedi* **divo**

diva'gare *vi* to digress

divam'pare *vi* to flare up, blaze up

di'vano *sm* sofa; divan

divari'care *vt* to open wide

di'vario *sm* difference

dive'nire *vi* = **diventare**

dive'nuto, a *pp di* **divenire**

diven'tare *vi* to become; **~ famoso/professore** to become famous/a teacher

di'verbio *sm* altercation

di'vergere [di'verdʒere] *vi* to diverge

diversifi'care *vt* to diversify, vary; to differentiate

diversi'one *sf* diversion

diversità *sf inv* difference, diversity;

(varietà) variety

diver'sivo sm diversion, distraction

di'verso, a ag (differente): ~ (da) different (from); ~i, e det pl several, various; (COMM) sundry ♦ pron pl several (people), many (people)

diver'tente ag amusing

diverti'mento sm amusement, pleasure; (passatempo) pastime, recreation

diver'tire vt to amuse, entertain; ~rsi vr to amuse o enjoy o.s.

divi'dendo sm dividend

di'videre vt (anche MAT) to divide; (distribuire, ripartire) to divide (up), split (up); ~rsi vr (separarsi) to separate; (strade) to fork

divi'eto sm prohibition; "~ di sosta" (AUT) "no parking"

divinco'larsi vr to wriggle, writhe

divinità sf inv divinity

di'vino, a ag divine

di'visa sf (MIL etc) uniform; (COMM) foreign currency

divisi'one sf division

di'viso, a pp di dividere

'divo, a sm/f star

divo'rare vt to devour

divorzi'are [divor'tsjare] vi: ~ (da qn) to divorce (sb); **divorzi'ato, a** sm/f divorcee

di'vorzio [di'vortsjo] sm divorce

divul'gare vt to divulge, disclose; (rendere comprensibile) to popularize; ~rsi vr to spread

dizio'nario [ditsjo'narjo] sm dictionary

dizi'one [dit'tsjone] sf diction; pronunciation

do sm (MUS) C; (: solfeggiando la scala) do(h)

DOC [dɔk] abbr (= denominazione di origine controllata) label guaranteeing the quality of wine

'doccia, ce ['dɔttʃa] sf (bagno) shower; (condotto) pipe; **fare la ~** to have a shower

do'cente [do'tʃɛnte] ag teaching ♦ sm/f teacher; (di università) lectur-

er; **do'cenza** sf university teaching o lecturing

'docile ['dɔtʃile] ag docile

documen'tare vt to document; ~rsi vr: ~rsi (su) to gather information o material (about)

documen'tario sm documentary

docu'mento sm document; ~i smpl (d'identità etc) papers

'dodici ['dodidʒi] num twelve

do'gana sf (ufficio) customs pl; (tassa) (customs) duty; **passare la ~** to go through customs; **doga'nale** ag customs cpd; **dogani'ere** sm customs officer

'doglie ['dɔʎʎe] sfpl (MED) labour sg, labour pains

'dolce ['doltʃe] ag sweet; (colore) soft; (carattere, persona) gentle, mild; (fig: mite: clima) mild; (non ripido: pendio) gentle ♦ sm (sapore dolce) sweetness, sweet taste; (CUC: portata) sweet, dessert; (: torta) cake; **dol'cezza** sf sweetness; softness; mildness; gentleness; **dolci'umi** smpl sweets

do'lente ag sorrowful, sad

do'lere vi to be sore, hurt, ache; ~rsi vr to complain; (essere spiacente): ~rsi di to be sorry for; **mi duole la testa** my head aches, I've got a headache

'dollaro sm dollar

'dolo sm (DIR) malice

Dolo'miti sfpl: **le ~** the Dolomites

do'lore sm (fisico) pain; (morale) sorrow, grief; **dolo'roso, a** ag painful; sorrowful, sad

do'loso, a ag (DIR) malicious

do'manda sf (interrogazione) question; (richiesta) demand; (: cortese) request; (DIR: richiesta scritta) application; (ECON): **la ~** demand; **fare una ~ a qn** to ask sb a question; **fare ~ (per un lavoro)** to apply (for a job)

doman'dare vt (per avere) to ask for; (per sapere) to ask; (esigere) to demand; ~rsi vr to wonder; to ask o.s.; ~ **qc a qn** to ask sb for sth; to ask sb sth

do'mani *av* tomorrow ♦ *sm*: il ~ (*il futuro*) the future; (*il giorno successivo*) the next day; ~ **l'altro** the day after tomorrow

do'mare *vt* to tame

domat'tina *av* tomorrow morning

do'menica, che *sf* Sunday; **di** o Sunday; ~ **on Sundays; domeni'cale** *ag* Sunday *cpd*

do'mestica, che *sf vedi* **domestico**

do'mestico, a, ci, che *ag* domestic ♦ *smlf* servant, domestic

domi'cilio [domi'tʃiljo] *sm* (*DIR*) domicile, place of residence

domi'nare *vt* to dominate; (*fig: sentimenti*) to control, master ♦ *vi* to be in the dominant position; **~rsi** *vr* (*controllarsi*) to control o.s.; ~ **su** (*fig*) to surpass, outclass; **dominazi'one** *sf* domination

do'minio *sm* dominion; (*fig: campo*) field, domain

do'nare *vt* to give, present; (*per beneficenza etc*) to donate ♦ *vi* (*fig*): ~ **a** to suit, become; ~ **sangue** to give blood; **dona'tore, 'trice** *smlf* donor; **donatore di sangue/di organi** blood/organ donor

dondo'lare *vt* (*cullare*) to rock; **~rsi** *vr* to swing, sway; **'dondolo** *sm*: **sedia/cavallo a dondolo** rocking chair/horse

'donna *sf* woman; ~ **di casa** housewife; home-loving woman; ~ **di servizio** maid

donnai'olo *sm* ladykiller

don'nesco, a, schi, sche *ag* women's, woman's

'donnola *sf* weasel

'dono *sm* gift

'dopo *av* (*tempo*) afterwards; (*: più tardi*) later; (*luogo*) after, next ♦ *prep* after ♦ *cong* (*temporale*): ~ **aver studiato** after having studied; ~ **mangiato** va a dormire after having eaten o after a meal he goes for a sleep ♦ *ag inv*: **il giorno** ~ the following day; **un anno** ~ a year later; ~ **di me/lui** after me/him

dopo'barba *sm inv* after-shave

dopodo'mani *av* the day after tomorrow

dopogu'erra *sm* postwar years *pl*

dopo'pranzo [dopo'prandzo] *av* after lunch (o dinner)

doposcì [dopoʃ'ʃi] *sm inv* après-ski outfit

doposcu'ola *sm inv* school club offering extra tuition and recreational facilities

dopo'tutto *av* (*tutto considerato*) after all

doppi'aggio [dop'pjaddʒo] *sm* (*CINEMA*) dubbing

doppi'are *vt* (*NAUT*) to round; (*SPORT*) to lap; (*CINEMA*) to dub

'doppio, a *ag* double; (*fig: falso*) double-dealing, deceitful ♦ *av* (*quantità*): **il** ~ (**di**) twice as much (o many), double the amount (o number) of; (*SPORT*) doubles *pl* ♦ *av* double

doppi'one *sm* duplicate (copy)

doppio'petto *sm* double-breasted jacket

do'rare *vt* to gild; (*CUC*) to brown; **do'rato, a** *ag* golden; (*ricoperto d'oro*) gilt, gilded; **dora'tura** *sf* gilding

dormicchi'are [dormik'kjare] *vi* to doze

dormigli'one, a [dormiʎ'ʎone] *smlf* sleepyhead

dor'mire *vt, vi* to sleep; **dor'mita** *sf*: **farsi una dormita** to have a good sleep

dormi'torio *sm* dormitory

dormi'veglia [dormi've ʎʎa] *sm* drowsiness

'dorso *sm* back; (*di montagna*) ridge, crest; (*di libro*) spine; **a** ~ **di cavallo** on horseback

do'sare *vt* to measure out; (*MED*) to dose

'dose *sf* quantity, amount; (*MED*) dose

'dosso *sm* (*rilievo*) rise; (*di strada*) bump; (*dorso*): **levarsi di** ~ **i vestiti** to take one's clothes off

do'tare vt: ~ di to provide o supply with; (fig) to endow with; **dotazi'one** sf (insieme di beni) endowment; (di macchine etc) equipment
'dote sf (di sposa) dowry; (assegnata a un ente) endowment; (fig) gift, talent

Dott. abbr (= dottore) Dr

'dotto, a ag (colto) learned ♦ sm (sapiente) scholar; (ANAT) duct

dotto'rato sm degree; ~ di ricerca doctorate, doctor's degree

dot'tore, essa smf doctor

dot'trina sf doctrine

Dott.ssa abbr (= dottoressa) Dr.

'dove av (gen) where; (in cui) where, in which; (dovunque) wherever ♦ cong (mentre, laddove) whereas; ~ sei?/vai? where are you?/are you going?; **dimmi dov'è** tell me where it is; **di ~ sei?** where are you from?; **per ~ si passa?** which way should we go?; **la città ~ abito** the town where o in which I live; **siediti ~ vuoi** sit wherever youlike

do'vere sm (obbligo) duty ♦ vt (essere debitore): ~ qc (a qn) to owe (sb) sth ♦ vi (seguito dall'infinito: obbligo) to have to; **rivolgersi a chi di ~** to apply to the appropriate authority o person; **lui deve farlo** he has to do it, he must do it; **è dovuto partire** he had to leave; **ha dovuto pagare** he had to pay; (: intenzione): **devo partire domani** I'm (due) to leave tomorrow; (: probabilità): **dev'essere tardi** it must be late; **come si deve** (lavorare, comportarsi) properly; **una persona come si deve** a respectable person

dove'roso, a ag (right and) proper

do'vunque av (in qualunque luogo) wherever; (dappertutto) everywhere; ~ io vada wherever I go

do'vuto, a ag (causato): ~ a due to

doz'zina [dod'dzina] sf dozen; **una** ~ **di uova** a dozen eggs

dozzi'nale [doddzi'nale] ag cheap, second-rate

dra'gare vt to dredge

'drago, ghi sm dragon

'dramma, i sm drama; **dram'-matico, a, ci, che** ag dramatic; **drammatiz'zare** vt to dramatize; **dramma'turgo, ghi** sm playwright, dramatist

drappeggi'are [draped'dʒare] vt o to drape

drap'pello sm (MIL) squad; (gruppo) band, group

'drastico, a, ci, che ag drastic

dre'naggio [dre'naddʒo] sm drainage

dre'nare vt to drain

'dritto, a ag, av = diritto

driz'zare [drit'tsare] vt (far tornare diritto) to straighten; (volgere: sguardo, occhi) to turn, direct; (innalzare: antenna, muro) to erect; ~rsi vr: ~rsi (in piedi) to stand up; ~ **le orecchie** to prick up one's ears

'droga, ghe sf (sostanza aromatica) spice; (stupefacente) drug; **dro'gare** vt to season, spice; to drug, dope; **drogarsi** vr to take drugs; **dro'gato, a** smf drug addict

droghe'ria [droge'ria] sf grocer's shop (BRIT), grocery (store) (US)

'dubbio, a ag (incerto) doubtful, dubious; (ambiguo) dubious ♦ sm (incertezza) doubt; **avere il ~ che** to be afraid that, suspect that; **mettere in ~ qc** to question sth; **dubbi'oso, a** ag doubtful, dubious

dubi'tare vi: ~ **di** to doubt; (risultato) to be doubtful of

Dub'lino sf Dublin

'duca, chi sm duke

du'chessa [du'kessa] sf duchess

'due num two

due'cento [due'tʃɛnto] num two hundred ♦ sm: **il D~** the thirteenth century

due'pezzi [due'pettsi] sm (costume da bagno) two-piece swimsuit; (abito femminile) two-piece suit

du'etto sm duet

'dunque cong (perciò) so, therefore;

(riprendendo il discorso) well (then) ♦ *sm inv:* **venire al** ~ to come to the point

du'omo *sm* cathedral

'duplex *sm inv (TEL)* party line

dupli'cato *sm* duplicate

'duplice ['duplitʃe] *ag* double, two-fold; **in** ~ **copia** in duplicate

du'rante *prep* during

du'rare *vi* to last; ~ **fatica a** to have difficulty in; **du'rata** *sf* length (of time); duration; **dura'turo, a** *ag* lasting; **du'revole** *ag* lasting

du'rezza · [du'rettsa] *sf* hardness; stubbornness; harshness; toughness

'duro, a *ag (pietra, lavoro, materasso, problema)* hard; *(persona: ostinato)* stubborn, obstinate; *(: severo)* harsh, hard; *(: voce)* harsh; *(carne)* tough ♦ *sm* hardness; *(difficoltà)* hard part; *(persona)* tough guy; **tener** ~ to stand firm, hold out; ~ **d'orecchi** hard of hearing

du'rone *sm* hard skin

E

e *(dav V spesso* **ed)** *cong* and; ~ **lui?** what about him?; ~ **compralo!** well buy it then!

E. *abbr (= est)* E

è *vb vedi* **essere**

'ebano *sm* ebony

eb'bene *cong* well (then)

eb'brezza [eb'brettsa] *sf* intoxication

'ebbro, a *ag* drunk; ~ **di** *(gioia etc)* beside o.s. with

'ebete *ag* stupid, idiotic

ebolli'zione [ebollit'tsjone] *sf* boiling; **punto di** ~ boiling point

e'braico, a, ci, che *ag* Hebrew, Hebraic ♦ *sm (LING)* Hebrew

e'breo, a *ag* Jewish ♦ *sm/f* Jew/Jewess

'Ebridi *sfpl:* **le (isole)** ~ the Hebrides

ecc *av abbr (= eccetera)* etc

ecce'denza [ettʃe'dɛntsa] *sf* excess, surplus

ec'cedere [et'tʃedere] *vt* to exceed ♦ *vi* to go too far; ~ **nel bere/mangiare** to indulge in drink/food to excess

eccel'lente [ettʃel'lɛnte] *ag* excellent; **eccel'lenza** *sf* excellence; *(titolo)* Excellency

ec'cellere [et'tʃellere] *vi:* ~ **(in)** to excel (at); **ec'celso, a** *pp di* **eccellere**

ec'centrico, a, ci, che [et'tʃɛntriko] *ag* eccentric

ec'cesso *sm* excess; **all'** ~ *(gentile, generoso)* to excess, excessively; ~ **di velocità** *(AUT)* speeding

ec'cessivo, a [ettʃes'sivo] *ag* excessive

ec'cetera [et'tʃetera] *av* et cetera, and so on

ec'cetto [et'tʃetto] *prep* except, with the exception of; ~ **che** except, other than; ~ **che (non)** unless

eccettu'are [ettʃettu'are] *vt* to except

eccezio'nale [ettʃettsjo'nale] *ag* exceptional

eccezi'one [ettʃet'tsjone] *sf* exception; *(DIR)* objection; **a** ~ **di** with the exception of, except for; **d'** ~ exceptional

ec'cidio [et'tʃidio] *sm* massacre

ecci'tare [ettʃi'tare] *vt (curiosità, interesse)* to excite, arouse; *(folla)* to incite; ~**rsi** *vr* to get excited; *(sessualmente)* to become aroused; **ecci-tazi'one** *sf* excitement

'ecco *av (per dimostrare):* ~ **il treno!** here's o here comes the train!; *(dav pron):* ~**mi!** here I am!; ~**ne uno!** here's one (of them)!; *(dav pp):* ~ **fatto!** there, that's it done!

echeggi'are [eked'dʒare] *vi* to echo

e'clissi *sf* eclipse

'eco *(pl(m)* **'echi)** *sm o f* echo

ecolo'gia [ekolo'dʒia] *sf* ecology

econo'mia *sf* economy; *(scienza)* economics *sg*; *(risparmio: azione)* saving; **fare** ~ to economize, make economies; **eco'nomico, a, ci, che**

ag economic; (*poco costoso*) economical; **econo'mista, i** *sm* economist; **economiz'zare** *vt, vi* to save; **e'conomo, a** *ag* thrifty ♦ *sm/f* (*INS*) bursar

E'CU [e'ku] *sm inv* (*Unità monetaria europea*) ECU *n*

ed *cong vedi* **e**

'edera *sf* ivy

e'dicola *sf* newspaper kiosk *o* stand (*US*)

edifi'care *vt* to build; (*fig: teoria, azienda*) to establish; (*indurre al bene*) to edify

edi'ficio [edi'fitʃo] *sm* building; (*fig*) structure

e'dile *ag* building *cpd*; **edi'lizia** *sf* building, building trade; **edi'lizio, a** *ag* building *cpd*

Edim'burgo *sf* Edinburgh

edi'tore, 'trice *ag* publishing *cpd* ♦ *sm/f* publisher; (*curatore*) editor; **edito'ria** *sf* publishing; **editori'ale** *ag* publishing *cpd* ♦ *sm* editorial, leader

edizi'one [edit'tsjone] *sf* edition; (*tiratura*) printing; (*di manifestazioni, feste etc*) production

edu'care *vt* to educate; (*gusto, mente*) to train; ~ **qn a fare** to train sb to do; **edu'cato, a** *ag* polite, well-mannered; **educazi'one** *sf* education; (*familiare*) upbringing; (*comportamento*) (good) manners *pl*; **educazione fisica** (*INS*) physical training *o* education

effemi'nato, a *ag* effeminate

effet'tivo, a *ag* (*reale*) real, actual; (*impiegato, professore*) permanent; (*MIL*) regular ♦ *sm* (*MIL*) strength; (*di patrimonio etc*) sum total

ef'fetto *sm* effect; (*COMM: cambiale*) bill; (*fig: impressione*) impression; **in ~i** in fact, actually; ~ **serra** greenhouse effect; **effettu'are** *vt* to effect, carry out

effi'cace [effi'katʃe] *ag* effective

effici'ente [effi'tʃɛnte] *ag* efficient; **effici'enza** *sf* efficiency

e'fimero, a *ag* ephemeral

E'geo [e'dʒɛo] *sm*: **l'~, il mare ~** the Aegean (Sea)

E'gitto [e'dʒitto] *sm*: **l'~** Egypt

egizi'ano, a [edʒit'tsjano] *ag, sm/f* Egyptian

'egli ['eʎʎi] *pron* he; ~ **stesso** he himself

ego'ismo *sm* selfishness, egoism; **ego'ista, i, e** *ag* selfish, egoistic ♦ *sm/f* egoist

egr. *abbr* = **egregio**

e'gregio, a, gi, gie [e'grɛdʒo] *ag* distinguished; (*nelle lettere*): **E~ Signore** Dear Sir

eguagli'anza etc [egwaʎ'ʎantsa] = **uguaglianza** etc

E.I. *abbr* = **Esercito Italiano**

elabo'rare *vt* (*progetto*) to work out, elaborate; (*dati*) to process; (*digerire*) to digest; **elabora'tore** *sm* (*INFORM*): **elaboratore elettronico** computer; **elaborazi'one** *sf* elaboration; digestion; **elaborazione dei dati** data processing

e'lastico, a, ci, che *ag* elastic; (*fig: andatura*) springy; (*: decisione, vedute*) flexible ♦ *sm* (*gomma*) rubber band; (*per il cucito*) elastic *no pl*

ele'fante *sm* elephant

ele'gante *ag* elegant

e'leggere [e'lɛddʒere] *vt* to elect

elemen'tare *ag* elementary; **le** (*scuole*) **~i** *sfpl* primary (*BRIT*) *o* grade (*US*) school

ele'mento *sm* element; (*parte componente*) element, component, part; **~i** *smpl* (*della scienza etc*) elements, rudiments

ele'mosina *sf* charity, alms *pl*; **chiedere l'~** to beg

elen'care *vt* to list

e'lenco, chi *sm* list; ~ **telefonico** telephone directory

e'letto, a *pp di* **eleggere** ♦ *sm/f* (*nominato*) elected member; **elet'to'rale** *ag* electoral, election *cpd*; **eletto'rato** *sm* electorate; **elet'tore, 'trice** *sm/f* voter, elector

elet'trauto *sm inv* workshop for car

electrical repairs; (*tecnico*) car electrician

elettri'cista, i [elettri'tʃista] *sm* electrician

elettricità [elettritʃi'ta] *sf* electricity

e'lettrico, a, ci, che *ag* electric(al)

elettriz'zare [elettrid'dzare] *vt* to electrify

elettro... *prefisso*: **elettrocardio-'gramma, i** *sm* electrocardiogram; **elettrodo'mestico, a, ci, che** *ag*: **apparecchi elettrodomestici** domestic (electrical) appliances; **elet'trone** *sm* electron; **elet'tronica** *sf* electronics *sg*; **elet'tronico, a, ci, che** *ag* electronic

ele'vare *vt* to raise; (*edificio*) to erect; (*multa*) to impose

elezi'one [elet'tsjone] *sf* election; ~**i** *sfpl* (*POL*) election(s)

'elica, che *sf* propeller

eli'cottero *sm* helicopter

elimi'nare *vt* to eliminate; **elimina'toria** *sf* eliminating round

'elio *sm* helium

'ella *pron* she; (*forma di cortesia*) you; ~ **stessa** she herself; you yourself

el'metto *sm* helmet

e'logio [e'lɔdʒo] *sm* (*discorso, scritto*) eulogy; (*lode*) praise (*di solito no pl*)

elo'quente *ag* eloquent

e'ludere *vt* to evade; **elu'sivo, a** *ag* evasive

ema'nare *vt* to send out, give off; (*fig*: *leggi, decreti*) to issue ♦ *vi*: ~ **da** to come from

emanci'pare [emantʃi'pare] *vt* to emancipate; ~**rsi** *vr* (*fig*) to become liberated *o* emancipated

embri'one *sm* embryo

emenda'mento *sm* amendment

emen'dare *vt* to amend

emer'genza [emer'dʒentsa] *sf* emergency; **in caso di** ~ in an emergency

e'mergere [e'merdʒere] *vi* to

emerge; (*sommergibile*) to surface; (*fig*: *distinguersi*) to stand out; **e'merso, a** *pp di* **emergere**

e'messo, a *pp di* **emettere**

e'mettere *vt* (*suono, luce*) to give out, emit; (*onde radio*) to send out; (*assegno, francobollo, ordine*) to issue; (*fig*: *giudizio*) to express, voice

emi'crania *sf* migraine

emi'grare *vi* to emigrate; **emigra-zi'one** *sf* emigration

emi'nente *ag* eminent, distinguished

emis'fero *sm* hemisphere; ~ **boreale/australe** northern/southern hemisphere

emissi'one *sf* (*vedi* **emettere**) emission; sending out; issue; (*RADIO*) broadcast

emit'tente *ag* (*banca*) issuing; (*RADIO*) broadcasting, transmitting ♦ *sf* (*RADIO*) transmitter

emorra'gia, 'gie [emorra'dʒia] *sf* haemorrhage

emo'tivo, a *ag* emotional

emozio'nante [emottsjo'nante] *ag* exciting, thrilling

emozio'nare [emottsjo'nare] *vt* (*appassionare*) to thrill, excite; (*commuovere*) to move; (*innervosire*) to upset; ~**rsi** *vr* to be excited; to be moved; to be upset

emozi'one [emot'tsjone] *sf* emotion; (*agitazione*) excitement

'empio, a *ag* (*sacrilego*) impious; (*spietato*) cruel, pitiless; (*malvagio*) wicked, evil

emulsi'one *sf* emulsion

enciclope'dia [entʃiklope'dia] *sf* encyclopaedia

endove'noso, a *ag* (*MED*) intravenous

'ENEL ['enel] *sigla m* (= *Ente Nazionale per l'Energia Elettrica*) ≈ C.E.G.B. (= *Central Electricity Generating Board*)

ener'gia, 'gie [ener'dʒia] *sf* (*FISICA*) energy; (*fig*) energy, strength, vigour; ~ **eolica** wind power; ~ **solare** solar energy, solar power; **e'nergico, a, ci, che** *ag* energetic,

enfasi

enfasi *sf* emphasis; (*peg*) bombast, pomposity; **en'fatico, a, ci, che** *ag* emphatic; pompous

'ENIT ['enit] *sigla m* = Ente Nazionale Italiano per il Turismo

en'nesimo, a *ag* (*MAT*, *fig*) nth; **per l'~a volta** for the umpteenth time

e'norme *ag* enormous, huge; **enormità** *sf inv* enormity, huge size; (*assurdità*) absurdity; **non dire enormità!** don't talk nonsense!

'ente *sm* (*istituzione*) body, board, corporation; (*FILOSOFIA*) being

en'trambi, e *pron pl* both (of them) ♦ *ag pl:* **~ i ragazzi** both boys, both of the boys

en'trare *vi* to enter, go (*o* come) in; **~ in** (*luogo*) to enter, go (*o* come) into; (*trovar posto, poter stare*) to fit into; (*essere ammesso a: club etc*) to join, become a member of; **~ in automobile** to get into the car; **far ~ qn** (*visitatore etc*) to show sb in; **questo non c'entra** (*fig*) that's got nothing to do with it; **en'trata** *sf* entrance, entry; **entrate** *sfpl* (*COMM*) receipts, takings; (*ECON*) income *sg*

'entro *prep* (*temporale*) within

entusias'mare *vt* to excite, fill with enthusiasm; **~rsi (per qc/qn)** to become enthusiastic (about sth/sb); **entusi'asmo** *sm* enthusiasm; **entusi'asta, i, e** *ag* enthusiastic ♦ *sm/f* enthusiast; **entusi'astico, a, ci, che** *ag* enthusiastic

enunci'are [enun'tʃare] *vt* (*teoria*) to enunciate, set out

'epico, a, ci, che *ag* epic

epide'mia *sf* epidemic

epi'dermide *sf* skin, epidermis

Epifa'nia *sf* Epiphany

epiles'sia *sf* epilepsy

e'pilogo, ghi *sm* conclusion

epi'sodio *sm* episode

e'piteto *sm* epithet

'epoca, che *sf* (*periodo storico*) age, era; (*tempo*) time; (*GEO*) age

ep'pure *cong* and yet, nevertheless

epu'rare *vt* (*POL*) to purge

equa'tore *sm* equator

equazi'one [ekwat'tsjone] *sf* (*MAT*) equation

e'questre *ag* equestrian

equi'latero, a *ag* equilateral

equili'brare *vt* to balance; **equi'librio** *sm* balance, equilibrium; **perdere l'~** to lose one's balance

e'quino, a *ag* horse *cpd*, equine

equipaggi'are [ekwipad'dʒare] *vt* (*di persone*) to man; (*di mezzi*) to equip; **equi'paggio** *sm* crew

equipa'rare *vt* to make equal

equità *sf* equity, fairness

equitazi'one [ekwitat'tsjone] *sf* (*horse-*)riding

equiva'lente *ag*, *sm* equivalent; **equiva'lenza** *sf* equivalence

equivo'care *vi* to misunderstand; **e'quivoco, a, ci, che** *ag* equivocal, ambiguous; (*sospetto*) dubious ♦ *sm* misunderstanding; **a scanso di equivoci** to avoid any misunderstanding; **giocare sull'equivoco** to equivocate

'equo, a *ag* fair, just

'era *sf* era

'erba *sf* grass; (*aromatica, medicinale*) herb; **in ~** (*fig*) budding; **er'baccia, ce** *sf* weed

e'rede *sm/f* heir; **eredità** *sf* (*DIR*) inheritance; (*BIOL*) heredity; **lasciare qc in eredità a qn** to leave *o* bequeath sth to sb; **eredi'tare** *vt* to inherit; **eredi'tario, a** *ag* hereditary

ere'mita *i* *sm* hermit

ere'sia *sf* heresy; **e'retico, a, ci, che** *ag* heretical ♦ *sm/f* heretic

e'retto, a *pp di* **erigere** ♦ *ag* erect, upright; **erezi'one** *sf* (*FISIOL*) erection

er'gastolo *sm* (*DIR: pena*) life imprisonment

'erica *sf* heather

e'rigere [e'ridʒere] *vt* to erect, raise; (*fig: fondare*) to found

ERM *sigla* (= Meccanismo dei tassi di cambio) ERM *n*

ermel'lino *sm* ermine

er'metico, a, ci, che *ag* hermetic

'ernia *sf* (*MED*) hernia

e'roe *sm* hero

ero'gare *vt* (*somme*) to distribute; (: *per beneficenza*) to donate; (*gas, servizi*) to supply

e'roico, a, ci, che *ag* heroic

ero'ina *sf* heroine; (*droga*) heroin

ero'ismo *sm* heroism

erosi'one *sf* erosion

e'rotico, a, ci, che *ag* erotic

er'rare *vi* (*vagare*) to wander, roam; (*sbagliare*) to be mistaken

er'rore *sm* error, mistake; (*morale*) error; **per ~** by mistake

'erta *sf* steep slope; **stare all'~** to be on the alert

erut'tare *vt* (*sog: vulcano*) to throw out, belch

eruzi'one [erut'tsjone] *sf* eruption

esacer'bare [ezatʃer'bare] *vt* to exacerbate

esage'rare [ezadʒe'rare] *vt* to exaggerate ♦ *vi* to exaggerate; (*eccedere*) to go too far; **esagerazi'one** *sf* exaggeration

e'sagono *sm* hexagon

esal'tare *vt* to exalt; (*entusiasmare*) to excite, stir; **esal'tato, a** *sm/f* fanatic

e'same *sm* examination; (*INS*) exam, examination; **fare** *o* **dare un ~** to sit *o* take an exam; **~ del sangue** blood test

esami'nare *vt* to examine

e'sanime *ag* lifeless

esaspe'rare *vt* to exasperate; to exacerbate; **~rsi** *vr* to become annoyed *o* exasperated; **esasperazi'one** *sf* exasperation

esatta'mente *av* exactly; accurately, precisely

esat'tezza [ezat'tettsa] *sf* exactitude, accuracy, precision

e'satto, a *pp di* **esigere** ♦ *ag* (*calcolo, ora*) correct, right, exact; (*preciso*) accurate, precise; (*puntuale*) punctual

esat'tore *sm* (*di imposte etc*) collector

esau'dire *vt* to grant, fulfil

esauri'ente *ag* exhaustive

esauri'mento *sm* exhaustion; **~ nervoso** nervous breakdown

esau'rire *vt* (*stancare*) to exhaust, wear out; (*provviste, miniera*) to exhaust; **~rsi** *vr* to exhaust o.s., wear o.s. out; (*provviste*) to run out; **esau'rito, a** *ag* exhausted; (*merci*) sold out; (*libri*) out of print; **registrare il tutto esaurito** (*TEATRO*) to have a full house; **e'sausto, a** *ag* exhausted

'esca (*pl* **esche**) *sf* bait

escande'scenza [eskandeʃ'ʃentsa] *sf*: **dare in ~e** to lose one's temper, fly into a rage

'esce *etc vb vedi* **uscire**

eschi'mese [eski'mese] *ag, sm/f* Eskimo

escla'mare *vi* to exclaim, cry out; **esclamazi'one** *sf* exclamation

es'cludere *vt* to exclude

esclu'siva *sf* (*DIR, COMM*) exclusive *o* sole rights *pl*

esclu'sivo, a *ag* exclusive

es'cluso, a *pp di* **escludere**

'esco *etc vb vedi* **uscire**

escogi'tare [eskodʒi'tare] *vt* to devise, think up

escursi'one *sf* (*gita*) excursion, trip; (: *a piedi*) hike, walk; (*METEOR*) range

ese'crare *vt* to loathe, abhor

esecu'tivo, a *ag, sm* executive

esecu'tore, 'trice *sm/f* (*MUS*) performer; (*DIR*) executor

esecuzi'one [ezekut'tsjone] *sf* execution, carrying out; (*MUS*) performance; **~ capitale** execution

esegu'ire *vt* to carry out, execute; (*MUS*) to perform, execute

e'sempio *sm* example; **per ~** for example, for instance; **fare** *o* **dare un ~** to give an example; **esem'plare** *ag* exemplary ♦ *sm* example; (*copia*) copy; **esemplifi'care** *vt* to exemplify

esen'tare *vt*: **~ qn/qc da** to exempt sb/sth from

e'sente *ag*: **~ da** (*dispensato da*)

exempt from; (privo di) free from; **esenzi'one** sf exemption

e'sequie sfpl funeral rites; funeral service sg

eser'cente [ezer'tʃɛnte] smf trader, dealer; shopkeeper

eserci'tare [ezertʃi'tare] vt (professione) to practise (BRIT), practice (US); (allenare: corpo, mente) to exercise, train; (diritto) to exercise; (influenza, pressione) to exert; ~rsi vr to practise; ~rsi alla lotta to practise fighting; **esercitazi'one** sf (scolastica, militare) exercise

e'sercito [e'zɛrtʃito] sm army

eser'cizio [ezer'tʃittsjo] sm practice; exercising; (fisico, di matematica) exercise; (ECON) financial year; (azienda) business, concern; **in** ~ (medico etc) practising

esi'bire vt to exhibit, display; (documenti) to produce, present; ~rsi vr (attore) to perform; (fig) to show off; **esibizi'one** sf exhibition; (di documento) presentation; (spettacolo) show, performance

esi'gente [ezi'dʒɛnte] ag demanding; **esi'genza** sf demand, requirement

e'sigere [e'zidʒere] vt (pretendere) to demand; (richiedere) to demand, require; (imposte) to collect

e'siguo, a ag small, slight

e'sile ag (persona) slender, slim; (stelo) thin; (voce) faint

esili'are vt to exile; **e'silio** sm exile

e'simere vt: ~ qn/qc da to exempt sb/sth from; ~rsi vr: ~rsi da to get out of

esis'tenza [ezis'tɛntsa] sf existence

e'sistere vi to exist

esis'tito, a pp di esistere

esi'tare vi to hesitate; **esitazi'one** sf hesitation

'esito sm result, outcome

'esodo sm exodus

esone'rare vt to exempt

e'sordio sm début

esor'tare vt: ~ qn a fare to urge sb to do

e'sotico, a, ci, che ag exotic

es'pandere vt to expand; (confini) to extend; (influenza) to extend, spread; ~rsi vr to expand; **espansi'one** sf expansion; **espan'sivo, a** ag expansive, communicative

espatri'are vi to leave one's country

espedi'ente sm expedient

es'pellere vt to expel

esperi'enza [espe'rjɛntsa] sf experience; (SCIENZA: prova) experiment

esperi'mento sm experiment

es'perto, a ag, sm expert

espi'are vt to atone for

espi'rare vt, vi to breathe out

espli'care vt (attività) to carry out, perform

es'plicito, a [es'plitʃito] ag explicit

es'plodere vi (anche fig) to explode ♦ vt to fire

esplo'rare vt to explore; **esplo'ratore** sm explorer; (anche: giovane esploratore) (boy) scout; (NAUT) scout (ship)

esplosi'one sf explosion; **esplo'sivo, a** ag, sm explosive; **es'ploso, a** pp di esplodere

espo'nente smf (rappresentante) representative

es'porre vt (merci) to display; (quadro) to exhibit, show; (fatti, idee) to explain, set out; (porre in pericolo, FOT) to expose

espor'tare vt to export; **esporta-zi'one** sf exportation; export

esposizi'one [espozit'tsjone] sf displaying; exhibiting; setting out; (anche FOT) exposure; (mostra) exhibition; (narrazione) explanation, exposition

es'posto, a pp di esporre ♦ ag: ~ a nord facing north ♦ sm (AMM) statement, account; (: petizione) petition

espressi'one sf expression

espres'sivo, a ag expressive

es'presso, a pp di esprimere ♦ ag express ♦ sm (lettera) express letter; (anche: treno ~) express train; (anche: caffè ~) espresso

es'primere vt to express

espuls'ione sf expulsion; **es'pulso, a** pp di **espellere**

'essa (pl 'esse) pron f vedi **esso**

es'senza [es'sɛntsa] sf essence; **essenzi'ale** ag essential; **l'essenziale** the main o most important thing

---

PAROLA CHIAVE

'essere sm being; ~ **umano** human being

♦ vb copulativo **1** (con attributo, sostantivo) to be; **sei giovane/simpatico** you are o you're young/nice; **è medico** he is o he's a doctor

2 (+di: appartenere) to be; **di chi è la penna?** whose pen is it?; **è di Carla** it is o it's Carla's, it belongs to Carla

3 (+di: provenire) to be; **è di Venezia** he is o he's from Venice

4 (data, ora): **è il 15 agosto/lunedì** it is o it's the 15th of August/Monday; **che ora è?, che ore sono?** what time is it?; **è l'una** it is o it's one o'clock; **sono le due** it is o it's two o'clock

5 (costare): **quant'è?** how much is it?; **sono 20.000 lire** it's 20,000 lire

♦ vb aus **1** (attivo): ~ **arrivato/venuto** to have arrived/come; **è gia partita** she has already left

2 (passivo) to be; ~ **fatto da** to be made by; **è stata uccisa** she has been killed

3 (riflessivo): **si sono lavati** they washed, they got washed

4 (+da +infinito): **è da farsi subito** it must be o is to be done immediately

♦ vi **1** (esistere, trovarsi) to be; **sono a casa** I'm at home; ~ **in piedi/seduto** to be standing/sitting

2 (esserci): **c'è** there is; **ci sono** there are; **che c'è?** what's the matter?, what is it?; **ci sono!** (fig: ho capito) I've got it!; vedi anche **ci**

♦ vb impers: **è tardi/Pasqua** it's late/Easter; **è possibile che venga** he may come; **è così** that's the way it is

---

'esso, a pron it; (riferito a persona: soggetto) he/she; (: complemento) him/her; ~**i, e** pron pl they; (complemento) them

est sm east

'estasi sf ecstasy

es'tate sf summer

es'tendere vt to extend; ~**rsi** vr (diffondersi) to spread; (territorio, confini) to extend; **estensi'one** sf extension; (di superficie) expanse; (di voce) range

esteri'ore ag outward, external

ester'nare vt to express

es'terno, a ag (porta, muro) outer, outside; (scala) outside; (alunno, impressione) external ♦ sm outside, exterior ♦ sm/f (allievo) day pupil; **per uso** ~ for external use only

'estero, a ag foreign ♦ sm: **all'**~ abroad

es'teso, a pp di **estendere** ag extensive, large; **scrivere per** ~ to write in full

es'tetico, a, ci, che ag aesthetic ♦ sf (disciplina) aesthetics sg; (bellezza) attractiveness; **este'tista, i, e** sm/f beautician

'estimo sm valuation; (disciplina) surveying

es'tinguere vt to extinguish, put out; (debito) to pay off; ~**rsi** vr to go out; (specie) to become extinct; **es'tinto, a** pp di **estinguere**; **estin'tore** sm (fire) extinguisher; **estinzi'one** sf putting out; (di specie) extinction

estir'pare vt (pianta) to uproot, pull up; (fig: vizio) to eradicate

es'tivo, a ag summer cpd

es'torcere [es'tɔrtʃere] vt: ~ **qc (a qn)** to extort sth (from sb); **estorsi'one** sf extortion

estradizi'one [estradit'tsjone] sf extradition

es'traneo, a ag foreign; (discorso) extraneous, unrelated ♦ sm/f stranger; **rimanere ~ a qc** to take no part in sth

es'trarre vt to extract; (minerali) to mine; (sorteggiare) to draw; **es'tratto, a** pp di **estrarre ♦** sm extract; (di documento (CUC) meat extract; estratto di carne (CUC) meat extract; estratto di nascita birth certificate; **estrazi'one** sf extraction; mining; drawing no pl; draw

estremità sf inv extremity, end ♦ sfpl (ANAT) extremities

es'tremo, a ag extreme; (ultimo: ora, tentativo) final, last ♦ sm extreme; (di pazienza, forze) limit, end; ~i smpl (AMM: dati essenziali) details, particulars; l'~ Oriente the Far East

'estro sm (capriccio) whim, fancy; (ispirazione creativa) inspiration; **es'troso, a** ag whimsical, capricious; inspired

estro'verso, a ag, sm extrovert

'esule sm/f exile

età sf inv age; **all'~ di 8 anni** at the age of 8, at 8 years of age; **ha la mia ~** he (o she) is the same age as me o as I am; **raggiungere la maggiore ~** to come of age; **essere in ~ minore** to be under age

'etere sm ether; **e'tereo, a** ag ethereal

eternità sf eternity

e'terno, a ag eternal

etero'geneo, a [etero'dʒɛneo] ag heterogeneous

'etica sf ethics sg; vedi anche **etico**

eti'chetta [eti'ketta] sf label; (cerimoniale): **l'~** etiquette

'etico, a, ci, che ag ethical

etimolo'gia, 'gie [etimolo'dʒia] sf etymology

Eti'opia sf: **l'~** Ethiopia

'Etna sm: **l'~** Etna

'etnico, a, ci, che ag ethnic

e'trusco, a, schi, sche ag, sm/f Etruscan

'ettaro sm hectare (= 10,000 m²)

'etto sm abbr = **ettogrammo**

etto'grammo sm hectogram(me) (= 100 grams)

Eucaris'tia sf: **l'~** the Eucharist

Eu'ropa sf: **l'~** Europe; **euro'peo, a** ag, sm/f European

evacu'are vt to evacuate

e'vadere vi (fuggire): **~ da** to escape from ♦ vt (sbrigare) to deal with, dispatch; (tasse) to evade

evan'gelico, a, ci, che [evan'dʒɛliko] ag evangelical

evapo'rare vi to evaporate; **evapo-razi'one** sf evaporation

evasi'one sf (vedi evadere) escape; dispatch; **~ fiscale** tax evasion

eva'sivo, a ag evasive

e'vaso, a pp di **evadere** ♦ sm escapee

eveni'enza [eve'njɛntsa] sf: **pronto(a) per ogni ~** ready for any eventuality

e'vento sm event

eventu'ale ag possible

evi'dente ag evident, obvious; **evi'denza** sf obviousness; **mettere in evidenza** to point out, highlight; **evidenzi'are** vt to emphasize; (con evidenziatore) to highlight; **eviden-zia'tore** sm highlighter (pen)

evi'tare vt to avoid; **~ di fare** to avoid doing; **~ qc a qn** to spare sb sth

'evo sm age, epoch

evo'care vt to evoke

evo'luto, a pp di **evolvere** ♦ ag (civiltà) (highly) developed, advanced; (persona) independent

evoluzi'one [evolut'tsjone] sf evolution

e'volversi vr to evolve

ev'viva escl hurrah!; **~ il re!** long live the king!, hurrah for the king!

ex prefisso ex, former

'extra ag inv first-rate; top-quality ♦ sm inv extra; **extracomuni'tario, a** ag from outside the EC ♦ sm/f non-EC citizen; **extraconiu'gale** ag extramarital

F

fa *vb vedi* **fare** ♦ *sm inv* (*MUS*) F; (: *solfeggiando la scala*) **fa** ♦ *av*: **10 anni** ~ 10 years ago

fabbi'sogno [fabbi'zoɲɲo] *sm* needs *pl*, requirements *pl*

'fabbrica *sf* factory; **fabbri'cante** *sm* manufacturer; maker; **fabbri'care** *vt* to build; (*produrre*) to manufacture, make; (*fig*) to fabricate, invent

'fabbro *sm* (black)smith

fac'cenda [fat'tʃɛnda] *sf* matter, affair; (*cosa da fare*) task, chore

fac'chino [fak'kino] *sm* porter

'faccia, ce [fattʃa] *sf* face; (*di moneta, medaglia*) side; ~ **a** ~ face to face

facci'ata [fat'tʃata] *sf* façade; (*di pagina*) side

'faccio ['fattʃo] *vb vedi* **fare**

fa'ceto, a [fa'tʃeto] *ag* witty, humorous

'facile ['fatʃile] *ag* easy; (*affabile*) easy-going; (*disposto*): ~ **a** inclined to, prone to; (*probabile*): **è** ~ **che piova** it's likely to rain; **facilità** *sf* easiness; (*disposizione, dono*) aptitude; **facili'tare** *vt* to make easier

facino'roso, a [fatʃino'roso] *ag* violent

facoltà *sf inv* faculty; (*CHIMICA*) property; (*autorità*) power

facolta'tivo, a *ag* optional; (*fermata d'autobus*) request *cpd*

fac'simile *sm* facsimile

'faggio ['faddʒo] *sm* beech

fagi'ano [fa'dʒano] *sm* pheasant

fagio'lino [fadʒo'lino] *sm* French (*BRIT*) o string bean

fagi'olo [fa'dʒɔlo] *sm* bean

fa'gotto *sm* bundle; (*MUS*) bassoon; **far** ~ (*fig*) to pack up and go

'fai *vb vedi* **fare**

'falce ['faltʃe] *sf* scythe; **fal'cetto** *sm* sickle; **falci'are** *vt* to cut; (*fig*) to mow down

'falco, chi *sm* hawk

fal'cone *sm* falcon

'falda *sf* layer, stratum; (*di cappello*) brim; (*di cappotto*) tails *pl*; (*di monte*) lower slope; (*di tetto*) pitch; **nevica a larghe** ~**e** the snow is falling in large flakes; **abito a** ~**e** tails *pl*

fale'gname [faleɲ'ɲame] *sm* joiner

fal'lace [fal'latʃe] *ag* misleading

falli'mento *sm* failure; bankruptcy

fal'lire *vi* (*non riuscire*): ~ **(in)** to fail (in); (*DIR*) to go bankrupt ♦ *vt* (*colpo, bersaglio*) to miss; **fal'lito, a** *ag* unsuccessful; bankrupt ♦ *smlf* bankrupt

'fallo *sm* error, mistake; (*imperfezione*) defect, flaw; (*SPORT*) foul; fault; **senza** ~ without fail

falò *sm inv* bonfire

fal'sare *vt* to distort, misrepresent; **fal'sario** *sm* forger; counterfeiter; **falsifi'care** *vt* to forge; (*monete*) to forge, counterfeit

'falso, a *ag* false; (*errato*) wrong; (*falsificato*) forged; fake; (: *oro, gioielli*) imitation *cpd* ♦ *sm* forgery; **giurare il** ~ to commit perjury

'fama *sf* fame; (*reputazione*) reputation, name

'fame *sf* hunger; **aver** ~ to be hungry; **fa'melico, a, ci, che** *ag* ravenous

fa'miglia [fa'miʎʎa] *sf* family

famili'are *ag* (*della famiglia*) family *cpd*; (*ben noto*) familiar; (*rapporti, atmosfera*) friendly; (*LING*) informal, colloquial ♦ *smlf* relative, relation; **familiarità** *sf* familiarity; friendliness; informality

fa'moso, a *ag* famous, well-known

fa'nale *sm* (*AUT*) light, lamp (*BRIT*); (*luce stradale, NAUT*) light; (*di faro*) beacon

fa'natico, a, ci, che *ag* fanatical; (*del teatro, calcio etc*): ~ **di** o **per** mad o crazy about ♦ *smlf* fanatic; (*tifoso*) fan

fanci'ullo, a [fan'tʃullo] *smlf* child

fan'donia *sf* tall story; ~**e** *sfpl* (as-

surdità) nonsense *sg*

fan'fara *sf* brass band; (*musica*) fanfare

'fango, ghi *sm* mud; **fan'goso, a** *ag* muddy

'fanno *vb vedi* **fare**

fannul'lone, a *smlf* idler, loafer

fantasci'enza [fanta∫'∫ɛntsa] *sf* science fiction

fanta'sia *sf* fantasy, imagination; (*capriccio*) whim, caprice ♦ *ag inv*: *vestito* ~ patterned

fan'tasma, i *sm* ghost, phantom

fan'tastico, a, ci, che *ag* fantastic; (*potenza, ingegno*) imaginative

'fante *sm* infantryman; (*CARTE*) jack, knave (*BRIT*); **fante'ria** *sf* infantry

fan'toccio [fan'tɔttʃo] *sm* puppet

fara'butto *sm* crook

far'dello *sm* bundle; (*fig*) burden

PAROLA CHIAVE

'fare *sm* 1 (*modo di fare*): **con ~ distratto** absent-mindedly; **ha un ~ simpatico** he has a pleasant manner
2: **sul far del giorno/della notte** at daybreak/nightfall

♦ *vt* **1** (*fabbricare, creare*) to make; (: *casa*) to build; (: *assegno*) to make out; ~ **un pasto/una promessa/un film** to make a meal/a promise/a film; ~ **rumore** to make a noise

2 (*effettuare: lavoro, attività, studi*) to do; (: *sport*) to play; **cosa fa?** (*adesso*) what are you doing?; (*di professione*) what do you do?; ~ **psicologia/italiano** (*INS*) to do psychology/Italian; ~ **un viaggio** to go on a trip *o* journey; ~ **una passeggiata** to go for a walk; ~ **la spesa** to do the shopping

3 (*funzione*) to be; (*TEATRO*) to play, be; ~ **il medico** to be a doctor; ~ **il malato** (*fingere*) to act the invalid

4 (*suscitare: sentimenti*): ~ **paura a qn** to frighten sb; (**non**) **fa niente** (*non importa*) it doesn't matter

5 (*ammontare*): **3 più 3 fa 6** 3 and 3 are *o* make 6; **fanno 6.000 lire** that's 6,000 lire; **Roma fa 2.000.000 di abitanti** Rome has 2,000,000 inhabitants; **che ora fai?** what time do you make it?

6 (+*infinito*): **far** ~ **qc a qn** (*obbligare*) to make sb do sth; (*permettere*) to let sb do sth; **fammi vedere** let me see; **far partire il motore** to start (up) the engine; **far riparare la macchina/costruire una casa** to get *o* have the car repaired/a house built

7: ~**rsi**: ~**rsi una gonna** to make o.s. a skirt; ~**rsi un nome** to make a name for o.s.; ~**rsi la permanente** to get a perm; ~**rsi tagliare i capelli** to get one's hair cut; ~**rsi operare** to have an operation

8 (*fraseologia*): **farcela** to succeed, manage; **non ce la faccio più** I can't go on; **ce la faremo** we'll make it; **me l'hanno fatta!** (*imbrogliare*) I've been done!; **lo facevo più giovane** I thought he was younger; **fare sì/no con la testa** to nod/shake one's head

♦ *vi* **1** (*agire*) to act, do; **fate come volete** do as you like; ~ **presto** to be quick; ~ **da** to act as; **non c'è niente da** ~ it's no use; **saperci** ~ **con qn/qc** to know how to deal with sb/sth; **faccia pure!** go ahead!

2 (*dire*) to say; **"davvero?" fece** "really?" he said

3: ~ **per** (*essere adatto*) to be suitable for; ~ **per** ~ **qc** to be about to do sth; **fece per andarsene** he made as if to leave

4: ~**rsi**: **si fa così** you do it like this, this is the way it's done; **non si fa così!** (*rimprovero*) that's no way to behave!; **la festa non si fa** the party is off

5: ~ **a gara con qn** to compete *o* vie with sb; ~ **a pugni** to come to blows; ~ **in tempo a** ~ to be in time to do

♦ *vb impers*: **fa bel tempo** the

far'falla sf butterfly

fa'rina sf flour

farma'cia, 'cie [farma'tʃia] sf pharmacy; (negozio) chemist's (shop) (BRIT), pharmacy; **farma'cista, i, e** sm/f chemist (BRIT), pharmacist

'farmaco, ci o **chi** sm drug, medicine

'faro sm (NAUT) lighthouse; (AER) beacon; (AUT) headlight

'farsa sf farce

'fascia, sce ['faʃʃa] sf band, strip; (MED) bandage; (di sindaco, ufficiale) sash; (parte di territorio) strip, belt; (di contribuenti etc) group, band; **essere in ~sce** (anche fig) to be in one's infancy; **~ oraria** time band

fasci'are [faʃ'ʃare] vt to bind; (MED) to bandage; (bambino) to put a nappy (BRIT) o diaper (US) on

fa'scicolo [fa'ʃikolo] sm (di documenti) file, dossier; (di rivista) issue, number; (opuscolo) booklet, pamphlet

fa'scino ['faʃʃino] sm charm, fascination

'fascio ['faʃʃo] sm bundle, sheaf; (di fiori) bunch; (di luce) beam; (POL): **il F~** the Fascist Party

fa'scismo [faʃ'ʃizmo] sm fascism

'fase sf phase; (TECN) stroke; **fuori ~** (motore) rough

fas'tidio sm bother, trouble; **dare ~ a qn** to bother o annoy sb; **sento ~ allo stomaco** my stomach's upset; **avere ~i con la polizia** to have trouble o bother with the police; **fastidi'oso, a** ag annoying, tiresome; (schifiltoso) fastidious

'fasto sm pomp, splendour

'fata sf fairy

fa'tale ag fatal; (inevitabile) inevitable; (fig) irresistible; **fatalità** sf inv inevitability; (avversità) misfortune; (fato) fate, destiny

'fato sm fate, destiny

fa'tica, che sf hard work, toil; (sforzo) effort; (di metalli) fatigue; **a ~** with difficulty; **fare ~ a fare qc** to have a job doing sth; **fati'care** vi to have difficulty doing sth; **faticare a fare qc** to have difficulty doing sth; **fati'coso, a** ag tiring, exhausting; (lavoro) laborious

'fatto, a pp di **fare** ♦ ag: **un uomo ~** a grown man; **~ a mano/in casa** hand-/home-made ♦ sm fact; (azione) deed; (avvenimento) event, occurrence; (di romanzo, film) action, story; **cogliere qn sul ~** to catch sb red-handed; **il ~ sta** o **che** the fact remains o is that; **in ~ di** as for, as far as ... is concerned

fat'tore sm (AGR) farm manager; (MAT, elemento costitutivo) factor

fatto'ria sf farm; farmhouse

fatto'rino sm errand-boy; (di ufficio) office-boy; (d'albergo) porter

fat'tura sf (COMM) invoice; (di abito) tailoring; (malia) spell

fattu'rare vt (COMM) to invoice; (prodotto) to produce; (vino) to adulterate

fattu'rato sm (COMM) turnover

'fatuo, a ag vain, fatuous

'fauna sf fauna

fau'tore, trice sm/f advocate, supporter

fa'vella sf speech

fa'villa sf spark

'favola sf (fiaba) fairy tale; (d'intento morale) fable; (fandonia) yarn; **favo'loso, a** ag fabulous; (incredibile) incredible

fa'vore sm favour; **per ~** please; **fare un ~ a qn** to do sb a favour; **favo'revole** ag favourable

favo'rire vt to favour; (il commercio, l'industria, le arti) to promote, encourage; **vuole ~?** won't you help yourself?; **favorisca in salotto**

please come into the sitting room; **favo'rito, a** ag, sm/f favourite

fazzo'letto [fattso'letto] sm handkerchief; (per la testa) (head)scarf

feb'braio sm February

'febbre sf fever; aver la ~ to have a high temperature; ~ da fieno hay fever; **feb'brile** ag (anche fig) feverish

'feccia, ce ['fɛttʃa] sf dregs pl

'fecola sf potato flour

fecondazi'one [fekondat'tsjone] sf fertilization; ~ **artificiale** artificial insemination

fe'condo, a ag fertile

'fede sf (credenza) belief, faith; (REL) faith; (fiducia) faith, trust; (fedeltà) loyalty; (anello) wedding ring; (attestato) certificate; aver ~ in qn to have faith in sb; in buona/cattiva ~ in good/bad faith; "in ~" (DIR) "in witness whereof"; **fe'dele** ag: fedele (a) faithful (to) ♦ sm/f follower; i fedeli (REL) the faithful; **fedeltà** sf faithfulness; (coniugale) fidelity; alta fedeltà (RADIO) high fidelity

'federa sf pillowslip, pillowcase

fede'rale ag federal

'fegato sm liver; (fig) guts pl, nerve

'felce ['fɛltʃe] sf fern

fe'lice [fe'litʃe] ag happy; (fortunato) lucky; **felicità** sf happiness; **felici'tarsi** [felitʃi'tarsi] vr (congratularsi): ~ con qn per qc to congratulate sb on sth

fe'lino, a ag, sm feline

'feltro sm felt

'femmina sf (ZOOL, TECN) female; (figlia) girl, daughter; (spesso peg) woman; **femmi'nile** ag feminine; (sesso) female; (lavoro, giornale, moda) woman's ♦ sm (LING) feminine; **femmi'nismo** sm feminism

'fendere vt to cut through; **fendi'nebbia** sm inv (AUT) fog lamp

fe'nomeno sm phenomenon

'feretro sm coffin

feri'ale ag working cpd, work cpd, week cpd; giorno ~ weekday

'ferie sfpl holidays (BRIT), vacation sg (US); andare in ~ to go on holiday o vacation

fe'rire vt to injure; (deliberatamente: MIL etc) to wound; (colpire) to hurt; **fe'rita** sf injury, wound; **fe'rito, a** sm/f wounded o injured man/woman

'ferma sf (MIL) (period of) service; (CACCIA): cane da ~ pointer

fer'maglio [fer'maʎʎo] sm clasp; (gioiello) brooch; (per documenti) clip

fer'mare vt to stop, halt; (POLIZIA) to detain, hold; (bottone etc) to fasten, fix ♦ vi to stop; ~rsi vr to stop, halt; ~rsi a fare qc to stop to do sth

fer'mata sf stop; ~ dell'autobus bus stop

fer'mento sm (anche fig) ferment; (lievito) yeast

fer'mezza [fer'mettsa] sf (fig) firmness, steadfastness

'fermo, a ag still, motionless; (veicolo) stationary; (orologio) not working; (saldo: anche fig) firm; (voce, mano) steady ♦ escl stop!; keep still! ♦ sm (chiusura) catch, lock; (DIR): ~ di polizia police detention

'fermo 'posta av, sm inv poste restante (BRIT), general delivery (US)

fe'roce [fe'rotʃe] ag (animale) wild, fierce, ferocious; (persona) cruel, fierce; (fame, dolore) raging

ferra'gosto sm (festa) feast of the Assumption; (periodo) August holidays pl

ferra'menta sfpl ironmongery sg (BRIT), hardware sg; negozio di ~ ironmonger's (BRIT), hardware shop o store (US)

fer'rato, a ag (FERR): strada ~a railway (BRIT) o railroad (US) line; (fig): essere ~ in to be well up in

'ferreo, a ag iron cpd

'ferro sm iron; una bistecca ai ~i a grilled steak; ~ battuto wrought iron; ~ da calza knitting needle; ~ di cavallo horseshoe; ~ da stiro iron

ferro'via *sf* railway (BRIT), railroad (US); **ferrovi'ario, a** *ag* railway *cpd* (BRIT), railroad *cpd* (US); **ferro-vi'ere** *sm* railwayman (BRIT), rail-road man (US)

'**fertile** *ag* fertile; **fertiliz'zante** *sm* fertilizer

'**fervido, a** *ag* fervent

fer'vore *sm* fervour, ardour; (*punto culminante*) height

'**fesso, a** *pp* di **fendere ♦** *ag* (*fam*: *sciocco*) crazy, cracked

fes'sura *sf* crack, split; (*per gettone, moneta*) slot

'**festa** *sf* (*religiosa*) feast; (*pubblica*) holiday; (*compleanno*) birthday; (*onomastico*) name day; (*ricevimen-to*) celebration, party; **far ~** to have a holiday; to live it up; **far ~ a qn** to give sb a warm welcome

festeggi'are [fested'dʒare] *vt* to cel-ebrate; (*persona*) to have a celebra-tion for

fes'tino *sm* party; (*con balli*) ball

fes'tivo, a *ag* (*atmosfera*) festive; **giorno ~** holiday

fes'toso, a *ag* merry, joyful

fe'ticcio [fe'tittʃo] *sm* fetish

'**feto** *sm* foetus (BRIT), fetus (US)

'**fetta** *sf* slice

fettuc'cine [fettut'tʃine] *sfpl* (CUC) ribbon-shaped pasta

FF.SS. *abbr* = **Ferrovie dello Stato**

fi'aba *sf* fairy tale

fi'acca *sf* weariness; (*svogliatezza*) listlessness

fiac'care *vt* to weaken

fi'acco, a, chi, che *ag* (*stanco*) tired, weary; (*svogliato*) listless; (*de-bole*) weak; (*mercato*) slack

fi'accola *sf* torch

fi'ala *sf* phial

fi'amma *sf* flame

fiam'mante *ag* (*colore*) flaming; **nuovo ~** brand new

fiammeggi'are [fjammed'dʒare] *vi* to blaze

fiam'mifero *sm* match

fiam'mingo, a, ghi, ‿ ghe *ag*

Flemish **♦** *sm/f* Fleming ~ *sm* (LING) Flemish; (ZOOL) flamingo; **i F~ghi** the Flemish

fiancheggi'are [fjanked'dʒare] *vt* to border; (*fig*) to support, back (up); (MIL) to flank

fi'anco, chi *sm* side; (MIL) flank; **di ~** sideways, from the side; **a ~ a ~** side by side

fi'asco, schi *sm* flask; (*fig*) fiasco; **fare ~** to be a fiasco

fi'ato *sm* breath; (*resistenza*) stami-na; **avere il ~ grosso** to be out of breath; **prendere ~** to catch one's breath; **~i** *smpl* (MUS) wind instru-ments; **strumento a ~** wind instru-ment

'**fibbia** *sf* buckle

'**fibra** *sf* fibre; (*fig*) constitution

fic'care *vt* to push, thrust, drive; **~rsi** *vr* (*andare a finire*) to get to

'**fico, chi** *sm* (*pianta*) fig tree; (*frut-to*) fig; **~ d'India** prickly pear; **~ secco** dried fig

fidanza'mento [fidantsa'mento] *sm* engagement

fidan'zarsi [fidan'tsarsi] *vr* to get en-gaged; **fidan'zato, a** *sm/f* fiancé/fiancée

fi'darsi *vr*: **~ di** to trust; **fi'dato, a** *ag* reliable, trustworthy

'**fido, a** *ag* faithful, loyal **♦** *sm* (COMM) credit

fi'ducia [fi'dutʃa] *sf* confidence, trust; **incarico di ~** position of trust, responsible position; **persona di ~** reliable person

fi'ele *sm* (MED) bile; (*fig*) bitterness

fi'eno *sm* hay; hayloft

fi'era *sf* fair

fie'rezza [fje'rettsa] *sf* pride

fi'ero, a *ag* proud; (*crudele*) fierce, cruel; (*audace*) bold

'**fifa** (*fam*) *sf*: **aver ~** to have the jit-ters

'**figlia** ['fiʎʎa] *sf* daughter

figli'astro, a [fiʎ'ʎastro] *sm/f* stepson/daughter

'**figlio** ['fiʎʎo] *sm* son; (*senza di-*

figura 102 **finlandese**

stinzione di sesso) child; ~ **di papà** spoilt, wealthy young man; ~ **unico** only child; **figli'occio, a, ci, ce** *smif* godchild, godson/daughter

fi'gura *sf* figure; (*forma, aspetto esterno*) form, shape; (*illustrazione*) picture, illustration; **far ~** to look smart; **fare una brutta ~** to make a bad impression

figu'rare *vi* to appear ♦ *vt:* ~**rsi qc** to imagine sth; ~**rsi** *vr:* **figurati!** imagine that!; **ti do noia? — ma figurati!** am I disturbing you? — not at all!

figura'tivo, a *ag* figurative

figu'rina *sf* figurine; (*cartoncino*) picture card

'fila *sf* row, line; (*coda*) queue; (*serie*) series, string; **di ~** in succession; **fare la ~** to queue; **in ~ indiana** in single file

filantro'pia *sf* philanthropy

fi'lare *vt* to spin ♦ *vi* (*baco, ragno*) to spin; (*formaggio fuso*) to go stringy; (*discorso*) to hang together; (*fam: amoreggiare*) to go steady; (*muoversi a forte velocità*) to go at full speed; (: *andarsene lentamente*) to make o.s. scarce; ~ **diritto** (*fig*) to toe the line

filas'trocca, che *sf* nursery rhyme

filate'lia *sf* philately, stamp collecting

fi'lato, a *ag* spun ♦ *sm* yarn; **3 giorni** ~**i** 3 days running o on end; **fila'tura** *sf* spinning; (*luogo*) spinning mill

fi'letto *sm* (*di vite*) thread; (*di carne*) fillet

fili'ale *ag* filial ♦ *sf* (*di impresa*) branch

fili'grana *sf* (*in oreficeria*) filigree; (*su carta*) watermark

film *sm inv* film; **fil'mare** *vt* to film

'filo *sm* (*anche fig*) thread; (*filato*) yarn; (*metallico*) wire; (*di lama, rasoio*) edge; **per ~ e per segno** in detail; ~ **d'erba** blade of grass; ~ **di perle** string of pearls; ~ **spinato** barbed wire; **con un** ~ **di voce** in a

whisper

'filobus *sm inv* trolley bus

filon'cino [filon'tʃino] *sm* ≈ French stick

fi'lone *sm* (*di minerali*) seam, vein; (*pane*) ≈ Vienna loaf; (*fig*) trend

filoso'fia *sf* philosophy; **fi'losofo, a** *smif* philosopher

fil'trare *vt, vi* to filter

'filtro *sm* filter; ~ **dell'olio** (*AUT*) oil filter

'filza ['filtsa] *sf* (*anche fig*) string

fin *av, prep* = **fino**

fi'nale *ag* final ♦ *sm* (*di opera*) end, ending; (: *MUS*) finale ♦ *sf* (*SPORT*) final; **finalità** *sf* (*scopo*) aim, purpose; **final'mente** *av* finally, at last

fi'nanza [fi'nantsa] *sf* finance; ~**e** *sfpl* (*di individuo, Stato*) finances; **finanzi'ario, a** *ag* financial; **finanzi'ere** *sm* financier; (*guardia di finanza: doganale*) customs officer; (: *tributaria*) inland revenue official

finché [fin'ke] *cong* (*per tutto il tempo che*) as long as; (*fino al momento in cui*) until; **aspetta ~ io (non) sia ritornato** wait until I get back

'fine *ag* (*lamina, carta*) thin; (*capelli, polvere*) fine; (*vista, udito*) keen, sharp; (*persona: raffinata*) refined, distinguished; (*osservazione*) subtle ♦ *sf* end ♦ *sm* aim, purpose; (*esito*) result, outcome; **secondo** ~ ulterior motive; **in o alla** ~ in the end, finally; ~ **settimana** *sm o f inv* weekend

fi'nestra *sf* window; **fines'trino** *sm* (*di treno, auto*) window

'fingere ['findʒere] *vt* to feign; (*supporre*) to imagine, suppose; ~**rsi** *vr:* ~**rsi ubriaco/pazzo** to pretend to be drunk/mad; ~ **di fare** to pretend to do

fini'mondo *sm* pandemonium

fi'nire *vt* to finish ♦ *vi* to finish, end; ~ **di fare** (*compiere*) to finish doing; (*smettere*) to stop doing; ~ **in galera** to end up o finish up in prison; **fini'tura** *sf* finish

finlan'dese *ag, sm* (*LING*) Finnish

♦ *sm/f* Finn

Fin'landia *sf*: la ~ Finland

'fino, a *ag* (*capelli, seta*) fine; (*oro*) pure; (*fig: acuto*) shrewd ♦ *av* (*spesso troncato in* fin: *pure, anche*) even ♦ *prep* (*spesso troncato in* fin: *tempo*): **fin quando?** till when?; (: *luogo*): **fin qui** as far as here; ~ a (*tempo*) until, till; (*luogo*) as far as, (up) to; **fin da domani** from tomorrow onwards; **fin da ieri** since yesterday; **fin dalla nascita** from *o* since birth

fi'nocchio [fi'nɔkkjo] *sm* fennel; (*fam: peg: pederasta*) queer

fi'nora *av* up till now

'finta *sf* pretence, sham; (*SPORT*) feint; **far** ~a **(di fare)** to pretend (to do)

'finto, a *pp di* fingere ♦ *ag* false; artificial

finzi'one [fin'tsjone] *sf* pretence, sham

fi'occo, chi *sm* (*di nastro*) bow; (*di stoffa, lana*) flock; (*di neve*) flake; (*NAUT*) jib; **coi** ~**chi** (*fig*) first-rate; ~**chi di granoturco** cornflakes

fi'ocina ['fjɔʃina] *sf* harpoon

fi'oco, a, chi, che *ag* faint, dim

fi'onda *sf* catapult

fio'raio, a *sm/f* florist

fi'ore *sm* flower; ~**i** *smpl* (*CARTE*) clubs; **a fior d'acqua** on the surface of the water; **avere i nervi a fior di pelle** to be on edge

fioren'tino, a *ag* Florentine

fio'retto *sm* (*SCHERMA*) foil

fio'rire *vi* (*rosa*) to flower; (*albero*) to blossom; (*fig*) to flourish

Fi'renze [fi'rɛntse] *sf* Florence

'firma *sf* signature; (*reputazione*) name

fir'mare *vt* to sign

fisar'monica, che *sf* accordion

fis'cale *ag* fiscal, tax *cpd*; **medico** ~ doctor employed by Social Security to verify cases of sick leave

fischi'are [fis'kjare] *vi* to whistle ♦ *vt* to whistle; (*attore*) to boo, hiss

'fischio ['fiskjo] *sm* whistle

'fisco *sm* tax authorities *pl*, ≈ Inland Revenue (*BRIT*), ≈ Internal Revenue Service (*US*)

'fisica *sf* physics *sg*

'fisico, a, ci, che *ag* physical ♦ *sm/f* physicist ♦ *sm* physique

fisio'logia [fizjolo'dʒia] *sf* physiology

fisiono'mia *sf* face, physiognomy

fisiotera'pia *sf* physiotherapy

fis'sare *vt* to fix, fasten; (*guardare intensamente*) to stare at; (*data, condizioni*) to fix, establish, set; (*prenotare*) to book; ~**rsi su** (*sog: sguardo, attenzione*) to focus on; (*fig: idea*) to become obsessed with; **fissazi'one** *sf* (*PSIC*) fixation

'fisso, a *ag* fixed; (*stipendio, impiego*) regular ♦ *av*: **guardare** ~ **qc**/**qn** to stare at sth/sb

'fitta *sf* sharp pain; *vedi anche* fitto

fit'tizio, a *ag* fictitious, imaginary

'fitto, a *ag* thick, dense; (*pioggia*) heavy ♦ *sm* depths *pl*, middle; (*affitto, pigione*) rent

fi'ume *sm* river

fiu'tare *vt* to smell, sniff; (*sog: animale*) to scent; (*fig: inganno*) to get wind of, smell; ~ **tabacco/cocaina** to take snuff/cocaine; **fi'uto** *sm* (*sense of*) smell; (*fig*) nose

fla'gello [fla'dʒɛllo] *sm* scourge

fla'grante *ag* flagrant; **cogliere qn in** ~ to catch sb red-handed

fla'nella *sf* flannel

flash [flaʃ] *sm inv* (*FOT*) flash; (*giornalistico*) newsflash

'flauto *sm* flute

'flebile *ag* faint, feeble

'flemma *sf* (*calma*) coolness, phlegm; (*MED*) phlegm

fles'sibile *ag* pliable; (*fig: che si adatta*) flexible

'flesso, a *pp di* flettere

flessu'oso, a *ag* supple, lithe; (*andatura*) flowing, graceful

'flettere *vt* to bend

F.lli *abbr* (= *fratelli*) Bros.

'flora *sf* flora

'florido, a *ag* flourishing; (*fig*) glowing with health

'floscio, a, sci, sce ['flɔʃʃo] ag *(cappello)* floppy, soft; *(muscoli)* flabby

'flotta sf fleet

'fluido, a ag, sm fluid

flu'ire vi to flow

flu'oro sm fluorine

fluo'ruro sm fluoride

'flusso sm flow; *(FISICA, MED)* flux; ~ **e riflusso** ebb and flow

fluttu'are vi to rise and fall; *(ECON)* to fluctuate

fluvi'ale ag river cpd, fluvial

'foca, che sf *(ZOOL)* seal

fo'caccia, ce [fo'kattʃa] sf kind of pizza; *(dolce)* bun

'foce ['fotʃe] sf *(GEO)* mouth

foco'laio sm *(MED)* centre of infection; *(fig)* hotbed

foco'lare sm hearth, fireside; *(TECN)* furnace

'fodera sf *(di vestito)* lining; *(di libro, poltrona)* cover; **fode'rare** vt to line; to cover

'fodero sm *(di spada)* scabbard; *(di pugnale)* sheath; *(di pistola)* holster

'foga sf enthusiasm, ardour

'foggia, ge ['fɔddʒa] sf *(maniera)* style; *(aspetto)* form, shape; *(moda)* fashion, style

'foglia ['fɔʎʎa] sf leaf; ~ **d'argento/d'oro** silver/gold leaf; **fogli'ame** sm foliage, leaves pl

'foglio ['fɔʎʎo] sm *(di carta)* sheet (of paper); *(di metallo)* sheet; *(documento)* document; *(banconota)* (bank)note; ~ **rosa** *(AUT)* provisional licence; ~ **di via** *(DIR)* expulsion order; ~ **volante** pamphlet

'fogna ['foɲɲa] sf drain, sewer; **fogna'tura** sf drainage, sewerage

föhn [føːn] sm inv hair dryer

folgo'rare vt *(sog: fulmine)* to strike down; *(: alta tensione)* to electrocute

'folla sf crowd, throng

'folle ag mad, insane; *(TECN)* idle; **in** ~ *(AUT)* in neutral

fol'lia sf folly, foolishness; foolish act; *(pazzia)* madness, lunacy

'folto, a ag thick

fomen'tare vt to stir up, foment

fondamen'tale ag fundamental, basic

fonda'mento sm foundation; ~**a** sfpl *(EDIL)* foundations

fon'dare vt to found; *(fig: dar base)*: ~ **qc su** to base sth on; **fondazi'one** sf foundation

'fondere vt *(neve)* to melt; *(metallo)* to fuse, melt; *(fig: colori)* to merge, blend; *(: imprese, gruppi)* to merge ♦ vi to melt; ~**rsi** vr to melt; *(fig: partiti, correnti)* to unite, merge; **fonde'ria** sf foundry

'fondo, a ag deep ♦ sm *(di recipiente, pozzo)* bottom; *(di stanza)* back; *(quantità di liquido che resta, deposito)* dregs pl; *(sfondo)* background; *(unità immobiliare)* property, estate; *(somma di denaro)* fund; *(SPORT)* long-distance race; ~**i** smpl *(denaro)* funds; **a notte** ~**a** at dead of night; **in** ~ **a** at the bottom of; at the back of; *(strada)* at the end of; **andare a** ~ *(nave)* to sink; **conoscere a** ~ to know inside out; **dar** ~ **a** *(fig: provviste, soldi)* to use up; **in** ~ *(fig)* after all, all things considered; **andare fino in** ~ **a** *(fig)* to examine thoroughly; **a** ~ **perduto** *(COMM)* without security; ~**i di caffè** coffee grounds; ~**i di magazzino** old o unsold stock sg

fo'netica sf phonetics sg

fon'tana sf fountain

'fonte sf spring, source; *(fig)* source ♦ sm: ~ **battesimale** *(REL)* font

fon'tina sf sweet full-fat hard cheese from Val d'Aosta

fo'raggio [fo'raddʒo] sm fodder, forage

fo'rare vt to pierce, make a hole in; *(pallone)* to burst; *(biglietto)* to punch; ~ **una gomma** to burst a tyre *(BRIT)* o tire *(US)*

'forbici ['fɔrbitʃi] sfpl scissors

'forca, che sf *(AGR)* fork, pitchfork; *(patibolo)* gallows sg

for'cella [for'tʃɛlla] sf *(TECN)* fork;

(di monte) pass

for'chetta [for'ketta] sf fork

for'cina [for'tʃina] sf hairpin

'forcipe ['fortʃipe] sm forceps pl

fo'resta sf forest

foresti'ero, a ag foreign ♦ sm/f foreigner

'forfora sf dandruff

'forgia, ge ['fordʒa] sf forge; **for-gi'are** vt to forge

'forma sf form; (aspetto esteriore) form, shape; (DIR: procedura) procedure; (per calzature) last; (stampo da cucina) mould; ~e sfpl (del corpo) figure, shape; le ~e (convenzioni) appearances; **essere in ~** to be in good shape

formag'gino [format'dʒino] sm processed cheese

for'maggio [for'maddʒo] sm cheese

for'male ag formal; **formalità** sf inv formality

for'mare vt to form, shape, make; (numero di telefono) to dial; (fig: carattere) to form, mould; **~rsi** vr to form, take shape; **for'mato** sm format, size; **formazi'one** sf formation; (fig: educazione) training

for'mica, che [s'ant; ant; formiche] sm anthill

formico'lare vi (gamba, braccio) to tingle; (brulicare: anche fig): **~ di** to be swarming with; **mi formicola la gamba** I've got pins and needles in my leg, my leg's tingling; **formi-co'lio** sm pins and needles pl; swarming

formi'dabile ag powerful, formidable; (straordinario) remarkable

'formula sf formula; **~ di cortesia** courtesy form

formu'lare vt to formulate; to express

for'nace [for'natʃe] sf (per laterizi etc) kiln; (per metalli) furnace

for'naio sm baker

for'nello sm (elettrico, a gas) ring; (di pipa) bowl

for'nire vt: **~ qn di qc, ~ qc a qn** to provide o supply sb with sth, to supply sth to sb

'forno sm (di cucina) oven; (panetteria) bakery; (TECN: per calce etc) kiln; (: per metalli) furnace

'foro sm (buco) hole; (STORIA) forum; (tribunale) (law) court

'forse av perhaps, maybe; (circa) about; **essere in ~** to be in doubt

forsen'nato, a ag mad, insane

'forte ag strong; (suono) loud; (spesa) considerable, great; (passione, dolore) great, deep ♦ av strongly; (velocemente) fast; (a voce alta) loud(ly); (violentemente) hard ♦ sm (edificio) fort; (specialità) forte, strong point; **essere ~ in qc** to be good at sth

for'tezza [for'tettsa] sf (morale) strength; (luogo fortificato) fortress

for'tuito, a ag fortuitous, chance

for'tuna sf (destino) fortune, luck; (buona sorte) success, fortune; (eredità, averi) fortune; **per ~** luckily, fortunately; **di ~** makeshift, improvised; **atterraggio di ~** emergency landing; **fortu'nato, a** ag lucky, fortunate; (coronato da successo) successful

forvi'are vt, vi = **fuorviare**

'forza [s'fortsa] sf strength; (potere) power; (FISICA) force; **~e** sfpl (fisiche) strength sg; (MIL) forces ♦ escl come on!; **per ~** against one's will; (naturalmente) of course; **~ viva** ~ by force; **a ~ di** by dint of; **~ maggiore** circumstances beyond one's control; **la ~ pubblica** the police pl; **le ~e armate** the armed forces; **~e dell'ordine** the forces of law and order

for'zare [for'tsare] vt to force; **~ a fare** to force sb to do; **for'zato, a** ag forced ♦ sm (DIR) prisoner sentenced to hard labour

fos'chia [fos'kia] sf mist, haze

'fosco, a, schi, sche ag dark, gloomy

'fosforo sm phosphorous

'fossa sf pit; (di cimitero) grave; **~ biologica** septic tank

fos'sato *sm* ditch; (*di fortezza*) moat

fos'setta *sf* dimple

'fossile *ag*, *sm* fossil

'fosso *sm* ditch; (*MIL*) trench

'foto *sf photo ♦ prefisso*: **foto'copia** *sf* photocopy; **fotocopi'are** *vt* to photocopy; **fotogra'fare** *vt* to photograph; **fotogra'fia** *sf* (*procedimento*) photography; (*immagine*) photograph; **fare una fotografia** to take a photograph; **una fotografia a colori/in bianco e nero** a colour/ black and white photograph; **fo'tografo, a** *smf* photographer; **foto'romanzo** *sm* romantic picture story

fra *prep* = **tra**

fracas'sare *vt* to shatter, smash; **~rsi** *vr* to shatter, smash; (*veicolo*) to crash; **fra'casso** *sm* smash; crash; (*baccano*) din, racket

'fradicio, a, ci, ce ['fraditʃo] *ag* (*molto bagnato*) soaking (wet); **ubriaco ~** blind drunk

'fragile ['fradʒile] *ag* fragile; (*fig*: *salute*) delicate

'fragola *sf* strawberry

fra'gore *sm* roar; (*di tuono*) rumble

frago'roso, a *ag* deafening

fra'grante *ag* fragrant

frain'tendere *vt* to misunderstand; **frain'teso, a** *pp di* **fraintendere**

fram'mento *sm* fragment

'frana *sf* landslide; (*fig*: *persona*): **essere una ~** to be useless; **fra'nare** *vi* to slip, slide down

fran'cese [fran'tʃeze] *ag* French ♦ *smf* Frenchman/woman ♦ *sm* (*LING*) French; **i F~i** the French

fran'chezza [fran'kettsa] *sf* frankness, openness

'Francia ['frantʃa] *sf*: **la ~** France

'franco, a, chi, che *ag* (*COMM*) free; (*sincero*) frank, open, sincere ♦ *sm* (*moneta*) franc; **farla ~a** (*fig*) to get off scot-free; **~ di dogana** duty-free; **~ a domicilio** delivered free of charge; **prezzo ~ fabbrica** ex-works price; **~ tiratore** *sm* sniper

franco'bollo *sm* (postage) stamp

fran'gente [fran'dʒɛnte] *sm* (*onda*) breaker; (*scoglio emergente*) reef; (*circostanza*) situation, circumstance

'frangia, ge ['frandʒa] *sf* fringe

frantu'mare *vt* to break into pieces, shatter; **~rsi** *vr* to break into pieces, shatter

frap'pé *sm* milk shake

'frasca, sche *sf* (leafy) branch

'frase *sf* (*LING*) sentence; (*locuzione, espressione, MUS*) phrase; **~ fatta** set phrase

'frassino *sm* ash (tree)

frastagli'ato, a [frastaʎʎato] *ag* (*costa*) indented, jagged

frastor'nare *vt* to daze; to befuddle

frastu'ono *sm* hubbub, din

'frate *sm* friar, monk

fratel'lanza [fratel'lantsa] *sf* brotherhood; (*associazione*) fraternity

fratel'lastro *sm* stepbrother

fra'tello *sm* brother; **~i** *smpl* brothers; (*nel senso di fratelli e sorelle*) brothers and sisters

fra'terno, a *ag* fraternal, brotherly

frat'tanto *av* in the meantime, meanwhile

frat'tempo *sm*: **nel ~** in the meantime, meanwhile

frat'tura *sf* fracture; (*fig*) split, break

frazi'one [frat'tsjone] *sf* fraction; **~ di comune** small town

'freccia, ce ['frettʃa] *sf* arrow; **~ di direzione** (*AUT*) indicator

fred'dare *vt* to shoot dead

fred'dezza [fred'dettsa] *sf* coldness

'freddo, a *ag*, *sm* cold; **fa ~** it's cold; **aver ~** to be cold; **a ~** (*fig*) deliberately; **freddo'loso, a** *ag* sensitive to the cold

fred'dura *sf* pun

fre'gare *vt* to rub; (*fam*: *truffare*) to take in, cheat; (: *rubare*) to swipe, pinch; **fregarsene** (*fam!*): **chi se ne frega?** who gives a damn (about it)?

fre'gata *sf* rub; (*fam*) swindle; (*NAUT*) frigate

'fregio ['fredʒo] sm (ARCHIT) frieze; (ornamento) decoration

'fremere vi: ~ **di** to tremble o quiver with; **'fremito** sm tremor, quiver

fre'nare vt (veicolo) to slow down; (cavallo) to rein in; (lacrime) to restrain, hold back ♦ vi to brake; **~rsi** vr (fig) to restrain o.s., control o.s.; **fre'nata** sf: **fare una frenata** to brake

frene'sia sf frenzy

'freno sm brake; (morso) bit; ~ **a disco** disc brake; ~ **a mano** handbrake; **tenere a** ~ to restrain

frequen'tare vt (scuola, corso) to attend; (locale, bar) to go to, frequent; (persone) to see (often)

fre'quente ag frequent; **di** ~ frequently; **fre'quenza** sf frequency; (INS) attendance

fres'chezza [fres'kettsa] sf freshness

'fresco, a, schi, sche ag fresh; (temperatura) cool; (notizia) recent, fresh ♦ sm: **godere il** ~ to enjoy the cool air; **stare** ~ (fig) to be in for it; **mettere al** ~ to put in a cool place

'fretta sf hurry, haste; **in** ~ in a hurry; **in** ~ **e furia** in a mad rush; **aver** ~ to be in a hurry; **fret'toloso, a** ag (persona) in a hurry; (lavoro etc) hurried, rushed

fri'abile ag (terreno) friable; (pasta) crumbly

'friggere ['friddʒere] vt to fry ♦ vi (olio etc) to sizzle

'frigido, a ['fridʒido] ag (MED) frigid

'frigo sm fridge

frigo'rifero, a ag refrigerating ♦ sm refrigerator

fringu'ello sm chaffinch

frit'tata sf omelette; **fare una** ~ (fig) to make a mess of things

frit'tella sf (CUC) pancake; (: ripiena) fritter

'fritto, a pp di **friggere** ♦ ag fried ♦ sm fried food; ~ **misto** mixed fry

frit'tura sf (CUC): ~ **di pesce** mixed fried fish

'frivolo, a ag frivolous

frizi'one [frit'tsjone] sf friction; (di pelle) rub, rub-down; (AUT) clutch

friz'zante [frid'dzante] ag (anche fig) sparkling

'frizzo ['friddzo] sm witticism

fro'dare vt to defraud, cheat

'frode sf fraud; ~ **fiscale** tax evasion

'frollo, a ag (carne) tender; (: di selvaggina) high; (fig: persona) soft; **pasta** ~a short (crust) pastry

'fronda sf (leafy) branch; (di partito politico) internal opposition

fron'tale ag frontal; (scontro) head-on

'fronte sf (ANAT) forehead; (di edificio) front, façade ♦ sm (MIL, POL, METEOR) front; **a** ~, **di** ~ facing, opposite; **di** ~ **a** (posizione) opposite, facing, in front of; (a paragone di) compared with

fronteggi'are [fronted'dʒare] vt (avversari, difficoltà) to face, stand up to; (spese) to cope with

fronti'era sf border, frontier

fronzolo ['frondzolo] sm frill

frottola sf fib; ~**e** sfpl (assurdità) nonsense sg

fru'gare vi to rummage ♦ vt to search

frul'lare vt (CUC) to whisk ♦ vi (uccelli) to flutter; **frul'lato** sm milk shake; fruit drink; **frulla'tore** sm electric mixer; **frul'lino** sm whisk

fru'mento sm wheat

fru'scio [fruʃ'ʃio] sm rustle; rustling; (di acque) murmur

'frusta sf whip; (CUC) whisk

frus'tare vt to whip

frus'tino sm riding crop

frus'trare vt to frustrate

'frutta sf fruit; (portata) dessert; ~ **candita/secca** candied/dried fruit

frut'tare vi to bear dividends, give a return

frut'teto sm orchard

frutti'vendolo, a smf greengrocer (BRIT), produce dealer (US)

'frutto sm fruit; (fig: risultato) result(s); (*ECON: interesse*) interest; (: *reddito*) income; ~i di mare seafood *sg*

FS *abbr* = **Ferrovie dello Stato**

fu *vb vedi* **essere** ♦ *ag inv*: il ~ Paolo Bianchi the late Paolo Bianchi

fuci'lare [futʃi'lare] *vt* to shoot; **fuci'lata** *sf* rifle shot

fu'cile [fu'tʃile] *sm* rifle, gun; (*da caccia*) shotgun, gun

fu'cina [fu'tʃina] *sf* forge

'fuga *sf* escape, flight; (*di gas, liquidi*) leak; (*MUS*) fugue; ~ **di cervelli** brain drain

fu'gace [fu'gatʃe] *ag* fleeting, transient

fug'gevole [fud'dʒevole] *ag* fleeting

fuggi'asco, a, schi, sche [fud'dʒasko] *ag, sm/f* fugitive

fuggi'fuggi [fuddʒi'fuddʒi] *sm* scramble, stampede

fug'gire [fud'dʒire] *vi* to flee, run away; (*fig: passar veloce*) to fly ♦ *vt* to avoid; **fuggi'tivo, a** *sm/f* fugitive, runaway

ful'gore *sm* brilliance, splendour

fu'liggine [fu'liddʒine] *sf* soot

fulmi'nare *vt* (*sog: fulmine*) to strike; (: *elettricità*) to electrocute; (*con arma da fuoco*) to shoot dead; (*fig: con lo sguardo*) to look daggers at

'fulmine *sm* thunderbolt; lightning *no pl*

fumai'olo *sm* (*di nave*) funnel; (*di fabbrica*) chimney

fu'mare *vi* to smoke; (*emettere vapore*) to steam ♦ *vt* to smoke; **fu'mata** *sf* (*segnale*) smoke signal; **farsi una fumata** to have a smoke; **fuma'tore, 'trice** *sm/f* smoker

fu'metto *sm* comic strip; **giornale** *sm* a ~**i** comic

'fumo *sm* smoke; (*vapore*) steam; (*il fumare tabacco*) smoking; ~**i** *smpl* (*industriali etc*) fumes; **i** ~**i dell'alcool** the after-effects of drink; **vendere** ~ to deceive, cheat; **fu'moso, a** *ag* smoky; (*fig*) muddled

fu'nambolo, a *sm/f* tightrope walker

'fune *sf* rope, cord; (*più grossa*) cable

'funebre *ag* (*rito*) funeral; (*aspetto*) gloomy, funereal

fune'rale *sm* funeral

'fungere ['fundʒere] *vi*: ~ **da** to act as

'fungo, ghi *sm* fungus; (*commestibile*) mushroom; ~ **velenoso** toadstool

funico'lare *sf* funicular railway

funi'via *sf* cable railway

funzio'nare [funtsjo'nare] *vi* to work, function; (*fungere*): ~ **da** to act as

funzio'nario [funtsjo'narjo] *sm* official

funzi'one [fun'tsjone] *sf* function; (*carica*) post, position; (*REL*) service; **in** ~ (*meccanismo*) in operation; **in** ~ **di** (*come*) as; **fare la** ~ **di qn** (*farne le veci*) to take sb's place

fu'oco, chi *sm* fire; (*fornello*) ring; (*FOT, FISICA*) focus; **dare** ~ **a qc** to set fire to sth; **far** ~ (*sparare*) to fire; ~ **d'artificio** firework

fuorché [fwor'ke] *cong, prep* except

fu'ori *av* outside; (*all'aperto*) outdoors, outside; (*fuori di casa, SPORT*) out; (*esclamativo*) get out! ♦ *prep*: ~ (**di**) out of, outside ♦ *sm* outside; **lasciar** ~ **qc/qn** to leave sth/sb out; **far** ~ **qn** (*fam*) to kill sb, do sb in; **essere** ~ **di sé** to be beside o.s.; ~ **luogo** (*inopportuno*) out of place, uncalled for; ~ **mano** out of the/way, remote; ~ **pericolo** out of danger; ~ **uso** old-fashioned; obsolete

fu'ori... *prefisso*: **fuori'bordo** *sm inv* speedboat (with outboard motor); outboard motor; **fuori'classe** *sm/f inv* (undisputed) champion; **fuori'gioco** *sm* offside; **fuori'legge** *sm/f inv* outlaw; **fuori'serie** *ag inv* (*auto etc*) custom-built ♦ *sf* custom-built car; **fuori'strada** sm (AUT) cross-country vehicle; **fuor(i)u'scito**, a smf exile; **fuorvi'are** vt to mislead; (fig) to lead astray ♦ vi to go astray

'furbo, a ag clever, smart; (peg) cunning

fu'rente ag: ~ (**contro**) furious (with)

fur'fante sm rascal, scoundrel

fur'gone sm van

'furia sf (ira) fury, rage; (fig: impeto) fury, violence; (fretta) rush; a ~ di by dint of; **andare su tutte le ~e** to get into a towering rage; **furi'bondo**, a ag furious

furi'oso, a ag furious; (mare, vento) raging

fu'rore sm fury; (esaltazione) frenzy; **far ~** to be all the rage

fur'tivo, a ag furtive

'furto sm theft; ~ **con scasso** burglary

'fusa sfpl: **fare le ~** to purr

fu'sibile sm (ELETTR) fuse

fusi'one sf (di metalli) fusion, melting; (colata) casting; (COMM) merger; (fig) merging

'fuso, a pp di **fondere** ♦ sm (FILATURA) spindle; ~ **orario** time zone

fus'tagno [fus'taɲɲo] sm corduroy

fus'tino sm (di detersivo) tub

'fusto sm stem; (ANAT, di albero) trunk; (recipiente) drum, can

fu'turo, a ag, sm future

G

gab'bare vt to take in, dupe; ~**rsi** vr: ~**rsi di qn** to make fun of sb

'gabbia sf cage; (DIR) dock; (da imballaggio) crate; ~ **dell'ascensore** lift (BRIT) o elevator (US) shaft; ~ **toracica** (ANAT) rib cage

gabbi'ano sm (sea)gull

gabi'netto sm (MED etc) consulting room; (POL) ministry; (di decenza) toilet, lavatory; (INS: di fisica etc) laboratory

'gaffe [gaf] sf inv blunder

gagli'ardo, a [gaʎ'ʎardo] ag strong, vigorous

'gaio, a ag cheerful, gay

'gala sf (sfarzo) pomp; (festa) gala

ga'lante ag gallant, courteous; (avventura) amorous; **galante'ria** sf gallantry

galantu'omo (pl **galantu'omini**) sm gentleman

ga'lassia sf galaxy

gala'teo sm (good) manners pl

gale'otto sm (rematore) galley slave; (carcerato) convict

ga'lera sf (NAUT) galley; (prigione) prison

'galla sf: a ~ afloat; **venire a ~** to surface, come to the surface; (fig: verità) to come out

galleggi'ante [galled'dʒante] ag floating ♦ sm (natante) barge; (di pescatore, lenza, TECN) float

galleggi'are [galled'dʒare] vi to float

galle'ria sf (traforo) tunnel; (ARCHIT, d'arte) gallery; (TEATRO) circle; (strada coperta con negozi) arcade

'Galles sm: **il ~** Wales; **gal'lese** ag, sm (LING) Welsh ♦ smf Welshman/woman

gal'letta sf cracker

gal'lina sf hen

'gallo sm cock

gal'lone sm piece of braid; (MIL) stripe; (unità di misura) gallon

galop'pare vi to gallop

ga'loppo sm gallop; **al o di ~** at a gallop

'gamba sf leg; (asta: di lettera) stem; in ~ (in buona salute) well; (bravo, sveglio) bright, smart; **prendere qc sotto ~** (fig) to treat sth too lightly

gambe'retto sm shrimp

'gambero sm (di acqua dolce) crayfish; (di mare) prawn

'gambo sm stem; (di frutta) stalk

'gamma sf (MUS) scale; (di colori, fig) range

ga'nascia, sce [ga'naʃʃa] sf jaw; ~**sce del freno** (AUT) brake shoes

'gancio ['gantʃo] *sm* hook

'gangheri ['gangeri] *smpl*: **uscire dai ~** (*fig*) to fly into a temper

'gara *sf* competition; (*SPORT*) competition; contest; match; (: *corsa*) race; **fare a ~** to compete, vie

ga'rage [ga'raʒ] *sm inv* garage

garan'tire *vt* to guarantee; (*debito*) to stand surety for; (*dare per certo*) to assure

garan'zia [garan'tsia] *sf* guarantee; (*pegno*) security

gar'bato, a *ag* courteous, polite

'garbo *sm* (*buone maniere*) politeness, courtesy; (*di vestito etc*) grace, style

gareggi'are [gared'dʒare] *vi* to compete

garga'rismo *sm* gargle; **fare i ~i** to gargle

ga'rofano *sm* carnation; **chiodo di ~** clove

'garza ['gardza] *sf* (*per bende*) gauze

gar'zone [gar'dzone] *sm* (*di negozio*) boy

gas *sm inv* gas; **a tutto ~** at full speed; **dare ~** (*AUT*) to accelerate

ga'solio *sm* diesel (oil)

ga's(s)ato, a *ag* (*bibita*) aerated, fizzy

gas'sosa *sf* fizzy drink

gas'soso, a *ag* gaseous; gassy

gastrono'mia *sf* gastronomy

gat'tino *sm* kitten

'gatto, a *sm/f* cat, tomcat/she-cat; **~ selvatico** wildcat; **~ delle nevi** (*AUT*, *SCI*) snowcat

gatto'pardo *sm*: **~ africano** serval; **~ americano** ocelot

'gaudio *sm* joy, happiness

ga'vetta *sf* (*MIL*) mess tin; **venire dalla ~** (*MIL*, *fig*) to rise from the ranks

'gazza ['gaddza] *sf* magpie

gaz'zella [gad'dzella] *sf* gazelle; (*dei carabinieri*) (high-speed) police car

gaz'zetta [gad'dzetta] *sf* news sheet; **G~ Ufficiale** official publication containing details of new laws

gel [dʒɛl] *sm inv* gel

ge'lare [dʒe'lare] *vt*, *vi*, *vb impers* to freeze; **ge'lata** *sf* frost

gelate'ria [dʒelate'ria] *sf* ice-cream shop

gela'tina [dʒela'tina] *sf* gelatine; **~ esplosiva** dynamite; **~ di frutta** fruit jelly

ge'lato, a *ag* frozen ♦ *sm* ice cream

'gelido, a ['dʒɛlido] *ag* icy, ice-cold

'gelo ['dʒɛlo] *sm* (*temperatura*) intense cold; (*brina*) frost; (*fig*) chill; **ge'lone** *sm* chilblain

gelo'sia [dʒelo'sia] *sf* jealousy

ge'loso, a [dʒe'loso] *ag* jealous

'gelso ['dʒɛlso] *sm* mulberry (tree)

gelso'mino [dʒelso'mino] *sm* jasmine

ge'mello, a [dʒe'mɛllo] *ag*, *sm/f* twin; **~i** *smpl* (*di camicia*) cufflinks; (*dello zodiaco*): **G~i** Gemini *sg*

'gemere ['dʒɛmere] *vi* to moan, groan; (*cigolare*) to creak; (*gocciolare*) to drip, ooze; **'gemito** *sm* moan, groan

'gemma ['dʒɛmma] *sf* (*BOT*) bud; (*pietra preziosa*) gem

gene'rale [dʒene'rale] *ag*, *sm* general; **in ~** (*per sommi capi*) in general terms; (*di solito*) usually, in general; **a ~ richiesta** by popular request; **generalità** *sfpl* (*dati d'identità*) particulars; **generaliz'zare** *vt*, *vi* to generalize; **general'mente** *av* generally

gene'rare [dʒene'rare] *vt* (*dar vita*) to give birth to; (*produrre*) to produce; (*causare*) to arouse; (*TECN*) to produce, generate; **genera'tore** *sm* (*TECN*) generator; **genera-zi'one** *sf* generation

'genere ['dʒɛnere] *sm* kind, type, sort; (*BIOL*) genus; (*merce*) article, product; (*LING*) gender; (*ARTE*, *LETTERATURA*) genre; **in ~** generally, as a rule; **il ~ umano** mankind; **~i alimentari** foodstuffs

ge'nerico, a, ci, che [dʒe'nɛriko] *ag* generic; (*vago*) vague, imprecise

'genero ['dʒɛnero] *sm* son-in-law

generosità [dʒenerosi'ta] *sf* generosity

gene'roso, a [dʒene'roso] *ag* generous

ge'netica [dʒe'nɛtika] *sf* genetics *sg*

ge'netico, a, ci, che [dʒe'nɛtiko] *ag* genetic

gen'giva [dʒen'dʒiva] *sf* (*ANAT*) gum

geni'ale [dʒen'jale] *ag* (*persona*) of genius; (*idea*) ingenious, brilliant

'genio ['dʒɛnjo] *sm* genius; **andare a ~ a qn** to be to sb's liking, appeal to sb

geni'tale [dʒeni'tale] *ag* genital; **~i** *smpl* genitals

geni'tore [dʒeni'tore] *sm* parent, father *o* mother; **i miei ~i** my parents, my father and mother

gen'naio [dʒen'najo] *sm* January

'Genova ['dʒɛnova] *sf* Genoa

gen'taglia [dʒen'taʎʎa] (*peg*) *sf* rabble

'gente ['dʒɛnte] *sf* people *pl*

gen'tile [dʒen'tile] *ag* (*persona, atto*) kind; (: *garbato*) courteous, polite; (*nelle lettere*): **G~ Signore** Dear Sir; (: *sulla busta*): **G~ Signor Fernando Villa** Mr Fernando Villa; **genti'lezza** *sf* kindness; courtesy, politeness; **per gentilezza** (*per favore*) please

gentil'uomo [dʒentil'lwɔmo] (*pl* gentil'uomini) *sm* gentleman

genu'ino, a [dʒenu'ino] *ag* (*prodotto*) natural; (*persona, sentimento*) genuine, sincere

geogra'fia [dʒeogra'fia] *sf* geography

geolo'gia [dʒeolo'dʒia] *sf* geology

ge'ometra, i, e [dʒe'ɔmetra] *smf* (*professionista*) surveyor

geome'tria [dʒeome'tria] *sf* geometry; **geo'metrico, a, ci, che** *ag* geometric(al)

gerar'chia [dʒerar'kia] *sf* hierarchy

ge'rente [dʒe'rɛnte] *smf* manager/manageress

'gergo, ghi ['dʒɛrgo] *sm* jargon; slang

geria'tria [dʒerja'tria] *sf* geriatrics *sg*

Ger'mania [dʒer'manja] *sf:* **la ~** Germany; **la ~ occidentale/orientale** West/East Germany

'germe ['dʒɛrme] *sm* germ; (*fig*) seed

germogli'are [dʒermoʎ'ʎare] *vi* to sprout, to germinate; **ger'moglio** *sm* shoot; bud

gero'glifico, ci [dʒero'glifiko] *sm* hieroglyphic

'gesso ['dʒɛsso] *sm* chalk; (*SCULTURA, MED, EDIL*) plaster; (*statua*) plaster figure; (*minerale*) gypsum

gesti'one [dʒes'tjone] *sf* management

ges'tire [dʒes'tire] *vt* to run, manage

'gesto ['dʒɛsto] *sm* gesture

ges'tore [dʒes'tore] *sm* manager

Gesù [dʒe'zu] *sm* Jesus

gesu'ita [dʒezu'ita] *sm* Jesuit

get'tare [dʒet'tare] *vt* to throw; (*anche*: **~ via**) to throw away *o* out; (*SCULTURA*) to cast; (*EDIL*) to lay; (*acqua*) to spout; (*grido*) to utter; **~rsi** *vr*: **~rsi in** (*sog: fiume*) to flow into; **~ uno sguardo su** to take a quick look at; **get'tata** *sf* (*di cemento, gesso, metalli*) cast; (*diga*) jetty

'getto ['dʒɛtto] *sm* (*di gas, liquido, AER*) jet; **a ~** continuo uninterruptedly; **di ~** (*fig*) straight off, in one go

get'tone [dʒet'tone] *sm* token; (*per giochi*) counter; (: *roulette etc*) chip; **~ telefonico** telephone token

ghiacci'aio [gjat'tʃajo] *sm* glacier

ghiacci'are [gjat'tʃare] *vt* to freeze; (*fig*): **~ qn** to make sb's blood run cold ♦ *vi* to freeze, ice over; **ghiacci'ato, a** *ag* frozen; (*bevanda*) ice-cold

ghi'accio [gi'attʃo] *sm* ice

ghiacci'olo [gjat'tʃɔlo] *sm* icicle; (*tipo di gelato*) ice lolly (*BRIT*), popsicle (*US*)

ghi'aia [gi'aja] *sf* gravel

ghi'anda [gi'anda] *sf* (*BOT*) acorn

ghi'andola [gi'andola] *sf* gland

ghigliot'tina [giʎʎot'tina] *sf* guillotine

ghi'gnare [giɲˈɲare] *vi* to sneer

ghi'otto, a [ˈgjɔtto] *ag* greedy; *(cibo)* delicious, appetizing; **ghiot'tone, a** *smf* glutton

ghiri'bizzo [giriˈbiddzo] *sm* whim

ghiri'goro [giriˈgoro] *sm* scribble, squiggle

ghir'landa [girˈlanda] *sf* garland, wreath

'ghiro [ˈgiro] *sm* dormouse

'ghisa [ˈgiza] *sf* cast iron

già [dʒa] *av* already; *(ex, in precedenza)* formerly ♦ *escl* of course!, yes indeed!

gi'acca, che [ˈdʒakka] *sf* jacket; ~ **a vento** windcheater *(BRIT)*, windbreaker *(US)*

giacché [dʒakˈke] *cong* since, as

giac'chetta [dʒakˈketta] *sf* (light) jacket

gia'cenza [dʒaˈtʃɛntsa] *sf*: **merce in ~ goods in stock**; **~e di magazzino** unsold stock

gia'cere [dʒaˈtʃere] *vi* to lie; **giaci'mento** *sm* deposit

gia'cinto [dʒaˈtʃinto] *sm* hyacinth

gi'ada [ˈdʒada] *sf* jade

giaggi'olo [dʒadˈdʒɔlo] *sm* iris

giagu'aro [dʒaˈgwaro] *sm* jaguar

gi'allo [ˈdʒallo] *ag* yellow; *(carnagione)* sallow ♦ *sm* yellow; *(anche: romanzo ~)* detective novel; *(anche: film ~)* detective film; ~ **dell'uovo** yolk

giam'mai [dʒamˈmai] *av* never

Giap'pone [dʒapˈpone] *sm* Japan; **giappo'nese** *ag, smf, sm* Japanese *inv*

gi'ara [ˈdʒara] *sf* jar

giardi'naggio [dʒardiˈnaddʒo] *sm* gardening

giardi'netta [dʒardiˈnetta] *sf* estate car *(BRIT)*, station wagon *(US)*

giardi'niera [dʒardiˈnjera] *sf (misto di sottaceti)* mixed pickles *pl*; *(automobile)* = **giardinetta**

giardini'ere, a [dʒardiˈnjere] *smf* gardener

giar'dino [dʒarˈdino] *sm* garden; ~

d'infanzia nursery school; ~ **pubblico** public gardens *pl*, (public) park; ~ **zoologico** zoo

giarretti'era [dʒarretˈtjera] *sf* garter

giavel'lotto [dʒavelˈlotto] *sm* javelin

gi'gante, 'essa [dʒiˈgante] *sm/f* giant ♦ *ag* giant, gigantic; *(COMM)* giant-size; **gigan'tesco, a, schi, sche** *ag* gigantic

'giglio [ˈdʒiʎʎo] *sm* lily

gilè [dʒiˈlɛ] *sm inv* waistcoat

gin [dʒin] *sm inv* gin

gine'cologo, a, gi, ghe [dʒineˈkɔlogo] *sm/f* gynaecologist

gi'nepro [dʒiˈnepro] *sm* juniper

gi'nestra [dʒiˈnɛstra] *sf (BOT)* broom

Gi'nevra [dʒiˈnevra] *sf* Geneva

gingil'larsi [dʒindʒilˈlarsi] *vr* to fritter away one's time; *(giocare)*: ~ **con** to fiddle with

gin'gillo [dʒinˈdʒillo] *sm* plaything

gin'nasio [dʒinˈnazjo] *sm the 4th and 5th year of secondary school in Italy*

gin'nasta, i, e [dʒinˈnasta] *sm/f* gymnast; **gin'nastica** *sf* gymnastics *sg*; *(esercizio fisico)* keep-fit exercises; *(INS)* physical education

gi'nocchio [dʒiˈnɔkkjo] *sm (pl(m) gi'nocchi o pl(f) gi'nocchia)* knee; **stare in ~** to kneel, be on one's knees; **mettersi in ~** to kneel (down); **ginocchi'oni** *av* on one's knees

gio'care [dʒoˈkare] *vt* to play; *(scommettere)* to stake, wager, bet; *(ingannare)* to take in ♦ *vi* to play; *(a roulette etc)* to gamble; *(fig)* to play a part, be important; *(TECN: meccanismo)* to be loose; ~ **a** *(giochi, sport)* to play; *(cavalli)* to bet on; ~**rsi la carriera** to put one's career at risk; **gioca'tore, 'trice** *sm/f* player; gambler

gio'cattolo [dʒoˈkattolo] *sm* toy

gio'chetto [dʒoˈketto] *sm (tranello)* trick; *(fig)*: **è un ~** it's child's play

gi'oco, chi [ˈdʒɔko] *sm* game; *(divertimento, TECN)* play; *(al casinò)* gambling; *(CARTE)* hand; *(insieme* *di pezzi etc necessari per un gioco)* set; **per ~** for fun; **fare il doppio ~ con qn** to double-cross sb; **~ d'azzardo** game of chance; **~ della palla** football; **~ degli scacchi** chess set; **i Giochi Olimpici** the Olympic Games

giocoli'ere [dʒoko'ljɛre] *sm* juggler

gio'coso, a [dʒo'koso] *ag* playful, jesting

gi'ogo, ghi ['dʒɔgo] *sm* yoke

gi'oia ['dʒɔja] *sf* joy, delight; *(pietra preziosa)* jewel, precious stone

gioielle'ria [dʒojelle'ria] *sf* jeweller's craft; jeweller's (shop)

gioielli'ere, a [dʒojel'ljɛre] *smf* jeweller

gioi'ello [dʒo'jɛllo] *sm* jewel, piece of jewellery; **i ~i di una donna** a woman's jewels o jewellery

gioi'oso, a [dʒo'joso] *ag* joyful

Gior'dania [dʒor'danja] *sf*: **la ~** Jordan

giorna'laio, a [dʒorna'lajo] *smf* newsagent *(BRIT)*, newsdealer *(US)*

gior'nale [dʒor'nale] *sm* (news) paper; *(diario)* journal, diary; *(COMM)* journal; **~ di bordo** log; **~ radio** radio news *sg*

giornali'ero, a [dʒorna'ljɛro] *ag* daily; *(che varia: umore)* changeable ♦ *sm* day labourer

giorna'lismo [dʒorna'lizmo] *sm* journalism

giorna'lista, i, e [dʒorna'lista] *smf* journalist

gior'nata [dʒor'nata] *sf* day; **~ lavorativa** working day

gi'orno ['dʒorno] *sm* day; *(opposto alla notte)* day, daytime; *(luce del ~)* daylight; **al ~** per day; **di ~** by day; **al ~ d'oggi** nowadays

gi'ostra ['dʒɔstra] *sf (per bimbi* merry-go-round; *(torneo storico)* joust

gio'vane ['dʒovane] *ag* young; *(aspetto)* youthful ♦ *smf* youth/girl, young man/woman; **i ~i** young people; **giova'nile** *ag* youthful; *(scritti)* early; *(errore)* of youth;

giova'notto *sm* young man

gio'vare [dʒo'vare] *vi*: **~ a** *(essere utile)* to be useful to; *(far bene)* to be good for ♦ *vb impers (essere utile)* to be useful; **~rsi di qc** to make use of sth

giovedì [dʒove'di] *sm inv* Thursday; **di o il ~** on Thursdays

gioventù [dʒoven'tu] *sf (periodo)* youth; *(i giovani)* young people *pl*, youth

giovi'ale [dʒo'vjale] *ag* jovial, jolly

giovi'nezza [dʒovi'nettsa] *sf* youth

gira'dischi [dʒira'diski] *sm inv* record player

gi'raffa [dʒi'raffa] *sf* giraffe

gi'randola [dʒi'randola] *sf (fuoco d'artificio)* Catherine wheel; *(giocattolo)* toy windmill; *(banderuola)* weather vane, weathercock

gi'rare [dʒi'rare] *vt (far ruotare)* to turn; *(percorrere, visitare)* to go round; *(CINEMA)* to shoot; to make; *(COMM)* to endorse ♦ *vi* to turn; *(più veloce)* to spin; *(andare in giro)* to wander, go around; **~rsi** *vr* to turn; **~ attorno a** to go round: to revolve round; **far ~ la testa a qn** to make sb dizzy; *(fig)* to turn sb's head

gira'rrosto [dʒira'rrɔsto] *sm (CUC)* spit

gira'sole [dʒira'sole] *sm* sunflower

gi'rata [dʒi'rata] *sf (passeggiata)* stroll; *(con veicolo)* drive; *(COMM)* endorsement

gira'volta [dʒira'vɔlta] *sf* twirl, turn; *(curva)* sharp bend; *(fig)* about-turn

gi'revole [dʒi'revole] *ag* revolving, turning

gi'rino [dʒi'rino] *sm* tadpole

'giro ['dʒiro] *sm (circuito, cerchio)* circle; *(di chiave, manovella)* turn; *(viaggio)* tour, excursion; *(passeggiata)* stroll, walk; *(in macchina)* drive; *(in bicicletta)* ride; *(SPORT: della pista)* lap; *(di denaro)* circulation; *(CARTE)* hand; *(TECN)* revolution; **prendere in ~ qn** *(fig)* to pull sb's leg; **fare un ~** to go for a walk *(o a drive o a ride)*; **andare in**

~ to go about, walk around; a stretto ~ di posta by return of post; **nel ~ di un mese** in a month's time; **essere nel ~** (*fig*) to belong to a circle (of friends); **~ d'affari** (*COMM*) turnover; **~ di parole** circumlocution; **~ di prova** (*AUT*) test drive; **~ turistico** sightseeing tour; **giro'collo** *sm*: **a girocollo** crewneck *cpd*

gironzo'lare [dʒirondzo'lare] *vi* to stroll about

'gita ['dʒita] *sf* excursion, trip; **fare una ~** to go for a trip, go on an outing

gi'tano, a [dʒi'tano] *smf* gipsy

giù [dʒu] *av* down; (*dabbasso*) downstairs; **in ~** downwards, down; **~ di lì** (*pressappoco*) thereabouts; **bambini dai 6 anni in ~** children aged 6 and under; **~ per: cadere ~ per le scale** to fall down the stairs; **essere ~** (*fig: di salute*) to be run down; (: *di spirito*) to be depressed

giub'botto [dʒub'botto] *sm* jerkin; **~ antiproiettile** bulletproof vest

gi'ubilo ['dʒubilo] *sm* rejoicing

giudi'care [dʒudi'kare] *vt* to judge; (*accusato*) to try; (*lite*) to arbitrate in; **~ qn/qc bello** to consider sb/sth (to be) beautiful

gi'udice ['dʒuditʃe] *sm* judge; **~ conciliatore** justice of the peace; **~ istruttore** examining magistrate; **~ popolare** member of a jury

giu'dizio [dʒu'dittsjo] *sm* judgment; (*opinione*) opinion; (*DIR*) judgment, sentence; (: *processo*) trial; (: *verdetto*) verdict; **aver ~** to be wise o prudent; **citare in ~** to summons; **giudizi'oso, a** *ag* prudent, judicious

gi'ugno ['dʒuɲɲo] *sm* June

giul'lare [dʒul'lare] *sm* jester

giu'menta [dʒu'menta] *sf* mare

gi'unco, chi ['dʒunko] *sm* rush

gi'ungere ['dʒundʒere] *vi* to arrive ♦ *vt* (*mani etc*) to join; **~ a** to arrive at, reach

gi'ungla ['dʒungla] *sf* jungle

gi'unta ['dʒunta] *sf* addition; (*organo*

esecutivo, amministrativo*) council, board; **per ~ into the bargain, in addition; **~a militare** military junta

gi'unto, a ['dʒunto] *pp di* giungere ♦ *sm* (*TECN*) coupling, joint; **giun'tura** *sf* joint

giuo'care [dʒwo'kare] *vt, vi* = giocare; **giu'oco** *sm* = gioco

giura'mento [dʒura'mento] *sm* oath; **~ falso** perjury

giu'rare [dʒu'rare] *vt* to swear ♦ *vi* to swear, take an oath; **nemico giurato** sworn enemy ♦ *smf* juror, juryman/woman

giu'ria [dʒu'ria] *sf* jury

giu'ridico, a, ci, che [dʒu'ridiko] *ag* legal

giustifi'care [dʒustifi'kare] *vt* to justify; **giustificazi'one** *sf* justification; (*INS*) (note) of excuse

gius'tizia [dʒus'tittsja] *sf* justice; **giustizi'are** *vt* to execute, put to death; **giustizi'ere** *sm* executioner

gi'usto, a ['dʒusto] *ag* (*equo*) fair, just; (*vero*) true, correct; (*adatto*) right, suitable; (*preciso*) exact, correct ♦ *av* (*esattamente*) exactly, precisely; (*per l'appunto, appena*) just; **arrivare ~** to arrive just in time; **ho ~ bisogno di te** you're just the person I need

glaci'ale [gla'tʃale] *ag* glacial

'glandola *sf* = ghiandola

gli [ʎi] (*dav V, s impura, gn, pn, ps, x, z*) *det mpl* the ♦ *pron* (*a lui*) to him; (*a esso*) to it; (*in coppia con lo, la, li, le, ne: a lui, a lei, a loro etc*): **glielo do** I'm giving them to him (o her o them)

gli'ela ['ʎela] *etc vedi* gli

glo'bale *ag* overall

'globo *sm* globe

'globulo *sm* (*ANAT*): **~ rosso/bianco** red/white corpuscle

'gloria *sf* glory; **glori'oso, a** *ag* glorious

glos'sario *sm* glossary

'gnocchi ['ɲɔkki] *smpl* (*CUC*) small dumplings made of semolina pasta or potato

'gobba *sf* (ANAT) hump; (*protuberanza*) bump

'gobbo, a *ag* hunchbacked; (*ricurvo*) round-shouldered ♦ *sm/f* hunchback

'goccia, ce ['gottʃa] *sf* drop; **goccio'lare** *vi*, *vt* to drip

go'dere *vi* (*compiacersi*): ~ **(di)** to be delighted (at), rejoice (at); (*trarre vantaggio*): ~ **di** to enjoy, benefit from ♦ *vt* to enjoy; ~**rsi la vita** to enjoy life; ~**sela** to have a good time, enjoy o.s.; **godi'mento** *sm* enjoyment

'goffo, a *ag* clumsy, awkward

'gola *sf* (ANAT) throat; (*golosità*) gluttony, greed; (*di camino*) flue; (*di monte*) gorge; **fare** ~ (*anche fig*) to tempt

golf *sm inv* (SPORT) golf; (*maglia*) cardigan

'golfo *sm* gulf

go'loso, a *ag* greedy

'gomito *sm* elbow; (*di strada etc*) sharp bend

go'mitolo *sm* ball

'gomma *sf* rubber; (*colla*) gum; (*per cancellare*) rubber, eraser; (*di veicolo*) tyre (BRIT), tire (US); ~ **americana** *o* **da masticare** chewing gum; ~ **a terra** flat tyre (BRIT) *o* tire (US); **gommapi'uma** ® *o* *sf* foam rubber

'gondola *sf* gondola; **gondoli'ere** *sm* gondolier

gonfa'lone *sm* banner

gonfi'are *vt* (*pallone*) to blow up, inflate; (*dilatare, ingrossare*) to swell; (*fig: notizia*) to exaggerate; ~**rsi** *vr* to swell; (*fiume*) to rise; **'gonfio, a** *ag* swollen; (*stomaco*) bloated; (*vela*) full; **gonfi'ore** *sm* swelling

gongo'lare *vi* to look pleased with o.s.; ~ **di gioia** to be overjoyed

'gonna *sf* skirt; ~ **pantalone** culottes *pl*

'gonzo ['gondzo] *sm* simpleton, fool

gorgheggi'are [gorged'dʒare] *vi* to warble; to trill

'gorgo, ghi *sm* whirlpool

gorgogli'are [gorgoʎ'ʎare] *vi* to gurgle

go'rilla *sm inv* gorilla; (*guardia del corpo*) bodyguard

'gotta *sf* gout

gover'nante *sm/f* ruler ♦ *sf* (*di bambini*) governess; (*donna di servizio*) housekeeper

gover'nare *vt* (*stato*) to govern, rule; (*pilotare, guidare*) to steer; (*bestiame*) to tend, look after; **governa'tivo, a** *ag* government *cpd*; **governa'tore** *sm* governor

go'verno *sm* government

gozzovigli'are [gottsoviʎ'ʎare] *vi* to make merry, carouse

gracchi'are [grak'kjare] *vi* to caw

graci'dare [gratʃi'dare] *vi* to croak

'gracile ['gratʃile] *ag* frail, delicate

gra'dasso *sm* boaster

gradazi'one [gradat'tsjone] *sf* (*sfumatura*) gradation; ~ **alcolica** alcoholic content, strength

gra'devole *ag* pleasant, agreeable

gradi'mento *sm* pleasure, satisfaction; **è di suo** ~? is it to your liking?

gradi'nata *sf* flight of steps; (*in teatro, stadio*) tiers *pl*

gra'dino *sm* step; (ALPINISMO) foothold

gra'dire *vt* (*accettare con piacere*) to accept; (*desiderare*) to wish, like; **gradisce una tazza di tè?** would you like a cup of tea?; **gra'dito, a** *ag* pleasing; welcome

'grado *sm* (MAT, FISICA etc) degree; (*stadio*) degree, level; (MIL, *sociale*) rank; **essere in** ~ **di fare** to be in a position to do

gradu'ale *ag* gradual

gradu'are *vt* to grade; **gradu'ato, a** *ag* (*esercizi*) graded; (*scala, termometro*) graduated ♦ *sm* (MIL) non-commissioned officer

'graffa *sf* (*gancio*) clip; (*segno grafico*) brace

graffi'are *vt* to scratch

'graffio *sm* scratch

gra'fia *sf* spelling; (*scrittura*) hand-

writing
'grafica *sf* graphic arts *pl*
'grafico, a, ci, che *ag* graphic ♦ *sm* graph; (*persona*) graphic designer
gra'migna [gra'miɲɲa] *sf* weed; couch grass
gram'matica, che *sf* grammar; **grammati'cale** *ag* grammatical
'grammo *sm* gram(me)
gran *ag vedi* **grande**
'grana *sf* (*granello, di minerali, corpi spezzati*) grain; (*fam: seccatura*) trouble; (: *soldi*) cash ♦ *sm inv* Parmesan (*cheese*)
gra'naio *sm* granary, barn
gra'nata *sf* (*frutto*) pomegranate; (*pietra preziosa*) garnet; (*proiettile*) grenade
Gran Bre'tagna [-bre'taɲɲa] *sf*: **la ~** Great Britain
'granchio ['grankjo] *sm* crab; (*fig*) blunder; **prendere un ~** (*fig*) to blunder
grandango'lare *sm* wide-angle lens *sg*
'grande (*qualche volta* **gran** +*C*, **grand'** +*V*) *ag* (*grosso, largo, vasto*) big, large; (*alto*) tall; (*lungo*) long; (*in sensi astratti*) great ♦ *sm/f* (*persona adulta*) adult, grown-up; (*chi ha ingegno e potenza*) great man/woman; **fare le cose in ~** to do things in style; **una gran bella donna** a very beautiful woman; **non è una gran cosa o un gran che** it's nothing special; **non ne so gran che** I don't know very much about it
grandeggi'are [grandede'dʒare] *vi* (*emergere per grandezza*): **~ su** to tower over; (*darsi arie*) to put on airs
gran'dezza [gran'dettsa] *sf* (*dimensione*) size; magnitude; (*fig*) greatness; **in ~ naturale** lifesize
grandi'nare *vb impers* to hail
'grandine *sf* hail
gran'duca, chi *sm* grand duke
gra'nello *sm* (*di cereali, uva*) seed; (*di frutta*) pip; (*di sabbia, sale etc*)

grain
gra'nita *sf* kind of water ice
gra'nito *sm* granite
'grano *sm* (*in quasi tutti i sensi*) grain; (*frumento*) wheat; (*di rosario, collana*) bead; **~ di pepe** peppercorn
gran'turco *sm* maize
'granulo *sm* granule; (*MED*) pellet
'grappa *sf* rough, strong brandy
'grappolo *sm* bunch, cluster
gras'setto *sm* (*TIP*) bold (type)
'grasso, a *ag* fat; (*cibo*) fatty; (*pelle*) greasy; (*terreno*) rich; (*fig: guadagno, annata*) plentiful; (: *volgare*) coarse, lewd ♦ *sm* (*di persona, animale*) fat; (*sostanza che unge*) grease; **gras'soccio, a, ci, ce** *ag* plump
'grata *sf* grating
gra'ticola *sf* grill
gra'tifica, che *sf* bonus
'gratis *av* free, for nothing
grati'tudine *sf* gratitude
'grato, a *ag* grateful; (*gradito*) pleasant, agreeable
gratta'capo *sm* worry, headache
gratta'cielo [gratta'tʃɛlo] *sm* skyscraper
grat'tare *vt* (*pelle*) to scratch; (*raschiare*) to scrape; (*pane, formaggio, carote*) to grate; (*fam: rubare*) to pinch ♦ *vi* (*stridere*) to grate; (*AUT*) to grind; **~rsi** *vr* to scratch o.s
grat'tugia, gie [grat'tudʒa] *sf* grater; **grattugi'are** *vt* to grate; **pane grattugiato** breadcrumbs *pl*
gra'tuito, a *ag* free; (*fig*) gratuitous
gra'vare *vt* to burden ♦ *vi*: **~ su** to weigh on
'grave *ag* (*danno, pericolo, peccato etc*) grave, serious; (*responsabilità*) heavy, grave; (*contegno*) grave, solemn; (*voce, suono*) deep, low-pitched; (*LING*): **accento ~** grave accent; **un malato ~** a person who is seriously ill
gravi'danza [gravi'dantsa] *sf* pregnancy
'gravido, a *ag* pregnant

gravità *sf* seriousness; *(anche FISI-CA)* gravity

gra'voso, a *ag* heavy, onerous

grazia ['grattsja] *sf* grace; *(favore)* favour; *(DIR)* pardon; **grazi'are** *vt (DIR)* to pardon

'grazie ['grattsje] *escl* thank you!; ~ **mille!** *o* **tante!** *o* **infinite!** thank you very much!; ~ **a** thanks to

grazi'oso, a [grat'tsjoso] *ag* charming, delightful; *(gentile)* gracious

'Grecia ['grɛtʃa] *sf:* **la** ~ Greece; **'greco, a, ci, che** *ag, sm/f, sm* Greek

'gregge ['greddʒe] *(pl(f)* **-i)** *sm* flock

'greggio, a, gi, ge ['greddʒo] *ag* raw, unrefined; *(diamante)* rough, uncut; *(tessuto)* unbleached ♦ *sm (anche: petrolio ~)* crude (oil)

grembi'ule *sm* apron; *(sopravveste)* overall

'grembo *sm* lap; *(ventre della madre)* womb

gre'mito, a *ag:* ~ **(di)** packed *o* crowded (with)

'gretto, a *ag* mean, stingy; *(fig)* narrow-minded

'greve *ag* heavy

'grezzo, a ['greddzo] *ag* = **greggio**

gri'dare *vi (per chiamare)* to shout, cry (out); *(strillare)* to scream, yell ♦ *vt* to shout (out), yell (out); ~ **aiuto** to cry *o* shout for help

'grido *(pl(m)* **-i** *o pl(f)* **-a)** *sm* shout, cry; scream, yell; *(di animale)* cry; **di** ~ famous

'grigio, a, gi, gie ['gridʒo] *ag, sm* grey

'griglia ['griʎʎa] *sf (per arrostire)* grill; *(ELETTR)* grid; *(inferriata)* grating; **alla** ~ *(CUC)* grilled; **gri-gli'ata** *sf (CUC)* grill

gril'letto *sm* trigger

'grillo *sm (ZOOL)* cricket; *(fig)* whim

grimal'dello *sm* picklock

'grinta *sf* grim expression; *(SPORT)* fighting spirit

'grinza ['grintsa] *sf* crease, wrinkle; *(ruga)* wrinkle; **non fare una** ~

(fig: ragionamento) to be faultless;
grin'zoso, a *ag* creased; wrinkled

grip'pare *vi (TECN)* to seize

gris'sino *sm* bread-stick

'gronda *sf* eaves *pl*

gron'daia *sf* gutter

gron'dare *vi* to pour; *(essere bagnato):* ~ **di** to be dripping with ♦ *vt* to drip with

'groppa *sf (di animale)* back, rump; *(fam: dell'uomo)* back, shoulders *pl*

'groppo *sm* tangle; **avere un** ~ **alla gola** *(fig)* to have a lump in one's throat

gros'sezza [gros'settsa] *sf* size; thickness

gros'sista, i, e *sm/f (COMM)* wholesaler

'grosso, a *ag* big, large; *(di spessore)* thick; *(grossolano: anche fig)* coarse; *(grave, insopportabile)* serious, great; *(tempo, mare)* rough ♦ *sm:* **il** ~ **di** the bulk of; **un pezzo** ~ *(fig)* a VIP, a bigwig; **farla** ~**a** to do something very stupid; **dirle** ~**e** to tell tall stories; **sbagliarsi di** ~ to be completely wrong

grosso'lano, a *ag* rough, coarse; *(fig)* coarse, crude; *(: errore)* stupid

grosso'modo *av* roughly

'grotta *sf* cave; grotto

grot'tesco, a, schi, sche *ag* grotesque

grovi'era *sm o f* gruyère (cheese)

gro'viglio [gro'viʎʎo] *sm* tangle; *(fig)* muddle

gru *sf inv* crane

'gruccia, ce ['gruttʃa] *sf (per cam-minare)* crutch; *(per abiti)* coat-hanger

gru'gnire [grun'nire] *vi* to grunt; **gru'gnito** *sm* grunt

'grugno ['grunno] *sm* snout; *(fam: faccia)* mug

'grullo, a *ag* silly, stupid

'grumo *sm (di sangue)* clot; *(di fa-rina etc)* lump

'gruppo *sm* group; ~ **sanguigno** blood group

gruvi'era *sm o f* = **groviera**

guada'gnare [gwadaɲˈɲare] vt (ottenere) to gain; (soldi, stipendio) to earn; (vincere) to win; (raggiungere) to reach

gua'dagno [gwaˈdaɲɲo] sm earnings pl; (COMM) profit; (vantaggio, utile) advantage, gain; ~ lordo/netto gross/net earnings pl

gu'ado sm ford; passare a ~ to ford

gu'ai escl: ~ a te (o lui etc)! woe betide you (o him etc)!

gua'ina sf (fodero) sheath; (indumento per donna) girdle

gu'aio sm trouble, mishap; (inconveniente) trouble, snag

gua'ire vi to whine, yelp

gu'ancia, ce [ˈgwantʃa] sf cheek

guanci'ale [gwanˈtʃale] sm pillow

gu'anto sm glove

guarda... prefisso: ~'**boschi** sm inv forester; ~'**caccia** sm inv gamekeeper; ~'**coste** sm inv coastguard; (nave) coastguard patrol vessel; ~'**linee** sm inv (SPORT) linesman

guar'dare (con lo sguardo: osservare) to look at; (film, televisione) to watch; (custodire) to look after, take care of ♦ vi to look; (badare): ~ a to pay attention to; (luoghi: esser orientato): ~ a to face; ~rsi vr to look at o.s.; ~rsi da (astenersi) to refrain from; (stare in guardia) to beware of; ~rsi da fare to take care not to do; guarda di non sbagliare try not to make a mistake; ~ a vista qn to keep a close watch on sb

guarda'roba sm inv wardrobe; (locale) cloakroom; **guardarobi'ere, a** smf cloakroom attendant

gu'ardia sf (individuo, corpo) guard; (sorveglianza) watch; fare la ~ a qc/qn to guard sth/sb; stare in ~ (fig) to be on one's guard; ~ (medico) on call; ~ carceraria (prison) warder; ~ del corpo bodyguard; ~ di finanza (corpo) customs pl; (persona) customs officer; ~ medica emergency doctor service

guardi'ano, a smf (di carcere) warder; (di villa etc) caretaker; (di museo) custodian; (di zoo) keeper; ~ notturno night watchman

guar'dingo, a, ghi, ghe ag wary, cautious

guardi'ola sf porter's lodge; (MIL) look-out tower

guarigi'one [gwariˈdʒone] sf recovery

gua'rire vt (persona, malattia) to cure; (ferita) to heal ♦ vi to recover, be cured; to heal (up)

guarnigi'one [gwarniˈdʒone] sf garrison

guar'nire vt (ornare: abiti) to trim; (CUC) to garnish; **guarnizi'one** sf trimming; garnish; (TECN) gasket

guasta'feste smf inv spoilsport

guas'tare vt to spoil, ruin; (meccanismo) to break; ~rsi vr (cibo) to go bad; (meccanismo) to break down; (tempo) to change for the worse; (amici) to quarrel, fall out

gu'asto, a ag (non funzionante) broken; (: telefono etc) out of order; (andato a male) bad, rotten; (: dente) decayed, bad; (fig: corrotto) depraved ♦ sm breakdown; (avaria) failure; ~ al motore engine failure

guazza'buglio [gwattsaˈbuʎʎo] sm muddle

gu'ercio, a, ci, ce [ˈgwertʃo] ag cross-eyed

gu'erra sf war; (tecnica: atomica, chimica etc) warfare; fare la ~ (a) to wage war (against); ~ mondiale world war; **guerreggi'are** vi to wage war; **guerri'ero, a** ag warlike ♦ sm warrior; **guer'riglia** sf guerrilla warfare; **guerrigli'ero** sm guerrilla

'gufo sm owl

gu'ida sf guide; (comando, direzione) guidance, direction; (AUT) driving; (: sterzo) steering; (tappeto, di tenda, cassetto) runner; ~ a destra/sinistra (AUT) right-/left-hand drive; ~ telefonica telephone directory; ~ turistica tourist guide

gui'dare vt to guide; (condurre a capo) to lead; (auto) to drive; (aereo, nave) to pilot; **sai ~?** can you drive?; **guida'tore, trice** smf (conducente) driver

guin'zaglio [gwin'tsaʎʎo] sm leash, lead

gu'isa sf: **a ~ di** like, in the manner of

guiz'zare [gwit'tsare] vi to dart; to flicker; to leap; **~ via** (fuggire) to slip away

'guscio ['guʃʃo] sm shell

gus'tare vt (cibi) to taste; (: assaporare con piacere) to enjoy, savour; (fig) to enjoy, appreciate ♦ vi: **~ a** to please; **non mi gusta affatto** I don't like it at all

'gusto sm taste; (sapore) flavour; (godimento) enjoyment; **al ~ di fragola** strawberry-flavoured; **mangiare di ~** to eat heartily; **prenderci ~**: **ci ha preso ~** he's acquired a taste for it, he's got to like it; **gus'toso, a** ag tasty; (fig) agreeable

H

h abbr = **ora**; **altezza**

ha etc [a] vb vedi **avere**

ha'cker [hæ'kəʳ] sm inv hacker

hall [hɔl] sf inv hall, foyer

'handicap ['handikap] sm inv handicap; **handicap'pato, a** ag handicapped ♦ smf handicapped person, disabled person

'hanno ['anno] vb vedi **avere**

hascisc ['haʃiʃ] sm hashish

herpes ['ɛrpɛs] sm (MED) herpes sg; **~ zoster** shingles sg

ho [ɔ] vb vedi **avere**

'hobby ['hɔbi] sm inv hobby

'hockey ['hɔki] sm hockey; **~ su ghiaccio** ice hockey

'hostess ['houstis] sf inv air hostess (BRIT) o stewardess

ho'tel sm inv hotel

I

i det mpl the

i'ato sm hiatus

ibernazi'one [ibernat'tsjone] sf hibernation

'ibrido, a ag, sm hybrid

Id'dio sm God

i'dea sf idea; (opinione) opinion, view; (ideale) ideal; **dare l'~ di** to seem, look like; **~ fissa** obsession; **neanche o neppure per ~!** certainly not!

ide'ale ag, sm ideal

ide'are vt (immaginare) to think up, conceive; (progettare) to plan

i'dentico, a, ci, che ag identical

identifi'care vt to identify; **identificazi'one** sf identification

identità sf inv identity

ideolo'gia, 'gie [ideolo'dʒia] sf ideology

idi'oma, i sm idiom, language; **idio'matico, a, ci, che** ag idiomatic; **frase idiomatica** idiom

idi'ota, i, e ag idiotic ♦ smf idiot

idola'trare vt to worship; (fig) to idolize

'idolo sm idol

idoneità sf suitability

i'doneo, a ag: **~ a** suitable for, fit for; (MIL) fit for; (qualificato) qualified for

i'drante sm hydrant

i'draulica sf hydraulics sg

i'draulico, a, ci, che ag hydraulic ♦ sm plumber

idroe'lettrico, a, ci, che ag hydroelectric

i'drofilo, a ag vedi **cotone**

i'drogeno [i'drɔdʒeno] sm hydrogen

idros'calo sm seaplane base

idrovo'lante sm seaplane

i'ena sf hyena

i'eri av, sm yesterday; **il giornale di ~** yesterday's paper; **~ l'altro** the day before yesterday; **~ sera** yesterday evening

igi'ene [i'dʒɛne] sf hygiene; ~ pubblica public health; **igi'enico, a, ci, che** ag hygienic; (salubre) healthy

i'gnaro, a [iɲ'naro] ag: ~ di unaware of, ignorant of

i'gnobile [iɲ'nɔbile] ag despicable, vile

igno'rante [iɲɲo'rante] ag ignorant

igno'rare [iɲɲo'rare] vt (non sapere, conoscere) to be ignorant o unaware of, not to know; (fingere di non vedere, sentire) to ignore

i'gnoto, a [iɲ'nɔto] ag unknown

PAROLA CHIAVE

il (pl (m) **i**; diventa **lo** (pl **gli**) davanti a s impura, gn, pn, ps, x, z; f la (pl **le**)) det m **1** the; ~ libro/lo studente/l'acqua the book/the student/the water; **gli** scolari the pupils

2 (astrazione): ~ coraggio/l'amore/la giovinezza courage/love/youth

3 (tempo): ~ mattino/la sera in the morning/evening; ~ venerdì etc (abitualmente) on Fridays etc; (quel giorno) on (the) Friday etc; la settimana prossima next week

4 (distributivo) a, an; 2.500 lire ~ chilo/paio 2,500 lire a o per kilo/pair

5 (partitivo) some, any; hai messo lo zucchero? have you added sugar?; hai comprato ~ latte? did you buy (some o any) milk?

6 (possesso): aprire gli occhi to open one's eyes; rompersi la gamba to break one's leg; avere i capelli neri/~ naso rosso to have dark hair/a red nose

7 (con nomi propri): ~ Petrarca Petrarch; ~ Presidente Reagan President Reagan; dov'è la Francesca? where's Francesca?

8 (con nomi geografici): ~ Tevere the Tiber; l'Italia Italy; ~ Regno Unito the United Kingdom; l'Everest Everest

---

'ilare ag cheerful; **ilarità** sf hilarity,

mirth

illangui'dire vi to grow weak o feeble

illazi'one [illat'tsjone] sf inference, deduction

ille'gale ag illegal

illeg'gibile [illed'dʒibile] ag illegible

ille'gittimo, a [ille'dʒittimo] ag illegitimate

il'leso, a ag unhurt, unharmed

illette'rato, a ag illiterate

illi'bato, a ag: donna ~a virgin

illimi'tato, a ag boundless; unlimited

ill.mo abbr = **illustrissimo**

il'ludere vt to deceive, delude; ~rsi vr to deceive o.s., delude o.s.

illumi'nare vt to light up, illuminate; (fig) to enlighten; ~rsi vr to light up; ~ a giorno to floodlight; **illuminazi'one** sf lighting; illumination; floodlighting; (fig) flash of inspiration

illusi'one sf illusion; farsi delle ~i to delude o.s.

illusio'nismo sm conjuring

il'luso, a pp di illudere

illus'trare vt to illustrate; **illus'trativo, a** ag illustrative; **illustrazi'one** sf illustration

il'lustre ag eminent, renowned; **il'lustrissimo, a** ag (negli indirizzi) very revered

imbacuc'care vt to wrap up; ~rsi vr to wrap up

imbal'laggio [imbal'laddʒo] sm packing no pl

imbal'lare vt to pack; (AUT) to race; ~rsi vr (AUT) to race

imbalsa'mare vt to embalm

imbambo'lato, a ag (sguardo) vacant, blank

imban'dire vt: ~ un pranzo to prepare a lavish meal

imbaraz'zare [imbarat'tsare] vt (mettere a disagio) to embarrass; (ostacolare: movimenti) to hamper; (: stomaco) to lie heavily on

imba'razzo [imba'rattso] sm (disagio) embarrassment; (perplessità) puzzlement, bewilderment; ~ **di sto-maco** indigestion

imbarca'dero *sm* landing stage

imbar'care *vt* (*passeggeri*) to embark; (*merci*) to load; ~**rsi** *vr*: ~**rsi su** to board; ~**rsi per l'America** to sail for America; ~**rsi in** (*fig: affare etc*) to embark on

imbarcazi'one [imbarkat'tsjone] *sf* (small) boat, (small) craft *inv*; ~ **di salvataggio** lifeboat

im'barco, chi *sm* embarkation; loading; boarding; (*banchina*) landing stage

imbas'tire *vt* (*cucire*) to tack; (*fig: abbozzare*) to sketch, outline

im'battersi *vr*: ~ **in** (*incontrare*) to bump o run into

imbat'tibile *ag* unbeatable, invincible

imbavagli'are [imbavaʎ'ʎare] *vt* to gag

imbec'cata *sf* (*TEATRO*) prompt

imbe'cille [imbe't∫ille] *ag* idiotic ♦ *smf* idiot; (*MED*) imbecile

imbel'lire *vt* to adorn, embellish ♦ *vi* to grow more beautiful

im'berbe *ag* beardless

im'bevere *vt* to soak; ~**rsi** *vr*: ~**rsi di** to soak up, absorb

imbian'care *vt* to whiten; (*muro*) to whitewash ♦ *vi* to become o turn white

imbian'chino [imbjan'kino] *sm* (house) painter, painter and decorator

imboc'care *vt* (*bambino*) to feed; (*entrare: strada*) to enter, turn into ♦ *vi*: ~ **in** (*sog: strada*) to lead into; (*: fiume*) to flow into

imbocca'tura *sf* mouth; (*di strada, porto*) entrance; (*MUS, del morso*) mouthpiece

im'bocco, chi *sm* entrance

imbos'care *vt* to hide; ~**rsi** *vr* (*MIL*) to evade military service

imbos'cata *sf* ambush

imbottigli'are [imbottiʎ'ʎare] *vt* to bottle; (*NAUT*) to blockade; (*MIL*) to hem in; ~**rsi** *vr* to be stuck in a

traffic jam

imbot'tire *vt* to stuff; (*giacca*) to pad; **imbot'tita** *sf* quilt; **imbotti'tura** *sf* stuffing; padding

imbrat'tare *vt* to dirty, smear, daub

imbrigli'are [imbriʎ'ʎare] *vt* to bridle

imbroc'care *vt* (*fig*) to guess correctly

imbrogli'are [imbroʎ'ʎare] *vt* to mix up; (*fig: raggirare*) to deceive, cheat; (*: confondere*) to confuse, mix up; ~**rsi** *vr* to get tangled; (*fig*) to become confused; **im'broglio** *sm* (*groviglio*) tangle; (*situazione confusa*) mess; (*truffa*) swindle, trick; **imbrogli'one, a** *smf* cheat, swindler

imbronci'are [imbron't∫are] *vi* (*anche*: ~**rsi**) to sulk; **imbronci'ato, a** *ag* sulky

imbru'nire *vi, vb impers* to grow dark; **all'**~ at dusk

imbrut'tire *vt* to make ugly ♦ *vi* to become ugly

imbu'care *vt* to post

imbur'rare *vt* to butter

im'buto *sm* funnel

imi'tare *vt* to imitate; (*riprodurre*) to copy; (*assomigliare*) to look like; **imitazi'one** *sf* imitation

immaco'lato, a *ag* spotless; immaculate

immagazzi'nare [immagaddzi'nare] *vt* to store

immagi'nare [immadʒi'nare] *vt* to imagine; (*supporre*) to suppose; (*inventare*) to invent; **s'immagini!** don't mention it!, not at all!; **immagi'nario, a** *ag* imaginary; **immaginazi'one** *sf* imagination; (*cosa immaginata*) fancy

im'magine [im'madʒine] *sf* image; (*rappresentazione grafica, mentale*) picture

imman'cabile *ag* certain; unfailing

imma'nente *ag* (*smisurato*) enormous; (*spaventoso*) terrible

immangi'abile [imman'dʒabile] *ag* inedible

immatrico'lare vt to register; **~rsi** vr (INS) to matriculate, enrol; **immatricolazi'one** sf registration; matriculation, enrolment

imma'turo, a ag (frutto) unripe; (persona) immature; (prematuro) premature

immedesi'marsi vr: **~ in** to identify with

immediata'mente av immediately, at once

immedi'ato, a ag immediate

im'memore ag: **~ di** forgetful of

im'menso, a ag immense

im'mergere [im'mɛrdʒere] vt to immerse, plunge; **~rsi** vr to plunge; (sommergibile) to dive, submerge; (dedicarsi a): **~rsi in** to immerse o.s. in

immeri'tato, a ag undeserved

immeri'tevole ag undeserving, unworthy

immersi'one sf immersion; (di sommergibile) submersion, dive; (di palombaro) dive

im'merso, a pp di immergere

im'mettere vt: **~ (in)** to introduce (into); **~ dati in un computer** to enter data on a computer

immi'grato, a smf immigrant; **immigrazi'one** sf immigration

immi'nente ag imminent

immischi'are [immis'kjare] vt: **~ qn in** to involve sb in; **~rsi in** to interfere o meddle in

immissi'one sf (di aria, gas) intake; **~ di dati** (INFORM) data entry

im'mobile ag motionless, still; **~i** smpl (anche: beni **~i**) real estate sg; **immobili'are** ag (DIR) property cpd; **immobilità** sf stillness; immobility

immo'desto, a ag immodest

immo'lare vt to sacrifice, immolate

immon'dizia [immon'dittsja] sf dirt, filth; (spesso al pl: spazzatura, rifiuti) rubbish no pl, refuse no pl

im'mondo, a ag filthy, foul

immo'rale ag immoral

immor'tale ag immortal

im'mune ag (esente) exempt; (MED, DIR) immune; **immunità** sf immunity; **immunità parlamentare** parliamentary privilege

immu'tabile ag immutable; unchanging

impacchet'tare [impakket'tare] vt to pack up

impacci'are [impat'tʃare] vt to hinder, hamper; **impacci'ato, a** ag awkward, clumsy; (imbarazzato) embarrassed; **im'paccio** sm obstacle; (imbarazzo) embarrassment; (situazione imbarazzante) awkward situation

im'pacco, chi sm (MED) compress

impadro'nirsi vr: **~ di** to seize, take possession of; (fig: apprendere a fondo) to master

impa'gabile ag priceless

impagi'nare [impadʒi'nare] vt (TIP) to paginate, page (up)

impagli'are [impaʎ'ʎare] vt to stuff (with straw)

impa'lato, a ag (fig) stiff as a board

impalca'tura sf scaffolding

impal'lidire vi to turn pale; (fig) to fade

impa'nare vt (CUC) to dip in breadcrumbs

impan'tanarsi vr to sink (in the mud); (fig) to get bogged down

impappi'narsi vr to stammer, falter

impa'rare vt to learn

imparen'tarsi vr: **~ con** to marry into

im'pari ag inv (disuguale) unequal; (dispari) odd

impar'tire vt to bestow, give

imparzi'ale [impar'tsjale] ag impartial, unbiased

impas'sibile ag impassive

impas'tare vt (pasta) to knead; (colori) to mix

im'pasto sm (l'impastare: di pane) kneading; (: di cemento) mixing; (pasta) dough; (anche fig) mixture

im'patto sm impact

impau'rire vt to scare, frighten ♦ vi (anche: ~rsi) to become scared o frightened

im'pavido, a ag intrepid, fearless

impazi'ente [impat'tsjɛnte] ag impatient; **impazi'enza** sf impatience

impaz'zata [impat'tsata] sf: all'~ (precipitosamente) at breakneck speed

impaz'zire [impat'tsire] vi to go mad; ~ **per qn/qc** to be crazy about sb/sth

impec'cabile ag impeccable

impedi'mento sm obstacle, hindrance

impe'dire vt (vietare): ~ **a qn di fare** to prevent sb from doing; (ostruire) to obstruct; (impacciare) to hamper, hinder

impe'gnare [impeɲ'ɲare] vt (dare in pegno) to pawn; (onore etc) to pledge; (prenotare) to book, reserve; (obbligare) to oblige; (occupare) to keep busy; (MIL: nemico) to engage; ~rsi vr (vincolarsi): ~rsi a fare to undertake to do; (mettersi risolutamente): ~rsi in qc to devote o.s. to; ~rsi con qn (accordarsi) to come to an agreement with sb; **impegna'tivo, a** ag binding; (lavoro) demanding, exacting; **impe'gna-to, a** ag (occupato) busy; (fig: romanzo, autore) committed, engagé

im'pegno [im'peɲɲo] sm (obbligo) obligation; (promessa) promise, pledge; (zelo) diligence, zeal; (compito, d'autore) commitment

impel'lente ag pressing, urgent

impene'trabile ag impenetrable

impen'narsi vr (cavallo) to rear up; (AER) to nose up; (fig) to bridle

impen'sato, a ag unforeseen, unexpected

impensie'rire vt to worry; ~rsi vr to worry

impe'rare vi (anche fig) to reign, rule

impera'tivo, a ag, sm imperative

impera'tore, 'trice sm/f emperor/

empress

imperdo'nabile ag unforgivable, unpardonable

imper'fetto, a ag imperfect ♦ sm (LING) imperfect (tense); **imperfezi'one** sf imperfection

imperi'ale ag imperial

imperi'oso, a ag (persona) imperious; (motivo, esigenza) urgent, pressing

impe'rizia [impe'rittsja] sf lack of experience

imperma'lirsi vr to take offence

imperme'abile ag waterproof ♦ sm raincoat

imperni'are vt: ~ **qc su** to hinge sth on; (fig) to base sth on; ~rsi vr (fig): ~rsi su to be based on

im'pero sm empire; (forza, autorità) rule, control

imperscru'tabile ag inscrutable

imperso'nale ag impersonal

imperso'nare vt to personify; (TEATRO) to play, act (the part of)

imper'territo, a ag fearless, undaunted; impassive

imperti'nente ag impertinent

imperver'sare vi to rage

im'peto sm (moto, forza) force, impetus; (assalto) onslaught; (fig: impulso) impulse; (: slancio) transport; **con** ~ energetically; vehemently

impet'tito, a ag stiff, erect

impetu'oso, a ag (vento) strong, raging; (persona) impetuous

impian'tare vt (motore) to install; (azienda, discussione) to establish, start

impi'anto sm (installazione) installation; (apparecchiature) plant; (sistema) system; ~ **elettrico** wiring; ~ **sportivo** sports complex; ~i **di risalita** (SCI) ski lifts

impiastricci'are [impjastrit'tʃare] vt = **impiastrare**

impi'astro sm poultice

impic'care vt to hang; ~rsi vr to hang o.s.

impicci'are [impit'tʃare] vt to hinder, hamper; ~rsi vr to meddle, interfere; **im'piccio** *sm* (*ostacolo*) hindrance; (*seccatura*) trouble, bother; (*affare imbrogliato*) mess; **essere d'impiccio** to be in the way

impie'gare *vt* (*usare*) to use, employ; (*assumere*) to employ, take on; (*spendere: denaro, tempo*) to spend; (*investire*) to invest; ~**rsi** *vr* to get a job, obtain employment; **im-pie'gato, a** *sm/f* employee

impi'ego, ghi *sm* (*uso*) use; (*occupazione*) employment; (*posto di lavoro*) (regular) job, post; (*ECON*) investment

impieto'sire *vt* to move to pity; ~**rsi** *vr* to be moved to pity

impie'trire *vt* (*fig*) to petrify

impigli'are [impiʎ'ʎare] *vt* to catch, entangle; ~**rsi** *vr* to get caught up o entangled

impi'grire *vt* to make lazy ♦ *vi* (*anche*: ~**rsi**) to grow lazy

impli'care *vt* to imply; (*coinvolgere*) to involve; ~**rsi** *vr*: ~**rsi** (**in**) to become involved (in); **implica-zi'one** *sf* implication

im'plicito, a [im'plitʃito] *ag* implicit

implo'rare *vt* to implore; (*pietà etc*) to beg for

impolve'rare *vt* to cover with dust; ~**rsi** *vr* to get dusty

impo'nente *ag* imposing, impressive

impo'nibile *ag* taxable ♦ *sm* taxable income

impopo'lare *ag* unpopular

im'porre *vt* to impose; (*costringere*) to force, make; (*far valere*) to impose, enforce; **imporsi** *vr* (*persona*) to assert o.s.; (*cosa: rendersi necessario*) to become necessary; (*aver successo: moda, attore*) to become popular; ~ **a qn di fare** to force sb to do, make sb do

impor'tante *ag* important; **impor-'tanza** *sf* importance; **dare impor-tanza a qc** to attach importance to sth; **darsi importanza** to give o.s. airs

impor'tare *vt* (*introdurre dall'e-*

stero) to import ♦ *vi* to matter, be important ♦ *vb impers* (*essere necessario*) to be necessary; (*interessare*) to matter; **non importa!** it doesn't matter!; **non me ne importa!** I don't care!; **importazi'one** *sf* importation; (*merci importate*) imports *pl*

im'porto *sm* (*total*) amount

importu'nare *vt* to bother

impor'tuno, a *ag* irksome, annoying

imposizi'one [impozit'tsjone] *sf* imposition; order, command; (*onere, imposta*) tax

imposses'sarsi *vr*: ~ **di** to seize, take possession of

impos'sibile *ag* impossible; **fare l'~** to do one's utmost, do all one can; **impossibilità** *sf* impossibility; **essere nell'impossibilità di fare qc** to be unable to do sth

im'posta *sf* (*di finestra*) shutter; (*tassa*) tax; ~ **sul reddito** income tax; ~ **sul valore aggiunto** value added tax (*BRIT*), sales tax (*US*)

impos'tare *vt* (*imbucare*) to post; (*preparare*) to plan, set out; (*avviare*) to begin, start off; (*voce*) to pitch

im'posto, a *pp di* **imporre**

impo'tente *ag* weak, powerless; (*anche MED*) impotent

impove'rire *vt* to impoverish ♦ *vi* (*anche*: ~**rsi**) to become poor

imprati'cabile *ag* (*strada*) impassable; (*campo da gioco*) unplayable

imprati'chire [imprati'kire] *vt* to train; ~**rsi** **in qc** to practise (*BRIT*) o practice (*US*) sth

impre'gnare [impreɲ'ɲare] *vt*: ~ (**di**) (*imbevere*) to soak o impregnate (with); (*riempire: anche fig*) to fill (with)

imprendi'tore *sm* (*industriale*) entrepreneur; (*appaltatore*) contractor; **piccolo** ~ small businessman

im'presa *sf* (*iniziativa*) enterprise; (*azione*) exploit; (*azienda*) firm, concern

impre'sario sm (TEATRO) manager, impresario; ~ di pompe funebri funeral director

imprescin'dibile [impreʃʃin'dibile] ag not to be ignored

impressio'nante ag impressive; upsetting

impressio'nare vt to impress; (turbare) to upset; (FOT) to expose; ~rsi vr to be easily upset

impressi'one sf impression; (fig: sensazione) sensation, feeling; (stampa) printing; fare ~ (colpire) to impress; (turbare) to frighten, upset; fare buona/cattiva ~ a to make a good/bad impression on

im'presso, a pp di **imprimere**

impres'tare vt: ~ qc a qn to lend sth to sb

impreve'dibile ag unforeseeable; (persona) unpredictable

imprevi'dente ag lacking in foresight

impre'visto, a ag unexpected, unforeseen ♦ sm unforeseen event; salvo ~i unless anything unexpected happens

imprigio'nare [impridʒo'nare] vt to imprison

im'primere vt (anche fig) to impress, stamp; (comunicare: movimento) to transmit, give

impro'babile ag improbable, unlikely

im'pronta sf imprint, impression, sign; (di piede, mano) print; (fig) mark, stamp; ~ digitale fingerprint

impro'perio sm insult

im'proprio, a ag improper; arma ~a offensive weapon

improvvisa'mente av suddenly, unexpectedly

improvvi'sare vt to improvise; ~rsi vr: ~rsi cuoco to (decide to) act as cook; **improvvi'sata** sf (pleasant) surprise

improv'viso, a ag (improvviso) unexpected; (subitaneo) sudden; all'~ unexpectedly; suddenly

impru'dente ag unwise, rash

impu'dente ag impudent

impu'dico, a, chi, che ag immodest

impu'gnare [impuɲ'ɲare] vt to grasp, grip; (DIR) to contest

impul'sivo, a ag impulsive

im'pulso sm impulse

impun'tarsi vr to stop dead, refuse to budge; (fig) to be obstinate

impu'tare vt (ascrivere): ~ qc a to attribute sth to; (DIR: accusare): ~ qn di to charge sb with, accuse sb of; **impu'tato, a** sm/f (DIR) accused, defendant; **imputazi'one** sf (DIR) charge

imputri'dire vi to rot

in (in+il = **nel**, in+lo = **nello**, in+l' = **nell'**, in+la = **nella**, in+i = **nei**, in+gli = **negli**, in+le = **nelle**) prep **1** (stato in luogo): in; vivere ~ Italia/città to live in Italy/town; essere ~ casa/ufficio to be at home/the office; se fossi ~ te if I were you

2 (moto a luogo): to; (: dentro) into; andare ~ Germania/città to go to Germany/town; andare ~ ufficio to go to the office; entrare ~ macchina/casa to get into the car/go into the house

3 (tempo): in; nel 1989 in 1989; ~ giugno/estate in June/summer

4 (modo, maniera) in; ~ silenzio in silence; ~ abito da sera in evening dress; ~ guerra at war; ~ vacanza on holiday; Maria Bianchi ~ Rossi Maria Rossi née Bianchi

5 (mezzo) by; viaggiare ~ autobus/treno to travel by bus/train

6 (materia) made of; ~ marmo made of marble, marble cpd; una collana ~ oro a gold necklace

7 (misura) in; siamo ~ quattro there are four of us; ~ tutto in all

8 (fine): dare ~ dono to give as a gift; spende tutto ~ alcool he spends all his money on drink; ~ onore di in honour of

inabi'tabile *ag* uninhabitable

inacces'sibile [inattʃes'sibile] *ag* (*luogo*) inaccessible; (*persona*) unapproachable; (*mistero*) unfathomable

inaccet'tabile [inattʃet'tabile] *ag* unacceptable

ina'datto, a *ag*: ~ (a) unsuitable *o* unfit (for)

inadegu'ato, a *ag* inadequate

inadempi'enza [inadem'pjɛntsa] *sf*: ~ (a) non-fulfilment (of)

inaffer'rabile *ag* elusive; (*concetto, senso*) difficult to grasp

ina'lare *vt* to inhale

inalbe'rare *vt* (*NAUT*) to hoist, raise; ~**rsi** *vr* (*fig*) to flare up, fly off the handle

inalte'rabile *ag* unchangeable; (*colore*) fast, permanent; (*affetto*) constant

inalte'rato, a *ag* unchanged

inami'dato, a *ag* starched

inani'mato, a *ag* inanimate; (*senza vita: corpo*) lifeless

inappa'gabile *ag* insatiable

inappel'labile *ag* (*decisione*) final, irrevocable; (*DIR*) final, not open to appeal

inappe'tenza [inappe'tɛntsa] *sf* (*MED*) lack of appetite

inappun'tabile *ag* irreproachable

inar'care *vt* (*schiena*) to arch; (*sopracciglia*) to raise; ~**rsi** *vr* to arch

inari'dire *vt* to make arid, dry up ♦ *vi* (*anche*: ~**rsi**) to dry up, become arid

inaspet'tato, a *ag* unexpected

inas'prire *vt* (*disciplina*) to tighten up, make harsher; (*carattere*) to embitter; ~**rsi** *vr* to become harsher; to become bitter; to become worse

inattac'cabile *ag* (*anche fig*) unassailable; (*alibi*) cast-iron

inatten'dibile *ag* unreliable

inat'teso, a *ag* unexpected

inatu'abile *ag* impracticable

inau'dito, a *ag* unheard of

inaugu'rare *vt* to inaugurate, open; (*monumento*) to unveil

inavve'duto, a *ag* careless, inad-

vertent

inavver'tenza [inavver'tɛntsa] *sf* carelessness, inadvertence

incagli'are [inkaʎ'ʎare] *vi* (*NAUT: anche*: ~**rsi**) to run aground

incal'lito, a *ag* calloused; (*fig*) hardened, inveterate; (: *insensibile*) hard

incal'zare [inkal'tsare] *vt* to follow *o* pursue closely; (*fig*) to press ♦ *vi* (*urgere*) to be pressing; (*essere imminente*) to be imminent

incame'rare *vt* (*DIR*) to expropriate

incammi'nare *vt* (*fig: avviare*) to start up; ~**rsi** *vr* to set off

incande'scente [inkandeʃ'ʃɛnte] *ag* incandescent, white-hot

incan'tare *vt* to enchant, bewitch; ~**rsi** *vr* (*rimanere intontito*) to be spellbound; to be in a daze; (*meccanismo: bloccarsi*) to jam; **incanta'tore, 'trice** *ag* enchanting, bewitching ♦ *smf* enchanter/enchantress; **incan'tesimo** *sm* spell, charm; **incan'tevole** *ag* charming, enchanting

in'canto *sm* spell, charm, enchantment; (*asta*) auction; **come per** ~ as if by magic; **mettere all'**~ to put up for auction

incanu'tire *vi* to go white

inca'pace [inka'patʃe] *ag* incapable; **incapacità** *sf* inability; (*DIR*) incapacity

incapo'nirsi *vr* to be stubborn, be determined

incap'pare *vi*: ~ **in qc/qn** (*anche fig*) to run into sth/sb

incapricci'arsi [inkaprit'tʃarsi] *vr*: ~ **di** to take a fancy to *o* for

incapsu'lare *vt* (*dente*) to crown

incarce'rare [inkartʃe'rare] *vt* to imprison

incari'care *vt*: ~ **qn di fare** to give sb the responsibility of doing; ~**rsi di** to take care *o* charge of; **inca-ri'cato, a** *ag*: **incaricato (di) in** charge (of), responsible (for) ♦ *smf* delegate, representative; **professore incaricato** *teacher with a temporary* appointment; **incaricato d'affari** (*POL*) chargé d'affaires

in'carico, chi *sm* task, job

incar'nare *vt* to embody; **~rsi** *vr* to be embodied; (*REL*) to become incarnate

incarta'mento *sm* dossier, file

incar'tare *vt* to wrap (in paper)

incas'sare *vt* (*merce*) to pack (in cases); (*gemma: incastonare*) to set; (*ECON: riscuotere*) to collect; (*PUGILATO: colpi*) to take, stand up to; **in'casso** *sm* cashing, encashment; (*introito*) takings *pl*

incasto'nare *vt* to set; **incastona'tura** *sf* setting

incas'trare *vt* to fit in, insert; (*fig: intrappolare*) to catch; **~rsi** *vr* (*combaciare*) to fit together; (*restare bloccato*) to become stuck; **in'castro** *sm* slot, groove; (*punto di unione*) joint

incate'nare *vt* to chain up

incatra'mare *vt* to tar

incatti'vire *vt* to make wicked; **~rsi** *vr* to turn nasty

in'cauto, a *ag* imprudent, rash

inca'vare *vt* to hollow out; **in'cavo** *sm* hollow; (*solco*) groove

incendi'are [intʃen'djare] *vt* to set fire to; **~rsi** *vr* to catch fire, burst into flames

incendi'ario, a [intʃen'djarjo] *ag* incendiary ♦ *sm/f* arsonist

in'cendio [in'tʃendjo] *sm* fire

incene'rire [intʃene'rire] *vt* to burn to ashes, incinerate; (*cadavere*) to cremate; **~rsi** *vr* to be burnt to ashes

in'censo [in'tʃenso] *sm* incense

incensu'rato, a [intʃensu'rato] *ag* (*DIR*): **essere ~** to have a clean record

incen'tivo [intʃen'tivo] *sm* incentive

incep'pare [intʃep'pare] *vt* to obstruct, hamper; **~rsi** *vr* to jam

ince'rata [intʃe'rata] *sf* (*tela*) tarpaulin; (*impermeabile*) oilskins *pl*

incer'tezza [intʃer'tettsa] *sf* uncertainty

in'certo, a [in'tʃerto] *ag* uncertain;

(*irresoluto*) undecided, hesitating ♦ *sm* uncertainty

in'cetta [in'tʃetta] *sf* buying up; **fare ~ di qc** to buy up sth

inchi'esta [in'kjɛsta] *sf* investigation, inquiry

inchi'nare [inki'nare] *vt* to bow; **~rsi** *vr* to bend down; (*per riverenza*) to bow; (*: donna*) to curtsy; **in'chino** *sm* bow; curtsy

inchio'dare [inkjo'dare] *vt* to nail (down); **~ la macchina** (*AUT*) to jam on the brakes

inchi'ostro [in'kjɔstro] *sm* ink; **~ simpatico** invisible ink

inciam'pare [intʃam'pare] *vi* to trip, stumble

inci'ampo [in'tʃampo] *sm* obstacle; **essere d'~ a qn** (*fig*) to be in sb's way

inci'dente [intʃi'dente] *sm* accident; **~ d'auto** car accident

inci'denza [intʃi'dentsa] *sf* incidence; **avere una forte ~ su qc** to affect sth greatly

in'cidere [in'tʃidere] *vi*: **~ su** to bear upon, affect ♦ *vt* (*tagliare incavando*) to cut into; (*ARTE*) to engrave; to etch; (*canzone*) to record

in'cinta [in'tʃinta] *ag f* pregnant

incipri'are [intʃi'prjare] *vt* to powder

in'circa [in'tʃirka] *av*: **all'~** more or less, very nearly

incisi'one [intʃi'zjone] *sf* cut; (*disegno*) engraving; etching; (*registrazione*) recording; (*MED*) incision

in'ciso, a [in'tʃizo] *pp di* **incidere**; **per ~** incidentally, by the way

inci'tare [intʃi'tare] *vt* to incite

inci'vile [intʃi'vile] *ag* uncivilized; (*villano*) impolite

incivi'lire [intʃivi'lire] *vt* to civilize

incl. *abbr* (= *incluso*) encl.

incli'nare *vt* to tilt ♦ *vi* (*fig*): **~ a qc/a fare** to incline towards sth/ doing; to tend towards sth/to do; **~rsi** *vr* (*barca*) to list; (*aereo*) to bank; **incli'nato, a** *ag* sloping; **in-**

clinazi'one sf slope; (fig) inclination, tendency; **in'cline** ag: incline a inclined to

in'cludere vt to include; (accludere) to enclose; **in'cluso, a** pp di **includere** ♦ ag included; enclosed

incoe'rente ag incoherent; (contraddittorio) inconsistent

in'cognita [in'kɔɲɲita] sf (MAT, fig) unknown quantity

in'cognito, a [in'kɔɲɲito] ag unknown ♦ sm: **in** ~ incognito

incol'lare vt to glue, gum; (unire con colla) to stick together

incolon'nare vt to draw up in columns

inco'lore ag colourless

incol'pare vt: ~ **qn di** to charge sb with

in'colto, a ag (terreno) uncultivated; (trascurato: capelli) neglected; (persona) uneducated

in'colume ag safe and sound, unhurt

incom'benza [inkom'bentsa] sf duty, task

in'combere vi (sovrastare minacciando): ~ **su** to threaten, hang over

incomin'ciare [inkomin'tʃare] vi, vt to begin, start

in'comodo, a ag uncomfortable; (inopportuno) inconvenient ♦ sm inconvenience, bother

incompe'tente ag incompetent

incompi'uto, a ag unfinished, incomplete

incom'pleto, a ag incomplete

incompren'sibile ag incomprehensible

incom'preso, a ag not understood; misunderstood

inconce'pibile [inkontʃe'pibile] ag inconceivable

inconcili'abile [inkontʃi'ljabile] ag irreconcilable

inconclu'dente ag inconclusive; (persona) ineffectual

incondizio'nato, a [inkondittsjo'nato] ag unconditional

inconfu'tabile ag irrefutable

incongru'ente ag inconsistent

inconsa'pevole ag: ~ **di** unaware of, ignorant of

in'conscio, a, sci, sce [in'kɔnʃo] ag unconscious ♦ sm (PSIC): **l'**~ the unconscious

inconsis'tente ag insubstantial; unfounded

inconsu'eto, a ag unusual

incon'sulto, a ag rash

incon'trare vt to meet; (difficoltà) to meet with; ~**rsi** vr to meet

incontras'tabile ag incontrovertible, indisputable

in'contro av: ~ **a** (verso) towards ♦ sm meeting; (SPORT) match; meeting; ~ **di calcio** football match

inconveni'ente sm drawback, snag

incoraggia'mento [inkoraddʒa'mento] sm encouragement

incoraggi'are [inkorad'dʒare] vt to encourage

incornici'are [inkorni'tʃare] vt to frame

incoro'nare vt to crown; **incorona-zi'one** sf coronation

incorpo'rare vt to incorporate; (fig: annettere) to annex

in'correre vi: ~ **in** to meet with, run into

incosci'ente [inkoʃ'ʃente] ag (inconscio) unconscious; (irresponsabile) reckless, thoughtless; **incosci'enza** sf unconsciousness; recklessness, thoughtlessness

incre'dibile ag incredible, unbelievable

in'credulo, a ag incredulous, disbelieving

incremen'tare vt to increase; (dar sviluppo a) to promote

incre'mento sm (sviluppo) development; (aumento numerico) increase, growth

incresci'oso, a [inkreʃ'ʃoso] ag (incidente etc) regrettable

incres'parsi vr (acqua) to ripple; (capelli) to go frizzy; (pelle, tessuto) to wrinkle

incrimi'nare vt (DIR) to charge

incri'nare vt to crack; (fig: rapporti,

amicizia) to cause to deteriorate; **~rsi** *vr* to crack; to deteriorate; **incrina'tura** *sf* crack; (*fig*) rift

incroci'are [iŋkro'tʃare] *vt* to cross; (*incontrare*) to meet ♦ *vi* (NAUT, AER) to cruise; **~rsi** *vr* (*strade*) to cross, intersect; (*persone, veicoli*) to pass each other; ~ **le braccia/le gambe** to fold one's arms/cross one's legs; **incrocia'tore** *sm* cruiser

in'crocio [iŋ'krotʃo] *sm* (*anche* FERR) crossing; (*di strade*) crossroads

incros'tare *vt* to encrust

incuba'trice [iŋkuba'tritʃe] *sf* incubator

'incubo *sm* nightmare

in'cudine *sf* anvil

incu'rante *ag*: ~ (**di**) heedless (of), careless (of)

incurio'sire *vt* to make curious; **~rsi** *vr* to become curious

incursi'one *sf* raid

incur'vare *vt* to bend, curve; **~rsi** *vr* to bend, curve

in'cusso, a *pp di* **incutere**

incus'todito, a *ag* unguarded, unattended

in'cutere *vt* to arouse; ~ **timore/ rispetto a qn** to strike fear into sb/ command sb's respect

'indaco *sm* indigo

indaffa'rato, a *ag* busy

inda'gare *vt* to investigate

in'dagine [in'dadʒine] *sf* investigation, inquiry; (*ricerca*) research, study

indebi'tarsi *vr* to run *o* get into debt

in'debito, a *ag* undue; undeserved

indebo'lire *vt, vi* (*anche*: **~rsi**) to weaken

inde'cente [inde'tʃɛnte] *ag* indecent; **inde'cenza** [inde'tʃɛntsa] *sf* indecency

inde'ciso, a [inde'tʃizo] *ag* indecisive; (*irrisoluto*) undecided

inde'fesso, a *ag* untiring, indefatigable

indefi'nito, a *ag* (*anche* LING) indefinite; (*impreciso, non determinato*) undefined

in'degno, a [in'deɲɲo] *ag* (*atto*) shameful; (*persona*) unworthy

indeli'catezza [indelika'tettsa] *sf* tactlessness

indemoni'ato, a *ag* possessed (by the devil)

in'denne *ag* unhurt, uninjured; **indennità** *sf inv* (*rimborso: di spese*) allowance; (: *di perdita*) compensation, indemnity; **indennità di contingenza** cost-of-living allowance; **indennità di trasferta** travel expenses *pl*

indenniz'zare [indennid'dzare] *vt* to compensate; **inden'nizzo** *sm* (*somma*) compensation, indemnity

indero'gabile *ag* binding

'India *sf*: l'~ India; **indi'ano, a** *ag* Indian ♦ *sm/f* (*d'India*) Indian; (*d'America*) Red Indian

indiavo'lato, a *ag* possessed (by the devil); (*vivace, violento*) wild

indi'care *vt* (*mostrare*) to show, indicate; (: *col dito*) to point to, point out; (*consigliare*) to suggest, recommend; **indica'tivo, a** *ag* indicative ♦ *sm* (LING) indicative (mood); **indica'tore** *sm* (*elenco*) guide; directory; (TECN) gauge; indicator; **cartello indicatore** sign; **indicatore di velocità** (AUT) speedometer; **indicatore della benzina** fuel gauge; **indicazi'one** *sf* indication; (*informazione*) piece of information

'indice [indiʃe] *sm* (ANAT: *dito*) index finger, forefinger; (*lancetta*) needle, pointer; (*fig: indizio*) sign; (TECN, MAT, *nei libri*) index; ~ **di gradimento** (RADIO, TV) popularity rating

indi'cibile [indi'tʃibile] *ag* inexpressible

indietreggi'are [indietred'dʒare] *vi* to draw back, retreat

indi'etro *av* back; (*guardare*) behind, back; (*andare, cadere: anche*: *all'~*) backwards; **rimanere** ~ to be left behind; **essere** ~ (*col lavoro*) to be behind; (*orologio*) to be slow; **rimandare qc** ~ to send sth back

indi'feso, a *ag* (*città etc*) undefended; (*persona*) defenceless

indiffe'rente *ag* indifferent; **indiffe'renza** *sf* indifference

in'digeno, a [in'didʒeno] *ag* indigenous, native ♦ *smlf* native

indi'gente [indi'dʒɛnte] *ag* poverty-stricken, destitute; **indi'genza** *sf* extreme poverty

indigesti'one [indidʒes'tjone] *sf* indigestion

indi'gesto, a [indi'dʒesto] *ag* indigestible

indi'gnare [indin'nare] *vt* to fill with indignation; **~rsi** *vr* to be (o get) indignant

indimenti'cabile *ag* unforgettable

indipen'dente *ag* independent; **indipen'denza** *sf* independence

in'dire *vt* (*concorso*) to announce; (*elezioni*) to call

indi'retto, a *ag* indirect

indiriz'zare [indirit'tsare] *vt* (*dirigere*) to direct; (*mandare*) to send; (*lettera*) to address

indi'rizzo [indi'rittso] *sm* address; (*direzione*) direction; (*avvio*) trend, course

indis'creto, a *ag* indiscreet

indis'cusso, a *ag* unquestioned

indispen'sabile *ag* indispensable, essential

indispet'tire *vt* to irritate, annoy ♦ *vi* (*anche*: **~rsi**) to get irritated o annoyed

in'divia *sf* endive

individu'ale *ag* individual; **individualità** *sf* individuality

individu'are *vt* (*dar forma distinta a*) to characterize; (*determinare*) to locate; (*riconoscere*) to single out

indi'viduo *sm* individual

indizi'are [indit'tsjare] *vt*: **~ qn di qc** to cast suspicion on sb for sth; **indizi'ato, a** *ag* suspected ♦ *smlf* suspect

in'dizio [in'dittsjo] *sm* (*segno*) sign, indication; (*POLIZIA*) clue; (*DIR*) piece of evidence

'indole *sf* nature, character

indolen'zito, a [indolen'tsito] *ag* stiff, aching; (*intorpidito*) numb

indo'lore *ag* painless

indo'mani *sm*: **l'~** the next day, the following day

Indo'nesia *sf*: **l'~** Indonesia

indos'sare *vt* (*mettere indosso*) to put on; (*avere indosso*) to have on; **indossa'tore, 'trice** *smlf* model

in'dotto, a *pp di* indurre

indottri'nare *vt* to indoctrinate

indovi'nare *vt* (*scoprire*) to guess; (*immaginare*) to imagine, guess; (*il futuro*) to foretell; **indovi'nato, a** *ag* successful; (*scelta*) inspired; **indovi'nello** *sm* riddle; **indovi'no, a** *smlf* fortuneteller

indubbia'mente *av* undoubtedly

in'dubbio, a *ag* certain, undoubted

indugi'are [indu'dʒare] *vi* to take one's time, delay

in'dugio [in'dudʒo] *sm* (*ritardo*) delay; **senza ~** without delay

indul'gente [indul'dʒɛnte] *ag* indulgent; (*giudice*) lenient; **indul'genza** *sf* indulgence; leniency

in'dulgere [in'duldʒere] *vi*: **~ a** (*accondiscendere*) to comply with; (*abbandonarsi*) to indulge in; **in'dulto, a** *pp di* indulgere ♦ *sm* (*DIR*) pardon

indu'mento *sm* article of clothing, garment; **~i** *smpl* (*vestiti*) clothes

indu'rire *vt* to harden ♦ *vi* (*anche*: **~rsi**) to harden, become hard

in'durre *vt*: **~ qn a fare qc** to induce o persuade sb to do sth; **~ qn in errore** to mislead sb

in'dustria *sf* industry; **industri'ale** *ag* industrial ♦ *sm* industrialist

industri'arsi *vr* to do one's best, try hard

industri'oso, a *ag* industrious, hard-working

induzi'one [indut'tsjone] *sf* induction

inebe'tito, a *ag* dazed, stunned

inebri'are *vt* (*anche fig*) to intoxicate; **~rsi** *vr* to become intoxicated

inecce'pibile [inettʃe'pibile] *ag* unexceptionable

i'nedia *sf* starvation

i'nedito, a *ag* unpublished

ineffi'cace [ineffi'katʃe] *ag* ineffective

ineffici'ente [ineffi'tʃɛnte] *ag* inefficient

inegu'ale *ag* unequal; (*irregolare*) uneven

ine'rente *ag*: ~ a concerning, regarding

i'nerme *ag* unarmed; defenceless

inerpi'carsi *vr*: ~ (**su**) to clamber (up)

i'nerte *ag* inert; (*inattivo*) indolent, sluggish; i'nerzia *sf* inertia; indolence, sluggishness

ine'satto, a *ag* (*impreciso*) inexact; (*erroneo*) incorrect; (*AMM: non riscosso*) uncollected

inesis'tente *ag* non-existent

inesperi'enza [inespe'rjɛntsa] *sf* inexperience

ines'perto, a *ag* inexperienced

i'netto, a *ag* (*incapace*) inept; (*che non ha attitudine*): ~ (**a**) unsuited (to)

ine'vaso, a *ag* (*ordine, corrispondenza*) outstanding

inevi'tabile *ag* inevitable

i'nezia [i'nɛttsja] *sf* trifle, thing of no importance

infagot'tare *vt* to bundle up, wrap up; ~**rsi** *vr* to wrap up

infal'libile *ag* infallible

infa'mare *vt* to defame

in'fame *ag* infamous; (*fig: cosa, compito*) awful, dreadful

infan'gare *vt* to cover with mud; (*fig: reputazione*) to sully

infan'tile *ag* child *cpd*; childlike; (*adulto, azione*) childish; letteratura ~ children's books *pl*

in'fanzia [in'fantsja] *sf* childhood; (*bambini*) children *pl*; prima ~ babyhood, infancy

infari'nare *vt* to cover with (*o* sprinkle with *o* dip in) flour; ~ **di** zucchero to sprinkle with sugar; infari'natura *sf* (*fig*) smattering

in'farto *sm* (*MED*): ~ (**cardiaco**)

coronary

infasti'dire *vt* to annoy, irritate; ~**rsi** *vr* to get annoyed *o* irritated

infati'cabile *ag* tireless, untiring

in'fatti *cong* as a matter of fact, in fact, actually

infatu'arsi *vr*: ~ **di** *o* **per** to become infatuated with, fall for; infatu'azi'one *sf* infatuation

in'fausto, a *ag* unpropitious, unfavourable

infe'condo, a *ag* infertile

infe'dele *ag* unfaithful; infedeltà *sf* infidelity

infe'lice [infe'litʃe] *ag* unhappy; (*sfortunato*) unlucky, unfortunate; (*inopportuno*) inopportune, ill-timed; (*mal riuscito: lavoro*) bad, poor; infelicità *sf* unhappiness

inferi'ore *ag* lower; (*per intelligenza, qualità*) inferior ♦ *smf* inferior; ~ a (*numero, quantità*) less *o* smaller than; (*meno buono*) inferior to; ~ alla media below average; inferiorità *sf* inferiority

inferme'ria *sf* infirmary; (*di scuola, nave*) sick bay

infermi'ere, a *smf* nurse

infermità *sf inv* illness; infirmity

in'fermo, a *ag* (*ammalato*) ill; (*debole*) infirm

infer'nale *ag* infernal; (*proposito, complotto*) diabolical

in'ferno *sm* hell

inferri'ata *sf* grating

infervo'rare *vt* to arouse enthusiasm in; ~**rsi** *vr* to get excited, get carried away

infes'tare *vt* to infest

infet'tare *vt* to infect; ~**rsi** *vr* to become infected; infet'tivo, a *ag* infectious; in'fetto, a *ag* infected; (*acque*) polluted, contaminated; infezi'one *sf* infection

infiac'chire [infjak'kire] *vt* to weaken ♦ *vi* (*anche*: ~**rsi**) to grow weak

infiam'mabile *ag* inflammable

infiam'mare *vt* to set alight; (*fig, MED*) to inflame; ~**rsi** *vr* to catch fire; (*MED*) to become inflamed;

(*fig*): ~**rsi di** to be fired with; **infiammazi'one** *sf* (*MED*) inflammation

in'**fido, a** *ag* unreliable, treacherous

infie'rire *vi*: ~ **su** (*fisicamente*) to attack furiously; (*verbalmente*) to rage at; (*epidemia*) to rage over

in'**figgere** [in'fiddʒere] *vt*: ~ **qc in** to thrust *o* drive sth into

infi'**lare** *vt* (*ago*) to thread; (*mettere: chiave*) to insert; (: *anello, vestito*) to slip *o* put on; (*strada*) to turn into, take; ~**rsi** *vr*: ~**rsi in** to slip into; (*indossare*) to slip on; ~ **l'uscio** to slip in; to slip out

infil'**trarsi** *vr* to penetrate, seep through; (*MIL*) to infiltrate; **infiltrazi'one** *sf* infiltration

infil'**zare** [infil'tsare] *vt* (*infilare*) to string together; (*trafiggere*) to pierce

in'**fimo, a** *ag* lowest

in'**fine** *av* finally; (*insomma*) in short

infi**nità** *sf* infinity; (*in quantità*): un'~ **di** an infinite number of

infi**ni'to, a** *ag* infinite; (*LING*) infinitive ♦ *sm* infinity; (*LING*) infinitive; **all'**~ (*senza fine*) endlessly

infinocchi'**are** [infinok'kjare] (*fam*) *vt* to hoodwink

infischi'**arsi** [infis'kjarsi] *vr*: ~ **di** not to care about

in'**fisso, a** *pp di* **infiggere** ♦ *sm* fixture; (*di porta, finestra*) frame

infit'**tire** *vt, vi* (*anche*: ~**rsi**) to thicken

inflazi'**one** [inflat'tsjone] *sf* inflation

in'**fliggere** [in'fliddʒere] *vt* to inflict; **in'flitto, a** *pp di* **infliggere**

influ'**ente** *ag* influential; **influ'enza** *sf* influence; (*MED*) influenza, flu

influ'**ire** *vi*: ~ **su** to influence

in'**flusso** *sm* influence

infol'**tire** *vt, vi* to thicken

infon'**dato, a** *ag* unfounded, groundless

in'**fondere** *vt*: ~ **qc in qn** to instill sth in sb

infor'**care** *vt* to fork (up); (*bicicletta, cavallo*) to get on; (*occhiali*) to put on

infor'**mare** *vt* to inform, tell; ~**rsi** *vr*: ~**rsi** (**di** *o* **su**) to inquire (about)

infor'**matica** *sf* computer science

informa'**tivo, a** *ag* informative

informa'**tore** *sm* informer

informazi'**one** [informat'tsjone] *sf* piece of information; **prendere** ~**i sul conto di qn** to get information about sb; **chiedere un'**~ to ask for (some) information

in'**forme** *ag* shapeless

informico'**larsi** *vr* = **informicolirsi**

informico'**lirsi** *vr* to have pins or needles

infor'**tunio** *sm* accident; ~ **sul lavoro** industrial accident, accident at work

infos'**sarsi** *vr* (*terreno*) to sink; (*guance*) to become hollow; **infos'sato, a** *ag* hollow; (*occhi*) deepset; (: *per malattia*) sunken

in'**frangere** [in'frandʒere] *vt* to smash; (*fig: legge, patti*) to break; ~**rsi** *vr* to smash, break; **infran'gibile** *ag* unbreakable; **in'franto, a** *pp di* **infrangere** ♦ *ag* broken

infrazi'**one** [infrat'tsjone] *sf*: ~ **a** breaking of, violation of

infredda'**tura** *sf* slight cold

infred'**dolito, a** *ag* cold, chilled

infruttu'**oso, a** *ag* fruitless

infu'**ori** *av* out; **all'**~ outwards; **all'**~ **di** (*eccetto*) except, with the exception of

infuri'**are** *vi* to rage; ~**rsi** *vr* to fly into a rage

infusi'**one** *sf* infusion

in'**fuso, a** *pp di* **infondere** ♦ *sm* infusion

Ing. *abbr* = **ingegnere**

ingabbi'**are** *vt* to cage

ingaggi'**are** [ingad'dʒare] *vt* (*assumere con compenso*) to take on, hire; (*SPORT*) to sign on; (*MIL*) to engage; **in'gaggio** *sm* hiring; signing on

ingan'**nare** *vt* to deceive; (*coniuge*) to be unfaithful to; (*fisco*) to cheat; (*eludere*) to dodge, elude; (*fig: tem-*

po) to while away ♦ *vi* (*apparenza*) to be deceptive; ~**rsi** *vr* to be mistaken, be wrong; **ingan'nevole** *ag* deceptive

in'ganno *sm* deceit, deception; (*azione*) trick; (*menzogna*, *frode*) cheat, swindle; (*illusione*) illusion

ingarbugli'are [ingarbuʎ'ʎare] *vt* to tangle; (*fig*) to confuse, muddle; ~**rsi** *vr* to become confused *o* muddled

inge'gnarsi [indʒeɲ'narsi] *vr* to do one's best, try hard; ~ **per vivere** to scrape a living by one's wits

inge'gnere [indʒeɲ'nɛre] *sm* engineer; ~ **civile/navale** civil/naval engineer; **ingegne'ria** *sf* engineering; ~ **genetica** genetic engineering

in'gegno [in'dʒeɲɲo] *sm* (*intelligenza*) intelligence, brains *pl*; (*capacità creativa*) ingenuity; (*disposizione*) talent; **inge'gnoso, a** *ag* ingenious, clever

ingelo'sire [indʒelo'zire] *vt* to make jealous ♦ *vi* (*anche*: ~**rsi**) to become jealous

in'gente [in'dʒɛnte] *ag* huge, enormous

ingenuità [indʒenui'ta] *sf* ingenuousness

in'genuo, a [in'dʒɛnuo] *ag* ingenuous, naïve

inge'rire [indʒe'rire] *vt* to ingest

inges'sare [indʒes'sare] *vt* (*MED*) to put in plaster; **ingessa'tura** *sf* plaster

Inghil'terra [ingil'tɛrra] *sf*: **l'~** England

inghiot'tire [ingjot'tire] *vt* to swallow

ingial'lire [indʒal'lire] *vi* to go yellow

ingigan'tire [indʒigan'tire] *vt* to enlarge, magnify ♦ *vi* to become gigantic *o* enormous

inginocchi'arsi [indʒinok'kjarsi] *vr* to kneel (down)

ingiù [in'dʒu] *av* down, downwards

ingiunzi'one [indʒun'tsjone] *sf* injunction

ingi'uria [in'dʒurja] *sf* insult; (*fig*:

danno) damage; **ingiuri'are** *vt* to insult, abuse; **ingiuri'oso, a** *ag* insulting, abusive

ingius'tizia [indʒus'tittsja] *sf* injustice

ingi'usto, a [in'dʒusto] *ag* unjust, unfair

in'glese *ag* English ♦ *sm/f* Englishman/woman ♦ *sm* (*LING*) English; **gli I~i** the English; **andarsene** *o* **filare all'~** to take French leave

ingoi'are *vt* to gulp (down); (*fig*) to swallow (up)

ingol'fare *vt* (*motore*) to flood; ~**rsi** *vr* to flood

ingom'brare *vt* (*strada*) to block; (*stanza*) to clutter up; **in'gombro, a** *ag* (*strada*, *passaggio*) blocked ♦ *sm* obstacle; **essere d'ingombro** to be in the way

in'gordo, a *ag*: ~ **di** greedy for; (*fig*) greedy *o* avid for

in'gorgo, ghi *sm* blockage, obstruction; (*anche*: ~ **stradale**) traffic jam

ingoz'zare [ingot'tsare] *vt* (*animali*) to fatten; (*fig*: *persona*) to stuff; ~**rsi** *vr*: ~**rsi (di)** to stuff o.s. (with)

ingra'naggio [ingra'naddʒo] *sm* (*TECN*) gear; (*di orologio*) mechanism; **gli ~i della burocrazia** the bureaucratic machinery

ingra'nare *vi* to mesh, engage ♦ *vt* to engage; ~ **la marcia** to get into gear

ingrandi'mento *sm* enlargement; extension

ingran'dire *vt* (*anche FOT*) to enlarge; (*estendere*) to extend; (*OTTICA*, *fig*) to magnify ♦ *vi* (*anche*: ~**rsi**) to become larger *o* bigger; (*aumentare*) to grow, increase; (*espandersi*) to expand

ingras'sare *vt* to make fat; (*animali*) to fatten; (*AGR*: *terreno*) to manure; (*lubrificare*) to oil, lubricate ♦ *vi* (*anche*: ~**rsi**) to get fat, put on weight

in'grato, a *ag* ungrateful; (*lavoro*

thankless, unrewarding

ingredi'ente sm ingredient

in'gresso sm (porta) entrance; (atrio) hall; (l'entrare) entrance, entry; (facoltà di entrare) admission; "~ libero" "admission free"

ingros'sare vt to increase; (folla, livello) to swell ♦ vi (anche: ~rsi) to increase; to swell

in'grosso av: all'~ (COMM) wholesale; (all'incirca) roughly, about

ingual'cibile [ingwal'tʃibile] ag crease-resistant

ingua'ribile ag incurable

'inguine sm (ANAT) groin

ini'bire vt to forbid, prohibit; (PSIC) to inhibit; **inibizi'one** sf prohibition, inhibition

iniet'tare vt to inject; ~rsi vr: ~rsi di sangue (occhi) to become bloodshot; **iniezi'one** sf injection

inimi'carsi vr: ~ con qn to fall out with sb

inimi'cizia [inimi'tʃittsja] sf animosity

ininter'rotto, a ag unbroken; uninterrupted

iniquità sf inv iniquity; (atto) wicked action

inizi'ale [init'tsjale] ag, sf initial

inizi'are [init'tsjare] vi, vt to begin, start; ~ qn to initiate sb into; (pittura etc) to introduce sb to; ~ a fare qc to start doing sth

inizia'tiva [inittsja'tiva] sf initiative; ~ privata private enterprise

i'nizio [i'nittsjo] sm beginning; all'~ at the beginning, at the start; dare ~ a qc to start sth, get sth going

innaffi'are etc = annaffiare etc

innal'zare [innal'tsare] vt (sollevare, alzare) to raise; (rizzare) to erect; ~rsi vr to rise

innamo'rare vt to enchant, charm; ~rsi vr: ~rsi (di qn) to fall in love (with sb); **innamo'rato, a** ag (che nutre amore): innamorato (di) in love (with); (appassionato): innamorato di very fond of ♦ sm/f lover; sweetheart

in'nanzi [in'nantsi] av (stato in luogo) in front, ahead; (moto a luogo) forward, on; (tempo: prima) before ♦ prep (prima) before; ~ a in front of

in'nato, a ag innate

innatu'rale ag unnatural

inne'gabile ag undeniable

innervo'sire vt: ~ qn to get on sb's nerves; ~rsi vr to get irritated o upset

innes'care vt to prime; **in'nesco, schi** sm primer

innes'tare vt (BOT, MED) to graft; (TECN) to engage; (inserire: presa) to insert; **in'nesto** sm graft; grafting no pl; (TECN) clutch; (ELETTR) connection

'inno sm hymn; ~ nazionale national anthem

inno'cente [inno'tʃɛnte] ag innocent; **inno'cenza** sf innocence

in'nocuo, a ag innocuous, harmless

inno'vare vt to change, make innovations in

innume'revole ag innumerable

ino'doro, a ag odourless

inol'trare vt (AMM) to pass on, forward; ~rsi vr (addentrarsi) to advance, go forward

i'noltre av besides, moreover

inon'dare vt to flood; **inondazi'one** sf flooding no pl; flood

inope'roso, a ag inactive, idle

inoppor'tuno, a ag untimely, illtimed; inappropriate; (momento) inopportune

inorgo'glire [inorgoʎ'ʎire] vt to make proud ♦ vi (anche: ~rsi) to become proud; ~rsi di qc to pride o.s. on sth

inor'ridire vt to horrify ♦ vi to be horrified

inospi'tale ag inhospitable

inosser'vato, a ag (non notato) unobserved; (non rispettato) not observed, not kept

inos'sidabile ag stainless

inqua'drare vt (foto, immagine) to frame; (fig) to situate, set

inquie'tare vt (turbare) to disturb, worry; ~rsi vr to worry, become anxious; (impazientirsi) to get upset

inquie'to, a ag restless; (preoccupato) worried, anxious; **inquie'tudine** sf anxiety, worry

inqui'lino, a smf tenant

inquina'mento sm pollution

inqui'nare vt to pollute

inqui'sire vt, vi to investigate; **inquisi'tore, 'trice** ag (sguardo) inquiring; **inquisizi'one** sf (STORIA) inquisition

insabbi'are vt (fig: pratica) to shelve; ~rsi vr (arenarsi: barca) to run aground; (fig: pratica) to be shelved

insac'cati smpl (CUC) sausages

insa'lata sf salad; ~ **mista** mixed salad; **insala'tiera** sf salad bowl

insa'lubre ag unhealthy

insa'nabile ag (piaga) which cannot be healed; (situazione) irremediable; (odio) implacable

insangui'nare vt to stain with blood

insa'puta sf: all'~ **di qn** without sb knowing

insce'nare [inʃe'nare] vt (TEATRO) to stage, put on; (fig) to stage

insedi'are vt to install; ~rsi vr to take up office; (popolo, colonia) to settle

in'segna [in'seɲɲa] sf sign; (emblema) sign, emblem; (bandiera) flag, banner; ~e sfpl (decorazioni) insignia pl

insegna'mento [inseɲɲa'mento] sm teaching

inse'gnante [inse'ɲɲante] ag teaching ♦ smf teacher

inse'gnare [inse'ɲɲare] vt, vi to teach; ~ **a qn qc** to teach sb sth; ~ **a qn a fare qc** to teach sb (how) to do sth

insegui'mento sm pursuit, chase

insegu'ire vt to pursue, chase

inselvati'chire [inselvati'kire] vi (anche: ~rsi) to grow wild

insena'tura sf inlet, creek

insen'sato, a ag senseless, stupid

insen'sibile ag (nervo) insensible; (persona) indifferent

inse'rire vt to insert; (ELETTR) to connect; (allegare) to enclose; (annuncio) to put in, place; ~rsi vr (fig): ~rsi **in** to become part of; **in'serto** sm (pubblicazione) insert

inservi'ente smf attendant

inserzi'one [inser'tsjone] sf insertion; (avviso) advertisement; **fare un'~ sul giornale** to put an advertisement in the paper

insetti'cida, i [insetti'tʃida] sm insecticide

in'setto sm insect

in'sidia sf snare, trap; (pericolo) hidden danger; **insidi'are** vt: ~ **la vita di qn** to make an attempt on sb's life

insi'eme av together ♦ prep: ~ **a** o **con** together with ♦ sm whole; (MAT, servizio, assortimento) set; (MODA) ensemble, outfit; **tutti** ~ all together; **tutto** ~ all together; (in una volta) at one go; **nell'~** on the whole; **d'~** (veduta etc) overall

in'signe [in'siɲɲe] ag (persona) famous, distinguished; (città, monumento) notable

insignifi'cante [insiɲɲifi'kante] ag insignificant

insi'gnire [insiɲ'ɲire] vt: ~ **qn di** to honour o decorate sb with

insin'cero, a [insin'tʃero] ag insincere

insinda'cabile ag unquestionable

insinu'are vt (introdurre): ~ **qc in** to slip o slide sth into; (fig) to insinuate, imply; ~rsi vr: ~rsi **in** to seep into; (fig) to creep into; to worm one's way into

insis'tente ag insistent; persistent

in'sistere vi: ~ **su** **qc** to insist on sth; ~ **in** **qc/a fare** (perseverare) to persist in sth/in doing; **insis'tito, a** pp di **insistere**

insoddis'fatto, a ag dissatisfied

insoffe'rente ag intolerant

insolazi'one [insolat'tsjone] sf (MED) sunstroke

inso'lente *ag* insolent; **insolen'tire** *vi* to grow insolent ♦ *vt* to insult, be rude to

in'solito, a *ag* unusual, out of the ordinary

inso'luto, a *ag* (*non risolto*) unsolved; (*non pagato*) unpaid, outstanding

in'somma *av* (*in breve, in conclusione*) in short; (*dunque*) well ♦ *escl* for heaven's sake!

in'sonne *ag* sleepless; **in'sonnia** *sf* insomnia, sleeplessness

insonno'lito, a *ag* sleepy, drowsy

insoppor'tabile *ag* unbearable

in'sorgere [in'sɔrdʒere] *vi* (*ribellarsi*) to rise up, rebel; (*apparire*) to come up, arise

in'sorto, a *pp di* **insorgere** ♦ *smif* rebel, insurgent

insospet'tire *vt* to make suspicious ♦ *vi* (*anche*: ~*rsi*) to become suspicious

inspi'rare *vt* to breathe in, inhale

in'stabile *ag* (*carico, indole*) unstable; (*tempo*) unsettled; (*equilibrio*) unsteady

instal'lare *vt* to install; ~*rsi* *vr* (*sistemarsi*): ~*rsi* in to settle in; **installazi'one** *sf* installation

instan'cabile *ag* untiring, indefatigable

instau'rare *vt* to introduce, institute

instra'dare *vt*: ~ (*verso*) to direct (towards)

insuc'cesso [insut'tʃɛsso] *sm* failure, flop

insudici'are [insudi'tʃare] *vt* to dirty; ~*rsi* *vr* to get dirty

insuffici'ente [insuffi'tʃɛnte] *ag* insufficient; (*compito, allievo*) inadequate; **insuffici'enza** *sf* insufficiency; inadequacy; (*INS*) fail

insu'lare *ag* insular

insu'lina *sf* insulin

in'sulso, a *ag* (*sciocco*) inane, silly; (*persona*) dull, insipid

insul'tare *vt* to insult, affront

in'sulto *sm* insult, affront

insussis'tente *ag* non-existent

intac'care *vt* (*fare tacche*) to cut into; (*corrodere*) to corrode; (*fig: cominciare ad usare: risparmi*) to break into; (: *ledere*) to damage

intagli'are [intaʎ'ʎare] *vt* to carve; **in'taglio** *sm* carving

intan'gibile [intan'dʒibile] *ag* untouchable; inviolable

in'tanto *av* (*nel frattempo*) meanwhile, in the meantime; (*per cominciare*) just to begin with; ~ **che** while

in'tarsio *sm* inlaying *no pl*, marquetry *no pl*; inlay

inta'sare *vt* to choke (up), block (up); (*AUT*) to obstruct, block; ~*rsi* *vr* to become choked *o* blocked

intas'care *vt* to pocket

in'tatto, a *ag* intact; (*puro*) unsullied

intavo'lare *vt* to start, enter into

inte'grale *ag* complete; (*pane, farina*) wholemeal (*BRIT*), wholewheat (*US*); (*MAT*): **calcolo** ~ integral calculus

inte'grante *ag*: **parte** ~ integral part

inte'grare *vt* to complete; (*MAT*) to integrate; ~*rsi* *vr* (*persona*) to become integrated

integrità *sf* integrity

'integro, a *ag* (*intatto, intero*) complete, whole; (*retto*) upright

intela'iatura *sf* frame; (*fig*) structure, framework

intel'letto *sm* intellect; **intellettu'ale** *ag, smif* intellectual

intelli'gente [intelli'dʒɛnte] *ag* intelligent; **intelli'genza** *sf* intelligence

intem'perie *sfpl* bad weather *sg*

intempes'tivo, a *ag* untimely

inten'dente *sm*: ~ **di Finanza** inland (*BRIT*) *o* internal (*US*) revenue officer; **inten'denza** *sf*: **intendenza di Finanza** inland (*BRIT*) *o* internal (*US*) revenue office

in'tendere *vt* (*avere intenzione*): ~ **fare qc** to intend *o* mean to do sth; (*comprendere*) to understand; (*udire*) to hear; (*significare*) to

mean; ~**rsi** *vr* (*conoscere*): ~**rsi di**
to know a lot about, be a connoisseur
of; (*accordarsi*) to get on (well); **in-**
tendersela con qn (*avere una relazione amorosa*) to have an affair with
sb; **intendi'mento** *sm* (*intelligenza*) understanding; (*proposito*) intention; **intendi'tore, 'trice** *smf* connoisseur, expert

intene'rire *vt* (*fig*) to move (to
pity); ~**rsi** *vr* (*fig*) to be moved

inten'sivo, a *ag* intensive

in'tenso, a *ag* intense

in'tento, a *ag* (*teso, assorto*): ~
(a) intent (on), absorbed (in) ♦ *sm*
aim, purpose

intenzio'nale [intentsjo'nale] *ag* intentional

intenzi'one [inten'tsjone] *sf* intention; (*DIR*) intent; **avere** ~ **di fare**
qc to intend to do sth, have the intention of doing sth

interat'tivo, a *ag* interactive

interca'lare *sm* pet phrase, stock
phrase ♦ *vt* to insert

interca'pedine *sf* gap, cavity

intercet'tare [intertʃet'tare] *vt* to in-
tercept

intercity [intɑsɪ'tɪ] *sm inv* (*FERR*) ~
intercity (train)

inter'detto, a *pp di* **interdire** ♦ *ag*
forbidden, prohibited; (*sconcertato*)
dumbfounded ♦ *sm* (*REL*) interdict

inter'dire *vt* to forbid, prohibit, ban;
(*REL*) to interdict; (*DIR*) to deprive
of civil rights; **interdizi'one** *sf* prohibition, ban

interessa'mento *sm* interest

interes'sante *ag* interesting; **essere in stato** ~ to be expecting (a
baby)

interes'sare *vt* to interest; (*concernere*) to concern, be of interest to;
(*far intervenire*): ~ **qn a** to draw
sb's attention to ♦ *vi*: ~ **a** to interest, matter to; ~**rsi** *vr* (*mostrare
interesse*): ~**rsi a** to take an interest
in, be interested in; (*occuparsi*):
~**rsi di** to take care of

inte'resse *sm* (*anche COMM*) inter-

est

inter'faccia, ce [inter'fattʃa] *sf* (*IN-
FORM*) interface

interfe'renza [interfe'rentsa] *sf* interference

interfe'rire *vi* to interfere

interiezi'one [interjet'tsjone] *sf* exclamation, interjection

interi'ora *sfpl* entrails

interi'ore *ag* interior, inner, inside,
internal; (*fig*) inner

inter'ludio *sm* (*MUS*) interlude

inter'medio, a *ag* intermediate

inter'mezzo [inter'meddzo] *sm* (*intervallo*) interval; (*breve spettacolo*)
intermezzo

inter'nare *vt* (*arrestare*) to intern;
(*MED*) to commit (to a mental institution)

internazio'nale [internattsjo'nale]
ag international

in'terno, a *ag* (*di dentro*) internal,
interior, inner; (: *mare*) inland; (*nazionale*) domestic; (*allievo*) boarding
♦ *sm* inside, interior; (*di paese*) interior; (*fodera*) lining; (*di appartamento*) flat (number); (*TEL*) extension ♦ *smf* (*INS*) boarder; ~**i** *smpl*
(*CINEMA*) interior shots; **all'**~ inside; **Ministero degli I~i** Ministry
of the Interior, ≈ Home Office
(*BRIT*), ≈ Department of the Interior
(*US*)

in'tero, a *ag* (*integro, intatto*)
whole, entire; (*completo, totale*)
complete; (*numero*) whole; (*non ridotto: biglietto*) full

interpel'lare *vt* to consult

inter'porre *vt* (*ostacolo*): ~ **qc a**
qc to put sth in the way of sth; (*influenza*) to use; ~ **appello** (*DIR*) to
appeal; **interporsi** *vr* to intervene;
interporsi fra (*mettersi in mezzo*)
to come between; **inter'posto, a** *pp*
di **interporre**

interpre'tare *vt* to interpret;
in'terprete *smf* interpreter; (*TEA-
TRO*) actor/actress, performer;
(*MUS*) performer

interro'gare *vt* to question; (*INS*) to

test; **interroga'tivo, a** ag (occhi, sguardo) questioning, inquiring; (LING) interrogative ♦ sm question; (fig) mystery; **interroga'torio, a** ag interrogatory, questioning ♦ sm (DIR) questioning no pl; **interrogazi'one** sf questioning no pl; (INS) oral test

inter'rompere vt to interrupt; (studi, trattative) to break off, interrupt; ~rsi vr to break off, stop; **inter'rotto, a** pp di **interrompere**

interrut'tore sm switch

interruzi'one [interrut'tsjone] sf interruption; break

interse'care vt to intersect; ~rsi vr to intersect

inter'stizio [inter'stittsjo] sm interstice, crack

interur'bana sf trunk call, long-distance call

interur'bano, a ag inter-city; (TEL: chiamata) trunk cpd, long-distance; (: telefono) long-distance

inter'vallo sm interval; (spazio) space, gap

interve'nire vi (partecipare): ~ a to take part in; (intromettersi: anche POL) to intervene; (MED: operare) to operate; **inter'vento** sm participation; (intromissione) intervention; (MED) operation; fare un intervento nel corso di (dibattito, programma) to take part in

inter'vista sf interview; **intervi'stare** vt to interview

in'tesa sf understanding; (accordo) agreement, understanding

in'teso, a pp di **intendere** ♦ ag agreed; non darsi per ~ di qc to take no notice of sth

intes'tare vt (lettera) to address; (proprietà): ~ a to register in the name of; ~ un assegno a qn to make out a cheque to sb; **intestazi'one** sf heading; (su carta da lettere) letterhead; (registrazione) registration

intes'tino, a ag (lotte) internal, civil ♦ sm (ANAT) intestine

inti'mare vt to order, command; **intimazi'one** sf order, command

intimidazi'one [intimidat'tsjone] sf intimidation

intimi'dire vt to intimidate ♦ vi (anche: ~rsi) to grow shy

intimità sf intimacy; privacy; (familiarità) familiarity

'intimo, a ag intimate; (affetti, vita) private; (fig: profondo) inmost ♦ sm (persona) intimate o close friend; (dell'animo) bottom, depths pl; parti ~e (ANAT) private parts

intimo'rire vt to frighten; ~rsi vr to become frightened

in'tingolo sm sauce; (pietanza) stew

intiriz'zire [intirid'dzire] vt to numb ♦ vi (anche: ~rsi) to go numb

intito'lare vt to give a title to; (dedicare) to dedicate

intolle'rabile ag intolerable

intolle'rante ag intolerant

in'tonaco, o chi sm plaster

into'nare vt (canto) to start to sing; (armonizzare) to match; ~rsi vr (colori) to go together; ~rsi a (carnagione) to suit; (abito) to go with, match

inton'tire vt to stun, daze ♦ vi to be stunned o dazed; ~rsi vr to be stunned o dazed

in'toppo sm stumbling block, obstacle

in'torno av around; ~ a (attorno a) around; (riguardo, circa) about

intorpi'dire vt to numb; (fig) to make sluggish ♦ vi (anche: ~rsi) to grow numb; (fig) to become sluggish

intossi'care vt to poison; **intossicazi'one** sf poisoning

intral'ciare [intral'tfare] vt to hamper, hold up

intransi'tivo, a ag, sm intransitive

intrapren'dente ag enterprising, go-ahead

intra'prendere vt to undertake

intrat'tabile ag intractable

intratte'nere vt to entertain; to engage in conversation; ~rsi vr to linger; ~**rsi su qc** to dwell on sth

intrave'dere vt to catch a glimpse of; (fig) to foresee

intrecci'are [intret'tʃare] vt (capelli) to plait, braid; (intessere: anche fig) to weave, interweave, intertwine; ~**rsi** vr to intertwine, become interwoven; ~ **le mani** to clasp one's hands; **in'treccio** sm (fig: trama) plot, story

intri'gare vi to manoeuvre (BRIT), maneuver (US); scheme; **in'trigo, ghi** sm plot, intrigue

in'trinseco, a, ci, che ag intrinsic

in'triso, a ag: ~ (di) soaked in(in)

intro'durre vt to introduce; (chiave etc): ~ **qc** to insert sth into; (persone: far entrare) to show in; **introdursi** vr (moda, tecniche) to be introduced; (introdursi in (persona: penetrare) to enter; (: entrare furtivamente) to steal o slip into; **introduzi'one** sf introduction

in'troito sm income, revenue

intro'mettersi vr to interfere, meddle; (interporsi) to intervene

in'truglio [in'truʎʎo] sm concoction

intrusi'one sf intrusion; interference

in'truso, a smf intruder

intu'ire vt to perceive by intuition; (rendersi conto) to realize; **in'tuito** sm intuition; (perspicacia) perspicacity; **intuizi'one** sf intuition

inu'mano, a ag inhuman

inumi'dire vt to dampen, moisten; ~**rsi** vr to become damp o wet

i'nutile ag useless; (superfluo) pointless, unnecessary; **inutilità** sf uselessness; pointlessness

inva'dente ag (fig) interfering, nosey

in'vadere vt to invade; (affollare) to swarm into, overrun; (sog: acque) to flood

inva'ghirsi [inva'girsi] vr: ~ **di** to take a fancy to

invalidità sf infirmity; disability; (DIR) invalidity

in'valido, a ag (inferno) infirm, in-

valid; (al lavoro) disabled; (DIR: nullo) invalid ♦ smif invalid; disabled person

in'vano av in vain

invasi'one sf invasion

in'vaso, a pp di **invadere**

inva'sore, invaди'trice [invadi-'tritʃe] ag invading ♦ sm invader

invecchi'are [invek'kjare] vi (persona) to grow old; (vino, popolazione) to age; (moda) to become dated ♦ vt to age; (far apparire più vecchio) to make look older

in'vece [in'vetʃe] av instead; (al contrario) on the contrary; ~ **di** instead of

inve'ire vi: ~ **contro** to rail against

inven'tare vt to invent; (pericoli, pettegolezzi) to make up, invent

inven'tario sm inventory; (COMM) stocktaking no pl

inven'tivo, a ag inventive ♦ sf inventiveness

inven'tore sm inventor

invenzi'one [inven'tsjone] sf invention; (bugia) lie, story

inver'nale ag winter cpd; (simile all'inverno) wintry

in'verno sm winter

invero'simile ag unlikely

inversi'one sf inversion; reversal; "divieto d'~" (AUT) "no U-turns"

in'verso, a ag opposite; (MAT) inverse ♦ sm contrary, opposite; **in senso** ~ in the opposite direction; **in ordine** ~ in reverse order

inver'tire vt to invert, reverse; ~ **la marcia** (AUT) to do a U-turn; **inver'tito, a** smf homosexual

investi'gare vt, vi to investigate; **investiga'tore, trice** smf investigator, detective; **investigazi'one** sf investigation, inquiry

investi'mento sm (ECON) investment; (scontro, urto) crash, collision; (incidente stradale) road accident

inves'tire vt (denaro) to invest; (sog: veicolo: pedone) to knock down; (: altro veicolo) to crash into;

(apostrofare) to assail; *(incaricare)*: ~ qn di to invest sb with

invi'are vt to send; **invi'ato, a** smf envoy; *(STAMPA)* correspondent

in'vidia sf envy; **invidi'are** vt: invidiare qn (per qc) to envy sb for sth; **invidiare qc a qn** to envy sb sth; **invidi'oso, a** ag envious

in'vio, 'vii sm sending; *(insieme di merci)* consignment

invipe'rito, a ag furious

invischi'are [invis'kjare] vt *(fig)*: ~ qn in to involve sb in; ~rsi vr: ~rsi (con qn/in qc) to get mixed up o involved (with sb/in sth)

invi'sibile ag invisible

invi'tare vt to invite; ~ qn a fare to invite sb to do; **invi'tato, a** smf guest; **in'vito** sm invitation

invo'care vt *(chiedere: aiuto, pace)* to cry out for; *(appellarsi: la legge, Dio)* to appeal to, invoke

invogli'are [invoʎ'ʎare] vt: ~ qn a fare to tempt sb to do, induce sb to do

involon'tario, a ag *(errore)* unintentional; *(gesto)* involuntary

invol'tino sm *(CUC)* roulade

in'volto sm *(pacco)* parcel; *(fagotto)* bundle

in'volucro sm cover, wrapping

involuzi'one [involut'tsjone] sf *(di stile)* convolutedness; *(regresso)*: subire un'~ to regress

inzacche'rare [intsakke'rare] vt to spatter with mud

inzup'pare [intsup'pare] vt to soak; ~rsi vr to get soaked

'io pron I ♦ sm inv: l'~ the ego, the self; ~ stesso(a) I myself

i'odio sm iodine

l'onio sm: lo ~, il mar ~ the Ionian (Sea)

ipermer'cato sm hypermarket

ipertensi'one sf high blood pressure, hypertension

ip'nosi sf hypnosis; **ipno'tismo** sm hypnotism; **ipnotiz'zare** vt to hypnotize

ipocri'sia sf hypocrisy

i'pocrita, i, e ag hypocritical ♦ smf hypocrite

ipo'teca, che sf mortgage; **ipote'care** vt to mortgage

i'potesi sf inv hypothesis; ipo'tetico, a, ci, che ag hypothetical

'ippica sf horseracing

'ippico, a, ci, che ag horse cpd

ippocas'tano sm horse chestnut

ip'podromo sm racecourse

ippo'potamo sm hippopotamus

'ira sf anger, wrath

l'ran sm: l'~ Iran

l'raq sm: l'~ Iraq

'iride sf *(arcobaleno)* rainbow; *(ANAT, BOT)* iris

Ir'landa sf: l'~ Ireland; l'~ del Nord Northern Ireland, Ulster; la Repubblica d'~ Eire, the Republic of Ireland; **irlan'dese** ag Irish ♦ smf Irishman/woman; gli Irlandesi the Irish

iro'nia sf irony; **i'ronico, a, ci, che** ag ironic(al)

irradi'are vt to radiate; *(sog: raggi di luce: illuminare)* to shine on ♦ vi *(diffondersi: anche: ~rsi)* to radiate; **irradiazi'one** sf radiation

irragio'nevole [irradʒo'nevole] ag irrational; unreasonable

irrazio'nale [irrattsjo'nale] ag irrational

irre'ale ag unreal

irrecupe'rabile ag irretrievable; *(fig: persona)* irredeemable

irrecu'sabile *(offerta)* not to be refused; *(prova)* irrefutable

irrego'lare ag irregular; *(terreno)* uneven

irremo'vibile ag *(fig)* unshakeable, unyielding

irrepa'rabile ag irreparable; *(fig)* inevitable

irrepe'ribile ag nowhere to be found

irrequi'eto, a ag restless

irresis'tibile ag irresistible

irrespon'sabile ag irresponsible

irridu'cibile [irridu'tʃibile] ag irreducible; *(fig)* indomitable

irri'gare vt *(annaffiare)* to irrigate;

(*sog: fiume etc*) to flow through; **irrigazi'one** *sf* irrigation

irrigi'dire [irridʒi'dire] *vt* to stiffen; ~rsi *vr* to stiffen

irri'sorio, a *ag* derisory

irri'tare *vt* (*mettere di malumore*) to irritate, annoy; (*MED*) to irritate; ~rsi *vr* (*stizzirsi*) to become irritated *o* annoyed; (*MED*) to become irritated; **irritazi'one** *sf* irritation, annoyance

ir'rompere *vi*: ~ **in** to burst into

irro'rare *vt* to sprinkle; (*AGR*) to spray

irru'ente *ag* (*fig*) impetuous, violent

irruzi'one [irrut'tsjone] *sf*: **fare** ~ **in** to burst into; (*sog: polizia*) to raid

'irto, a *ag* bristly; ~ **di** bristling with

is'critto, a *pp di* **iscrivere ♦** *sm/f* member; **per** *o* **in** ~ in writing

is'crivere *vt* to register, enter; (*persona*): ~ **(a)** to register (in), enrol (in); ~**rsi** *vr*: ~**rsi (a)** (*club, partito*) to join; (*università*) to register *o* enrol (at); (*esame, concorso*) to register *o* enter (for); **iscrizi'one** *sf* (*epigrafe etc*) inscription; (*a scuola, società*) enrolment, registration; (*registrazione*) registration

Is'lam *sm*: **l'**~ Islam

Is'landa *sf*: **l'**~ Iceland

'isola *sf* island; ~ **pedonale** (*AUT*) pedestrian precinct

isola'mento *sm* isolation; (*TECN*) insulation

iso'lante *ag* insulating **♦** *sm* insulator

iso'lare *vt* to isolate; (*TECN*) to insulate; (: *acusticamente*) to soundproof; **iso'lato, a** *ag* isolated; insulated **♦** *sm* (*edificio*) block

ispetto'rato *sm* inspectorate

ispet'tore *sm* inspector

ispezio'nare [ispettsjo'nare] *vt* to inspect

ispezi'one [ispet'tsjone] *sf* inspection

'ispido, a *ag* bristly, shaggy

ispi'rare *vt* to inspire; ~**rsi** *vr*: ~**rsi a** to draw one's inspiration from

Isra'ele *sm*: **l'**~ Israel; **israeli'ano, a, ag, sm/f** Israeli

is'sare *vt* to hoist

istan'taneo, a *ag* instantaneous **♦** *sf* (*FOT*) snapshot

is'tante *sm* instant, moment; **all'**~, **sull'**~ instantly, immediately

is'tanza [is'tantsa] *sf* petition, request

is'terico, a, ci, che *ag* hysterical

iste'rismo *sm* hysteria

isti'gare *vt* to incite; **istigazi'one** *sf* incitement; **istigazione a delinquere** (*DIR*) incitement to crime

is'tinto *sm* instinct

istitu'ire *vt* (*fondare*) to institute, found; (*porre: confronto*) to establish; (*intraprendere: inchiesta*) to set up

isti'tuto *sm* institute; (*di università*) department; (*ente, DIR*) institution; ~ **di bellezza** beauty salon

istituzi'one [istitut'tsjone] *sf* institution

'istmo *sm* (*GEO*) isthmus

istra'dare *vt* = **instradare**

'istrice ['istritʃe] *sm* porcupine

istri'one (*peg*) *sm* ham actor

istru'ire *vt* (*insegnare*) to teach; (*ammaestrare*) to train; (*informare*) to instruct, inform; (*DIR*) to prepare; **istrut'tore, 'trice** *sm/f* instructor **♦** *ag*: **giudice istruttore** examining (*BRIT*) *o* committing (*US*) magistrate; **istrut'toria** *sf* (*DIR*) (preliminary) investigation and hearing; **istruzi'one** *sf* education; training; (*direttiva*) instruction; (*DIR*) = **istruttoria**

I'talia *sf*: **l'**~ Italy

itali'ano, a *ag* Italian **♦** *sm/f* Italian **♦** *sm* (*LING*) Italian; **gli I~i** the Italians

itine'rario *sm* itinerary

itte'rizia [itte'rittsja] *sf* (*MED*) jaundice

'ittico, a, ci, che *ag* fish *cpd*; fishing *cpd*

Iugos'lavia *sf* = Jugoslavia

iugos'lavo, a *ag, sm/f* = **jugoslavo, a**

i'uta *sf* jute

I.V.A. ['iva] *sigla f* (= *imposta sul valore aggiunto*) VAT

J

jazz [dʒaz] *sm* jazz

jeans [dʒinz] *smpl* jeans

Jugos'lavia [jugoz'lavja] *sf*: la ~ Yugoslavia; **jugos'lavo, a** *ag*, *sm/f* Yugoslav(ian)

'juta ['juta] *sf* = iuta

K

K *abbr* (*INFORM*) K

k *abbr* (= *kilo*) k

karatè *sm* karate

Kg *abbr* (= *chilogrammo*) kg

'killer *sm inv* gunman, hired gun

km *abbr* (= *chilometro*) km

'krapfen *sm inv* (*CUC*) doughnut

L

l' *det vedi* **la**; **lo**

la[1] (*dav* **l'** **l'**) *det f* the ♦ *pron* (*oggetto*: *persona*) her; (: *cosa*) it; (: *forma di cortesia*) you

la[2] *sm inv* (*MUS*) A; (: *solfeggiando la scala*) la

là *av* there; **di** ~ (*da quel luogo*) from there; (*in quel luogo*) in there; (*dall'altra parte*) over there; **di** ~ **di** beyond; **per di** ~ that way; **più in** ~ further on; (*tempo*) later on; **fatti in** ~ move up; ~ **dentro/sopra/sotto** in/up (*o on*)/under there; *vedi* **quello**

'labbro (*pl(f)*: **labbra**: *solo nel senso ANAT*) *sm* lip

labi'rinto *sm* labyrinth, maze

labora'torio *sm* (*di ricerca*) laboratory; (*di arti, mestieri*) workshop; ~ **linguistico** language laboratory

labori'oso, a *ag* (*faticoso*) laborious; (*attivo*) hard-working

labu'rista, i, e *ag* Labour (*BRIT*) ♦ *smf* Labour Party member (*BRIT*)

'lacca, che *sf* lacquer

'laccio ['lattʃo] *sm* noose; (*legaccio*, *tirante*) lasso; (*di scarpa*) lace; ~ **emostatico** tourniquet

lace'rare [latʃe'rare] *vt* to tear to shreds, lacerate; **~rsi** *vr* to tear; **'lacero, a** *ag* (*logoro*) torn, tattered; (*MED*) lacerated

'lacrima *sf* tear; **in** ~**e** in tears; **la-cri'mare** *vi* to water; **la-cri'mogeno, a** *ag*: **gas lacrimogeno** tear gas

la'cuna *sf* (*fig*) gap

'ladro *sm* thief; **ladro'cinio** *sm* theft, larceny

laggiù [lad'dʒu] *av* down there; (*di là*) over there

la'gnarsi [laɲ'narsi] *vr*: ~ **(di)** to complain (about)

'lago, ghi *sm* lake

'lagrima *etc* = lacrima *etc*

la'guna *sf* lagoon

'laico, a, ci, che *ag* (*apostolato*) lay; (*vita*) secular; (*scuola*) non-denominational ♦ *smf/m* layman/woman ♦ *sm* lay brother

'lama *sm inv* (*ZOOL*) llama; (*REL*) lama ♦ *sf* blade

lam'bire *vt* to lick; to lap

lamen'tare *vt* to lament; **~rsi** *vr* (*emettere lamenti*) to moan, groan; (*rammaricarsi*): **~rsi (di)** to complain (about); **lamen'tela** *sf* complaining *no pl*; **lamen'tevole** *ag* (*voce*) complaining, plaintive; (*destino*) pitiful; **la'mento** *sm* moan, groan; wail; **lamen'toso, a** *ag* plaintive

la'metta *sf* razor blade

lami'era *sf* sheet metal

'lamina *sf* (*lastra sottile*) thin sheet (*o* layer *o* plate); ~ **d'oro** gold leaf; gold foil; **lami'nare** *vt* to laminate; **lami'nato, a** *ag* laminated; (*tessuto*) lamé ♦ *sm* laminate

'lampada *sf* lamp; ~ **a gas** gas lamp; ~ **a spirito** blow lamp;

(BRIT), blow torch (US); ~ **da tavolo** table lamp

lampa'dario sm chandelier

lampa'dina sf light bulb; ~ **tascabile** pocket torch (BRIT) o flashlight (US)

lam'pante ag (fig: evidente) crystal clear, evident

lampeggi'are [lamped'dʒare] vi (luce, fari) to flash; ~i smpl: **lampeggia** there's lightning; **lampeggia'tore** sm (AUT) indicator

lampi'one sm street light o lamp (BRIT)

'lampo sm (METEOR) flash of lightning; (di luce, fig) flash; ~i smpl lightning no pl ♦ ag inv: **cerniera** ~ zip (fastener) (BRIT), zipper (US); **guerra** ~ blitzkrieg

lam'pone sm raspberry

'lana sf wool; ~ **d'acciaio** steel wool; **pura** ~ **vergine** pure new wool; ~ **di vetro** glass wool

lan'cetta [lan'tʃetta] sf (indice) pointer, needle; (di orologio) hand

'lancia ['lantʃa] sf (arma) lance; (: picca) spear; (di pompa antincendio) nozzle; (imbarcazione) launch

lanciafi'amme [lantʃa'fjamme] sm inv flamethrower

lanci'are [lan'tʃare] vt to throw, hurl, fling; (SPORT) to throw; (far partire: automobile) to get up to full speed; (bombe) to drop; (razzo, prodotto, moda) to launch; ~**rsi** vr: ~**rsi contro/su** to throw o hurl o fling o.s. against/on; ~**rsi in** (fig) to embark on

lanci'nante [lantʃi'nante] ag (dolore) shooting, throbbing; (grido) piercing

'lancio ['lantʃo] sm throwing no pl; throw; dropping no pl; drop; launching no pl; launch; ~ **del peso** putting the shot

'landa sf (GEO) moor

langu'ido, a ag (fiacco) languid, weak; (tenero, malinconico) languishing

langu'ore sm weakness, languor

lani'ficio [lani'fitʃo] sm woollen mill

la'noso, a ag woolly

lan'terna sf lantern; (faro) lighthouse

la'nugine [la'nudʒine] sf down

lapi'dare vt to stone

lapi'dario, a ag (fig) terse

'lapide sf (di sepolcro) tombstone; (commemorativa) plaque

'lapis sm inv pencil

Lap'ponia sf Lapland

'lapsus sm inv slip

la'ptop [læ'ptɔp] sm inv laptop (computer)

'lardo sm bacon fat, lard

lar'ghezza [lar'gettsa] sf width; breadth; looseness; generosity; ~ **di vedute** broad-mindedness

'largo, a, ghi, ghe ag wide; broad; (maniche) wide; (abito: troppo ampio) loose; (fig) generous ♦ sm width; breadth; (mare aperto): **il** ~ the open sea ♦ sf: **stare o tenersi alla** ~**a** (da qn/qc) to keep one's distance (from sb/sth), keep away (from sb/sth); ~ **due metri** two metres wide; ~ **di spalle** broadshouldered; (fig) ~ **di vedute** broadminded; **su** ~**a scala** on a large scale; **di manica** ~**a** generous, open-handed; **al** ~ **di Genova** off (the coast of) Genoa; **farsi** ~ **tra la folla** to push one's way through the crowd

'larice ['laritʃe] sm (BOT) larch

larin'gite [larin'dʒite] sf laryngitis

'larva sf larva; (fig) shadow

la'sagne [la'zaɲɲe] sfpl lasagna sg

lasci'are [laʃ'ʃare] vt to leave; (abbandonare) to leave, abandon, give up; (cessare di tenere) to let go of ♦ vb aus: ~ **fare qn** to let sb do ♦ vi: ~ **di fare** (smettere) to stop doing; ~**rsi andare/truffare** to let o.s. go/ be cheated; ~ **andare** o **correre** o **perdere** to let things go their own way; ~ **stare qc/qn** to leave sth/sb alone

'lascito ['laʃʃito] sm (DIR) legacy

laser ['lazer] ag, sm inv: (raggio) ~ laser (beam)

lassa'tivo, a *ag, sm* laxative

'lasso *sm*: ~ **di tempo** interval, lapse of time

lassù *av* up there

'lastra *sf* (*di pietra*) slab; (*di metallo, FOT*) plate; (*di ghiaccio, vetro*) sheet; (*radiografica*) X-ray (plate)

lastri'cato *sm*, **'lastrico, ci** o **chi** *sm* paving

late'rale *ag* lateral, side *cpd*; (*uscita, ingresso etc*) side *cpd* ♦ *sm* (*CALCIO*) half-back

late'rizio [late'rittsjo] *sm* (perforated) brick

lati'fondo *sm* large estate

la'tino, a *ag, sm* Latin; **~ americano, a** *ag* Latin-American

lati'tante *smf* fugitive (from justice)

lati'tudine *sf* latitude

'lato, a *ag* (*fig*) wide, broad ♦ *sm* side; (*fig*) aspect, point of view; **in senso** ~ broadly speaking

la'trare *vi* to bark

la'trina *sf* public lavatory

'latta *sf* tin (plate); (*recipiente*) tin, can

lat'taio, a *smf* milkman/woman; dairyman/woman

lat'tante *ag* unweaned

'latte *sm* milk; ~ **detergente** cleansing milk o lotion; ~ **in polvere** dried o powdered milk; ~ **scremato** skimmed milk; **latte'ria** *sf* dairy; **latti'cini** *smpl* dairy products

lat'tina *sf* (*di birra etc*) can

lat'tuga, ghe *sf* lettuce

'laurea *sf* degree; **laure'are** *vt* to confer a degree on; **laurearsi** *vr* to graduate; **laure'ato, a** *ag, smf* graduate

'lauro *sm* laurel

'lauto, a *ag* (*pranzo, mancia*) lavish

'lava *sf* lava

la'vabo *sm* washbasin

la'vaggio [la'vaddʒo] *sm* washing *no pl*; ~ **del cervello** brainwashing *no pl*

la'vagna [la'vaɲɲa] *sf* (*GEO*) slate; (*di scuola*) blackboard

la'vanda *sf* (*anche MED*) wash; (*BOT*) lavender; **lavan'daia** *sf* washerwoman; **lavande'ria** *sf* laundry; **lavanderia automatica** launderette; **lavanderia a secco** dry-cleaner's; **lavan'dino** *sm* sink

lavapi'atti *smf* dishwasher

la'vare *vt* to wash; **~rsi** *vr* to wash, have a wash; ~ **a secco** to dry-clean; **~rsi le mani/i denti** to wash one's hands/clean one's teeth

lava'secco *sm* o *f inv* drycleaner's

lavasto'viglie [lavasto'viʎʎe] *sm* o *f inv* (*macchina*) dishwasher

lava'toio *sm* (public) washhouse

lava'trice [lava'tritʃe] *sf* washing machine

lava'tura *sf* washing *no pl*; ~ **di piatti** dishwater

lavo'rante *smf* worker

lavo'rare *vi* to work; (*fig: bar, studio etc*) to do good business ♦ *vt* to work; **~rsi qn** (*persuaderlo*) to work on sb; ~ **a** to work on; ~ **a maglia** to knit; **lavora'tivo, a** *ag* working; **lavora'tore, 'trice** *smf* worker ♦ *ag* working; **lavorazi'one** *sf* (*gen*) working; (*di legno, pietra*) carving; (*di film*) making; (*di prodotto*) manufacture; (*modo di esecuzione*) workmanship; **lavo'rio** *sm* intense activity

la'voro *sm* work; (*occupazione*) job, work *no pl*; (*opera*) piece of work, job; (*ECON*) labour; **~i forzati** hard labour *sg*; **~i pubblici** public works

le *det* fpl ♦ *pron* (*oggetto*) them; (: *a lei, a essa*) (to) her; (: *forma di cortesia*) (to) you

le'ale *ag* loyal; (*sincero*) sincere; (*onesto*) fair; **lealtà** *sf* loyalty; sincerity; fairness

'lebbra *sf* leprosy

'lecca 'lecca *sm inv* lollipop

leccapi'edi (*peg*) *smf inv* toady, bootlicker

lec'care *vt* to lick; (*sog: gatto: latte etc*) to lick o lap up; (*fig*) to flatter; **~rsi i baffi** to lick one's lips

'leccio ['lettʃo] *sm* holm oak, ilex

leccor'nia *sf* titbit, delicacy

'lecito, a ['lɛtʃito] *ag* permitted, allowed

'ledere *vt* to damage, injure

'lega, ghe *sf* league; (*di metalli*) alloy

le'gaccio [le'gattʃo] *sm* string, lace

le'gale *ag* legal ♦ *sm* lawyer; **legaliz'zare** *vt* to authenticate; (*regolarizzare*) to legalize

le'game *sm* (*corda, fig: affettivo*) tie, bond; (*nesso logico*) link, connection

le'gare *vt* (*prigioniero, capelli, cane*) to tie (up); (*libro*) to bind; (CHIM) to alloy; (*fig: collegare*) to bind, join ♦ *vi* (*far lega*) to unite; (*fig*) to get on well

lega'tario, a *sm/f* (DIR) legatee

le'gato *sm* (REL) legate; (DIR) legacy, bequest

lega'tura *sf* (*di libro*) binding; (MUS) ligature

le'genda [le'dʒɛnda] *sf* (*di carta geografica etc*) = **leggenda**

'legge ['leddʒe] *sf* law

leg'genda [led'dʒɛnda] *sf* (*narrazione*) legend; (*di carta geografica etc*) key, legend

'leggere ['lɛddʒere] *vt, vi* to read

legge'rezza [leddʒe'rettsa] *sf* lightness; thoughtlessness; fickleness

leg'gero, a [led'dʒero] *ag* light; (*agile, snello*) nimble, agile, light; (*tè, caffè*) weak; (*fig: non grave, piccolo*) slight; (: *spensierato*) thoughtless; (: *incostante*) fickle; free and easy; **alla ~a** thoughtlessly

leggi'adro, a [led'dʒadro] *ag* pretty, lovely; (*movimenti*) graceful

leg'gio, 'gii [led'dʒio] *sm* lectern; (MUS) music stand

legisla'tura [ledʒizla'tura] *sf* legislature

legislazi'one [ledʒizlat'tsjone] *sf* legislation

le'gittimo, a [le'dʒittimo] *ag* legitimate; (*fig: giustificato, lecito*) justified, legitimate; **~a difesa** (DIR) self-defence

'legna ['lɛɲɲa] *sf* firewood; **le'gname** *sm* wood, timber

'legno ['lɛɲɲo] *sm* wood; (*pezzo di ~*) piece of wood; **di ~** wooden; **~ compensato** plywood; **le'gnoso, a** *ag* wooden; woody; (*carne*) tough

le'gumi *smpl* (BOT) pulses

'lei *pron* (*soggetto*) she; (*oggetto: per dare rilievo, con preposizione*) her; (*forma di cortesia: anche: L~*) you ♦ *sm*: **dare del ~ a qn** to address sb as "lei"; **~ stessa** she herself; **you yourself**

'lembo *sm* (*di abito, strada*) edge; (*striscia sottile: di terra*) strip

'lemma, i *sm* headword

'lemme 'lemme *av* (very) very slowly

'lena *sf* (*fig*) energy, stamina

le'nire *vt* to soothe

'lente *sf* (OTTICA) lens *sg*; **~ d'ingrandimento** magnifying glass; **~i a contatto** *o* **corneali** contact lenses

len'tezza [len'tettsa] *sf* slowness

len'ticchia [len'tikkja] *sf* (BOT) lentil

len'tiggine [len'tiddʒine] *sf* freckle

'lento, a *ag* slow; (*molle: fune*) slack; (*non stretto: vite, abito*) loose ♦ *sm* (*ballo*) slow dance

'lenza ['lɛntsa] *sf* fishing-line

lenzu'olo [len'tswɔlo] *sm* sheet; **~a** *sfpl* pair of sheets

le'one *sm* lion; (*dello zodiaco*): **L~** Leo

lepo'rino, a *ag*: **labbro ~** harelip

'lepre *sf* hare

'lercio, a, ci, cie ['lɛrtʃo] *ag* filthy

'lesbica, che *sf* lesbian

lesi'nare *vt* to be stingy with ♦ *vi*: **~ (su)** to skimp (on), be stingy (with)

lesi'one *sf* (MED) lesion; (DIR) injury, damage; (EDIL) crack

'leso, a *pp di* **ledere** ♦ *ag* (*offeso*) injured; **parte ~a** (DIR) injured party

les'sare *vt* (CUC) to boil

'lessico, ci *sm* vocabulary; lexicon

'lesso, a *ag* boiled ♦ *sm* boiled meat

'lesto, a *ag* quick; *(agile)* nimble; ~ **di mano** *(per rubare)* light-fingered; *(per picchiare)* free with one's fists

le'tale *ag* lethal; fatal

leta'maio *sm* dunghill

le'tame *sm* manure, dung

le'targo, ghi *sm* lethargy; *(ZOOL)* hibernation

le'tizia [le'tittsja] *sf* joy, happiness

'lettera *sf* letter; ~**e** *sfpl (letteratura)* literature *sg*; *(studi umanistici)* arts (subjects); **alla** ~ literally; **in** ~**e** in words, in full; **lette'rale** *ag* literal

lette'rario, a *ag* literary

lette'rato, a *ag* well-read, scholarly

lettera'tura *sf* literature

let'tiga, ghe *sf (portantina)* litter; *(barella)* stretcher

let'tino *sm* cot *(BRIT)*, crib *(US)*

'letto, a *pp di* **leggere ♦** *sm* bed; **andare a** ~ to go to bed; ~ **a castello** bunk beds *pl*; ~ **a una piazza/a due piazze** *o* **matrimoniale** single/double bed

let'tore, 'trice *sm/f* reader; *(INS)* (foreign language) assistant *(BRIT)*, (foreign) teaching assistant *(US)* **♦** *sm (TECN)*: ~ **ottico** optical character reader

let'tura *sf* reading

leuce'mia [leutfe'mia] *sf* leukaemia

'leva *sf* lever; *(MIL)* conscription; **far** ~ **su qn** to work on sb; ~ **del cambio** *(AUT)* gear lever

le'vante *sm* east; *(vento)* East wind; **il L**~ the Levant

le'vare *vt (occhi, braccio)* to raise; *(sollevare, togliere: tassa, divieto)* to lift; *(indumenti)* to take off, remove; *(rimuovere)* to take away; (: *dal di sopra)* to take off; (: *dal di dentro)* to take out; ~**rsi** *vr* to get up; *(sole)* to rise; **la'vata** *sf (di posta)* collection

leva'toio, a *ag*: **ponte** ~ drawbridge

leva'tura *sf* intelligence, mental capacity

levi'gare *vt* to smooth; *(con carta vetrata)* to sand

levri'ere *sm* greyhound

lezi'one [let'tsjone] *sf* lesson; *(all'università, sgridata)* lecture; **fare** ~ to teach; to lecture

lezi'oso, a [let'tsjoso] *ag* affected; simpering

'lezzo ['leddzo] *sm* stench, stink

li *pron pl (oggetto)* them

lì *av* there; **di** *o* **da** ~ from there; **per di** ~ that way; **di** ~ **a pochi giorni** a few days later; ~ **per** ~ there and then; at first; **essere** ~ (~) **per fare** to be on the point of doing, be about to do; ~ **dentro** in there; ~ **sotto** under there; ~ **sopra** on there; up there; *vedi* **quello**

liba'nese *ag, sm/f* Lebanese *inv*

Li'bano *sm*: **il** ~ the Lebanon

'libbra *sf (peso)* pound

li'beccio [li'bettfo] *sm* south-west wind

li'bello *sm* libel

li'bellula *sf* dragonfly

libe'rale *ag, sm/f* liberal

liberaliz'zare [liberalid'dzare] *vt* to liberalize

libe'rare *vt (rendere libero: prigioniero)* to release; (: *popolo)* to free, liberate; *(sgombrare: passaggio)* to clear; (: *stanza)* to vacate; *(produrre: energia)* to release; ~**rsi** *vr*: ~**rsi di qc/qn** to get rid of sth/sb; **libera'tore, 'trice** *ag* liberating **♦** *sm/f* liberator; **liberazi'one** *sf* liberation, freeing; release; rescuing

'libero, a *ag* free; *(strada)* clear; *(non occupato: posto etc)* vacant; not taken; empty; not engaged; ~ **di fare qc** free to do sth; ~ **da** free from; ~ **arbitrio** free will; ~ **professionista** self-employed professional person; ~ **scambio** free trade; **libertà** *sf inv* freedom; *(tempo disponibile)* free time **♦** *sfpl (licenza)* liberties; **in libertà provvisoria/vigilata** released without bail/on probation

'Libia *sf*: **la** ~ Libya; **'libico, a, ci, che** *ag, sm/f* Libyan

li'bidine *sf* lust

li'braio sm bookseller

li'brario, a ag book cpd

li'brarsi vr to hover

libre'ria sf (bottega) bookshop; (stanza) library; (mobile) bookcase

li'bretto sm booklet; (taccuino) notebook; (MUS) libretto; ~ **degli assegni** cheque book; ~ **di circolazione** (AUT) logbook; ~ **di risparmio** (savings) bank-book, passbook; ~ **universitario** student's report book

'libro sm book; ~ **bianco** (POL) white paper; ~ **di cassa** cash book; ~ **mastro** ledger; ~ **paga** payroll

li'cenza [li'tʃɛntsa] sf (permesso) permission, leave; (di pesca, caccia, circolazione) permit, licence; (MIL) leave; (INS) school leaving certificate; (libertà) liberty; licence; licentiousness; **andare in** ~ (MIL) to go on leave

licenzia'mento [litʃɛntsja'mento] sm dismissal

licenzi'are [litʃen'tsjare] vt (impiegato) to dismiss; (INS) to award a certificate to; ~**rsi** vr (impiegato) to resign, hand in one's notice; (INS) to obtain one's school-leaving certificate

li'ceo [li'tʃɛo] sm (INS) secondary (BRIT) o high (US) school (for 14- to 19-year-olds)

'lido sm beach, shore

li'eto, a ag happy, glad; "**molto** ~" (nelle presentazioni) "pleased to meet you"

li'eve ag light; (di poco conto) slight; (sommesso: voce) faint, soft

lievi'tare vi (anche fig) to rise ♦ vt to leaven

li'evito sm yeast; ~ **di birra** brewer's yeast

'ligio, a, gi, gie ['lidʒo] ag faithful, loyal

'lilla sm inv lilac

'lillà sm inv = lilla

'lima sf file

limacci'oso, a [limat'tʃoso] ag slimy; muddy

li'mare vt to file (down); (fig) to polish

'limbo sm (REL) limbo

li'metta sf nail file

limi'tare vt to limit, restrict; (circoscrivere) to bound, surround; **limita'tivo, a** ag limiting, restricting; **limi'tato, a** ag limited, restricted

'limite sm limit; (confine) border, boundary; ~ **di velocità** speed limit

li'mitrofo, a ag neighbouring

limo'nata sf lemonade (BRIT), (lemon) soda (US); lemon squash (BRIT), lemonade (US)

li'mone sm (pianta) lemon tree; (frutto) lemon

'limpido, a ag clear; (acqua) limpid, clear

'lince ['lintʃe] sf lynx

linci'are vt to lynch

'lindo, a ag tidy, spick and span; (biancheria) clean

'linea sf line; (di mezzi pubblici di trasporto: itinerario) route; (: servizio) service; **a grandi** ~**e** in outline; **mantenere la** ~ to look after one's figure; **aereo di** ~ airliner; **nave di** ~ liner; **volo di** ~ scheduled flight; ~ **aerea** airline; ~ **di partenza/d'arrivo** (SPORT) starting/finishing line; ~ **di tiro** line of fire

linea'menti smpl features; (fig) outlines

line'are ag linear; (fig) coherent, logical

line'etta sf (trattino) dash; (d'unione) hyphen

lin'gotto sm ingot, bar

'lingua sf (ANAT, CUC) tongue; (idioma) language; **mostrare la** ~ to stick out one's tongue; **di** ~ **italiana** Italian-speaking; ~ **madre** mother tongue; **una** ~ **di terra** a spit of land

lingu'aggio [lin'gwaddʒo] sm language

lingu'etta sf (di strumento) reed; (di scarpa, TECN) tongue; (di busta) flap

lingu'istica sf linguistics sg

'lino sm (pianta) flax; (tessuto) linen

li'noleum sm inv linoleum, lino

lique'fare vt (render liquido) to liquefy; (fondere) to melt; ~**rsi** vr to liquefy; to melt

liqui'dare vt (società, beni; persona: uccidere) to liquidate; (persona: sbarazzarsene) to get rid of; (conto, problema) to settle; (COMM: merce) to sell off, clear; **liquidazi'one** sf liquidation; settlement; clearance sale

liquidità sf liquidity

'liquido, a ag, sm liquid; ~ **per freni** brake fluid

liqui'rizia [likwi'rittsja] sf liquorice

li'quore sm liqueur

'lira sf (unità monetaria) lira; (MUS) lyre; ~ **sterlina** pound sterling

'lirica, che sf (poesia) lyric poetry; (componimento poetico) lyric; (MUS) opera

'lirico, a, ci, che ag lyric(al); (MUS) lyric; **cantante/teatro** ~ opera singer/house

'lisca, sche sf (di pesce) fishbone

lisci'are [liʃ'ʃare] vt to smooth; (fig) to flatter

'liscio, a, sci, sce ['liʃʃo] ag smooth; (capelli) straight; (mobile) plain; (bevanda alcolica) neat; (fig) straightforward, simple ♦ av: **andare** ~ to go smoothly; **passarla** ~**a** to get away with it

'liso, a ag worn out, threadbare

'lista sf (striscia) strip; (elenco) list; ~ **elettorale** electoral roll; ~ **delle vivande** menu

lis'tino sm list; ~ **dei cambi** (foreign) exchange rate; ~ **dei prezzi** price list

'lite sf quarrel, argument; (DIR) lawsuit

liti'gare vi to quarrel; (DIR) to litigate

li'tigio [li'tidʒo] sm quarrel; **litigi'oso, a** ag quarrelsome; (DIR) litigious

litogra'fia sf (sistema) lithography; (stampa) lithograph

lito'rale ag coastal, coast cpd ♦ sm coast

'litro sm litre

livel'lare vt to level, make level; ~**rsi** vr to become level; (fig) to level out, balance out

li'vello sm level; (fig) level, standard; **ad alto** ~ (fig) high-level; ~ **del mare** sea level

'livido, a ag livid; (per percosse) bruised, black and blue; (cielo) leaden ♦ sm bruise

li'vore sm malice, spite

Li'vorno sf Livorno, Leghorn

li'vrea sf livery

'lizza ['littsa] sf lists pl; **scendere in** ~ (anche fig) to enter the lists

lo (dav s impura, gn, pn, ps, x, z; dav V l') det m the ♦ pron (oggetto: persona) him; (: cosa) it; ~ **sapevo** I knew it; ~ **so** I know; **sii buono, anche se lui non** ~ **è** be good, even if he isn't

lo'cale ag local ♦ sm room; (luogo pubblico) premises pl; ~ **notturno** nightclub; **località** sf inv locality;

localiz'zare vt (circoscrivere) to confine, localize; (accertare) to locate, place

lo'canda sf inn; **locandi'ere, a** smf innkeeper

loca'tario, a smf tenant

loca'tore, 'trice smf landlord/lady

locazi'one [lokat'tsjone] sf (da parte del locatario) renting no pl; (da parte del locatore) renting out no pl, letting no pl; (contratto di) ~ lease; (canone di) ~ rent; **dare in** ~ to rent out, let

locomo'tiva sf locomotive

locomo'tore sm electric locomotive

locomozi'one [lokomot'tsjone] sf locomotion; **mezzi di** ~ vehicles, means of transport

lo'custa sf locust

locuzi'one [lokut'tsjone] sf phrase, expression

lo'dare vt to praise

'lode sf praise; (INS): **laurearsi con 110 e** ~ ≈ to graduate with a first-class honours degree (BRIT), graduate summa cum laude (US)

'loden sm inv (stoffa) loden; (cap-

potto) loden overcoat

lo'devole *ag* praiseworthy

loga'ritmo *sm* logarithm

'loggia, ge [ˈlɔddʒa] *sf* (ARCHIT) loggia; (*circolo massonico*) lodge; **loggi'one** *sm* (*di teatro*): **il loggione the Gods** *sg*

'logica *sf* logic

'logico, a, ci, che [ˈlɔdʒiko] *ag* logical

logo'rare *vt* to wear out; (*sciupare*) to waste; **~rsi** *vr* to wear out; (*fig*) to wear o.s. out

logo'rio *sm* wear and tear; (*fig*) strain

'logoro, a *ag* (*stoffa*) worn out, threadbare; (*persona*) worn out

lom'baggine [lomˈbaddʒine] *sf* lumbago

Lombar'dia *sf*: **la ~** Lombardy

lom'bata *sf* (*taglio di carne*) loin

'lombo *sm* (ANAT) loin

lom'brico, chi *sm* earthworm

londi'nese *ag* London *cpd* ♦ *smf* Londoner

'Londra *sf* London

lon'gevo, a [lonˈdʒεvo] *ag* long-lived

longi'tudine [londʒiˈtudine] *sf* longitude

lonta'nanza [lontaˈnantsa] *sf* distance; absence

lon'tano, a *ag* (*distante*) distant, faraway; (*assente*) absent; (*vago: sospetto*) slight, remote; (*tempo: remoto*) far-off, distant; (*parente*) distant, remote ♦ *av* far; **è ~a la casa?** is it far to the house?, is the house far from here?; **è ~ un chilometro** it's a kilometre away *o* a kilometre from here; **più ~** farther; **da o di ~** from a distance; (*fig*) **da o da ~** a long way from; **alla ~a** slightly, vaguely

'lontra *sf* otter

lo'quace [loˈkwatʃe] *ag* talkative, loquacious; (*fig*: *gesto etc*) eloquent

'lordo, a *ag* dirty, filthy; (*peso, stipendio*) gross

'loro *pron pl* (*oggetto, con preposizione*) them; (*complemento di termine*) to them; (*parente*) theirs; (*for-*

ma di cortesia: anche: L~) you; to you; **il(la) ~, i(le) ~** *det* their; (*forma di cortesia*: anche: L~) your ♦ *pron* theirs; (*forma di cortesia*: anche: L~) yours; **~ stessi(e)** they themselves; you yourselves

'losco, a, schi, sche *ag* (*fig*) shady, suspicious

'lotta *sf* struggle, fight; (SPORT) wrestling; **~ libera** all-in wrestling; **lot'tare** *vi* to fight, struggle; to wrestle; **lotta'tore, trice** *smf* wrestler

lotte'ria *sf* lottery; (*di gara ippica*) sweepstake

'lotto *sm* (*gioco*) (state) lottery; (*parte*) lot; (EDIL) site

lozi'one [lotˈtsjone] *sf* lotion

lubrifi'cante *sm* lubricant

lubrifi'care *vt* to lubricate

luc'chetto [lukˈketto] *sm* padlock

lucci'care [luttʃiˈkare] *vi* to sparkle, glitter, twinkle

'luccio [ˈluttʃo] *sm* (ZOOL) pike

'lucciola [ˈluttʃola] *sf* (ZOOL) firefly; glowworm

'luce [ˈlutʃe] *sf* light; (*finestra*) window; **alla ~ di** by the light of; **fare ~ su qc** (*fig*) to shed *o* throw light on sth; **~ del sole/della luna** sun/moonlight; **lu'cente** *ag* shining

lu'cerna [luˈtʃεrna] *sf* oil-lamp

lucer'nario [lutʃerˈnarjo] *sm* skylight

lu'certola [luˈtʃεrtola] *sf* lizard

luci'dare [lutʃiˈdare] *vt* to polish; (*ricalcare*) to trace

lucida'trice [lutʃidaˈtritʃe] *sf* floor polisher

'lucido, a [ˈlutʃido] *ag* shining, bright; (*lucidato*) polished; (*fig*) lucid ♦ *sm* shine, lustre; (*per scarpe etc*) polish; (*disegno*) tracing

'lucro *sm* profit, gain; **lu'croso, a** *ag* lucrative, profitable

lu'dibrio *sm* mockery *no pl*; (*oggetto di scherno*) laughing-stock

'luglio [ˈluʎʎo] *sm* July

'lugubre *ag* gloomy

'lui *pronome* (*soggetto*) he; (*oggetto: per dare rilievo, con preposizione*) him; **~ stesso** he himself

lu'maca, che sf slug; (chiocciola) snail

'lume sm light; (lampada) lamp; (fig): **chiedere ~i a qn** to ask sb for advice; **a ~ di naso** (fig) by rule of thumb

lumi'naria sf (per feste) illuminations pl

lumi'noso, a ag (che emette luce) luminous; (cielo, colore, stanza) bright; (sorgente) of light, light cpd; (fig: sorriso) bright, radiant

'luna sf moon; **~ nuova/piena** new/full moon; **~ di miele** honeymoon

'luna park sm inv amusement park, funfair

lu'nare ag lunar, moon cpd

lu'nario sm almanac; **sbarcare il ~** to make ends meet

lu'natico, a, ci, che ag whimsical, temperamental

lunedì sm inv Monday; **di o il ~** on Mondays

lun'gaggine [lun'gaddʒine] sf slowness; **~i della burocrazia** red tape

lun'ghezza [lun'gettsa] sf length; **~ d'onda** (FISICA) wavelength

'lungi ['lundʒi]: **~ da** prep far from

'lungo, a, ghi, ghe ag long; (lento: persona) slow; (diluito: caffè, brodo) weak, watery, thin ♦ sm length ♦ prep along; **~ 3 metri** 3 metres long; **a ~** for a long time; **a ~ andare** in the long run; **di gran ~a** (molto) by far; **andare in ~** o **per le lunghe** to drag on; **saperla ~a** to know what's what; **in ~ e in largo** far and wide, all over; **~ il corso dei secoli** throughout the centuries

lungo'mare sm promenade

lu'notto sm (AUT) rear o back window; **~ termico** heated rear window

lu'ogo, ghi sm place; (posto: di incidente etc) scene, site; (punto, passo di libro) passage; **in ~ di** instead of; **in primo ~** in the first place; **aver ~** to take place; **dar ~ a** to give rise to; **~ comune** commonplace; **~ di nascita** birthplace; (AMM) place

of birth; **~ di provenienza** place of origin

luogote'nente sm (MIL) lieutenant

lu'para sf sawn-off shotgun

'lupo, a sm/f wolf

'luppolo sm (BOT) hop

'lurido, a ag filthy

lu'singa, ghe sf (spesso al pl) flattery no pl

lusin'gare vt to flatter; **lusin'ghi'ero, a** ag flattering, gratifying

lus'sare vt (MED) to dislocate

Lussem'burgo sm (stato): **il ~** Luxembourg ♦ sf (città) Luxembourg

'lusso sm luxury; **di ~** luxury cpd; **lussu'oso, a** ag luxurious

lussureggi'are [lussured'dʒare] vi to be luxuriant

lus'suria sf lust

lus'trare vt to polish, shine

lustra'scarpe sm/f inv shoeshine

lus'trino sm sequin

'lustro, a ag shiny; (pelliccia) glossy ♦ sm shine, gloss; (fig) prestige, glory; (quinquennio) five-year period

'lutto sm mourning; **essere in/portare il ~** to be in/wear mourning; **luttu'oso, a** ag mournful, sad

M

ma cong but; **~ insomma!** for goodness sake!; **~ no!** of course not!

'macabro, a ag gruesome, macabre

macché [mak'ke] escl not at all!, certainly not!

macche'roni [makke'roni] smpl macaroni sg

'macchia ['makkja] sf stain, spot; (chiazza di diverso colore) spot; splash, patch; (tipo di boscaglia) scrub; **alla ~** (fig) in hiding; **macchi'are** vt (sporcare) to stain, mark; **macchiarsi** vr (persona) to get o.s. dirty; (stoffa) to stain; to get stained o marked

'macchina ['makkina] sf machine; (motore, locomotiva) engine; (auto-

mobile) car; *(fig: meccanismo)* machinery; **andare in ~** *(AUT)* to go by car; *(STAMPA)* to go to press; **~ da cucire** sewing machine; **~ fotografica** camera; **~ da presa** cine *o* movie camera; **~ da scrivere** typewriter; **~ a vapore** steam engine

macchi'nare [makki'nare] *vt* to plot

macchi'nario [makki'narjo] *sm* machinery

macchi'netta [makki'netta] *(fam) sf (caffettiera)* percolator; *(accendino)* lighter

macchi'nista, i [makki'nista] *sm (di treno)* engine-driver; *(di nave)* engineer; *(TEATRO, TV)* stagehand

macchi'noso, a [makki'noso] *ag* complex, complicated

mace'donia [matʃe'dɔnja] *sf* fruit salad

macel'laio [matʃel'lajo] *sm* butcher

macel'lare [matʃel'lare] *vt* to slaughter, butcher; **macelle'ria** *sf* butcher's (shop); **ma'cello** *sm (mattatoio)* slaughterhouse, abattoir *(BRIT); (fig)* slaughter, massacre; *(: disastro)* shambles *sg*

mace'rare [matʃe'rare] *vt* to macerate; *(CUC)* to marinate; **~rsi** *vr (fig):* **~rsi in** to be consumed with

ma'cerie [ma'tʃɛrje] *sfpl* rubble *sg*, debris *sg*

ma'cigno [ma'tʃiɲɲo] *sm (masso)* rock, boulder

maci'lento, a [matʃi'lɛnto] *ag* emaciated

'macina ['matʃina] *sf (pietra)* millstone; *(macchina)* grinder; **macina-caffè** *sm inv* coffee grinder; **macina'pepe** *sm inv* peppermill

maci'nare [matʃi'nare] *vt* to grind; *(carne)* to mince *(BRIT)*, grind *(US)*; **maci'nato** *sm* meal, flour; *(carne)* minced *(BRIT) o* ground *(US)* meat

maci'nino [matʃi'nino] *sm* coffee grinder; peppermill

'madido, a *ag:* **~ (di)** wet *o* moist (with)

Ma'donna *sf (REL)* Our Lady

mador'nale *ag* enormous, huge

'madre *sf* mother; *(matrice di bolletta)* counterfoil ♦ *ag inv* mother *cpd:* **ragazza ~** unmarried mother; **scena ~** *(TEATRO)* principal scene; *(fig)* terrible scene

madre'lingua *sf* mother tongue, native language

madre'perla *sf* mother-of-pearl

ma'drina *sf* godmother

maestà *sf inv* majesty; **maes'toso, a** *ag* majestic

ma'estra *sf vedi* **maestro**

maes'trale *sm* north-west wind, mistral

maes'tranze [maes'trantse] *sfpl* workforce *sg*

maes'tria *sf* mastery, skill

ma'estro, a *smf (INS: anche: ~ di scuola o elementare)* primary *(BRIT) o* grade school *(US)* teacher; *(esperto)* expert ♦ *sm (artigiano, fig: guida)* master; *(MUS)* maestro ♦ *ag (principale)* main; *(di grande abilità)* masterly, skilful; **~a d'asilo** nursery teacher; **~ di cerimonie** master of ceremonies

'mafia *sf* Mafia; **mafi'oso** *sm* member of the Mafia

'maga *sf* sorceress

ma'gagna [ma'gaɲɲa] *sf* defect, flaw, blemish; *(noia, guaio)* problem

ma'gari *escl (esprime desiderio):* **~ fosse vero!** if only it were true!; **ti piacerebbe andare in Scozia? — ~!** would you like to go to Scotland? — and how! ♦ *av (anche)* even; *(forse)* perhaps

magaz'zino [magad'dzino] *sm* warehouse; **grande ~** department store

'maggio ['maddʒo] *sm* May

maggio'rana [maddʒo'rana] *sf (BOT)* (sweet) marjoram

maggio'ranza [maddʒo'rantsa] *sf* majority

maggio'rare [maddʒo'rare] *vt* to increase, raise

maggior'domo [maddʒor'dɔmo] *sm* butler

maggi'ore [mad'dʒore] *ag* (*comparativo: più grande*) bigger, larger; taller; greater; (*: più vecchio: sorella, fratello*) older, elder; (*: di grado superiore*) senior; (*: più importante, MIL, MUS*) major; (*superlativo*) biggest, largest; tallest; greatest; oldest, eldest ♦ *smf* (*di grado*) superior; (*di età*) elder; (*MIL*) major; (*: AER*) squadron leader; la **maggior parte** the majority; **andare per la ~** (*cantante etc*) to be very popular; **maggio'renne** *ag* of age ♦ *smf* person who has come of age; **maggior'mente** *av* much more; (*con senso superlativo*) most

ma'gia [ma'dʒia] *sf* magic; **'magico, a, ci, che** *ag* magic; (*fig*) fascinating, charming, magical

'magio ['madʒo] *sm* (*REL*): **i re Magi** the Magi, the Three Wise Men

magis'tero [madʒis'tɛro] *sm* teaching; (*fig: maestria*) skill; (*INS*): **facoltà di M~** ≈ teachers' training college; **magis'trale** *ag* primary (*BRIT*) *o* grade school (*US*) teachers', primary (*BRIT*) *o* grade school (*US*) teaching *cpd*; skilful

magis'trato [madʒis'trato] *sm* magistrate; **magistra'tura** *sf* magistrature; (*magistrati*): **la magistratura** the Bench

'maglia ['maʎʎa] *sf* stitch; (*lavoro ai ferri*) knitting *no pl*; (*tessuto, SPORT*) jersey; (*maglione*) jersey, sweater; (*di catena*) link; (*di rete*) mesh; ~ **diritta/rovescia** plain/purl; **maglie'ria** *sf* knitwear; (*negozio*) knitwear shop; **magli'etta** *sf* (*canottiera*) vest; (*tipo camicia*) T-shirt; **magli'ficio** *sm* knitwear factory

'maglio ['maʎʎo] *sm* mallet; (*macchina*) power hammer

ma'gnanimo, a [ma'ɲanimo, a] *ag* magnanimous

ma'gnete [ma'ɲete] *sm* magnet; **ma'gnetico, a, ci, che** *ag* magnetic

magne'tofono [maɲɲe'tɔfono] *sm* tape recorder

ma'gnifico, a, ci, che [maɲ'ɲifiko] *ag* magnificent, splendid; (*ospite*) generous

'magno, a ['maɲɲo] *ag*: **aula ~a** main hall

ma'gnolia [maɲ'ɲɔlja] *sf* magnolia

'mago, ghi *sm* (*stregone*) magician, wizard; (*illusionista*) magician

ma'grezza [ma'grettsa] *sf* thinness

'magro, a *ag* (*very*) thin, skinny; (*carne*) lean; (*formaggio*) low-fat; (*fig: scarso, misero*) meagre, poor; (*: meschino: scusa*) poor, lame; **mangiare di ~** not to eat meat

'mai *av* (*nessuna volta*) never; (*talvolta*) ever; **non ... ~** never; ~ **più** never again; **come ~?** why (*o* how) on earth?; **chi/dove/quando ~?** whoever/wherever/whenever?

mai'ale *sm* (*ZOOL*) pig; (*carne*) pork

maio'nese *sf* mayonnaise

'mais *sm inv* maize

mai'uscola *sf* capital letter

mai'uscolo, a *ag* (*lettera*) capital; (*fig*) enormous, huge

mal *av, sm vedi* **male**

malac'corto, a *ag* rash, careless

mala'fede *sf* bad faith

mala'lingua (*pl* **male'lingue**) *sf* gossip(monger)

mala'mente *av* badly; dangerously

malan'dato, a *ag* (*persona: di salute*) in poor health; (*: di condizioni finanziarie*) badly off; (*trascurato*) shabby

ma'lanno *sm* (*disgrazia*) misfortune; (*malattia*) ailment

mala'pena *sf*: **a ~** hardly, scarcely

ma'laria *sf* (*MED*) malaria

mala'sorte *sf* bad luck

mala'ticcio, a [mala'tittʃo] *ag* sickly

ma'lato, a *ag* ill, sick; (*gamba*) bad; (*pianta*) diseased ♦ *smf* sick person; (*in ospedale*) patient; **ma'lattia** *sf* (*infettiva etc*) illness, disease; (*cattiva salute*) illness, sickness; (*di pianta*) disease

malau'gurio *sm* bad *o* ill omen

mala'vita *sf* underworld

mala'voglia [mala'vɔʎʎa] *sf*: di ~ unwillingly, reluctantly

mal'concio, a, ci, ce [mal'kontʃo] *ag* in a sorry state

malcon'tento *sm* discontent

malcos'tume *sm* immorality

mal'destro, a *ag* (*inabile*) inexpert, inexperienced); (*goffo*) awkward

maldi'cenza [maldi'tʃentsa] *sf* malicious gossip

maldis'posto, a *ag*: ~ (*verso*) ill-disposed (towards)

'male *av* badly ♦ *sm* (*ciò che è ingiusto, disonesto*) evil; (*danno, svantaggio*) harm; (*sventura*) misfortune; (*dolore fisico, morale*) pain, ache; di ~ in peggio from bad to worse; sentirsi ~ to feel ill; far ~ (*dolere*) to hurt; far del ~ a qn to hurt *o* harm sb; restare *o* rimanere ~ to be sorry; to be disappointed; to be hurt; andare a ~ to go bad; come va? — non c'è ~ how are you? — not bad; mal di cuore heart trouble; ~ di dente toothache; mal di mare seasickness; avere mal di gola/testa to have a sore throat/a headache; aver ~ ai piedi to have sore feet

male'detto, a *pp di* maledire ♦ *ag* cursed, damned; (*fig: fam*) damned, blasted

male'dire *vt* to curse; **maledizi'one** *sf* curse; **maledizione!** damn it!

male'ducato, a *ag* rude, ill-mannered

male'fatta *sf* misdeed

male'ficio [male'fitʃo] *sm* witchcraft

ma'lefico, a, ci, che *ag* (*aria, cibo*) harmful, bad; (*influsso, azione*) evil

ma'lessere *sm* indisposition, slight illness; (*fig*) uneasiness

ma'levolo, a *ag* malevolent

malfa'mato, a *ag* notorious

mal'fatto, a *ag* (*persona*) deformed; (*oggetto*) badly made; (*lavoro*) badly done

malfat'tore, 'trice *smf* wrongdoer

mal'fermo, a *ag* unsteady, shaky; (*salute*) poor, delicate

malformazi'one [malformat'tsjone] *sf* malformation

malgo'verno *sm* maladministration

mal'grado *prep* in spite of, despite ♦ *cong* although; **mio** (*o* **tuo** *etc*) ~ against my (*o* your *etc*) will

ma'lia *sf* spell; (*fig: fascino*) charm

mali'gnare [maliɲ'ɲare] *vi*: ~ **su** to malign, speak ill of

ma'ligno, a [ma'liɲɲo] *ag* (*malvagio*) malicious, malignant; (*MED*) malignant

malinco'nia *sf* melancholy, gloom; **malin'conico, a, ci, che** *ag* melancholy

malincu'ore: a ~ *av* reluctantly, unwillingly

malintenzio'nato, a [malintentsjo'nato] *ag* ill-intentioned

malin'teso, a *ag* misunderstood; (*riguardo, senso del dovere*) mistaken, wrong ♦ *sm* misunderstanding

ma'lizia [ma'littsja] *sf* (*malignità*) malice; (*furbizia*) cunning; (*espediente*) trick; **malizi'oso, a** *ag* malicious; cunning; (*vivace, birichino*) mischievous

mal'loppo *sm* (*involto*) bundle; (*fam: refurtiva*) loot

malme'nare *vt* to beat up; (*fig*) to ill-treat

mal'messo, a *ag* shabby

malnu'trito, a *ag* undernourished

ma'locchio [ma'lɔkkjo] *sm* evil eye

ma'lora *sf*: andare in ~ to go to the dogs

ma'lore *sm* (sudden) illness

mal'sano, a *ag* unhealthy

malsi'curo, a *ag* unsafe

'Malta *sf*: la ~ Malta

'malta *sf* (*EDIL*) mortar

mal'tempo *sm* bad weather

'malto *sm* malt

maltrat'tare *vt* to ill-treat

malu'more *sm* bad mood; (*irritabilità*) bad temper; (*discordia*) ill feeling; **di** ~ in a bad mood

mal'vagio, a, gi, gie [mal'vadʒo] *ag* wicked, evil

malversazi'one [malversat'tsjone] *sf* (*DIR*) embezzlement

mal'visto, a *ag*: ~ (**da**) disliked (by), unpopular (with)

malvi'vente *sm* criminal

malvolenti'eri *av* unwillingly, reluctantly

'mamma *sf* mummy, mum; ~ **mia!** my goodness!

mam'mella *sf* (*ANAT*) breast; (*di vacca, capra etc*) udder

mam'mifero *sm* mammal

'mammola *sf* (*BOT*) violet

ma'nata *sf* (*colpo*) slap; (*quantità*) handful

'manca *sf* left (hand); **a destra e a ~** left, right and centre, on all sides

man'canza [man'kantsa] *sf* lack; (*carenza*) shortage, scarcity; (*fallo*) fault; (*imperfezione*) failing, shortcoming; **per ~ di tempo** through lack of time; **in ~ di meglio** for lack of anything better

man'care *vi* (*essere insufficiente*) to be lacking; (*venir meno*) to fail; (*sbagliare*) to be wrong, make a mistake; (*non esserci*) to be missing, not to be there; (*essere lontano*): ~ (**da**) to be away (from) ♦ *vt* to miss; ~ **di** to lack; ~ **a** (*promessa*) to fail to keep; **tu mi manchi** I miss you; **mancò poco che morisse** he very nearly died; **mancano ancora 10 sterline** we're still £10 short; **manca un quarto alle 6** it's a quarter to 6; **man'cato, a** *ag* (*tentativo*) unsuccessful; (*artista*) failed

'mancia, ce ['mantʃa] *sf* tip; ~ **competente** reward

manci'ata [man'tʃata] *sf* handful

man'cino, a [man'tʃino] *ag* (*braccio*) left; (*persona*) left-handed; (*fig*) underhand

'manco *av* (*nemmeno*) ~ **per sogno o per idea!** not on your life!

man'dante *sm/f* (*di delitto*) instigator

man'dare *vt* to send; (*far funzio-*

nare: macchina) to drive; (*emettere*) to send out; (: *grido*) to give, utter, let out; ~ **a chiamare qn** to send for sb; ~ **avanti** (*fig: famiglia*) to provide for; (: *fabbrica*) to run, look after; ~ **giù** to send down; (*anche fig*) to swallow; ~ **via** to send away; (*licenziare*) to fire

manda'rino *sm* mandarin (orange); (*cinese*) mandarin

man'data *sf* (*quantità*) lot, batch; (*di chiave*) turn; **chiudere a doppia ~** to double-lock

manda'tario *sm* (*DIR*) representative, agent

man'dato *sm* (*incarico*) commission; (*DIR: provvedimento*) warrant; (*di deputato etc*) mandate; (*ordine di pagamento*) postal o money order; ~ **d'arresto** warrant for arrest

man'dibola *sf* mandible, jaw

'mandorla *sf* almond; **'mandorlo** *sm* almond tree

'mandria *sf* herd

maneggi'are [maned'dʒare] *vt* (*creta, cera*) to mould, work, fashion; (*arnesi, utensili*) to handle; (: *adoperare*) to use; (*fig: persone, denaro*) to handle, deal with; **ma'neggio** [ma'neddʒo] *sm* moulding; handling; use; (*intrigo*) plot, scheme; (*per cavalli*) riding school

ma'nesco, a, schi, sche *ag* free with one's fists

ma'nette *sfpl* handcuffs

manga'nello *sm* club

manga'nese *sm* manganese

mange'reccio, a, ci, ce [mandʒe'rettʃo] *ag* edible

mangia'dischi [mandʒa'diski] *sm inv* record player

mangi'are [man'dʒare] *vt* to eat; (*intaccare*) to eat into o away; (*CARTE, SCACCHI etc*) to take ♦ *vi* to eat ♦ *sm* eating; (*cibo*) food; (*cucina*) cooking; ~**rsi le parole** to mumble; ~**rsi le unghie** to bite one's nails; **mangia'toia** *sf* feeding-trough

man'gime [man'dʒime] *sm* fodder

'**mango, ghi** sm mango

ma'nia sf (PSIC) mania; (fig) obsession, craze; **ma'niaco, a, ci, che** ag suffering from a mania; **maniaco (di)** obsessed (by), crazy (about)

'**manica** sf sleeve; (fig: gruppo) gang, bunch; (GEO): **la M~, il Canale della M~** the (English) Channel; **essere di ~ larga/stretta** to be easy-going/strict; **~ a vento** (AER) wind sock

mani'chino [mani'kino] sm (di sarto, vetrina) dummy

'**manico, ci** sm handle; (MUS) neck

mani'comio sm mental hospital; (fig) madhouse

mani'cotto sm muff; (TECN) coupling; sleeve

mani'cure sm o f inv manicure ♦ sf inv manicurist

mani'era sf way, manner; (stile) style, manner; **~e** sfpl (comportamento) manners; **in ~ da** so as to; **in ~ che** so that; **in tutte le ~e** at all costs

manie'rato, a ag affected

manifat'tura sf (lavorazione) manufacture; (stabilimento) factory

manifes'tare vt to show, display; (esprimere) to express; (rivelare) to reveal, disclose ♦ vi to demonstrate; **~rsi** vr to show o.s.; **~rsi amico** to prove o.s. (to be) a friend; **manifestazi'one** sf show, display, expression; (sintomo) sign, symptom; (dimostrazione pubblica) demonstration; (cerimonia) event

mani'festo, a ag obvious, evident ♦ sm poster, bill; (scritto ideologico) manifesto

ma'niglia [ma'niʎʎa] sf handle; (sostegno: negli autobus etc) strap

manipo'lare vt to manipulate; (alterare: vino) to adulterate; **manipolazi'one** sf manipulation; adulteration

manis'calco, chi sm blacksmith

'**manna** sf (REL) manna

man'naia sf (del boia) (executioner's) axe; (per carni) cleaver

man'naro: lupo ~ sm werewolf

'**mano, i** sf hand; (strato: di vernice etc) coat; **di prima ~** (notizia) first-hand; **di seconda ~** second-hand; **man ~** little by little, gradually; **man ~ che** as; **darsi o stringersi la ~** to shake hands; **mettere le ~i avanti** (fig) to safeguard o.s.; **restare a ~i vuote** to be left empty-handed; **venire alle ~i** to come to blows; **a ~ by hand**; **~i in alto!** hands up!

mano'dopera sf labour

mano'messo, a pp di manomettere

ma'nometro sm gauge, manometer

mano'mettere vt (alterare) to tamper with; (aprire indebitamente) to break open illegally

ma'nopola sf (dell'armatura) gauntlet; (guanto) mitt; (di impugnatura) hand-grip; (pomello) knob

manos'critto, a ag handwritten ♦ sm manuscript

mano'vale sm labourer

mano'vella sf handle; (TECN) crank

ma'novra sf manoeuvre (BRIT), maneuver (US); (FERR) shunting; **mano'vrare** vt (veicolo) to manoeuvre (BRIT), maneuver (US); (macchina, congegno) to operate; (fig: persona) to manipulate ♦ vi to manoeuvre

manro'vescio [manro'veʃʃo] sm slap (with back of hand)

man'sarda sf attic

mansi'one sf task, duty, job

mansu'eto, a ag gentle, docile

man'tello sm cloak; (fig: di neve etc) blanket, mantle; (TECN: involucro) casing, shell; (ZOOL) coat

mante'nere vt to maintain; (adempiere: promesse) to keep, abide by; (provvedere a) to support, maintain; **~rsi** vr: **~rsi calmo/giovane** to stay calm/young; **manteni'mento** sm maintenance

'**mantice** ['mantitʃe] sm bellows pl; (di carrozza, automobile) hood

'manto *sm* cloak; ~ **stradale** road surface

manu'ale *ag* manual ♦ *sm* (*testo*) manual, handbook

ma'nubrio *sm* handle; (*di bicicletta etc*) handlebars *pl*; (*SPORT*) dumbbell

manu'fatto *sm* manufactured article

manutenzi'one [manuten'tsjone] *sf* maintenance, upkeep; (*d'impianti*) maintenance, servicing

'manzo ['mandzo] *sm* (*ZOOL*) steer; (*carne*) beef

'mappa *sf* (*GEO*) map; **mappa'mondo** *sm* map of the world; (*globo girevole*) globe

ma'rasma, i *sm* (*fig*) decay, decline

mara'tona *sf* marathon

'marca, che *sf* mark; (*bollo*) stamp; (*COMM: di prodotti*) brand; (*contrassegno, scontrino*) ticket, check; **prodotto di** ~ (*di buona qualità*) high-class product; ~ **da bollo** official stamp

mar'care *vt* (*munire di contrassegno*) to mark; (*a fuoco*) to brand; (*SPORT: gol*) to score; (: *avversario*) to mark; (*accentuare*) to stress; ~ **visita** (*MIL*) to report sick

'Marche ['marke] *sfpl*: **le** ~ the Marches (*region of central Italy*)

mar'chese, a [mar'keze] *sm/f* marquis *o* marquess/marchioness

marchi'are [mar'kjare] *vt* to brand; **'marchio** *sm* (*di bestiame, COMM, fig*) brand; **marchio depositato** registered trademark; **marchio di fabbrica** trademark

'marcia, ce ['martʃa] *sf* (*anche MUS, MIL*) march; (*funzionamento*) running; (*il camminare*) walking; (*AUT*) gear; **mettere in** ~ to start; **mettersi in** ~ to get moving; **far** ~ **indietro** (*AUT*) to reverse; (*fig*) to back-pedal

marciapi'ede [martʃa'pjɛde] *sm* (*di strada*) pavement (*BRIT*), sidewalk (*US*); (*FERR*) platform

marci'are [mar'tʃare] *vi* to march;

(*andare: treno, macchina*) to go; (*funzionare*) to run, work

'marcio, a, ci, ce ['martʃo] *ag* (*frutta, legno*) rotten, bad; (*MED*) festering; (*fig*) corrupt, rotten

mar'cire [mar'tʃire] *vi* (*andare a male*) to go bad, rot; (*suppurare*) to fester; (*fig*) to rot, waste away

'marco, chi *sm* (*unità monetaria*) mark

'mare *sm* sea; **in** ~ at sea; **andare al** ~ (*in vacanza etc*) to go to the seaside; **il M~ del Nord** the North Sea

ma'rea *sf* tide; **alta/bassa** ~ high/low tide

mareggi'ata [mared'dʒata] *sf* heavy sea

ma'remma *sf* (*GEO*) maremma, swampy coastal area

mare'moto *sm* seaquake

maresci'allo [mareʃ'ʃallo] *sm* (*MIL*) marshal; (: *sottufficiale*) warrant officer

marga'rina *sf* margarine

marghe'rita [marge'rita] *sf* (ox-eye) daisy, marguerite; (*di stampante*) daisy wheel

'margine ['mardʒine] *sm* margin; (*di bosco, via*) edge, border

ma'rina *sf* navy; (*costa*) coast; (*quadro*) seascape; ~ **militare/ mercantile** navy/merchant navy (*BRIT*) *o* marine (*US*)

mari'naio *sm* sailor

mari'nare *vt* (*CUC*) to marinate; ~ **la scuola** to play truant; **mari'nata** *sf* marinade

ma'rino, a *ag* sea *cpd*, marine

mario'netta *sf* puppet

mari'tare *vt* to marry; ~**rsi** *vr*: ~**rsi a** *o* **con qn** to marry sb, get married to sb

ma'rito *sm* husband

ma'rittimo, a *ag* maritime, sea *cpd*

mar'maglia [mar'maʎʎa] *sf* mob, riff-raff

marmel'lata *sf* jam; (*di agrumi*) marmalade

mar'mitta *sf* (*recipiente*) pot;

(AUT) silencer; ~ **catalitica** catalytic convertor

'marmo sm marble

mar'mocchio [mar'mɔkkjo] (fam) sm tot, kid

mar'motta sf (ZOOL) marmot

Ma'rocco sm: il ~ Morocco

ma'roso sm breaker

mar'rone ag inv brown ♦ sm (BOT) chestnut

mar'sala sf inv (vino) Marsala

mar'sina sf (tails pl, tail coat)

martedì sm inv Tuesday; **di** o **il** ~ on Tuesdays; ~ **grasso** Shrove Tuesday

martel'lare vt to hammer ♦ vi (pulsare) to throb; (: cuore) to thump

mar'tello sm hammer; (di uscio) knocker

marti'netto sm (TECN) jack

'martire sm/f martyr; **mar'tirio** sm martyrdom; (fig) agony, torture

'martora sf marten

martori'are vt to torment, torture

mar'xista, i, e ag, sm/f Marxist

marza'pane [martsa'pane] sm marzipan

'marzo ['martso] sm March

mascal'zone [maskal'tsone] sm rascal, scoundrel

ma'scella [maʃ'ʃella] sf (ANAT) jaw

'maschera ['maskera] sf mask; (travestimento) disguise; (: per un ballo etc) fancy dress; (TEATRO, CINEMA) usher/usherette; (personaggio del teatro) stock character; **mas-che'rare** vt to mask; (travestire) to disguise; to dress up; (fig: celare) to hide, conceal; (MIL) to camouflage; ~**rsi da** to disguise o.s. as; to dress up as; (fig) to masquerade as

mas'chile [mas'kile] ag masculine; (sesso, popolazione) male; (abiti) men's; (per ragazzi: scuola) boys'

'maschio, a ['maskjo] ag (BIOL) male; (virile) manly ♦ sm (anche ZOOL, TECN) male; (uomo) man; (ragazzo) boy; (figlio) son

masco'lino, a ag masculine

'massa sf mass; (di errori etc): **una** ~ **di** heaps of, masses of; (di gente) mass, multitude; (ELETTR) earth; **in** ~ (COMM) in bulk; (tutti insieme) en masse; **adunata in** ~ mass meeting; **di** ~ (cultura, manifestazione) mass cpd; **la** ~ **del popolo** the masses pl

mas'sacro sm massacre, slaughter; (fig) mess, disaster

mas'saggio [mas'saddʒo] sm massage

mas'saia sf housewife

masse'rizie [masse'rittsje] sfpl (household) furnishings

mas'siccio, a, ci, ce [mas'sittʃo] ag (oro, legno) solid; (palazzo) massive; (corporatura) stout ♦ sm (GEO) massif

'massima sf (sentenza, regola) maxim; (METEOR) maximum temperature; **in linea di** ~ generally speaking; vedi anche **massimo**

massi'male sm maximum

'massimo, a ag, sm maximum; **al** ~ at (the) most

'masso sm rock, boulder

mas'sone sm freemason; **masso-ne'ria** sf freemasonry

mas'tello sm tub

masti'care vt to chew

'mastice ['mastitʃe] sm mastic; (per vetri) putty

mas'tino sm mastiff

ma'tassa sf skein

mate'matica sf mathematics sg

mate'matico, a, ci, che ag mathematical ♦ sm/f mathematician

mate'rasso sm mattress; ~ **a molle** spring o interior-sprung mattress

ma'teria sf (FISICA) matter; (TECN, COMM) material, matter no pl; (disciplina) subject; (argomento) subject matter, material; ~**e prime** raw materials; **in** ~ **di** (per quanto concerne) on the subject of; **mate-ri'ale** ag material; (fig: grossolano) rough, rude ♦ sm material; (insieme di strumenti etc) equipment no pl, materials pl

maternità sf motherhood, maternity; (clinica) maternity hospital

ma'terno, a ag (amore, cura etc) maternal, motherly; (nonno) maternal; (lingua, terra) mother cpd

ma'tita sf pencil

ma'trice [ma'tritʃe] sf matrix; (COMM) counterfoil; (fig: origine) background

ma'tricola sf (registro) register; (numero) registration number; (nell'università) freshman, fresher

ma'trigna [ma'triɲɲa] sf stepmother

matrimoni'ale ag matrimonial, marriage cpd

matri'monio sm marriage, matrimony; (durata) marriage, married life; (cerimonia) wedding

ma'trona sf (fig) matronly woman

mat'tina sf morning; **matti'nata** sf morning; (spettacolo) matinée, afternoon performance; **mattini'ero, a** ag: **essere mattiniero** to be an early riser; **mat'tino** sm morning

'matto, a ag mad, crazy; (fig: falso) false, imitation; (: opaco) matt, dull ♦ sm/f madman/woman; **avere una voglia ~a di qc** to be dying for sth

mat'tone sm brick; (fig): **questo libro/film è un ~** this book/film is heavy going

matto'nella sf tile

matu'rare vi (anche: ~rsi) (frutta, grano) to ripen; (ascesso) to come to a head; (fig: persona, idea, ECON) to mature ♦ vt to ripen; to (make) mature

maturità sf maturity; (di frutta) ripeness, maturity; (INS) school-leaving examination, ≈ GCE A-levels (BRIT)

ma'turo, a ag mature; (frutto) ripe, mature

'mazza ['mattsa] sf (bastone) club; (martello) sledge-hammer; (SPORT: da golf) club; (: da baseball, cricket) bat

maz'zata [mat'tsata] sf (anche fig) heavy blow

'mazzo ['mattso] sm (di fiori, chiavi

etc) bunch; (di carte da gioco) pack

me pron me; ~ **stesso(a)** myself; **sei bravo quanto ~** you are as clever as I (am) o as me

me'andro sm meander

M.E.C. [mɛk] sigla m (= Mercato Comune Europeo) EEC

mec'canica, che sf mechanics sg; (attività tecnologica) mechanical engineering; (meccanismo) mechanism

mec'canico, a, ci, che ag mechanical ♦ sm mechanic

mecca'nismo sm mechanism

me'daglia [me'daʎʎa] sf medal; **medagli'one** sm (ARCHIT) medallion; (gioiello) locket

me'desimo, a ag same; (in persona): **io ~ I** myself

'media sf average; (MAT) mean; (INS: voto) end-of-term average; **in ~** on average; vedi anche **medio**

medi'ano, a ag median; (valore) mean ♦ sm (CALCIO) half-back

medi'ante prep by means of

medi'are vt (fare da mediatore) to act as mediator in; (MAT) to average

media'tore, trice sm/f mediator; (COMM) middle man, agent

medica'mento sm medicine, drug

medi'care vt to treat; (ferita) to dress; **medicazi'one** sf treatment, medication; dressing

medi'cina [medi'tʃina] sf medicine; ~ **legale** forensic medicine; **medi'cinale** ag medicinal ♦ sm drug, medicine

'medico, a, ci, che ag medical ♦ sm doctor; ~ **generico** general practitioner, GP

medie'vale ag medieval

'medio, a ag average; (punto, ceto) middle; (altezza, statura) medium ♦ sm (dito) middle finger; **licenza** ~a leaving certificate awarded at the end of 3 years of secondary education; **scuola** ~a first 3 years of secondary school

medi'ocre ag mediocre, poor

medioe'vale ag = **medievale**

medio'evo *sm* Middle Ages *pl*

medi'tare *vt* to ponder over, meditate on; (*progettare*) to plan, think out ♦ *vi* to meditate

mediter'raneo, a *ag* Mediterranean; **il (mare) M~** the Mediterranean (Sea)

me'dusa *sf* (*ZOOL*) jellyfish

me'gafono *sm* megaphone

'meglio ['mɛʎʎo] *av, ag inv* better; (*con senso superlativo*) best ♦ *sm* (*la cosa migliore*) the best (thing); **faresti ~ ad andartene** you had better leave; **alla ~** as best one can; **andar di bene in ~** to get better and better; **fare del proprio ~** to do one's best; **per il ~** for the best; **aver la ~ su qn** to get the better of sb

'mela *sf* apple; **~ cotogna** quince

mela'grana *sf* pomegranate

melan'zana [melan'dzana] *sf* aubergine (*BRIT*), eggplant (*US*)

me'lenso, a *ag* dull, stupid

mel'lifluo, a (*peg*) *ag* sugary, honeyed

'melma *sf* mud, mire

'melo *sm* apple tree

melo'dia *sf* melody

me'lone *sm* (musk)melon

'membra *sfpl vedi* **membro**

'membro *sm* member; (*pl(f) ~a:* *arto*) limb

memo'randum *sm inv* memorandum

me'moria *sf* memory; **~e** *sfpl* (*opera autobiografica*) memoirs; **a ~** (*imparare, sapere*) by heart; **a ~ d'uomo** within living memory; **memori'ale** *sm* (*raccolta di memorie*) memoirs *pl*; (*DIR*) memorial

mena'dito: a ~ *av* perfectly, thoroughly; **sapere qc a ~** to have sth at one's fingertips

me'nare *vt* to lead; (*picchiare*) to hit, beat; (*dare: colpi*) to deal; **~ la coda** (*cane*) to wag its tail

mendi'cante *sm/f* beggar

mendi'care *vt* to beg for ♦ *vi* to beg

'meno *av* **1** (*in minore misura*) less; **dovresti mangiare ~** you should eat less, you shouldn't eat so much

2 (*comparativo*): **~ ... di** not as ..., as, less ... than; **sono ~ alto di te** I'm not as tall as you (are), I'm less tall than you (are); **~ ... che** not as ... as, less ... than; **~ che mai** less than ever; **è ~ intelligente che ricco** he's more rich than intelligent; **~ fumo più mangio** the less I smoke the more I eat

3 (*superlativo*) least; **il ~ dotato degli studenti** the least gifted of the students; **è quello che compro ~ spesso** it's the one I buy least often

4 (*MAT*) minus; **8 ~ 5** 8 minus 5, 8 take away 5; **sono le 8 ~ un quarto** it's a quarter to 8; **~ 5 gradi** 5 degrees below zero, minus 5 degrees; **mille lire in ~** a thousand lire less

5 (*fraseologia*): **quanto ~ poteva telefonare** he could at least have phoned; **non so se accettare o ~** I don't know whether to accept or not; **fare a ~ di qc/qn** to do without sth/sb; **non potevo fare a ~ di ridere** I couldn't help laughing; **~ male!** thank goodness!; **~ male che sei arrivato** it's a good job that you've come

♦ *ag inv* (*tempo, denaro*) less; (*errori, persone*) fewer; **ha fatto ~ errori di tutti** he made fewer mistakes than anyone, he made the fewest mistakes of all

♦ *sm inv* **1**: **il ~** (*il minimo*) the least; **parlare del più e del ~** to talk about this and that

2 (*MAT*) minus

♦ *prep* (*eccetto*) except (for), apart from; **a ~ che**, **a ~ di** unless; **a ~ che non piova** unless it rains; **non posso, a ~ di prendere ferie** I can't, unless I take some leave

meno'mare *vt* (*danneggiare*) to maim, disable

meno'pausa *sf* menopause

'**mensa** *sf* (*locale*) canteen; (: *MIL*) mess; (: *nelle università*) refectory

men'sile *ag* monthly ♦ *sm* (*periodico*) monthly (magazine); (*stipendio*) monthly salary

'**mensola** *sf* bracket; (*ripiano*) shelf; (*ARCHIT*) corbel

'**menta** *sf* mint; (*anche*: ~ *piperita*) peppermint; (*bibita*) peppermint cordial; (*caramella*) mint, peppermint

men'tale *ag* mental; **mentalità** *sf inv* mentality

'**mente** *sf* mind; **imparare/sapere** qc a ~ to learn/know sth by heart; **avere in** ~ qc to have sth in mind; **passare di** ~ a qn to slip sb's mind

men'tire *vi* to lie

'**mento** *sm* chin

men'tolo *sm* menthol

'**mentre** *cong* (*temporale*) while; (*avversativo*) whereas

menù *sm inv* menu; ~ **turistico** set menu

menzio'nare [mentsjo'nare] *vt* to mention

menzi'one [men'tsjone] *sf* mention; **fare** ~ **di** to mention

men'zogna [men'tsɔɲɲa] *sf* lie

mera'viglia [mera'viʎʎa] *sf* amazement, wonder; (*persona, cosa*) marvel, wonder; **a** ~ perfectly, wonderfully; **meravigli'are** *vt* to amaze, astonish; **meravigliarsi (di)** *vb* to marvel (at); (*stupirsi*) to be amazed (at), be astonished (at); **meraviglio'so, a** *ag* wonderful, marvellous

mer'cante *sm* merchant; ~ **d'arte** art dealer; **mercanteggi'are** *vt* (*onore, voto*) to sell ♦ *vi* to bargain, haggle; **mercan'tile** *ag* commercial, mercantile; (*nave, marina*) merchant *cpd* ♦ *sm* (*nave*) merchantman; **mercan'zia** *sf* merchandise, goods *pl*

mer'cato *sm* market; ~ **dei cambi** exchange market; **M~ Comune (Europeo)** (European) Common Market; ~ **nero** black market

'**merce** ['mertʃe] *sf* goods *pl*,

merchandise; ~ **deperibile** perishable goods *pl*

mercé [mer'tʃe] *sf* mercy

merce'nario, a [mertʃe'narjo] *ag*, *sm* mercenary

merce'ria [mertʃe'ria] *sf* (*articoli*) haberdashery (*BRIT*), notions *pl* (*US*); (*bottega*) haberdasher's shop (*BRIT*), notions store (*US*)

mercoledì *sm inv* Wednesday; **di** ○ **il** ~ on Wednesdays; ~ **delle Ceneri** Ash Wednesday

mer'curio *sm* mercury

'**merda** (*fam!*) *sf* shit (!)

me'renda *sf* afternoon snack

meridi'ana *sf* (*orologio*) sundial

meridi'ano, a *ag* meridian; midday *cpd*, noonday ♦ *sm* meridian

meridio'nale *ag* southern ♦ *sm/f* southerner

meridi'one *sm* south

me'ringa, ghe *sf* (*CUC*) meringue

meri'tare *vt* to deserve, merit ♦ *vb impers*: **merita andare** it's worth going

meri'tevole *ag* worthy

me'rito *sm* merit; (*valore*) worth; **in** ~ **a** as regards, with regard to; **dare** ~ **a qn** to give sb credit for; **finire a pari** ~ to finish joint first (*o* second *etc*); **to tie**; **meri'torio, a** *ag* praiseworthy

mer'letto *sm* lace

'**merlo** *sm* (*ZOOL*) blackbird; (*ARCHIT*) battlement

mer'luzzo [mer'luttso] *sm* (*ZOOL*) cod

mes'chino, a [mes'kino] *ag* wretched; (*scarso*) scanty, poor; (*persona*: *gretta*) mean; (: *limitata*) narrow-minded, petty

mesco'lanza [mesko'lantsa] *sf* mixture

mesco'lare *vt* to mix; (*vini, colori*) to blend; (*mettere in disordine*) to mix up, muddle up; (*carte*) to shuffle; ~**rsi** *vb* to mix; to blend; to get mixed up; (*fig*): ~**rsi in** to get mixed up in, meddle in

'**mese** *sm* month

'**messa** *sf* (*REL*) mass; (*il mettere*): ~ **in moto** starting; ~ **in piega** set; ~ **a punto** (*TECN*) adjustment; (*AUT*) tuning; (*fig*) clarification; ~ **in scena** = **messinscena**

messag'gero [messad'dʒɛro] *sm* messenger

mes'saggio [mes'saddʒo] *sm* message

mes'sale *sm* (*REL*) missal

'**messe** *sf* harvest

Mes'sia *sm inv* (*REL*): **il** ~ **the** Messiah

'**Messico** *sm*: **il** ~ Mexico

messin'scena [messin'ʃɛna] *sf* (*TEATRO*) production

'**messo, a** *pp di* **mettere** ♦ *sm* messenger

mesti'ere *sm* (*professione*) job; (: *manuale*) trade; (: *artigianale*) craft; (*fig*: *abilità nel lavoro*) skill, technique; **essere del** ~ **to** know the tricks of the trade

'**mesto, a** *ag* sad, melancholy

mestola *sf* (*CUC*) ladle; (*EDIL*) trowel

mestolo *sm* (*CUC*) ladle

mestruazi'one [mestruat'tsjone] *sf* menstruation

'**meta** *sf* destination; (*fig*) aim, goal

metà *sf inv* half; (*punto di mezzo*) middle; **dividere qc a o per** ~ **to** divide sth in half, halve sth; **fare a** ~ (**di qc con qn**) **to go halves** (*with sb in sth*); **a** ~ **prezzo at half price**; **a** ~ **strada halfway**

me'tafora *sf* metaphor

me'tallico, a, ci, che *ag* (*di metallo*) metal *cpd*; (*splendore, rumore etc*) metallic

me'tallo *sm* metal

metalmec'canico, a, ci, che *ag* engineering *cpd* ♦ *sm* engineering worker

me'tano *sm* methane

meteorolo'gia [meteorolo'dʒia] *sf* meteorology; **meteoro'logico, a, ci, che** *ag* meteorological, weather *cpd*

me'ticcio, a, ci, ce [me'tittʃo] *sm/f*

---

half-caste, half-breed

me'todico, a, ci, che *ag* methodical

'**metodo** *sm* method; (*manuale*) tutor (*BRIT*), manual

'**metrica** *sf* metrics *sg*

'**metrico, a, ci, che** *ag* metric; (*POESIA*) metrical

'**metro** *sm* metre; (*nastro*) tape measure; (*asta*) (metre) rule

metropoli'tana *sf* underground, subway

metropoli'tano, a *ag* metropolitan

'**mettere** *vt* to put; (*abito*) to put on; (: *portare*) to wear; (*installare*: *telefono*) to put in; (*fig*: *provocare*): ~ **fame/allegria a qn** to make sb hungry/happy; (*supporre*): **mettiamo che** ... let's suppose o say that ... ; ~**rsi** *vr* (*persona*) to put o.s.; (*oggetto*) to go; (*disporsi*: *faccenda*) to turn out; ~**rsi a sedere** to sit down; ~**rsi a letto** to get into bed; (*per malattia*) to take to one's bed; ~**rsi il cappello** to put on one's hat; ~**rsi a** (*cominciare*) to begin to, start to; ~**rsi al lavoro** to set to work; ~**rsi con qn** (*in società*) to team up with sb; (*in coppia*) to start going out with sb; ~**rci**: ~**rci molta cura/molto tempo** to take a lot of care/a lot of time; **ci ho messo 3 ore per venire** it's taken me 3 hours to get here; ~**rcela tutta** to do one's best; ~**a tacere qn/qc** to keep sb/ sth quiet; ~**su casa** to set up house; ~**su un negozio** to start a shop; ~ **via** to put away

'**mezza** ['mɛddza] *sf*: **la** ~ half-past twelve (*in the afternoon*); *vedi anche* **mezzo**

mez'zadro [med'dzadro] *sm* (*AGR*) sharecropper

mezza'luna [meddza'luna] *sf* half-moon; (*dell'islamismo*) crescent; (*coltello*) (semicircular) chopping knife

mezza'nino [meddza'nino] *sm* mezzanine (floor)

mez'zano, a [med'dzano] *ag*

(medio) average, medium; *(figlio)* middle cpd ♦ *sm/f (intermediario)* go-between; *(ruffiano)* pimp

mezza'notte [meddza'nɔtte] *sf* midnight

'mezzo, a ['mɛddzo] *ag* half; **un ~ litro/panino** half a litre/roll ♦ *av* half-; **~ morto** half-dead ♦ *sm (metà)* half; *(parte centrale: di strada etc)* middle; *(per raggiungere un fine)* means *sg*; *(veicolo)* vehicle; *(nell'indicare l'ora)*: **le nove e ~** half past nine; **mezzogiorno e ~** half past twelve; **~i** *smpl (possibilità economiche)* means; **di ~a età** middle-aged; **un soprabito di ~a stagione** a spring *o* autumn coat; **di ~, in mezzo**, in the middle; **andarci di ~** *(patir danno)* to suffer; **levarsi** *o* **togliersi di ~** to get out of the way; **in ~ a** in the middle of; **per** *o* **a ~ di** by means of; **~i di comunicazione di massa** mass media *pl*; **~i pubblici** public transport *sg*; **~i di trasporto** means of transport

mezzogi'orno [meddzo'dʒorno] *sm* midday, noon; *(GEO)* south; **a ~ at 12** (o'clock) *o* midday *o* noon; **il ~ d'Italia** southern Italy

mez'z'ora [med'dzora] *sf* half-hour, half an hour

mez'zora [med'dzora] *sf* = **mezz'ora**

mi *(dav lo, la, li, le, ne diventa* **me)** *pron (oggetto)* me; *(complemento di termine)* to me; *(riflessivo)* myself ♦ *sm (MUS)* E; *(: solfeggiando la scala)* mi

'mia *vedi* **mio**

miago'lare *vi* to miaow, mew

'mica *sf (CHIM)* mica ♦ *av (fam)*: **non ... ~** not ... at all; **non sono ~ stanco** I'm not a bit tired; **non sarà ~ partito?** he wouldn't have left, would he?; **~ male** not bad

'miccia, ce ['mittʃa] *sf* fuse

micidi'ale [mitʃi'djale] *ag* fatal; *(dannosissimo)* deadly

mi'crofono *sm* microphone

micros'copio *sm* microscope

mi'dollo *(pl(f)* **~a)** *sm (ANAT)* marrow

'mie *vedi* **mio**

mi'ele *sm* honey

mi'ei *vedi* **mio**

mi'etere *vt (AGR)* to reap, harvest; *(fig: vite)* to take, claim

'miglia ['miʎʎa] *sfpl di* **miglio**

migli'aio [miʎ'ʎajo] *(pl(f)* **~a)** *sm* thousand; **un ~ (di)** about a thousand; **a ~a** by the thousand, in thousands

'miglio ['miʎʎo] *sm (BOT)* millet; *(pl(f)* **~a**: *unità di misura)* mile; **~ marino** *o* **nautico** nautical mile

miglicra'mento [miʎʎora'mento] *sm* improvement

miglio'rare [miʎʎo'rare] *vt, vi* to improve

migli'ore [miʎ'ʎore] *ag (comparativo)* better; *(superlativo)* best ♦ *sm*: **il ~** the best (thing) ♦ *sm/f*: **il(la) ~** the best (person); **il miglior vino di questa regione** the best wine in this area

'mignolo ['miɲɲolo] *sm (ANAT)* little finger, pinkie; *(: dito del piede)* little toe

mi'grare *vi* to migrate

'mila *pl di* **mille**

Mi'lano *sf* Milan

miliar'dario, a *sm/f* millionaire

mili'ardo *sm* thousand million, billion *(US)*

mili'are *ag*: **pietra ~** milestone

mili'one *sm* million; **un ~ di lire** a million lire

mili'tante *ag, sm/f* militant

mili'tare *vi (MIL)* to be a soldier, serve; *(fig: in un partito)* to be a militant ♦ *ag* military ♦ *sm* serviceman; **fare il ~** to do one's military service

'milite *sm* soldier

millan'ta'tore, 'trice *sm/f* boaster

'mille *(pl* **mila)** *num a* **o** one thousand; **dieci mila** ten thousand

mille'foglie [mille'fɔʎʎe] *sm inv (CUC)* cream *o* vanilla slice

mil'lennio *sm* millennium

millepi'edi *sm inv* centipede

mil'lesimo, a *ag, sm* thousandth

milli'grammo *sm* milligram(me)

mil'limetro *sm* millimetre

'milza ['miltsa] *sf* (*ANAT*) spleen

mimetiz'zare [mimetid'dzare] *vt* to camouflage; **~rsi** *vr* to camouflage o.s.

'mimica *sf* (*arte*) mime

'mimo *sm* (*attore, componimento*) mime

mi'mosa *sf* mimosa

'mina *sf* (*esplosiva*) mine; (*di matita*) lead

mi'naccia, ce [mi'nattʃa] *sf* threat; **minacci'are** *vt* to threaten; **minacciare qn di morte** to threaten to kill sb; **minacciare di fare qc** to threaten to do sth; **minacci'oso, a** *ag* threatening

mi'nare *vt* (*MIL*) to mine; (*fig*) to undermine

mina'tore *sm* miner

mina'torio, a *ag* threatening

mine'rale *ag, sm* mineral

mine'rario, a *ag* (*delle miniere*) mining; (*dei minerali*) ore *cpd*

mi'nestra *sf* soup; **~ in brodo/di verdure** noodle/vegetable soup; **mi-nes'trone** *sm* thick vegetable and pasta soup

mingher'lino, a [minger'lino] *ag* thin, slender

'mini *ag inv* mini ♦ *sf inv* miniskirt

minia'tura *sf* miniature

mini'era *sf* mine

mini'gonna *sf* miniskirt

'minimo, a *ag* minimum, least, slightest; (*piccolissimo*) very small, slight; (*il più basso*) lowest, minimum ♦ *sm* minimum; **al ~** at least; **girare al ~** (*AUT*) to idle

minis'tero *sm* (*POL, REL*) ministry; (*governo*) government; **M~ delle Finanze** Ministry of Finance, ≈ Treasury

mi'nistro *sm* (*POL, REL*) minister; **M~ delle Finanze** Minister of Finance, ≈ Chancellor of the Exchequer

mino'ranza [mino'rantsa] *sf* minority

mino'rato, a *ag* handicapped ♦ *sm/f* physically (*o* mentally) handicapped person

mi'nore *ag* (*comparativo*) less; (*più piccolo*) smaller; (*numero*) lower; (*inferiore*) lower, inferior; (*meno importante*) minor; (*più giovane*) younger; (*superlativo*) least; smallest; lowest; youngest ♦ *sm/f* (*minorenne*) minor, person under age

mino'renne *ag* under age ♦ *sm/f* minor, person under age

mi'nuscolo, a *ag* (*scrittura, carattere*) small; (*piccolissimo*) tiny ♦ *sf* small letter

mi'nuta *sf* rough copy, draft

mi'nuto, a *ag* tiny, minute; (*pioggia*) fine; (*corporatura*) delicate, fine; (*lavoro*) detailed ♦ *sm* (*unità di misura*) minute; **al ~** (*COMM*) retail

'mio (*f* **'mia**, *pl* **mi'ei, 'mie**) *det*: **il ~, la mia** *etc* my ♦ *pron*: **il ~, la mia** *etc* mine; **i miei** my family; **un ~ amico** a friend of mine

'miope *ag* short-sighted

'mira (*f* **'mira**, *anche fig*) aim; **prendere la ~** to take aim; **prendere di ~ qn** (*fig*) to pick on sb

mi'rabile *ag* admirable, wonderful

mi'racolo *sm* miracle

mi'raggio [mi'raddʒo] *sm* mirage

mi'rare *vi*: **~ a** to aim at

mi'rino *sm* (*TECN*) sight; (*FOT*) viewer, viewfinder

mir'tillo *sm* bilberry (*BRIT*), blueberry (*US*), whortleberry

mi'scela [miʃ'ʃela] *sf* mixture; (*di caffè*) blend

miscel'lanea [miʃʃel'lanea] *sf* miscellany

'mischia ['miskja] *sf* scuffle; (*RUGBY*) scrum, scrummage

mischi'are [mis'kjare] *vt* to mix, blend; **~rsi** *vr* to mix, blend

mis'cuglio [mis'kuʎʎo] *sm* mixture, hotchpotch, jumble

mise'rabile *ag* (*infelice*) miserable,

wretched; (*povero*) poverty-stricken; (*di scarso valore*) miserable

mi'seria *sf* extreme poverty; (*infelicità*) misery; ~e *sfpl* (*del mondo etc*) misfortunes, t•roubles; **porca** ~! (*fam*) blast!, damn!

miseri'cordia *sf* mercy, pity

'misero, a *ag* miserable, wretched; (*povero*) poverty-stricken; (*insufficiente*) miserable

mis'fatto *sm* misdeed, crime

mi'sogino [mi'zɔdʒino] *sm* misogynist

'missile *sm* missile

missio'nario, a *ag*, *smlf* missionary

missi'one *sf* mission

misteri'oso, a *ag* mysterious

mis'tero *sm* mystery

mistifi'care *vt* to fool, bamboozle

'misto, a *ag* mixed; (*scuola*) mixed, coeducational ♦ *sm* mixture

mis'tura *sf* mixture

mi'sura *sf* measure; (*misurazione*, *dimensione*) measurement; (*taglia*) size; (*provvedimento*) measure, step; (*moderazione*) moderation; (*MUS*) time; (: *divisione*) bar; (*fig*: *limite*) bounds *pl*, limit; **nella** ~ **in cui** inasmuch as, insofar as; **su** ~ made to measure

misu'rare *vt* (*ambiente*, *stoffa*) to measure; (*terreno*) to survey; (*abito*) to try on; (*pesare*) to weigh; (*fig*: *parole etc*) to weigh up; (: *spese*, *cibo*) to limit ♦ *vi* to measure; ~**rsi** *vr*: ~**rsi con qn** to have a confrontation with sb; to compete with sb's

misu'rato, a *ag* (*ponderato*) measured; (*prudente*) cautious; (*moderato*) moderate

'mite *ag* mild; (*prezzo*) moderate, reasonable

miti'gare *vt* to mitigate, lessen; (*lenire*) to soothe, relieve; ~**rsi** *vr* (*odio*) to subside; (*tempo*) to become milder

'mito *sm* myth; **mitolo'gia, 'gie** *sf* mythology

'mitra *sf* (*REL*) mitre ♦ *sm inv* (*arma*) sub-machine gun

mitraglia'trice [mitraʎʎa'tritʃe] *sf* machine gun

mit'tente *smlf* sender

'mobile *ag* mobile; (*parte di macchina*) moving; (*DIR*: *bene*) movable, personal ♦ *sm* (*arredamento*) piece of furniture; ~**i** *smpl* (*mobilia*) furniture *sg*

mo'bilia *sf* furniture

mobili'are *ag* (*DIR*) personal, movable

mo'bilio *sm* = **mobilia**

mobili'tare *vt* to mobilize

mocas'sino *sm* moccasin

mocci'oso, a *sm/f* [mot'tʃoso, a] (*peg*) snotty(-nosed) kid

'moccolo *sm* (*di candela*) candleend; (*fam*: *bestemmia*) oath; (: *moccio*) snot; **reggere il** ~ to play gooseberry (*BRIT*), act as chaperon

'moda *sf* fashion; **alla** ~, **di** ~ fashionable, in fashion

modalità *sf inv* formality

mo'della *sf* model

model'lare *vt* (*creta*) to model, shape; ~**rsi** *vr*: ~**rsi su** to model o.s. on

mo'dello *sm* model; (*stampo*) mould ♦ *ag inv* model *cpd*

'modem *sm inv* modem

mode'rare *vt* to moderate; ~**rsi** *vr* to restrain o.s.; **mode'rato, a** *ag* moderate

modera'tore, 'trice *sm/f* moderator

mo'derno, a *ag* modern

mo'destia *sf* modesty

mo'desto, a *ag* modest

'modico, a, ci, che *ag* reasonable, moderate

mo'difica *sf* modification

modifi'care *vt* to modify, alter; ~**rsi** *vr* to alter, change

mo'dista *sf* milliner

'modo *sm* way, manner; (*mezzo*) means, way; (*occasione*) opportunity; (*LING*: *mood*) (*MUS*) mode; ~**i** *smpl* (*comportamento*) manners; **a suo** ~, **a** ~ **suo** in his own way; **ad** *o* **in ogni** ~ anyway; **di** *o* **in**

che so that; **in ~ da** so as to; **in tutti i ~i** at all costs; (*comunque sia*) anyway; (*in ogni caso*) in any case; **in qualche ~** somehow or other; **~ di dire** turn of phrase; **per ~ di dire** so to speak

modu'lare *vt* to modulate; **modulazi'one** *sf* modulation; **modulazione di frequenza** frequency modulation

'modulo *sm* (*modello*) form; (*AR-CHIT, lunare, di comando*) module

'mogano *sm* mahogany

'mogio, a, gi, gie ['mɔdʒo] *ag* down in the dumps, dejected

'moglie ['mɔʎʎe] *sf* wife

mo'ine *sfpl* cajolery *sg*; (*leziosità*) affectation *sg*

'mola *sf* millstone; (*utensile abrasivo*) grindstone

mo'lare *sm* (*dente*) molar

'mole *sf* mass; (*dimensioni*) size; (*edificio grandioso*) massive structure

moles'tare *vt* to bother, annoy; **mo'lestia** *sf* annoyance, bother; **recar molestia a qn** to bother sb; **mo'lesto, a** *ag* annoying

'molla *sf* spring; **~e** *sfpl* (*per camino*) tongs

mol'lare *vt* to release, let go; (*NAUT*) to ease; (*fig: ceffone*) to give ♦ *vi* (*cedere*) to give in

'molle *ag* soft; (*muscoli*) flabby; (*fig: debole*) weak, feeble

mol'letta *sf* (*per capelli*) hairgrip; (*per panni stesi*) clothes peg; **~e** *sfpl* (*per zucchero*) tongs

'mollica, che *sf* crumb, soft part

mol'lusco, schi *sm* mollusc

'molo *sm* mole, breakwater; jetty

mol'teplice [mol'teplitʃe] *ag* (*formato di più elementi*) complex; **~i pl** (*svariati: interessi, attività*) numerous, various

moltipli'care *vt* to multiply; **~rsi** *vr* to multiply; to increase in number; **moltiplicazi'one** *sf* multiplication

PAROLA CHIAVE

'molto, a *det* (*quantità*) a lot of, much; (*numero*) a lot of, many; **~ pane/carbone** a lot of bread/coal; **~a gente** a lot of people, many people; **~i libri** a lot of books, many books; **non ho ~ tempo** I haven't got much time; **per ~ (tempo)** for a long time

♦ *av* **1** a lot, (very) much; **viaggia ~** he travels a lot; **non viaggio ~** he doesn't travel much *o* a lot

2 (*intensivo: con aggettivi, avverbi*) very; (*: con participio passato*) (very) much; **~ buono** very good; **~ migliore, ~ meglio** much *o* a lot better

♦ *pron* much, a lot; **~i, e** *pron pl* many, a lot; **~i pensano che ...** many (people) think ...

momen'taneo, a *ag* momentary, fleeting

mo'mento *sm* moment; **da un ~ all'altro** at any moment; (*all'improvviso*) suddenly; **al ~ di fare** just as I was (*o* you were *o* he was *etc*) doing; **per il ~** for the time being; **dal ~ che** ever since; (*dato che*) since; **a ~i** (*da un ~ all'altro*) any time *o* moment now; (*quasi*) nearly

'monaca, che *sf* nun

'Monaco *sf* Monaco; **~ (di Baviera)** Munich

'monaco, ci *sm* monk

mo'narca, chi *sm* monarch; **mo-nar'chia** *sf* monarchy

monas'tero *sm* (*di monaci*) monastery; (*di monache*) convent; **mo'nastico, a, ci, che** *ag* monastic

'monco, a, chi, che *ag* maimed; (*fig*) incomplete; **~ d'un braccio** one-armed

mon'dana *sf* prostitute

mon'dano, a *ag* (*anche fig*) worldly; (*dell'alta società*) society *cpd*; fashionable

mon'dare *vt* (*frutta, patate*) to

peel; (piselli) to shell; (pulire) to clean

mondi'ale ag (campionato, popolazione) world cpd; (influenza) worldwide

'**mondo** sm world; (grande quantità): **un** ~ **di** lots of, a host of; **il bel** ~ high society

mo'nello, a sm/f street urchin; (ragazzo vivace) scamp, imp

mo'neta sf coin; (ECON: valuta) currency; (denaro spicciolo) (small) change; ~ **estera** foreign currency; ~ **legale** legal tender; **mone'tario, a** ag monetary

mongo'loide ag, sm/f (MED) mongol

mongo'lico ag mongol

'**monito** sm warning

'**monitor** sm inv (TECN, TV) monitor

monoco'lore ag (POL): **governo** ~ one-party government

mono'polio sm monopoly

mo'notono, a ag monotonous

monsi'gnore [monsin'nore] sm (REL: titolo) Your (o His) Grace

mon'sone sm monsoon

monta'carichi [monta'kariki] sm inv hoist, goods lift

mon'taggio [mon'taddʒo] sm (TECN) assembly; (CINEMA) editing

mon'tagna [mon'taɲɲa] sf mountain; (zona montuosa): **la** ~ **the mountains** pl; **andare in** ~ to go to the mountains; ~ **e russe** roller coaster sg, big dipper sg (BRIT); **monta'gnoso, a** ag mountainous

monta'naro, a ag mountain cpd ♦ sm/f mountain dweller

mon'tano, a ag mountain cpd; (alpino) alpine

mon'tare vt to go to (o come) up; (cavallo) to ride; (apparecchiatura) to set up, assemble; (CUC) to whip; (ZOOL) to cover; (incastonare) to mount, set; (CINEMA) to edit; (FOT) to mount ♦ vi to go to (o come) up; (a cavallo): ~ **bene/male** to ride well/badly; (aumentare di livel-

lo, volume) to rise; ~ **rsi** vr to become big-headed; ~ **qc** to exaggerate sth; ~ **qn** **a** **la testa a qn** to turn sb's head; ~ **in bicicletta/macchina/treno** to get on a bicycle/into a car/on a train; ~ **a cavallo** to get on o mount a horse

monta'tura sf assembling no pl; (di occhiali) frames pl; (di gioiello) mounting, setting; (fig): ~ **pubblicitaria** publicity stunt

'**monte** sm mountain; **a** ~ upstream; **mandare a** ~ **qc** to upset sth, cause sth to fail; **il M~ Bianco** Mont Blanc; ~ **di pietà** pawnshop

mon'tone sm (ZOOL) ram; **carne di** ~ mutton

montu'oso, a ag mountainous

monu'mento sm monument

'**mora** sf (del rovo) blackberry; (del gelso) mulberry; (DIR) delay; (: somma) arrears pl

mo'rale ag moral ♦ sf (scienza) ethics sg, moral philosophy; (complesso di norme) moral standards pl, morality; (condotta) morals pl; (insegnamento morale) moral ♦ sm morale; **essere giù di** ~ to be feeling down; **moralità** sf morality; (condotta) morals pl

'**morbido, a** ag soft; (pelle) soft, smooth

mor'billo sm (MED) measles sg

'**morbo** sm disease

mor'boso, a ag (fig) morbid

mor'dace [mor'datʃe] ag biting, cutting

mor'dente sm (fig: di satira, critica) bite; (: di persona) drive

'**mordere** vt to bite; (addentare) to bite into; (corrodere) to eat into

mori'bondo, a ag dying, moribund

morige'rato, a [moridʒe'rato] ag of good morals

mo'rire vi to die; (abitudine, civiltà) to die out; ~ **di fame** to die of hunger; (fig) to be starving; ~ **di noia/paura** to be bored/scared to death; **fa un caldo da** ~ it's terribly hot

mormo'rare vi to murmur; (bronto-

lare) to grumble

'**moro, a** *ag* dark(-haired); dark(-complexioned); **i M~i** *smpl* (*STORIA*) the Moors

mo'**roso, a** *ag* in arrears ♦ *sm/f* (*fam: innamorato*) sweetheart

'**morsa** *sf* (*TECN*) vice; (*fig: stretta*) grip

morsi'**care** *vt* to nibble (at), gnaw (at); (*sog: insetto*) to bite

'**morso, a** *pp di* **mordere** ♦ *sm* bite; (*di insetto*) sting; (*parte della briglia*) bit; **~i della fame** pangs of hunger

mor'**taio** *sm* mortar

mor'**tale** *ag, sm* mortal; **mortalità** *sf* mortality, death rate

'**morte** *sf* death

mortifi'**care** *vt* to mortify

'**morto, a** *pp di* **morire** ♦ *ag* dead ♦ *sm/f* dead man/woman; **i ~i** the dead; **fare il ~** (*nell'acqua*) to float on one's back; **il Mar M~** the Dead Sea

mor'**torio** *sm* (*anche fig*) funeral

mo'**saico, ci** *sm* mosaic

'**Mosca** *sf* Moscow

'**mosca, sche** *sf* fly; **~ cieca** blind-man's-buff

mos'**cato** *sm* muscatel (wine)

mosce'**rino** [moʃʃe'rino] *sm* midge, gnat

mos'**chea** [mos'kɛa] *sf* mosque

mos'**chetto** [mos'ketto] *sm* musket

'**moscio, a, sci, sce** ['mɔʃʃo] *ag* (*fig*) lifeless

mos'**cone** *sm* (*ZOOL*) bluebottle; (*barca*) pedalo; (*: a remi*) kind of pedalo with oars

'**mossa** *sf* movement; (*nel gioco*) move

'**mosso, a** *pp di* **muovere** ♦ *ag* (*mare*) rough; (*capelli*) wavy; (*FOT*) blurred; (*ritmo, prosa*) animated

mos'**tarda** *sf* mustard

'**mostra** *sf* exhibition, show; (*ostentazione*) show; **in ~** on show; **far ~ di** (*fingere*) to pretend; **far ~ di sé** to show off

mos'**trare** *vt* to show ♦ *vi*: **~ di fare** to pretend to do; **~rsi** *vr* to appear

'**mostro** *sm* monster; **mostru'oso, a** *ag* monstrous

mo'**tel** *sm inv* motel

moti'**vare** *vt* (*causare*) to cause; (*giustificare*) to justify, account for; **motivazi'one** *sf* justification; motive; (*PSIC*) motivation

mo'**tivo** *sm* (*causa*) reason, cause; (*movente*) motive; (*letterario*) (central) theme; (*disegno*) motif, design, pattern; (*MUS*) motif; **per quale ~**? why?, for what reason?

'**moto** *sm* (*anche FISICA*) motion; (*movimento, gesto*) movement; (*esercizio fisico*) exercise; (*sommossa*) rising, revolt; (*commozione*) feeling, impulse ♦ *sf inv* (*motocicletta*) motorbike; **mettere in ~** to set in motion; (*AUT*) to start up

motoci'**cletta** [mototʃi'kletta] *sf* motorcycle; **motoci'clismo** *sm* motorcycling, motorcycle racing; **motoci'clista, i, e** *sm/f* motorcyclist

mo'**tore, 'trice** *ag* motor; (*TECN*) driving ♦ *sm* engine, motor; **a ~** motor *cpd*, power-driven; **~ a combustione interna/a reazione** internal combustion/jet engine; **moto'rino** *sm* moped; **motorino di avviamento** (*AUT*) starter; **motoriz'zato, a** *ag* (*truppe*) motorized; (*persona*) having a car *o* transport

motos'**cafo** *sm* motorboat

'**motto** *sm* (*battuta scherzosa*) witty remark; (*frase emblematica*) motto, maxim

mo'**vente** *sm* motive

movimen'**tare** *vt* to liven up

movi'**mento** *sm* movement; (*fig*) activity, hustle and bustle; (*MUS*) tempo, movement

mozi'**one** [mot'tsjone] *sf* (*POL*) motion

moz'**zare** [mot'tsare] *vt* to cut off; (*coda*) to dock; **~ il fiato** *o* **il respiro a qn** (*fig*) to take sb's breath away

mozza'rella [mottsa'rɛlla] *sf* mozzarella (*a moist Neapolitan curd cheese*)

mozzi'cone [mottsi'kone] *sm* stub, butt, end; (*anche:* ~ *di sigaretta*) cigarette end

'**mozzo**[1] ['mɔddzo] *sm* (*MECCANICA*) hub

'**mozzo**[2] ['mottso] *sm* (*NAUT*) ship's boy; ~ **di stalla** stable boy

'**mucca, che** *sf* cow

'**mucchio** ['mukkjo] *sm* pile, heap; (*fig*): **un** ~ **di** lots of, heaps of

'**muco, chi** *sm* mucus

'**muffa** *sf* mould, mildew

mug'gire [mud'dʒire] *vi* (*vacca*) to low, moo; (*toro*) to bellow; (*fig*) to roar; **mug'gito** *sm* low, moo; bellow; roar

mu'ghetto [mu'getto] *sm* lily of the valley

mu'gnaio, a [muɲ'najo] *sm/f* miller

mugo'lare *vi* (*cane*) to whimper, whine; (*fig*: *persona*) to moan

muli'nare *vi* to whirl, spin (round and round)

muli'nello *sm* (*moto vorticoso*) eddy, whirl; (*di canna da pesca*) reel; (*NAUT*) windlass

mu'lino *sm* mill; ~ **a vento** windmill

'**mulo** *sm* mule

'**multa** *sf* fine; **mul'tare** *vt* to fine

'**multiplo, a** *ag*, *sm* multiple

mummia *sf* mummy

mungere ['mundʒere] *vt* (*anche fig*) to milk

munici'pale [munitʃi'pale] *ag* municipal; town *cpd*

muni'cipio [muni'tʃipjo] *sm* town council, corporation; (*edificio*) town hall

mu'nire *vt*: ~ **qc/qn di** to equip sth/sb with

munizi'oni [munit'tsjoni] *sfpl* (*MIL*) ammunition *sg*

'**munto, a** *pp di* mungere

mu'overe *vt* to move; (*ruota, macchina*) to drive; (*sollevare: questione, obiezione*) to raise, bring up; (: *accusa*) to make, bring forward; ~**rsi** *vr* to move; **muoviti!** hurry up!, get a move on!

'**mura** *sfpl vedi* muro

mu'raglia [mu'raʎʎa] *sf* (high) wall

mu'rale *ag* wall *cpd*; mural

mu'rare *vt* (*persona, porta*) to wall up

mura'tore *sm* mason; bricklayer

'**muro** *sm* wall; ~**a** *sfpl* (*cinta cittadina*) walls; **che** ~ **a** wall *cpd*; (*armadio etc*) built-in; ~ **del suono** sound barrier; **mettere al** ~ (*fucilare*) to shoot *o* execute (by firing squad)

'**muschio** ['muskjo] *sm* (*ZOOL*) musk; (*BOT*) moss

musco'lare *ag* muscular, muscle *cpd*

'**muscolo** *sm* (*ANAT*) muscle

mu'seo *sm* museum

museru'ola *sf* muzzle

'**musica** *sf* music; ~ **da ballo/camera** dance/chamber music; **musi'cale** *ag* musical; **musi'cista, i, e** *sm/f* musician

'**muso** *sm* muzzle; (*di auto, aereo*) nose; **tenere il** ~ to sulk; **mu'sone, a** *sm/f* sulky person

'**muta** *sf* (*di animali*) moulting; (*di serpenti*) sloughing; (*per immersioni subacquee*) diving suit; (*gruppo di cani*) pack

muta'mento *sm* change

mu'tande *sfpl* (*da uomo*) (under)pants; **mutan'dine** *sfpl* (*da donna, bambino*) pants (*BRIT*), briefs

mu'tare *vt*, *vi* to change, alter; **mutazi'one** *sf* change, alteration; (*BIOL*) mutation; **mu'tevole** *ag* changeable

muti'lare *vt* to mutilate, maim; (*fig*) to mutilate, deface; **muti'lato, a** *sm/f* disabled person (*through loss of limbs*)

mu'tismo *sm* (*MED*) mutism; (*atteggiamento*) (stubborn) silence

'**muto, a** *ag* (*MED*) dumb; (*emozione, dolore, CINEMA*) silent;

(*LING*) silent, mute; (*carta geografica*) blank; ~ **per lo stupore** *etc* speechless with amazement *etc*

'mutua (*anche: cassa* ~) health insurance scheme

mutu'are *vt* (*fig*) to borrow

mutu'ato, a *smf* member of a health insurance scheme

'mutuo, a *ag* (*reciproco*) mutual ♦ *sm* (*ECON*) (long-term) loan

N

N. *abbr* (= *nord*) N

'nacchere ['nakkere] *sfpl* castanets

'nafta *sf* naphtha; (*per motori diesel*) diesel oil

nafta'lina *sf* (*CHIM*) naphthalene; (*tarmicida*) mothballs *pl*

'naia *sf* (*ZOOL*) cobra; (*MIL*) slang term for national service

'nailon *sm* nylon

'nanna *sf* (*linguaggio infantile*): andare a ~ to go to beddy-byes

'nano, a *ag, smf* dwarf

napole'tano, a *ag, smf* Neapolitan

'Napoli *sf* Naples

'nappa *sf* tassel

nar'ciso [nar'tʃizo] *sm* narcissus

nar'cosi *sf* narcosis

nar'cotico, ci *sm* narcotic

na'rice [na'ritʃe] *sf* nostril

nar'rare *vt* to tell the story of, recount; **narra'tiva** *sf* (*branca letteraria*) fiction; **narra'tivo, a** *ag* narrative; **narra'tore, 'trice** *smf* narrator; **narrazi'one** *sf* narration; (*racconto*) story, tale

na'sale *ag* nasal

'nascere ['naʃʃere] *vi* (*bambino*) to be born; (*pianta*) to come *o* spring up; (*fiume*) to rise, have its source; (*sole*) to rise; (*dente*) to come through; (*fig: derivare, conseguire*): ~ **da** to arise from, be born out of; **è nata nel 1952** she was born in 1952; **'nascita** *sf* birth

nas'condere *vt* to hide, conceal; **~rsi** *vr* to hide; **nascon'diglio** *sm*

hiding place; **nascon'dino** *sm* (*gioco*) hide-and-seek; **nas'costo, a** *pp di* nascondere ♦ *ag* hidden; **di nascosto** secretly

na'sello *sm* (*ZOOL*) hake

'naso *sm* nose

'nastro *sm* ribbon; (*magnetico, isolante, SPORT*) tape; ~ **adesivo** adhesive tape; ~ **trasportatore** conveyor belt

nas'turzio [nas'turtsjo] *sm* nasturtium

na'tale *ag* of one's birth ♦ *sm* (*REL*): N~ Christmas; (*giorno della nascita*) birthday; **natalità** *sf* birth rate; **nata'lizio, a** *ag* (*del Natale*) Christmas *cpd*

na'tante *sm* craft *inv*, boat

'natica, che *sf* (*ANAT*) buttock

na'tio, a, 'tii, 'tie *ag* native

Natività *sf* (*REL*) Nativity

na'tivo, a *ag, smf* native

'nato, a *pp di* nascere ♦ *ag*: **un attore** ~ a born actor; **~a Pieri** née Pieri

na'tura *sf* nature; **pagare in** ~ to pay in kind; ~ **morta** still life

natu'rale *ag* natural; **natura'lezza** *sf* naturalness; **natura'lista, i, e** *smf* naturalist

naturaliz'zare [naturalid'dzare] *vt* to naturalize

natural'mente *av* naturally; (*certamente, sì*) of course

naufra'gare *vi* (*nave*) to be wrecked; (*persona*) to be shipwrecked; (*fig*) to fall through; **nau'fragio** *sm* shipwreck; (*fig*) ruin, failure; **'naufrago, ghi** *sm* castaway, shipwreck victim

'nausea *sf* nausea; **nausea'bondo, a** *ag* nauseating, sickening; **nause'are** *vt* to nauseate, make (feel) sick

'nautica *sf* (art of) navigation

'nautico, a, ci, che *ag* nautical

na'vale *ag* naval

na'vata *sf* (*anche:* ~ *centrale*) nave; (*anche:* ~ *laterale*) aisle

'nave *sf* ship, vessel; ~ **cisterna**

tanker; ~ **da guerra** warship; ~ **passeggeri** passenger ship; ~ **spaziale** spaceship

na'**vetta** *sf* shuttle; (*servizio di collegamento*) shuttle (service)

navi'**cella** [navi'tʃɛlla] *sf* (*di aerostato*) gondola

navi'**gare** *vi* to sail; **navigazi'one** *sf* navigation

na'**viglio** [na'viʎʎo] *sm* fleet, ships *pl*; (*canale artificiale*) canal; ~ **da pesca** fishing fleet

nazio'**nale** [nattsjo'nale] *ag* national ♦ *sf* (*SPORT*) national team; **nazio-na'lismo** *sm* nationalism; **naziona-lità** *sf inv* nationality

nazi'**one** [nat'tsjone] *sf* nation

PAROLA CHIAVE

ne *pron* **1** (*di lui, lei, loro*) of him/her/them; about him/her/them; ~ **riconosco la voce** I recognize his (*o* her) voice

2 (*di questa, quella cosa*) of it; about it; ~ **voglio ancora** I want some more (of it *o* them); **non parliamone più!** let's not talk about it any more!

3 (*con valore partitivo*): **hai dei libri?** — **sì,** ~ **ho** have you any books? — yes, I have (some); **hai del pane?** — **no, non** ~ **ho** have you any bread? — no, I haven't any; **quanti anni hai?** — ~ **ho 17** how old are you? — I'm 17

♦ *av* (*moto a luogo: da lì*) from there; ~ **vengo ora** I've just come from there

---

né *cong*: ~ ... ~ neither ... nor; ~ **l'uno** ~ **l'altro lo vuole** neither of them wants it; **non parla** ~ **l'italiano** ~ **il tedesco** he speaks neither Italian nor German, he doesn't speak either Italian or German; **non piove** ~ **nevica** it isn't raining or snowing

ne'**anche** [ne'anke] *av, cong* not even; **non** ... ~ not even; ~ **se volesse potrebbe venire** he couldn't come even if he wanted to; **non l'ho**

visto — ~ **io** I didn't see him — neither did I *o* I didn't either; ~ **per idea** *o* **sogno!** not on your life!

'**nebbia** *sf* fog; (*foschia*) mist; **neb-bi'oso, a** *ag* foggy; misty

nebu'**loso, a** *ag* (*atmosfera*) hazy; (*fig*) hazy, vague

necessaria'**mente** [netʃessa-rja'mente] *av* necessarily

neces'**sario, a** [netʃes'sarjo] *ag* necessary

necessità [netʃessi'ta] *sf inv* necessity; (*povertà*) need, poverty; **ne-cessi'tare** *vt* to require ♦ *vi* (*aver bisogno*): **necessitare di** to need

necro'**logio** [nekro'lɔdʒo] *sm* obituary notice; (*registro*) register of deaths

ne'**fando, a** *ag* infamous, wicked

ne'**fasto, a** *ag* inauspicious, ill-omened

ne'**gare** *vt* to deny; (*rifiutare*) to deny, refuse; ~ **di aver fatto/che** to deny having done/that; **nega'tivo, a** *ag, sf, sm* negative; **negazi'one** *sf* negation

ne'**gletto, a** [ne'gletto] *ag* (*trascurato*) neglected

'**negli** ['neʎʎi] *prep* +*det vedi* **in**

negli'**gente** [negli'dʒɛnte] *ag* negligent, careless; **negli'genza** *sf* negligence, carelessness

negozi'**ante** [negot'tsjante] *sm/f* trader, dealer; (*bottegaio*) shopkeeper (*BRIT*), storekeeper (*US*)

negozi'**are** [negot'tsjare] *vt* to negotiate ♦ *vi*: ~ **in** to trade *o* deal in; **negozi'ato** *sm* negotiation

ne'**gozio** [ne'gɔttsjo] *sm* (*locale*) shop (*BRIT*), store (*US*); (*affare*) (piece of) business *no pl*

'**negro, a** *ag, sm/f* Negro

'**nei** *prep* + *det vedi* **in**

nel *prep* + *det vedi* **in**

nell' *prep* + *det vedi* **in**

'**nella** *prep* + *det vedi* **in**

'**nelle** *prep* + *det vedi* **in**

'**nello** *prep* + *det vedi* **in**

'**nembo** *sm* (*METEOR*) nimbus

ne'**mico, a, ci, che** *ag* hostile;

(MIL) enemy cpd ♦ sm/f enemy: essere ~ di to be strongly averse o opposed to

nem'meno av, cong = **neanche**

'nenia sf dirge; (motivo monotono) monotonous tune

neo sm mole; (fig) (slight) flaw

'neo... prefisso neo...

'neon sm (CHIM) neon

neo'nato, a ag newborn ♦ sm/f newborn baby

neozelan'dese [neoddzelan'dese] ag New Zealand cpd ♦ sm/f New Zealander

nep'pure av, cong = **neanche**

'nerbo sm lash; (fig) strength, backbone; **nerbo'ruto, a** ag muscular; robust

ne'retto sm (TIP) bold type

'nero, a ag black; (scuro) dark ♦ sm black; **il Mar N~** the Black Sea

nerva'tura sf (ANAT) nervous system; (BOT) veining; (ARCHIT, TECN) rib

'nervo sm (ANAT) nerve; (BOT) vein; avere i ~i to be on edge; dare sui ~i a qn to get on sb's nerves; **ner'voso, a** ag nervous; (irritabile) irritable ♦ sm (fam): far venire il nervoso a qn to get on sb's nerves

'nespola sf (BOT) medlar; (fig) blow, punch; **'nespolo** sm medlar tree

'nesso sm connection, link

PAROLA CHIAVE

nes'suno, a (det: dav sm nessun +C, V, nessuno +s impura, gn, pn, ps, x, z; dav sf nessuna +C, nessun' +V) det **1** (non uno) no, nessuna espressione negativa +any; non c'è nessun libro there isn't any book, there is no book; nessun altro no one else, nobody else; nessun'altra cosa nothing else; in nessun luogo nowhere **2** (qualche) any; hai ~a obiezione? do you have any objections?

♦ pron **1** (non uno) no one, nobody, espressione negativa +any(one); (: cosa) none, espressione negativa

+any; ~ è venuto, non è venuto = nobody came

2 (qualcuno) anyone, anybody; ha telefonato ~? did anyone phone?

---

net'tare[1] vt to clean

'nettare[2] sm nectar

net'tezza [net'tettsa] sf cleanness, cleanliness; ~ **urbana** cleansing department

'netto, a ag (pulito) clean; (chiaro) clear, clear-cut; (deciso) definite; (ECON) net

nettur'bino sm dustman (BRIT), garbage collector (US)

neu'rosi sf = **nevrosi**

neu'trale ag neutral; **neutralità** sf neutrality; **neutraliz'zare** vt to neutralize

'neutro, a ag neutral; (LING) neuter ♦ sm (LING) neuter

ne'vaio sm snowfield

'neve sf snow; **nevi'care** vb impers to snow; **nevi'cata** sf snowfall

ne'vischio [ne'viskjo] sm sleet

ne'voso, a ag snowy; snow-covered

nevral'gia [nevral'dʒia] sf neuralgia

nevras'tenico, a, ci, che ag (MED) neurasthenic; (fig) hot-tempered

ne'vrosi sf neurosis

'nibbio sm (ZOOL) kite

'nicchia ['nikkja] sf niche; (naturale) cavity, hollow

nicchi'are [nik'kjare] vi to shilly-shally, hesitate

'nichel ['nikel] sm nickel

nico'tina sf nicotine

'nido sm nest; **a ~ d'ape** (tessuto etc) honeycomb cpd

PAROLA CHIAVE

ni'ente pron **1** (nessuna cosa) nothing; ~ **può fermarlo** nothing can stop him; ~ **di** ~ absolutely nothing; **nient'altro** nothing else; **nient'altro che** nothing but, just, only; ~ **affatto** not at all, not in the least; come se ~ **fosse** as if nothing had happened; cose da ~ trivial matters;

per ~ (gratis, invano) for nothing 2 (qualcosa): **hai bisogno di** ~? do you need anything? 3: **non ...** ~ nothing, espressione negativa + anything; **non l'ho** ~ **visto** I didn't see anything; **non ho** ~ **da dire** I have nothing o haven't anything to say ♦ sm nothing; **un bel** ~ absolutely nothing; **basta un** ~ **per farla piangere** the slightest thing is enough to make her cry ♦ av (in nessuna misura): **non ...** ~ not ... at all; **non è (per)** ~ **buono** it isn't good at all

nientedi'meno av actually, even ♦ escl really!, I say!

niente'meno av, escl = **nientedimeno**

'Nilo sm: **il** ~ **the Nile**

'ninfa sf nymph

nin'fea sf water lily

ninna-'nanna sf lullaby

'ninnolo sm (balocco) plaything; (gingillo) knick-knack

ni'pote smf (di zii) nephew/niece; (di nonni) grandson/daughter, grandchild

'nitido, a ag clear; (specchio) bright

ni'trato sm nitrate

'nitrico, a, ci, che ag nitric

ni'trire vi to neigh

ni'trito sm (di cavallo) neighing no pl; neigh; (CHIM) nitrite

nitroglice'rina [nitroglitʃe'rina] sf nitroglycerine

no av (risposta) no; **vieni o** ~? are you coming or not?; **perché** ~? why not?; **lo conosciamo?** — **tu** — **ma io sì do we know him?** — you don't but I do; **verrai,** ~? you'll come, won't you?

'nobile ag noble ♦ smf noble, nobleman/woman; **nobil'are** ag noble; **nobiltà** sf nobility; (di azione etc) nobleness

'nocca, che sf (ANAT) knuckle

nocci'ola [not'tʃɔla] ag inv (colore) hazel, light brown ♦ sf hazelnut

'nocciolo¹ [ˈnɔttʃolo] sm (di frutto) stone; (fig) heart, core

noc'ciolo² [not'tʃɔlo] sm (albero) hazel

'noce [ˈnotʃe] sm (albero) walnut tree ♦ sf (frutto) walnut; ~ **moscata** nutmeg

no'civo, a [no'tʃivo] ag harmful, noxious

'nodo sm (di cravatta, legname, NAUT) knot; (AUT, FERR) junction; (MED, ASTR, BOT) node; (fig: legame) bond, tie; (: punto centrale) heart, crux; **avere un** ~ **alla gola** to have a lump in one's throat; **no'doso, a** ag (tronco) gnarled

'noi pron (soggetto) we; (oggetto: per dare rilievo, con preposizione) us; ~ **stessi(e)** we ourselves; (oggetto) ourselves

'noia sf boredom; (disturbo, impaccio) bother no pl, trouble no pl; **avere qn/qc a** ~ not to like sb/sth; **mi è venuto a** ~ I'm tired of it; **dare** ~ **a** to annoy; **avere delle** ~**e con qn** to have trouble with sb

noi'altri pron we

noi'oso, a ag boring; (fastidioso) annoying, troublesome

noleggi'are [noled'dʒare] vt (prendere a noleggio) to hire (BRIT), rent; (dare a noleggio) to hire out (BRIT), rent (out); (aereo, nave) to charter; **no'leggio** sm hire (BRIT), rental; charter

'nolo sm hire (BRIT), rental; charter; (per trasporto merci) freight; **prendere/dare a** ~ **qc** to hire/hire out sth

'nomade ag nomadic ♦ smf nomad

'nome sm name; (LING) noun; **in/a** ~ **di** in the name of; **di** o **per** ~ (chiamato) called, named; **conoscere qn di** ~ to know sb by name; **d'arte** stage name; ~ **di battesimo** Christian name; ~ **di famiglia** surname

no'mea sf notoriety

no'mignolo [no'miɲɲolo] sm nickname

'nomina sf appointment

nomi'nale ag nominal; (LING) noun cpd

nomi'nare vt to name; (eleggere) to appoint; (citare) to mention

nomina'tivo, a ag (LING) nominative; (ECON) registered ♦ sm (LING: anche: caso ~) nominative (case); (AMM) name

non av not ♦ prefisso non-; vedi affatto; appena etc

nonché [non'ke] cong (tanto più, tanto meno) let alone; (e inoltre) as well as

noncu'rante ag: ~ (di) careless (of), indifferent (to); **noncu'ranza** sf carelessness, indifference

nondi'meno cong (tuttavia) however; (nonostante) nevertheless

'nonno, a sm/f grandfather/mother; (in senso più familiare) grandma/grandpa; ~i smpl grandparents

non'nulla sm inv: **un** ~ nothing, a trifle

'nono, a ag, sm ninth

nonos'tante prep in spite of, notwithstanding ♦ cong although, even though

nontiscordardimé sm inv (BOT) forget-me-not

nord sm North ♦ ag inv north; northern; **il Mare del N**~ the North Sea; **nor'dest** sm north-east; **'nordico, a, ci, che** ag nordic, northern European; **nor'dovest** sm north-west

'norma sf (principio) norm; (regola) regulation, rule; (consuetudine) custom, rule; **a** ~ **di legge** according to law, as laid down by law

nor'male ag normal; standard cpd; **normalità** sf normality; **norma-liz'zare** vt to normalize, bring back to normal

normal'mente av normally

norve'gese [norve'dʒese] ag, sm/f, sm Norwegian

Nor'vegia [nor'vedʒa] sf: **la** ~ Norway

nostal'gia [nostal'dʒia] sf (di casa, paese) homesickness; (del passato)

nostalgia; **nos'talgico, a, ci, che** ag homesick; nostalgic

nos'trano, a ag local; national; home-produced

'nostro, a det: **il(la)** ~(a) etc our ♦ pron: **il(la)** ~(a) etc ours ♦ sm: **il** ~ our money; our belongings; **i** ~**i** our family; our own people; **è dei** ~**i** he's one of us

'nota sf (segno) mark; (comunicazione scritta, MUS) note; (fattura) bill; (elenco) list; **degno di** ~ noteworthy, worthy of note

no'tabile ag notable; (persona) important ♦ sm prominent citizen

no'taio sm notary

no'tare vt (segnare: errori) to mark; (registrare) to note (down), write down; (rilevare, osservare) to note, notice; **farsi** ~ to get o.s. noticed

notazi'one [notat'tsjone] sf (MUS) notation

no'tevole ag (talento) notable, remarkable; (peso) considerable

no'tifica, che sf notification

notifi'care vt (DIR): ~ **qc a qn** to notify sb of sth, give sb notice of sth

no'tizia [no'tittsja] sf (piece) of news sg; (informazione) piece of information; ~**e** sfpl (informazioni) news sg; information sg; **notizi'ario** (RADIO, TV, STAMPA) news sg

'noto, a ag (well-)known

notorietà sf fame; notoriety

no'torio, a ag well-known; (peg) notorious

not'tambulo, a sm/f night-bird (fig)

not'tata sf night

'notte sf night; **di** ~ at night; (durante la notte) in the night, during the night; **peggio che andar di** ~ worse than ever; ~ **bianca** sleepless night; **notte'tempo** av at night; during the night

not'turno, a ag nocturnal; (servizio, guardiano) night cpd

no'vanta num ninety; **no-van'tesimo, a** num ninetieth; no-

van'tina sf: **una novantina (di)** about ninety

'nove sm inv nine

nove'cento [nove'tʃɛnto] num nine hundred ♦ sm: **il N~** the twentieth century

no'vella sf (LETTERATURA) short story

novel'lino, a ag (pivello) green, inexperienced

no'vello, a ag (piante, patate) new; (insalata, verdura) early; (sposo) newly-married

no'vembre sm November

novi'lunio sm (ASTR) new moon

novità sf inv novelty; (innovazione) innovation; (cosa originale, insolita) something new; (notizia) (piece of) news sg; **le ~ della moda** the latest fashions

novizi'ato [novit'tsjato] sm (REL) novitiate; (tirocinio) apprenticeship

no'vizio, a [no'vittsjo] smlf (REL) novice; (tirocinante) beginner, apprentice

nozi'one [not'tsjone] sf notion, idea; **~i** sfpl (rudimenti) basic knowledge sg, rudiments

'nozze ['nɔttse] sfpl wedding sg, marriage sg; **~ d'argento/d'oro** silver/golden wedding sg

ns. abbr (COMM) = **nostro**

'nube sf cloud; **nubi'fragio** sm cloudburst

'nubile ag (donna) unmarried, single

'nuca sf nape of the neck

nucle'are ag nuclear

'nucleo sm nucleus; (gruppo) team, unit, group; (MIL, POLIZIA) squad; **il ~ familiare** the family unit

nu'dista, i, e smlf nudist

'nudo, a ag (persona) bare, naked, nude; (membra) bare, naked; (montagna) bare ♦ sm (ARTE) nude

'nugolo sm: **un ~ di** a whole host of

'nulla pron, av = **niente** ♦ sm: **il ~** nothing

nulla'osta sm inv authorization

nullità sf inv nullity; (persona) non-

entity

'nullo, a ag useless, worthless; (DIR) null (and void); (SPORT): **in-contro ~** draw

nume'rale ag, sm numeral

nume'rare vt to number; **nume-razi'one** sf numbering; (araba, decimale) notation

nu'merico, a, ci, che ag numerical

'numero sm number; (romano, arabo) numeral; (di spettacolo) act, turn; **~ civico** house number; **~ di telefono** telephone number; **nume'roso, a** ag numerous, many; (con sostantivo sg: adunanza etc) large

'nunzio ['nuntsjo] sm (REL) nuncio

nu'ocere ['nwɔtʃere] vi: **~ a** to harm, damage; **nuoci'uto, a** pp di **nuocere**

nu'ora sf daughter-in-law

nuo'tare vi to swim; (galleggiare: oggetti) to float; **nuota'tore, 'trice** smlf swimmer; **nu'oto** sm swimming

nu'ova sf (notizia) (piece of) news sg; vedi anche **nuovo**

nuova'mente av again

Nu'ova Ze'landa [-dze'landa] sf: **la ~** New Zealand

nu'ovo, a ag new; **di ~** again; **~ fiammante** o **di zecca** brand-new

nutri'ente ag nutritious, nourishing

nutri'mento sm food, nourishment

nu'trire vt to feed; (fig: sentimenti) to harbour, nurse; **nutri'tivo, a** ag nutritional; (alimento) nutritious; **nutrizi'one** sf nutrition

'nuvola sf cloud; **'nuvolo, a** ag, **nuvo'loso, a** ag cloudy

nuzi'ale [nut'tsjale] ag nuptial; wedding cpd

O

o (*dav V spesso* **od**) *cong* or; ~ ... ~ either ... or; ~ **l'uno** ~ **l'altro** either (of them)

O. *abbr* (= *ovest*) W

'oasi *sf inv* oasis

obbedi'ente *etc* = **ubbidiente** *etc*

obbli'gare *vt* (*costringere*): ~ **qn a fare** to force o oblige sb to do; (*DIR*) to bind; ~**rsi** *vr*: ~**rsi a fare** to undertake to do; **obbli'gato, a** *ag* (*costretto, grato*) obliged; (*percorso, tappa*) set, fixed; **obbliga'torio, a** *ag* compulsory, obligatory; **obbliga-zi'one** *sf* obligation; (*COMM*) bond, debenture; **'obbligo, ghi** *sm* obligation; (*dovere*) duty; **avere l'obbligo di fare**, **essere nell'obbligo di fare** to be obliged to do; **essere d'obbligo** (*discorso, applauso*) to be called for

ob'brobrio *sm* disgrace; (*fig*) mess, eyesore

o'beso, a *ag* obese

obiet'tare *vt*: ~ **che** to object that; ~ **su qc** to object to sth, raise objections concerning sth

obiet'tivo, a *ag* objective ♦ *sm* (*OTTICA, FOT*) lens *sg*, objective; (*MIL, fig*) objective

obiet'tore *sm* objector; ~ **di coscienza** conscientious objector

obiezi'one [objet'tsjone] *sf* objection

obi'torio *sm* morgue, mortuary

o'bliquo, a *ag* oblique; (*inclinato*) slanting; (*fig*) devious, underhand; **sguardo** ~ sidelong glance

oblite'rare *vt* (*biglietto*) to stamp; (*francobollo*) to cancel

oblò *sm inv* porthole

o'blungo, a ghi, ghe *ag* oblong

'oboe *sm* (*MUS*) oboe

'oca (*pl* **'oche**) *sf* goose

occasi'one *sf* (*caso favorevole*) opportunity; (*causa, motivo, circostanza*) occasion; (*COMM*) bargain; **d'**~ (*a buon prezzo*) bargain *cpd*; (*usato*) secondhand

occhi'aia [ok'kjaja] *sf* eye socket; **avere le** ~**e** to have shadows under one's eyes

occhi'ali [ok'kjali] *smpl* glasses, spectacles; ~ **da sole** sunglasses; ~ **da vista** (prescription) glasses

occhi'ata [ok'kjata] *sf* look, glance; **dare un'**~ **a** to have a look at

occhieggi'are [okkjed'dʒare] *vi* (*apparire qua e là*) to peep (out)

occhi'ello [ok'kjɛllo] *sm* buttonhole; (*asola*) eyelet

'occhio ['ɔkkjo] *sm* eye; ~! careful!, watch out!; **a** ~ **nudo** with the naked eye; **a quattr'**~**i** privately, tête-à-tête; **dare all'**~ o **nell'**~ **a qn** to catch sb's eye; **fare l'**~ **a qc** to get used to sth; **tenere d'**~ **qn** to keep an eye on sb; **vedere di buon/mal** ~ **qc** to look favourably/unfavourably on sth

occhio'lino [okkjo'lino] *sm*: **fare l'**~ **a qn** to wink at sb

occi'dente [ottʃiden'tale] *ag* western ♦ *sm/f* Westerner

occi'dente [ottʃi'dɛnte] *sm* west; (*POL*): **l'O**~ the West; **a** ~ **in the west**

oc'cipite [ot'tʃipite] *sm* back of the head, occiput

oc'cludere *vt* to block; **occlusi'one** *sf* blockage, obstruction; **oc'cluso, a** *pp di* **occludere**

occor'rente *ag* necessary ♦ *sm* all that is necessary

occor'renza [okkor'rentsa] *sf* necessity, need; **all'**~ **in case of need**

oc'correre *vi* to be needed, be required ♦ *vb impers*: **occorre farlo** it must be done; **occorre che tu parta** you must leave, you'll have to leave; **mi occorrono i soldi** I need the money; **oc'corso, a** *pp di* **occorrere**

occul'tare *vt* to hide, conceal

oc'culto, a *ag* hidden, concealed; (*scienze, forze*) occult

occu'pare *vt* to occupy; (*manodopera*) to employ; (*ingombrare*) to occupy, take up; ~**rsi** *vr* to occupy

o.s., keep o.s. busy; (*impiegarsi*) to
get a job; **~rsi di** (*interessarsi*) to
take an interest in; (*prendersi cura
di*) to look after, take care of;
occu'pato, a *ag* (MIL, POL) occu-
pied; (*persona: affaccendato*) busy;
(*posto, sedia*) taken; (*toilette, TEL*)
engaged; **occupazi'one** *sf* occupation; (*impiego, lavoro*) job; (ECON)
employment

o'ceano [o'tʃeano] *sm* ocean

'ocra *sf* ochre

ocu'lare *ag* ocular, eye *cpd*; **testimone ~** eye witness

ocu'lato, a *ag* (*attento*) cautious,
prudent; (*accorto*) shrewd

ocu'lista, i, e *sm/f* eye specialist,
oculist

'ode *sf* ode

odi'are *vt* to hate, detest

odi'erno, a *ag* today's, of today;
(*attuale*) present

'odio *sm* hatred; **avere in ~** qc/qn
to hate *o* detest sth/sb; **odi'oso, a**
ag hateful, odious

odo'rare *vt* (*annusare*) to smell;
(*profumare*) to perfume, scent ♦ *vi*:
~ (di) to smell (of); **odo'rato** *sm*
sense of smell

o'dore *sm* smell; **gli ~i** *smpl* (CUC)
(aromatic) herbs; **odo'roso, a** *ag*
sweet-smelling

of'fendere *vt* to offend; (*violare*) to
break, violate; (*insultare*) to insult;
(*ferire*) to hurt; **~rsi** *vr* (*con senso
reciproco*) to insult one another; (*risentirsi*): **~rsi (di)** to take offence
(at), be offended (by); **offen'sivo, a**
ag, sf offensive

offe'rente *sm* (*in aste*): **al maggior
~** to the highest bidder

of'ferta *sf* offer; (*donazione, anche
REL*) offering; (*in gara d'appalto*)
tender; (*in aste*) bid; (ECON) supply; **"~ d'impiego"** "situations vacant"; **fare un'~a** to make an offer;
**to tender; to bid

of'ferto, a *pp di* **offrire**

of'fesa *sf* insult, affront; (MIL) attack; (DIR) offence; *vedi anche* **offe-**

so

of'feso, a *pp di* **offendere** ♦ *ag* offended; (*fisicamente*) hurt, injured ♦
sm/f offended party; **essere ~ con
qn** to be annoyed with sb; **parte ~a**
(DIR) plaintiff

offi'cina [offi'tʃina] *sf* workshop

of'frire *vt* to offer; **~rsi** *vr* (*proporr-
si*) to offer (o.s.), volunteer; (*occasione*) to present itself; (*esporsi*):
~rsi a to expose o.s. to; **ti offro da
bere** I'll buy you a drink

offus'care *vt* to obscure, darken;
(*fig: intelletto*) to dim, cloud; (:
fama) to obscure, overshadow; **~rsi**
vr to grow dark; to cloud, grow dim;
to be obscured

ogget'tivo, a [oddʒet'tivo] *ag* objective

og'getto [od'dʒɛtto] *sm* object;
(*materia, argomento*) subject (matter); **~i smarriti** lost property *sg*

'oggi ['oddʒi] *av, sm* today; **~ a otto**
a week today; **oggigi'orno** *av*
nowadays

'ogni ['oɲi] *det* every, each; (*tutti*)
all; (*con valore distributivo*) every;
~ uomo è mortale all men are
mortal; **viene ~ due giorni** he
comes every two days; **~ cosa**
everything; **ad ~ costo** at all costs,
at any price; **in ~ luogo** everywhere; **~ tanto** so often; **~
volta che** every time that

Ognis'santi [oɲis'santi] *sm* All
Saints' Day

o'gnuno [oɲ'ɲuno] *pron* everyone,
everybody

'ohi *escl* oh!; (*esprimere dolore*)
ow!

ohimè *escl* oh dear!

O'landa *sf*: **l'~** Holland; **olan'dese**
ag Dutch ♦ *sm* (LING) Dutch ♦ *sm/f*
Dutchman/woman; **gli Olandesi**
the Dutch

oleo'dotto *sm* oil pipeline

ole'oso, a *ag* oily; (*che contiene
olio*) oil-yielding

ol'fatto *sm* sense of smell

oli'are *vt* to oil

oli'era *sf* oil cruet

olim'piadi *sfpl* Olympic games; **o'limpico, a, ci, che** *ag* Olympic

'olio *sm* oil; **sott'~** (*CUC*) in oil; **~ di fegato di merluzzo** cod liver oil; **~ d'oliva** olive oil; **~ di semi** vegetable oil

o'liva *sf* olive; **oli'vastro, a** *ag* olive(-coloured); (*carnagione*) sallow; **oli'veto** *sm* olive grove; **o'livo** *sm* olive tree

'olmo *sm* elm

oltraggi'are [oltrad'dʒare] *vt* to outrage; to offend gravely

ol'traggio [ol'traddʒo] *sm* outrage; offence, insult; **~ a pubblico ufficiale** (*DIR*) insulting a public official; **~ al pudore** (*DIR*) indecent behaviour; **oltraggi'oso, a** *ag* offensive

ol'tralpe *av* beyond the Alps

ol'tranza [ol'trantsa] *sf*: **a ~** to the last, to the bitter end

'oltre *av* (*più in là*) further; (*di più: aspettare*) longer, more ♦ *prep* (*di là da*) beyond, over, on the other side of; (*più di*) more than, over; (*in aggiunta a*) besides; (*eccetto*): **~ a** except, apart from; **oltre'mare** *av* overseas; **oltre'modo** *av* extremely; **oltre'passare** *vt* to go beyond, exceed

o'maggio [o'maddʒo] *sm* (*dono*) gift; (*segno di rispetto*) homage, tribute; **~i** *smpl* (*complimenti*) respects; **rendere ~ a** to pay homage o tribute to; **in ~** (*copia, biglietto*) complimentary

ombeli'cale *ag* umbilical

ombe'lico, chi *sm* navel

'ombra *sf* (*zona non assolata, fantasma*) shade; (*sagoma scura*) shadow; **sedere all'~** to sit in the shade; **restare nell'~** (*fig*) to remain in obscurity

ombreggi'are [ombred'dʒare] *vt* to shade

om'brello *sm* umbrella; **ombrel'lone** *sm* beach umbrella

om'bretto *sm* eyeshadow

om'broso, a *ag* shady, shaded; (*cavallo*) nervous, skittish; (*persona*) touchy, easily offended

ome'lia *sf* (*REL*) homily, sermon

omeopa'tia *sf* homoeopathy

omertà *sf* conspiracy of silence

o'messo, a *pp di* omettere

o'mettere *vt* to omit, leave out; **~ di fare** to omit o fail to do

omi'cida, i, e [omi'tʃida] *ag* homicidal, murderous ♦ *smf* murderer/eress

omi'cidio [omi'tʃidjo] *sm* murder; **~ colposo** culpable homicide

omissi'one *sf* omission; **~ di soccorso** (*DIR*) failure to stop and give assistance

omogeneiz'zato [omodʒeneid'dza-toj *sm* baby food

omo'geneo, a [omo'dʒɛneo] *ag* homogeneous

omolo'gare *vt* to approve, recognize; to ratify

o'monimo, a *sm/f* namesake ♦ *sm* (*LING*) homonym

omosessu'ale *ag, smf* homosexual

'oncia, ce [ʹontʃa] *sf* ounce

'onda *sf* wave; **mettere** o **mandare in ~** (*RADIO, TV*) to broadcast; **andare in ~** (*RADIO, TV*) to go on the air; **~e corte/medie/lunghe** short/medium/long wave; **on'data** *sf* wave, billow; (*fig*) wave, surge; **a ondate** in waves; **ondata di caldo** heatwave

'onde *cong* (*affinché: con il congiuntivo*) so that, in order that; (*: con l'infinito*) so as to, in order to

ondeggi'are [onded'dʒare] *vi* (*acqua*) to ripple; (*muoversi sulle onde: barca*) to rock, roll; (*fig: muoversi come le onde, barcollare*) to sway; (*: essere incerto*) to waver

ondulazi'one [ondulat'tsjone] *sf* undulation; (*acconciatura*) wave

'onere *sm* burden; **~i fiscali** taxes; **one'roso, a** *ag* (*fig*) heavy, onerous

onestà *sf* honesty

o'nesto, a *ag* (*probo, retto*) honest; (*giusto*) fair; (*casto*) chaste, virtuous

'onice ['ɔnitʃe] *sf* onyx

onnipo'tente *ag* omnipotent

onniveg'gente [onnived'dʒɛnte] *ag* all-seeing

ono'mastico, ci *sm* name-day

ono'ranze [ono'rantse] *sfpl* honours; ~ **funebri** funeral (service)

ono'rare *vt* to honour; (*far onore a*) to do credit to; ~**rsi** *vr*: ~**rsi di** to feel honoured at, be proud of

ono'rario, a *ag* honorary ♦ *sm* fee

o'nore *sm* honour; **in** ~ **di** in honour of; **fare gli** ~i **di casa** to play host (*o* hostess); **fare** ~ **a** to honour; (*pranzo*) to do justice to; (*famiglia*) to be a credit to; **farsi** ~ to distinguish o.s.; **ono'revole** *ag* honourable ♦ *smif* (*POL*) ≈ Member of Parliament (*BRIT*), ≈ Congressman/woman (*US*); **onorifi'cenza** *sf* honour; decoration; **ono'rifico, a, ci, che** *ag* honorary

'onta *sf* shame, disgrace

on'tano *sm* (*BOT*) alder

'O.N.U. ['ɔnu] *sigla f* (= *Organizzazione delle Nazioni Unite*) UN, UNO

o'paco, a, chi, che *ag* (*vetro*) opaque; (*metallo*) dull, matt

o'pale *sm o f* opal

'opera *sf* work; (*azione rilevante*) action, deed, work; (*MUS*) work; opus; (: *melodramma*) opera; (: *teatro*) opera house; (*ente*) institution, organization; ~ **d'arte** work of art; ~ **lirica** (grand) opera; ~e **pubbliche** public works

ope'raio, a *ag* working-class; workers' ♦ *smif* worker; **classe** ~**a** working class

ope'rare *vt* to carry out, make; (*MED*) to operate on ♦ *vi* to operate, work; (*rimedio*) to act, work; (*MED*) to operate; ~**rsi** *vr* to occur, take place; (*MED*) to have an operation; ~**rsi d'appendicite** to have one's appendix out; **opera'tivo, a** *ag* operative, operating; **opera'tore, 'trice** *smif* operator; (*TV, CINEMA*) cameraman; **operatore economico** agent, broker; **operatore turistico**

tour operator; **opera'torio, a** *ag* (*MED*) operating; **operazi'one** *sf* operation

ope'retta *sf* (*MUS*) operetta, light opera

ope'roso, a *ag* busy, active, hardworking

opi'ficio [opi'fitʃo] *sm* factory, works *pl*

opini'one *sf* opinion; ~ **pubblica** public opinion

'oppio *sm* opium

oppo'nente *ag* opposing ♦ *smif* opponent

op'porre *vt* to oppose; **opporsi** *vr*: **opporsi (a qc)** to oppose (sth); to object (to sth); ~ **resistenza/un rifiuto** to offer resistance/refuse

opportu'nista, i, e *smif* opportunist

opportunità *sf inv* opportunity; (*convenienza*) opportuneness, timeliness

oppor'tuno, a *ag* timely, opportune

opposi'tore, 'trice *smif* opposer, opponent

opposizi'one [oppozit'tsjone] *sf* opposition; (*DIR*) objection

op'posto, a *pp di* **opporre** ♦ *ag* opposite; (*opinioni*) conflicting ♦ *sm* opposite, contrary; **all'** ~ on the contrary

oppressi'one *sf* oppression

oppres'sivo, a *ag* oppressive

op'presso, a *pp di* **opprimere**

oppres'sore *sm* oppressor

op'primere *vt* (*premere, gravare*) to weigh down; (*estenuare*: *sog*: *caldo*) to suffocate, oppress; (*tiranneggiare*: *popolo*) to oppress

oppu'gnare [oppuɲ'ɲare] *vt* (*fig*) to refute

op'pure *cong* or (else)

op'tare *vi*: ~ **per** to opt for

o'puscolo *sm* booklet, pamphlet

opzi'one [op'tsjone] *sf* option

'ora¹ *sf* (60 *minuti*) hour; (*momento*) time; **che** ~ **è?, che** ~**e sono?** what time is it?; **non veder l'**~ **di fare** to long to do, look forward to doing; **di buon'~** early; **alla buon'~!** at last!; **~ legale** o **estiva** summer time (BRIT), daylight saving time (US); **~ locale** local time; **~ di punta** (AUT) rush hour

ora² av (adesso) now; (poco fa): **è uscito proprio ~** he's just gone out; (tra poco) presently, in a minute; (correlativo): **~ ... ~** now ... now; **d'~ in avanti** o **poi** from now on; or **~ just** now, a moment ago; **5 anni** or **sono 5 years ago; **~ come ~** right now, at present

o'racolo sm oracle

'orafo sm goldsmith

o'rale ag, sm oral

ora'mai av = ormai

o'rario, a ag hourly; (fuso, segnale) time cpd; (velocità) per hour ♦ sm timetable, schedule; (di ufficio, visite etc) hours pl, time(s pl)

o'rata sf (ZOOL) sea bream

ora'tore, 'trice sm/f speaker; orator

ora'toria sf (arte) oratory

ora'torio, a ag oratorical ♦ sm (REL) oratory; (MUS) oratorio

ora'zione [orat'tsjone] sf (REL) prayer; (discorso) speech, oration

or'bene cong so, well (then)

'orbita sf (ASTR, FISICA) orbit; (ANAT) (eye-)socket

or'chestra [or'kestra] sf orchestra; **orches'trare** vt to orchestrate; (fig) to mount, stage-manage

orchi'dea [orki'dɛa] sf orchid

'orco, chi sm ogre

'orda sf horde

or'digno [or'diɲɲo] sm (esplosivo) explosive device

ordi'nale ag, sm ordinal

ordina'mento sm order, arrangement; (regolamento) regulations pl, rules pl; **~ scolastico/giuridico** education/legal system

ordi'nanza [ordi'nantsa] sf (DIR, MIL) order; (persona: MIL) orderly, batman; **d'~** (MIL) regulation cpd

ordi'nare vt (mettere in ordine) to arrange, organize; (COMM) to

(prescrivere: medicina) to prescribe; (comandare): **~ a qn di fare qc** to order o command sb to do sth; (REL) to ordain

ordi'nario, a ag (comune) ordinary; everyday; standard; (grossolano) coarse, common ♦ sm ordinary; (INS: di università) full professor

ordi'nato, a ag tidy, orderly

ordinazi'one [ordinat'tsjone] sf (COMM) order; (REL) ordination; **eseguire qc su ~** to make sth to order

'ordine sm order; (carattere): **d'~ pratico** of a practical nature; **all'~** (COMM): assegno to order; **di prim'~** first-class; **fino a nuovo ~** until further notice; **essere in ~** (documenti) to be in order; (stanza, persona) to be tidy; **mettere in ~** to put in order, tidy (up); **~ del giorno** (di seduta) agenda; (MIL) order of the day; **~ di pagamento** (COMM) order for payment; **l'~ pubblico** law and order; **~i (sacri)** (REL) holy orders

or'dire vt (fig) to plot, scheme; **or'dito** sm (di tessuto) warp

orec'chino [orek'kino] sm earring

o'recchio [o'rekkjo] (pl(f) **o'recchie**) sm (ANAT) ear

orecchi'oni [orek'kjoni] smpl (MED) mumps sg

o'refice [o'refitfe] sm goldsmith; jeweller; **orefice'ria** sf (arte) goldsmith's art; (negozio) jeweller's (shop)

'orfano, a ag orphan(ed) ♦ sm/f orphan; **~ di padre/madre** fatherless/motherless; **orfano'trofio** sm orphanage

orga'netto sm barrel organ; (fam: armonica a bocca) mouth organ; (: fisarmonica) accordion

or'ganico, a, ci, che ag organic ♦ sm personnel, staff

organi'gramma, i sm organization chart

orga'nismo sm (BIOL) organism; (corpo umano) body; (AMM) body, organism

organiz'zare [organid'dzare] *vt* to organize; **~rsi** *vr* to get organized; **organizza'tore, 'trice** *sf* organizing ♦ *sm/f* organizer; **organizza-zi'one** *sf* organization

'organo *sm* organ; (*di congegno*) part; (*portavoce*) spokesman, mouthpiece

or'gasmo *sm* (*FISIOL*) orgasm; (*fig*) agitation, anxiety

'orgia, ge ['ɔrdʒa] *sf* orgy

or'goglio [or'gɔʎʎo] *sm* pride; **orgogli'oso, a** *ag* proud

orien'tale *ag* oriental; eastern; east

orienta'mento *sm* positioning; orientation; direction; **senso di ~** sense of direction; **perdere l'~** to lose one's bearings; **~ professionale** careers guidance

orien'tare *vt* (*situare*) to position; (*fig*) to direct, orientate; **~rsi** *vr* to find one's bearings; (*fig: tendere*) to tend, lean; (: *indirizzarsi*): **~rsi verso** to take up, go in for

ori'ente *sm* east; **l'O~** the East, the Orient; **a ~** in the east

o'rigano *sm* oregano

origi'nale [oridʒi'nale] *ag* original; (*bizzarro*) eccentric ♦ *sm* original; **originalità** *sf* originality; eccentricity

origi'nare [oridʒi'nare] *vt* to bring about, produce ♦ *vi*: **~ da** to arise o spring from

origi'nario, a [oridʒi'narjo] *ag* original; essere **~ di** to be a native of; (*provenire da*) to originate from; to be native to

o'rigine [o'ridʒine] *sf* origin; **all'~** originally; **d'~ inglese** of English origin; **dare ~ a** to give rise to

origli'are [oriʎ'ʎare] *vi*: **~ (a)** to eavesdrop (on)

o'rina *sf* urine

ori'nare *vi* to urinate ♦ *vt* to pass; **orina'toio** *sm* (public) urinal

ori'undo, a *ag*: **essere ~ di Milano** *etc* to be of Milanese *etc* extraction *o* origin ♦ *sm/f* person of foreign

extraction *o* origin

orizzon'tale [oriddzon'tale] *ag* horizontal

oriz'zonte [orid'dzonte] *sm* horizon

or'lare *vt* to hem

'orlo *sm* edge, border; (*di recipiente*) rim, brim; (*di vestito etc*) hem

'orma *sf* (*di persona*) footprint; (*di animale*) track; (*impronta, traccia*) mark, trace

or'mai *av* by now, by this time; (*adesso*) now; (*quasi*) almost, nearly

ormeggi'are [ormed'dʒare] *vt* (*NAUT*) to moor; **or'meggio** *sm* (*atto*) mooring *no pl*; (*luogo*) moorings *pl*

or'mone *sm* hormone

ornamen'tale *ag* ornamental, decorative

orna'mento *sm* ornament, decoration

or'nare *vt* to adorn, decorate; **~rsi** *vr*: **~rsi (di)** to deck o.s. (out) (with); **or'nato, a** *ag* ornate

ornitolo'gia [ornitolo'dʒia] *sf* ornithology

'oro *sm* gold; **d'~, in ~** gold *cpd*; **d'~** (*colore, occasione*) golden; (*persona*) marvellous

orolo'geria [orolodʒe'ria] *sf* watchmaking *no pl*; watchmaker's (shop); clockmaker's (shop); **bomba a ~** time bomb

orologi'aio [orolo'dʒajo] *sm* watchmaker; clockmaker

oro'logio [oro'lɔdʒo] *sm* clock; (*da tasca, da polso*) watch; **~ da polso** wristwatch; **~ al quarzo** quartz watch

o'roscopo *sm* horoscope

or'rendo, a *ag* (*spaventoso*) horrible, awful; (*bruttissimo*) hideous

or'ribile *ag* horrible

'orrido, a *ag* fearful, horrid

orripi'lante *ag* hair-raising, horrifying

or'rore *sm* horror; avere in **~ qn/qc** to loathe *o* detest sb/sth; **mi fanno ~** I loathe *o* detest them

orsacchi'otto [orsak'kjɔtto] *sm* teddy bear

'orso *sm* bear; **~ bruno/bianco** brown/polar bear

or'taggio [or'taddʒo] *sm* vegetable

or'tensia *sf* hydrangea

or'tica, che *sf* (stinging) nettle

orti'caria *sf* nettle rash

'orto *sm* vegetable garden, kitchen garden; (*AGR*) market garden (*BRIT*), truck farm (*US*)

orto'dosso, a *ag* orthodox

ortogra'fia *sf* spelling

orto'lano, a *smif* (*venditore*) greengrocer (*BRIT*), produce dealer (*US*)

ortope'dia *sf* orthopaedics *sg*; **orto'pedico, a, ci, che** *ag* orthopaedic ♦ *sm* orthopaedic specialist

orzai'olo [ordza'jɔlo] *sm* (*MED*) stye

or'zata [or'dzata] *sf* barley water

'orzo ['ordzo] *sm* barley

o'sare *vt, vi* to dare; **~ fare** to dare (to) do

oscenità [ɔʃʃeni'ta] *sf inv* obscenity

o'sceno, a [ɔʃ'ʃɛno] *ag* obscene; (*ripugnante*) ghastly

oscil'lare [ɔʃʃil'lare] *vi* (*pendolo*) to swing; (*dondolare: al vento etc*) to rock; (*variare*) to fluctuate; (*TECN*) to oscillate; (*fig*): **~ fra** to waver *o* hesitate between; **oscillazi'one** *sf* oscillation; (*di prezzi, temperatura*) fluctuation

oscura'mento *sm* darkening; obscuring; (*in tempo di guerra*) blackout

oscu'rare *vt* to darken, obscure; (*fig*) to obscure; **~rsi** *vr* (*cielo*) to darken, cloud over; (*persona*): **si oscurò in volto** his face clouded over

os'curo, a *ag* dark; (*fig*) obscure; humble, lowly ♦ *sm*: **all'~** in the dark; **tenere qn all'~ di qc** to keep sb in the dark about sth

ospe'dale *sm* hospital; **ospeda-li'ero, a** *ag* hospital *cpd*

ospi'tale *ag* hospitable; **ospitalità** *sf* hospitality

ospi'tare *vt* to give hospitality to; (*sog: albergo*) to accommodate

'ospite *smif* (*persona che ospita*) host/hostess; (*persona ospitata*) guest

os'pizio [os'pittsjo] *sm* (*per vecchi etc*) home

'ossa *sfpl vedi* osso

ossa'tura *sf* (*ANAT*) skeletal structure, frame; (*TECN, fig*) framework

'osseo, a *ag* bony; (*tessuto etc*) bone *cpd*

os'sequio *sm* deference, respect; **~i** *smpl* (*saluto*) respects, regards; **ossequi'oso, a** *ag* obsequious

osser'vanza [osser'vantsa] *sf* observance

osser'vare *vt* to observe, watch; (*esaminare*) to examine; (*notare, rilevare*) to notice, observe; (*DIR: la legge*) to observe, respect; (*mantenere: silenzio*) to keep, observe; **far ~ qc a qn** to point sth out to sb; **osserva'tore, 'trice** *ag* observant, perceptive ♦ *smif* observer; **osserva'torio** *sm* (*ASTR*) observatory; (*MIL*) observation post; **osservazi'one** *sf* observation; (*di legge etc*) observance; (*considerazione critica*) observation, remark; (*rimprovero*) reproof; **in osservazione** under observation

ossessi'onare *vt* to obsess, haunt; (*tormentare*) to torment, harass

ossessi'one *sf* obsession

os'sesso, a *ag* (*spiritato*) possessed

os'sia *cong* that is, to be precise

ossi'buchi [ɔssi'buki] *smpl di* ossobuco

ossi'dare *vt* to oxidize; **~rsi** *vr* to oxidize

'ossido *sm* oxide; **~ di carbonio** carbon monoxide

ossige'nare [ɔssidʒe'nare] *vt* to oxygenate; (*decolorare*) to bleach; **acqua ossigenata** hydrogen peroxide

os'sigeno *sm* oxygen

'osso (*pl(f) ossa nel senso ANAT*) *sm* bone; **d'~** (*bottone etc*) of bone, bone *cpd*

osso'buco (*pl* **ossi'buchi**) *sm* (*CUC*) marrowbone; (: *piatto*) stew *made with knuckle of veal in tomato sauce*

os'suto, a *ag* bony

ostaco'lare *vt* to block, obstruct

os'tacolo *sm* obstacle; (*EQUITA-ZIONE*) hurdle, jump

os'taggio [os'taddʒo] *sm* hostage

'oste, os'tessa *sm/f* innkeeper

osteggi'are [osted'dʒare] *vt* to oppose, be opposed to

os'tello *sm*: ~ della gioventù youth hostel

osten'tare *vt* to make a show of, flaunt; ostentazi'one *sf* ostentation, show

oste'ria *sf* inn

os'tessa *sf vedi* oste

os'tetrica *sf* midwife

os'tetrico, a, ci, che *ag* obstetric ♦ *sm* obstetrician

'ostia *sf* (*REL*) host; (*per medicinali*) wafer

'ostico, a, ci, che *ag* (*fig*) harsh; hard, difficult; unpleasant

os'tile *ag* hostile; ostilità *sf inv* hostility ♦ *sfpl* (*MIL*) hostilities

osti'narsi *vr* to insist, dig one's heels in; ~ a fare to persist (obstinately) in doing; osti'nato, a *ag* (*caparbio*) obstinate; (*tenace*) persistent, determined; ostinazi'one *sf* obstinacy; persistence

'ostrica, che *sf* oyster

ostru'ire *vt* to obstruct, block; ostruzi'one *sf* obstruction, blockage

'otre *sm* (*recipiente*) goatskin

otta'gonale *ag* octagonal

ot'tagono *sm* octagon

ot'tanta *num* eighty; ottan'tesimo, a *num* eightieth; ottan'tina *sf*: una ottantina (di) about eighty

ot'tava *sf* octave

ot'tavo, a *num* eighth

ottempe'rare *vi*: ~ a to comply with, obey

otte'nere *vt* to obtain, get; (*risultato*) to achieve, obtain

'ottica *sf* (*scienza*) optics *sg*; (*FOT: lenti, prismi etc*) optics *pl*

'ottico, a, ci, che *ag* (*della vista:*

nervo) optic; (*dell'ottica*) optical ♦ *sm* optician

ottima'mente *av* excellently, very well

otti'mismo *sm* optimism; otti'mista, i, e *sm/f* optimist

'ottimo, a *ag* excellent, very good

'otto *num* eight

ot'tobre *sm* October

otto'cento [otto'tʃɛnto] *num* eight hundred ♦ *sm*: l'O~ the nineteenth century

ot'tone *sm* brass; gli ~i (*MUS*) brass

ottu'rare *vt* to close (up); (*dente*) to fill; ottura'tore *sm* (*FOT*) shutter; (*nelle armi*) breechblock; otturazi'one *sf* closing (up); (*dentaria*) filling

ot'tuso, a *ag* (*MAT*, *fig*) obtuse; (*suono*) dull

o'vaia *sf* (*ANAT*) ovary

o'vaio *sm* = ovaia

o'vale *ag*, *sm* oval

o'vatta *sf* cotton wool; (*per imbottire*) padding, wadding; ovat'tare *vt* (*fig: smorzare*) to muffle

ovazi'one [ovat'tsjone] *sf* ovation

'ovest *sm* west

o'vile *sm* pen, enclosure

o'vino, a *ag* sheep *cpd*; ovine

ovulazi'one [ovulat'tsjone] *sf* ovulation

'ovulo *sm* (*FISIOL*) ovum

o'vunque *av* = dovunque

ov'vero *cong* (*ossia*) that is, to be precise; (*oppure*) or (else)

ovvi'are *vi*: ~ a to obviate

'ovvio, a *ag* obvious

ozi'are [ot'tsjare] *vi* to laze, idle

'ozio ['ɔttsjo] *sm* idleness; (*tempo libero*) leisure; ore d'~ leisure time; stare in ~ to be idle; ozi'oso, a *ag* idle

o'zono [o'dzɔno] *sm* ozone

P

pa'cato, a *ag* quiet, calm

pac'chetto [pak'ketto] *sm* packet; ~ **azionario** (*COMM*) shareholding

pacchi'ano, a [pak'kjano, a] *ag* vulgar

'pacco, chi *sm* parcel; (*involto*) bundle

'pace ['patʃe] *sf* peace; **darsi** ~ **to** resign o.s.

pacifi'care [patʃifi'kare] *vt* (*riconciliare*) to reconcile, make peace between; (*mettere in pace*) to pacify

pa'cifico, a, ci, che [pa'tʃi:fiko] *ag* (*persona*) peaceable; (*vita*) peaceful; (*fig: indiscusso*) indisputable; (: *ovvio*) obvious, clear ♦ *sm:* **il P~, l'Oceano P~** the Pacific (Ocean)

paci'fista, i, e [patʃi'fista] *smf* pacifist

pa'della *sf* frying pan; (*per infermi*) bedpan

padigli'one [padiʎ'ʎone] *sm* pavilion; (*AUT*) roof

'Padova *sf* Padua

'padre *sm* father; **~i** *smpl* (*antenati*) forefathers; **pa'drino** *sm* godfather

padro'nanza [padro'nantsa] *sf* command, mastery

pa'drone, a *smf* master/mistress; (*proprietario*) owner; (*datore di lavoro*) employer; **essere ~ di sé** to be in control of o.s.; ~ **di casa** (*ospite*) host/hostess; (*per gli inquilini*) landlord/lady; **padroneggi'are** *vt* (*fig: sentimenti*) to master, control; (: *materia*) to master, know thoroughly; **padroneggi'arsi** *vr* to control o.s.

pae'saggio [pae'zaddʒo] *sm* landscape

pae'sano, a *ag* country *cpd* ♦ *smf* villager; countryman/woman

pa'ese *sm* (*nazione*) country, nation; (*terra*) country, land; (*villaggio*) village; ~ **di provenienza** country of

origin; **i P~i Bassi** the Netherlands

paf'futo, a *ag* chubby, plump

'paga, ghe *sf* pay, wages *pl*

paga'mento *sm* payment

pa'gano, a *ag, smf* pagan

pa'gare *vt* to pay; (*acquisto, fig: colpa*) to pay for; (*contraccambiare*) to repay, pay back ♦ *vi* to pay; **quanto l'hai pagato?** how much did you pay for it?; ~ **con carta di credito** to pay by credit card; ~ **in contanti** to pay cash

pa'gella [pa'dʒɛlla] *sf* (*INS*) report card

'paggio ['paddʒo] *sm* page(boy)

paghe'rò [page'rɔ] *sm inv* acknowledgement of a debt, IOU

'pagina [pa'dʒina] *sf* page; **~e gialle** Yellow Pages

'paglia ['paʎʎa] *sf* straw

pagli'accetto [paʎʎat'tʃetto] *sm* (*per bambini*) rompers *pl*

pagli'accio [paʎ'ʎattʃo] *sm* clown

pagli'etta [paʎ'ʎetta] *sf* (*cappello per uomo*) (straw) boater; (*per tegami etc*) steel wool

pa'gnotta [paɲ'ɲɔtta] *sf* round loaf

'paio (*pl(f)* **'paia**) *sm* pair; **un ~ di** (*alcuni*) a couple of

pai'olo *sm* (copper) pot

'pala *sf* shovel; (*di remo, ventilatore, elica*) blade; (*di ruota*) paddle

pa'lato *sm* palate

pa'lazzo [pa'lattso] *sm* (*reggia*) palace; (*edificio*) building; ~ **di giustizia** courthouse; ~ **dello sport** sports stadium

pal'chetto [pal'ketto] *sm* shelf

'palco, chi *sm* (*TEATRO*) box; (*tavolato*) platform, stand; (*ripiano*) layer

palco'scenico, ci [palko'ʃeniko] *sm* (*TEATRO*) stage

pale'sare *vt* to reveal, disclose; **~rsi** *vr* to reveal *o* show o.s.

pa'lese *ag* clear, evident

Pales'tina *sf:* **la ~** Palestine

pa'lestra *sf* gymnasium; (*esercizio atletico*) exercise; training; (*fig*) training ground, school

pa'letta sf spade; (per il focolare) shovel; (del capostazione) signalling disc

pa'letto sm stake, peg; (spranga) bolt

'palio sm (gara): **il P~** horserace run at Siena; **mettere qc in ~** to offer sth as a prize

'palla sf (ball); (pallottola) bullet; **~ canestro** sm basketball; **~ nuoto** sm water polo; **~ ovale** rugby ball; **~ volo** sm volleyball

palleggi'are [palled'dʒare] vi (CALCIO) to practise with the ball; (TENNIS) to knock up

pallia'tivo sm palliative; (fig) stopgap measure

'pallido, a ag pale

pal'lina sf (bilia) marble

pallon'cino [pallon'tʃino] sm balloon; (lampioncino) Chinese lantern

pal'lone sm (palla) ball; (CALCIO) football; (aerostato) balloon; **gioco del ~** football

pal'lore sm pallor, paleness

pal'lottola sf pellet; (proiettile) bullet

'palma sf (ANAT) = **palmo**; (BOT, simbolo) palm; **~ da datteri** date palm

'palmo sm (ANAT) palm; **restare con un ~ di naso** to be badly disappointed

'palo sm (legno appuntito) stake; (sostegno) pole; **fare da o il ~** (fig) to act as look-out

palom'baro sm diver

pa'lombo sm (pesce) dogfish

pal'pare vt to feel, finger

'palpebra sf eyelid

palpi'tare vi (cuore, polso) to beat; (: più forte) to pound, throb; (fremere) to quiver; **'palpito** sm (del cuore) beat; (fig: d'amore etc) throb

paltò sm inv overcoat

pa'lude sf marsh, swamp; **palu'doso, a** ag marshy, swampy

pa'lustre ag marsh cpd, swamp cpd

pam'pino sm vine leaf

pancarrè sm sliced square bread (used mainly for toasted sandwiches)

'panca, che sf bench

pan'cetta [pan'tʃetta] sf (CUC) bacon

pan'chetto [pan'ketto] sm stool; footstool

pan'china [pan'kina] sf garden seat; (di giardino pubblico) (park) bench

'pancia, ce ['pantʃa] sf belly, stomach; **mettere o fare ~** to be getting a paunch; **avere mal di ~** to have stomachache o a sore stomach

panci'otto [pan'tʃɔtto] sm waistcoat

'pancreas sm inv pancreas

'panda sm inv panda

pande'monio sm pandemonium

'pane sm bread; (pagnotta) loaf (of bread); (forma): **un ~ di burro/cera** etc a pat of butter/bar of wax etc; **guadagnarsi il ~** to earn one's living; **~ a cassetta** sliced bread; **~ di Spagna** sponge cake; **~ integrale** wholemeal bread; **~ tostato** toast

panette'ria sf (forno) bakery; (negozio) baker's (shop), bakery

panetti'ere, a sm/f baker

panet'tone sm a kind of spiced brioche with sultanas, eaten at Christmas

'panfilo sm yacht

pangrat'tato sm breadcrumbs pl

'panico, a [ci, che ag, sm panic

pani'ere sm basket

pani'ficio [pani'fitʃo] sm (forno) bakery; (negozio) baker's (shop), bakery

pa'nino sm roll; **~ caldo** toasted sandwich; **~ imbottito** filled roll; sandwich; **panino'teca** sf sandwich bar

'panna sf (CUC) cream; (TECN) = **panne**; **~ da cucina** cooking cream; **~ montata** whipped cream

'panne sf inv: **essere in ~** (AUT) to have broken down

pan'nello sm panel; **~ solare** solar panel

'panno sm cloth; **~i** smpl (abiti) clothes; **mettiti nei miei ~i** (fig) put yourself in my shoes

pan'nocchia [pan'nɔkkja] sf (di

mais etc) ear

panno'lino *sm* (*per bambini*) nappy (*BRIT*), diaper (*US*)

pano'rama, i *sm* panorama; **pano'ramico, a, ci, che** *ag* panoramic; **strada panoramica** scenic route

panta'loni *smpl* trousers (*BRIT*), pants (*US*), pair *sg* of trousers *o* pants

pan'tano *sm* bog

pan'tera *sf* panther

pan'tofola *sf* slipper

panto'mima *sf* pantomime

pan'zana [pan'tsana] *sf* fib, tall story

pao'nazzo, a [pao'nattso] *ag* purple

papa, i *sm* pope

papà *sm inv* dad(dy)

pa'pale *ag* papal

pa'pato *sm* papacy

pa'pavero *sm* poppy

papera *sf* (*fig*) slip of the tongue, blunder; *vedi anche* papero

papero, a *smf* (*ZOOL*) gosling

pa'piro *sm* papyrus

pappa *sf* baby cereal

pappa'gallo *sm* parrot; (*fig: uomo*) Romeo, wolf

pappa'gorgia, ge [pappa'gɔrdʒa] *sf* double chin

pap'pare *vt* (*fam: anche: ~rsi*) to gobble up

'para *sf*: **suole di ~** crepe soles

pa'rabola *sf* (*MAT*) parabola; (*REL*) parable

para'brezza [para'breddza] *sm inv* (*AUT*) windscreen (*BRIT*), windshield (*US*)

paraca'dute *sm inv* parachute

para'carro *sm* kerbstone (*BRIT*), curbstone (*US*)

para'diso *sm* paradise

parados'sale *ag* paradoxical

para'dosso *sm* paradox

para'fango, ghi *sm* mudguard

paraf'fina *sf* paraffin, paraffin wax

para'fulmine *sm* lightning conductor

pa'raggi [pa'raddʒi] *smpl*: **nei ~ in** the vicinity, in the neighbourhood

parago'nare *vt*: **~ con/a** to compare with/to

para'gone *sm* comparison; (*esempio analogo*) analogy, parallel; **reggere al ~** to stand comparison

pa'ragrafo *sm* paragraph

pa'ralisi *sf* paralysis; **para'litico, a, ci, che** *sm/f* paralytic

paraliz'zare [paralid'dzare] *vt* to paralyze

paral'lela *sf* parallel (line); **~e** *sfpl* (*attrezzo ginnico*) parallel bars

paral'lelo, a *ag* parallel ♦ *sm* (*GEO*) parallel; (*comparazione*): **fare un ~ tra** to draw a parallel between

para'lume *sm* lampshade

pa'rametro *sm* parameter

para'noia *sf* paranoia; **para'noico, a, ci, che** *ag, sm/f* paranoid

para'occhi [para'ɔkki] *smpl* blinkers

para'petto *sm* balustrade

para'piglia [para'piʎʎa] *sm* commotion, uproar

pa'rare *vt* (*addobbare*) to adorn, deck; (*proteggere*) to shield, protect; (*scansare: colpo*) to parry; (*CALCIO*) to save ♦ *vi*: **dove vuole andare a ~?** what are you driving at?; **~rsi** *vr* (*presentarsi*) to appear, present o.s.

para'sole *sm inv* parasol, sunshade

paras'sita, i *sm* parasite

pa'rata *sf* (*SPORT*) save; (*MIL*) review, parade

para'tia *sf* (*di nave*) bulkhead

para'urti *sm inv* (*AUT*) bumper

para'vento *sm* folding screen; **fare da ~ a qn** (*fig*) to shield sb

par'cella [par'tʃɛlla] *sf* account, fee (*of lawyer etc*)

parcheggi'are [parked'dʒare] *vt* to park; **par'cheggio** *sm* parking *no pl*; (*luogo*) car park; (*singolo posto*) parking space

par'chimetro [par'kimetro] *sm* parking meter

'parco[1], chi *sm* park; (*spazio per deposito*) depot; (*complesso di veicoli*) fleet '**parco²**, a, chi, che *ag*: ~ (in) (*sobrio*) moderate (in); (*avaro*) sparing (with)

pa'recchio, a [pa'rekkjo] *det* quite a lot of; (*tempo*) quite a lot of, a long; ~i, e *det pl* quite a lot of, several ♦ *pron* quite a lot, quite a bit; (*tempo*) quite a while, a long time; ~i, e *pron pl* quite a lot, several ♦ *av* (*con ag*) quite a lot, quite a bit

pareggi'are [pared'dʒare] *vt* to make equal; (*terreno*) to level, make level; (*bilancio, conti*) to balance ♦ *vi* (*SPORT*) to draw; **pa'reggio** *sm* (*ECON*) balance; (*SPORT*) draw

pa'rente *smlf* relative, relation

paren'tela *sf* (*vincolo di sangue, fig*) relationship; (*insieme dei parenti*) relations *pl*, relatives *pl*

pa'rentesi *sf* (*segno grafico*) bracket, parenthesis; (*frase incisa*) parenthesis; (*digressione*) parenthesis, digression

pa'rere *sm* (*opinione*) opinion; (*consiglio*) advice, opinion; a mio ~ in my opinion ♦ *vi* to seem, appear ♦ *vb impers*: pare che it seems o appears that, they say that; mi pare che it seems o that; mi pare di sì I think so; fai come ti pare do as you like; che ti pare del mio libro? what do you think of my book?

pa'rete *sf* wall

'**pari** *ag inv* (*uguale*) equal, same; (*in giochi*) equal; drawn, tied; (*MAT*) even ♦ *sm inv* (*POL: di Gran Bretagna*) peer ♦ *smlf inv* peer, equal; copiato ~ ~ copied word for word; alla ~ on the same level; ragazza alla ~ au pair girl; mettersi alla ~ con to place o.s. on the same level as; mettersi in ~ con to catch up with; andare di ~ passo con qn to keep pace with

Pa'rigi [pa'ridʒi] *sf* Paris

pa'riglia [pa'riʎʎa] *sf* pair; rendere la ~ to give tit for tat

parità *sf* parity, equality; (*SPORT*) draw, tie

parlamen'tare *ag* parliamentary ♦ *smlf* ≈ Member of Parliament (*BRIT*), ≈ Congressman/woman (*US*) ♦ *vi* to negotiate, parley

parla'mento *sm* parliament

parlan'tina (*fam*) *sf* talkativeness; avere una buona ~ to have the gift of the gab

par'lare *vi* to speak, talk; (*confidare cose segrete*) to talk ♦ *vt* to speak; ~ (a qn) di to speak o talk (to sb) about; **parla'torio** *sm* (*di carcere etc*) visiting room; (*REL*) parlour

parmigi'ano [parmi'dʒano] *sm* (*grana*) Parmesan (cheese)

paro'dia *sf* parody

pa'rola *sf* word; (*facoltà*) speech; ~e *sfpl* (*chiacchiere*) talk *sg*; chiedere la ~ to ask permission to speak; prendere la ~ to take the floor; ~ d'onore word of honour; ~ d'ordine (*MIL*) password; ~e incrociate crossword (puzzle) *sg*; **paro'laccia, ce** *sf* bad word, swearword

par'rocchia [par'rokkja] *sf* parish; parish church

'**parroco, ci** *sm* parish priest

par'rucca, che *sf* wig

parrucchi'ere, a [parruk'kjere] *smlf* hairdresser ♦ *sm* barber

parsi'monia *sf* frugality, thrift

'**parso, a** *pp di* parere

'**parte** *sf* part; (*lato*) side; (*quota spettante a ciascuno*) share; (*direzione*) direction; (*POL*) party; faction; (*DIR*) party; a ~ *ag* separate ♦ *av* separately; scherzi a ~ joking aside; a ~ ciò apart from that; da ~ (*in disparte*) to one side, aside; d'altra ~ on the other hand; da ~ di (*per conto di*) on behalf of; da ~ mia as far as I'm concerned, as for me; da ~ a ~ right through; da ogni ~ on all sides, everywhere; (*moto a luogo*) from all sides; da nessuna ~ nowhere; da questa ~ (*in questa direzione*) this way; prendere ~ a qc to take part in sth; mettere qc da ~ to put aside; mettere

qn a ~ **di** qc to inform sb of sth
parteci'pare [partetʃi'pare] vi: ~ a
to take part in, participate in; (utili
etc) to share in; (spese etc) to contribute to; (dolore, successo di qn) to
share (in); **partecipazi'one** sf participation; sharing; (ECON) interest;
partecipazione agli utili profit-
sharing; **partecipazioni di nozze**
wedding announcement card;
par'tecipe ag participating; **essere
partecipe di** to take part in, participate in; to share (in); (consapevole)
to be aware of
parteggi'are [parted'dʒare] vi: ~
per to side with, be on the side of
par'tenza [par'tentsa] sf departure;
(SPORT) start; **essere in ~** to be
about to leave, be leaving
parti'cella [parti'tʃella] sf particle
parti'cipio [parti'tʃipjo] sm participle
partico'lare ag (specifico) particular; (proprio) personal, private;
(speciale) special, particular; (carat-
teristico) distinctive, characteristic;
(fuori dal comune) peculiar ♦ sm detail, particular; **in ~** in particular,
particularly; **particolarità** sf inv
particularity; detail; characteristic,
feature
partigi'ano, a [parti'dʒano] ag partisan ♦ sm (fautore) supporter,
champion; (MIL) partisan
par'tire vi to go, leave; (allontanarsi) to go o (drive etc) away o off;
(petardo, colpo) to go off; (fig: avere
inizio, SPORT) to start; **sono partita da Roma alle 7** I left Rome at 7;
il volo parte da Ciampino the flight
leaves from Ciampino; **a ~ da** from
par'tita sf (COMM) lot, consignment; (ECON: registrazione) entry,
item; (CARTE, SPORT: gioco)
game; (: competizione) match,
game; ~ **di caccia** hunting party; ~
IVA VAT registration number
par'tito sm (POL) party; (decisione)
decision, resolution; (persona da ma-
ritare) match

parti'tura sf (MUS) score
'parto sm (MED) delivery,
(child)birth; labour; **parto'rire** vt to
give birth to; (fig) to produce
parzi'ale ag (limitato) partial;
(non obiettivo) biased, partial
'pascere ['paʃʃere] vi to graze ♦ vt
(brucare) to graze on; (far pascolare) to graze, pasture; **pasci'uto, a**
pp di **pascere**
pasco'lare vt, vi to graze
pascolo sm pasture
'Pasqua sf Easter; **pas'quale** ag
Easter cpd
pas'sabile ag fairly good, passable
pas'saggio [pas'saddʒo] sm passing
no pl, passage; (traversata) crossing
no pl, passage; (luogo, prezzo della
traversata, brano di libro etc) passage; (su veicolo altrui) lift (BRIT),
ride; (SPORT) pass; **di ~** (persona)
passing through; ~ **pedonale/a livello** pedestrian/level (BRIT) o
grade (US) crossing
pas'sante sm/f passer-by ♦ sm loop
passa'porto sm passport
pas'sare vi (andare) to go; (veicolo,
pedone) to pass (by), go by; (fare
una breve sosta: postino etc) to
come, call; (: amico: per fare una
visita) to call o drop in; (sole, aria,
luce) to get through; (trascorrere:
giorni, tempo) to pass, go by; (fig:
proposta di legge) to be passed; (:
dolore) to pass, go away; (CARTE)
to pass ♦ vt (attraversare) to cross;
(trasmettere: messaggio): ~ **qc a
qn** to pass sth on to sb; (dare): ~ **qc
a qn** to pass sth to sb, give sb sth;
(trascorrere: tempo) to spend; (superare: esame) to pass; (triturare:
verdura) to strain; (approvare) to
pass, approve; (oltrepassare, sorpassare: anche fig) to go beyond, pass;
(fig: subire) to go through; ~ **da ...
a** to pass from ... to; ~ **di padre in
figlio** to be handed down o to pass
from father to son; ~ **per** (anche
fig) to go through; ~ **per stupido/in**

genio to be taken for a fool/a genius; **~ sopra** (*anche fig*) to pass over; **~ attraverso** (*anche fig*) to go through; **~ alla storia** to pass into history; **~ a un esame** to go up (to the next class) after an exam; **~ inosservato** to go unnoticed; **~ di moda** to go out of fashion; **le passo il Signor X** (*al telefono*) here is Mr X; I'm putting you through to Mr X; **lasciar ~ qn/qc** to let sb/sth through; **passarsela: come te la passi?** how are you getting on o along?

pas'sata *sf*: **dare una ~ di vernice a qc** to give sth a coat of paint; **dare una ~ al giornale** to have a look at the paper, skim through the paper

passa'tempo *sm* pastime, hobby

pas'sato, a *ag* past; (*sfiorito*) faded ♦ *sm* past; (*LING*) past (tense); **~ prossimo** (*LING*) present perfect; **~ remoto** (*LING*) past historic; **~ di verdura** (*CUC*) vegetable purée

passaver'dura *sm inv* vegetable mill

passeg'gero, a [passed'dʒero] *ag* passing ♦ *smlf* passenger

passeggi'are [passed'dʒare] *vi* to go for a walk; (*in veicolo*) to go for a drive; (*luogo*) promenade; **fare una passeggiata** to go for a walk o drive; **passeg'gino** *sm* pushchair (*BRIT*), stroller (*US*); **pas'seggio** *sm* walk, stroll; (*luogo*) promenade

passe'rella *sf* footbridge; (*di nave, aereo*) gangway; (*pedana*) catwalk

'passero *sm* sparrow

pas'sibile *ag*: **~ di** liable to

passi'one *sf* passion

pas'sivo, a *ag* passive ♦ *sm* (*LING*) passive; (*ECON*) debit; (: *complesso dei debiti*) liabilities *pl*

'passo *sm* step; (*andatura*) pace; (*rumore*) foot'step; (*orma*) foot'print; (*passaggio, fig*: *brano*) passage; (*valico*) pass; **a ~ d'uomo** at walking pace; **~ (a) ~** step by step;

fare due *o* **quattro ~i** to go for a walk *o* a stroll; **di questo ~** at this rate; **"~ carraio"** "vehicle entrance — keep clear"

'pasta *sf* (*CUC*) dough; (: *impasto per dolce*) pastry; (: *anche*: **~ alimentare**) pasta; (*massa molle di materia*) paste; (*fig*: *indole*) nature; **~e** *spl* (*pasticcini*) pastries; **~ in brodo** noodle soup

pastasci'utta [pastaʃ'ʃutta] *sf* pasta

pas'tella *sf* batter

pas'tello *sm* pastel

pas'ticca, che *sf* = **pastiglia**

pasticce'ria [pastittʃe'ria] *sf* (*pasticcini*) pastries *pl*, cakes *pl*; (*negozio*) cake shop; (*arte*) confectionery

pasticci'are [pastit'tʃare] *vt* to mess up, make a mess of ♦ *vi* to make a mess

pasticci'ere, a [pastit'tʃere] *smlf* pastrycook; confectioner

pas'ticcio [pas'tittʃo] *sm* (*CUC*) pie; (*lavoro disordinato, imbroglio*) mess; **trovarsi nei ~i** to get into trouble

pasti'ficio [pasti'fitʃo] *sm* pasta factory

pas'tiglia [pas'tiʎʎa] *sf* pastille, lozenge

pas'tina *sf* small pasta shapes used in soup

'pasto *sm* meal

pas'tore *sm* shepherd; (*REL*) pastor, minister; (*anche*: **cane ~**) sheepdog; **~ tedesco** (*ZOOL*) Alsatian, German shepherd

pastoriz'zare [pastorid'dzare] *vt* to pasteurize

pas'toso, a *ag* doughy; pasty; (*fig*: *voce, colore*) mellow, soft

pas'trano *sm* greatcoat

pas'tura *sf* pasture

pa'tata *sf* potato; **~e fritte** chips (*BRIT*), French fries; **pata'tine** *sfpl* (*potato*) crisps; **~ fritte** chips

pata'trac *sm* (*crollo*: *anche fig*) crash

pa'tella *sf* (*ZOOL*) limpet

pa'tema, i *sm* anxiety, worry

pa'tente *sf* licence; (*anche*: **~ di**

guida) driving licence (*BRIT*), driver's license (*US*)

pater'nità *sf* paternity, fatherhood

pa'terno, a *ag* (*affetto, consigli*) fatherly; (*casa, autorità*) paternal

pa'tetico, a, ci, che *ag* pathetic; (*commovente*) moving, touching

pa'tibolo *sm* gallows *sg*, scaffold

'patina *sf* (*su rame etc*) patina; (*sulla lingua*) fur, coating

pa'tire *vt, vi* to suffer

pa'tito, a *sm/f* enthusiast, fan, lover

patolo'gia [patolo'dʒia] *sf* pathology; **pato'logico, a, ci, che** *ag* pathological

'patria *sf* homeland

patri'arca, chi *sm* patriarch

pa'trigno [pa'triɲɲo] *sm* stepfather

patri'monio *sm* estate, property; (*fig*) heritage

patri'ota, i, e *sm/f* patriot; **patri'ottico, a, ci, che** *ag* patriotic; **patriot'tismo** *sm* patriotism

patroci'nare [patrotʃi'nare] *vt* (*DIR: difendere*) to defend; (*sostenere*) to sponsor, support; **patro'cinio** *sm* defence; support, sponsorship

patro'nato *sm* patronage; (*istituzione benefica*) charitable institution *o* society

pa'trono *sm* (*REL*) patron saint; (*socio di patronato*) patron; (*DIR*) counsel

'patta *sf* flap; (*dei pantaloni*) fly

patteggi'are [patted'dʒare] *vt, vi* to negotiate

patti'naggio [patti'naddʒo] *sm* skating

patti'nare *vi* to skate; ~ *sul ghiaccio* to ice-skate; **pattina'tore, 'trice** *sm/f* skater; **'pattino**[^1] *sm* skate; (*di slitta*) runner; (*AER*) skid; (*TECN*) sliding block; **pattini (da ghiaccio)** (ice) skates; **pattini a rotelle** roller skates; **pat'tino**[^2] *sm* (*barca*) kind of pedalo *with* oars

'patto *sm* (*accordo*) pact, agreement; (*condizione*) term, condition; *a* ~ *che* on condition that

pat'tuglia [pat'tuʎʎa] *sf* (*MIL*) patrol

pattu'ire *vt* to reach an agreement on

pattumi'era *sf* (*dust*)bin (*BRIT*), ashcan (*US*)

pa'ura *sf* fear; *aver* ~ *di/di fare/che* to be frightened *o* afraid of/of doing/that; *far* ~ *a* to frighten; *per* ~ *di/che* for fear of/that; **pau'roso, a** *ag* (*che fa paura*) frightening; (*che ha paura*) fearful, timorous

'pausa *sf* (*sosta*) break; (*nel parlare, MUS*) pause

pavi'mento *sm* floor

pa'vone *sm* peacock; **pavoneggi'arsi** *vr* to strut about, show off

pazien'tare [pattsjen'tare] *vi* to be patient

pazi'ente [pat'tsjɛnte] *ag, sm/f* patient; **pazi'enza** *sf* patience

paz'zesco, a, schi, sche [pat'tsesko] *ag* mad, crazy

paz'zia [pat'tsia] *sf* (*MED*) madness, insanity; (*azione*) folly; (*di azione, decisione*) madness, folly

'pazzo, a [pat'tsɔ] *ag* (*MED*) mad, insane; (*strano*) wild, mad ♦ *sm/f* madman/woman; ~ *di* (*gioia, amore etc*) mad *o* crazy with; ~ *per qc/qn* mad *o* crazy about sth/sb

PCI *sigla m* = Partito Comunista Italiano

'pecca, che *sf* defect, flaw, fault

peccami'noso, a *ag* sinful

pec'care *vi* to sin; (*fig*) to err

pec'cato *sm* sin; *è un* ~ *che* it's a pity that; *che* ~! what a shame *o* pity!

pecca'tore, 'trice *sm/f* sinner

'pece ['petʃe] *sf* pitch

Pe'chino [pe'kino] *sf* Peking

'pecora *sf* sheep; **peco'raio** *sm* shepherd; **peco'rino** *sm* sheep's milk cheese

peculi'are *ag*: ~ *di* peculiar to

pe'daggio [pe'daddʒo] *sm* toll

pedago'gia [pedago'dʒia] *sf* pedagogy, educational methods *pl*

peda'lare *vi* to pedal; (*andare in bicicletta*) to cycle

[^1]: **'pattino**
[^2]: **pat'tino**

pe'dale sm pedal

pe'dana sf footboard; (SPORT: nel salto) springboard; (: nella scherma) piste

pe'dante ag pedantic ♦ smf pedant

pe'data sf (impronta) footprint; (colpo) kick; **prendere a ~e** qn/qc to kick sb/sth

pede'rasta, i sm pederast; homosexual

pedi'atra, i sm paediatrician; **pedia'tria** sf paediatrics sg

pedi'cure smf inv chiropodist

pe'dina sf (della dama) draughtsman (BRIT), draftsman (US); (fig) pawn

pedi'nare vt to shadow, tail

pedo'nale ag pedestrian

pe'done, a sm/f pedestrian ♦ sm (SCACCHI) pawn

'peggio ['pɛddʒo] av, ag inv worse ♦ sm o f: **il o la** ~ the worst; **alla** ~ at worst, if the worst comes to the worst; **peggiora'mento** sm worsening; **peggio'rare** vi to make worse, worsen ♦ vi to grow worse, worsen; **peggiora'tivo, a** ag pejorative; **peggi'ore** ag (comparativo) worse; (superlativo) worst ♦ smf: **il(la) peggiore** the worst (person)

'pegno ['peɲɲo] sm (DIR) security, pledge; (nei giochi di società) forfeit; (fig) pledge, token; **dare in** ~ qc to pawn sth

pe'lare vt (spennare) to pluck; (spellare) to skin; (sbucciare) to peel; (fig) to make pay through the nose; **~rsi** vr to go bald

pe'lato, a ag: **pomodori** ~**i** tinned tomatoes

pel'lame sm skins pl, hides pl

'pelle sf skin; (di animale) skin, hide; (cuoio) leather; **avere la** ~ **d'oca** to have goose pimples o gooseflesh

pellegri'naggio [pellegri'naddʒo] sm pilgrimage

pelle'grino, a sm/f pilgrim

pelle'rossa (pl **pelli'rosse**) sm/f Red Indian

pelli'rossa sm/f = pellerossa

pellette'ria sf leather goods pl; (negozio) leather goods shop

pelli'cano sm pelican

pellic'ceria [pellittʃe'ria] sf (negozio) furrier's (shop); (quantità di pellicce) furs pl

pel'liccia, ce [pel'littʃa] sf (mantello di animale) coat, fur; (indumento) fur coat

pel'licola sf (membrana sottile) film, layer; (FOT, CINEMA) film

'pelo sm hair; (pelame) coat, hair; (pelliccia) fur; (di tappeto) pile; (di liquido) surface; **per un** ~: **per un** ~ **non ho perduto il treno** I very nearly missed the train; **c'è mancato un** ~ **che affogasse** he escaped drowning by the skin of his teeth; **pe'loso, a** ag hairy

'peltro sm pewter

pe'luria sf down

'pena sf (DIR) sentence; (punizione) punishment; (sofferenza) sadness no pl, sorrow; (fatica) trouble no pl, effort; (difficoltà) difficulty; **far** ~ to be pitiful; **mi fai** ~ I feel sorry for you; **prendersi o darsi la** ~ **di fare** to go to the trouble of doing; ~ **di morte** death sentence; ~ **pecuniaria** fine; **pe'nale** ag penal; **penalità** sf inv penalty; **penaliz'zare** vt (SPORT) to penalize

pe'nare vi (patire) to suffer; (faticare) to struggle

pen'dente ag hanging; leaning ♦ sm (ciondolo) pendant; (orecchino) drop earring; **pen'denza** sf slope, slant; (grado d'inclinazione) gradient; (ECON) outstanding account

'pendere vi (essere appeso): ~ **da** to hang from; (essere inclinato) to lean; (fig: incombere): ~ **su** to hang over

pen'dice [pen'ditʃe] sf: **alle** ~**i del monte** at the foot of the mountain

pen'dio, 'dii sm slope, slant; (luogo in pendenza) slope

'pendola sf pendulum clock

pendo'lare smf commuter

'pendolo *sm (peso)* pendulum; *(anche: orologio a ~)* pendulum clock

'pene *sm* penis

pene'trante *ag* piercing, penetrating

pene'trare *vi* to come o get in ♦ *vt* to penetrate; ~ in to enter; *(sog: proiettile)* to penetrate; *(: acqua, aria)* to go o come into

penicil'lina [penitʃil'lina] *sf* penicillin

pe'nisola *sf* peninsula

peni'tenza [peni'tɛntsa] *sf* penitence; *(punizione)* penance

penitenzi'ario [peniten'tsjarjo] *sm* prison

'penna *sf (di uccello)* feather; *(per scrivere)* pen; ~e *sfpl (CUC)* quills *(type of pasta)*; ~ a feltro/ stilografica/a sfera felt-tip/fountain/ ballpoint pen

penna'rello *sm* felt(-tip) pen

pennel'lare *vi* to paint

pen'nello *sm* brush; *(per dipingere)* (paint)brush; a ~ *(perfettamente)* to perfection, perfectly; ~ per la barba shaving brush

pen'nino *sm* nib

pen'none *sm (NAUT)* yard; *(stendardo)* banner, standard

pe'nombra *sf* half-light, dim light

pe'noso, a *ag* painful, distressing; *(faticoso)* tiring, laborious

pen'sare *vi* to think ♦ *vt* to think; *(inventare, escogitare)* to think out; ~ a to think of; *(amico, vacanze)* to think of o about; *(problema)* to think about; ~ di fare qc to think of doing sth; ci penso io I'll see to o take care of it

pensi'ero *sm* thought; *(modo di pensare, dottrina)* thinking *no pl; (preoccupazione)* worry, care, trouble; stare in ~ per qn to be worried about sb; **pensie'roso, a** *ag* thoughtful

'pensile *ag* hanging

pensio'nante *sm/f (presso una famiglia)* lodger; *(di albergo)* guest

pensio'nato, a *sm/f* pensioner

pensi'one *sf (al prestatore di la-*

voro) pension; *(vitto e alloggio)* board and lodging; *(albergo)* boarding house; **andare in** ~ to retire; **mezza** ~ half board; ~ **completa** full board

pen'soso, a *ag* thoughtful, pensive, lost in thought

pentapar'tito *sm* five-party government

Pente'coste *sf* Pentecost, Whit Sunday *(BRIT)*

penti'mento *sm* repentance, contrition

pen'tirsi *vr:* ~ di to repent of; *(rammaricarsi)* to regret, be sorry for

'pentola *sf* pot; ~ a pressione pressure cooker

pe'nultimo, a *ag* last but one *(BRIT)*, next to last, penultimate

pe'nuria *sf* shortage

penzo'lare [pendzo'lare] *vi* to dangle, hang loosely; **penzo'loni** *av* dangling, hanging down; **stare penzoloni** to dangle, hang down

'pepe *sm* pepper; ~ macinato/in grani ground/whole pepper

pepero'nata *sf (CUC)* stewed peppers, tomatoes and onions

pepe'rone *sm* pepper, capsicum; *(piccante)* chili

pe'pita *sf* nugget

PAROLA CHIAVE

per *prep* 1 *(moto attraverso luogo)* through; **i ladri sono passati ~ la finestra** the thieves got in (o out) through the window; **l'ho cercato ~ tutta la casa** I've searched the whole house o all over the house for it

2 *(moto a luogo)* for, to; **partire ~ la Germania/il mare** to leave for Germany/the sea; **il treno ~ Roma** the Rome train, the train for o to Rome

3 *(stato in luogo)*: **seduto/sdraiato ~ terra** sitting/lying on the ground

4 *(tempo)* for; ~ **anni/lungo tempo** for years/a long time; ~ **tutta**

l'estate throughout the summer, all summer long; **lo rividi ~ Natale** I saw him again at Christmas; **lo faccio ~ lunedì** I'll do it for Monday

5 (*mezzo, maniera*) by; **~ lettera/via aerea/ferrovia** by letter/airmail/rail; **prendere qn ~ un braccio** to take sb by the arm

6 (*causa, scopo*) for; **assente ~ malattia** absent because of *o* through *o* owing to illness; **ottimo ~ il mal di gola** excellent for sore throats

7 (*limitazione*) for; **è troppo difficile ~ lui** it's too difficult for him; **~ quel che mi riguarda** as far as I'm concerned; **~ poco che sia** however little it may be; **~ questa volta ti perdono** I'll forgive you this time

8 (*prezzo, misura*) for; (*distributivo*) a, per; **venduto ~ 3 milioni** sold for 3 million; **1000 lire ~ persona** 1000 lire a *o* per person; **uno ~ volta** one at a time; **uno ~ uno** one by one; **5 ~ cento** 5 per cent; **3 ~ 4 fa 12** 3 times 4 equals 12; **dividere/moltiplicare 12 ~ 4** to divide/multiply 12 by 4

9 (*in qualità di*) as; (*al posto di*) for; **avere qn ~ professore** to have sb as a teacher; **ti ho preso ~ Mario** I mistook you for Mario, I thought you were Mario; **dare ~ morto qn** to give sb up for dead

10 (*seguito da vb: finale*): **~ fare qc** (so as) to do sth, in order to do sth; (*: causale*): **~ aver fatto qc** for having done sth; (*: consecutivo*): **è abbastanza grande ~ andarci da solo** he's big enough to go on his own

'pera *sf* pear

pe'raltro *av* moreover, what's more

per'bene *ag inv* respectable, decent ♦ *av* (*con cura*) properly, well

percentu'ale [pertʃentu'ale] *sf* percentage

perce'pire [pertʃe'pire] *vt* (*sentire*) to perceive; (*ricevere*) to receive;

percezi'one *sf* perception

PAROLA CHIAVE

perché [per'ke] *av* why; **~ no?** why not?; **~ non vuoi andarci?** why don't you want to go?; **spiegami ~ l'hai fatto** tell me why you did it

♦ *cong* **1** (*causale*) because; **non posso uscire ~ ho da fare** I can't go out because *o* as I've a lot to do

2 (*finale*) in order that, so that; **te lo do ~ tu legga** I'm giving it to you so (that) you can read it

3 (*consecutivo*): **è troppo forte ~ si possa batterlo** he's too strong to be beaten

♦ *sm inv* reason; **il ~ di** the reason for

perciò [per'tʃɔ] *cong* so, for this *o* that) reason

per'correre *vt* (*luogo*) to go all over; (*: paese*) to travel up and down, go all over; (*distanza*) to cover

per'corso, a *pp di* **percorrere** ♦ *sm* (*tragitto*) journey; (*tratto*) route

per'cossa *sf* blow

per'cosso, a *pp di* **percuotere**

percu'otere *vt* to hit, strike

percussi'one *sf* percussion; **strumenti a ~** (*MUS*) percussion instruments

'perdere *vt* to lose; (*lasciarsi sfuggire*) to miss; (*sprecare: tempo, denaro*) to waste; (*mandare in rovina: persona*) to ruin ♦ *vi* to lose; (*serbatoio etc*) to leak; **~rsi** *vr* (*smarrirsi*) to get lost; (*svanire*) to disappear, vanish; **saper ~** to be a good loser; **lascia ~!** forget it!, never mind!

perdigi'orno [perdi'dʒorno] *sm/f inv* idler, waster

'perdita *sf* loss; (*spreco*) waste; (*fuoriuscita*) leak; **siamo in ~** (*COMM*) we are running at a loss; **a ~ d'occhio** as far as the eye can see

perdo'nare *vt* to pardon, forgive; (*scusare*) to excuse, pardon

per'dono *sm* forgiveness; (*DIR*) pardon

perdu'rare *vi* to go on, last;

(*perseverare*) to persist

perduta'mente *av* desperately, passionately

per'duto, a *pp di* **perdere**

peregri'nare *vi* to wander, roam

pe'renne *ag* eternal, perpetual, perennial; (*BOT*) perennial

peren'torio, a *ag* peremptory; (*definitivo*) final

per'fetto, a *ag* perfect ♦ *sm* (*LING*) perfect (tense)

perfezio'nare [perfettsjo'nare] *vt* to improve, perfect; ~**rsi** *vr* to improve

perfezi'one [perfet'tsjone] *sf* perfection

'perfido, a *ag* perfidious, treacherous

per'fino *av* even

perfo'rare *vt* to perforate; to punch a hole (*o* holes) in; (*banda, schede*) to punch; (*trivellare*) to drill; **perfora'tore, 'trice** *sm/f* punch-card operator ♦ *sm* (*utensile*) punch; (*INFORM*): **perforatore di schede** card punch; **perfora'trice** *sf* (*TECN*) boring *o* drilling machine; (*INFORM*) card punch; *vedi anche* **perforatore**; **perfora-zi'one** *sf* perforation; punching; drilling; (*INFORM*) punch; (*MED*) perforation

perga'mena *sf* parchment

'pergola *sf* (*per rampicanti*) pergola

perico'lante *ag* precarious

pe'ricolo *sm* danger; **mettere in** ~ to endanger, put in danger; **peri-co'loso, a** *ag* dangerous

perife'ria *sf* periphery; (*di città*) outskirts *pl*

pe'rifrasi *sf* circumlocution

pe'rimetro *sm* perimeter

peri'odico, a, ci, che *ag* periodic(al); (*MAT*) recurring ♦ *sm* periodical

pe'riodo *sm* period

peripe'zie [peripet'tsie] *sfpl* ups and downs, vicissitudes

pe'rire *vi* to perish, die

pe'rito, a *ag* expert, skilled ♦ *sm/f* expert; (*agronomo, navale*) surveyor; **un** ~ **chimico** a qualified chem-

ist

pe'rizia [pe'rittsja] *sf* (*abilità*) ability; (*giudizio tecnico*) expert opinion; expert's report

'perla *sf* pearl; **per'lina** *sf* bead

perlu'strare *vt* to patrol

perma'loso, a *ag* touchy

perma'nente *ag* permanent ♦ *sf* permanent wave, perm; **perma'nenza** *sf* permanence; (*soggiorno*) stay

perma'nere *vi* to remain

perme'are *vt* to permeate

per'messo, a *pp di* **permettere** ♦ *sm* (*autorizzazione*) permission, leave; (*dato a militare, impiegato*) leave; (*licenza*) licence, permit; (*MIL: foglio*) pass; ~?, è ~? (*posso entrare?*) may I come in?; (*posso passare?*) excuse me; ~ **di lavoro/pesca** work/fishing permit; ~ **di soggiorno** residence permit

per'mettere *vt* to allow, permit; ~ **a qn qc/di fare** to allow sb sth/to do; ~**rsi** qc/di fare to allow o.s. sth/to do; (*avere la possibilità*) to afford sth/to do

per'nacchia [per'nakkja] (*fam*) *sf*: **fare una** ~ to blow a raspberry

per'nice [per'nitʃe] *sf* partridge

'perno *sm* pivot

pernot'tare *vi* to spend the night, stay overnight

'pero *sm* pear tree

però *cong* (*ma*) but; (*tuttavia*) however, nevertheless

pero'rare *vt* (*DIR, fig*): ~ **la causa di qn** to plead sb's case

perpendico'lare *ag, sf* perpendicular

perpe'trare *vt* to perpetrate

perpetu'are *vt* to perpetuate

per'petuo, a *ag* perpetual

per'plesso, a *ag* perplexed; uncertain, undecided

perqui'sire *vt* to search; **perquisi-zi'one** *sf* (*police*) search

persecu'tore *sm* persecutor

persecuzi'one [persekut'tsjone] *sf* persecution

persegu'ire *vt* to pursue

persegui'tare *vt* to persecute

perseve'rante *ag* persevering

perseve'rare *vi* to persevere

'Persia *sf*: la ~ Persia

persi'ana *sf* shutter; ~ avvolgibile Venetian blind

persi'ano, a *ag, sm/f* Persian

'persico, a, ci, che *ag*: il golfo P~ the Persian Gulf

per'sino *av* = perfino

persis'tente *ag* persistent

per'sistere *vi* to persist; ~ a fare to persist in doing; **persis'tito, a** *pp di* **persistere**

'perso, a *pp di* **perdere**

per'sona *sf* person; (*qualcuno*): una ~ someone, somebody, *espressione interrogativa* +anyone *o* anybody; ~e *sfpl* people; **non c'è** ~ **che** ..., there's nobody who ..., there isn't anybody who ...

perso'naggio [perso'naddʒo] *sm* (*persona ragguardevole*) personality, figure; (*tipo*) character, individual; (*LETTERATURA*) character

perso'nale *ag* personal ♦ *sm* staff; personnel; (*figura fisica*) build

personalità *sf inv* personality

personifi'care *vt* to personify; to embody

perspi'cace [perspi'katʃe] *ag* shrewd, discerning

persu'adere *vt*: ~ **qn** (**di qc/a fare**) to persuade sb (of sth/to do); **persuasi'one** *sf* persuasion; **per'suasivo, a** *ag* persuasive; **per'suaso, a** *pp di* **persuadere**

per'tanto *cong* (*quindi*) so, therefore

'pertica, che *sf* pole

perti'nente *ag*: ~ **(a)** relevant (to), pertinent (to)

per'tosse *sf* whooping cough

per'tugio [per'tudʒo] *sm* hole, opening

perturbazi'one [perturbat'tsjone] *sf* disruption; perturbation; ~ **atmosferica** atmospheric disturbance

per'vadere *vt* to pervade;

per'vaso, a *pp di* **pervadere**

perve'nire *vi*: ~ **a** to reach, arrive at, come to; (*venire in possesso*): **gli pervenne una fortuna** he inherited a fortune; **far** ~ **qc a** to have sth sent to; **perve'nuto, a** *pp di* **pervenire**

per'verso, a *ag* depraved; perverse

p. es. *abbr* (= *per esempio*) e.g.

'pesa *sf* weighing *no pl*; weighbridge

pe'sante *ag* heavy; (*fig: noioso*) dull, boring

pe'sare *vt* to weigh ♦ *vi* (*avere un peso*) to weigh; (*essere pesante*) to be heavy; (*fig*) to carry weight; ~ **su** (*fig*) to lie heavy on; to influence; ~ **a:** **mi pesa sgridarlo** I find it hard to scold him

'pesca (*pl* **pesche:** *frutto*) *sf* peach; (*il pescare*) fishing; **andare a** ~ to go fishing; ~ **di beneficenza** (*lotteria*) lucky dip; ~ **con la lenza** angling

pes'care *vt* (*pesce*) to fish for; to catch; (*qc nell'acqua*) to fish out; (*fig*) (*trovare*) to get hold of, find

pesca'tore *sm* fisherman; angler

'pesce ['peʃʃe] *sm* fish *gen inv*; P~**i** (*dello zodiaco*) Pisces; **d'aprile!** April Fool!; ~ **spada** swordfish; **pe-sce'cane** *sm* shark

pesche'reccio [peske'rettʃo] *sm* fishing boat

pesche'ria [peske'ria] *sf* fishmonger's (shop) (*BRIT*), fish store (*US*)

pesci'vendolo, a [peʃʃi'vendolo] *sm/f* fishmonger (*BRIT*), fish merchant (*US*)

'pesco, schi *sm* peach tree

pes'coso, a *ag* abounding in fish

'peso *sm* weight; (*SPORT*) shot; **ru-bare sul** ~ to give short weight; **essere di** ~ **a qn** (*fig*) to be a burden to sb; ~ **lordo/netto** gross/net weight; ~ **piuma/mosca/gallo/medio/massimo** (*PUGILATO*) feather/fly/bantam/middle/heavyweight

pessi'mismo *sm* pessimism; **pes-si'mista, i, e** *ag* pessimistic ♦ *sm/f* pessimist

'**pessimo, a** *ag* very bad, awful

pes'tare *vt* to tread on, trample on; (*sale, pepe*) to grind; (*uva, aglio*) to crush; (*fig: picchiare*): ~ **qn** to beat sb up

'**peste** *sf* plague; (*persona*) nuisance, pest

pes'tello *sm* pestle

pesti'lenza [pesti'lɛntsa] *sf* pestilence; (*fetore*) stench

'**pesto, a** *ag*: **c'è buio** ~ it's pitch-dark; **occhio** ~ black eye ♦ *sm* (*CUC*) sauce made with basil, garlic, cheese and oil

'**petalo** *sm* (*BOT*) petal

pe'tardo *sm* firecracker, banger (*BRIT*)

petizi'one [petit'tsjone] *sf* petition

'**peto** (*fam!*) *sm* fart (*!*)

petrol'chimica [petrol'kimika] *sf* petrochemical industry

petroli'era *sf* (*nave*) oil tanker

petro'lifero, a *ag* oil-bearing; oil cpd

pe'trolio *sm* oil, petroleum; (*per lampada, fornello*) paraffin

pettego'lare *vi* to gossip

pettego'lezzo [pettego'leddzo] *sm* gossip *no pl*; **fare** ~**i** to gossip

pet'tegolo, a *ag* gossipy ♦ *sm/f* gossip

petti'nare *vt* to comb (the hair of); ~**rsi** *vr* to comb one's hair; **petti-na'tura** *sf* (*acconciatura*) hairstyle

'**pettine** *sm* comb; (*ZOOL*) scallop

petti'rosso *sm* robin

'**petto** *sm* chest; (*seno*) breast, bust; (*CUC: di carne bovina*) brisket; (: *di pollo etc*) breast; **a doppio** ~ (*abito*) double-breasted; **petto'ruto, a** *ag* broad-chested; full-breasted

petu'lante *ag* insolent

pe'tunia *sf* (*BOT*) petunia

'**pezza** ['pettsa] *sf* piece of cloth; (*toppa*) patch; (*cencio*) rag, cloth

pez'zato, a [pet'tsato] *ag* piebald

pez'zente [pet'tsɛnte] *sm/f* beggar

'**pezzo** ['pettso] *sm* (*gen*) piece; (*brandello, frammento*) piece, bit;

(*di macchina, arnese etc*) part; (*STAMPA*) article; (*di tempo*): **aspettare un** ~ to wait quite a while o some time; **in** *o* **a** ~**i** in pieces; **andare in** ~**i** to break into pieces; **un bel** ~ **d'uomo** a fine figure of a man; **abito a due** ~**i** two-piece suit; ~ **di cronaca** (*STAMPA*) report; ~ **grosso** (*fig*) bigwig; ~ **di ricambio** spare part

pia'cente [pja'tʃɛnte] *ag* attractive, pleasant

pia'cere [pja'tʃere] *vi* to please; **una ragazza che piace** a likeable girl; **an attractive girl**; ~ **a: mi piace** I like it; **quei ragazzi non mi piacciono** I don't like those boys; **gli piacerebbe andare al cinema** he would like to go to the cinema ♦ *sm* pleasure; (*favore*) favour; "~!" (*nelle presentazioni*) "pleased to meet you!"; **con** ~ certainly, with pleasure; **per** ~! please; **fare un** ~ **a qn** to do sb a favour; **pia'cevole** *ag* pleasant, agreeable; **piaci'uto, a** *pp di* **piacere**

pi'aga, ghe *sf* (*lesione*) sore; (*ferita: anche fig*) wound; (*fig: flagello*) scourge, curse; (: *persona*) pest, nuisance

piagnis'teo [pjaɲɲis'tɛo] *sm* whining, whimpering

piagnuco'lare [pjaɲɲuko'lare] *vi* to whimper

pi'alla *sf* (*arnese*) plane; **pial'lare** *vt* to plane

pi'ana *sf* stretch of level ground; (*più esteso*) plain

pianeg'giante [pjaned'dʒante] *ag* flat, level

piane'rottolo *sm* landing

pia'neta *sm* (*ASTR*) planet

pi'angere [pjandʒere] *vi* to cry, weep; (*occhi*) to water ♦ *vt* to cry, weep; (*lamentare*) to bewail, lament; ~ **la morte di qn** to mourn sb's death

pianifi'care *vt* to plan; **pianifica-zi'one** *sf* planning

pia'nista, i, e *sm/f* pianist

pi'ano, a *ag* (*piatto*) flat, level; (*MAT*) plane; (*facile*) straightforward, simple; (*chiaro*) clear, plain ♦ *av* (*adagio*) slowly; (*a bassa voce*) softly; (*con cautela*) slowly, carefully ♦ *sm* (*MAT*) plane; (*GEO*) plain; (*livello*) level, plane; (*di edificio*) floor; (*programma*) plan; (*MUS*) piano; **pian** ~ very slowly; (*poco a poco*) little by little; **in primo/secondo** ~ in the foreground/background; **di primo** ~ (*fig*) prominent, high-ranking

piano'forte *sm* piano, pianoforte

pi'anta *sf* (*BOT*) plant; (*ANAT: anche:* ~ **del piede**) sole (of the foot); (*grafico*) plan; (*topografica*) map; **in** ~ **stabile** on the permanent staff; **piantagi'one** *sf* plantation; **pian'tare** *vt* to plant; (*conficcare*) to drive o hammer in; (*tenda*) to put up, pitch; (*fig: lasciare*) to leave, desert; ~**rsi** *vr*: ~**rsi davanti a qn** to plant o.s. in front of sb; **piantala!** (*fam*) cut it out!

pianter'reno *sm* ground floor

pi'anto, a *pp di* **piangere** ♦ *sm* tears *pl*, crying

pian'tone *sm* (*vigilante*) sentry, guard; (*soldato*) orderly; (*AUT*) steering column

pia'nura *sf* plain

pi'astra *sf* plate; (*di pietra*) slab; (*di fornello*) hotplate; ~ **di registrazione** tape deck; **panino alla** ~ ≈ toasted sandwich

pias'trella *sf* tile

pias'trina *sf* (*MIL*) identity disc

piatta'forma *sf* (*anche fig*) platform

piat'tino *sm* saucer

pi'atto, a *ag* flat; (*fig: scialbo*) dull ♦ *sm* (*recipiente, vivanda*) dish; (*portata*) course; (*parte piana*) flat (part); ~ **i** *smpl* (*MUS*) cymbals; ~ **fondo** soup dish; ~ **forte** main course; ~ **del giorno** dish of the day, plat du jour; ~ **del giradischi** turntable

pi'azza ['pjattsa] *sf* square; (*COMM*) market; **far** ~ **pulita** to make a clean sweep; ~ **d'armi** (*MIL*) parade ground; **piaz'zale** *sm* (*large*) square

piaz'zare [pjat'tsare] *vt* to place; (*COMM*) to market, sell; ~**rsi** *vr* (*SPORT*) to be placed

piaz'zista, i [pjat'tsista] *sm* (*COMM*) commercial traveller

piaz'zola [pjat'tsɔla] *sf* (*AUT*) lay-by

'picca, che *sf* pike; ~**che** *sfpl* (*CARTE*) spades

pic'cante *ag* hot, pungent; (*fig*) racy; biting

pic'carsi *vr*: ~ **di fare** to pride o.s. on one's ability to do; ~ **per qc** to take offence at sth

pic'chetto [pik'ketto] *sm* (*MIL, di scioperanti*) picket

picchi'are [pik'kjare] *vt* (*persona: colpire*) to hit, strike; (*: prendere a botte*) to beat (up); (*battere*) to beat; (*sbattere*) to bang ♦ *vi* (*bussare*) to knock; (*: con forza*) to bang; (*colpire*) to hit, strike; (*sole*) to beat down; **picchi'ata** *sf* (*percosse*) beating, thrashing; (*AER*) dive

picchiet'tare [pikkjet'tare] *vt* (*punteggiare*) to spot, dot; (*colpire*) to tap

'picchio ['pikkjo] *sm* woodpecker

pic'cino, a [pit'tʃino] *ag* tiny, very small

piccio'naia [pittʃo'naja] *sf* pigeonloft; (*TEATRO*): **la** ~ the gods *sg*

picci'one [pit'tʃone] *sm* pigeon

'picco, chi *sm* peak; **a** ~ vertically

'piccolo, a *ag* small; (*oggetto, mano, di età: bambino*) small, little (*dav sostantivo*); (*di breve durata: viaggio*) short; (*fig*) mean, petty ♦ *smf* child, little one; ~**i** *smpl* (*di animale*) young *pl*; **in** ~ in miniature

pic'cone *sm* pick(-axe)

pic'cozza [pik'kɔttsa] *sf* ice-axe

pic'nic *sm inv* picnic

pi'docchio [pi'dɔkkjo] *sm* louse

pi'ede *sm* foot; (*di mobile*) leg; **in** ~**i** standing; **a** ~**i** on foot; **a** ~**i nudi** barefoot; **su due** ~**i** (*fig*) at once; **prendere** ~ (*fig*) to gain ground, catch on; **sul ~ di guerra** (MIL) ready for action; **~ di porco** crowbar

piedes'tallo sm = **piedistallo**

piedipi'atti sm inv (peg) cop

piedis'tallo sm pedestal

pi'ega, ghe sf (piegatura, GEO) fold; (di gonna) pleat; (di pantaloni) crease; (grinza) wrinkle, crease; **prendere una brutta ~** (avvenimento) to take a turn for the worse

pie'gare vt to fold; (braccio, gambe, testa) to bend ♦ vi to bend; **~rsi** vr to bend; (fig): **~rsi (a)** to yield (to), submit (to); **pieghet'tare** vt to pleat; **pie'ghevole** ag pliable, flexible; (porta) folding; (fig) yielding, docile

Pie'monte sm: **il ~** Piedmont

pi'ena sf (di fiume) flood, spate; (gran folla) crowd, throng

pi'eno, a ag full; (muro, mattone) solid ♦ sm (colmo) height, peak; (carico) full load; **~ di** full of; **in ~ giorno** in broad daylight; **fare il ~** (di benzina) to fill up (with petrol)

pietà sf inv (pity) (REL) piety; **senza ~** pitiless, merciless; **avere ~ di** (compassione) to pity, feel sorry for; (misericordia) to have pity o mercy on

pie'tanza sf (pje'tantsa) sf dish; (main) course

pie'toso, a ag (compassionevole) pitying, compassionate; (che desta pietà) pitiful

pie'tra sf stone; **~ preziosa** precious stone, gem; **pie'traia** sf (terreno) stony ground; **pietrifi'care** vt to petrify; (fig) to transfix, paralyze

'piffero sm (MUS) pipe

pigi'ama, i (pi'dʒama) sm pyjamas pl

'pigia 'pigia ('pidʒa'pidʒa) sm crowd, press

pigi'are (pi'dʒare) vt to press

pigi'one (pi'dʒone) sf rent

pigli'are (piʎ'ʎare) vt to take, grab; (afferrare) to catch

'piglio ('piʎʎo) sm look, expression

pig'meo, a smf pygmy

'pigna ('piɲɲa) sf pine cone

pi'gnolo, a (piɲ'ɲɔlo) ag pernickety

pigo'lare vi to cheep, chirp

pigno'rare (piɲɲo'rare) vt to distrain

pi'grizia (pi'grittsja) sf laziness

'pigro, a ag lazy

'pila sf (catasta, di ponte) pile; (ELETTR) battery; (fam: torcia) torch (BRIT), flashlight

pi'lastro sm pillar

'pillola sf pill; **prendere la ~** to be on the pill

pi'lone sm (di ponte) pier; (di linea elettrica) pylon

pi'lota, i, e smf pilot; (AUT) driver ♦ ag inv pilot cpd; **~ automatico** automatic pilot; **pilo'tare** vt to pilot; to drive

pi'mento sm pimento, allspice

pina'co'teca, che sf art gallery

pi'neta sf pinewood

ping-'pong (pɪŋ'pɔŋ) sm table tennis

'pingue ag fat, corpulent

pingu'ino sm (ZOOL) penguin

'pinna sf fin; (di pinguino, spatola di gomma) flipper

'pino sm pine (tree); **pi'nolo** sm pine kernel

'pinza ('pintsa) sf pliers pl; (MED) forceps pl; (ZOOL) pincer

pin'zette (pin'tsette) sfpl tweezers

'pio, a, 'pii, 'pie ag pious; (opere, istituzione) charitable, charity cpd

pi'oggia, ge (pi'jɔddʒa) sf rain; **~ acida** acid rain

pi'olo sm peg; (di scala) rung

piom'bare vi to fall heavily; (gettarsi con impeto): **~ su** to fall upon, assail ♦ vt (dente) to fill; **piomba'tura** sf (di dente) filling

piom'bino sm (sigillo) (lead) seal; (del filo a piombo) plummet; (PESCA) sinker

pi'ombo sm (CHIM) lead; (sigillo) (lead) seal; (proiettile) (lead) shot; **a ~** (cadere) straight down

pioni'ere, a smf pioneer

pi'oppo sm poplar

pi'overe *vb impers* to rain ♦ *vi* (*fig: scendere dall'alto*) to rain down; (: *affluire in gran numero*): ~ **in** to pour into; **piovigg'nare** *vb impers* to drizzle; **pio'voso, a** *ag* rainy

pi'ovra *sf* octopus

'pipa *sf* pipe

pipì (*fam*) *sf*: **fare** ~ to have a wee (wee)

pipis'trello *sm* (*ZOOL*) bat

pi'ramide *sf* pyramid

pi'rata, i *sm* pirate; ~ **della strada** hit-and-run driver

Pire'nei *smpl*: **i** ~ the Pyrenees

'pirico, a, ci, che *ag*: **polvere** ~**a** gunpowder

pi'rite *sf* pyrite

pi'rofilo, a *ag* heat-resistant; **pi'rofila** *sf* heat-resistant dish

pi'roga, ghe *sf* dug-out canoe

pi'romane *smf* pyromaniac; arsonist

pi'roscafo *sm* steamer, steamship

pisci'are [piʃ'ʃare] (*fam!*) *vi* to piss (!), pee (!)

pi'scina [piʃ'ʃina] *sf* (swimming) pool; (*stabilimento*) (swimming) baths *pl*

pi'sello *sm* pea

piso'lino *sm* nap

'pista *sf* (*traccia*) track, trail; (*di stadio*) track; (*di pattinaggio*) rink; (*da sci*) run; (*AER*) runway; (*di circo*) ring; ~ **da ballo** dance floor

pis'tacchio [pis'takkjo] *sm* pistachio (tree); pistachio (nut)

pis'tola *sf* pistol, gun

pis'tone *sm* piston

pi'tone *sm* python

pit'tore, 'trice *smf* painter; **pit-to'resco, a, schi, sche** *ag* picturesque

pit'tura *sf* painting; **pittu'rare** *vt* to paint

PAROLA CHIAVE

più *av* **1** (*in maggiore quantità*) more; ~ **del solito** more than usual; **in** ~, **di** ~ more; **ne voglio di** ~ I want some more; **ci sono 3 persone**

in *o* **di** ~ there are 3 more *o* extra people; ~ **o meno** more or less; **per di** ~ (*inoltre*) what's more, moreover

2 (*comparativo*) more, aggettivo corto +...er; ~ ... **di/che** more ... than; **lavoro** ~ **di te/Paola** I work harder than you/Paola; **è** ~ **intelligente che ricco** he's more intelligent than rich

3 (*superlativo*) most, aggettivo corto +...est; **il** ~ **grande/intelligente** the biggest/most intelligent; **è quello che compro** ~ **spesso** that's the one I buy most often; **al** ~ **presto** as soon as possible; **al** ~ **tardi** at the latest

4 (*negazione*): **non** ... ~ no more, no longer; **non ho** ~ **soldi** I've got no more money, I don't have any more money; **non lavoro** ~ I'm no longer working, I don't work any more; **a** ~ **non posso** (*gridare*) at the top of one's voice; (*correre*) as fast as one can

5 (*MAT*) plus; **4** ~ **5 fa 9** 4 plus 5 equals 9; ~ **5 gradi** 5 degrees above freezing, plus 5

♦ *prep* plus

♦ *ag inv* **1**: ~ ... (**di**) more ... (than); ~ **denaro/tempo** more money/time; ~ **persone di quante ci aspettassimo** more people than we expected

2 (*numerosi, diversi*) several; **l'aspettai per** ~ **giorni** I waited for it for several days

♦ *sm* **1** (*la maggior parte*): **il** ~ **è fatto** most of it is done

2 (*MAT*) plus (sign)

3: **i** ~ the majority

---

piucchepper'fetto [pjukkepper'fɛtto] *sm* (*LING*) pluperfect, past perfect

pi'uma *sf* feather; **piu'maggio** *sm* plumage, feathers *pl*; **piu'mino** *sm* (*eider*)down; (*per letto*) eiderdown; (: *tipo danese*) duvet, continental quilt; (*giacca*) quilted jacket (with _goose-feather_ padding); (_per cipria_) powder puff; (_per spolverare_) feather duster

piut'tosto _av_ rather; ~ che (_anziché_) rather than

pi'vello, a _sm/f_ greenhorn

pizza ['pittsa] _sf_ pizza; **pizze'ria** _sf_ place where pizzas are made, sold or eaten

pizzi'cagnolo, a [pittsi'kappolo] _sm/f_ specialist grocer

pizzi'care [pittsi'kare] _vt_ (_stringere_) to nip, pinch; (_pungere_) to sting; to bite; (_MUS_) to pluck ♦ _vi_ (_prudere_) to itch, be itchy; (_cibo_) to be hot _o_ spicy

pizziche'ria [pittsike'ria] _sf_ delicatessen (shop)

'pizzico, chi ['pittsiko] _sm_ (_pizzicotto_) pinch, nip; (_piccola quantità_) pinch, dash; (_d'insetto_) sting; bite

pizzi'cotto [pittsi'kɔtto] _sm_ pinch, nip

'pizzo ['pittso] _sm_ (_merletto_) lace; (_barbetta_) goatee beard

pla'care _vt_ to placate, soothe; ~**rsi** _vr_ to calm down

'placca, che _sf_ plate; (_con iscrizione_) plaque; (_anche:_ ~ **dentaria**) (dental) plaque; **plac'care** _vt_ to plate; **placcato in oro/argento** gold-/silver-plated

'placido, a ['platʃido] _ag_ placid, calm

plagi'are [pla'dʒare] _vt_ (_copiare_) to plagiarize; **'plagio** _sm_ plagiarism

pla'nare _vi_ (_AER_) to glide

'plancia, ce ['plantʃa] _sf_ (_NAUT_) bridge

plane'tario, a _ag_ planetary ♦ _sm_ (_locale_) planetarium

'plasma _sm_ plasma

plas'mare _vt_ to mould, shape

'plastica, che _sf_ (_arte_) plastic arts _pl_; (_MED_) plastic surgery; (_sostanza_) plastic

'plastico, a, ci, che _ag_ plastic ♦ _sm_ (_rappresentazione_) relief model; (_esplosivo_): **bomba al** ~ plastic bomb

plasti'lina ® _sf_ plasticine ®

'platano _sm_ plane tree

pla'tea _sf_ (_TEATRO_) stalls _pl_

'platino _sm_ platinum

pla'tonico, a, ci, che _ag_ platonic

plau'sibile _ag_ plausible

'plauso _sm_ (_fig_) approval

ple'baglia [ple'baʎʎa] (_peg_) _sf_ rabble, mob

'plebe _sf_ common people; **ple'beo, a** _ag_ plebeian; (_volgare_) coarse, common

ple'nario, a _ag_ plenary

pleni'lunio _sm_ full moon

'plettro _sm_ plectrum

pleu'rite _sf_ pleurisy

'plico, chi _sm_ (_pacco_) parcel; **in ~ a parte** (_COMM_) under separate cover

plo'tone _sm_ (_MIL_) platoon; ~ **d'esecuzione** firing squad

'plumbeo, a _ag_ leaden

plu'rale _ag, sm_ plural; **pluralità** _sf_ plurality; (_maggioranza_) majority

plusva'lore _sm_ (_ECON_) surplus

pneu'matico, a, ci, che _ag_ inflatable; pneumatic ♦ _sm_ (_AUT_) tyre (_BRIT_), tire (_US_)

po' _av, sm vedi_ **poco**

PAROLA CHIAVE

'poco, a, chi, che _ag_ (_quantità_) little, not much; (_numero_) few, not many; ~ **pane/denaro/spazio** little _o_ not much bread/money/space; ~**che persone/idee** few _o_ not many people/ideas; **ci vediamo tra** ~ (_soltinteso: tempo_) see you soon

♦ _av_ **1** (_in piccola quantità_) little, not much; (_numero limitato_) few, not many; **guadagna** ~ he doesn't earn much, he earns little

2 (_con ag, av_) (_a_) little, not very; **sta** ~ **bene** he isn't very well; **è** ~ **più vecchia di lui** she's a little _o_ slightly older than him

3 (_tempo_): **dopo/prima** shortly afterwards/before; **il film dura** ~ the film doesn't last very long; **ci vediamo molto** ~ we don't see each other very often, we hardly ever see each other

4: **un po'** a little, a bit; **è un po' corto** it's a little o a bit short; **arriverà fra un po'** he'll arrive shortly o in a little while

5: **a dir ~** to say the least; **a ~ a ~** little by little; **per ~ non cadevo** I nearly fell; **è una cosa da ~** it's nothing, it's of no importance; **una persona da ~** a worthless person

♦ *pron* (a) little; **~chi, che** *pron pl* (*persone*) few (people); (*cose*) few ♦ *sm* **1** little; **vive del ~** on the little he has

2: un po' di zucchero a little sugar; **un bel po' di denaro** quite a lot of money; **un po' per ciascuno** a bit each

po'dere *sm* (*AGR*) farm
pode'roso, a *ag* powerful
podestà *sm inv* (*nel fascismo*) podesta, mayor
'**podio** *sm* dais, platform; (*MUS*) podium
po'dismo *sm* (*SPORT*) track events *pl*
po'ema, i *sm* poem
poe'sia *sf* (*arte*) poetry; (*componimento*) poem
po'eta, 'essa *smf* poet/poetess; **po'etico, a, ci, che** *ag* poetic(al)
poggi'are [pod'dʒare] *vt* to lean, rest; (*posare*) to lay, place; **poggia'testa** *sm inv* (*AUT*) headrest
'**poggio** ['pɔddʒo] *sm* hillock, knoll
poggi'olo [pod'dʒɔlo] *sm* balcony
'**poi** *av* then; (*alla fine*) finally, at last; **e ~** (*inoltre*) and besides; **questa ~ (è bella)!** (*ironico*) that's a good one!
poiché [poi'ke] *cong* since, as
'**poker** *sm* poker
po'lacco, a, chi, che *ag* Polish ♦ *smf* Pole
po'lare *ag* polar
po'lemica, che *sf* controversy
po'lemico, a, ci, che *ag* polemic(al), controversial

po'lenta *sf* (*CUC*) sort of thick porridge made with maize flour
poli'clinico, ci *sm* general hospital, polyclinic
poli'estere *sm* polyester
'**polio(mie'lite)** *sf* polio(myelitis)
'**polipo** *sm* polyp
polisti'rolo *sm* polystyrene
poli'tecnico, ci *sm* postgraduate technical college
po'litica, che *sf* (*SCIENZA*) politics *sg*; (*linea di condotta*) policy; *vedi anche* **politico**
politiciz'zare [politit∫id'dzare] *vt* to politicize
po'litico, a, ci, che *ag* political ♦ *smf* politician
poli'zia [polit'tsia] *sf* police; **~ giudiziaria** ≈ Criminal Investigation Department (*BRIT*) = Federal Bureau of Investigation (*US*); **~ stradale** traffic police; **polizi'esco, a, schi, sche** *ag* police *cpd*; (*film, romanzo*) detective *cpd*; **polizi'otto** *sm* policeman; **cane poliziotto** police dog; **donna poliziotto** policewoman
'**polizza** ['pɔlittsa] *sf* (*COMM*) bill; **~ di assicurazione** insurance policy; **~ di carico** bill of lading
pol'laio *sm* henhouse
pol'lame *sm* poultry
pol'lastro *sm* (*ZOOL*) cockerel
'**pollice** ['pɔllit∫e] *sm* thumb
'**polline** *sm* pollen
'**pollo** *sm* chicken
pol'mone *sm* lung; **~ d'acciaio** (*MED*) iron lung; **polmo'nite** *sf* pneumonia
'**polo** *sm* (*GEO, FISICA*) pole; (*gioco*) polo; **il ~ sud/nord** the South/North Pole
Po'lonia *sf:* **la ~** Poland
'**polpa** *sf* flesh, pulp; (*carne*) lean meat
pol'paccio [pol'patt∫o] *sm* (*ANAT*) calf
polpas'trello *sm* fingertip
pol'petta *sf* (*CUC*) meatball; **pol-pet'tone** *sm* (*CUC*) meatloaf
'**polpo** *sm* octopus

pol'poso, a ag fleshy

pol'sino sm cuff

'polso sm (ANAT) wrist; (pulsazione) pulse; (fig: forza) drive, vigour

pol'tiglia [pol'tiʎʎa] sf (composto) mash, mush; (di fango e neve) slush

pol'trire vi to laze about

pol'trona sf armchair; (TEATRO: posto) seat in the front stalls (BRIT) o orchestra (US)

pol'trone ag lazy, slothful

'polvere sf dust; (anche: ~ da sparo) (gun)powder; (sostanza ridotta minutissima) powder, dust; **latte in ~** dried o powdered milk; **caffè in ~** instant coffee; **sapone in ~** soap powder; **polveri'era** sf powder magazine; **polveriz'zare** vt to pulverize; (nebulizzare) to atomize; (fig) to crush, pulverize; to smash; **polve'rone** sm thick cloud of dust; **polve'roso, a** ag dusty

po'mata sf ointment, cream

po'mello sm knob

pomeridi'ano, a ag afternoon cpd; **nelle ore ~e** in the afternoon

pome'riggio [pome'riddʒo] sm afternoon

'pomice ['pomitʃe] sf pumice

'pomo sm (mela) apple; (ornamentale) knob; (di sella) pommel; ~ **d'Adamo** (ANAT) Adam's apple

pomo'doro sm tomato

'pompa sf pump; (sfarzo) pomp (and ceremony); ~e **funebri** funeral parlour sg (BRIT), undertaker's sg; **pom'pare** vt to pump; (trarre) to pump out; (gonfiare d'aria) to pump up

pom'pelmo sm grapefruit

pompi'ere sm fireman

pom'poso, a ag pompous

ponde'rare vt to ponder over, consider carefully

ponde'roso, a ag (anche fig) weighty

po'nente sm west

'ponte sm bridge; (di nave) deck; (: anche: ~ **di comando**) bridge; (impalcatura) scaffold; **fare il ~** (fig) to take the extra day off (between 2 public holidays); **governo** ~ interim government; ~ **aereo** airlift; ~ **sospeso** suspension bridge

pon'tefice [pon'tefitʃe] sm (REL) pontiff

pontifi'care vi (anche fig) to pontificate

ponti'ficio, a, ci, cie [ponti'fitʃo] ag papal

popo'lano, a ag popular, of the people

popo'lare ag popular; (quartiere, clientela) working-class ♦ vt (rendere abitato) to populate; ~**rsi** vr to fill with people, get crowded; **popolarità** sf popularity; **popolazi'one** sf population

'popolo sm people; **popo'loso, a** ag densely populated

po'pone sm melon

'poppa sf (di nave) stern; (mammella) breast

pop'pare vt to suck

poppa'toio sm (feeding) bottle

porcel'lana [portʃel'lana] sf porcelain, china; piece of china

porcel'lino sm [portʃel'lino] smf piglet

porche'ria [porke'ria] sf filth, muck; (fig: oscenità) obscenity; (: azione disonesta) dirty trick; (: cosa mal fatta) rubbish

por'cile [por'tʃile] sm pigsty

por'cino, a [por'tʃino] ag of pigs, pork cpd ♦ sm (fungo) type of edible mushroom

'porco, ci sm pig; (carne) pork

porcos'pino sm porcupine

'porgere ['pordʒere] vt to hand, give; (tendere) to hold out

pornogra'fia sf pornography; **porno'grafico, a, ci, che** ag pornographic

'poro sm pore; **po'roso, a** ag porous

'porpora sf purple

'porre vt (mettere) to put; (collocare) to place; (posare) to lay

(down), put (down); (fig: supporre):
poniamo (il caso) che ... let's suppose that ...; **porsi** vr (mettersi):
porsi a sedere/in cammino to sit
down/set off; ~ **una domanda a qn**
to ask sb a question, put a question to
sb

'porro sm (BOT) leek; (MED) wart

'porta sf door; (SPORT) goal; ~e
sfpl (di città) gates; **a ~e chiuse**
(DIR) in camera

'porta... prefisso: **portaba'gagli** sm
inv (facchino) porter; (AUT, FERR)
luggage rack; **porta'cenere** sm inv
ashtray; **portachi'avi** sm inv key-
ring; **porta'cipria** sf inv powder
compact; **porta'erei** sf inv (nave)
aircraft carrier ♦ sm inv (aereo) aircraft transporter; **portafi'nestra** (pl
portefi'nestre) sf French window;
porta'foglio sm (busta) wallet;
(cartella) briefcase; (POL, BORSA)
portfolio; **portafor'tuna** sm inv
lucky charm; mascot; **portagi'oie** or
sm inv jewellery box; **porta-
gioi'elli** sm inv = portagioie

porta'lettere smf/inv postman/
woman (BRIT), mailman/woman
(US)

porta'mento sm carriage, bearing

portamo'nete sm inv purse

por'tante ag (muro etc) supporting,
load-bearing

portan'tina sf sedan chair; (per
ammalati) stretcher

por'tare vt (sostenere, sorreggere:
peso, bambino, pacco) to carry; (indossare: abito, occhiali) to wear; (:
capelli lunghi) to have; (avere:
nome, titolo) to have, bear; (recare):
~ **qc a qn** to take (o bring) sth to
sb; (fig: sentimenti) to bear; **~rsi** vr
(recarsi) to go; ~ **avanti** (discorso,
idea) to pursue; ~ **via** to take away;
(rubare) to take; ~ **i bambini a
spasso** to take the children for a
walk; ~ **fortuna** to bring good luck

portasiga'rette sm inv cigarette
case

por'tata sf (vivanda) course; (AUT)

carrying (o loading) capacity; (di
arma) range; (volume d'acqua) (rate
of) flow; (fig: limite) scope, capability; (: importanza) impact, import; **alla ~ di tutti** (conoscenza)
within everybody's capabilities;
(prezzo) within everybody's means;
a/fuori ~ (di) within/out of reach
(of); **a ~ di mano** within (arm's)
reach

por'tatile ag portable

por'tato, a ag (incline): ~ **a** inclined o apt to

porta'tore, 'trice smf (anche
COMM) bearer; (MED) carrier

portau'ovo sm inv eggcup

porta'voce [porta'votʃe] smf/inv
spokesman/woman

por'tento sm wonder, marvel

'portico, ci sm portico

porti'era sf (AUT) door

porti'ere sm (portinaio) concierge,
caretaker; (di hotel) porter; (nel calcio) goalkeeper

porti'naio, a smf/inv concierge, caretaker

portine'ria sf caretaker's lodge

'porto, a pp di **porgere** ♦ sm
(NAUT) harbour, port; (spesa di trasporto) carriage ♦ sm inv port
(wine); ~ **d'armi** (documento) gun
licence

Porto'gallo sm: **il ~** Portugal

porto'ghese ag, smf/, sm Portuguese inv

por'tone sm main entrance, main
door

portu'ale ag harbour cpd, port cpd
♦ sm dock worker

porzi'one [por'tsjone] sf portion,
share; (di cibo) portion, helping

'posa sf (FOT) exposure; (atteggiamento, di modello) pose

posa'cenere [posa'tʃenere] sm inv
ashtray

po'sare vt to put (down), lay (down)
♦ vi (ponte, edificio, teoria): ~ **su** to
rest on; (FOT, atteggiarsi) to pose;
~rsi vr (aereo) to land; (uccello) to
alight; (sguardo) to settle

po'sata sf piece of cutlery; ~e sfpl (servizio) cutlery sg

po'sato, a ag serious

pos'critto sm postscript

posi'tivo, a ag positive

posizi'one [pozit'tsjone] sf position; **prendere** ~ (fig) to take a stand; **luci di** ~ (AUT) sidelights

posolo'gia, 'gie [pozolo'dʒia] sf dosage, directions pl for use

pos'porre vt to place after; (differire) to postpone, defer; **pos'posto, a** pp di **posporre**

posse'dere vt to own, possess; (qualità, virtù) to have, possess; (conoscere a fondo: lingua etc) to have a thorough knowledge of; (sog: ira etc) to possess; **possedi'mento** sm possession

posses'sivo, a ag possessive

pos'sesso sm ownership no pl; possession

posses'sore sm owner

pos'sibile ag possible ♦ sm: **fare tutto il** ~ to do everything possible; **nei limiti del** ~ as far as possible; **al più tardi** ~ as late as possible; **possibilità** sf inv possibility ♦ sfpl (mezzi) means; **aver la possibilità di fare** to be in a position to do; to have the opportunity to do

possi'dente sm/f landowner

'posta sf (servizio) post, postal service; (corrispondenza) post, mail; (ufficio postale) post office; (nei giochi d'azzardo) stake; ~e sfpl (amministrazione) post office; ~ **aerea** airmail; **ministro delle P~e e Telecomunicazioni** Postmaster General; **posta'giro** sm post office cheque, postal giro (BRIT); **pos'tale** ag postal, post office cpd

post'bellico, a, ci, che ag post-war

posteggi'are [posted'dʒare] vt, vi to park; **pos'teggio** sm car park (BRIT), parking lot (US); (di taxi) rank (BRIT), stand (US)

postelegra'fonico, a, ci, che ag postal and telecommunications cpd

posteri'ore ag (dietro) back; (dopo) later ♦ sm (fam: sedere) behind

pos'ticcio, a, ci, ce [pos'tittʃo] ag false ♦ sm hairpiece

postici'pare [postitʃi'pare] vt to defer, postpone

pos'tilla sf marginal note

pos'tino sm postman (BRIT), mailman (US)

'posto, a pp di **porre** ♦ sm (sito, posizione) place; (impiego) job; (spazio libero) room, space; (di parcheggio) space; (sedile: al teatro, in treno etc) seat; (MIL) post; a ~ (in ordine) in place, tidy; (fig) settled; (: persona) reliable; **al** ~ **di** in place of; **sul** ~ on the spot; **mettere a** ~ to tidy (up), put in order; (faccende) to straighten out; ~ **di blocco** roadblock; ~ **di polizia** police station

pos'tribolo sm brothel

'postumo, a ag posthumous; (tardivo) belated; ~**i** smpl (conseguenze) after-effects, consequences

po'tabile ag drinkable; **acqua** ~ drinking water

po'tare vt to prune

po'tassio sm potassium

po'tente ag (nazione) strong, powerful; (veleno, farmaco) potent, strong; **po'tenza** sf power; (forza) strength

potenzi'ale [poten'tsjale] ag, sm potential

po'tere sm power; **al** ~ (partito etc) in power; ~ **d'acquisto** purchasing power

♦ vb aus **1** (essere in grado di) can, be able to; **non ha potuto ripararlo** he couldn't o he wasn't able to repair it; **non è potuto venire** he couldn't o he wasn't able to come; **spiacente di non poter aiutare** sorry not to be able to help

2 (avere il permesso) can, may, be allowed to; **posso entrare?** can o may I come in?; **si può sapere dove sei stato?** where on earth have

you been?
3 (*eventualità*) may, might, could; **potrebbe essere vero** it might *o* could be true; **può aver avuto un incidente** he may *o* might *o* could have had an accident; **può darsi** perhaps; **può darsi** *o* **essere che non venga** he may *o* might not come **4** (*augurio*): **potessi almeno parlargli!** if only I could speak to him! **5** (*suggerimento*): **potrsi almeno scusarti!** you could at least apologize!
♦ *vt* can, be able to; **può molto per noi** he can do a lot for us; **non ne posso più** (*per stanchezza*) I'm exhausted; (*per rabbia*) I can't take any more

potestà *sf* (*potere*) power; (*DIR*) authority
'povero, a *ag* poor; (*disadorno*) plain, bare ♦ *smif* poor man/woman; **i ~i** the poor; **~ di** lacking in, having little; **povertà** *sf* poverty
'pozza ['pottsa] *sf* pool
poz'zanghera [pot'tsangera] *sf* puddle
'pozzo ['pottso] *sm* well; (*cava: di carbone*) pit; (*di miniera*) shaft; **~ petrolifero** oil well
pran'zare [pran'dzare] *vi* to dine, have dinner; *(a mezzogiorno)* to lunch, have lunch
'pranzo ['prandzo] *sm* dinner; (*a mezzogiorno*) lunch
'prassi *sf* usual procedure
'pratica, che *sf* practice; (*esperienza*) experience; (*conoscenza*) knowledge, familiarity; (*tirocinio*) training, practice; (*AMM: affare*) matter, case; (: *incartamento*) file, dossier; **in ~** (*praticamente*) in practice; **mettere in ~** to put into practice
prati'cabile *ag* (*progetto*) practicable, feasible; (*luogo*) passable, practicable
prati'cante *smif* apprentice, trainee; (*REL*) (regular) churchgoer
prati'care *vt* to practise; (*SPORT*:

tennis etc) to play; (: *nuoto, scherma etc*) to go in for; (*eseguire: apertura, buco*) to make; **~ uno sconto** to give a discount
'pratico, a ci, che *ag* practical; **~ di** (*esperto*) experienced *o* skilled in; (*familiare*) familiar with
'prato *sm* meadow; (*di giardino*) lawn
preav'viso *sm* notice; **telefonata con ~** personal *o* person to person call
pre'cario, a *ag* precarious; (*INS*) temporary
precauzi'one [prekaut'tsjone] *sf* caution, care; (*misura*) precaution
prece'dente [pretfe'dente] *ag* previous ♦ *sm* precedent; **il discorso/film ~** the previous *o* preceding speech/film; **senza ~i** unprecedented; **~i penali** criminal record *sg*; **prece'denza** *sf* priority, precedence; (*AUT*) right of way
pre'cedere [pre'tfedere] *vt* to precede, go (*o* come) before
pre'cetto [pre'tfetto] *sm* precept; (*MIL*) call-up notice
precet'tore [pretfet'tore] *sm* (*private*) tutor
precipi'tare [pretfipi'tare] *vi* (*cadere*) to fall headlong; (*fig: situazione*) to get out of control ♦ *vt* (*gettare: dall'alto in basso*) to hurl, fling; (*fig: affrettare*) to rush; **~rsi** *vr* (*gettarsi*) to hurl *o* fling o.s.; (*affrettarsi*) to rush; **precipitazi'one** *sf* (*METEOR*) precipitation; (*fig*) haste; **precipi'toso, a** *ag* (*caduta, fuga*) headlong; (*fig: avventato*) rash, reckless; (: *affrettato*) hasty, rushed
preci'pizio [pretfi'pittsjo] *sm* precipice; **a ~** (*fig: correre*) headlong
preci'sare [pretfi'zare] *vt* to state, specify; (*spiegare*) to explain (in detail)
precisi'one [pretfi'zjone] *sf* precision; accuracy
pre'ciso, a [pre'tfizo] *ag* (*esatto*) precise; (*accurato*) accurate, pre-

cise; (*deciso: idee*) precise, definite; (*uguale*): 2 **vestiti** ~i 2 dresses exactly the same; **sono le 9** ~e it's exactly 9 o'clock

pre'cludere *vt* to block, obstruct; **pre'cluso, a** *pp di* precludere

pre'coce [pre'kɔtʃe] *ag* early; (*bambino*) precocious; (*vecchiaia*) premature

precon'cetto [prekon'tʃetto] *sm* preconceived idea, prejudice

precur'sore *sm* forerunner, precursor

'preda *sf* (*bottino*) booty; (*animale, fig*) prey; **essere** ~ **di** to fall prey to; **essere in** ~ **a** to be prey to; **preda'tore** *sm* predator

predeces'sore, a [predetʃes'sore] *sm/f* predecessor

predesti'nare *vt* to predestine

pre'detto, a *pp di* predire

'predica, che [*pl* 'predike] *sf* (*fig*) sermon; (*fig*) lecture, talking-to

predi'care *vt, vi* to preach

predi'cato *sm* (*LING*) predicate

prediletto, a *pp di* prediligere ♦ *ag, sm/f* favourite

predilezi'one [predilet'tsjone] *sf* fondness, partiality; **avere una** ~ **per qc/qn** to be partial to sth/fond of sb

predi'ligere [predi'lidʒere] *vt* to prefer, have a preference for

pre'dire *vt* to foretell, predict

predis'porre *vt* to get ready, prepare; ~ **qn a qc** to predispose sb to sth; **predis'posto, a** *pp di* predisporre

predizi'one [predit'tsjone] *sf* prediction

predomi'nare *vi* to predominate; **predo'minio** *sm* predominance; supremacy

prefabbri'cato, a *ag* (*EDIL*) prefabricated

prefazi'one [prefat'tsjone] *sf* preface, foreword

prefe'renza [prefe'rentsa] *sf* preference; **preferenzi'ale** *ag* preferential; **corsia** ~ bus and taxi lane

prefe'rire *vt* to prefer, like better; ~ **il caffè al tè** to prefer coffee to tea, like coffee better than tea

pre'fetto *sm* prefect; **prefet'tura** *sf* prefecture

pre'figgersi [pre'fiddʒersi] *vr*: ~**rsi uno scopo** to set o.s. a goal

pre'fisso, a *pp di* prefiggere ♦ *sm* (*LING*) prefix; (*TEL*) dialling (*BRIT*) o dial (*US*) code

pre'gare *vi* to pray ♦ *vt* (*REL*) to pray to; (*implorare*) to beg; (*chiedere*): ~ **qn di fare** to ask sb to do; **farsi** ~ to need coaxing o persuading

pre'gevole [pre'dʒevole] *ag* valuable

preghi'era [pre'gjɛra] *sf* (*REL*) prayer; (*domanda*) request

pregi'ato, a [pre'dʒato] *ag* (*di valore*) valuable; **vino** ~ vintage wine

'pregio ['predʒo] *sm* (*stima*) esteem, regard; (*qualità*) (good) quality, merit; (*valore*) value, worth

pregiudi'care [predʒudi'kare] *vt* to prejudice, harm, be detrimental to; **pregiudi'cato, a** *sm/f* (*DIR*) previous offender

pregiu'dizio [predʒu'dittsjo] *sm* (*idea errata*) prejudice; (*danno*) harm *no pl*

'pregno, a ['preɲɲo] *ag* (*gravido*) pregnant; (*saturo*): ~ **di** full of, saturated with

'prego *escl* (*a chi ringrazia*) don't mention it!; (*invitando qn ad accomodarsi*) please sit down!; (*invitando qn ad andare prima*) after you!

pregus'tare *vt* to look forward to

preis'torico, a, ci, che *ag* prehistoric

pre'lato *sm* prelate

prele'vare *vt* (*denaro*) to withdraw; (*campione*) to take; (*sog: polizia*) to take, capture

preli'evo *sm* (*MED*): **fare un** ~ (**di**) to take a sample (of)

prelimi'nare *ag* preliminary; ~**i** *smpl* preliminary talks; preliminaries

pre'ludio *sm* prelude

pré-ma'man [prema'mã] *sm inv* maternity dress

prema'turo, a ag premature

premeditazi'one [premeditat-'tsjone] sf (DIR) premeditation: **con ~ ag** premeditated ♦ av with intent

'premere vt to press ♦ vi: **~ su** to press down on; (fig) to put pressure on; **~ a** (fig: importare) to matter to

pre'messa sf introductory statement, introduction

pre'messo, a pp di **premettere**

pre'mettere vt to put before; (dire prima) to start by saying, state first

premi'are vt to give a prize to; (fig: merito, onestà) to reward

'premio sm prize; (ricompensa) reward; (COMM) premium; (AMM: indennità) bonus

premu'nirsi vr: **~ di** to provide o.s. with; **~ contro** to protect o.s. from, guard o.s. against

pre'mura sf (fretta) haste, hurry; (riguardo) attention, care; **premu-'roso, a** ag thoughtful, considerate

prena'tale ag antenatal

'prendere vt to take; (andare a prendere) to get, fetch; (ottenere) to get; (guadagnare) to get, earn; (catturare: ladro, pesce) to catch; (collaboratore, dipendente) to take on; (passeggero) to pick up; (chiedere: somma, prezzo) to charge, ask; (trattare: persona) to handle ♦ vi (colla, cemento) to set; (pianta) to take; (fuoco: nel camino) to catch; (voltare): **~ a destra** to turn to the right; **~rsi** vr (azzuffarsi): **~rsi a pugni** to come to blows; **prendi qualcosa?** (da bere, da mangiare) would you like something to eat (o drink)?; **prendo un caffè** I'll have a coffee; **~ a fare qc** to start doing sth; **~ qn/qc per** (scambiare) to take sb/sth for; **~ fuoco** to catch fire; **~ parte a** to take part in; **~rsi cura di qn/qc** to look after sb/sth; **prendersela** (adirarsi) to get annoyed; (preoccuparsi) to get upset, worry

prendi'sole sm inv sundress

preno'tare vt to book, reserve; **pre-**

notazi'one sf booking, reservation

preoccu'pare vt to worry; to preoccupy; **~rsi** vr: **~rsi di qn/qc** to worry about sb/sth; **~rsi per qn** to be anxious for sb; **preoccupazi'one** sf worry, anxiety

prepa'rare vt to prepare; (esame, concorso) to prepare for; **~rsi** vr (vestirsi) to get ready; **~rsi a qc/a fare** to get ready o prepare (o.s.) for sth/to do; **~ da mangiare** to prepare a meal; **prepa'tivi** smpl preparations; **prepa'rato** sm (prodotto) preparation; **preparazi'one** sf preparation

preposizi'one [prepozit'tsjone] sf (LING) preposition

prepo'tente ag (persona) domineering, arrogant; (bisogno, desiderio) overwhelming, pressing ♦ sm/f bully; **prepo'tenza** sf arrogance; arrogant behaviour

'presa sf taking no pl; catching no pl; (di città) capture; (indurimento: di cemento) setting; (appiglio, SPORT) hold; (di acqua, gas) supply) point; (ELETTR): **~ (di corrente)** socket; (: al muro) point; (piccola quantità: di sale etc) pinch; (CARTE) trick; **far ~ (colla)** to set; **far ~ sul pubblico** to catch the public's imagination; **~ d'aria** air inlet; **essere alle ~e con qc** (fig) to be struggling with sth

pre'sagio [pre'zadʒo] sm omen

presa'gire [preza'dʒire] vt to foresee

pre'sbite ag long-sighted

presbi'terio sm presbytery

pre'scindere [pref'ʃindere] vi: **~ da** to leave out of consideration; **a ~ da** apart from

pres'critto, a pp di **prescrivere**

pres'crivere vt to prescribe; **pre-scrizi'one** sf (MED, DIR) prescription; (norma) rule, regulation

presen'tare vt to present; (far conoscere): **~ qn (a)** to introduce sb (to); (AMM: inoltrare) to submit; **~rsi** vr (recarsi, farsi vedere) to present o.s., appear; (farsi co-

noscere) to introduce o.s.; (*occasione*) to arise; ~**rsi come candidato** (*POL*) to stand as a candidate; ~**rsi bene/male** to have a good/poor appearance; **presentazi'one** *sf* presentation; introduction

pre'sente *ag* present; (*questo*) this ♦ *sm* present; **i ~i** those present; **aver ~ qc/qn** to remember sth/sb

presenti'mento *sm* premonition

pre'senza [pre'zɛntsa] *sf* presence; (*aspetto esteriore*) appearance; ~ **di spirito** presence of mind

pre'sepe *sm* = presepio

pre'sepio *sm* crib

preser'vare *vt* to protect; to save; **preserva'tivo** *sm* sheath, condom

'preside *smif* (*INS*) head (teacher) (*BRIT*), principal (*US*); (*di facoltà universitaria*) dean

presi'dente *sm* (*POL*) president; (*di assemblea, COMM*) chairman; ~ **del consiglio** prime minister; **presiden'tessa** *sf* president; president's wife;chairwoman; **presi'denza** *sf* presidency; office of president; chairmanship

presidi'are *vt* to garrison; **pre'sidio** *sm* garrison

presi'edere *vt* to preside over ♦ *vi*: ~ **a** to direct, be in charge of

'preso, a *pp* di prendere

'pressa *sf* (*TECN*) press

pressap'poco *av* about, roughly

pres'sare *vt* to press

pressi'one *sf* pressure; **far ~ su qn** to put pressure on sb; ~ **sanguigna** blood pressure

'presso *av* (*vicino*) nearby, close at hand ♦ *prep* (*vicino a*) near; (*accanto a*) beside, next to; (*in casa di*): ~ **qn** at sb's home; (*nelle lettere*) care of, c/o; (*alle dipendenze di*): **lavora ~ di noi** he works for *o* with us ♦ *smpl*: **nei ~i di** near, in the vicinity of

pressuriz'zare [pressurid'dzare] *vt* to pressurize

presta'nome (*peg*) *smif inv* figurehead

pres'tante *ag* good-looking

pres'tare *vt*: ~ **(qc a qn)** to lend (sb sth *o* sth to sb); ~**rsi** *vr* (*offrirsi*): ~**rsi a fare** to offer to do; (*essere adatto*): ~**rsi a** to lend itself to, be suitable for; ~ **aiuto** to lend a hand; ~ **attenzione** to pay attention; ~ **fede a qc/qn** to give credence to sth/sb; ~ **orecchio** to listen; **prestazi'one** *sf* (*TECN, SPORT*) performance; **prestazioni** *sfpl* (*di persona; servizi*) services

prestigia'tore, 'trice [prestidʒa'tore] *smif* conjurer

pres'tigio [pres'tidʒo] *sm* (*potere*) prestige; (*illusione*): **gioco di ~** conjuring trick

pres'tito *sm* lending *no pl*; loan; **dar in ~** to lend; **prendere in ~** to borrow

'presto *av* (*tra poco*) soon; (*in fretta*) quickly; (*di buon'ora*) early; **a ~** see you soon; **fare ~ a fare qc** to hurry up and do sth; (*non costare fatica*) to have no trouble doing sth; **si fa ~ a criticare** it's easy to criticize

pre'sumere *vt* to presume, assume; **pre'sunto, a** *pp* di presumere

presuntu'oso, a *ag* presumptuous

presunzi'one [prezun'tsjone] *sf* presumption

presup'porre *vt* to suppose; to presuppose

'prete *sm* priest

preten'dente *smif* pretender ♦ *sm* (*corteggiatore*) suitor

pre'tendere *vt* (*esigere*) to demand, require; (*sostenere*): ~ **che** to claim that; **pretende di aver sempre ragione** he thinks he's always right

pretenzi'oso, a [preten'tsjoso] *ag* pretentious

pre'tesa *sf* (*esigenza*) claim, demand; (*presunzione, sfarzo*) pretentiousness; **senza ~e** unpretentious; *vedi anche* preteso

pre'teso, a *pp* di pretendere

pre'testo *sm* pretext, excuse

pre'tore *sm* magistrate

pre'tura *sf* magistracy; (*sede*) magistrate's court

preva'lente *ag* prevailing; **preva'lenza** *sf* predominance

preva'lere *vi* to prevail; **pre'valso, a** *pp di* **prevalere**

preve'dere *vt* (*indovinare*) to foresee; (*presagire*) to foretell; (*considerare*) to make provision for

preve'nire *vt* (*anticipare*) to forestall; to anticipate; (*evitare*) to avoid, prevent; (*avvertire*): ~ qn (di) to warn sb (of); to inform sb (of)

preven'tivo, a *ag* preventive ♦ *sm* (*COMM*) estimate

prevenzi'one *sf* prevention; (*preconcetto*) prejudice

previ'dente *ag* showing foresight; prudent; **previ'denza** *sf* foresight; istituto di previdenza provident institution; **previdenza sociale** social security (*BRIT*), welfare (*US*)

previsi'one *sf* forecast, prediction; ~i meteorologiche *o* del tempo weather forecast *sg*

pre'visto, a *pp di* **prevedere** ♦ *sm*: più/meno del ~ more/less than expected

prezi'oso, a [pret'tsjoso] *ag* precious; invaluable ♦ *sm* jewel; valuable

prez'zemolo [pret'tsemolo] *sm* parsley

'prezzo ['prettso] *sm* price; ~ d'acquisto *o* di vendita buying/selling price

prigi'one [pri'dʒone] *sf* prison; **prigio'nia** *sf* imprisonment; **prigio-ni'ero, a** *ag* captive ♦ *sm/f* prisoner

'prima (*TEATRO*) first night; (*CI-NEMA*) première; (*AUT*) first gear; *vedi anche* **primo** ♦ *av* before; (*in anticipo*) in advance, beforehand; (*per l'addietro*) at one time, formerly; (*più presto*) sooner, earlier; (*in primo luogo*) first ♦ *cong*: ~ **di fare/che** before doing/he leaves; ~ **di** before; ~ **o poi** sooner or later

pri'mario, a *ag* primary; (*princi-*

pale) chief, leading, primary ♦ *sm* (*MED*) chief physician

pri'mato *sm* supremacy; (*SPORT*) record

prima'vera *sf* spring; **prima've'rile** *ag* spring *cpd*

primeggi'are [primed'dʒare] *vi* to excel, be one of the best

primi'tivo, a *ag* primitive; original

pri'mizie [pri'mittsje] *sfpl* early produce *sg*

'primo, a *ag* first; (*fig*) initial; basic; prime ♦ *sm/f* first (one) ♦ *sm* (*CUC*) first course; (*in date*): il ~ luglio the first of July; le ~e ore del mattino the early hours of the morning; ai ~i di maggio at the beginning of May; viaggiare in ~a to travel first-class; in ~ luogo first of all, in the first place; di prim'ordine *o* ~a qualità first-class, first-rate; in un ~ tempo at first; ~a donna leading lady; (*di opera lirica*) prima donna

primo'genito, a [primo'dʒenito] *ag*, *sm/f* firstborn

primordi'ale *ag* primordial

'primula *sf* primrose

princi'pale [printʃi'pale] *ag* main, principal ♦ *sm* manager, boss

princi'pato [printʃi'pato] *sm* principality

'principe ['printʃipe] *sm* prince; ~ **ereditario** crown prince; **princi-'pessa** *sf* princess

principi'ante [printʃi'pjante] *sm/f* beginner

prin'cipio [prin'tʃipjo] *sm* (*inizio*) beginning, start; (*origine*) origin, cause; (*concetto, norma*) principle; al *o* in ~ at first; per ~ on principle

pri'ore *sm* (*REL*) prior

priorità *sf* priority

'prisma, i *sm* prism

pri'vare *vt*: ~ **qn di** to deprive sb of; ~**rsi di** to go *o* do without

pri'vato, a *ag* private; (*cittadino*) private citizen; **in** ~ in private

privazi'one [privat'tsjone] *sf* privation, hardship

privilegi'are [privile'dʒare] vt to grant a privilege to

privi'legio [privi'ledʒo] sm privilege

'privo, a ag: ~ **di** without, lacking

pro prep for, on behalf of ♦ sm inv (utilità) advantage, benefit; **a che** ~? what's the use?; **il** ~ **e il contro** the pros and cons

pro'babile ag probable, likely; **probabilità** sf inv probability

pro'blema, i sm problem

pro'boscide [pro'bɔʃʃide] sf (di elefante) trunk

procacci'are [prokat'tʃare] vt to get, obtain

pro'cedere [pro'tʃedere] vi to proceed; (comportarsi) to behave; (iniziare): ~ **a** to start; ~ **contro** (DIR) to start legal proceedings against; **procedi'mento** sm (modo di condurre) procedure; (di avvenimenti) course; (TECN) process; **procedimento penale** (DIR) criminal proceedings; **proce'dura** sf (DIR) procedure

proces'sare [protʃes'sare] vt (DIR) to try

processi'one [protʃes'sjone] sf procession

pro'cesso [pro'tʃɛsso] sm (DIR) trial; proceedings pl; (metodo) process

pro'cinto [pro'tʃinto] sm: **in** ~ **di fare** about to do, on the point of doing

pro'clama, i sm proclamation

procla'mare vt to proclaim

procre'are vt to procreate

pro'cura sf (DIR) proxy; power of attorney; (ufficio) attorney's office

procu'rare vt: ~ **qc a qn** (fornire) to get o obtain sth for sb; (causare: noie etc) to bring o give sb sth

procura'tore, 'trice sm/f (DIR) ≈ solicitor; (: chi ha la procura) attorney; proxy; ~ **generale** (in corte d'appello) public prosecutor; (in corte di cassazione) Attorney General; ~ **della Repubblica** (in corte d'assise, tribunale) public prosecutor

prodi'gare vt to be lavish with; ~**rsi per qn** to do all one can for sb

pro'digio [pro'didʒo] sm marvel, wonder; (persona) prodigy; **prodigi'oso, a** ag prodigious; phenomenal

'prodigo, a, ghi, ghe ag lavish, extravagant

pro'dotto, a pp di **produrre** ♦ sm product; ~**i agricoli** farm produce

pro'durre vt to produce; **produttività** sf productivity; **produt'tivo, a** ag productive; **produt'tore, 'trice** sm/f producer; **produzi'one** sf production; (rendimento) output

pro'emio sm introduction, preface

Prof. abbr (= professore) Prof

profa'nare vt to desecrate

pro'fano, a ag (mondano) secular; profane; (sacrilego) profane

profe'rire vt to utter

profes'sare vt to profess; (medicina etc) to practise

professio'nale ag professional

professi'one sf profession; **professio'nista, i, e** sm/f professional

profes'sore, 'essa sm/f (INS) teacher; (: di università) lecturer; (: titolare di cattedra) professor

pro'feta, i sm prophet; **profe'zia** sf prophecy

pro'ficuo, a ag useful, profitable

profi'larsi vr to stand out, be silhouetted; to loom up

profi'lattico sm condom

pro'filo sm profile; (breve descrizione) sketch, outline; **di** ~ in profile

profit'tare vi: ~ **di** (trarre profitto) to profit by; (approfittare) to take advantage of

pro'fitto sm advantage, profit, benefit; (fig: progresso) progress; (COMM) profit

profondità sf inv depth

pro'fondo, a ag deep; (rancore, meditazione) profound ♦ sm depth(s pl), bottom; ~ **8 metri** 8 metres deep

'profugo, a, ghi, ghe sm/f refugee

profu'mare vt to perfume ♦ vi to be fragrant; **~rsi** vr to put on perfume o scent

profume'ria sf perfumery; (negozio) perfume shop

pro'fumo sm (prodotto) perfume, scent; (fragranza) scent, fragrance

profusi'one sf profusion; **a ~** in plenty

proget'tare [prodʒet'tare] vt to plan; (TECN: edificio) to plan, design; **pro'getto** sm plan; (idea) plan, project; **progetto di legge** bill

pro'gramma, i sm programme; (TV, RADIO) programmes pl; (INS) syllabus, curriculum; (INFORM) program; **program'mare** vt (TV, RADIO) to put on; (INFORM) to program; (ECON) to plan; **programma'tore, 'trice** smf (INFORM) computer programmer

progre'dire vi to progress, make progress

progres'sivo, a ag progressive

pro'gresso sm progress no pl; **fare ~i** to make progress

proi'bire vt to forbid, prohibit; **proibi'tivo, a** ag prohibitive; **proibizi'one** sf prohibition

proiet'tare vt (gen, GEOM, CINEMA) to project; (: presentare) to show, screen; (luce, ombra) to throw, cast, project; **proi'ettile** sm projectile, bullet (o shell etc); **proiet'tore** sm (CINEMA) projector; (AUT) headlamp; (MIL) searchlight; **proiezi'one** sf (CINEMA) projection; showing

'prole sf children pl, offspring

prole'tario, a ag, sm proletarian

prolife'rare vi (fig) to proliferate

pro'lisso, a ag verbose

'prologo, ghi sm prologue

pro'lunga, ghe sf (di cavo elettrico etc) extension

prolun'gare vt (discorso, attesa) to prolong; (linea, termine) to extend

prome'moria sm inv memorandum

pro'messa sf promise

pro'messo, a pp di promettere

pro'mettere vt to promise ♦ vi to be o look promising; **~ a qn di fare** to promise sb that one will do

promi'nente ag prominent

promiscuità sf promiscuousness

promon'torio sm promontory, headland

pro'mosso, a pp di promuovere

promo'tore, 'trice smf promoter, organizer

promozi'one [promot'tsjone] sf promotion

promul'gare vt to promulgate

promu'overe vt to promote ♦ vi

proni'pote smf (di nonni) greatgrandchild, great-grandson/granddaughter; (di zii) great-nephew/niece; **~i** smpl (discendenti) descendants

pro'nome sm (LING) pronoun

pro'nostico, ci sm forecast, prediction

pron'tezza [pron'tettsa] sf readiness; quickness, promptness

'pronto, a ag ready; (rapido) fast, quick, prompt; **~!** (TEL) hello!; **~ all'ira** quick-tempered; **~ soccorso** first aid

prontu'ario sm manual, handbook

pro'nuncia [pro'nuntʃa] sf pronunciation

pronunci'are [pronun'tʃare] vt (parola, sentenza) to pronounce; (discorso) to utter; (discorso) to deliver; **~rsi** vr to declare one's opinion; **pronunci'ato, a** ag (spiccato) pronounced, marked; (sporgente) prominent

pro'nunzia etc [pro'nuntsja] = **pronuncia** etc

propa'ganda sf propaganda

propa'gare vt (notizia, malattia) to spread; (REL, BIOL) to propagate; **~rsi** vr to spread; (BIOL) to propagate; (FISICA) to be propagated

pro'pendere vi: **~ per** to favour, lean towards; **propensi'one** sf inclination, propensity; **pro'penso, a** pp di propendere

propi'nare vt to administer

pro'pizio, a [pro'pittsjo] ag favourable

pro'porre vt (suggerire): ~ qc (a qn) to suggest sth (to sb); (candidato) to put forward; (legge, brindisi) to propose; ~ **di fare** to suggest o propose doing; **proporsi di fare** o propose o intend to do; **proporsi una meta** to set o.s. a goal

proporzio'nale [proportsjo'nale] ag proportional

proporzio'nare [proportsjo'nare] vt: ~ qc a to proportion o adjust sth to

proporzi'one [propor'tsjone] sf proportion; **in** ~ a in proportion to

pro'posito sm (intenzione) intention, aim; (argomento) subject, matter; a ~ di regarding, with regard to; **di** ~ (apposta) deliberately, on purpose; a ~ by the way; **capitare a** ~ (cosa, persona) to turn up at the right time

proposizi'one [propozit'tsjone] sf (LING) clause; (: periodo) sentence

pro'posta sf proposal; (suggerimento) suggestion; ~ **a di legge** bill

pro'posto, a pp di **proporre**

proprietà sf inv (ciò che si possiede) property gen no pl, estate; (caratteristica) property; (correttezza) correctness; **proprie'tario, a** sm/f owner; (di albergo etc) proprietor, owner; (per l'inquilino) landlord/lady

'proprio, a ag (possessivo) own; (: impersonale) one's; (esatto) exact, correct, proper; (senso, significato) literal; (LING: nome) proper; (particolare): ~ **di** characteristic of, peculiar to ♦ av (precisamente) just, exactly; (davvero) really; (affatto): **non** ... ~ not ... at all; **l'ha visto con i (suoi) ~i occhi** he saw it with his own eyes

'prora sf (NAUT) bow(s pl), prow

'proroga, ghe sf extension; postponement; **proro'gare** vt to extend; (differire) to postpone, defer

pro'rompere vi to burst out; **pro'rotto, a** pp di **prorompere**

che ag (fig) prosaic, mundane

pro'sciogliere [prof'ʃɔʎʎere] vt to release; (DIR) to acquit; **pro-sci'olto, a** pp di **prosciogliere**

prosciu'gare [proʃʃu'gare] vt (terreni) to drain, reclaim; ~**rsi** vr to dry up

prosci'utto [proʃ'ʃutto] sm ham; ~ **cotto/crudo** cooked/cured ham

prosegui'mento sm continuation; **buon** ~! all the best!; (a chi viaggia) enjoy the rest of your journey!

prosegu'ire vt to carry on with, continue ♦ vi to carry on, go on

prospe'rare vi to thrive; **prosperità** sf prosperity; **'prospero, a** ag (fiorente) flourishing, thriving, prosperous; **prospe'roso, a** ag (robusto) hale and hearty; (: ragazza) buxom

prospet'tare vt (esporre) to point out, show; ~**rsi** vr to look, appear

prospet'tiva sf (ARTE) perspective; (veduta) view; (fig: previsione, possibilità) prospect

pros'petto sm (DISEGNO) elevation; (veduta) view, prospect; (facciata) façade, front; (tabella) table; (sommario) summary

prospici'ente [prospi'ʃɛnte] ag: ~ qc facing o overlooking sth

prossimità sf nearness, proximity; **in** ~ **di** near (to), close to

'prossimo, a ag (vicino): ~ a near (to), close to; (che viene subito dopo) next; (parente) close ♦ sm neighbour, fellow man

prosti'tuta sf prostitute; **prostitu-zi'one** sf prostitution

pros'trare vt (fig) to exhaust, wear out; ~**rsi** vr (fig) to humble o.s

protago'nista, i, e sm/f protagonist

pro'teggere [pro'tɛddʒere] vt to protect

prote'ina sf protein

pro'tendere vt to stretch out; **pro'teso, a** pp di **protendere**

pro'testa sf protest

protes'tante ag, sm/f Protestant

protes'tare vt, vi to protest; **~rsi** vr: **~rsi innocente** etc to protest one's innocence o that one is innocent etc

protet'tivo, a ag protective

protet'tore, 'trice sm/f protector; (sostenitore) patron

protezi'one [protet'tsjone] sf protection; (patrocinio) patronage

protocol'lare vt to register ♦ ag formal; of protocol

proto'collo sm protocol; (registro) register of documents

pro'totipo sm prototype

pro'trarre vt (prolungare) to prolong; **pro'tratto, a** pp di **protrarre**

protube'ranza [protube'rantsa] sf protuberance, bulge

'prova sf (esperimento, cimento) test, trial; (tentativo) attempt, try; (MAT, testimonianza, documento etc) proof; (DIR) evidence no pl, proof; (INS) exam, test; (TEATRO) rehearsal; (di abito) fitting; **a ~ di** (in testimonianza di) as proof of; **a ~ di fuoco** fireproof; **fino a ~ contraria** until it is proved otherwise; **mettere alla ~** to put to the test; **giro di ~** test o trial run; **~ generale** (TEATRO) dress rehearsal

pro'vare vt (sperimentare) to test; (tentare) to try, attempt; (assaggiare) to try, taste; (sperimentare in sé) to experience; (sentire) to feel; (cimentare) to put to the test; (dimostrare) to prove; (abito) to try on; **~ a fare** to try o attempt to do

proveni'enza [prove'njentsa] sf origin, source

prove'nire vi: **~ da** to come from

pro'venti smpl revenue sg

prove'nuto, a pp di **provenire**

pro'verbio sm proverb

pro'vetta sf test tube; **bambino in ~** test-tube baby

pro'vetto, a ag skilled, experienced

pro'vincia, ce o **cie** [pro'vintʃa] sf province; **provinci'ale** ag provincial; **(strada) provinciale** main

road (BRIT), highway (US)

pro'vino sm (CINEMA) screen test; (campione) specimen

provo'cante ag (attraente) provocative

provo'care vt (causare) to cause, bring about; (eccitare: riso, pietà) to arouse; (irritare, sfidare) to provoke; **provoca'torio, a** ag provocative; **provocazi'one** sf provocation

provve'dere vi (disporre): **~ (a)** to provide (for); (prendere un provvedimento) to take steps, act ♦ vt: **~ qc a qn** to supply sth to sb; **~rsi di**: **~rsi di** to provide o.s. with; **provvedi'mento** sm measure; (di previdenza) precaution

provvi'denza [provvi'dentsa] sf: **la ~** providence; **provvidenzi'ale** ag providential

provvigi'one [provvi'dʒone] sf (COMM) commission

provvi'sorio, a ag temporary

prov'vista sf provision, supply

'prua sf (NAUT) = **prora**

pru'dente ag cautious, prudent; (assennato) sensible, wise; **pru'denza** sf prudence, caution; wisdom

'prudere vi to itch, be itchy

'prugna ['pruɲɲa] sf plum; **~ secca** prune

pruri'ginoso, a [pruridʒi'noso] ag itchy

pru'rito sm itchiness no pl; itch

P.S. abbr (= postscriptum) P.S.; (POLIZIA) = **Pubblica Sicurezza**

pseu'donimo sm pseudonym

PSI sigla m = **Partito Socialista Italiano**

psicana'lista, i, e sm/f psychoanalyst

'psiche ['psike] sf (PSIC) psyche

psichi'atra, i, e [psi'kjatra] sm/f psychiatrist; **psichi'atrico, a, ci, che** ag psychiatric

'psichico, a, ci, che ['psikiko] ag psychological

psicolo'gia [psikolo'dʒia] sf psychology; **psico'logico, a, ci, che** ag psychological; **psi'cologo, a, gi,**

ghe *sm/f* psychologist

psico'patico, a, ci, che *ag* psychopathic ♦ *sm/f* psychopath

P.T. *abbr* ♦ **Posta e Telegrafi**

pubbli'care *vt* to publish

pubblicazi'one [pubblikat'tsjone] *sf* publication; **~i (matrimoniali)** *sfpl* (marriage) banns

pubbli'cista, i, e [pubbli'tʃista] *sm/f* (*STAMPA*) occasional contributor

pubblicità [pubblitʃi'ta] *sf* (*diffusione*) publicity; (*attività*) advertising; (*annunci nei giornali*) advertisements *pl*; **pubbli'citario, a** *ag* advertising *cpd*; (*trovata, film*) publicity *cpd*

'pubblico, a, ci, che *ag* public; (*statale: scuola etc*) state *cpd* ♦ *sm* public; (*spettatori*) audience; **in ~** in public; **~ funzionario** civil servant; **P~ Ministero** Public Prosecutor's Office; **la P~a Sicurezza** the police

'pube *sm* (*ANAT*) pubis

pubertà *sf* puberty

pu'dico, a, ci, che *ag* modest

pu'dore *sm* modesty

puericul'tura *sf* paediatric nursing; infant care

pue'rile *ag* childish

pugi'lato [pudʒi'lato] *sm* boxing

'pugile ['pudʒile] *sm* boxer

pugna'lare [puɲɲa'lare] *vt* to stab

pu'gnale [pu'ɲɲale] *sm* dagger

'pugno ['puɲɲo] *sm* fist; (*colpo*) punch; (*quantità*) fistful

'pulce ['pultʃe] *sf* flea

pul'cino [pul'tʃino] *sm* chick

pu'ledro, a *sm/f* colt/filly

pu'leggia, ge [pu'leddʒa] *sf* pulley

pu'lire *vt* to clean; (*lucidare*) to polish; **pu'lita** *sf* quick clean; **pu'lito, a** *ag* (*anche fig*) clean; (*ordinato*) neat, tidy; **puli'tura** *sf* cleaning; pulitura a secco dry cleaning; **puli'zia** *sf* cleaning; cleanness; **fare le pulizie** to do the cleaning, do the housework

'pullman *sm inv* coach

pul'lover *sm inv* pullover, jumper

pullu'lare *vi* to swarm, teem

pul'mino *sm* minibus

'pulpito *sm* pulpit

pul'sante *sm* (push-)button

pul'sare *vi* to pulsate, beat; **pulsazi'one** *sf* beat

pul'viscolo *sm* fine dust

'puma *sm inv* puma

pun'gente [pun'dʒente] *ag* prickly; stinging; (*anche fig*) biting

'pungere ['pundʒere] *vt* to prick; (*sog: insetto, ortica*) to sting; (: *freddo*) to bite

pungigli'one [pundʒiʎ'ʎone] *sm* sting

pu'nire *vt* to punish; **punizi'one** *sf* punishment; (*SPORT*) penalty

'punta *sf* point; (*parte terminale*) tip, end; (*di monte*) peak; (*di costa*) promontory; (*minima parte*) touch, trace; **in ~ di piedi** on tip-toe; **ore di ~** peak hours; **uomo di ~** front-rank o leading man

pun'tare *vt* (*piedi a terra, gomiti sul tavolo*) to plant; (*dirigere: pistola*) to point; (*scommettere*) to bet ♦ *vi* (*mirare*): **~ a** to aim at; (*avviarsi*): **~ su** to head o make for; (*fig: contare*): **~ su** to count o rely on

pun'tata *sf* (*gita*) short trip; (*scommessa*) bet; (*parte di opera*) instalment; **romanzo a ~e** serial

punteggia'tura [punteddʒa'tura] *sf* (*LING*) punctuation

pun'teggio [pun'teddʒo] *sm* score

puntel'lare *vt* to support

pun'tello *sm* prop, support

puntigli'oso [puntiʎ'ʎoso] *ag* punctilious

pun'tina *sf*: **~ da disegno** drawing pin

pun'tino *sm* dot; **fare qc a ~** to do sth properly

'punto, a *pp di* **pungere** ♦ *sm* (*segno, macchiolina*) dot; (*LING*) full stop; (*MAT, momento, di punteggio, fig: argomento*) point; (*posto*) spot; (*a scuola*) mark; (*nel cucire, nella maglia, MED*) stitch ♦ *av*: **non ... ~** not at all; **due ~i** *sm* (*LING*) colon; **sul ~ di fare** (just) about to do;

fare il ~ (*NAUT*) to take a bearing; (*fig*): fare il ~ della situazione to take stock of the situation; to sum up the situation; alle 6 in ~ at 6 o'clock sharp *o* on the dot; essere a buon ~ to have reached a satisfactory stage; mettere a ~ to adjust; (*motore*) to tune; (*cannocchiale*) to focus; (*fig*) to settle; di ~ in bianco point-blank; ~ cardinale point of the compass, cardinal point; ~ debole weak point; ~ esclamativo/interrogativo exclamation/question mark; ~ di riferimento landmark; (*fig*) point of reference; ~ di vendita retail outlet; ~ e virgola semicolon; ~ di vista (*fig*) point of view; ~i di sospensione suspension points

puntu'ale *ag* punctual; **puntualità** *sf* punctuality

pun'tura *sf* (*di ago*) prick; (*di insetto*) sting, bite; (*MED*) puncture; (: *iniezione*) injection; (*dolore*) sharp pain

punzecchi'are [puntsek'kjare] *vt* to prick; (*fig*) to tease

pun'zone [pun'tsone] *sm* (*per metalli*) stamp, die

'pupa *sf* doll

pu'pazzo [pu'pattso] *sm* puppet

pu'pilla (*ANAT*) pupil; *vedi anche* pupillo

pu'pillo, a *sm/f* (*DIR*) ward; (*prediletto*) favourite, pet

purché [pur'ke] *cong* provided that, on condition that

'pure *cong* (*tuttavia*) and yet, nevertheless; (*anche se*) even if ♦ *av* (*anche*) too, also; *pur di* (*al fine di*) just to; faccia ~! go ahead!, please do!

purè *sm* (*CUC*) purée; (: *di patate*) mashed potatoes

pu'rea *sf* = purè

pu'rezza [pu'rettsa] *sf* purity

'purga, ghe *sf* (*MED*) purging *no pl*; purge; (*POL*) purge

pur'gante *sm* (*MED*) purgative, purge

pur'gare *vt* (*MED*, *POL*) to purge;

(*pulire*) to clean

purga'torio *sm* purgatory

purifi'care *vt* to purify; (*metallo*) to refine

puri'tano, a *ag*, *sm/f* puritan

'puro, a *ag* pure; (*acqua*) clear, limpid; (*vino*) undiluted; **puro'sangue** *sm/f inv* thoroughbred

pur'troppo *av* unfortunately

'pustola *sf* pimple

puti'ferio *sm* rumpus, row

putre'fare *vi* to putrefy, rot; **putre'fatto, a** *pp di* putrefare

'putrido, a *ag* putrid, rotten

put'tana (*fam!*) *sf* whore (!)

'puzza ['puttsa] *sf* = puzzo

puz'zare [put'tsare] *vi* to stink

'puzzo ['puttso] *sm* stink, foul smell

'puzzola ['puttsola] *sf* polecat

puzzo'lente [puttso'lɛnte] *ag* stinking

Q

qua *av* here; in ~ (*verso questa parte*) this way; da un anno in ~ for a year now; da quando in ~? since when?; per di ~ (*passare*) this way; al di ~ di (*fiume, strada*) on this side of; ~ dentro/fuori *etc* in/out here *etc*; *vedi anche* questo

qua'derno *sm* notebook; (*per scuola*) exercise book

qua'drante *sm* quadrant; (*di orologio*) face

qua'drare *vi* (*bilancio*) to balance, tally; (*descrizione*) to correspond; (*fig*): ~ a to please, be to one's liking ♦ *vt* (*MAT*) to square; non mi quadra I don't like it; **qua'drato, a** *ag* square; (*fig*: *equilibrato*) level-headed, sensible; (: *peg*) square ♦ *sm* (*MAT*) square; (*PUGILATO*) ring; 5 al quadrato 5 squared

qua'dretto *sm*: a ~i (*tessuto*) checked; (*foglio*) squared

quadri'foglio [kwadri'fɔʎʎo] *sm* four-leaf clover

'quadro *sm* (*pittura*) painting, picture; (*quadrato*) square; (*tabella*) table, chart; (*TECN*) board, panel; (*TEATRO*) scene; (*fig*: scena, spettacolo) sight; (: *descrizione*) outline, description; ~i *smpl* (*POL*) party organizers; (*MIL*) cadres; (*COMM*) managerial staff; (*CARTE*) diamonds

'quadruplo, a *ag, sm* quadruple

quaggiù [kwad'dʒu] *av* down here

'quaglia ['kwaʎʎa] *sf* quail

PAROLA CHIAVE

'qualche ['kwalke] *det* **1** some, a few; (*in interrogative*) any; **ho comprato ~ libro** I've bought some *o* a few books; **~ volta** sometimes; **hai ~ sigaretta?** have you any cigarettes?

2 (*uno*): **c'è ~ medico?** is there a doctor?; **in ~ modo** somehow

3 (*un certo, parecchio*) some; **un personaggio di ~ rilievo** a figure of some importance

4: **~ cosa** = qualcosa

qualche'duno [kwalke'duno] *pron* = qualcuno

qual'cosa *pron* something, (*in espressioni interrogative*) anything; **qualcos'altro** something else; **anything else**; **~ di nuovo** something new; **anything new**; **~ da mangiare** something to eat; **anything to eat**; **c'è ~ che non va?** is there something *o* anything wrong?

qual'cuno *pron* (*persona*) someone, somebody; (: *in espressioni interrogative*) anyone, anybody; (*alcuni*) some; **~ è favorevole a noi** some are on our side; **qualcun altro** someone *o* somebody else; **anyone** *o* anybody else

---

PAROLA CHIAVE

'quale (*spesso troncato in* **qual**) *det* **1** (*interrogativo*) what *o* which; (: *scegliendo tra due o più cose o persone*) which; **~ uomo/denaro?** what man/money?; **which man/money?**; **~i**

sono i tuoi programmi? what are your plans?; **~ stanza preferisci?** which room do you prefer?

2 (*relativo: come*): **il risultato fu ~ ci si aspettava** the result was as expected

3 (*esclamativo*) what; **~ disgrazia!** what bad luck!

◆ *pron* **1** (*interrogativo*) which; **~ dei due scegli?** which of the two do you want?

2 (*relativo*): **il(la) ~** (*persona: soggetto*) who; (: *oggetto, con preposizione*) whom; (*cosa*) which; (*possessivo*) whose; **suo padre, il ~ è avvocato, ...** his father, who is a lawyer, ...; **il signore con il ~ parlavo** the gentleman to whom I was speaking; **l'albergo al ~ ci siamo fermati** the hotel where we stayed *o* which we stayed at; **la signora della ~ ammiriamo la bellezza** the lady whose beauty we admire

3 (*relativo: in elenchi*) such as, like; **piante ~i l'edera** plants like *o* such as ivy; **~ sindaco di questa città** as mayor of this town

qua'lifica, che *sf* qualification; (*titolo*) title

qualifi'care *vt* to qualify; (*definire*): **~ qn/qc come** to describe sb/sth as; **~rsi** *vr* (*anche SPORT*) to qualify; **qualifica'tivo, a** *ag* qualifying; **gara di qualificazione** (*SPORT*) qualifying event

qualità *sf inv* quality; **in ~ di** in one's capacity as

qua'lora *cong* in case, if

qual'siasi *det inv* = qualunque

qua'lunque *det inv* any; (*quale che sia*) whatever; (*discriminativo*) whichever; (*posposto: mediocre*) poor, indifferent; ordinary; **mettiti un vestito ~** put on any old dress; **~ cosa** anything; **~ cosa accada** whatever happens; **a ~ costo** at any cost, whatever the cost; **l'uomo ~** the man in the street; **~ persona** anyone, anybody

'quando *cong, av* when; ~ sarò ricco when I'm rich; **da** ~ *(dacché)* since; *(interrogativo):* **da** ~ **sei qui?** how long have you been here?; **quand'anche** even if

quantità *sf inv* quantity; *(gran numero):* **una** ~ **di** a great deal of; a lot of; **in grande** ~ in large quantities; **quanti'tativo** *sm (COMM)* amount, quantity

---

PAROLA CHIAVE

'quanto, a *det* **1** *(interrogativo: quantità)* how much; *(: numero)* how many; ~ **pane/denaro?** how much bread/money?; ~ **libri/ragazzi?** how many books/boys?; ~ **tempo?** how long?; ~ **i anni hai?** how old are you?

2 *(esclamativo):* ~e **storie!** what a lot of nonsense!; ~ **tempo sprecato!** what a waste of time!

3 *(relativo: quantità)* as much as; *(: numero)* as many ... as; **ho ~ denaro mi occorre** I have as much money as I need; **prendi ~i libri vuoi** take as many books as you like

♦ *pron* **1** *(interrogativo: quantità)* how much; *(: numero)* how many; *(: tempo)* how long; ~ **mi dai?** how much will you give me?; ~**i me ne hai portati?** how many did you bring me?; **da** ~ **sei qui?** how long have you been here?; ~**i ne abbiamo oggi?** what's the date today?

2 *(relativo: quantità)* as much as; *(: numero)* as many as; **farò** ~ **posso** I'll do as much as I can; **possono venire** ~**i sono stati invitati** all those who have been invited can come

♦ *av* **1** *(interrogativo: con ag, av)* how; *(: con vb)* how much; ~ **stanco ti sembrava?** how tired did he seem to you?; ~ **corre la tua moto?** how fast can your motorbike go?; ~ **costa?** how much does it cost?; **quant'è?** how much is it?

2 *(esclamativo: con ag, av)* how; *(: con vb)* how much; ~ **sono felice!**

how happy I am!; **sapessi** ~ **siamo camminato!** if you knew how far we've walked!; **studierò** ~ **posso** I'll study as much as *o* all I can; ~ **prima** as soon as possible

3: **in** ~ *(in qualità di)* as; *(perché, per il fatto che)* as, since; **(in)** ~ **a** *(per ciò che riguarda)* as for, as regards

4: **per** ~ *(nonostante, anche se)* however; **per** ~ **si sforzi, non ce la farà** try as he may, he won't manage it; **per** ~ **sia brava, fa degli errori** however good she may be, she makes mistakes; **per** ~ **io sappia** as far as I know

quan'tunque *cong* although, though

qua'ranta *num* forty

quaran'tena *sf* quarantine

quaran'tesimo, a *num* fortieth

quaran'tina *sf*: **una** ~ **(di)** about forty

qua'resima *sf*: **la** ~ Lent

'quarta *sf (AUT)* fourth (gear); *vedi anche* **quarto**

quar'tetto *sm* quartet(te)

quar'tiere *sm* district, area; *(MIL)* quarters *pl*; ~ **generale** headquarters *pl*, HQ

'quarto, a *ag* fourth ♦ *sm* fourth; *(quarta parte)* quarter; **le 6 e un** ~ a quarter past six; ~ **d'ora** quarter of an hour; ~**i di finale** quarter final

'quarzo ['kwartso] *sm* quartz

'quasi *av* almost, nearly ♦ *cong (anche:* ~ **che)** as if; **(non)** ... ~ **mai** hardly ever; ~ ~ **me ne andrei** I've half a mind to leave

quas'sù *av* up here

'quatto, a *ag* crouched, squatting; *(silenzioso)* silent; ~ ~ very quietly; stealthily

quat'tordici [kwat'torditʃi] *num* fourteen

quat'trini *smpl* money *sg*, cash *sg*

'quattro *num* four; **in** ~ **e quatt'rotto** in less than no time; **quattro'cento** *num* four hundred ♦ *sm*: **il Quattrocento** the fifteenth century; **quattro'mila** *num* four thousand

'quello, a (*dav sm* quel +*C*, quell' +*V*, quello +*s impura, gn, pn, ps, x, z; pl* quei +*C*, quegli +*V o s impura, gn, pn, ps, x, z; dav sf* quella +*C*, quell' +*V; pl* quelle) *det that;* those *pl;* ~a casa that house; quegli uomini those men; voglio ~ la camicia (**lì** *o* **là**) I want that shirt

♦ *pron* **1** (*dimostrativo*) that (one); those (ones) *pl;* (*ciò*) that; conosci ~a? do you know that woman?; prendo ~ bianco I'll take the white one; chi è ~? who's that?; prendiamo ~ (**lì** *o* **là**) let's take that one (there)

2 (*relativo*): ~(a) che the one (who); (*cosa*) the one (which), the one (that); ~i(e) che *(persone)* those who; (*cose*) those which; è lui ~ che non voleva venire he's the one who didn't want to come; ho fatto ~ che potevo I did what I could

'quercia, ce ['kwɛrtʃa] *sf* oak (tree); (*legno*) oak

que'rela *sf* (*DIR*) (legal) action; **quere'lare** *vt* to bring an action against

que'sito *sm* question, query; problem

questio'nario *sm* questionnaire

questi'one *sf* problem, question; (*controversia*) issue; (*litigio*) quarrel; **in** ~ in question; **fuori di** ~ out of the question; **è** ~ **di tempo** it's a matter *o* question of time

'questo, a *det* **1** (*dimostrativo*) this; these *pl;* ~ **libro** (**qui** *o* **qua**) this book; **io prendo** ~ **cappotto, io quello** I'll take this coat, you take that one; **quest'oggi** today; ~a **sera** this evening

2 (*enfatico*): **non fatemi più prendere di** ~**e paure** don't frighten me

like that again

♦ *pron* (*dimostrativo*) this (one); these (ones) *pl;* (*ciò*) this; **prendo** ~ (**qui** *o* **qua**) I'll take this one; **preferisci** ~**i** *o* **quelli?** do you prefer these (ones) or those (ones)?; ~ **intendevo io** this is what I meant; **vengono Paolo e Luca:** ~ **da Roma,** quello **da Palermo** Paolo and Luca are coming: the former from Palermo, the latter from Rome

ques'tore *sm* ≈ chief constable (*BRIT*), ≈ police commissioner (*US*)

'questua *sf* collection of (alms)

ques'tura *sf* police headquarters *pl*

qui *av* here; **da** *o* **di** ~ from here; **di** ~ **in avanti** from now on; **di** ~ **a poco/una settimana** in a little while/a week's time; ~ **dentro/sopra/vicino** in/up/near here; *vedi* **questo**

quie'tanza [kwje'tantsa] *sf* receipt

quie'tare *vt* to calm, soothe

qui'ete *sf* quiet, quietness; calmness; stillness; peace

qui'eto, a *ag* quiet; (*notte*) calm, still; (*mare*) calm

'quindi *av* then ♦ *cong* therefore, so

'quindici ['kwinditʃi] *num* fifteen; ~ **giorni** a fortnight (*BRIT*), two weeks

quindi'cina [kwindi'tʃina] *sf* (*serie*): **una** ~ (**di**) about fifteen; **fra una** ~ **di giorni** in a fortnight

quin'quennio *sm* period of five years

quin'tale *sm* quintal (*100 kg*)

'quinte *sfpl* (*TEATRO*) wings

'quinto, a *num* fifth

'quota *sf* (*parte*) quota, share; (*AER*) height, altitude; (*IPPICA*) odds *pl;* **prendere/perdere** ~ (*AER*) to gain/lose height *o* altitude; ~ **d'iscrizione** enrolment fee; (*ad un club*) membership fee

quo'tare *vt* (*BORSA*) to quote; **quotazi'one** *sf* quotation

quotidi'ano, a *ag* daily; (*banale*) everyday ♦ *sm* (*giornale*) daily (paper)

quozi'ente [kwot'tsjɛnte] *sm* (*MAT*) quotient; ~ **d'intelligenza** intelligence quotient, IQ

R

ra'barbaro *sm* rhubarb

'rabbia *sf* (*ira*) anger, rage; (*accanimento, furia*) fury; (*MED: idrofobia*) rabies *sg*

rab'bino *sm* rabbi

rabbi'oso, a *ag* angry, furious; (*facile all'ira*) quick-tempered; (*forze, acqua etc*) furious, raging; (*MED*) rabid, mad

rabbo'nire *vt* to calm down; ~rsi *vr* to calm down

rabbrivi'dire *vi* to shudder, shiver

rabbui'arsi *vr* to grow dark

raccapez'zarsi [rakkapet'tsarsi] *vr*: **non** ~ to be at a loss

raccapricci'ante [rakkaprit'tʃante] *ag* horrifying

raccatta'palle *sm inv* (*SPORT*) ballboy

raccat'tare *vt* to pick up

rac'chetta [rak'ketta] *sf* (*per tennis*) racket; (*per ping-pong*) bat; ~ **da neve** snowshoe; ~ **da sci** ski stick

racchi'udere [rak'kjudere] *vt* to contain; **racchi'uso, a** *pp di* racchiudere

rac'cogliere [rak'kɔʎʎere] *vt* to collect; (*raccattare*) to pick up; (*frutti, fiori*) to pick, pluck; (*AGR*) to harvest; (*approvazione, voti*) to win; (*profughi*) to take in; ~rsi *vr* to gather; (*fig*) to gather one's thoughts; to meditate; **raccogli'mento** *sm* meditation; **raccogli'tore** *sm* (*cartella*) folder, binder; **raccoglitore a fogli mobili** looseleaf binder

rac'colta *sf* collecting *no pl*; collection; (*AGR*) harvesting *no pl*, gathering *no pl*; harvest, crop; (*adunata*) gathering

rac'colto, a *pp di* raccogliere ♦ *ag* (*persona: pensoso*) pensive; (*luogo: appartato*) secluded, quiet ♦ *sm* (*AGR*) crop, harvest

raccoman'dare *vt* to recommend; (*affidare*) to entrust; (*esortare*): ~ **a qn di non fare** to tell o warn sb not to do; ~rsi *vr*: ~rsi **a qn** to commend o.s. to sb; **mi raccomando!** don't forget!; **raccoman'data** *sf* (*anche: lettera raccomandata*) recorded-delivery letter; **raccomandazi'one** *sf* recommendation

raccon'tare *vt*: ~ **(a qn)** (*dire*) to tell (sb); (*narrare*) to relate to (sb), tell (sb) about; **rac'conto** *sm* telling *no pl*, relating *no pl*; (*fatto raccontato*) story, tale

raccorci'are [rakkor'tʃare] *vt* to shorten

rac'cordo *sm* (*TECN: giunzione*) connection, joint; (*AUT: di autostrada*) slip road (*BRIT*), entrance (*o* exit) ramp (*US*); ~ **anulare** (*AUT*) ring road (*BRIT*), beltway (*US*)

ra'chitico, a, ci, che [ra'kitiko] *ag* suffering from rickets; (*fig*) scraggy, scrawny

racimo'lare [ratʃimo'lare] *vt* (*fig*) to scrape together, glean

'rada *sf* (*natural*) harbour

'radar *sm* radar

raddol'cire [raddol'tʃire] *vt* (*persona, carattere*) to soften; ~rsi *vr* (*tempo*) to grow milder; (*persona*) to soften, mellow

raddoppi'are *vt, vi* to double

raddriz'zare [raddrit'tsare] *vt* to straighten; (*fig: correggere*) to put straight, correct

'radere *vt* (*barba*) to shave off; (*mento*) to shave; (*fig: rasentare*) to graze; to skim; ~rsi *vr* to shave (o.s.); ~ **al suolo** to raze to the ground

radi'are *vt* to strike off

radia'tore *sm* radiator

radiazi'one *sf* (*FISICA*) radiation; (*cancellazione*) striking off

radi'cale *ag* radical ♦ *sm* (*LING*) root

ra'dicchio [ra'dikkjo] sm chicory

ra'dice [ra'ditʃe] sf root

'radio sf inv radio ♦ sm (CHIM) radium; **radioat'tivo, a** ag radioactive; **radiodiffusi'one** sf (radio) broadcasting; **radiogra'fare** vt to X-ray; **radiogra'fia** sf radiography; (foto) X-ray photograph

radi'oso, a ag radiant

radiostazi'one [radjostat'tsjone] sf radio station

'rado, a ag (capelli) sparse, thin; (visite) infrequent; **di ~** rarely

radu'nare vt, to gather, assemble; **~rsi** vr to gather, assemble

ra'dura sf clearing

raffazzo'nare [raffattso'nare] vt to patch up

raf'fermo, a ag stale

'raffica, che sf (METEOR) gust of wind; (di colpi: scarica) burst of gunfire

raffigu'rare vt to represent

raffi'nare vt to refine; **raffina'tezza** sf refinement; **raffi'nato, a** ag refined; **raffine'ria** sf refinery

raffor'zare [raffor'tsare] vt to reinforce

raffredda'mento sm cooling

raffred'dare vt to cool; (fig) to dampen, have a cooling effect on; **~rsi** vr to grow cool o cold; (prendere un raffreddore) to catch a cold; (fig) to cool (off)

raffred'dato, a ag (MED): **essere ~** to have a cold

raffred'dore sm (MED) cold

raf'fronto sm comparison

'rafia sf (fibra) raffia

ra'gazzo, a [ra'gattso] sm/f boy/girl; (fam: fidanzato) boyfriend/girlfriend

raggi'ante [rad'dʒante] ag radiant, shining

'raggio ['raddʒo] sm (di sole etc) ray; (MAT, distanza) radius; (di ruota etc) spoke; **~ d'azione** range; **~i X** X-rays

raggi'rare [raddʒi'rare] vt to take in, trick; **rag'giro** sm trick

raggi'ungere [rad'dʒundʒere] vt to

reach; (persona: riprendere) to catch up (with); (bersaglio) to hit; (fig: meta) to achieve; **raggi'unto, a** pp di raggiungere

raggomi'tolarsi vr to curl up

raggranel'lare vt to scrape together

raggrup'pare vt to group (together)

raggu'aglio [rag'gwaʎʎo] sm comparison; (informazione, relazione) piece of information

ragguar'devole ag (degno di riguardo) distinguished, notable; (notevole: somma) considerable

ragiona'mento [radʒona'mento] sm reasoning no pl; arguing no pl; argument

ragio'nare [radʒo'nare] vi (usare la ragione) to reason; (discorrere): **~ (di)** to argue (about)

ragi'one [ra'dʒone] sf reason; (dimostrazione, prova) argument; reason; (diritto) right; **aver ~** to be right; **aver ~ di qn** to get the better of sb; **dare ~ a qn** to agree with sb; to prove sb right; **perdere la ~** to become insane; (fig) to take leave of one's senses; **in ~ di** at the rate of; to the amount of; according to; **a o con ~** rightly, justly; **~ sociale** (COMM) corporate name; **a ragion veduta** after due consideration

ragione'ria [radʒone'ria] sf accountancy; accounts department

ragio'nevole [radʒo'nevole] ag reasonable

ragioni'ere, a [radʒo'njɛre] sm/f accountant

ragli'are [raʎ'ʎare] vi to bray

ragna'tela [raɲɲa'tela] sf cobweb, spider's web

'ragno ['raɲɲo] sm spider

ragù sm inv (CUC) meat sauce; stew

RAI-TV [raiti'vu] sigla f = **Radio televisione italiana**

rallegra'menti smpl congratulations

ralle'grare vt to cheer up; **~rsi** vr to cheer up; (provare allegrezza) to rejoice; **~rsi con qn** to congratulate sb

rallen'tare vt to slow down; (fig) to lessen, slacken ♦ vi to slow down

raman'zina [raman'dzina] sf lecture, telling-off

'rame sm (CHIM) copper

rammari'carsi vr: ~ (di) (rincrescersi) to be sorry (about), regret; (lamentarsi) to complain (about); **ram'marico, chi** sm regret

rammen'dare vt to mend; (calza) to darn; **ram'mendo** sm mending no pl; darning no pl; mend; darn

rammen'tare vt to remember, recall; (richiamare alla memoria): ~ qc a qn to remind sb of sth; ~rsi vr: ~rsi (di qc) to remember (sth)

rammol'lire vt to soften ♦ vi (anche: ~rsi) to go soft

'ramo sm branch

ramo'scello [ramoʃ'ʃɛllo] sm twig

'rampa sf flight (of stairs); ~ di lancio launching pad

rampi'cante ag (BOT) climbing

ram'pone sm harpoon; (ALPINISMO) crampon

'rana sf frog

'rancido, a ['rantʃido] ag rancid

ran'core sm rancour, resentment

ran'dagio, a, gi, gie o **ge** [ran'dadʒo] ag (gatto, cane) stray

ran'dello sm club, cudgel

'rango, ghi sm (condizione sociale, MIL: riga) rank

rannicchi'arsi [rannik'kjarsi] vr to crouch, huddle

rannuvo'larsi vr to cloud over, become overcast

ra'nocchio [ra'nɔkkjo] sm (edible) frog

'rantolo sm wheeze; (di agonizzanti) death rattle

'rapa sf (BOT) turnip

ra'pace [ra'patʃe] ag (animale) predatory; (fig) rapacious, grasping ♦ sm bird of prey

ra'pare vt (capelli) to crop, cut very short

'rapida sf (di fiume) rapid; vedi anche **rapido**

rapida'mente av quickly, rapidly

rapidità sf speed

'rapido, a ag fast; (esame, occhiata) quick, rapid ♦ sm (FERR) express (train)

rapi'mento sm kidnapping; (fig) rapture

ra'pina sf robbery; ~ a mano armata armed robbery; **rapi'nare** vt to rob; **rapina'tore, 'trice** sm/f robber

ra'pire vt (cose) to steal; (persone) to kidnap; (fig) to enrapture, delight; **rapi'tore, 'trice** sm/f kidnapper

rappor'tare vt (confrontare) to compare; (riprodurre) to reproduce

rap'porto sm (resoconto) report; (legame) relationship; (MAT, TECN) ratio; ~i smpl (fra persone, paesi) relations; ~i sessuali sexual intercourse sg

rap'prendersi vr to coagulate, clot; (latte) to curdle

rappre'saglia [rappre'saʎʎa] sf reprisal, retaliation

rappresen'tante sm/f representative; **rappresen'tanza** sf delegation, deputation; (COMM: ufficio, sede) agency

rappresen'tare vt to represent; (TEATRO) to perform; **rappresentazi'one** sf representation; performing no pl; (spettacolo) performance

rap'preso, a pp di **rapprendere**

rapso'dia sf rhapsody

rara'mente av seldom, rarely

rare'fatto, a ag rarefied

'raro, a ag rare

ra'sare vt (barba etc) to shave off; (siepi, erba) to trim, cut; ~rsi vr to shave (o.s.)

raschi'are [ras'kjare] vt to scrape; (macchia, fango) to scrape off ♦ vi to clear one's throat

rasen'tare vt (andar rasente) to keep close to; (sfiorare) to skim along (o over); (fig) to border on

ra'sente prep: ~ (a) close to, very near

'raso, a pp di **radere** ♦ ag (barba) shaved; (capelli) cropped; (con misure *di capacità*) level; (*pieno: bicchiere*) full to the brim ♦ *sm* (*tessuto*) satin; ~ **terra** close to the ground; **un cucchiaio** ~ a level spoonful

ra'soio *sm* razor; ~ **elettrico** electric shaver *o* razor

ras'segna [ras'seɲɲa] *sf* (MIL) inspection, review; (*esame*) inspection; (*resoconto*) review, survey; (*pubblicazione letteraria etc*) review; (*mostra*) exhibition, show; **passare in** ~ (MIL, *fig*) to review

rasse'gnare [rasseɲ'ɲare] *vt*: ~ **le dimissioni** to resign, hand in one's resignation; ~**rsi** *vr* (*accettare*): ~**rsi (a qc/a fare)** to resign o.s. (to sth/to doing); **rassegnazi'one** *sf* resignation

rasse'renarsi *vr* (*tempo*) to clear up

rasset'tare *vt* to tidy, put in order; (*aggiustare*) to repair, mend

rassicu'rare *vt* to reassure

rasso'dare *vt* to harden, stiffen

rassomigli'anza [rassomiʎ'ʎantsa] *sf* resemblance

rassomigli'are [rassomiʎ'ʎare] *vi*: ~ **a** to resemble, look like

rastrel'lare *vt* to rake; (*fig: perlustrare*) to comb

rastrelli'era *sf* rack; (*per piatti*) dish rack

ras'trello *sm* rake

'rata *sf* (*quota*) instalment; **pagare a** ~**e** to pay by instalments *o* on hire purchase (BRIT)

ratifi'care *vt* (DIR) to ratify

'ratto *sm* (DIR) abduction; (ZOOL) rat

rattop'pare *vt* to patch; **rat'toppo** *sm* patching *no pl*; patch

rattrap'pire *vt* to make stiff; ~**rsi** *vr* to be stiff

rattris'tare *vt* to sadden; ~**rsi** *vr* to become sad

'rauco, a, chi, che *ag* hoarse

rava'nello *sm* radish

ravi'oli *smpl* ravioli *sg*

ravve'dersi *vr* to mend one's ways

ravvici'nare [ravvitʃi'nare] *vt* (*avvicinare*): ~ **qc** to bring sth nearer to; (: *due tubi*) to bring closer together; (*riconciliare*) to reconcile, bring together

ravvi'sare *vt* to recognize

ravvi'vare *vt* to revive; (*fig*) to brighten up, enliven; ~**rsi** *vr* to revive; to brighten up

razio'cinio [ratsjo'tʃinjo] *sm* reasoning *no pl*; reason; (*buon senso*) common sense

razio'nale [rattsjo'nale] *ag* rational

razio'nare [rattsjo'nare] *vt* to ration

razi'one [rat'tsjone] *sf* ration; (*porzione*) portion, share

'razza ['rattsa] *sf* race; (ZOOL) breed; (*discendenza, stirpe*) stock, race; (*sorta*) sort, kind

raz'zia [rat'tsia] *sf* raid, foray

razzi'ale [rat'tsjale] *ag* racial

raz'zismo [rat'tsizmo] *sm* racism, racialism

raz'zista, i, e [rat'tsista] *ag*, *smf* racist, racialist

razzo'lare [rattso'lare] *vi* (*galline*) to scratch about

'razzo ['raddzo] *sm* rocket

re *sm inv* king; (MUS) D; (: *solfeggiando la scala*) re

rea'gire [rea'dʒire] *vi* to react

re'ale *ag* real; (*di, da re*) royal ♦ *sm*: **il** ~ reality; **rea'lismo** *sm* realism; **rea'lista, i, e** *smf* realist; (POL) royalist

realiz'zare [realid'dzare] *vt* (*progetto etc*) to realize, carry out; (*sogno, desiderio*) to realize, fulfil; (*scopo*) to achieve; (COMM: *titoli etc*) to realize; (CALCIO *etc*) to score; ~**rsi** *vr* to be realized; **realizzazi'one** *sf* realization; fulfilment; achievement

real'mente *av* really, actually

realtà *sf inv* reality

re'ato *sm* offence

reat'tore *sm* (FISICA) reactor; (AER: *aereo*) jet; (: *motore*) jet engine

reazio'nario, a [reattsjo'narjo] *ag* (POL) reactionary

reazi'one [reat'tsjone] *sf* reaction

recapi'tare *vt* to deliver

re'capito *sm* (*indirizzo*) address; (*consegna*) delivery

re'care *vt* (*portare*) to bring; (*avere su di sé*) to carry, bear; (*cagionare*) to cause, bring; **~rsi** *vr* to go

re'cedere [re'tʃɛdere] *vi* to withdraw

recensi'one [retʃen'sjone] *sf* review; **recen'sire** *vt* to review

re'cente [re'tʃɛnte] *ag* recent; **di ~** recently; **recente'mente** *av* recently

recessi'one [retʃes'sjone] *sf* (ECON) recession

re'cidere [re'tʃidere] *vt* to cut off, chop off

reci'divo, a [retʃi'divo] *smf* (DIR) second (*o habitual*) offender, recidivist

re'cinto [re'tʃinto] *sm* enclosure; (*ciò che recinge*) fence; surrounding wall

recipi'ente [retʃi'pjɛnte] *sm* container

re'ciproco, a, ci, che [re'tʃiproko] *ag* reciprocal

re'ciso, a [re'tʃizo] *pp di* recidere

'recita [ˈrɛtʃita] *sf* performance

reci'tare [retʃi'tare] *vt* (*poesia, lezione*) to recite; (*dramma*) to perform; (*ruolo*) to play *o* act (the part of); **recitazi'one** *sf* recitation; (*di attore*) acting

recla'mare *vi* to complain ♦ *vt* (*richiedere*) to demand

ré'clame [reˈklam] *sf inv* advertising *no pl*; advertisement, advert (BRIT), ad (*fam*)

re'clamo *sm* complaint

reclusi'one (DIR) imprisonment

'recluta *sf* recruit; **reclu'tare** *vt* to recruit

re'condito, a *ag* secluded; (*fig*) secret, hidden

recriminazi'one [rekriminat'tsjone] *sf* recrimination

recrude'scenza [rekrudeʃˈʃentsa] *sf* fresh outbreak

recupe'rare *vt* = ricuperare

redargu'ire *vt* to rebuke

re'datto, a *pp di* redigere; **re'dattore, 'trice** *smf* (STAMPA) editor; (: *di articolo*) writer; (*di dizionario etc*) compiler; **redattore capo** chief editor; **redazi'one** *sf* editing; writing; (*sede*) editorial office(s); (*personale*) editorial staff; (*versione*) version

reddi'tizio, a [reddi'tittsjo] *ag* profitable

'reddito *sm* income; (*dello Stato*) revenue; (*di un capitale*) yield

re'dento, a *pp di* redimere

redenzi'one [reden'tsjone] *sf* redemption

re'digere [re'didʒere] *vt* to write; (*contratto*) to draw up

re'dimere *vt* to deliver; (REL) to redeem

'redini *sfpl* reins

'reduce [ˈrɛdutʃe] *ag*: ~ **da** returning from, back from ♦ *smf* survivor

refe'rendum *sm inv* referendum

refe'renza [refe'rɛntsa] *sf* reference

re'ferto *sm* medical report

refet'torio *sm* refectory

refrat'tario, a *ag* refractory

refrige'rare [refridʒe'rare] *vt* to refrigerate; (*rinfrescare*) to cool, refresh

rega'lare *vt* to give (as a present), make a present of

re'gale *ag* regal

re'galo *sm* gift, present

re'gata *sf* regatta

reg'gente [red'dʒɛnte] *smf* regent

'reggere [ˈreddʒere] *vt* (*tenere*) to hold; (*sostenere*) to support, bear, hold up; (*portare*) to carry, bear; (*resistere*) to withstand; (*dirigere: impresa*) to manage, run; (*governare*) to rule, govern; (LING) to take, be followed by ♦ *vi* (*resistere*): ~ **a** to stand up to, hold out against; (*sopportare*): ~ **a** to stand; (*durare*) to last; (*fig: teoria etc*) to hold water; **~rsi** *vr* (*stare ritto*) to stand; (*fig: dominarsi*) to control o.s.; **~rsi sulle gambe in piedi** to stand up

'reggia, ge ['rɛddʒa] sf royal palace
reggi'calze [reddʒi'kaltse] sm inv suspender belt
reggi'mento [reddʒi'mento] sm (MIL) regiment
reggi'petto [reddʒi'pɛtto] sm = **reggiseno**
reggi'seno [reddʒi'seno] sm bra
re'gia, 'gie [re'dʒia] sf (TV, CINEMA etc) direction
re'gime [re'dʒime] sm (POL) regime; (DIR: aureo, patrimoniale etc) system; (MED) diet; (TECN) (engine) speed
re'gina [re'dʒina] sf queen
'regio, a, gi, gie ['rɛdʒo] ag royal
regio'nale [redʒo'nale] ag regional
regi'one [re'dʒone] sf region; (territorio) region, district, area
re'gista, i, e [re'dʒista] smf (TV, CINEMA etc) director
regis'trare [redʒis'trare] vt (AMM) to register; (COMM) to enter; (notare) to note, take note of; (canzone, conversazione, sog: strumento di misura) to record; (mettere a punto) to adjust, regulate; (bagagli) to check in; **registra'tore** sm (strumento) recorder; (magnetofono) tape recorder; **registratore di cassa** cash register; **registrazi'one** sf recording; (AMM) registration; (COMM) entry; (di bagagli) check-in
re'gistro [re'dʒistro] sm (libro) register; ledger; logbook; (DIR) registry; (MUS, TECN) register
re'gnare [reɲ'ɲare] vi to reign, rule; (fig) to reign
'regno ['reɲɲo] sm kingdom; (periodo) reign; (fig) realm; **il ~ animale/vegetale** the animal/vegetable kingdom; **il R~ Unito** the United Kingdom
'regola sf rule; **a ~ d'arte** duly; perfectly; **in ~** in order
regola'mento sm (complesso di norme) regulations pl; (di debito) settlement; **~ di conti** (fig) settling of scores
rego'lare ag regular; (in regola: do-manda) in order, lawful ♦ vt to regulate, control; (apparecchio) to adjust, regulate; (questione, conto, debito) to settle; **~rsi** vr (moderarsi); **~rsi nel bere/nello spendere** to control one's drinking/spending; (comportarsi) to behave, act; **regolarità** sf inv regularity
'regolo sm ruler; **~ calcolatore** slide rule
reinte'grare vt (energie) to recover; (in una carica) to reinstate
rela'tivo, a ag relative
relazi'one sf (fra cose, persone) relation(ship); (resoconto) report, account; **~i** sfpl (conoscenze) connections
rele'gare vt to banish; (fig) to relegate
religi'one [reli'dʒone] sf religion; **religi'oso, a** ag religious ♦ smf monk/nun
re'liquia sf relic
re'litto sm wreck; (fig) down-and-out
re'mare vi to row
remini'scenze [reminiʃ'ʃɛntse] sfpl reminiscences
remissi'one sf remission
remis'sivo, a ag submissive, compliant
'remo sm oar
re'moto, a ag remote
'rendere vt (ridare) to return, give back; (: saluto etc) to return; (produrre) to yield, bring in; (esprimere, tradurre) to render; (far diventare): **~ qc possibile** to make sth possible; **~ grazie a qn** to thank sb; **~rsi utile** to make o.s. useful; **~rsi conto di qc** to realize sth
rendi'conto sm (rapporto) report, account; (AMM, COMM) statement of account
rendi'mento sm (reddito) yield; (di manodopera, TECN) efficiency; (capacità di produrre) output; (di studenti) performance
'rendita sf (di individuo) private o unearned income; (COMM) revenue; **~ annua** annuity

'**rene** *sm* kidney

'**reni** *sfpl* back *sg*

reni'tente *ag* reluctant, unwilling; ~ ai consigli di qn unwilling to follow sb's advice; essere ~ alla leva (MIL) to fail to report for military service

'**renna** *sf* reindeer *inv*

'**Reno** *sm*: il ~ the Rhine

'**reo, a** *smf* (DIR) offender

re'parto *sm* department, section; (MIL) detachment

repel'lente *ag* repulsive

repen'taglio [repen'taʎʎo] *sm*: mettere a ~ to jeopardize, risk

repen'tino, a *ag* sudden, unexpected

repe'rire *vt* to find, trace

re'perto *sm* (ARCHEOLOGIA) find; (MED) report; (DIR: anche: ~ giudiziario) exhibit

reper'torio *sm* (TEATRO) repertory; (elenco) index, (alphabetical) list

'replica, che *sf* repetition; reply, answer; (obiezione) objection; (TEATRO, CINEMA) repeat performance; (copia) replica

repli'care *vt* (ripetere) to repeat; (rispondere) to answer, reply

repressi'one *sf* repression

re'presso, a *pp di* reprimere

re'primere *vt* to suppress, repress

re'pubblica, che *sf* republic; repubbli'cano, a *ag, smf* republican

repu'tare *vt* to consider, judge

reputazi'one [reputat'tsjone] *sf* reputation

'requie *sf*: senza ~ unceasingly

requi'sire *vt* to requisition

requi'sito *sm* requirement

requisizi'one [rekwizit'tsjone] *sf* requisition

'resa (l'arrendersi) surrender; (restituzione, rendimento) return; ~ dei conti rendering of accounts; (fig) day of reckoning

resi'dente *ag* resident; resi'denza *sf* residence; residenzi'ale *ag* residential

re'siduo, a *ag* residual, remaining

♦ *sm* remainder; (CHIM) residue

'**resina** *sf* resin

resis'tente *ag* (che resiste): ~ a resistant to; (forte) strong; (duraturo) long-lasting, durable; ~ al caldo heat-resistant; resis'tenza *sf* resistance; (di persona: fisica) stamina, endurance; (: mentale) endurance, resistance

re'sistere *vi* to resist; ~ a (assalto, tentazioni) to resist; (dolore, soggetto: pianta) to withstand; (non patir danno) to be resistant to; resis'tito, a *pp di* resistere

'**reso, a** *pp di* rendere

reso'conto *sm* report, account

res'pingere [res'pindʒere] *vt* to drive back, repel; (rifiutare) to reject; (INS: bocciare) to fail; res'pinto, a *pp di* respingere

respi'rare *vi* to breathe; (fig) to get one's breath; to breathe again ♦ *vt* to breathe (in), inhale; respira'tore *sm* respirator; respirazi'one *sf* breathing; respirazione artificiale artificial respiration; res'piro *sm* breathing *no pl*; (singolo atto) breath; (fig) respite, rest; mandare un respiro di sollievo to give a sigh of relief

respon'sabile *ag* responsible ♦ *sm/ f* person responsible; (capo) person in charge; ~ di responsible for; (DIR) liable for; responsabilità *sf inv* responsibility; (legale) liability

res'ponso *sm* answer

'**ressa** *sf* crowd, throng

res'tare *vi* (rimanere) to remain, stay; (diventare): ~ orfano/cieco to become o be left an orphan/become blind; (trovarsi): ~ sorpreso to be surprised; (avanzare) to be left, remain; ~ d'accordo to agree; non resta più niente there's nothing left; restano pochi giorni there are only a few days left

restau'rare *vt* to restore; restaurazi'one *sf* (POL) restoration; res'tauro *sm* (di edifici etc) restoration

res'tio, a, 'tii, 'tie *ag* restive; (*persona*): ~ a reluctant to

restitu'ire *vt* to return, give back; (*energie, forze*) to restore

'resto *sm* remainder, rest; (*denaro*) change; (*MAT*) remainder; ~**i** *smpl* (*di cibo*) leftovers; (*di città*) remains; **del** ~ moreover, besides; ~**i mortali** (*mortal*) remains

res'tringere [res'trindʒere] *vt* to reduce; (*vestito*) to take in; (*stoffa*) to shrink; (*fig*) to restrict, limit; ~**rsi** *vr* (*strada*) to narrow; (*stoffa*) to shrink; **restrizi'one** *sf* restriction

'rete *sf* net; (*fig*) trap, snare; (*di recinzione*) wire netting; (*AUT, FERR, di spionaggio etc*) network; **segnare una** ~ (*CALCIO*) to score a goal; ~ **del letto** (sprung) bed base

reti'cente [reti'tʃɛnte] *ag* reticent

retico'lato *sm* grid; (*rete metallica*) wire netting; (*di filo spinato*) barbed wire (fence)

'retina (*ANAT*) retina

re'torica *sf* rhetoric

re'torico, a, ci, che *ag* rhetorical

retribu'ire *vt* to pay; (*premiare*) to reward; **retribuzi'one** *sf* payment; reward

'retro *sm inv* back ♦ *av* (*dietro*): **vedi** ~ see over(leaf)

retro'cedere [retro'tʃɛdere] *vi* to withdraw ♦ *vt* (*CALCIO*) to relegate; (*MIL*) to degrade

re'trogrado, a *ag* (*fig*) reactionary, backward-looking

retro'marcia [retro'martʃa] *sf* (*AUT*) reverse; (: *dispositivo*) reverse gear

retro'scena [retroʃ'ʃɛna] *sm inv* (*TEATRO*) backstage; **i** ~ (*fig*) the behind-the-scenes activities

retrospet'tivo, a *ag* retrospective

retrovi'sore *sm* (*AUT*) (rear-view) mirror

'retta *sf* (*MAT*) straight line; (*di convitto*) charge for bed and board; (*fig: ascolto*): **dar** ~ **a** to listen to, pay attention to

rettango'lare *ag* rectangular

ret'tangolo, a *ag* right-angled ♦ *sm* rectangle

ret'tifica, che *sf* rectification, correction

rettifi'care *vt* (*curva*) to straighten; (*fig*) to rectify, correct

'rettile *sm* reptile

retti'lineo, a *ag* rectilinear

retti'tudine *sf* rectitude, uprightness

'retto, a *pp* *di* **reggere** ♦ *ag* straight; (*MAT*): **angolo** ~ right angle; (*onesto*) honest, upright; (*giusto, esatto*) correct, proper, right

ret'tore *sm* (*REL*) rector; (*di università*) ≈ chancellor

reuma'tismo *sm* rheumatism

reve'rendo, a *ag*: **il** ~ **padre Belli** the Reverend Father Belli

rever'sibile *ag* reversible

revisio'nare *vt* (*conti*) to audit; (*TECN*) to overhaul, service; (*DIR: processo*) to review; (*componimento*) to revise

revisi'one *sf* auditing *no pl*; audit; servicing *no pl*; overhaul; review; revision

revi'sore *sm*: ~ **di conti/bozze** auditor/proofreader

'revoca *sf* revocation

revo'care *vt* to revoke

re'volver *sm inv* revolver

riabili'tare *vt* to rehabilitate; (*fig*) to restore to favour

rial'zare [rial'tsare] *vt* to raise, lift; (*alzare di più*) to heighten, raise; (*aumentare: prezzi*) to increase, raise ♦ *vi* (*prezzi*) to rise, increase; **ri'alzo** *sm* (*di prezzi*) increase, rise; (*sporgenza*) rise

rianimazi'one [rianimat'tsjone] *sf* (*MED*) resuscitation; **centro di** ~ intensive care unit

riap'pendere *vt* to rehang; (*TEL*) to hang up

ria'prire *vt* to reopen, open again; ~**rsi** *vr* to reopen, open again

ri'armo *sm* (*MIL*) rearmament

riasset'tare *vt* (*stanza*) to tidy (up)

rias'setto *sm* (*di stanza etc*) rearrangement; (*ordinamento*) reorganization

rias'sumere vt (riprendere) to resume; (impiegare di nuovo) to re-employ; (sintetizzare) to summarize; **rias'sunto, a** pp di **riassumere** ♦ sm summary

ria'vere vt to have again; (avere indietro) to get back; (riacquistare) to recover; **~rsi** vr to recover

riba'dire vt (fig) to confirm

ri'balta sf flap; (TEATRO: proscenio) front of the stage; (: apparecchio d'illuminazione) footlights pl; (fig) limelight

ribal'tabile ag (sedile) tip-up

ribal'tare vt, vi (anche: ~rsi) to turn over, tip over

ribas'sare vt to lower, bring down ♦ vi to come down, fall; **ri'basso** sm reduction, fall

ri'battere vt to return, hit back; (confutare) to refute; **~** che to retort that

ribel'larsi vr: **~ (a)** to rebel (against); **ri'belle** ag (soldati) rebel; (ragazzo) rebellious ♦ sm/f rebel; **ribelli'one** sf rebellion

'ribes sm inv currant; **~ nero** blackcurrant; **~ rosso** redcurrant

ribol'lire vi (fermentare) to ferment; (fare bolle) to bubble, boil; (fig) to seethe

ri'brezzo [ri'breddzo] sm disgust, loathing; **far ~ a** to disgust

ribut'tante ag disgusting, revolting

rica'dere vi to fall again; (scendere a terra, fig: nel peccato etc) to fall back; (vestiti, capelli etc) to hang down; (riversarsi: fatiche, colpe): **~ su** to fall on; **rica'duta** sf (MED) relapse

rical'care vt (disegni) to trace; (fig) to follow faithfully

rica'mare vt to embroider

ricam'biare vt to change again; (contraccambiare) to repay, return; **ri'cambio** sm exchange, return; (FISIOL) metabolism; **ricambi** smpl (TECN) spare parts

ri'camo sm embroidery

ricapito'lare vt to recapitulate, sum up

ricari'care vt (arma, macchina fotografica) to reload; (pipa) to refill; (orologio) to rewind; (batteria) to recharge

ricat'tare vt to blackmail; **ricat'tatore, 'trice** sm/f blackmailer; **ri'catto** sm blackmail

rica'vare vt (estrarre) to draw out, extract; (ottenere) to obtain, gain; **ri'cavo** sm proceeds pl

ric'chezza [rik'kettsa] sf wealth; (fig) richness; **~e** sfpl (beni) wealth sg, riches

'riccio, a ['rittʃo] ag curly ♦ sm (ZOOL) hedgehog; (: anche: **~ di mare**) sea urchin; **'ricciolo** sm curl; **ricci'uto, a** ag curly

'ricco, a, chi, che ag rich; (persona, paese) rich, wealthy ♦ sm/f rich man/woman; **i ~chi** the rich; **~ di** full of; rich in

ri'cerca, che [ri'tʃerka] sf search; (indagine) investigation, inquiry; (studio): **la ~** research; **una ~** piece of research

ricer'care [ritʃer'kare] vt (motivi, cause) to look for, try to determine; (successo, piacere) to pursue; (onore, gloria) to seek; **ricer'cato, a** ag (apprezzato) much sought-after; (affettato) studied, affected ♦ sm/f (POLIZIA) wanted man/woman

ri'cetta [ri'tʃetta] sf (MED) prescription; (CUC) recipe

ricettazi'one [ritʃettat'tsjone] sf (DIR) receiving (stolen goods)

ri'cevere [ri'tʃevere] vt to receive; (stipendio, lettera) to get, receive; (accogliere: ospite) to welcome; (vedere: cliente, rappresentante etc) to see; **ricevi'mento** sm receiving no pl; (trattenimento) reception; **rice-vi'tore** sm (TECN) receiver; **ricevito'ria** sf lottery o pools office; **rice'vuta** sf receipt; **ricevuta fiscale** receipt for tax purposes; **ricezi'one** sf (RADIO, TV) reception

richia'mare vt (chia-

mare indietro, ritelefonare) to call back; *(ambasciatore, truppe)* to recall; *(rimproverare)* to reprimand; *(attirare)* to attract, draw; ~**rsi a** *(riferirsi a)* to refer to; **richi'amo** *sm* call; recall; reprimand; attraction

richi'edere [ri'kjɛdere] *vt* to ask again for; *(chiedere indietro)*: ~ **qc** to ask for sth back; *(chiedere: per sapere)* to ask; *(: per avere)* to ask for; *(AMM: documenti)* to apply for; *(esigere)* to need, require; **richi'esta** *sf (domanda)* request; *(AMM)* application, request; *(esigenza)* demand, request; **a richiesta** on request; **ri-chi'esto, a** *pp di* **richiedere**

rici'clare [ritʃi'klare] *vt* to recycle

'ricino ['ritʃino] *sm*: **olio di** ~ castor oil

riconizi'one [rikonnit'tsjone] *sf (MIL)* reconnaissance; *(DIR)* recognition, acknowledgement

ricominci'are [rikomin'tʃare] *vt, vi* to start again, begin again

ricom'pensa *sf* reward

ricompen'sare *vt* to reward

riconcili'are [rikontʃi'ljare] *vt* to reconcile; ~**rsi** *vr* to be reconciled; **riconciliazi'one** *sf* reconciliation

ricono'scente [rikono'ʃʃɛnte] *ag* grateful; **ricono'scenza** *sf* gratitude

rico'noscere [riko'noʃʃere] *vt* to recognize; *(DIR: figlio, debito)* to acknowledge; *(ammettere: errore)* to admit, acknowledge; **riconosci'mento** *sm* recognition; acknowledgement; *(identificazione)* identification; **riconosci'uto, a** *pp di* **riconoscere**

ricopi'are *vt* to copy

rico'prire *vt (coprire)* to cover; *(occupare: carica)* to hold

ricor'dare *vt* to remember, recall; *(richiamare alla memoria)*: ~ **qc a qn** to remind sb of sth; ~**rsi** *vr*; ~**rsi (di)** to remember; ~**rsi di qc/ di aver fatto** to remember sth/ having done

ri'cordo *sm* memory; *(regalo)* keep-

sake, souvenir; *(di viaggio)* souvenir; ~**i** *smpl (memorie)* memoirs

ricor'rente *ag* recurrent, recurring; **ricor'renza** *sf* recurrence; *(festività)* anniversary

ri'correre *vi (ripetersi)* to recur; ~ **a** *(rivolgersi)* to turn to; *(: DIR)* to appeal to; *(servirsi di)* to have recourse to; **ri'corso, a** *pp di* **ricorrere ♦** *sm* recurrence; *(DIR)* appeal; **far ricorso a** = **ricorrere a**

ricostitu'ente *ag (MED)*: **cura** ~ tonic

ricostru'ire *vt (casa)* to rebuild; *(fatti)* to reconstruct; **ricostruzi'one** *sf* rebuilding *no pl*; reconstruction

ri'cotta *sf* soft white unsalted cheese made from sheep's milk

ricove'rare *vt* to give shelter to; ~ **qn in ospedale** to admit sb to hospital

ri'covero *sm* shelter, refuge; *(MIL)* shelter; *(MED)* admission (to hospital)

ricre'are *vt* to recreate; *(rinvigorire)* to restore; *(fig: distrarre)* to amuse **ricreazi'one** [rikreat'tsjone] *sf* recreation, entertainment; *(INS)* break

ri'credersi *vr* to change one's mind

ricupe'rare *vt (rientrare in possesso di)* to recover, get back; *(tempo perduto)* to make up for; *(NAUT)* to salvage; *(: naufraghi)* to rescue; *(delinquente)* to rehabilitate; ~ **lo svantaggio** *(SPORT)* to close the gap

ridacchi'are [ridak'kjare] *vi* to snigger

ri'dare *vt* to return, give back

'ridere *vi* to laugh; *(deridere, beffare)*: ~ **di** to laugh at, make fun of

ri'detto, a *pp di* **ridire**

ri'dicolo, a *ag* ridiculous, absurd

ridimensio'nare *vt* to reorganize; *(fig)* to see in the right perspective

ri'dire *vt* to repeat; *(criticare)* to find fault with; to object to; **trova sempre qualcosa da** ~ **he** always manages to find fault

ridon'dante *ag* redundant

ri'dotto, a pp di **ridurre**

ri'durre vt (anche CHIM, MAT) to reduce; (prezzo, spese) to cut, reduce; (accorciare: opera letteraria) to abridge; (: RADIO, TV) to adapt; **ridursi** vr (diminuirsi) to be reduced, shrink; **ridursi a** to be reduced to; **ridursi pelle e ossa** to be reduced to skin and bone; **ridu-zi'one** sf reduction; abridgement; adaptation

riem'pire vt to fill (up); (modulo) to fill in o out; **~rsi** vr to fill (up); (mangiare troppo) to stuff o.s.; **~ qc di** to fill sth (up) with

rien'tranza [rien'trantsa] sf recess; indentation

rien'trare vi (entrare di nuovo) to go (o come) back in; (tornare) to return; (fare una rientranza) to go in, curve inwards; to be indented; (ri-guardare): **~ in** to be included among, form part of; **ri'entro** sm (ritorno) return; (di astronave) re-entry

riepilo'gare vt to summarize ♦ vi to recapitulate

ri'fare vt to do again; (ricostruire) to make again; (nodo) to tie again, do up again; (imitare) to imitate, copy; **~rsi** vr (risarcirsi): **~rsi di** to make up for; (vendicarsi): **~rsi di qc su qn** to get one's own back on sb for sth; (riferirsi): **~rsi a** to go back to; to follow; **~ il letto** to make the bed; **~rsi una vita** to make a new life for o.s.; **ri'fatto, a** pp di **rifare**

riferi'mento sm reference; in o con **~ a** with reference to

rife'rire vt (riportare) to report; (ascrivere): **~ qc a** to attribute sth to ♦ vi to do a report; **~rsi** vr: **~rsi a** to refer to

rifi'nire vt to finish off, put the finishing touches to; **rifini'tura** sf finishing touch; **rifiniture** sfpl (di mobile, auto) finish sg

rifiu'tare vt to refuse; **~ di fare** to refuse to do; **ri'fiuto** sm refusal; **rifiuti** smpl (spazzatura) rubbish sg,

refuse sg

riflessi'one sf (FISICA, meditazione) reflection; (il pensare) thought, reflection; (osservazione) remark

rifles'sivo, a ag (persona) thoughtful, reflective; (LING) reflexive

ri'flesso, a pp di **riflettere** ♦ sm (di luce, rispecchiamento) reflection; (FISIOL) reflex; **di o per ~** indirectly

ri'flettere vt to reflect ♦ vi to think; **~rsi** vr to be reflected; **~ su** to think over

riflet'tore sm reflector; (proiettore) floodlight; searchlight

ri'flusso sm flowing back; (della marea) ebb; **un'epoca di ~** an era of nostalgia

ri'fondere vt (rimborsare) to refund, repay

ri'forma sf reform; **la R~** (REL) the Reformation

rifor'mare vt to re-form; (cambiare, innovare) to reform; (MIL: recluta) to declare unfit for service; (: soldato) to invalid out, discharge; **rifor-ma'torio** sm (DIR) community home (BRIT), reformatory (US)

riforni'mento sm supplying, providing; restocking; **~i** smpl (provviste) supplies, provisions

rifor'nire vt (provvedere): **~ di** to supply o provide with; (fornire di nuovo: casa etc) to restock

rifrazi'one [rifrat'tsjone] sf refraction

rifug'gire [rifud'dʒire] vi to escape again; (fig): **~ da** to shun

rifugi'arsi [rifu'dʒarsi] vr to take refuge; **rifugi'ato, a** sm/f refugee

ri'fugio [ri'fudʒo] sm refuge, shelter; (in montagna) shelter; **~ antiaereo** air-raid shelter

'riga, ghe sf line; (striscia) stripe; (di persone, cose) line, row; (regolo) ruler; (scriminatura) parting; **mettersi in ~** to line up; **a ~ghe** (foglio) lined; (vestito) striped

ri'gagnolo [ri'gaɲɲolo] sm rivulet

ri'gare vt (foglio) to rule ♦ vi: **~ di-**

ritto (fig) to toe the line

rigatti'ere sm junk dealer

riget'tare [ridʒet'tare] vt (gettare indietro) to throw back; (fig: respingere) to reject; (vomitare) to bring o throw up; **ri'getto** sm (anche MED) rejection

rigidità [ridʒidi'ta] sf rigidity; stiffness; severity, rigours pl; strictness

'rigido, a ['ridʒido] ag rigid, stiff; (membra etc: indurite) stiff; (METEOR) harsh, severe; (fig) strict

rigi'rare [ridʒi'rare] vt to turn; ~rsi vr to turn round; (nel letto) to turn over; ~ qc tra le mani to turn sth over in one's hands; ~ il discorso to change the subject

'rigo, ghi sm line; (MUS) stave, stave

rigogli'oso, a [rigoʎ'ʎoso] ag (pianta) luxuriant; (fig: commercio, sviluppo) thriving

ri'gonfio, a ag swollen

ri'gore sm (METEOR) harshness, rigours pl; (fig) severity, strictness; (anche: calcio di ~) penalty; **di** ~ compulsory; **a rigor di termini** strictly speaking; **rigo'roso, a** ag (severo: persona, ordine) strict; (preciso) rigorous

rigover'nare vt to wash (up)

riguar'dare vt to look at again; (considerare) to regard, consider; (concernere) to regard, concern; ~**rsi** vr (aver cura di sé) to look after o.s.

rigu'ardo sm (attenzione) care; (considerazione) regard, respect; ~ a concerning, with regard to; **non aver ~i nell'agire/nel parlare** to act/speak freely

rilasci'are [rilaʃ'ʃare] vt (rimettere in libertà) to release; (AMM: documenti) to issue; **ri'lascio** sm release; issue

rilas'sare vt to relax; ~**rsi** vr to relax; (fig: disciplina) to become slack

rile'gare vt (libro) to bind; **rile'gatura** sf binding

ri'leggere [ri'ledₔere] vt to reread,

read again; (rivedere) to read over

ri'lento: a ~ av slowly

rileva'mento sm (topografico, statistico) survey; (NAUT) bearing

rile'vante ag considerable; important

rile'vare vt (ricavare) to find; (notare) to notice; (mettere in evidenza) to point out; (venire a conoscere: notizia) to learn; (raccogliere: dati) to gather, collect; (TOPOGRAFIA) to survey; (MIL) to relieve; (COMM) to take over

rili'evo sm (ARTE, GEO) relief; (fig: rilevanza) importance; (osservazione) point, remark; (TOPOGRAFIA) survey; **dar** ~ **a** o **mettere in** ~ **qc** (fig) to bring sth out, highlight sth

rilut'tante ag reluctant; **rilut'tanza** sf reluctance

'rima sf rhyme; (verso) verse

riman'dare vt to send again; (restituire, rinviare) to send back, return; (differire) to postpone; ~ **qc** (a) to postpone sth o put sth off (till); (fare riferimento): ~ **qn a** to refer sb to; **essere rimandato** (INS) to have to repeat one's exams; **ri'mando** sm (rinvio) return; (dilazione) postponement; (riferimento) cross-reference

rima'nente ag remaining ♦ sm rest, remainder; **i** ~**i** (persone) the rest of them, the others; **rima'nenza** sf rest, remainder; **rimanenze** sfpl (COMM) unsold stock sg

rima'nere vi (restare) to remain, stay; (avanzare) to be left, remain; (restare stupito) to be amazed; (restare, mancare): **rimangono poche settimane a Pasqua** there are only a few weeks left till Easter; **rimane da vedere se** it remains to be seen whether; (diventare): ~ **vedovo** to be a widower; (trovarsi): ~ **confuso/sorpreso** to be confused/surprised

ri'mare vt, vi to rhyme

rimargi'nare [rimardʒi'nare] vt, vi (anche: ~rsi) to heal

ri'masto, a pp di rimanere

rima'sugli [rima'suʎʎi] smpl leftovers

rimbal'zare [rimbal'tsare] vi to bounce back, rebound; (proiettile) to ricochet; **rim'balzo** sm rebound; ricochet

rimbam'bito, a ag senile, in one's dotage

rimboc'care vt (orlo) to turn up; (coperta) to tuck in; (maniche, pantaloni) to turn o roll up

rimbom'bare vi to resound

rimbor'sare vt to pay back, repay; **rim'borso** sm repayment

rime'diare vi: ~ a to remedy ♦ vt (fam: procurarsi) to get o scrape together

ri'medio sm (medicina) medicine; (cura, fig) remedy, cure

rimesco'lare vt to mix quickly, stir well; (carte) to shuffle; **sentirsi ~ il sangue** (per paura) to feel one's blood run cold; (per rabbia) to feel one's blood boil

ri'messa sf (locale: per veicoli) garage; (: per aerei) hangar; (COMM: di merce) consignment; (: di denaro) remittance; (TENNIS) return; (CALCIO: anche: ~ in gioco) throw-in

ri'messo, a pp di rimettere

ri'mettere vt (mettere di nuovo) to put back; (indossare di nuovo): ~ qc to put sth back on, put sth on again; (restituire) to return, give back; (affidare) to entrust; (: decisione) to refer; (condonare) to remit; (COMM: merci) to deliver; (: denaro) to remit; (vomitare) to bring up; (perdere: anche: rimetterci) to lose; ~rsi al bello (tempo) to clear up; ~rsi in salute to get better, recover one's health

'rimmel ® sm inv mascara

rimoder'nare vt to modernize

rimon'tare vt (meccanismo) to reassemble; (: tenda) to put up again ♦ vi (salire di nuovo): ~ in (macchina, treno) to get back into; (SPORT) to close the gap

rimorchi'are [rimor'kjare] vt to tow; (fig: ragazza) to pick up; **rimorchia'tore** sm (NAUT) tug(boat)

ri'morchio [ri'mɔrkjo] sm tow; (veicolo) trailer

ri'morso sm remorse

rimozi'one [rimot'tsjone] sf removal; (da un impiego) dismissal; (PSIC) repression

rim'pasto sm (POL) reshuffle

rimpatri'are vi to return home ♦ vt to repatriate; **rim'patrio** sm repatriation

rimpi'angere [rim'pjandʒere] vt to regret; (persona) to miss; **rimpi'anto, a** pp di rimpiangere ♦ sm regret

rimpiat'tino sm hide-and-seek

rimpiaz'zare [rimpjat'tsare] vt to replace

rimpiccio'lire [rimpittʃo'lire] vt to make smaller ♦ vi (anche: ~rsi) to become smaller

rimpin'zare [rimpin'tsare] vt: ~ di to cram o stuff with

rimprove'rare vt to rebuke, reprimand; **rim'provero** sm rebuke, reprimand

rimugi'nare [rimudʒi'nare] vt (fig) to turn over in one's mind

rimunerazi'one [rimunerat'tsjone] sf remuneration; (premio) reward

rimu'overe vt to remove; (destituire) to dismiss

Rinasci'mento [rinaʃʃi'mento] sm: **il ~** the Renaissance

ri'nascita [ri'naʃʃita] sf rebirth, revival

rincal'zare [rinkal'tsare] vt (palo, albero) to support, prop up; (lenzuola) to tuck in

rinca'rare vt to increase the price of ♦ vi to go up, become more expensive

rinca'sare vi to go home

rinchi'udere [rin'kjudere] vt to shut (o lock) up; ~**rsi** vr: ~**rsi in** to shut o.s. up in; ~**rsi in se stesso** to withdraw into o.s.; **rinchi'uso, a** pp di rinchiudere

rin'correre *vt* to chase, run after; **rin'corsa** *sf* short run; **rin'corso, a** *pp di* **rincorrere**

rin'crescere [rin'kreʃʃere] *vb impers:* **mi rincresce che/di non poter fare** I'm sorry that/I can't do, I regret that/being unable to do; **rincresci'mento** *sm* regret; **rincresci'uto, a** *pp di* **rincrescere**

rincu'lare *vi* to draw back; *(arma)* to recoil

rinfacci'are [rinfat'tʃare] *vt (fig):* ~ **qc a qn** to throw sth in sb's face

rinfor'zare [rinfor'tsare] *vt* to reinforce, strengthen ♦ *vi (anche: ~rsi)* to grow stronger; **rin'forzo** *sm:* **mettere un rinforzo a** to strengthen; **di rinforzo** *(asse, sbarra)* strengthening; *(esercito)* supporting; *(personale)* extra, additional; **rinforzi** *smpl (MIL)* reinforcements

rinfran'care *vt* to encourage, reassure

rinfres'care *vt (atmosfera, temperatura)* to cool (down); *(abito, pareti)* to freshen up ♦ *vi (tempo)* to grow cooler; **~rsi** *vr (ristorarsi)* to refresh o.s.; *(lavarsi)* to freshen up; **rin'fresco, schi** *sm (festa)* party; **rinfreschi** *smpl* refreshments

rin'fusa *sf:* **alla** ~ in confusion, higgledy-piggledy

ringhi'are [rin'gjare] *vi* to growl, snarl

ringhi'era [rin'gjɛra] *sf* railing; *(delle scale)* banister(s *pl*)

ringiova'nire [rindʒova'nire] *vt (sog: vestito, acconciatura etc):* ~ **qn** to make sb look younger; *(: vacanze etc)* to rejuvenate ♦ *vi (anche: ~rsi)* to become (o look) younger

ringrazia'mento [ringrattsja'mento] *sm* thanks *pl*

ringrazi'are [ringrat'tsjare] *vt* to thank; ~ **qn di qc** to thank sb for sth

rinne'gare *vt (fede)* to renounce; *(figlio)* to disown, repudiate; **rin-negato, a** *sm/f* renegade

rinnova'mento *sm* renewal; *(eco-nomico)* revival

rinno'vare *vt* to renew; *(ripetere)* to repeat, renew; **rin'novo** *sm (di contratto)* renewal; **"chiuso per rinnovo dei locali"** "closed for alterations"

rinoce'ronte [rinotʃe'ronte] *sm* rhinoceros

rino'mato, a *ag* renowned, celebrated

rinsal'dare *vt* to strengthen

rintoc'care *vi (campana)* to toll; *(orologio)* to strike

rintracci'are [rintrat'tʃare] *vt* to track down

rintro'nare *vi* to boom, roar ♦ *vt (assordare)* to deafen; *(stordire)* to stun

ri'nuncia [ri'nuntʃa] *etc* = **rinunzia**

ri'nunzia [ri'nuntsja] *sf* renunciation

rinunzi'are [rinun'tsjare] *vi:* ~ **a** to give up, renounce

rinve'nire *vt* to find, recover; *(scoprire)* to discover, find out ♦ *vi (riprendere i sensi)* to come round; *(riprendere l'aspetto naturale)* to revive

rinvi'are *vt (rimandare indietro)* to send back, return; *(differire):* ~ **qc (a)** to postpone sth *o* put sth off (till); to adjourn sth (till); *(fare un\ rimando):* ~ **qn a** to refer sb to

rinvigo'rire *vt* to strengthen

rin'vio, 'vii *sm (rimando)* return; *(differimento)* postponement; *(: di seduta)* adjournment; *(in un testo)* cross-reference

ri'one *sm* district, quarter

riordi'nare *vt (rimettere in ordine)* to tidy; *(riorganizzare)* to reorganize

riorganiz'zare [riorganid'dzare] *vt* to reorganize

ripa'gare *vt* to repay

ripa'rare *vt (proteggere)* to protect, defend; *(correggere: male, torto)* to make up for; *(: errore)* to put right; *(aggiustare)* to repair ♦ *vi (mettere rimedio):* ~ **a** to make up for; **~rsi** *vr (rifugiarsi)* to take refuge *o* shelter; **riparazi'one** *sf (di un torto)* reparation; (di guasto, scarpe) repairing no pl; repair; (risarcimento) compensation

ri'paro sm (protezione) shelter, protection; (rimedio) remedy

ripar'tire vt (dividere) to divide up; (distribuire) to share out ♦ vi to set off again; to leave again

ripas'sare vi to come (o go) back ♦ vt (scritto, lezione) to go over (again)

ripen'sare vi to think; (cambiare pensiero) to change one's mind; (tornare col pensiero): ~ a to recall

ripercu'otersi vr: ~ su (fig) to have repercussions on

ripercussi'one sf (fig): avere una ~ o delle ~i su to have repercussions on

ripes'care vt (pesce) to catch again; (persona, cosa) to fish out; (fig: ritrovare) to dig out

ri'petere vt to repeat; (ripassare) to go over; **ripetizi'one** sf repetition; (di lezione) revision; **ripetizioni** sfpl (INS) private tutoring o coaching sg

ripi'ano sm (GEO) terrace; (di mobile) shelf

ri'picca sf: per ~ out of spite

'ripido, a ag steep

ripie'gare vt to refold; (piegare più volte) to fold (up) ♦ vi (MIL) to retreat, fall back; (fig: accontentarsi): ~ su to make do with; **ripi'ego, ghi** sm expedient

ripi'eno, a ag full; (CUC) stuffed; (: panino) filled ♦ sm (CUC) stuffing

ri'porre vt (porre al suo posto) to put back, replace; (mettere via) to put away; (fiducia, speranza): ~ qc in qn to place o put sth in sth

ripor'tare vt (portare indietro) to bring (o take) back; (riferire) to report; (citare) to quote; (ricevere) to receive, get; (vittoria) to gain; (successo) to have; (MAT) to carry; ~rsi a (anche fig) to refer to; (riferirsi a) to refer to; ~ danni to suffer damage

ripo'sare vt (bicchiere, valigia) to put down; (dare sollievo) to rest ♦ vi to rest; ~rsi vr to rest; **ri'poso** sm rest; (MIL): **riposo!** at ease!; **a riposo** (in pensione) retired; **giorno di riposo** day off

ripos'tiglio [ripos'tiλλo] sm lumberroom

ri'posto, a pp di **riporre**

ri'prendere vt (prigioniero, fortezza) to recapture; (prendere indietro) to take back; (ricominciare: lavoro) to resume; (andare a prendere) to fetch, come back for; (assumere di nuovo: impiegati) to take on again, re-employ; (rimproverare) to tell off; (restringere: abito) to take in; (CINEMA) to shoot; ~rsi vr to recover; (correggersi) to correct o.s.; **ri'presa** sf recapture; resumption; (economica, da malattia, emozione) recovery; (AUT) acceleration no pl; (TEATRO, CINEMA) rerun; (CINEMA: presa) shooting no pl; shot; (SPORT) second half; (: PUGILATO) round; **a più riprese** on several occasions, several times; **ripreso, a** pp di **riprendere**

ripristi'nare vt to restore

ripro'durre vt to reproduce; **riprodursi** vr (BIOL) to reproduce; (riformarsi) to form again; **riproduzi'one** sf reproduction; **riproduzione vietata** all rights reserved

ripudi'are vt to repudiate, disown

ripu'gnante [ripun'nante] ag disgusting, repulsive

ripu'gnare [ripun'nare] vi: ~ a qn to repel o disgust sb

ripu'lire vt to clean up; (sog: ladri) to clean out; (perfezionare) to polish, refine

ri'quadro sm square; (ARCHIT) panel

ri'saia sf paddy field

risa'lire vi (ritornare in su) to go back up; ~ a (ritornare con la mente) to go back to; (datare da) to date back to, go back to

risal'tare vi (fig: distinguersi) to stand out; (ARCHIT) to project, jut out; **ri'salto** sm prominence; (sporgenza) projection; **mettere** o **porre in risalto** to make sth stand out

risa'nare vt (guarire) to heal, cure; (palude) to reclaim; (economia) to improve; (bilancio) to reorganize

risa'puto, a ag: è ~ che ... everyone knows that ..., it is common knowledge that ...

risarci'mento [risartʃi'mento] sm: ~ (di) compensation (for)

risar'cire [risar'tʃire] vt (cose) to pay compensation for; (persona): ~ qn di qc to compensate sb for sth

ri'sata sf laugh

riscalda'mento sm heating; ~ **centrale** central heating

riscal'dare vt (scaldare) to heat; (: mani, persona) to warm; (minestra) to reheat; ~**rsi** vr to warm up

riscat'tare vt (prigioniero) to ransom, pay a ransom for; (DIR) to redeem; ~**rsi** vr (da disonore) to redeem o.s.; **ris'catto** sm ransom; redemption

rischia'rare [riskja'rare] vt (illuminare) to light up; (colore) to make lighter; ~**rsi** vr (tempo) to clear up; (cielo) to clear; (fig: volto) to brighten up; ~**rsi la voce** to clear one's throat

rischi'are [ris'kjare] vt to risk ♦ vi: ~ **di fare qc** to risk o run the risk of doing sth

'rischio ['riskjo] sm risk; **rischi'oso, a** ag risky, dangerous

riscia'cquare [riʃʃa'kware] vt to rinse

riscon'trare vt (confrontare: due cose) to compare; (esaminare) to check, verify; (rilevare) to find; **ris'contro** sm comparison; check, verification; (AMM: lettera di risposta) reply

ris'cossa sf (riconquista) recovery, reconquest; vedi anche **riscosso**

riscossi'one sf collection

ris'cosso, a pp di **riscuotere**

ris'cuotere vt (ritirare una somma dovuta) to collect; (: stipendio) to

draw, collect; (assegno) to cash; (fig: successo etc) to win, earn; ~**rsi** vr: ~**rsi (da)** to shake o.s. (out of), rouse o.s. (from)

risenti'mento sm resentment

risen'tire vt to hear again; (provare) to feel ♦ vi: ~ **di** to feel (o show) the effects of; ~**rsi** vr: ~**rsi di** o **per** to take offence at, resent; **risen'tito, a** ag resentful

ri'serbo sm reserve

ri'serva sf reserve; (di caccia, pesca) preserve; (restrizione, di indigeni) reservation; **di** ~ (provviste etc) in reserve

riser'vare vt (tenere in serbo) to keep, put aside; (prenotare) to book, reserve; ~**rsi** vr: ~**rsi di fare qc** to intend to do sth; **riser'vato, a** ag (prenotato, fig: persona) reserved; (confidenziale) confidential; **riserva'tezza** sf reserve

risi'edere vi: ~ **a** o **in** to reside in

'risma sf (di carta) ream; (fig) kind, sort

'riso (pl(f) ~**a**: il ridere; risa: un ~ a laugh; il ~ laughter; (pianta) rice ♦ pp di **ridere**

riso'lino sm snigger

ri'solto, a pp di **risolvere**

risolu'tezza [risolu'tettsa] sf determination

riso'luto, a ag determined, resolute

risoluzi'one [risolut'tsjone] sf solving no pl; (MAT) solution; (decisione, di immagine) resolution

ri'solvere vt (difficoltà, controversia) to resolve; (problema) to solve; (decidere): ~ **di fare** to resolve to do; ~**rsi** vr (decidersi): ~**rsi a fare** to make up one's mind to do; (andare a finire): ~**rsi in** to end up, turn out; ~**rsi in nulla** to come to nothing

riso'nanza [riso'nantsa] sf resonance; **aver vasta** ~ (fig: fatto etc) to be known far and wide

riso'nare vt, vi = **risuonare**

ri'sorgere [ri'sordʒere] vi to rise again; **risorgi'mento** sm revival; il

Risorgimento *(STORIA)* the Risorgimento

ri'sorsa *sf* expedient, resort; **~e** *sfpl (naturali, finanziarie etc)* resources; **persona piena di ~e** resourceful person

ri'sorto, a *pp di* risorgere

ri'sotto *sm (CUC)* risotto

risparmi'are *vt* to save; *(non uccidere)* to spare ♦ *vi* to save; **~ qc a qn** to spare sb sth

ris'parmio *sm* saving *no pl*; *(denaro)* savings *pl*

rispec'chiare [rispek'kjare] *vt* to reflect

rispet'tabile *ag* respectable

rispet'tare *vt* to respect; **farsi ~** to command respect

rispet'tivo, a *ag* respective

ris'petto *sm* respect; **~i** *smpl (saluti)* respects, regards; **~a** *(in paragone a)* compared to; *(in relazione a)* as regards, as for; **rispet'toso, a** *ag* respectful

ris'plendere *vi* to shine

ris'pondere *vi* to answer, reply; *(freni)* to respond; **~ a** *(domanda)* to answer, reply to; *(persona)* to answer; *(invito)* to reply to; *(provocazione, sog: veicolo, apparecchio)* to respond to; *(corrispondere a)* to correspond to; *(: speranze, bisogno)* to answer; **~ di** to answer for; **ris'posta** *sf* answer, reply; **in risposta a** in reply to; **risposto, a** *pp di* rispondere

'rissa *sf* brawl

ristabi'lire *vt* to re-establish, restore; *(persona: sog: riposo etc)* to restore to health; **~rsi** *vr* to recover

rista'gnare [ristaɲ'ɲare] *vi (acqua)* to become stagnant; *(sangue)* to cease flowing; *(fig: industria)* to stagnate; **ris'tagno** *sm* stagnation

ris'tampa *sf* reprinting *no pl*; reprint

risto'rante *sm* restaurant

risto'rarsi *vr* to have something to eat and drink; *(riposarsi)* to rest, have a rest; **ris'toro** *sm (bevanda,* *cibo)* refreshment; **servizio di ristoro** *(FERR)* refreshments *pl*

ristret'tezza [ristret'tettsa] *sf (strettezza)* narrowness; *(fig: scarsezza)* scarcity, lack; *(: meschinità)* meanness; **~e** *sfpl (povertà)* financial straits

ris'tretto, a *pp di* restringere ♦ *ag (racchiuso)* enclosed, hemmed in; *(angusto)* narrow; *(limitato)*: **~ (a)** restricted o limited (to); *(CUC: brodo)* thick; *(: caffè)* extra strong

risucchi'are [risuk'kjare] *vt* to suck in

risul'tare *vi (dimostrarsi)* to prove (to be), turn out (to be); *(riuscire)*: **~ vincitore** to emerge as the winner; **~ da** *(provenire)* to result from, be the result of; **mi risulta che ...** I understand that ...; **non mi risulta** not as far as I know; **risul'tato** *sm* result

risuo'nare *vi (rimbombare)* to resound

risurrezi'one [risurret'tsjone] *sf (REL)* resurrection

risusci'tare [risuʃʃi'tare] *vt* to resuscitate, restore to life; *(fig)* to revive, bring back ♦ *vi* to rise (from the dead)

ris'veglio [riz'veʎʎo] *sm* waking up; *(fig)* revival

ris'volto *sm (di giacca)* lapel; *(di pantaloni)* turn-up; *(di manica)* cuff; *(di tasca)* flap; *(di libro)* inside flap; *(fig)* implication

ritagli'are [ritaʎ'ʎare] *vt (tagliar via)* to cut out; **ri'taglio** *sm (di giornale)* cutting, clipping; *(di stoffa etc)* scrap; **nei ritagli di tempo** in one's spare time

ritar'dare *vi (persona, treno)* to be late; *(orologio)* to be slow ♦ *vt (rallentare)* to slow down; *(impedire)* to delay, hold up; *(differire)* to postpone, delay; **ritarda'tario, a** *smf* latecomer

ri'tardo *sm* delay; *(di persona aspettata)* lateness *no pl*; *(fig: mentale)* backwardness; **in ~** late

ri'tegno [ri'teɲɲo] *sm* restraint

rite'nere *vt* (*trattenere*) to hold back; (: *somma*) to deduct; (*giudicare*) to consider, believe; **rite'nuta** *sf* (*sul salario*) deduction

riti'rare *vt* to withdraw; (POL: *richiamare*) to recall; (*andare a prendere*: *pacco etc*) to collect, pick up; ~**rsi** *vr* to withdraw; (*da un'attività*) to retire; (*stoffa*) to shrink; (*marea*) to recede; **riti'rata** *sf* (MIL) retreat; (*latrina*) lavatory; **ri'tiro** *sm* withdrawal; recall; collection; (*luogo appartato*) retreat

'ritmo *sm* rhythm; (*fig*) rate; (: *della vita*) pace, tempo

'rito *sm* rite; **di** ~ usual, customary

ritoc'care *vt* (*disegno*, *fotografia*) to touch up; (*testo*) to alter; **ri'tocco, chi** *sm* touching up *no pl*; alteration

ritor'nare *vi* to return, go (*o* come) back; (*ripresentarsi*) to recur; (*ridiventare*): ~ **ricco** to become rich again ♦ *vt* (*restituire*) to return, give back

ritor'nello *sm* refrain

ri'torno *sm* return; **essere di** ~ to be back; **avere un** ~ **di fiamma** (AUT) to backfire; (*fig*: *persona*) to be back in love again

ritorsi'one *sf* retaliation

ritrarre *vt* (*trarre indietro*, *via*) to withdraw; (*distogliere*: *sguardo*) to turn away; (*rappresentare*) to portray, depict; (*ricavare*) to get, obtain

ritrat'tare *vt* (*disdire*) to retract, take back; (*trattare nuovamente*) to deal with again

ri'tratto, a *pp di* **ritrarre** ♦ *sm* portrait

ri'troso, a *ag* (*restio*) ~ **(a)** reluctant (to); (*schivo*) shy; **andare a** ~ to go backwards

ritro'vare *vt* to find; (*salute*) to regain; (*persona*) to find; to meet again; ~**rsi** *vr* (*essere, capitare*) to find o.s.; (*raccapezzarsi*) to find one's way; (*con senso reciproco*) to meet (again); **ri'trovo** *sm* meeting place; **ritrovo notturno** night club

'ritto, a *ag* (*in piedi*) standing, on one's feet; (*levato in alto*) erect, raised; (: *capelli*) standing on end; (*posto verticalmente*) upright

ritu'ale *ag, sm* ritual

riuni'one *sf* (*adunanza*) meeting; (*riconciliazione*) reunion

riu'nire *vt* (*ricongiungere*) to join (together); (*riconciliare*) to reunite, bring together (again); ~**rsi** *vr* (*adunarsi*) to meet; (*tornare a stare insieme*) to be reunited

riu'scire [riuʃ'ʃire] *vi* (*uscire di nuovo*) to go out again, go back out; (*aver esito*: *fatti, azioni*) to go, turn out; (*aver successo*) to succeed, be successful; (*essere, apparire*) to be; (*raggiungere il fine*) to make, manage, succeed; ~ **a fare qc** to manage to do *o* succeed in doing *o* be able to do sth; **questo mi riesce nuovo** this is new to me; **riu'scita** *sf* (*esito*) result, outcome; (*buon esito*) success

'riva *sf* (*di fiume*) bank; (*di lago, mare*) shore

ri'vale *smf* rival; **rivalità** *sf* rivalry

ri'valsa *sf* (*rivincita*) revenge; (*risarcimento*) compensation

rivalu'tare *vt* (ECON) to revalue

rivan'gare *vt* (*ricordi etc*) to dig up (again)

rive'dere *vt* to see again; (*ripassare*) to revise; (*verificare*) to check

rive'lare *vt* to reveal; (*divulgare*) to reveal, disclose; (*dare indizio*) to reveal, show; ~**rsi** *vr* (*manifestarsi*) to be revealed; ~**rsi onesto** *etc* to prove to be honest *etc*; **rivela'tore, trice** *ag* revealing ♦ *sm* (TECN) detector; (FOT) developer; **rivelazi'one** *sf* revelation

rivendi'care *vt* to claim, demand

riven'dita *sf* (*bottega*) retailer's (shop)

rivendi'tore, trice *smf* retailer; ~ **autorizzato** (COMM) authorized dealer

ri'verbero *sm* (*di luce, calore*) reflection; (*di suono*) reverberation

rive'renza [rive'rɛntsa] *sf* reverence;

(*inchino*) bow; curtsey

rive'rire *vt* (*rispettare*) to revere; (*salutare*) to pay one's respects to

river'sare *vt* (*anche fig*) to pour; ~rsi *vr* (*fig: persone*) to pour out

rivesti'mento *sm* covering; coating

rives'tire *vt* to dress again; (*ricoprire*) to cover; to coat; (*fig: carica*) to hold; ~rsi *vr* to get dressed again; to change (one's clothes)

rivi'era *sf* coast; **la ~ italiana** the Italian Riviera

ri'vincita [ri'vintʃita] *sf* (*SPORT*) return match; (*fig*) revenge

rivis'suto, a *pp di* **rivivere**

ri'vista *sf* review; (*periodico*) magazine, review; (*TEATRO*) revue; variety show

ri'vivere *vi* (*riacquistare forza*) to come alive again; (*tornare in uso*) to be revived ♦ *vt* to relive

ri'volgere [ri'vɔldʒere] *vt* (*attenzione, sguardo*) to turn, direct; (*parole*) to address; ~rsi *vr* to turn round; (*fig: dirigersi per informazioni*): ~rsi a to go and see, go and speak to; (: *ufficio*) to enquire at

ri'volta *sf* revolt, rebellion

rivol'tare *vt* to turn over; (*con l'interno all'esterno*) to turn inside out; (*disgustare: stomaco*) to upset, turn; ~rsi *vr* (*ribellarsi*) to rebel (against)

rivol'tella *sf* revolver

ri'volto, a *pp di* **rivolgere**

rivoluzio'nare [rivoluttsjo'nare] *vt* to revolutionize

rivoluzio'nario, a [rivoluttsjo'narjo] *ag, sm/f* revolutionary

rivoluzi'one [rivolut'tsjone] *sf* revolution

riz'zare [rit'tsare] *vt* to raise, erect; ~rsi *vr* to stand up; (*capelli*) to stand on end

'roba *sf* stuff, things *pl*; (*possessi, beni*) belongings *pl*, things *pl*, possessions *pl*; ~ **da mangiare** things *pl* to eat, food; ~ **da matti sheer madness** *o* lunacy

'robot *sm inv* robot

ro'busto, a *ag* robust, sturdy; (*solido: catena*) strong

'rocca, che *sf* fortress

rocca'forte *sf* stronghold

roc'chetto [rok'ketto] *sm* reel, spool

'roccia, ce ['rɔttʃa] *sf* rock; **fare ~** (*SPORT*) to go rock climbing; **roc'cioso, a** *ag* rocky

ro'daggio [ro'daddʒo] *sm* running (*BRIT*) *o* breaking (*US*) in; **in ~** running (*BRIT*) *o* breaking (*US*) in

'Rodano *sm*: **il ~** the Rhone

'rodere *vt* to gnaw (at); (*distruggere poco a poco*) to eat into

rodi'tore *sm* (*ZOOL*) rodent

rodo'dendro [rok'kletto] *sm* rhododendron

'rogna ['rɔŋŋa] *sf* (*MED*) scabies *sg*; (*fig*) bother, nuisance

ro'gnone [roŋ'ŋone] *sm* (*CUC*) kidney

'rogo, ghi *sm* (*per cadaveri*) (funeral) pyre; (*supplizio*): **il ~** the stake

rol'lio *sm* roll(ing)

'Roma *sf* Rome

Roma'nia *sf*: **la ~** Romania

ro'manico, a, ci, che *ag* Romanesque

ro'mano, a *ag, sm/f* Roman

romanti'cismo [romanti'tʃizmo] *sm* romanticism

ro'mantico, a, ci, che *ag* romantic

ro'manza [ro'mandza] *sf* (*MUS, LETTERATURA*) romance

roman'zesco, a, schi, sche [roman'dzesko] *ag* (*stile, personaggi*) fictional; (*fig*) storybook *cpd*

romanzi'ere [roman'dzjere] *sm* novelist

ro'manzo, a [ro'mandzo] *ag* (*LING*) romance *cpd* ♦ *sm* (*medievale*) romance; (*moderno*) novel; ~ **d'appendice** serial (story)

rom'bare *vi* to rumble, thunder, roar

'rombo *sm* rumble, thunder, roar; (*MAT*) rhombus; (*ZOOL*) turbot; brill

ro'meno, a *ag, sm/f, sm* = **ru-**

meno, a

'**rompere** *vt* to break; (*conversazione, fidanzamento*) to break off ♦ *vi* to break; ~**rsi** *vr* to break; **mi rompe le scatole** (*fam*) he (*o* she) is a pain in the neck; ~**rsi un braccio** to break an arm; **rompi'capo** *sm* worry, headache; (*indovinello*) puzzle; (*in enigmistica*) brainteaser; **rompighi'accio** *sm* (*NAUT*) icebreaker; **rompis'catole** (*fam*) *sm/f inv* pest, pain in the neck

'**ronda** *sf* (*MIL*) rounds *pl*, patrol

ron'della *sf* (*TECN*) washer

'**rondine** *sf* (*ZOOL*) swallow

ron'done *sm* (*ZOOL*) swift

ron'zare [ron'dzare] *vi* to buzz, hum

ron'zino [ron'dzino] *sm* (*peg: cavallo*) nag

'**rosa** ♦ *sf* rose ♦ *ag inv*, *sm* pink; **ro'saio** *sm* (*pianta*) rosebush, rose tree; (*giardino*) rose garden; **ro-'sario** *sm* (*REL*) rosary; **ro'sato, a** *ag* pink, rosy ♦ *sm* (*vino*) rosé (*wine*); **ro'seo, a** *ag* (*anche fig*) rosy

rosicchi'are [rosik'kjare] *vt* to gnaw (at); (*mangiucchiare*) to nibble (at)

rosma'rino *sm* rosemary

'**roso, a** *pp di* **rodere**

roso'lare *vt* (*CUC*) to brown

roso'lia *sf* (*MED*) German measles *sg*, rubella

ro'sone *sm* rosette; (*vetrata*) rose window

'**rospo** *sm* (*ZOOL*) toad

ros'setto *sm* (*per labbra*) lipstick; (*per guance*) rouge

'**rosso, a** *ag*, *sm*, *sm/f* red; **il mar R~** the Red Sea; ~ **d'uovo** egg yolk; **ros'sore** *sm* flush, blush

rosticce'ria [rostittʃe'ria] *sf* shop selling roast meat and other cooked food

ro'tabile *ag* (*percorribile*): **strada ~** roadway; (*FERR*): **materiale ~** rolling stock

ro'taia *sf* rut, track; (*FERR*) rail

ro'tare *vt*, *vi* to rotate; **rotazi'one** *sf* rotation

rote'are *vt*, *vi* to whirl; ~ **gli occhi** to roll one's eyes

ro'tella *sf* small wheel; (*di mobile*) castor

roto'lare *vt*, *vi* to roll; ~**rsi** *vr* to roll (*about*)

'**rotolo** *sm* roll; **andare a ~i** (*fig*) to go to rack and ruin

ro'tonda *sf* rotunda

ro'tondo, a *ag* round

ro'tore *sm* rotor

'**rotta** *sf* (*AER, NAUT*) course, route; (*MIL*) rout; **a ~ di collo** at breakneck speed; **essere in ~ con qn** to be on bad terms with sb

rot'tame *sm* fragment, scrap, broken bit; ~**i** *smpl* (*di nave, aereo etc*) wreckage *sg*

'**rotto, a** *pp di* **rompere** ♦ *ag* broken; (*calzoni*) torn, split; (*persona: pratico, resistente*): ~ **a** accustomed *o* inured to; **per il ~ della cuffia** by the skin of one's teeth

rot'tura *sf* breaking *no pl*; break; breaking off; (*MED*) fracture, break

rou'lotte [ru'lɔt] *sf* caravan

ro'vente *ag* red-hot

'**rovere** *sm* oak

rovesci'are [rovef'fare] *vt* (*versare in giù*) to pour; (: *accidentalmente*) to spill; (*capovolgere*) to turn upside down; (*gettare a terra*) to knock down; (: *fig: governo*) to overthrow; (*piegare all'indietro: testa*) to throw back; ~**rsi** *vr* (*sedia, macchina*) to overturn; (*barca*) to capsize; (*liquido*) to spill; (*fig: situazione*) to be reversed

ro'vescio, sci [ro'veffo] *sm* other side, wrong side; (*della mano*) back; (*di moneta*) reverse; (*pioggia*) sudden downpour; (*fig*) setback; (*MAGLIA: anche: punto ~*) purl (stitch); (*TENNIS*) backhand (stroke); **a ~** upside-down; inside-out; **capire qc a ~** to misunderstand sth

ro'vina *sf* ruin; **andare in ~** (*andare a pezzi*) to collapse; (*fig*) to go to rack and ruin

rovi'nare *vi* to collapse, fall down ♦

vt (far cadere giù: casa) to demolish; *(danneggiare, fig)* to ruin; **rovi'noso, a** *ag* disastrous; damaging; violent

rovis'tare *vt (casa)* to ransack; *(tasche)* to rummage in (o through)

'rovo *sm (BOT)* blackberry bush, bramble bush

'rozzo, a ['roddzo] *ag* rough, coarse

'ruba *sf:* andare a ~ to sell like hot cakes

ru'bare *vt* to steal; ~ qc a qn to steal sth from sb

rubi'netto *sm* tap, faucet (US)

ru'bino *sm* ruby

ru'brica, che *sf (STAMPA)* column; *(quadernetto)* index book; address book

'rude *ag* tough, rough

'rudere *sm (rovina)* ruins *pl*

rudimen'tale *ag* rudimentary, basic

rudi'menti *smpl* rudiments; basic principles; basic knowledge *sg*

ruffi'ano *sm* pimp

'ruga, ghe *sf* wrinkle

'ruggine ['ruddʒine] *sf* rust

rug'gire [rud'dʒire] *vi* to roar

rugi'ada [ru'dʒada] *sf* dew

ru'goso, a *ag* wrinkled

rul'lare *vi (tamburo, nave)* to roll; *(aereo)* to taxi

rul'lino *sm (FOT)* spool; *(: pellicola)* film

'rullo *sm (di tamburi)* roll; *(arnese cilindrico, TIP)* roller; ~ compressore steam roller; ~ di pellicola roll of film

rum *sm* rum

ru'meno, a *ag, sm/f, sm* Romanian

rumi'nare *vt (ZOOL)* to ruminate

ru'more *sm:* un ~ a noise, a sound; *(fig)* a rumour; il ~ noise; **rumo'roso, a** *ag* noisy

ru'olo *sm (TEATRO, fig)* role, part; *(elenco)* roll, register, list; di ~ permanent, on the permanent staff

ru'ota *sf (wheel);* a ~ *(forma)* circular; ~ anteriore/posteriore front/back wheel; ~ di scorta spare wheel

ruo'tare *vt, vi =* rotare

'rupe *sf* cliff

ru'rale *ag* rural, country *cpd*

ru'scello [ruʃ'ʃɛllo] *sm* stream

'ruspa *sf* excavator

rus'pare *vi* to snore

'Russia *sf:* la ~ Russia; **'russo, a** *ag, sm/f, sm* Russian

'rustico, a, ci, che *ag* rustic; *(fig)* rough, unrefined

rut'tare *vi* to belch; **'rutto** *sm* belch

'ruvido, a *ag* rough, coarse

ruzzo'lare [ruttso'lare] *vi* to tumble down; **ruzzo'loni** *av:* cadere ruzzoloni to tumble down; fare le scale ruzzoloni to tumble down the stairs

S

S. *abbr (= sud)* S

sa *vb vedi* sapere

'sabato *sm* Saturday; di o il ~ on Saturdays

'sabbia *sf* sand; ~e mobili quicksand(s); **sabbi'oso, a** *ag* sandy

sabo'taggio [sabo'taddʒo] *sm* sabotage

sabo'tare *vt* to sabotage

'sacca, che *sf* bag; *(bisaccia)* haversack; *(insenatura)* inlet; ~ da viaggio travelling bag

sacca'rina *sf* saccharin(e)

sac'cente [sat'tʃɛnte] *sm/f* know-all (BRIT), know-it-all (US)

saccheggi'are [sakked'dʒare] *vt* to sack, plunder; **sac'cheggio** *sm* sack(ing)

sac'chetto [sak'ketto] *sm (small) bag;* (small) sack

'sacco, chi *sm* bag; *(per carbone etc)* sack; *(ANAT, BIOL)* sac; *(tela)* sacking; *(saccheggio)* sack(ing); *(fig: grande quantità):* un ~ di lots of, heaps of; ~ a pelo sleeping bag; ~ per i rifiuti bin bag

sacer'dote [satʃer'dɔte] *sm* priest; **sacer'dozio** *sm* priesthood

sacra'mento *sm* sacrament

sacrifi'care *vt* to sacrifice; ~rsi *vr*

to sacrifice o.s.; (*privarsi di qc*) to make sacrifices

sacri'ficio [sakri'fitʃo] *sm* sacrifice

sacri'legio [sakri'ledʒo] *sm* sacrilege

'sacro, a *ag* sacred

'sadico, a, ci, che *ag* sadistic ♦ *sm/f* sadist

sa'etta *sf* arrow; (*fulmine: anche fig*) thunderbolt; flash of lightning

sa'fari *sm inv* safari

sa'gace [sa'gatʃe] *ag* shrewd, sagacious

sag'gezza [sad'dʒettsa] *sf* wisdom

saggi'are [sad'dʒare] *vt* (*metalli*) to assay; (*fig*) to test

'saggio, a, gi, ge ['saddʒo] *ag* wise ♦ *sm* (*persona*) sage; (*operazione sperimentale*) test; (: *dell'oro*) assay; (*fig: prova*) proof; (*campione indicativo*) sample; (*ricerca, esame critico*) essay

Sagit'tario [sadʒit'tarjo] *sm* Sagittarius

'sagoma *sf* (*profilo*) outline, profile; (*forma*) form, shape; (*TECN*) template; (*bersaglio*) target; (*fig: persona*) character

'sagra *sf* festival

sagres'tano *sm* sacristan; sexton

sagres'tia *sf* sacristy; (*culto protestante*) vestry

Sa'hara [sa'ara] *sm*: **il** (*deserto del*) ~ the Sahara (Desert)

'sai *vb vedi* **sapere**

'sala *sf* hall; (*stanza*) room; ~ **d'aspetto** waiting room; ~ **da ballo** ballroom; ~ **per concerti** concert hall; ~ **da gioco** gaming room; ~ **operatoria** operating theatre; ~ **da pranzo** dining room

sa'lame *sm* salami *no pl*, salami sausage

sala'moia *sf* (*CUC*) brine

sa'lare *vt* to salt

salari'ato, a *sm/f* wage-earner

sa'lario *sm* pay, wages *pl*

sa'lato, a, g (*sapore*) salty; (*CUC*) salted, salt *cpd*; (*fig: discorso etc*) biting, sharp; (: *prezzi*) steep, stiff

sal'dare *vt* (*congiungere*) to join,

bind; (*parti metalliche*) to solder; (: *con saldatura autogena*) to weld; (*conto*) to settle, pay; **salda'tura** *sf* soldering; welding; (*punto saldato*) soldered joint; weld

sal'dezza [sal'dettsa] *sf* firmness; strength

'saldo, a *ag* (*resistente, forte*) strong, firm; (*fermo*) firm, steady, stable; (*fig*) firm, steadfast ♦ *sm* (*svendita*) sale; (*di conto*) settlement; (*ECON*) balance

'sale *sm* salt; (*fig*): **ha poco** ~ **in zucca** he doesn't have much sense; ~ **fino/grosso** table/cooking salt

'salice ['salitʃe] *sm* willow; ~ **piangente** weeping willow

sali'ente *ag* (*fig*) salient, main

sali'era *sf* salt cellar

sa'lina *sf* saltworks *sg*

sa'lino, a *ag* saline

sa'lire *vi* to go (*o* come) up; (*aereo etc*) to climb, go up; (*passeggero*) to get on; (*sentiero, prezzi, livello*) to go up, rise ♦ *vt* (*scale, gradini*) to go (*o* come) up; ~ **su** to climb (up); ~ **sul treno/sull'autobus** to board the train/the bus; ~ **in macchina** to get into the car; **sa'lita** *sf* climb, ascent; (*erta*) hill, slope; **in salita** *ag, av* uphill

sa'liva *sf* saliva

'salma *sf* corpse

'salmo *sm* psalm

sal'mone *sm* salmon

sa'lone *sm* (*stanza*) sitting room, lounge; (*in albergo*) lounge; (*su nave*) lounge, saloon; (*mostra*) show, exhibition; ~ **di bellezza** beauty salon

sa'lotto *sm* lounge, sitting room; (*mobilio*) lounge suite

sal'pare *vi* (*NAUT*) to set sail; (*anche*: ~ **l'ancora**) to weigh anchor

'salsa *sf* (*CUC*) sauce; ~ **di pomodoro** tomato sauce

sal'siccia, ce [sal'sittʃa] *sf* pork sausage

sal'tare *vi* to jump, leap; (*esplodere*) to blow up, explode; (: *valvola*) to blow; (*venir via*) to pop off; (*non aver luogo: corso etc*) to be cancelled ♦ *vt* to jump (over), leap (over); (*fig: pranzo, capitolo*) to skip, miss (out); (*CUC*) to sauté; **far ~** to blow up; to burst open; **~ fuori** (*fig: apparire all'improvviso*) to turn up

saltel'lare *vi* to skip; to hop

saltim'banco *sm* acrobat

'**salto** *sm* jump; (*SPORT*) jumping; **fare un ~** to jump, leap; **fare un ~ da qn** to pop over to sb's (place); **~ in alto/lungo** high/long jump; **~ con l'asta** pole vaulting; **~ mortale** somersault

saltu'ario, a *ag* occasional, irregular

sa'lubre *ag* healthy, salubrious

salume'ria *sf* delicatessen

sa'lumi *smpl* salted pork meats

salu'tare *ag* healthy; (*fig*) salutary, beneficial ♦ *vt* (*per dire buon giorno*, *fig*) to greet; (*per dire addio*) to say goodbye to; (*MIL*) to salute

sa'lute *sf* health; **~!** (*a chi starnutisce*) bless you!; (*nei brindisi*) cheers!; **bere alla ~ di qn** to drink (to) sb's health

sa'luto *sm* (*gesto*) wave; (*parola*) greeting; (*MIL*) salute; **~i** *smpl* (*formula di cortesia*) greetings; **cari ~i** best regards; **vogliate gradire i nostri più distinti ~i** Yours faithfully

salvacon'dotto *sm* (*MIL*) safe-conduct

salva'gente [salva'dʒɛnte] *sm* (*NAUT*) lifebuoy; (*stradale*) traffic island; **~ a ciambella** life belt; **~ a giubbotto** lifejacket

salvaguar'dare *vt* to safeguard

sal'vare *vt* to save; (*trarre da un pericolo*) to rescue; (*proteggere*) to protect; **~rsi** *vr* to save o.s.; to escape; **salva'taggio** *sm* rescue; **sal'va'tore, 'trice** *smf* saviour

'salve (*fam*) *escl* hi!

sal'vezza [sal'vettsa] *sf* salvation; (*sicurezza*) safety

'salvia *sf* (*BOT*) sage

'salvo, a *ag* safe, unhurt, unharmed;

(*fuori pericolo*) safe, out of danger ♦ *sm*: **in ~** safe ♦ *prep* (*eccetto*) except; **mettere qc in ~** to put sth in a safe place; **~ che** (*a meno che*) unless; (*eccetto che*) except (that); **~ imprevisti** barring accidents

sam'buco *sm* elder (tree)

san *ag vedi* **santo**

sa'nare *vt* to heal, cure; (*economia*) to put right

san'cire [san'tʃire] *vt* to sanction

'sandalo *sm* (*BOT*) sandalwood; (*calzatura*) sandal

'sangue *sm* blood; **farsi cattivo ~** to fret, get in a state; **~ freddo** (*fig*) sang-froid, calm; **a ~ freddo** in cold blood; **sangu'igno, a** *ag* blood cpd; (*colore*) blood-red; **sangui'nare** *vi* to bleed; **sangui'noso, a** *ag* bloody; **sangui'suga** *sf* leech

sanità *sf* health; (*salubrità*) healthiness; **Ministero della S~** Department of Health; **~ mentale** sanity

sani'tario, a *ag* health cpd; (*condizioni*) sanitary ♦ *sm* (*AMM*) doctor; (*impianti*) **~i** *smpl* bathroom *o* sanitary fittings

'sanno *vb vedi* **sapere**

'sano, a *ag* healthy; (*denti, costituzione*) healthy, sound; (*integro*) whole, unbroken; (*fig: politica, consigli*) sound; **~ di mente** sane; **di ~ a pianta** completely, entirely; **~ e salvo** safe and sound

sant' *ag vedi* **santo**

santifi'care *vt* to sanctify; (*feste*) to observe

santità *sf* sanctity; holiness; **Sua/Vostra ~** (*titolo di Papa*) His/Your Holiness

'santo, a *ag* holy; (*fig*) saintly; (*seguito da nome proprio*) saint ♦ *sm/f* saint; **la S~a Sede** the Holy See

santu'ario *sm* sanctuary

sanzio'nare [santsjo'nare] *vt* to sanction

sanzi'one [san'tsjone] *sf* sanction; (*penale, civile*) sanction, penalty

sa'pere *vt* to know; (*essere capace di*): **so nuotare** I know how to swim,

I can swim ♦ vi: ~ **di** (aver sapore) to taste of; (aver odore) to smell of ♦ sm knowledge; **far** ~ **a qn** to inform sb about sth, let sb know sth; **mi sa che non sia vero** I don't think that's true

sapi'enza [sa'pjentsa] sf wisdom

sa'pone sm soap; ~ **da bucato** washing soap; **sapo'netta** sf cake o bar o tablet of soap

sa'pore sm taste, flavour; **sapo'rito, a** ag tasty

sappi'amo vb vedi **sapere**

saraci'nesca [saratʃi'neska] sf (serranda) rolling shutter

sar'casmo sm sarcasm no pl; sarcastic remark

Sar'degna [sar'deɲɲa] sf: **la** ~ Sardinia

sar'dina sf sardine

'sardo, a ag, sm/f Sardinian

'sarto, a sm/f tailor/dressmaker; **sarto'ria** sf tailor's (shop); dressmaker's (shop); (casa di moda) fashion house; (arte) couture

'sasso sm stone; (ciottolo) pebble; (masso) rock

sas'sofono sm saxophone

sas'soso, a ag stony; pebbly

'Satana sm Satan; **sa'tanico, a, ci, che** ag satanic, fiendish

sa'tellite sm, ag satellite

'satira sf satire

'saturo, a ag saturated; (fig): ~ **di** full of

S.A.U.B. ['saub] sigla f (= Struttura Amministrativa Unificata di Base) state welfare system

'sauna sf sauna

Sa'voia sf: **la** ~ Savoy

savoi'ardo, a ag of Savoy, Savoyard ♦ sm (biscotto) sponge finger

sazi'are [sat'tsjare] vt to satisfy, satiate; ~**rsi** vr (riempirsi di cibo): ~**rsi (di)** to eat one's fill (of); (fig): ~**rsi di** to grow tired o weary of

'sazio, a ['sattsjo] ag: ~ **(di)** sated (with), full (of); (fig: stufo) fed up (with), sick (of)

sba'dato, a ag careless, inattentive

sbadigli'are [zbadiʎ'ʎare] vi to yawn; **sba'diglio** sm yawn

sbagli'are [zbaʎ'ʎare] vt to make a mistake in, get wrong ♦ vi to make a mistake, be mistaken, be wrong; (operare in modo non giusto) to err; ~**rsi** vr to make a mistake, be mistaken, be wrong; ~ **la mira/strada** to miss one's aim/take the wrong road; **'sbaglio** sm mistake, error; (morale) error; **fare uno sbaglio** to make a mistake

sbal'lare vt (merce) to unpack ♦ vi (nel fare un conto) to overestimate; (fam: gergo della droga) to get high

sballot'tare vt to toss about

sbalor'dire vt to stun, amaze ♦ vi to be stunned, be amazed; **sbalordi'tivo, a** ag amazing; (prezzo) incredible, absurd

sbal'zare [zbal'tsare] vt to throw, hurl ♦ vi (balzare) to bounce; (saltare) to leap, bound; **'sbalzo** sm (spostamento improvviso) jolt, jerk; **a sbalzi** jerkily; (fig) in fits and starts; **uno sbalzo di temperatura** a sudden change in temperature

sban'dare vi (NAUT) to list; (AER) to bank; (AUT) to skid; ~**rsi** vr (folla) to disperse; (fig: famiglia) to break up

sbandie'rare vt (bandiera) to wave; (fig) to parade, show off

sbaragli'are [zbaraʎ'ʎare] vt (MIL) to rout; (in gare sportive etc) to beat, defeat

sba'raglio [zba'raʎʎo] sm rout; defeat; **gettarsi allo** ~ to risk everything

sbaraz'zarsi [zbarat'tsarsi] vr: ~ **di** to get rid of, rid o.s. of

sbar'care vt (passeggeri) to disembark; (merci) to unload ♦ vi to disembark; **'sbarco** sm disembarkation; unloading; (MIL) landing

'sbarra sf bar; (di passaggio a livello) barrier; (DIR): **presentarsi alla** ~ to appear before the court

sbarra'mento sm (stradale) barrier; (diga) dam, barrage; (MIL) barrage

sbar'rare vt (strada etc) to block, bar; (assegno) to cross; ~ **il passo** to bar the way; ~ **gli occhi** to open one's eyes wide

'**sbattere** vt (porta) to slam, bang; (tappeti, ali, CUC) to beat; (urtare) to knock, hit ♦ vi (porta, finestra) to bang; (agitarsi: ali, vele etc) to flap; **me ne sbatto!** (fam) I don't give a damn!; **sbat'tuto, a** ag (viso, aria) dejected, worn out; (uovo) beaten

sba'vare vi to dribble; (colore) to smear, smudge

sbia'dire vi, vt to fade; ~**rsi** vr to fade, **sbia'dito, a** ag faded; (fig) colourless, dull

sbian'care vt to whiten; (tessuto) to bleach ♦ vi (impallidire) to grow pale o white

sbi'eco, a, chi, che ag (storto) squint, askew; di ~: **guardare qn di** ~ (fig) to look askance at sb; **tagliare una stoffa di** ~ to cut a material on the bias

sbigot'tire vt to dismay, stun ♦ vi (anche: ~**rsi**) to be dismayed

sbilan'ciare [zbilan'tʃare] vt to throw off balance; ~**rsi** vr (perdere l'equilibrio) to overbalance, lose one's balance; (fig: compromettersi) to compromise o.s.

sbir'ciare [zbir'tʃare] vt to cast sidelong glances at, eye

'**sbirro** (peg) sm cop

sbizzar'rirsi [zbiddzar'rirsi] vr to indulge one's whims

sbloc'care vt to unblock, free; (freno) to release; (prezzi, affitti) to decontrol

sboc'care vi: ~ **in** (fiume) to flow into; (strada) to lead into; (persona) to come (out) into; (fig: concludersi) to end (up) in

sboc'cato, a ag (persona) foulmouthed; (linguaggio) foul

sbocci'are [zbot'tʃare] vi (fiore) to bloom, open (out)

'**sbocco, chi** sm (di fiume) mouth; (di strada) end; (di tubazione,

COMM) outlet; (uscita: anche fig) way out; **siamo in una situazione senza** ~**chi** there's no way out of this for us

sbol'lire vi (fig) to cool down, calm down

'**sbornia** (fam) sf: **prendersi una** ~ to get plastered

sbor'sare vt (denaro) to pay out

sbot'tare vi: ~ **in una risata/per la collera** to burst out laughing/ explode with anger

sbotto'nare vt to unbutton, undo

sbracci'ato, a [zbrat'tʃato] ag (camicia) sleeveless; (persona) barearmed

sbrai'tare vi to yell, bawl

sbra'nare vt to tear to pieces

sbricio'lare [zbritʃo'lare] vt to crumble; ~**rsi** vr to crumble

sbri'gare vt to deal with, get through; (cliente) to attend to, deal with; ~**rsi** vr to hurry (up); **sbri-ga'tivo, a** ag (persona, modo) quick, expeditious; (giudizio) hasty

sbrin'dello, a ag tattered, in tatters

sbrodo'lare vt to stain, dirty

'**sbronza** ['zbrontsa] (fam) sf (ubriaco): **prendersi una** ~ to get tight o plastered

'**sbronzo, a** ['zbrontso] (fam) ag (ubriaco) tight

sbruf'fone, a sm/f boaster

sbu'care vi to come out, emerge; (apparire improvvisamente) to pop out (o up)

sbucci'are [zbut'tʃare] vt (arancia, patata) to peel; (piselli) to shell; ~**rsi un ginocchio** to graze one's knee

sbudel'larsi vr: ~ **dalle risa** to split one's sides laughing

sbuf'fare vi (persona, cavallo) to snort; (: ansimare) to puff, pant; (treno) to puff; '**sbuffo** sm (di aria, fumo, vapore) puff; **maniche a sbuffo** puff(ed) sleeves

'**scabbia** sf (MED) scabies sg

sca'broso, a ag (fig: difficile) difficult, thorny; (: *imbarazzante*) embarrassing; (: *sconcio*) indecent

scacchi'era [skak'kjɛra] *sf* chessboard

scacci'are [skat'tʃare] *vt* to chase away *o* out, drive away *o* out

'scacco, chi *sm* (*pezzo del gioco*) chessman; (*quadretto di scacchiera*) square; (*fig*) setback, reverse; ~**chi** *smpl* (*gioco*) chess sg; **a ~chi** (*tessuto*) check(ed); **scacco'matto** *sm* checkmate

sca'dente *ag* shoddy, of poor quality

sca'denza [ska'dɛntsa] *sf* (*di cambiale, contratto*) maturity; (*di passaporto*) expiry date; (*di passaporto*) expiry date; **a breve/lunga ~** short-/long-term; **data di ~** expiry date

sca'dere *vi* (*contratto etc*) to expire; (*debito*) to fall due; (*valore, forze, peso*) to decline, go down

sca'fandro *sm* (*di palombaro*) diving suit; (*di astronauta*) space-suit

scaf'fale *sm* shelf; (*mobile*) set of shelves

'scafo *sm* (*NAUT, AER*) hull

scagio'nare [skadʒo'nare] *vt* to exonerate, free from blame

'scaglia ['skaʎʎa] *sf* (*ZOOL*) scale; (*scheggia*) chip, flake

scagli'are [skaʎ'ʎare] *vt* (*lanciare: anche fig*) to hurl, fling; **~rsi** *vr*: **~rsi su** *o* **contro** to hurl *o* fling o.s. at; (*fig*) to rail at

scaglio'nare [skaʎʎo'nare] *vt* (*pagamenti*) to space out, spread out; (*MIL*) to echelon; **scagli'one** *sm* echelon; (*GEO*) terrace; **a scaglioni** in groups

'scala *sf* (*a gradini etc*) staircase, stairs *pl*; (*a pioli, di corda*) ladder; (*MUS, GEO, di colori, valori, fig*) scale; **~e** *sfpl* (*scalinata*) stairs; su vasta ~/~ **ridotta** on a large/small scale; **~ a libretto** stepladder; **~ mobile** escalator; (*ECON*) sliding scale; **~ mobile (dei salari)** index-linked pay scale

sca'lare *vt* (*ALPINISMO, muro*) to climb, scale; (*debito*) to scale down,

reduce; **sca'lata** *sf* scaling *no pl*, climbing *no pl*; (*arrampicata, fig*) climb; **scala'tore, 'trice** *sm/f* climber

scalda'bagno [skalda'baɲɲo] *sm* water-heater

scal'dare *vt* to heat; **~rsi** *vr* to warm up, heat up; (*al fuoco, al sole*) to warm o.s.; (*fig*) to get excited

scal'fire *vt* to scratch

scali'nata *sf* staircase

sca'lino *sm* (*anche fig*) step; (*di scala a pioli*) rung

'scalo *sm* (*NAUT*) slipway; (: *porto d'approdo*) port of call; (*AER*) stopover; **fare ~ (a)** (*NAUT*) to call (at), put in (at); (*AER*) to land (at), make a stop (at); **~ merci** (*FERR*) goods (*BRIT*) *o* freight yard

scalop'pina *sf* (*CUC*) escalope

scal'pello *sm* chisel

scal'pore *sm* noise, row; **far ~** (*notizia*) to cause a sensation *o* a stir

scal'tro, a *ag* cunning, shrewd

scal'zare [skal'tsare] *vt* (*albero*) to bare the roots of; (*muro, fig: autorità*) to undermine

'scalzo, a ['skaltso] *ag* barefoot

scambi'are *vt* to exchange; (*confondere*): **~ qn/qc per** to take *o* mistake sb/sth for; **mi hanno scambiato il cappello** they've given me the wrong hat

scambi'evole *ag* mutual, reciprocal

'scambio *sm* exchange; (*FERR*) points *pl*; **fare (uno) ~** to make a swap

scampa'gnata [skampaɲ'ɲata] *sf* trip to the country

scam'pare *vt* (*salvare*) to rescue, save; (*evitare: morte, prigione*) to escape ♦ *vi*: **~ (a qc)** to survive (sth), escape (sth); **scamparla bella** to have a narrow escape

'scampo *sm* (*salvezza*) escape; (*ZOOL*) prawn; **cercare ~ nella fuga** to seek safety in flight

'scampolo *sm* remnant

scanala'tura *sf* (*incavo*) channel, groove

scandagli'are [skanda'ʎʎare] *vt* (NAUT) to sound; (fig) to sound out; to probe

scandaliz'zare [skandalid'dzare] *vt* to shock, scandalize; ~**rsi** *vr* to be shocked

'scandalo *sm* scandal

Scandi'navia *sf:* **la ~ Scandinavia;** **scandi'navo, a** *ag, sm/f* Scandinavian

scan'dire *vt* (*versi*) to scan; (*parole*) to articulate, pronounce distinctly; **~ il tempo** (*MUS*) to beat time

scan'nare *vt* (*animale*) to butcher, slaughter; (*persona*) to cut o slit the throat of

'scanno *sm* seat, bench

scansafa'tiche [skansafa'tike] *sm/f inv* idler, loafer

scan'sare *vt* (*rimuovere*) to move (aside), shift; (*schivare: schiaffo*) to dodge; (*sfuggire*) to avoid; ~**rsi** *vr* to move aside

scan'sia *sf* shelves *pl;* (*per libri*) bookcase

'scanso *sm:* **a ~ di** in order to avoid, as a precaution against

scanti'nato *sm* basement

scanto'nare *vi* to turn the corner; (*svignarsela*) to sneak off

scapacci'one [skapat'tʃone] *sm* clout

scapes'trato, a *ag* dissolute

'scapito *sm* (*perdita*) loss; (*danno*) damage, detriment; **a ~ di** to the detriment of

'scapola *sf* shoulder blade

'scapolo *sm* bachelor

scappa'mento *sm* (*AUT*) exhaust

scap'pare *vi* (*fuggire*) to escape; (*andare via in fretta*) to rush off; **lasciarsi ~ un'occasione** to let an opportunity go by; **~ di prigione** to escape from prison; **~ di mano** (*oggetto*) to slip out of one's hands; **~ di mente a qn** to slip sb's mind; **mi scappò detto** I let it slip; **scap'pata** *sf* quick visit o call; **scappa'tella** *sf* escapade; **scappa'toia** *sf* way out

scara'beo *sm* beetle

scarabocchi'are [skarabok'kjare] *vt* to scribble, scrawl; **scara'bocchio** *sm* scribble, scrawl

scara'faggio [skara'faddʒo] *sm* cockroach

scaraven'tare *vt* to fling, hurl

scardi'nare *vt:* **~ una porta** to take a door off its hinges

scarce'rare *vt* to release (from prison)

'scarica, che *sf* (*di più armi*) volley of shots; (*di sassi, pugni*) hail, shower; (*ELETTR*) discharge; **~ di mitra** burst of machine-gun fire

scari'care *vt* (*merci, camion etc*) to unload; (*passeggeri*) to set down, put off; (*arma*) to unload; (*: sparare, ELETTR*) to discharge; (*sog: corso d'acqua*) to empty, pour; (*fig: liberare da un peso*) to unburden, relieve; ~**rsi** *vr* (*orologio*) to run o wind down; (*batteria, accumulatore*) to go flat o dead; (*fig: rilassarsi*) to unwind; (*: sfogarsi*) to let off steam; **il fulmine si scaricò su un albero** the lightning struck a tree; **scari-ca'tore** *sm* loader; (*di porto*) docker

'scarico, a, chi, che *ag* unloaded; (*orologio*) run down; (*accumulatore*) dead, flat ♦ *sm* (*di merci, materiali*) unloading; (*di immondizie*) dumping, tipping (*BRIT*); (*: luogo*) rubbish dump; (*TECN: deflusso*) draining; (*: dispositivo*) drain; (*AUT*) exhaust

scarlat'tina *sf* scarlet fever

scar'latto, a *ag* scarlet

'scarno, a *ag* thin, bony

'scarpa *sf* shoe; ~**e da ginnastica/tennis** gym/tennis shoes

scar'pata *sf* escarpment

scarseggi'are [skarsed'dʒare] *vi* to be scarce; **~ di** to be short of, lack

scar'sezza [skar'settsa] *sf* scarcity, lack

'scarso, a *ag* (*insufficiente*) insufficient, meagre; (*povero: annata*) poor, lean; (*INS: voto*) poor; **~ di** lacking in; **3 chili ~i** just under 3 kilos, barely 3 kilos

scarta'mento *sm* (FERR) gauge; ~ **normale/ridotto** standard/narrow gauge

scar'tare *vt* (pacco) to unwrap; (idea) to reject; (MIL) to declare unfit for military service; (carte da gioco) to discard; (CALCIO) to dodge (past) ♦ *vi* to swerve

'scarto *sm* (cosa scartata, anche COMM) reject; (di veicolo) swerve; (differenza) gap, difference

scassi'nare *vt* to break, force

'scasso *sm vedi* **furto**

scate'nare *vt* (fig) to incite, stir up; ~**rsi** *vr* (temporale) to break; (rivolta) to break out; (persona: infuriarsi) to rage

'scatola *sf* box; (di latta) tin (BRIT), can; **cibi in** ~ tinned (BRIT) o canned foods; ~ **cranica** cranium

scat'tare *vt* (fotografia) to take ♦ *vi* (congegno, molla etc) to be released; (balzare) to spring up; (SPORT) to put on a spurt; (fig: dell'ira) to fly into a rage; ~ **in piedi** to spring to one's feet

'scatto *sm* (dispositivo) release; (: di arma da fuoco) trigger mechanism; (rumore) click; (balzo) jump, start; (SPORT) spurt; (fig: di ira etc) fit; (: di stipendio) increment; **di** ~ suddenly

scatu'rire *vi* to gush, spring

scaval'care *vt* (ostacolo) to pass (o climb) over; (fig) to get ahead of, overtake

sca'vare *vt* (terreno) to dig; (legno) to hollow out; (pozzo, galleria) to bore; (città sepolta etc) to excavate

'scavo *sm* excavating *no pl*; excavation

'scegliere ['ʃeʎʎere] *vt* to choose, select

sce'icco, chi [ʃe'ikko] *sm* sheik

scelle'rato, a [ʃelle'rato] *ag* wicked, evil

scel'lino [ʃel'lino] *sm* shilling

'scelta ['ʃelta] *sf* choice; selection; **di prima** ~ top grade o quality; **frutta**

o **formaggi a** ~ choice of fruit or cheese

'scelto, a ['ʃelto] *pp di* **scegliere** ♦ *ag* (gruppo) carefully selected; (frutta, verdura) choice, top quality; (MIL: specializzato) crack *cpd*, highly skilled

sce'mare [ʃe'mare] *vt, vi* to diminish

'scemo, a ['ʃemo] *ag* stupid, silly

'scempio ['ʃempjo] *sm* slaughter, massacre; (fig) ruin; **far** ~ **di** (fig) to play havoc with, ruin

'scena ['ʃɛna] *sf* (gen) scene; (palcoscenico) stage; **le** ~**e** (fig: teatro) the stage; **fare una** ~ to make a scene; **andare in** ~ to be staged o put on o performed; **mettere in** ~ to stage

sce'nario [ʃe'narjo] *sm* scenery; (di film) scenario

sce'nata [ʃe'nata] *sf* row, scene

'scendere ['ʃɛndere] *vi* to go (o come) down; (strada, sole) to go down; (notte) to fall; (passeggero: fermarsi) to get out, alight; (fig: temperatura, prezzi) to go o come down, fall, drop ♦ *vt* (scale, pendio) to go (o come) down; ~ **dalle scale** to go o come down the stairs; ~ **dal treno** to get off o out of the train; ~ **dalla macchina** to get out of the car; ~ **da cavallo** to dismount, get off one's horse

'scenico, a, ci, che ['ʃɛniko] *ag* stage *cpd*, scenic

scervel'lato, a [ʃervel'lato] *ag* feather-brained, scatterbrained

'sceso, a ['ʃeso] *pp di* **scendere**

'scettico, a, ci, che ['ʃɛttiko] *ag* sceptical

'scettro ['ʃɛttro] *sm* sceptre

'scheda ['skɛda] *sf* (index) card; ~ **elettorale** ballot paper; ~ **perfora'ta** punch card; ~ **telefonica** phone card; **sche'dare** *vt* (dati) to file; (libri) to catalogue; (registrare: anche POLIZIA) to put on one's files; **sche'dario** *sm* file; (mobile) filing cabinet

scheggia, ge ['skeddʒa] *sf* splinter,

sliver

'scheletro ['skɛletro] *sm* skeleton

'schema, i ['skɛma] *sm (diagramma)* diagram, sketch; *(progetto, abbozzo)* outline, plan

'scherma ['skɛrma] *sf* fencing

scher'maglia [sker'maʎʎa] *sf (fig)* skirmish

'schermo ['skɛrmo] *sm* shield, screen; *(CINEMA, TV)* screen

scher'nire [sker'nire] *vt* to mock, sneer at; **'scherno** *sm* mockery, derision

scher'zare [sker'tsare] *vi* to joke

'scherzo ['skɛrtso] *sm* joke; *(tiro)* trick; *(MUS)* scherzo; **è uno ~!** *(una cosa facile)* it's child's play!, it's easy!; **per ~** in jest; for a joke o a laugh; **fare un brutto ~ a qn** to play a nasty trick on sb; **scher'zoso, a** *ag (tono, gesto)* playful; *(osservazione)* facetious; **è un tipo scherzoso** he likes a joke

schiaccia'noci [skjattʃa'notʃi] *sm inv* nutcracker

schiacci'are [skjat'tʃare] *vt (dito)* to crush; *(noci)* to crack; **~ un pisolino** to have a nap

schiaffeggi'are [skjaffed'dʒare] *vt* to slap

schi'affo ['skjaffo] *sm* slap

schiamaz'zare [skjamat'tsare] *vi* to squawk, cackle

schian'tare [skjan'tare] *vt* to break, tear apart; **~rsi** *vr* to break (up), shatter; **schi'anto** *sm (rumore)* crash; tearing sound; **è uno schianto!** *(fam)* it's o he's o she's terrific!; **di schianto** all of a sudden

schia'rire [skja'rire] *vt* to lighten, make lighter ♦ *vi (anche: ~rsi)* to grow lighter; *(tornar sereno)* to clear, brighten up; **~rsi la voce** to clear one's throat

schiavitù [skjavi'tu] *sf* slavery

schi'avo, a ['skjavo] *sm/f* slave

schi'ena ['skjɛna] *sf (ANAT)* back; **schie'nale** *sm (di sedia)* back

schi'era ['skjɛra] *sf (MIL)* rank; *(gruppo)* group, band

schiera'mento [skjera'mento] *sm (MIL, SPORT)* formation; *(fig)* alliance

schie'rare [skje'rare] *vt (esercito)* to line up, draw up, marshal; **~rsi** *vr* to line up; *(fig)*: **~rsi con o dalla parte di/contro qn** to side with/ oppose sb

schi'etto, a [skj'etto] *ag (puro)* pure; *(fig)* frank, straightforward; sincere

'schifo ['skifo] *sm* disgust; **fare ~** *(essere fatto male, dare pessimi risultati)* to be awful; **mi fa ~** it makes me sick, it's disgusting; **quel libro è uno ~** that book's rotten; **schi'foso, a** *ag* disgusting, revolting; *(molto scadente)* rotten, lousy

schioc'care [skjok'kare] *vt (frusta)* to crack; *(dita)* to snap; *(lingua)* to click; **~ le labbra** to smack one's lips

schi'udere ['skjudere] *vt* to open; **~rsi** *vr* to open

schi'uma ['skjuma] *sf* foam; *(di sapone)* lather; *(di saliva)* froth; *(fig: feccia)* scum; **schiu'mare** *vt* to skim ♦ *vi* to foam

schi'uso, a [skj'uso] *pp di* **schiudere**

schi'vare [ski'vare] *vt* to dodge, avoid

'schivo, a ['skivo] *ag (ritroso)* stand-offish, reserved; *(timido)* shy

schiz'zare [skit'tsare] *vt (spruzzare)* to spurt, squirt; *(sporcare)* to splash, spatter; *(fig: abbozzare)* to sketch ♦ *vi* to spurt, squirt; *(saltar fuori)* to dart up (o off etc)

schizzi'noso, a [skittsi'noso] *ag* fussy, finicky

'schizzo ['skittso] *sm (di liquido)* spurt; splash, spatter; *(abbozzo)* sketch

sci [ʃi] *sm (attrezzo)* ski; *(attività)* skiing; **~ nautico** water-skiing

'scia ['ʃia] *sf (pl scie)* (di imbarcazione) wake; *(di profumo)* trail

scià [ʃa] *sm inv* shah

sci'abola ['ʃabola] *sf* sabre

scia'callo [ʃa'kallo] sm jackal

sciac'quare [ʃak'kware] vt to rinse

scia'gura [ʃa'gura] sf disaster, calamity; misfortune; **sciagu'rato, a** ag unfortunate; (malvagio) wicked

scialac'quare [ʃalak'kware] vt to squander

scia'lare [ʃa'lare] vi to lead a life of luxury

sci'albo, a ['ʃalbo] ag pale, dull; (fig) dull, colourless

sci'alle ['ʃalle] sm shawl

scia'luppa [ʃa'luppa] sf (NAUT) sloop; (anche: ~ di salvataggio) lifeboat

sci'ame ['ʃame] sm swarm

scian'cato, a [ʃan'kato] ag lame; (mobile) rickety

sci'are [ʃi'are] vi to ski

sci'arpa ['ʃarpa] sf scarf; (fascia) sash

scia'tore, 'trice [ʃia'tore] sm/f skier

sci'atto, a ['ʃatto] ag (persona: nell'aspetto) slovenly, unkempt; (: nel lavoro) sloppy, careless

scien'tifico, a, ci, che [ʃen'tifiko] ag scientific

sci'enza ['ʃentsa] sf science; (sapere) knowledge; **~e** sfpl (INS) science sg; **~e naturali** natural sciences; **scienzi'ato, a** sm/f scientist

'scimmia ['ʃimmja] sf monkey; **scimmiot'tare** vt to ape, mimic

scimpanzé [ʃimpan'tse] sm inv chimpanzee

scimu'nito, a [ʃimu'nito] ag silly, idiotic

'scindere ['ʃindere] vt to split (up); **~rsi** vr to split (up)

scin'tilla [ʃin'tilla] sf spark; **scintil'lare** vi to spark; (acqua, occhi) to sparkle

scioc'chezza [ʃok'kettsa] sf stupidity no pl; stupid o foolish thing; **dire ~e** to talk nonsense

sci'occo, a, chi, che ['ʃokko] ag stupid, foolish

sci'ogliere ['ʃɔʎʎere] vt (nodo) to untie; (capelli) to loosen; (persona, animale) to untie, release; (fig: persona): **~ da** to release from; (neve) to melt; (nell'acqua: zucchero etc) to dissolve; (fig: mistero) to solve; (porre fine a: contratto) to cancel; (: società, matrimonio) to dissolve; (: riunione) to bring to an end; **~rsi** vr to loosen, come untied; to melt; to dissolve; (assemblea etc) to break up; **~ i muscoli** to limber up

sciol'tezza [ʃol'tettsa] sf agility; suppleness; ease

sci'olto, a ['ʃolto] pp di sciogliere ♦ ag loose; (agile) agile, nimble; supple; (disinvolto) free and easy; **versi ~i** (POESIA) blank verse

sciope'rante [ʃope'rante] sm/f striker

sciope'rare [ʃope'rare] vi to strike, go on strike

sci'opero ['ʃopero] sm strike; **fare ~** to strike; **~ bianco** work-to-rule (BRIT), slowdown (US); **~ selvaggio** wildcat strike; **~ a singhiozzo** on-off strike

sci'rocco [ʃi'rokko] sm sirocco

sci'roppo [ʃi'roppo] sm syrup

'scisma, i ['ʃizma] sm (REL) schism

scissi'one [ʃis'sjone] sf (anche fig) split, division; (FISICA) fission

'scisso, a ['ʃisso] pp di scindere

sciu'pare [ʃu'pare] vt (abito, libro, appetito) to spoil, ruin; (tempo, denaro) to waste; **~rsi** vr to get spoilt o ruined; (rovinarsi la salute) to ruin one's health

scivo'lare [ʃivo'lare] vi to slide o glide along; (involontariamente) to slip, slide; **'scivolo** sm slide; (TECN) chute

scle'rosi [skle'rɔzi] sf sclerosis

scoc'care vt (freccia) to shoot ♦ vi (guizzare) to shoot up; (battere: ora) to strike

scocci'are [skot'tʃare] (fam) vt to bother, annoy; **~rsi** vr to be bothered o annoyed

sco'della sf bowl

scodinzo'lare [skodintso'lare] vi to wag its tail

scogli'era [skoʎ'ʎɛra] sf reef; cliff

'**scoglio** ['skɔʎʎo] *sm* (*al mare*) rock

scoi'attolo *sm* squirrel

sco'lare: *età* ~ school age ♦ *vt* to drain ♦ *vi* to drip

scola'resca *sf* schoolchildren *pl*, pupils *pl*

sco'laro, a *sm/f* pupil, schoolboy/girl

sco'lastico, a, ci, che *ag* school *cpd*; scholastic

scol'lare *vt* (*staccare*) to unstick; ~**rsi** *vr* to come unstuck

scolla'tura *sf* neckline

'**scolo** *sm* drainage

scolo'rire *vt* to fade; to discolour ♦ *vi* (*anche*: ~**rsi**) to fade; to become discoloured; (*impallidire*) to turn pale

scol'pire *vt* to carve, sculpt

scombi'nare *vt* to mess up, upset

scombus'solare *vt* to upset

scom'messa *sf* bet, wager

scom'messo, a *pp di* **scommettere**

scom'mettere *vt, vi* to bet

scomo'dare *vt* to trouble, bother; to disturb; ~**rsi** *vr* to put o.s. out; ~**rsi a fare** to go to the bother *o* trouble of doing

'**scomodo, a** *ag* uncomfortable; (*sistemazione, posto*) awkward, inconvenient

scompa'rire *vi* (*sparire*) to disappear, vanish; (*fig*) to be insignificant; **scom'parsa** *sf* disappearance; **scom'parso, a** *pp di* **scomparire**

scomparti'mento *sm* (*FERR*) compartment

scom'parto *sm* compartment, division

scompigli'are [skompiʎ'ʎare] *vt* (*cassetto, capelli*) to mess up, disarrange; (*fig: piani*) to upset; **scom'piglio** *sm* mess, confusion

scom'porre (*parola, numero*) to break up; (*CHIM*) to decompose; **scomporsi** *vr* (*fig*) to get upset, lose one's composure; **scom'posto, a** *pp di* **scomporre** ♦ *ag* (*gesto*) unseemly; (*capelli*) ruffled, dishevelled

sco'munica *sf* excommunication

scomuni'care *vt* to excommunicate

sconcer'tare [skontʃer'tare] *vt* to disconcert, bewilder

'**sconcio, a, ci, ce** ['skontʃo] *ag* (*osceno*) indecent, obscene ♦ *sm* (*cosa riprovevole, mal fatta*) disgrace

sconfes'sare *vt* to renounce, disavow; to repudiate

scon'figgere [skon'fiddʒere] *vt* to defeat, overcome

sconfi'nare *vi* to cross the border; (*in proprietà privata*) to trespass; (*fig*): ~ **da** to stray *o* digress from; **sconfi'nato, a** *ag* boundless, unlimited

scon'fitta *sf* defeat

scon'fitto, a *pp di* **sconfiggere**

scon'forto *sm* despondency

scongiu'rare [skondʒu'rare] *vt* (*implorare*) to entreat, beseech, implore; (*eludere: pericolo*) to ward off, avert; **scongi'uro** *sm* entreaty; (*esorcismo*) exorcism; **fare gli scongiuri** to touch wood (*BRIT*), knock on wood (*US*)

scon'nesso, a *ag* (*fig: discorso*) incoherent, rambling

sconosci'uto, a [skonoʃ'ʃuto] *ag* unknown; new, strange ♦ *sm/f* stranger; unknown person

sconquas'sare *vt* to shatter, smash

sconside'rato, a *ag* thoughtless, rash

sconsigli'are [skonsiʎ'ʎare] *vt*: ~ **qc a qn** to advise sb against sth; ~ **qn dal fare qc** to advise sb not to do *o* against doing sth

sconso'lato, a *ag* inconsolable; desolate

scon'tare *vt* (*COMM: detrarre*) to deduct; (: *debito*) to pay off; (: *cambiale*) to discount; (*pena*) to serve; (*colpa, errori*) to pay for, suffer for

scon'tato, a *ag* (*previsto*) foreseen, taken for granted; **dare per** ~ **che** to take it for granted that

scon'tento, a *ag*: ~ (**di**) discontented *o* dissatisfied (with) ♦ *sm* discontent, dissatisfaction

'sconto *sm* discount; **fare uno ~ to** give a discount

scon'trarsi *vr* (*treni etc*) to crash, collide; (*venire ad uno scontro*, *fig*) to clash; **~ con** to crash into, collide with

scon'trino *sm* ticket

'scontro *sm* clash, encounter; crash, collision

scon'troso, **a** *ag* sullen, surly; (*permaloso*) touchy

sconveni'ente *ag* unseemly, improper

scon'volgere [skon'vɔldʒere] *vt* to throw into confusion, upset; (*turbare*) to shake, disturb, upset; **scon'volto**, **a** *pp di* **sconvolgere**

'scopa *sf* broom; (*CARTE*) Italian card game; **sco'pare** *vt* to sweep

sco'perta *sf* discovery

sco'perto, **a** *pp di* **scoprire** ♦ *ag* uncovered; (*capo*) uncovered, bare; (*macchina*) open; (*MIL*) exposed, without cover; (*conto*) overdrawn

'scopo *sm* aim, purpose; **a che ~?** what for?

scoppi'are *vi* (*spaccarsi*) to burst; (*esplodere*) to explode; (*fig*) to break out; **~ in pianto o a piangere** to burst out crying; **~ dalle risa o dal ridere** to split one's sides laughing

scoppiet'tare *vi* to crackle

'scoppio *sm* explosion; (*di tuono*, *arma etc*) crash, bang; (*fig*: *di risa*, *ira*) fit, outburst; (: *di guerra*) outbreak; **a ~ ritardato** delayed-action

sco'prire *vt* to discover; (*liberare da ciò che copre*) to uncover; (: *monumento*) to unveil; **~rsi** *vr* to put on lighter clothes; (*fig*) to give o.s. away

scoraggi'are [skorad'dʒare] *vt* to discourage; **~rsi** *vr* to become discouraged, lose heart

scorcia'toia [skortʃa'toja] *sf* short cut

'scorcio ['skortʃo] *sm* (*ARTE*) foreshortening; (*di secolo*, *periodo*) end, close

scor'dare *vt* to forget; **~rsi** *vr*:

~rsi di qc/di fare to forget sth/to do

'scorgere ['skɔrdʒere] *vt* to make out, distinguish, see

'sco'ria *sf* (*di metalli*) slag; (*vulcanica*) scoria; **~e radioattive** (*FISICA*) radioactive waste *sg*

'scorno *sm* ignominy, disgrace

scorpacci'ata [skorpat'tʃata] *sf*: **fare una ~ (di)** to stuff o.s. (with), eat one's fill (of)

scorpi'one *sm* scorpion; (*dello zodiaco*): **S~** Scorpio

scorraz'zare [skorrat'tsare] *vi* to run about

'scorrere *vt* (*giornale*, *lettera*) to run o skim through ♦ *vi* (*liquido*, *fiume*) to run, flow; (*fune*) to run; (*cassetto*, *porta*) to slide easily; (*tempo*) to pass (by)

scor'retto, **a** *ag* incorrect; (*sgarbato*) impolite; (*sconveniente*) improper

scor'revole *ag* (*porta*) sliding; (*fig*: *stile*) fluent, flowing

scorri'banda *sf* (*MIL*) raid; (*escursione*) trip, excursion

'scorsa *sf* quick look, glance

'scorso, **a** *pp di* **scorrere** ♦ *ag* last

scor'soio, **a** *ag*: **nodo ~** noose

'scorta *sf* (*di personalità*, *convoglio*) escort; (*provvista*) supply, stock; **scor'tare** *vt* to escort

scor'tese *ag* discourteous, rude; **scorte'sia** *sf* discourtesy, rudeness; (*azione*) discourtesy

scorti'care *vt* to skin

'scorto, **a** *pp di* **scorgere**

'scorza ['skɔrdza] *sf* (*di albero*) bark; (*di agrumi*) peel, skin

sco'sceso, **a** [skoʃ'ʃeso] *ag* steep

'scossa *sf* jerk, jolt, shake; (*ELETTR*, *fig*) shock

'scosso, **a** *pp di* **scuotere** ♦ *ag* (*turbato*) shaken, upset

scos'tante *ag* (*fig*) off-putting (*BRIT*), unpleasant

scos'tare *vt* to move (away), shift; **~rsi** *vr* to move away

scostu'mato, **a** *ag* immoral, dissolute

scot'tare *vt* (*ustionare*) to burn; (:

con liquido bollente) to scald ♦ vi to burn; (caffè) to be too hot; **scotta'tura** sf burn; scald

'**scotto, a** ag overcooked ♦ sm (fig): pagare lo ~ (di) to pay the penalty (for)

sco'vare vt to drive out, flush out; (fig) to discover

'Scozia ['skɔttsja] sf: la ~ Scotland; scoz'zese ag Scottish ♦ sm/f Scot

scredi'tare vt to discredit

screpo'lare vt to crack; ~rsi vr to crack; screpola'tura sf cracking no pl; crack

screzi'ato, a [skret'tsjato] ag streaked

'screzio ['skrɛttsjo] sm disagreement

scricchio'lare [skrikkjo'lare] vi to creak, squeak

'scricciolo ['skrittʃolo] sm wren

'scrigno ['skriɲɲo] sm casket

scrimina'tura sf parting

'scritta sf inscription

'scritto, a pp di scrivere ♦ ag written ♦ sm writing; (lettera) letter, note; ~i smpl (letterari etc) writing sg; per o in ~ in writing

scrit'toio sm writing desk

scrit'tore, 'trice sm/f writer

scrit'tura sf writing; (COMM) entry; (contratto) contract; (REL): la Sacra S~ the Scriptures pl; ~e sfpl (COMM) accounts, books

scrittu'rare vt (TEATRO, CINEMA) to sign up, engage; (COMM) to enter

scriva'nia sf desk

scri'vente sm/f writer

'scrivere vt to write; come si scrive? how is it spelt?, how do you write it?

scroc'cone, a sm/f scrounger

'scrofa sf (ZOOL) sow

scrol'lare vt to shake; ~rsi vr vr (anche fig) to give o.s. a shake; ~ le spalle/il capo to shrug one's shoulders/shake one's head

scrosci'are [skroʃ'ʃare] vi (pioggia) to pour down, pelt down; (torrente, fig: applausi) to thunder, roar; 'scroscio sm pelting; thunder, roar;

(di applausi) burst

scros'tare vt (intonaco) to scrape off, strip; ~rsi vr to peel off, flake off

'scrupolo sm scruple; (meticolosità) care, conscientiousness

scru'tare vt to scrutinize; (intenzioni, causa) to examine, scrutinize

scruti'nare vt (voti) to count; scru'tinio sm (votazione) ballot; (insieme delle operazioni) poll; (INS) (meeting for) assignment of marks at end of a term or year

scu'cire [sku'tʃire] vt (orlo etc) to unpick, undo

scude'ria sf stable

scu'detto [sku'detto] sm (SPORT) (championship) shield; (distintivo) badge

'scudo sm shield

scul'tore, 'trice sm/f sculptor

scul'tura sf sculpture

scu'ola sf school; ~ elementare/materna/media primary/ nursery/secondary (BRIT) o grade o high (US) school; ~ guida driving school; ~ dell'obbligo compulsory education; ~e serali evening classes, night school sg; ~ tecnica technical college

scu'otere [sku'ɔtere] vt to shake; ~rsi vr to jump, be startled; (fig: muoversi) to rouse o.s., stir o.s.; (: turbarsi) to be shaken

'scure sf axe

'scuro, a ag dark; (fig: espressione) grim ♦ sm darkness; dark colour; (imposta) (window) shutter; verde/rosso etc ~ dark green/red etc

scur'rile ag scurrilous

'scusa sf apology; (pretesto) excuse; chiedere ~ a sb (per) to apologize to sb (for); chiedo ~ I'm sorry; (disturbando etc) excuse me

scu'sare vt to excuse; ~rsi vr: ~rsi (di) to apologize (for); (mi) scusi I'm sorry; (per richiamare l'attenzione) excuse me

sde'gnato, a [zdeɲ'ɲato] ag indignant, angry

'sdegno ['zdeɲɲo] sm scorn, disdain; **sde'gnoso, a** *ag* scornful, disdainful

sdoga'nare *vt* (*merci*) to clear through customs

sdolci'nato, a [zdoltʃi'nato] *ag* mawkish, oversentimental

sdoppi'are *vt* (*dividere*) to divide o split in two

sdrai'arsi *vr* to stretch out, lie down

'sdraio *sm*: **sedia a ~** deck chair

sdruccio'levole [zdruttʃo'levole] *ag* slippery

PAROLA CHIAVE
---

se *pron vedi* si
♦ *cong* **1** (*condizionale, ipotetica*) if; **~ nevica non vengo** I won't come if it snows; **sarei rimasto ~ me l'avessero chiesto** I would have stayed if they'd asked me; **non puoi fare altro ~ non telefonare** all you can do is phone; **~ mai** if, if ever; **siamo noi ~ mai che te le siamo grati** it is we who should be grateful to you; **~ no** (*altrimenti*) or (else), otherwise
2 (*in frasi dubitative, interrogative indirette*) if, whether; **non so ~ scrivere o telefonare** I don't know whether o if I should write or phone

sé *pron* (*gen*) oneself; (*esso, essa, lui, lei, loro*) itself; himself; herself; themselves; **~ stesso(a)** *pron* oneself; itself; himself; herself; **~ stessi(e)** *pron* pl themselves

seb'bene *cong* although, though

sec. *abbr* (= *secolo*) c

'secca *sf* (*del mare*) shallows pl; *vedi anche* secco

sec'care *vt* to dry; (*prosciugare*) to dry up; (*fig: importunare*) to annoy, bother ♦ *vi* to dry; to dry up; **~rsi** *vr* to dry; to dry up; (*fig*) to grow annoyed; **secca'tura** *sf* (*fig*) bother *no pl*, trouble *no pl*

'secchia ['sekkja] *sf* bucket, pail

'secco, a, chi, che *ag* dry; (*fichi, pesce*) dried; (*foglie, ramo*) withered; (*magro: persona*) thin, skinny;

(*fig: risposta, modo di fare*) curt, abrupt; (: *colpo*) clean, sharp ♦ *sm* (*siccità*) drought; **restarci ~** (*fig: morire sul colpo*) to drop dead; **mettere in ~** (*barca*) to beach; **rimanere in o a ~** (*NAUT*) to run aground; (*fig*) to be left in the lurch

seco'lare *ag* age-old, centuries-old; (*laico, mondano*) secular

'secolo *sm* century; (*epoca*) age

secon'dario, a *ag* secondary

se'conda *sf* (*AUT*) second (gear); **viaggiare in ~** to travel second-class; *vedi anche* **secondo**

se'condo, a *ag* second ♦ *sm* second; (*di pranzo*) main course ♦ *prep* according to; (*nel modo prescritto*) in accordance with; **~ me** in my opinion, to my mind; **di ~a classe** second-class; **di ~a mano** second-hand; **a ~a di** according to; in accordance with

'sedano *sm* celery

seda'tivo, a *ag, sm* sedative

'sede *sf* seat; (*di ditta*) head office; (*di organizzazione*) headquarters *pl*; **in ~ di** (*in occasione di*) during; **~ sociale** registered office

seden'tario, a *ag* sedentary

se'dere *vi* to sit, be seated; **~rsi** *vr* to sit down ♦ *sm* (*deretano*) behind, bottom

'sedia *sf* chair

sedi'cente [sedi'tʃɛnte] *ag* self-styled

'sedici ['seditʃi] *num* sixteen

se'dile *sm* seat; (*panchina*) bench

se'dotto, a *pp di* sedurre

sedu'cente [sedu'tʃɛnte] *ag* seductive; (*proposta*) very attractive

se'durre *vt* to seduce

se'duta *sf* session, sitting; (*riunione*) meeting; **~ spiritica** séance; **~ stante** (*fig*) immediately

seduzi'one [sedut'tsjone] *sf* seduction; (*fascino*) charm, appeal

'sega, ghe *sf* saw

'segale *sf* rye

se'gare *vt* to saw; (*recidere*) to saw off; **sega'tura** *sf* (*residuo*) sawdust

'seggio ['sɛddʒo] *sm* seat; **~ eletto-**

rale polling station

seg'giola ['seddʒola] sf chair; **seggio'lino** sm seat; (per bambini) child's chair; **seggio'lone** sm (per bambini) highchair

seggio'via [seddʒo'via] sf chairlift

seghe'ria [sege'ria] sf sawmill

segna'lare [seɲɲa'lare] vt (manovra etc) to signal; to indicate; (annunciare) to announce; to report; (fig: far conoscere) to point out; (: persona) to single out; **~rsi** vr (distinguersi) to distinguish o.s.

se'gnale [seɲ'nale] sm signal; (cartello): ~ **stradale** road sign; ~ **d'allarme** alarm; (FERR) communication cord; ~ **orario** (RADIO) time signal; **segna'letica** sf signalling, signposting; **segnaletica stradale** road signs pl

se'gnare [seɲ'nare] vt to mark; (prendere nota) to note; (indicare) to indicate, mark; (SPORT: goal) to score; **~rsi** vr (REL) to make the sign of the cross, cross o.s.

'segno ['seɲɲo] sm sign; (impronta, contrassegno) mark; (limite) limit, bounds pl; (bersaglio) target; **fare ~ di sì/no** to nod (one's head)/shake one's head; **fare ~ a qn** di fermarsi to motion (:) sb to stop; **cogliere o colpire nel ~** (fig) to hit the mark

segre'gare vt to segregate, isolate; **segregazi'one** sf segregation

segre'tario, a sm/f secretary; **~ comunale** town clerk; **S~ di Stato** Secretary of State

segrete'ria sf (di ditta, scuola) (secretary's) office; (d'organizzazione internazionale) secretariat; (POL etc: carica) office of Secretary; ~ **telefonica** answering service

segre'tezza sf (segrettesa] sf secrecy

se'greto, a ag secret ♦ sm secret; secrecy no pl; **in** ~ in secret, secretly

segu'ace [se'gwatʃe] sm/f follower, disciple

segu'ente ag following, next

segu'ire vt to follow; (frequentare:

corso) to attend ♦ vi to follow; (continuare: testo) to continue

segui'tare vt to continue, carry on with ♦ vi to continue, carry on

'seguito sm (scorta) suite, retinue; (discepoli) followers pl; (favore) following; (serie) sequence, series sg; (continuazione) continuation; (conseguenza) result; **di** ~ at a stretch, on end; **in** ~ later on; **in** ~ **a, a** ~ **di** following; (a causa di) as a result of, owing to

'sei vb vedi essere ♦ num six

sei'cento [sei'tʃɛnto] num six hundred ♦ sm: **il S~** the seventeenth century

sel'ciato [sel'tʃato] sm cobbled surface

selezio'nare [selettsjo'nare] vt to select

selezi'one [selet'tsjone] sf selection

'sella sf saddle; **sel'lare** vt to saddle

selvag'gina [selvad'dʒina] sf (animali) game

sel'vaggio, a, gi, ge [sel'vaddʒo] ag wild; (tribù) savage, uncivilized; (fig) savage, brutal ♦ sm/f savage, brutal

sel'vatico, a, ci, che ag wild

se'maforo sm (AUT) traffic lights pl

sem'brare vi to seem ♦ vb impers: **sembra che** it seems that; **mi sembra che** it seems to me that; **I think** (that); ~ **di essere** to seem to be

'seme sm seed; (sperma) semen; (CARTE) suit

se'mestre sm half-year, six-month period

'semi... prefisso semi...; **semi'cerchio** sm semicircle; **semifi'nale** sf semifinal; **semi'freddo, a** ag (CUC) chilled ♦ sm ice-cream cake

se'mina sf (AGR) sowing

semi'nare vt to sow

semi'nario sm seminar; (REL) seminary

seminter'rato sm basement; (appartamento) basement flat

se'mitico, a, ci, che ag semitic

sem'mai = se mai; vedi se

'**semola** sf bran; ~ **di grano duro**
durum wheat

semo'lino sm semolina

'**semplice** ['semplitʃe] ag simple; (di
un solo elemento) single; **semplice'mente** av simply; **semplicità** sf
simplicity

'**sempre** av always; (ancora) still;
posso ~ **tentare** I can always o still
try; **da** ~ always; **per** ~ forever;
una volta per ~ once and for all; ~
che provided (that); ~ **più** more
and more; ~ **meno** less and less

sempre'verde ag, sm o f (BOT)
evergreen

se'nape sf (CUC) mustard

se'nato sm senate; **sena'tore**, '**tri-**
ce sm/f senator

'**senno** sm judgment, (common)
sense; **col** ~ **di poi** with hindsight

sennò av = se no; vedi **se**

'**seno** sm (ANAT: petto, mammella)
breast; (: grembo, fig) womb; (: cavità) sinus; (GEO) inlet, creek;
(MAT) sine

sen'sato, **a** ag sensible

sensazio'nale [sensattsjo'nale] ag
sensational

sensazi'one [sensat'tsjone] sf feeling, sensation; **avere la** ~ **che** to
have a feeling that; **fare** ~ to cause
a sensation, create a stir

sen'sibile ag sensitive; (ai sensi)
perceptible; (rilevante, notevole) ap-
preciable, noticeable; ~ **a** sensitive
to; **sensibilità** sf sensitivity

'**senso** sm (FISIOL, istinto) sense;
(impressione, sensazione) feeling,
sensation; (significato) meaning,
sense; (direzione) direction; ~**i** smpl
(coscienza) consciousness sg; (sensualità) senses; **ciò non ha** ~ that
doesn't make sense; **fare** ~ **a** (ripugnare) to disgust, repel; ~ **comu-**
ne common sense; **in** ~ **orario/**
antiorario clockwise/anticlockwise;
a ~ **unico** one-way; "~
vietato" (AUT) "no entry"

sensu'ale ag sensual; sensuous;
sensualità sf sensuality; sensuous-
ness

sen'tenza [sen'tɛntsa] sf (DIR) sentence; (massima) maxim; **senten-**
zi'are vi (DIR) to pass judgment

senti'ero sm path

sentimen'tale ag sentimental;
(vita, avventura) love cpd

senti'mento sm feeling

senti'nella sf sentry

sen'tire vt (percepire al tatto, fig) to
feel; (udire) to hear; (ascoltare) to
listen to; (odore) to smell; (avvertire
con il gusto, assaggiare) to taste ♦
vi: ~ **di** (avere sapore) to taste of;
(avere odore) to smell of; ~**rsi** vr
(uso reciproco) to be in touch; ~**rsi**
bene/male to feel well/unwell o ill;
~**rsi di fare qc** (essere disposto) to
feel like doing sth

sen'tito, **a** ag (sincero) sincere,
warm; **per** ~ **dire** by hearsay

'**senza** ['sɛntsa] prep, cong without;
~ **dir nulla** without saying a word;
fare ~ **qc** to do without sth; ~ **di**
me without me; ~ **che io lo sapessi**
without me o my knowing; **senz'al-**
tro of course, certainly; ~ **dubbio**
no doubt; ~ **scrupoli** unscrupulous;
~ **amici** friendless; ~ **piombo** unleaded

sepa'rare vt to separate; (dividere)
to divide; (tenere distinto) to distinguish; ~**rsi** vr (coniugi) to separate,
part; (amici) to part, leave each
other; ~**rsi da** (coniuge) to separate
o part from; (amico, socio) to part
company with; (oggetto) to part
with; **sepa'rato**, **a** ag (letti, conto
etc) separate; (coniugi) separated;
separazi'one sf separation

se'polcro sm sepulchre

se'polto, **a** pp di **seppellire**

seppel'lire vt to bury

'**seppia** sf cuttlefish ♦ ag inv sepia

se'quenza [se'kwɛntsa] sf sequence

seques'trare vt (DIR) to impound;
(rapire) to kidnap; (costringere in un
luogo) to hold, confine; **se'questro**
sm (DIR) impoundment; **sequestro**
di persona kidnapping

'**sera** *sf* evening; **di** ~ in the evening; **domani** ~ tomorrow, evening, tomorrow night; **se'rale** *ag* evening *cpd*; **se'rata** *sf* evening; (*ricevimento*) party

ser'**bare** *vt* to keep; (*mettere da parte*) to put aside; ~ **rancore/odio verso qn** to bear sb a grudge/hate sb

serba'toio *sm* tank; (*cisterna*) cistern

'**serbo** *sm*: **mettere/tenere** *o* **avere in** ~ **qc** to put/keep sth aside

se'reno, a *ag* (*tempo, cielo*) clear; (*fig*) serene, calm

ser'gente [ser'dʒɛnte] *sm* (*MIL*) sergeant

'**serie** *sf inv* (*successione*) series *inv*; (*gruppo, collezione*: *di chiavi etc*) set; (*SPORT*) division; league; (*COMM*): **modello di** ~ **standard/custom-built model; in** ~ **in quick succession; (**COMM**) mass *cpd*

serietà *sf* seriousness; reliability

'**serio, a** *ag* serious; (*impiegato*) responsible, reliable; (*ditta, cliente*) reliable, dependable; **sul** ~ (*davvero*) really, truly; (*seriamente*) seriously, in earnest

ser'mone *sm* sermon

serpeggi'are [serped'dʒare] *vi* to wind; (*fig*) to spread

ser'pente *sm* snake; ~ **a sonagli** rattlesnake

'**serra** *sf* greenhouse; hothouse

ser'randa *sf* roller shutter

ser'rare *vt* to close, shut; (*a chiave*) to lock; (*stringere*) to tighten; (*premere*: *nemico*) to close in on; ~ **i pugni/i denti** to clench one's fists/ teeth; ~ **le file** to close ranks

serra'tura *sf* lock

'**serva** *sf vedi* **servo**

ser'vire *vt* to serve; (*clienti*: *al ristorante*) to wait on; (: *al negozio*) to serve, attend to; (*fig*: *giovare*) to aid, help; (*CARTE*) to deal ♦ *vi* (*TENNIS*) to serve; (*essere utile*): ~ **a qn** to be of use to sb; ~ **a qc/a fare** (*utensile etc*) to be used for sth/for doing; ~ **(a qn) da** to serve as (for

sb); ~**rsi** *vr* (*usare*): ~**rsi di** to use; (*prendere*: *cibo*): ~**rsi (di)** to help o.s. (to); (*essere cliente abituale*): ~**rsi da** to be a regular customer at, go to

servitù *sf* servitude; slavery; (*personale di servizio*) servants *pl*, domestic staff

servizi'evole [servit'tsjevole] *ag* obliging, willing to help

ser'vizio [ser'vittsjo] *sm* service; (*al ristorante*: **sul** **conto**) service (charge); (*STAMPA, TV, RADIO*) report; (*da tè, caffè etc*) set, service; ~**i** *smpl* (*di casa*) kitchen and bathroom; (*ECON*) services; **essere di** ~ to be on duty; **fuori** ~ (*telefono etc*) out of order; ~ **compreso** service included; ~ **militare** military service; ~**i segreti** secret service *sg*

'**servo, a** *sm/f* servant

ses'santa *num* sixty; **sessan'tesimo, a** *num* sixtieth

sessan'tina *sf*: **una** ~ **(di)** about sixty

sessi'one *sf* session

sesso *sm* sex; **sessu'ale** *ag* sexual, sex *cpd*

ses'tante *sm* sextant

'**sesto, a** *ag, sm* sixth

'**seta** *sf* silk

'**sete** *sf* thirst; **avere** ~ to be thirsty

setola *sf* bristle

'**setta** *sf* sect

set'tanta *num* seventy; **settan'tesimo, a** *num* seventieth

settan'tina *sf*: **una** ~ **(di)** about seventy

'**sette** *num* seven

sette'cento [sette'tʃento] *num* seven hundred ♦ *sm*: **il S~** the eighteenth century

set'tembre *sm* September

settentrio'nale *ag* northern

settentri'one *sm* north

setti'mana *sf* week; **settima'nale** *ag, sm* weekly

'**settimo, a** *ag, sm* seventh

set'tore *sm* sector

severità *sf* severity

se'vero, a ag severe

sevizi'are [sevit'tsjare] vt to torture

se'vizie [se'vittsje] sfpl torture sg

sezio'nare [settsjo'nare] vt to divide into sections; (MED) to dissect

sezi'one [set'tsjone] sf section; (MED) dissection

sfaccen'dato, a [sfattʃen'dato] ag idle

sfacci'ato, a [sfat'tʃato] ag (maleducato) cheeky, impudent; (vistoso) gaudy

sfa'celo [sfa'tʃelo] sm (fig) ruin, collapse

sfal'darsi vr to flake (off)

sfa'mare vt to feed; (sog: cibo) to fill

'sfarzo ['sfartso] sm pomp, splendour

sfasci'are [sfaʃ'ʃare] vt (ferita) to unbandage; (distruggere: porta) to smash, shatter; **~rsi** vr (rompersi) to smash, shatter

sfa'tare vt (leggenda) to explode

sfavil'lare vi to spark, send out sparks; (risplendere) to sparkle

sfavo'revole ag unfavourable

'sfera sf sphere; **'sferico, a, ci, che** ag spherical

sfer'rare vt (fig: colpo) to land, deal; (: attacco) to launch

sfer'zare [sfer'tsare] vt to whip; (fig) to lash out at

sfi'brare vt (indebolire) to exhaust, enervate

'sfida sf challenge; **sfi'dare** vt to challenge; (fig) to defy, brave

sfi'ducia [sfi'dutʃa] sf distrust, mistrust

sfigu'rare vt (persona) to disfigure; (quadro, statua) to deface ♦ vi (far cattiva figura) to make a bad impression

sfi'lare vt (ago) to unthread; (abito, scarpe) to slip off ♦ vi (truppe) to march past; (atleti) to parade; **~rsi** vr (perle etc) to come unstrung; (orlo, tessuto) to fray; (calza) to run, ladder; **sfi'lata** sf march past; parade; **sfilata di moda** fashion show

'sfinge ['sfindʒe] sf sphinx

sfi'nito, a ag exhausted

sfio'rare vt to brush (against); (argomento) to touch upon

sfio'rire vi to wither, fade

sfo'cato, a ag (FOT) out of focus

sfoci'are [sfo'tʃare] vi: **~ in** to flow into; (fig: malcontento) to develop into

sfo'gare vt to vent, pour out; **~rsi** vr (sfogare la propria rabbia) to give vent to one's anger; (confidarsi): **~rsi (con)** to pour out one's feelings (to); **non sfogarti su di me!** don't take your bad temper out on me!

sfoggi'are [sfod'dʒare] vt, vi to show off

'sfoglia ['sfoʎʎa] sf sheet of pasta dough; **pasta ~** (CUC) puff pastry

sfogli'are [sfoʎ'ʎare] vt (libro) to leaf through

'sfogo, ghi sm outlet; (eruzione cutanea) rash; (fig) outburst; **dare ~ a** (fig) to give vent to

sfol'gorante ag (luce) blazing; (fig: vittoria) brilliant

sfol'lare vt to empty, clear ♦ vi to disperse; **~ da** (città) to evacuate

sfon'dare vt (porta) to break down; (scarpe) to wear a hole in; (cesto, scatola) to burst, knock the bottom out of; (MIL) to break through ♦ vi (riuscire) to make a name for o.s.

'sfondo sm background

sfor'mato sm (CUC) type of soufflé

sfor'nare vt (pane etc) to take out of the oven; (fig) to churn out

sfor'nito, a ag: **~ di** lacking in, without; (negozio) cleaned out

sfor'tuna sf misfortune, ill luck no pl; **avere ~** to be unlucky; **sfortu'nato, a** ag unlucky; (impresa, film) unsuccessful

sfor'zare [sfor'tsare] vt to force; (voce, occhi) to strain; **~rsi** vr: **~rsi di o a o per fare** to try hard to do

'sforzo ['sfɔrtso] sm effort; (tensione eccessiva, TECN) strain; **fare uno ~** to make an effort

frat'tare vt to evict; **'sfratto** sm

eviction

sfrecci'are [sfret't∫are] *vi* to shoot *o* flash past

sfregi'are [sfre'dʒare] *vt* to slash, gash; (*persona*) to disfigure; (*quadro*) to deface; **'sfregio** *sm* gash; scar; (*fig*) insult

sfre'nato, a *ag* (*fig*) unrestrained, unbridled

sfron'tato, a *ag* shameless

sfrutta'mento *sm* exploitation

sfrut'tare *vt* (*terreno*) to overwork, exhaust; (*miniera*) to exploit, work; (*fig: operai, occasione, potere*) to exploit

sfug'gire [sfud'dʒire] *vi* to escape; ~ a (*custode*) to escape (from); (*morte*) to escape; ~ a qn (*dettaglio, nome*) to escape sb; ~ **di mano a qn** to slip out of sb's hand (*o* hands); **sfug'gita: di sfuggita** *ad* (*rapidamente, in fretta*) in passing

sfu'mare *vt* (*colori, contorni*) to soften, shade off ♦ *vi* to shade (off), fade; (*fig: svanire*) to vanish, disappear; (*: speranze*) to come to nothing; **sfuma'tura** *sf* shading off *no pl*; (*tonalità*) shade, tone; (*fig*) touch, hint

sfuri'ata *sf* (*scatto di collera*) fit of anger; (*rimprovero*) sharp rebuke

sga'bello *sm* stool

sgabuz'zino [zgabud'dzino] *sm* lumber room

sgambet'tare *vi* to kick one's legs about

sgam'betto *sm*: far lo ~ a qn to trip sb up; (*fig*) to oust sb

sganasci'arsi [zganaʃ'ʃarsi] *vr*: ~ **dalle risa** to roar with laughter

sganci'are [zgan't∫are] *vt* to unhook; (*FERR*) to uncouple; (*bombe: da aereo*) to release, drop; (*fig: fam: soldi*) to fork out; **~rsi** *vr* (*fig*): **~rsi (da)** to get away (from)

sganghe'rato, a [zgange'rato] *ag* (*porta*) off its hinges; (*auto*) ramshackle; (*risata*) wild, boisterous

sgar'bato, a *ag* rude, impolite

'sgarbo *sm*: fare uno ~ a qn to be rude to sb

sgattaio'lare *vi* to sneak away *o* off

sge'lare [zdʒe'lare] *vi, vt* to thaw

'sghembo, a ['zgembo] *ag* (*obliquo*) slanting; (*storto*) crooked

sghignaz'zare [zgiɲɲat'tsare] *vi* to laugh scornfully

sgob'bare (*fam*) *vi* (*scolaro*) to swot; (*operaio*) to slog

sgoccio'lare [zgottʃo'lare] *vt* (*vuotare*) to drain (to the last drop) ♦ *vi* (*acqua*) to drip; (*recipiente*) to drain; **'sgoccioli** *smpl*: essere agli ~ (*provviste*) to be nearly finished; (*periodo*) to be nearly over

sgo'larsi *vr* to talk (*o* shout *o* sing) o.s. hoarse

sgomb(e)'rare *vt* to clear; (*andarsene da: stanza*) to vacate; (*evacuare*) to evacuate

'sgombro, a *ag*: ~ (**di**) clear (of), free (from) ♦ *sm* (*ZOOL*) mackerel; (*anche: sgombero*) clearing; vacating; evacuation; (*: trasloco*) removal

sgomen'tare *vt* to dismay; **sgo'mento, a** *ag* dismayed ♦ *sm* dismay, consternation

sgonfi'are *vt* to let down, deflate; **~rsi** *vr* to go down

'sgorbio *sm* blot; scribble

sgor'gare *vi* to gush (out)

sgoz'zare [zgot'tsare] *vt* to cut the throat of

sgra'devole *ag* unpleasant, disagreeable

sgra'dito, a *ag* unpleasant, unwelcome

sgra'nare *vt* (*piselli*) to shell; ~ **gli occhi** to open one's eyes wide

sgran'chirsi [zgran'kirsi] *vr* to stretch; ~ **le gambe** to stretch one's legs

sgranocchi'are [zgranok'kjare] *vt* to munch

'sgravio *sm*: ~ fiscale tax relief

sgrazi'ato, a [zgrat'tsjato] *ag* clumsy, ungainly

sgreto'lare *vt* to cause to crumble; **~rsi** *vr* to crumble

sgri'dare *vt* to scold; **sgri'data** *sf*

scolding

sguai'ato, a ag coarse, vulgar

sgual'cire [zgwal'tʃire] vt to crumple (up), crease

sgual'drina (peg) sf slut

sgu'ardo sm (occhiata) look, glance; (espressione) look (in one's eye)

sguat'tero, a smf dishwasher (person)

sguaz'zare [zgwat'tsare] vi (nell'acqua) to splash about; (nella melma) to wallow; ~ **nell'oro** to be rolling in money

sguinzagli'are [zgwintsaʎ'ʎare] vt to let off the leash; (fig: persona): ~ **qn dietro a qn** to set sb on sb

sgusci'are [zguʃ'ʃare] vt to shell ♦ vi (sfuggire di mano) to slip; ~ **via** to slip o slink away

'shampoo ['ʃampo] sm inv shampoo

shock [ʃɔk] sm inv shock

PAROLA CHIAVE

---

si¹ (dav lo, la, li, le, ne diventa se) pron 1 (riflessivo: maschile) himself; (: femminile) herself; (: neutro) itself; (: impersonale) oneself; (: pl) themselves; **lavarsi** to wash (oneself); ~ **è tagliato** he has cut himself; ~ **credono importanti** they think a lot of themselves

2 (riflessivo: con complemento oggetto): **lavarsi le mani** to wash one's hands; ~ **sta lavando i capelli** (o she) is washing his (o her) hair

3 (reciproco) one another, each other; **si amano** they love one another o each other

4 (passivo): ~ **ripara facilmente** it is easily repaired

5 (impersonale): ~ **dice che ...** they o people say that ...; ~ **vede che è vecchio** one o you can see that it's old

6 (noi) we; **tra poco** ~ **parte** we're leaving soon

si² sm (MUS) B; (solfeggiando la scala) ti

sì av yes; **un giorno** ~ **e uno no** every other day

'sia cong: ~ ... ~ (o ... o): ~ **che lavori,** ~ **che non lavori** whether he works or not; (tanto ... quanto): **verranno** ~ **Luigi** ~ **suo fratello** both Luigi and his brother will be coming

si'amo vb vedi essere

sibi'lare vi to hiss; (fischiare) to whistle; **'sibilo** sm hiss; whistle

si'cario sm hired killer

sicché [sik'ke] cong (perciò) so (that), therefore; (e quindi) (and) so

siccità [sittʃi'ta] sf drought

sic'come cong since, as

Si'cilia [si'tʃilja] sf: **la** ~ Sicily; **sici-li'ano, a** ag, smf Sicilian

sicu'rezza [siku'rettsa] sf safety; security; (fiducia) confidence; (certezza) certainty; **di** ~ safety cpd; **la** ~ **stradale** road safety

si'curo, a ag safe; (ben difeso) secure; (fiducioso) confident; (certo) sure, certain; (notizia, amico) reliable; (esperto) skilled ♦ av (anche: **di** ~) certainly; **essere/mettere al** ~ to be safe/put in a safe place; ~ **di sé** self-confident, sure of o.s.; **sentir-si** ~ to feel safe o secure

siderur'gia [siderur'dʒia] sf iron and steel industry

'sidro sm cider

si'epe sf hedge

si'ero sm (MED) serum; **sieronega'tivo, a** ag HIV-negative; **sieroposi'tivo, a** ag HIV-positive

si'esta sf siesta, (afternoon) nap

si'ete vb vedi essere

si'filide sf syphilis

si'fone sm siphon

Sig. abbr (= signore) Mr

siga'retta sf cigarette

'sigaro sm cigar

Sigg. abbr (= signori) Messrs

sigil'lare [sidʒil'lare] vt to seal

si'gillo [si'dʒillo] sm seal

'sigla sf initials pl; acronym, abbreviation; ~ **automobilistica** abbreviation of province on vehicle number *plate*; ~ **musicale** signature tune

si'glare *vt* to initial

Sig.na *abbr* (= *signorina*) Miss

signifi'care [siɲɲifi'kare] *vt* to mean; **significa'tivo, a** *ag* significant; **signifi'cato** *sm* meaning

si'gnora [siɲ'ɲora] *sf* lady; **la ~ X** Mrs X; **buon giorno S~/Signore/ Signorina** good morning; (*deferente*) good morning Madam/Sir/Madam; (*quando si conosce il nome*) good morning Mrs/Mr/Miss X; **Gentile S~/Signore/Signorina** (*in una lettera*) Dear Madam/Sir/Madam; **il signor Rossi e ~** Mr Rossi and his wife; **~e i signori** ladies and gentlemen

si'gnore [siɲ'ɲore] *sm* gentleman; (*padrone*) lord, master; (*REL*): **il S~** the Lord; **il signor X** Mr X; **i ~i Bianchi** (*coniugi*) Mr and Mrs Bianchi; *vedi anche* **signora**

signo'rile [siɲɲo'rile] *ag* refined

signo'rina [siɲɲo'rina] *sf* young lady; **la ~ X** Miss X; *vedi anche* **signora**

Sig.ra *abbr* (= *signora*) Mrs

silenzia'tore [silentsja'tore] *sm* silencer

si'lenzio [si'lɛntsjo] *sm* silence; **fare ~** to be quiet, stop talking; **silenzi'oso, a** *ag* silent, quiet

si'licio [si'litʃo] *sm* silicon; **piastrina di ~** silicon chip

'sillaba *sf* syllable

silu'rare *vt* to torpedo; (*fig: privare del comando*) to oust

si'luro *sm* torpedo

simboleggi'are [simboled'dʒare] *vt* to symbolize

'simbolo *sm* symbol

'simile *ag* (*analogo*) similar; (*di questo tipo*): **un uomo ~** such a man, a man like this; **libri ~i** such books; ~ **a** similar to; **i suoi ~i** one's fellow men; one's peers

simme'tria *sf* symmetry

simpa'tia *sf* (*qualità*) pleasantness; (*inclinazione*) liking; **avere ~ per qn** to like sb, have a liking for sb;

sim'patico, a, ci, che *ag* (*persona*) nice, pleasant, likeable; (*casa, albergo etc*) nice, pleasant

simpatiz'zare [simpatid'dzare] *vi*: ~ **con** to take a liking to

sim'posio *sm* symposium

simu'lare *vt* to sham, simulate; (*TECN*) to simulate; **simulazi'one** *sf* shamming; simulation

simul'taneo, a *ag* simultaneous

sina'goga, ghe *sf* synagogue

since'rità [sintʃeri'ta] *sf* sincerity

sin'cero, a [sin'tʃero] *ag* sincere; genuine; heartfelt

'sincope *sf* syncopation; (*MED*) blackout

sinda'cale *ag* (trade-)union *cpd*; **sinda'calista, i, e** *sm/f* trade union-ist

sinda'cato *sm* (*di lavoratori*) (trade) union; (*AMM, ECON, DIR*) syndicate, trust, pool

'sindaco *sm* mayor

sinfo'nia *sf* (*MUS*) symphony

singhioz'zare [singjot'tsare] *vi* to sob; to hiccup

singhi'ozzo [sin'gjottso] *sm* sob; (*MED*) hiccup; **avere il ~** to have the hiccups; **a ~** (*fig*) by fits and starts

singo'lare *ag* (*insolito*) remarkable, singular; (*LING*) singular ♦ *sm* (*LING*) singular; (*TENNIS*): ~ **maschile/femminile** men's/women's singles

'singolo, a *ag* single, individual ♦ *sm* (*persona*) individual; (*TENNIS*) = **singolare**

si'nistra [si'nistra] *sf* (*POL*) left (wing); **a ~** on the left; (*direzione*) to the left

si'nistro, a *ag* left, left-hand; (*fig*) sinister ♦ *sm* (*incidente*) accident

'sino *prep* = **fino**

si'nonimo, a *ag* synonymous ♦ *sm* synonym; ~ **di** synonymous with

sin'tassi *sf* syntax

'sintesi *sf* synthesis; (*riassunto*) summary, résumé

sin'tetico, a, ci, che *ag* synthetic

sintetiz'zare [sintetid'dzare] *vt* to

synthesize; (*riassumere*) to summarize

sinto'matico, a, ci, che *ag* symptomatic

'sintomo *sm* symptom

sinu'oso, a *ag* (*strada*) winding

S.I.P. *sigla f* (= *Società italiana per l'esercizio telefonico*) Italian telephone company

si'pario *sm* (TEATRO) curtain

si'rena *sf* (*apparecchio*) siren; (*nella mitologia, fig*) siren, mermaid

'Siria *sf*: **la ~** Syria

si'ringa, ghe *sf* syringe

'sismico, a, ci, che *ag* seismic

sis'mografo *sm* seismograph

sis'tema, i *sm* system; method, way; **~ di vita** way of life

siste'mare (*mettere a posto*) to tidy, put in order; (*risolvere: questione*) to sort out, settle; (*procurare un lavoro a*) to find a job for; (*dare un alloggio a*) to settle, find accommodation for; **~rsi** *vr* (*problema*) to be settled; (*persona: trovare alloggio*) to find accommodation (BRIT) *o* accommodations (US); (: *trovarsi un lavoro*) to get fixed up with a job; **ti sistemo io!** I'll soon sort you out!

siste'matico, a, ci, che *ag* systematic

sistemazi'one [sistemat'tsjone] *sf* arrangement, order; settlement; employment; accommodation (BRIT), accommodations (US)

'sito *sm* (*letterario*) place

situ'are *vt* to site, situate; **situ'ato, a** *ag*: **situato a/su** situated at/on

situazi'one [situat'tsjone] *sf* situation

ski-lift ['skɪːlɪft] *sm inv* ski-lift

slacci'are [zlat'tʃare] *vt* to undo, unfasten

slanci'arsi [zlan'tʃarsi] *vr* to dash, fling o.s.; **slanci'ato, a** *ag* slender; **'slancio** *sm* dash, leap; (*fig*) surge; **di slancio** impetuously

sla'vato, a *ag* faded, washed out; (*fig: viso, occhi*) pale, colourless

'slavo, a *ag* Slav(onic), Slavic

sle'ale *ag* disloyal; (*concorrenza etc*) unfair

sle'gare *vt* to untie

slip [zlip] *sm inv* briefs *pl*

'slitta *sf* sledge; (*trainata*) sleigh

slit'tare *vi* to slip, slide; (AUT) to skid

slo'gare *vt* (MED) to dislocate

sloggi'are [zlod'dʒare] *vt* (*inquilino*) to turn out; (*nemico*) to drive out, dislodge ♦ *vi* to move out

Slovenia [zlo'venja] *sf* Slovenia

smacchi'are [zmak'kjare] *vt* to remove stains from

'smacco, chi *sm* humiliating defeat

smagli'ante [zmaʎ'ʎante] *ag* brilliant, dazzling

smagli'atura [zmaʎʎa'tura] *sf* (*su maglia, calza*) ladder; (*della pelle*) stretch mark

smalizi'ato, a [smalit'tsjato] *ag* shrewd, cunning

smal'tare *vt* to enamel; (*ceramica*) to glaze; (*unghie*) to varnish

smal'tire *vt* (*merce*) to sell off; (*rifiuti*) to dispose of; (*cibo*) to digest; (*peso*) to lose; (*rabbia*) to get over; **~ la sbornia** to sober up

'smalto *sm* (*anche: di denti*) enamel; (*per ceramica*) glaze; **~ per unghie** nail varnish

'smania *sf* agitation, restlessness; (*fig*): **~ di** thirst for, craving for; **avere la ~ addosso** to have the fidgets; **avere la ~ di fare** to be desperate to do

smantel'lare *vt* to dismantle

smarri'mento *sm* loss; (*fig*) bewilderment; dismay

smar'rire *vt* to lose; (*non riuscire a trovare*) to mislay; **~rsi** *vr* (*perdersi*) to lose one's way, get lost; (: *oggetto*) to go astray; **smar'rito, a** *ag* (*sbigottito*) bewildered

smasche'rare [zmaske'rare] *vt* to unmask

smemo'rato, a *ag* forgetful

smen'tire *vt* (*negare*) to deny; (*testimonianza*) to refute; (*reputazione*) to give the lie to; **~rsi** *vr* to be inconsistent; **smen'tita** *sf* denial;

retraction

sme'raldo sm emerald

smerci'are [zmer'tʃare] vt (COMM) to sell; (: svendere) to sell off

sme'riglio [zme'riʎʎo] sm emery

'smesso, a pp di smettere

'smettere vt to stop; (vestiti) to stop wearing ♦ vi to stop, cease; ~ **di fare** to stop doing

'smilzo, a ['zmiltso] ag thin, lean

sminu'ire vt to diminish, lessen; (fig) to belittle

sminuz'zare [zminut'tsare] vt to break into small pieces; to crumble

smis'tare vt (pacchi etc) to sort; (FERR) to shunt

smisu'rato, a ag boundless, immeasurable; (grandissimo) immense, enormous

smobili'tare vt to demobilize

smo'dato, a ag immoderate

smoking ['zmoukiŋ] sm inv dinner jacket

smon'tare vt (mobile, macchina etc) to take to pieces, dismantle; (fig: scoraggiare) to dishearten ♦ vi (scendere: da cavallo) to dismount; (: da treno) to get off; (terminare il lavoro) to stop (work); ~rsi vr to lose heart; to lose one's enthusiasm

'smorfia sf grimace; (atteggiamento lezioso) simpering; **fare ~e** to make faces; to simper; **smorfi'oso, a** ag simpering

'smorto, a ag (viso) pale, wan; (colore) dull

smor'zare [zmor'tsare] vt (suoni) to deaden; (colori) to tone down; (luce) to dim; (sete) to quench; (entusiasmo) to dampen; ~rsi vr (suono, luce) to fade; (entusiasmo) to dampen

'smosso, a pp di smuovere

smotta'mento sm landslide

'smunto, a ag haggard, pinched

smu'overe vt to move, shift; (fig: commuovere) to move; (: dall'inerzia) to rouse, stir; ~rsi vr to move, shift

smus'sare vt (angolo) to round off,

smooth; (lama etc) to blunt; ~rsi vr to become blunt

snatu'rato, a ag inhuman, heartless

'snello, a ag (agile) agile; (svelto) slender, slim

sner'vare vt to enervate, wear out; ~rsi vr to become enervated

sni'dare vt to drive out, flush out

snob'bare vt to snub

sno'bismo sm snobbery

snoccio'lare [znottʃo'lare] vt (frutta) to stone; (fig: orazioni) to rattle off; (: verità) to blab

sno'dare vt (rendere agile, mobile) to loosen; ~rsi vr to come loose; (articolarsi) to bend; (strada, fiume) to wind

so vb vedi sapere

sob'balzare [sobbal'tsare] vi to jolt, jerk; (trasalire) to jump; start; **sob'balzo** sm jerk, jolt; jump, start

sobbar'carsi vr: ~ **a** to take on, undertake

sob'borgo, ghi sm suburb

sobil'lare vt to stir up, incite

'sobrio, a ag sober

socchi'udere [sok'kjudere] vt (porta) to leave ajar; (occhi) to half-close; **socchi'uso, a** pp di **socchiudere**

soc'correre vt to help, assist; **soc'corso, a** pp di **soccorrere** ♦ sm help, aid, assistance; **soccorsi** smpl relief sg, aid sg; **soccorso stradale** breakdown service

socialdemo'cratico, a, ci, che [sotʃaldemo'kratiko] smf Social Democrat

soci'ale [so'tʃale] ag social; (di associazione) club cpd, association cpd

socia'lismo [sotʃa'lizmo] sm socialism; **socia'lista, i, e** ag, smf socialist

società [sotʃe'ta] sf inv society; (sportiva) club; (COMM) company; ~ **per azioni** limited (BRIT) o incorporated (US) company; ~ **a responsabilità limitata** type of limited liability company

soci'evole [so'tʃevole] ag sociable

'socio ['sɔtʃo] sm (DIR, COMM) partner; (membro di associazione) member

'soda sf (CHIM) soda; (acqua gassata) soda (water)

soda'lizio [soda'littsjo] sm association, society

soddisfa'cente [soddisfa'tʃente] ag satisfactory

soddis'fare vt, vi: ~ a to satisfy; (impegno) to fulfil; (debito) to pay off; (richiesta) to meet, comply with; (offesa) to make amends for; **soddis'fatto, a** pp di **soddisfare ♦** ag satisfied; **soddisfatto di** happy o satisfied with; pleased with; **soddisfazi'one** sf satisfaction

'sodo, a ag firm, hard **♦** av (picchiare, lavorare) hard; **dormire** ~ to sleep soundly

sofà sm inv sofa

soffe'renza [soffe'rentsa] sf suffering

sof'ferto, a pp di **soffrire**

soffi'are vt to blow; (notizia, segreto) to whisper **♦** vi to blow; (sbuffare) to puff (and blow); ~**rsi il naso** to blow one's nose; ~ **qc/qn a qn** (fig) to pinch o steal sth/sb from sb; ~ **via** qc to blow sth away

'soffice ['sɔffitʃe] ag soft

'soffio sm (di vento) breath; (di fumo) puff; (MED) murmur

sof'fitta sf attic

sof'fitto sm ceiling

soffo'care vi (anche: ~rsi) to suffocate, choke **♦** vt to suffocate, choke; (fig) to stifle, suppress

sof'friggere [sof'friddʒere] vt to fry lightly

sof'frire vt to suffer, endure; (sopportare) to bear, stand **♦** vi to suffer, to be in pain; ~ (di) qc (MED) to suffer from sth

sof'fritto, a pp di **soffriggere ♦** sm (CUC) fried mixture of herbs, bacon and onions

sofisti'cato, a ag sophisticated; (vino) adulterated

sogget'tivo, a [soddʒet'tivo] ag

subjective

sog'getto, a [sod'dʒetto] ag: ~ **a** (sottomesso) subject to; (esposto: a variazioni, danni etc) subject o liable to **♦** sm subject

soggezi'one [soddʒet'tsjone] sf subjection; (timidezza) awe; **avere ~ di qn** to stand in awe of sb; to be ill at ease in sb's presence

sogghi'gnare [soggin'ɲare] vi to sneer

soggior'nare [soddʒor'nare] vi to stay; **soggi'orno** sm (invernale, marino) stay; (stanza) living room

sog'giungere [sod'dʒundʒere] vt to add

'soglia ['sɔʎʎa] sf doorstep; (anche fig) threshold

'sogliola ['sɔʎʎola] sf (ZOOL) sole

so'gnare [son'ɲare] vt, vi to dream; ~ **a occhi aperti** to daydream; **so-gna'tore, 'trice** smf dreamer

'sogno ['sonɲo] sm dream

'soia sf (BOT) soya

sol sm (MUS) G; (: solfeggiando la scala) so(h)

so'laio sm (soffitta) attic

sola'mente av only, just

so'lare ag solar, sun cpd

'solco, chi sm (scavo, fig: ruga) furrow; (incavo) rut, track; (di disco) groove; (scia) wake

sol'dato sm soldier; ~ **semplice** private

'soldo sm (fig): **non avere un** ~ to be penniless; **non vale un** ~ it's not worth a penny; ~**i** smpl (denaro) money sg

'sole sm sun; (luce) sun(light); (tempo assolato) sun(shine); **prendere il** ~ to sunbathe

soleggi'ato, a [soled'dʒato] ag sunny

so'lenne ag solemn; **solennità** sf solemnity; (festività) holiday, feast day

sol'fato sm (CHIM) sulphate

soli'dale ag: essere ~ (con) to be in agreement (with)

solidarietà sf solidarity

'solido, a *ag* solid; (*forte, robusto*) sturdy, solid; (*fig: ditta*) sound, solid ♦ *sm* (MAT) solid

soli'loquio *sm* soliloquy

so'lista, i, e *ag solo* ♦ *smf* soloist

solita'mente *av* usually, as a rule

soli'tario, a *ag* (*senza compagnia*) solitary, lonely; (*solo, isolato*) solitary, lone; (*deserto*) lonely ♦ *sm* (*gioiello, gioco*) solitaire

'solito, a *ag* usual; **essere ~ fare** to be in the habit of doing; **di ~** usually; **più tardi del ~** later than usual; **come al ~** as usual

soli'tudine *sf* solitude

solleci'tare [solletʃi'tare] *vt* (*lavoro*) to speed up; (*persona*) to urge on; (*chiedere con insistenza*) to press for, request urgently; (*stimolare*): ~ **qn a fare** to urge sb to do; (TECN) to stress; **sollecitazi'one** *sf* entreaty, request; (*fig*) incentive; (TECN) stress

sol'lecito, a [sol'letʃito] *ag* prompt, quick ♦ *sm* (*lettera*) reminder; **solleci'tudine** *sf* promptness, speed

solleti'care *vt* to tickle

sol'letico *sm* tickling; **soffrire il ~** to be ticklish

solleva'mento *sm* raising; lifting; revolt; **~ pesi** (SPORT) weight-lifting

solle'vare *vt* to lift, raise; (*fig: persona: alleggerire*): ~ (**da**) to relieve (of); (*: dar conforto*) to comfort, relieve; (*: questione*) to raise; (*: far insorgere*) to stir (to revolt); **~rsi** *vr* to rise; (*fig: riprendersi*) to recover; (*: ribellarsi*) to rise up

solli'evo *sm* relief; (*conforto*) comfort

'solo, a *ag* alone; (*in senso spirituale: isolato*) lonely; (*unico*): **un ~** libro only one book, a single book; (*con ag numerale*): **veniamo noi tre ~i** just o only the three of us are coming ♦ *av* (*soltanto*) only, just; **non ~ ... ma anche** not only ... but also; **fare qc da ~** to do sth (all) by oneself; **da me ~** single-handed, on

my own

sol'tanto *av* only

so'lubile *ag* (*sostanza*) soluble

soluzi'one [solut'tsjone] *sf* solution

sol'vente *ag, sm* solvent

'soma *sf*: **bestia da ~** beast of burden

so'maro *sm* ass, donkey

somigli'anza [somiʎ'ʎantsa] *sf* resemblance

somigli'are [somiʎ'ʎare] *vi*: ~ **a** to be like, resemble; (*nell'aspetto fisico*) to look like; **~rsi** *vr* to be (o look) alike

'somma *sf* (MAT) sum; (*di denaro*) sum (of money); (*complesso di varie cose*) whole amount, sum total

som'mare *vt* to add up; (*aggiungere*) to add; **tutto sommato** all things considered

som'mario, a *ag* (*racconto, indagine*) brief; (*giustizia*) summary ♦ *sm* summary

som'mergere [som'mɛrdʒere] *vt* to submerge

sommer'gibile [sommer'dʒibile] *sm* submarine

som'merso, a *pp di* **sommergere**

som'messo, a *ag* (*voce*) soft, subdued

somminis'trare *vt* to give, administer

sommità *sf inv* summit, top; (*fig*) height

'sommo, a *ag* highest; (*rispetto etc*) highest, greatest; (*poeta, artista*) great, outstanding ♦ *sm* (*fig*) height; **per ~i capi** briefly, covering the main points

som'mossa *sf* uprising

so'nare *etc* = **suonare** *etc*

son'daggio [son'daddʒo] *sm* sounding; probe; boring, drilling; (*indagine*) survey; **~ d'opinioni** opinion poll

son'dare *vt* (NAUT) to sound; (*atmosfera, piaga*) to probe; (MINERALOGIA) to bore, drill; (*fig: opinione etc*) to survey, poll

so'netto *sm* sonnet

son'nambulo, a *smf* sleepwalker

sonnecchi'are [sonnek'kjare] *vi* to doze, nod

son'nifero *sm* sleeping drug (*o* pill)

'sonno *sm* sleep; **prendere** (*o* **fall asleep); aver ~** to be sleepy

'sono *vb vedi* **essere**

so'noro, a *ag* (*ambiente*) resonant; (*voce*) sonorous, ringing; (*onde, film*) sound *cpd*

sontu'oso, a *ag* sumptuous; lavish

sopo'rifero, a *ag* soporific

soppe'sare *vt* to weigh in one's hand(s), feel the weight of; (*fig*) to weigh up

soppi'atto: di ~ *av* secretly; furtively

soppor'tare *vt* (*reggere*) to support; (*subire: perdita, spese*) to bear, sustain; (*soffrire: dolore*) to bear, endure; (*sog: cosa: freddo*) to withstand; (*sog: persona: freddo, vino*) to take; (*tollerare*) to put up with, tolerate

sop'presso, a *pp di* **sopprimere**

sop'primere *vt* (*carica, privilegi, testimone*) to do away with; (*pubblicazione*) to suppress; (*parola, frase*) to delete

'sopra *prep* (*gen*) on; (*al di sopra di, più in alto di*) above; over; (*riguardo a*) on, about ♦ *av* on top; (*attaccato, scritto*) on it; (*al di sopra*) above; (*al piano superiore*) upstairs; **donne ~ i 30 anni** women over 30 (years of age); **abito di ~** I live upstairs; **dormirci ~** (*fig*) to sleep on it

so'prabito *sm* overcoat

sopracci'glio [soprat'tʃiʎʎo] (*pl(f)* **sopracc'ciglia**) *sm* eyebrow

sopracco'perta *sf* (*di letto*) bedspread; (*di libro*) jacket

soprad'detto, a *ag* aforesaid

sopraf'fare *vt* to overcome, overwhelm; **sopraf'fatto, a** *pp di* **sopraffare**

sopraf'fino, a *ag* (*pranzo, vino*) excellent

sopraggi'ungere [soprad'dʒundʒere] *vi* (*giungere all'improvviso*) to arrive (unexpectedly); (*accadere*) to occur (unexpectedly)

sopral'luogo, ghi *sm* (*di esperti*) inspection; (*di polizia*) on-the-spot investigation

sopram'mobile *sm* ornament

soprannatu'rale *ag* supernatural

sopran'nome *sm* nickname

so'prano, a *smf* (*persona*) soprano ♦ *sm* (*voce*) soprano

soprappensi'ero *av* lost in thought

sopras'salto *sm*: **di ~ with a start; suddenly

soprasse'dere *vi*: **~ a** to delay, put off

soprat'tutto *av* (*anzitutto*) above all; (*specialmente*) especially

soprav'vento *sm*: **avere/prendere il ~ su** to have/get the upper hand over

sopravvi'suto, a *pp di* **sopravvivere**

soprav'vivere *vi* to survive; (*continuare a vivere*): **~ (in)** to live on (in); **~ a** (*incidente etc*) to survive; (*persona*) to outlive

sopre'le'vata *sf* (*strada*) flyover; (*ferrovia*) elevated railway

soprinten'dente *smf* supervisor; (*statale: di belle arti etc*) keeper; **soprinten'denza** *sf* supervision; (*ente*): **soprintendenza alle Belle Arti** government department responsible for monuments and artistic treasures

so'pruso *sm* abuse of power; **subire un ~** to be abused

soq'quadro *sm*: **mettere a ~** to turn upside-down

sor'betto *sm* sorbet, water ice

sor'bire *vt* to sip; (*fig*) to put up with

'sorcio, ci [ˈsortʃo] *sm* mouse

sor'dido, a *ag* sordid; (*fig: gretto*) stingy

sor'dina *sf*: **in ~** softly; (*fig*) on the sly

sordità *sf* deafness

'sordo, a *ag* deaf; (*rumore*) muffled; (*dolore*) dull; (*odio, ran-*

core) veiled ♦ *smf* deaf person; **sordo'muto, a** *ag* deaf-and-dumb ♦ *smf* deaf-mute

so'rella *sf* sister; **sorel'lastra** *sf* stepsister

sor'gente [sor'dʒɛnte] *sf* (*acqua che sgorga*) spring; (*di fiume, FISICA, fig*) source

'sorgere ['sordʒere] *vi* to rise; (*scaturire*) to spring, rise; (*fig: difficoltà*) to arise

sormon'tare *vt* (*fig*) to overcome, surmount

sorni'one, a *ag* sly

sorpas'sare *vt* (*AUT*) to overtake; (*fig*) to surpass; (: *eccedere*) to exceed, go beyond; **~ in altezza** to be higher than; (*persona*) to be taller than

sorpren'dente *ag* surprising

sor'prendere *vt* (*cogliere: in flagrante etc*) to catch; (*stupire*) to surprise; **~rsi** *vr*: **~rsi** (**di**) to be surprised (at); **sor'presa** *sf* surprise; **fare una sorpresa a qn** to give sb a surprise; **sor'preso, a** *pp di* **sorprendere**

sor'reggere [sor'rɛddʒere] *vt* to support, hold up; (*fig*) to sustain; **sor'retto, a** *pp di* **sorreggere**

sor'ridere *vi* to smile; **sor'riso, a** *pp di* **sorridere** ♦ *sm* smile

'sorso *sm* sip

'sorta *sf* sort, kind; **di ~** whatever, of any kind, at all

'sorte *sf* (*fato*) fate, destiny; (*evento fortuito*) chance; **tirare a ~** to draw lots

sor'teggio [sor'tɛddʒo] *sm* draw

sorti'legio [sorti'lɛdʒo] *sm* witchcraft *no pl*; (*incantesimo*) spell; **fare un ~ a qn** to cast a spell on sb

sor'tita *sf* (*MIL*) sortie

'sorto, a *pp di* **sorgere**

sorvegli'anza [sorveʎ'ʎantsa] *sf* watch; supervision; (*POLIZIA, MIL*) surveillance

sorvegli'are [sorveʎ'ʎare] *vt* (*bambino, bagagli, prigioniero*) to watch, keep an eye on; (*malato*) to watch

over; (*territorio, casa*) to watch o keep watch over; (*lavori*) to supervise

sorvo'lare *vt* (*territorio*) to fly over ♦ *vi*: **~ su** (*fig*) to skim over

'sosia *sm inv* double

sos'pendere *vt* (*appendere*) to hang (up); (*interrompere, privare di una carica*) to suspend; (*rimandare*) to defer; **~ un quadro al muro/un lampadario al soffitto** to hang a picture on the wall/a chandelier from the ceiling; **sospensi'one** *sf* (*anche CHIM, AUT*) suspension; deferment;

sos'peso, a *pp di* **sospendere** ♦ *ag* (*appeso*) sospeso a hanging on (o from); (*treno, autobus*) cancelled; **in sospeso** in abeyance; (*conto*) outstanding; **tenere in sospeso** (*fig*) to keep in suspense

sospet'tare *vt* to suspect ♦ *vi*: **~ di** to suspect; (*diffidare*) to be suspicious of

sos'petto, a *ag* suspicious ♦ *sm* suspicion; **sospet'toso, a** *ag* suspicious

sos'pingere [sos'pindʒere] *vt* to drive, push; **sos'pinto, a** *pp di* **sospingere**

sospi'rare *vi* to sigh ♦ *vt* to long for, yearn for; **sos'piro** *sm* sigh

'sosta *sf* (*fermata*) stop, halt; (*pausa*) pause, break; **senza ~** non-stop, without a break

sostan'tivo *sm* noun, substantive

sos'tanza [sos'tantsa] *sf* substance; **~e** *sfpl* (*ricchezze*) wealth *sg*, possessions; **in ~** in short, to sum up; **sostanzi'oso, a** *ag* (*cibo*) nourishing, substantial

sos'tare *vi* (*fermarsi*) to stop (for a while), stay; (*fare una pausa*) to take a break

sos'tegno [sos'teɲɲo] *sm* support

soste'nere *vt* to support; (*prendere su di sé*) to take on, bear; (*resistere*) to withstand, stand up to; (*affermare*): **~ che** to maintain that; **~rsi** *vr* to hold o.s. up, support o.s.; (*fig*) to keep up one's strength; **~ gli esa-**

mi to sit exams; **soste'ni,tore, 'tri-ce** *smf* supporter

sostenta'mento *sm* maintenance, support

soste'nuto, a *ag* (*stile*) elevated; (*velocità, ritmo*) sustained; (*prezzo*) high ♦ *smf*: **fare il(la)** ~(**a**) to be standoffish, keep one's distance

sostitu'ire *vt* (*mettere al posto di*): ~ **qn/qc a** to substitute sb/sth for; (*prendere il posto di: persona*) to substitute for; (: *cosa*) to take the place of

sosti'tuto, a *smf* substitute

sostituzi'one [sostitut'tsjone] *sf* substitution; **in** ~ **di** as a substitute for, in place of

sotta'ceti [sotta'ʃeti] *smpl* pickles

sot'tana *sf* (*sottoveste*) underskirt; (*gonna*) skirt; (*REL*) soutane, cassock

sotter'fugio [sotter'fudʒo] *sm* subterfuge

sotter'raneo, a *ag* underground ♦ *sm* cellar

sotter'rare *vt* to bury

sottigli'ezza [sottiʎ'ʎettsa] *sf* thinness; slimness; (*fig*: *acutezza*) subtlety; shrewdness; ~**e** *sfpl* (*pedanteria*) quibbles

sot'tile *ag* thin; (*figura, caviglia*) thin, slim, slender; (*fine: polvere, capelli*) fine; (*fig: leggero*) light; (: *vista*) sharp, keen; (: *olfatto*) fine, discriminating; (: *mente*) subtle, shrewd ♦ *sm*: **non andare per il** ~ not to mince matters

sottin'tendere *vt* (*intendere qc non espresso*) to understand; (*implicare*) to imply; **sottin'teso, a** *pp di* **sottintendere** ♦ *sm* allusion; **parlare senza sottintesi** to speak plainly

'sotto *prep* (*gen*) under; (*più in basso di*) below ♦ *av* underneath, beneath; below; (*al piano inferiore*): **(al piano) di** ~ downstairs; (: *vista*) sharp, keen; ~ **for-ma di** in the form of; ~ **il monte** at the foot of the mountain; **siamo** ~ **Natale** it's nearly Christmas; ~ **la pioggia/il sole** in the rain/

sun(shine); ~ **terra** underground; ~ **voce** in a low voice; **chiuso** ~ **vuoto** vacuum-packed

sottoline'are *vt* to underline; (*fig*) to emphasize, stress

sotto'marino, a *ag* (*flora*) submarine; (*cavo, navigazione*) underwater ♦ *sm* (*NAUT*) submarine

sotto'messo, a *pp di* **sottomettere**

sotto'mettere *vt* to subdue, subjugate; ~**rsi** *vr* to submit

sottopas'saggio [sottopas'saddʒo] *sm* (*AUT*) underpass; (*pedonale*) subway, underpass

sotto'porre *vt* (*costringere*) to subject; (*fig: presentare*) to submit; **sottoporsi** *vr* to submit; **sottoporsi a** (*subire*) to undergo; **sotto'posto, a** *pp di* **sottoporre**

sottos'critto, a *pp di* **sottoscrivere**

sottos'crivere *vt* to sign ♦ *vi*: ~ **a** to subscribe to; **sottoscrizi'one** *sf* signing; subscription

sottosegre'tario *sm*: ~ **di Stato** Under-Secretary of State (*BRIT*), Assistant Secretary of State (*US*)

sotto'sopra *av* upside-down

sotto'terra *av* underground

sotto'titolo *sm* subtitle

sotto'veste *sf* underskirt

sotto'voce [sotto'votʃe] *av* in a low voice

sot'trarre *vt* (*MAT*) to subtract, take away; ~ **qn/qc a** (*togliere*) to remove sb/sth from; (*salvare*) to save *o* rescue sb/sth from; ~ **qc a qn** (*rubare*) to steal sth from sb; **sottrarsi** *vr*: **sottrarsi a** (*sfuggire*) to escape; (*evitare*) to avoid; **sot'tratto, a** *pp di* **sottrarre; sottrazi'one** *sf* subtraction; removal

sovi'etico, a, ci, che *ag* Soviet ♦ *smf* Soviet citizen

sovraccari'care *vt* to overload

sovrannatu'rale *ag* = **soprannaturale**

so'vrano, a *ag* sovereign; (*fig: sommo*) supreme ♦ *smf* sovereign, monarch

sovrap'porre vt to place on top of, put on top of

sovra'stare vi: ~ a (vallata, fiume) to overhang; (fig) to hang over, threaten ♦ vt to overhang; to hang over, threaten

sovrinten'dente smf = soprintendente; **sovrinten'denza** sf = soprintendenza

sovru'mano, a ag superhuman

sovvenzi'one [sovven'tsjone] sf subsidy, grant

sover'sivo, a ag subversive

'sozzo, a ['sottso] ag filthy, dirty

S.p.A. abbr = società per azioni

spac'care vt to split, break; (legna) to chop; **~rsi** vr to split, break; **spacca'tura** sf split

spacci'are [spat'tʃare] vt (vendere) to sell (off); (mettere in circolazione) to circulate; (droga) to peddle, push; **~rsi** vr: **~rsi per** (farsi credere) to pass o.s. off as, pretend to be; **spaccia'tore, 'trice** smf (di droga) pusher; (di denaro falso) dealer; **'spaccio** sm (di merce rubata, droga); spaccio (di) trafficking (in); (in denaro falso): smuggling (of); (vendita) sale; **spaccio (di)** passing (of); (vendita: bottega) shop

'spacco, chi sm (fenditura) split, crack; (strappo) tear; (di gonna) slit

spac'cone smf boaster, braggart

'spada sf sword

spae'sato, a ag disorientated, lost

spa'ghetti [spa'getti] smpl (CUC) spaghetti sg

'Spagna ['spaɲɲa] sf: **la ~** Spain; **spa'gnolo, a** ag Spanish ♦ smf Spaniard ♦ sm (LING) Spanish; **gli** Spagnoli the Spanish

'spago, ghi sm string, twine

spai'ato, a ag (calza, guanto) odd

spalan'care vt to open wide; **~rsi** vr to open wide

spa'lare vt to shovel

'spalla sf shoulder; (fig: TEATRO) stooge; **~e** sfpl (dorso) back; **spalleggi'are** vt to back up, support

spalli'era sf (di sedia etc) back; (di letto: da capo) head(board); (: da piedi) foot(board); (GINNASTICA) wall bars pl

spal'mare vt to spread

'spalti smpl (di stadio) terracing

'spandere vt to spread; (versare) to pour (out); **~rsi** vr to spread; **'spanto, a** pp di spandere

spa'rare vt to fire ♦ vi (far fuoco) to fire; (tirare) to shoot; **spara'tore** sm gunman; **spara'toria** sf exchange of shots

sparec'chiare [sparek'kjare] vt: ~ **(la tavola)** to clear the table

spa'reggio [spa'reddʒo] sm (SPORT) play-off

'spargere ['spardʒere] vt (sparpagliare) to scatter; (versare: vino) to spill; (: lacrime, sangue) to shed; (diffondere) to spread; (emanare) to give off (o out); **~rsi** vr to spread; **spargi'mento** sm scattering, strewing; spilling; shedding; **spargimento** di sangue bloodshed

spa'rire vi to disappear, vanish

spar'lare vi: ~ **di** to run down, speak ill of

'sparo sm shot

sparpagli'are [sparpaʎ'ʎare] vt to scatter; **~rsi** vr to scatter

'sparso, a pp di spargere ♦ ag scattered; (sciolto) loose

spar'tire vt (eredità, bottino) to share out; (avversari) to separate

spar'tito sm (MUS) score

sparti'traffico sm inv (AUT) central reservation (BRIT), median (strip) (US)

spa'ruto, a ag (viso etc) haggard

sparvi'ero sm (ZOOL) sparrowhawk

spa'simante sm suitor

spasi'mare vi to be in agony; ~ **di** fare (fig) to yearn to do; ~ **per** qn to be madly in love with sb

'spasimo sm pang; **'spasmo** sm (MED) spasm; **spas'modico, a, ci, che** ag (angoscioso) agonizing; (MED) spasmodic

spassio'nato, a ag dispassionate,

impartial

'**spasso** sm (divertimento) amusement, enjoyment; **andare a ~** to go out for a walk; **essere a ~** (fig) to be out of work; **mandare qn a ~** (fig) to give sb the sack

'**spatola** sf spatula; (di muratore) trowel

spau'racchio [spau'rakkjo] sm scarecrow

spau'rire vt to frighten, terrify

spa'valdo, a ag arrogant, bold

spaventa'passeri sm inv scarecrow

spaven'tare vt to frighten, scare; **~rsi** vr to be frightened, be scared; to get a fright; **spa'vento** sm fear, fright; **far spavento a qn** to give sb a fright; **spaven'toso, a** ag frightening, terrible; (fig: fam) tremendous, fantastic

spazien'tire [spattsjen'tire] vi (anche: ~rsi) to lose one's patience

'**spazio** ['spattsjo] sm space; **~ aereo** airspace; **spazi'oso, a** ag spacious

spazzaca'mino [spattsaka'mino] sm chimney sweep

spaz'zare [spat'tsare] vt to sweep; (foglie etc) to sweep up; (cacciare) to sweep away; **spazza'tura** sf sweepings pl; (immondizia) rubbish; **spaz'zino** sm street sweeper

'**spazzola** ['spattsola] sf brush; **~ per abiti** clothesbrush; **~ da capelli** hairbrush; **spazzo'lare** vt to brush; **spazzo'lino** sm (small) brush; **spazzolino da denti** toothbrush

specchi'arsi [spek'kjarsi] vr to look at o.s. in a mirror; (riflettersi) to be mirrored, be reflected

'**specchio** ['spekkjo] sm mirror

speci'ale [spe'tʃale] ag special; **specia'lista, i, e** smif specialist; **specialità** sf inv speciality; (branca di studio) special field, speciality; **specia'lizzarsi** vr: specializzarsi (in) to specialize (in); **special'mente** av especially, particularly

'**specie** ['spetʃe] sf inv (BIOL, BOT,

ZOOL) species inv; (tipo) kind, sort ♦ av especially, particularly; **una ~ di** a kind of; **fare ~ a qn** to surprise sb; **la ~ umana** mankind

specifi'care [spetʃifi'kare] vt to specify, state

spe'cifico, a, ci, che [spe'tʃifiko] ag specific

specu'lare vi: **~ su** (COMM) to speculate in; (sfruttare) to exploit; (meditare) to speculate on; **specula-zi'one** sf speculation

spe'dire vt to send; **spedizi'one** sf sending; (collo) consignment; (scientifica etc) expedition

'**spegnere** ['speɲɲere] vt (fuoco, sigaretta) to put out, extinguish; (apparecchio elettrico) to turn o switch off; (gas) to turn off; (fig: suoni, passioni) to stifle; (debito) to extinguish; **~rsi** vr to go out; to go off; (morire) to pass away

spel'lare vt (scuoiare) to skin; (scorticare) to graze; **~rsi** vr to peel

'**spendere** vt to spend

spen'nare vt to pluck

spensie'rato, a ag carefree

'**spento, a** pp di spegnere ♦ ag (suono) muffled; (colore) dull; (sigaretta) out; (civiltà, vulcano) extinct

spe'ranza [spe'rantsa] sf hope

spe'rare vt to hope for ♦ vi: **~ in** to trust in; **~ che/di fare** to hope that/to do; **lo spero, spero di sì** I hope so

sper'duto, a ag (isolato) out-of-the-way; (persona: smarrita, a disagio) lost

spergi'uro, a [sper'dʒuro] smif perjurer ♦ sm perjury

sperimen'tale ag experimental

sperimen'tare vt to experiment with, test; (fig) to test, put to the test

'**sperma, i** sm (BIOL) sperm

spe'rone sm spur

sperpe'rare vt to squander

'**spesa** sf (somma di denaro) expense; (costo) cost; (acquisto) purchase; (fam: acquisto del cibo quotidiano) shopping; ~e sfpl (soldi spesi) expenses; (COMM) costs; charges; **fare la ~** to do the shopping; **a ~e di** (a carico di) at the expense of; ~**e generali** overheads; ~**e postali** postage sg; ~**e di viaggio** travelling expenses

'speso, a pp di spendere

'spesso, a ag (fitto) thick; (frequente) frequent ♦ av often; ~**e volte** frequently, often

spes'sore sm thickness

spet'tabile (abbr: **Spett.**: in lettere) ag: ~ **ditta X** Messrs X and Co.

spet'tacolo sm (rappresentazione) performance, show; (vista, scena) sight; **dare ~ di sé** to make an exhibition o a spectacle of o.s.; **spettaco'loso, a** ag spectacular

spet'tare vi: ~ **a** (decisione) to be up to; (stipendio) to be due to; **spetta a te decidere** it's up to you to decide

spetta'tore, 'trice smf (CINEMA, TEATRO) member of the audience; (di avvenimento) onlooker, witness

spetti'nare vt: ~ **qn** to ruffle sb's hair; ~**rsi** vr to get one's hair in a mess

'spettro sm (fantasma) spectre; (FISICA) spectrum

'spezie ['spɛttsje] sfpl (CUC) spices

spez'zare [spet'tsare] vt (rompere) to break; (fig: interrompere) to break up; ~**rsi** vr to break

spezza'tino [spettsa'tino] sm (CUC) stew

spezzet'tare [spettset'tare] vt to break up o chop) into small pieces

'spia sf spy; (confidente della polizia) informer; (ELETTR) indicating light; warning light; (fessura) peephole; (fig: sintomo) sign, indication

spia'cente [spja'tʃɛnte] ag sorry; **essere ~ di qc/di fare qc** to be sorry about sth/for doing sth

spia'cevole [spja'tʃevole] ag unpleasant, disagreeable

spi'aggia, ge ['spjaddʒa] sf beach;

~ **libera** public beach

spia'nare vt (terreno) to level, make level; (edificio) to raze to the ground; (pasta) to roll out; (rendere liscio) to smooth (out)

spi'ano sm: **a tutto ~** (lavorare) non-stop, without a break; (spendere) lavishly

spian'tato, a ag penniless, ruined

spi'are vt to spy on; (occasione etc) to watch o wait for

spi'azzo [spi'attso] sm open space; (radura) clearing

spic'care vt (assegno, mandato di cattura) to issue ♦ vi (risaltare) to stand out; ~ **il volo** to fly off; (fig) to spread one's wings; ~ **un balzo** to leap; **spic'cato, a** ag (marcato) marked, strong; (notevole) remarkable

'spicchio ['spikkjo] sm (di agrumi) segment; (di aglio) clove; (parte) piece, slice

spicci'are [spit'tʃare] vt to finish off quickly; ~**rsi** vr to hurry up

spicciolo, a ['spittʃolo] ag: **moneta** ~**a**, ~**i** smpl (small) change

'spicco, chi sm: **di ~** outstanding; (tema) main, principal; **fare ~** to stand out

spi'edo sm (CUC) spit

spie'gare vt (far capire) to explain; (tovaglia) to unfold; (vele) to unfurl; ~**rsi** vr to explain o.s., make o.s. clear; ~ **qc a qn** to explain sth to sb; **il problema si spiega** one can understand the problem; **spiegazi'one** sf explanation

spiegaz'zare [spjegat'tsare] vt to crease, crumple

spie'tato, a ag ruthless, pitiless

spiffe'rare (fam) vt to blurt out, blab

'spiga, ghe sf (BOT) ear

spigli'ato, a [spiʎ'ʎato] ag self-possessed, self-confident

'spigolo sm corner; (MAT) edge

'spilla sf brooch; (da cravatta, cappello) pin

spil'lare vt (vino, fig) to tap; ~

denaro/notizie a qn to tap sb for
money/information

'spillo sm pin; (spilla) brooch; ~ **di
sicurezza** o **da balia** safety pin

spi'lorcio, a, ci, ce [spi'lortʃo] ag
mean, stingy

'spina sf (BOT) thorn; (ZOOL)
spine, prickle; (di pesce) bone;
(ELETTR) plug; (di botte) bunghole;
birra alla ~ draught beer; ~ **dorsale** (ANAT) backbone

spi'nacio [spi'natʃo] sm spinach
(CUC); ~**i spinach** sg

'spingere ['spindʒere] vt to push;
(condurre: anche fig) to drive; (stimolare): ~ **qn a fare** to urge o
press sb to do; ~**rsi** vr (inoltrarsi) to
push on, carry on; ~**rsi troppo lontano** (anche fig) to go too far

spi'noso, a ag thorny, prickly

'spinta sf (urto) push; (FISICA)
thrust; (fig: stimolo) incentive, spur;
(: appoggio) string-pulling no pl;
dare una ~**a a qn** (fig) to pull
strings for sb

'spinto, a pp di **spingere**

spio'naggio [spio'naddʒo] sm
espionage, spying

spi'overe vi (scorrere) to flow
down; (ricadere) to hang loose, fall

'spira sf coil

spi'raglio [spi'raʎʎo] sm (fessura)
chink, narrow opening; (raggio di
luce, fig) glimmer, gleam

spi'rale sf spiral; (contraccettivo)
coil; **a** ~ spiral(-shaped)

spi'rare vi (vento) to blow; (morire)
to expire, pass away

spiri'tato, a ag possessed; (fig: persona, espressione) wild

spiri'tismo sm spiritualism

'spirito sm (REL, CHIM, disposizione d'animo, di legge etc, fantasma) spirit; (pensiero, intelletto)
mind; (arguzia) wit; (umorismo) humour, wit; lo **S~ Santo** the Holy
Spirit o Ghost

spirito'saggine [spirito'saddʒine] sf
witticism; (peg) wisecrack

spiri'toso, a ag witty

spiritu'ale ag spiritual

'splendere vi to shine

splen'dido, a ag splendid; (splen-
dente) shining; (sfarzoso) magnificent, splendid

splen'dore sm splendour; (luce in-
tensa) brilliance, brightness

spodes'tare vt to deprive of power;
(sovrano) to depose

'spoglia ['spɔʎʎa] sf (ZOOL) skin,
hide; (: di rettile) slough; ~**e** sfpl
(salma) remains; (preda) spoils, booty sg; vedi anche **spoglio**

spogli'are [spoʎ'ʎare] vt (svestire)
to undress; (privare, fig: depredare):
~ **qn di qc** to deprive sb of sth; (togliere ornamenti: anche fig): ~ **qn/
qc di** to strip sb/sth of; ~**rsi** vr to
undress, strip; ~**rsi di** (ricchezze
etc) to deprive o.s. of, give up;
(pregiudizi) to rid o.s. of; **spoglia'toio** sm dressing room; (di
scuola etc) cloakroom; (SPORT)
changing room; **'spoglio, a** ag
(pianta, terreno) bare; (privo): **spoglio di** stripped of; lacking in, without ♦ sm (di voti) counting

'spola sf shuttle; (bobina di filo)
cop; **fare la** ~ (fra) to go to and fro
o shuttle (between)

spol'pare vt to strip the flesh off

spolve'rare vt (anche CUC) to dust;
(con spazzola) to brush; (con batti-
panni) to beat; (fig) to polish off ♦ vi
to dust

'sponda sf (di fiume) bank; (di
mare, lago) shore; (bordo) edge

spon'taneo, a ag spontaneous;
(persona) unaffected, natural

spopo'lare vt to depopulate ♦ vi
(attirare folla) to draw the crowds;
~**rsi** vr to become depopulated

spor'care vt to dirty, make dirty;
(fig) to sully, soil; ~**rsi** vr to get
dirty

spor'cizia [spor'tʃittsja] sf (stato)
dirtiness; (sudiciume) dirt, filth;
(cosa sporca) dirt no pl, something
dirty; (fig: cosa oscena) obscenity

'sporco, a, chi, che ag dirty, filthy

spor'genza [spor'dʒentsa] sf projection

'sporgere ['spɔrdʒere] vt to put out, stretch out ♦ vi (venire in fuori) to stick out; ~**rsi** vr to lean out; ~ **querela contro qn** (DIR) to take legal action against sb

sport sm inv sport

'sporta sf shopping bag

spor'tello sm (di treno, auto etc) door; (di banca, ufficio) window, counter; ~ **automatico** (BANCA) cash dispenser, automated telling machine

spor'tivo, a ag (gara, giornale) sports cpd; (persona) sporty; (abito) casual; (spirito, atteggiamento) sporting

'sporto, a pp di sporgere

'sposa sf bride; (moglie) wife

sposa'lizio [spoza'littsjo] sm wedding

spo'sare vt to marry; (fig: idea, fede) to espouse; ~**rsi** vr to get married, marry; ~**rsi con qn** to marry sb, get married to sb; **spo'sato, a** ag married

'sposo sm (bride)groom; (marito) husband; gli ~i smpl the newlyweds

spos'sato, a ag exhausted, weary

spos'tare vt to move, shift; (cambiare: orario) to change; ~**rsi** vr to move

'spranga, ghe sf (sbarra) bar

'sprazzo ['sprattso] sm (di sole etc) flash; (fig: di gioia etc) burst

spre'care vt to waste; ~**rsi** vr (persona) to waste one's energy; **'spreco** sm waste

spre'gevole [spre'dʒevole] ag contemptible, despicable

spregiudi'cato, a [spredʒudi'kato] ag unprejudiced, unbiased; (peg) unscrupulous

'spremere vt to squeeze

spre'muta sf fresh juice; ~ **d'arancia** fresh orange juice

sprez'zante [spret'tsante] ag scornful, contemptuous

sprigio'nare [spridʒo'nare] vt to

give off, emit; ~**rsi** vr to emanate; (uscire con impeto) to burst out

spriz'zare [sprit'tsare] vt, vi to spurt; ~ **gioia/salute** to be bursting with joy/health

sprofon'dare vi to sink; (casa) to collapse; (suolo) to give way, subside; ~**rsi** vr: ~**rsi in** (poltrona) to sink into; (fig) to become immersed o absorbed in

spro'nare vt to spur (on)

'sprone sm (sperone, fig) spur

sproporzio'nato, a [sproportsjo'nato] ag disproportionate, out of all proportion

sproporzi'one [spropor'tsjone] sf disproportion

sproposi'tato, a ag (lettera, discorso) full of mistakes; (fig: costo) excessive, enormous

spro'posito sm blunder; a ~ at the wrong time; (rispondere, parlare) irrelevantly

sprovve'duto, a ag inexperienced, naive

sprov'visto, a ag (mancante): ~ **di** lacking in, without; **alla ~a** unawares

spruz'zare [sprut'tsare] vt (a nebulizzazione) to spray; (aspergere) to sprinkle; (inzaccherare) to splash; **'spruzzo** sm spray; splash

'spugna ['spuɲɲa] sf (ZOOL) sponge; (tessuto) towelling; **spu'gnoso, a** ag spongy

'spuma sf (schiuma) foam; (bibita) mineral water

spu'mante sm sparkling wine

spumeggi'ante [spumed'dʒante] ag (birra) foaming; (vino, fig) sparkling

spu'mone sm (CUC) mousse

spun'tare vt (coltello) to break the point of; (capelli) to trim ♦ vi (uscire: germogli) to sprout; (: capelli) to begin to grow; (: denti) to come through; (apparire) to appear (suddenly); ~**rsi** vr to become blunt, lose its point; **spuntarla** (fig) to make it, win through

spun'tino sm snack

'spunto sm (TEATRO, MUS) cue; (fig) starting point; **dare lo ~ a** (fig) to give rise to

spur'gare vt (fogna) to clean, clear

spu'tare vt to spit out; (fig) to belch (out) ♦ vi to spit; 'sputo sm spittle no pl, spit no pl

'squadra sf (strumento) (set) square; (gruppo) team, squad; (di operai) gang, squad; (MIL) squad; (: AER, NAUT) squadron; (SPORT) team; **lavoro a ~e** teamwork

squa'drare vt to square, make square; (osservare) to look at closely

squa'driglia [skwa'driʎʎa] sf (AER) flight; (NAUT) squadron

squa'drone sm squadron

squagli'arsi [skwaʎ'ʎarsi] vr to melt; (fig) to sneak off

squa'lifica sf disqualification

squalifi'care vt to disqualify

'squallido, a ag wretched, bleak

squal'lore sm wretchedness, bleakness

'squalo sm shark

'squama sf scale; **squa'mare** vt to scale; **squamarsi** vr to flake o peel (off)

squarcia'gola [skwartʃa'gola]: **a ~** av at the top of one's voice

squarci'are [skwar'tʃare] vt to rip (open); (fig) to pierce

squar'tare vt to quarter, cut up

squattri'nato, a ag penniless

squili'brato, a ag (PSIC) unbalanced; **squi'librio** sm (differenza, sbilancio) imbalance; (PSIC) unbalance

squil'lante ag shrill, sharp

squil'lare vi (campanello, telefono) to ring (out); (tromba) to blare; **'squillo** sm ring, ringing no pl; blare; **ragazza f squillo** inv call girl

squi'sito, a ag exquisite; (cibo) delicious; (persona) delightful

squit'tire vi (uccello) to squawk; (topo) to squeak

sradi'care vt to uproot; (fig) to eradicate

sragio'nare [zradʒo'nare] vi to talk

nonsense, rave

srego'lato, a ag (senza ordine: vita) disorderly; (smodato) immoderate; (dissoluto) dissolute

S.r.l. abbr = società a responsabilità limitata

'stabile ag stable, steady; (tempo: non variabile) settled; (TEATRO: compagnia) resident ♦ sm (edificio) building

stabili'mento sm (edificio) establishment; (fabbrica) plant, factory

stabi'lire vt to establish; (fissare: prezzi, data) to fix; (decidere): ~ di to decide; **~rsi** vr (prendere dimora) to settle

stac'care vt (levare) to detach, remove; (separare: anche fig) to separate, divide; (strappare) to tear off (o out); (scandire: parole) to pronounce clearly; (SPORT) to leave behind; **~rsi** vr (bottone etc) to come off; (scostarsi): **~rsi (da)** to move away (from); (fig: separarsi): **~rsi da** to leave; **non ~ gli occhi da qn** not to take one's eyes off sb

'stadio sm (SPORT) stadium; (periodo, fase) phase, stage

'staffa sf (di sella, TECN) stirrup; **perdere le ~e** (fig) to fly off the handle

staf'fetta sf (messo) dispatch rider; (SPORT) relay race

stagio'nale [stadʒo'nale] ag seasonal

stagio'nare [stadʒo'nare] vt (legno) to season; (formaggi, vino) to mature

stagi'one [sta'dʒone] sf season; **alta/bassa ~** high/low season

stagli'arsi [staʎ'ʎarsi] vr to stand out, be silhouetted

sta'gnare [stan'ɲare] vt (vaso, tegame) to tin-plate; (barca, botte) to make watertight; (sangue) to stop ♦ vi to stagnate

'stagno, a ['stanɲo] ag watertight; (a tenuta d'aria) airtight ♦ sm (acquitrino) pond; (CHIM) tin

sta'gnola [stan'ɲola] sf tinfoil

'stalla sf (per bovini) cowshed; (per

cavalli) stable

stal'lone *sm* stallion

sta'mani *av* = stamattina

stamat'tina *av* this morning

stam'becco, chi *sm* ibex

'stampa *sf* (*TIP, FOT: tecnica*) printing; (*impressione, copia fotografica*) print; (*insieme di quotidiani, giornalisti etc*) press; "~e" *sfpl* "printed matter"

stam'pante *sf* (*INFORM*) printer

stam'pare *vt* to print; (*pubblicare*) to publish; (*coniare*) to strike, coin; (*imprimere: anche fig*) to impress

stampa'tello *sm* block letters *pl*

stam'pella *sf* crutch

'stampo *sm* mould; (*fig: indole*) type, kind, sort

sta'nare *vt* to drive out

stan'care *vt* to tire, make tired; (*annoiare*) to bore; (*infastidire*) to annoy; **~rsi** *vr* to get tired, tire o.s. out; **~rsi (di)** to grow weary (of), grow tired (of)

stan'chezza [stan'kettsa] *sf* tiredness, fatigue

'stanco, a, chi, che *ag* tired; **~ di** tired of, fed up with

'stanga, ghe *sm* bar; (*di carro*) shaft

stan'gata *sf* (*colpo: anche fig*) blow; (*cattivo risultato*) poor result; (*CALCIO*) shot

sta'notte *av* tonight; (*notte passata*) last night

'stante *prep*: a sé ~ (*appartamento, casa*) independent, separate

stan'tio, a, 'tii, 'tie *ag* stale; (*burro*) rancid; (*fig*) old

stan'tuffo *sm* piston

'stanza ['stantsa] *sf* room; (*POESIA*) stanza; ~ **da letto** bedroom

stanzi'are [stan'tsjare] *vt* to allocate

stap'pare *vt* to uncork; to uncap

'stare *vi* (*restare in un luogo*) to stay, remain; (*abitare*) to stay, live; (*essere situato*) to be, be situated; (*anche: ~ in piedi*) to be, stand; (*essere, trovarsi*) to be; (*dipendere*): **se stesse in me** if it were up to me, if

it depended on me; (*seguito da gerundio*): **sta studiando** he's studying; **starci** (*esserci spazio*): **nel baule non ci sta più niente** there's no more room in the boot; (*accettare*) to accept; **ci stai?** is that okay with you?; ~ **a** (*attenersi a*) to follow, stick to; (*seguito dall'infinito*): **stiamo a discutere** we're talking; (*toccare a*): **sta a te giocare** it's your turn to play; ~ **per fare qc** to be about to do sth; **come sta?** how are you?; **io sto bene/male** I'm very well/not very well; ~ **a qn** (*abiti etc*) to fit sb; **queste scarpe mi stanno strette** these shoes are tight for me; **il rosso ti sta bene** red suits you

starnu'tire *vi* to sneeze; **star'nuto** *sm* sneeze

sta'sera *av* this evening, tonight

sta'tale *ag* state *cpd*; government *cpd* ♦ *smf* state employee, local authority employee; (*nell'amministrazione*) ≈ civil servant

sta'tista, i *sm* statesman

sta'tistica *sf* statistics *sg*

'stato, a *pp di* essere; **stare** ♦ *sm* (*condizione*) state, condition; (*POL*) state; (*DIR*) status; **essere in ~ d'accusa** (*DIR*) to be committed for trial; ~ **d'assedio/d'emergenza** state of siege/emergency; ~ **civile** (*AMM*) marital status; ~ **maggiore** (*MIL*) staff; **gli S~i Uniti (d'America)** the United States (of America)

'statua *sf* statue

statuni'tense *ag* United States *cpd*, of the United States

sta'tura *sf* (*ANAT*) height, stature; (*fig*) stature

sta'tuto *sm* (*DIR*) statute; constitution

sta'volta *av* this time

stazio'nario, a [stattsjo'narjo] *ag* stationary; (*fig*) unchanged

stazi'one [stat'tsjone] *sf* station; (*balneare, termale*) resort; ~ **degli autobus** bus station; ~ **balneare** seaside resort; ~ **ferroviaria** railway (*BRIT*) *o* railroad (*US*) station;

~ invernale winter sports resort; **~ di polizia** police station (*in small town*); **~ di servizio** service *o* petrol (*BRIT*) *o* filling station

'stecca, che *sf* stick; (*di ombrello*) rib; (*di sigaretta*) carton; (*MED*) splint; (*stonatura*): **fare una ~** to sing (*o* play) a wrong note

stec'cato *sm* fence

stec'chito, a [stek'kito] *ag* dried up; (*persona*) skinny; **lasciar ~ qn** (*fig*) to leave sb flabbergasted; **morto ~** stone dead

'stella *sf* star; **~ alpina** (*BOT*) edelweiss; **~ di mare** (*ZOOL*) starfish

'stelo *sm* stem; (*asta*) rod; **lampada a ~** standard lamp

'stemma, i *sm* coat of arms

stempe'rare *vt* to dilute; to dissolve; (*colori*) to mix

sten'dardo *sm* standard

'stendere *vt* (*braccia, gambe*) to stretch (out); (*tovaglia*) to spread (out); (*bucato*) to hang out; (*mettere a giacere*) to lay (down); (*spalmare: colore*) to spread; (*mettere per iscritto*) to draw up; **~rsi** *vr* (*coricarsi*) to stretch out, lie down; (*estendersi*) to extend, stretch

stenodatti'lografo, a *smif* shorthand typist (*BRIT*), stenographer (*US*)

stenogra'fare *vt* to take down in shorthand; **stenogra'fia** *sf* shorthand

sten'tare *vi*: **~ a fare** to find it hard to do, have difficulty doing

'stento *sm* (*fatica*) difficulty; **~i** *smpl* (*privazioni*) hardship *sg*, privation *sg*; **a ~** with difficulty, barely

'sterco *sm* dung

'stereo('fonico, a, ci, che) ag stereo(phonic)

'sterile *ag* sterile; (*terra*) barren; (*fig*) futile, fruitless; **sterilità** *sf* sterility

sterilizzare [sterilid'dzare] *vt* to sterilize; **sterilizzazi'one** *sf* sterilization

ster'lina *sf* pound (sterling)

stermi'nare *vt* to exterminate, wipe out

stermi'nato, a *ag* immense; endless

ster'minio *sm* extermination, destruction

'sterno *sm* (*ANAT*) breastbone

'sterpo *sm* dry twig; **~i** *smpl* brushwood *sg*

ster'zare [ster'tsare] *vt, vi* (*AUT*) to steer; **'sterzo** *sm* steering; (*volante*) steering wheel

'steso, a *pp di* **stendere**

'stesso, a *ag* same; (*rafforzativo: in persona, proprio*): **il re ~** the king himself *o* in person ♦ *pron*: **lo(la) ~(a)** the same (one); **i suoi ~i av-versari** lo ammirano even his enemies admire him; **fa lo ~** it doesn't matter; **per me è lo ~** it's all the same to me, it doesn't matter to me; *vedi* **io; tu** *etc*

ste'sura *sf* drafting *no pl*, drawing up *no pl*; draft

stigma, i *sm* stigma

stig'mate *sfpl* (*REL*) stigmata

sti'lare *vt* to draw up, draft

'stile *sm* style; **sti'lista, i** *sm* designer

stil'lare *vi* (*trasudare*) to ooze; (*gocciolare*) to drip; **stilli'cidio** *sm* (*fig*) continual pestering (*o moaning etc*)

stilo'grafica, che *sf* (*anche*: **penna ~**) fountain pen

'stima *sf* esteem; valuation; assessment, estimate

sti'mare *vt* (*persona*) to esteem, hold in high regard; (*terreno, casa etc*) to value; (*stabilire in misura approssimativa*) to estimate, assess; (*ritenere*): **~ che** to consider that; **~rsi fortunato** to consider o.s. (to be) lucky

stimo'lare *vt* to stimulate; (*incitare*): **~ qn (a fare)** to spur sb on (to do)

'stimolo *sm* (*anche fig*) stimulus

'stinco, chi *sm* shin; shinbone

'stingere ['stindʒere] *vt, vi* (*anche: ~rsi*) to fade; **'stinto, a** *pp di* **stin-**

gere

sti'pare vt to cram, pack; ~**rsi** vr (accalcarsi) to crowd, throng

sti'pendio sm salary

'stipite sm (di porta, finestra) jamb

stipu'lare vt (redigere) to draw up

sti'rare vt (abito) to iron; (distendere) to stretch; (strappare: muscolo) to strain; ~**rsi** vr to stretch (o.s.); **stira'tura** sf ironing

'stirpe sf birth, stock; descendants pl

stiti'chezza [stiti'kettsa] sf constipation

'stitico, a, ci, chi ag constipated

'stiva sf (di nave) hold

sti'vale sm boot

'stizza ['stittsa] sf anger, vexation; **stiz'zirsi** vr to lose one's temper; **stiz'zoso, a** ag (persona) quick-tempered, irascible; (risposta) angry

stocca'fisso sm stockfish, dried cod

stoc'cata sf (colpo) stab, thrust; (fig) gibe, cutting remark

'stoffa sf material, fabric; (fig): aver la ~ di to have the makings of

'stola sf stole

'stolto, a ag stupid, foolish

'stomaco, chi sm stomach; dare di ~ to vomit, be sick

sto'nare vt to sing (o play) out of tune ♦ vi to be out of tune, sing (o play) out of tune; (fig) to be out of place, jar; (: colori) to clash; **stona'tura** sf (suono) false note

stop sm inv (TEL) stop; (AUT: cartello) stop sign; (: fanalino d'arresto) brake-light

'stoppa sf tow

'stoppia sf (AGR) stubble

stop'pino sm wick; (miccia) fuse

'storcere ['stortʃere] vt to twist; ~**rsi** vr to writhe, twist; ~ **il naso** (fig) to turn up one's nose; ~**rsi la caviglia** to twist one's ankle

stor'dire vt (intontire) to stun, daze; ~**rsi** vr: ~**rsi col bere** to dull one's senses with drink; **stor'dito, a** ag stunned; (sventato) scatterbrained, heedless

'storia sf (scienza, avvenimenti) his-

tory; (racconto, bugia) story; (faccenda, questione) business no pl; (pretesto) excuse, pretext; ~**e** sfpl (smancerie) fuss sg; **'storico, a, ci, che** ag historic(al) ♦ sm historian

stori'one sm (ZOOL) sturgeon

stor'mire vi to rustle

'stormo sm (di uccelli) flock

stor'nare vt (COMM) to transfer

'storno sm starling

storpi'are vt to cripple, maim; (fig: parole) to mangle; (: significato) to twist

'storpio, a ag crippled, maimed

'storta sf (distorsione) sprain, twist; (recipiente) retort

'storto, a pp di storcere ♦ ag (chiodo) twisted, bent; (gamba, quadro) crooked; (fig: ragionamento) false, wrong

sto'viglie [sto'viʎʎe] sfpl dishes pl, crockery

'strabico, a, ci, che ag squint-eyed; (occhi) squint

stra'bismo sm squinting

stra'carico, a, chi, che ag overloaded

strac'chino [strak'kino] sm type of soft cheese

stracci'are [strat'tʃare] vt to tear

'straccio, a, ci, ce ['strattʃo] ag: carta ~**a** waste paper ♦ sm rag; (per pulire) cloth, duster; **stracci'vendolo** sm ragman

stra'cotto, a ag overcooked ♦ sm (CUC) beef stew

'strada sf road; (di città) street; (cammino, via, fig) way; **farsi** ~ (fig) to do well for o.s.; **essere fuori** ~ (fig) to be on the wrong track; **facendo** o **sulla** ~ on the way; ~ **senza uscita** dead end; **stra'dale** ag road cpd

strafalci'one [strafal'tʃone] sm blunder, howler

stra'fare vi to overdo it; **stra'fatto, a** pp di strafare

strafot'tente ag: è ~ he doesn't give a damn, he couldn't care less

'strage ['stradʒe] sf massacre, slaughter

stralu'nato, a *ag* (*occhi*) rolling; (*persona*) beside o.s., very upset

stramaz'zare [stramat'tsare] *vi* to fall heavily

'strambo, a *ag* strange, queer

strampa'lato, a *ag* odd, eccentric

stra'nezza [stra'nettsa] *sf* strangeness

strango'lare *vt* to strangle; **~rsi** *vr* to choke

strani'ero, a *ag* foreign ♦ *smf* foreigner

'strano, a *ag* strange, odd

straordi'nario, a *ag* extraordinary; (*treno etc*) special ♦ *sm* (*lavoro*) overtime

strapaz'zare [strapat'tsare] *vt* to ill-treat; **~rsi** *vr* to tire o.s. out, overdo things; **stra'pazzo** *sm* strain, fatigue; **da strapazzo** (*fig*) third-rate

strapi'ombo *sm* overhanging rock; **a ~** overhanging

strapo'tere *sm* excessive power

strap'pare *vt* (*gen*) to tear, rip; (*pagina etc*) to tear off, tear out; (*sradicare*) to pull up; (*togliere*): **~ qc a qn** to snatch sth from sb; (*fig*) to wrest sth from sb; **~rsi** *vr* (*lacerarsi*) to rip, tear; (*rompersi*) to break; **~rsi un muscolo** to tear a muscle; **'strappo** *sm* pull, tug; tear, rip; **fare uno strappo alla regola** to make an exception to the rule; **strappo muscolare** torn muscle

strari'pare *vi* to overflow

strasci'care [straʃʃi'kare] *vt* to trail; (*piedi*) to drag; **~ le parole** to drawl

'strascico, chi [ʃtraʃʃiko] *sm* (*di abito*) train; (*conseguenza*) after-effect

strata'gemma, i [strata'dʒɛmma] *sm* stratagem

strate'gia, 'gie [strate'dʒia] *sf* strategy; **stra'tegico, a, ci, che** *ag* strategic

'strato *sm* layer; (*rivestimento*) coat, coating; (*GEO*, *fig*) stratum; (*METEOR*) stratus; **~ di ozono** ozone layer

stra'vagante *ag* odd, eccentric; **stra'vaganza** *sf* eccentricity

stra'vecchio, a [stra'vekkjo] *ag* very old

stra'vizio [stra'vittsjo] *sm* excess

stra'volgere [stra'vɔldʒere] *vt* (*volto*) to contort; (*fig*: *animo*) to trouble deeply; (: *verità*) to twist, distort; **stra'volto, a** *pp di* **stravolgere**

strazi'are [strat'tsjare] *vt* to torture, torment; **'strazio** *sm* torture; (*fig*: *cosa fatta male*): **essere uno ~** to be appalling

'strega, ghe *sf* witch

stre'gare *vt* to bewitch

stre'gone *sm* (*mago*) wizard; (*di tribù*) witch doctor

'streguna *sf*: **alla ~ di** by the same standard as

stre'mare *vt* to exhaust

'stremo *sm* very end; **essere allo ~** to be at the end of one's tether

'strenna *sf* Christmas present

'strenuo, a *ag* brave, courageous

strepi'toso, a *ag* clamorous, deafening; (*fig*: *successo*) resounding

stres'sante *ag* stressful

'stretta *sf* (*di mano*) grasp; (*finanziaria*) squeeze; (*fig*: *dolore*, *turbamento*) pang; **una ~a di mano** a handshake; **essere alle ~e** to have one's back to the wall; *vedi anche* **stretto**

stretta'mente *av* tightly; (*rigorosamente*) strictly

stret'tezza [stret'tettsa] *sf* narrowness

'stretto, a *pp di* **stringere** ♦ *ag* (*corridoio*, *limiti*) narrow; (*gonna*, *scarpe*, *nodo*, *curva*) tight; (*intimo*: *parente*, *amico*) close; (*rigoroso*: *osservanza*) strict; (*preciso*: *significato*) precise, exact ♦ *sm* (*braccio di mare*) strait; **a denti ~i** with clenched teeth; **lo ~ necessario** the bare minimum; **stret'toia** *sf* bottleneck; (*fig*) tricky situation

stri'ato, a *ag* streaked

'stridere *vi* (*porta*) to squeak; (*animale*) to screech, shriek; (*colori*) to

clash; **'strido** (pl(f) **strida**) sm
screech, shriek; **stri'dore** sm
screeching, shrieking; **'stridulo, a**
ag shrill

stril'lare vt, vi to scream, shriek;
'strillo sm scream, shriek

stril'lone sm newspaper seller

strimin'zito, a [strimin'tsito] ag
(misero) shabby; (molto magro)
skinny

strimpel'lare vt (MUS) to strum

'stringa, ghe sf lace

strin'gato, a ag (fig) concise

'stringere ['strindʒere] vt (avvicinare due cose) to press (together),
squeeze (together); (tenere stretto)
to hold tight, clasp, clutch; (pugno,
mascella, denti) to clench; (labbra)
to compress; (avvitare) to tighten;
(abito) to take in; (sog: scarpe) to
pinch, be tight for; (fig: concludere:
patto) to make; (: accelerare: passo,
tempo) to quicken ♦ vi (essere stretto) to be tight; (tempo: incalzare) to
be pressing; **~rsi** vr (accostarsi):
~rsi a to press o.s. up against; **~ la
mano a qn** to shake sb's hand; **~
gli occhi** to screw up one's eyes

'striscia, sce ['striʃʃa] sf (di carta,
tessuto etc) strip; (riga) stripe;
~sce (pedonali) zebra crossing sg

strisci'are [striʃ'ʃare] vt (piedi) to
drag; (muro, macchina) to graze ♦
vi to crawl, creep

'striscio ['striʃʃo] sm graze; (MED)
smear; **colpire di ~** to graze

strito'lare vt to grind

striz'zare [strit'tsare] vt (arancia) to
squeeze; (panni) to wring (out); **~
l'occhio** to wink

'strofa sf = strofe

'strofe sf inv strophe

strofi'naccio [strofi'nattʃo] sm
duster, cloth; (per piatti) dishcloth;
(per pavimenti) floorcloth

strofi'nare vt to rub

stron'care vt to break off; (fig: ribellione) to suppress, put down; (:
film, libro) to tear to pieces

stropicci'are [stropit'tʃare] vt to rub

stroz'zare [strot'tsare] vt (soffocare)
to choke, strangle; **~rsi** vr to choke;
strozza'tura sf (restringimento)
narrowing; (di strada etc) bottleneck

'struggersi ['struddʒersi] vr (fig): **~
di** to be consumed with

strumen'tale ag (MUS) instrumental

strumentaliz'zare [strumentalid-
'dzare] vt to exploit, use to one's own
ends

stru'mento sm (arnese, fig) instrument, tool; (MUS) instrument; **~ a
corda** o **ad arco/a fiato** stringed/
wind instrument

'strutto sm lard

strut'tura sf structure; **struttu'rare**
vt to structure

'struzzo ['struttso] sm ostrich

stuc'care vt (muro) to plaster; (vetro) to putty; (decorare con stucchi) vt
to stucco

stuc'chevole [stuk'kevole] ag
nauseating; (fig) tedious, boring

'stucco, chi sm plaster; (da vetri)
putty; (ornamentale) stucco; **rimanere di ~** (fig) to be dumbfounded

stu'dente, essa sm/f student;
(scolaro) pupil, schoolboy/girl; **studen'tesco, a, schi, sche** ag student cpd; school cpd

studi'are vt to study

'studio sm studying; (ricerca, saggio, stanza) study; (di professionista)
office; (di artista, CINEMA, TV,
RADIO) studio; **~** i smpl (INS)
studies; **~** medico doctor's surgery
(BRIT) o office (US)

studi'oso, a ag studious, hard-
working ♦ sm/f scholar

'stufa sf stove; **~ elettrica** electric
fire o heater

stu'fare vt (CUC) to stew; (fig: fam)
to bore; **stu'fato** sm (CUC) stew;
'stufo, a (fam) ag: **essere stufo di**
to be fed up with, be sick and tired of

stu'oia sf mat

stupefa'cente [stupefa'tʃɛnte] ag
stunning, astounding ♦ sm drug, narcotic

stu'pendo, a *ag* marvellous, wonderful

stupi'daggine [stupi'daddʒine] *sf* stupid thing (to do *o* say)

stupidità *sf* stupidity

'stupido, a *ag* stupid

stu'pire *vt* to amaze, stun ♦ *vi* (*anche:* ~rsi): ~ (**di**) to be amazed (at), be stunned (at)

stu'pore *sm* amazement, astonishment

'stupro *sm* rape

stu'rare (*lavandino*) to clear

stuzzica'denti [stuttsika'denti] *sm* toothpick

stuzzi'care [stuttsi'kare] *vt* (*ferita etc*) to poke (at), prod (at); (*fig*) to tease; (*: appetito*) to whet; (*: curiosità*) to stimulate; ~ **i denti** to pick one's teeth

---

PAROLA CHIAVE

su (*su +il* = **sul**, *su +lo* = **sullo**, *su +l'* = **sull'**, *su +la* = **sulla**, *su +i* = **sui**, *su +gli* = **sugli**, *su +le* = **sulle**) *prep* **1** (*gen*) on; (*moto*) on(to); (*in cima a*) on (top of); (*in cima a*) on top of); **mettilo sul tavolo** put it on the table; **un paesino sul mare** a village by the sea

2 (*argomento*) about, on; **un libro ~ Cesare** a book on *o* about Caesar

3 (*circa*) about; **costerà sui 3 milioni** it will cost about 3 million; **una ragazza sui 17 anni** a girl of about 17 (years of age)

4: ~ **misura** made to measure; ~ **richiesta** on request; **3 casi ~ dieci** 3 cases out of 10

♦ *av* **1** (*in alto, verso l'alto*) up; **vieni** ~ come on up; **guarda** ~ look up; ~ **le mani!** hands up!; **in** ~ (*verso l'alto*) up(wards); (*in poi*) onwards; **dai 20 anni in** ~ from the age of 20 onwards

2 (*addosso*) on; **cos'hai** ~? what have you got on?

♦ *escl* come on!; ~ **coraggio!** come on, cheer up!

'sua *vedi* **suo**

---

su'bacqueo, a *ag* underwater ♦ *sm* skindiver

sub'buglio [sub'buʎʎo] *sm* confusion, turmoil

subcosci'ente [subkoʃ'ʃente] *ag, sm* subconscious

'subdolo, a *ag* underhand, sneaky

suben'trare *vi*: ~ **a qn in qc** to take over sth from sb

su'bire *vt* to suffer, endure

subis'sare *vt* (*fig*): ~ **di** to overwhelm with, load with

subi'taneo, a *ag* sudden

'subito *av* immediately, at once, straight away

subo'dorare *vt* (*insidia etc*) to smell, suspect

subordi'nato, a *ag* subordinate; (*dipendente*): ~ **a** a dependent on, subject to

subur'bano, a *ag* suburban

succe'daneo [suttʃe'daneo] *sm* substitute

suc'cedere [sut'tʃedere] *vi* (*prendere il posto di qn*): ~ **a** to succeed; (*venire dopo*): ~ **a** to follow; (*accadere*) to happen; ~**rsi** *vr* to follow each other; ~ **al trono** to succeed to the throne; **successi'one** *sf* succession; **succes'sivo, a** *ag* successive; **suc'cesso, a** *pp di* **succedere** ♦ *sm* (*esito*) outcome; (*buona riuscita*) success; **di successo** (*libro, personaggio*) successful

succhi'are [suk'kjare] *vt* to suck (up)

suc'cinto, a [sut'tʃinto] *ag* (*discorso*) succinct; (*abito*) brief

'succo, chi *sm* juice; (*fig*) essence, gist; ~ **di frutta** fruit juice; **suc'coso, a** *ag* juicy; (*fig*) pithy

succur'sale *sf* branch (office)

sud *sm inv* south ♦ *ag inv* south; (*lato*) south, southern

Su'dafrica *sm*: **il** ~ South Africa; **sudafri'cano, a** *ag, smf* South African

Suda'merica *sm*: **il** ~ South America; **sudameri'cano, a** *ag, smf* South American

su'dare vi to perspire, sweat; ~ **freddo** to come out in a cold sweat; **su'data** sf sweat; **ho fatto una bella sudata per finirlo in tempo** it was a real sweat to get it finished in time

sud'detto, a ag above-mentioned

sud'dito, a smf subject

suddi'videre vt to subdivide

su'dest sm south-east

'sudicio, a, ci, ce ['suditʃo] ag dirty, filthy; **sudici'ume** sm dirt, filth

su'dore sm perspiration, sweat

su'dovest sm south-west

'sue vedi suo

suffici'ente [suffi'tʃɛnte] ag enough, sufficient; (borioso) self-important; (INS) satisfactory; **suffici'enza** sf self-importance; pass mark; **a sufficienza** enough; **ne ho avuto a sufficienza** I've had enough of this!

suf'fisso sm (LING) suffix

suf'fragio [suf'fradʒo] sm (voto) vote; ~ **universale** universal suffrage

suggel'lare [suddʒel'lare] vt (fig) to seal

suggeri'mento [suddʒeri'mento] sm suggestion; (consiglio) piece of advice, advice no pl

sugge'rire [suddʒe'rire] vt (risposta) to tell; (consigliare) to advise; (proporre) to suggest; (TEATRO) to prompt; **suggeri'tore, 'trice** smf (TEATRO) prompter

suggestio'nare [suddʒestjo'nare] vt to influence

suggesti'one [suddʒes'tjone] sf (PSIC) suggestion; (istigazione) instigation

sugges'tivo, a [suddʒes'tivo] ag (paesaggio) evocative; (teoria) interesting, attractive

'sughero [sugero] sm cork

'sugli ['suʎʎi] prep + det vedi su

'sugo, ghi sm (succo) juice; (di carne) gravy; (condimento) sauce; (fig) gist, essence

'sui prep + det vedi su

sui'cida, i, e [sui'tʃida] ag suicidal ♦ smf suicide

suici'darsi [suitʃi'darsi] vr to commit suicide

sui'cidio [sui'tʃidjo] sm suicide

su'ino, a ag: **carne** ~**a** pork ♦ sm pig; ~**i** smpl swine pl

sul prep + det vedi su

sull' prep + det vedi su

'sulla prep + det vedi su

'sulle prep + det vedi su

'sullo prep + det vedi su

sulta'nina ag f: **(uva)** ~ sultana

sul'tano, a smf sultan/sultana

'sunto sm summary

'suo (f 'sua, pl 'sue, su'oi) det: **il** ~, **la sua** etc (di lui) his; (di lei) her; (di esso) its; (con valore indefinito) one's, his/her; (forma di cortesia: anche: S~) your ♦ pron: **il** ~, **la sua** etc his; hers; yours; **i suoi** his (o her o one's own) family

su'ocero, a ['swɔtʃero] smf father/mother-in-law; **i** ~**i** smpl father-and mother-in-law

su'oi vedi suo

su'ola sf (di scarpa) sole

su'olo sm (terreno) ground; (terra) soil

suo'nare vt (MUS) to play; (campana) to ring; (ore) to strike; (clacson, allarme) to sound ♦ vi to play; (telefono, campana) to ring; (ore) to strike; (clacson, fig: parole) to sound

suone'ria sf alarm

su'ono sm sound

su'ora sf (REL) sister

'super sf (anche: benzina) ≈ four-star (petrol) (BRIT), premium (US)

supe'rare vt (oltrepassare: limite) to exceed, surpass; (percorrere) to cover; (attraversare: fiume) to cross; (sorpassare: veicolo) to overtake; (fig: essere più bravo di) to surpass, outdo; (: difficoltà) to overcome; (: esame) to get through; ~ **qn in altezza/peso** to be taller/heavier than sb; **ha superato la cinquantina** he's over fifty (years of age)

su'perbia *sf* pride

su'perbo, a *ag* proud; (*fig*) magnificent, superb

superfici'ale [superfit'ʃale] *ag* superficial

super'ficie, ci [super'fitʃe] *sf* surface

su'perfluo, a *ag* superfluous

superi'ore *ag* (*piano, arto, classi*) upper; (*più elevato: temperatura, livello*): ~ **(a)** higher (than); (*migliore*): ~ **(a)** superior (to); ~, **a** *smf* (*anche REL*) superior; **superiorità** *sf* superiority

superla'tivo, a *ag, sm* superlative

supermer'cato *sm* supermarket

su'perstite *ag* surviving ♦ *smf* survivor

superstizi'one [superstit'tsjone] *sf* superstition; **superstizi'oso, a** *ag* superstitious

su'pino, a *ag* supine

suppel'lettile *sf* furnishings *pl*

suppergiù [supper'dʒu] *av* more or less, roughly

supplemen'tare *ag* extra; (*treno*) relief *cpd*; (*entrate*) additional

supple'mento *sm* supplement

sup'plente *ag* temporary; (*insegnante*) supply *cpd* (*BRIT*), substitute *cpd* (*US*) ♦ *smf* temporary member of staff; supply (*o* substitute) teacher

'supplica, che *sf* (*preghiera*) plea; (*domanda scritta*) petition, request

suppli'care *vt* to implore, beseech

sup'plire *vi*: ~ **a** to make up for, compensate for

sup'plizio [sup'plittsjo] *sm* torture

sup'porre *vt* to suppose

sup'porto *sm* (*sostegno*) support

sup'posta *sf* (*MED*) suppository

sup'posto, a *pp di* supporre

su'premo, a *ag* supreme

surge'lare [surdʒe'lare] *vt* to (deep-) freeze; **surge'lati** *smpl* frozen food *sg*

sur'plus *sm inv* (*ECON*) surplus

surriscal'dare *vt* to overheat

surro'gato *sm* substitute

suscet'tibile [suʃʃet'tibile] *ag* (*sensibile*) touchy, sensitive; (*soggetto*): ~ **di miglioramento** that can be improved, open to improvement

susci'tare [suʃʃi'tare] *vt* to provoke, arouse

su'sina *sf* plum; **su'sino** *sm* plum (tree)

sussegu'ire *vt* to follow; ~**rsi** *vr* to follow one another

sussidi'ario, a *ag* subsidiary; auxiliary

sus'sidio *sm* subsidy

sus'sistere *vi* to exist; (*essere fondato*) to be valid *o* sound

sussul'tare *vi* to shudder

sussur'rare *vt, vi* to whisper, murmur; **sus'surro** *sm* whisper, murmur

sutu'rare *vt* (*MED*) to stitch up, suture

sva'gare *vt* (*distrarre*) to distract; (*divertire*) to amuse; ~**rsi** *vr* to amuse o.s.; to enjoy o.s.

'svago, ghi *sm* (*riposo*) relaxation; (*ricreazione*) amusement; (*passatempo*) pastime

svali'giare [zvali'dʒare] *vt* to rob, burgle (*BRIT*), burglarize (*US*)

svalu'tare *vt* (*ECON*) to devalue; (*fig*) to belittle; ~**rsi** *vr* (*ECON*) to be devalued; **svalutazi'one** *sf* devaluation

sva'nire *vi* to disappear, vanish

svan'taggio [zvan'taddʒo] *sm* disadvantage; (*inconveniente*) drawback, disadvantage

svapo'rare *vi* to evaporate

svari'ato, a *ag* varied; various

'svastica *sf* swastika

sve'dese *ag* Swedish ♦ *smf* Swede ♦ *sm* (*LING*) Swedish

'sveglia ['zveʎʎa] *sf* waking up; (*orologio*) alarm (clock); **suonare la** ~ (*MIL*) to sound the reveille; ~ **telefonica** alarm call

svegli'are [zveʎ'ʎare] *vt* to wake up; (*fig*) to awaken, arouse; ~**rsi** *vr* to wake up; (*fig*) to be revived, reawaken

'sveglio, a ['zveʎʎo] *ag* awake; (*fig*)

quick-witted

sve'lare vt to reveal

'svelto, a ag (passo) quick; (mente) quick, alert; (linea) slim, slender; **alla ~a** quickly

'svendita sf (COMM) (clearance) sale

sveni'mento sm fainting fit, faint

sve'nire vi to faint

sven'tare vt to foil, thwart

sven'tato, a ag (distratto) scatter-brained; (imprudente) rash

svento'lare vt, vi to wave, flutter

sven'trare vt to disembowel

sven'tura sf misfortune; **sventu'rato, a** ag unlucky, unfortunate

sve'nuto, a pp di **svenire**

svergo'gnato, a [zvergoɲ'ɲato] ag shameless

sver'nare vi to spend the winter

sves'tire vt to undress; **~rsi** vr to get undressed

'Svezia ['zvɛttsja] sf: **la ~** Sweden

svez'zare [zvet'tsare] vt to wean

svi'are vt to divert; (fig) to lead astray; **~rsi** vr to go astray

svi'gnarsela [zviɲ'ɲarsela] vr to slip away, sneak off

svilup'pare vt to develop; **~rsi** vr to develop

svi'luppo sm development

'svincolo sm (COMM) clearance; (stradale) motorway (BRIT) o expressway (US) intersection

svisce'rare [zviʃʃe'rare] vt (fig: argomento) to examine in depth; **svisce'rato, a** ag (amore) passionate; (lodi) obsequious

'svista sf oversight

svi'tare vt to unscrew

'Svizzera ['zvittsera] sf: **la ~** Swit-zerland

'svizzero, a ['zvittsero] ag, sm/f Swiss

svogli'ato, a [zvoʎ'ʎato] ag listless; (pigro) lazy

svolaz'zare [zvolat'tsare] vi to flutter

'svolgere ['zvoldʒere] vt to unwind; (srotolare) to unroll; (fig: argomento) to develop; (: piano, programma)

to carry out; **~rsi** vr to unwind; to unroll; (fig: aver luogo) to take place; (: procedere) to go on; **svol-gi'mento** sm development; carrying out; (andamento) course

'svolta sf (atto) turning no pl; (cur-va) turn, bend; (fig) turning-point

svol'tare vi to turn

'svolto, a pp di **svolgere**

svuo'tare vt to empty (out)

T

tabac'caio, a sm/f tobacconist

tabacche'ria [tabakke'ria] sf tobacconist's (shop)

ta'bacco, chi sm tobacco

ta'bella sf (tavola) table; (elenco) list

taber'nacolo sm tabernacle

tabu'lato sm (INFORM) printout

'tacca, che sf notch, nick; **di mez-za ~** (fig) mediocre

tac'cagno, a [tak'kaɲɲo] ag mean, stingy

tac'cheggio [tak'keddʒo] sm shop lifting

tac'chino [tak'kino] sm turkey

tacci'are [tat'tʃare] vt: **~ qn di** to accuse sb of

'tacco, chi sm heel; **~chi a spillo** stiletto heels

taccu'ino sm notebook

ta'cere [ta'tʃere] vi to be silent o quiet; (smettere di parlare) to fall si-lent ♦ vt to keep to oneself, say noth-ing; **far ~ qn** to make sb be quiet; (fig) to silence sb

ta'chimetro [ta'kimetro] sm speed-ometer

'tacito, a ['tatʃito] ag silent; (sottin-teso) tacit, unspoken

'tafano sm horsefly

taffe'ruglio [taffe'ruʎʎo] sm brawl, scuffle

taffettà sm taffeta

'taglia ['taʎʎa] sf (statura) height; (misura) size; (riscatto) ransom; (ri-compensa) reward; **~ forte** (di abi-

to) large size
taglia'carte [taʎʎa'karte] *sm inv*
paperknife
tagli'ando [taʎ'ʎando] *sm* coupon
tagli'are [taʎ'ʎare] *vt* to cut; *(recidere, interrompere)* to cut off; *(intersecare)* to cut across, intersect; *(carne)* to carve; *(vini)* to blend ♦ *vi* to cut; *(prendere una scorciatoia)* to take a short-cut; ~ **corto** *(fig)* to cut short
taglia'telle [taʎʎa'tɛlle] *sfpl* tagliatelle *pl*
tagli'ente [taʎ'ʎɛnte] *ag* sharp
'taglio ['taʎʎo] *sm* cutting *no pl*; cut; *(parte tagliente)* cutting edge; *(di abito)* cut, style; *(di stoffa: lunghezza)* length; *(di vini)* blending; **di** ~ on edge, edgeways; **banconote di piccolo/grosso** ~ notes of small/large denomination
tagli'ola [taʎ'ʎɔla] *sf* trap, snare
tagliuz'zare [taʎʎut'tsare] *vt* to cut into small pieces
'talco *sm* talcum powder

'tale *det* **1** *(simile, così grande)* such; **un(a)** ~ ... such (a) ...; **non accetto** ~**i discorsi** I won't allow such talk; **è di una** ~ **arroganza** he is so arrogant; **fa una** ~ **confusione!** he makes such a mess!
2 *(persona o cosa indeterminata)* such-and-such; **il giorno** ~ **all'ora** ~ on such-and-such a day at such-and-such a time; **la tal persona** that person; **ha telefonato una** ~ **Giovanna** somebody called Giovanna phoned
3 *(nelle similitudini)*: ~ ... ~ like ... like; ~ **padre** ~ **figlio** like father, like son; **hai il vestito** ~ **quale il mio** your dress is just *o* exactly like mine
♦ *pron (indefinito: persona)*: **un(a)** ~ someone; **quel** *(o* **quella)** ~ that man *(o* woman); **il tal dei** ~**i** what's-his-name

ta'lento *sm* talent
talis'mano *sm* talisman
tallon'cino [tallon'tʃino] *sm* counterfoil
tal'mente *av* so
ta'lora *av* = **talvolta**
'talpa *sf (ZOOL)* mole
tal'volta *av* sometimes, at times
tam'buro *sm* drum
Ta'migi [ta'midʒi] *sm*: **il** ~ **the** Thames
tampo'nare *vt (otturare)* to plug; *(urtare: macchina)* to crash *o* ram into
tam'pone *sm (MED)* wad, pad; *(per timbri)* ink-pad; *(respingente* buffer; ~ **assorbente** tampon
'tana *sf* lair, den
'tanfo *sm* stench; musty smell
tan'gente [tan'dʒɛnte] *ag (MAT)*: ~ **a** tangential to ♦ *sf* tangent; *(quota)* share
tan'tino: **un** ~ *av* a little, a bit

'tanto, a *det* **1** *(molto: quantità)* a lot of, much; *(: numero)* a lot of, many; *(così* ~: *quantità)* so much, such a lot of; *(: numero)* so many, such a lot of; ~**e volte** so many times, so often; ~**i auguri!** all the best!; ~**e grazie** many thanks; ~ **tempo** so long, such a long time; **ogni** ~ **i chilometri** every so many kilometres
2: ~ ... **quanto** *(quantità)* as much ... as; *(numero)* as many ... as; **ho** ~**a pazienza quanta ne hai tu** I have as much patience as you have *o* as you; **ha** ~**i amici quanti nemici** he has as many friends as he has enemies
3 *(rafforzativo)* such; **ho aspettato per** ~ **tempo** I waited so long *o* for such a long time
♦ *pron* **1** *(molto)* much, a lot; *(così* ~) so much, such a lot; ~**i, e** many, a lot; so many, such a lot; **credevo**

ce ne fosse ~ I thought there was (such) a lot, I thought there was plenty

2: ~ **quanto** (denaro) as much as; (cioccolatini) as many as; **ne ho** ~ **quanto basta** I have as much as I need; **due volte** ~ twice as much

3 (indeterminato) so much; ~ **per l'affitto,** ~ **per il gas** so much for the rent, so much for the gas; **costa un** ~ **al metro** it costs so much per metre; **di** ~ **in** ~, **ogni** ~ every so often; ~ **vale che ...** I (o we etc) may as well ...; ~ **meglio!** so much the better!; ~ **peggio per lui!** so much the worse for him!

♦ av **1** (molto) very; **vengo** ~ **volentieri** I'm so glad to come; **non ci vuole** ~ **a capirlo** it doesn't take much to understand it

2 (così ~: con ag, av) so; (: con vb) so much, such a lot; **è** ~ **bella!** she's so beautiful!; **non urlare** ~ don't shout so much; **sto** ~ **meglio adesso** I'm so much better now; ~ ... **che so** ... (that); ~ ... **da so** ...

3: ~ ... **quanto as** ... as; **conosco** ~ **Carlo quanto suo padre** I know both Carlo and his father; **non è poi** ~ **complicato quanto sembri** it's not as difficult as it seems; ~ **più insisti,** ~ **più non mollerà** the more you insist, the more stubborn he'll be; **quanto più** ... ~ **meno** the more ... the less

4 (solamente) just; ~ **per cambiare/scherzare** just for a change/a joke; **una volta** ~ **for once**

5 (a lungo) (for) long

♦ cong after all

'tappa sf (luogo di sosta, fermata) stop, halt; (parte di un percorso) stage, leg; (SPORT) lap; **a ~e** in stages

tap'pare vt to plug, stop up; (bottiglia) to cork

tap'peto sm carpet; (anche: tappetino) rug; (di tavolo) cloth; (SPORT)

andare al ~ to go down for the count; **mettere sul** ~ (fig) to bring up for discussion

tappez'zare [tappet'tsare] vt (con carta) to paper; (rivestire): ~ **qc (di)** to cover sth (with); **tappezze'ria** sf (tessuto) tapestry; (carta da parato) wallpaper; (arte) upholstery; **far da tappezzeria** (fig) to be a wallflower; **tappezzi'ere** sm upholsterer

'tappo sm stopper; (in sughero) cork; ~ **a fare** to delay doing

tarchi'ato, a [tar'kjato] ag stocky, thickset

tar'dare vi to be late ♦ vt to delay; ~ **a fare** to delay doing

'tardi av late; **più** ~ later (on); **al più** ~ at the latest; **sul** ~ (verso sera) late in the day; **far** ~ to be late; (restare alzato) to stay up late

tar'divo, a ag (primavera) late; (rimedio) belated, tardy; (fig: bambino) retarded

'tardo, a ag (lento, fig: ottuso) slow; (tempo: avanzato) late

'targa, ghe sf plate; (AUT) number (BRIT) o license (US) plate

ta'riffa sf (gen) rate, tariff; (di trasporti fare; (elenco) price list; tariff

'tarlo sm woodworm

'tarma sf moth

tar'rocco, chi sm tarot card; ~**chi** smpl (gioco) tarot sg

tartagli'are [tartaʎ'ʎare] vi to stutter, stammer

'tartaro, a ag, sm (in tutti i sensi) tartar

tarta'ruga, ghe sf tortoise; (di mare) turtle; (materiale) tortoiseshell

tar'tina sf canapé

tar'tufo sm (BOT) truffle

'tasca, sche sf pocket; **tas'cabile** ag (libro) pocket cpd; **tasca'pane** sm haversack; **tas'chino** sm breast pocket

'tassa sf (imposta) tax; (doganale) duty; (per iscrizione: a scuola etc) fee; ~ **di circolazione/di soggiorno** road/tourist tax

tas'sametro *sm* taximeter

tas'sare *vt* to tax; to levy a duty on

tassa'tivo, a *ag* peremptory

tassazi'one [tassat'tsjone] *sf* taxation

tas'sello *sm* plug; wedge

tassi *sm inv* = **taxi**; **tas'sista, i, e** *smf* taxi driver

'**tasso** *sm* (*di natalità, d'interesse etc*) rate; (*BOT*) yew; (*ZOOL*) badger; ~ **di cambio/d'interesse** rate of exchange/interest

tas'tare *vt* to feel; ~ **il terreno** (*fig*) to see how the land lies

tasti'era *sf* keyboard

'**tasto** *sm* key; (*tatto*) touch, feel

tas'toni *av*: **procedere** (**a**) ~ to grope one's way forward

'**tattica, che** *sf tactics pl*

'**tattico, a, ci, che** *ag* tactical

'**tatto** *sm* (*senso*) touch; (*fig*) tact; **duro al** ~ hard to the touch; **aver** ~ to be tactful, have tact

tatu'aggio [tatu'addʒo] *sm* tattooing; (*disegno*) tattoo

tatu'are *vt* to tattoo

'**tavola** *sf* table; (*asse*) plank, board; (*lastra*) tablet; (*quadro*) panel (painting); (*illustrazione*) plate; ~ **calda** snack bar

tavo'lato *sm* boarding; (*pavimento*) wooden floor

tavo'letta *sf* tablet, bar; **a** ~ (*AUT*) flat out

tavo'lino *sm* small table; (*scrivania*) desk

'**tavolo** *sm* table

tavo'lozza [tavo'lɔttsa] *sf* (*ARTE*) palette

'**taxi** *sm inv* taxi

'**tazza** ['tattsa] *sf* cup; ~ **da caffè/tè** coffee/tea cup; **una** ~ **di caffè/tè** a cup of coffee/tea

te *pron* (*soggetto: in forme comparative, oggetto*) you

tè *sm inv* tea; (*trattenimento*) tea party

tea'trale *ag* theatrical

te'atro *sm* theatre

'**tecnica, che** *sf* technique; (*tecnologia*) technology

'**tecnico, a, ci, che** *ag* technical ♦ *smf* technician

tecnolo'gia [teknolo'dʒia] *sf* technology

te'desco, a, schi, sche *ag, smf, sm* German

'**tedio** *sm* tedium, boredom

'**te'game** *sm* (*CUC*) pan

'**teglia** ['teʎʎa] *sf* (*per dolci*) (baking) tin; (*per arrosti*) (roasting) tin

'**tegola** *sf* tile

tei'era *sf* teapot

'**tela** *sf* (*tessuto*) cloth; (*per vele, quadri*) canvas; (*dipinto*) canvas, painting; **di** ~ (*calzoni*) (heavy) cotton *cpd*; (*scarpe, borsa*) canvas *cpd*; ~ **cerata** oilcloth; (*copertone*) tarpaulin

te'laio *sm* (*apparecchio*) loom; (*struttura*) frame

tele'camera *sf* television camera

tele'cronaca *sf* television report

tele'ferica, che *sf* cableway

telefo'nare *vi* to telephone, ring; to make a phone call ♦ *vt* to telephone; ~ **a** to phone up, ring up, call up

telefo'nata *sf* (*telephone*) call; ~ **a carico del destinatario** reverse charge (*BRIT*) o collect (*US*) call

tele'fonico, a, ci, che *ag* (*tele*)phone *cpd*

telefo'nino [telefo'nino] *sm* mobile phone

telefo'nista, i, e *smf* telephonist; (*d'impresa*) switchboard operator

te'lefono *sm* telephone; ~ **a gettoni** o **pay phone**

telegior'nale [teledʒor'nale] *sm* television news (programme)

te'legrafo *sm* telegraph; (*ufficio*) telegraph office

tele'gramma, i *sm* telegram

tele'matica *sf* data transmission; telematics *sg*

telepa'tia *sf* telepathy

teles'copio *sm* telescope

teleselezi'one [teleselet'tsjone] *sf* direct dialling

telespetta'tore, 'trice *smf* (television) viewer

televisi'one sf television

televi'sore sm television set

'telex sm inv telex

'tema, i sm theme; (INS) essay, composition

teme'rario, a ag rash, reckless

te'mere vt to fear, be afraid of; (essere sensibile a: freddo, calore) to be sensitive to ♦ vi to be afraid; (essere preoccupato): ~ **per** to worry about, fear for; ~ **di/che** to be afraid of/ that

temperama'tite sm inv pencil sharpener

tempera'mento sm temperament

tempe'rare vt (aguzzare) to sharpen; (fig) to moderate, control, temper

tempe'rato, a ag moderate, temperate; (clima) temperate

tempera'tura sf temperature

tempe'rino sm penknife

tem'pesta sf storm; ~ **di sabbia/ neve** sand/snowstorm

tempes'tare vt: ~ **qn di domande** to bombard sb with questions; ~ **qn di colpi** to rain blows on sb

tempes'tivo, a ag timely

tempes'toso, a ag stormy

'tempia sf (ANAT) temple

'tempio sm (edificio) temple

'tempo sm (METEOR) weather; (cronologico) time; (epoca) time, times pl; (di film, gioco: parte) part; (MUS) time; (: battuta) beat; (LING) tense; **un** ~ once; ~ **fa** some time ago; **al** ~ **stesso** o **a un** ~ at the same time; **per** ~ early; **aver fatto il suo** ~ to have had its (o his etc) day; **primo/secondo** ~ (TEATRO) first/second part; (SPORT) first/second half; **in** ~ **utile** in due time o course

tempo'rale ag temporal ♦ sm (METEOR) (thunder)storm

tempo'raneo, a ag temporary

temporeggi'are [tempored'dʒare] vi to play for time, temporize

tem'prare vt to temper

te'nace [te'natʃe] ag strong, tough; (fig) tenacious; **te'nacia** sf tenacity

te'naglie [te'naʎʎe] sfpl pincers pl

'tenda sf (riparo) awning; (di finestra) curtain; (per campeggio etc) tent

ten'denza [ten'dɛntsa] sf tendency; (orientamento) trend; **avere** ~ **a** o **per qc** to have a bent for sth

'tendere vt (allungare al massimo) to stretch, draw tight; (porgere: mano) to hold out; (fig: trappola) to lay, set ♦ vi: ~ **a qc/a fare** to tend towards sth/to do; ~ **l'orecchio** to prick up one's ears; **il tempo tende al caldo** the weather is getting hot; **un blu che tende al verde** a greenish blue

ten'dina sf curtain

'tendine sm tendon, sinew

ten'done sm (da circo) tent

'tenebre sfpl darkness sg; **tene'broso, a** ag dark, gloomy

te'nente sm lieutenant

te'nere vt to hold; (conservare, mantenere) to keep; (ritenere, considerare) to consider; (spazio: occupare) to take up, occupy; (seguire: strada) to keep to ♦ vi to hold; (colori) to be fast; (dare importanza): ~ **a** to care about; ~ **a fare** to want to do, be keen to do; ~**rsi** vr (stare in una determinata posizione) to stand; (stimarsi) to consider o.s.; (aggrapparsi): ~**rsi a** to hold on to; (attenersi): ~**rsi a** to stick to; ~ **una conferenza** to give a lecture; ~ **conto di qc** to take sth into consideration; ~ **presente qc** to bear sth in mind

'tenero, a ag tender; (pietra, cera, colore) soft; (fig) tender, loving

'tenia sf tapeworm

'tennis sm tennis

te'nore sm (tono) tone; (MUS) tenor; ~ **di vita** way of life; (livello) standard of living

tensi'one sf tension

ten'tare vt (indurre) to tempt; (provare): ~ **qc/di fare** to attempt o try sth/to do; **tenta'tivo** sm attempt;

tentazi'one sf temptation

tenten'nare vi to shake, be unsteady; (fig) to hesitate, waver ♦ vt: ~ **il capo** to shake one's head

ten'toni av: **andare a** ~ (anche fig) to grope one's way

'tenue ag (sottile) fine; (colore) soft; (fig) slender, slight

te'nuta sf (capacità) capacity; (divisa) uniform; (abito) dress; (AGR) estate; **a** ~ **d'aria** airtight; ~ **di strada** roadholding power

teolo'gia [teolo'dʒia] sf theology; **te'ologo, gi** sm theologian

teo'rema, i sm theorem

teo'ria sf theory; **te'orico, a, ci, che** ag theoretic(al)

'tepido, a ag = tiepido

te'pore sm warmth

'teppa sf mob, hooligans pl; **tep'pismo** sm hooliganism; **tep'pista, i** sm hooligan

tera'pia sf therapy

tergicris'tallo [terdʒikris'tallo] sm windscreen (BRIT) o windshield (US) wiper

tergiver'sare [terdʒiver'sare] vi to shilly-shally

'tergo sm: **a** ~ behind; **vedi a** ~ please turn over

ter'male ag thermal; **stazione** sf ~ spa

'terme sfpl thermal baths

'termico, a, ci, che ag thermic; (unità) thermal

termi'nale ag, sm terminal

termi'nare vt to end; (lavoro) to finish ♦ vi to end

'termine sm term; (fine, estremità) end; (di territorio) boundary, limit; **contratto a** ~ (COMM) forward contract; **a breve/lungo** ~ short-/long-term; **parlare senza mezzi** ~**i** to talk frankly, not to mince one's words

ter'mometro sm thermometer

termonucle'are ag thermonuclear

'termos sm inv = thermos

termosi'fone sm radiator; (riscaldamento a) ~ central heating

ter'mostato sm thermostat

'terra sf (gen, ELETTR) earth; (sostanza) soil, earth; (opposto al mare) land no pl; (regione, paese) land; (argilla) clay; ~**e** sfpl (possedimento) lands, land sg; **a o per** ~ (stato) on the ground (o floor); (moto) to the ground, down; **mettere a** ~ (ELETTR) to earth

terra'cotta sf terracotta; **vasellame** sm **di** ~ earthenware

terra'ferma sf dry land, terra firma; (continente) mainland

terrapi'eno sm embankment, bank

ter'razza [ter'rattsa] sf terrace

ter'razzo [ter'rattso] sm = **terrazza**

terre'moto sm earthquake

ter'reno, a ag (vita, beni) earthly ♦ sm (suolo, fig) ground; (COMM) land no pl, plot (of land); site; (SPORT, MIL) field

ter'restre ag (superficie) of the earth, earth's; (di terra: battaglia, animale) land cpd; (REL) earthly, worldly

ter'ribile ag terrible, dreadful

ter'rina sf tureen

territori'ale ag territorial

terri'torio sm territory

ter'rore sm terror; **terro'rismo** sm terrorism; **terro'rista, i, e** sm/f terrorist

'terso, a ag clear

'terzo, a ['tertso] ag third ♦ sm (frazione) third; (DIR) third party; ~**i** smpl (altri) others, other people; **la** ~**a pagina** (STAMPA) the Arts page

'tesa sf brim

'teschio ['teskjo] sm skull

'tesi sf thesis

'teso, a pp di **tendere** ♦ ag (tirato) taut, tight; (fig) tense

tesore'ria sf treasury

tesori'ere sm treasurer

te'soro sm treasure; **il Ministero del T**~ the Treasury

'tessera sf (documento) card

'tessere vt to weave; **'tessile** ag, sm textile; **tessi'tore, 'trice** sm/f weaver; **tessi'tura** *sf* weaving

tes'suto *sm* fabric, material; (BIOL) tissue; (fig) web

'**testa** *sf* head; (di cose: estremità, parte anteriore) head, front; **di ~** (vettura etc) front; **tenere ~ a qn** (nemico etc) to stand up to sb; **fare di ~ propria** to go one's own way; **in ~** (SPORT) in the lead; **~ o croce?** heads or tails?; **avere la ~ dura** to be stubborn; **~ di serie** (TENNIS) seed, seeded player

testa'mento *sm* (atto) will; **l'Antico/il Nuovo T~** (REL) the Old/New Testament

tes'tardo, a *ag* stubborn, pig-headed

tes'tata *sf* (parte anteriore) head; (intestazione) heading

'**teste** *smf* witness

tes'ticolo *sm* testicle

testi'mone *smf* (DIR) witness

testimoni'anza [testimo'njantsa] *sf* testimony

testimoni'are *vt* to testify; (fig) to bear witness to, to testify to ♦ *vi* to give evidence, testify

tes'tina *sf* (TECN) head

'**testo** *sm* text; (opera, autore) to be authoritative; **questo libro non fa ~** this book is not essential reading; **testu'ale** *ag* textual; literal, word for word

tes'tuggine [tes'tuddʒine] *sf* tortoise; (di mare) turtle

'**tetano** *sm* (MED) tetanus

'**tetro, a** *ag* gloomy

'**tetto** *sm* roof; **tet'toia** *sf* roofing; canopy

'**Tevere** *sm*: **il ~** the Tiber

Tg. *abbr* = **telegiornale**

'**thermos** ['tɛrmos] ® *sm inv* vacuum *o* Thermos ® flask

ti *pron* (dav lo, la, li, le, ne diventa **te**) *pron* (oggetto) you; (complemento di termine) (to) you; (riflessivo) yourself

ti'ara *sf* (REL) tiara

'**tibia** *sf* tibia, shinbone

tic *sm inv* tic, (nervous) twitch; (fig) mannerism

ticchet'tio [tikket'tio] *sm* (di macchina da scrivere) clatter; (di orologio) ticking; (della pioggia) patter

'**ticchio** ['tikkjo] *sm* (ghiribizzo) whim; (tic) tic, (nervous) twitch

ti'epido, a *ag* lukewarm, tepid

ti'fare *vi*: **~ per** to be a fan of; (parteggiare) to side with

'**tifo** *sm* (MED) typhus; (fig): **fare il ~ per** to be a fan of

tifoi'dea *sf* typhoid

ti'fone *sm* typhoon

ti'foso, a *smf* (SPORT etc) fan

'**tiglio** ['tiʎʎo] *sm* lime (tree), linden (tree)

'**tigre** *sf* tiger

tim'ballo *sm* (strumento) kettledrum; (CUC) timbale

'**timbro** *sm* stamp; (MUS) timbre, tone

'**timido, a** *ag* shy; timid

'**timo** *sm* thyme

ti'mone *sm* (NAUT) rudder; **timoni'ere** *sm* helmsman

ti'more *sm* (paura) fear; (rispetto) awe; **timo'roso, a** *ag* timid, timorous

'**timpano** *sm* (ANAT) eardrum; (MUS): **~i** *smpl* kettledrums, timpani

ti'nello *sm* small dining room

'**tingere** ['tindʒere] *vt* to dye

'**tino** *sm* vat

ti'nozza [ti'nɔttsa] *sf* tub

'**tinta** *sf* (materia colorante) dye; (colore) colour, shade; **tinta'rella** (fam) *sf* (sun)tan

tintin'nare *vi* to tinkle

'**tinto, a** *pp di* **tingere**

tinto'ria *sf* (officina colorante) dyeworks *sg*; (lavasecco) dry cleaner's (shop)

tin'tura *sf* (operazione) dyeing; (colorante) dye; **~ di iodio** tincture of iodine

'**tipico, a, ci, che** *ag* typical

'**tipo** *sm* type; (genere) kind, type; (fam) chap, fellow

tipogra'fia *sf* typography; (procedimento) letterpress (printing); (officina) printing house; **tipo'grafico, a,**

ci, che *ag* typographic(al); letterpress *cpd*; **ti'pografo** *sm* typographer

ti'ranno, a *ag* tyrannical ♦ *sm* tyrant

ti'rante *sm* (*per tenda*) guy

ti'rare *vt* (*gen*) to pull; (*estrarre*): ~ qc da to take o pull sth out of; to get sth out of; to extract sth from; (*chiudere: tenda etc*) to draw, pull; (*tracciare, disegnare*) to draw, trace; (*lanciare: sasso, palla*) to throw; (*stampare*) to print; (*pistola, freccia*) to fire ♦ *vi* (*pipa, camino*) to draw; (*vento*) to blow; (*abito*) to be tight; (*fare fuoco*) to fire; (*fare del tiro, CALCIO*) to shoot; ~ **avanti** *vi* to struggle on ♦ *vt* to keep going; ~ **fuori** (*estrarre*) to take out, pull out; ~ **giù** (*abbassare*) to bring down; ~ **su** to pull up; (*capelli*) to put up; (*fig: bambino*) to bring up; ~**rsi indietro** to move back

tira'tore *sm* gunman; **un buon** ~ a good shot; ~ **scelto** marksman

tira'tura *sf* (*azione*) printing; (*di libro*) (print) run; (*di giornale*) circulation

'tirchio, a ['tirkjo] *ag* mean, stingy

'tiro *sm* shooting *no pl*, firing *no pl*; (*colpo, sparo*) shot; (*di palla: lancio*) throwing *no pl*; throw; (*fig*) trick; **cavallo da** ~ draught (*BRIT*) o draft (*US*) horse; ~ **a segno** target shooting; (*luogo*) shooting range

tiro'cinio [tiro'tʃinjo] *sm* apprenticeship; (*professionale*) training

ti'roide *sf* thyroid (gland)

Tir'reno *sm*: **il** (*mar*) ~ the Tyrrhenian Sea

ti'sana *sf* herb tea

tito'lare *ag* appointed; (*sovrano*) titular ♦ *sm/f* incumbent; (*proprietario*) owner; (*CALCIO*) regular player

'titolo *sm* title; (*di giornale*) headline; (*diploma*) qualification; (*COMM*) security; (*c*) share; **a che** ~? for what reason?; **a** ~ **di amicizia** out of friendship; **a** ~ **di premio** as a prize; ~ **di credito**

share

titu'bante *ag* hesitant, irresolute

'tizio, a ['tittsjo] *sm/f* fellow, chap

tiz'zone [tit'tsone] *sm* brand

toc'cante *ag* touching

toc'care *vt* to touch; (*tastare*) to feel; (*fig: riguardare*) to concern; (*: commuovere*) to touch, move; (*: pungere*) to hurt, wound; (*: far cenno a: argomento*) to touch on, mention ♦ *vi*: ~ **a** (*accadere*) to happen to; (*spettare*) to be up to; ~ (**il fondo**) (*in acqua*) to touch the bottom; **tocca a te difenderci** it's up to you to defend us; **a chi tocca?** whose turn is it?; **mi toccò pagare** I had to pay

'tocco, chi *sm* touch; (*ARTE*) stroke, touch

'toga, ghe *sf* toga; (*di magistrato, professore*) gown

'togliere ['tɔʎʎere] *vt* (*rimuovere*) to take away (o off), remove; (*riprendere, non concedere più*) to take away, remove; (*MAT*) to take away, subtract; (*liberare*) to free; ~ **qc a qn** to take sth (away) from sb; **ciò non toglie che** nevertheless, be that as it may; ~**rsi il cappello** to take off one's hat

toi'lette [twa'lɛt] *sf inv* toilet; (*mobile*) dressing table

to'letta *sf* = **toilette**

tolle'ranza [tolle'rantsa] *sf* tolerance

tolle'rare *vt* to tolerate

'tolto, a *pp* di **togliere**

to'maia *sf* (*di scarpa*) upper

'tomba *sf* tomb

tom'bino *sm* manhole cover

'tombola *sf* (*gioco*) tombola; (*ruzzolone*) tumble

'tomo *sm* volume

to'naca, che *sf* (*REL*) habit

to'nare *vi* = **tuonare**

'tondo, a *ag* round

'tonfo *sm* splash; (*rumore sordo*) thud; (*caduta*): **fare un** ~ to take a tumble

'tonico, a, ci, che *ag, sm* tonic

tonifi'care *vt* (*muscoli, pelle*) to

tone up; (*irrobustire*) to invigorate, brace

tonnel'laggio [tonnel'laddʒo] *sm* (*NAUT*) tonnage

tonnel'lata *sf* ton

'tonno *sm* tuna (fish)

'tono *sm* (*gen*) tone; (*MUS: di pezzo*) key; (*di colore*) shade, tone

ton'silla *sf* tonsil; **tonsil'lite** *sf* tonsillitis

'tonto, a *ag* dull, stupid

to'pazio [to'pattsjo] *sm* topaz

'topo *sm* mouse

topogra'fia *sf* topography

'toppa *sf* (*serratura*) keyhole; (*pezza*) patch

to'race [to'ratʃe] *sm* chest

'torba *sf* peat

'torbido, a *ag* (*liquido*) cloudy; (*: fiume*) muddy; (*fig*) dark; troubled ♦ *sm*: **pescare nel ~** (*fig*) to fish in troubled water

'torcere ['tɔrtʃere] *vt* to twist; (*biancheria*) to wring (out); **~rsi** *vr* to twist, writhe

torchi'are [tor'kjare] *vt* to press; **'torchio** *sm* press

'torcia, ce ['tɔrtʃa] *sf* torch; ~ **elettrica** torch (*BRIT*), flashlight (*US*)

torci'collo [tortʃi'kɔllo] *sm* stiff neck

'tordo *sm* thrush

To'rino *sf* Turin

tor'menta *sf* snowstorm

tormen'tare *vt* to torment; **~rsi** *vr* to fret, worry o.s.; **tor'mento** *sm* torment

torna'conto *sm* advantage, benefit

tor'nado *sm* tornado

tor'nante *sm* hairpin bend

tor'nare *vi* to return, go (*o* come) back; (*ridiventare: anche fig*) to become (again); (*riuscire giusto, esatto: conto*) to work out; (*risultare*) to turn out (to be), prove (to be); ~ **utile** to prove *o* turn out (to be) useful; ~ **a casa** to go (*o* come) home

torna'sole *sm inv* litmus

tor'neo *sm* tournament

'tornio *sm* lathe

'toro *sm* bull; (*dello zodiaco*) **T~** Taurus

tor'pedine *sf* torpedo; **torpedini'era** *sf* torpedo boat

'torre *sf* tower; (*SCACCHI*) rook, castle; ~ **di controllo** (*AER*) control tower

torrefazi'one [torrefat'tsjone] *sf* roasting

tor'rente *sm* torrent

tor'retta *sf* turret

torri'one *sm* keep

tor'rone *sm* nougat

torsi'one *sf* twisting; torsion

'torso *sm* torso, trunk; (*ARTE*) torso

'torsolo *sm* (*di cavolo etc*) stump; (*di frutta*) core

'torta *sf* cake

'torto, a *pp di* **torcere** ♦ *ag* (*ritorto*) twisted; (*storto*) twisted, crooked ♦ *sm* (*ingiustizia*) wrong; (*colpa*) fault; **a ~** wrongly; **aver ~** to be wrong

tor'tora *sf* turtle dove

tortu'oso, a *ag* (*strada*) twisting; (*fig*) tortuous

tor'tura *sf* torture; **tortu'rare** *vt* to torture

'torvo, a *ag* menacing, grim

tosa'erba *sm o f inv* (lawn)mower

to'sare *vt* (*pecora*) to shear; (*siepe*) to clip, trim

Tos'cana *sf*: **la ~** Tuscany; **tos'cano, a** *ag, smf* Tuscan ♦ *sm* (*sigaro*) strong Italian cigar

'tosse *sf* cough

'tossico, a, ci, che *ag* toxic

tossicodipen'dente *smf* drug addict

tossi'comane *smf* drug addict

tos'sire *vi* to cough

tosta'pane *sm inv* toaster

tos'tare *vt* to toast; (*caffè*) to roast

'tosto, a *ag*: **faccia ~a** cheek

to'tale *ag, sm* total; **totalità** *sf*: **la totalità di** all of, the total amount (*o* number) of; **the whole** +*sg*; **totaliz'zare** *vt* to total; (*SPORT*: *punti*) to score

toto'calcio [toto'kaltʃo] *sm* gambling pool betting on football results,

≈ (football) pools pl (BRIT)

to'vaglia [to'vaʎʎa] sf tablecloth;
tovagli'olo sm napkin

'tozzo, a ['tɔttso] ag squat ♦ sm: ~
di pane crust of bread

tra prep (di due persone, cose) between; (di più persone, cose)
among(st); (tempo: entro) within,
in; ~ 5 giorni in 5 days' time; sia
detto ~ noi ... between you and me
...; litigano ~ (di) loro they're
fighting amongst themselves; ~ breve soon; ~ sé e sé (parlare etc) to
oneself

trabal'lare vi to stagger, totter

traboc'care vi to overflow

traboc'chetto [trabok'ketto] sm
(fig) trap

tracan'nare vt to gulp down

'traccia, ce ['trattʃa] sf (segno, striscia) trail, track; (orma) tracks pl;
(residuo, testimonianza) trace, sign;
(abbozzo) outline

tracci'are [trat'tʃare] vt to trace,
mark (out); (disegnare) to draw;
(fig: abbozzare) to outline; **tracci'ato** sm (grafico) layout, plan

tra'chea [tra'kɛa] sf windpipe,
trachea

tra'colla sf shoulder strap; **borsa a**
~ shoulder bag

tra'collo sm (fig) collapse, crash

traco'tante ag overbearing, arrogant

tradi'mento sm betrayal; (DIR,
MIL) treason

tra'dire vt to betray; (coniuge) to be
unfaithful to; (doveri: mancare) to
fail in; (rivelare) to give away, reveal; **tradi'tore, 'trice** smf traitor

tradizi'one [tradit'tsjone] sf tradition

tra'dotto, a pp di tradurre

tra'durre vt to translate; (spiegare)
to render, convey; **tradut'tore, 'trice** smf translator; **traduzi'one** sf
translation

tra'ente smf (ECON) drawer

trafe'lato, a ag out of breath

traffi'cante smf dealer; (peg)
trafficker

traffi'care vi (commerciare): ~
(in) to trade (in), deal (in); (affac-
cendarsi) to busy o.s. ♦ vt (peg) to
traffic in

'traffico, ci sm traffic; (commercio)
trade, traffic

tra'figgere [tra'fiddʒere] vt to run
through, stab; (fig) to pierce;
tra'fitto, a pp di trafiggere

tra'forare vt to bore, drill; **tra'foro**
sm (azione) boring, drilling; (galleria) tunnel

tra'gedia [tra'dʒɛdja] sf tragedy

tra'ghetto [tra'getto] sm crossing;
(barca) ferry(boat)

'tragico, a, ci, che ['tradʒiko] ag
tragic

tra'gitto [tra'dʒitto] sm (passaggio)
crossing; (viaggio) journey

tragu'ardo sm (SPORT) finishing
line; (fig) goal, aim

traiet'toria sf trajectory

trai'nare vt to drag, haul; (rimorchiare) to tow; **'traino** sm (carro) wagon; (slitta) sledge; (carico)
load

tralasci'are [tralaʃ'ʃare] vt (studi) to
neglect; (dettagli) to leave out, omit

'tralcio [tral't ʃo] sm (BOT) shoot

tra'liccio [tra'littʃo] sm (tela) ticking; (struttura) trellis; (ELETTR)
pylon

tram sm inv tram

'trama sf (filo) weft, woof; (fig: argomento, maneggio) plot

traman'dare vt to pass on, hand
down

tra'mare vt (fig) to scheme, plot

tram'busto sm turmoil

trames'tio sm bustle

tramez'zino [tramed'dzino] sm
sandwich

tra'mezzo [tra'mɛddzo] sm (EDIL)
partition

'tramite prep through

tramon'tare vi to set, go down;
tra'monto sm setting; (del sole)
sunset

tramor'tire vi to faint ♦ vt to stun

trampo'lino sm (per tuffi) springboard, diving board; (per lo sci) skijump

'trampolo sm stilt

tramu'tare vt: ~ in to change into, turn into

tra'nello sm trap

trangugi'are [trangu'dʒare] vt to gulp down

'tranne prep except (for), but (for); ~ che unless

tranquil'lante sm (MED) tranquillizer

tranquillità sf calm, stillness; quietness; peace of mind

tranquilliz'zare [trankwillid'dzare] vt to reassure

tran'quillo, a ag calm, quiet; (bambino, scolaro) quiet; (sereno) with one's mind at rest; **sta'** ~ don't worry

transat'lantico, a, ci, che ag transatlantic ♦ sm transatlantic liner

tran'satto, a pp di transigere

transi'tabile ag passable

transi'tare vi to pass

transi'tivo, a ag transitive

'transito sm transit; **di** ~ (merci) in transit; (stazione) transit cpd; "**divieto di** ~" "no entry"

transi'torio, a ag transitory, transient; (provvisorio) provisional

tran'via sf tramway (BRIT), streetcar line (US)

'trapano sm (utensile) drill; (: MED) trepan

trapas'sare vt to pierce

tra'passo sm passage

trape'lare vi to leak, drip; (fig) to leak out

tra'pezio [tra'pɛttsjo] sm (MAT) trapezium; (attrezzo ginnico) trapeze

trapian'tare vt to transplant; **tra-pi'anto** sm transplanting; (MED) transplant

'trappola sf trap

tra'punta sf quilt

'trarre vt to draw, pull; (portare) to take; (prendere, tirare fuori) to take (out), draw; (derivare) to obtain; ~ **origine da** qc to have its origins o originate in sth

trasa'lire vi to start, jump

trasan'dato, a ag shabby

trasbor'dare vt to transfer; (NAUT) to tran(s)ship ♦ vi (NAUT) to change ship; (AER) to change plane; [FERR] to change (trains)

trasci'nare [traffi'nare] vt to drag; ~rsi vr to drag o drag o.s. along; (fig) to drag on

tras'correre vt (tempo) to spend, pass ♦ vi to pass; **tras'corso, a** pp di trascorrere

tras'critto, a pp di trascrivere

tras'crivere vt to transcribe

trascu'rare vt to neglect; (non considerare) to disregard; **trascura-'tezza** sf carelessness, negligence; **trascu'rato, a** ag (casa) neglected; (persona) careless, negligent

traseco'lato, a ag astounded, amazed

trasferi'mento sm transfer; (trasloco) removal, move

trasfe'rire vt to transfer; ~rsi vr to move; **tras'ferta** sf transfer; (indennità) travelling expenses pl; (SPORT) away game

trasfigu'rare vt to transfigure

trasfor'mare vt to transform, change

trasfusi'one sf (MED) transfusion

trasgre'dire vt to disobey, contravene

tras'lato, a ag metaphorical, figurative

traslo'care vt to move, transfer; ~rsi vr to move; **tras'loco, chi** sm removal

tras'messo, a *pp di* trasmettere
tras'mettere *vt* (*passare*): ~ qc a qn to pass sth on to sb; (*mandare*) to send; (*TECN, TEL, MED*) to transmit; (*TV, RADIO*) to broadcast; **trasmetti'tore** *sm* transmitter; **tra'smissi'one** *sf* (*gen, FISICA, TECN*) transmission; (*passaggio*) transmission, passing on; (*TV, RADIO*) broadcast; **trasmit'tente** *sf* transmitting *o* broadcasting station
traso'gnato, a [trasoɲ'ɲato] *ag* dreamy
traspa'rente *ag* transparent
traspa'rire *vi* to show (through)
traspi'rare *vi* to perspire; (*fig*) to come to light, leak out; **traspirazi'one** *sf* perspiration
traspor'tare *vt* to transport, move; (*merce*) to transport, convey; lasciarsi ~ (da qc) (*fig*) to let o.s. be carried away (by sth); **tras'porto** *sm* transport
trastul'lare *vt* to amuse; ~**rsi** *vr* to amuse o.s.
trasu'dare *vi* (*filtrare*) to ooze; (*sudare*) to sweat ♦ *vt* to ooze with
trasver'sale *ag* transverse, cross(-); running at right angles
trasvo'lare *vt* to fly over
'tratta *sf* (*ECON*) draft; (*di persone*): **la** ~ **delle bianche** the white slave trade
tratta'mento *sm* treatment; (*servizio*) service
trat'tare *vt* (*gen*) to treat; (*commerciare*) to deal in; (*svolgere: argomento*) to discuss, deal with; (*negoziare*) to negotiate ♦ *vi*: ~ **di** to deal with; ~ **con** (*persona*) to deal with; **si tratta di ... it's about ...; trat'tative** *sfpl* negotiations; **trat'tato** *sm* (*testo*) treatise; (*accordo*) treaty; **trattazi'one** *sf* treatment
tratteggi'are [tratted'dʒare] *vt* (*disegnare: a tratti*) to sketch, outline; (: *col tratteggio*) to hatch
tratte'nere *vt* (*far rimanere: persona*) to detain; (*intrattenere: ospiti*) to entertain; (*tenere, frenare, repri-*

mere) to hold back, keep back; (*astenersi dal consegnare*) to hold, keep; (*detrarre: somma*) to deduct; ~**rsi** *vr* (*astenersi*) to restrain o.s., stop o.s.; (*soffermarsi*) to stay, remain
tratteni'mento *sm* entertainment; (*festa*) party
tratte'nuta *sf* deduction
trat'tino *sm* dash; (*in parole composte*) hyphen
'tratto, a *pp di* trarre ♦ *sm* (*di penna, matita*) stroke; (*parte*) part, piece; (*di strada*) stretch; (*di mare, cielo*) expanse; (*di tempo*) period (of time); ~**i** *smpl* (*caratteristiche*) features; (*modo di fare*) ways, manners; **a un** ~, **d'un** ~ suddenly
trat'tore *sm* tractor
tratto'ria *sf* restaurant
'trauma, a *sm* trauma; **trau'matico, a, ci, che** *ag* traumatic
tra'vaglio [tra'vaʎʎo] *sm* (*angoscia*) pain, suffering; (*MED*) pains *pl*
trava'sare *vt* to decant
'trave *sf* beam
tra'versa *sf* (*trave*) crosspiece; (*via*) sidestreet; (*FERR*) (railroad) tie (*US*); (*CALCIO*) crossbar
traver'sare *vt* to cross; **traver'sata** *sf* crossing; (*AER*) flight, trip
traver'sie *sfpl* mishaps, misfortunes
traver'sina *sf* (*FERR*) sleeper (*BRIT*), (railroad) tie (*US*)
tra'verso, a *ag* oblique; **di** ~ *ag* askew ♦ *av* sideways; **andare di** ~ (*cibo*) to go down the wrong way; **guardare di** ~ to look askance at
travesti'mento *sm* disguise
traves'tire *vt* to disguise; ~**rsi** *vr* to disguise o.s.
travi'are *vt* (*fig*) to lead astray
travi'sare *vt* (*fig*) to distort, misrepresent
tra'volgere [tra'vɔldʒere] *vt* to sweep away, carry away; (*fig*) to overwhelm; **tra'volto, a** *pp di* travolgere
tre *num* three
trebbi'are *vt* to thresh

'treccia, ce ['trettʃa] sf plait, braid

tre'cento [tre'tʃento] num three hundred ♦ sm: **il T~** the fourteenth century

'tredici ['treditʃi] num thirteen

'tregua sf truce; (fig) respite

tre'mare vi: **~ di** (freddo etc) to shiver o tremble with; (paura, rabbia) to shake o tremble with

tre'mendo, a ag terrible, awful

tre'mila num three thousand

'tremito sm trembling no pl; shaking no pl; shivering no pl

tremo'lare vi to tremble; (luce) to flicker; (foglie) to quiver

tre'more sm tremor

'treno sm train; **~ di gomme** set of tyres (BRIT) o tires (US); **~ merci** goods (BRIT) o freight train; **~ viaggiatori** passenger train

'trenta num thirty; **tren'tesimo, a** num thirtieth; **tren'tina** sf: **una trentina (di)** thirty or so, about thirty

'trepido, a ag anxious

treppi'ede sm tripod; (CUC) trivet

'tresca, sche sf (fig) intrigue; (: relazione amorosa) affair

'trespolo sm trestle

tri'angolo sm triangle

tribù sf inv tribe

tri'buna sf (podio) platform; (in aule etc) gallery; (di stadio) stand

tribu'nale sm court

tribu'tare vt to bestow

tri'buto sm tax; (fig) tribute

tri'checo, chi [tri'kɛko] sm (ZOOL) walrus

tri'ciclo [tri'tʃiklo] sm tricycle

trico'lore ag three-coloured ♦ sm tricolour; (bandiera italiana) Italian flag

tri'dente sm trident

tri'foglio [tri'fɔʎʎo] sm clover

'triglia [tri'ʎʎa] sf red mullet

tril'lare vi (MUS) to trill

tri'mestre sm period of three months; (INS) term, quarter (US); (COMM) quarter

'trina sf lace

trin'cea [trin'tʃea] sf trench; **trin-ce'rare** vt to entrench

trinci'are [trin'tʃare] vt to cut up

trion'fare vi to triumph, win; **~ su** to triumph over, overcome; **tri'onfo** sm triumph

tripli'care vt to triple

'triplice ['triplitʃe] ag triple; **in ~ copia** in triplicate

'triplo, a ag triple; treble ♦ sm: **il ~ (di)** three times as much (as); **la spesa è ~a** it costs three times as much

'tripode sm tripod

'trippa sf (CUC) tripe

'triste ag sad; (luogo) dreary, gloomy; **tris'tezza** sf sadness; gloominess

trita'carne sm inv mincer, grinder (US)

tri'tare vt to mince, grind (US)

'trito, a ag (tritato) minced, ground (US); **~ e ritrito** (fig) trite, hackneyed

'trittico, ci sm (ARTE) triptych

trivel'lare vt to drill

tri'vio sm (fig) triangle

trivi'ale ag vulgar, low

tro'feo sm trophy

'trogolo sm (per maiali) trough

'tromba sf (MUS) trumpet; (AUT) horn; **~ d'aria** whirlwind; **~ delle scale** stairwell

trom'bone sm trombone

trom'bosi sf thrombosis

tron'care vt to cut off; (spezzare) to break off

'tronco, a, chi, che ag cut off; broken off; (LING) truncated; (fig) cut short ♦ sm (BOT, ANAT) trunk; (fig: tratto) section; (: pezzo: di lancia) stump; **licenziare qn in ~** to fire sb on the spot

troneggi'are [troned'dʒare] vi: **~ (su)** to tower (over)

'tronfio, a ag conceited

'trono sm throne

tropi'cale ag tropical

'tropico, ci sm tropic; **~ci** smpl (GEO) tropics

PAROLA CHIAVE

'troppo, a det (in eccesso: quantità) too much; (: numero) too many; c'era ~a gente there were too many people; fa ~ caldo it's too hot
◆ pron (in eccesso: quantità) too much; (: numero) too many; ne hai messo ~ you've put in too much; meglio ~ i che pochi better too many than too few
◆ av (eccessivamente: con ag, av) too; (: con vb) too much; ~ amaro/tardi too bitter/late; lavora ~ he works too much; di ~ too much; too many; qualche tazza di ~ a few cups too many; 3000 lire di ~ 3000 lire too much; essere di ~ to be in the way

'trota sf trout
trot'tare vi to trot; **trotterel'lare** vi to trot along; (bambino) to toddle; **'trotto** sm trot
'trottola sf spinning top
tro'vare vt to find; (giudicare): **trovo che** I find o think that; ~rsi vr (reciproco: incontrarsi) to meet; (essere, stare) to be; (arrivare, capitare) to find o.s.; **andare a ~ qn** to go and see sb; ~rsi **colpevole** to find sb guilty; ~rsi **bene** (in un luogo, con qn) to get on well; **tro'vata** sf good idea

truc'care vt (falsare) to fake; (attore etc) to make up; (travestire) to disguise; (SPORT) to fix; (AUT) to soup up; ~rsi vr to make up (one's face); **trucca'tore, 'trice** smf (CINEMA, TEATRO) make-up artist
'trucco, chi sm trick; (cosmesi) make-up
'truce ['trutʃe] ag fierce
truci'dare [trutʃi'dare] vt to slaughter
'truciolo ['trutʃolo] sm shaving
'truffa sf fraud, swindle; **truf'fare** vt to swindle, cheat
'truppa sf troop
tu pron you; ~ **stesso(a)** you your-

self; **dare del ~ a qn** to address sb as "tu"

'tua vedi **tuo**
'tuba sf (MUS) tuba; (cappello) top hat
tu'bare vi to coo
tuba'tura sf piping q, pipes pl
tubazi'one [tubat'tsjone] sf = **tubatura**
tu'betto sm tube
'tubo sm tube; pipe; ~ **digerente** (ANAT) alimentary canal, digestive tract; ~ **di scappamento** (AUT) exhaust pipe
'tue vedi **tuo**
tuf'fare vt to plunge, dip; ~rsi vr to plunge, dive; **'tuffo** sm dive; (breve bagno) dip
tu'gurio sm hovel
tuli'pano sm tulip
tume'farsi vr (MED) to swell
'tumido, a ag swollen
tu'more sm (MED) tumour
tu'multo sm uproar, commotion; (sommossa) riot; (fig) turmoil; **tumultu'oso, a** ag rowdy, unruly; (fig) turbulent, stormy
'tunica, che sf tunic
Tuni'sia sf la ~ Tunisia
'tuo (f 'tua, pl tu'oi, 'tue) det: il ~, la tua etc your ◆ pron: il ~, la tua etc yours
tuo'nare vi to thunder; **tuona** it is thundering, there's some thunder
tu'ono sm thunder
tu'orlo sm yolk
tu'racciolo [tu'rattʃolo] sm cap, top; (di sughero) cork
tu'rare vt to stop, plug; (con sughero) to cork; ~rsi **il naso** to hold one's nose
turba'mento sm disturbance; (di animo) anxiety, agitation
tur'bante sm turban
tur'bare vt to disturb, trouble
'turbine sm whirlwind
turbo'lento, a ag turbulent; (ragazzo) boisterous, unruly
turbo'lenza [turbo'lɛntsa] sf turbulence

tur'chese [tur'kese] *sf* turquoise

Tur'chia [tur'kia] *sf*: **la ~** Turkey

tur'chino, a [tur'kino] *ag* deep blue

'turco, a, chi, che *ag* Turkish ♦ *smf* Turk/Turkish woman ♦ *sm* (*LING*) Turkish; **parlare ~** (*fig*) to talk double-dutch

tu'rismo *sm* tourism; tourist industry; **tu'rista, i, e** *smf* tourist; **tu'ristico, a, ci, che** *ag* tourist *cpd*

'turno *sm* turn; (*di lavoro*) shift; **di ~** (*soldato, medico, custode*) on duty; **a ~** (*rispondere*) in turn; (*lavorare*) in shifts; **fare a ~ a fare qc** to take turns to do sth; **è il suo ~** it's your (*o* his *etc*) turn

'turpe *ag* filthy, vile; **turpi'loquio** *sm* obscene language

'tuta *sf* overalls *pl*; (*SPORT*) tracksuit

tu'tela *sf* (*DIR: di minore*) guardianship; (: *protezione*) protection; (*difesa*) defence; **tute'lare** *vt* to protect, defend

tu'tore, 'trice *smf* (*DIR*) guardian

tutta'via *cong* nevertheless, yet

PAROLA CHIAVE

'tutto, a *det* **1** (*intero*) all; **~ il latte** all the milk; **~a la notte** all night, the whole night; **~ il libro** the whole book; **~ a una bottiglia** a whole bottle

2 (*pl, collettivo*) all; every; **~i i libri** all the books; **~e le notti** every night; **~i i venerdì** every Friday; **~i gli uomini** all the men; (*collettivo*) all men; **~i e due** both *o* each of us (*o* them *o* you); **~i e cinque** all five of us (*o* them *o* you)

3 (*completamente*): **era ~a sporca** she was all dirty; **tremava ~** he was trembling all over; **è ~a sua madre** she's just *o* exactly like her mother

4: **a tutt'oggi** so far, up till now; **a ~a velocità** at full *o* top speed

♦ *pron* **1** (*ogni cosa*) everything, all; (*qualsiasi cosa*) anything; **ha mangiato ~** he's eaten everything; **~**

considerato all things considered; **in ~: 10,000 lire in ~** 10.000 lire in all; **in ~ eravamo 50** there were 50 of us in all

2: **~i, e** (*ognuno*) all, everybody; **vengono ~i** they are all coming, everybody's coming; **~i quanti** all and sundry

♦ *av* (*completamente*) entirely, quite; **è ~ il contrario** it's quite *o* exactly the opposite; **tutt'al più: saranno stati tutt'al più una cinquantina** there were about fifty of them at (*the very*) most; **tutt'al più possiamo prendere un treno** if the worst comes to the worst we can take a train; **tutt'altro** on the contrary; **è tutt'altro che felice** he's anything but happy; **tutt'a un tratto** suddenly

♦ *sm*: **il ~** the whole lot, all of it

---

tutto'fare *ag inv*: **domestica ~** general maid; **ragazzo ~** office boy ♦ *smf inv* handyman/woman

tut'tora *av* still

U

ubbidi'ente *ag* obedient; **ubbidi'enza** *sf* obedience

ubbi'dire *vi* to obey; **~ a** to obey; (*sog: veicolo, macchina*) to respond to

ubria'care *vt*: **~ qn** to make sb drunk; (*sog: alcool*) to make sb drunk; (*fig*) to make sb's head spin *o* reel; **~rsi** *vr* to get drunk; **~rsi di** (*fig*) to become intoxicated with

ubri'aco, a, chi, che *ag, smf* drunk

uccel'liera [uttʃelˈljɛra] *sf* aviary

uccel'lino [uttʃelˈlino] *sm* baby bird, chick

uc'cello [utˈtʃɛllo] *sm* bird

uc'cidere [utˈtʃidere] *vt* to kill; **~rsi** *vr* (*suicidarsi*) to kill o.s.; (*perdere la vita*) to be killed; **uccis'ione** *sf* killing; **uc'ciso, a** *pp* di **uccidere**; **ucci'sore** *sm* killer

udi'enza [u'djɛntsa] *sf* audience; (*DIR*) hearing; **dare ~ (a)** to grant an audience (to)

u'dire *vt* to hear; **udi'tivo, a** *ag* auditory; **u'dito** *sm* (sense of hearing; **udi'tore, 'trice** *smf* listener; (*INS*) unregistered student (*attending lectures*); **udi'torio** *sm* (*persone*) audience

uffa *escl* tut!

uffici'ale [uffi'tʃale] *ag* official ♦ *sm* (*AMM*) official, officer; (*MIL*) officer; **~ di stato civile** registrar

uf'ficio [uf'fitʃo] *sm* (*gen*) office; (*dovere*) duty; (*mansione*) task, function, job; (*agenzia*) agency, bureau; (*REL*) service; **d'~** *ag* office *cpd*; official ♦ *av* officially; **~ di collocamento** employment office; **~ informazioni** information bureau; **~ oggetti smarriti** lost property office (*BRIT*), lost and found (*US*); **~ postale** post office

uffici'oso, a [uffi'tʃoso] *ag* unofficial

'ufo: a ~ *av* free, for nothing

uggi'oso, a [ud'dʒoso] *ag* tiresome; (*tempo*) dull

uguagli'anza [ugwaʎ'ʎantsa] *sf* equality

uguagli'are [ugwaʎ'ʎare] *vt* to make equal; (*essere uguale*) to equal, be equal to; (*livellare*) to level; **~rsi a o con qn** (*paragonarsi*) to compare o.s. with sb

ugu'ale *ag* equal; (*identico*) identical, the same; (*uniforme*) level, even ♦ *av*: **costano ~** they cost the same; **sono bravi ~** they're equally good; **ugual'mente** *av* equally; (*lo stesso*) all the same

'ulcera [ˈultʃera] *sf* ulcer

u'liva *etc* = **oliva** *etc*

ulteri'ore *ag* further

ulti'mare *vt* to finish, complete

'ultimo, a *ag* (*finale*) last; (*estremo*) farthest, utmost; (*recente: notizia, moda*) latest; (*fig: sommo, fondamentale*) ultimate ♦ *sm/f* last (one); **fino all'~** to the last, until the end; **da ~, in ~** in the end; **abitare**

all'~ *piano* to live on the top floor; **per ~** (*entrare, arrivare*) last

ulu'lare *vi* to howl; **ulu'lato** *sm* howling *no pl*; howl

umanità *sf* humanity; **umani'tario, a** *ag* humanitarian

u'mano, a *ag* human; (*comprensivo*) humane

umbi'lico *sm* = **ombelico**

umet'tare *vt* to dampen, moisten

umidità *sf* dampness; humidity

'umido, a *ag* damp; (*mano, occhi*) moist; (*clima*) humid ♦ *sm* dampness, damp; **carne in ~** stew

'umile *ag* humble

umili'are *vt* to humiliate; **~rsi** *vr* to humble o.s.; **umiliazi'one** *sf* humiliation

umiltà *sf* humility, humbleness

u'more *sm* (*disposizione d'animo*) mood; (*carattere*) temper; **di buon/cattivo ~** in a good/bad mood

umo'rismo *sm* humour; **avere il senso dell'~** to have a sense of humour; **umo'rista, i, e** *smf* humorist; **umo'ristico, a, ci, che** *ag* humorous, funny

un *vedi* **uno**

un' *vedi* **uno**

una *vedi* **uno**

u'nanime *ag* unanimous; **unanimità** *sf* unanimity; **all'unanimità** unanimously

unci'netto [untʃi'netto] *sm* crochet hook

un'cino [un'tʃino] *sm* hook

'undici [ˈunditʃi] *num* eleven

'ungere [ˈundʒere] *vt* to grease, oil; (*REL*) to anoint; (*fig*) to flatter, butter up; **~rsi** *vr* (*sporcarsi*) to get covered in grease; **~rsi con la crema** to put on cream

unghe'rese [unge'rese] *ag, sm/f, sm* Hungarian

Unghe'ria [unge'ria] *sf*: **l'~** Hungary

'unghia [ˈungja] *sf* (*ANAT*) nail; (*di animale*) claw; (*di rapace*) talon; (*di cavallo*) hoof; **unghi'ata** *sf* (*graffio*) scratch

ungu'ento sm ointment

'unico, a, ci, che ag (solo) only; (ineguagliabile) unique; (singolo: binario) single; **figlio(a)** ~(a) only son/daughter, only child

unifi'care vt to unite, unify; (sistemi) to standardize; **unificazi'one** sf uniting; unification; standardization

uni'forme ag uniform; (superficie) even ♦ sf (divisa) uniform

unilate'rale ag one-sided; (DIR) unilateral

uni'one sf union; (fig: concordia) unity, harmony; l'U~ Sovietica the Soviet Union

u'nire vt to unite; (congiungere) to join, connect; (: ingredienti, colori) to combine; (in matrimonio) to unite, join together; ~rsi vr to unite; (in matrimonio) to be joined together; ~ qc a to unite sth with; to join o connect sth with; to combine sth with; ~rsi a (gruppo, società) to join

unità sf inv (unione, concordia) unity; (MAT, MIL, COMM, di misura) unit; **uni'tario, a** ag unitary; **prezzo unitario** price per unit

u'nito, a ag (paese) united; (amici, famiglia) close; **in tinta** ~a plain, self-coloured

univer'sale ag universal; general

università sf inv university; **universi'tario, a** ag university cpd ♦ sm/f (studente) university student; (insegnante) academic, university lecturer

uni'verso sm universe

PAROLA CHIAVE

'uno, a (dav sm un +C, V, uno +s impura, gn, pn, ps, x, z; dav sf un' +V, una +C) art indef **1** a; (dav vocale) an; **un bambino** a child; ~a **strada** a street; ~ **zingaro** a gypsy
2 (intensivo): **ho avuto** ~a **paura!** I got such a fright!
♦ pron **1** one; **prendine** ~ take one (of them); l'~ o l'altro either (of them); l'~ e l'altro both (of them);

aiutarsi l'un l'altro to help one another o each other; **sono entrati l'~ dopo l'altro** they came in one after the other
2 (un tale) someone, somebody
3 (con valore impersonale) one, you; **se** ~ **vuole** if one wants, if you want
♦ num one; ~a **mela e due pere** one apple and two pears; ~ **più** ~ **fa due** one plus one equals two, one and one are two
♦ sf: **è l'~a** it's one (o'clock)

'unto, a pp di ungere ♦ ag greasy, oily ♦ sm grease; **untu'oso, a** ag greasy, oily

u'omo (pl u'omini) sm man; **da** ~ (abito, scarpe) men's, for men; ~ **d'affari** businessman; ~ **di paglia** stooge; ~ **rana** frogman

u'opo sm: **all'~** if necessary

u'ovo (pl(f) uova) sm egg; ~ **al tegame** fried egg; ~ **alla coque** boiled egg; ~ **bazzotto/sodo** soft-/hard-boiled egg; ~ **di Pasqua** Easter egg; ~ **in camicia** poached egg; ~a **strapazzate** scrambled eggs

ura'gano sm hurricane

urba'nistica sf town planning

ur'bano, a ag urban, city cpd; (TEL: chiamata) local; (fig) urbane

ur'gente [ur'dʒɛnte] ag urgent; **ur'genza** sf urgency; **in caso d'urgenza** in (case of) an emergency; **d'urgenza** ag emergency ♦ av urgently, as a matter of urgency

'urgere ['urdʒere] vi to be urgent; to be needed urgently

u'rina sf = orina

ur'lare vi (persona) to scream, yell; (animale, vento) to howl ♦ vt to scream, yell

'urlo (pl(m) urli, pl(f) urla) sm scream, yell; howl

'urna sf urn; (elettorale) ballot-box; **andare alle** ~ to go to the polls

urrà escl hurrah!

U.R.S.S. abbr f: l'~ the USSR

ur'tare vt to bump into, knock against; (fig: irritare) to annoy ♦ vi: ~ **contro** o **in** to bump into, knock against, crash into; (fig: imbattersi) to come up against; **~rsi** vr (reciproco: scontrarsi) to collide; (: fig) to clash; (irritarsi) to get annoyed; **'urto** sm (colpo) knock, bump; (scontro) crash, collision; (fig) clash

U.S.A. ['uza] smpl: **gli** ~ the USA

u'sanza [u'zantsa] sf custom; (moda) fashion

u'sare vt to use, employ ♦ vi (servirsi); ~ **di** to use; (: diritto) to exercise; (essere di moda) to be fashionable; (essere solito): ~ **fare** to be in the habit of doing, be accustomed to doing ♦ vb impers: **qui usa così** it's the custom round here; **u'sato, a** ag used; (consumato) worn; (di seconda mano) used, second-hand ♦ sm second-hand goods pl

usci'ere [uʃ'ʃɛre] sm usher

'uscio ['uʃʃo] sm door

u'scire [uʃ'ʃire] vi (gen) to come out; (partire, andare a passeggio, a uno spettacolo etc) to go out; (essere sorteggiato: numero) to come up; ~ **da** (gen) to leave; (posto) to go o (come) out of, leave; (solco, vasca etc) to come out of; (muro) to stick out of; (competenza etc) to be outside; (infanzia, adolescenza) to leave behind; (famiglia nobile etc) to come from; ~ **da** o **di casa** to go out; (fig) to leave home; ~ **in automobile** to go out in the car, go for a drive; ~ **di strada** (AUT) to go off o leave the road

u'scita [uʃ'ʃita] sf (passaggio, varco) exit, way out; (per divertimento) outing; (ECON: somma) expenditure; (TEATRO) entrance; (fig: battuta) witty remark; ~ **di sicurezza** emergency exit

usi'gnolo [uziɲ'nɔlo] sm nightingale

U.S.L. [uzl] sigla f (= unità sanitaria locale) local health centre

'uso sm (utilizzazione) use; (esercizio) practice; (abitudine) custom; a

~ **di** for (the use of); **d'**~ (corrente) in use; **fuori** ~ out of use

usti'one sf burn

usu'ale ag common, everyday

u'sura sf usury; (logoramento) wear (and tear)

uten'sile sm tool, implement; **~i da cucina** kitchen utensils

u'tente sm/f user

'utero sm uterus

'utile ag useful ♦ sm (vantaggio) advantage, benefit; (ECON: profitto) profit; **utilità** sf usefulness no pl; use; (vantaggio) benefit; **utili'taria** sf (AUT) economy car; **utili'tario, a** ag utilitarian

utiliz'zare [utilid'dzare] vt to use, make use of, utilize

'uva sf grapes pl; ~ **passa** raisins pl; ~ **spina** gooseberry

V

v. abbr (= vedi) v

va vb vedi **andare**

va'cante ag vacant

va'canza [va'kantsa] sf (l'essere vacante) vacancy; (riposo, ferie) holiday(s pl) (BRIT), vacation (US); (giorno di permesso) day off, holiday; **~e** sfpl (periodo di ferie) holidays (BRIT), vacation (US); **essere/andare in** ~ to be/go on holiday o vacation; **~e estive** summer holiday(s) o vacation

'vacca, che sf cow

vacci'nare [vattʃi'nare] vt to vaccinate

vac'cino [vat'tʃino] sm (MED) vaccine

vacil'lare [vatʃil'lare] vi to sway, wobble; (luce) to flicker; (fig: memoria, coraggio) to be failing, falter

'vacuo, a ag (fig) empty, vacuous ♦ sm vacuum

'vado vb vedi **andare**

vaga'bondo, a sm/f tramp, vagrant; (fannullone) idler, loafer

va'gare vi to wander

vagheggi'are [vaged'dʒare] *vt* to long for, dream of

va'gina [va'dʒina] *sf* vagina

va'gire [va'dʒire] *vi* to whimper

va'gito [va'dʒito] *sm* cry

'vaglia ['vaλλa] *sm inv* money order; ~ **postale** postal order

vagli'are [vaλ'λare] *vt* to sift; (*fig*) to weigh up; **'vaglio** *sm* sieve

'vago, a, ghi, ghe *ag* vague

va'gone *sm* (*FERR: per passeggeri*) coach; (: *per merci*) truck, wagon; ~ **letto** sleeper, sleeping car; ~ **ristorante** dining *o* restaurant car

'vai *vb vedi* **andare**

vai'olo *sm* smallpox

va'langa, ghe *sf* avalanche

va'lente *ag* able, talented

va'lere *vi* (*avere forza, potenza*) to have influence; (*essere valido*) to be valid; (*avere vigore, autorità*) to hold, apply; (*essere capace: poeta, studente*) to be good, be able ♦ *vt* (*prezzo, sforzo*) to be worth; (*corrispondere*) to correspond to; (*procurare*): ~ **qc a qn** to earn sb sth; ~**rsi di** to make use of, take advantage of; **far** ~ (*autorità etc*) to assert; **vale a dire** that is to say; ~ **la pena** to be worth the effort *o* worth it

va'levole *ag* valid

vali'care *vt* to cross

'valico, chi *sm* (*passo*) pass

'valido, a *ag* valid; (*rimedio*) effective; (*aiuto*) real; (*persona*) worthwhile

valige'ria [validʒe'ria] *sf* leather goods *pl*; leather goods factory; leather goods shop

va'ligia, gie *o* **ge** [va'lidʒa] *sf* (suit)case; **fare la** ~**gie** to pack (up); ~ **diplomatica** diplomatic bag

val'lata *sf* valley

'valle *sf* valley; a ~ (*di fiume*) downstream; **scendere a** ~ to go downhill

val'letto *sm* valet

va'lore *sm* (*gen*) value; (*merito*) merit, worth; (*coraggio*) valour, courage; (*COMM: titolo*) security; ~**i** *smpl* (*oggetti preziosi*) valuables

valoriz'zare [valorid'dzare] *vt* (*terreno*) to develop; (*fig*) to make the most of

'valso, a *pp di* **valere**

va'luta *sf* currency, money; (*BANCA*): ~ **15 gennaio** interest to run from January 15th

valu'tare *vt* (*casa, gioiello, fig*) to value; (*stabilire: peso, entrate, fig*) to estimate; **valutazi'one** *sf* valuation; estimate

'valvola *sf* (*TECN, ANAT*) valve; (*ELETTR*) fuse

'valzer ['valtser] *sm inv* waltz

vam'pata *sf* (*di fiamma*) blaze; (*di calore*) blast; (: *al viso*) flush

vam'piro *sm* vampire

vanda'lismo *sm* vandalism

'vandalo *sm* vandal

vaneggi'are [vaned'dʒare] *vi* to rave

'vanga, ghe *sf* spade; **van'gare** *vt* to dig

van'gelo [van'dʒɛlo] *sm* gospel

va'niglia [va'niλλa] *sf* vanilla

vanità *sf* vanity; (*di promessa*) emptiness; (*di sforzo*) futility; **vani'toso, a** *ag* vain, conceited

'vanno *vb vedi* **andare**

'vano, a *ag* vain ♦ *sm* (*spazio*) space; (*apertura*) opening; (*stanza*) room

van'taggio [van'taddʒo] *sm* advantage; **essere/portarsi in** ~ (*SPORT*) to be in/take the lead; **vantag-gi'oso, a** *ag* advantageous; favourable

van'tare *vt* to praise, speak highly of; ~**rsi** *vr*: ~**rsi (di/di aver fatto)** to boast *o* brag (about/about having done); **vante'ria** *sf* boasting; **'vanto** *sm* boasting; (*merito*) virtue, merit; (*gloria*) pride

'vanvera *sf*: a ~ haphazardly; **parlare a** ~ to talk nonsense

va'pore *sm* vapour; (*anche*: ~ **acqueo**) steam; (*nave*) steamer; **a** ~ (*turbina etc*) steam *cpd*; **al** ~ (*CUC*) steamed; **vapo'retto** *sm* steamer;

vapori'era sf (FERR) steam engine; **vaporiz'zare** vt to vaporize; **vapo'roso, a** ag (tessuto) filmy; (capelli) soft and full

va'rare vt (NAUT, fig) to launch; (DIR) to pass

var'care vt to cross

'varco, chi sm passage; **aprirsi un ~ tra la folla** to push one's way through the crowd

vari'abile ag variable; (tempo, umore) changeable, variable ♦ sf (MAT) variable

vari'are vt, vi to vary; **~ di opinione** to change one's mind; **variazi'one** sf variation; change

va'rice [va'ritʃe] sf varicose vein

vari'cella [vari'tʃella] sf chickenpox

vari'coso, a ag varicose

varie'gato, a ag variegated

varie'tà sf inv variety ♦ sm inv variety show

'vario, a ag varied; (parecchi: col sostantivo al pl) various; (mutevole: umore) changeable; **vario'pinto, a** ag multicoloured

'varo sm (NAUT, fig) launch; (di leggi) passing

va'saio sm potter

'vasca, sche sf basin; (anche: ~ da bagno) bathtub, bath

va'scello [vaʃ'fello] sm (NAUT) vessel, ship

vase'lina sf vaseline

vasel'lame sm (stoviglie) crockery; (: di porcellana) china; ~ **d'oro/d'argento** gold/silver plate

'vaso sm (recipiente) pot; (: barattolo) jar; (: decorativo) vase; (ANAT) vessel; ~ **da fiori** vase; (per piante) flowerpot

vas'soio sm tray

'vasto, a ag vast, immense

Vati'cano sm: **il ~ the Vatican**

ve pron, av vedi **vi**

vecchi'aia [vek'kjaja] sf old age

'vecchio, a ['vekkjo] ag old ♦ sm/f old man/woman; **i ~i** the old

'vece ['vetʃe] sf: **in ~ di** in the place of, for; **fare le ~i di qn** to take sb's place

ve'dere vt, vi to see; **~rsi** vr to meet, see one another; **avere a che ~ con** to have something to do with; **far ~ a qn** to show sb sth; **farsi ~** to show o.s.; (farsi vivo) to show one's face; **vedi di non farlo** make sure o see you don't; **non (ci) si vede** (è buio etc) you can't see a thing; **non lo posso ~** (fig) I can't stand him

ve'detta sf (sentinella, posto) lookout; (NAUT) patrol boat

'vedovo, a sm/f widower/widow

ve'duta sf view

vee'mente ag vehement; violent

vege'tale [vedʒe'tale] ag, sm vegetable

vegetari'ano, a [vedʒeta'rjano] ag, sm/f vegetarian

'vegeto, a ['vedʒeto] ag (pianta) thriving; (persona) strong, vigorous

'veglia ['veʎʎa] sf wakefulness; (sorveglianza) watch; (trattenimento) evening gathering; **fare la ~ a un malato** to watch over a sick person

vegli'are [veʎ'ʎare] vi to be awake; to stay o sit up; (stare vigile) to watch; to keep watch ♦ vt (malato, morto) to watch over, sit up with

ve'icolo sm vehicle; ~ **spaziale** spacecraft inv

'vela sf (NAUT: tela) sail; (sport) sailing

ve'lare vt to veil; **~rsi** vr (occhi, luna) to mist over; (voce) to become husky; **~rsi il viso** to cover one's face (with a veil); **ve'lato, a** ag veiled

veleggi'are [veled'dʒare] vi to sail; (AER) to glide

ve'leno sm poison; **vele'noso, a** ag poisonous

veli'ero sm sailing ship

ve'lina sf (anche: carta ~: per imballare) tissue paper; (: per copie) flimsy paper; (copia) carbon copy

ve'livolo sm aircraft

velleità sf inv vain ambition, vain desire

'**vello** *sm* fleece

vel'luto *sm* velvet; **~ a coste** cord

'**velo** *sm* veil; (*tessuto*) voile

ve'loce [ve'lotʃe] *ag* fast, quick, ♦ *av* fast, quickly; **velo'cista, i, e** *smf* (SPORT) sprinter; **velocità** *sf* speed; **a forte velocità** at high speed; **velocità di crociera** cruising speed

ve'lodromo *sm* velodrome

'**vena** *sf* (*gen*) vein; (*filone*) vein, seam; (*fig: ispirazione*) inspiration; (: *umore*) mood; **essere in ~ di qc** to be in the mood for sth

ve'nale *ag* (*prezzo, valore*) market *cpd*; (*fig*) venal; mercenary

ven'demmia *sf* (*raccolta*) grape harvest; (*quantità d'uva*) grape crop, grapes *pl*; (*vino ottenuto*) vintage; **vendemmi'are** *vt* to harvest ♦ *vi* to harvest the grapes

'vendere *vt* to sell; **"vendesi"** "for sale"

ven'detta *sf* revenge

vendi'care *vt* to avenge; **~rsi** *vr*: **~rsi (di)** to avenge o.s. (for); (*per rancore*) to take one's revenge (for); **~rsi su qn** to revenge o.s. on sb; **vendica'tivo, a** *ag* vindictive

ven'dita *sf* sale; **la ~** (*attività*) selling; (*smercio*) sales *pl*; **in ~** on sale; **~ all'asta** sale by auction; **vendi'tore** *sm* seller, vendor; (*gestore di negozio*) trader, dealer

ve'nefico, a, ci, che *ag* poisonous

vene'rabile *ag* venerable

venerando, a *ag* = **venerabile**

vene'rare *vt* to venerate

venerdì *sm inv* Friday; **di o il ~** on Fridays; **V~ Santo** Good Friday

ve'nereo, a *ag* venereal

'veneto, a *ag, smf* Venetian

Ve'nezia [ve'nɛttsja] *sf* Venice; **ve-nezi'ano, a** *ag, smf* Venetian

veni'ale *ag* venial

ve'nire *vi* to come; (*riuscire: dolce, fotografia*) to turn out; (*come ausiliare: essere*): **viene ammirato da tutti** he is admired by everyone; **~ da** to come from; **quanto viene?**

how much does it cost?; **far ~** (*mandare a chiamare*) to send for; **~ giù** to come down; **~ meno** (*svenire*) to faint; **~ meno a qc** not to fulfil sth; **~ su** to come up; **~ a trovare qn** to come and see sb; **~ via** to come away

ven'taglio [ven'taʎʎo] *sm* fan

ven'tata *sf* gust (of wind)

ven'tenne *ag*: **una ragazza ~** a twenty-year-old girl, a girl of twenty

ven'tesimo, a *num* twentieth

'venti *num* twenty

venti'lare *vt* (*stanza*) to air, ventilate; (*fig: idea, proposta*) to air; **ventila'tore** *sm* ventilator, fan

ven'tina *sf*: **una ~ (di)** around twenty, twenty or so

venti'sette *num* twenty-seven; **il ~** (*giorno di paga*) (monthly) pay day

'vento *sm* wind

ven'tola *sf* (AUT, TECN) fan

ven'tosa *sf* (ZOOL) sucker; (*di gomma*) suction pad

ven'toso, a *ag* windy

'ventre *sm* stomach

ven'tura *sf*: **andare alla ~** to trust to luck; **soldato di ~** mercenary

ven'turo, a *ag* next, coming

ve'nuta *sf* coming, arrival

ve'nuto, a *pp* di **venire**

vera'mente *av* really

ver'bale *ag* verbal ♦ *sm* (*di riunione*) minutes *pl*

'verbo *sm* (LING) verb; (*parola*) word; (REL): **il V~** the Word

'verde *ag, sm* green; **essere al ~** to be broke; **~ bottiglia/oliva** bottle/ olive green

verde'rame *sm* verdigris

ver'detto *sm* verdict

ver'dura *sf* vegetables *pl*

vere'condo, a *ag* modest

'verga, ghe *sf* rod

ver'gato, a *ag* (*foglio*) ruled

'vergine ['verdʒine] *sf* virgin; (*dello zodiaco*): **V~** Virgo ♦ *ag* virgin; (*ragazza*): **essere ~** to be a virgin

ver'gogna [ver'goɲɲa] *sf* shame; (*timidezza*) shyness, embarrassment

vergo'gnarsi vr: **vergognarsi (di)** to be o feel ashamed (of); to be shy (about), be embarrassed (about); **vergo'gnoso, a** ag ashamed; (timido) shy, embarrassed; (causa di vergogna: azione) shameful

ve'rifica, che sf checking no pl, check

verifi'care vt (controllare) to check; (confermare) to confirm, bear out

verità sf inv truth

veriti'ero, a ag (che dice la verità) truthful; (conforme a verità) true

'verme sm worm

vermi'celli [vermi'tʃelli] smpl vermicelli sg

ver'miglio [ver'miʎʎo] sm vermilion, scarlet

'vermut sm inv vermouth

ver'nice [ver'nitʃe] sf (colorazione) paint; (trasparente) varnish; (pelle) patent leather; "~ fresca" "wet paint"; **vernici'are** vt to paint; to varnish

'vero, a ag (veridico: fatti, testimonianza) true; (autentico) real ♦ sm (verità) truth; (realtà) reality; **un ~ e proprio delinquente** a real criminal, an out-and-out criminal

vero'simile ag likely, probable

ver'ruca sf wart

versa'mento sm (pagamento) payment; (deposito di denaro) deposit

ver'sante sm slopes pl, side

ver'sare vt (fare uscire: vino, farina) to pour (out); (spargere: lacrime, sangue) to shed; (rovesciare) to spill; (ECON) to pay; (depositare) to deposit, pay in; ~rsi vr (rovesciarsi) to spill; (fiume, folla): ~rsi (in) to pour (into)

versa'tile ag versatile

ver'setto sm (REL) verse

versi'one sf version; (traduzione) translation

'verso sm (di poesia) verse, line; (di animale, uccello, venditore ambulante) cry; (direzione) direction; (modo) way; (di foglio di carta) verso; (di moneta) reverse; ~i smpl (poe-

sia) verse sg; **non c'è ~ di persuaderlo** there's no way of persuading him, he can't be persuaded ♦ prep (in direzione di) toward(s); (nei pressi di) near, around (about); (in senso temporale) about, around; (nei confronti di) for; ~ **di me** towards me; ~ **sera** towards evening

'vertebra sf vertebra

verti'cale ag, sf vertical

'vertice ['vertitʃe] sm summit, top; (MAT) vertex; **conferenza al ~** (POL) summit conference

ver'tigine [ver'tidʒine] sf dizziness no pl; dizzy spell; (MED) vertigo; **avere le ~i** to feel dizzy; **vertigi'noso, a** ag (altezza) dizzy; (fig) breathtakingly high (o deep etc)

ve'scica, che [veʃ'ʃika] sf (ANAT) bladder; (MED) blister

'vescovo sm bishop

'vespa sf wasp

'vespro sm (REL) vespers pl

ves'sillo sm standard; (bandiera) flag

ves'taglia [ves'taʎʎa] sf dressing gown

'veste sf garment; (rivestimento) covering; (qualità, facoltà) capacity; **in ~ ufficiale** (fig) in an official capacity; **in ~ di** in the guise of, as; **vesti'ario** sm wardrobe, clothes pl

ves'tibolo sm (entrance) hall

ves'tire vt (bambino, malato) to dress; (avere indosso) to have on, wear; ~rsi vr to dress, get dressed; **ves'tito, a** ag dressed ♦ sm garment; (da donna) dress; (da uomo) suit; vestiti smpl (indumenti) clothes; **vestito di bianco** dressed in white

Ve'suvio sm: **il** ~ Vesuvius

vete'rano, a ag, sm/f veteran

veteri'naria sf veterinary medicine

veteri'nario, a ag veterinary ♦ sm veterinary surgeon (BRIT), veterinarian (US), vet

'veto sm inv veto

ve'traio sm glassmaker; glazier

ve'trata sf glass door (o window)

(di chiesa) stained glass window

ve'trato, a *ag (porta, finestra)* glazed; *(che contiene vetro)* glass *cpd*

vetre'ria *sf (stabilimento)* glassworks *sg*; *(oggetti di vetro)* glassware

ve'trina *sf (di negozio)* (shop) window; *(armadio)* display cabinet; **vetri'nista, i, e** *smf* window dresser

vetri'olo *sm* vitriol

'vetro *sm* glass; *(per finestra, porta)* pane (of glass)

'vetta *sf* peak, summit, top

vet'tore *sm (MAT, FISICA)* vector; *(chi trasporta)* carrier

vetto'vaglie [vetto'vaʎʎe] *sfpl* supplies

vet'tura *sf (carrozza)* carriage; *(FERR)* carriage (BRIT), car (US); *(auto)* car (BRIT), automobile (US)

vezzeggi'are [vettsed'dʒare] *vt* to fondle, caress; **vezzeggia'tivo** *sm (LING)* term of endearment

'vezzo ['vettso] *sm* habit; **~i** *smpl (smancerie)* affected ways; *(leggiadria)* charms; **vez'zoso, a** *ag (grazioso)* charming, pretty; *(lezioso)* affected

vi *(dav lo, la, li, le, ne diventa ve)* *pron (oggetto) you; (complemento di termine)* (to) you; *(riflessivo)* yourselves; *(reciproco)* each other ♦ *av (li)* there; *(qui)* here; *(per questo/quel luogo)* through here/there; **~ è/sono** there is/are

'via *sf (gen)* way; *(strada)* street; *(sentiero, pista)* path, track; *(AMM: procedimento)* channels *pl* ♦ *prep (passando per)* via, by way of ♦ *av* away ♦ *escl* go away!; *(suvvia)* come on!; *(SPORT)* go! ♦ *sm (SPORT)* starting signal; **in ~ di guarigione** on the road to recovery; **per ~ di** *(a causa di)* because of, on account of; **in o per ~** on the way; **per ~ aerea** by air; *(lettere)* by airmail; **andare/essere ~** to go/be away; **~ ~ che** *(a mano a mano)* as; **dare il ~** *(SPORT)* to give the

starting signal; **dare il ~ a** *(fig)* to start; **V~ lattea** *(ASTR)* Milky Way; **~ di mezzo** middle course; **in ~ provvisoria** provisionally

viabilità *sf (di strada)* practicability; *(rete stradale)* roads *pl*, road network

via'dotto *sm* viaduct

viaggi'are [viad'dʒare] *vi* to travel; **viaggia'tore, 'trice** *ag* travelling ♦ *sm* traveller; *(passeggero)* passenger

vi'aggio ['vjaddʒo] *sm* travel(ling); *(tragitto)* journey, trip; **buon ~!** have a good trip!; **~ di nozze** honeymoon

vi'ale *sm* avenue

via'vai *sm* coming and going, bustle

vi'brare *vi* to vibrate; *(agitarsi)*: **~** *(di)* to quiver (with)

vi'cario *sm (apostolico etc)* vicar

'vice ['vitʃe] *smf* deputy ♦ *prefisso*: **~'console** *sm* vice-consul; **~di'rettore** *sm* assistant manager

vi'cenda [vi'tʃenda] *sf* event; **a ~** in turn; **vicen'devole** *ag* mutual, reciprocal

vice'versa [vitʃe'vɛrsa] *av* vice versa; **da Roma a Pisa e ~** from Rome to Pisa and back

vici'nanza [vitʃi'nantsa] *sf* nearness, closeness; **~e** *sfpl (paraggi)* neighbourhood, vicinity

vici'nato [vitʃi'nato] *sm* neighbourhood; *(vicini)* neighbours *pl*

vi'cino, a [vi'tʃino] *ag (gen)* near; *(nello spazio)* near, nearby; *(accanto)* next; *(nel tempo)* near, close at hand ♦ *smf* neighbour ♦ *av* near, close; **da ~** *(guardare)* close up; *(esaminare, seguire)* closely; *(conoscere)* well, intimately; **~ a** near (to), close to; *(accanto a)* beside; **~ di casa** neighbour

'vicolo *sm* alley; **~ cieco** blind alley

'video *sm inv (TV: schermo)* screen; **~'camera** *sf* camcorder; **~cas'setta** *sf* videocassette; **~regi stra'tore** *sm* video (recorder)

vie'tare *vt* to forbid; *(AMM)* to prohibit; **~ a qn di fare** to forbid sb to do; to prohibit sb from doing; "**vie-tato fumare/l'ingresso**" "no smoking/admittance"

Viet'nam sm: il ~ Vietnam; **viet-na'mita, i, e** ag, smif, sm Vietnamese inv

vi'gente [vi'dʒɛnte] ag in force

vigi'lante [vidʒi'lante] ag vigilant, watchful

vigi'lare [vidʒi'lare] vt to watch over, keep an eye on; ~ **che** to make sure that, see to it that

'vigile ['vidʒile] ag watchful ♦ sm (anche: ~ urbano) policeman (in towns); ~ **del fuoco** fireman

vi'gilia [vi'dʒilja] sf (giorno antecedente) eve; la ~ **di Natale** Christmas Eve

vigliac'co, a, chi, che [viʎ'ʎakko] ag cowardly ♦ smif coward

'vigna ['vippa] sf = **vi'gneto**

vi'gneto [vip'peto] sm vineyard

vi'gnetta [vip'petta] sf cartoon

vi'gore sm vigour; (DIR): **essere/entrare in** ~ to be in/come into force; **vigo'roso, a** ag vigorous

'vile ag (spregevole) low, mean, base; (codardo) cowardly

vili'pendio sm contempt, scorn; public insult

'villa sf villa

vil'laggio [vil'laddʒo] sm village

villa'nia sf rudeness, lack of manners; **fare** (o **dire**) **una** ~ **a qn** to be rude to sb

vil'lano, a ag rude, ill-mannered ♦ sm boor

villeggia'tura [villeddʒa'tura] sf holiday(s pl) (BRIT), vacation (US)

vil'lino sm small house (with a garden), cottage

vil'loso, a ag hairy

viltà sf cowardice no pl; cowardly act

'vimine sm wicker; **mobili di** ~**i** wicker furniture sg

'vincere ['vintʃere] vt (in guerra, al gioco, a una gara) to defeat, beat; (premio, guerra, partita) to win; (fig) to overcome, conquer ♦ vi to win; ~ **qn in bellezza** to be better-

looking than sb; **'vincita** sf win; (denaro vinto) winnings pl; **vinci'tore** sm winner; (MIL) victor

vinco'lare vt to bind; (COMM: denaro) to tie up; **'vincolo** sm (fig) bond, tie; (DIR: servitù) obligation

vi'nicolo, a ag wine cpd

'vino sm wine; ~ **bianco/rosso** white/red wine; ~ **da pasto** table wine

'vinto, a pp di **vincere**

vi'ola sf (BOT) violet; (MUS) viola ♦ ag, sm inv (colore) purple

vio'lare vt (chiesa) to desecrate, violate; (giuramento, legge) to violate

violen'tare vt to use violence on; (donna) to rape

vio'lento, a ag violent; **vio'lenza** sf violence; **violenza carnale** rape

vio'letta sf (BOT) violet

vio'letto, a ag, sm (colore) violet

violi'nista, i, e smif violinist

vio'lino sm violin

violon'cello [violon'tʃɛllo] sm cello

vi'ottolo sm path, track

'vipera sf viper, adder

vi'rare vt (NAUT) to haul (in), heave (in) ♦ vi (NAUT, AER) to turn; (FOT) to tone; ~ **di bordo** (NAUT) to tack

'virgola sf (LING) comma; (MAT) point; **virgo'lette** sfpl inverted commas, quotation marks

vi'rile ag (proprio dell'uomo) masculine; (non puerile, da uomo) manly, virile

virtù sf inv virtue; **in** o **per** ~ **di** by virtue of, by

virtu'ale ag virtual

virtu'oso, a ag virtuous ♦ smif (MUS etc) virtuoso

'virus sm inv (anche COMPUT) virus

'viscere ['viʃʃere] sm (ANAT) internal organ ♦ sfpl (di animale) entrails pl; (fig) bowels pl

'vischio ['viskjo] sm (BOT) mistletoe; (pania) birdlime; **vischi'oso, a** ag sticky

'viscido, a ['viʃʃido] ag slimy

vi'sibile *ag* visible

visi'bilio *sm*: **andare in ~ to** go into raptures

visibilità *sf* visibility

visi'era *sf* (*di elmo*) visor; (*di berretto*) peak

visi'one *sf* vision; **prendere ~ di qc** to examine sth, look sth over; **prima/seconda ~** (*CINEMA*) first/second showing

'visita *sf* visit; (*MED*) visit, call; (*: esame*) examination; **visi'tare** *vt* to visit; (*MED*) to visit, call on; (*: esaminare*) to examine; **visita'tore, 'trice** *smf* visitor

vi'sivo, a *ag* visual

'viso *sm* face

vi'sone *sm* mink

'vispo, a *ag* quick, lively

vis'suto, a *pp di* **vivere** ♦ *ag* (*aria, modo di fare*) experienced

'vista *sf* (*facoltà*) (eye)sight; (*fatto di vedere*): **la ~ di** the sight of; (*veduta*) view; **sparare a ~** to shoot on sight; **in ~** in sight; **perdere qn di ~** to lose sight of sb; (*fig*) to lose touch with sb; **a ~ d'occhio** as far as the eye can see; (*fig*) before one's very eyes; **far ~ di fare** to pretend to do

'visto, a *pp di* **vedere** ♦ *sm* visa; **~ che** seeing (that)

vis'toso, a *ag* gaudy, garish; (*ingente*) considerable

visu'ale *ag* visual; **visualizza'tore** *sm* (*INFORM*) visual display unit, VDU

'vita *sf* life; (*ANAT*) waist; **a ~ for life**

vi'tale *ag* vital; **vita'lizio, a** *ag* life *cpd* ♦ *sm* life annuity

vita'mina *sf* vitamin

'vite *sf* (*BOT*) vine; (*TECN*) screw

vi'tello *sm* (*ZOOL*) calf; (*carne*) veal; (*pelle*) calfskin

vi'ticcio [viˈtittʃo] *sm* (*BOT*) tendril

viticol'tore *sm* wine grower; **viticol'tura** *sf* wine growing

'vitreo, a *ag* vitreous; (*occhio, sguardo*) glassy

'vittima *sf* victim

'vitto *sm* food; (*in un albergo etc*) board; **~ e alloggio** board and lodging

vit'toria *sf* victory

'viva *escl*: **~ il re!** long live the king!

vi'vace [viˈvatʃe] *ag* (*vivo, animato*) lively; (*: mente*) lively, sharp; (*colore*) bright; **vivacità** *sf* vivacity, liveliness; brightness

vi'vaio *sm* (*di pesci*) hatchery; (*AGR*) nursery

vi'vanda *sf* food; (*piatto*) dish

vi'vente *ag* living, alive; **i ~i** the living

'vivere *vi* to live ♦ *vt* to live; (*passare: brutto momento*) to live through, go through; (*sentire: gioie, pene di qn*) to share ♦ *sm* life; (*anche: modo di ~*) way of life; **~i** *smpl* (*cibo*) food sg, provisions; **~ di** to live on

vi'vido, a *ag* (*colore*) vivid, bright

'vivo, a *ag* (*vivente*) alive, living; (*: animale*) live; (*fig*) lively; (*: colore*) bright, brilliant; **i ~i** the living; **~ e vegeto** hale and hearty; **farsi ~** to show one's face; to be heard from; **ritrarre dal ~** to paint from life; **pungere qn nel ~** (*fig*) to cut sb to the quick

vizi'are [vitˈtsjare] *vt* (*bambino*) to spoil; (*corrompere moralmente*) to corrupt; **vizi'ato, a** *ag* spoilt; (*aria, acqua*) polluted

'vizio [ˈvittsjo] *sm* (*morale*) vice; (*cattiva abitudine*) bad habit; (*imperfezione*) flaw, defect; (*errore*) fault, mistake; **vizi'oso, a** *ag* depraved; defective; (*inesatto*) incorrect, wrong

vocabo'lario *sm* (*dizionario*) dictionary; (*lessico*) vocabulary

vo'cabolo *sm* word

vo'cale *ag* vocal ♦ *sf* vowel

vocazi'one [vokatˈtsjone] *sf* vocation; (*fig*) natural bent

'voce [ˈvotʃe] *sf* voice; (*diceria*) rumour; (*di un elenco, in bilancio,*

item; **aver ~ in capitolo** (*fig*) to
have a say in the matter

voci'are [vo'tʃare] *vi* to shout, yell

'voga *sf* (*NAUT*) rowing; (*usanza*):
essere **in ~** to be in fashion *o* in
vogue

vo'gare *vi* to row

'voglia ['vɔʎʎa] *sf* desire, wish;
(*macchia*) birthmark; **aver ~ di**
qc/di fare to feel like sth/like doing;
(*più forte*) to want sth/to do

'voi *pron* you; **voi'altri** *pron* you

vo'lano *sm* (*SPORT*) shuttlecock;
(*TECN*) flywheel

vo'lante *ag* flying ♦ *sm* (steering)
wheel

volan'tino *sm* leaflet

vo'lare *vi* (*uccello, aereo, fig*) to fly;
(*cappello*) to blow away *o* off, fly
away *o* off; **~ via** to fly away *o* off

vo'latile *ag* (*CHIM*) volatile ♦ *sm*
(*ZOOL*) bird

volente'roso, a *ag* willing

volenti'eri *av* willingly; **"~"** "with
pleasure", "I'd be glad to"

---

vo'lere *sm* will, wish(es); **contro il**
~ di against the wishes of; **per ~ di**
qn in obedience to sb's will *o* wishes
♦ *vt* **1** (*esigere, desiderare*) to
want; **voler fare/che qn faccia** to
want to do/sb to do; **volete del caf-**
fè? would you like *o* do you want
some coffee?; **vorrei questo/fare I**
would *o* I'd like this/to do; **come**
vuoi as you like; **senza ~** (*inav-*
vertitamente) without meaning to,
unintentionally

2 (*consentire*): **vogliate attendere,**
per piacere please wait; **vogliamo**
andare? shall we go?; **vuole essere**
così gentile da ...? would you be so
kind as to ...?; **non ha voluto rice-**
vermi he wouldn't see me

3: **volerci** (*essere necessario: mate-*
riale, attenzione) to need; (: *tempo*)
to take; **quanta farina ci vuole per**
questa torta? how much flour do
you need for this cake?; **ci vuole**

un'ora per arrivare a Venezia it
takes an hour to get to Venice

4: **voler bene a qn** (*amore*) to love
sb; (*affetto*) to be fond of sb, like sb
very much; **voler male a qn** to dislike sb; **volerne a qn** to bear sb a
grudge; **voler dire** to mean

vol'gare *ag* vulgar; **volgariz'zare**
vt to popularize

'volgere ['vɔldʒere] *vt* to turn ♦ *vi* to
turn; (*tendere*): **~ a:** **il tempo vol-**
ge al brutto the weather is breaking; **un rosso che volge al viola** a
red verging on purple; **~rsi** *vr* to
turn; **~ al peggio** to take a turn for
the worse; **~ al termine** to draw to
an end

'volgo *sm* common people

voli'era *sf* aviary

voli'tivo, a *ag* strong-willed

'volo *sm* flight; **al ~: colpire qc al**
~ to hit sth as it flies past; **capire al**
~ to understand straight away

volontà *sf* will; **a ~** (*mangiare,*
bere) as much as one likes; **buona/**
cattiva ~ goodwill/lack of goodwill

volon'tario, a *ag* voluntary ♦ *sm*
(*MIL*) volunteer

'volpe *sf* fox

'volta *sf* (*momento, circostanza*)
time; (*turno, giro*) turn; (*curva*)
turn, bend; (*ARCHIT*) vault; (*di-*
rezione): **partire alla ~ di** to set off
for; **a mia** (*o* **tua etc**) **~** in turn;
una ~ once; **una ~ sola** only once;
due ~e twice; **una cosa per ~** one
thing at a time; **una ~ per tutte**
once and for all; **a ~e** at times,
sometimes; **una ~ che** (*temporale*)
once; (*causale*) since; **3 ~e 4 3**
times 4

volta'faccia [volta'fattʃa] *sm inv*
(*fig*) volte-face

vol'taggio [vol'taddʒo] *sm*
(*ELETTR*) voltage

vol'tare *vt* to turn; (*girare: moneta*)
to turn over; (*rigirare*) to turn round
♦ *vi* to turn; **~rsi** *vr* to turn; to turn
over; to turn round

volteggi'are [volted'dʒare] vi (volare) to circle; (in equitazione) to do trick riding; (in ginnastica) to vault; to perform acrobatics

'volto, a pp di **volgere ♦** sm face

vo'lubile ag changeable, fickle

vo'lume sm volume; **volumi'noso, a** ag voluminous, bulky

volut'tà sf sensual pleasure o delight; **voluttu'oso, a** ag voluptuous

vomi'tare vt, vi to vomit; **'vomito** sm vomiting no pl; vomit

'vongola sf clam

vo'race [vo'ratʃe] ag voracious, greedy

vo'ragine [vo'radʒine] sf abyss, chasm

'vortice ['vortitʃe] sm whirlwind; whirlpool; (fig) whirl

'vostro, a det: **il(la)** ~**(a)** etc your ♦ pron: **il(la)** ~**(a)** etc yours

vo'tante sm/f voter

vo'tare vi to vote ♦ vt (sottoporre a votazione) to take a vote on; (approvare) to vote for; (REL): ~ **qc** a to dedicate sth to; **votazi'one** sf vote, voting; **votazi'oni** sfpl (POL) votes; (INS) marks

'voto sm (POL) vote; (INS) mark; (REL) vow; (: offerta) votive offering; aver ~**i belli/brutti** (INS) to get good/bad marks

vs. abbr (COMM) = **vostro**

vul'cano sm volcano

vulne'rabile ag vulnerable

vuo'tare vt to empty; ~**rsi** vr to empty

vu'oto, a ag empty; (fig: privo): ~ **di** (senso etc) devoid of ♦ sm empty space, gap; (spazio in bianco) blank; (FISICA) vacuum; (fig: mancanza) gap, void; **a mani** ~**e** empty-handed; ~ **d'aria** air pocket; ~ **a rendere** returnable bottle

W X Y

watt [vat] sm inv watt

'weekend ['wi:kend] sm inv weekend

'whisky ['wiski] sm inv whisky

'xeres ['kseres] sm inv sherry

xero'copia [ksero'kɔpja] sf xerox ®, photocopy

xi'lofono [ksi'lɔfono] sm xylophone

yacht [jɔt] sm inv yacht

'yoghurt ['jɔgurt] sm inv yoghourt

Z

zabai'one [dzaba'jone] sm dessert made of egg yolks, sugar and marsala

zaf'fata [tsaf'fata] sf (tanfo) stench

zaffe'rano [dzaffe'rano] sm saffron

zaf'firo [dzaf'firo] sm sapphire

'zaino ['dzaino] sm rucksack

'zampa ['tsampa] sf (di animale: gamba) leg; (: piede) paw; **a quattro** ~**e** on all fours

zampil'lare [tsampil'lare] vi to gush, spurt; **zam'pillo** sm gush, spurt

zam'pogna [tsam'pɔɲɲa] sf instrument similar to bagpipes

'zanna ['tsanna] sf (di elefante) tusk; (di carnivori) fang

zan'zara [dzan'dzara] sf mosquito; **zanzari'era** sf mosquito net

'zappa ['tsappa] sf hoe; **zap'pare** vt to hoe

zar, za'rina [tsar, tsa'rina] sm/f tsar/tsarina

'zattera ['dzattera] sf raft

za'vorra [dza'vɔrra] sf ballast

'zazzera ['tsattsera] sf shock of hair

'zebra ['dzɛbra] sf zebra; ~**e** sfpl (AUT) zebra crossing sg (BRIT), crosswalk sg (US)

'zecca, che ['tsekka] sf (ZOOL) tick; (officina di monete) mint

'zelo ['dzɛlo] sm zeal

'zenit ['dzenit] sm zenith

ENGLISH - ITALIAN
INGLESE - ITALIANO
A

A |eɪ| n (MUS) la m

> **KEYWORD**

a |ə| (before vowel or silent h: **an**) indef art **1** un (uno +s impure, gn, pn, ps, x, z), f una (un' +vowel); ~ **book** un libro; ~ **mirror** uno specchio; **an apple** una mela; **she's** ~ **doctor** è medico
2 (instead of the number "one") un(o), f un(a); ~ **year ago** un anno fa; ~ **hundred/thousand** etc **pounds** cento/mille etc sterline
3 (in expressing ratios, prices etc) a, per; ~ **3** ~ **day/week** 3 al giorno/alla settimana; **10 km an hour** 10 km all'ora; £5 ~ **person** 5 sterline a persona or per persona

A.A. n abbr (= Alcoholics Anonymous) AA; (BRIT: = Automobile Association) ≈ A.C.I. m
A.A.A. (US) n abbr (= American Automobile Association) ≈ A.C.I. m
aback |əˈbæk| adv: **to be taken** ~ essere sbalordito(a)
abandon |əˈbændən| vt abbandonare ♦ n: **with** ~ sfrenatamente, spensieratamente
abashed |əˈbæʃt| adj imbarazzato(a)
abate |əˈbeɪt| vi calmarsi
abattoir |ˈæbətwɑː*| (BRIT) n mattatoio
abbey |ˈæbɪ| n abbazia, badia
abbot |ˈæbət| n abate m
abbreviation |əˌbriːvɪˈeɪʃən| n abbreviazione f
abdicate |ˈæbdɪkeɪt| vt abdicare a ♦ vi abdicare
abdomen |ˈæbdəmən| n addome m
abduct |æbˈdʌkt| vt rapire
aberration |æbəˈreɪʃən| n aberrazione f
abet |əˈbet| vt see **aid**

abeyance |əˈbeɪəns| n: **in** ~ (law) in disuso; (matter) in sospeso
abide |əˈbaɪd| vt: **I can't** ~ **it/him** non lo posso soffrire or sopportare; ~ **by** vt fus conformarsi a
ability |əˈbɪlɪtɪ| n abilità f inv
abject |ˈæbdʒekt| adj (poverty) abietto(a); (apology) umiliante
ablaze |əˈbleɪz| adj in fiamme
able |ˈeɪbl| adj capace; **to be** ~ **to do sth** essere capace di fare qc; poter fare qc; ~**-bodied** adj robusto(a); **ably** adv abilmente
abnormal |æbˈnɔːml| adj anormale
aboard |əˈbɔːd| adv a bordo ♦ prep a bordo di
abode |əˈbəud| n: **of no fixed** ~ senza fissa dimora
abolish |əˈbɒlɪʃ| vt abolire
abominable |əˈbɒmɪnəbl| adj abominevole
aborigine |æbəˈrɪdʒɪnɪ| n aborigeno/a
abort |əˈbɔːt| vt abortire; ~**ion** |əˈbɔːʃən| n aborto; **to have an** ~**ion** abortire; ~**ive** adj abortivo(a)
abound |əˈbaund| vi abbondare; **to** ~ **in** or **with** abbondare di

> **KEYWORD**

about |əˈbaut| adv **1** (approximately) circa, quasi; ~ **a hundred/thousand** etc un centinaio/migliaio etc, circa cento/mille etc; **it takes** ~ **10 hours** ci vogliono circa 10 ore; **at** ~ **2 o'clock** verso le 2; **I've just** ~ **finished** ho quasi finito
2 (referring to place) qua e là, in giro; **to leave things lying** ~ lasciare delle cose in giro; **to run** ~ correre qua e là; **to walk** ~ camminare
3: to be ~ **to do sth** stare per fare qc

♦ *prep* **1** (*relating to*) su, di; **a book ~ London** un libro su Londra; **what is it ~?** di che si tratta?; (*book, film etc*) di cosa tratta?; **we talked ~ it** ne abbiamo parlato; **what or how ~ doing this?** che ne dici di fare questo?

2 (*referring to place*): **to walk ~ the town** camminare per la città; **her clothes were scattered ~ the room** i suoi vestiti erano sparsi *or* in giro per tutta la stanza

about-face *n* dietro front *m inv*
about-turn *n* dietro front *m inv*
above [ə'bʌv] *adv, prep* sopra; **mentioned ~** suddetto; **~ all** soprattutto; **~board** *adj* aperto(a); onesto(a)
abrasive [ə'breɪzɪv] *adj* abrasivo(a); (*fig*) caustico(a)
abreast [ə'brɛst] *adv* di fianco; **to keep ~ of** tenersi aggiornato su
abridge [ə'brɪdʒ] *vt* ridurre
abroad [ə'brɔːd] *adv* all'estero
abrupt [ə'brʌpt] *adj* (*sudden*) improvviso(a); (*gruff, blunt*) brusco(a)
abscess ['æbsɪs] *n* ascesso
abscond [əb'skɔnd] *vi* scappare
absence ['æbsəns] *n* assenza
absent ['æbsənt] *adj* assente; **~ee** [-'tiː] *n* assente *m/f*; **~-minded** *adj* distratto(a)
absolute ['æbsəluːt] *adj* assoluto(a); **~ly** [-'luːtlɪ] *adv* assolutamente
absolve [əb'zɔlv] *vt*: **to ~ sb (from)** (*sin*) assolvere qn (da); (*oath*) sciogliere qn (da)
absorb [əb'zɔːb] *vt* assorbire; **to be ~ed in a book** essere immerso in un libro; **~ent cotton** (*US*) *n* cotone *m* idrofilo; **~ing** *adj* avvincente
absorption [əb'zɔːpʃən] *n* assorbimento
abstain [əb'steɪn] *vi*: **to ~ (from)** astenersi (da)
abstemious [əb'stiːmɪəs] *adj* astemio(a)
abstract ['æbstrækt] *adj* astratto(a)
absurd [əb'sɜːd] *adj* assurdo(a)
abuse [n ə'bjuːs, vb ə'bjuːz] *n* abuso;

(*insults*) ingiurie *fpl* ♦ *vt* abusare di; **abusive** *adj* ingiurioso(a)
abysmal [ə'bɪzməl] *adj* spaventoso(a)
abyss [ə'bɪs] *n* abisso
AC *abbr* (= *alternating current*) c.a
academic [ækə'dɛmɪk] *adj* accademico(a); (*pej: issue*) puramente formale ♦ *n* universitario/a
academy [ə'kædəmɪ] *n* (*learned body*) accademia; (*school*) scuola privata; **~ of music** conservatorio
accelerate [æk'sɛləreɪt] *vt, vi* accelerare; **accelerator** *n* acceleratore *m*
accent ['æksɛnt] *n* accento
accept [ək'sɛpt] *vt* accettare; **~able** *adj* accettabile; **~ance** *n* accettazione *f*
access ['æksɛs] *n* accesso; **~ible** [æk'sɛsəbl] *adj* accessibile
accessory [æk'sɛsərɪ] *n* accessorio; (*LAW*): **~ to** complice *m/f* di
accident ['æksɪdənt] *n* incidente *m*; (*chance*) caso; **by ~** per caso; (*accidentally*) accidentalmente; **~al** [-'dɛntl] *adj* accidentale; **~ally** [-'dɛntəlɪ] *adv* per caso; **~-prone** *adj*: **he's very ~-prone** è un vero passaguai
acclaim [ə'kleɪm] *n* acclamazione *f*
accolade ['ækəleɪd] *n* encomio
accommodate [ə'kɔmədeɪt] *vt* alloggiare; (*oblige, help*) favorire
accommodating [ə'kɔmədeɪtɪŋ] *adj* compiacente
accommodation [əkɔmə'deɪʃən] *n* alloggio; **~s** (*US*) *npl* alloggio
accompany [ə'kʌmpənɪ] *vt* accompagnare
accomplice [ə'kʌmplɪs] *n* complice *m/f*
accomplish [ə'kʌmplɪʃ] *vt* compiere; (*goal*) raggiungere; **~ed** *adj* esperto(a); **~ment** *n* compimento; realizzazione *f*; **~ments** *npl* (*skills*) doti *fpl*
accord [ə'kɔːd] *n* accordo ♦ *vt* accordare; **of his own ~** di propria iniziativa; **~ance** *n*: **in ~ance with** in conformità con; **~ing**: **~ing to** *prep* secondo; **~ingly** *adv* in conformità

'**zenzero** ['dzendzero] *sm* ginger

'**zeppa** ['tseppa] *sf* wedge

'**zeppo, a** ['tseppo] *ag:* ~ **di** crammed *o* packed with

zer'bino [dzer'bino] *sm* doormat

'**zero** ['dzɛro] *sm* zero, nought; **vincere per tre a** ~ (*SPORT*) to win three-nil

'**zeta** ['dzɛta] *sm o f* zed, (the letter) z

'**zia** ['tsia] *sf* aunt

zibel'lino [dzibel'lino] *sm* sable

'**zigomo** ['dzigomo] *sm* cheekbone

zig'zag [dzig'dzag] *sm inv* zigzag; **andare a** ~ to zigzag

zim'bello [dzim'bɛllo] *sm* (*oggetto di burle*) laughing-stock

'**zinco** ['dzinko] *sm* zinc

'**zingaro, a** ['dzingaro] *sm/f* gipsy

'**zio** ['tsio] (*pl* '**zii**) *sm* uncle; **zii** *smpl* (*zio e zia*) uncle and aunt

zi'tella [dzi'tɛlla] *sf* spinster; (*peg*) old maid

'**zitto, a** ['tsitto] *ag* quiet, silent; **sta'** ~! be quiet!

ziz'zania [dzid'dzanja] *sf* (*fig*): **gettare** *o* **seminare** ~ to sow discord

'**zoccolo** ['tsɔkkolo] *sm* (*calzatura*) clog; (*di cavallo etc*) hoof; (*basamento*) base; plinth

zo'diaco [dzo'diako] *sm* zodiac

'**zolfo** ['tsolfo] *sm* sulphur

'**zolla** ['dzɔlla] *sf* clod (of earth)

zol'letta [dzol'letta] *sf* sugar lump

'**zona** ['dzɔna] *sf* zone, area; ~ **di depressione** (*METEOR*) trough of low pressure; ~ **disco** (*AUT*) ≈ me-

ter zone; ~ **pedonale** pedestrian precinct; ~ **verde** (*di abitato*) green area

'**zonzo** ['dzondzo]: **a** ~ *av:* **andare a** ~ to wander about, stroll about

zoo ['dzɔo] *sm inv* zoo

zoolo'gia [dzoolo'dʒia] *sf* zoology

zoppi'care [tsoppi'kare] *vi* to limp; to be shaky, rickety

'**zoppo, a** ['tsoppo] *ag* lame; (*fig: mobile*) shaky, rickety

zoti'cone [dzoti'kone] *sm* lout

'**zucca, che** ['tsukka] *sf* (*BOT*) marrow; pumpkin

zucche'rare [tsukke'rare] *vt* to put sugar in; **zucche'rato, a** *ag* sweet, sweetened

zuccheri'era [tsukke'rjɛra] *sf* sugar bowl

zuccheri'ficio [tsukkeri'fitʃo] *sm* sugar refinery

zucche'rino, a [tsukke'rino] *ag* sugary, sweet

'**zucchero** ['tsukkero] *sm* sugar

zuc'china [tsuk'kina] *sf* courgette (*BRIT*), zucchini (*US*)

zuc'chino [tsuk'kino] *sm* = **zucchina**

'**zuffa** ['tsuffa] *sf* brawl

'**zuppa** ['tsuppa] *sf* soup; (*fig*) mixture, muddle; ~ **inglese** (*CUC*) dessert made with sponge cake, custard and chocolate, ≈ trifle (*BRIT*); **zuppi'era** *sf* soup tureen

'**zuppo, a** ['tsuppo] *ag:* ~ **(di)** drenched (with), soaked (with)

accordion [ə'kɔːdɪən] n fisarmonica

accost [ə'kɔst] vt avvicinare

account [ə'kaunt] n (COMM) conto; (report) descrizione f; ~s npl (COMM) conti mpl; **of no** ~ di nessuna importanza; **on** ~ in acconto; **on no** ~ per nessun motivo; **on** ~ **of** a causa di; **to take into** ~, **take** ~ **of** tener conto di; ~ **for** vt fus spiegare; giustificare; ~**able** adj: ~**able (to)** responsabile (verso)

accountancy [ə'kauntənsɪ] n ragioneria

accountant [ə'kauntənt] n ragioniere/a

account number n numero di conto

accrued interest [ə'kruːd-] n interesse m maturato

accumulate [ə'kjuːmjuleɪt] vt accumulare ♦ vi accumularsi

accuracy ['ækjurəsɪ] n precisione f

accurate ['ækjurɪt] adj preciso(a); ~**ly** adv precisamente

accusation [ækju'zeɪʃən] n accusa

accuse [ə'kjuːz] vt accusare; ~**d** n accusato/a

accustom [ə'kʌstəm] vt abituare; ~**ed** adj: ~**ed to** abituato(a) a

ace [eɪs] n asso

ache [eɪk] n male m, dolore m ♦ vi (be sore) far male, dolere; **my head** ~**s** mi fa male la testa

achieve [ə'tʃiːv] vt (aim) raggiungere; (victory, success) ottenere; ~**ment** n compimento; successo

acid ['æsɪd] adj acido(a) ♦ n acido; ~ **rain** n pioggia acida

acknowledge [ək'nɔlɪdʒ] vt (letter: also: ~ receipt of) confermare la ricevuta di; (fact) riconoscere; ~**ment** n conferma; riconoscimento

acne ['æknɪ] n acne f

acorn ['eɪkɔːn] n ghianda

acoustic [ə'kuːstɪk] adj acustico(a); ~**s** n, npl acustica

acquaint [ə'kweɪnt] vt: **to** ~ **sb with sth** far sapere qc a qn; **to be** ~**ed with** (person) conoscere; ~**ance** n conoscenza; (person) cono-

scente m/f

acquiesce [ækwɪ'es] vi: **to** ~ **(to)** acconsentire (a)

acquire [ə'kwaɪə*] vt acquistare

acquisition [ækwɪ'zɪʃən] n acquisto

acquit [ə'kwɪt] vt assolvere; **to** ~ **o.s. well** comportarsi bene; ~**tal** n assoluzione f

acre ['eɪkə*] n acro (= 4047 m2)

acrid ['ækrɪd] adj acre; pungente

acrimonious [ækrɪ'məunɪəs] adj astioso(a)

acrobat ['ækrəbæt] n acrobata m/f

across [ə'krɔs] prep (on the other side) dall'altra parte di; (crosswise) attraverso ♦ adv dall'altra parte; in larghezza; **to run/swim** ~ attraversare di corsa/a nuoto; ~ **from** di fronte a

acrylic [ə'krɪlɪk] adj acrilico(a)

act [ækt] n atto; (in music-hall etc) numero; (LAW) decreto ♦ vi agire; (THEATRE) recitare; (pretend) fingere ♦ vt (part) recitare; **to** ~ **as** agire da; ~**ing** adj che fa le funzioni di ♦ n (of actor) recitazione f; (activity): **to do some** ~**ing** fare del teatro (or del cinema)

action ['ækʃən] n azione f; (MIL) combattimento; (LAW) processo; **out of** ~ fuori combattimento; fuori servizio; **to take** ~ agire; ~ **replay** n (TV) replay m inv

activate ['æktɪveɪt] vt (mechanism) attivare

active ['æktɪv] adj attivo(a); ~**ly** adv (participate) attivamente; (discourage, dislike) vivamente

activity [æk'tɪvɪtɪ] n attività f inv

actor ['æktə*] n attore m

actress ['æktrɪs] n attrice f

actual ['æktjuəl] adj reale, vero(a); ~**ly** adv veramente; (even) addirittura

acumen ['ækjumən] n acume m

acute [ə'kjuːt] adj acuto(a); (mind, person) perspicace

ad [æd] n abbr = advertisement

A.D. adv abbr (= Anno Domini) d.C

adamant ['ædəmənt] adj irremovibile

adapt [ə'dæpt] vt adattare ♦ vi: to ~ (to) adattarsi (a); **~able** adj (device) adattabile; (person) che sa adattarsi; **~er** or **~or** n (ELEC) adattatore m

add [æd] vt aggiungere; (figures: also: ~ up) addizionare ♦ vi: to ~ to (increase) aumentare; it doesn't ~ up (fig) non quadra, non ha senso

adder ['ædə'] n vipera

addict ['ædɪkt] n tossicomane m/f; (fig) fanatico/a; **~ed** [ə'dɪktɪd] adj: to be ~ed to (drink etc) essere dedito(a) a; (fig: football etc) essere tifoso(a) di; **~ion** [ə'dɪkʃən] n (MED) tossicodipendenza; **~ive** [ə'dɪktɪv] adj che dà assuefazione

addition [ə'dɪʃən] n addizione f; (thing added) aggiunta; in ~ inoltre; in ~ to oltre; **~al** adj supplementare

additive ['ædɪtɪv] n additivo

address [ə'dres] n indirizzo; (talk) discorso ♦ vt indirizzare; (speak to) fare un discorso a; (issue) affrontare

adept ['ædept] adj: ~ at esperto(a) in

adequate ['ædɪkwɪt] adj adeguato(a); sufficiente

adhere [əd'hɪə'] vi: to ~ to aderire a; (fig: rule, decision) seguire

adhesive [əd'hi:zɪv] n adesivo; ~ tape n (BRIT: for parcels etc) nastro adesivo; (US: MED) cerotto adesivo

adjacent ['ædʒektɪv] n aggettivo

adjoining [ə'dʒɔɪnɪŋ] adj accanto inv, adiacente

adjourn [ə'dʒə:n] vt rimandare ♦ vi essere aggiornato(a)

adjudicate [ə'dʒu:dɪkeɪt] vi (contest) giudicare; (claim) decidere su

adjust [ə'dʒʌst] vt aggiustare; (change) rettificare ♦ vi: to ~ (to) adattarsi (a); **~able** adj regolabile; **~ment** n (PSYCH) adattamento; (of machine) regolazione f; (of prices, wages) modifica

ad-lib [æd'lɪb] vi improvvisare ♦

adv: ad lib a piacere, a volontà

administer [əd'mɪnɪstə'] vt amministrare; (justice, drug) somministrare

administration [ədmɪnɪs'treɪʃən] n amministrazione f

administrative [əd'mɪnɪstrətɪv] adj amministrativo(a)

admiral ['ædmərəl] n ammiraglio; **A~ty** (BRIT) n Ministero della Marina

admiration [ædmə'reɪʃən] n ammirazione f

admire [əd'maɪə'] vt ammirare

admission [əd'mɪʃən] n ammissione f; (to exhibition, night club etc) ingresso; (confession) confessione f

admit [əd'mɪt] vt ammettere; far entrare; (agree) riconoscere; to ~ to riconoscere; **~tance** n ingresso; **~tedly** adv bisogna per riconoscere (che)

admonish [əd'mɔnɪʃ] vt ammonire

ad nauseam [æd'nɔ:sɪæm] adv fino alla nausea, a non finire

ado [ə'du:] n: without (any) more ~ senza più indugi

adolescence [ædəu'lesns] n adolescenza

adolescent [ædəu'lesnt] adj, n adolescente m/f

adopt [ə'dɔpt] vt adottare; **~ed** adj adottivo(a); **~ion** [ə'dɔpʃən] n adozione f

adore [ə'dɔ:'] vt adorare

Adriatic [eɪdrɪ'ætɪk] n: the ~ (Sea) il mare Adriatico, l'Adriatico

adrift [ə'drɪft] adv alla deriva

adult ['ædʌlt] adj adulto(a); (work, education) per adulti ♦ n adulto/a

adultery [ə'dʌltərɪ] n adulterio

advance [əd'vɑ:ns] n avanzamento; (money) anticipo ♦ adj (booking etc) in anticipo ♦ vt (money) anticipare ♦ vi avanzare; in ~ in anticipo; **~d** adj avanzato(a); (SCOL: studies) superiore

advantage [əd'vɑ:ntɪdʒ] n (also: TENNIS) vantaggio; to take ~ of approfittarsi di

advent ['ædvənt] n avvento; (REL):

A~ Avvenno

adventure [əd'vɛntʃə*] n avventura

adverb [ˈædvəːb] n avverbio

adverse [ˈædvəːs] adj avverso(a)

advert [ˈædvəːt] (BRIT) n abbr = **advertisement**

advertise [ˈædvətaiz] vi (vt) fare pubblicità or réclame (a); fare un'inserzione (per vendere); **to ~ for** (staff) mettere un annuncio sul giornale per trovare

advertisement [əd'vəːtismənt] n (COMM) réclame f inv, pubblicità f inv; (in classified ads) inserzione f

advertiser [ˈædvətaizə*] n (in newspaper etc) inserzionista m/f

advertising [ˈædvətaiziŋ] n pubblicità

advice [ədˈvais] n consigli mpl; (notification) avviso; **piece of ~** consiglio; **to take legal ~** consultare un avvocato

advisable [ədˈvaizəbl] adj consigliabile

advise [ədˈvaiz] vt consigliare; **to ~ sb of sth** informare qn di qc; **to ~ sb against sth/doing sth** sconsigliare qc a qn/a qn di fare qc; **~dly** [ˈʌdli] adv (deliberately) di proposito; **~r** or **advisor** n consigliere/a; advisory [-əri] adj consultivo(a)

advocate [n ˈædvəkit, vb ˈædvəkeit] n (upholder) sostenitore/trice; (LAW) avvocato difensore ♦ vt propugnare

Aegean [iˈdʒiːən] n: **the ~** (Sea) il mar Egeo, l'Egeo

aerial [ˈɛəriəl] n antenna ♦ adj aereo(a)

aerobics [ɛəˈrəubiks] n aerobica

aeroplane [ˈɛərəplein] (BRIT) n aeroplano

aerosol [ˈɛərəsɔl] (BRIT) n aerosol m inv

aesthetic [iːsˈθɛtik] adj estetico(a)

afar [əˈfaː*] adv: **from ~** da lontano

affair [əˈfɛə*] n affare m; (also: love ~) relazione f amorosa

affect [əˈfɛkt] vt toccare; (influence) influire su, incidere su; (feign) fingere; **~ed** adj affettato(a)

affection [əˈfɛkʃən] n affezione f; **~ate** adj affettuoso(a)

affix [əˈfiks] vt apporre; attaccare

afflict [əˈflikt] vt affliggere

affluence [ˈæfluəns] n abbondanza; opulenza

affluent [ˈæfluənt] adj ricco(a); **the ~ society** la società del benessere

afford [əˈfɔːd] vt permettersi; (provide) fornire

afield [əˈfiːld] adv: **far ~** lontano

afloat [əˈfləut] adv a galla

afoot [əˈfut] adv: **there is something ~** si sta preparando qualcosa

afraid [əˈfreid] adj impaurito(a); **to be ~ of** or **to/that** aver paura di/che; **I am ~ so/not** ho paura di sì/no

afresh [əˈfrɛʃ] adv di nuovo

Africa [ˈæfrikə] n Africa; **~n** adj, n africano/a

aft [aːft] adv a poppa, verso poppa

after [ˈaːftə*] prep, adv dopo ♦ conj dopo che; **what/who are you ~?** che/chi cerca?; **~ he left/having done** dopo che se ne fu andato/dopo aver fatto; **to name sb ~ sb** dare a qn il nome di qn; **it's twenty ~ eight** (US) sono le otto e venti; **to ask ~ sb** chiedere di qn; **~ all** dopo tutto; **~ you!** dopo di lei!; **~-effects** npl conseguenze fpl; (of illness) postumi mpl; **~math** n conseguenze fpl; **in the ~math of** nel periodo dopo; **~noon** n pomeriggio; **~s** n (inf: dessert) dessert m inv; **~-sales service** (BRIT) n servizio assistenza clienti; **~-shave (lotion)** n dopobarba m inv; **~thought** n: **as an ~thought** come aggiunta; **~wards** (US **~ward**) adv dopo

again [əˈgɛn] adv di nuovo; **to begin/see ~** ricominciare/rivedere; **not ... ~** non ... più; **~ and ~** ripetutamente

against [əˈgɛnst] prep contro

age [eidʒ] n età f inv ♦ vt, vi invecchiare; **it's been ~s since** sono secoli che; **he is 20 years of ~** ha 20 anni; **to come of ~** diventare maggiorenne; **~d 10** di 10 anni; **the ~d**

['eɪdʒɪd] gli anziani; ~ **group** n generazione f; ~ **limit** n limite m d'età

agency ['eɪdʒənsɪ] n agenzia

agenda [ə'dʒɛndə] n ordine m del giorno

agent ['eɪdʒənt] n agente m

aggravate ['ægrəveɪt] vt aggravare; (person) irritare

aggregate ['ægrɪgeɪt] n aggregato

aggressive [ə'grɛsɪv] adj aggressivo(a)

aggrieved [ə'griːvd] adj addolorato(a)

aghast [ə'gɑːst] adj sbigottito(a)

agitate ['ædʒɪteɪt] vt turbare; agitare ♦ vi: to ~ for agitarsi per

AGM n abbr = **annual general meeting**

ago [ə'gəʊ] adv: 2 days ~ 2 giorni fa; not long ~ poco tempo fa; how long ~? quanto tempo fa?

agog [ə'gɔg] adj ansioso(a), emozionato(a)

agonizing ['ægənaɪzɪŋ] adj straziante

agony ['ægənɪ] n dolore m atroce; to be in ~ avere dolori atroci

agree [ə'griː] vt (price) pattuire ♦ vi: to ~ (with) essere d'accordo (con); (LING) concordare (con); to ~ to sth/to do sth accettare qc/di fare qc; to ~ that (admit) ammettere che; to ~ on sth accordarsi su qc; garlic doesn't ~ with me l'aglio non mi va; ~able adj gradevole; (willing) disposto(a); ~d adj (time, place) stabilito(a); in ~ment n accordo; in ~ment d'accordo

agricultural [ægrɪ'kʌltʃərəl] adj agricolo(a)

agriculture ['ægrɪkʌltʃə*] n agricoltura

aground [ə'graʊnd] adv: to run ~ arenarsi

ahead [ə'hɛd] adv avanti; davanti; ~ of davanti a; (fig: schedule etc) in anticipo su; ~ of time in anticipo; go right or straight ~ tiri diritto

aid [eɪd] n aiuto ♦ vt aiutare; in ~

of a favore di; to ~ and abet (LAW) essere complice di

aide [eɪd] n (person) aiutante m

AIDS [eɪdz] n abbr (= acquired immune deficiency syndrome) AIDS f

ailing ['eɪlɪŋ] adj sofferente

ailment ['eɪlmənt] n indisposizione f

aim [eɪm] vt: to ~ sth at (such as gun) mirare qc a, puntare qc a; (camera) rivolgere qc a; (missile) lanciare qc contro ♦ vi (also: to take ~) prendere la mira ♦ n mira; to ~ at mirare; to ~ to do aver l'intenzione di fare; ~less adj senza scopo

ain't [eɪnt] (inf) = am not; aren't; isn't

air [ɛə*] n aria ♦ vt arieggiare; (room) areare; (clothes) far prendere aria a; (grievances, ideas) esprimere pubblicamente ♦ cpd (currents) d'aria; (attack) aereo(a); to throw sth into the ~ lanciare qc in aria; by ~ (travel) in aereo; on the ~ (RADIO, TV) in onda; ~bed (BRIT) n materassino; ~borne adj in volo; aerotrasportato(a); ~-conditioning n condizionamento d'aria; ~craft n inv apparecchio; ~craft carrier n portaerei f inv; ~field n campo d'aviazione; A~ Force n aviazione f militare; ~ freshener n deodorante m per ambienti; ~gun n fucile m ad aria compressa; ~ hostess (BRIT) n hostess f inv; ~ letter (BRIT) n aerogramma m; ~lift n ponte m aereo; ~line n linea aerea; ~liner n aereo di linea; ~mail n: by ~mail per via aerea; ~plane (US) n aeroplano; ~port n aeroporto; ~ raid n incursione f aerea; ~sick adj: to be ~sick soffrire di mal d'aria; ~ terminal n air-terminal m inv; ~tight adj ermetico(a); ~ traffic controller n controllore m del traffico aereo; ~y adj arioso(a); (manners) noncurante

aisle [aɪl] n (of church) navata laterale; navata centrale; (of plane) corridoio

ajar [ə'dʒɑː*] adj socchiuso(a)

akin [əˈkɪn] *adj*: ~ **to** simile a

alacrity [əˈlækrɪtɪ] *n*: **with** ~ con prontezza

alarm [əˈlɑːm] *n* allarme *m* ♦ *vt* allarmare; ~ **call** *n* (*in hotel etc*) sveglia; ~ **clock** *n* sveglia

alas [əˈlæs] *excl* ohimè!, ahimè!

albeit [ɔːlˈbiːɪt] *conj* sebbene +*sub*, benché +*sub*

album [ˈælbəm] *n* album *m inv*

alcohol [ˈælkəhɒl] *n* alcool *m*; ~**ic** [-ˈhɒlɪk] *adj* alcolico/a ♦ *n* alcolizzato/a

ale [eɪl] *n* birra

alert [əˈlɜːt] *adj* vigile ♦ *n* allarme *m* ♦ *vt* avvertire; mettere in guardia; **on the** ~ all'erta

algebra [ˈældʒɪbrə] *n* algebra

alias [ˈeɪlɪəs] *adv* alias ♦ *n* pseudonimo, falso nome *m*

alibi [ˈælɪbaɪ] *n* alibi *m inv*

alien [ˈeɪlɪən] *n* straniero/a; (*extraterrestrial*) alieno/a ♦ *adj*: ~ (**to**) estraneo/a (a); ~**ate** *vt* alienare

alight [əˈlaɪt] *adj* acceso/a ♦ *vi* scendere; (*bird*) posarsi

align [əˈlaɪn] *vt* allineare

alike [əˈlaɪk] *adj* simile ♦ *adv* sia ... sia; **to look** ~ assomigliarsi

alimony [ˈælɪmənɪ] *n* (*payment*) alimenti *mpl*

alive [əˈlaɪv] *adj* vivo/a; (*lively*) vivace

KEYWORD
---

all [ɔːl] *adj* tutto/a; ~ **day** tutto il giorno; ~ **night** tutta la notte; ~ **men** tutti gli uomini; ~ **five came** sono venuti tutti e cinque; ~ **the books** tutti i libri; ~ **the food** tutto il cibo; ~ **the time** sempre; tutto il tempo; ~ **his life** tutta la vita

♦ *pron* **1** tutto/a; **I ate it** ~, **I ate** ~ **of it** l'ho mangiato tutto; ~ **of us went** tutti noi siamo andati; ~ **of the boys went** tutti i ragazzi sono andati

2 (*in phrases*): **above** ~ soprattutto; **after** ~ dopotutto; **at** ~: **not at** ~ (*in answer to question*) niente affat-

to; (*in answer to thanks*) prego!, di niente!, s'immagini!; **I'm not at** ~ **tired** non sono affatto stanco(a); **anything at** ~ **will do** andrà bene qualsiasi cosa; ~ **in** ~ tutto sommato

♦ *adv*: ~ **alone** tutto(a) solo(a); **it's not as hard as** ~ **that** non è poi così difficile; ~ **the more/the better** tanto più/meglio; ~ **but** quasi; **the score is two** ~ il punteggio è di due a due

allay [əˈleɪ] *vt* (*fears*) dissipare

all clear *n* (*also fig*) segnale *m* di cessato allarme

allegation [ælɪˈɡeɪʃən] *n* asserzione *f*

allege [əˈledʒ] *vt* asserire; ~**dly** [əˈledʒɪdlɪ] *adv* secondo quanto si asserisce

allegiance [əˈliːdʒəns] *n* fedeltà

allergic [əˈlɜːdʒɪk] *adj*: ~ **to** allergico(a)

allergy [ˈælədʒɪ] *n* allergia

alleviate [əˈliːvɪeɪt] *vt* sollevare

alley [ˈælɪ] *n* vicolo

alliance [əˈlaɪəns] *n* alleanza

allied [ˈælaɪd] *adj* alleato/a

all-in *adj* (*BRIT*: *also adv*: *charge*) tutto compreso; ~ **wrestling** *n* lotta americana

all-night *adj* aperto(a) (*or che dura*) tutta la notte

allocate [ˈæləkeɪt] *vt* assegnare

allot [əˈlɒt] *vt* assegnare; ~**ment** *n* assegnazione *f*; (*garden*) lotto di terra

all-out *adj* (*effort etc*) totale ♦ *adv*: **to go all out for** mettercela tutta per

allow [əˈlau] *vt* (*practice*, *behaviour*) permettere; (*sum to spend etc*) accordare; (*sum*, *time estimated*) dare; (*concede*): **to** ~ **that** ammettere che; **to** ~ **sb to do** permettere a qn di fare; **he is** ~**ed to** lo può fare; ~ **for** *vt fus* tener conto di; ~**ance** *n* (*money received*) assegno; indennità *f inv*; (*TAX*) detrazione *f* di imposta; **to make** ~**ances for**

conto di
alloy ['ælɔɪ] n lega
all right adv (feel, work) bene; (as answer) va bene
all-round adj completo(a)
all-time adj (record) assoluto(a)
allude [ə'luːd] vi: to ~ to alludere a
alluring [ə'ljuərɪŋ] adj seducente
ally ['ælaɪ] n alleato
almighty [ɔːl'maɪtɪ] adj onnipotente; (row etc) colossale
almond ['aːmənd] n mandorla
almost ['ɔːlməʊst] adv quasi
alms [aːmz] npl elemosina sg
aloft [ə'lɒft] adv in alto
alone [ə'ləʊn] adj, adv solo(a); to leave sb ~ lasciare qn in pace; to leave sth ~ lasciare stare qc; let ~ ... figuriamoci poi ..., tanto meno ...
along [ə'lɒŋ] prep lungo ♦ adv: is he coming ~? viene con noi?; he was limping ~ veniva zoppicando; ~ with insieme con; all ~ (all the time) sempre, fin dall'inizio; ~side prep accanto a; lungo ♦ adv accanto
aloof [ə'luːf] adj distaccato(a) ♦ adv: to stand ~ tenersi a distanza or in disparte
aloud [ə'laʊd] adv ad alta voce
alphabet ['ælfəbɛt] n alfabeto
alpine ['ælpaɪn] adj alpino(a)
Alps [ælps] npl: the ~ le Alpi
already [ɔːl'rɛdɪ] adv già
alright ['ɔːl'raɪt] (BRIT) adv = all right
Alsatian [æl'seɪʃən] (BRIT) n (dog) pastore m tedesco, (cane m) lupo
also ['ɔːlsəʊ] adv anche
altar ['ɔltə*] n altare m
alter ['ɔltə*] vt, vi alterare
alternate [adj ɔl'təːnɪt, vb 'ɔltəːneɪt] adj alterno(a); (US: plan etc) alternativo(a) ♦ vi: to ~ (with) alternarsi (a); on ~ days ogni due giorni; **alternating** adj (current) alternato(a)
alternative [ɔl'təːnətɪv] adj alternativo(a) ♦ n (choice) alternativa; **~ly** adv: ~ly one could ... come alter-

nativa si potrebbe ....
alternator ['ɔltəːneɪtə*] n (AUT) alternatore m
although [ɔːl'ðəʊ] conj benché +sub, sebbene +sub
altitude ['æltɪtjuːd] n altitudine f
alto ['æltəʊ] n contralto; (male) contraltino
altogether [ɔːltə'gɛðə*] adv del tutto, completamente; (on the whole) tutto considerato; (in all) in tutto
aluminium ['ælju'mɪnɪəm] n alluminio
aluminum [ə'luːmɪnəm] (US) n = **aluminium**
always ['ɔːlweɪz] adv sempre
Alzheimer's (disease) ['æltshaɪməz-] n (malattia di) Alzheimer
am [æm] vb see **be**
a.m. adv abbr (= ante meridiem) della mattina
amalgamate [ə'mælgəmeɪt] vt amalgamare ♦ vi amalgamarsi
amateur ['æmətə*] n dilettante m/f ♦ adj (SPORT) dilettante; **~ish** (pej) adj da dilettante
amaze [ə'meɪz] vt stupire; to be ~d (at) essere sbalordito (da); **~ment** n stupore m; **amazing** adj sorprendente, sbalorditivo(a)
ambassador [æm'bæsədə*] n ambasciatore/trice
amber ['æmbə*] n ambra; at ~ (BRIT: AUT) giallo
ambiguous [æm'bɪgjuəs] adj ambiguo(a)
ambition [æm'bɪʃən] n ambizione f
ambitious [æm'bɪʃəs] adj ambizioso(a)
amble ['æmbl] vi (gen: to ~ along) camminare tranquillamente
ambulance ['æmbjuləns] n ambulanza
ambush ['æmbuʃ] n imboscata ♦ vt fare un'imboscata a
amenable [ə'miːnəbl] adj: ~ to (advice etc) ben disposto(a) a
amend [ə'mɛnd] vt (law) emendare; (text) correggere; to make ~s fare ammenda

amenities [əˈmiːnɪtɪz] npl attrezzature fpl ricreative e culturali

America [əˈmɛrɪkə] n America; **~n** adj, n americano(a)

amiable [ˈeɪmɪəbl] adj amabile, gentile

amicable [ˈæmɪkəbl] adj amichevole

amid(st) [əˈmɪd(st)] prep fra, tra, in mezzo a

amiss [əˈmɪs] adj, adv: **there's something ~** c'è qualcosa che non va bene; **don't take it ~** non prendertela (a male)

ammonia [əˈməʊnɪə] n ammoniaca

ammunition [æmjuˈnɪʃən] n munizioni fpl

amok [əˈmɒk] adv: **to run ~** diventare pazzo(a) furioso(a)

among(st) [əˈmʌŋ(st)] prep fra, tra, in mezzo a

amorous [ˈæmərəs] adj amoroso(a)

amount [əˈmaʊnt] n somma; ammontare m; quantità f inv ♦ vi: **to ~ to** (total) ammontare a; (be same as) essere come

amp(ère) [ˈæmp(ɛə*)] n ampère m inv

ample [ˈæmpl] adj ampio(a); spazioso(a); (enough): **this is ~** questo è più che sufficiente

amplifier [ˈæmplɪfaɪə*] n amplificatore m

amuck [əˈmʌk] adv = amok

amuse [əˈmjuːz] vt divertire; **~ment** n divertimento; **~ment arcade** n sala giochi

an [æn] indef art see **a**

anaemic [əˈniːmɪk] adj anemico(a)

anaesthetic [ænɪsˈθɛtɪk] adj anestetico(a) ♦ n anestetico

analog(ue) [ˈænəlɒɡ] adj (watch, computer) analogico(a)

analyse [ˈænəlaɪz] (BRIT) vt analizzare

analyses [əˈnæləsiːz] npl of **analysis**

analysis [əˈnæləsɪs] (pl **analyses**) n analisi f inv

analyst [ˈænəlɪst] n (POL etc) analista m/f; (US) (psic)analista m/f

analyze [ˈænəlaɪz] (US) vt = analyse

anarchist [ˈænəkɪst] n anarchico/a

anarchy [ˈænəkɪ] n anarchia

anathema [əˈnæθɪmə] n: **that is ~ to him** non vuole nemmeno sentirne parlare

anatomy [əˈnætəmɪ] n anatomia

ancestor [ˈænsɪstə*] n antenato/a

anchor [ˈæŋkə*] n ancora ♦ vi (also: **to drop ~**) gettare l'ancora ♦ vt ancorare; **to weigh ~** salpare or levare l'ancora

anchovy [ˈæntʃəvɪ] n acciuga

ancient [ˈeɪnʃənt] adj antico(a); (person, car) vecchissimo(a)

ancillary [ænˈsɪlərɪ] adj ausiliario(a)

and [ænd] conj e (often ed before vowel); **~ so on** e così via; **try ~ come** cerca di venire; **he talked ~ talked** non la finiva di parlare; **better ~ better** sempre meglio

anemic [əˈniːmɪk] (US) adj = **anaemic**

anesthetic [ænɪsˈθɛtɪk] (US) adj, n = **anaesthetic**

anew [əˈnjuː] adv di nuovo

angel [ˈeɪndʒəl] n angelo

anger [ˈæŋɡə*] n rabbia

angina [ænˈdʒaɪnə] n angina pectoris

angle [ˈæŋɡl] n angolo; **from their ~** dal loro punto di vista

Anglican [ˈæŋɡlɪkən] adj, n anglicano(a)

angling [ˈæŋɡlɪŋ] n pesca con la lenza

Anglo- [ˈæŋɡləʊ] prefix anglo....

angrily [ˈæŋɡrɪlɪ] adv con rabbia

angry [ˈæŋɡrɪ] adj arrabbiato(a), furioso(a); (wound) infiammato(a); **to be ~ with sb/at sth** essere in collera con qn/per qc; **to get ~** arrabbiarsi; **to make sb ~** fare arrabbiare qn

anguish [ˈæŋɡwɪʃ] n angoscia

animal [ˈænɪməl] adj animale ♦ n animale m

animate [ˈænɪmɪt] adj animato(a)

animated [ˈænɪmeɪtɪd] adj animato(a)

aniseed [ˈænɪsiːd] n semi mpl di anice

ankle [ˈæŋkl] n caviglia; ~ **sock** n calzino

annex [n ˈænɛks, vb əˈnɛks] n (also: BRIT: annexe) (edificio) annesso ♦ vt annettere

annihilate [əˈnaɪəleɪt] vt annientare

anniversary [ænɪˈvəːsərɪ] n anniversario

announce [əˈnauns] vt annunciare; ~**ment** n annuncio; (letter, card) partecipazione f; ~**r** n (RADIO, TV: between programmes) annunciatore/trice; (: in a programme) presentatore/trice

annoy [əˈnɔɪ] vt dare fastidio a; **don't get** ~**ed!** non irritarti!; ~**ance** n fastidio; (cause of ~ance) noia; ~**ing** adj noioso(a)

annual [ˈænjuəl] adj annuale ♦ n (BOT) pianta annua; (book) annuario

annul [əˈnʌl] vt annullare

annum [ˈænəm] n see per

anonymous [əˈnɒnɪməs] adj anonimo(a)

anorak [ˈænəræk] n giacca a vento

another [əˈnʌðə*] adj: ~ **book** (one more) un altro libro, ancora un libro; (a different one) un altro libro ♦ pron un altro(un'altra), ancora uno(a); see also **one**

answer [ˈɑːnsə*] n risposta; soluzione f ♦ vi rispondere ♦ vt (reply to) rispondere a; (problem) risolvere; (prayer) esaudire; **in** ~ **to your letter** in risposta alla sua lettera; **to** ~ **the phone** rispondere (al telefono); **to** ~ **the bell** rispondere al campanello; **to** ~ **the door** aprire la porta; ~ **back** vi ribattere; ~ **for** vt fus essere responsabile di; ~ **to** vt fus (description) corrispondere a; ~**able** adj: ~**able** (**to sb/for sth**) responsabile (verso qn/di qc); ~**ing machine** n segreteria (telefonica) automatica

ant [ænt] n formica

antagonism [ænˈtægənɪzəm] n antagonismo

antagonize [ænˈtægənaɪz] vt provo-

care l'ostilità di

Antarctic [æntˈɑːktɪk] n: **the** ~ l'Antartide f

antenatal [ˈæntɪˈneɪtl] adj prenatale; ~ **clinic** n assistenza medica preparto

anthem [ˈænθəm] n: **national** ~ inno nazionale

anthology [ænˈθɒlədʒɪ] n antologia

antibiotic [ˈæntɪbaɪˈɒtɪk] n antibiotico

antibody [ˈæntɪbɒdɪ] n anticorpo

anticipate [ænˈtɪsɪpeɪt] vt prevedere; pregustare; (wishes, request) prevenire

anticipation [æntɪsɪˈpeɪʃən] n anticipazione f; (expectation) aspettative fpl

anticlimax [ˈæntɪˈklaɪmæks] n: **it was an** ~ fu una completa delusione

anticlockwise [ˈæntɪˈklɒkwaɪz] adj, adv in senso antiorario

antics [ˈæntɪks] npl buffonerie fpl

antifreeze [ˈæntɪˈfriːz] n anticongelante m

antihistamine [ˈæntɪˈhɪstəmɪn] n antistaminico

antiquated [ˈæntɪkweɪtɪd] adj antiquato(a)

antique [ænˈtiːk] n antichità f inv ♦ adj antico(a); ~ **dealer** n antiquario/a; ~ **shop** n negozio d'antichità

antiquity [ænˈtɪkwɪtɪ] n antichità f inv

anti-Semitism [ˈæntɪˈsɛmɪtɪzəm] n antisemitismo

antiseptic [ˈæntɪˈsɛptɪk] n antisettico

antisocial [ˈæntɪˈsəuʃəl] adj asociale

antlers [ˈæntləz] npl palchi mpl

anvil [ˈænvɪl] n incudine f

anxiety [æŋˈzaɪətɪ] n ansia; (keenness): ~ **to do** smania di fare

anxious [ˈæŋkʃəs] adj ansioso(a), inquieto(a); (worrying) angosciante; (keen): ~ **to do/that** impaziente di fare/che +sub

KEYWORD

any [ˈɛnɪ] adj **1** (in questions etc):

have you ~ butter? hai del burro?, hai un po' di burro?; **have you ~ children?** hai bambini?; **if there are ~ tickets left** se ci sono ancora (dei) biglietti, se c'è ancora qualche biglietto

2 (*with negative*): **I haven't ~ money/books** non ho soldi/libri

3 (*no matter which*) qualsiasi, qualunque; **choose ~ book you like** scegli un libro qualsiasi

4 (*in phrases*): **in ~ case** in ogni caso; **~ day now** da un giorno all'altro; **at ~ moment** in qualsiasi momento, da un momento all'altro; **at ~ rate** ad ogni modo

♦ **pron 1** (*in questions, with negative*): **have you got ~?** ne hai?; **can ~ of you sing?** qualcuno di voi sa cantare?; **I haven't ~ (of them)** non ne ho

2 (*no matter which one(s)*): **take ~ of those books (you like)** prendi uno qualsiasi di quei libri

♦ **adv 1** (*in questions etc*): **do you want ~ more soup/sandwiches?** vuoi ancora un po' di minestra/degli altri panini?; **are you feeling ~ better?** ti senti meglio?

2 (*with negative*): **I can't hear him ~ more** non lo sento più; **don't wait ~ longer** non aspettare più

anybody ['ɛnɪbɔdɪ] *pron* (*in questions etc*) qualcuno, nessuno; (*with negative*) nessuno; (*no matter who*) chiunque; **can you see ~?** vedi qualcuno or nessuno?; **if ~ should phone ...** se telefona qualcuno ...; **I can't see ~** non vedo nessuno; **~ could do it** chiunque potrebbe farlo

anyhow ['ɛnɪhaʊ] *adv* (*at any rate*) ad ogni modo, comunque; (*haphazard*): **do it ~ you like** fallo come ti pare; **I shall go ~** ci andrò lo stesso or comunque; **she leaves things just ~** lascia tutto come capita

anyone ['ɛnɪwʌn] *pron* = anybody

anything ['ɛnɪθɪŋ] *pron* (*in question*

etc) qualcosa, niente; (*with negative*) niente; (*no matter what*): **you can say ~** you like puoi dire quello che ti pare; **can you see ~?** vedi niente or qualcosa?; **if ~ happens to me ...** se mi dovesse succedere qualcosa ...; **I can't see ~** non vedo niente; **~ will do** va bene qualsiasi cosa *or* tutto

anyway ['ɛnɪweɪ] *adv* (*at any rate*) ad ogni modo, comunque; (*besides*) ad ogni modo

anywhere ['ɛnɪwɛə*] *adv* (*in questions etc*) da qualche parte; (*with negative*) da nessuna parte; (*no matter where*) da qualsiasi *or* qualunque parte, dovunque; **can you see him ~?** lo vedi da qualche parte?; **I can't see him ~** non lo vedo da nessuna parte; **~ in the world** dovunque nel mondo

apart [ə'pɑːt] *adv* (*to one side*) a parte; (*separately*) separatamente; **with one's legs ~** con le gambe divaricate; **10 miles ~** a 10 miglia di distanza (l'uno dall'altro); **to take ~** smontare; **~ from** a parte, eccetto

apartheid [ə'pɑːteɪt] *n* apartheid *f*

apartment [ə'pɑːtmənt] *n* (*US*) appartamento; (*room*) locale *m*; **~ building** (*US*) *n* stabile *m*, caseggiato

apathetic [æpə'θɛtɪk] *adj* apatico/a

ape [eɪp] *n* scimmia ♦ *vt* scimmiottare

apéritif [ə'pɛrɪtɪf] *n* aperitivo

aperture ['æpətʃjʊə*] *n* apertura

apex ['eɪpɛks] *n* apice *m*

apiece [ə'piːs] *adv* ciascuno/a

aplomb [ə'plɔm] *n* disinvoltura

apologetic [əpɔlə'dʒɛtɪk] *adj* (*tone, letter*) di scusa

apologize [ə'pɔlədʒaɪz] *vi*: **to ~ (for sth to sb)** scusarsi (di qc a qn), chiedere scusa (a qn per qc)

apology [ə'pɔlədʒɪ] *n* scuse *fpl*

apostle [ə'pɔsl] *n* apostolo

apostrophe [ə'pɔstrəfɪ] *n* (*sign*) apostrofo

appal [ə'pɔːl] *vt* scioccare; **~ing** *adj*

spaventoso(a)

apparatus [æpə'reɪtəs] n apparato; (in gymnasium) attrezzatura

apparel [ə'pærl] (US) n abbigliamento, confezioni fpl

apparent [ə'pærənt] adj evidente; ~ly adv evidentemente

apparition [æpə'rɪʃən] n apparizione f

appeal [ə'piːl] vi (LAW) appellarsi alla legge ♦ n (LAW) appello; (request) richiesta; (charm) attrattiva; to ~ for chiedere (con insistenza); to ~ to (subj: person) appellarsi a; (subj: thing) piacere a; it doesn't ~ to me mi dice poco; ~ing adj (nice) attraente

appear [ə'pɪə*] vi apparire; (LAW) comparire; (publication) essere pubblicato(a); (seem) sembrare; it would ~ that sembra che; ~ance n apparizione f; apparenza; (look, aspect) aspetto

appease [ə'piːz] vt calmare, appagare

appendices [ə'pendɪsiːz] npl of appendix

appendicitis [əpendɪ'saɪtɪs] n appendicite f

appendix [ə'pendɪks] (pl appendices) n appendice f

appetite ['æpɪtaɪt] n appetito

appetizer ['æpɪtaɪzə*] n stuzzichino

applaud [ə'plɔːd] vt, vi applaudire

applause [ə'plɔːz] n applauso

apple ['æpl] n mela; ~ tree n melo

appliance [ə'plaɪəns] n apparecchio

applicant ['æplɪkənt] n candidato/a

application [æplɪ'keɪʃən] n applicazione f; (for a job, a grant etc) domanda; ~ form n modulo per la domanda

applied [ə'plaɪd] adj applicato(a)

apply [ə'plaɪ] vt: to ~ (to) (paint, ointment) dare (a); (theory, technique) applicare (a) ♦ vi: to ~ to (ask) rivolgersi a; (be suitable for, relevant to) riguardare, riferirsi a; to ~ (for) (permit, grant, job) fare domanda (per); to ~ o.s. to dedi-

carsi a

appoint [ə'pɔɪnt] vt nominare; ~ed adj: at the ~ed time all'ora stabilita; ~ment n nomina; (arrangement to meet) appuntamento; to make an ~ment (with) prendere un appuntamento (con)

appraisal [ə'preɪzl] n valutazione f

appreciate [ə'priːʃɪeɪt] vt (like) apprezzare; (be grateful for) essere riconoscente di; (be aware of) rendersi conto di ♦ vi (FINANCE) aumentare

appreciation [əpriːʃɪ'eɪʃən] n apprezzamento; (FINANCE) aumento del valore

appreciative [ə'priːʃɪətɪv] adj (person) sensibile; (comment) elogiativo(a)

apprehend [æprɪ'hɛnd] vt (arrest) arrestare

apprehension [æprɪ'hɛnʃən] n (fear) inquietudine f

apprehensive [æprɪ'hɛnsɪv] adj apprensivo(a)

apprentice [ə'prɛntɪs] n apprendista m/f; ~ship n apprendistato

approach [ə'prəʊtʃ] vi avvicinarsi ♦ vt (come near) avvicinarsi a; (ask, apply to) rivolgersi a; (subject, passer-by) avvicinare ♦ n approccio; accesso; (to problem) modo di affrontare; ~able adj accessibile

appropriate [adj ə'prəʊprɪɪt, vb ə'prəʊprɪeɪt] adj appropriato(a), adatto(a) ♦ vt (take) appropriarsi

approval [ə'pruːvl] n approvazione f; on ~ (COMM) in prova, in esame

approve [ə'pruːv] vt, vi approvare; ~ of vt fus approvare

approximate [ə'prɒksɪmɪt] adj approssimativo(a); ~ly adv circa

apricot ['eɪprɪkɒt] n albicocca

April ['eɪprəl] n aprile m; ~ fool! pesce d'aprile!

apron ['eɪprən] n grembiule m

apt [æpt] adj (suitable) adatto(a); (able) capace; (likely): to be ~ to do avere tendenza a fare

aptitude ['æptɪtjuːd] n abilità f inv

aquarium [ə'kwɛərɪəm] n acquario

Aquarius [əˈkwεərɪəs] n Acquario

Arab [ˈærəb] adj, n arabo(a)

Arabian [əˈreɪbɪən] adj arabo(a)

Arabic [ˈærəbɪk] adj arabico(a), arabo(a) ♦ n arabo; ~ **numerals** numeri mpl arabi, numerazione f araba

arbitrary [ˈɑːbɪtrərɪ] adj arbitrario(a)

arbitration [ɑːbɪˈtreɪʃən] n (LAW) arbitrato; (INDUSTRY) arbitraggio

arcade [ɑːˈkeɪd] n portico, (passage with shops) galleria

arch [ɑːtʃ] n arco; (of foot) arco plantare ♦ vt inarcare

archaeologist [ɑːkɪˈɔlədʒɪst] n archeologo/a

archaeology [ɑːkɪˈɔlədʒɪ] n archeologia

archbishop [ɑːtʃˈbɪʃəp] n arcivescovo

arch-enemy n arcinemico/a

archeology [ɑːkɪˈɔlədʒɪ] etc (US) = **archaeology** etc

archery [ˈɑːtʃərɪ] n tiro all'arco

architect [ˈɑːkɪtεkt] n architetto; ~**ure** [ˈɑːkɪtεktʃəˈ] n architettura

archives [ˈɑːkaɪvz] npl archivi mpl

Arctic [ˈɑːktɪk] adj artico(a) ♦ n: **the** ~ l'Artico

ardent [ˈɑːdənt] adj ardente

are [ɑː*] vb see **be**

area [ˈεərɪə] n (GEOM) area; (zone) zona; (: smaller) settore m

aren't [ɑːnt] = **are not**

Argentina [ɑːdʒənˈtiːnə] n Argentina; **Argentinian** [-ˈtɪnɪən] adj, n argentino(a)

arguably [ˈɑːgjuəblɪ] adv: **it is ~** ... si può sostenere che sia ....

argue [ˈɑːgjuː] vi (quarrel) litigare; (reason) ragionare; **to ~ that** sostenere che

argument [ˈɑːgjumənt] n (reasons) argomento; (quarrel) lite f; ~**ative** [ɑːgjuˈmεntətɪv] adj litigioso(a)

Aries [ˈεərɪz] n Ariete m

arise [əˈraɪz] (pt **arose**, pp **arisen**) vi (opportunity, problem) presentarsi; **arisen** [əˈrɪzn] pp of **arise**

aristocrat [ˈærɪstəkræt] n aristocrati-

co/a

arithmetic [əˈrɪθmətɪk] n aritmetica

ark [ɑːk] n: **Noah's A~** l'arca di Noè

arm [ɑːm] n braccio ♦ vt armare; ~**s** npl (weapons) armi fpl; ~ **in** ~ a braccetto

armaments [ˈɑːməmənts] npl armamenti mpl

arm: ~**chair** n poltrona; ~ed adj armato(a); ~**ed robbery** n rapina a mano armata

armour [ˈɑːməˈ] (US **armor**) n armatura; (MIL: tanks) mezzi mpl blindati; ~**ed car** n autoblinda f inv

armpit [ˈɑːmpɪt] n ascella

armrest [ˈɑːmrεst] n bracciolo

army [ˈɑːmɪ] n esercito

aroma [əˈrəumə] n aroma

arose [əˈrəuz] pt of **arise**

around [əˈraund] adv attorno, intorno ♦ prep intorno a; (fig: about): ~ £5/3 o'clock circa 5 sterline/le 3; is he ~? è in giro?

arouse [əˈrauz] vt (sleeper) svegliare; (curiosity, passions) suscitare

arrange [əˈreɪndʒ] vt sistemare; (programme) preparare; **to ~ to do sth** mettersi d'accordo per fare qc; ~**ment** n sistemazione f; (agreement) accordo; ~**ments** npl (plans) progetti mpl, piani mpl

array [əˈreɪ] n: ~ **of** fila di

arrears [əˈrɪəz] npl arretrati mpl; **to be in** ~ **with one's rent** essere in arretrato con l'affitto

arrest [əˈrεst] vt arrestare; (sb's attention) attirare ♦ n arresto; **under** ~ in arresto

arrival [əˈraɪvl] n arrivo; (person) arrivato/a; **a new** ~ un nuovo venuto; (baby) un neonato

arrive [əˈraɪv] vi arrivare

arrogant [ˈærəgənt] adj arrogante

arrow [ˈærəu] n freccia

arse [ɑːs] (inf!) n culo (!)

arson [ˈɑːsn] n incendio doloso

art [ɑːt] n arte f; (craft) mestiere m; **A~s** npl (SCOL) Lettere fpl

artefact [ˈɑːtɪfækt] n manufatto

artery [ˈɑːtərɪ] n arteria

artful ['ɑ:tful] *adj* abile

art gallery *n* galleria d'arte

arthritis [ɑ:'θraɪtɪs] *n* artrite *f*

artichoke ['ɑ:tɪtʃəuk] *n* carciofo; Jerusalem ~ topinambur *m inv*

article ['ɑ:tɪkl] *n* articolo; ~s *npl* (BRIT: LAW: training) contratto di tirocinio; ~ of clothing capo di vestiario

articulate [*adj* ɑ:'tɪkjulɪt, *vb* ɑ:'tɪkjuleɪt] *adj* (person) che si esprime forbitamente; (speech) articolato(a) ♦ *vi* articolare; **~d** (BRIT) *n* autotreno

artificial [ɑ:tɪ'fɪʃl] *adj* artificiale; ~ **respiration** *n* respirazione *f* artificiale

artillery [ɑ:'tɪlərɪ] *n* artiglieria

artisan ['ɑ:tɪzæn] *n* artigiano/a

artist ['ɑ:tɪst] *n* artista *m/f*; ~**ic** [ɑ:'tɪstɪk] *adj* artistico(a); ~**ry** *n* arte *f*

artless ['ɑ:tlɪs] *adj* semplice, ingenuo(a)

art school *n* scuola d'arte

KEYWORD

as [æz] *conj* **1** (referring to time) mentre; ~ **the years went by** col passare degli anni; **he came in ~ I was leaving** arrivò mentre stavo uscendo; ~ **from tomorrow** da domani

2 (in comparisons): ~ **big** ~ grande come; **twice** ~ **big** ~ due volte più grande di; ~ **much/many** ~ tanto quanto/tanti quanti; ~ **soon** ~ **possible** prima possibile

3 (since, because) dal momento che, siccome

4 (referring to manner, way) come; **do** ~ **you wish** fa' come vuoi; ~ **she said** come ha detto lei

5 (concerning): ~ **for** or **to that** per quanto riguarda or quanto a quello

6: ~ **if** or **though** come se; **he looked** ~ **if he was ill** sembrava stare male; see also **long**; **such**; **well**

♦ *prep*: **he works** ~ **a driver** è

l'autista; ~ **chairman of the company, he ...** come presidente della compagnia, lui ...; **he gave me it** ~ **a present** me lo ha regalato

a.s.a.p. *abbr* = **as soon as possible**

ascend [ə'sɛnd] *vt* salire; ~**ancy** *n* ascendente *m*

ascent [ə'sɛnt] *n* salita; (of mountain) ascensione *f*

ascertain [æsə'teɪn] *vt* accertare

ascribe [ə'skraɪb] *vt*: **to** ~ **sth to** attribuire qc a

ash [æʃ] *n* (dust) cenere *f*; (wood, tree) frassino

ashamed [ə'feɪmd] *adj* vergognoso(a); **to be** ~ **of** vergognarsi di

ashen ['æʃn] *adj* (pale) livido(a)

ashore [ə'ʃɔ:] *adv* a terra

ashtray ['æʃtreɪ] *n* portacenere *m*

Ash Wednesday *n* mercoledì *m inv* delle Ceneri

Asia ['eɪʃə] *n* Asia; ~**n** *adj*, *n* asiatico(a)

aside [ə'saɪd] *adv* da parte ♦ *n* a parte *m*

ask [ɑ:sk] *vt* (question) domandare; (invite) invitare; **to** ~ **sb sth/sb to do sth** chiedere qc a qn/a qn di fare qc; **to** ~ **sb about sth** chiedere a qn di qc; **to** ~ **(sb) a question** fare una domanda (a qn); **to** ~ **sb out to dinner** invitare qn a mangiare fuori; ~ **after** *vt fus* chiedere di; ~ **for** *vt fus* chiedere; (trouble etc) cercare

askance [ə'skɑ:ns] *adv*: **to look** ~ **at sb** guardare qn di traverso

askew [ə'skju:] *adv* di traverso, storto

asleep [ə'sli:p] *adj* addormentato(a); **to be** ~ dormire; **to fall** ~ addormentarsi

asparagus [əs'pærəgəs] *n* asparagi *mpl*

aspect ['æspɛkt] *n* aspetto

aspersions [əs'pə:ʃənz] *npl*: **to cast** ~ **on** diffamare

asphyxiation [æsfɪksɪ'eɪʃən] *n* asfissia

aspire [əs'paɪə] *vi*: **to** ~ **to** aspirare

a

aspirin [ˈæsprɪn] n aspirina

ass [æs] n asino; (inf) scemo/a; (US: inf!) culo (!)

assailant [əˈseɪlənt] n assalitore m

assassinate [əˈsæsɪneɪt] vt assassinare; **assassination** [əsæsɪˈneɪʃən] n assassinio

assault [əˈsɔːlt] n (MIL) assalto; (gen: attack) aggressione f ♦ vt assaltare; aggredire; (sexually) violentare

assemble [əˈsɛmbl] vt riunire; (TECH) montare ♦ vi riunirsi

assembly [əˈsɛmblɪ] n (meeting) assemblea; (construction) montaggio; ~ **line** n catena di montaggio

assent [əˈsɛnt] n assenso, consenso

assert [əˈsɜːt] vt asserire; (insist on) far valere

assess [əˈsɛs] vt valutare; ~**ment** n valutazione f

asset [ˈæsɛt] n vantaggio; ~s npl (FINANCE: of individual) beni mpl; (: of company) attivo

assign [əˈsaɪn] vt: **to ~** (**to**) (task) assegnare (a); (resources) riservare (a); (cause, meaning) attribuire (a); **to ~ a date to sth** fissare la data di qc; ~**ment** n compito

assist [əˈsɪst] vt assistere, aiutare; ~**ance** n assistenza, aiuto; ~**ant** n assistente m/f; (BRIT: also: shop ~ant) commesso/a

associate [adj, n əˈsəʊʃɪɪt, vb əˈsəʊʃɪeɪt] adj associato(a); (member) aggiunto(a) ♦ n collega m/f ♦ vt associare ♦ vi: **to ~ with sb** frequentare qn

association [əsəʊsɪˈeɪʃən] n associazione f

assorted [əˈsɔːtɪd] adj assortito(a)

assortment [əˈsɔːtmənt] n assortimento

assume [əˈsjuːm] vt supporre; (responsibilities etc) assumere; (attitude, name) prendere; ~**d name** n nome m falso

assumption [əˈsʌmpʃən] n supposizione f, ipotesi f inv; (of power) as-

sunzione f

assurance [əˈʃʊərəns] n assicurazione f; (self-confidence) fiducia in se stesso

assure [əˈʃʊə*] vt assicurare

asthma [ˈæsmə] n asma

astonish [əˈstɒnɪʃ] vt stupire; ~**ment** n stupore m

astound [əˈstaʊnd] vt sbalordire

astray [əˈstreɪ] adv: **to go** ~ smarrirsi; **to lead** ~ portare sulla cattiva strada

astride [əˈstraɪd] prep a cavalcioni di

astrology [əsˈtrɒlədʒɪ] n astrologia

astronaut [ˈæstrənɔːt] n astronauta m/f

astronomy [əsˈtrɒnəmɪ] n astronomia

astute [əsˈtjuːt] adj astuto(a)

asylum [əˈsaɪləm] n asilo; (building) manicomio

KEYWORD

---

at [æt] prep **1** (referring to position, direction) a; ~ **the top** in cima; ~ **the desk** al banco, alla scrivania; ~ **home/school** a casa/scuola; ~ **the baker's** dal panettiere; **to look** ~ **sth** guardare qc; **to throw sth** ~ **sb** lanciare qc a qn

2 (referring to time) a; ~ **4 o'clock** alle 4; ~ **night** di notte; ~ **Christmas** a Natale; ~ **times** a volte

3 (referring to rates, speed etc) a; **£1 a kilo** a 1 sterlina al chilo; **two** ~ **a time** due alla volta, due per volta; ~ **50 km/h** a 50 km/h

4 (referring to manner): ~ **a stroke** d'un solo colpo; ~ **peace** in pace

5 (referring to activity): **to be** ~ **work** essere al lavoro; **to play** ~ **cowboys** giocare ai cowboy; **to be good** ~ **sth/doing sth** essere bravo in qc/a fare qc

6 (referring to cause): **shocked/surprised/annoyed** ~ **sth** colpito da/sorpreso da/arrabbiato per qc; **I went** ~ **his suggestion** ci sono andato dietro suo consiglio

ate [eɪt] *pt of* eat

atheist ['eɪθɪɪst] *n* ateo/a

Athens ['æθɪnz] *n* Atene *f*

athlete ['æθliːt] *n* atleta *m/f*

athletic [æθ'lɛtɪk] *adj* atletico(a); **~s** *n* atletica

Atlantic [ət'læntɪk] *adj* atlantico(a)
♦ *n*: the ~ (Ocean) l'Atlantico, l'Oceano Atlantico

atlas ['ætləs] *n* atlante *m*

atmosphere ['ætməsfɪə*] *n* atmosfera

atom ['ætəm] *n* atomo; **~ic** [ə'tɔmɪk] *adj* atomico(a); **~(ic) bomb** *n* bomba atomica; **~izer** ['ætəmaɪzə*] *n* atomizzatore *m*

atone [ə'təun] *vi*: to ~ for espiare

atrocious [ə'trəuʃəs] *adj* pessimo(a), atroce

attach [ə'tætʃ] *vt* attaccare; (document, letter) allegare; (importance etc) attribuire; to be **~ed to** sb/sth (to like) essere affezionato/a a qn/qc

attaché case [ə'tæʃeɪ-] *n* valigetta per documenti

attachment [ə'tætʃmənt] *n* (tool) accessorio; (love): ~ (to) affetto (per)

attack [ə'tæk] *vt* attaccare; (person) aggredire; (task etc) iniziare; (problem) affrontare ♦ *n* attacco; **heart** ~ infarto; **~er** *n* aggressore *m*

attain [ə'teɪn] *vt* (also: to ~ to) arrivare a, raggiungere; **~ments** *npl* cognizioni *fpl*

attempt [ə'tɛmpt] *n* tentativo ♦ *vt* tentare; to **make an** ~ **on sb's life** attentare alla vita di qn

attend [ə'tɛnd] *vt* frequentare; (meeting, talk) andare a; (patient) assistere; **to** ~ *vt fus* (needs, affairs etc) prendersi cura di; (customer) occuparsi di; **~ance** *n* (being present) presenza; (people present) gente *f* presente; **~ant** *n* custode *m/f*; persona di servizio ♦ *adj* concomitante

attention [ə'tɛnʃən] *n* attenzione *f* ♦ *excl* (MIL) attenti!; **for the** ~ **of** (ADMIN) per l'attenzione di

attentive [ə'tɛntɪv] *adj* attento(a);

(kind) premuroso(a)

attic ['ætɪk] *n* soffitta

attitude ['ætɪtjuːd] *n* atteggiamento; posa

attorney [ə'tɜːnɪ] *n* (lawyer) avvocato; (having proxy) mandatario; **A~ General** *n* (BRIT) Procuratore *m* Generale; (US) Ministro della Giustizia

attract [ə'trækt] *vt* attirare; **~ion** [ə'trækʃən] *n* (gen pl: pleasant things) attrattiva; (PHYSICS, fig: towards sth) attrazione *f*; **~ive** *adj* attraente

attribute [n 'ætrɪbjuːt, vb ə'trɪbjuːt] *n* attributo ♦ *vt*: to ~ **sth to** attribuire qc a

attrition [ə'trɪʃən] *n*: **war of** ~ guerra di logoramento

aubergine ['əubəʒiːn] *n* melanzana

auburn ['ɔːbən] *adj* tizianesco(a)

auction ['ɔːkʃən] *n* (also: sale by ~) asta ♦ *vt* (also: to sell by ~) vendere all'asta; (also: to put up for ~) mettere all'asta; **~eer** [-'nɪə*] *n* banditore *m*

audible ['ɔːdɪbl] *adj* udibile

audience ['ɔːdɪəns] *n* (people) pubblico; spettatori *mpl*; ascoltatori *mpl*; (interview) udienza

audio-typist ['ɔːdɪəu'taɪpɪst] *n* dattilografo/a che trascrive da nastro

audio-visual [ɔːdɪəu'vɪzjuəl] *adj* audiovisivo(a); ~ **aid** *n* sussidio audiovisivo

audit ['ɔːdɪt] *vt* rivedere, verificare

audition [ɔː'dɪʃən] *n* audizione *f*

auditor ['ɔːdɪtə*] *n* revisore *m*

augment [ɔːg'mɛnt] *vt, vi* aumentare

augur ['ɔːgə*] *vi*: **it ~s well** promette bene

August ['ɔːgəst] *n* agosto

aunt [ɑːnt] *n* zia; **~ie** *n* zietta; **~y** *n* zietta

au pair ['əu'pɛə*] *n* (also: ~ **girl**) (ragazza *f*) alla pari *inv*

aura ['ɔːrə] *n* aura

auspicious [ɔːs'pɪʃəs] *adj* propizio(a)

austerity [ɔs'tɛrɪtɪ] n austerità

Australia [ɔs'treɪlɪə] n Australia; **~n**
adj, n australiano(a)

Austria ['ɒstrɪə] n Austria; **~n** adj,
n austriaco(a)

authentic [ɔː'θɛntɪk] adj autenti-
co(a)

author ['ɔːθə*] n autore/trice

authoritarian [ɔːθɔrɪ'tɛərɪən] adj
autoritario(a)

authoritative [ɔː'θɔrɪtətɪv] adj (account etc) autorevole; (manner) au-
toritario(a)

authority [ɔː'θɔrɪtɪ] n autorità f inv;
(permission) autorizzazione f; **the
authorities** npl (government etc) le
autorità

authorize ['ɔːθəraɪz] vt autorizzare

auto ['ɔːtəʊ] (US) n auto f inv

autobiography [ɔːtəbaɪ'ɒɡrəfɪ] n
autobiografia

autograph ['ɔːtəɡrɑːf] n autografo ♦
vt firmare

automata [ɔː'tɒmətə] npl of automaton

automatic [ɔːtə'mætɪk] adj automa-
tico(a) ♦ n (gun) arma automatica;
(washing machine) lavatrice f automatica; (car) automobile f con cambio automatico; **~ally** adv automati-
camente

automation [ɔːtə'meɪʃən] n automazione f

automaton [ɔː'tɒmətən] (pl automata) n automa m

automobile ['ɔːtəməbiːl] (US) n automobile f

autonomy [ɔː'tɒnəmɪ] n autonomia

autumn ['ɔːtəm] n autunno

auxiliary [ɔːɡ'zɪlɪərɪ] adj ausilia-
rio(a) ♦ n ausiliare m/f

Av. abbr = avenue

avail [ə'veɪl] vt: to ~ o.s. of servirsi
di; approfittarsi di ♦ n: to no ~ inutilmente

available [ə'veɪləbl] adj disponibile

avalanche ['ævəlɑːnʃ] n valanga

avant-garde ['ævɑŋ'ɡɑːd] adj d'avanguardia

Ave. abbr = avenue

avenge [ə'vɛndʒ] vt vendicare

avenue ['ævənjuː] n viale m; (fig)
strada, via

average ['ævərɪdʒ] n media ♦ adj
medio(a) ♦ vt (a certain figure) fare
di or in media; **on ~** in media; **~**
out vi: **to ~ out at** aggirarsi in media su, essere in media di

averse [ə'vɜːs] adj: **to be ~ to sth/**
doing essere contrario a qc/a fare

avert [ə'vɜːt] vt (danger) evitare, prevenire;
(one's eyes) distogliere

aviary ['eɪvɪərɪ] n voliera, uccelliera

avid ['ævɪd] adj (supporter etc) acca-
nito(a)

avocado [ævə'kɑːdəʊ] n (also:
BRIT: ~ pear) avocado m inv

avoid [ə'vɔɪd] vt evitare

avuncular [ə'vʌŋkjʊlə*] adj pater-
no(a)

await [ə'weɪt] vt aspettare

awake [ə'weɪk] (pt awoke, pp awok-
en, awaked) adj sveglio(a) ♦ vt svegliare ♦ vi svegliarsi; **~ning**
[ə'weɪknɪŋ] n risveglio

award [ə'wɔːd] n premio; (LAW) risarcimento ♦ vt assegnare; (LAW:
damages) accordare

aware [ə'wɛə*] adj: **~ of** (conscious)
conscio(a) di; (informed) informa-
to(a) di; **to become ~ of** accorgersi
di; **~ness** n consapevolezza

awash [ə'wɒʃ] adj: **~ (with)** inonda-
to(a) (da)

away [ə'weɪ] adj, adv via; lonta-
no(a); **two kilometres ~** a due chilometri di distanza; **two hours ~ by**
car a due ore di distanza in macchina; **the holiday was two weeks ~**
mancavano due settimane alle vacanze; **he's ~ for a week** è andato via
per una settimana; **to take ~** togliere; **to work away/pedalling** etc
~ la particella indica la continuità e
l'energia dell'azione: **lavorava/peda-**
lava etc più che poteva; **to fade/**
wither etc ~ la particella rinforza
l'idea della diminuzione; **~ game** n
(SPORT) partita fuori casa

awe [ɔː] n timore m; **~-inspiring**

imponente; ~**some** adj imponente

awful ['ɔːfəl] adj terribile; **an ~ lot of** un mucchio di; **~ly** adv (very) terribilmente

awhile [ə'waɪl] adv (per) un po'

awkward ['ɔːkwəd] adj (clumsy) goffo(a); (inconvenient) scomodo(a); (embarrassing) imbarazzante

awning ['ɔːnɪŋ] n (of shop, hotel etc) tenda

awoke [ə'wəuk] pt of awake

awoken [ə'wəukn] pp of awake

awry [ə'raɪ] adv di traverso; **to go ~** andare a monte

axe [æks] (US **ax**) n scure f ♦ vt (project etc) abolire; (jobs) sopprimere

axes ['æksiːz] npl of axis

axis ['æksɪs] (pl **axes**) n asse m

axle ['æksl] n (also: ~-tree) asse m

ay(e) [aɪ] excl (yes) sì

B

B [biː] n (MUS) si m

B.A. n abbr = Bachelor of Arts

babble ['bæbl] vi (person, voices) farfugliare; (brook) gorgogliare

baby ['beɪbɪ] n bambino/a; ~ **carriage** (US) n carrozzina; ~**-sit** vi fare il (or la) babysitter; ~**-sitter** n baby-sitter m/f inv

bachelor ['bætʃələ*] n scapolo; **B~ of Arts/Science** n = laureato/a in lettere/scienze

back [bæk] n (of person, horse) dorso, schiena; (as opposed to front) dietro; (of hand) dorso; (of train) coda; (of chair) schienale m; (of page) rovescio; (of book) retro; (FOOTBALL) difensore m ♦ vt (candidate: also: ~ **up**) appoggiare; (horse: at races) puntare su; (car) guidare a marcia indietro ♦ vi indietreggiare; (car etc) fare marcia indietro ♦ cpd posteriore, di dietro; (AUT: seat, wheels) posteriore ♦ adv (not forward) indietro; (returned): **he's ~** è tornato; **he ran ~** tornò indietro di

corsa; (restitution): **throw the ball ~** ritira la palla; **can I have it ~?** posso riaverlo?; (again): **he called ~** ha richiamato; ~ **down** vi fare marcia indietro; ~ **out** vi (of promise) tirarsi indietro; ~ **up** vt (support) appoggiare, sostenere; (COMPUT) fare una copia di riserva di; ~**bencher** (BRIT) n membro del Parlamento senza potere amministrativo; ~**bone** n spina dorsale; ~**cloth** n scena di sfondo; ~**date** vt (letter) retrodatare; ~**dated pay rise** aumento retroattivo; ~**drop** n = ~**cloth**; ~**fire** vi (AUT) dar ritorni di fiamma; (plans) fallire; ~**ground** n sfondo; (of events) background m inv; (basic knowledge) base f; (experience) esperienza; **family** ~**ground** ambiente m familiare; ~**hand** n (TENNIS: also: ~**hand stroke**) rovescio; ~**handed** adj (fig) ambiguo(a); ~**hander** (BRIT) n (bribe) bustarella; ~**ing** n (fig) appoggio; ~**lash** n contraccolpo, ripercussione f; ~**log** n: ~**log of work** lavoro arretrato; ~ **number** n (of magazine etc) numero arretrato; ~**pack** n zaino; ~ **pay** n arretrato di paga; ~**payments** npl arretrati mpl; ~**side** (inf) n sedere m; ~**stage** adv nel retroscena; ~**stroke** n nuoto sul dorso; ~**up** adj (train, plane) supplementare; (COMPUT) di riserva ♦ n (support) appoggio, sostegno; (also: ~**up file**) file m inv di riserva; ~**ward** adj (movement) indietro inv; (person) tardivo(a); (country) arretrato(a); ~**wards** adv indietro; (fall, walk) all'indietro; ~**water** n (fig) posto morto; ~**yard** n cortile m dietro la casa

bacon ['beɪkən] n pancetta

bad [bæd] adj cattivo(a); (accident, injury) brutto(a); (meat, food) andato(a) a male; **his ~ leg** la sua gamba malata; **to go ~** andare a male

bade [bæd] pt of bid

badge [bædʒ] n insegna; (of police-

badger 19 bank

man) stemma *m*

badger ['bædʒə*] *n* tasso

badly ['bædlɪ] *adv* (*work, dress etc*) male; ~ **wounded** gravemente ferito; **he needs it** ~ ne ha un gran bisogno; ~ **off** *adj* povero(a)

badminton ['bædmɪntən] *n* badminton *m*

bad-tempered ['bæd'tɛmpəd] *adj* irritabile; di malumore

baffle ['bæfl] *vt* (*puzzle*) confondere

bag [bæg] *n* sacco; (*handbag etc*) borsa; ~**s of** (*inf: lots of*) un sacco di; ~**gage** *n* bagagli *mpl*; ~**gy** *adj* largo(a), sformato(a); ~**pipes** *npl* cornamusa

bail [beɪl] *n* cauzione *f* ♦ *vt* (*prisoner: also: grant* ~ *to*) concedere la libertà provvisoria su cauzione a; (*boat: also* ~ *out*) aggottare; **on** ~ in libertà provvisoria su cauzione; ~ **out** *vt* (*prisoner*) ottenere la libertà provvisoria su cauzione di; *see also* **bale**

bailiff ['beɪlɪf] *n* (*LAW: BRIT*) ufficiale *m* giudiziario; (: *US*) usciere *m*

bait [beɪt] *n* esca ♦ *vt* (*hook*) innescare; (*trap*) munire di esca; (*fig*) tormentare

bake [beɪk] *vt* cuocere al forno ♦ *vi* cuocersi al forno; ~**d beans** *npl* fagioli *mpl* in salsa di pomodoro; ~**r** *n* fornaio/a, panettiere/a; ~**ry** *n* panetteria; **baking** *n* cottura (al forno); **baking powder** *n* lievito in polvere

balance ['bæləns] *n* equilibrio; (*COMM: sum*) bilancio; (*remainder*) resto; (*scales*) bilancia ♦ *vt* tenere in equilibrio; (*budget*) far quadrare; (*account*) pareggiare; (*compensate*) contrappesare; ~ **of trade/payments** bilancia commerciale/dei pagamenti; ~**d** *adj* (*personality, diet*) equilibrato(a); ~ **sheet** *n* bilancio

balcony ['bælkənɪ] *n* balcone *m*; (*in theatre*) balconata

bald [bɔːld] *adj* calvo(a); (*tyre*) liscio(a)

bale [beɪl] *n* balla; ~ **out** *vi* (*of a*

plane) gettarsi col paracadute

baleful ['beɪlful] *adj* funesto(a)

ball [bɔːl] *n* palla; (*football*) pallone *m*; (*for golf*) pallina; (*of wool, string*) gomitolo; (*dance*) ballo; **to play** ~ (*fig*) stare al gioco

ballast ['bæləst] *n* zavorra

ball bearings *npl* cuscinetti a sfere

ballerina [bælə'riːnə] *n* ballerina

ballet ['bæleɪ] *n* balletto; ~ **dancer** *n* ballerino/a classico(a)

balloon [bə'luːn] *n* pallone *m*

ballot paper ['bælət-] *n* scheda

ball-point pen *n* penna a sfera

ballroom ['bɔːlrum] *n* sala da ballo

balm [baːm] *n* balsamo

ban [bæn] *n* interdizione *f* ♦ *vt* interdire

banana [bə'nɑːnə] *n* banana

band [bænd] *n* banda; (*at a dance*) orchestra; (*MIL*) fanfara; ~ **together** *vi* collegarsi

bandage ['bændɪdʒ] *n* benda, fascia

bandaid ['bændeɪd] ® (*US*) *n* cerotto

bandwagon ['bændwægən] *n:* **to jump on the** ~ (*fig*) seguire la corrente

bandy ['bændɪ] *vt* (*jokes, insults*) scambiare

bandy-legged [-'lɛgɪd] *adj* dalle gambe storte

bang [bæŋ] *n* (*of door*) lo sbattere; (*of gun, blow*) colpo ♦ *vt* battere (violentemente); (*door*) sbattere ♦ *vi* scoppiare; sbattere

Bangladesh [bɑːŋglə'dɛʃ] *n* Bangladesh *m*

bangle ['bæŋgl] *n* braccialetto

bangs [bæŋz] (*US*) *npl* (*fringe*) frangia, frangetta

banish ['bænɪʃ] *vt* bandire

banister(s) ['bænɪstə(z)] *n*(*pl*) ringhiera

bank [bæŋk] *n* banca, banco; (*of river, lake*) riva, sponda; (*of earth*) banco ♦ *vi* (*AVIAT*) inclinarsi in virata; ~ **on** *vt fus* contare su; ~ **account** *n* conto in banca; ~ **card** *n* carta assegni; ~**er** *n* banchiere *m*; ~**er's card** (*BRIT*) *n* = ~ **card**;

B~ **holiday** (BRIT) n giorno di festa (in cui le banche sono chiuse); ~**ing** n attività bancaria; professione f di banchiere; ~**note** n banconota; ~ **rate** n tasso bancario

bankrupt ['bæŋkrʌpt] adj fallito(a); to go ~ fallire; ~**cy** n fallimento

bank statement n estratto conto

banner ['bænə*] n striscione m

banns [bænz] npl pubblicazioni fpl di matrimonio

baptism ['bæptɪzəm] n battesimo

bar [ba:*] n (place) bar m inv; (counter) banco; (rod) barra; (of window etc) sbarra; (of chocolate) tavoletta; (fig) ostacolo, restrizione f; (MUS) battuta ♦ vt (road, window) sbarrare; (person) escludere; (activity) interdire; ~ of soap saponetta; the B~ (LAW) l'Ordine m degli avvocati; **behind** ~s (prisoner) dietro le sbarre; ~ **none** senza eccezione

barbaric [ba:'bærik] adj barbarico(a)

barbecue ['ba:bɪkju:] n barbecue m inv

barbed wire ['ba:bd-] n filo spinato

barber ['ba:bə*] n barbiere m

bar code n (on goods) codice m a barre

bare [bɛə*] adj nudo(a) ♦ vt scoprire, denudare; (teeth) mostrare; **the ~ necessities** lo stretto necessario; ~**back** adv senza sella; ~**faced** adj sfacciato(a); ~**foot** adj, adv scalzo(a); ~**ly** adv appena

bargain ['ba:gɪn] n (transaction) contratto; (good buy) affare m ♦ vi trattare; **into the** ~ per giunta; ~ **for** vt fus: **he got more than he ~ed for** gli è andata peggio di quel che si aspettava

barge [ba:dʒ] n chiatta; ~ **in** vi (walk in) piombare dentro; (interrupt talk) intromettersi a sproposito

bark [ba:k] n (of tree) corteccia; (of dog) abbaio ♦ vi abbaiare

barley ['ba:li] n orzo

barmaid ['ba:meɪd] n cameriera al banco

barman ['ba:mən] n barista m

barn [ba:n] n granaio

barometer [bə'rɒmɪtə*] n barometro

baron ['bærən] n barone m; ~**ess** n baronessa

barracks ['bærəks] npl caserma

barrage ['bæra:ʒ] n (MIL, dam) sbarramento; (fig) fiume m

barrel ['bærəl] n barile m; (of gun) canna

barren ['bærən] adj sterile; (soil) arido(a)

barricade [bærɪ'keɪd] n barricata

barrier ['bærɪə*] n barriera

barring ['ba:rɪŋ] prep salvo

barrister ['bærɪstə*] (BRIT) n avvocato/essa (con diritto di parlare davanti a tutte le corti)

barrow ['bærəu] n (cart) carriola

bartender ['ba:tendə*] (US) n barista m

barter ['ba:tə*] vt: **to** ~ **sth for** barattare qc con

base [beɪs] n base f ♦ vt: **to** ~ **sth on** basare qc su ♦ adj vile

baseball ['beɪsbɔ:l] n baseball m

basement ['beɪsmənt] n seminterrato; (of shop) interrato

bases[1] ['beɪsi:z] npl of **base**

bases[2] ['beɪsɪz] npl of **basis**

bash [bæʃ] (inf) vt picchiare

bashful ['bæʃful] adj timido(a)

basic ['beɪsɪk] adj rudimentale; essenziale; ~**ally** [-li] adv fondamentalmente; sostanzialmente; ~**s** npl: **the** ~**s** l'essenziale m

basil ['bæzl] n basilico

basin ['beɪsn] n (vessel, also GEO) bacino; (also: wash~) lavabo

basis ['beɪsɪs] (pl **bases**) n base f; **on a part-time** ~ part-time; **on a trial** ~ in prova

bask [ba:sk] vi: **to** ~ **in the sun** crogiolarsi al sole

basket ['ba:skɪt] n cesta; (smaller) cestino; (with handle) paniere m; ~**ball** n pallacanestro f

bass [beɪs] n (MUS) basso

bassoon [bə'su:n] n fagotto

bastard ['bɑ:stəd] n bastardo/a; (infl!) stronzo (!)

bat [bæt] n pipistrello; (for baseball etc) mazza; (BRIT: for table tennis) racchetta ♦ vt: he didn't ~ an eyelid non batté ciglio

batch [bætʃ] n (of bread) infornata; (of papers) cumulo

bated ['beɪtɪd] adj: with ~ breath col fiato sospeso

bath [bɑ:θ] n bagno; (bathtub) vasca da bagno ♦ vt far fare il bagno a; to have a ~ fare un bagno; see also baths

bathe [beɪð] vi fare il bagno ♦ vt (wound) lavare; ~r n bagnante m/f

bathing ['beɪðɪŋ] n bagni mpl; ~ cap n cuffia da bagno; ~ costume (US = suit) n costume m da bagno

bathrobe ['bɑ:θrəub] n accappatoio

bathroom ['bɑ:θrum] n stanza da bagno

baths [bɑ:ðz] npl bagni mpl pubblici

bath towel n asciugamano da bagno

baton ['bætən] n (MUS) bacchetta; (ATHLETICS) testimone m; (club) manganello

batter ['bætə*] vt battere ♦ n pastetta; ~ed adj (hat) sformato/a; (pan) ammaccato/a

battery ['bætərɪ] n batteria; (of torch) pila

battle ['bætl] n battaglia ♦ vi battagliare, lottare; ~field n campo di battaglia; ~ship n nave f da guerra

bawdy ['bɔ:dɪ] adj piccante

bawl [bɔ:l] vi urlare

bay [beɪ] n (of sea) baia; to hold sb at ~ tenere qn a bada; ~ leaf n foglia d'alloro; ~ window n bovindo

bazaar [bə'zɑ:*] n bazar m inv; vendita di beneficenza

B. & B. abbr = bed and breakfast

BBC n abbr (= British Broadcasting Corporation) rete nazionale di radiotelevisione in Gran Bretagna

B.C. adv abbr (= before Christ) a.C

be [bi:] (pt was, were, pp been) aux vb 1 (with present participle: forming continuous tenses): what are you doing? che fa?, che sta facendo?; they're coming tomorrow vengono domani; I've been waiting for her for hours sono ore che l'aspetto

2 (with pp: forming passives) essere; to ~ killed essere or venire ucciso(a); the box had been opened la scatola era stata aperta; the thief was nowhere to ~ seen il ladro non si trovava da nessuna parte

3 (in tag questions): it was fun, wasn't it? è stato divertente, no?; he's good-looking, isn't he? è un bell'uomo, vero?; she's back, is she? così è tornata, eh?

4 (+ to + infinitive): the house is to ~ sold abbiamo (or hanno etc) intenzione di vendere casa; you're to ~ congratulated for all your work dovremo farvi i complimenti per tutto il vostro lavoro; he's not to open it non deve aprirlo

♦ vb + complement 1 (gen) essere; I'm English sono inglese; I'm tired sono stanco(a); I'm hot/cold ho caldo/freddo; he's a doctor è medico; 2 and 2 are 4 2 più 2 fa 4; ~ careful! sta attento(a)!; ~ good! sii buono/a

2 (of health): how are you? come sta?; he's very ill sta molto male

3 (of age): how old are you? quanti anni hai?; I'm sixteen (years old) ho sedici anni

4 (cost): costare; how much was the meal? quant'era or quanto costava il pranzo?; that'll ~ £5, please (fig) 5 sterline, per favore

♦ vi (exist, occur etc) essere, esistere; the best singer that ever was il migliore cantante mai esistito or di tutti tempi; ~ that as it may comunque sia, sia come sia; so ~ it

sia pure, e sia
2 (*referring to place*) essere, trovarsi; **I won't ~ here tomorrow** non ci sarò domani; **Edinburgh is in Scotland** Edimburgo si trova in Scozia
3 (*referring to movement*): **where have you been?** dov'è stato?; **I've been to China** sono stato in Cina
♦ *impers vb* **1** (*referring to time, distance*) essere; **it's 5 o'clock** sono le 5; **it's the 28th of April** è il 28 aprile; **it's 10 km to the village** di qui al paese sono 10 km
2 (*referring to the weather*) fare; **it's too hot/cold** fa troppo caldo/freddo; **it's windy** c'è vento
3 (*emphatic*): **it's me** sono io; **it was Maria who paid the bill** è stata Maria che ha pagato il conto

beach [biːtʃ] *n* spiaggia ♦ *vt* tirare in secco
beacon ['biːkən] *n* (*lighthouse*) faro; (*marker*) segnale *m*
bead [biːd] *n* perlina
beak [biːk] *n* becco
beaker ['biːkə'] *n* coppa
beam [biːm] *n* trave *f*; (*of light*) raggio ♦ *vi* brillare
bean [biːn] *n* fagiolo; (*of coffee*) chicco; **runner ~** fagiolino; **broad ~** fava; **~sprouts** *npl* germogli *mpl* di soia
bear [bɛə'] *n* (*pt* **bore**, *pp* **borne**) *n* orso ♦ *vt* portare; (*endure*) sopportare; (*produce*) generare ♦ *vi*: **to ~ right/left** piegare a destra/sinistra; **~ out** *vt* (*suspicions*) confermare, convalidare; (*person*) dare il proprio appoggio a; **~ up** *vi* (*person*) fare buon viso a cattiva sorte
beard [bɪəd] *n* barba
bearer ['bɛərə'] *n* portatore *m*
bearing ['bɛərɪŋ] *n* portamento; (*connection*) rapporto; **~s** *npl* (*also*: **ball ~s**) cuscinetti *mpl* a sfere; **to take a ~** fare un rilevamento; **to find one's ~s** orientarsi
beast [biːst] *n* bestia; **~ly** *adj* meschino(a); (*weather*) da cani

beat [biːt] (*pt* **beat**, *pp* **beaten**) *n* colpo; (*of heart*) battito; (*MUS*) tempo; battuta; (*of policeman*) giro ♦ *vt* battere; (*eggs, cream*) sbattere ♦ *vi* battere; **off the ~en track** fuori mano; **~ it!** (*inf*) fila!, fuori dai piedi!; **~ off** *vt* respingere; **~ up** *vt* (*person*) picchiare; (*eggs*) sbattere; **beaten** *pp* of **beat**; **~ing** *n* bastonata
beautiful ['bjuːtɪful] *adj* bello(a); **~ly** *adv* splendidamente
beauty ['bjuːtɪ] *n* bellezza; **~ salon** *n* istituto di bellezza; **~ spot** (*BRIT*) *n* (*TOURISM*) luogo pittoresco
beaver ['biːvə'] *n* castoro
became [bɪ'keɪm] *pt* of **become**
because [bɪ'kɔz] *conj* perché; **~ of** a causa di
beck [bɛk] *n*: **to be at sb's ~ and call** essere a completa disposizione di qn
beckon ['bɛkən] *vt* (*also*: **~ to**) chiamare con un cenno
become [bɪ'kʌm] (*irreg: like* **come**) *vt* diventare; **to ~ fat/thin** ingrassarsi/dimagrire
becoming [bɪ'kʌmɪŋ] *adj* (*behaviour*) che si conviene; (*clothes*) grazioso(a)
bed [bɛd] *n* letto; (*of flowers*) aiuola; (*of coal, clay*) strato; **single/double ~** letto a una piazza/a due piazze o matrimoniale; **~ and breakfast** *n* (*place*) ≈ pensione *f* familiare; (*terms*) camera con colazione; **~clothes** *npl* biancheria e coperte *fpl* da letto; **~ding** *n* coperte e lenzuola *fpl*
bedlam ['bɛdləm] *n* baraonda
bedraggled [bɪ'drægld] *adj* fradicio(a)
bed: **~ridden** *adj* costretto(a) a letto; **~room** *n* camera da letto; **~side** *n*: **at sb's ~side** al capezzale di qn; **~sit(ter)** (*BRIT*) *n* monolocale *m*; **~spread** *n* copriletto; **~time** *n*: **it's ~time** è ora di andare a letto
bee [biː] *n* ape *f*

beech [biːtʃ] n faggio

beef [biːf] n manzo; **roast** ~ arrosto di manzo; **~burger** n hamburger m inv; **B~eater** n guardia della Torre di Londra

beehive ['biːhaɪv] n alveare m

beeline ['biːlaɪn] n: **to make a** ~ **for** buttarsi a capo fitto verso

been [biːn] pp of **be**

beer [bɪə*] n birra

beetle ['biːtl] n scarafaggio; coleottero

beetroot ['biːtruːt] (BRIT) n barbabietola

before [bɪ'fɔː*] prep (in time) prima di; (in space) davanti a ♦ conj prima che (+ sub); prima di ♦ adv prima; ~ **going** prima di andare; ~ **she goes** prima che vada; **the week** ~ la settimana prima; **I've seen it** ~ l'ho già visto; **I've never seen it** ~ è la prima volta che lo vedo; **~hand** adv in anticipo

beg [bɛg] vi chiedere l'elemosina ♦ vt (also: ~ for) chiedere in elemosina; (: favour) chiedere; **to** ~ **sb to do** pregare qn di fare

began [bɪ'gæn] pt of **begin**

beggar ['bɛgə*] n mendicante m/f

begin [bɪ'gɪn] (pt **began**, pp **begun**) vt, vi cominciare; **to** ~ **doing** or **to do sth** incominciare or iniziare a fare qc; **~ner** n principiante m/f; **~ning** n inizio, principio

begun [bɪ'gʌn] pp of **begin**

behalf [bɪ'hɑːf] n: **on** ~ **of** per conto di; a nome di

behave [bɪ'heɪv] vi comportarsi; (well: also: ~ o.s.) comportarsi bene

behaviour [bɪ'heɪvjə*] (US **behavior**) n comportamento, condotta

behead [bɪ'hɛd] vt decapitare

beheld [bɪ'hɛld] pt, pp of **behold**

behind [bɪ'haɪnd] prep dietro; (followed by pronoun) dietro di; (time) in ritardo con ♦ adv dietro; (leave, stay) indietro ♦ n didietro; **to be** ~ (schedule) essere in ritardo rispetto al programma; ~ **the scenes** (fig) dietro le quinte

behold [bɪ'həuld] (irreg: like **hold**) vt vedere, scorgere

beige [beɪʒ] adj beige inv

Beijing [beɪ'dʒɪŋ] n Pechino f

being ['biːɪŋ] n essere m

belated [bɪ'leɪtɪd] adj tardo(a)

belch [bɛltʃ] vi ruttare ♦ vt (gen: ~ out: smoke etc) eruttare

belfry ['bɛlfrɪ] n campanile m

Belgian ['bɛldʒən] adj, a belga m/f

Belgium ['bɛldʒəm] n Belgio

belie [bɪ'laɪ] vt smentire

belief [bɪ'liːf] n (opinion) opinione f, convinzione f; (trust, faith) fede f

believe [bɪ'liːv] vt, vi credere; **to** ~ **in** (God) credere in; (ghosts) credere a; (method) avere fiducia in; **~r** n (REL) credente m/f; (in idea, activity): **to be a** ~**r in** credere in

belittle [bɪ'lɪtl] vt sminuire

bell [bɛl] n campana; (small, on door, electric) campanello

belligerent [bɪ'lɪdʒərənt] adj bellicoso(a)

bellow ['bɛləu] vi muggire

bellows ['bɛləuz] npl soffietto

belly ['bɛlɪ] n pancia

belong [bɪ'lɔŋ] vi: **to** ~ **to** appartenere a; (club etc) essere socio di; **this book** ~**s here** questo libro va qui; **~ings** npl cose fpl, roba

beloved [bɪ'lʌvɪd] adj adorato(a)

below [bɪ'ləu] prep sotto, al di sotto di ♦ adv sotto, di sotto; giù; **see** ~ vedi sotto or oltre

belt [bɛlt] n cintura; (TECH) cinghia ♦ vt (thrash) picchiare ♦ vi (inf) filarsela; **~way** (US) n (AUT: ring road) circonvallazione f; (: motorway) autostrada

bemused [bɪ'mjuːzd] adj perplesso(a), stupito(a)

bench [bɛntʃ] n panca; (in workshop, POL) banco; **the B~** (LAW) la Corte

bend [bɛnd] (pt, pp **bent**) vt curvare; (leg, arm) piegare ♦ vi curvarsi; piegarsi ♦ n (BRIT: in road) curva; (in pipe, river) gomito; ~ **down** vi chinarsi; ~ **over** vi piegarsi

beneath [bɪ'ni:θ] prep sotto, al di sotto di; (*unworthy of*) indegno(a) di ♦ adv sotto, di sotto

benefactor ['bɛnɪfæktə*] n benefattore m

beneficial [bɛnɪ'fɪʃəl] adj che fa bene; vantaggioso(a)

benefit ['bɛnɪfɪt] n beneficio, vantaggio; (*allowance of money*) indennità f inv ♦ vt far bene a ♦ vi: **he'll ~ from it** ne trarrà beneficio or profitto

benevolent [bɪ'nɛvələnt] adj benevolo(a)

benign [bɪ'naɪn] adj (*person, smile*) benevolo(a); (MED) benigno(a)

bent [bɛnt] pt, pp of **bend** ♦ n inclinazione f ♦ adj (inf: *dishonest*) losco(a); **to be ~ on** essere deciso(a) a

bequest [bɪ'kwɛst] n lascito

bereaved [bɪ'ri:vd] n: **the ~** i familiari in lutto

beret ['bɛreɪ] n berretto

berm [bə:m] (US) n (AUT) corsia d'emergenza

berry ['bɛrɪ] n bacca

berserk [bə'sə:k] adj: **to go ~** montare su tutte le furie

berth [bə:θ] n (*bed*) cuccetta; (*for ship*) ormeggio ♦ vi (*in harbour*) entrare in porto; (*at anchor*) gettare l'ancora

beseech [bɪ'si:tʃ] (pt, pp **besought**) vt implorare

beset [bɪ'sɛt] (pt, pp **beset**) vt assalire

beside [bɪ'saɪd] prep accanto a; **to be ~ o.s. (with anger)** essere fuori di sé (dalla rabbia); **that's ~ the point** non c'entra

besides [bɪ'saɪdz] adv inoltre, per di più ♦ prep oltre a; a parte

besiege [bɪ'si:dʒ] vt (*town*) assediare; (*fig*) tempestare

besought [bɪ'sɔ:t] pt, pp of **beseech**

best [bɛst] adj migliore ♦ adv meglio; **the ~ part of** (*quantity*) la maggior parte di; **at ~** tutt'al più; **to make the ~ of sth** cavare il mas-

glio possibile da qc; **to do one's ~** fare del proprio meglio; **to the ~ of my knowledge** per quel che ne so; **to the ~ of my ability** al massimo delle mie capacità; **~ man** n testimone m dello sposo

bestow [bɪ'stəu] vt accordare; (*title*) conferire

bet [bɛt] (pt, pp **bet** or **betted**) n scommessa ♦ vt, vi scommettere; **to ~ sb sth** scommettere qc con qn

betray [bɪ'treɪ] vt tradire; **~al** n tradimento

better ['bɛtə*] adj migliore ♦ adv meglio ♦ vt migliorare ♦ n: **to get the ~ of** avere la meglio su; **you had ~ do it** è meglio che lo faccia; **he thought ~ of it** cambiò idea; **to get ~** migliorare; **~ off** adj più ricco(a); (*fig*): **you'd be ~ off this way** starebbe meglio così

betting ['bɛtɪŋ] n scommesse fpl; **~ shop** (BRIT) n ufficio dell'allibratore

between [bɪ'twi:n] prep tra ♦ adv in mezzo, nel mezzo

beverage ['bɛvərɪdʒ] n bevanda

beware [bɪ'wɛə*] vt, vi: **to ~ (of)** stare attento(a) (a); **"~ of the dog"** "attenti al cane"

bewildered [bɪ'wɪldəd] adj sconcertato(a), confuso(a)

bewitching [bɪ'wɪtʃɪŋ] adj affascinante

beyond [bɪ'jɔnd] prep (*in space*) oltre; (*exceeding*) al di sopra di ♦ adv di là; **~ doubt** senza dubbio; **~ repair** irreparabile

bias ['baɪəs] n (*prejudice*) pregiudizio; (*preference*) preferenza; **~(s)ed** adj parziale

bib [bɪb] n bavaglino

Bible ['baɪbl] n Bibbia

bicarbonate of soda [baɪ'kɑ:bənɪt-] n bicarbonato (di sodio)

bicker ['bɪkə*] vi bisticciare

bicycle ['baɪsɪkl] n bicicletta

bid [bɪd] (pt **bade** or **bid**, pp **bidden** or **bid**) n offerta; (*attempt*) tentativo

♦ *vi* fare un'offerta ♦ *vt* fare un'offerta di; **to ~ sb good day** dire buon giorno a qn; **bidden** *pp of* **bid**; **~der** *n*: **the highest ~der** il maggior offerente; **~ding** *n* offerte *fpl*

bide [baɪd] *vt*: **to ~ one's time** aspettare il momento giusto

bifocals [baɪˈfəʊklz] *npl* occhiali *mpl* bifocali

big [bɪg] *adj* grande; grosso(a)

big dipper [-ˈdɪpə*] *n* montagne *fpl* russe, otto *m inv* volante

bigheaded [ˈbɪgˈhɛdɪd] *adj* presuntuoso(a)

bigot [ˈbɪgət] *n* persona gretta; **~ed** *adj* gretto(a); **~ry** *n* grettezza

big top *n* tendone *m* del circo

bike [baɪk] *n* bici *f inv*

bikini [bɪˈkiːnɪ] *n* bikini *m inv*

bilingual [baɪˈlɪŋgwəl] *adj* bilingue

bill [bɪl] *n* conto; (*POL*) atto; (*US: banknote*) banconota; (*of bird*) becco; (*of show*) locandina; **"post no ~s"** "divieto di affissione"; **to fit** or **fill the ~** (*fig*) fare al caso; **~board** *n* tabellone *m*

billet [ˈbɪlɪt] *n* alloggio

billfold [ˈbɪlfəʊld] (*US*) *n* portafoglio

billiards [ˈbɪljədz] *n* biliardo

billion [ˈbɪljən] *n* (*BRIT*) bilione *m*; (*US*) miliardo

bin [bɪn] *n* (*for coal, rubbish*) bidone *m*; (*for bread*) cassetta; (*dust~*) pattumiera; (*litter ~*) cestino

bind [baɪnd] (*pt, pp* **bound**) *vt* legare; (*oblige*) obbligare ♦ *n* (*inf*) scocciatura; **~ing** *adj* (*contract*) vincolante

binge [bɪndʒ] (*inf*) *n*: **to go on a ~** fare baldoria

bingo [ˈbɪngəʊ] *n* gioco simile alla tombola

binoculars [bɪˈnɔkjuləz] *npl* binocolo *m*

bio... [baɪə'...] *prefix*: **~chemistry** *n* biochimica; **~graphy** [baɪˈɔgrəfɪ] *n* biografia; **~logical** *adj* biologico(a); **~logy** [baɪˈɔlədʒɪ] *n* biologia

birch [bɜːtʃ] *n* betulla

bird [bɜːd] *n* uccello; (*BRIT: inf: girl*) bambola; **~'s eye view** *n* vista panoramica; **~ watcher** *n* ornitologo/a dilettante

Biro [ˈbaɪrəʊ] ® *n* biro *f inv* ®

birth [bɜːθ] *n* nascita; **to give ~ to** partorire; **~ certificate** *n* certificato di nascita; **~ control** *n* controllo delle nascite; contraccezione *f*; **~day** *n* compleanno ♦ *cpd* di compleanno; **~ rate** *n* indice *m* di natalità

biscuit [ˈbɪskɪt] (*BRIT*) *n* biscotto

bisect [baɪˈsɛkt] *vt* tagliare in due (parti)

bishop [ˈbɪʃəp] *n* vescovo

bit [bɪt] *pt of* **bite** ♦ *n* pezzo; (*COMPUT*) bit *m inv*; (*of horse*) morso; **a ~ of** un po' di; **a ~ mad** un po' matto; **~ by ~** a poco a poco

bitch [bɪtʃ] *n* (*dog*) cagna; (*inf!*) vacca

bite [baɪt] (*pt* **bit**, *pp* **bitten**) *vt, vi* mordere; (*subj: insect*) pungere ♦ *n* morso; (*insect ~*) puntura; (*mouthful*) boccone *m*; **let's have a ~** (**to eat**) mangiamo un boccone; **to ~ one's nails** mangiarsi le unghie; **bitten** [ˈbɪtn] *pp of* **bite**

bitter [ˈbɪtə*] *adj* amaro(a); (*wind, criticism*) pungente ♦ *n* (*BRIT: beer*) birra amara; gusto amaro; **~ness** *n* amarezza; gusto amaro

blab [blæb] *vi* parlare troppo

black [blæk] *adj* nero(a) ♦ *n* nero; (*person*): **B~** negro/a ♦ *vt* (*BRIT: INDUSTRY*) boicottare; **to give sb a ~ eye** fare un occhio nero a qn; **in the ~** (*bank account*) in attivo; **~ and blue** *adj* tutto(a) pesto(a); **~berry** *n* mora; **~bird** *n* merlo; **~board** *n* lavagna; **~currant** *n* ribes *m inv*; **~en** *vt* annerire; **~ ice** *n* strato trasparente di ghiaccio; **~leg** (*BRIT*) *n* crumiro; **~list** *n* lista nera; **~mail** *n* ricatto ♦ *vt* ricattare; **~ market** *n* mercato nero; **~out** *n* oscuramento; (*TV, RADIO*) interruzione *f* delle trasmissioni; (*fainting*) svenimento; **B~ Sea** *n*: **the B~ Sea** il Mar Nero; **~ sheep** *n* pecora nera; **~smith** *n* fabbro ferraio; ~ **spot** n (AUT) luogo famigerato per gli incidenti; (for unemployment etc) zona critica

bladder ['blædə*] n vescica

blade [bleɪd] n lama; (of oar) pala; ~ **of grass** filo d'erba

blame [bleɪm] n colpa ♦ vt: to ~ sb/sth for sth dare la colpa di qc a qn/qc; who's to ~? chi è colpevole?

bland [blænd] adj mite; (taste) blando(a)

blank [blæŋk] adj bianco(a); (look) distratto(a) ♦ n spazio vuoto; (cartridge) cartuccia a salve; ~ **cheque** n assegno in bianco

blanket ['blæŋkɪt] n coperta

blare [blɛə*] vi strombettare

blasphemy ['blæsfɪmɪ] n bestemmia

blast [blɑːst] n (of wind) raffica; (of bomb etc) esplosione f ♦ vt far saltare; ~**off** n (SPACE) lancio

blatant ['bleɪtənt] adj flagrante

blaze [bleɪz] n (fire) incendio; (fig) vampata; splendore m ♦ vi (fire) ardere, fiammeggiare; (guns) sparare senza sosta; (fig: eyes) ardere ♦ vt: to ~ **a trail** (fig) tracciare una via nuova; in **a** ~ **of publicity** circondato da grande pubblicità

blazer ['bleɪzə*] n blazer m inv

bleach [bliːtʃ] n (also: household ~) varechina ♦ vt (material) candeggiare; ~**ed** adj (hair) decolorato(a); ~**ers** (US) npl (SPORT) posti mpl di gradinata

bleak [bliːk] adj tetro(a)

bleary-eyed ['blɪərɪ'aɪd] adj dagli occhi offuscati

bleat [bliːt] vi belare

bled [bled] pt, pp of **bleed**

bleed [bliːd] (pt, pp bled) vi sanguinare; **my nose is** ~**ing** mi viene fuori sangue dal naso

bleeper ['bliːpə*] n (device) cicalino

blemish ['blemɪʃ] n macchia

blend [blend] n miscela ♦ vt mescolare ♦ vi (colours etc: also: ~ **in**) armonizzare

bless [bles] (pt, pp blessed or blest) vt benedire; ~ **you!** (after sneeze)

salute!; ~**ing** n benedizione f; fortuna; **blest** [blest] pt, pp of **bless**

blew [bluː] pt of **blow**

blight [blaɪt] vt (hopes etc) deludere; (life) rovinare

blimey ['blaɪmɪ] (BRIT: inf) excl accidenti!

blind [blaɪnd] adj cieco(a) ♦ n (for window) avvolgibile m; (Venetian ~) veneziana ♦ vt accecare; **the** ~ npl i ciechi; ~ **alley** n vicolo cieco; ~**corner** (BRIT) n svolta cieca; ~**fold** n benda ♦ adj, adv bendato(a) ♦ vt bendare gli occhi a; ~**ly** adv ciecamente; ~**ness** n cecità; ~ **spot** n (AUT etc) punto cieco; (fig) punto debole

blink [blɪŋk] vi battere gli occhi; (light) lampeggiare; ~**ers** npl paraocchi mpl

bliss [blɪs] n estasi f

blister ['blɪstə*] n (on skin) vescica; (on paintwork) bolla ♦ vi (paint) coprirsi di bolle

blithely ['blaɪðlɪ] adv allegramente

blizzard ['blɪzəd] n bufera di neve

bloated ['bləʊtɪd] adj gonfio(a)

blob [blɒb] n (drop) goccia; (stain, spot) macchia

bloc [blɒk] n (POL) blocco

block [blɒk] n blocco; (in pipes) ingombro; (toy) cubo; (of buildings) isolato ♦ vt bloccare; ~ **of flats** (BRIT) n caseggiato; ~**ade** [-'keɪd] n blocco; ~**age** n ostacolo; ~**buster** n (film, book) grande successo; ~ **letters** npl stampatello

bloke [bləʊk] (BRIT: inf) n tizio

blonde [blɒnd] adj, n biondo(a)

blood [blʌd] n sangue m; ~ **donor** n donatore/trice di sangue; ~ **group** n gruppo sanguigno; ~**hound** n segugio; ~ **poisoning** n setticemia; ~ **pressure** n pressione f sanguigna; ~**shed** n spargimento di sangue; ~**shot** adj: ~**shot eyes** occhi iniettati di sangue; ~**stream** n flusso del sangue; ~ **test** n analisi f inv del sangue; ~**thirsty** adj assetato(a) di sangue; ~**y** adj (fight) sanguinoso(a); (*nose*) sanguinante; (*BRIT: inf!*): **this ~y ...** questo maledetto ...; **~y awful/good** (*inf!*) veramente terribile/forte; **~y-minded** (*BRIT: inf*) adj indisponente

bloom [bluːm] n fiore m ♦ vi (*tree*) essere in fiore; (*flower*) aprirsi

blossom ['blɒsəm] n fiore m; (*with pl sense*) fiori mpl ♦ vi essere in fiore

blot [blɒt] n macchia ♦ vt macchiare; **~ out** vt (*memories*) cancellare; (*view*) nascondere

blotchy ['blɒtʃi] adj (*complexion*) coperto(a) di macchie

blotting paper ['blɒtɪŋ-] n carta assorbente

blouse [blauz] n (*feminine garment*) camicetta

blow [bləu] (*pt* **blew**, *pp* **blown**) n colpo ♦ vi soffiare ♦ vt (*fuse*) far saltare; (*subj: wind*) spingere; (*instrument*) suonare; **to ~ one's nose** soffiarsi il naso; **to ~ a whistle** fischiare; **~ away** vt portare via; **~ down** vt abbattere; **~ off** vt far volare via; **~ out** vi scoppiare; **~ over** vi calmarsi; **~ up** vi saltare in aria ♦ vt far saltare in aria; (*tyre*) gonfiare; (*PHOT*) ingrandire; **~-dry** n messa in piega a föhn; **~lamp** (*BRIT*) n lampada a benzina per saldare; **blown** pp of **blow**; **~out** n (*of tyre*) scoppio; **~torch** n = **~lamp**

blue [bluː] adj azzurro(a); (*depressed*) giù inv; **~ film/joke** film/barzelletta pornografico(a); **out of the ~** (*fig*) all'improvviso; **~bell** n giacinto dei boschi; **~bottle** n moscone m; **~print** n (*fig*): **~print (for)** formula (di)

bluff [blʌf] vi bluffare ♦ n bluff m inv ♦ adj (*person*) brusco(a); **to call sb's ~** mettere alla prova il bluff di qn

blunder ['blʌndə*] n abbaglio ♦ vi prendere un abbaglio

blunt [blʌnt] adj smussato(a); spuntato(a); (*person*) brusco(a)

blur [bləː*] n forma indistinta ♦ vt offuscare

blurb [bləːb] n trafiletto pubblicitario

blurt out [bləːt-] vt lasciarsi sfuggire

blush [blʌʃ] vi arrossire ♦ n rossore m

blustering ['blʌstərɪŋ] adj infuriato(a)

blustery ['blʌstərɪ] adj (*weather*) burrascoso(a)

boar [bɔː*] n cinghiale m

board [bɔːd] n tavola; (*on wall*) tabellone m; (*committee*) consiglio, comitato; (*in firm*) consiglio d'amministrazione; (*NAUT, AVIAT*): **on ~** a bordo ♦ vt (*ship*) salire a bordo di; (*train*) salire su; **full ~** (*BRIT*) pensione completa; **half ~** (*BRIT*) mezza pensione; **~ and lodging** vitto e alloggio; **which goes by the ~** (*fig*) che viene abbandonato; **~ up** vt (*door*) chiudere con assi; **~er** n (*SCOL*) convittore/trice; **~ing card** n = **~ing pass**; **~ing house** n pensione f; **~ing pass** n (*AVIAT, NAUT*) carta d'imbarco; **~ing school** n collegio; **~ room** n sala del consiglio

boast [bəust] vi: **to ~ (about or of)** vantarsi (di)

boat [bəut] n nave f; (*small*) barca; **~er** n (*hat*) paglietta; **~swain** ['bəusn] n nostromo

bob [bɒb] vi (*boat, cork on water: also: ~ up and down*) andare su e giù; **~ up** vi saltare fuori

bobby ['bɒbɪ] (*BRIT: inf*) n poliziotto

bobsleigh ['bɒbslei] n bob m inv

bode [bəud] vi: **to ~ well/ill (for)** essere di buon/cattivo auspicio (per)

bodily ['bɒdɪlɪ] adj fisico(a), corporale ♦ adv corporalmente; interamente; in persona

body ['bɒdɪ] n corpo; (*of car*) carrozzeria; (*of plane*) fusoliera; (*fig: group*) gruppo; (: *organization*) organizzazione f; (: *quantity*) quantità f inv; **~-building** n culturismo

~guard n guardia del corpo;
~work n carrozzeria

bog [bɔg] n palude f ♦ vt: **to get
~ged down** (fig) impantanarsi

boggle ['bɔgl] vi: **the mind ~s** è incredibile

bogus ['bəugəs] adj falso(a); finto(a)

boil [bɔɪl] vt, vi bollire ♦ n (MED)
foruncolo; **to come to the** (BRIT) or
a (US) **~** raggiungere l'ebollizione;
~ down to vt fus (fig) ridursi a; **~
over** vi traboccare (bollendo); **~ed
egg** n uovo alla coque; **~ed potatoes** npl patate fpl bollite or lesse;
~er n caldaia; **~er suit** (BRIT) n
tuta; **~ing point** n punto di ebollizione

boisterous ['bɔɪstərəs] adj chiassoso(a)

bold [bəuld] adj audace; (child) impudente; (colour) deciso(a)

bollard ['bɔləd] (BRIT) n (AUT) colonnina luminosa

bolster ['bəulstə*] vt: **~ up** sostenere

bolt [bəult] n chiavistello; (with nut)
bullone m ♦ adv: **~ upright** diritto(a) come un fuso ♦ vt serrare;
(also: **~ together**) imbullonare;
(food) mangiare in fretta ♦ vi scappare via

bomb [bɔm] n bomba ♦ vt bombardare

bombastic [bɔm'bæstɪk] adj magniloquente

bomb~ disposal unit n corpo
degli artificieri; **~er** n (AVIAT)
bombardiere m; **~shell** n (fig) notizia bomba

bona fide ['bəunə'faɪdɪ] adj sincero(a); (offer) onesto(a)

bond [bɔnd] n legame m; (binding
promise, FINANCE) obbligazione f;
(COMM): **in ~** in attesa di sdoganamento

bondage ['bɔndɪdʒ] n schiavitù f

bone [bəun] n osso; (of fish) spina,
lisca ♦ vt disossare; togliere le spine
a; **~ idle** adj pigrissimo(a)

bonfire ['bɔnfaɪə*] n falò m inv

bonnet ['bɔnɪt] n cuffia; (BRIT: of
car) cofano

bonus ['bəunəs] n premio; (fig) sovrappiù m inv

bony ['bəunɪ] adj (MED: tissue) osseo(a); (arm, face) ossuto(a);
(meat) pieno(a) di ossi; (fish) pieno(a) di spine

boo [buː] excl ba! ♦ vt fischiare

booby trap ['buːbɪ-] n trappola

book [buk] n libro; (of stamps etc)
blocchetto ♦ vt (ticket, seat, room)
prenotare; (driver) multare; (football player) ammonire; **~s** npl
(COMM) conti mpl; **~case** n scaffale m; **~ing office** (BRIT) n (RAIL)
biglietteria; (THEATRE) botteghino;
~keeping n contabilità; **~let** n libricino; **~maker** n allibratore m;
~seller n libraio; **~shop, ~store**
n libreria

boom [buːm] n (noise) rimbombo;
(in prices etc) boom m inv ♦ vi rimbombare; andare a gonfie vele

boon [buːn] n vantaggio

boost [buːst] n spinta ♦ vt spingere;
~er n (MED) richiamo

boot [buːt] n stivale m; (for hiking)
scarpone m da montagna; (for football etc) scarpa; (BRIT: of car) portabagagli m inv ♦ vt (COMPUT) inizializzare; **to ~** (in addition) per
giunta, in più

booth [buːð] n cabina; (at fair) baraccone m

booty ['buːtɪ] n bottino

booze [buːz] (inf) n alcool m

border ['bɔːdə*] n orlo; margine m;
(of a country) frontiera; (for flowers)
aiuola (laterale) ♦ vt (road) costeggiare; (another country: also: **~ on**)
confinare con; **the B~**s la zona di
confine tra l'Inghilterra e la Scozia;
~ on vt fus (fig: insanity etc) sfiorare; **~line** n (fig): **on the ~line** incerto(a); **~line case** n caso incerto

bore [bɔː*] pt of **bear** ♦ vt (hole etc)
scavare; (person) annoiare ♦ n (person) seccatore/trice; (of gun) calibro; **to be ~d** annoiarsi; **~dom** n

noia; **boring** adj noioso(a)

born [bɔːn] adj: **to be ~** nascere; **I was ~ in 1960** sono nato nel 1960

borne [bɔːn] pp of **bear**

borough ['bʌrə] n comune m

borrow ['bɔrəu] vt: **to ~ sth (from sb)** prendere in prestito qc (da qn)

bosom ['buzəm] n petto; **~ friend** n amico/a del cuore

boss [bɔs] n capo ♦ vt comandare; **~y** adj prepotente

bosun ['bəusn] n nostromo

botany ['bɔtənɪ] n botanica

botch [bɔtʃ] vt (also: **~ up**) fare un pasticcio di

both [bəuθ] adj entrambi(e), tutt'e due ♦ pron: **~ (of them)** entrambi(e); **~ of us went, we ~ went** ci siamo andati tutt'e due ♦ adv: **they sell ~ meat and poultry** vendono insieme la carne ed il pollame

bother ['bɔðə*] vt (worry) preoccupare; (annoy) infastidire ♦ vi (also: **~ o.s.**) preoccuparsi ♦ n: **it is a ~ to have to do** è una seccatura dover fare; **it was no ~** non c'era problema; **to ~ doing sth** darsi la pena di fare qc

bottle ['bɔtl] n bottiglia; (baby's) biberon m inv ♦ vt imbottigliare; **~ up** vt contenere; **~ bank** n contenitore m per la raccolta del vetro; **~neck** n imbottigliamento; **~-opener** n apribottiglie m inv

bottom ['bɔtəm] n fondo; (buttocks) sedere m ♦ adj più basso(a); ultimo(a); **at the ~ of** in fondo a

bough [bau] n ramo

bought [bɔːt] pt, pp of **buy**

boulder ['bəuldə*] n masso (tondeggiante)

bounce [bauns] vi (ball) rimbalzare; (cheque) essere restituito(a) ♦ vt far rimbalzare ♦ n (rebound) rimbalzo; **~r** (inf) n buttafuori m inv

bound [baund] pt, pp of **bind** ♦ n (gen pl) limite m; (leap) salto ♦ vi saltare ♦ vt (limit) delimitare ♦ adj: **~ by law** obbligato(a) per legge; **to be ~ to do sth** (obliged) essere co-

stretto(a) a fare qc; **he's ~ to fail** (likely) fallirà di certo; **~ for** diretto(a) a; **out of ~s** il cui accesso è vietato

boundary ['baundrɪ] n confine m

boundless ['baundlɪs] adj senza limiti

bourgeois ['buəʒwɑː] adj borghese

bout [baut] n periodo; (of malaria etc) attacco; (BOXING etc) incontro

bow¹ [bəu] n nodo; (weapon) arco; (MUS) archetto

bow² [bau] n (with body) inchino; (NAUT: also: **~s**) prua ♦ vi inchinarsi; (yield): **to ~ to or before** sottomettersi a

bowels ['bauəlz] npl intestini mpl; (fig) viscere fpl

bowl [bəul] n (for eating) scodella; (for washing) bacino; (ball) boccia ♦ vi (CRICKET) servire (la palla)

bow-legged ['bəu'legɪd] adj dalle gambe storte

bowler ['bəulə*] n (CRICKET, BASEBALL) lanciatore m; (BRIT: also: **~ hat**) bombetta

bowling ['bəulɪŋ] n (game) gioco delle bocce; **~ alley** n pista da bowling; **~ green** n campo di bocce

bowls [bəulz] n gioco delle bocce

bow tie n cravatta a farfalla

box [bɔks] n scatola; (also: cardboard **~**) cartone m; (THEATRE) palco ♦ vt inscatolare ♦ vi fare del pugilato; **~er** n (person) pugile m; **~ing** n (SPORT) pugilato; **B~ing Day** (BRIT) n Santo Stefano; **~ing gloves** npl guantoni mpl da pugile; **~ing ring** n ring m inv; **~ office** n biglietteria; **~ room** n ripostiglio

boy [bɔɪ] n ragazzo

boycott ['bɔɪkɔt] n boicottaggio ♦ vt boicottare

boyfriend ['bɔɪfrend] n ragazzo

boyish ['bɔɪɪʃ] adj da ragazzo

B.R. abbr = **British Rail**

bra [brɑː] n reggipetto, reggiseno

brace [breɪs] n (on teeth) apparecchio correttore; (tool) trapano ♦ vt rinforzare, sostenere; **~s** (BRIT) npl

(DRESS) bretelle fpl; **to ~ o.s.** (also fig) tenersi forte

bracelet ['breɪslɪt] n braccialetto

bracing ['breɪsɪŋ] adj invigorante

bracken ['brækən] n felce f

bracket ['brækɪt] n (TECH) mensola; (group) gruppo; (TYP) parentesi f inv ♦ vt mettere fra parentesi

brag [bræg] vi vantarsi

braid [breɪd] n (trimming) passamano; (of hair) treccia

brain [breɪn] n cervello; **~s** npl (intelligence) cervella fpl; **he's got ~s** è intelligente; **~child** n creatura, creazione f; **~wash** vt fare un lavaggio di cervello a; **~wave** n lampo di genio; **~y** adj intelligente

braise [breɪz] vt brasare

brake [breɪk] n (on vehicle) freno ♦ vi frenare; **~ fluid** n liquido dei freni; **~ light** n (fanalino dello) stop m inv

bramble ['bræmbl] n rovo

bran [bræn] n crusca

branch [brɑːntʃ] n ramo; (COMM) succursale f; **~ out** vi (fig) intraprendere una nuova attività

brand [brænd] n (also: **~ name**) marca; (fig) tipo ♦ vt (cattle) marcare (a ferro rovente)

brand-new adj nuovo(a) di zecca

brandy ['brændɪ] n brandy m inv

brash [bræʃ] adj sfacciato(a)

brass [brɑːs] n ottone m; **the ~** (MUS) gli ottoni; **~ band** n fanfara

brassière ['bræsɪə'] n reggipetto, reggiseno

brat [bræt] (pej) n marmocchio, monello(a)

bravado [brə'vɑːdəʊ] n spavalderia

brave [breɪv] adj coraggioso(a) ♦ vt affrontare; **~ry** n coraggio

brawl [brɔːl] n rissa

brawny ['brɔːnɪ] adj muscoloso(a)

bray [breɪ] vi ragliare

brazen ['breɪzn] adj sfacciato(a) ♦ vt: **to ~ it out** fare lo sfacciato

brazier ['breɪzɪə'] n braciere m

Brazil [brə'zɪl] n Brasile m

breach [briːtʃ] vt aprire una breccia

in ♦ n (gap) breccia, varco; (breaking): **~ of contract** rottura di contratto; **~ of the peace** violazione f dell'ordine pubblico

bread [bred] n pane m; **~ and butter** n pane e burro; (fig) mezzi mpl di sussistenza; **~bin** (US **~box**) n cassetta f portapane inv; **~crumbs** npl briciole fpl; (CULIN) pangrattato; **~line** n: **to be on the ~line** avere appena il denaro per vivere

breadth [bretθ] n larghezza; (fig: of knowledge etc) ampiezza

breadwinner ['bredwɪnə'] n chi guadagna il pane per tutta la famiglia

break [breɪk] (pt **broke**, pp **broken**) vt rompere; (law) violare; (record) battere ♦ vi rompersi; (storm) scoppiare; (weather) cambiare; (dawn) spuntare; (news) saltare fuori ♦ n (gap) breccia; (fracture) rottura; (rest, also SCOL) intervallo; (: short) pausa; (chance) possibilità f inv; **to ~ one's leg** etc rompersi la gamba etc; **to ~ the news to sb** comunicare per primo la notizia a qn; **to ~ even** coprire le spese; **to ~ free** or **loose** spezzare i legami; **to ~ open** (door etc) sfondare; **~ down** vt (figures, data) analizzare ♦ vi (person) avere un esaurimento (nervoso); (AUT) guastarsi; **~ in** vt (horse etc) domare ♦ vi (burglar) fare irruzione; (interrupt) interrompere; **~ into** vt fus (house) fare irruzione in; **~ off** vi (speaker) interrompersi; (branch) troncarsi; **~ out** vi evadere; (war, fight) scoppiare; **to ~ out in spots** coprirsi di macchie; **~ up** vi (ship) sfondarsi; (meeting) sciogliersi; (crowd) disperdersi; (marriage) andare a pezzi; (SCOL) chiudere ♦ vt fare a pezzi, spaccare; (fight etc) interrompere, far cessare; **~age** n rottura; (object broken) cosa rotta; **~down** n (AUT) guasto; (in communications) interruzione f; (of marriage) rottura; (MED: also: **nervous ~down**) esaurimento nervoso; (of statistics) resoconto; ~**down van** (BRIT) n carro m attrezzi inv; ~**er** n frangente m

breakfast ['brɛkfəst] n colazione f

break: ~**-in** n irruzione f; ~**ing and entering** n (LAW) violazione f di domicilio con scasso; ~**through** n (fig) passo avanti; ~**water** n frangiflutti m inv

breast [brɛst] n (of woman) seno; (chest, CULIN) petto; ~**-feed** (irreg: like feed) vt, vi allattare (al seno); ~**-stroke** n nuoto a rana

breath [brɛθ] n respiro; **out of** ~ senza fiato

Breathalyser ['brɛθəlaɪzə⁎] ®️ (BRIT) n alcoltest m inv

breathe [bri:ð] vt, vi respirare; ~ **in** vi respirare ♦ vi inspirare; ~ **out** vi, vi espirare; ♦ vi espirare; ~**r** n attimo di respiro; **breathing** n respiro, respirazione f

breathless ['brɛθlɪs] adj senza fiato

breathtaking ['brɛθteɪkɪŋ] adj mozzafiato inv

bred [brɛd] pt, pp of **breed**

breed [bri:d] (pt, pp bred) vt allevare ♦ vi riprodursi ♦ n razza; (type, class) varietà f inv; ~**ing** n riproduzione f; allevamento; (upbringing) educazione f

breeze [bri:z] n brezza

breezy ['bri:zɪ] adj allegro(a); ventilato(a)

brew [bru:] vt (tea) fare un infuso di; (beer) fare ♦ vi (storm, fig: trouble etc) prepararsi; ~**er** n birraio; ~**ery** n fabbrica di birra

bribe [braɪb] n bustarella ♦ vt comprare; ~**ry** n corruzione f

brick [brɪk] n mattone m; ~**layer** n muratore m

bridal ['braɪdl] adj nuziale

bride [braɪd] n sposa; ~**groom** n sposo; ~**smaid** n damigella d'onore

bridge [brɪdʒ] n ponte m; (NAUT) ponte di comando; (of nose) dorso; (CARDS) bridge m inv ♦ vt (fig: gap) colmare

bridle ['braɪdl] n briglia; ~ **path** n

sentiero (per cavalli)

brief [bri:f] adj breve ♦ n (LAW) comparsa; (gen) istruzioni fpl ♦ vt mettere al corrente; ~**s** npl (underwear) mutande fpl; ~**case** n cartella; ~**ing** n briefing m inv; ~**ly** adv (glance) di sfuggita; (explain, say) brevemente

bright [braɪt] adj luminoso(a); (clever) sveglio(a); (lively) vivace; ~**en** (also: ~en up) vt (room) rendere luminoso(a) ♦ vi schiarirsi; (person) rallegrarsi

brilliance ['brɪljəns] n splendore m

brilliant ['brɪljənt] adj brillante; (light, smile) radioso(a); (inf) splendido(a)

brim [brɪm] n orlo

brine [braɪn] n (CULIN) salamoia

bring [brɪŋ] (pt, pp brought) vt portare; ~ **about** vt causare; ~ **back** vt riportare; ~ **down** vt portare giù; abbattere; ~ **forward** vt (proposal) avanzare; (meeting) anticipare; ~ **off** vt (task, plan) portare a compimento; ~ **out** vt tirar fuori; (meaning) mettere in evidenza; (book, album) far uscire; ~ **round** vt (unconscious person) far rinvenire; ~ **up** vt (carry up) portare su; (child) allevare; (question) introdurre; (food: vomit) rimettere, rigurgitare

brink [brɪŋk] n orlo

brisk [brɪsk] adj (manner) spiccio(a); (trade) vivace; (pace) svelto(a)

bristle ['brɪsl] n setola ♦ vi rizzarsi; **bristling with** irto(a) di

Britain ['brɪtən] n (also: Great ~) Gran Bretagna

British ['brɪtɪʃ] adj britannico(a); **the** ~ npl i Britannici; **the** ~ **Isles** npl le Isole Britanniche; **the** ~ **Rail** n compagnia ferroviaria britannica, ≈ Ferrovie fpl dello Stato

Briton ['brɪtən] n britannico/a

brittle ['brɪtl] adj fragile

broach [brəutʃ] vt (subject) affrontare

broad [brɔːd] *adj* largo(a); (*distinction*) generale; (*accent*) spiccato(a); in ~ **daylight** in pieno giorno; ~**cast** (*pt, pp* ~**cast**) *n* trasmissione *f* ♦ *vt* trasmettere per radio (or per televisione) ♦ *vi* fare una trasmissione; ~**en** *vt* allargare ♦ *vi* allargarsi; ~**ly** *adv* (*fig*) in generale; ~**minded** *adj* di mente aperta

broccoli [ˈbrɔkəlɪ] *n* broccoli *mpl*

brochure [ˈbrəʊʃjuəˈ] *n* dépliant *m inv*

broil [brɔɪl] *vt* cuocere a fuoco vivo

broke [brəʊk] *pt* of **break** ♦ *adj* (*inf*) squattrinato(a)

broken [ˈbrəʊkn] *pp* of **break** ♦ *adj* rotto(a); a ~ **leg** una gamba rotta; in ~ **English** in un inglese stentato; ~**-hearted** *adj*: to be ~**-hearted** avere il cuore spezzato

broker [ˈbrəʊkəˈ] *n* agente *m*

brolly [ˈbrɔlɪ] *n* (*BRIT: inf*) *n* ombrello

bronchitis [brɔŋˈkaɪtɪs] *n* bronchite *f*

bronze [brɔnz] *n* bronzo

brooch [brəʊtʃ] *n* spilla

brood [bruːd] *n* covata ♦ *vi* (*person*) rimuginare

brook [brʊk] *n* ruscello

broom [brʊm] *n* scopa; (*BOT*) ginestra; ~**stick** *n* manico di scopa

Bros. *abbr* (= *Brothers*) F.lli

broth [brɔθ] *n* brodo

brothel [ˈbrɔθl] *n* bordello

brother [ˈbrʌðəˈ] *n* fratello; ~**-in-law** *n* cognato

brought [brɔːt] *pt, pp* of **bring**

brow [braʊ] *n* fronte *f*; (*rare, gen: eye*~) sopracciglio; (of *hill*) cima

brown [braʊn] *adj* bruno(a), marrone; (*tanned*) abbronzato(a) ♦ *n* (*colour*) color *m* bruno or marrone ♦ *vt* (*CULIN*) rosolare; ~ **bread** *n* pane *m* integrale, pane nero

brownie [ˈbraʊnɪ] *n* giovane esploratrice *f*; (*US: cake*) dolce al cioccolato e nocciole

brown paper *n* carta da pacchi or da imballaggio

brown sugar *n* zucchero greggio

browse [braʊz] *vi* (*among books*) curiosare fra i libri; to ~ **through** a **book** sfogliare un libro

bruise [bruːz] *n* (*on person*) livido ♦ *vt* farsi un livido a

brunette [bruːˈnet] *n* bruna

brunt [brʌnt] *n*: the ~ of (*attack, criticism etc*) il peso maggiore di

brush [brʌʃ] *n* spazzola; (*for painting, shaving*) pennello; (*quarrel*) schermaglia ♦ *vt* spazzolare; (*also*: ~ *against*) sfiorare; ~ **aside** *vt* scostare; ~ **up** *vt* (*knowledge*) rinfrescare; ~**wood** *n* macchia

Brussels [ˈbrʌslz] *n* Bruxelles *f*; ~ **sprout** *n* cavolo di Bruxelles

brutal [ˈbruːtl] *adj* brutale

brute [bruːt] *n* bestia ♦ *adj*: by ~ **force** con la forza, a viva forza

B.Sc. *n abbr* = **Bachelor of Science**

bubble [ˈbʌbl] *n* bolla ♦ *vi* ribollire; (*sparkle, fig*) essere effervescente; ~ **bath** *n* bagnoschiuma *m inv*; ~ **gum** *n* gomma americana

buck [bʌk] *n* maschio (di *camoscio, caprone, coniglio etc*); (*US: inf*) dollaro ♦ *vi* sgroppare; to **pass the** ~ (to *sb*) scaricare (su di qn) la propria responsabilità; ~ **up** *vi* (*cheer up*) rianimarsi

bucket [ˈbʌkɪt] *n* secchio

buckle [ˈbʌkl] *n* fibbia ♦ *vt* allacciare ♦ *vi* (*wheel etc*) piegarsi

bud [bʌd] *n* gemma; (of *flower*) bocciolo ♦ *vi* germogliare; (*flower*) sbocciare

Buddhism [ˈbʊdɪzəm] *n* buddismo

budding [ˈbʌdɪŋ] *adj* (*poet etc*) in erba

buddy [ˈbʌdɪ] (*US*) *n* compagno

budge [bʌdʒ] *vt* scostare; (*fig*) smuovere ♦ *vi* spostarsi; smuoversi

budgerigar [ˈbʌdʒərɪɡɑːˈ] *n* pappagallino

budget [ˈbʌdʒɪt] *n* bilancio preventivo ♦ *vi*: to ~ **for sth** fare il bilancio per qc

budgie [ˈbʌdʒɪ] *n* = **budgerigar**

buff [bʌf] *adj* color camoscio ♦ *n* (*inf: enthusiast*) appassionato/a

buffalo [ˈbʌfələʊ] (*pl* ~ *or* ~**es**) *n*

bufalo; (US) bisonte m

buffer ['bʌfə*] n respingente m; (COMPUT) memoria tampone, buffer m inv

buffet[1] ['bufeɪ] n (food, BRIT: bar) buffet m inv; ~ **car** (BRIT) n (RAIL) ≈ servizio ristoro

buffet[2] ['bʌfɪt] vt sferzare

bug [bʌg] n (esp US: insect) insetto; (COMPUT, fig: germ) virus m inv; (spy device) microfono spia ♦ vt mettere sotto controllo; (inf: annoy) scocciare

buggy ['bʌgɪ] n (baby ~) passeggino

bugle ['bju:gl] n tromba

build [bɪld] (pt, pp built) n (of person) corporatura ♦ vt costruire; ~ **up** vt accumulare; aumentare; ~**er** n costruttore m; ~**ing** n costruzione f; edificio; (industry) edilizia; ~**ing society** (BRIT) n società f inv immobiliare

built [bɪlt] pt, pp of build ♦ adj: ~-**in** (cupboard) a muro; (device) incorporato(a); ~-**up area** n abitato

bulb [bʌlb] n (BOT) bulbo; (ELEC) lampadina

bulge [bʌldʒ] n rigonfiamento ♦ vi essere protuberante or rigonfio(a) ♦ to be bulging with essere pieno(a) or zeppo(a) di

bulk [bʌlk] n massa, volume m; in ~ a pacchi (or cassette etc); (COMM) all'ingrosso; the ~ of il grosso di; ~**y** adj grosso(a); voluminoso(a)

bull [bul] n toro; (male elephant, whale) maschio; ~**dog** n bulldog m inv

bulldozer ['buldəuzə*] n bulldozer m inv

bullet ['bulɪt] n pallottola

bulletin ['bulɪtɪn] n bollettino

bulletproof ['bulɪtpru:f] adj (car) blindato(a); (vest etc) antiproiettile m inv

bullfight ['bulfaɪt] n corrida; ~**er** n torero; ~**ing** n tauromachia

bullion ['buljən] n oro or argento in lingotti

bullock ['bulək] n manzo

bullring ['bulrɪŋ] n arena (per corride)

bull's-eye ['bulzaɪ] n centro del bersaglio

bully ['bulɪ] n prepotente m ♦ vt angariare; (frighten) intimidire

bum [bʌm] (inf) n (backside) culo; (tramp) vagabondo/a

bumblebee ['bʌmblbi:] n bombo

bump [bʌmp] n (in car) piccolo tamponamento; (jolt) scossa; (on road etc) protuberanza; (on head) bernoccolo ♦ vt battere; ~ **into** vt fus scontrarsi con; (person) imbattersi in; ~**er** n paraurti m inv ♦ adj: ~**er harvest** raccolto eccezionale; ~**er cars** npl autoscontri mpl

bumptious ['bʌmpʃəs] adj presuntuoso(a)

bumpy ['bʌmpɪ] adj (road) dissestato(a)

bun [bʌn] n focaccia; (of hair) crocchia

bunch [bʌntʃ] n (of flowers, keys) mazzo; (of bananas) casco; (of people) gruppo; ~ **of grapes** grappolo d'uva; ~**es** npl (in hair) codine fpl

bundle ['bʌndl] n fascio ♦ vt (also: ~ **up**) legare in un fascio; (put): **to ~ sth/sb into** spingere qc/qn in

bungalow ['bʌŋgələu] n bungalow m inv

bungle ['bʌŋgl] vt fare un pasticcio di

bunion ['bʌnjən] n callo (al piede)

bunk [bʌŋk] n cuccetta; ~ **beds** npl letti mpl a castello

bunker ['bʌŋkə*] n (coal store) ripostiglio per il carbone; (MIL, GOLF) bunker m inv

bunny ['bʌnɪ] n (also: ~ rabbit) coniglietto

bunting ['bʌntɪŋ] n pavesi mpl, bandierine fpl

buoy [bɔɪ] n boa; ~ **up** vt (fig) sostenere; ~**ant** adj galleggiante; (fig) vivace

burden ['bə:dn] n carico, fardello ♦ vt: to ~ **sb with** caricare di

bureau [bjuə'rəu] (pl **bureaux**) n

(BRIT: writing desk) scrivania; (US: chest of drawers) cassettone m; (office) ufficio, agenzia

bureaucracy [bjuə'rɔkrəsɪ] n burocrazia

bureaux [bjuə'rəuz] npl of **bureau**

burglar ['bəːglə*] n scassinatore m; ~ **alarm** n campanello antifurto; ~**y** n furto con scasso

burial ['berɪəl] n sepoltura

burly ['bəːlɪ] adj robusto(a)

Burma ['bəːmə] n Birmania

burn [bəːn] (pt, pp **burned** or **burnt**) vt, vi bruciare ♦ n bruciatura, scottatura; ~ **down** vt distruggere col fuoco; ~**er** n (on cooker) fornello; (TECH) bruciatore m, becco (a gas); ~**ing** adj in fiamme; (sand) che scotta; (ambition) bruciante; **burnt** pt, pp of **burn**

burrow ['bʌrəu] n tana ♦ vt scavare

bursary ['bəːsərɪ] n (BRIT) (SCOL) borsa di studio

burst [bəːst] (pt, pp **burst**) vt far scoppiare ♦ vi esplodere; (tyre) scoppiare ♦ n scoppio; (also: ~ **pipe**) rottura nel tubo, perdita; **a** ~ **of speed** uno scatto di velocità; **to** ~ **into flames/tears** scoppiare in fiamme/lacrime; **to** ~ **out laughing** scoppiare a ridere; **to be** ~**ing with** scoppiare di; ~ **into** vt fus (room etc) irrompere in

bury ['berɪ] vt seppellire

bus [bʌs] (pl ~**es**) n autobus m inv

buses ['bʌsɪz] npl of **bus**

bush [buʃ] n cespuglio; (scrub land) macchia; **to beat about the** ~ menare il cane per l'aia

bushy ['buʃɪ] adj cespuglioso(a)

busily ['bɪzɪlɪ] adv con impegno, alacremente

business ['bɪznɪs] n (matter) affare m; (trading) affari mpl; (firm) azienda; (job, duty) lavoro; **to be away on** ~ essere andato via per affari; **it's none of my** ~ questo non mi riguarda; **he means** ~ non scherza; ~**like** adj serio(a); efficiente; ~**man/woman** n uomo/donna

d'affari; ~ **trip** n viaggio d'affari

busker ['bʌskə*] (BRIT) n suonatore/trice ambulante

bus-stop n fermata d'autobus

bust [bʌst] n busto; (ANAT) seno ♦ adj (inf: broken) rotto(a); **to go** ♦ fallire

bustle ['bʌsl] n movimento, attività ♦ vi darsi da fare; **bustling** adj movimentato(a)

busy ['bɪzɪ] adj occupato(a); (shop, street) molto frequentato(a) ♦ vt: **to** ~ **o.s. darsi da fare**; ~**body** n ficcanaso m/f inv; ~ **signal** (US) n (TEL) segnale m di occupato

KEYWORD

but [bʌt] conj ma; **I'd love to come,** ~ **I'm busy** vorrei tanto venire, ma ho da fare

♦ prep (apart from, except) eccetto, tranne, meno; **he was nothing** ~ **trouble** non dava altro che guai; **no-one** ~ **him can do it** nessuno può farlo tranne lui; ~ **for your/your help** se non fosse per te/per il tuo aiuto; **anything** ~ **that** tutto ma non questo

♦ adv (just, only) solo, soltanto; **she's** ~ **a child** è solo una bambina; **had I** ~ **known** se solo avessi saputo; **I can** ~ **try** tentar non nuoce; **all** ~ **finished** quasi finito

butcher ['butʃə*] n macellaio ♦ vt macellare; ~'**s (shop)** n macelleria

butler ['bʌtlə*] n maggiordomo

butt [bʌt] n (cask) grossa botte f; (of gun) calcio; (of cigarette) mozzicone m; (BRIT: fig: target) oggetto ♦ vt cozzare; ~ **in** vi (interrupt) interrompere

butter ['bʌtə*] n burro ♦ vt imburrare; ~**cup** n ranuncolo

butterfly ['bʌtəflaɪ] n farfalla; (SWIMMING: also: ~ **stroke**) (nuoto a) farfalla

buttocks ['bʌtəks] npl natiche fpl

button ['bʌtn] n bottone m; (US: badge) distintivo ♦ vt (also: ~ **up**) abbottonare ♦ *vi* abbottonarsi

buttress ['bʌtrɪs] *n* contrafforte *f*

buxom ['bʌksəm] *adj* formoso(a)

buy [baɪ] (*pt, pp* **bought**) *vt* comprare ♦ *n* acquisto; **to ~ sb sth/sth from sb** comprare qc per qn/qc da qn; **to ~ sb a drink** offrire da bere a qn; **~er** *n* compratore/trice

buzz [bʌz] *n* ronzio; (*inf: phone call*) colpo di telefono ♦ *vi* ronzare

buzzer ['bʌzə*] *n* cicalino

buzz word (*inf*) *n* termine *m* di gran moda

KEYWORD

by [baɪ] *prep* **1** (*referring to cause, agent*) da; **killed ~ lightning** ucciso da un fulmine; **surrounded ~ a fence** circondato da uno steccato; **a painting ~ Picasso** un quadro di Picasso

2 (*referring to method, manner, means*): **~ bus/car/train** in autobus/macchina/treno, con l'autobus/la macchina/il treno; **to pay ~ cheque** pagare con (un) assegno; **~ moonlight** al chiaro di luna; **~ saving hard, he ...** risparmiando molto, lui ...

3 (*via, through*) per; **we came ~ Dover** siamo venuti via Dover

4 (*close to, past*) accanto a; **the house ~ the river** la casa sul fiume; **a holiday ~ the sea** una vacanza al mare; **she sat ~ his bed** si sedette accanto al suo letto; **she rushed ~ me** mi è passata accanto correndo; **I go ~ the post office every day** passo davanti all'ufficio postale ogni giorno

5 (*not later than*) per, entro; **~ 4 o'clock** per *or* entro le 4; **~ this time tomorrow** domani a quest'ora; **~ the time I got here it was too late** quando sono arrivato era ormai troppo tardi

6 (*during*): **~ day/night** di giorno/notte

7 (*amount*) a; **~ the kilo/metre** a chili/metri; **paid ~ the hour** pagato

all'ora; **one ~ one** uno per uno; **little ~ little** a poco a poco

8 (*MATH, measure*): **to divide/multiply ~ 3** dividere/moltiplicare per 3; **it's broader ~ a metre** è un metro più largo, è più largo di un metro

9 (*according to*) per; **to play ~ the rules** attenersi alle regole; **it's all right ~ me** per me va bene

10: (*all*) **~ oneself** etc (*tutto*(a)) solo(a); **he did it** (*all*) **~ himself** lo ha fatto (tutto) da solo

11: **~ the way** a proposito; **this wasn't my idea ~ the way** tra l'altro l'idea non è stata mia

♦ *adv* **1** *see* go; pass *etc*

2: **~ and ~** (*in past*) poco dopo; (*in future*) fra breve; **~ and large** nel complesso

---

bye(-bye) ['baɪ('baɪ)] *excl* ciao!, arrivederci!

by(e)-law *n* legge *f* locale

by-election (*BRIT*) *n* elezione *f* straordinaria

bygone ['baɪgɒn] *adj* passato(a) ♦ *n*: **let ~s be** *se* mettiamoci una pietra sopra

bypass ['baɪpɑːs] *n* circonvallazione *f*; (*MED*) by-pass *m inv* ♦ *vt* fare una deviazione intorno a

by-product *n* sottoprodotto; (*fig*) conseguenza secondaria

bystander ['baɪstændə*] *n* spettatore/trice

byte [baɪt] *n* (*COMPUT*) byte *m inv*, bicarattere *m*

byword ['baɪwɜːd] *n*: **to be a ~ for** essere sinonimo di

by-your-leave *n*: **without so much as a ~** senza nemmeno chiedere il permesso

C

C [siː] *n* (*MUS*) do

C.A. *n abbr* = **chartered accountant**

cab [kæb] *n* taxi *m inv*; (*of train, truck*) cabina

cabaret ['kæbəreɪ] *n* cabaret *m inv*

cabbage ['kæbɪdʒ] *n* cavolo

cabin ['kæbɪn] *n* capanna; (*on ship*) cabina; ~ **cruiser** *n* cabinato

cabinet ['kæbɪnɪt] *n* (*POL*) consiglio dei ministri; (*furniture*) armadietto; (*also: display* ~) vetrinetta

cable ['keɪbl] *n* cavo; fune *f*; (*TEL*) cablogramma *m* ♦ *vt* telegrafare; ~-**car** *n* funivia; ~ **television** *n* televisione *f* via cavo

cache [kæʃ] *n* deposito segreto

cackle ['kækl] *vi* schiamazzare

cacti ['kæktaɪ] *npl of* **cactus**

cactus ['kæktəs] (*pl* **cacti**) *n* cactus *m inv*

cadet [kə'dɛt] *n* (*MIL*) cadetto

cadge [kædʒ] (*inf*) *vt* scroccare

café ['kæfeɪ] *n* caffè *m inv*

cafeteria [kæfɪ'tɪərɪə] *n* self-service *m inv*

cage [keɪdʒ] *n* gabbia

cagey ['keɪdʒɪ] (*inf*) *adj* chiuso(a); guardingo(a)

cagoule [kə'guːl] *n* K-way *m inv* ®

cajole [kə'dʒəul] *vt* allettare

cake [keɪk] *n* (*large*, *torta*; (*small*) pasticcino; ~ **of soap** saponetta; ~**d** *adj*: ~**d with** incrostato(a) di

calculate ['kælkjuleɪt] *vt* calcolare; **calculation** [-'leɪʃən] *n* calcolo; **calculator** *n* calcolatrice *f*

calendar ['kæləndə*] *n* calendario; ~ **year** *n* anno civile

calf [kɑːf] (*pl* **calves**) *n* (*of cow*) vitello; (*of other animals*) piccolo; (*also:* ~**skin**) (pelle *f* di) vitello; (*ANAT*) polpaccio

calibre ['kælɪbə*] (*US* **caliber**) *n* calibro

call [kɔːl] *vt* (*gen*, *also TEL*) chiama-

re; (*meeting*) indire ♦ *vi* chiamare; (*visit: also:* ~ **in**, ~ **round**) passare ♦ *n* (*shout*) grido, urlo; (*TEL*) telefonata; **to be** ~**ed** (*person*, *object*) chiamarsi; **to be on** ~ a disposizione; ~ **back** *vi* (*return*) ritornare; (*TEL*) ritelefonare, richiamare; ~ **for** *vt fus* richiedere; (*fetch*) passare a prendere; ~ **off** *vt* disdire; ~ **on** *vt fus* (*visit*) passare da; (*appeal to*) chiedere a; ~ **out** *vi* (*in pain*) urlare; (*to person*) chiamare; ~ **up** *vt* (*MIL*) richiamare; (*TEL*) telefonare a; ~**box** (*BRIT*) *n* cabina telefonica; ~**er** *n* persona che chiama; visitatore/trice; ~ **girl** *n* ragazza *f* squillo *inv*; ~-**in** (*US*) *n* (*phone-in*) trasmissione *f* a filo diretto con gli ascoltatori; ~**ing** *n* vocazione *f*; ~**ing card** (*US*) *n* biglietto da visita

callous ['kæləs] *adj* indurito(a), insensibile

calm [kɑːm] *adj* calmo(a) ♦ *n* calma ♦ *vt* calmare; ~ **down** *vi* calmarsi ♦ *vt* calmare

Calor gas ['kælə*-] ® *n* butano

calorie ['kælərɪ] *n* caloria

calves [kɑːvz] *npl of* **calf**

camber ['kæmbə*] *n* (*of road*) bombatura

Cambodia [kæm'bəudjə] *n* Cambogia

camcorder ['kæmkɔːdə*] *n* videocamera

came [keɪm] *pt of* **come**

camel ['kæml] *n* cammello

camera ['kæmərə] *n* macchina fotografica; (*CINEMA*, *TV*) cinepresa; **in** ~ a porte chiuse; ~**man** *n* cameraman *m inv*

camouflage ['kæməflɑːʒ] *n* (*MIL*, *ZOOL*) mimetizzazione *f* ♦ *vt* mimetizzare

camp [kæmp] *n* campeggio; (*MIL*) campo ♦ *vi* accamparsi ♦ *adj* effeminato(a)

campaign [kæm'peɪn] *n* (*MIL*, *POL etc*) campagna ♦ *vi* (*also fig*) fare una campagna

camp bed (*BRIT*) *n* brandina

camper ['kæmpə*] n campeggiatore/
trice; (vehicle) camper m inv

camping ['kæmpɪŋ] n campeggio; **to
go ~** andare in campeggio

campsite ['kæmpsaɪt] n campeggio

campus ['kæmpəs] n campus m inv

can[1] [kæn] n (of milk) scatola; (of
oil) bidone m; (of water) tanica;
(tin) scatola ♦ vt mettere in scatola

KEYWORD

---

can[2] [kæn] (negative **cannot, can't**;
conditional and pt **could**) aux vb **1**
(be able to) potere; **I ~'t go any
further** non posso andare oltre; **you
~ do it if you try** sei in grado di
farlo — basta provarci; **I'll help you
all I ~** ti aiuterò come potrò; **I ~'t
see you** non ti vedo

2 (know how to) sapere, essere capace di; **I ~ swim** so nuotare; **~ you
speak French?** parla francese?

3 (may) potere; **could I have a
word with you?** posso parlarle un
momento?

4 (expressing disbelief, puzzlement
etc): **it ~'t be true!** non può essere
vero!; **what CAN he want?** cosa può
mai volere?

5 (expressing possibility, suggestion
etc): **he could be in the library**
può darsi che sia in biblioteca; **she
could have been delayed** può aver
avuto un contrattempo

Canada ['kænədə] n Canada m

Canadian [kə'neɪdɪən] adj, n canadese m/f

canal [kə'næl] n canale m

canary [kə'neərɪ] n canarino

cancel ['kænsəl] vt annullare; (train)
sopprimere; (cross out) cancellare;
~lation [-'leɪʃən] n annullamento,
soppressione f; cancellazione f;
(TOURISM) prenotazione f annullata

cancer ['kænsə*] n cancro; **C~**
(sign) Cancro

candid ['kændɪd] adj onesto(a)

candidate ['kændɪdeɪt] n candidato/a

candle ['kændl] n candela; (in
church) cero; **~light** n: **by ~light** a
lume di candela; **~stick** n bugia;
(bigger, ornate) candeliere m

candour ['kændə*] (US **candor**) n
sincerità

candy ['kændɪ] n zucchero candito;
(US) caramella; caramelle fpl; **~-
floss** (BRIT) n zucchero filato

cane [keɪn] n canna; (for furniture)
bambù m; (stick) verga ♦ vt (BRIT:
SCOL) punire a colpi di verga

canister ['kænɪstə*] n scatola metallica

cannabis ['kænəbɪs] n canapa indiana

canned ['kænd] adj (food) in scatola

cannon ['kænən] (pl ~ or ~s) n
(gun) cannone m

cannot ['kænɔt] = **can not**

canny ['kænɪ] adj furbo(a)

canoe [kə'nu:] n canoa

canon ['kænən] n (clergyman) cano-
nico; (standard) canone m

can opener [-'əupnə*] n apriscatole
m inv

canopy ['kænəpɪ] n baldacchino

can't [kænt] = **can not**

cantankerous [kæn'tæŋkərəs] adj
stizzoso(a)

canteen [kæn'ti:n] n mensa; (BRIT:
of cutlery) portaposate m inv

canter ['kæntə*] vi andare al piccolo
galoppo

canvas ['kænvəs] n tela

canvass ['kænvəs] vi (POL): **to ~
for** raccogliere voti per ♦ vt fare un
sondaggio di

canyon ['kænjən] n canyon m inv

cap [kæp] n (hat) berretto; (of pen)
coperchio; (of bottle, toy gun) tappo;
(contraceptive) diaframma m ♦ vt
(outdo) superare; (limit) fissare un
tetto (a)

capability [keɪpə'bɪlɪtɪ] n capacità f
inv, abilità f inv

capable ['keɪpəbl] adj capace

capacity [kə'pæsɪtɪ] n capacità f inv;
(of lift etc) capienza

cape [keɪp] n (garment) cappa;
(GEO) capo

caper ['keɪpə*] n (CULIN) cappero; (prank) scherzetto

capital ['kæpɪtl] n (also: ~ city) capitale f; (money) capitale m; (also: ~ letter) (lettera) maiuscola; ~ **gains tax** n imposta sulla plusvalenza; ~**ism** n capitalismo; ~**ist** adj, n capitalista (m/f); ~**ize**: to ~**ize on** vt fus trarre vantaggio da; ~ **punishment** n pena capitale

Capricorn ['kæprɪkɔ:n] n Capricorno

capsize [kæp'saɪz] vt capovolgere ♦ vi capovolgersi

capsule ['kæpsju:l] n capsula

captain ['kæptɪn] n capitano

caption ['kæpʃən] n leggenda

captivate ['kæptɪveɪt] vt avvincere

captive ['kæptɪv] adj, n prigioniero(a)

captivity [kæp'tɪvɪtɪ] n cattività

capture ['kæptʃə*] vt catturare; (COMPUT) registrare ♦ n cattura; (data ~) registrazione f or rilevazione f di dati

car [kɑ:*] n (AUT) macchina, automobile f; (RAIL) vagone m

carafe [kə'ræf] n caraffa

caramel ['kærəməl] n caramello

caravan ['kærəvæn] n (BRIT) roulotte f inv; (of camels) carovana; ~ **site** (BRIT) n campeggio per roulotte

carbohydrates [kɑ:bəʊ'haɪdreɪts] npl (foods) carboidrati mpl

carbon ['kɑ:bən] n carbonio; ~ **paper** n carta carbone

carburettor [kɑ:bjʊ'retə*] (US **carburetor**) n carburatore n

card [kɑ:d] n carta; (visiting ~ etc) biglietto; (Christmas ~ etc) cartolina; ~**board** n cartone m; ~ **game** n gioco di carte

cardiac ['kɑ:dɪæk] adj cardiaco(a)

cardigan ['kɑ:dɪgən] n cardigan m inv

cardinal ['kɑ:dɪnl] adj cardinale ♦ n cardinale m

card index n schedario

care [kɛə*] n cura, attenzione f; (worry) preoccupazione f ♦ vi: to ~

about curarsi di; (thing, idea) interessarsi di; ~ **of** presso; **in sb's** ~ alle cure di qn; **to take** ~ (**to do**) fare attenzione (a fare); **to take** ~ **of** curarsi di; (bill, problem) occuparsi di; **I don't** ~ non me ne importa; **I couldn't** ~ less non m'interessa affatto; ~ **for** vt fus aver cura di; (like) volere bene a

career [kə'rɪə*] n carriera ♦ vi (also: ~ along) andare di (gran) carriera

carefree ['kɛəfri:] adj sgombro(a) di preoccupazioni

careful ['kɛəful] adj attento(a); (cautious) cauto(a); (**be**) ~! attenzione!; ~**ly** adv con cura; cautamente

careless ['kɛəlɪs] adj negligente; (heedless) spensierato(a)

carer ['kɛərə*] n assistente m/f (di persone malata o handicappata)

caress [kə'rɛs] n carezza ♦ vt accarezzare

caretaker ['kɛəteɪkə*] n custode m

car-ferry n traghetto

cargo ['kɑ:gəʊ] (pl ~**es**) n carico

car hire n autonoleggio

Caribbean [kærɪ'bi:ən] adj: **the** ~ (**Sea**) il Mar dei Caraibi

caring ['kɛərɪŋ] adj (person) premuroso(a); (society, organization) umanitario(a)

carnage ['kɑ:nɪdʒ] n carneficina

carnation [kɑ:'neɪʃən] n garofano

carnival ['kɑ:nɪvəl] n (public celebration) carnevale m; (US: funfair) luna park m inv

carol ['kærəl] n: (**Christmas**) ~ canto di Natale

carp [kɑ:p] n (fish) carpa; ~ **at** vt fus trovare da ridire su

car park (BRIT) n parcheggio

carpenter ['kɑ:pɪntə*] n carpentiere m

carpentry ['kɑ:pɪntrɪ] n carpenteria

carpet ['kɑ:pɪt] n tappeto ♦ vt coprire con tappeto; ~ **slippers** npl pantofole fpl; ~ **sweeper** n scopatappeti m inv

car phone n telefonino per auto, cellulare *m* per auto

carriage ['kærɪdʒ] *n* vettura; (*of goods*) trasporto; ~ **return** *n* (*on typewriter etc*) leva (*or* tasto) del ritorno a capo; ~**way** (*BRIT*) *n* (*part of road*) carreggiata

carrier ['kærɪə*] *n* (*of disease*) portatore/trice; (*COMM*) impresa di trasporti; ~ **bag** (*BRIT*) *n* sacchetto

carrot ['kærət] *n* carota

carry ['kærɪ] *vt* (*subj: person*) portare; (: *vehicle*) trasportare; (*involve: responsibilities etc*) comportare; (*MED*) essere portatore/trice di ♦ *vi* (*sound*) farsi sentire; **to be** *or* **get carried away** (*fig*) entusiasmarsi; ~ **on** *vi*: **to** ~ **on with sth/doing** continuare qc/a fare ♦ *vt* mandare avanti; ~ **out** *vt* (*orders*) eseguire; (*investigation*) svolgere; ~**cot** (*BRIT*) *n* culla portabile; ~**on** (*inf*) *n* (*fuss*) casino, confusione *f*

cart [kɑ:t] *n* carro ♦ *vt* (*inf*) trascinare

carton ['kɑ:tən] *n* (*box*) scatola di cartone; (*of yogurt*) cartone *m*; (*of cigarettes*) stecca

cartoon [kɑ:'tu:n] *n* (*PRESS*) disegno umoristico; (*comic strip*) fumetto; (*CINEMA*) disegno animato

cartridge ['kɑ:trɪdʒ] *n* (*for gun, pen*) cartuccia; (*music tape*) cassetta

carve [kɑ:v] *vt* (*meat*) trinciare; (*wood, stone*) intagliare; ~ **up** *vt* (*fig: country*) suddividere; **carving** *n* (*in wood etc*) scultura; **carving knife** *n* trinciante *m*

car wash *n* lavaggio auto

cascade [kæs'keɪd] *n* cascata

case [keɪs] *n* caso; (*LAW*) causa, processo; (*box*) scatola; (*BRIT: also: suit~*) valigia; **in** ~ **of** in caso di; **in** ~ **he comes** mai lui; **in any** ~ in ogni caso; **just in** ~ in caso di bisogno

cash [kæʃ] *n* denaro; (*coins, notes*) denaro liquido ♦ *vt* incassare; **to pay (in)** ~ pagare in contanti; ~ **on delivery** pagamento alla consegna; ~**book** *n* giornale *m* di cassa;

~ **card** (*BRIT*) *n* tesserino di prelievo; ~ **desk** (*BRIT*) *n* cassa; ~ **dispenser** (*BRIT*) *n* sportello automatico

cashew [kæ'ʃu:] *n* (*also:* ~ **nut**) anacardio

cashier [kæ'ʃɪə*] *n* cassiere/a

cashmere [kæʃ'mɪə*] *n* cachemire *m*

cash register *n* registratore *m* di cassa

casing ['keɪsɪŋ] *n* rivestimento

casino [kə'si:nəʊ] *n* casinò *m inv*

cask [kɑ:sk] *n* botte *f*

casket ['kɑ:skɪt] *n* cofanetto; (*US: coffin*) bara

casserole ['kæsərəʊl] *n* casseruola; (*food*): **chicken** ~ pollo in casseruola

cassette [kæ'set] *n* cassetta; ~ **player** *n* riproduttore *m* a cassette; ~ **recorder** *n* registratore *m* a cassette

cast [kɑ:st] (*pt, pp* **cast**) *vt* (*throw*) gettare; (*metal*) gettare, fondere; (*THEATRE*): **to** ~ **sb as Hamlet** scegliere qn per la parte di Amleto ♦ *n* (*THEATRE*) cast *m inv*; (*also: plaster* ~) ingessatura; **to** ~ **one's vote** votare, dare il voto; ~ **off** *vi* (*NAUT*) salpare; (*KNITTING*) calare; ~ **on** *vi* (*KNITTING*) avviare le maglie

castaway ['kɑ:stəweɪ] *n* naufrago/a

caster sugar ['kɑ:stə*-] (*BRIT*) *n* zucchero semolato

casting vote ['kɑ:stɪŋ-] (*BRIT*) *n* voto decisivo

cast iron *n* ghisa

castle ['kɑ:sl] *n* castello

castor ['kɑ:stə*] *n* (*wheel*) rotella; ~ **oil** *n* olio di ricino

castrate [kæs'treɪt] *vt* castrare

casual ['kæʒʊl] *adj* (*by chance*) casuale, fortuito(a); (*irregular: work etc*) avventizio(a); (*unconcerned*) noncurante, indifferente; ~ **wear** casual *m*; ~**ly** *adv* (*in a relaxed way*) con noncuranza; (*dress*) casual

casualty ['kæʒjʊltɪ] *n* ferito/a; (*dead*) morto/a, vittima; (*MED: department*) pronto soccorso

cat [kæt] n gatto

catalogue ['kætələg] (US **catalog**) n catalogo ♦ vt catalogare

catalyst ['kætəlɪst] n catalizzatore m

catalytic convertor [kætəlɪtɪk-] n marmitta catalitica

catapult ['kætəpʌlt] n catapulta; fionda

cataract ['kætərækt] n (also MED) cateratta

catarrh [kə'tɑː*] n catarro

catastrophe [kə'tæstrəfɪ] n catastrofe f

catch [kætʃ] (pt, pp **caught**) vt prendere; (ball) afferrare; (surprise: person) sorprendere; (attention) attirare; (comment, whisper) cogliere; (person: also: ~ **up**) raggiungere ♦ vi (fire) prendere ♦ n (fish etc caught) retata; (of ball) presa; (trick) trappola; (TECH) gancio; (game) catch m inv; **to ~ fire** prendere fuoco; **to ~ sight of** scorgere; **~ on** vi capire; (become popular) affermarsi, far presa; **~ up** vi mettersi in pari ♦ vt (also: **~ up with**) raggiungere

catching ['kætʃɪŋ] adj (MED) contagioso(a)

catchment area ['kætʃmənt-] (BRIT) n (SCOL) circoscrizione f scolare

catch phrase n slogan m inv; frase f fatta

catchy ['kætʃɪ] adj orecchiabile

category ['kætɪgərɪ] n categoria

cater ['keɪtə*] vi: **~ for** (BRIT: needs) provvedere a; (: readers, consumers) incontrare i gusti di; (COMM: provide food) provvedere alla ristorazione di; **~er** n fornitore m; **~ing** n approvvigionamento

caterpillar ['kætəpɪlə*] n bruco; **~ track** n catena a cingoli

cathedral [kə'θiːdrəl] n cattedrale f, duomo

catholic ['kæθəlɪk] adj universale; aperto(a); eclettico(a); **C~** adj, n (REL) cattolico(a)

cat's-eye [kæts'aɪ] (BRIT) n (AUT)

catarifrangente m

cattle ['kætl] npl bestiame m, bestie fpl

catty ['kætɪ] adj maligno(a), dispettoso(a)

caucus ['kɔːkəs] n (POL: group) comitato di dirigenti; (: US) (riunione f del) comitato elettorale

caught [kɔːt] pt, pp of **catch**

cauliflower ['kɔlɪflauə*] n cavolfiore m

cause [kɔːz] n causa ♦ vt causare

caution ['kɔːʃən] n prudenza; (warning) avvertimento ♦ vt avvertire; ammonire

cautious ['kɔːʃəs] adj cauto(a), prudente

cavalier [kævə'lɪə*] adj brusco(a)

cavalry ['kævəlrɪ] n cavalleria

cave [keɪv] n caverna, grotta; **~ in** vi (roof etc) crollare; **~man** n uomo delle caverne

caviar(e) ['kævɪɑː*] n caviale m

cavort [kə'vɔːt] vi far capriole

CB n abbr (= Citizens' Band (Radio)): **~ radio** (set) baracchino

CBI n abbr (= Confederation of British Industries) ≈ Confindustria

cc abbr = cubic centimetres; carbon copy

CD abbr (disc) CD m inv; (player) lettore m CD inv

CD-ROM [-rɔm] n abbr CD-ROM m inv

cease [siːs] vt, vi cessare; **~fire** n cessate il fuoco m inv; **~less** adj incessante, continuo(a)

cedar ['siːdə*] n cedro

ceiling ['siːlɪŋ] n soffitto; (on wages etc) tetto

celebrate ['sɛlɪbreɪt] vt, vi celebrare; **~d** adj celebre; **celebration** [-'breɪʃən] n celebrazione f

celery ['sɛlərɪ] n sedano

cell [sɛl] n cella; (of revolutionaries, BIOL) cellula; (ELEC) elemento (di batteria)

cellar ['sɛlə*] n sottosuolo; cantina

'cello ['tʃɛləu] n violoncello

cellphone [sɛl,fəun] n cellulare m

Celt [kɛlt, sɛlt] n celta m/f

Celtic ['kɛltɪk, 'sɛltɪk] adj celtico(a)

cement [sə'mɛnt] n cemento; ~ **mixer** n betoniera

cemetery ['sɛmɪtrɪ] n cimitero

censor ['sɛnsə*] n censore m ♦ vt censurare; ~**ship** n censura

censure ['sɛnʃə*] vt riprovare, censurare

census ['sɛnsəs] n censimento

cent [sɛnt] n (US: coin) centesimo (= 1:100 di un dollaro); see also **per**

centenary [sɛn'tiːnərɪ] n centenario

center ['sɛntə*] (US) n, vt = **centre**

centigrade ['sɛntɪgreɪd] adj centigrado(a)

centimetre ['sɛntɪmiːtə*] (US **centimeter**) n centimetro

centipede ['sɛntɪpiːd] n centopiedi m inv

central ['sɛntrəl] adj centrale; **C~ America** n America centrale; ~ **heating** n riscaldamento centrale; ~**ize** vt accentrare

centre ['sɛntə*] (US **center**) n centro ♦ vt centrare; ~**-forward** n (SPORT) centroavanti m inv; ~**-half** n (SPORT) centromediano

century ['sɛntjʊrɪ] n secolo; **20th ~** ventesimo secolo

ceramic [sɪ'ræmɪk] adj ceramico(a); ~**s** npl ceramica

cereal ['sɪːrɪəl] n cereale m

ceremony ['sɛrɪmənɪ] n cerimonia; **to stand on ~** fare complimenti

certain ['sɜːtən] adj certo(a); **to make ~ of** assicurarsi di; **for ~** per certo, di sicuro; ~**ly** adv certamente, certo; ~**ty** n certezza

certificate [sə'tɪfɪkɪt] n certificato; diploma m

certified ['sɜːtɪfaɪd]: ~ **mail** (US) n posta raccomandata con ricevuta di ritorno; ~ **public accountant** (US) n ≈ commercialista m/f

certify ['sɜːtɪfaɪ] vt certificare; (award diploma to) conferire un diploma a; (declare insane) dichiarare pazzo(a)

cervical ['sɜːvɪkl] adj: ~ **cancer**

cancro della cervice; ~ **smear** Pap test m inv

cervix ['sɜːvɪks] n cervice f

cesspit ['sɛspɪt] n pozzo nero

cf. abbr (= compare) cfr

CFC n (= chlorofluorocarbon) CFC m inv

ch. abbr (= chapter) cap

chafe [tʃeɪf] vt fregare, irritare

chagrin ['ʃægrɪn] n disappunto

chain [tʃeɪn] n catena ♦ vt (also: ~ up) incatenare; ~ **reaction** n reazione f a catena; ~**-smoke** vi fumare una sigaretta dopo l'altra; ~ **store** n negozio a catena

chair [tʃɛə*] n sedia; (armchair) poltrona; (of university) cattedra; (of meeting) presidenza ♦ vt (meeting) presiedere; ~**lift** n seggiovia; ~**man** n presidente m

chalice ['tʃælɪs] n calice m

chalk [tʃɔːk] n gesso

challenge ['tʃælɪndʒ] n sfida ♦ vt sfidare; (statement, right) mettere in dubbio; **to ~ sb to do** sfidare qn a fare; **challenging** adj (task) impegnativo(a); (look) di sfida

chamber ['tʃeɪmbə*] n camera; ~ **of commerce** n camera di commercio; ~**maid** n cameriera; ~ **music** n musica da camera

chamois ['ʃæmwɑː] n camoscio; (also: ~ leather) panno in pelle di camoscio

champagne [ʃæm'peɪn] n champagne m inv

champion ['tʃæmpɪən] n campione/essa; ~**ship** n campionato

chance [tʃɑːns] n caso; (opportunity) occasione f; (likelihood) possibilità f inv ♦ vt: **to ~ it** rischiare, provarci ♦ adj fortuito(a); **to take a ~** rischiare; **by ~** per caso

chancellor ['tʃɑːnsələ*] n cancelliere m; **C~ of the Exchequer** (BRIT) n Cancelliere dello Scacchiere

chandelier [ʃændə'lɪə*] n lampadario

change [tʃeɪndʒ] vt cambiare; (transform): **to ~ sb into** trasformare qn in ♦ *vi* cambiare; (~ *one's clothes*) cambiarsi; (*be transformed*): **to ~ into** trasformarsi in ♦ *n* cambiamento; (*of clothes*) cambio; (*money*) resto; **to ~ one's mind** cambiare idea; **for a ~** tanto per cambiare; **~able** *adj* (*weather*) variabile; **~ machine** *n* distributore automatico di monete; **~over** *n* cambiamento, passaggio

changing ['tʃeɪndʒɪŋ] *adj* che cambia; (*colours*) cangiante; **~ room** *n* (*BRIT*: *in shop*) camerino; (: *SPORT*) spogliatoio

channel ['tʃænl] *n* canale *m*; (*of river, sea*) alveo ♦ *vt* canalizzare; **the (English) C~** la Manica; **the C~ Islands** *npl* le Isole Normanne

chant [tʃɑːnt] *n* canto; salmodia ♦ *vt* cantare; salmodiare

chaos ['keɪɒs] *n* caos *m*

chap [tʃæp] (*BRIT*: *inf*) *n* (*man*) tipo

chapel ['tʃæpəl] *n* cappella

chaperone ['ʃæpərəun] *n* accompagnatrice *f* ♦ *vt* accompagnare

chaplain ['tʃæplɪn] *n* cappellano

chapped [tʃæpt] *adj* (*skin, lips*) screpolato(a)

chapter ['tʃæptə*] *n* capitolo

char [tʃɑː*] *vt* (*burn*) carbonizzare ♦ *n* (*BRIT*) = **charlady**

character ['kærɪktə*] *n* carattere *m*; (*in novel, film*) personaggio; **~istic** [-'rɪstɪk] *adj* caratteristico(a) ♦ *n* caratteristica

charade [ʃə'rɑːd] *n* sciarada

charcoal ['tʃɑːkəul] *n* carbone *m* di legna

charge [tʃɑːdʒ] *n* accusa; (*cost*) prezzo; (*responsibility*) responsabilità ♦ *vt* (*gun, battery, MIL: enemy*) caricare; (*customer*) fare pagare a; (*sum*) fare pagare; (*LAW*): **to ~** (**with**) accusare qn (di) ♦ *vi* (*gen with: up, down*) lanciarsi; **~s** *npl* (*bank ~s etc*) tariffe *fpl*; **to reverse the ~s** (*TEL*) fare una telefonata a carico del destinatario; **to take ~ of** incaricarsi di; **to be in ~ of** essere responsabile per; **how much do you**

~? quanto chiedete?; **to ~ an expense (up) to sb** addebitare una spesa a qn; **~ card** *n* carta *f* clienti *inv*

charitable ['tʃærɪtəbl] *adj* caritatevole

charity ['tʃærɪtɪ] *n* carità; (*organization*) opera pia

charlady ['tʃɑːleɪdɪ] (*BRIT*) *n* domestica a ore

charlatan ['ʃɑːlətən] *n* ciarlatano

charm [tʃɑːm] *n* fascino; (*on bracelet*) ciondolo ♦ *vt* affascinare, incantare; **~ing** *adj* affascinante

chart [tʃɑːt] *n* tabella; grafico; (*map*) carta nautica ♦ *vt* fare una carta nautica di; **~s** *npl* (*MUS*) hit parade *f*

charter ['tʃɑːtə*] *vt* (*plane*) noleggiare ♦ *n* (*document*) carta; **~ed accountant** (*BRIT*) *n* ragioniere/a professionista; **~ flight** *n* volo *m* charter *inv*

charwoman ['tʃɑːwumən] *n* = **charlady**

chase [tʃeɪs] *vt* inseguire; (*also*: **~ away**) cacciare ♦ *n* caccia

chasm ['kæzəm] *n* abisso

chassis ['ʃæsɪ] *n* telaio

chastity ['tʃæstɪtɪ] *n* castità

chat [tʃæt] *vi* (*also*: *have a ~*) chiacchierare ♦ *n* chiacchierata; **~ show** (*BRIT*) *n* talk show *m inv*

chatter ['tʃætə*] *vi* (*person*) ciarlare; (*bird*) cinguettare; (*teeth*) battere ♦ *n* ciarle *fpl*; cinguettio; **~box** (*inf*) *n* chiacchierone/a

chatty ['tʃætɪ] *adj* (*style*) familiare; (*person*) chiacchierino(a)

chauffeur ['ʃəufə*] *n* autista *m*

chauvinist ['ʃəuvɪnɪst] *n* (*male ~*) maschilista *m*; (*nationalist*) sciovinista *m/f*

cheap [tʃiːp] *adj* a buon mercato; (*joke*) grossolano(a); (*poor quality*) di cattiva qualità ♦ *adv* a buon mercato; **~er** *adj* meno caro(a); **~ly** *adv* a buon prezzo, a buon mercato

cheat [tʃiːt] *vi* imbrogliare; (*at school*) copiare ♦ *vt* ingannare ♦ *n* imbroglione *m*; **to ~ sb out of sth** defraudare qn di qc

check [tʃɛk] *vt* verificare; *(passport, ticket)* controllare; *(halt)* fermare; *(restrain)* contenere ♦ *n* verifica; controllo; *(curb)* freno; *(US: bill)* conto; *(pattern: gen pl)* quadretti *mpl*; *(US)* = **cheque** ♦ *adj (pattern, cloth)* a quadretti; **~ in** *vi (in hotel)* registrare; *(at airport)* presentarsi all'accettazione ♦ *vt (luggage)* depositare; **~ out** *vi (in hotel)* saldare il conto; **~ up** *vi:* **to ~ up (on sth)** investigare (qc); **to ~ up on sb** informarsi sul conto di qn; **~ered** *(US) adj* = **chequered**; **~ers** *(US) n dama*; **~in (desk)** *n* check-in *m inv*, accettazione *f* (bagagli *inv*); **~ing account** *(US)* *n* conto corrente; **~mate** *n* scaccomatto; **~out** *n (in supermarket)* cassa; **~point** *n* posto di blocco; **~room** *(US)* *n* deposito *m* bagagli *inv*; **~up** *n (MED)* controllo medico

cheek [tʃiːk] *n* guancia; *(impudence)* faccia tosta; **~bone** *n* zigomo; **~y** *adj* sfacciato(a)

cheep [tʃiːp] *vi* pigolare

cheer [tʃɪə*] *vt* applaudire; *(gladden)* rallegrare ♦ *vi* applaudire ♦ *n* grido (di incoraggiamento); **~s** *npl (of approval, encouragement)* applausi *mpl*; evviva *mpl*; **~s!** salute!; **~ up** *vi* rallegrarsi, farsi animo ♦ *vt* rallegrare; **~ful** *adj* allegro(a)

cheerio [tʃɪərɪ'əu] *(BRIT)* *excl* ciao!

cheese [tʃiːz] *n* formaggio; **~board** *n* piatto del (or per il) formaggio

cheetah [tʃiːtə] *n* ghepardo

chef [ʃɛf] *n* capocuoco

chemical ['kɛmɪkəl] *adj* chimico(a) ♦ *n* prodotto chimico

chemist ['kɛmɪst] *n (BRIT: pharmacist)* farmacista *m/f*; *(scientist)* chimico(a); **~ry** *n* chimica; **~'s (shop)** *(BRIT)* *n* farmacia

cheque [tʃɛk] *(BRIT)* *n* assegno; **~book** *n* libretto degli assegni; **~ card** *n* carta *f* assegni *inv*

chequered ['tʃɛkəd] *(US* check-

ered) *adj (fig)* movimentato(a)

cherish ['tʃɛrɪʃ] *vt* aver caro

cherry ['tʃɛrɪ] *n* ciliegia; *(also: ~ tree)* ciliegio

chess [tʃɛs] *n* scacchi *mpl*; **~board** *n* scacchiera

chest [tʃɛst] *n* petto; *(box)* cassa; **~ of drawers** *n* cassettone *m*

chestnut ['tʃɛsnʌt] *n* castagna; *(also: ~ tree)* castagno

chew [tʃuː] *vt* masticare; **~ing gum** *n* chewing gum *m*

chic [ʃiːk] *adj* elegante

chick [tʃɪk] *n* pulcino; *(inf)* pollastrella

chicken ['tʃɪkɪn] *n* pollo; *(inf: coward)* coniglio; **~ out** *(inf)* *vi* avere fifa; **~pox** *n* varicella

chicory ['tʃɪkərɪ] *n* cicoria

chief [tʃiːf] *n* capo ♦ *adj* principale; **~ executive** *n* direttore *m* generale; **~ly** *adv* per lo più, soprattutto

chilblain ['tʃɪlbleɪn] *n* gelone *m*

child [tʃaɪld] *(pl* **~ren**) *n* bambino/a; **~birth** *n* parto; **~hood** *n* infanzia; **~ish** *adj* puerile; **~like** *adj* fanciullesco(a); **~ minder** *(BRIT)* *n* bambinaia

children ['tʃɪldrən] *npl of* **child**

Chile ['tʃɪlɪ] *n* Cile *m*

chill [tʃɪl] *n* freddo; *(MED)* infreddatura ♦ *vt* raffreddare

chil(l)i ['tʃɪlɪ] *n* peperoncino

chilly ['tʃɪlɪ] *adj* freddo(a), fresco(a); **to feel ~** sentirsi infreddolito(a)

chime [tʃaɪm] *n* carillon *m inv* ♦ *vi* suonare, scampanare

chimney ['tʃɪmnɪ] *n* camino; **~ sweep** *n* spazzacamino

chimpanzee [tʃɪmpæn'ziː] *n* scimpanzé *m inv*

chin [tʃɪn] *n* mento

China ['tʃaɪnə] *n* Cina

china ['tʃaɪnə] *n* porcellana

Chinese [tʃaɪ'niːz] *adj* cinese ♦ *n inv* cinese *m/f*; *(LING)* cinese *m*

chink [tʃɪŋk] *n (opening)* fessura; *(noise)* tintinnio

chip [tʃɪp] *n (gen pl: CULIN)* patatina fritta; *(: US: also: potato ~)* patatina; (of wood, glass, stone) scheggia; (also: micro~) chip m inv ♦ vt (cup, plate) scheggiare; ~ in (inf) vi (contribute) contribuire; (interrupt) intromettersi

chiropodist [kɪˈrɔpədɪst] (BRIT) n pedicure m/f inv

chirp [tʃɜːp] vi cinguettare; fare cri cri

chisel [ˈtʃɪzl] n cesello

chit [tʃɪt] n biglietto

chitchat [ˈtʃɪtʃæt] n chiacchiere fpl

chivalry [ˈʃɪvəlrɪ] n cavalleria; cortesia

chives [tʃaɪvz] npl erba cipollina

chock-a-block [ˈtʃɔk-] adj pieno(a) zeppo(a)

chock-full [ˈtʃɔk-] adj = chock-a-block

chocolate [ˈtʃɔklɪt] n (substance) cioccolato, cioccolata; (drink) cioccolata; (a sweet) cioccolatino

choice [tʃɔɪs] n scelta ♦ adj scelto(a)

choir [ˈkwaɪə*] n coro; ~**boy** n corista m fanciullo

choke [tʃəʊk] vi soffocare ♦ vt soffocare; (block): **to be ~d with** essere intasato(a) di ♦ n (AUT) valvola dell'aria

cholera [ˈkɔlərə] n colera m

cholesterol [kəˈlestərɔl] n colesterolo

choose [tʃuːz] (pt chose, pp chosen) vt scegliere; **to ~ to do** decidere di fare; preferire fare

choosy [ˈtʃuːzɪ] adj schizzinoso(a)

chop [tʃɔp] vt (wood) spaccare; (CULIN: also: ~ up) tritare ♦ n (CULIN) costoletta; ~**s** npl (jaws) mascelle fpl

chopper [ˈtʃɔpə*] n (helicopter) elicottero

choppy [ˈtʃɔpɪ] adj (sea) mosso(a)

chopsticks [ˈtʃɔpstɪks] npl bastoncini mpl cinesi

choral [ˈkɔːrəl] adj corale

chord [kɔːd] n (MUS) accordo

chore [tʃɔː*] n faccenda; household ~s faccende fpl domestiche

choreographer [kɔrɪˈɔɡrəfə*] n coreografo/a

chortle [ˈtʃɔːtl] vi ridacchiare

chorus [ˈkɔːrəs] n coro; (repeated part of song, also fig) ritornello

chose [tʃəʊz] pt of **choose**

chosen [ˈtʃəʊzn] pp of **choose**

Christ [kraɪst] n Cristo

christen [ˈkrɪsn] vt battezzare

Christian [ˈkrɪstɪən] adj, n cristiano(a); ~**ity** [-ˈænɪtɪ] n cristianesimo; ~ **name** n nome m (di battesimo)

Christmas [ˈkrɪsməs] n Natale m; Merry ~! Buon Natale!; ~ **card** n cartolina di Natale; ~ **Day** n il giorno di Natale; ~ **Eve** n la vigilia di Natale; ~ **tree** n albero di Natale

chrome [krəʊm] n cromo

chromium [ˈkrəʊmɪəm] n cromo

chronic [ˈkrɔnɪk] adj cronico(a)

chronicle [ˈkrɔnɪkl] n cronaca

chronological [krɔnəˈlɔdʒɪkəl] adj cronologico(a)

chrysanthemum [krɪˈsænθəməm] n crisantemo

chubby [ˈtʃʌbɪ] adj paffuto(a)

chuck [tʃʌk] (inf) vt buttare, gettare; (BRIT: also: ~ up) piantare; ~ **out** vt buttar fuori

chuckle [ˈtʃʌkl] vi ridere sommessamente

chug [tʃʌɡ] vi fare ciuf ciuf

chum [tʃʌm] n compagno/a

chunk [tʃʌŋk] n pezzo

church [tʃɜːtʃ] n chiesa; ~**yard** n sagrato

churlish [ˈtʃɜːlɪʃ] adj rozzo(a), sgarbato(a)

churn [tʃɜːn] n (for butter) zangola; (for milk) bidone m; ~ **out** vt sfornare

chute [ʃuːt] n (also: rubbish ~) canale m di scarico; (BRIT: children's slide) scivolo

chutney [ˈtʃʌtnɪ] n salsa piccante (di frutta, zucchero e spezie)

CIA (US) n abbr (= Central Intelligence Agency) CIA f

CID (BRIT) n abbr (= Criminal Investigation Department) ≈ polizia giudiziaria

cider ['saɪdə*] n sidro

cigar [sɪ'gɑː*] n sigaro

cigarette [sɪgə'rɛt] n sigaretta; ~ **case** n portasigarette m inv; ~ **end** n mozzicone m

Cinderella [sɪndə'rɛlə] n Cenerentola

cinders ['sɪndəz] npl ceneri fpl

cine camera ['sɪnɪ-] (BRIT) n cinepresa

cine-film ['sɪnɪ-] (BRIT) n pellicola

cinema ['sɪnəmə] n cinema m inv

cinnamon ['sɪnəmən] n cannella

cipher ['saɪfə*] n cifra

circle ['səːkl] n cerchio; (of friends etc) circolo; (in cinema) galleria ♦ vi girare in circolo ♦ vt (surround) circondare; (move round) girare intorno a

circuit ['səːkɪt] n circuito; ~ous [səː'kjuːɪtəs] adj indiretto(a)

circular ['səːkjulə*] adj circolare ♦ n circolare f

circulate ['səːkjuleɪt] vi circolare ♦ vt far circolare; **circulation** [-'leɪʃən] n circolazione f; (of newspaper) tiratura

circumstances ['səːkəmstənsɪz] npl circostanze fpl; (financial condition) condizioni fpl finanziarie

circumvent [səːkəm'vɛnt] vt aggirare

circus ['səːkəs] n circo

CIS n abbr (= Commonwealth of Independent States) CSI f

cistern ['sɪstən] n cisterna; (in toilet) serbatoio d'acqua

citizen ['sɪtɪzn] n (of country) cittadino/a; (of town) abitante m/f; ~**ship** n cittadinanza

citrus fruit ['sɪtrəs-] n agrume m

city ['sɪtɪ] n città f inv; the C~ la Città di Londra (centro commerciale)

civic ['sɪvɪk] adj civico(a); ~ **centre** (BRIT) n centro civico

civil ['sɪvɪl] adj civile; ~ **engineer** n ingegnere m civile; ~**ian** [sɪ'vɪlɪən] adj, n borghese m/f

civilization [sɪvɪlaɪ'zeɪʃən] n civiltà f inv

civilized ['sɪvɪlaɪzd] adj civilizza-

to(a); (fig) cortese

civil: ~ **law** n codice m civile; (study) diritto civile; ~ **servant** n impiegato/a statale; **C~ Service** n amministrazione f statale; ~ **war** n guerra civile

clad [klæd] adj: ~ (in) vestito(a) (di)

claim [kleɪm] vt (assert): to ~ (that)/to sostenere (che)/di essere; (credit, rights etc) rivendicare; (damages) richiedere ♦ vi (for insurance) fare una domanda d'indennizzo ♦ n pretesa; rivendicazione f; richiesta; ~**ant** n (ADMIN, LAW) richiedente m/f

clairvoyant [klɛə'vɔɪənt] n chiaroveggente m/f

clam [klæm] n vongola

clamber ['klæmbə*] vi arrampicarsi

clammy ['klæmɪ] adj (weather) caldo(a) umido(a); (hands) viscido(a)

clamour ['klæmə*] (US clamor) vi: to ~ for chiedere a gran voce

clamp [klæmp] n pinza, morsa ♦ vt stringere con una morsa; ~ **down on** vt fus dare un giro di vite a

clan [klæn] n clan m inv

clang [klæŋ] vi emettere un suono metallico

clap [klæp] vi applaudire; ~**ping** n applausi mpl

claret ['klærət] n vino di Bordeaux

clarify ['klærɪfaɪ] vt chiarificare, chiarire

clarinet ['klærɪ'nɛt] n clarinetto

clarity ['klærɪtɪ] n clarità f

clash [klæʃ] n frastuono; (fig) scontro ♦ vi scontrarsi; cozzare

clasp [klɑːsp] n (hold) stretta; (of necklace, bag) fermaglio, fibbia ♦ vt stringere

class [klɑːs] n classe f ♦ vt classificare

classic ['klæsɪk] adj classico(a) ♦ n classico; ~**al** adj classico(a)

classified ['klæsɪfaɪd] adj (information) segreto(a), riservato(a); ~ **advertisement** n annuncio economico

classmate ['klɑːsmeɪt] n compagno/a

di classe
classroom ['klɑːsrum] n aula
clatter ['klætə*] n tintinnio; scalpitio
♦ vi tintinnare; scalpitare
clause [klɔːz] n clausola; (LING)
proposizione f
claw [klɔː] n (of bird of prey) artiglio; (of lobster) pinza; ~ **at** vt fus
graffiare; afferrare
clay [kleɪ] n argilla
clean [kliːn] adj pulito(a); (clear,
smooth) liscio(a) ♦ vt pulire; ~ **out**
vt ripulire; ~ **up** vt (also fig) ripulire; ~**cut** adj (man) curato(a); ~**er**
n (person) addetto/a delle pulizie; ~**er's**
n (also: dry ~er's) tintoria; ~**ing** n
pulizia; ~**liness** ['klɛnlɪnɪs] n pulizia
cleanse [klɛnz] vt pulire; purificare;
~**r** n detergente m
clean-shaven [-'ʃeɪvn] adj sbarbato(a)
cleansing department ['klɛnzɪŋ-]
(BRIT) n nettezza urbana
clear [klɪə*] adj chiaro(a); (glass
etc) trasparente; (road, way) libero(a); (conscience) pulito(a) ♦ vt
sgombrare; liberare; (table) sparecchiare; (cheque) far compensazione di; (LAW: suspect) discolpare;
(obstacle) superare ♦ vi (weather)
rasserenarsi; (fog) andarsene ♦ adv:
~ **of** distante da; ~ **up** vt mettere
in ordine; (mystery) risolvere;
~**ance** n (removal) sgombro; (permission) autorizzazione f, permesso;
~**cut** adj ben delineato(a); ~**ing** n
radura; ~**ing bank** (BRIT) n banca (che fa uso della camera di compensazione); ~**ly** adv
chiaramente; ~**way** (BRIT) n strada con divieto di sosta
cleaver ['kliːvə*] n mannaia
clef [klɛf] n (MUS) chiave f
cleft [klɛft] n (in rock) crepa, fenditura
clench [klɛntʃ] vt stringere
clergy ['klɜːdʒɪ] n clero; ~**man** n
ecclesiastico
clerical ['klɛrɪkəl] adj d'impiegato;
(REL) cleiricale

clerk [klɑːk, (US) klɜːrk] n (BRIT)
impiegato/a; (US) commesso/a
clever ['klɛvə*] adj (mentally) intelligente; (deft, skilful) abile; (device,
arrangement) ingegnoso(a)
click [klɪk] vi scattare ♦ vt (heels
etc) battere; (tongue) far schioccare
client ['klaɪənt] n cliente m/f
cliff [klɪf] n scogliera scoscesa, rupe f
climate ['klaɪmɪt] n clima m
climax ['klaɪmæks] n culmine m;
(sexual) orgasmo
climb [klaɪm] vi salire; (clamber) arrampicarsi ♦ vt salire; (CLIMBING)
scalare ♦ n salita; arrampicata; scalata; ~**down** n marcia indietro;
~**er** n rocciatore/trice; alpinista m/f;
~**ing** n alpinismo
clinch [klɪntʃ] vt (deal) concludere
cling [klɪŋ] (pt, pp clung) vi: to ~
(**to**) aggrapparsi (a); (of clothes)
aderire strettamente (a)
clinic ['klɪnɪk] n clinica; ~**al** adj clinico(a); (fig) distaccato(a); (: room)
freddo(a)
clink [klɪŋk] vi tintinnare
clip [klɪp] n (for hair) forcina; (also:
paper ~) graffetta; (TV, CINEMA)
sequenza ♦ vt attaccare insieme;
(hair, nails) tagliare; (hedge) tosare;
~**pers** npl (for gardening) cesoie
fpl; (also: nail ~pers) forbicine fpl
per le unghie; ~**ping** n (from newspaper) ritaglio
clique [kliːk] n cricca
cloak [kləuk] n mantello ♦ vt avvolgere; ~**room** n (for coats etc) guardaroba m inv; (BRIT: W.C.) gabinetti
mpl
clock [klɔk] n orologio; ~ **in** or **on**
vi timbrare il cartellino (all'entrata);
~ **off** or **out** vi timbrare il cartellino (all'uscita); ~**wise** adv in senso
orario; ~**work** n movimento or meccanismo a orologeria ♦ adj a molla
clog [klɔg] n zoccolo ♦ vt intasare
♦ vi (also: ~ up) intasarsi, bloccarsi
cloister ['klɔɪstə*] n chiostro
clone [kləun] n clone m
close¹ [kləus] adj: ~ (**to**) vicino(a),

(a); (*watch, link, relative*) stretto(a); (*examination*) attento(a); (*contest*) combattuto(a); (*weather*) afoso(a) ♦ *adv* vicino, dappresso; ~ to vicino a; ~ **by**, ~ **at hand** a portata di mano; a ~ **friend** un amico intimo; **to have a** ~ **shave** (*fig*) scamparla bella

close² [kləʊz] *vt* chiudere ♦ *vi* (*shop etc*) chiudere; (*lid, door etc*) chiudersi; (*end*) finire ♦ *n* (*end*) fine *f*; ~ **down** *vi* cessare (definitivamente); ~**d** *adj* chiuso(a); ~**d shop** *n* azienda o fabbrica che impiega solo aderenti ai sindacati

close-knit [kləʊs'nɪt] *adj* (*family, community*) molto unito(a)

closely ['kləʊslɪ] *adv* (*examine, watch*) da vicino; (*related*) strettamente

closet ['klɒzɪt] *n* (*cupboard*) armadio

close-up ['kləʊsʌp] *n* primo piano

closure ['kləʊʒə*] *n* chiusura

clot [klɒt] *n* (*also: blood* ~) coagulo; (*inf: idiot*) scemo/a ♦ *vi* coagularsi

cloth [klɒθ] *n* (*material*) tessuto, stoffa; (*rag*) strofinaccio

clothe [kləʊð] *vt* vestire; ~**s** *npl* abiti *mpl*, vestiti *mpl*; ~**s brush** *n* spazzola per abiti; ~**s line** *n* corda (per stendere il bucato); ~**s peg** (*US* ~**s pin**) *n* molletta

clothing ['kləʊðɪŋ] *n* = **clothes**

cloud [klaʊd] *n* nuvola; ~**burst** *n* acquazzone *m*; ~**y** *adj* nuvoloso(a); (*liquid*) torbido(a)

clout [klaʊt] *vt* dare un colpo a

clove [kləʊv] *n* chiodo di garofano; ~ **of garlic** spicchio d'aglio

clover ['kləʊvə*] *n* trifoglio

clown [klaʊn] *n* pagliaccio ♦ *vi* (*also:* ~ *about,* ~ *around*) fare il pagliaccio

cloying ['klɔɪŋ] *adj* (*taste, smell*) nauseabondo(a)

club [klʌb] *n* (*society*) club *m inv*, circolo; (*weapon, GOLF*) mazza ♦ *vt* bastonare ♦ *vi*: **to** ~ **together** associarsi; ~**s** *npl* (*CARDS*) fiori *mpl*; ~ **car** (*US*) *n* (*RAIL*) vagone *m* risto-

rante; ~**house** *n* sede *f* del circolo

cluck [klʌk] *vi* chiocciare

clue [kluː] *n* indizio; (*in crosswords*) definizione *f*; **I haven't a** ~ non ho la minima idea

clump [klʌmp] *n* (*of flowers, trees*) gruppo; (*of grass*) ciuffo

clumsy ['klʌmzɪ] *adj* goffo(a)

clung [klʌŋ] *pt, pp of* **cling**

cluster ['klʌstə*] *n* gruppo ♦ *vi* raggrupparsi

clutch [klʌtʃ] *n* (*grip, grasp*) presa, stretta; (*AUT*) frizione *f* ♦ *vt* afferrare, stringere forte

clutter ['klʌtə*] *vt* ingombrare

CND *n abbr* = **Campaign for Nuclear Disarmament**

Co. *abbr* = **county**; **company**

c/o *abbr* (= *care of*) presso

coach [kəʊtʃ] *n* (*bus*) pullman *m inv*; (*horse-drawn, of train*) carrozza; (*SPORT*) allenatore/trice; (*tutor*) chi dà ripetizioni ♦ *vt* allenare; dare ripetizioni a; ~ **trip** *n* viaggio in pullman

coal [kəʊl] *n* carbone *m*; ~ **face** *n* fronte *f*; ~**field** *n* bacino carbonifero

coalition [kəʊə'lɪʃən] *n* coalizione *f*

coal: ~**man** *n* negoziante *m* di carbone; ~ **merchant** *n* = ~**man**; ~**mine** *n* miniera di carbone

coarse [kɔːs] *adj* (*salt, sand etc*) grosso(a); (*cloth, person*) rozzo(a)

coast [kəʊst] *n* costa ♦ *vi* (*with cycle etc*) scendere a ruota libera; ~**al** *adj* costiero(a); ~**guard** *n* guardia costiera; ~**line** *n* linea costiera

coat [kəʊt] *n* cappotto; (*of animal*) pelo; (*of paint*) mano *f* ♦ *vt* coprire; ~ **of arms** *n* stemma *m*; ~**hanger** *n* attaccapanni *m inv*; ~**ing** *n* rivestimento

coax [kəʊks] *vt* indurre (con moine)

cob [kɒb] *n see* **corn**

cobbler ['kɒblə*] *n* calzolaio

cobbles ['kɒblz] *npl* ciottoli *mpl*

cobblestones ['kɒblstəʊnz] *npl* ciottoli *mpl*

cobweb ['kɒbweb] *n* ragnatela

cocaine [kə'keɪn] *n* cocaina

cock 48 **colour**

cock [kɔk] n (rooster) gallo; (male bird) maschio ♦ vt (gun) armare; ~**erel** n galletto; ~**-eyed** adj (fig) storto(a); strampalato(a)

cockle ['kɔkl] n cardio

cockney ['kɔknɪ] n cockney m/f inv (abitante dei quartieri popolari dell'East End di Londra)

cockpit ['kɔkpɪt] n abitacolo

cockroach ['kɔkrəutʃ] n blatta

cocktail ['kɔkteɪl] n cocktail m inv; ~ **cabinet** n mobile m bar inv; ~ **party** n cocktail m inv

cocoa ['kəukəu] n cacao

coconut ['kəukənʌt] n noce f di cocco

cocoon [kə'ku:n] n bozzolo

cod [kɔd] n merluzzo

C.O.D. abbr = cash on delivery

code [kəud] n codice m

cod-liver oil n olio di fegato di merluzzo

coercion [kəu'ə:ʃən] n coercizione f

coffee ['kɔfɪ] n caffè m inv; ~ **bar** (BRIT) n caffè m inv; ~ **break** n pausa per il caffè; ~**pot** n caffettiera; ~ **table** n tavolino

coffin ['kɔfɪn] n bara

cog [kɔg] n dente m

cogent ['kəudʒənt] adj convincente

coherent [kəu'hɪərənt] adj coerente

coil [kɔɪl] n rotolo; (ELEC) bobina; (contraceptive) spirale f ♦ vt avvolgere

coin [kɔɪn] n moneta ♦ vt (word) coniare; ~**age** n sistema m monetario; ~**-box** (BRIT) n telefono a gettoni

coincide [kəuɪn'saɪd] vi coincidere; ~**nce** [kəu'ɪnsɪdəns] n combinazione f

Coke [kəuk] ® n coca

coke [kəuk] n coke m

colander ['kɔləndə*] n colino

cold [kəuld] adj freddo(a) ♦ n freddo; (MED) raffreddore m; it's ~ fa freddo; to be ~ (person) aver freddo; (object) essere freddo(a); to catch ~ prendere freddo; to catch a ~ prendere un raffreddore; in ~

blood a sangue freddo; ~**-shoulder** vt trattare con freddezza; ~ **sore** n erpete m

coleslaw ['kəulslɔ:] n insalata di cavolo bianco

colic ['kɔlɪk] n colica

collapse [kə'læps] vi crollare ♦ n crollo; (MED) collasso

collapsible [kə'læpsəbl] adj pieghevole

collar ['kɔlə*] n (of coat, shirt) colletto; (of dog, cat) collare m; ~**bone** n clavicola

collateral [kɔ'lætərl] n garanzia

colleague ['kɔli:g] n collega m/f

collect [kə'lekt] vt (gen) raccogliere; (as a hobby) fare collezione di; (BRIT: call and pick up) prendere; (money owed, pension) riscuotere; (donations, subscriptions) fare una colletta di ♦ vi adunarsi, riunirsi; ammucchiarsi; to call ~ (US: TEL) fare una chiamata a carico del destinatario; ~**ion** [kə'lekʃən] n raccolta; collezione f; (for money) colletta

collector [kə'lektə*] n collezionista m/f

college ['kɔlɪdʒ] n college m inv; (of technology etc) istituto superiore

collide [kə'laɪd] vi: to ~ (with) scontrarsi (con)

collie ['kɔlɪ] n (dog) collie m inv

colliery ['kɔliərɪ] (BRIT) n miniera di carbone

collision [kə'lɪʒən] n collisione f, scontro

colloquial [kə'ləukwɪəl] adj familiare

colon ['kəulən] n (sign) due punti mpl; (MED) colon m inv

colonel ['kə:nl] n colonnello

colonial [kə'ləunɪəl] adj coloniale

colony ['kɔlənɪ] n colonia

colour ['kʌlə*] (US **color**) n colore m ♦ vt colorare; (tint, dye) tingere; (fig: affect) influenzare ♦ vi (blush) arrossire; ~**s** npl (of party, club) colori mpl; **in** ~ a colori; ~ **in** vt colorare; ~ **bar** n discriminazione f razziale (in locali etc); ~**-blind** adj daltonico(a); **~ed** adj (photo) a colori; (person) di colore; **~ film** n (for camera) pellicola a colori; **~ful** adj pieno(a) di colore, a vivaci colori; (personality) colorante m; **~ing** n (substance) colorante m; (complexion) colorito; **~ scheme** n combinazione f di colori; **~ television** n televisione f a colori

colt [kəʊlt] n puledro

column ['kɒləm] n colonna; **~ist** ['kɒləmnɪst] n articolista m/f

coma ['kəʊmə] n coma m inv

comb [kəʊm] n pettine n ♦ vt (hair) pettinare; (area) battere a tappeto

combat ['kɒmbæt] n combattimento ♦ vt combattere, lottare contro

combination [kɒmbɪ'neɪʃən] n combinazione f

combine [vb kəm'baɪn, n 'kɒmbaɪn] vt: to **~** (with) combinare (con); (one quality with another) unire (a) ♦ vi unirsi; (CHEM) combinarsi ♦ n (ECON) associazione f; **~ (harvester)** n mietitrebbia

come [kʌm] (pt came, pp come) vi venire; arrivare; to **~ to** (decision etc) raggiungere; **I've ~ to** like him ha cominciato a piacermi; to **~ undone** slacciarsi; to **~ loose** allentarsi; **~ about** vi succedere; **~ across** vt fus trovare per caso; **~ away** vi venire via; staccarsi; **~ back** vi ritornare; **~ by** vt fus (acquire) procurarsi; **~ down** vi scendere; (prices) calare; (buildings) essere demolito(a); **~ forward** vi farsi avanti; presentarsi; **~ from** vt fus venire da; provenire da; **~ in** vi entrare; **~ in for** vt fus (criticism etc) ricevere; **~ into** vt fus (money) ereditare; **~ off** vi (button) staccarsi; (stain) andar via; (attempt) riuscire; **~ on** vi (pupil, work, project) fare progressi; (lights) accendersi; (electricity) entrare in funzione; **~ on!** avanti!, andiamo!, forza!; **~ out** vi uscire; (stain) andare via; **~ round** vi (after faint, operation) riprendere cono-

scenza, rinvenire; **~ to** vi rinvenire; **~ up** vi (sun) salire; (problem) sorgere; (event) essere in arrivo; (in conversation) saltar fuori; **~ up against** vt fus (resistance, difficulties) urtare contro; **~ up with** vt fus: he came up with an idea venne fuori con un'idea; **~ upon** vt fus trovare per caso; **~back** n (THEATRE etc) ritorno

comedian [kə'miːdɪən] n comico

comedienne [kəmiːdɪ'ɛn] n attrice f comica

comedy ['kɒmɪdɪ] n commedia

comeuppance [kʌm'ʌpəns] n: to get one's **~** ricevere ciò che si merita

comfort ['kʌmfət] n comodità f inv, benessere m; (relief) consolazione f, conforto ♦ vt consolare, confortare; **~s** npl comodità fpl; **~able** adj comodo(a); (financially) agiato(a); **~ably** adv (sit etc) comodamente; (live) bene; **~ station** n (US) n gabinetti mpl

comic ['kɒmɪk] adj (also: **~al**) comico(a) ♦ n comico; (BRIT: magazine) giornaletto; **~ strip** n fumetto

coming ['kʌmɪŋ] n arrivo ♦ adj (next) prossimo(a); (future) futuro(a); **~(s) and going(s)** n(pl) andirivieni m inv

comma ['kɒmə] n virgola

command [kə'mɑːnd] n ordine m, comando; (MIL: authority) comando; (mastery) padronanza ♦ vt comandare; to **~ sb to do** ordinare a qn di fare; **~er** [kəmən'dɪə[?]] vt requisire; **~er** n capo; (MIL) comandante m

commando [kə'mɑːndəʊ] n commando m inv; membro di un commando

commence [kə'mɛns] vt, vi cominciare

commend [kə'mɛnd] vt lodare; raccomandare

commensurate [kə'mɛnʃərɪt] adj: **~ with** proporzionato(a) a

comment ['kɒmɛnt] n commento ♦

vi: to ~ (**on**) fare commenti (su); **~ary** [kə'mentəri] *n* commentario; (*SPORT*) radiocronaca; telecronaca; **~ator** [kə'menteitə*] *n* commentatore/trice; radiocronista *m/f*; telecronista *m/f*

commerce ['kɒmə:s] *n* commercio

commercial [kə'mə:ʃəl] *adj* commerciale ♦ *n* (*TV*, *RADIO*: *advertisement*) pubblicità *f inv*; ~ **radio/television** *n* radio *f inv*/televisione *f* privata

commiserate [kə'mizəreit] *vi:* to ~ **with** partecipare al dolore di

commission [kə'miʃən] *n* commissione *f* ♦ *vt* (*work of art*) commissionare; **out of** ~ (*NAUT*) in disarmo; **~aire** [kəmiʃə'nɛə*] *n* (*BRIT*) *n* (*at shop, cinema etc*) portiere *m* in livrea; **~er** *n* (*POLICE*) questore *m*

commit [kə'mit] *vt* (*act*) commettere; (*to sb's care*) affidare; to ~ **o.s.** (**to do**) impegnarsi (a fare); to ~ **suicide** suicidarsi; **~ment** *n* impegno; promessa

committee [kə'miti] *n* comitato

commodity [kə'mɒditi] *n* prodotto, articolo

common ['kɒmən] *adj* comune; (*pej*) volgare; (*usual*) normale ♦ *n* terreno comune; **the C~s** (*BRIT*) *npl* la Camera dei Comuni; **in** ~ in comune; **~er** *n* cittadino/a (non nobile); ~ **law** *n* diritto consuetudinario; **~ly** *adv* comunemente, usualmente; **C~ Market** *n* Mercato Comune; **~place** *adj* banale, ordinario/a; **~room** *n* sala di riunione; (*SCOL*) sala dei professori; ~ **sense** *n* buon senso; **the C~wealth** *n* il Commonwealth

commotion [kə'məuʃən] *n* confusione *f*, tumulto

communal ['kɒmju:nl] *adj* (*for common use*) pubblico(a)

commune [*n* 'kɒmju:n. *vb* kə'mju:n] *n* (*group*) comune *f* ♦ *vi:* to ~ **with** mettersi in comunione con

communicate [kə'mju:nikeit] *vt* comunicare, trasmettere ♦ *vi:* to ~

(**with**) comunicare (con)

communication [kəmju:ni'keiʃən] *n* comunicazione *f*; ~ **cord** (*BRIT*) *n* segnale *m* d'allarme

communion [kə'mju:niən] *n* (*also: Holy C~*) comunione *f*

communiqué [kə'mju:nikei] *n* comunicato

communism ['kɒmjunizəm] *n* comunismo; **communist** *adj, n* comunista *m/f*

community [kə'mju:niti] *n* comunità *f inv*; ~ **centre** *n* circolo ricreativo; ~ **chest** (*US*) *n* fondo di beneficenza; ~ **home** (*BRIT*) *n* riformatorio

commutation ticket [kɒmju-'teiʃən-] (*US*) *n* biglietto di abbonamento

commute [kə'mju:t] *vi* fare il pendolare ♦ *vt* (*LAW*) commutare; **~r** *n* pendolare *m/f*

compact [*adj* kəm'pækt. *n* 'kɒmpækt] *adj* compatto(a) ♦ *n* (*also: powder* ~) portacipria *m inv*; ~ **disc** *n* compact disc *m inv*; ~ **disc player** *n* lettore *m* CD *inv*

companion [kəm'pæniən] *n* compagno/a; **~ship** *n* compagnia

company ['kʌmpəni] *n* (*also: COMM, MIL, THEATRE*) compagnia; to **keep sb** ~ tenere compagnia a qn; ~ **secretary** (*BRIT*) *n* segretario/a generale

comparable ['kɒmpərəbl] *adj* simile

comparative [kəm'pærətiv] *adj* relativo(a); (*adjective etc*) comparativo(a); **~ly** *adv* relativamente

compare [kəm'pɛə*] *vt:* to ~ **sth/sb with/to** confrontare qc/qn con/a ♦ *vi:* to ~ (**with**) reggere il confronto (con); **comparison** [-'pærisn] *n* confronto; **in comparison** (**with**) in confronto (a)

compartment [kəm'pɑ:tmənt] *n* compartimento; (*RAIL*) scompartimento

compass ['kʌmpəs] *n* bussola; **~es** *npl* (*MATH*) compasso

compassion [kəm'pæʃən] *n* compassione *f*

compatible [kəm'pætɪbl] adj compatibile

compel [kəm'pɛl] vt costringere, obbligare; **~ling** adj (fig: argument) irresistibile

compensate ['kɔmpənseɪt] vt risarcire ♦ vi: **to ~ for** compensare; **compensation** [-'seɪʃən] n compensazione f; (money) risarcimento

compère ['kɔmpɛə*] n presentatore/trice

compete [kəm'piːt] vi (take part) concorrere; (vie): **to ~ (with)** fare concorrenza (a)

competent ['kɔmpɪtənt] adj competente

competition [kɔmpɪ'tɪʃən] n gara; concorso; (ECON) concorrenza

competitive [kəm'pɛtɪtɪv] adj (ECON) concorrenziale; (sport) agonistico(a); (person) che ha spirito di competizione; che ha spirito agonistico

competitor [kəm'pɛtɪtə*] n concorrente m/f

complacency [kəm'pleɪsnsɪ] n compiacenza di sé

complain [kəm'pleɪn] vi lagnarsi, lamentarsi; **~t** n lamento; (in shop etc) reclamo; (MED) malattia

complement [n 'kɔmplɪmənt, vb 'kɔmplɪmɛnt] n complemento; (especially of ship's crew etc) effettivo ♦ vt (enhance) accompagnarsi bene a; **~ary** [kɔmplɪ'mɛntərɪ] adj complementare

complete [kəm'pliːt] adj completo(a) ♦ vt completare; (a form) riempire; **~ly** adv completamente; **completion** n completamento

complex ['kɔmplɛks] adj complesso(a) ♦ n (PSYCH, buildings etc) complesso

complexion [kəm'plɛkʃən] n (of face) carnagione f

compliance [kəm'plaɪəns] n acquiescenza; **in ~ with** (orders, wishes etc) in conformità con

complicate [kəm'plɪkeɪt] vt complicare; **~d** adj complicato(a); **com-**

plication [-'keɪʃən] n complicazione f

compliment [n 'kɔmplɪmənt, vb 'kɔmplɪmɛnt] n complimento ♦ vt fare un complimento a; **~s** npl (greetings) complimenti mpl; rispetti mpl; **to pay sb a ~** fare un complimento a qn; **~ary** [-'mɛntərɪ] adj complimentoso(a), elogiativo(a); (free) in omaggio; **~ary ticket** n biglietto omaggio

comply [kəm'plaɪ] vi: **to ~ with** assentire a; conformarsi a

component [kəm'pəunənt] a componente ♦ n componente m

compose [kəm'pəuz] vt (form): **to be ~d of** essere composto di; (music, poem etc) comporre; **to ~ o.s.** ricomporsi; **~d** adj calmo(a); **~r** n (MUS) compositore/trice

composition [kɔmpə'zɪʃən] n composizione f

composure [kəm'pəuʒə*] n calma

compound ['kɔmpaund] n (CHEM, LING) composto; (enclosure) recinto ♦ adj composto(a); **~ fracture** n frattura esposta

comprehend [kɔmprɪ'hɛnd] vt comprendere, capire; **comprehension** [-'hɛnʃən] n comprensione f

comprehensive [kɔmprɪ'hɛnsɪv] adj comprensivo(a); **~ policy** n (INSURANCE) polizza che copre tutti i rischi; **~ (school)** (BRIT) n scuola secondaria aperta a tutti

compress [vb kəm'prɛs, n 'kɔmprɛs] vt comprimere ♦ n (MED) compressa

comprise [kəm'praɪz] vt (also: be **~d of**) comprendere

compromise ['kɔmprəmaɪz] n compromesso ♦ vt compromettere ♦ vi venire a un compromesso

compulsion [kəm'pʌlʃən] n costrizione f

compulsive [kəm'pʌlsɪv] adj (liar, gambler) che non riesce a controllarsi; (viewing, reading) cui non si può fare a meno

compulsory [kəm'pʌlsərɪ] adj obbligatorio(a)

computer [kəm'pju:tə*] n computer m inv, elaboratore m elettronico; ~ **game** n gioco per computer; ~**ize** vt computerizzare; ~ **programmer** n programmatore/trice; ~ **programming** n programmazione f di computer; ~ **science** n informatica; **computing** n informatica

comrade ['kɔmrɪd] n compagno/a; ~**ship** n cameratismo

con [kɔn] (inf) vt truffare ♦ n truffa

conceal [kən'si:l] vt nascondere

concede [kən'si:d] vt ammettere

conceit [kən'si:t] n presunzione f, vanità; ~**ed** adj presuntuoso(a), vanitoso(a)

conceive [kən'si:v] vt concepire ♦ vi concepire un bambino

concentrate ['kɔnsəntreɪt] vi concentrarsi ♦ vt concentrare

concentration [kɔnsən'treɪʃən] n concentrazione f; ~ **camp** n campo di concentramento

concept ['kɔnsɛpt] n concetto

concern [kən'sə:n] n affare m; (COMM) azienda, ditta; (anxiety) preoccupazione f ♦ vt riguardare; to be ~**ed** (about) preoccuparsi (di); ~**ing** prep riguardo a, circa

concert ['kɔnsət] n concerto; ~**ed** [kən'sə:tɪd] adj concertato(a); ~ **hall** n sala da concerti

concertina [kɔnsə'ti:nə] n piccola fisarmonica

concerto [kən'tʃə:təu] n concerto

conclude [kən'klu:d] vt concludere; **conclusion** [-'klu:ʒən] n conclusione f; **conclusive** [-'klu:sɪv] adj conclusivo(a)

concoct [kən'kɔkt] vt inventare; ~**ion** [-'kɔkʃən] n miscuglio

concourse ['kɔŋkɔ:s] n (hall) atrio

concrete ['kɔŋkri:t] n calcestruzzo ♦ adj concreto(a); di calcestruzzo

concur [kən'kə:*] vi concordare

concurrently [kən'kʌrntlɪ] adv simultaneamente

concussion [kən'kʌʃən] n commozione f cerebrale

condemn [kən'dɛm] vt condannare; (building) dichiarare pericoloso(a)

condensation [kɔndɛn'seɪʃən] n condensazione f

condense [kən'dɛns] vi condensarsi ♦ vt condensare; ~**d milk** n latte m condensato

condescending [kɔndɪ'sɛndɪŋ] adj (person) che ha un'aria di superiorità

condition [kən'dɪʃən] n condizione f; (MED) malattia ♦ vt condizionare; **on** ~ **that** a condizione che + sub, a condizione di; ~**al** adj condizionale; ~**er** n (for hair) balsamo; (for fabrics) ammorbidente m

condolences [kən'dəulənsɪz] npl condoglianze fpl

condom ['kɔndəm] n preservativo

condominium [kɔndə'mɪnɪəm] (US) n condominio

conducive [kən'dju:sɪv] adj: ~ to favorevole a

conduct [n 'kɔndʌkt, vb kən'dʌkt] n condotta ♦ vt condurre; (manage) dirigere; amministrare; (MUS) dirigere; to ~ o.s. comportarsi; ~**ed tour** n gita accompagnata; ~**or** n (of orchestra) direttore m d'orchestra; (on bus) bigliettaio; (US: on train) controllore m; (ELEC) conduttore m; ~**ress** n (on bus) bigliettaia

cone [kəun] n cono; (BOT) pigna; (traffic ~) birillo

confectioner [kən'fɛkʃənə*] n pasticciere m; ~**'s (shop)** n ≈ pasticceria; ~**y** n dolciumi mpl

confer [kən'fə:*] vt: to ~ sth on conferire qc a ♦ vi conferire

conference ['kɔnfərns] n congresso

confess [kən'fɛs] vt confessare, ammettere ♦ vi confessare; ~**ion** [-'fɛʃən] n confessione f

confetti [kən'fɛtɪ] n coriandoli mpl

confide [kən'faɪd] vi: to ~ in confidarsi con

confidence ['kɔnfɪdns] n confidenza; (trust) fiducia; (self-assurance) sicurezza di sé; **in** ~ (speak, write) in confidenza, confidenzialmente; ~ **trick** n truffa; **confident** adj sicuro(a); sicuro(a) di sé; **confidential** [kɒnfɪ'denʃəl] adj riservato(a), confidenziale

confine [kən'faɪn] vt limitare; (shut up) rinchiudere; ~**d** adj (space) ristretto(a); ~**ment** n prigionia; ~**s** ['kɒnfaɪnz] npl confini mpl

confirm [kən'fɔːm] vt confermare; ~**ation** [kɒnfə'meɪʃən] n conferma; (REL) cresima; ~**ed** adj inveterato(a)

confiscate ['kɒnfɪskeɪt] vt confiscare

conflict [n 'kɒnflɪkt, vb kən'flɪkt] n conflitto ♦ vi essere in conflitto; ~**ing** adj contrastante

conform [kən'fɔːm] vi: to ~ (to) conformarsi a

confound [kən'faund] vt confondere

confront [kən'frʌnt] vt (enemy, danger) affrontare; ~**ation** [kɒnfrən'teɪʃən] n scontro

confuse [kən'fjuːz] vt (one thing with another) confondere; ~**d** adj confuso(a); **confusing** adj che fa confondere; **confusion** [-'fjuːʒən] n confusione f

congeal [kən'dʒiːl] vi (blood) congelarsi

congenial [kən'dʒiːnɪəl] adj (person) simpatico(a); (thing) congeniale

congested [kən'dʒestɪd] adj congestionato(a)

congestion [kən'dʒestʃən] n congestione f

congratulate [kən'grætjuleɪt] vt: to ~ sb (on) congratularsi con qn (per or di); **congratulations** [-'leɪʃənz] npl auguri mpl; (on success) complimenti mpl, congratulations fpl

congregate ['kɒŋgrɪgeɪt] vi congregarsi, riunirsi

congress ['kɒŋgres] n congresso; ~**man** (US) n membro del Congresso

conjecture [kən'dʒektʃə*] n congettura

conjunction [kən'dʒʌŋkʃən] n congiunzione f

conjunctivitis [kəndʒʌŋktɪ'vaɪtɪs] n congiuntivite f

conjure ['kʌndʒə*] vi fare giochi di prestigio; ~ **up** vt (ghost, spirit) evocare; (memories) rievocare; ~**r** n prestidigitatore/trice, prestigiatore/trice

conk out [kɒŋk-] (inf) vi andare in panne

con man n truffatore m

connect [kə'nekt] vt connettere, collegare; (ELEC, TEL) collegare; (fig) associare ♦ vi (train): to ~ **with** be essere in coincidenza con; **to be ~ed with** (associated) aver rapporti con; ~**ion** [-ʃən] n relazione f, rapporto; (ELEC) connessione f; (train, plane) coincidenza; (TEL) collegamento

connive [kə'naɪv] vi: to ~ **at** essere conivente in

connoisseur [kɒnɪ'sə*] n conoscitore/trice

conquer ['kɒŋkə*] vt conquistare; (feelings) vincere

conquest ['kɒŋkwest] n conquista

cons [kɒnz] npl see **convenience**; **pro**

conscience ['kɒnʃəns] n coscienza

conscientious [kɒnʃɪ'enʃəs] adj coscienzioso(a)

conscious ['kɒnʃəs] adj consapevole; (MED) cosciente; ~**ness** n consapevolezza, coscienza

conscript ['kɒnskrɪpt] n coscritto; ~**ion** [-'skrɪpʃən] n arruolamento (obbligatorio)

consent [kən'sent] n consenso ♦ vi: to ~ (to) acconsentire (a)

consequence ['kɒnsɪkwəns] n conseguenza, risultato; importanza

consequently ['kɒnsɪkwəntlɪ] adv di conseguenza, dunque

conservation [kɒnsə'veɪʃən] n conservazione f

conservative [kən'sɜːvətɪv] adj conservatore(trice); (cautious) cauto(a); **C**~ (BRIT) adj, n (POL) conservatore(trice)

conservatory [kən'sɜːvətrɪ] n (greenhouse) serra; (MUS) conservatorio

conserve [kən'sɜːv] vt conservare ♦

n conserva

consider [kən'sɪdə*] *vt* considerare; (*take into account*) tener conto di; **to ~ doing sth** considerare la possibilità di fare qc

considerable [kən'sɪdərəbl] *adj* considerevole, notevole; **considerably** *adv* notevolmente, decisamente

considerate [kən'sɪdərɪt] *adj* premuroso(a)

consideration [kənsɪdə'reɪʃən] *n* considerazione *f*

considering [kən'sɪdərɪŋ] *prep* in considerazione di

consign [kən'saɪn] *vt*: **to ~ to** (*sth unwanted*) relegare in; (*person: to sb's care*) consegnare a; (: *to poverty*) condannare a; **~ment** (: *of goods*) consegna; spedizione *f*

consist [kən'sɪst] *vi*: **to ~ of** constare di, essere composto(a) di

consistency [kən'sɪstənsɪ] *n* consistenza; (*fig*) coerenza

consistent [kən'sɪstənt] *adj* coerente

consolation [kɒnsə'leɪʃən] *n* consolazione *f*

console[1] [kən'səul] *vt* consolare

console[2] ['kɒnsəul] *n* quadro di comando

consonant ['kɒnsənənt] *n* consonante *f*

consortium [kən'sɔːtɪəm] *n* consorzio

conspicuous [kən'spɪkjuəs] *adj* cospicuo(a)

conspiracy [kən'spɪrəsɪ] *n* congiura, cospirazione *f*

constable ['kʌnstəbl] (*BRIT*) *n* ≈ poliziotto, agente *m* di polizia; **chief ~** ≈ questore *m*

constabulary [kən'stæbjulərɪ] *n* forze *fpl* dell'ordine

constant ['kɒnstənt] *adj* costante, continuo(a); **~ly** *adv* costantemente, continuamente

constipated ['kɒnstɪpeɪtd] *adj* stitico(a)

constipation [kɒnstɪ'peɪʃən] *n* stitichezza

constituency [kən'stɪtjuənsɪ] *n* collegio elettorale

constituent [kən'stɪtjuənt] *n* elettore/trice; (*part*) elemento componente

constitution [kɒnstɪ'tjuːʃən] *n* costituzione *f*; **~al** *adj* costituzionale

constraint [kən'streɪnt] *n* costrizione *f*

construct [kən'strʌkt] *vt* costruire; **~ion** [-ʃən] *n* costruzione *f*; **~ive** *adj* costruttivo(a)

construe [kən'struː] *vt* interpretare

consul ['kɒnsl] *n* console *m*; **~ate** ['kɒnsjulɪt] *n* consolato

consult [kən'sʌlt] *vt* consultare; **~ant** *n* (*MED*) consulente *m* medico; (*other specialist*) consulente; **~ation** [-'teɪʃən] *n* (*MED*) consulto; (*discussion*) consultazione *f*; **~ing room** (*BRIT*) *n* ambulatorio

consume [kən'sjuːm] *vt* consumare; **~r** *n* consumatore/trice; **~r goods** *npl* beni *mpl* di consumo; **~r society** *n* società dei consumi

consumption [kən'sʌmpʃən] *n* consumo

cont. *abbr* = **continued**

contact ['kɒntækt] *n* contatto; (*person*) conoscenza ♦ *vt* mettersi in contatto con; **~ lenses** *npl* lenti *fpl* a contatto

contagious [kən'teɪdʒəs] *adj* (*also fig*) contagioso(a)

contain [kən'teɪn] *vt* contenere; **to ~ o.s.** contenersi; **~er** *n* recipiente *m*; (*for shipping etc*) container *m inv*

contaminate [kən'tæmɪneɪt] *vt* contaminare

cont'd *abbr* = **continued**

contemplate ['kɒntəmpleɪt] *vt* contemplare; (*consider*) pensare a (*or* di)

contemporary [kən'tempərərɪ] *adj*, *n* contemporaneo(a)

contempt [kən'tempt] *n* disprezzo; **~ of court** (*LAW*) oltraggio alla Corte; **~ible** *adj* disprezzabile; **~uous** *adj* sdegnoso(a)

contend [kən'tend] *vt*: **to ~ that** sostenere che ♦ *vi*: **to ~ with** lottare contro; ~**er** *n* contendente *m/f*; concorrente *m/f*

content[1] ['kɔntɛnt] *n* contenuto; ~**s** *npl* (*of box, case etc*) contenuto; (**table of**) ~**s** indice *m*

content[2] [kən'tɛnt] *adj* contento(a), soddisfatto(a) ♦ *vt* contentare, soddisfare; ~**ed** *adj* contento(a), soddisfatto(a)

contention [kən'tɛnʃən] *n* contesa; (*assertion*) tesi *f inv*

contentment [kən'tɛntmənt] *n* contentezza

contest [*n* 'kɔntɛst, *vb* kən'tɛst] *n* lotta; (*competition*) gara, concorso ♦ *vt* contestare; impugnare; (*compete for*) essere in lizza per; ~**ant** [kən'tɛstənt] *n* concorrente *m/f*; (*in fight*) avversario/a

context ['kɔntɛkst] *n* contesto

continent ['kɔntɪnənt] *n* continente *m*; **the C**~ (*BRIT*) l'Europa continentale; ~**al** [-'nɛntl] *adj* continentale; ~**al quilt** (*BRIT*) *n* piumino

contingency [kən'tɪndʒənsɪ] *n* eventualità *f inv*

continual [kən'tɪnjuəl] *adj* continuo(a)

continuation [kəntɪnju'eɪʃən] *n* continuazione *f*; (*after interruption*) ripresa; (*of story*) seguito

continue [kən'tɪnju:] *vi* continuare ♦ *vt* continuare; (*start again*) riprendere

continuity [kɔntɪ'nju:ɪtɪ] *n* continuità; (*TV, CINEMA*) (ordine *m* della) sceneggiatura

continuous [kən'tɪnjuəs] *adj* continuo(a); ininterrotto(a); ~ **stationery** *n* carta a moduli continui

contort [kən'tɔːt] *vt* contorcere

contour ['kɔntuə'] *n* contorno, profilo; (*also*: ~ **line**) curva di livello

contraband ['kɔntrəbænd] *n* contrabbando

contraceptive [kɔntrə'sɛptɪv] *adj* contraccettivo(a) ♦ *n* contraccettivo

contract [*n* 'kɔntrækt, *vb* kən'trækt] *n* contratto ♦ *vi* (*become smaller*) contrarsi; (*COMM*): **to** ~ **to do sth**

fare un contratto per fare qc ♦ *vt* (*illness*) contrarre; ~**ion** [-ʃən] *n* contrazione *f*; ~**or** *n* imprenditore *m*

contradict [kɔntrə'dɪkt] *vt* contraddire

contraption [kən'træpʃən] (*pej*) *n* aggeggio

contrary[1] ['kɔntrərɪ] *adj* contrario(a); (*unfavourable*) avverso(a), contrario(a) ♦ *n* contrario; **on the** ~ al contrario; **unless you hear to the** ~ salvo contrordine

contrary[2] [kən'trɛərɪ] *adj* (*perverse*) bisbetico(a)

contrast [*n* 'kɔntrɑːst, *vb* kən'trɑːst] *n* contrasto ♦ *vt* mettere in contrasto; **in** ~ **to** contrariamente a

contribute [kən'trɪbjuːt] *vi* contribuire ♦ *vt*: **to** ~ **£10/an article to** dare 10 sterline/un articolo a; **to** ~ **to** contribuire a; (*newspaper*) scrivere per; ~**ion** [kɔntrɪ'bjuːʃən] *n* contributo; **contributor** *n* (*to newspaper*) collaboratore/trice

contrivance [kən'traɪvəns] *n* congegno; espediente *m*

contrive [kən'traɪv] *vi*: **to** ~ **to do** fare in modo di fare

control [kən'trəul] *vt* controllare; (*firm, operation etc*) dirigere ♦ *n* controllo; ~**s** *npl* (*of vehicle etc*) comandi *mpl*; (*governmental*) controlli *mpl*; **under** ~ sotto controllo; **to be in** ~ **of** avere il controllo di; **to go out of** ~ (*car*) non rispondere ai comandi; (*situation*) sfuggire di mano; ~ **panel** *n* quadro dei comandi; ~ **room** *n* (*NAUT, MIL*) sala di comando; (*RADIO, TV*) sala di regia; ~ **tower** *n* (*AVIAT*) torre *f* di controllo

controversial [kɔntrə'vəːʃl] *adj* controverso(a), polemico(a)

controversy ['kɔntrəvəːsɪ] *n*, controversia, polemica

convalesce [kɔnvə'lɛs] *vi* rimettersi in salute

convene [kən'viːn] *vt* convocare ♦ *vi* convenire, adunarsi

convenience [kən'viːnɪəns] *n* comodità *f inv*; **at your ~** a suo comodo; **all modern ~s**, (BRIT) **all mod cons** tutte le comodità moderne

convenient [kən'viːnɪənt] *adj* conveniente, comodo(a)

convent ['kɒnvənt] *n* convento

convention [kən'venʃən] *n* convenzione *f*; (*meeting*) convegno; **~al** *adj* convenzionale

conversant [kən'vəːsnt] *adj*: **to be ~ with** essere al corrente di; essere pratico(a) di

conversation [kɒnvə'seɪʃən] *n* conversazione *f*; **~al** *adj* non formale

converse¹ [kən'vəːs] *vi* conversare

converse² ['kɒnvəːs] *n* contrario, opposto; **~ly** [-'vəːslɪ] *adv* al contrario, per contro

convert [*vb* kən'vəːt, *n* 'kɒnvəːt] *vt* (COMM, REL) convertire; (*alter*) trasformare ♦ *n* convertito/a; **~ible** *n* macchina decappottabile

convex ['kɒnveks] *adj* convesso(a)

convey [kən'veɪ] *vt* trasportare; (*thanks*) comunicare; (*idea*) dare; **~or belt** *n* nastro trasportatore

convict [*vb* kən'vɪkt, *n* 'kɒnvɪkt] *vt* dichiarare colpevole ♦ *n* carcerato/a; **~ion** [-ʃən] *n* condanna; (*belief*) convinzione *f*

convince [kən'vɪns] *vt* convincere, persuadere; **convincing** *adj* convincente

convoluted [kɒnvə'luːtɪd] *adj* (*argument etc*) involuto(a)

convoy ['kɒnvɔɪ] *n* convoglio

convulse [kən'vʌls] *vt*: **to be ~d with laughter** contorcersi dalle risa

coo [kuː] *vi* tubare

cook [kuk] *vt* cucinare, cuocere ♦ *vi* cuocere; (*person*) cucinare ♦ *n* cuoco/a; **~book** *n* libro di cucina; **~er** *n* fornello, cucina; **~ery** *n* cucina; **~ery book** (BRIT) *n* = **~book**; **~ie** (US) *n* biscotto; **~ing** *n* cucina

cool [kuːl] *adj* fresco(a); (*not afraid, calm*) calmo(a); (*unfriendly*) freddo(a) ♦ *vt* raffreddare; (*room*) rinfrescare ♦ *vi* (*water*) raffreddarsi; (*air*) rinfrescarsi

coop [kuːp] *n* stia ♦ *vt*: **to ~ up** (*fig*) rinchiudere

cooperate [kəʊ'ɒpəreɪt] *vi* cooperare, collaborare; **cooperation** [-'reɪʃən] *n* cooperazione *f*, collaborazione *f*

cooperative [kəʊ'ɒpərətɪv] *adj* cooperativo(a) ♦ *n* cooperativa

coordinate [*vb* kəʊ'ɔːdɪneɪt, *n* kəʊ'ɔːdɪnət] *vt* coordinare ♦ *n* (MATH) coordinata; **~s** *npl* (*clothes*) coordinati *mpl*

co-ownership [kəʊ'əʊnəʃɪp] *n* comproprietà

cop [kɒp] (*inf*) *n* sbirro

cope [kəʊp] *vi*: **to ~ with** (*problems*) far fronte a

copper ['kɒpə*] *n* rame *m*; (*inf*: *policeman*) sbirro; **~s** *npl* (*coins*) spiccioli *mpl*

coppice ['kɒpɪs] *n* bosco ceduo

copse [kɒps] *n* bosco ceduo

copulate ['kɒpjuleɪt] *vi* accoppiarsi

copy ['kɒpɪ] *n* copia ♦ *vt* copiare; **~right** *n* diritto d'autore

coral ['kɒrəl] *n* corallo; **~ reef** *n* barriera corallina

cord [kɔːd] *n* corda; (ELEC) filo; (*fabric*) velluto a coste

cordial ['kɔːdɪəl] *adj* cordiale ♦ *n* (BRIT) cordiale *m*

cordon ['kɔːdn] *n* cordone *m*; **~ off** *vt* fare cordone a

corduroy ['kɔːdərɔɪ] *n* fustagno

core [kɔː*] *n* (*of fruit*) torsolo; (*of organization etc*) cuore *m* ♦ *vt* estrarre il torsolo da

cork [kɔːk] *n* sughero; (*of bottle*) tappo; **~screw** *n* cavatappi *m inv*

corn [kɔːn] *n* (BRIT: *wheat*) grano; (US: *maize*) granturco; (*on foot*) callo; **~ on the cob** (CULIN) pannocchia cotta

corned beef ['kɔːnd-] *n* carne *f* di manzo in scatola

corner ['kɔːnə*] *n* angolo; (AUT) curva ♦ *vt* intrappolare; mettere con le spalle al muro; (COMM: *market*) accaparrare ♦ *vi* prendere una curva; **~stone** *n* pietra angolare

cornet ['kɔːnɪt] n (MUS) cornetta; (BRIT: of ice-cream) cono

cornflakes ['kɔːnfleɪks] npl fiocchi mpl di granturco

cornflour ['kɔːnflauə*] (BRIT) n farina finissima di granturco

cornstarch ['kɔːnstɑːtʃ] (US) n = cornflour

Cornwall ['kɔːnwəl] n Cornovaglia

corny ['kɔːnɪ] (inf) adj trito(a)

coronary ['kɔrənərɪ] n: ~ (thrombosis) trombosi f coronaria

coronation [kɔrə'neɪʃən] n incoronazione f

coroner ['kɔrənə*] n magistrato incaricato di indagare la causa di morte in circostanze sospette

coronet ['kɔrənɪt] n diadema m

corporal ['kɔːpərl] n caporalmaggiore m ♦ adj: ~ punishment pena corporale

corporate ['kɔːpərɪt] adj costituito(a) (in corporazione); comune

corporation [kɔːpə'reɪʃən] n (of town) consiglio comunale; (COMM) ente m

corps [kɔː*, pl kɔːz] n inv corpo

corpse [kɔːps] n cadavere m

corral [kə'rɑːl] n recinto

correct [kə'rɛkt] adj (accurate) corretto(a), esatto(a); (proper) corretto(a) ♦ vt correggere; ~ion [-ʃən] n correzione f

correspond [kɔrɪs'pɔnd] vi corrispondere; ~ence n corrispondenza; ~ence course n corso per corrispondenza; ~ent n corrispondente m/f

corridor ['kɔrɪdɔː*] n corridoio

corrode [kə'rəud] vt corrodere ♦ vi corrodersi

corrugated ['kɔrəgeɪtɪd] adj increspato(a); ondulato(a); ~ iron n lamiera di ferro ondulata

corrupt [kə'rʌpt] adj corrotto(a); (COMPUT) alterato(a) ♦ vt corrompere; ~ion [-ʃən] n corruzione f

corset ['kɔːsɪt] n busto

Corsica ['kɔːsɪkə] n Corsica

cosh [kɔʃ] (BRIT) n randello (corto)

cosmetic [kɔz'mɛtɪk] n cosmetico ♦ adj (fig: measure etc) superficiale

cosset ['kɔsɪt] vt vezzeggiare

cost [kɔst] (pt, pp cost) n costo ♦ vt costare; (find out the ~ of) stabilire il prezzo di; ~s npl (COMM, LAW) spese fpl; how much does it ~? quanto costa?; at all ~s a ogni costo

co-star ['kəu-] n attore/trice della stessa importanza del protagonista

cost-effective adj conveniente

costly ['kɔstlɪ] adj costoso(a), caro(a)

cost-of-living adj: ~ allowance indennità f inv di contingenza

cost price (BRIT) n prezzo all'ingrosso

costume ['kɔstjuːm] n costume m; (lady's suit) tailleur m inv; (BRIT: also: swimming ~) costume da bagno; ~ jewellery n bigiotteria

cosy ['kəuzɪ] (US cozy) adj intimo(a); I'm very ~ here sto proprio bene qui

cot [kɔt] n (BRIT: child's) lettino; (US: campbed) brandina

cottage ['kɔtɪdʒ] n cottage m inv; ~ cheese n fiocchi npl di latte magro

cotton ['kɔtn] n cotone m; ~ on to (inf) vt fus afferrare; ~ candy (US) n zucchero filato; ~ wool (BRIT) n cotone idrofilo

couch [kautʃ] n sofà m inv

couchette [kuː'ʃɛt] n (on train, boat) cuccetta

cough [kɔf] vi tossire ♦ n tosse f; ~ drop n pasticca per la tosse

could [kud] pt of can; ~n't = could not

council ['kaunsl] n consiglio; city or town ~ consiglio comunale; ~ estate (BRIT) n quartiere m di case popolari; ~ house (BRIT) n casa popolare; ~lor n consigliere/a

counsel ['kaunsl] n avvocato; consultazione f ♦ vt consigliare; ~lor n consigliere/a; (US) avvocato

count [kaunt] vt, vi contare ♦ n (of votes etc) conteggio; (of pollen etc) livello; (nobleman) conte m; ~ on *vt fus* contare su; **~down** *n* conto alla rovescia

countenance ['kauntɪnəns] *n* volto, aspetto ♦ *vt* approvare

counter ['kauntə*] *n* banco ♦ *vt* opporsi a ♦ *adv:* ~ **to** contro; in opposizione a; *(poison etc)* annullare gli effetti di; **~act** *vt* agire in opposizione a; *(poison etc)* annullare gli effetti di; **~espionage** *n* controspionaggio

counterfeit ['kauntəfɪt] *n* contraffazione *f*, falso ♦ *vt* contraffare, falsificare ♦ *adj* falso(a)

counterfoil ['kauntəfɔɪl] *n* matrice *f*

countermand [kauntə'maːnd] *vt* annullare

counterpart ['kauntəpaːt] *n (of document etc)* copia; *(of person)* corrispondente *m/f*

counter-productive [-prə'dʌktɪv] *adj* controproducente

countersign ['kauntəsaɪn] *vt* controfirmare

countess ['kauntɪs] *n* contessa

countless ['kauntlɪs] *adj* innumerevole

country ['kʌntrɪ] *n* paese *m*; *(native land)* patria; *(as opposed to town)* campagna; *(region)* regione *f*; ~ **dancing** *(BRIT)* *n* danza popolare; ~ **house** *n* villa in campagna; **~man** *n (national)* compatriota *m*; *(rural)* contadino; **~side** *n* campagna

county ['kauntɪ] *n* contea

coup [kuː] *(pl* coups*)* *n* colpo; *(also:* ~ *d'état)* colpo di Stato

couple ['kʌpl] *n* coppia; **a ~ of** un paio di

coupon ['kuːpɔn] *n* buono; *(detachable form)* coupon *m inv*

courage ['kʌrɪdʒ] *n* coraggio

courgette [kuə'ʒɛt] *(BRIT)* *n* zucchina

courier ['kurɪə*] *n* corriere *m*; *(for tourists)* guida

course [kɔːs] *n* corso; *(of ship)* rotta; *(for golf)* campo; *(part of meal)* piatto; **of** ~ senz'altro, naturalmente; **of** ~ **action** modo d'agire; **a ~ of treatment** *(MED)* una cura

court [kɔːt] *n* corte *f*; *(TENNIS)* campo ♦ *vt (woman)* fare la corte a; **to take to** ~ citare in tribunale

courteous ['kɜːtɪəs] *adj* cortese

courtesan [kɔːtɪ'zæn] *n* cortigiana

courtesy ['kɜːtəsɪ] *n* cortesia; **(by)** ~ **of** per gentile concessione di

court-house *(US)* *n* palazzo di giustizia

courtier ['kɔːtɪə*] *n* cortigiano/a

court-martial [-'mɑːʃəl] *(pl* courts-martial*)* *n* corte *f* marziale

courtroom ['kɔːtrum] *n* tribunale *m*

courtyard ['kɔːtjɑːd] *n* cortile *m*

cousin ['kʌzn] *n* cugino/a; **first** ~ cugino di primo grado

cove [kəuv] *n* piccola baia

covenant ['kʌvənənt] *n* accordo

cover ['kʌvə*] *vt* coprire; *(book, table)* rivestire; *(include)* comprendere; *(PRESS)* fare un servizio su ♦ *n (of pan)* coperchio; *(over furniture)* fodera; *(of bed)* copriletto; *(of book)* copertina; *(shelter)* riparo; *(COMM, INSURANCE, of spy)* copertura; **to take** ~ *(shelter)* ripararsi; **under** ~ al riparo; **under** ~ **of darkness** protetto dall'oscurità; **under separate** ~ *(COMM)* a parte, in plico separato; **to** ~ **up** *vi:* **to** ~ **up for sb** coprire qn; **~age** *n (PRESS, RADIO, TV):* **to give full ~age to sth** fare un ampio servizio su qc; ~ **charge** *n* coperto; **~ing** *n* copertura; **~ing letter** *(US* ~ **letter)** *n* lettera d'accompagnamento; ~ **note** *n (INSURANCE)* polizza *(di assicurazione)* provvisoria

covert ['kʌvət] *adj (hidden)* nascosto(a); *(glance)* furtivo(a)

cover-up *n* occultamento *(di informazioni)*

covet ['kʌvɪt] *vt* bramare

cow [kau] *n* vacca ♦ *vt (person)* intimidire

coward ['kauəd] *n* vigliacco/a; **~ice** [-ɪs] *n* vigliaccheria; **~ly** *adj* vigliacco(a)

cowboy ['kaubɔɪ] *n* cow-boy *m inv*

cower ['kauə*] *vi* acquattarsi

coxswain ['kɔksn] (abbr: **cox**) n timoniere m

coy [kɔɪ] adj falsamente timido(a)

cozy ['kəuzɪ] (US) adj = cosy

CPA (US) n abbr = certified public accountant

crab [kræb] n granchio; ~ **apple** n mela selvatica

crack [kræk] n fessura, crepa; incrinatura; (noise) schiocco; (: of gun) scoppio; (drug) crack m inv ♦ vt spaccare; incrinare; (whip) schioccare; (nut) schiacciare; (problem) risolvere; (code) decifrare ♦ adj (troops) fuori classe; **to ~ a joke** fare una battuta; ~ **down on** vt fus porre freno a; ~ **up** vi crollare; **~er** n cracker m inv; petardo

crackle ['krækl] vi crepitare

cradle ['kreɪdl] n culla

craft [krɑːft] n mestiere m; (cunning) astuzia; (boat) naviglio; **~sman** n artigiano; **~smanship** n abilità; **~y** adj furbo(a), astuto(a)

crag [kræg] n roccia

cram [kræm] vt (fill): **to ~ sth with** riempire qc di; (put): **to ~ sth into** stipare qc in ♦ vi (for exams) prepararsi (in gran fretta)

cramp [kræmp] n crampo; **~ed** adj ristretto(a)

crampon ['kræmpən] n (CLIMBING) rampone m

cranberry ['krænbərɪ] n mirtillo

crane [kreɪn] n gru f inv

crank [kræŋk] n manovella; (person) persona stramba; **~shaft** n albero a gomiti

cranny ['krænɪ] n see **nook**

crash [kræʃ] n fragore m; (of car) incidente m; (of plane) caduta; (of business etc) crollo ♦ vt fracassare ♦ vi (plane) fracassarsi; (car) avere un incidente; (two cars) scontrarsi; (business etc) fallire, andare in rovina; ~ **course** n corso intensivo; ~ **helmet** n casco; ~ **landing** n atterraggio di fortuna

crate [kreɪt] n cassa

cravat(e) [krə'væt] n fazzoletto da

collo

crave [kreɪv] vt, vi: **to ~ (for)** desiderare ardentemente

crawl [krɔːl] vi strisciare carponi; (vehicle) avanzare lentamente ♦ n (SWIMMING) crawl m

crayfish ['kreɪfɪʃ] n inv (freshwater) gambero (d'acqua dolce); (saltwater) gambero

crayon ['kreɪən] n matita colorata

craze [kreɪz] n mania

crazy ['kreɪzɪ] adj matto(a); (inf: keen): ~ **about sb** pazzo(a) di qn; ~ **about sth** matto(a) per qc; ~ **paving** (BRIT) n lastricato a mosaico irregolare

creak [kriːk] vi cigolare, scricchiolare

cream [kriːm] n crema; (fresh) panna ♦ adj (colour) color crema inv; ~ **cake** n torta alla panna; ~ **cheese** n formaggio fresco; **~y** adj cremoso(a)

crease [kriːs] n grinza; (deliberate) piega ♦ vt sgualcire ♦ vi sgualcirsi

create [kriː'eɪt] vt creare; **creation** [-ʃən] n creazione f; **creative** adj creativo(a)

creature ['kriːtʃə'] n creatura

crèche [krɛʃ] n asilo infantile

credence ['kriːdns] n: **to lend** or **give ~** to prestar fede a

credentials [krɪ'denʃlz] npl credenziali fpl

credit ['krɛdɪt] n credito; onore m ♦ vt (COMM) accreditare; (believe: also: **give ~ to**) credere, prestar fede a; **~s** npl (CINEMA) titoli mpl; **to ~ sb with** (fig) attribuire a qn; **to be in** ~ (person) essere creditore (trice); (bank account) essere coperto(a); ~ **card** n carta di credito; **~or** n creditore/trice

creed [kriːd] n credo; dottrina

creek [kriːk] n insenatura; (US) piccolo fiume m

creep [kriːp] (pt, pp **crept**) vi avanzare furtivamente (or pian piano); **~er** n pianta rampicante; **~y** adj (frightening) che fa accapponare la pelle

crematoria [krɛməˈtɔːrɪə] npl of **crematorium**

crematorium [krɛməˈtɔːrɪəm] (pl **crematoria**) n forno crematorio

crêpe [kreɪp] n crespo; ~ **bandage** (BRIT) n fascia elastica

crept [krɛpt] pt, pp of **creep**

crescent ['krɛsnt] n (shape) mezzaluna; (street) strada semicircolare

cress [krɛs] n crescione n

crest [krɛst] n cresta; (of coat of arms) cimiero; **~fallen** adj mortificato(a)

Crete [kriːt] n Creta

crevasse [krɪˈvæs] n crepaccio

crevice ['krɛvɪs] n fessura, crepa

crew [kruː] n equipaggio; **to have a ~-cut** avere i capelli a spazzola; **~-neck** n girocollo

crib [krɪb] n culla ♦ vt (inf) copiare

crick [krɪk] n crampo

cricket ['krɪkɪt] n (insect) grillo; (game) cricket m

crime [kraɪm] n crimine m; **criminal** ['krɪmɪnl] adj, n criminale m/f

crimson ['krɪmzn] adj color cremisi inv

cringe [krɪndʒ] vi acquattarsi; (in embarrassment) sentirsi sprofondare

crinkle ['krɪŋkl] vt arricciare, increspare

cripple ['krɪpl] n zoppo/a ♦ vt azzoppare

crises ['kraɪsiːz] npl of **crisis**

crisis ['kraɪsɪs] (pl **crises**) n crisi f inv

crisp [krɪsp] adj croccante; (fig) frizzante; vivace; deciso(a); **~s** (BRIT) npl patatine fpl

criss-cross ['krɪs-] adj incrociato(a)

criteria [kraɪˈtɪərɪə] npl of **criterion**

criterion [kraɪˈtɪərɪən] (pl **criteria**) n criterio

critic ['krɪtɪk] n critico; **~al** adj critico(a); **~ally** adv (speak etc) criticamente; **~ally ill** gravemente malato; **~ism** ['krɪtɪsɪzm] n critica; **~ize** ['krɪtɪsaɪz] vt criticare

croak [krəʊk] vi gracchiare; (frog) gracidare

Croatia [krəʊˈeɪʃə] n Croazia

crochet ['krəʊʃeɪ] n lavoro all'uncinetto

crockery ['krɒkərɪ] n vasellame m

crocodile ['krɒkədaɪl] n coccodrillo

crocus ['krəʊkəs] n croco

croft [krɒft] (BRIT) n piccolo podere m

crony ['krəʊnɪ] (inf: pej) n compare m

crook [krʊk] n truffatore m; (of shepherd) bastone m; **~ed** ['krʊkɪd] adj curvo(a), storto(a); (action) disonesto(a)

crop [krɒp] n (produce) coltivazione f; (amount produced) raccolto; (riding ~) frustino ♦ vt (hair) rapare; **~ up** vi presentarsi

croquette [krɒˈkɛt] n crocchetta

cross [krɒs] n croce f; (BIOL) incrocio ♦ vt (street etc) attraversare; (arms, legs, BIOL) incrociare; (cheque) sbarrare ♦ adj di cattivo umore; **~ out** vt cancellare; **~ over** vi attraversare; **~bar** n traversa; **~country (race)** n crosscountry m inv; **~-examine** vt (LAW) interrogare in contraddittorio; **~-eyed** adj strabico(a); **~fire** n fuoco incrociato; **~ing** n incrocio; (sea passage) traversata; (also: pedestrian ~ing) passaggio pedonale; **~ing guard** (US) n dipendente comunale che aiuta i bambini ad attraversare la strada; **~ purposes** npl: **to be at ~ purposes** non parlare della stessa cosa; **~-reference** n rinvio, rimando; **~roads** n incrocio; **~-section** n sezione f trasversale; (in population) settore m rappresentativo; **~walk** (US) n strisce fpl pedonali, passaggio pedonale; **~wind** n vento di traverso; **~word** n cruciverba m inv

crotch [krɒtʃ] n (ANAT) inforcatura; (of garment) pattina

crotchet ['krɒtʃɪt] n (MUS) semiminima

crotchety ['krɒtʃɪtɪ] adj (person) burbero(a)

crouch [krautʃ] vi acquattarsi; rannicchiarsi

crow [krəu] n (bird) cornacchia; (of cock) canto del gallo ♦ vi (cock) cantare

crowbar ['krəubɑ:*] n piede m di porco

crowd [kraud] n folla ♦ vt affollare, stipare ♦ vi: to ~ **round/in** affollarsi intorno a/in; ~**ed** affollato(a); ~**ed with** stipato(a) di

crown [kraun] n corona; (of head) calotta cranica; (of tooth) cuccuzolo; (of hill) cima ♦ vt incoronare; (fig: career) coronare; ~ **jewels** npl gioielli mpl della Corona; ~ **prince** n principe m ereditario

crow's feet npl zampe fpl di gallina

crucial ['kru:ʃl] adj cruciale, decisivo(a)

crucifix ['kru:sifiks] n crocifisso; ~**ion** [-'fikʃən] n crocifissione f

crude [kru:d] adj (materials) greggio(a); non raffinato(a); (fig: basic) crudo(a), primitivo(a); (: vulgar) rozzo(a), grossolano(a); ~ (**oil**) n (petrolio) greggio

cruel ['kruəl] adj crudele; ~**ty** n crudeltà f inv

cruise [kru:z] n crociera ♦ vi andare a velocità di crociera; (taxi) circolare; ~**r** n incrociatore m

crumb [krʌm] n briciola

crumble ['krʌmbl] vt sbriciolare ♦ vi sbriciolarsi; (plaster etc) screttolarsi; (land, earth) franare; (building, fig) crollare; **crumbly** adj friabile

crumpet ['krʌmpit] n specie di frittella

crumple ['krʌmpl] vt raggrinzare, spiegazzare

crunch [krʌntʃ] vt sgranocchiare; (underfoot) scricchiolare ♦ n (fig) punto o momento cruciale; ~**y** adj croccante

crusade [kru:'seid] n crociata

crush [krʌʃ] n folla; (love): to have a ~ **on sb** avere una cotta per qn; (drink): **lemon** ~ spremuta di limone ♦ vt schiacciare; (crumple) sgualcire

crust [krʌst] n crosta

crutch [krʌtʃ] n gruccia

crux [krʌks] n nodo

cry [krai] vi (weep) piangere; (shout: also: ~ **out**) urlare ♦ n urlo, grido; ~ **off** vi ritirarsi

cryptic ['kriptik] adj ermetico(a)

crystal ['kristl] n cristallo; ~**-clear** adj cristallino(a)

cub [kʌb] n cucciolo; (also: ~ **scout**) lupetto

Cuba ['kju:bə] n Cuba

cubbyhole ['kʌbihəul] n angolino

cube [kju:b] n cubo ♦ vt (MATH) elevare al cubo; **cubic** adj cubico(a); (metre, foot) cubo(a); **cubic capacity** n cilindrata

cubicle ['kju:bikl] n scompartimento separato; cabina

cuckoo ['kuku:] n cucù m inv; ~ **clock** n orologio a cucù

cucumber ['kju:kʌmbə*] n cetriolo

cuddle ['kʌdl] vt abbracciare, coccolare ♦ vi abbracciarsi

cue [kju:] n (snooker ~) stecca; (THEATRE etc) segnale m

cuff [kʌf] n (BRIT: of shirt, coat etc) polsino; (US: of trousers) risvolto; **off the** ~ improvvisando; ~**link** n gemello

cuisine [kwi'zi:n] n cucina

cul-de-sac ['kʌldəsæk] n vicolo cieco

cull [kʌl] vt (ideas etc) scegliere ♦ n (of animals) abbattimento selettivo

culminate ['kʌlmineit] vi: to ~ **in** culminare con; **culmination** [-'neiʃən] n culmine m

culottes [kju:'lɔts] npl gonna f pantalone inv

culpable ['kʌlpəbl] adj colpevole

culprit ['kʌlprit] n colpevole m/f

cult [kʌlt] n culto

cultivate ['kʌltiveit] vt (also fig) coltivare; **cultivation** [-'veiʃən] n coltivazione f

cultural ['kʌltʃərəl] adj culturale

culture ['kʌltʃə*] n (also fig) cultura; ~**d** adj colto(a)

cumbersome ['kʌmbəsəm] adj ingombrante

cunning ['kʌnɪŋ] n astuzia, furberia ♦ adj astuto(a), furbo(a)

cup [kʌp] n tazza; (prize, of bra) coppa

cupboard ['kʌbəd] n armadio

cup-tie (BRIT) n partita di coppa

curate ['kjuərɪt] n cappellano

curator [kjuə'reɪtə*] n direttore m (di museo etc)

curb [kə:b] vt tenere a freno ♦ n freno; (US) bordo del marciapiede

curdle ['kə:dl] vi cagliare

cure [kjuə*] vt guarire; (CULIN) trattare; affumicare; essiccare ♦ n rimedio

curfew ['kə:fju:] n coprifuoco

curio ['kjuərɪəu] n curiosità f inv

curiosity [kjuərɪ'ɔsɪtɪ] n curiosità

curious ['kjuərɪəs] adj curioso(a)

curl [kə:l] n riccio ♦ vt ondulare; (tightly) arricciare ♦ vi arricciarsi; ~ up vi rannicchiarsi; ~er n bigodino

curly ['kə:lɪ] adj ricciuto(a)

currant ['kʌrnt] n (dried) sultanina; (bush, fruit) ribes m inv

currency ['kʌrnsɪ] n moneta; to gain ~ (fig) acquistare larga diffusione

current ['kʌrnt] adj corrente ♦ n corrente f; ~ account (BRIT) n conto corrente; ~ affairs npl attualità f; ~ly adv attualmente

curricula [kə'rɪkjulə] npl of **curriculum**

curriculum [kə'rɪkjuləm] (pl ~s or **curricula**) n curriculum m inv; ~ vitae n curriculum vitae m inv

curry ['kʌrɪ] n curry m inv ♦ vt: to ~ favour with cercare di attirarsi i favori di; ~ powder n curry m

curse [kə:s] vi maledire ♦ vi bestemmiare ♦ n maledizione f; bestemmia

cursor ['kə:sə*] n (COMPUT) cursore m

cursory ['kə:sərɪ] adj superficiale

curt [kə:t] adj secco(a)

curtail [kə:'teɪl] vt (freedom etc) limitare; (visit etc) accorciare; (ex-

penses etc) ridurre, decurtare

curtain ['kə:tn] n tenda; (THEATRE) sipario

curts(e)y ['kə:tsɪ] vi fare un inchino or una riverenza

curve [kə:v] n curva ♦ vi curvarsi

cushion ['kuʃən] n cuscino ♦ vt (shock) fare da cuscinetto a

custard ['kʌstəd] n (for pouring) crema

custodian [kʌs'təudɪən] n custode m/f

custody ['kʌstədɪ] n (of child) tutela; to take into ~ (suspect) mettere in detenzione preventiva

custom ['kʌstəm] n costume m, consuetudine f; (COMM) clientela; ~ary adj consueto(a)

customer ['kʌstəmə*] n cliente m/f

customized ['kʌstəmaɪzd] adj (car etc) fuoriserie inv

custom-made adj (clothes) fatto(a) su misura; (other goods) fatto(a) su ordinazione

customs ['kʌstəmz] npl dogana; ~ duty n tassa doganale; ~ officer n doganiere m

cut [kʌt] (pt, pp cut) vt tagliare; (shape, make) intagliare; (reduce) ridurre ♦ vi tagliare ♦ n taglio; (in salary etc) riduzione f; to ~ a tooth mettere un dente; ~ down vt (tree etc) abbattere ♦ vt fus (also: ~ down on) ridurre; ~ off vt tagliare; (fig) isolare; ~ out vt tagliare fuori; eliminare; ritagliare; ~ up vt (paper, meat) tagliare a pezzi; ~back n riduzione f

cute [kju:t] adj (sweet) carino(a)

cuticle ['kju:tɪkl] n (on nail) pellicina, cuticola

cutlery ['kʌtlərɪ] n posate fpl

cutlet ['kʌtlɪt] n costoletta; (nut etc ~) cotoletta vegetariana

cut: ~out n interruttore m; (cardboard ~out) ritaglio; ~-price (US ~-rate) adj a prezzo ridotto; ~throat n assassino ♦ adj (competition) spietato(a)

cutting ['kʌtɪŋ] adj tagliente ♦ n

(from newspaper) ritaglio (di giornale); *(from plant)* talea
CV *n abbr* = **curriculum vitae**
cwt *abbr* = **hundredweight(s)**
cyanide ['saɪənaɪd] *n* cianuro
cycle ['saɪkl] *n* ciclo; *(bicycle)* bicicletta ♦ *vi* andare in bicicletta
cycling ['saɪklɪŋ] *n* ciclismo
cyclist ['saɪklɪst] *n* ciclista *m/f*
cygnet ['sɪgnɪt] *n* cigno giovane
cylinder ['sɪlɪndə*] *n* cilindro; **~ head gasket** *n* guarnizione *f* della testata del cilindro
cymbals ['sɪmblz] *npl* cembali *mpl*
cynic ['sɪnɪk] *n* cinico/a; **~al** *adj* cinico(a); **~ism** ['sɪnɪsɪzəm] *n* cinismo
Cyprus ['saɪprəs] *n* Cipro
cyst [sɪst] *n* cisti *f inv*
cystitis [sɪs'taɪtɪs] *n* cistite *f*
czar [zɑ:*] *n* zar *m inv*
Czech [tʃɛk] *adj* ceco(a) ♦ *n* ceco/a; *(LING)* ceco
Czechoslovakia [tʃɛkəslə'vækɪə] *n* Cecoslovacchia; **~n** *adj, n* cecoslovacco(a)

D

D [di:] *n (MUS)* re *m*
dab [dæb] *vt (eyes, wound)* tamponare; *(paint, cream)* applicare (con leggeri colpetti)
dabble ['dæbl] *vi*: **to ~ in** occuparsi (da dilettante) di
dad(dy) [dæd(ɪ)] *(inf)* *n* babbo, papà *m inv*
daffodil ['dæfədɪl] *n* trombone *m*, giunchiglia
daft [dɑ:ft] *adj* sciocco(a)
dagger ['dægə*] *n* pugnale *m*
daily ['deɪlɪ] *adj* quotidiano(a), giornaliero(a) ♦ *n* quotidiano ♦ *adv* tutti i giorni
dainty ['deɪntɪ] *adj* delicato(a), grazioso(a)
dairy ['dɛərɪ] *n (BRIT: shop)* latteria; *(on farm)* caseificio ♦ *adj* caseario(a); **~ farm** *n* caseificio; **~ products** *npl* latticini *mpl*; **~ store**

(US) *n* latteria
dais ['deɪɪs] *n* pedana, palco
daisy ['deɪzɪ] *n* margherita; **~ wheel** *n (on printer)* margherita
dale [deɪl] *(BRIT)* *n* valle *f*
dam [dæm] *n* diga ♦ *vt* sbarrare; costruire dighe su
damage ['dæmɪdʒ] *n* danno, danni *mpl; (fig)* danno ♦ *vt* danneggiare; **~s** *npl (LAW)* danni
damn [dæm] *vt* condannare; *(curse)* maledire ♦ *n (inf)*: **I don't give a ~** non me ne frega niente ♦ *adj (inf: also: ~ed)*: **this ~ ...** questo maledetto ...; **~ (it)!** accidenti!; **~ing** *adj (evidence)* schiacciante
damp [dæmp] *adj* umido(a) ♦ *n* umidità, umido ♦ *vt (also: ~en: cloth, rag)* inumidire, bagnare; *(: enthusiasm etc)* spegnere
damson ['dæmzən] *n* susina damaschina
dance [dɑ:ns] *n* danza, ballo; *(ball)* ballo ♦ *vi* ballare; **~ hall** *n* dancing *m inv*, sala da ballo; **~r** *n* danzatore/trice; *(professional)* ballerino/a
dancing ['dɑ:nsɪŋ] *n* danza, ballo
dandelion ['dændɪlaɪən] *n* dente *m* di leone
dandruff ['dændrəf] *n* forfora
Dane [deɪn] *n* danese *m/f*
danger ['deɪndʒə*] *n* pericolo; **there is a ~ of fire** c'è pericolo di incendio; **in ~** in pericolo; **he was in ~ of falling** rischiava di cadere; **~ous** *adj* pericoloso(a)
dangle ['dæŋgl] *vt* dondolare; *(fig)* far balenare ♦ *vi* pendolare
Danish ['deɪnɪʃ] *adj* danese ♦ *n (LING)* danese *m*
dapper ['dæpə*] *adj* lindo(a)
dare [dɛə*] *vt*: **to ~ sb to do** sfidare qn a fare qc ♦ *vi*: **to ~ (to) do sth** osare fare qc; **I ~ say** *(I suppose)* immagino (che); **~devil** *n* scavezzacollo *m/f*; **daring** *adj* audace, ardito(a) ♦ *n* audacia
dark [dɑ:k] *adj (night, room)* buio(a), scuro(a); *(colour, complexion)* scu-

ro(a); *(fig)* cupo(a), tetro(a), nero(a) ♦ *n*: **in the ~** al buio; **in the ~ about** *(fig)* all'oscuro di; **after ~** a notte fatta; **~en** *vt (colour)* scurire ♦ *vi (sky, room)* oscurarsi; **~ glasses** *npl* occhiali *mpl* scuri; **~ness** *n* oscurità, buio; **~ room** *n* camera oscura

darling ['dɑ:lɪŋ] *adj* caro(a) ♦ *n* tesoro

darn [dɑ:n] *vt* rammendare

dart [dɑ:t] *n* freccetta, *(SEWING)* pince *f inv* ♦ *vi*: **to ~ towards** precipitarsi verso; **to ~ away/along** sfrecciare via/lungo; **~board** *n* bersaglio (per freccette); **~s** *n* tiro al bersaglio (con freccette)

dash [dæʃ] *n (sign)* lineetta, *(small quantity)* punta ♦ *vt (missile)* gettare; *(hopes)* infrangere ♦ *vi*: **to ~ towards** precipitarsi verso; **~ away** *or* **off** *vi* scappare via

dashboard ['dæʃbɔːd] *n (AUT)* cruscotto

dashing ['dæʃɪŋ] *adj* ardito(a)

data ['deɪtə] *npl* dati *mpl*; **~base** *n* base *f* di dati, data base *m inv*; **~ processing** *n* elaborazione *f* (elettronica) dei dati

date [deɪt] *n* data; appuntamento; *(fruit)* dattero ♦ *vt* datare; *(person)* uscire con; **~ of birth** data di nascita; **to ~** *(until now)* fino a oggi; **~d** *adj* passato(a) di moda

daub [dɔːb] *vt* imbrattare

daughter ['dɔːtə*] *n* figlia; **~-in-law** *n* nuora

daunting ['dɔːntɪŋ] *adj* non invidiabile

dawdle ['dɔːdl] *vi* bighellonare

dawn [dɔːn] *n* alba ♦ *vi (day)* spuntare; *(fig)*: **it ~ed on him that ...** gli è venuto in mente che ...

day [deɪ] *n* giorno; *(as duration)* giornata; *(period of time, age)* tempo, epoca; **the ~ before** il giorno avanti *or* prima; **the ~ after, the following ~** il giorno dopo *or* seguente; **the ~ after tomorrow** dopodomani; **the ~ before yesterday** l'altroieri; **by**

~ di giorno; **~break *n* spuntar *m* del giorno; **~dream** *vi* sognare a occhi aperti; **(: blow)** stordire ♦ *n*: **in a ~** inebetito(a); stordito(a)

~time *n* giorno; **~-to-** *adj (life, organization)* quotidiano(a)

daze [deɪz] *vt (subject: drug)* inebetire; *(: blow)* stordire ♦ *n*: **in a ~** inebetito(a); stordito(a)

dazzle ['dæzl] *vt* abbagliare

DC *abbr* (= *direct current*) c.c

D-day *n* il giorno dello sbarco alleato in Normandia

dead [dɛd] *adj* morto(a); *(numb)* intirizzito(a); *(telephone)* muto(a); *(battery)* scarico(a) ♦ *adv* assolutamente, perfettamente ♦ *npl*: **the ~** i morti; **he was shot ~** fu colpito a morte; **~ tired** stanco(a) morto(a); **to stop ~** fermarsi di colpo; **~en** *vt (blow, sound)* ammortire; **~ end** *n* vicolo cieco; **~ heat** *n (SPORT)*: **to finish in a ~ heat** finire alla pari; **~line** *n* scadenza; **~lock** *n* punto morto; **~ loss** *n*: **to be a ~ loss** *(inf: person, thing)* non valere niente; **~ly** *adj* mortale; *(weapon, poison)* micidiale; **~pan** *adj* a faccia impassibile

deaf [dɛf] *adj* sordo(a); **~en** *vt* assordare; **~ness** *n* sordità

deal [diːl] *n (pt, pp* **dealt***)* accordo; *(business ~)* affare *m* ♦ *vt (blow, cards)* dare; **a great ~ (of)** molto(a); **~ in** *vt fus* occuparsi di; **~ with** *vt fus (COMM)* fare affari con, trattare con; *(handle)* occuparsi di; *(be about: book etc)* trattare di; **~er** *n* commerciante *m/f*; **~ings** *npl* *(COMM)* relazioni *fpl*; *(relations)* rapporti *mpl*; **dealt** [dɛlt] *pt, pp of* **deal**

dean [diːn] *n (REL)* decano; *(SCOL)* preside *m* di facoltà *(or* di collegio)

dear [dɪə*] *adj* caro(a) ♦ *n*: **my ~** caro mio/cara mia; **(: ~ me!** che! Dio mio!; **D~ Sir/Madam** *(in letter)* Egregio Signore/Egregia Signora, **D~ Mr/Mrs X** Gentile Signor/

Signora X; **~ly** adv (love) moltissimo; (pay) a caro prezzo

death [deθ] n morte f; (ADMIN) decesso; **~ certificate** n atto di decesso; **~ly** adj di morte; **~ penalty** n pena di morte; **~ rate** n indice m di mortalità; **~ toll** n vittime fpl

debacle [dɪ'bækl] n fiasco

debar [dɪ'baː] vt: **to ~ sb from doing** impedire a qn di fare

debase [dɪ'beɪs] vt (currency) adulterare; (person) degradare

debatable [dɪ'beɪtəbl] adj discutibile

debate [dɪ'beɪt] n dibattito ♦ vt dibattere; discutere

debauchery [dɪ'bɔːtʃərɪ] n dissolutezza

debit ['debɪt] n debito ♦ vt: **to ~ a sum to sb** or **to sb's account** addebitare una somma a qn

debris ['debriː] n detriti mpl

debt [det] n debito; **to be in ~** essere indebitato(a); **~or** n debitore/trice

debunk [diː'bʌŋk] vt (theory, claim) smentire

début ['deɪbjuː] n debutto

decade ['dekeɪd] n decennio

decadence ['dekədəns] n decadenza

decaffeinated [dɪ'kæfɪneɪtɪd] adj decaffeinizzato(a)

decanter [dɪ'kæntə*] n caraffa

decay [dɪ'keɪ] n decadimento; (also: **tooth ~**) carie f ♦ vi (rot) imputridire

deceased [dɪ'siːst] n defunto/a

deceit [dɪ'siːt] n inganno; **~ful** adj ingannevole, perfido(a)

deceive [dɪ'siːv] vt ingannare

December [dɪ'sembə*] n dicembre m

decent ['diːsənt] adj decente; (respectable) per bene; (kind) gentile

deception [dɪ'sepʃən] n inganno

deceptive [dɪ'septɪv] adj ingannevole

decide [dɪ'saɪd] vt (person) far prendere una decisione a; (question, argument) risolvere, decidere ♦ vi decidere, decidersi; **to ~ to do/that** decidere di fare/che; **to ~ on** decide-

re per; **~d** adj (resolute) deciso(a); (clear, definite) netto(a), chiaro(a); **~dly** [-dɪdlɪ] adv indubbiamente; decisamente

decimal ['desɪməl] adj decimale ♦ n decimale m; **~ point** n = virgola

decipher [dɪ'saɪfə*] vt decifrare

decision [dɪ'sɪʒən] n decisione f

decisive [dɪ'saɪsɪv] adj decisivo(a); (person) deciso(a)

deck [dek] n (NAUT) ponte m; (of bus): **top ~** imperiale m; (record ~) ,piatto; (of cards) mazzo; **~chair** n sedia a sdraio

declaration [deklə'reɪʃən] n dichiarazione f

declare [dɪ'klɛə*] vt dichiarare

decline [dɪ'klaɪn] n (decay) declino; (lessening) ribasso ♦ vt declinare; rifiutare ♦ vi declinare; diminuire

decode [diː'kəud] vt decifrare

decoder [diː'kəudə*] n (TV) decodificatore m

decompose [diːkəm'pəuz] vi decomporre

décor ['deɪkɔː*] n decorazione f

decorate ['dekəreɪt] vt (adorn, give a medal to) decorare; (paint and paper) tinteggiare e tappezzare; **decoration** [-'reɪʃən] n (medal etc, adornment) decorazione f; **decorator** n decoratore m

decorum [dɪ'kɔːrəm] n decoro

decoy ['diːkɔɪ] n zimbello

decrease [n 'diːkriːs, vb diː'kriːs] n diminuzione f ♦ vt, vi diminuire

decree [dɪ'kriː] n decreto; **~ nisi** [-'naɪsaɪ] n sentenza provvisoria di divorzio

dedicate ['dedɪkeɪt] vt consacrare; (book etc) dedicare

dedication [dedɪ'keɪʃən] n (devotion) dedizione f; (in book etc) dedica

deduce [dɪ'djuːs] vt dedurre

deduct [dɪ'dʌkt] vt: **to ~ sth (from)** dedurre qc (da); **~ion** [dɪ'dʌkʃən] n deduzione f

deed [diːd] n azione f, atto; (LAW) atto

deem [diːm] vt giudicare, ritenere

deep [di:p] *adj* profondo(a); **4 me-**
tres ~ profondo(a) 4 metri ♦
adv: **spectators stood 20** ~ c'erano
20 file di spettatori; ~**en** *vt* (*hole*)
approfondire ♦ *vi* approfondirsi;
(*darkness*) farsi più buio; ~**freeze**
n congelatore *m*; ~**fry** *vt* friggere
in olio abbondante; ~**ly** *adv* profondamente; ~**sea diving** *n* immersione *f* in alto mare; ~**seated** *adj* ra-
dicato(a)

deer [dɪə*] *n inv:* **the** ~ i cervidi;
(**red**) ~ cervo; (**fallow**) ~ daino
(**roe**) ~ capriolo; ~**skin** *n* pelle *f* di
daino

deface [dɪ'feɪs] *vt* imbrattare

default [dɪ'fɔːlt] *n* (*COMPUT: also:*
~ **value**) default *m inv*; **by** ~
(*SPORT*) per abbandono

defeat [dɪ'fiːt] *n* sconfitta ♦ *vt* (*team*,
opponents) sconfiggere; ~**ist** *adj, n*
disfattista *m/f*

defect [*n* 'diːfɛkt, *vb* dɪ'fɛkt] *n* difetto ♦ *vi:* **to** ~ **to the enemy** passare
al nemico; ~**ive** [dɪ'fɛktɪv] *adj* difet-
toso(a)

defence [dɪ'fɛns] (*US* **defense**) *n* difesa; ~**less** *adj* senza difesa

defend [dɪ'fɛnd] *vt* difendere; ~**ant**
n imputato/a; ~**er** *n* difensore/a

defense [dɪ'fɛns] (*US*) *n* = **defence**

defensive [dɪ'fɛnsɪv] *adj* difensi-
vo(a) ♦ *n:* **on the** ~ sulla difensiva

defer [dɪ'fəː*] *vt* (*postpone*) differire,
rinviare

defiance [dɪ'faɪəns] *n* sfida; **in** ~ **of**
a dispetto di

defiant [dɪ'faɪənt] *adj* (*attitude*) di
sfida; (*person*) ribelle

deficiency [dɪ'fɪʃənsɪ] *n* deficienza,
carenza

deficit ['dɛfɪsɪt] *n* deficit *m inv*

defile [dɪ'faɪl] *vt* deturpare

define [dɪ'faɪn] *vt* definire

definite ['dɛfɪnɪt] *adj* (*fixed*) defini-
to(a), preciso(a); (*clear, obvious*)
ben definito(a), esatto(a); (*LING*)
determinativo(a); **he was** ~ **about**
it ne era sicuro; ~**ly** *adv* indubbiamente

definition [dɛfɪ'nɪʃən] *n* definizione *f*

deflate [di:'fleɪt] *vt* sgonfiare

deflect [dɪ'flɛkt] *vt* deflettere, deviare

deformed [dɪ'fɔːmd] *adj* deforme

defraud [dɪ'frɔːd] *vt* defraudare

defrost [di:'frɔst] *vt* (*fridge*) disgela-
re; ~**er** (*US*) *n* (*demister*) sbrinatore *m*

deft [dɛft] *adj* svelto(a), destro(a)

defunct [dɪ'fʌŋkt] *adj* che non esiste
più

defuse [di:'fjuːz] *vt* disinnescare;
(*fig*) distendere

defy [dɪ'faɪ] *vt* sfidare; (*efforts etc*)
resistere a; **it defies description** su-
pera ogni descrizione

degenerate [*vb* dɪ'dʒɛnəreɪt, *adj*
dɪ'dʒɛnərɪt] *vi* degenerare ♦ *adj* de-
genere

degree [dɪ'griː] *n* grado; (*SCOL*) laurea (universitaria); **a** (**first**) ~ **in**
maths una laurea in matematica;
by ~**s** (*gradually*) gradualmente, a
poco a poco; **to some** ~ fino a un
certo punto, in certa misura

dehydrated [di:haɪ'dreɪtɪd] *adj* disi-
dratato(a); (*milk, eggs*) in polvere

de-ice [di:'aɪs] *vt* (*windscreen*) disge-
lare

deign [deɪn] *vi:* **to** ~ **to do** degnarsi
di fare

deity ['di:ɪtɪ] *n* divinità *f inv*

dejected [dɪ'dʒɛktɪd] *adj* abbattu-
to(a), avvilito(a)

delay [dɪ'leɪ] *vt* ritardare ♦ *vi:* **to** ~
(**in doing sth**) ritardare (a fare qc)
♦ *n* ritardo; **to be** ~**ed** subire un ritardo; (*person*) essere trattenuto(a)

delectable [dɪ'lɛktəbl] *adj* (*person*,
food) delizioso(a)

delegate [*n* 'dɛlɪgɪt, *vb* 'dɛlɪgeɪt] *n*
delegato/a ♦ *vt* delegare; **delega-**
tion [-'geɪʃən] *n* (*group*) delegazione
f; (*by manager*) delega

delete [dɪ'li:t] *vt* cancellare

deliberate [*adj* dɪ'lɪbərɪt, *vb* dɪ'lɪbər-
eɪt] *adj* (*intentional*) intenzionale; (*slow*) misurato(a) ♦ *vi* delibe-
rare, riflettere; ~**ly** *adv* (*on purpo-*
se) deliberatamente

delicacy ['dɛlɪkəsɪ] n delicatezza

delicate ['dɛlɪkɪt] adj delicato(a)

delicatessen [dɛlɪkə'tɛsn] n = salumeria

delicious [dɪ'lɪʃəs] adj delizioso(a), squisito(a)

delight [dɪ'laɪt] n delizia, gran piacere m ♦ vt dilettare; **to take (a) ~ in** dilettarsi in; **~ed** adj: **~ed (at** or **with)** contentissimo(a) (di), felice (di); **~ed to do** felice di fare; **~ful** adj delizioso(a); incantevole

delinquent [dɪ'lɪŋkwənt] adj, n delinquente m/f

delirious [dɪ'lɪrɪəs] adj: **to be ~** delirare

deliver [dɪ'lɪvə*] vt (mail) distribuire; (goods) consegnare; (speech) pronunciare; (MED) far partorire; **~y** n distribuzione f; consegna; (of speaker) dizione f; (MED) parto

delude [dɪ'lu:d] vt illudere

deluge ['dɛlju:dʒ] n diluvio

delusion [dɪ'lu:ʒən] n illusione f

delve [dɛlv] vi: **to ~ into** frugare in; (subject) far ricerche in

demand [dɪ'mɑ:nd] vt richiedere; (rights) rivendicare ♦ n domanda; (claim) rivendicazione f; **in ~** ricercato(a), richiesto(a); **on ~** a richiesta; **~ing** adj (boss) esigente; (work) impegnativo(a)

demean [dɪ'mi:n] vt: **to ~ o.s.** umiliarsi

demeanour [dɪ'mi:nə*] (US demeanor) n comportamento; contegno

demented [dɪ'mɛntɪd] adj demente, impazzito(a)

demise [dɪ'maɪz] n decesso

demister [dɪ'mɪstə*] (BRIT) n (AUT) sbrinatore m

demo ['dɛməu] (inf) n abbr (= demonstration) manifestazione f

democracy [dɪ'mɔkrəsɪ] n democrazia

democrat ['dɛməkræt] n democratico/a; **~ic** [dɛmə'krætɪk] adj democratico(a)

demolish [dɪ'mɔlɪʃ] vt demolire

demonstrate ['dɛmənstreɪt] vt di-

mostrare, provare ♦ vi dimostrare, manifestare; **demonstration** [-'streɪʃən] n dimostrazione f; (POL) dimostrazione, manifestazione f; **demonstrator** n (POL) dimostrante m/f; (COMM) dimostratore/trice

demote [dɪ'məut] vt far retrocedere

demure [dɪ'mjuə*] adj contegnoso(a)

den [dɛn] n tana, covo; (room) buco

denatured alcohol [diː'neɪtʃəd-] (US) n alcool m inv denaturato

denial [dɪ'naɪəl] n diniego; rifiuto

denim ['dɛnɪm] n tessuto di cotone ritorto; **~s** npl (jeans) blue jeans mpl

Denmark ['dɛnmɑ:k] n Danimarca

denomination [dɪnɔmɪ'neɪʃən] n (money) valore m; (REL) confessione f

denounce [dɪ'nauns] vt denunciare

dense [dɛns] adj fitto(a); (smoke) denso(a); (inf: person) ottuso(a), duro(a)

density ['dɛnsɪtɪ] n densità f inv

dent [dɛnt] n ammaccatura ♦ vt (also: **make a ~ in**) ammaccare

dental ['dɛntl] adj dentale; **~ surgeon** n medico/a dentista

dentist ['dɛntɪst] n dentista m/f; **~ry** n odontoiatria

dentures ['dɛntʃəz] npl dentiera

deny [dɪ'naɪ] vt negare; (refuse) rifiutare

deodorant [diː'əudərənt] n deodorante m

depart [dɪ'pɑ:t] vi partire; **to ~ from** (fig) deviare da

department [dɪ'pɑ:tmənt] n (COMM) reparto; (SCOL) sezione f; dipartimento; (POL) ministero; **~ store** n grande magazzino

departure [dɪ'pɑ:tʃə*] n partenza; (fig): **~ from** deviazione f da; **a new ~** una svolta (decisiva); **~ lounge** n (at airport) sala d'attesa

depend [dɪ'pɛnd] vi: **to ~ on** dipendere da; (rely on) contare su; **it ~s** dipende; **~ing on the result ...** a seconda del risultato ...; **~able** adj fidato(a); (car etc) affidabile; **~ant** n persona a carico; **~ent** adj: **to be**

~ent on dipendere da; (child, relative) essere a carico di ♦ n = ~ant

depict [dɪ'pɪkt] vt (in picture) dipingere; (in words) descrivere

depleted [dɪ'pliːtɪd] adj diminuito(a)

deploy [dɪ'plɔɪ] vt dispiegare

depopulation ['diːpɔpju'leɪʃən] n spopolamento

deport [dɪ'pɔːt] vt deportare; espellere

deportment [dɪ'pɔːtmənt] n portamento

depose [dɪ'pəuz] vt deporre

deposit [dɪ'pɔzɪt] n (COMM, GEO) deposito; (of ore, oil) giacimento; (CHEM) sedimento; (part payment) acconto; (for hired goods etc) cauzione f ♦ vt depositare; dare in acconto; mettere o lasciare in deposito; ~ **account** n conto vincolato

depot ['depəu] n deposito; (US) stazione f ferroviaria

depreciate [dɪ'priːʃɪeɪt] vi svalutarsi

depress [dɪ'prɛs] vt deprimere; (price, wages) abbassare; (press down) premere; ~**ed** adj (person) depresso(a), abbattuto(a); (price) in ribasso; (industry) in crisi; ~**ing** adj deprimente; ~**ion** [dɪ'prɛʃən] n depressione f

deprivation [deprɪ'veɪʃən] n privazione f

deprive [dɪ'praɪv] vt: to ~ sb of privare qn di; ~**d** adj disgraziato(a)

depth [dɛpθ] n profondità f inv; in the ~s of nel profondo di; nel cuore di; out of one's ~ (in water) dove non si tocca; (fig) a disagio

deputize ['depjutaiz] vi: to ~ for svolgere le funzioni di

deputy ['depjuti] adj: ~ head (BRIT: SCOL) vicepreside m/f ♦ n (assistant) vice m/f inv; (US: also: ~ sheriff) vice-sceriffo

derail [dɪ'reɪl] vt: to be ~ed deragliare

deranged [dɪ'reɪndʒd] adj: to be ~ (mentally) ~ essere pazzo(a)

derby ['dɑːbɪ] (US) n (bowler hat) bombetta

derelict ['dɛrɪlɪkt] adj abbandonato(a)

derisory [dɪ'raɪsərɪ] adj (sum) irrisorio(a); (laughter, person) beffardo(a)

derive [dɪ'raɪv] vt: to ~ sth from derivare qc da; trarre qc da ♦ vi: to ~ **from** derivare da

derogatory [dɪ'rɔgətərɪ] adj denigratorio(a)

derv [dəːv] (BRIT) n gasolio

descend [dɪ'sɛnd] vt, vi discendere, scendere; to ~ **from** discendere da; to ~ **to** (lying, begging) abbassarsi a; ~**ant** n discendente m/f

descent [dɪ'sɛnt] n (in descesa; (origin) discendenza, famiglia

describe [dɪs'kraɪb] vt descrivere; **description** [-'krɪpʃən] n descrizione f; (sort) genere m, specie f

desecrate ['dɛsɪkreɪt] vt profanare

desert [n 'dɛzət, vb dɪ'zəːt] n deserto ♦ vt lasciare, abbandonare ♦ vi (MIL) disertare; ~**er** n disertore m; ~**ion** [dɪ'zəːʃən] n (MIL) diserzione f; (LAW) abbandono del tetto coniugale; ~ **island** n isola deserta; ~**s** [dɪ'zəːts] npl: to get one's just ~s avere ciò che si merita

deserve [dɪ'zəːv] vt meritare; **deserving** adj (person) meritevole, degno(a); (cause) meritorio(a)

design [dɪ'zaɪn] n (art, sketch) disegno; (layout, shape) linea; (pattern) fantasia; (intention) intenzione f ♦ vt disegnare; progettare

designer [dɪ'zaɪnə*] n (ART, TECH) disegnatore/trice; (of fashion) modellista m/f

desire [dɪ'zaɪə*] n desiderio, voglia ♦ vt desiderare, volere

desk [dɛsk] n (in office) scrivania; (for pupil) banco; (BRIT: in shop, restaurant) cassa; (in hotel) ricevimento; (at airport) accettazione f

desolate ['dɛsəlɪt] adj desolato(a)

despair [dɪs'pɛə*] n disperazione f ♦ vi: to ~ **of** disperare di

despatch [dɪs'pætʃ] n, vt = dispatch

desperate ['dɛspərɪt] adj disperato(a); *(fugitive)* capace di tutto; **to be ~ for sth/to do** volere disperatamente qc/fare; **~ly** *adv* disperatamente; *(very)* terribilmente, estremamente

desperation |dɛspəˈreɪʃən| *n* disperazione *f*

despicable |dɪsˈpɪkəbl| *adj* disprezzabile

despise |dɪsˈpaɪz| *vt* disprezzare, sdegnare

despite |dɪsˈpaɪt| *prep* malgrado, a dispetto di, nonostante

despondent |dɪsˈpɔndənt| *adj* abbattuto(a), scoraggiato(a)

dessert |dɪˈzɜːt| *n* dolce *m*; frutta; **~spoon** *n* cucchiaio da dolci

destination |dɛstɪˈneɪʃən| *n* destinazione *f*

destined |ˈdɛstɪnd| *adj*: **to be ~ to do/for** essere destinato(a) a fare/di

destiny |ˈdɛstɪnɪ| *n* destino

destitute |ˈdɛstɪtjuːt| *adj* indigente, bisognoso(a)

destroy |dɪsˈtrɔɪ| *vt* distruggere; **~er** *n* *(NAUT)* cacciatorpediniere *m*

destruction |dɪsˈtrʌkʃən| *n* distruzione *f*

detach |dɪˈtætʃ| *vt* staccare, distaccare; **~ed** *adj* *(attitude)* distante; **~ed house** *n* villa; **~ment** *n* *(MIL)* distaccamento; *(fig)* distacco

detail |ˈdiːteɪl| *n* particolare *m*, dettaglio ♦ *vt* dettagliare, particolareggiare; **in ~** nei particolari; **~ed** *adj* particolareggiato(a)

detain |dɪˈteɪn| *vt* trattenere; *(in captivity)* detenere

detect |dɪˈtɛkt| *vt* scoprire, scorgere; *(MED, POLICE, RADAR etc)* individuare; **~ion** |dɪˈtɛkʃən| *n* scoperta; individuazione *f*; **~ive** *n* investigatore/trice; **~ive story** *n* giallo

détente |deɪˈtɑːnt| *n* *(POL)* distensione *f*

detention |dɪˈtɛnʃən| *n* detenzione *f*; *(SCOL)* permanenza forzata per punizione

deter |dɪˈtɜː*| *vt* dissuadere

detergent |dɪˈtɜːdʒənt| *n* detersivo

deteriorate |dɪˈtɪərɪəreɪt| *vi* deteriorarsi

determine |dɪˈtɜːmɪn| *vt* determinare; **~d** *adj* *(person)* risoluto(a), deciso(a); **~d to do** deciso(a) a fare

detour |ˈdiːtuə*| *n* deviazione *f*

detract |dɪˈtrækt| *vi*: **to ~ from** detrarre da

detriment |ˈdɛtrɪmənt| *n*: **to the ~ of** a detrimento di; **~al** |dɛtrɪˈmɛntl| *adj*: **~al to** dannoso(a), nocivo(a) a

devaluation |dɪvæljuˈeɪʃən| *n* svalutazione *f*

devastate |ˈdɛvəsteɪt| *vt* devastare; *(fig)*: **~d by** sconvolto(a) da; **devastating** *adj* devastatore(trice); sconvolgente

develop |dɪˈvɛləp| *vt* sviluppare; *(habit)* prendere (gradualmente) ♦ *vi* svilupparsi; *(facts, symptoms: appear)* manifestarsi, rivelarsi; **~er** *n* *(also: property ~er)* costruttore *m* edile; **~ing country** *n* paese *m* in via di sviluppo; **~ment** *n* sviluppo

device |dɪˈvaɪs| *n* *(apparatus)* congegno

devil |ˈdɛvl| *n* diavolo; demonio

devious |ˈdiːvɪəs| *adj* *(person)* subdolo(a)

devise |dɪˈvaɪz| *vt* escogitare, concepire

devoid |dɪˈvɔɪd| *adj*: **~ of** privo(a) di

devolution |diːvəˈluːʃən| *n* *(POL)* decentramento

devote |dɪˈvəut| *vt*: **to ~ sth to do** dedicare qc a; **~d** *adj* devoto(a); **to be ~d to sb** essere molto affezionato(a) a qn; **~e** |dɛvəuˈtiː| *n* *(MUS, SPORT)* appassionato/a

devotion |dɪˈvəuʃən| *n* devozione *f*, attaccamento; *(REL)* atto di devozione, preghiera

devour |dɪˈvauə*| *vt* divorare

devout |dɪˈvaut| *adj* pio(a), devoto(a)

dew |djuː| *n* rugiada

dexterity |dɛksˈtɛrɪtɪ| *n* destrezza

diabetes [daɪə'biːtiːz] n diabete m;
  diabetic [-'bɛtɪk] adj, n diabetico(a)

diabolical [daɪə'bɔlɪk] (inf) adj
(weather, behaviour) orribile

diagnoses [daɪəg'nəusiːz] npl of diagnosis

diagnosis [daɪəg'nəusɪs] (pl diagnoses) n diagnosi f inv

diagonal [daɪ'ægənl] adj diagonale ♦
n diagonale f

diagram ['daɪəgræm] n diagramma
m

dial ['daɪəl] n quadrante m; (on radio) lancetta; (on telephone) disco
combinatore ♦ vt (number) fare

dialect ['daɪəlɛkt] n dialetto

dialling code ['daɪəlɪŋ-] (US dial
code) n prefisso

dialling tone ['daɪəlɪŋ-] (US dial
tone) n segnale m di linea libera

dialogue ['daɪəlɔg] (US dialog) n
dialogo

diameter [daɪ'æmɪtə*] n diametro

diamond ['daɪəmənd] n diamante m;
(shape) rombo; **~s** npl (CARDS)
quadri mpl

diaper ['daɪəpə*] (US) n pannolino

diaphragm ['daɪəfræm] n diaframma m

diarrhoea [daɪə'riːə] (US diarrhea)
n diarrea

diary ['daɪərɪ] n (daily account) diario; (book) agenda

dice [daɪs] n inv dado ♦ vt (CULIN)
tagliare a dadini

Dictaphone ['dɪktəfəun] ® n dittafo-
no ®

dictate [dɪk'teɪt] vt dettare

dictation [dɪk'teɪʃən] n dettatura;
(SCOL) dettato

dictator [dɪk'teɪtə*] n dittatore m;
  ~ship n dittatura

dictionary ['dɪkʃənrɪ] n dizionario

did [dɪd] pt of do

didn't = did not

die [daɪ] vi morire; to be dying for
sth/to do sth morire dalla voglia di
qc/di fare qc; **~ away** vi spegnersi
a poco a poco; **~ down** vi abbassarsi; **~ out** vi estinguersi

diehard ['daɪhɑːd] n reazionario/a

diesel ['diːzəl] n (vehicle) diesel m
inv; **~ engine** n motore m diesel
inv; **~ (oil)** n gasolio (per motori
diesel), diesel m inv

diet ['daɪət] n alimentazione f; (restricted food) dieta ♦ vi (also: be on
a ~) stare a dieta

differ ['dɪfə*] vi: to ~ from sth differire da qc; essere diverso(a) da
qc; to ~ from sb over sth essere in
disaccordo con qn su qc; **~ence** n
differenza; (disagreement) screzio;
~ent adj diverso(a); **~entiate**
[-'rɛnʃɪeɪt] vi: to ~entiate between
discriminare or fare differenza fra

difficult ['dɪfɪkəlt] adj difficile; **~y** n
difficoltà f inv

diffident ['dɪfɪdənt] adj sfiduciato(a)

diffuse [adj dɪ'fjuːs, vb dɪ'fjuːz] adj
diffuso(a) ♦ vt diffondere

dig [dɪg] (pt, pp dug) vt (hole) scavare; (garden) vangare ♦ n (prod) gomitata; (archaeological) scavo; (fig)
frecciata; **~ into** vt fus (savings)
scavare in; to ~ one's nails into
conficcare le unghie in; **~ up** vt
(tree etc) sradicare; (information)
scavare fuori

digest [vb daɪ'dʒɛst, n 'daɪdʒɛst] vt
digerire ♦ n compendio; **~ion**
[dɪ'dʒɛstʃən] n digestione f; **~ive**
(juices, system) digerente

digit ['dɪdʒɪt] n cifra; (finger) dito;
~al adj digitale

dignified ['dɪgnɪfaɪd] adj dignito-
so(a)

dignity ['dɪgnɪtɪ] n dignità

digress [daɪ'grɛs] vi: to ~ from divagare da

digs [dɪgz] (BRIT: inf) npl camera
ammobiliata

dike [daɪk] n = dyke

dilapidated [dɪ'læpɪdeɪtɪd] adj cadente

dilemma [daɪ'lɛmə] n dilemma m

diligent ['dɪlɪdʒənt] adj diligente

dilute [daɪ'luːt] vt diluire; (with water) annacquare

dim [dɪm] adj (light) debole; (outline,

figure) vago(a); (*room*) in penombra; (*inf: person*) tonto(a) ♦ *vt* (*light*) abbassare

dime [daɪm] (*US*) *n* = 10 cents

dimension [daɪˈmɛnʃən] *n* dimensione *f*

diminish [dɪˈmɪnɪʃ] *vt, vi* diminuire

diminutive [dɪˈmɪnjʊtɪv] *adj* minuscolo(a) ♦ *n* (*LING*) diminutivo

dimmers [ˈdɪməz] (*US*) *npl* (*AUT*) anabbaglianti *mpl*; luci *fpl* di posizione

dimple [ˈdɪmpl] *n* fossetta

din [dɪn] *n* chiasso, fracasso

dine [daɪn] *vi* pranzare; ~**r** *n* (*person*) cliente *m/f*; (*US: place*) tavola calda

dinghy [ˈdɪŋgɪ] *n* battello pneumatico; (*also: rubber* ~) gommone *m*

dingy [ˈdɪndʒɪ] *adj* grigio(a)

dining car [ˈdaɪnɪŋ-] (*BRIT*) *n* vagone *m* ristorante

dining room [ˈdaɪnɪŋ-] *n* sala da pranzo

dinner [ˈdɪnə*] *n* (*lunch*) pranzo; (*evening meal*) cena; (*public*) banchetto; ~ **jacket** *n* smoking *m inv*; ~ **party** *n* cena; ~ **time** *n* ora di pranzo (*or* cena)

dint [dɪnt] *n*: **by** ~ **of** a forza di

dip [dɪp] *n* discesa; (*in sea*) bagno; (*CULIN*) salsetta ♦ *vt* immergere; bagnare; (*BRIT: AUT: lights*) abbassare ♦ *vi* abbassarsi

diphthong [ˈdɪfθɒŋ] *n* dittongo

diploma [dɪˈpləumə] *n* diploma *m*

diplomacy [dɪˈpləuməsɪ] *n* diplomazia

diplomat [ˈdɪpləmæt] *n* diplomatico; ~**ic** [dɪpləˈmætɪk] *adj* diplomatico(a)

diprod [ˈdɪprɒd] (*US*) *n* = **dipstick**

dipstick [ˈdɪpstɪk] *n* (*AUT*) indicatore *m* di livello dell'olio

dipswitch [ˈdɪpswɪtʃ] (*BRIT*) *n* (*AUT*) levetta dei fari

dire [daɪə*] *adj* terribile; estremo(a)

direct [daɪˈrɛkt] *adj* diretto(a) ♦ *vt* dirigere; (*order*): **to** ~ **sb to do sth** dare direttive a qn di fare qc ♦ *adv* direttamente; **can you** ~ **me to ...?**

mi può indicare la strada per ...?

direction [dɪˈrɛkʃən] *n* direzione *f*; ~**s** *npl* (*advice*) chiarimenti *mpl*; **sense of** ~ senso dell'orientamento; ~**s for use** istruzioni *fpl*

directly [dɪˈrɛktlɪ] *adv* (*in straight line*) direttamente; (*at once*) subito

director [dɪˈrɛktə*] *n* direttore/trice; amministratore/trice; (*THEATRE, CINEMA*) regista *m/f*

directory [dɪˈrɛktərɪ] *n* elenco

dirt [dəːt] *n* sporcizia; immondizia; (*earth*) terra; ~**-cheap** *adj* da due soldi; ~**y** *adj* sporco(a) ♦ *vt* sporcare; ~**y trick** *n* brutto scherzo

disability [dɪsəˈbɪlɪtɪ] *n* invalidità *f inv*; (*LAW*) incapacità *f inv*

disabled [dɪsˈeɪbld] *adj* invalido(a); (*mentally*) ritardato(a) ♦ *npl*: **the** ~ gli invalidi

disadvantage [dɪsədˈvɑːntɪdʒ] *n* svantaggio

disaffection [dɪsəˈfɛkʃən] *n*: ~ (**with**) allontanamento (da)

disagree [dɪsəˈgriː] *vi* (*differ*) discordare; (*be against, think otherwise*): **to** ~ (**with**) essere in disaccordo (con), dissentire (da); ~**able** *adj* sgradevole; (*person*) antipatico(a); ~**ment** *n* disaccordo; (*argument*) dissapore *m*

disallow [dɪsəˈlau] *vt* (*appeal*) respingere

disappear [dɪsəˈpɪə*] *vi* scomparire; ~**ance** *n* scomparsa

disappoint [dɪsəˈpɔɪnt] *vt* deludere; ~**ed** *adj* deluso(a); ~**ing** *adj* deludente; ~**ment** *n* delusione *f*

disapproval [dɪsəˈpruːvəl] *n* disapprovazione *f*

disapprove [dɪsəˈpruːv] *vi*: **to** ~ **of** disapprovare

disarm [dɪsˈɑːm] *vt* disarmare; ~**ament** *n* disarmo

disarray [dɪsəˈreɪ] *n*: **in** ~ (*army*) in rotta; (*organization*) in uno stato di confusione; (*clothes, hair*) in disordine

disaster [dɪˈzɑːstə*] *n* disastro

disband [dɪsˈbænd] *vt* sbandare;

(MIL) congedare ♦ *vi* sciogliersi

disbelief [dɪsbə'liːf] *n* incredulità

disc [dɪsk] *n* disco; *(COMPUT)* = **disk**

discard [dɪs'kɑːd] *vt (old things)* scartare; *(fig)* abbandonare

discern [dɪ'səːn] *vt* discernere, distinguere; **~ing** *adj* perspicace

discharge [*vb* dɪs'tʃɑːdʒ, *n* 'dɪstʃɑːdʒ] *vt (duties)* compiere; *(ELEC, waste etc)* scaricare; *(MED)* emettere; *(patient)* dimettere; *(employee)* licenziare; *(soldier)* congedare; *(defendant)* liberare ♦ *n (ELEC)* scarica; *(MED)* emissione *f*; *(dismissal)* licenziamento; congedo; liberazione *f*

disciple [dɪ'saɪpl] *n* discepolo

discipline ['dɪsɪplɪn] *n* disciplina ♦ *vt* disciplinare; *(punish)* punire

disc jockey *n* disc jockey *m inv*

disclaim [dɪs'kleɪm] *vt* negare, smentire

disclose [dɪs'kləʊz] *vt* rivelare, svelare; **disclosure** [-'kləʊʒə*] *n* rivelazione *f*

disco ['dɪskəʊ] *n abbr* = **discothèque**

discoloured [dɪs'kʌləd] *(US* **discolored**) *adj* scolorito(a); ingiallito(a)

discomfort [dɪs'kʌmfət] *n* disagio; *(lack of comfort)* scomodità *f inv*

disconcert [dɪskən'səːt] *vt* sconcertare

disconnect [dɪskə'nekt] *vt* sconnettere, staccare; *(ELEC, RADIO)* staccare; *(gas, water)* chiudere

discontent [dɪskən'tent] *n* scontentezza; **~ed** *adj* scontento(a)

discontinue [dɪskən'tɪnjuː] *vt* smettere, cessare; **"~d"** *(COMM)* "fuori produzione"

discord ['dɪskɔːd] *n* disaccordo; *(MUS)* dissonanza

discothèque ['dɪskəʊtek] *n* discoteca

discount [*n* 'dɪskaʊnt, *vb* dɪs'kaʊnt] *n* sconto ♦ *vt* scontare; *(idea)* non badare a

discourage [dɪs'kʌrɪdʒ] *vt* scoraggiare

discourteous [dɪs'kəːtɪəs] *adj* scortese

discover [dɪs'kʌvə*] *vt* scoprire; **~y** *n* scoperta

discredit [dɪs'kredɪt] *vt* screditare; mettere in dubbio

discreet [dɪs'kriːt] *adj* discreto(a)

discrepancy [dɪ'skrepənsɪ] *n* discrepanza

discriminate [dɪ'skrɪmɪneɪt] *vi*: to **~ between** distinguere tra; to **~ against** discriminare contro; **discriminating** *adj* fine, giudizioso(a); **discrimination** [-'neɪʃən] *n* discriminazione *f*; *(judgment)* discernimento

discuss [dɪ'skʌs] *vt* discutere; *(debate)* dibattere; **~ion** [dɪ'skʌʃən] *n* discussione *f*

disdain [dɪs'deɪn] *n* disdegno

disease [dɪ'ziːz] *n* malattia

disembark [dɪsɪm'bɑːk] *vt, vi* sbarcare

disengage [dɪsɪn'geɪdʒ] *vt (AUT: clutch)* disinnestare

disentangle [dɪsɪn'tæŋgl] *vt* liberare; *(wool etc)* sbrogliare

disfigure [dɪs'fɪgə*] *vt* sfigurare

disgrace [dɪs'greɪs] *n* vergogna; *(disfavour)* disgrazia ♦ *vt* disonorare, far cadere in disgrazia; **~ful** *adj* scandaloso(a), vergognoso(a)

disgruntled [dɪs'grʌntld] *adj* scontento(a), di cattivo umore

disguise [dɪs'gaɪz] *n* travestimento ♦ *vt*: to **~ (as)** travestire (da); **in ~** travestito(a)

disgust [dɪs'gʌst] *n* disgusto, nausea ♦ *vt* disgustare, far schifo a; **~ing** *adj* disgustoso(a); ripugnante

dish [dɪʃ] *n* piatto; **to do** *or* **wash the ~es** fare i piatti; **~ out** *vt* distribuire; **~ up** *vt* servire; **~cloth** *n* strofinaccio

dishearten [dɪs'hɑːtn] *vt* scoraggiare

dishevelled [dɪ'ʃevəld] *adj* arruffato(a); scapigliato(a)

dishonest [dɪs'ɒnɪst] *adj* disonesto(a)

dishonour [dɪs'ɒnə*] *(US* **dishonor**)

n disonore *m*; ~**able** *adj* disonorevole

dishtowel ['dɪʃtaʊəl] (*US*) *n* strofinaccio dei piatti

dishwasher ['dɪʃwɔʃə*] *n* lavastoviglie *f inv*

disillusion [dɪsɪ'luːʒən] *vt* disilludere, disingannare

disincentive [dɪsɪn'sɛntɪv] *n*: to be a ~ non essere un incentivo

disinfect [dɪsɪn'fɛkt] *vt* disinfettare; ~**ant** *n* disinfettante *m*

disintegrate [dɪs'ɪntɪɡreɪt] *vi* disintegrarsi

disinterested [dɪs'ɪntrəstɪd] *adj* disinteressato(a)

disjointed [dɪs'dʒɔɪntɪd] *adj* sconnesso(a)

disk [dɪsk] *n* (*COMPUT*) disco; single-/double-sided ~ disco a facciata singola/doppia; ~ **drive** *n* lettore *m*; ~**ette** (*US*) *n* = **disk**

dislike [dɪs'laɪk] *n* antipatia, avversione *f*; (*gen pl*) cosa che non piace ♦ *vt*: he ~**s** it non gli piace

dislocate ['dɪsləkeɪt] *vt* slogare

dislodge [dɪs'lɔdʒ] *vt* rimuovere

disloyal [dɪs'lɔɪəl] *adj* sleale

dismal ['dɪzməl] *adj* triste, cupo(a)

dismantle [dɪs'mæntl] *vt* (*machine*) smontare

dismay [dɪs'meɪ] *n* costernazione *f* ♦ *vt* sgomentare

dismiss [dɪs'mɪs] *vt* congedare; (*employee*) licenziare; (*idea*) scacciare; (*LAW*) respingere; ~**al** *n* congedo, licenziamento

dismount [dɪs'maʊnt] *vi* scendere

disobedience [dɪsə'biːdɪəns] *n* disubbidienza

disobedient [dɪsə'biːdɪənt] *adj* disubbidiente

disobey [dɪsə'beɪ] *vt* disubbidire a

disorder [dɪs'ɔːdə*] *n* disordine *m*; (*rioting*) tumulto; (*MED*) disturbo; ~**ly** *adj* disordinato(a); tumultuoso(a)

disorientated [dɪs'ɔːrɪenteɪtɪd] *adj* disorientato(a)

disown [dɪs'əʊn] *vt* rinnegare

disparaging [dɪs'pærɪdʒɪŋ] *adj* spregiativo(a), sprezzante

dispassionate [dɪs'pæʃənət] *adj* calmo(a), freddo(a); imparziale

dispatch [dɪs'pætʃ] *vt* spedire, inviare ♦ *n* spedizione *f*, invio; (*MIL*, *PRESS*) dispaccio

dispel [dɪs'pɛl] *vt* dissipare, scacciare

dispense [dɪs'pɛns] *vt* distribuire, amministrare; ~ **with** *vt fus* fare a meno di; ~**r** *n* (*container*) distributore *m*; **dispensing chemist** (*BRIT*) *n* farmacista *m/f*

disperse [dɪs'pɜːs] *vt* disperdere; (*knowledge*) disseminare ♦ *vi* disperdersi

dispirited [dɪs'pɪrɪtɪd] *adj* scoraggiato(a), abbattuto(a)

displace [dɪs'pleɪs] *vt* spostare; ~**d person** *n* (*POL*) profugo/a

display [dɪs'pleɪ] *n* esposizione *f*; (*of feeling etc*) manifestazione *f*; (*screen*) schermo ♦ *vt* mostrare; (*goods*) esporre; (*pej*) ostentare

displease [dɪs'pliːz] *vt* dispiacere a, scontentare; ~**d with** scontento di; **displeasure** [-'plɛʒə*] *n* dispiacere *m*

disposable [dɪs'pəʊzəbl] *adj* (*pack etc*) a perdere; (*income*) disponibile; ~ **nappy** *n* pannolino di carta

disposal [dɪs'pəʊzl] *n* eliminazione *f*; (*of property*) cessione *f*; **at one's** ~ a sua disposizione

dispose [dɪs'pəʊz] *vi*: ~ **of** sbarazzarsi di; ~**d** *adj*: ~**d to do** disposto(a) a fare; **disposition** [-'zɪʃən] *n* disposizione *f*; (*temperament*) carattere *m*

disproportionate [dɪsprə'pɔːʃənət] *adj* sproporzionato(a)

disprove [dɪs'pruːv] *vt* confutare

dispute [dɪs'pjuːt] *n* disputa; (*also*: **industrial** ~) controversia (sindacale) ♦ *vt* contestare; (*matter*) discutere; (*victory*) disputare

disqualify [dɪs'kwɔlɪfaɪ] *vt* (*SPORT*) squalificare; **to** ~ **sb from sth/from doing** rendere qn incapace a qualcosa/

fare; squalificare qn da qc/da fare; **to ~ sb from driving** ritirare la patente a qn

disquiet [dɪs'kwaɪət] n inquietudine f

disregard [dɪsrɪ'gɑːd] vt non far caso a, non badare a

disrepair [dɪsrɪ'pɛə*] n: **to fall into ~** (building) andare in rovina; (machine) deteriorarsi

disreputable [dɪs'rɛpjutəbl] adj poco raccomandabile; indecente

disrupt [dɪs'rʌpt] vt disturbare; creare scompiglio in

dissatisfaction [dɪssætɪs'fækʃən] n scontentezza, insoddisfazione f

dissect [dɪ'sɛkt] vt sezionare

dissent [dɪ'sɛnt] n dissenso

dissertation [dɪsə'teɪʃən] n tesi f inv, dissertazione f

disservice [dɪs'səːvɪs] n: **to do sb a ~** fare un cattivo servizio a qn

dissimilar [dɪ'sɪmɪlə*] adj: **~ (to)** dissimile or diverso(a) (da)

dissipate [dɪsɪpeɪt] vt dissipare

dissolute [dɪsəluːt] adj dissoluto(a), licenzioso(a)

dissolution [dɪsə'luːʃən] n (of organization, marriage, POL) scioglimento

dissolve [dɪ'zɔlv] vt dissolvere, sciogliere; (POL, marriage etc) sciogliere ♦ vi dissolversi, sciogliersi

distance [dɪstns] n distanza; **in the ~** in lontananza

distant [dɪstnt] adj lontano(a), distante; (manner) riservato(a), freddo(a)

distaste [dɪs'teɪst] n ripugnanza; **~ful** adj ripugnante, sgradevole

distended [dɪs'tɛndɪd] adj (stomach) dilatato(a)

distil [dɪs'tɪl] (US **distill**) vt distillare; **~lery** n distilleria

distinct [dɪs'tɪŋkt] adj distinto(a); **as ~ from** a differenza di; **~ion** [dɪs'tɪŋkʃən] n distinzione f; (in exam) lode f; **~ive** adj distintivo(a)

distinguish [dɪs'tɪŋgwɪʃ] vt distinguere; discernere; **~ed** adj (eminent) eminente; **~ing** adj (feature)

distort [dɪs'tɔːt] vt distorcere; (TECH) deformare

distract [dɪs'trækt] vt distrarre; **~ed** adj distratto(a); **~ion** [dɪs'trækʃən] n distrazione f

distraught [dɪs'trɔːt] adj stravolto(a)

distress [dɪs'trɛs] n angoscia ♦ vt affliggere; **~ing** adj doloroso(a); **~ signal** n segnale m di soccorso

distribute [dɪs'trɪbjuːt] vt distribuire; **distribution** [-'bjuːʃən] n distribuzione f; **distributor** n distributore m

district [dɪstrɪkt] n (of country) regione f; (of town) quartiere m; (ADMIN) distretto; **~ attorney** (US) n ≈ sostituto procuratore m della Repubblica; **~ nurse** (BRIT) n infermiera di quartiere

distrust [dɪs'trʌst] n diffidenza, sfiducia ♦ vt non aver fiducia in

disturb [dɪs'təːb] vt disturbare; **~ance** n disturbo; (political etc) disordini mpl; **~ed** adj (worried, upset) turbato(a); **emotionally ~ed** con turbe emotive; **~ing** adj sconvolgente

disuse [dɪs'juːs] n: **to fall into ~** cadere in disuso

disused [dɪs'juːzd] adj abbandonato(a)

ditch [dɪtʃ] n fossa ♦ vt (inf) piantare in asso

dither [dɪðə*] (pej) vi vacillare

ditto [dɪtəu] adv idem

dive [daɪv] n tuffo; (of submarine) immersione f ♦ vi tuffarsi; immergersi; **~r** n tuffatore/trice; palombaro

diverse [daɪ'vəːs] adj vario(a)

diversion [daɪ'vəːʃən] n (BRIT: AUT) deviazione f; (distraction) divertimento

divert [daɪ'vəːt] vt deviare

divide [dɪ'vaɪd] vt dividere; (separate) separare ♦ vi dividersi; **~d highway** (US) n strada a doppia carreggiata

dividend ['dɪvɪdend] *n* dividendo; *(fig)*: **to pay ~** dare dei frutti

divine [dɪ'vaɪn] *adj* divino(a)

diving ['daɪvɪŋ] *n* tuffo; ~ **board** *n* trampolino

divinity [dɪ'vɪnɪtɪ] *n* divinità *f inv*; teologia

division [dɪ'vɪʒən] *n* divisione *f*; separazione *f*; *(esp FOOTBALL)* serie *f*

divorce [dɪ'vɔːs] *n* divorzio ♦ *vt* divorziare da; *(dissociate)* separare; **~d** *adj* divorziato(a); **~e** [-'siː] *n* divorziato/a

D.I.Y. *(BRIT) n abbr* = do-it-yourself

dizzy ['dɪzɪ] *adj*: **to feel ~** avere il capogiro

DJ *n abbr* = disc jockey

do [duː] *(pt* did, *pp* done*) n (inf:* party etc*)* festa; **it was rather a grand ~** è stato un ricevimento piuttosto importante
♦ *vb* **1** *(in negative constructions)* non tradotto; **I don't understand** non capisco
2 *(to form questions)* non tradotto; **didn't you know?** non lo sapevi?; **why didn't you come?** perché non sei venuto?
3 *(for emphasis, in polite expressions)*: **she does seem rather late** sembra essere piuttosto in ritardo; ~ **sit down** si accomodi la prego, prego si sieda; ~ **take care!** mi raccomando, sta attento!
4 *(used to avoid repeating vb)*: **she swims better than I ~** lei nuota meglio di me; ~ **you agree?** — **yes, I ~/no, I don't** sei d'accordo? — sì/no; **she lives in Glasgow** — **so ~ I** lei vive a Glasgow — anch'io; **he asked me to help him and I did** mi ha chiesto di aiutarlo ed io l'ho fatto
5 *(in question tags)*: **you like him, don't you?** ti piace, vero?; **I don't know him, ~ I?** non lo conosco, vero?

♦ *vt (gen, carry out, perform etc)* fare; **what are you ~ing tonight?** che fa stasera?; **to ~ the cooking** cucinare; **to ~ the washing-up** fare i piatti; **to ~ one's teeth** lavarsi i denti; **to ~ one's hair/nails** farsi i capelli/le unghie; **the car was ~ing 100** la macchina faceva i 100 all'ora
♦ *vi* **1** *(act, behave)* fare; ~ **as I ~** faccia come me, faccia come faccio io
2 *(get on, fare)* andare; **he's ~ing well/badly at school** va bene/male a scuola; **how ~ you ~?** piacere!
3 *(suit)* andare bene; **this room will ~** questa stanza va bene
4 *(be sufficient)* bastare; **will £10 ~?** basteranno 10 sterline?; **that'll ~** basta così; **that'll ~!** *(in annoyance)* ora basta!; **to make ~ (with)** arrangiarsi (con)

do away with *vt fus (kill)* far fuori; *(abolish)* abolire

do up *vt (laces)* allacciare; *(dress, buttons)* abbottonare; *(renovate: room, house)* rimettere a nuovo, rifare

do with *vt fus (need)* aver bisogno di; *(be connected)*: **what has it got to ~ with you?** e tu che c'entri?; **I won't have anything to ~ with it** non voglio avere niente a che farci; **it has to ~ with money** si tratta di soldi

do without *vi* fare senza ♦ *vt fus* fare a meno di

dock [dɔk] *n (NAUT)* bacino; *(LAW)* banco degli imputati ♦ *vi* entrare in bacino; *(SPACE)* agganciarsi; **~s** *npl (NAUT)* dock *m inv*; **~er** *n* scaricatore *m*; **~yard** *n* cantiere *m* (navale)

doctor ['dɔktə*] *n* medico/a; *(Ph.D. etc)* dottore/essa ♦ *vt (drink etc)* adulterare; **D~ of Philosophy** *n* dottorato di ricerca; *(person)* titolare *m/f* di un dottorato di ricerca

doctrine ['dɔktrɪn] *n* dottrina

document ['dɔkjumənt] *n* documen-

dodge   76   doubt

to; **~ary** [-'mɛntərɪ] adj (evidence)
documentato(a) ♦ n documentario
dodge [dɔdʒ] n trucco; schivata ♦ vt
schivare, eludere
dodgems ['dɔdʒəmz] (BRIT) npl autoscontri mpl
doe [dəu] n (deer) femmina di daino;
(rabbit) coniglia
does [dʌz] vb see do; **doesn't** =
does not
dog [dɔg] n cane m ♦ vt (follow
closely) pedinare; (fig: memory etc)
perseguitare; **~ collar** n collare m
di cane; (fig) collarino; **~-eared** adj
(book) con orecchie
dogged ['dɔgɪd] adj ostinato(a), tenace
dogsbody ['dɔgzbɔdɪ] (BRIT: inf) n
factotum m inv
doings ['duɪŋz] npl attività fpl
do-it-yourself n il far da sé
doldrums ['dɔldrəmz] npl (fig): to
be in the ~ avere un brutto periodo
dole [dəul] (BRIT) n sussidio di disoccupazione; **to be on the ~** vivere
del sussidio; **~ out** vt distribuire
doleful ['dəulful] adj triste
doll [dɔl] n bambola; **~ed up** (inf)
adj in ghingheri
dollar ['dɔlə*] n dollaro
dolphin ['dɔlfɪn] n delfino
domain [də'meɪn] n dominio
dome [dəum] n cupola
domestic [də'mɛstɪk] adj (duty, happiness, animal) domestico(a); (policy, affairs, flights) nazionale; **~ated**
adj addomesticato(a)
dominate ['dɔmɪneɪt] vt dominare
domineering [dɔmɪ'nɪərɪŋ] adj di-
spotico(a), autoritario(a)
dominion [də'mɪnɪən] n dominio; so-
vranità; dominion m inv
domino ['dɔmɪnəu] (pl ~es) n domino; **~es** n (game) gioco del domino
don [dɔn] (BRIT) n docente m/f uni-
versitario(a)
donate [də'neɪt] vt donare
done [dʌn] pp of do
donkey ['dɔŋkɪ] n asino
donor ['dəunə*] n donatore/trice

don't [dəunt] = do not
doodle ['duːdl] vi scarabocchiare
doom [duːm] n destino; rovina ♦ vt:
to be ~ed (to failure) essere prede-
stinato(a) (a fallire); **~sday** n il
giorno del Giudizio
door [dɔː*] n porta; **~bell** n campanello; **~ handle** n maniglia; **~man**
n (in hotel) portiere m in livrea;
~mat n stuoia della porta; **~step** n
gradino della porta; **~way** n porta
dope [dəup] n (inf: drugs) roba ♦ vt
(horse etc) drogare
dopey ['dəupɪ] (inf) adj inebetito(a)
dormant ['dɔːmənt] adj inattivo(a)
dormice ['dɔːmaɪs] npl of **dormouse**
dormitory ['dɔːmɪtrɪ] n dormitorio;
(US) casa dello studente
dormouse ['dɔːmaus] (pl **dormice**) n
ghiro
dosage ['dəusɪdʒ] n posologia
dose [dəus] n dose f; (bout) attacco
doss house ['dɔs-] (BRIT) n asilo
notturno
dot [dɔt] n punto; macchiolina ♦ vt:
~ted with punteggiato(a) di; on the
~ in punto
dote [dəut]: **~ on** vt fus essere infa-
tuato(a) di
dot-matrix printer [dɔt'meɪtrɪks-]
n stampante f a matrice a punti
dotted line ['dɔtɪd-] n linea puntegg-
giata
double ['dʌbl] adj doppio(a) ♦ adv
(twice): **to cost ~ (sth)** costare il
doppio (di qc) ♦ n sosia m inv ♦ vt
raddoppiare; (fold) piegare doppio or
in due ♦ vi raddoppiarsi; **at the ~**
(BRIT), **on the ~** a passo di corsa;
~ bass n contrabbasso; **~ bed** n
letto matrimoniale; **~-breasted** adj
a doppio petto; **~cross** vt fare il
doppio gioco con; **~decker** n autobus m inv a due piani; **~ glazing**
(BRIT) n doppi vetri mpl; **~ room**
n camera per due; **~s** n (TENNIS)
doppio; **doubly** adv doppiamente
doubt [daut] n dubbio ♦ vt dubitare
di; **to ~ that** dubitare che + sub;
~ful adj dubbioso(a), incerto(a);

(*person*) equivoca(o); ~**less** *adv* indubbiamente

dough [dəu] *n* pasta, impasto; ~**nut** *n* bombolone *m*

douse [dauz] *vt* (*drench*) inzuppare; (*extinguish*) spegnere

dove [dʌv] *n* colombo/a

dovetail ['dʌvteɪl] *vi* (*fig*) combaciare

dowdy ['daudɪ] *adj* trasandato(a); malvestito(a)

down [daun] *n* piume *fpl* ♦ *adv* giù, di sotto ♦ *prep* giù per ♦ *vt* (*inf*: *drink*) scolarsi; ~ **with X!** abbasso X!; ~**-and-out** *n* barbone *m*; ~ **at-heel** *adj* scalcagnato(a); ~**cast** *adj* abbattuto(a); ~**fall** *n* caduta; rovina; ~**hearted** *adj* scoraggiato(a); ~**hill** *adv*: **to go** ~**hill** andare in discesa; (*fig*) lasciarsi andare; andare a rotoli; ~ **payment** *n* acconto; ~**pour** *n* scroscio di pioggia; ~**right** *adj* franco(a); (*refusal*) assoluto(a); ~**stairs** *adv* di sotto; al piano inferiore; ~**stream** *adv* a valle; ~**-to-earth** *adj* pratico(a); ~**town** *adv* in città; ~ **under** *adv* (*Australia etc*) agli antipodi; ~**ward** ['daunwəd] *adj*, *adv* in giù, in discesa; ~**wards** ['daunwədz] *adv* = ~**ward**

dowry ['dauri] *n* dote *f*

doz. *abbr* = **dozen**

doze [dauz] *vi* sonnecchiare; ~ **off** *vi* appisolarsi

dozen ['dʌzn] *n* dozzina; **a** ~ **books** una dozzina di libri; ~**s of** decine *fpl* di

Dr. *abbr* (= *doctor*) dott.; (*in street names*) = **drive** *n*

drab [dræb] *adj* tetro(a), grigio(a)

draft [drɑ:ft] *n* abbozzo; (*POL*) bozza; (*COMM*) tratta; (*US*: *call-up*) leva ♦ *vt* abbozzare; *see also* **draught**

draftsman ['drɑ:ftsmən] (*US*) *n* = **draughtsman**

drag [dræg] *vt* trascinare; (*river*) dragare ♦ *vi* trascinarsi ♦ *n* (*inf*) noioso/a; noia, fatica; (*women's*

---

clothing): **in** ~ travestito (da donna); ~ **on** *vi* tirar avanti lentamente

dragon ['drægən] *n* drago

dragonfly ['drægənflai] *n* libellula

drain [dreɪn] *n* (*for sewage*) fogna; (*on resources*) salasso ♦ *vt* (*land*, *marshes*) prosciugare; (*vegetables*) scolare ♦ *vi* (*water*) defluire (via); ~**age** *n* prosciugamento; fognatura; ~**ing board** (*US* ~**board**) *n* piano del lavello; ~**pipe** *n* tubo di scarico

drama ['drɑ:mə] *n* (*art*) dramma *m*, teatro; (*play*) commedia; (*event*) dramma; ~**tic** [drə'mætɪk] *adj* drammatico(a); ~**tist** ['dræmətɪst] *n* drammaturgo/a; ~**tize** *vt* (*events*) drammatizzare; (*adapt*: *for TV/cinema*) ridurre or adattare per la televisione/lo schermo

drank [dræŋk] *pt of* **drink**

drape [dreɪp] *vt* drappeggiare; ~**r** (*BRIT*) *n* negoziante *m/f* di stoffe; ~**s** (*US*) *npl* (*curtains*) tende *fpl*

drastic ['dræstɪk] *adj* drastico(a)

draught [drɑ:ft] (*US* **draft**) *n* corrente *f* d'aria; (*NAUT*) pescaggio; (*beer*) alla spina; ~**board** (*BRIT*) *n* scacchiera; ~**s** (*BRIT*) *n* (*gioco della*) dama

draughtsman ['drɑ:ftsmən] *n* disegnatore *m*

draw [drɔ:] (*pt* **drew**, *pp* **drawn**) *vt* tirare; (*take out*) estrarre; (*attract*) attirare; (*picture*) disegnare; (*line*, *circle*) tracciare; (*money*) ritirare ♦ *vi* (*SPORT*) pareggiare ♦ *n* pareggio; (*in lottery*) estrazione *f*; **to** ~ **near** avvicinarsi; ~ **out** *vi* (*lengthen*) allungarsi ♦ *vt* (*money*) ritirare; ~ **up** *vi* (*stop*) arrestarsi, fermarsi ♦ *vt* (*chair*) avvicinare; (*document*) compilare; ~**back** *n* svantaggio, inconveniente *m*; ~**bridge** *n* ponte *m* levatoio

drawer [drɔ:*] *n* cassetto

drawing ['drɔ:ɪŋ] *n* disegno; ~ **board** *n* tavola da disegno; ~ **pin** (*BRIT*) *n* puntina da disegno; ~ **room** *n* salotto

drawl [drɔ:l] *n* pronuncia strascicata

drawn [drɔːn] pp of **draw**

dread [drɛd] n terrore m ♦ vt tremare all'idea di; **~ful** adj terribile

dream [driːm] (pt, pp **dreamed** or **dreamt**) n sogno ♦ vt, vi sognare; **dreamt** [drɛmt] pt, pp of **dream**; **~y** adj sognante

dreary ['drɪərɪ] adj tetro(a); monotono(a)

dredge [drɛdʒ] vt dragare

dregs [drɛgz] npl feccia

drench [drɛntʃ] vt inzuppare

dress [drɛs] n vestito; (no pl: clothing) abbigliamento ♦ vt vestire; (wound) fasciare ♦ vi vestirsi; to get **~ed** vestirsi; **~ up** vi vestirsi a festa; (in fancy dress) vestirsi in costume; **~ circle** (BRIT) n prima galleria; **~er** n (BRIT: cupboard) credenza; (US) cassettone m; **~ing** n (MED) benda; (CULIN) condimento; **~ing gown** (BRIT) n vestaglia; **~ing room** n (THEATRE) camerino; (SPORT) spogliatoio; **~ing table** n toilette f inv; **~maker** n sarta; **~ rehearsal** n prova generale; **~y** (inf) adj elegante

drew [druː] pt of **draw**

dribble ['drɪbl] vi (baby) sbavare ♦ vt (ball) dribblare

dried [draɪd] adj (fruit, beans) secco(a); (eggs, milk) in polvere

drier ['draɪə*] n = **dryer**

drift [drɪft] n (of current etc) direzione f; forza; (of snow) cumulo; turbine m; (general meaning) senso ♦ vi (boat) essere trasportato(a) dalla corrente; (sand, snow) ammucchiarsi; **~wood** n resti mpl della mareggiata

drill [drɪl] n trapano; (MIL) esercitazione f ♦ vt trapanare; (troops) addestrare ♦ vi (for oil) fare trivellazioni

drink [drɪŋk] (pt **drank**, pp **drunk**) n bevanda, bibita; (alcoholic **~**) bicchierino; (sip) sorso ♦ vt, vi bere; to have a **~** bere qualcosa; a **~ of** water un po' d'acqua; **~er** n bevitore/trice; **~ing water** n acqua

potabile

drip [drɪp] n goccia; gocciolamento; (MED) fleboclisi f inv ♦ vi gocciolare; (tap) sgocciolare; **~-dry** adj (shirt) che non si stira; **~ping** n grasso d'arrosto

drive [draɪv] (pt **drove**, pp **driven**) n passeggiata or giro m in macchina; (also: **~way**) viale m d'accesso; (energy) energia; (campaign) campagna; (also: disk **~**) lettore m ♦ vt guidare; (nail) piantare; (push) cacciare, spingere; (TECH: motor) azionare; far funzionare ♦ vi (AUT: at controls) guidare; (: travel) andare in macchina; **left-/right-hand ~** guida a sinistra/destra; to **~ sb mad** far impazzire qn

drivel ['drɪvl] (inf) n idiozie fpl

driven ['drɪvn] pp of **drive**

driver ['draɪvə*] n conducente m/f; (of taxi) tassista m; (chauffeur, of bus) autista m/f; **~'s license** (US) n patente f di guida

driveway ['draɪvweɪ] n viale m d'accesso

driving ['draɪvɪŋ] n guida; **~ instructor** n istruttore/trice di scuola guida; **~ lesson** n lezione f di guida; **~ licence** (BRIT) n patente f di guida; **~ mirror** n specchietto retrovisore; **~ school** n scuola f guida inv; **~ test** n esame m di guida

drizzle ['drɪzl] n pioggerella

drone [drəʊn] n ronzio; (male bee) fuco

drool [druːl] vi sbavare

droop [druːp] vi (flower) appassire; (head, shoulders) chinarsi

drop [drɒp] n (of water) goccia; (lessening) diminuzione f; (fall) caduta ♦ vt lasciare cadere; (voice, eyes, price) abbassare; (set down from car) far scendere; (name from list) lasciare fuori ♦ vi cascare; (wind) abbassarsi; **~s** npl (MED) gocce fpl; **~ off** vi (sleep) addormentarsi ♦ vt (passenger) far scendere; **~ out** vi (withdraw) ritirarsi; (student etc) smettere di studiare;

drought   79   dungeon

~-out n (from society/from university) chi ha abbandonato (la società/gli studi); **~per** n contagocce m inv; **~pings** npl sterco

drought [draut] n siccità f inv

drove [drǝuv] pt of **drive**

drown [draun] vt affogare; (fig: noise) soffocare ♦ vi affogare

drowsy ['drauzı] adj sonnolento(a), assonnato(a)

drudgery ['drʌdʒǝrı] n lavoro faticoso

drug [drʌg] n farmaco; (narcotic) droga ♦ vt drogare; **to be on ~s** drogarsi; (MED) prendere medicinali; **hard/soft** ~s droghe pesanti/leggere; ~ **addict** n tossicomane m/f; ~**gist** (US) n persona che gestisce un drugstore; ~**store** (US) n drugstore m inv

drum [drʌm] n tamburo; (for oil, petrol) fusto ♦ vt tamburellare; ~s npl (set of ~s) batteria; ~**mer** n batterista m/f

drunk [drʌŋk] pp of **drink** ♦ adj ubriaco(a); ebbro(a) ♦ n (also: ~ard) ubriacone/a; ~**en** adj ubriaco(a); da ubriaco

dry [draı] adj secco(a); (day, clothes) asciutto(a) ♦ vt seccare; (clothes, hair, hands) asciugare ♦ vi asciugarsi; ~ **up** vi seccarsi; ~-**cleaner's** n lavasecco m inv; ~-**cleaning** n pulitura a secco; ~**er** n (for hair) föhn m inv, asciugacapelli m inv; (for clothes) asciugabiancheria; (US: spin-dryer) centrifuga; ~ **goods store** (US) n negozio di stoffe; ~ **rot** n fungo del legno

DSS n abbr (= Department of Social Security) ministero della Previdenza sociale

dual ['djuǝl] adj doppio(a); ~ **carriageway** (BRIT) n strada a doppia carreggiata; ~-**purpose** adj a doppio uso

dubbed [dʌbd] adj (CINEMA) doppiato(a)

dubious ['dju:bıǝs] adj dubbio(a)

Dublin ['dʌblın] n Dublino f

duchess ['dʌtʃıs] n duchessa

duck [dʌk] n anatra ♦ vi abbassare la testa; ~**ling** n anatroccolo

duct [dʌkt] n condotto; (ANAT) canale m

dud [dʌd] n (object, tool): **it's a ~** è inutile, non funziona ♦ adj: ~ **cheque** (BRIT) assegno a vuoto

due [dju:] adj dovuto(a); (expected) atteso(a); (fitting) giusto(a) ♦ n dovuto ♦ adv: ~ **north** diritto verso nord; ~**s** npl (for club, union) quota; (in harbour) diritti mpl di porto; **in ~ course** a tempo debito; finalmente; ~ **to** dovuto a, a causa di; **to be ~ to do** dover fare

duet [dju:'et] n duetto

duffel bag ['dʌfl-] n sacca da viaggio di tela

duffel coat ['dʌfl-] n montgomery m inv

dug [dʌg] pt, pp of **dig**

duke [dju:k] n duca m

dull [dʌl] adj (light) debole; (boring) noioso(a); (slow-witted) ottuso(a); (sound, pain) sordo(a); (weather, day) fosco(a), scuro(a) ♦ vt (pain, grief) attutire; (mind, senses) intorpidire

duly ['dju:lı] adv (on time) a tempo debito; (as expected) debitamente

dumb [dʌm] adj muto(a); (pej) stupido(a); ~-**founded** [dʌm'faundıd] adj stupito(a), stordito(a)

dummy ['dʌmı] n (tailor's model) manichino; (TECH, COMM) riproduzione f; (BRIT: for baby) tettarella ♦ adj falso(a), finto(a)

dump [dʌmp] n (also: rubbish ~) discarica di rifiuti; (inf: place) buco ♦ vt (put down) scaricare; mettere giù; (get rid of) buttar via

dumpling ['dʌmplıŋ] n specie di gnocco

dumpy ['dʌmpı] adj tracagnotto(a)

dunce [dʌns] n (SCOL) somaro/a

dung [dʌŋ] n concime m

dungarees [dʌŋgǝ'ri:z] npl tuta

dungeon ['dʌndʒǝn] n prigione f sotterranea

dupe [dju:p] n zimbello ♦ vt gabbare, ingannare

duplex ['dju:plɛks] (US) n (house) casa con muro divisorio in comune con un'altra; (apartment) appartamento su due piani

duplicate [n 'dju:plɪkət, vb 'dju:plɪkeɪt] n doppio ♦ vt duplicare; **in ~** in doppia copia

durable ['djuərəbl] adj durevole; (clothes, metal) resistente

duration [djuə'reɪʃən] n durata

duress [djuə'rɛs] n: **under ~** sotto costrizione

during ['djuərɪŋ] prep durante, nel corso di

dusk [dʌsk] n crepuscolo

dust [dʌst] n polvere f ♦ vt (furniture) spolverare; (cake etc) to ~ **with** cospargere con; **~bin** (BRIT) n pattumiera; **~er** n straccio per la polvere; **~man** (BRIT) n netturbino; **~y** adj polveroso(a)

Dutch [dʌtʃ] adj olandese ♦ n (LING) olandese m; **the ~** npl gli Olandesi; **to go ~** (inf) fare alla romana; **~man/woman** n olandese m/f

dutiful ['dju:tɪful] adj (child) rispettoso(a)

duty ['dju:tɪ] n dovere m; (tax) dazio, tassa; **on ~** di servizio; **off ~** libero(a), fuori servizio; **~-free** adj esente da dazio

duvet ['du:veɪ] (BRIT) n piumino, piumone m

dwarf [dwɔ:f] n nano/a ♦ vt far apparire piccolo

dwell [dwɛl] (pt, pp dwelt) vi dimorare; **~ on** vt fus indugiare su; **~ing** n dimora; **dwelt** pt, pp of dwell

dwindle ['dwɪndl] vi diminuire, decrescere

dye [daɪ] n tinta ♦ vt tingere

dying ['daɪɪŋ] adj morente, moribondo(a)

dyke [daɪk] (BRIT) n diga

dynamic [daɪ'næmɪk] adj dinamico(a)

dynamite ['daɪnəmaɪt] n dinamite f

dynamo ['daɪnəməu] n dinamo f inv

dyslexia [dɪs'lɛksɪə] n dislessia

E

E [i:] n (MUS) mi m

each [i:tʃ] adj ogni, ciascuna(a) ♦ pron ciascuno(a), ognuno(a); **~ one** ognuno(a); **~ other** si (or ci etc); **they hate ~ other** si odiano (l'un l'altro); **you are jealous of ~ other** siete gelosi l'uno dell'altro; **they have 2 books ~** hanno 2 libri ciascuno

eager ['i:gə'] adj impaziente; desideroso(a); ardente; **to be ~ for** essere desideroso di, aver gran voglia di

eagle ['i:gl] n aquila

ear [ɪə'] n orecchio; (of corn) pannocchia; **~ache** n mal m d'orecchi; **~drum** n timpano

earl [ə:l] n conte m

earlier ['ə:lɪə'] adj precedente ♦ adv prima

early ['ə:lɪ] adv presto, di buon'ora; (ahead of time) in anticipo ♦ adj (near the beginning) primo(a); (sooner than expected) prematuro(a); (quick: reply) veloce; **at an ~ hour** di buon'ora; **to have an ~ night** andare a letto presto; **in the ~ or ~ in the spring/19th century** all'inizio della primavera/dell'Ottocento; **~ retirement** n ritiro anticipato

earmark ['ɪəmɑ:k] vt: **to ~ sth for** destinare qc a

earn [ə:n] vt guadagnare; (rest, reward) meritare

earnest ['ə:nɪst] adj serio(a); **in ~** sul serio

earnings ['ə:nɪŋz] npl guadagni mpl; (salary) stipendio

earphones ['ɪəfəunz] npl cuffia

earring ['ɪərɪŋ] n orecchino

earshot ['ɪəʃɔt] n: **within ~** a portata d'orecchio

earth [ə:θ] n terra ♦ vt (BRIT: ELEC) mettere a terra; **~enware** n

terracotta; stoviglie *fpl* di terracotta;
~quake *n* terremoto; **~y** *adj* (*fig*)
grossolano(a)

ease [izz] *n* agio, comodo ♦ *vt*
(*soothe*) calmare; (*loosen*) allentare;
to ~ sth out/in tirare fuori/infilare
qc con delicatezza; facilitare l'usci-
ta/l'entrata di qc; **at ~** a proprio a-
gio; (*MIL*) a riposo; **~ off** or **up** *vi*
diminuire; (*slow down*) rallentare

easel ['iizl] *n* cavalletto

easily ['izzili] *adv* facilmente

east [iist] *n* est *m* ♦ *adj* dell'est ♦
adv a oriente; **the E~** l'Oriente *m*;
(*POL*) l'Est

Easter ['iistə*] *n* Pasqua; **~ egg** *n*
uovo di Pasqua

easterly ['iistəli] *adj* dall'est, d'oriente

eastern ['iistən] *adj* orientale,
d'oriente; dell'est

East Germany *n* Germania dell'Est

eastward(s) ['iistwəd(z)] *adv* verso
est, verso levante

easy ['izzi] *adj* facile; (*manner*) disin-
volto(a) ♦ *adv*: **to take it** or **things**
~ prendersela con calma; **~ chair** *n*
poltrona; **~-going** *adj* accomodante

eat [iit] (*pt* ate, *pp* eaten) *vt*, *vi*
mangiare; **~ away at** *vt fus* rodere; **~ into** *vt fus* rodere; **~en** ['iitn]
pp of eat

eaves [iivz] *npl* gronda

eavesdrop ['iivzdrop] *vi*: **to ~** (**on**
a conversation) origliare (una conversazione)

ebb [εb] *n* riflusso ♦ *vi* rifluire; (*fig:
also: ~ away*) declinare

ebony ['εbəni] *n* ebano

EC *n abbr* (= *European Community*)
CEE *f*

eccentric [ik'sεntrik] *adj*, *n* eccentri-
co(a)

echo ['εkəu] (*pl* **~es**) *n* eco *m* or *f* ♦
vt ripetere; fare eco ♦ *vi* echeggia-
re; dare un eco

éclair [ei'klεə*] *n* = bignè *m* inv

eclipse [i'klips] *n* eclissi *f inv*

ecology [i'kɔlədʒi] *n* ecologia

economic [iːkə'nɔmik] *adj* economi-

co(a); **~al** *adj* economico(a); (*person*) economo(a); **~s** *n* economia ♦
npl lato finanziario

economize [i'kɔnəmaiz] *vi* risparmiare, fare economia

economy [i'kɔnəmi] *n* economia; **~**
class *n* (*AVIAT*) classe *f* turistica;
~ size *n* (*COMM*) confezione *f* economica

ecstasy ['εkstəsi] *n* estasi *f inv*

ECU ['eikju:] *n abbr* (= *European
Currency Unit*) ECU *m inv*

eczema ['εksimə] *n* eczema *m*

edge [εdʒ] *n* margine *m*; (*of table,
plate, cup*) orlo; (*of knife etc*) taglio
♦ *vt* bordare; **on ~** (*fig*) = edgy; **to**
~ away from scattaiolare da;
~ways *adv*: **he couldn't get a**
word in ~ways non riuscì a dire
una parola; **edgy** *adj* nervoso(a)

edible ['εdibl] *adj* commestibile;
(*meal*) mangiabile

edict ['iːdikt] *n* editto

Edinburgh ['εdinbərə] *n* Edimburgo
f

edit ['εdit] *vt* curare; **~ion** [i'diʃən]
n edizione *f*; **~or** *n* (*in newspaper*)
redattore/trice; redattore/trice capo;
(*of sb's work*) curatore/trice; **~orial**
[-'tɔːriəl] *adj* redazionale, editoriale ♦
n editoriale *m*

educate ['εdjukeit] *vt* istruire; educa-
re

education [εdju'keiʃən] *n* educazione *f*; (*schooling*) istruzione *f*; **~al**
adj pedagogico(a); scolastico(a);
istruttivo(a)

EEC *n abbr* = EC

eel [iːl] *n* anguilla

eerie ['iəri] *adj* che fa accapponare la
pelle

effect [i'fεkt] *n* effetto ♦ *vt* effettuare; **to take ~** (*law*) entrare in vigore; (*drug*) fare effetto; **in ~** in effettivamente; **~ive** *adj* efficace; (*actual*)
effettivo(a); **~ively** *adv* efficace-
mente; effettivamente; **~iveness** *n*
efficacia

effeminate [i'fεminit] *adj* effemina-
to(a)

efficiency [ɪ'fɪʃənsɪ] n efficienza; rendimento effettivo

efficient [ɪ'fɪʃənt] adj efficiente

effort ['efət] n sforzo

effrontery [ɪ'frʌntərɪ] n sfrontatezza

effusive [ɪ'fjuːsɪv] adj (handshake, welcome) caloroso(a)

e.g. adv abbr (= exempli gratia) per esempio, p.es

egg [eg] n uovo; **hard-boiled/soft-boiled** ~ uovo sodo/alla coque; ~ **on** vt incitare; ~**cup** n portauovo m inv; ~**plant** n (especially US) melanzana; ~**shell** n guscio d'uovo

ego ['iːgəu] n ego m inv

egotism ['egəutɪzəm] n egotismo

Egypt ['iːdʒɪpt] n Egitto; ~**ian** [ɪ'dʒɪpʃən] adj, n egiziano(a)

eiderdown ['aɪdədaun] n piumino

eight [eɪt] num otto; ~**een** num diciotto; **eighth** [eɪtθ] num ottavo(a); ~**y** num ottanta

Eire ['ɛərə] n Repubblica d'Irlanda

either ['aɪðə] adj l'uno o l'altro(a); (both, each) ciascuno(a) ♦ pron: ~ (**of them**) (o) l'uno(a) o l'altro(a) ♦ adv neanche ♦ conj: ~ good or bad o buono o cattivo; on ~ side su ciascun lato; **I don't like** ~ non mi piace né l'uno né l'altro; **no, I don't** ~ no, neanch'io

eject [ɪ'dʒɛkt] vt espellere; lanciare

eke [iːk]: **to** ~ **out** vt far durare; aumentare

elaborate [adj ɪ'læbərɪt, vb ɪ'læbəreɪt] adj elaborato(a), minuzioso(a) ♦ vt elaborare ♦ vi fornire i particolari

elapse [ɪ'læps] vi trascorrere, passare

elastic [ɪ'læstɪk] adj elastico(a) ♦ n elastico; ~ **band** (BRIT) n elastico

elated [ɪ'leɪtɪd] adj pieno(a) di gioia

elbow ['ɛlbəu] n gomito

elder ['ɛldə] adj maggiore, più vecchio(a) ♦ n (tree) sambuco; **one's** ~s i più anziani; ~**ly** adj anziano(a) ♦ npl: **the** ~**ly** gli anziani

eldest ['ɛldɪst] adj, n: **the** ~ (**child**) il(la) maggiore (dei bambini)

elect [ɪ'lɛkt] vt eleggere ♦ adj: **the president** ~ il presidente designato; **to** ~ **to do** decidere di fare; ~**ion** [ɪ'lɛkʃən] n elezione f; ~**ioneering** [ɪlɛkʃə'nɪərɪŋ] n propaganda elettorale; ~**or** n elettore/trice; ~**orate** n elettorato

electric [ɪ'lɛktrɪk] adj elettrico(a); ~**al** adj elettrico(a); ~ **blanket** n coperta elettrica; ~ **fire** n stufa elettrica

electrician [ɪlɛk'trɪʃən] n elettricista m

electricity [ɪlɛk'trɪsɪtɪ] n elettricità

electrify [ɪ'lɛktrɪfaɪ] vt (RAIL) elettrificare; (audience) elettrizzare

electrocute [ɪ'lɛktrəukjuːt] vt fulminare

electronic [ɪlɛk'trɔnɪk] adj elettronico(a); ~ **mail** n posta elettronica; ~**s** n elettronica

elegant ['ɛlɪgənt] adj elegante

element ['ɛlɪmənt] n elemento; (of heater, kettle etc) resistenza; ~**ary** [-'mɛntərɪ] adj elementare

elephant ['ɛlɪfənt] n elefante/essa

elevation [ɛlɪ'veɪʃən] n elevazione f

elevator ['ɛlɪveɪtə] n elevatore m; (US: lift) ascensore m

eleven [ɪ'lɛvn] num undici; ~**ses** (BRIT) n caffè m a metà mattina; ~**th** adj undicesimo(a)

elicit [ɪ'lɪsɪt] vt: **to** ~ (**from**) trarre (da), cavare fuori (da)

eligible ['ɛlɪdʒəbl] adj eleggibile; (for membership) che ha i requisiti

elm [ɛlm] n olmo

elocution [ɛlə'kjuːʃən] n dizione f

elongated ['iːlɔŋgeɪtɪd] adj allungato(a)

elope [ɪ'ləup] vi (lovers) scappare; ~**ment** n fuga

eloquent ['ɛlɔkwənt] adj eloquente

else [ɛls] adv altro; **something** ~ qualcos'altro; **somewhere** ~ altrove; **everywhere** ~ in qualsiasi altro luogo; **nobody** ~ nessun altro; **where** ~ in quale altro luogo?; **little** ~ poco altro; ~**where** adv altrove

elucidate [ɪˈluːsɪdeɪt] *vt* delucidare

elude [ɪˈluːd] *vt* eludere

elusive [ɪˈluːsɪv] *adj* elusivo(a)

emaciated [ɪˈmeɪsɪeɪtɪd] *adj* emaciato(a)

emanate [ˈemǝneɪt] *vi:* to ~ from provenire da

emancipate [ɪˈmænsɪpeɪt] *vt* emancipare

embankment [ɪmˈbæŋkmǝnt] *n (of road, railway)* terrapieno

embark [ɪmˈbɑːk] *vi:* to ~ (on) imbarcarsi (su) ♦ *vt* imbarcare; to ~ on (fig) imbarcarsi in; ~ation [ɛmbɑːˈkeɪʃǝn] *n* imbarco

embarrass [ɪmˈbærǝs] *vt* imbarazzare; ~ed *adj* imbarazzato(a); ~ing *adj* imbarazzante; ~ment *n* imbarazzo

embassy [ˈembǝsɪ] *n* ambasciata

embedded [ɪmˈbedɪd] *adj* incastrato(a)

embellish [ɪmˈbelɪʃ] *vt* abbellire

embers [ˈembǝz] *npl* braci *fpl*

embezzle [ɪmˈbezl] *vt* appropriarsi indebitamente di

embitter [ɪmˈbɪtǝ*] *vt* amareggiare; inasprire

embody [ɪmˈbɔdɪ] *vt (features)* racchiudere, comprendere; *(ideas)* dar forma concreta a, esprimere

embossed [ɪmˈbɔst] *adj* in rilievo; goffrato(a)

embrace [ɪmˈbreɪs] *vt* abbracciare ♦ *vi* abbracciarsi ♦ *n* abbraccio

embroider [ɪmˈbrɔɪdǝ*] *vt* ricamare; ~y *n* ricamo

embryo [ˈembrɪǝu] *n* embrione *m*

emerald [ˈemǝrǝld] *n* smeraldo

emerge [ɪˈmɜːdʒ] *vi* emergere

emergency [ɪˈmɜːdʒǝnsɪ] *n* emergenza; in an ~ in caso di emergenza; ~ cord (US) *n* segnale *m* d'allarme; ~ exit *n* uscita di sicurezza; ~ landing *n* atterraggio forzato; ~ services *npl* (fire, police, ambulance) servizi *mpl* di pronto intervento

emery board [ˈemǝrɪ-] *n* limetta di carta smerigliata

emigrate [ˈemɪgreɪt] *vi* emigrare

eminent [ˈemɪnǝnt] *adj* eminente

emissions [ɪˈmɪʃǝnz] *npl* emissioni *fpl*

emit [ɪˈmɪt] *vt* emettere

emotion [ɪˈmǝuʃǝn] *n* emozione *f;* ~al *adj (person)* emotivo(a); *(scene)* commovente; *(tone, speech)* carico(a) d'emozione

emperor [ˈempǝrǝ*] *n* imperatore *m*

emphases [ˈemfǝsiːz] *npl of* **emphasis**

emphasis [ˈemfǝsɪs] *(pl* **-ases**) *n* enfasi *f inv;* importanza

emphasize [ˈemfǝsaɪz] *vt (word, point)* sottolineare; *(feature)* mettere in evidenza

emphatic [emˈfætɪk] *adj (strong)* vigoroso(a); *(unambiguous, clear)* netto(a); ~ally *adv* vigorosamente; nettamente

empire [ˈempaɪǝ*] *n* impero

employ [ɪmˈplɔɪ] *vt* impiegare; ~ee [-ˈiː] *n* impiegato/a; ~er *n* principale *m/f,* datore *m* di lavoro; ~ment *n* impiego; ~ment agency *n* agenzia di collocamento

empower [ɪmˈpauǝ*] *vt:* to ~ sb to do concedere autorità a qn di fare

empress [ˈemprɪs] *n* imperatrice *f*

emptiness [ˈemptɪnɪs] *n* vuoto

empty [ˈemptɪ] *adj* vuoto(a); *(threat, promise)* vano(a) ♦ *vt* vuotare ♦ *vi* vuotarsi; *(liquid)* scaricarsi; ~handed *adj* a mani vuote

emulate [ˈemjuleɪt] *vt* emulare

emulsion [ɪˈmʌlʃǝn] *n* emulsione *f;* ~ (paint) *n* colore *m* a tempera

enable [ɪˈneɪbl] *vt:* to ~ sb to do permettere a qn di fare

enact [ɪnˈækt] *vt (law)* emanare; *(play, scene)* rappresentare

enamel [ɪˈnæml] *n* smalto; *(also:* ~ paint) vernice *f* a smalto

encased [ɪnˈkeɪst] *adj:* ~ in racchiuso(a) in; rivestito(a) di

enchant [ɪnˈtʃɑːnt] *vt* incantare; *(subj: magic spell)* catturare; ~ing *adj* incantevole, affascinante

encircle [ɪnˈsɜːkl] *vt* accerchiare

encl. *abbr* (= *enclosed*) all

enclave [ˈenkleɪv] *n* enclave *f*

enclose [ɪnˈkləʊz] vt (land) circondare, recingere; (letter etc): to ~ (with) allegare (con); please find ~d trovi qui accluso

enclosure [ɪnˈkləʊʒə*] n recinto

encompass [ɪnˈkʌmpəs] vt comprendere

encore [ɔŋˈkɔ:*] excl bis ♦ n bis m inv

encounter [ɪnˈkaʊntə*] n incontro ♦ vt incontrare

encourage [ɪnˈkʌrɪdʒ] vt incoraggiare; ~ment n incoraggiamento

encroach [ɪnˈkrəʊtʃ] vi: to ~ (up)on (rights) usurpare; (time) abusare di; (land) oltrepassare i limiti di

encumber [ɪnˈkʌmbə*] vt: to be ~ed with essere carico(a) di

encyclop(a)edia [ensaɪkləʊˈpi:dɪə] n enciclopedia

end [end] n fine f; (aim) fine m; (of table) bordo estremo; (of pointed object) punta ♦ vt finire; (also: bring to an ~, put an ~ to) mettere fine a ♦ vi finire; in the ~ alla fine; on ~ (object) ritto(a); to stand on ~ (hair) rizzarsi; for hours on ~ per ore ed ore; ~ up vi: to ~ up in finire in

endanger [ɪnˈdeɪndʒə*] vt mettere in pericolo

endearing [ɪnˈdɪərɪŋ] adj accattivante

endeavour [ɪnˈdevə*] (US **endeavor**) n sforzo, tentativo ♦ vi: to ~ to do cercare or sforzarsi di fare

ending [ˈendɪŋ] n fine f, conclusione f; (LING) desinenza

endive [ˈendaɪv] n (curly) indivia (riccia); (smooth, flat) indivia belga

endless [ˈendlɪs] adj senza fine

endorse [ɪnˈdɔːs] vt (cheque) girare; (approve) approvare, appoggiare; ~ment n approvazione f; (on driving licence) contravvenzione registrata sulla patente

endow [ɪnˈdaʊ] vt (provide with money) devolvere denaro a; (equip): to ~ with fornire di, dotare di

endurance [ɪnˈdjʊərəns] n resistenza; pazienza

endure [ɪnˈdjʊə*] vt sopportare, resistere a ♦ vi durare

enemy [ˈenəmɪ] adj, n nemico(a)

energetic [enəˈdʒetɪk] adj energico(a); attivo(a)

energy [ˈenədʒɪ] n energia

enforce [ɪnˈfɔːs] vt (LAW) applicare, far osservare

engage [ɪnˈgeɪdʒ] vt (hire) assumere; (lawyer) incaricare; (attention, interest) assorbire; (TECH): to ~ gear/the clutch innestare la marcia/la frizione ♦ vi (TECH) ingranare; to ~ in impegnarsi in; ~d adj (BRIT: busy, in use) occupato(a); (betrothed) fidanzato(a); to get ~d fidanzarsi; ~d tone (BRIT) n (TEL) segnale m di occupato; ~ment n impegno, obbligo; appuntamento; (to marry) fidanzamento; ~ment ring n anello di fidanzamento

engaging [ɪnˈgeɪdʒɪŋ] adj attraente

engender [ɪnˈdʒendə*] vt produrre, causare

engine [ˈendʒɪn] n (AUT) motore m; (RAIL) locomotiva; ~ **driver** n (of train) macchinista m

engineer [endʒɪˈnɪə*] n ingegnere m; (BRIT: for repairs) tecnico; (on ship, US: RAIL) macchinista m; ~ing n ingegneria

England [ˈɪŋglənd] n Inghilterra

English [ˈɪŋglɪʃ] adj inglese ♦ n (LING) inglese m; the ~ npl gli inglesi; the ~ Channel n la Manica; ~man/woman n inglese m/f

engraving [ɪnˈgreɪvɪŋ] n incisione f

engrossed [ɪnˈgrəʊst] adj: ~ in assorbito(a) da, preso(a) da

engulf [ɪnˈgʌlf] vt inghiottire

enhance [ɪnˈhɑːns] vt accrescere

enjoy [ɪnˈdʒɔɪ] vt godere; (have: success, fortune) avere; ~ o.s. godersela, divertirsi; ~able adj piacevole; ~ment n piacere m, godimento

enlarge [ɪnˈlɑːdʒ] vt ingrandire ♦ vi:

to ~ on (*subject*) dilungarsi su

enlighten [ɪn'laɪtn] *vt* illuminare; dare schiarimenti a; ~**ed** *adj* illuminato(a); ~**ment** *n*: the E~ment (*HISTORY*) l'Illuminismo

enlist [ɪn'lɪst] *vt* arruolare; (*support*) procurare ♦ *vi* arruolarsi

enmity ['ɛnmɪtɪ] *n* inimicizia

enormous [ɪ'nɔːməs] *adj* enorme

enough [ɪ'nʌf] *adj, n*: ~ **time/books** assai tempo/libri; **have you got** ~? ne ha abbastanza or a sufficienza? ♦ *adv*: **big** ~ abbastanza grande; **he has not worked** ~ non ha lavorato abbastanza; ~! basta!; **that's** ~, **thanks** basta così, grazie; **I've had** ~ **of him** ne ho abbastanza di lui; ... **which, funnily or oddly** ~ ... che, strano a dirsi

enquire [ɪn'kwaɪə*] *vt, vi* = **inquire**

enrage [ɪn'reɪdʒ] *vt* fare arrabbiare

enrich [ɪn'rɪtʃ] *vt* arricchire

enrol [ɪn'rəul] *vt* iscrivere ♦ *vi* iscriversi; ~**ment** *n* iscrizione *f*

ensue [ɪn'sjuː] *vi* seguire, risultare

ensure [ɪn'ʃuə*] *vt* assicurare; garantire

entail [ɪn'teɪl] *vt* comportare

entangled [ɪn'tæŋgld] *adj*: **to become** ~ (**in**) impigliarsi (in)

enter ['ɛntə*] *vt* entrare in; (*army*) arruolarsi in; (*competition*) partecipare a; (*sb for a competition*) iscrivere; (*write down*) registrare; (*COMPUT*) inserire ♦ *vi* entrare; ~ **for** *vt fus* iscriversi a; ~ **into** *vt fus* (*explanation*) cominciare a dare; (*debate*) partecipare a; (*agreement*) concludere

enterprise ['ɛntəpraɪz] *n* (*undertaking, company*) impresa; (*spirit*) iniziativa; **free** ~ liberalismo economico; **private** ~ iniziativa privata

enterprising ['ɛntəpraɪzɪŋ] *adj* intraprendente

entertain [ɛntə'teɪn] *vt* divertire; (*invite*) ricevere; (*idea, plan*) nutrire; ~**er** *n* comico/a; ~**ing** *adj* divertente; ~**ment** *n* (*amusement*) divertimento; (*show*) spettacolo

enthralled [ɪn'θrɔːld] *adj* affascinato(a)

enthusiasm [ɪn'θuːzɪæzəm] *n* entusiasmo

enthusiast [ɪn'θuːzɪæst] *n* entusiasta *m/f*; ~**ic** [-'æstɪk] *adj* entusiasta, entusiastico(a); **to be** ~**ic about sth/ sb** essere appassionato/a di qc/ qn

entice [ɪn'taɪs] *vt* allettare, sedurre

entire [ɪn'taɪə*] *adj* intero(a); ~**ly** *adv* completamente, interamente; ~**ty** [ɪn'taɪərətɪ] *n*: **in its** ~**ty** nel suo complesso

entitle [ɪn'taɪtl] *vt* (*give right*): **to** ~ **sb to sth/to do** dare diritto a qn a qc/a fare; ~**d** *adj* (*book*) che si intitola; **to be** ~**d to do** avere il diritto di fare

entrails ['ɛntreɪlz] *npl* interiora *fpl*

entrance [*n* 'ɛntrns, *vb* ɪn'trɑːns] *n* entrata, ingresso; (*of person*) entrata ♦ *vt* incantare, rapire; **to gain** ~ **to** (*university etc*) essere ammesso a; ~ **examination** *n* esame *m* di ammissione; ~ **fee** *n* tassa d'iscrizione; (*to museum etc*) prezzo d'ingresso; ~ **ramp** (*US*) *n* (*AUT*) rampa di accesso

entrant ['ɛntrnt] *n* partecipante *m/f*; concorrente *m/f*

entreat [ɛn'triːt] *vt* supplicare

entrenched [ɛn'trɛntʃt] *adj* radicato(a)

entrepreneur [ɔntrəprə'nəː*] *n* imprenditore *m*

entrust [ɪn'trʌst] *vt*: **to** ~ **sth to** affidare qc a

entry ['ɛntrɪ] *n* entrata; (*way in*) entrata, ingresso; (*item: on list*) iscrizione *f*; (*in dictionary*) voce *f*; **no** ~ vietato l'ingresso; (*AUT*) divieto di accesso; ~ **form** *n* modulo d'iscrizione; ~ **phone** *n* citofono

envelop [ɪn'vɛləp] *vt* avvolgere, avviluppare

envelope ['ɛnvələup] *n* busta

envious ['ɛnvɪəs] *adj* invidioso(a)

environment [ɪn'vaɪərnmənt] *n* ambiente *m*; ~**al** [-'mɛntl] *adj* ecologi-

co(a); ambientale; ~**-friendly** adj
che rispetta l'ambiente

envisage [ɪn'vɪzɪdʒ] vt immaginare;
prevedere

envoy ['envɔɪ] n inviato/a

envy ['envɪ] n invidia ♦ vt invidiare;
to ~ sb sth invidiare qn per qc

epic ['epɪk] n poema m epico ♦ adj
epico(a)

epidemic [epɪ'demɪk] n epidemia

epilepsy ['epɪlepsɪ] n epilessia

episode ['epɪsəud] n episodio

epistle [ɪ'pɪsl] n epistola

epitome [ɪ'pɪtəmɪ] n epitome f; quin-
tessenza; **epitomize** vt (fig) incar-
nare

equable ['ekwəbl] adj uniforme;
equilibrato(a)

equal ['iːkwl] adj uguale ♦ n pari m/f
inv ♦ vt uguagliare; ~ to (task)
all'altezza di; ~**ity** [iː'kwɔlɪtɪ] n
uguaglianza; ~**ize** vi pareggiare;
~**ly** adv ugualmente

equanimity [ekwə'nɪmɪtɪ] n serenità

equate [ɪ'kweɪt] vt: to ~ sth with
considerare qc uguale a; (compare)
paragonare qc con; **equation**
[ɪ'kweɪʃən] n (MATH) equazione f

equator [ɪ'kweɪtə*] n equatore m

equilibrium [iːkwɪ'lɪbrɪəm] n equilibrio

equip [ɪ'kwɪp] vt equipaggiare, attrezzare; to ~ sb/sth with fornire
qn/qc di; to be well ~**ped** (office
etc) essere ben attrezzato(a); he is
well ~**ped** for the job ha i requisiti
necessari per quel lavoro; ~**ment** n
attrezzatura; (electrical etc) apparecchiatura

equitable ['ekwɪtəbl] adj equo(a),
giusto(a)

equities ['ekwɪtɪz] (BRIT) npl
(COMM) azioni fpl ordinarie

equivalent [ɪ'kwɪvəlnt] adj equivalente ♦ n equivalente m; to be ~ to
equivalere a

equivocal [ɪ'kwɪvəkl] adj equivo-
co(a); (open to suspicion) dubbio(a)

era ['ɪərə] n era, età f inv

eradicate [ɪ'rædɪkeɪt] vt sradicare

erase [ɪ'reɪz] vt cancellare; ~**r** n
gomma

erect [ɪ'rekt] adj eretto(a) ♦ vt costruire; (assemble) montare; ~**ion**
[ɪ'rekʃən] n costruzione f; montaggio;
(PHYSIOL) erezione f

ERM n (= Exchange Rate Mechanism) ERM m

ermine ['əːmɪn] n ermellino

erode [ɪ'rəud] vt erodere; (metal)
corrodere

erotic [ɪ'rɔtɪk] adj erotico(a)

err [əː*] vi errare

errand ['ernd] n commissione f

erratic [ɪ'rætɪk] adj imprevedibile;
(person, mood) incostante

error ['erə*] n errore m

erupt [ɪ'rʌpt] vi (volcano) mettersi
(or essere) in eruzione; (war, crisis)
scoppiare; ~**ion** [ɪ'rʌpʃən] n eruzione f; scoppio

escalate ['eskəleɪt] vi intensificarsi

escalator ['eskəleɪtə*] n scala mobile

escapade [eskə'peɪd] n scappatella;
avventura

escape [ɪ'skeɪp] n evasione f; fuga;
(of gas etc) fuga, fuoriuscita ♦ vi
fuggire; (from jail) evadere, scappare; (leak) uscire ♦ vt sfuggire a; to
~ **from** (place) fuggire da; (person)
sfuggire a; **escapism** n evasione f
(dalla realtà)

escort [n 'eskɔːt, vb ɪ'skɔːt] n scorta;
(male companion) cavaliere m ♦ vt
scortare; accompagnare

Eskimo ['eskɪməu] n eschimese m/f

especially [ɪ'speʃlɪ] adv specialmente; soprattutto; espressamente

espionage ['espɪənɑːʒ] n spionaggio

esplanade [esplə'neɪd] n lungomare
m inv

Esq. abbr = Esquire

Esquire [ɪ'skwaɪə*] n: J. Brown, ~
Signor J. Brown

essay ['eseɪ] n (SCOL) composizione
f; (LITERATURE) saggio

essence ['esns] n essenza

essential [ɪ'senʃl] adj essenziale ♦ n
elemento essenziale; ~**ly** adv essenzialmente

establish [ɪˈstæblɪʃ] vt stabilire; (business) mettere su; (one's power etc) affermare; ~**ed** adj (business etc) affermato; ~**ment** n stabilimento; **the E~ment** la classe dirigente, l'establishment m

estate [ɪˈsteɪt] n proprietà f inv; beni mpl, patrimonio; (BRIT: also: housing ~) complesso edilizio; ~ **agent** (BRIT) n agente m immobiliare; ~ **car** (BRIT) n giardiniera

esteem [ɪˈstiːm] n stima ♦ vt (think highly of) stimare; (consider) considerare

esthetic [ɪsˈθetɪk] (US) adj = **aesthetic**

estimate [n ˈestɪmət, vb ˈestɪmeɪt] n stima; (COMM) preventivo ♦ vt stimare, valutare; **estimation** [-ˈmeɪʃən] n stima; opinione f

estranged [ɪˈstreɪndʒd] adj separato(a)

etc abbr (= et cetera) etc, ecc

etching [ˈetʃɪŋ] n acquaforte f

eternal [ɪˈtɜːnl] adj eterno(a)

eternity [ɪˈtɜːnɪtɪ] n eternità f

ether [ˈiːθə*] n etere m

ethical [ˈeθɪkl] adj etico(a), morale

ethics [ˈeθɪks] n etica ♦ npl morale f

Ethiopia [iːθɪˈəupɪə] n Etiopia f

ethnic [ˈeθnɪk] adj etnico(a)

ethos [ˈiːθɒs] n norma di vita

etiquette [ˈetɪket] n etichetta f

Eurocheque [ˈjuərəutʃek] n eurochèque m inv

Europe [ˈjuərəp] n Europa; ~**an** [-ˈpiːən] adj, n europeo(a)

evacuate [ɪˈvækjueɪt] vt evacuare

evade [ɪˈveɪd] vt (tax) evadere; (duties etc) sottrarsi a; (person) schivare

evaluate [ɪˈvæljueɪt] vt valutare

evaporate [ɪˈvæpəreɪt] vi evaporare; ~**d milk** n latte m concentrato

evasion [ɪˈveɪʒən] n evasione f

evasive [ɪˈveɪsɪv] adj evasivo(a)

eve [iːv] n: **on the ~ of** alla vigilia di

even [ˈiːvn] adj regolare; (number) pari inv ♦ adv anche, perfino; ~ **if**,

~ **though** anche se; ~ **more** ancora di più; ~ **so** ciò nonostante; **not** ~ nemmeno; **to get** ~ **with sb** dare la pari a qn; ~ **out** vi pareggiare

evening [ˈiːvnɪŋ] n sera; (as duration, event) serata; **in the** ~ la sera; ~ **class** n corso serale; ~ **dress** n (woman's) abito da sera; (man) in abito scuro; (woman) in abito lungo

event [ɪˈvent] n avvenimento; (SPORT) gara; **in the** ~ **of** in caso di; ~**ful** adj denso(a) di eventi

eventual [ɪˈventʃuəl] adj finale; ~**ity** [-ˈælɪtɪ] n possibilità f inv, eventualità f inv; ~**ly** adv alla fine

ever [ˈevə*] adv mai; (at all times) sempre; **the best** ~ il migliore che ci sia mai stato; **have you** ~ **seen it?** l'ha mai visto?; ~ **since** adv da allora ♦ conj sin da quando; ~ **so pretty** così bello(a); ~**green** n sempreverde m; ~**lasting** adj eterno(a)

every [ˈevrɪ] adj ogni; ~ **day** tutti i giorni, ogni giorno; ~ **other/third day** ogni due/tre giorni; ~ **other car** una macchina su due; ~ **now and then** ogni tanto, di quando in quando; ~**body** pron ~**one**; ~**day** adj quotidiano(a); di ogni giorno; ~**one** pron ognuno, tutti pl; ~**thing** pron tutto, ogni cosa; ~**where** adv (gen) dappertutto; (wherever) ovunque

evict [ɪˈvɪkt] vt sfrattare

evidence [ˈevɪdns] n (proof) prova; (of witness) testimonianza; (sign) to show ~ of dare segni di; **to give** ~ deporre

evident [ˈevɪdnt] adj evidente; ~**ly** adv evidentemente

evil [ˈiːvl] adj cattivo(a), maligno(a) ♦ n male m

evoke [ɪˈvəuk] vt evocare

evolution [iːvəˈluːʃən] n evoluzione f

evolve [ɪˈvɒlv] vt elaborare ♦ vi svilupparsi, evolversi

ewe [juː] n pecora

ex- [eks] prefix ex

exacerbate [eksˈæsəbeɪt] vt aggravare

exact [ɪgˈzækt] adj esatto(a) ♦ vt: to ~ sth (from) estorcere qc (da); esigere qc (da); ~**ing** adj esigente; (work) faticoso(a); ~**ly** adv esattamente

exaggerate [ɪgˈzædʒəreɪt] vt, vi esagerare; **exaggeration** [-ˈreɪʃən] n esagerazione f

exalted [ɪgˈzɔːltɪd] adj esaltato(a); elevato(a)

exam [ɪgˈzæm] n abbr (SCOL) = examination

examination [ɪgzæmɪˈneɪʃən] n (SCOL) esame m; (MED) controllo

examine [ɪgˈzæmɪn] vt esaminare; ~**r** n esaminatore/trice

example [ɪgˈzɑːmpl] n esempio; for ~ ad or per esempio

exasperate [ɪgˈzɑːspəreɪt] vt esasperare; **exasperating** adj esasperante; **exasperation** [-ˈreɪʃən] n esasperazione f

excavate [ˈekskəveɪt] vt scavare

exceed [ɪkˈsiːd] vt superare; (one's powers, time limit) oltrepassare; ~**ingly** adv eccessivamente

excellent [ˈeksələnt] adj eccellente

except [ɪkˈsept] prep (also: ~ for, ~ing) salvo, all'infuori di, eccetto ♦ vt escludere; ~ **if/when** salvo se/quando; ~ **that** salvo che; ~**ion** [ɪkˈsepʃən] n eccezione f; to **take** ~**ion to** trovare a ridire su; ~**ional** [ɪkˈsepʃənl] adj eccezionale

excerpt [ˈeksɜːpt] n estratto

excess [ɪkˈses] n eccesso; ~ **baggage** n bagaglio in eccedenza; ~ **fare** n supplemento; ~**ive** adj eccessivo(a)

exchange [ɪksˈtʃeɪndʒ] n scambio; (also: **telephone** ~) centralino ♦ vt to ~ (**for**) scambiare (con); ~ **rate** n tasso di cambio

Exchequer [ɪksˈtʃekəˈ] n: the ~ (BRIT) lo Scacchiere, ≈ il ministero delle Finanze

excise [ˈeksaɪz] n imposta, dazio

excite [ɪkˈsaɪt] vt eccitare; to get ~**d** eccitarsi; ~**ment** n eccitazione f; agitazione f; **exciting** adj avven-

turoso(a); (film, book) appassionante

exclaim [ɪkˈskleɪm] vi esclamare; **exclamation** [eksklaˈmeɪʃən] n esclamazione f; **exclamation mark** n punto esclamativo

exclude [ɪkˈskluːd] vt escludere

exclusive [ɪkˈskluːsɪv] adj esclusivo(a); ~ **of VAT** I.V.A. esclusa

excommunicate [ekskəˈmjuːnɪkeɪt] vt scomunicare

excruciating [ɪkˈskruːʃɪeɪtɪŋ] adj straziante, atroce

excursion [ɪkˈskəːʃən] n escursione f, gita

excuse [n ɪkˈskjuːs, vb ɪkˈskjuːz] n scusa ♦ vt scusare; to ~ **sb from** (activity) dispensare qn da; ~ **me!** mi scusi!; **now, if you will** ~ me ... ora, mi scusi ma ....

ex-directory [BRIT] adj (TEL): to **be** ~ non essere sull'elenco

execute [ˈeksɪkjuːt] vt (prisoner) giustiziare; (plan etc) eseguire

execution [eksɪˈkjuːʃən] n esecuzione f; ~**er** n boia m inv

executive [ɪgˈzekjutɪv] n (COMM) dirigente m; (POL) esecutivo ♦ adj esecutivo(a)

exemplify [ɪgˈzemplɪfaɪ] vt esemplificare

exempt [ɪgˈzempt] adj esentato(a) ♦ vt: to ~ **sb from** esentare qn da; ~**ion** [ɪgˈzempʃən] n esenzione f

exercise [ˈeksəsaɪz] n (keep fit) moto; (SCOL, MIL etc) esercizio ♦ vt esercitare; (patience) usare; (dog) portar fuori ♦ vi (also: **take** ~) fare del moto; ~**bike** n cyclette f inv; ~ **book** n quaderno

exert [ɪgˈzəːt] vt esercitare; to ~ **o.s.** sforzarsi; ~**ion** [-ʃən] n sforzo

exhale [eksˈheɪl] vt, vi espirare

exhaust [ɪgˈzɔːst] n (also: ~ **fumes**) scappamento; (also: ~ **pipe**) tubo di scappamento ♦ vt esaurire; ~**ed** adj esaurito(a); ~**ion** [ɪgˈzɔːstʃən] n esaurimento; **nervous** ~**ion** sovraffaticamento mentale; ~**ive** adj esauriente

exhibit [ɪgˈzɪbɪt] n (ART) oggetto

esposto; (LAW) documento or oggetto esibito ♦ vt esporre; (courage, skill) dimostrare; ~ion [ɛksɪˈbɪʃən] n mostra, esposizione f

exhilarating [ɪɡˈzɪləreɪtɪŋ] adj esilarante; stimolante

exhort [ɪɡˈzɔːt] vt esortare

exile [ˈɛksaɪl] n esilio; (person) esiliato/a ♦ vt esiliare

exist [ɪɡˈzɪst] vi esistere; ~ence n esistenza; ~ing adj esistente

exit [ˈɛksɪt] n uscita ♦ vi (THEATRE, COMPUT) uscire; ~ ramp (US) n (AUT) rampa di uscita

exodus [ˈɛksədəs] n esodo

exonerate [ɪɡˈzɒnəreɪt] vt: to ~ from discolparsi da

exotic [ɪɡˈzɒtɪk] adj esotico(a)

expand [ɪkˈspænd] vt espandere; estendere; allargare ♦ vi (business, gas) espandersi; (metal) dilatarsi

expanse [ɪkˈspæns] n distesa, estensione f

expansion [ɪkˈspænʃən] n (gen) espansione f; (of town, economy) sviluppo; (of metal) dilatazione f

expect [ɪkˈspɛkt] vt (anticipate) prevedere, aspettarsi, prevedere or aspettarsi che + sub; (require) richiedere, esigere; (suppose) supporre; (await, also baby) aspettare ♦ vi: to be ~ing essere in stato interessante; to ~ sb to do aspettarsi che qn faccia; (anticipation) attesa; life ~ancy probabilità fpl di vita; ~ant mother n gestante f; ~ancy n (anticipation) attesa; ~ation [ɛkspɛkˈteɪʃən] n aspettativa; speranza

expedience [ɪkˈspiːdɪəns] n convenienza

expediency [ɪkˈspiːdɪənsɪ] n convenienza

expedient [ɪkˈspiːdɪənt] adj conveniente; vantaggioso(a) ♦ n espediente m

expedition [ɛkspəˈdɪʃən] n spedizione f

expel [ɪkˈspɛl] vt espellere

expend [ɪkˈspɛnd] vt spendere; (use up) consumare; ~able adj sacrifica-

bile; ~iture [ɪkˈspɛndɪtʃə*] n spesa

expense [ɪkˈspɛns] n spesa; (high cost) costo; ~s npl (COMM) spese fpl, indennità fpl; at the ~ of a spese di; ~ account n conto m spese inv

expensive [ɪkˈspɛnsɪv] adj caro(a), costoso(a)

experience [ɪkˈspɪərɪəns] n esperienza ♦ vt (pleasure) provare; (hardship) soffrire; ~d adj esperto(a)

experiment [n ɪkˈspɛrɪmənt. vb ɪkˈspɛrɪment] n esperimento, esperienza ♦ vi: to ~ (with/on) fare esperimenti (con/su)

expert [ˈɛkspəːt] adj, n esperto(a); ~ise [-ˈtiːz] n competenza

expire [ɪkˈspaɪə*] vi (period of time, licence) scadere; **expiry** n scadenza

explain [ɪkˈspleɪn] vt spiegare; **explanation** [ɛkspləˈneɪʃən] n spiegazione f; **explanatory** [ɪkˈsplænətrɪ] adj esplicativo(a)

explicit [ɪkˈsplɪsɪt] adj esplicito(a)

explode [ɪkˈspləud] vi esplodere

exploit [n ˈɛksplɔɪt. vb ɪkˈsplɔɪt] n impresa ♦ vt sfruttare; ~ation [-ˈteɪʃən] n sfruttamento

exploratory [ɪkˈsplɔrətrɪ] adj esplorativo(a)

explore [ɪkˈsplɔː*] vt esplorare; (possibilities) esaminare; ~r n esploratore/trice

explosion [ɪkˈspləuʒən] n esplosione f

explosive [ɪkˈspləusɪv] adj esplosivo(a) ♦ n esplosivo

exponent [ɪkˈspəunənt] n esponente m/f

export [vb ɛkˈspɔːt. n ˈɛkspɔːt] vt esportare ♦ n esportazione f; articolo di esportazione ♦ cpd di esportazione; ~er n esportatore m

expose [ɪkˈspəuz] vt esporre; (unmask) smascherare; ~d adj (position) esposto(a)

exposure [ɪkˈspəuʒə*] n esposizione f; (PHOT) posa; (MED) assideramento; ~ meter n esposimetro

expound [ɪkˈspaund] vt esporre

express [ɪk'sprɛs] adj (definite) chiaro(a), espresso(a); (BRIT: letter etc) espresso inv ♦ n (train) espresso ♦ vt esprimere; ~ion [ɪk'sprɛʃən] n espressione f; ~ive adj espressivo(a); ~ly adv espressamente; ~way (US) n (urban motorway) autostrada che attraversa la città

exquisite [ɛk'skwɪzɪt] adj squisito(a)

extend [ɪk'stɛnd] vt (visit) protrarre; (road, deadline) prolungare; (building) ampliare; (offer) offrire, porgere ♦ vi (land, period) estendersi

extension [ɪk'stɛnʃən] n (of road, term) prolungamento; (of contract, deadline) proroga; (building) annesso; (to wire, table) prolunga; (telephone) interno; (: in private house) apparecchio supplementare

extensive [ɪk'stɛnsɪv] adj esteso(a), ampio(a); (damage) su larga scala; (coverage, discussion) esauriente; (use) grande; ~ly adv: he's travelled ~ly ha viaggiato molto

extent [ɪk'stɛnt] n estensione f; to some ~ fino a un certo punto; to such an ~ that ... a un tal punto che ...; to what ~? fino a che punto?; to the ~ of ... fino al punto di ...

extenuating [ɪks'tɛnjueɪtɪŋ] adj: ~ circumstances attenuanti fpl

exterior [ɛk'stɪərɪə*] adj esteriore, esterno(a) ♦ n esteriore m, esterno, aspetto (esteriore)

exterminate [ɪk'stɜːmɪneɪt] vt sterminare

external [ɛk'stɜːnl] adj esterno(a), esteriore

extinct [ɪk'stɪŋkt] adj estinto(a)

extinguish [ɪk'stɪŋgwɪʃ] vt estinguere; ~er n estintore m

extort [ɪk'stɔːt] vt: to ~ sth (from) estorcere qc (da); ~ionate [ɪk'stɔːʃnət] adj esorbitante

extra ['ɛkstrə] adj extra inv, supplementare ♦ adv (in addition) di più ♦ n extra m inv; (surcharge) supplemento; (CINEMA, THEATRE) comparsa

extra... ['ɛkstrə] prefix extra...

extract [vb ɪk'strækt, n 'ɛkstrækt] vt estrarre; (money, promise) strappare ♦ n estratto; (passage) brano

extracurricular ['ɛkstrəkə'rɪkjulə*] adj extrascolastico(a)

extradite ['ɛkstrədaɪt] vt estradare

extramarital [ɛkstrə'mærɪtl] adj extraconiugale

extramural [ɛkstrə'mjuərl] adj fuori dell'università

extraordinary [ɪk'strɔːdnrɪ] adj straordinario(a)

extravagance [ɪk'strævəgəns] n sperpero; stravaganza

extravagant [ɪk'strævəgənt] adj (lavish) prodigo(a); (wasteful) dispendioso(a)

extreme [ɪk'striːm] adj estremo(a) ♦ n estremo; ~ly adv estremamente

extricate ['ɛkstrɪkeɪt] vt: to ~ sth (from) districare qc (da)

extrovert ['ɛkstrəvɜːt] n estroverso/a

exude [ɪg'zjuːd] vt trasudare; (fig) emanare

eye [aɪ] n occhio; (of needle) cruna ♦ vt osservare; to keep an ~ on tenere d'occhio; ~ball n il globo dell'occhio; ~bath n occhio; ~brow n sopracciglio; ~brow pencil n matita per le sopracciglia; ~drops npl gocce fpl oculari, collirio; ~lash n ciglio; ~lid n palpebra; ~liner n eye-liner m inv; ~opener n rivelazione f; ~shadow n ombretto; ~sight n vista; ~sore n pugno nell'occhio; ~ witness n testimone m/f oculare

F

F [ɛf] n (MUS) fa m

fable ['feɪbl] n favola

fabric ['fæbrɪk] n stoffa, tessuto

fabrication [fæbrɪ'keɪʃən] n fabbricazione f; falsificazione f

fabulous ['fæbjuləs] adj favoloso(a); (super) favoloso(a), fantastico(a)

façade [fə'saːd] *n* (*also fig*) facciata

face [feɪs] *n* faccia, viso, volto; (*expression*) faccia; (*of clock*) quadrante *m*; (*of building*) facciata ♦ *vt* essere di fronte a; (*facts, situation*) affrontare; ~ **down** a faccia in giù; **to make** *or* **pull a** ~ fare una smorfia; **in the** ~ **of** (*difficulties etc*) di fronte a; **on the** ~ **of it** a prima vista; ~ **to** ~ faccia a faccia; ~ **up to** *vt fus* affrontare, far fronte a; ~ **cloth** (*BRIT*) *n* guanto di spugna; ~ **cream** *n* crema per il viso; ~ **lift** *n* lifting *m inv*; (*of façade etc*) ripulita; ~ **powder** *n* cipria; ~**saving** *adj* per salvare la faccia

facet ['fæsɪt] *n* sfaccettatura

facetious [fə'siːʃəs] *adj* faceto(a)

face value *n* (*of coin*) valore *m* facciale *or* nominale; **to take sth at** ~ (*fig*) giudicare qc dalle apparenze

facial ['feɪʃəl] *adj* del viso

facile ['fæsaɪl] *adj* superficiale

facilities [fə'sɪlɪtɪz] *npl* attrezzature *fpl*; **credit** ~ facilitazioni *fpl* di credito

facing ['feɪsɪŋ] *prep* di fronte a

facsimile [fæk'sɪmɪlɪ] *n* facsimile *m inv*; ~ **machine** *n* telecopiatrice *f*

fact [fækt] *n* fatto; **in** ~ infatti

factor ['fæktə*] *n* fattore *m*

factory ['fæktərɪ] *n* fabbrica, stabilimento

factual ['fæktjuəl] *adj* che si attiene ai fatti

faculty ['fækəltɪ] *n* facoltà *f inv*; (*US*) corpo insegnante

fad [fæd] *n* mania; capriccio

fade [feɪd] *vi* sbiadire, sbiadirsi; (*light, sound, hope*) attenuarsi, affievolirsi; (*flower*) appassire

fag [fæg] (*BRIT: inf*) *n* (*cigarette*) cicca

fail [feɪl] *vt* (*exam*) non superare; (*candidate*) bocciare; (*subj: courage, memory*) mancare a ♦ *vi* fallire; (*student*) essere respinto(a); (*eyesight, health, light*) venire a mancare; **to** ~ **to do sth** (*neglect*) non riuscire a fare qc; (*be unable to*) non

re a fare qc; **without** ~ senza fallo; certamente; ~**ing** *n* difetto ♦ *prep* in mancanza di; ~**ure** ['feɪljə*] *n* fallimento; (*person*) fallito/a; (*mechanical etc*) guasto

faint [feɪnt] *adj* debole; (*recollection*) vago(a); (*mark*) indistinto(a) ♦ *n* (*MED*) svenimento ♦ *vi* svenire; **to feel** ~ sentirsi svenire

fair [fɛə*] *adj* (*person, decision*) giusto(a), equo(a); (*quite large, quite good*) discreto(a); (*hair etc*) biondo(a); (*skin, complexion*) chiaro(a); (*weather*) bello(a), clemente ♦ *adv* (*play*) lealmente ♦ *n* fiera; (*BRIT: funfair*) luna park *m inv*; ~**ly** *adv* equamente; (*quite*) abbastanza; ~**ness** *n* equità, giustizia; ~ **play** *n* correttezza

fairy ['fɛərɪ] *n* fata; ~ **tale** *n* fiaba

faith [feɪθ] *n* fede *f*; (*trust*) fiducia; (*sect*) religione *f*, fede *f*; ~**ful** *adj* fedele; ~**fully** *adv* fedelmente; **yours** ~**fully** (*BRIT: in letters*) distinti saluti

fake [feɪk] *n* imitazione *f*; (*picture*) falso; (*person*) impostore/a ♦ *adj* falso(a) ♦ *vt* (*accounts*) falsificare; (*illness*) fingere; (*painting*) contraffare

falcon ['fɔːlkən] *n* falco, falcone *m*

fall [fɔːl] (*pt* **fell**, *pp* **fallen**) *n* caduta; (*in temperature*) abbassamento; (*in price*) ribasso; (*US: autumn*) autunno ♦ *vi* cadere; (*temperature, price, night*) scendere; ~**s** *npl* (*waterfall*) cascate *fpl*; **to** ~ **flat** (*on one's face*) cadere bocconi; (*joke*) fare cilecca; (*plan*) fallire; ~ **back** *vi* (*retreat*) indietreggiare; (*MIL*) ritirarsi; ~ **back on** *vt fus* (*remedy etc*) ripiegare su; ~ **behind** *vi* rimanere indietro; ~ **down** *vi* (*person*) cadere; (*building*) crollare; ~ **for** *vt fus* (*person*) prendere una cotta per; **to** ~ **for a trick** (*or a story etc*) cascarci; ~ **in** *vi* crollare; (*MIL*) mettersi in riga; ~ **off** *vi* cadere; (*diminish*) diminuire, abbassarsi; ~ **out** *vi* (*hair, teeth*) cadere; (*friends etc*) litigare; ~ **through** *vi* (*plan, pro-

ject) fallire

fallacy ['fæləsı] *n* errore *m*

fallen ['fɔːlən] *pp of* **fall**

fallout ['fɔːlaut] *n* fall-out *m*; ~ **shelter** *n* rifugio antiatomico

fallow ['fæləu] *adj* incolto(a), a maggese

false [fɔːls] *adj* falso(a); **under** ~ **pretences** con l'inganno; ~ **teeth** *(BRIT) npl* denti *mpl* finti

falter ['fɔːltə*] *vi* esitare, vacillare

fame [feɪm] *n* fama, celebrità

familiar [fə'mılıə*] *adj* familiare; *(close)* intimo(a); **to be** ~ **with** *(subject)* conoscere; ~**ize** [fə'mılıəraız] *vt*: **to** ~**ize o.s. with** familiarizzare con

family ['fæmılı] *n* famiglia; ~ **business** *n* ditta a conduzione familiare

famine ['fæmın] *n* carestia

famished ['fæmıʃt] *adj* affamato(a)

famous ['feıməs] *adj* famoso(a); ~**ly** *adv (get on)* a meraviglia

fan [fæn] *n (folding)* ventaglio; *(ELEC)* ventilatore *m*; *(person)* ammiratore/trice; tifoso/a ♦ *vt* far vento a; *(fire, quarrel)* alimentare; ~ **out** *vi* spargersi a ventaglio

fanatic [fə'nætık] *n* fanatico/a

fan belt *n* cinghia del ventilatore

fanciful ['fænsıful] *adj* fantasioso(a)

fancy ['fænsı] *n* immaginazione *f*, fantasia; *(whim)* capriccio ♦ *adj (hat)* stravagante; *(hotel, food)* speciale ♦ *vt (feel like, want)* aver voglia di; *(imagine, think)* immaginare; **to take a** ~ **to** incapricciarsi di; **he fancies her** *(inf)* gli piace; ~ **dress** *n* costume *m* (per maschera); ~ **dress ball** *n* ballo in maschera

fang [fæŋ] *n* zanna; *(of snake)* dente *m*

fantastic [fæn'tæstık] *adj* fantastico(a)

fantasy ['fæntəsı] *n* fantasia, immaginazione *f*; fantasticheria; chimera

far [fɑː*] *adj* lontano(a) ♦ *adv* lontano; *(much, greatly)* molto; ~ **away**, ~ **off** lontano, distante; ~ **better** assai migliore; ~ **from** lontano da; **by**

~ **di gran lunga**; **go as** ~ **as the farm** vada fino alla fattoria; **as** ~ **as I know** per quel che so; **how** ~? quanto lontano?; *(referring to activity etc)* fino a dove?; ~**away** *adj* lontano(a)

farce [fɑːs] *n* farsa

farcical ['fɑːsıkəl] *adj* farsesco(a)

fare [fɛə*] *n (on trains, buses)* tariffa; *(in taxi)* prezzo della corsa; *(food)* vitto, cibo; **half** ~ metà tariffa; **full** ~ tariffa intera

Far East *n*: **the** ~ l'Estremo Oriente

farewell [fɛə'wɛl] *excl, n* addio

farm [fɑːm] *n* fattoria, podere *m* ♦ *vt* coltivare; ~**er** *n* coltivatore/trice; agricoltore/trice; ~**hand** *n* bracciante *m* agricolo; ~**house** *n* fattoria; ~**ing** *n (gen)* agricoltura; *(of crops)* coltivazione *f*; *(of animals)* allevamento; ~**land** *n* terreno coltivabile; ~ **worker** *n* =**hand**; ~**yard** *n* aia

far-reaching [-'riːtʃıŋ] *adj* di vasta portata

fart [fɑːt] *(inf!) vi* scoreggiare *(!)*

farther ['fɑːðə*] *adv* più lontano ♦ *adj* più lontano(a)

farthest ['fɑːðıst] *superl of* **far**

fascinate ['fæsıneıt] *vt* affascinare

fascinating *adj* affascinante; **fascination** [-'neıʃən] *n* fascino

fascism ['fæʃızəm] *n* fascismo

fashion ['fæʃən] *n* moda; *(manner)* maniera, modo ♦ *vt* foggiare, formare; **in** ~ alla moda; **out of** ~ passato(a) di moda; ~**able** *adj* alla moda, di moda; ~ **show** *n* sfilata di moda

fast [fɑːst] *adj* rapido(a), svelto(a), veloce; *(clock)*: **to be** ~ andare avanti; *(dye, colour)* solido(a) ♦ *adv* rapidamente; *(stuck, held)* saldamente ♦ *n* digiuno ♦ *vi* digiunare; ~ **asleep** profondamente addormentato

fasten ['fɑːsn] *vt* chiudere, fissare; *(coat)* abbottonare, allacciare ♦ *vi* chiudersi, fissarsi; abbottonarsi, allacciarsi; ~**er** *n* fermaglio, chiusura; ~**ing** *n* = ~**er**

fast food n fast food m

fastidious [fæs'tɪdɪəs] adj esigente, difficile

fat [fæt] adj grasso(a); (book, profit etc) grosso(a) ♦ n grasso m

fatal ['feɪtl] adj fatale; mortale; disastroso(a); **~ity** [fə'tælɪtɪ] n (road death etc) morto/a, vittima; **~ly** adv a morte

fate [feɪt] n destino; (of person) sorte f; **~ful** adj fatidico(a)

father ['fɑːðə*] n padre m; **~-in-law** n suocero; **~ly** adj paterno(a)

fathom ['fæðəm] n braccio (= 1828 mm) ♦ vt (mystery) penetrare, sondare

fatigue [fə'tiːg] n stanchezza

fatten ['fætn] vt, vi ingrassare

fatty ['fætɪ] adj (food) grasso(a) ♦ n (inf) ciccione/a

fatuous ['fætjʊəs] adj fatuo(a)

faucet ['fɔːsɪt] (US) n rubinetto

fault [fɔːlt] n colpa; (TENNIS) n (defect) difetto; (GEO) faglia ♦ vt criticare; **it's my ~** è colpa mia; **to find ~ with** trovare da ridire su; **at ~** in fallo; **~y** adj difettoso(a)

fauna ['fɔːnə] n fauna

faux pas ['fəʊ'pɑː] n gaffe f inv

favour ['feɪvə*] (US **favor**) n favore m ♦ vt (proposition) favorire, essere favorevole a; (pupil etc) favorire; (team, horse) dare per vincente; **to do sb a ~** fare un favore or una cortesia a qn; **to find ~ with** (subj: person) entrare nelle buone grazie di; (: suggestion) avere l'approvazione di; **in ~ of** in favore di; **~able** adj favorevole; **~ite** [-rɪt] adj, n favorito/a

fawn [fɔːn] n daino ♦ adj (also: **~-coloured**) marrone chiaro inv ♦ vi: **to ~ (up)on** adulare servilmente

fax [fæks] n (document) facsimile m inv, telecopia; (machine) telecopiatrice f ♦ vt telecopiare, trasmettere in facsimile

FBI (US) n abbr (= Federal Bureau of Investigation) F.B.I. f

fear [fɪə*] n paura, timore m ♦ vt

aver paura di, temere; **for ~ of** per paura di; **~ful** adj pauroso(a); (sight, noise) terribile, spaventoso(a)

feasible ['fiːzəbl] adj possibile, realizzabile

feast [fiːst] n festa, banchetto; (REL: also: **~ day**) festa ♦ vi banchettare

feat [fiːt] n impresa, fatto insigne

feather ['feðə*] n penna

feature ['fiːtʃə*] n caratteristica; (PRESS, TV) articolo ♦ vt (subj: film) avere come protagonista ♦ vi figurare; **~s** npl (of face) fisionomia; **~ film** n film m inv principale

February ['februərɪ] n febbraio

fed [fed] pt, pp of **feed**

federal ['fedərəl] adj federale

fed-up adj: **to be ~** essere stufo(a)

fee [fiː] n pagamento; (of doctor, lawyer) onorario; (for examination) tassa d'esame; **school ~s** tasse fpl scolastiche

feeble ['fiːbl] adj debole

feed [fiːd] (pt, pp **fed**) n (of baby) pappa; (of animal) mangime m; (on printer) meccanismo di alimentazione ♦ vt nutrire; (baby) allattare; (horse etc) dare da mangiare a; (fire, machine) alimentare; (data, information): **to ~ into** inserire in; **~ on** vt fus nutrirsi di; **~back** n feedback m; **~ing bottle** (BRIT) n biberon m inv

feel [fiːl] (pt, pp **felt**) n consistenza; (sense of touch) tatto ♦ vt toccare; palpare; tastare; (cold, pain, anger) sentire; (think, believe): **to ~ (that)** pensare che; **to ~ hungry/cold** aver fame/freddo; **to ~ lonely/better** sentirsi solo/meglio; **I don't ~ well** non mi sento bene; **it ~s soft** è morbido al tatto; **to ~ like** (want) aver voglia di; **to ~ about** or **around for** cercare a tastoni; **~er** n (of insect) antenna; **to put out a ~er** or **~ers** (fig) fare un sondaggio; **~ing** n sensazione f; (emotion) sentimento

feet [fiːt] npl of **foot**

feign [feɪn] vt fingere, simulare

fell [fel] pt of **fall** ♦ vt (tree) abbattere

re

fellow ['fɛləu] n individuo, tipo; compagno; (of learned society) membro
♦ cpd: ~ **citizen** n concittadino/a; ~ **countryman** n compatriota m; ~ **men** npl simili mpl; ~**ship** n associazione f; compagnia; specie di borsa di studio universitaria

felony ['fɛlənɪ] n reato, crimine m

felt [fɛlt] pt, pp of **feel** ♦ n feltro; ~**-tip pen** n pennarello

female ['fiːmeɪl] n (ZOOL) femmina; (pej: woman) donna, femmina ♦ adj (BIOL, ELEC) femmina inv; (sex, character) femminile; (vote etc) di donne

feminine ['fɛmɪnɪn] adj femminile

feminist ['fɛmɪnɪst] n femminista m/f

fence [fɛns] n recinto ♦ vt (also: ~ in) recingere ♦ vi (SPORT) tirare di scherma; **fencing** n (SPORT) scherma

fend [fɛnd] vi: **to ~ for o.s.** arrangiarsi; **~ off** (attack, questions) respingere, difendersi da

fender ['fɛndə*] n parafuoco; (on boat) parabordo; (US) parafango; paraurti m inv

ferment [vb fə'mɛnt, n 'fɜːmɛnt] vi fermentare ♦ n (fig) agitazione f, eccitazione f

fern [fɜːn] n felce f

ferocious [fə'rəuʃəs] adj feroce

ferret ['fɛrɪt] n furetto; **~ out** vt (information) scovare

ferry ['fɛrɪ] n (small) traghetto; (large: also: ~**boat**) nave f traghetto inv ♦ vt traghettare

fertile ['fɜːtaɪl] adj fertile; (BIOL) fecondo(a); **fertilizer** ['fɜːtɪlaɪzə*] n fertilizzante m

fester ['fɛstə*] vi suppurare

festival ['fɛstɪvəl] n (REL) festa; (ART, MUS) festival m inv

festive ['fɛstɪv] adj di festa; **the ~ season** (BRIT: Christmas) il periodo delle feste

festivities [fɛs'tɪvɪtɪz] npl festeggiamenti mpl

festoon [fɛs'tuːn] vt: **to ~ with** or-

nare di

fetch [fɛtʃ] vt andare a prendere; (sell for) essere venduto(a) per

fetching ['fɛtʃɪŋ] adj attraente

fête [feɪt] n festa

fetish ['fɛtɪʃ] n feticcio

fetus ['fiːtəs] (US) n = **foetus**

feud [fjuːd] n contesa, lotta

feudal ['fjuːdl] adj feudale

fever ['fiːvə*] n febbre f; **~ish** adj febbrile

few [fjuː] adj pochi(e); **a ~** adj qualche inv ♦ pron alcuni(e); **~er** adj meno inv; meno numerosi(e); **~est** adj il minor numero di

fiancé [fɪ'ɑ̃ːŋseɪ] n fidanzato; **~e** n fidanzata

fib [fɪb] n piccola bugia

fibre ['faɪbə*] (US **fiber**) n fibra; **F~glass** ® n fibra di vetro

fickle ['fɪkl] adj incostante, capriccioso(a)

fiction ['fɪkʃən] n narrativa, romanzi mpl; (sth made up) finzione f; **~al** adj immaginario(a)

fictitious [fɪk'tɪʃəs] adj fittizio(a)

fiddle ['fɪdl] n (MUS) violino; (cheating) imbroglio; truffa ♦ vt (BRIT: accounts) falsificare, falsare; **~ with** vt fus gingillarsi con

fidelity [fɪ'dɛlɪtɪ] n fedeltà; (accuracy) esattezza

fidget ['fɪdʒɪt] vi agitarsi

field [fiːld] n campo; **~ marshal** n feldmaresciallo; **~work** n ricerche fpl esterne

fiend [fiːnd] n demonio; **~ish** ['fiːndɪʃ] adj (person, problem) diabolico(a)

fierce [fɪəs] adj (animal, person, fighting) feroce; (loyalty) assoluto(a); (wind) furioso(a); (heat) intenso(a)

fiery ['faɪərɪ] adj ardente; infocato(a)

fifteen [fɪf'tiːn] num quindici

fifth [fɪfθ] num quinto(a)

fifty ['fɪftɪ] num cinquanta; **~-~** adj: **a ~-~ chance** una possibilità su due ♦ adv fifty-fifty, metà per ciascuno

fig [fɪg] n fico

fight [faɪt] (*pt, pp* **fought**) *n* zuffa,
rissa; (*MIL*) battaglia, combattimen-
to; (*against cancer etc*) lotta ♦ *vt*
(*person*) azzuffarsi con; (*enemy:
also: MIL*) combattere; (*cancer, alcoholism, emotion*) lottare contro;
(*election*) partecipare a ♦ *vi* combattere; **~er** *n* combattente
m; (*plane*) aeroplano da caccia; **~ing** *n* combattimento

figment ['fɪɡmənt] *n*: **a ~ of the
imagination** un parto della fantasia

figurative ['fɪɡjʊrətɪv] *adj* figura-
to(a)

figure ['fɪɡə*] *n* figura; (*number, cipher*) cifra ♦ *vt* (*think: esp US*) pensare ♦ *vi* (*appear*) figurare; **~ out**
vt riuscire a capire; calcolare;
~head *n* (*NAUT*) polena; (*pej*) pre-
stanome *m/f inv*; **~ of speech** *n*
figura retorica

filch [fɪltʃ] (*inf*) *vt* sgraffignare

file [faɪl] *n* (*tool*) lima; (*dossier*) incartamento; (*folder*) cartellina,
(*COMPUT*) archivio; (*row*) fila ♦ *vt*
(*nails, wood*) limare; (*papers*) archi-
viare; (*LAW: claim*) presentare;
passare agli atti; **~ in/out** *vi*
entrare/uscire in fila

filing cabinet ['faɪlɪŋ-] *n* casellario

fill [fɪl] *vt* riempire; (*job*) coprire ♦
n: **to eat one's ~** mangiare a sazie-
tà; **~ in** *vt* (*hole*) riempire; (*form*)
compilare; **~ up** *vt* riempire ♦ *vi*
(*AUT*) fare il pieno

fillet ['fɪlɪt] *n* filetto; **~ steak** *n* bistecca di filetto

filling ['fɪlɪŋ] *n* (*CULIN*) impasto, ripieno; (*for tooth*) otturazione *f*; **~
station** *n* stazione *f* di rifornimento

film [fɪlm] *n* (*CINEMA*) film *m inv*;
(*PHOT*) pellicola; (*of powder, liquid*)
sottile strato ♦ *vt, vi* girare; **~ star**
n diva/o dello schermo; **~ strip** *n*
filmina

filter ['fɪltə*] *n* filtro ♦ *vt* filtrare; **~
lane** (*BRIT*) *n* (*AUT*) corsia di svincolo; **~-tipped** *adj* con filtro

filth [fɪlθ] *n* sporcizia; **~y** *adj* lor-
do(a), sozzo(a); (*language*) osce-

no(a)

fin [fɪn] *n* (*of fish*) pinna

final ['faɪnl] *adj* finale, ultimo(a);
definitivo(a) ♦ *n* (*SPORT*) finale *f*;
~s *npl* (*SCOL*) esami *mpl* finali

finale [fɪ'nɑːlɪ] *n* finale *m*

finalize ['faɪnəlaɪz] *vt* mettere a punto

finally ['faɪnəlɪ] *adv* (*lastly*) alla fine;
(*eventually*) finalmente

finance [faɪ'næns] *n* finanza; (*capital*) capitale *m* ♦ *vt* finanziare; **~s**
npl (*funds*) finanze *fpl*

financial [faɪ'nænʃəl] *adj* finan-
ziario(a)

financier [faɪ'nænsɪə*] *n* finanziatore
m

find [faɪnd] (*pt, pp* **found**) *vt* trovare; (*lost object*) ritrovare ♦ *n* trovata, scoperta; **to ~ sb guilty** (*LAW*)
giudicare qn colpevole; **~ out** *vt*
(*truth, secret*) scoprire; (*person*)
cogliere in fallo; **to ~ out about** informarsi su; (*by chance*) scoprire;
~ings *npl* (*LAW*) sentenza, conclusioni *fpl*; (*of report*) conclusioni

fine [faɪn] *adj* bello(a); ottimo(a);
(*thin, subtle*) fine ♦ *adv* (*well*) molto
bene ♦ *n* (*LAW*) multa ♦ *vt* (*LAW*)
multare; **to be ~** (*person*) stare
bene; (*weather*) far bello; **~ arts**
npl belle arti *fpl*

finery ['faɪnərɪ] *n* abiti *mpl* eleganti

finger ['fɪŋɡə*] *n* dito ♦ *vt* toccare,
tastare; **little/index ~** mignolo/(dito)
indice *m*; **~nail** *n* unghia; **~print** *n*
impronta digitale; **~tip** *n* punta del
dito

finicky ['fɪnɪkɪ] *adj* esigente, pigno-
lo(a); minuzioso(a)

finish ['fɪnɪʃ] *n* fine *f*; (*polish etc*)
finitura ♦ *vt, vi* finire; **to ~ doing
sth** finire di fare qc; **to ~ third** arrivare terzo(a); **~ off** *vt* compiere;
(*kill*) uccidere; **~ up** *vi, vt* finire;
~ing line *n* linea d'arrivo; **~ing
school** *n* scuola privata di perfezio-
namento (*per signorine*)

finite ['faɪnaɪt] *adj* limitato(a);
(*verb*) finito(a)

Finland ['fɪnlənd] n Finlandia
Finn [fɪn] n finlandese m/f; **~ish** adj
finlandese ♦ n (LING) finlandese m
fir [fəː*] n abete m
fire [faɪə*] n fuoco; (destructive)
incendio; (gas ~, electric ~) stufa ♦ vt
(gun) far fuoco con; (arrow) sparare; (fig) infiammare; (inf: dismiss)
licenziare ♦ vi sparare, far fuoco; on
~ in fiamme; **~ alarm** n allarme m
d'incendio; **~arm** n arma da fuoco;
~ brigade (US ~ **department**) n
(corpo dei) pompieri mpl; **~ engine**
n autopompa; **~ escape** n scala di
sicurezza; **~ extinguisher** n estintore m; **~guard** n parafuoco;
~man n pompiere m; **~place** n focolare m; **~side** n angolo del focolare; **~ station** n caserma dei pompieri; **~wood** n legna; **~works** npl
fuochi mpl d'artificio
firing squad ['faɪərɪŋ-] n plotone m
d'esecuzione
firm [fəːm] adj fermo(a) ♦ n ditta,
azienda; **~ly** adv fermamente
first [fəːst] adj primo(a) ♦ adv (before others) il primo, la prima; (before other things) per primo; (when
listing reasons etc) per prima cosa ♦
n (person: in race) primo/a; (AUT)
SCOL) laurea con lode; (AUT) prima; at ~ dapprima, all'inizio; ~ of
all prima di tutto; **~ aid** n pronto
soccorso; **~-aid kit** n cassetta pronto soccorso; **~-class** adj di prima
classe; **~hand** adj di prima mano;
~ **lady** (US) n moglie f del presidente; **~ly** adv in primo luogo; **~-
name** n prenome m; **~-rate** adj di
prima qualità, ottimo(a)
fish [fɪʃ] n inv pesce m ♦ vt (river,
area) pescare in ♦ vi pescare; to go
~ing andare a pesca; **~erman** n
pescatore m; **~ farm** n vivaio; **~
fingers** (BRIT) npl bastoncini mpl
di pesce (surgelati); **~ing boat** n
barca da pesca; **~ing line** n lenza;
~ing rod n canna da pesca;
~monger n pescivendolo; **~mon-
ger's (shop)** n pescheria; **~ sticks**

(US) npl = ~ **fingers**; **~y** (inf) adj
(tale, story) sospetto(a)
fist [fɪst] n pugno
fit [fɪt] adj (MED, SPORT) in forma;
(proper) adatto(a), appropriato(a);
conveniente ♦ vt (subj: clothes) stare bene a; (put in, attach) mettere;
installare; (equip) fornire, equipaggiare ♦ vi (clothes) stare bene;
(parts) andare bene, adattarsi; (in
space, gap) entrare ♦ n (MED) accesso, attacco; ~ to in grado di; ~
for adatto(a) a; degno(a) di; a ~ of
anger un accesso d'ira; this dress
is a good ~ questo vestito sta bene;
by ~s and starts a sbalzi; ~ in vi
accordarsi; adattarsi; ~ful adj (sleep
etc) agitato(a); **~ment** n mobile m
componibile; **~ness** n (MED) forma fisica; **~ted
carpet** n moquette f; **~ted kitchen**
n cucina componibile; **~ter** n aggiu-
statore m or montatore m meccanico; **~ting** adj appropriato(a) ♦ n
(of dress) prova; (of piece of equipment) montaggio, aggiustaggio;
~tings npl (in building) impianti
mpl; **~ting room** n camerino
five [faɪv] num cinque; **~r** (inf) n
(BRIT) biglietto da cinque sterline;
(US) biglietto da cinque dollari
fix [fɪks] vt fissare; (mend) riparare;
(meal, drink) preparare ♦ n: to be
in a ~ essere nei guai; **~ up** vt
(meeting) fissare; to ~ sb up with
sth procurare qc a qn; **~ation** n
fissazione f; **~ed** [fɪkst] adj (prices
etc) fisso(a); **~ture** ['fɪkstʃə*] n impianto (fisso); (SPORT) incontro (del
calendario sportivo)
fizzle out ['fɪzl-] vi finire in nulla
fizzy ['fɪzɪ] adj frizzante; gassato(a)
flabbergasted ['flæbəgɑːstɪd] adj
sbalordito(a)
flabby ['flæbɪ] adj flaccido(a)
flag [flæg] n bandiera; (also: ~stone)
pietra da lastricare ♦ vi stancarsi;
affievolirsi; **~ down** vt fare segno
(di fermarsi) a
flagpole ['flægpəul] n albero
flagship ['flægʃɪp] n nave f ammira-

glia

flair [flɛə*] n (for business etc) fiuto; (for languages etc) facilità; (style) stile m

flak [flæk] n (MIL) fuoco d'artiglieria; (inf: criticism) critiche fpl

flake [fleɪk] n (of rust, paint) scaglia; (of snow, soap powder) fiocco ♦ vi (also: ~ off) sfaldarsi

flamboyant [flæm'bɔɪənt] adj sgargiante

flame [fleɪm] n fiamma

flamingo [flə'mɪŋɡəu] n fenicottero, fiammingo

flammable ['flæməbl] adj infiammabile

flan [flæn] (BRIT) n flan m inv

flank [flæŋk] n fianco ♦ vt fiancheggiare

flannel ['flænl] n (BRIT: also: face ~) guanto di spugna; (fabric) flanella; ~s npl (trousers) pantaloni mpl di flanella

flap [flæp] n (of pocket) patta; (of envelope) lembo ♦ vt (wings) battere ♦ vi (sail, flag) sbattere; (inf: also: be in a ~) essere in agitazione

flare [flɛə*] n razzo; (in skirt etc) svasatura; ~ **up** vi andare in fiamme; (fig: person) infiammarsi di rabbia; (: revolt) scoppiare

flash [flæʃ] n vampata; (also: news ~) notizia f lampo inv; (PHOT) flash m inv ♦ vt accendere e spegnere; (send: message) trasmettere; (: look, smile) lanciare ♦ vi brillare; (light on ambulance, eyes etc) lampeggiare; in a ~ in un lampo; to ~ one's headlights lampeggiare; he ~ed by or past ci passò davanti come un lampo; ~**bulb** n cubo m flash inv; ~**cube** n flash m inv; ~**light** n lampadina tascabile

flashy ['flæʃɪ] (pej) adj vistoso(a)

flask [flɑ:sk] n fiasco; (also: vacuum ~) thermos m inv ®

flat [flæt] adj piatto(a); (tyre) sgonfio(a), a terra; (battery) scarico(a); (beer) svampito(a); (denial) netto(a); (MUS) bemolle inv; (: voice) stonato(a); (rate, fee) unico(a) ♦ n (BRIT: rooms) appartamento; (AUT) pneumatico sgonfio; (MUS) bemolle m; to **work** ~ **out** lavorare a più non posso; ~**ly** adv categoricamente; ~**ten** vt (also: ~ten out) appiattire; (building, city) spianare

flatter ['flætə*] vt lusingare; ~**ing** adj lusinghiero(a); (dress) che dona; ~**y** n adulazione f

flaunt [flɔ:nt] vt fare mostra di

flavour ['fleɪvə*] (US **flavor**) n gusto ♦ vt insaporire, aggiungere sapore a; **strawberry-~ed** al gusto di fragola; ~**ing** n essenza (artificiale)

flaw [flɔ:] n difetto

flax [flæks] n lino; ~**en** adj biondo(a)

flea [fli:] n pulce f

fleck [flɛk] n (mark) macchiolina; (pattern) screziatura

fled [flɛd] pt, pp of **flee**

flee [fli:] (pt, pp **fled**) vt fuggire da ♦ vi fuggire, scappare

fleece [fli:s] n vello ♦ vt (inf) pelare

fleet [fli:t] n flotta; (of lorries etc) convoglio; parco

fleeting ['fli:tɪŋ] adj fugace, fuggitivo(a); (visit) volante

Flemish ['flɛmɪʃ] adj fiammingo(a)

flesh [flɛʃ] n carne f; (of fruit) polpa; ~ **wound** n ferita superficiale

flew [flu:] pt of **fly**

flex [flɛks] n filo (flessibile) ♦ vt flettere; (muscles) contrarre; ~**ible** adj flessibile

flick [flɪk] n colpetto; scarto ♦ vt dare un colpetto a; ~ **through** vt fus sfogliare

flicker ['flɪkə*] vi tremolare

flier ['flaɪə*] n aviatore m

flight [flaɪt] n volo; (escape) fuga; (also: ~ of steps) scalinata; ~ **attendant** (US) n steward m inv, hostess f inv; ~ **deck** n (AVIAT) cabina di controllo; (NAUT) ponte m di comando

flimsy ['flɪmzɪ] adj (shoes, clothes) leggero(a); (building) poco solido(a); (excuse) che non regge

flinch [flɪntʃ] vi ritirarsi; to ~ **from**

tirarsi indietro di fronte a

fling [flɪŋ] (*pt, pp* **flung**) *vt* lanciare, gettare

flint [flɪnt] *n* selce *f*; (*in lighter*) pietrina

flip [flɪp] *vt* (*switch*) far scattare; (*coin*) lanciare in aria

flippant ['flɪpənt] *adj* senza rispetto, irriverente

flipper ['flɪpə*] *n* pinna

flirt [flɜːt] *vi* flirtare ♦ *n* civetta

flit [flɪt] *vi* svolazzare

float [fləut] *n* galleggiante *m*; (*in procession*) carro; (*money*) somma ♦ *vi* galleggiare

flock [flɔk] *n* (*of sheep, REL*) gregge *m*; (*of birds*) stormo ♦ *vi*: **to ~ to** accorrere in massa a

flog [flɔg] *vt* flagellare

flood [flʌd] *n* alluvione *m*; (*of letters etc*) marea ♦ *vt* allagare; (*subj: people*) invadere ♦ *vi* (*place*) allagarsi; (*people*): **to ~ into** riversarsi in; **~ing** *n* inondazione *f*; **~light** *n* riflettore *m* ♦ *vt* illuminare a giorno

floor [flɔː*] *n* pavimento; (*storey*) piano; (*of sea, valley*) fondo ♦ *vt* (*subj: blow*) atterrare; (: *question*) ridurre al silenzio; **ground ~**, (*US*) **first ~** pianterreno; **first ~**, (*US*) **second ~** primo piano; **~board** *n* tavellone *m* di legno; **~ show** *n* spettacolo di varietà

flop [flɔp] *n* fiasco ♦ *vi* far fiasco; (*fall*) lasciarsi cadere

floppy ['flɔpɪ] *adj* floscio(a), molle; **~ (disk)** *n* (*COMPUT*) floppy disk *m inv*

flora ['flɔːrə] *n* flora

Florence ['flɔrəns] *n* Firenze *f*; **Florentine** ['flɔrəntaɪn] *adj* fiorentino(a)

florid ['flɔrɪd] *adj* (*complexion*) florido(a); (*style*) fiorito(a)

florist ['flɔrɪst] *n* fioraio/a

flounce [flauns] *n* balzo; **~ out** *vi* uscire stizzito(a)

flounder ['flaundə*] *vi* annaspare ♦ *n* (*ZOOL*) passera di mare

flour ['flauə*] *n* farina

flourish ['flʌrɪʃ] *vi* fiorire ♦ *n* (*bold*

gesture): **with a ~** con ostentazione; **~ing** *adj* florido(a)

flout [flaut] *vt* (*order*) contravvenire a

flow [fləu] *n* flusso; circolazione *f* ♦ *vi* fluire; (*traffic, blood in veins*) circolare; (*hair*) scendere; **~ chart** *n* schema *m* di flusso

flower ['flauə*] *n* fiore *m* ♦ *vi* fiorire; **~ bed** *n* aiuola; **~pot** *n* vaso da fiori; **~y** *adj* (*perfume*) di fiori; (*pattern*) a fiori; (*speech*) fiorito(a)

flown [fləun] *pp* of **fly**

flu [fluː] *n* influenza

fluctuate ['flʌktjueɪt] *vi* fluttuare, oscillare

fluent ['fluːənt] *adj* (*speech*) facile, sciolto(a); corrente; **he speaks ~ Italian, he's ~ in Italian** parla l'italiano correntemente

fluff [flʌf] *n* lanugine *f*; **~y** *adj* lanuginoso(a); (*toy*) di peluche

fluid ['fluːɪd] *adj* fluido(a) ♦ *n* fluido

fluke [fluːk] (*inf*) *n* colpo di fortuna

flung [flʌŋ] *pt, pp* of **fling**

fluoride ['fluəraɪd] *n* fluoruro; **~ toothpaste** dentifricio al fluoro

flurry ['flʌrɪ] *n* (*of snow*) tempesta; **a ~ of activity** uno scoppio di attività

flush [flʌʃ] *n* rossore *m*; (*fig: of youth, beauty etc*) rigoglio, pieno vigore ♦ *vt* ripulire con un getto d'acqua ♦ *vi* arrossire ♦ *adj*: **~ with** a livello di, pari a; **to ~ the toilet** tirare l'acqua; **~ out** *vt* (*birds*) far alzare in volo; (*animals, fig*) stanare; **~ed** *adj* tutto(a) rosso(a)

flustered ['flʌstəd] *adj* sconvolto(a)

flute [fluːt] *n* flauto

flutter ['flʌtə*] *n* agitazione *f*; (*of wings*) battito ♦ *vi* (*bird*) battere le ali

flux [flʌks] *n*: **in a state of ~** in continuo mutamento

fly [flaɪ] (*pt* **flew**, *pp* **flown**) *n* (*insect*) mosca; (*on trousers: also*: **flies**) chiusura ♦ *vt* pilotare; (*passengers, cargo*) trasportare (in aereo); (*distances*) percorrere ♦ *vi* volare;

(*passengers*) andare in aereo; (*escape*) fuggire; (*flag*) sventolare; ~ **away** *or* **off** *vi* volare via; ~**ing** *n* (*activity*) aviazione *f*; (*action*) volo ♦ *adj*: ~**ing** visita volante; **with** ~**ing colours** con risultati brillanti; ~**ing saucer** *n* disco volante; ~**ing start** *n*: **to get off to a** ~**ing start** partire come un razzo; ~**over** (*BRIT*) *n* (*bridge*) cavalcavia *m inv*; ~**sheet** *n* (*TYP for tent*) soprattetto

foal [fəul] *n* puledro

foam [fəum] *n* schiuma; (*also*: ~ *rubber*) gommapiuma ® ♦ *vi* schiumare; (*soapy water*) fare la schiuma

fob [fɔb] *vt*: **to** ~ **sb off with** rifilare a qn

focus ['fəukəs] (*pl* ~**es**) *n* fuoco; (*of interest*) centro ♦ *vt* (*field glasses etc*) mettere a fuoco ♦ *vi*: **to** ~ **on** (*with camera*) mettere a fuoco; (*person*) fissare lo sguardo su; **in** ~ a fuoco; **out of** ~ sfocato(a)

fodder ['fɔdə*] *n* foraggio

foe [fəu] *n* nemico

foetus ['fiːtəs] (*US* **fetus**) *n* feto

fog [fɔg] *n* nebbia; ~**gy** *adj*: **it's** ~**gy** c'è nebbia; ~ **lamp** (*US* ~ **light**) *n* (*AUT*) faro *m* antinebbia *inv*

foil [fɔil] *vt* confondere, frustrare ♦ *n* lamina di metallo; (*kitchen* ~) foglio di alluminio; (*FENCING*) fioretto; **to act as a** ~ **to** (*fig*) far risaltare

fold [fəuld] *n* (*bend, crease*) piega; (*AGR*) ovile *m*; (*fig*) gregge *m* ♦ *vt* piegare; (*arms*) incrociare; ~ **up** *vi* (*map, bed, table*) piegarsi; (*business*) crollare ♦ *vt* (*map etc*) piegare, ripiegare; ~**er** *n* (*for papers*) cartella; cartellina; ~**ing** *adj* (*chair, bed*) pieghevole

foliage ['fəuliidʒ] *n* fogliame *m*

folk [fəuk] *npl* gente *f* ♦ *adj* popolare; ~**s** *npl* (*family*) famiglia; ~**lore** ['fəuklɔː*] *n* folclore *m*; ~ **song** *n* canto popolare

follow ['fɔləu] *vt* seguire ♦ *vi* seguire; (*result*) conseguire, risultare; **to** ~ **suit** fare lo stesso; ~ **up** *vt* (*letter, offer*) fare seguito a; (*case*) se-

guire; ~**er** *n* seguace *m/f*, discepolo/a; ~**ing** *adj* seguente ♦ *n* seguito, discepoli *mpl*

folly ['fɔli] *n* pazzia, follia

fond [fɔnd] *adj* (*memory, look*) tenero(a), affettuoso(a); **to be** ~ **of sb** volere bene a qn; **he's** ~ **of walking** gli piace fare camminate

fondle ['fɔndl] *vt* accarezzare

font [fɔnt] *n* (*in church*) fonte *m* battesimale; (*TYP*) caratteri *mpl*

food [fuːd] *n* cibo; ~ **mixer** *n* frullatore *m*; ~ **poisoning** *n* intossicazione *f*; ~ **processor** *n* tritatutto *m inv* elettrico; ~**stuffs** *npl* generi *fpl* alimentari

fool [fuːl] *n* sciocco/a; (*CULIN*) frullato ♦ *vt* ingannare ♦ *vi* (*gen*: ~ *around*) fare lo sciocco; ~**hardy** *adj* avventato(a); ~**ish** *adj* scemo(a), stupido(a); imprudente; ~**proof** *adj* (*plan etc*) sicurissimo(a)

foot [fut] (*pl* **feet**) *n* piede *m*; (*measure*) piede (= 304 *mm*; 12 *inches*); (*of animal*) zampa ♦ *vt* (*bill*) pagare; **on** ~ a piedi; ~**age** *n* (*CINEMA*: *length*) = metraggio; (: *material*) sequenza; ~**ball** *n* pallone *m*; (*sport*: *BRIT*) calcio; (: *US*) football *m* americano; ~**ball player** *n* (*BRIT*: *also*: ~**baller**) calciatore *m*; (*US*) giocatore *m* di football americano; ~**brake** *n* freno a pedale; ~**bridge** *n* passerella; ~**hills** *npl* contrafforti *mpl*; ~**hold** *n* punto d'appoggio; ~**ing** *n* (*fig*) posizione *f*; **to lose one's** ~**ing** mettere un piede in fallo; ~**lights** *npl* luci *fpl* della ribalta; ~**man** *n* lacchè *m inv*; ~**note** *n* nota (a piè di pagina); ~**path** *n* sentiero; (*in street*) marciapiede *m*; ~**print** *n* orma, impronta; ~**step** *n* passo; (~*print*) orma, impronta; ~**wear** *n* calzatura

KEYWORD

for [fɔː*] *prep* **1** (*indicating destination, intention, purpose*) per; **the train** ~ **London** il treno per Londra; **he went** ~ **the paper** è andato a prendere il giornale; **it's time ~ lunch** è ora di pranzo; **what's it ~?** a che serve?; **what ~?** (why) perché?

2 (on behalf of, representing) per; **to work ~ sb/sth** lavorare per qn/qc; **I'll ask him ~ you** glielo chiederò a nome tuo; **G ~ George** G come George

3 (because of) per, a causa di; **~ this reason** per questo motivo

4 (with regard to) per; **it's cold ~ July** è freddo per luglio; **~ everyone who voted yes, 50 voted no** per ogni voto a favore ce n'erano 50 contro

5 (in exchange for) per; **I sold it ~ £5** l'ho venduto per 5 sterline

6 (in favour of) per, a favore di; **are you ~ or against us?** è con noi o contro di noi?; **I'm all ~ it** sono completamente a favore

7 (referring to distance, time) per; **there are roadworks ~ 5 km** ci sono lavori in corso per 5 km; **he was away ~ 2 years** è stato via per 2 anni; **she will be away ~ a month** starà via un mese; **it hasn't rained ~ 3 weeks** non piove da 3 settimane; **can you do it ~ tomorrow?** può farlo per domani?

8 (with infinitive clauses): **it isn't ~ me to decide** non sta a me decidere; **it would be best ~ you to leave** sarebbe meglio che lei se ne andasse; **there is still time ~ you to do it** ha ancora tempo per farlo; **~ this to be possible ...** perché ciò sia possibile ...

9 (in spite of) nonostante; **~ all his complaints, he's very fond of her** nonostante tutte le sue lamentele, le vuole molto bene

♦ conj (since, as: rather formal) dal momento che, poiché

forage ['fɔrɪdʒ] vi: **to ~ (for)** andare in cerca (di)

foray ['fɔreɪ] n incursione f

forbad(e) [fə'bæd] pt of **forbid**

forbid [fə'bɪd] (pt **forbad(e)**, pp **forbidden**) vt vietare, interdire; **to ~ sb to do sth** proibire a qn di fare qc; **~den** pp of forbid; **~ding** adj minaccioso(a)

force [fɔːs] n forza ♦ vt forzare; **the F~s** (BRIT) npl le forze armate; **to ~ o.s. to do** costringersi a fare; **in ~** (in large numbers) in gran numero; (law) in vigore; **~d** adj forzato(a); **~-feed** vt (animal, prisoner) sottoporre ad alimentazione forzata; **~ful** adj forte, vigoroso(a)

forceps ['fɔːseps] npl forcipe m

forcibly ['fɔːsəblɪ] adv con la forza; (vigorously) vigorosamente

ford [fɔːd] n guado

fore [fɔː*] n: **to come to the ~** mettersi in evidenza

forearm ['fɔːrɑːm] n avambraccio

foreboding [fɔː'bəudɪŋ] n cattivo presagio

forecast ['fɔːkɑːst] (irreg: like **cast**) n previsione f ♦ vt prevedere

forecourt ['fɔːkɔːt] n (of garage) corte f esterna

forefathers ['fɔːfɑːðəz] npl antenati mpl, avi mpl

forefinger ['fɔːfɪŋgə*] n (dito) indice m

forefront ['fɔːfrʌnt] n: **in the ~ of** all'avanguardia in

forego [fɔː'gəu] (irreg: like **go**) vt rinunciare a

foregone ['fɔːgɔn] pp of **forego** ♦ adj: **it's a ~ conclusion** è una conclusione scontata

foreground ['fɔːgraund] n primo piano

forehead ['fɔrɪd] n fronte f

foreign ['fɔrɪn] adj straniero(a); (trade) estero(a); (object, matter) estraneo(a); **~er** n straniero/a; **~ exchange** n cambio con l'estero; (currency) valuta estera; **F~ Office** (BRIT) n Ministero degli Esteri; **F~ Secretary** (BRIT) n ministro degli Affari esteri

foreleg ['fɔːleg] n zampa anteriore

foreman ['fɔːmən] n caposquadra m

foremost ['fɔːməust] adj principale; più in vista ♦ adv: **first and ~ in**nanzitutto

forensic [fə'rɛnsɪk] adj: ~ **medicine** medicina legale

forerunner ['fɔːrʌnə*] n precursore m

foresaw [fɔː'sɔː] pt of **foresee**

foresee [fɔː'siː] (irreg: like see) vt prevedere; ~**able** adj prevedibile;

foreseen pp of **foresee**

foreshadow [fɔː'ʃædəu] vt presagire, far prevedere

foresight ['fɔːsaɪt] n previdenza f

forest ['fɔrɪst] n foresta

forestall [fɔː'stɔːl] vt prevenire

forestry ['fɔrɪstrɪ] n silvicoltura

foretaste ['fɔːteɪst] n pregustazione f

foretell [fɔː'tɛl] (irreg: like tell) vt predire; **foretold** [fɔː'təuld] pt, pp of **foretell**

forever [fə'rɛvə*] adv per sempre; (endlessly) sempre, di continuo

forewent [fɔː'wɛnt] pt of **forego**

foreword ['fɔːwəːd] n prefazione f

forfeit ['fɔːfɪt] vt perdere; (one's happiness, health) giocarsi

forgave [fə'geɪv] pt of **forgive**

forge [fɔːdʒ] n fucina ♦ vt (signature, money) contraffare, falsificare; (wrought iron) fucinare, foggiare; ~ **ahead** vi tirare avanti; ~ **r** n contraffattore m; ~**ry** n falso; (activity) contraffazione f

forget [fə'gɛt] (pt **forgot**, pp **forgotten**) vt, vi dimenticare; ~**ful** adj di corta memoria; ~**ful of** dimentico di; ~**-me-not** n nontiscordardimé m inv

forgive [fə'gɪv] (pt **forgave**, pp **forgiven**) vt perdonare; **to** ~ **sb for sth** perdonare qc a qn; **forgiven** pp of **forgive**; ~**ness** n perdono

forgo [fɔː'gəu] = **forego**

forgot [fə'gɔt] pt of **forget**

forgotten [fə'gɔtn] pp of **forget**

fork [fɔːk] n (for eating) forchetta; (for gardening) forca; (of roads, rivers, railways) biforcazione f ♦ vi (road etc) biforcarsi; ~ **out** (inf) vt

(pay) sborsare; ~**-lift truck** n carrello elevatore

forlorn [fə'lɔːn] adj (person) sconsolato(a); (place) abbandonato(a); (attempt) disperato(a); (hope) vano(a)

form [fɔːm] n forma; (SCOL) classe f; (questionnaire) scheda ♦ vt formare; **in top** ~ in gran forma

formal ['fɔːməl] adj formale; (gardens) simmetrico(a), regolare; ~**ly** adv formalmente

format ['fɔːmæt] n formato ♦ vt (COMPUT) formattare

formation [fɔː'meɪʃən] n formazione f

formative ['fɔːmətɪv] adj: ~ **years** anni mpl formativi

former ['fɔːmə*] adj vecchio(a) (before n), ex inv (before n); **the** ~ ... **the latter** quello ... questo; ~**ly** adv in passato

formula ['fɔːmjulə] n formula

forsake [fə'seɪk] (pt **forsook**, pp **forsaken**) vt abbandonare; **forsaken** pp of **forsake**; **forsook** [fə'suk] pt of **forsake**

fort [fɔːt] n forte m

forth [fɔːθ] adv in avanti; **back and** ~ avanti e indietro; **and so** ~ e così via; ~**coming** adj (event) prossimo(a); (help) disponibile; (character) aperto(a), comunicativo(a); ~**right** adj franco(a), schietto(a); ~**with** adv immediatamente, subito

fortify ['fɔːtɪfaɪ] vt (city) fortificare; (person) armare

fortitude ['fɔːtɪtjuːd] n forza d'animo

fortnight ['fɔːtnaɪt] (BRIT) n quindici giorni mpl, due settimane fpl; ~**ly** adj bimensile ♦ adv ogni quindici giorni

fortress ['fɔːtrɪs] n fortezza, rocca

fortunate ['fɔːtʃənɪt] adj fortunato(a); **it is** ~ **that** è una fortuna che; ~**ly** adv fortunatamente

fortune ['fɔːtʃən] n fortuna; ~**teller** n indovino/a

forty ['fɔːtɪ] num quaranta

forum ['fɔːrəm] n foro

forward ['fɔːwəd] adj (ahead of

schedule) in anticipo; (*movement, position*) in avanti; (*not shy*) aperto(a); diretto(a) ♦ *n* (*SPORT*) avanti *m inv* ♦ *vt* (*letter*) inoltrare; (*parcel, goods*) spedire; (*career, plans*) promuovere, appoggiare; **to move ~** avanzare; **~(s)** *adv* avanti

fossil ['fɔsl] *adj* fossile ♦ *n* fossile *m*

foster ['fɔstə*] *vt* incoraggiare, nutrire; (*child*) avere in affidamento; **~ child** *n* bambino(a) preso(a) in affidamento

fought [fɔ:t] *pt, pp* of *fight*

foul [faul] *adj* (*smell, food, temper etc*) cattivo(a); (*weather*) brutto(a); (*language*) osceno(a) ♦ *n* (*SPORT*) fallo ♦ *vt* sporcare; **~ play** *n* (*LAW*): **the police suspect ~ play** la polizia sospetta un atto criminale

found [faund] *pt, pp* of *find* ♦ *vt* (*establish*) fondare; **~ation** [-'deɪʃən] *n* (*act*) fondazione *f*; (*base*) base *f*; (*also*: **~ation cream**) fondo tinta; **~ations** *npl* (*of building*) fondamenta *fpl*

founder ['faundə*] *n* fondatore/trice ♦ *vi* affondare

foundry ['faundrɪ] *n* fonderia

fountain ['fauntɪn] *n* fontana; **~ pen** *n* penna stilografica

four [fɔ:*] *num* quattro; **on all ~s** a carponi; **~-poster** *n* (*also*: **~-poster bed**) letto a quattro colonne; **~some** ['fɔ:səm] *n*. partita a quattro; uscita in quattro; **~teen** *num* quattordici; **~th** *num* quarto(a)

fowl [faul] *n* pollame *m*; volatile *m*

fox [fɔks] *n* volpe *f* ♦ *vt* confondere

foyer ['fɔɪeɪ] *n* atrio; (*THEATRE*) ridotto

fraction ['frækʃən] *n* frazione *f*

fracture ['fræktʃə*] *n* frattura

fragile ['frædʒaɪl] *adj* fragile

fragment ['frægmənt] *n* frammento

fragrant ['freɪgrənt] *adj* fragrante, profumato(a)

frail [freɪl] *adj* debole, delicato(a)

frame [freɪm] *n* (*of building*) armatura; (*of human, animal*) ossatura, corpo; (*of picture*) cornice *f*; (*of door,*

window) telaio; (*of spectacles: also*: **~s**) montatura ♦ *vt* (*picture*) incorniciare; **~ of mind** *n* stato d'animo; **~work** *n* struttura

France [frɑ:ns] *n* Francia

franchise ['fræntʃaɪz] *n* (*POL*) diritto di voto; (*COMM*) concessione *f*

frank [fræŋk] *adj* franco(a), aperto(a) ♦ *vt* (*letter*) affrancare; **~ly** *adv* francamente, sinceramente

frantic ['fræntɪk] *adj* frenetico(a)

fraternity [frə'tɜ:nɪtɪ] *n* (*club*) associazione *f*; (*spirit*) fratellanza

fraud [frɔ:d] *n* truffa; (*LAW*) frode *f*; (*person*) impostore/a

fraught [frɔ:t] *adj*: **~ with** pieno di, intriso(a) da

fray [freɪ] *n* baruffa ♦ *vt* logorare ♦ *vi* logorarsi; **her nerves were ~ed** aveva i nervi a pezzi

freak [fri:k] *n* fenomeno, mostro

freckle ['frekl] *n* lentiggine *f*

free [fri:] *adj* libero(a); (*gratis*) gratuito(a) ♦ *vt* (*prisoner, jammed person*) liberare; (*jammed object*) districare; **~ of charge, for ~** gratuitamente; **~dom** ['fri:dəm] *n* libertà; **~-for-all** *n* parapiglia *m* generale; **~ gift** *n* regalo, omaggio; **~hold** *n* proprietà assoluta; **~ kick** *n* calcio libero; **~lance** *adj* indipendente; **~ly** *adv* liberamente; (*liberally*) liberalmente; **F~mason** *n* massone *m*; **F~post** ® *n* affrancatura a carico del destinatario; **~range** *adj* (*hen*) ruspante; (*eggs*) di gallina ruspante; **~ trade** *n* libero scambio; **~way** (*US*) *n* superstrada; **~ will** *n* libero arbitrio; **of one's own ~ will** di spontanea volontà

freeze [fri:z] (*pt* froze, *pp* frozen) *vi* gelare ♦ *vt* gelare; (*food*) congelare; (*prices, salaries*) bloccare ♦ *n* gelo; blocco; **~-dried** *adj* liofilizzato(a); **~r** *n* congelatore *m*

freezing ['fri:zɪŋ] *adj* (*wind, weather*) gelido(a); **~** *n* punto di congelamento; **3 degrees below ~ point** 3 gradi sotto zero

freight [freɪt] *n* (*goods*) merce *f*

merci *fpl*; (*money charged*) spese *fpl* di trasporto; ~ **train** (*US*) *n* treno *m* merci *inv*

French [frɛntʃ] *adj* francese ♦ *n* (*LING*) francese *m*; **the** ~ *npl* i Francesi; ~ **bean** *n* fagiolino *m*; **~ fried potatoes** (*US* ~ **fries**) *npl* patate *fpl* fritte; **~man** *n* francese *m*; ~ **window** *n* portafinestra; **~woman** *n* francese *f*

frenzy [ˈfrɛnzɪ] *n* frenesia

frequent [*adj* ˈfriːkwənt, *vb* frɪˈkwɛnt] *adj* frequente ♦ *vt* frequentare; **~ly** *adv* frequentemente, spesso

fresco [ˈfrɛskəu] *n* affresco

fresh [frɛʃ] *adj* fresco(a); (*new*) nuovo(a); (*cheeky*) sfacciato(a); **~en** *vi* (*wind, air*) rinfrescare; **~en up** *vi* rinfrescarsi; **~er** *n* (*BRIT: inf*) *n* (*SCOL*) matricola; **~ly** *adv* di recente, di fresco; **~man** (*US*) *n* = **~er**; **~ness** *n* freschezza; **~water** *adj* (*fish*) d'acqua dolce

fret [frɛt] *vi* agitarsi, affliggersi

friar [ˈfraɪə*] *n* frate *m*

friction [ˈfrɪkʃən] *n* frizione *f*, attrito

Friday [ˈfraɪdɪ] *n* venerdì *m inv*

fridge [frɪdʒ] (*BRIT*) *n* frigo, frigorifero

fried [fraɪd] *pt*, *pp* of **fry** ♦ *adj* fritto(a)

friend [frɛnd] *n* amico/a; **~ly** *adj* amichevole; **~ship** *n* amicizia

frieze [friːz] *n* fregio

fright [fraɪt] *n* paura, spavento; **to take** ~ spaventarsi; **~en** *vt* spaventare, far paura a; **~ened** *adj* spaventato(a); **~ening** *adj* spaventoso(a), pauroso(a); **~ful** *adj* orribile

frigid [ˈfrɪdʒɪd] *adj* (*woman*) frigido(a)

frill [frɪl] *n* balza

fringe [frɪndʒ] *n* (*decoration, BRIT: of hair*) frangia; (*edge: of forest etc*) margine *m*; **~ benefits** *npl* vantaggi *mpl*

frisk [frɪsk] *vt* perquisire

frisky [ˈfrɪskɪ] *adj* vivace, vispo(a)

fritter [ˈfrɪtə*] *n* frittella; ~ **away** *vt* sprecare

frivolous [ˈfrɪvələs] *adj* frivolo(a)

frizzy [ˈfrɪzɪ] *adj* crespo(a)

fro [frəu] *see* **to**

frock [frɔk] *n* vestito

frog [frɔg] *n* rana; **~man** *n* uomo *m* rana *inv*

frolic [ˈfrɔlɪk] *vi* sgambettare

KEYWORD

from [frɔm] *prep* **1** (*indicating starting place, origin etc*) da; **where do you come** ~?, **where are you** ~? da dove viene?, di dov'è?; ~ **London to Glasgow** da Londra a Glasgow; **a letter** ~ **my sister** una lettera da mia sorella; **tell him** ~ **me that ...** gli dica da parte mia che ...

2 (*indicating time*) da; ~ **one o'clock to** *or* **until** *or* **till two** dall'una alle due; ~ **January** (**on**) da gennaio, a partire da gennaio

3 (*indicating distance*) da; **the hotel is 1 km** ~ **the beach** l'albergo è a 1 km dalla spiaggia

4 (*indicating price, number etc*) da; **prices range** ~ **£10 to £50** i prezzi vanno dalle 10 alle 50 sterline

5 (*indicating difference*) da; **he can't tell red** ~ **green** non sa distinguere il rosso dal verde

6 (*because of, on the basis of*): ~ **what he says** da quanto dice lui; ~ **weak** ~ **hunger** debole per la fame

---

front [frʌnt] *n* (*of house, dress*) davanti *m inv*; (*of train*) testa; (*of book*) copertina; (*promenade: also:* **sea** ~) lungomare *m*; (*MIL, POL, METEOR*) fronte *m*; (*fig: appearances*) fronte *f* ♦ *adj* primo(a); anteriore, davanti *inv*; **in** ~ **of** davanti a; **~age** *n* facciata; ~ **door** *n* porta d'entrata; (*of car*) sportello anteriore; **~ier** [ˈfrʌntɪə*] *n* frontiera; ~ **page** *n* prima pagina; ~ **room** (*BRIT*) *n* salotto; **~-wheel drive** *n* trasmissione *f* anteriore

frost [frɔst] *n* gelo; (*also:* **hoar**~) brina; ~**bite** n congelamento; ~**ed** adj (glass) smerigliato(a); ~**y** adj (weather, look) gelido(a)

froth ['frɔθ] n spuma; schiuma

frown [fraun] vi accigliarsi

froze [frəuz] pt of **freeze; frozen** pp of **freeze**

fruit [fruːt] n inv (also fig) frutto; (collectively) frutta; ~**erer** n fruttivendolo; ~**erer's (shop)** n: at the ~**erer's (shop)** dal fruttivendolo; ~**ful** adj fruttuoso(a); ~**ion** [fruː'ɪʃən] n: to come to ~**ion** realizzarsi; ~ **juice** n succo di frutta; ~ **machine** (BRIT) n macchina f mangiasoldi inv; ~ **salad** n macedonia

frustrate (BRIT) vt frustrare

fry [fraɪ] (pt, pp **fried**) vt friggere; see also **small**; ~**ing pan** n padella

ft. abbr = **foot; feet**

fuddy-duddy ['fʌdɪdʌdɪ] n matusa

fudge [fʌdʒ] n (CULIN) specie di caramella a base di latte, burro e zucchero

fuel [fjuəl] n (for heating) combustibile m; (for propelling) carburante m; ~ **tank** n deposito m nafta inv; (on vehicle) serbatoio (della benzina)

fugitive ['fjuːdʒɪtɪv] n fuggitivo/a, profugo/a

fulfil [ful'fɪl] vt (function) compiere; (order) eseguire; (wish, desire) soddisfare, appagare; ~**ment** (of wishes) soddisfazione f, appagamento; sense of ~**ment** soddisfazione f

full [ful] adj pieno(a); (details, skirt) ampio(a) ♦ adv: to know ~ **well** that sapere benissimo che; I'm ~ (up) sono pieno(a); a ~ **two hours** due ore intere; at ~ **speed** a tutta velocità; in ~ per intero; ~ **employment** n piena occupazione; ~ **length** adj (film) a lungometraggio; (coat, novel) lungo(a); (portrait) in piedi; ~ **moon** n luna piena; ~ **scale** adj (attack, war) su larga scala; (model) in grandezza naturale; ~ **stop** n punto; ~**time** adj, adv (work) a tempo pieno; ~**y** adv interamente, pienamente, completamen-

te; (at least) almeno; ~**y-fledged** adj (teacher, member etc) a tutti gli effetti

fulsome ['fulsəm] (pej) adj (praise, compliments) esagerato(a)

fumble ['fʌmbl] vi: to ~ **with** sth armeggiare con qc

fume [fjuːm] vi essere furioso(a); ~**s** npl esalazioni fpl, vapori mpl

fun [fʌn] n divertimento, spasso; to have ~ divertirsi; for ~ per scherzo; to make ~ **of** prendersi gioco di

function ['fʌŋkʃən] n funzione f; cerimonia, ricevimento ♦ vi funzionare; ~**al** adj funzionale

fund [fʌnd] n fondo, cassa; (source) fondo; (store) riserva; ~**s** npl (money) fondi mpl

fundamental [fʌndə'mɛntl] adj fondamentale

funeral ['fjuːnərəl] n funerale m; ~ **parlour** n impresa di pompe funebri; ~ **service** n ufficio funebre

fun fair (BRIT) n luna park m inv

fungi ['fʌŋgaɪ] npl of **fungus**

fungus ['fʌŋgəs] (pl **fungi**) n fungo; (mould) muffa

funnel ['fʌnl] n imbuto; (of ship) ciminiera

funny ['fʌnɪ] adj divertente, buffo(a); (strange) strano(a), bizzarro(a)

fur [fəː*] n pelo; pelliccia; (BRIT: in kettle etc) deposito calcare; ~ **coat** n pelliccia

furious ['fjuərɪəs] adj furioso(a); (effort) accanito(a)

furlong ['fəːlɔŋ] n = 201.17 m (termine ippico)

furlough ['fəːləu] n congedo, permesso

furnace ['fəːnɪs] n fornace f

furnish ['fəːnɪʃ] vt ammobiliare; (supply) fornire; ~**ings** npl mobili mpl, mobilia

furniture ['fəːnɪtʃə*] n mobili mpl; piece of ~ mobile m

furrow ['fʌrəu] n solco

furry ['fəːrɪ] adj (animal) peloso(a)

further ['fəːðə*] adj supplementare,

altro(a); nuovo(a); più lontano(a) ♦
adv più lontano; (more) di più;
(moreover) inoltre ♦ vt favorire, promuovere; **college of ~ education**
n istituto statale con corsi specializzati (di formazione professionale,
aggiornamento professionale etc);
~more [fə:ðə'mɔ:*] adv inoltre, per
di più

furthest [fə:ðɪst] superl of **far**

fury [fjuərɪ] n furore m

fuse [fju:z] n fusibile m, (for bomb
etc) miccia, spoletta ♦ vt fondere ♦
vi fondersi; **to ~ the lights** (BRIT:
ELEC) far saltare i fusibili; **~ box**
n cassetta dei fusibili

fuselage [fju:zəlɑ:ʒ] n fusoliera

fuss [fʌs] n agitazione f; (complaining) storie fpl; **to make a ~** fare
delle storie; **~y** adj (person) puntiglioso(a), esigente; che fa le storie;
(dress) carico(a) di fronzoli; (style)
elaborato(a)

future [fju:tʃə*] adj futuro(a) ♦ n
futuro, avvenire m; (LING) futuro;
in ~ in futuro

fuze [fju:z] (US) = **fuse**

fuzzy [fʌzɪ] adj (PHOT) indistinto(a), sfocato(a); (hair) crespo(a)

G

G [dʒi:] n (MUS) sol m

G7 abbr (= Group of Seven) G7

gabble [gæbl] vi borbottare; farfugliare

gable [geɪbl] n frontone m

gadget [gædʒɪt] n aggeggio

Gaelic [geɪlɪk] adj gaelico(a) ♦ n
(LING) gaelico

gag [gæg] n bavaglio; (joke) facezia,
scherzo ♦ vt imbavagliare

gaiety [geɪtɪ] n gaiezza

gaily [geɪlɪ] adv allegramente

gain [geɪn] n guadagno, profitto ♦ vt
guadagnare ♦ vi (clock, watch) andare avanti; (benefit): **to ~ (from)**
trarre beneficio (da); **to ~ 3lbs (in
weight)** aumentare di 3 libbre; **to ~**

on sb (in race etc) guadagnare su qn

gait [geɪt] n andatura

gal. abbr = **gallon**

galaxy [gæləksɪ] n galassia

gale [geɪl] n vento forte; burrasca

gallant [gælənt] adj valoroso(a); (towards ladies) galante, cortese

gall bladder [gɔ:l-] n cistifellea

gallery [gælərɪ] n galleria

galley [gælɪ] n (ship's kitchen) cambusa

gallon [gælən] n gallone m (= 8
pints; BRIT = 4.543l; US = 3.785l)

gallop [gæləp] n galoppo ♦ vi galoppare

gallows [gæləuz] n forca

gallstone [gɔ:lstəun] n calcolo biliare

galore [gə'lɔ:*] adv a iosa, a profusione

galvanize [gælvənaɪz] vt galvanizzare

gambit [gæmbɪt] n (fig): (opening)
~ prima mossa

gamble [gæmbl] n azzardo, rischio
calcolato ♦ vt, vi giocare; **to ~ on**
(fig) giocare su; **~r** n giocatore/trice
d'azzardo; **gambling** n gioco d'azzardo

game [geɪm] n gioco; (event) partita; (TENNIS) game m inv; (CULIN,
HUNTING) selvaggina ♦ adj
(ready): **to be ~ (for sth/to do)** essere pronto(a) (a qc/a fare); **big ~**
selvaggina grossa; **~keeper** n guardacaccia m inv

gammon [gæmən] n (bacon) quarto
di maiale; (ham) prosciutto affumicato

gamut [gæmət] n gamma

gang [gæŋ] n banda, squadra ♦ vi:
to ~ up on sb far combutta contro
qn

gangrene [gæŋgri:n] n cancrena

gangster [gæŋstə*] n gangster m
inv

gangway [gæŋweɪ] n passerella;
(BRIT: of bus) corridoio

gaol [dʒeɪl] (BRIT) n, vt = **jail**

gap [gæp] n (space) buco; (in

intervallo; *(difference):* ~ *(between)* divario (tra)

gape [geɪp] *vi (person)* restare a bocca aperta; *(shirt, hole)* essere spa-
lancato(a); **gaping** *adj* spalan-
cato(a)

garage ['gærɑːʒ] *n* garage *m inv*

garbage ['gɑːbɪdʒ] *n (US)* immondizie *fpl*, rifiuti *mpl*; *(inf)* sciocchezze
fpl; ~ **can** *(US)* *n* bidone *m* della
spazzatura

garbled ['gɑːbld] *adj* deformato(a);
ingarbugliato(a)

garden ['gɑːdn] *n* giardino; ~**s** *mpl
(public park)* giardini pubblici; ~**er**
n giardiniere(a); ~**ing** *n* giardinaggio

gargle ['gɑːgl] *vi* fare gargarismi

garish ['gɛərɪʃ] *adj* vistoso(a)

garland ['gɑːlənd] *n* ghirlanda; corona

garlic ['gɑːlɪk] *n* aglio

garment ['gɑːmənt] *n* indumento

garnish ['gɑːnɪʃ] *vt (food)* guarnire

garrison ['gærɪsn] *n* guarnigione *f*

garrulous ['gærjuləs] *adj* ciarlie-
ro(a), loquace

garter ['gɑːtə*] *n* giarrettiera

gas [gæs] *n* gas *m inv; (US: gasoline)*
benzina ♦ *vt* asfissiare con il gas; ~
cooker *(BRIT)* *n* cucina a gas; ~
cylinder *n* bombola del gas; ~ **fire**
(BRIT) *n* radiatore *m* a gas

gash [gæʃ] *n* sfregio ♦ *vt* sfregiare

gasket ['gæskɪt] *n (AUT)* guarnizione
f

gas mask *n* maschera *f* antigas *inv*

gas meter *n* contatore *m* del gas

gasoline ['gæsəliːn] *(US)* *n* benzina

gasp [gɑːsp] *n* respiro affannoso, an-
sito ♦ *vi* ansare, ansimare; *(in surprise)* restare senza fiato; ~ **out** *vt*
dire affannosamente

gas station *n* distributore *m*
di benzina

gassy ['gæsɪ] *adj* gassoso(a)

gate [geɪt] *n* cancello; *(at airport)*
uscita; ~**crash** *(BRIT)* *vt* partecipare senza invito a; ~**way** *n* porta

gather ['gæðə*] *vt (flowers, fruit)* cogliere; *(pick up)* raccogliere; *(as-*

semble) radunare; raccogliere; *(understand)* capire; *(SEWING)* increspare ♦ *vi (assemble)* radunarsi; to
~ **speed** acquistare velocità; ~**ing**
n adunanza

gauche [gəʊʃ] *adj* goffo(a), maldc-
stro(a)

gaudy ['gɔːdɪ] *adj* vistoso(a)

gauge [geɪdʒ] *n (instrument)* indicatore *m* ♦ *vt* misurare; *(fig)* valutare

gaunt [gɔːnt] *adj* scarno(a); *(grim,
desolate)* desolato(a)

gauntlet ['gɔːntlɪt] *n* guanto; *(fig):*
to run the ~ through an angry
crowd passare sotto il fuoco di una
folla ostile; to throw down the ~
gettare il guanto

gauze [gɔːz] *n* garza

gave [geɪv] *pt of* give

gay [geɪ] *adj (homosexual)* omosessuale; *(cheerful)* gaio(a), allegro(a);
(colour) vivace, vivo(a)

gaze [geɪz] *n* sguardo fisso ♦ *vi:* to ~
at guardare fisso

gazetteer [gæzɪ'tɪə*] *n* indice *m* dei
nomi geografici

GB *abbr* = Great Britain

GCE *(BRIT)* *n abbr = General Certificate of Education)* ≈ maturità

GCSE *(BRIT)* *n abbr = General Certificate of Secondary Education*

gear [gɪə*] *n* attrezzi *mpl*, equipaggiamento; *(TECH)* ingranaggio;
(AUT) marcia ♦ *vt (fig: adapt):* to
~ **sth** to adattare qc a; **in top** *or
(US)* **high/low** ~ in quarta *(or
quinta)/seconda; in ~ in marcia; ~
box *n* scatola del cambio; ~ **lever**
(US ~ **shift)** *n* leva del cambio

geese [giːs] *npl of* goose

gelignite ['dʒelɪgnaɪt] *n* nitroglice-
na

gem [dʒem] *n* gemma

Gemini ['dʒemɪnaɪ] *n* Gemelli *mpl*

gender ['dʒendə*] *n* genere *m*

general ['dʒenərl] *n* generale *m* ♦
adj generale; **in** ~ in genere; ~ **delivery** *(US)* *n* fermo posta *m*; ~
election *n* elezioni *fpl* generali; ~**ly**

adv generalmente; ~ **practitioner** *n* medico generico

generate ['dʒɛnəreɪt] *vt* generare

generation [dʒɛnə'reɪʃən] *n* generazione *f*

generator ['dʒɛnəreɪtə*] *n* generatore *m*

generosity [dʒɛnə'rɔsɪtɪ] *n* generosità

generous ['dʒɛnərəs] *adj* generoso(a); (*copious*) abbondante

genetic engineering [dʒɪ'nɛtɪk-ɛndʒɪ'nɪərɪŋ] *n* ingegneria genetica

Geneva [dʒɪ'niːvə] *n* Ginevra

genial ['dʒiːnɪəl] *adj* geniale, cordiale

genitals ['dʒɛnɪtlz] *npl* genitali *mpl*

genius ['dʒiːnɪəs] *n* genio

Genoa ['dʒɛnəuə] *n* Genova

gent [dʒɛnt] *n abbr* = gentleman

genteel [dʒɛn'tiːl] *adj* raffinato(a), distinto(a)

gentle ['dʒɛntl] *adj* delicato(a); (*person*) dolce

gentleman ['dʒɛntlmən] *n* signore *m*; (*well-bred man*) gentiluomo

gently ['dʒɛntlɪ] *adv* delicatamente

gentry ['dʒɛntrɪ] *n* nobiltà minore

gents [dʒɛnts] *n* W.C. *m* (per signori)

genuine ['dʒɛnjuɪn] *adj* autentico(a); sincero(a)

geography [dʒɪ'ɔgrəfɪ] *n* geografia

geology [dʒɪ'ɔlədʒɪ] *n* geologia

geometric(al) [dʒɪə'mɛtrɪk(l)] *adj* geometrico(a)

geometry [dʒɪ'ɔmətrɪ] *n* geometria

geranium [dʒɪ'reɪnjəm] *n* geranio

geriatric [dʒɛrɪ'ætrɪk] *adj* geriatrico(a)

germ [dʒəːm] *n* (*MED*) microbo; (*BIOL, fig*) germe *m*

German ['dʒəːmən] *adj* tedesco(a) ♦ *n* tedesco(a); (*LING*) tedesco; ~ **measles** (*BRIT*) *n* rosolia

Germany ['dʒəːmənɪ] *n* Germania

gesture ['dʒɛstjə*] *n* gesto

KEYWORD

get [gɛt] (*pt, pp* **got**, (*US*) *pp* **gotten**)

vi **1** (*become, be*) diventare, farsi; **to ~ old** invecchiare; **to ~ tired** stancarsi; **to ~ drunk** ubriacarsi; **to ~ killed** venire *or* rimanere ucciso(a); **when do I ~ paid?** quando mi pagate?; **it's ~ting late** si sta facendo tardi

2 (*go*): **to ~ to/from** andare a/da; **to ~ home** arrivare *or* tornare a casa; **how did you ~ here?** come sei venuto?

3 (*begin*) mettersi a, cominciare a; **to ~ to know sb** incominciare a conoscere qn; **let's ~ going** *or* **started** muoviamoci

4 (*modal aux vb*): **you've got to do it** devi farlo

♦ *vt* **1**: **to ~ sth done** (*do*) fare qc; (*have done*) far fare qc; **to ~ one's hair cut** farsi tagliare i capelli; **to ~ sb to do sth** far fare qc a qn

2 (*obtain: money, permission, results*) ottenere; (*find: job, flat*) trovare; (*fetch: person, doctor*) chiamare; (*: object*) prendere; **to ~ sth for sb** prendere *or* procurare qc a qn; **~ me Mr Jones, please** (*TEL*) mi passi il signor Jones, per favore; **can I ~ you a drink?** le posso offrire da bere?

3 (*receive: present, letter, prize*) ricevere; (*acquire: reputation*) farsi; **how much did you ~ for the painting?** quanto le hanno dato per il quadro?

4 (*catch*) prendere; (*hit: target etc*) colpire; **to ~ sb by the arm/throat** afferrare qn per un braccio/alla gola; **~ him!** prendetelo!

5 (*take, move*) portare; **to ~ sth to sb** far avere qc a qn; **do you think we'll ~ it through the door?** pensi che riusciremo a farlo passare per la porta?

6 (*catch, take: plane, bus etc*) prendere

7 (*understand*) afferrare; (*hear*) sentire; **I've got it!** ci sono arrivato!, ci sono!; **I'm sorry, I didn't ~ your name** scusi, non ho capito (*or* sentito) il suo nome

8 (have, possess): **to have got** avere; **how many have you got?** quanti ne ha?

get about vi muoversi; (news) diffondersi

get along vi (agree) andare d'accordo; (depart) andarsene; (manage) = get by

get at vt fus (attack) prendersela con; (reach) raggiungere, arrivare a

get away vi partire, andarsene; (escape) scappare

get away with vt fus cavarsela; farla franca

get back vi (return) ritornare, tornare ♦ vt riottenere, riavere

get by vi (pass) passare; (manage) farcela

get down vi, vt fus scendere ♦ vt far scendere; (depress) buttare giù

get down to vt fus (work) mettersi a (fare)

get in vi entrare; (train) arrivare; (arrive home) ritornare, tornare

get into vt fus entrare in; **to ~ into a rage** incavolarsi

get off vi (from train etc) scendere; (depart: person, car) andare via; (escape) cavarsela ♦ vt (remove: clothes, stain) levare ♦ vt fus (train, bus) scendere da

get on vi (at exam etc) andare; (agree): **to ~ on (with)** andare d'accordo (con) ♦ vt fus montare in; (horse) montare su

get out vi uscire; (of vehicle) scendere ♦ vt tirar fuori, far uscire

get out of vt fus uscire da; (duty etc) evitare

get over vt fus (illness) riaversi da

get round vt fus aggirare; (fig: person) rigirare

get through vi (TEL) avere la linea

get through to vt fus (TEL) parlare a

get together vi riunirsi ♦ vt raccogliere; (people) adunare

get up vi (rise) alzarsi ♦ vt fus sa-

lire su per

get up to vt fus (reach) raggiungere; (prank etc) fare

getaway ['gɛtəweɪ] n fuga

geyser ['giːzə°] n (BRIT) scaldabagno; (GEO) geyser m inv

Ghana ['gɑːnə] n Ghana m

ghastly ['gɑːstlɪ] adj orribile, orrendo(a); (pale) spettrale

gherkin ['gəːkɪn] n cetriolino

ghetto blaster ['gɛtəʊblɑːstə°] n maxistereo m inv portatile

ghost [gəʊst] n fantasma m, spettro

giant ['dʒaɪənt] n gigante m ♦ adj gigantesco(a), enorme

gibberish ['dʒɪbərɪʃ] n parole fpl senza senso

gibe [dʒaɪb] n = jibe

giblets ['dʒɪblɪts] npl frattaglie fpl

Gibraltar [dʒɪ'brɔːltə°] n Gibilterra

giddy ['gɪdɪ] adj (dizzy): **to be ~** aver le vertigini

gift [gɪft] n regalo; (donation, ability) dono; **~ed** adj dotato(a); **~ token** n buono m omaggio inv; **~ voucher** n = **~ token**

gigantic [dʒaɪ'gæntɪk] adj gigantesco(a)

giggle ['gɪgl] vi ridere scioccamente

gill [dʒɪl] n (measure) = 0.25 pints (BRIT = 0.148l, US = 0.118l)

gills [gɪlz] npl (of fish) branchie fpl

gilt [gɪlt] n doratura ♦ adj dorato(a); **~-edged** adj (COMM) della massima sicurezza

gimmick ['gɪmɪk] n trucco

gin [dʒɪn] n (liquor) gin m inv

ginger ['dʒɪndʒə°] n zenzero; **~ ale** n bibita gassosa allo zenzero; **~ beer** n = **~ ale**; **~bread** n pan m di zenzero

gingerly ['dʒɪndʒəlɪ] adv cautamente

gipsy ['dʒɪpsɪ] n zingaro/a

giraffe [dʒɪ'rɑːf] n giraffa

girder ['gəːdə°] n trave f

girdle ['gəːdl] n (corset) guaina

girl [gəːl] n ragazza; (young unmarried woman) signorina; (daughter) figlia, figliola; **~friend** n (of amica; (of boy) ragazza; ~**ish** adj da ragazza

giro ['dʒaɪrəu] n (bank ~) versamento bancario; (post office ~) postagiro; (BRIT: welfare cheque) assegno del sussidio di assistenza sociale

girth [gɜ:θ] n circonferenza; (of horse) cinghia

gist [dʒɪst] n succo

give [gɪv] (pt gave, pp given) vt dare ♦ vi cedere; to ~ sb sth, ~ sth to sb dare qc a qn; I'll ~ you £5 for it te lo pago 5 sterline; to ~ a cry/sigh emettere un grido/sospiro; to ~ a speech fare un discorso; to ~ away vt dare via; (disclose) rivelare; (bride) condurre all'altare; ~ **back** vt rendere; ~ **in** vi cedere ♦ vt consegnare; ~ **off** vt emettere; ~ **out** vt distribuire; annunciare; ~ **up** vi rinunciare ♦ vt rinunciare a; to ~ up smoking smettere di fumare; to ~ o.s. up arrendersi; ~ **way** vi cedere; (BRIT: AUT) dare la precedenza; **given** pp of **give**

glacier ['glæsɪə*] n ghiacciaio

glad [glæd] adj lieto(a), contento(a)

gladly ['glædlɪ] adv volentieri

glamorous ['glæmərəs] adj affascinante, seducente

glamour ['glæmə*] n fascino

glance [glɑ:ns] n occhiata, sguardo ♦ vi: to ~ at dare un'occhiata a; to ~ off (bullet) rimbalzare su; **glancing** adj (blow) che colpisce di striscio

gland [glænd] n ghiandola

glare [glɛə*] n (of anger) sguardo furioso; (of light) riverbero, luce f abbagliante; (of publicity) chiasso ♦ vi abbagliare; to ~ at guardare male; **glaring** adj (mistake) madornale

glass [glɑ:s] n (substance) vetro; (tumbler) bicchiere m; ~**es** npl (spectacles) occhiali mpl; ~**house** n serra; ~**ware** n vetrame m; ~**y** adj (eyes) vitreo(a)

glaze [gleɪz] vt (door) fornire di vetri; (pottery) smaltare ♦ n smalto; ~**d** adj (eyes) vitreo(a); (pottery) smaltato(a)

glazier ['gleɪzɪə*] n vetraio

gleam [gli:m] vi luccicare

glean [gli:n] vt (information) racimolare

glee [gli:] n allegrezza, gioia

glen [glɛn] n valletta

glib [glɪb] adj dalla parola facile; facile

glide [glaɪd] vi scivolare; (AVIAT, birds) planare; ~**r** n (AVIAT) aliante m; **gliding** n (AVIAT) volo a vela

glimmer ['glɪmə*] n barlume m

glimpse [glɪmps] n impressione f fugace ♦ vt vedere al volo

glint [glɪnt] vi luccicare

glisten ['glɪsn] vi luccicare

glitter ['glɪtə*] vi scintillare

gloat [gləut] vi: to ~ (over) gongolare di piacere (per)

global ['gləubl] adj globale

globe [gləub] n globo, sfera

gloom [glu:m] n oscurità, buio; (sadness) tristezza, malinconia; ~**y** adj scuro(a); fosco(a), triste

glorious ['glɔ:rɪəs] adj glorioso(a); magnifico(a)

glory ['glɔ:rɪ] n gloria; splendore m

gloss [glɔs] n (shine) lucentezza; (also: ~ paint) vernice f a olio; ~ **over** vt fus scivolare su

glossary ['glɔsərɪ] n glossario

glossy ['glɔsɪ] adj lucente

glove [glʌv] n guanto; ~ **compartment** n (AUT) vano portaoggetti

glow [gləu] vi ardere; (face) essere luminoso(a)

glower ['glauə*] vi: to ~ (at sb) guardare (qn) in cagnesco

glue [glu:] n colla ♦ vt incollare

glum [glʌm] adj abbattuto(a)

glut [glʌt] n eccesso

glutton ['glʌtn] n ghiottone(a); a ~ for work un(a) patito(a) del lavoro

gnarled [nɑ:ld] adj nodoso(a)

gnat [næt] n moscerino

gnaw [nɔ:] vt rodere

go [gəu] (pt went, pp gone; pl ~es) vi andare; (depart) partire, andarsene; (work) funzionare; (time) passare; (break etc) rompersi; (be sold):

to ~ for £10 essere venduto per 10 sterline; (*fit, suit*): to ~ **with** andare bene con; (*become*): to ~ **pale** diventare pallido(a); to ~ **mouldy** ammuffire ♦ *n*: to have a ~ (**at**) provare; to be on the ~ essere in moto; whose ~ is it? a chi tocca?; he's going to do sta per fare; to ~ **for a walk** andare a fare una passeggiata; to ~ **dancing/shopping** andare a ballare/fare la spesa; just then the bell went proprio allora suonò il campanello; how did it ~? com'è andato?; to ~ **round** the back/by the shop passare da dietro/davanti al negozio; ~ **about** *vi* (*also*: ~ round: *rumour*) correre, circolare ♦ *vt fus*: how do I ~ about this? qual'è la prassi per questo?; ~ **ahead** *vi* andare avanti; ~ **along** *vi* andare, avanzare ♦ *vt fus* percorrere; to ~ **along with** (*plan, idea*) appoggiare; ~ **away** *vi* partire, andarsene; ~ **back** *vi* tornare, ritornare; ~ **back on** *vt fus* (*promise*) non mantenere; ~ **by** *vi* (*years, time*) scorrere ♦ *vt fus* attenersi a, seguire (alla lettera); prestar fede a; ~ **down** *vi* scendere; (*ship*) affondare; (*sun*) tramontare ♦ *vt fus* scendere; ~ **for** *vt fus* (*fetch*) andare a prendere; (*like*) andar matto(a) per; (*attack*) attaccare; saltare addosso a; ~ **in** *vi* entrare; ~ **in for** *vt fus* (*competition*) iscriversi a; (*be interested in*) interessarsi di; ~ **into** *vt fus* entrare in; (*investigate*) indagare, esaminare; (*embark on*) lanciarsi in; ~ **off** *vi* partire, andar via; (*food*) guastarsi; (*explode*) esplodere, scoppiare; (*event*) passare ♦ *vt fus*: I've gone off chocolate la cioccolata non mi piace più; the gun went off il fucile si scaricò; ~ **on** *vi* continuare; (*happen*) succedere; to ~ **on doing** continuare a fare; ~ **out** *vi* uscire; (*couple*): they went out for 3 years sono stati insieme per 3 anni; (*fire, light*) spegnersi; ~ **over** *vi* (*ship*) ribaltarsi ♦ *vt fus*

(*check*) esaminare; ~ **through** *vt fus* (*town etc*) attraversare; (*files, papers*) passare in rassegna; (*examine: list etc*) leggere da cima a fondo; ~ **up** *vi* salire; ~ **without** *vt fus* fare a meno di

goad [gəʊd] *vt* spronare

go-ahead *adj* intraprendente ♦ *n* via *m*

goal [gəʊl] *n* (*SPORT*) gol *m*, rete *f*; (: *place*) porta; (*fig: aim*) fine *m*, scopo; ~**keeper** *n* portiere *m*; ~**post** *n* palo (della porta)

goat [gəʊt] *n* capra

gobble ['gɔbl] *vt* (*also*: ~ down, ~ up) ingoiare

go-between *n* intermediario/a

god [gɔd] *n* dio; G~ *n* Dio; ~**child** *n* figlioccio/a; ~**daughter** *n* figlioccia; ~**dess** *n* dea; ~**father** *n* padrino; ~**forsaken** *adj* desolato(a), sperduto(a); ~**mother** *n* madrina; ~**send** *n* dono del cielo; ~**son** *n* figlioccio

goggles ['gɔglz] *npl* occhiali *mpl* (di protezione)

going ['gəʊɪŋ] *n* (*conditions*) andare *m*, stato del terreno ♦ *adj*: the ~ **rate** la tariffa in vigore

gold [gəʊld] *n* oro ♦ *adj* d'oro; ~**en** *adj* (*made of* ~) d'oro; (*in colour*) dorato(a); ~**fish** *n* pesce *m* dorato o rosso; ~**mine** *n* (*also fig*) miniera d'oro; ~**plated** *adj* placcato(a) oro; ~**smith** *n* orefice *m*, orafo

golf [gɔlf] *n* golf *m*; ~ **ball** *n* (*for game*) pallina da golf; (*on typewriter*) pallina; ~ **club** *n* circolo da golf; (*stick*) bastone *m* o mazza da golf; ~ **course** *n* campo di golf; ~**er** *n* giocatore/trice di golf

gondola ['gɔndələ] *n* gondola

gone [gɔn] *pp of* **go** ♦ *adj* partito(a)

gong [gɔŋ] *n* gong *m inv*

good [gʊd] *adj* buono(a); (*kind*) buono(a), gentile; (*child*) bravo(a) ♦ *n* bene *m*; ~s *npl* (*COMM etc*) merci *mpl*; merci *fpl*; ~! bene!, ottimo!; to be ~ at essere bravo(a) in; to be ~ **for** andare bene per; it's ~ for

you fa bene; **would you be ~ enough to ...?** avrebbe la gentilezza di
...?; **a ~ deal (of)** molto(a), una
buona quantità (di); **a ~ many** molti(e); **to make ~** (loss, damage)
compensare; **it's no ~ complaining**
brontolare non serve a niente; **for ~
per sempre, definitivamente; ~
morning!** buon giorno!; **~
afternoon/evening!** buona sera!; **~
night!** buona notte!; **~bye** excl arrivederci!; **G~ Friday** n Venerdì
Santo; **~looking** adj bello(a); **~-
natured** adj affabile; **~ness** n (of
person) bontà; **~ness sake!** per
amor di Dio!; **~ness gracious!** santo cielo!, mamma mia!; **~ train**
(BRIT) n treno m merci inv; **~will**
n amicizia, benevolenza

goose [guːs] (pl **geese**) n oca
gooseberry ['guzbəri] n uva spina;
to play ~ (BRIT) tenere la candela
gooseflesh ['guːsfleʃ] n pelle f d'oca
goose pimples npl pelle f d'oca
gore [gɔːʳ] vt incornare ♦ n sangue
m (coagulato)
gorge [gɔːdʒ] n gola ♦ vt: **to ~ o.s.
(on)** ingozzarsi (di)
gorgeous ['gɔːdʒəs] adj magnifico(a)
gorilla [gə'rɪlə] n gorilla m inv
gorse [gɔːs] n ginestrone m
gory ['gɔːrɪ] adj sanguinoso(a)
go-slow [gəʊ'sləʊ] n rallentamento dei
lavori (per agitazione sindacale)
gospel ['gɒspl] n vangelo
gossip ['gɒsɪp] n chiacchiere fpl; pettegolezzi mpl; (person) pettegolo/a ♦
vi chiacchierare
got [gɒt] pt, pp of **get**; **~ten** (US) pp
of **get**
gout [gaut] n gotta
govern ['gʌvən] vt governare
governess ['gʌvənɪs] n governante f
government ['gʌvnmənt] n governo
governor ['gʌvənəʳ] n (of state,
bank) governatore m; (of school,
hospital) amministratore m; (BRIT:
of prison) direttore/trice
gown [gaun] n vestito lungo; (of

teacher, BRIT: of judge) toga
G.P. n abbr = general practitioner
grab [græb] vt afferrare, ghermire;
(property, power) impadronirsi di ♦
vt: **to ~ at** cercare di afferrare
grace [greɪs] n grazia ♦ vt onorare; **5
days' ~** dilazione f di 5 giorni; **~ful**
adj elegante, aggraziato(a); **gra-
cious** ['greɪʃəs] adj grazioso(a); misericordioso(a)
grade [greɪd] n (COMM) qualità f
inv; classe f; categoria; (in hierarchy) grado; (SCOL: mark) voto; (US: school class) classe ♦ vt classificare; ordinare; graduare; **~
crossing** (US) n passaggio a livello;
~ school (US) n scuola elementare
gradient ['greɪdɪənt] n pendenza, inclinazione f
gradual ['grædjuəl] adj graduale; **~ly** adv man mano, a poco a poco
graduate [n 'grædjuɪt, vb 'grædjueɪt]
n (of university) laureato/a; (US: of
high school) diplomato/a ♦ vi laurearsi; diplomarsi; **graduation** [-'eɪʃən] n (ceremony) consegna delle
lauree (or dei diplomi)
graffiti [grə'fiːtɪ] npl graffiti mpl
graft [grɑːft] n (AGR, MED) innesto;
(bribery) corruzione f; (BRIT: hard
work): **it's hard ~** è un lavoraccio
♦ vt innestare
grain [greɪn] n grano; (of sand) granello; (of wood) venatura
gram [græm] n grammo
grammar ['græməʳ] n grammatica; **~
school** (BRIT) n liceo
grammatical [grə'mætɪkl] adj grammaticale
gramme [græm] n = **gram**
grand [grænd] adj grande, magnifico(a); grandioso(a); **~children** npl
nipoti mpl; **~dad** (inf) n nonno;
~daughter n nipote f; **~eur**
['grændjəʳ] n grandiosità; **~father** n
nonno; **~ma** (inf) n nonna;
~mother n nonna; **~pa** (inf) n =
~dad; **~parents** npl nonni mpl; **~
piano** n pianoforte m a coda; **~son**
n nipote m; **~stand** n (SPORT) tri-

buna

granite ['grænɪt] *n* granito

granny ['grænɪ] (*inf*) *n* nonna

grant [graːnt] *vt* accordare; (*a request*) accogliere; (*admit*) ammettere, concedere ♦ *n* (*SCOL*) borsa; (*ADMIN*) sussidio, sovvenzione *f*; to **take sth for** ~**ed** dare qc per scontato; to **take sb for** ~**ed** dare per scontata la presenza di qn

granulated ['grænjuleɪtɪd] *adj*: ~ **sugar** zucchero cristallizzato

granule ['grænjuːl] *n* granello

grape [greɪp] *n* chicco d'uva, acino

grapefruit ['greɪpfruːt] *n* pompelmo

graph [graːf] *n* grafico; ~**ic** *adj* grafico(a); (*vivid*) vivido(a); ~**ics** *n* grafica ♦ *npl* illustrazioni *fpl*

grapple ['græpl] *vi*: to ~ **with** essere alle prese con

grasp [graːsp] *vt* afferrare ♦ *n* (*grip*) presa; (*fig*) potere *m*; comprensione *f*; ~**ing** *adj* avido(a)

grass [graːs] *n* erba; ~**hopper** *n* cavalletta; ~**-roots** *adj* di base

grate [greɪt] *n* graticola (del focolare) ♦ *vi* cigolare, stridere ♦ *vt* (*CULIN*) grattugiare

grateful ['greɪtful] *adj* grato(a), riconoscente

grater ['greɪtə*] *n* grattugia

grating ['greɪtɪŋ] *n* (*iron bars*) grata ♦ *adj* (*noise*) stridente, stridulo(a)

gratitude ['grætɪtjuːd] *n* gratitudine *f*

gratuity [grə'tjuːɪtɪ] *n* mancia

grave [greɪv] *n* tomba ♦ *adj* grave, serio(a)

gravel ['grævl] *n* ghiaia

gravestone ['greɪvstəʊn] *n* pietra tombale

graveyard ['greɪvjɑːd] *n* cimitero

gravity ['grævɪtɪ] *n* (*PHYSICS*) gravità; pesantezza; (*seriousness*) gravità, serietà

gravy ['greɪvɪ] *n* intingolo della carne; salsa

gray [greɪ] *adj* = **grey**

graze [greɪz] *vi* pascolare, pascere ♦ *vt* (*touch lightly*) sfiorare; (*scrape*) escoriare ♦ *n* (*MED*) escoriazione *f*

grease [griːs] *n* (*fat*) grasso; (*lubricant*) lubrificante *m* ♦ *vt* ingrassare; lubrificare; ~**proof paper** (*BRIT*) *n* carta oleata; **greasy** *adj* grasso(a), untuoso(a)

great [greɪt] *adj* grande; (*inf*) magnifico(a), meraviglioso(a); **G~ Britain** *n* Gran Bretagna; ~**grandfather** *n* bisnonno; ~**grandmother** *n* bisnonna; ~**ly** *adv* molto; ~**ness** *n* grandezza

Greece [griːs] *n* Grecia

greed [griːd] *n* (*also*: ~**iness**) avarizia; (*for food*) golosità, ghiottoneria; ~**y** *adj* avido(a); goloso(a), ghiotto(a)

Greek [griːk] *adj* greco(a) ♦ *n* greco/a; (*LING*) greco

green [griːn] *adj* verde; (*inexperienced*) inesperto(a), ingenuo(a) ♦ *n* verde *m*; (*stretch of grass*) prato; (*on golf course*) area *m* inv; ~**s** *npl* (*vegetables*) verdura; ~ **belt** *n* (*round town*) cintura *f* di verde; ~ **card** *n* (*BRIT*: *AUT*) carta verde; (*US*: *ADMIN*) permesso di soggiorno e di lavoro; ~**ery** *n* verde *m*; ~**grocer** (*BRIT*) *n* fruttivendolo/a, erbivendolo/a; ~**house** *n* serra; ~**house effect** *n* effetto serra; ~**house gas** *n* gas responsabile dell'effetto serra; ~**ish** *adj* verdastro(a)

Greenland ['griːnlənd] *n* Groenlandia

greet [griːt] *vt* salutare; ~**ing** *n* saluto; ~**ing(s) card** *n* cartolina d'auguri

gregarious [grə'gɛərɪəs] *adj* (*person*) socievole

grenade [grə'neɪd] *n* (*also*: **hand** ~) granata

grew [gruː] *pt of* **grow**

grey [greɪ] *adj* grigio(a); ~**haired** *adj* dai capelli grigi; ~**hound** *n* levriere *m*

grid [grɪd] *n* grata; (*ELEC*) rete *f*

grief [griːf] *n* dolore *m*

grievance ['griːvəns] *n* lagnanza

grieve [griːv] *vi* addolorarsi; rattristarsi ♦ vt addolorare; **to ~ for sb** (dead person) piangere qn

grievous ['gri:vəs] adj: **~ bodily harm** (LAW) aggressione f

grill [grɪl] n (on cooker) griglia; (also: mixed ~) grigliata mista ♦ vt (BRIT) cuocere ai ferri; (inf: question) interrogare senza sosta

grille [grɪl] n grata; (AUT) griglia

grim [grɪm] adj sinistro(a), brutto(a)

grimace [grɪ'meɪs] n smorfia ♦ vi fare smorfie; fare boccacce

grime [graɪm] n sudiciume m

grin [grɪn] n sorriso smagliante ♦ vi fare un gran sorriso

grind [graɪnd] (pt, pp **ground**) vt macinare; (make sharp) arrotare ♦ n (work) sgobbata

grip [grɪp] n impugnatura; presa; (holdall) borsa da viaggio ♦ vt (object) afferrare; (attention) catturare; **to come to ~s with** affrontare, cercare di risolvere

gripping ['grɪpɪŋ] adj avvincente

grisly ['grɪzlɪ] adj macabro(a), orrido(a)

gristle ['grɪsl] n cartilagine f

grit [grɪt] n ghiaia; (courage) fegato ♦ vt (road) coprire di sabbia; **to ~ one's teeth** stringere i denti

groan [grəun] n gemito ♦ vi gemere

grocer ['grəusə*] n negoziante m di generi alimentari; **~ies** npl provviste fpl; **~'s (shop)** n negozio di (generi) alimentari

groggy ['grɔgɪ] adj barcollante

groin [grɔɪn] n inguine m

groom [gru:m] n palafreniere m; (also: bride~) sposo ♦ vt (horse) strigliare; (fig): **to ~ sb for** avviare qn a; **well~ed** (person) curato(a)

groove [gru:v] n scanalatura, solco

grope [grəup] vi: **to ~ for** cercare a tastoni

gross [grəus] adj grossolano(a); (COMM) lordo(a); **~ly** adv (greatly) molto

grotesque [grəu'tɛsk] adj grottesco(a)

grotto ['grɔtəu] n grotta

grotty ['grɔtɪ] (inf) adj terribile

ground [graund] pt, pp of **grind** ♦ n suolo, terra; (land) terreno; (SPORT) campo; (reason: gen pl) ragione f; (US: also: ~ wire) terra ♦ vt (plane) tenere a terra; (US: ELEC) mettere la presa a terra a; **~s** npl (of coffee etc) fondi mpl; (gardens etc) terreno, giardini mpl; **on/to the ~** per/a terra; **to gain/lose ~** guadagnare/perdere terreno; **~ cloth** (US) n = ~sheet; **~ing** n (in education) basi fpl; **~less** adj infondato(a); **~sheet** (BRIT) n telone m impermeabile; **~ staff** n personale m di terra; **~ swell** n (fig) movimento; **~work** n preparazione f

group [gru:p] n gruppo ♦ vt (also: ~ together) raggruppare ♦ vi (also: ~ together) raggrupparsi

grouse [graus] n inv (bird) tetraone m ♦ vi (complain) brontolare

grove [grəuv] n boschetto

grovel ['grɔvl] vi (fig): **to ~** (before) strisciare (di fronte a)

grow [grəu] (pt **grew**, pp **grown**) vi crescere; (increase) aumentare; (develop) svilupparsi; (become): **to ~ rich/weak** arricchirsi/indebolirsi ♦ vt coltivare, far crescere; **~ up** vi farsi grande, crescere; **~er** n coltivatore/trice; **~ing** adj (fear, amount) crescente

growl [graul] vi ringhiare

grown [grəun] pp of **grow**; **~-up** n adulto/a, grande m/f

growth [grəuθ] n crescita, sviluppo; (what has grown) crescita; (MED) escrescenza, tumore m

grub [grʌb] n larva; (inf: food) roba (da mangiare)

grubby ['grʌbɪ] adj sporco(a)

grudge [grʌdʒ] n rancore m ♦ vt: **to ~ sb sth** dare qc a qn di malavoglia; invidiare qc a qn; **to bear sb a ~ (for)** serbar rancore a qn (per)

gruelling ['gruəlɪŋ] adj estenuante

gruesome ['gru:səm] adj orribile

gruff [grʌf] adj rozzo(a)

grumble ['grʌmbl] vi brontolare, lagnarsi

grumpy ['grʌmpɪ] adj scorbutico(a)

grunt [grʌnt] vi grugnire

G-string n tanga m inv

guarantee [gærən'tiː] n garanzia ♦ vt garantire

guard [gɑːd] n guardia; (one man) guardia, sentinella; (BRIT: RAIL) capotreno; (on machine) schermo protettivo; (also: fire~) parafuoco ♦ vt fare la guardia a; (protect): to ~ (against) proteggere (da); **to be on one's ~** stare in guardia; **~ against** vt fus guardarsi da; **~ed** adj (fig) cauto(a), guardingo(a); **~ian** n custode m; (of minor) tutore/trice; **~'s van** (BRIT) n (RAIL) vagone m di servizio

guerrilla [gə'rɪlə] n guerrigliero

guess [gɛs] vi indovinare ♦ vt indovinare; (US) credere, pensare ♦ vi: to take o have a ~ provare a indovinare; **~work** n: I got the answer by **~work** ho azzeccato la risposta

guest [gɛst] n ospite m/f; (in hotel) cliente m/f; **~-house** n pensione f; **~ room** n camera degli ospiti

guffaw [gʌ'fɔː] vi scoppiare in una risata sonora

guidance ['gaɪdəns] n guida, direzione f

guide [gaɪd] n (person, book etc) guida; (BRIT: also: girl ~) giovane esploratrice f ♦ vt guidare; **~book** n guida; **~ dog** n cane m guida inv; **~lines** npl (fig) indicazioni fpl, linee fpl direttive

guild [gɪld] n arte f, corporazione f; associazione f

guile [gaɪl] n astuzia

guillotine ['gɪlətiːn] n ghigliottina; (for paper) taglierina

guilt [gɪlt] n colpevolezza; **~y** adj colpevole

guinea pig ['gɪnɪ-] n cavia

guise [gaɪz] n maschera

guitar [gɪ'tɑːʳ] n chitarra

gulf [gʌlf] n golfo; (abyss) abisso

gull [gʌl] n gabbiano

gullet ['gʌlɪt] n gola

gullible ['gʌlɪbl] adj credulo(a)

gully ['gʌlɪ] n burrone m; gola; canale m

gulp [gʌlp] vi deglutire; (from emotion) avere il nodo in gola ♦ vt (also: ~ down) tracannare, inghiottire

gum [gʌm] n (ANAT) gengiva; (glue) colla; (also: ~drop) caramella gommosa; (also: chewing ~) chewing-gum m ♦ vt: to ~ (together) incollare; **~boots** (BRIT) npl stivali mpl di gomma

gumption ['gʌmpʃən] n spirito d'iniziativa, buonsenso

gun [gʌn] n fucile m; (small) pistola, rivoltella; (rifle) carabina; (shotgun) fucile da caccia; (cannon) cannone m; **~boat** n cannoniera; **~fire** n spari mpl; **~man** n bandito armato; **~point** n: at ~point sotto minaccia di fucile; **~powder** n polvere f da sparo; **~shot** n sparo

gurgle ['gɜːgl] vi gorgogliare

guru ['guruː] n guru m inv

gush [gʌʃ] vi sgorgare; (fig) abbandonarsi ad effusioni

gusset ['gʌsɪt] n gherone m

gust [gʌst] n (of wind) raffica; (of smoke) buffata

gusto ['gʌstəu] n entusiasmo

gut [gʌt] n intestino, budello; **~s** npl (ANAT) interiora fpl; (courage) fegato

gutter ['gʌtəʳ] n (of roof) grondaia; (in street) cunetta

guy [gaɪ] n (inf: man) tipo, elemento; (also: ~rope) cavo or corda di fissaggio; (figure) effigie di Guy Fawkes

guzzle ['gʌzl] vt trangurgiare

gym [dʒɪm] n (also: gymnasium) palestra; (also: gymnastics) ginnastica

gymnast ['dʒɪmnæst] n ginnasta m/f; **~ics** [-'næstɪks] n, npl ginnastica

gym shoes npl scarpe fpl da ginnastica

gym slip (BRIT) n grembiule m da scuola (per ragazze)

gynaecologist [gaɪnɪ'kɒlədʒɪst] (US **gynecologist**) n ginecologo/a

gypsy ['dʒɪpsɪ] n = **gipsy**

gyrate [dʒaɪˈreɪt] vi girare

H

haberdashery [ˈhæbəˈdæʃərɪ] (BRIT) n merceria

habit [ˈhæbɪt] n abitudine f; (costume) abito; (REL) tonaca

habitual [həˈbɪtjuəl] adj abituale; (drinker, liar) inveterato(a)

hack [hæk] vt tagliare, fare a pezzi ♦ n (pej: writer) scribacchino/a

hacker [ˈhækəˈ] n (COMPUT) pirata m informatico

hackneyed [ˈhæknɪd] adj comune, trito(a)

had [hæd] pt, pp of **have**

haddock [ˈhædək] (pl ~ or ~s) n eglefino

hadn't [ˈhædnt] = **had not**

haemorrhage [ˈhɛmərɪdʒ] (US hemorrhage) n emorragia

haemorrhoids [ˈhɛmərɔɪdz] (US hemorrhoids) npl emorroidi fpl

haggard [ˈhægəd] adj smunto(a)

haggle [ˈhægl] vi mercanteggiare

Hague [heɪg] n: The ~ L'Aia

hail [heɪl] n grandine f; (of criticism etc) pioggia ♦ vt (call) chiamare; (flag down: taxi) fermare; (greet) salutare ♦ vi grandinare; **~stone** n chicco di grandine

hair [hɛəˈ] n capelli mpl; (single hair: on head) capello; (: on body) pelo; **to do one's ~** pettinarsi; **~brush** n spazzola per capelli; **~cut** n taglio m di capelli; **~do** [ˈhɛəduː] n acconciatura, pettinatura; **~dresser** n parrucchiere/a; **~ dryer** n asciugacapelli m inv; **~ grip** n forcina; **~net** n retina per capelli; **~pin** n forcina; **~pin bend** (US **~pin curve**) n tornante m; **~raising** adj orripilante; **~removing cream** n crema depilatoria; **~spray** n lacca per capelli; **~style** n pettinatura, acconciatura; **~y** adj irsuto(a); peloso(a); (inf: frightening) spaventoso(a)

hake [heɪk] (pl ~ or ~s) n nasello

half [hɑːf] (pl halves) n mezzo, metà f inv ♦ adj mezzo(a) ♦ adv a mezzo, a metà; **~ an hour** mezz'ora; **~ a dozen** mezza dozzina; **~ a pound** mezza libbra; **two and a ~** due e mezzo; **a week and a ~** una settimana e mezza; **~ (of it)** la metà; **~ (of)** la metà di; **to cut sth in ~** tagliare qc in due; **~-asleep** mezzo(a) addormentato(a); **~-baked** adj (scheme) che non sta in piedi; **~-caste** n meticcio/a; **~-hearted** adj tiepido(a); **~-hour** n mezz'ora; **~-mast**: at **~-mast** adv (flag) a mezz'asta; **~-penny** [ˈheɪpnɪ] (BRIT) n mezzo penny m inv; **~-price** adv a metà prezzo; **~ term** (BRIT) n (SCOL) vacanza a or di metà trimestre; **~-time** n (SPORT) intervallo; **~way** adv a metà strada

halibut [ˈhælɪbət] n inv ippoglosso

hall [hɔːl] n sala, salone m; (entrance way) entrata; **~ of residence** (BRIT) n casa dello studente

hallmark [ˈhɔːlmɑːk] n marchio di garanzia; (fig) caratteristica

hallo [həˈləʊ] excl = **hello**

Hallowe'en [ˈhæləʊˈiːn] n vigilia d'Ognissanti

hallucination [həluːsɪˈneɪʃən] n allucinazione f

hallway [ˈhɔːlweɪ] n corridoio; (entrance) ingresso

halo [ˈheɪləʊ] n (of saint etc) aureola

halt [hɔːlt] n fermata ♦ vt fermare ♦ vi fermarsi

halve [hɑːv] vt (apple etc) dividere a metà; (expense) ridurre di metà

halves [hɑːvz] npl of **half**

ham [hæm] n prosciutto

hamburger [ˈhæmbəːgəˈ] n hamburger m inv

hamlet [ˈhæmlɪt] n paesetto

hammer [ˈhæməˈ] n martello ♦ vt martellare ♦ vi: to ~ on or at the door picchiare alla porta

hammock [ˈhæmək] n amaca

hamper [ˈhæmpəˈ] vt impedire ♦ n cesta

hamster ['hæmstə*] n criceto

hand [hænd] n mano f; (of clock) lancetta; (handwriting) scrittura; (at cards) mano; (: game) partita; (worker) operaio/a ♦ vt dare, passare; to give sb a ~ dare una mano a qn; at ~ a portata di mano; in ~ a disposizione; (work) in corso; on ~ (person) disponibile; (services) pronto(a) a intervenire; to ~ (information etc) a portata di mano; on the one ~ ..., on the other ~ da un lato ..., dall'altro; ~ in vt consegnare; ~ out vt distribuire; ~ over vt passare; cedere; ~bag n borsetta; ~book n manuale m; ~brake n freno a mano; ~cuffs npl manette fpl; ~ful n manciata, pugno

handicap ['hændɪkæp] n handicap m inv ♦ vt handicappare; to be physically ~ped essere handicappato(a); to be mentally ~ped essere un(a) handicappato(a) mentale

handicraft ['hændɪwɜːk] n lavoro d'artigiano

handiwork ['hændɪwɜːk] n opera

handkerchief ['hæŋkətʃɪf] n fazzoletto

handle ['hændl] n (of door etc) maniglia; (of cup etc) ansa; (of knife etc) impugnatura; (of saucepan) manico; (for winding) manovella ♦ vt toccare, maneggiare; (deal with) occuparsi di; (treat: people) trattare; "~ with care" "fragile"; to fly off the ~ (fig) perdere le staffe, uscire dai gangheri; ~bar(s) n(pl) manubrio

hand: ~ luggage n bagagli mpl a mano; ~made adj fatto(a) a mano; ~out n (money, food) elemosina; (leaflet) volantino; (at lecture) prospetto; ~rail n corrimano; ~shake n stretta di mano

handsome ['hænsəm] adj bello(a); (profit, fortune) considerevole

handwriting ['hændraɪtɪŋ] n scrittura

handy ['hændɪ] adj (person) bravo(a); (close at hand) a portata di mano; (convenient) comodo(a);

~man n tuttofare m inv

hang [hæŋ] (pt, pp hung) vt appendere; (criminal: pt, pp hanged) impiccare ♦ vi (painting) essere appeso(a); (hair) scendere; (drapery) cadere; to get the ~ of sth (inf) capire come qc funziona; ~ about or around vi bighellonare, ciondolare; ~ on vi (wait) aspettare; ~ up vi (TEL) riattaccare ♦ vt appendere

hangar ['hæŋə*] n hangar m inv

hanger ['hæŋə*] n gruccia

hanger-on n parassita m

hang-gliding ['-glaɪdɪŋ] n volo col deltaplano

hangover ['hæŋəʊvə*] n (after drinking) postumi mpl di sbornia

hang-up n complesso

hanker ['hæŋkə*] vi: to ~ after bramare

hankie ['hæŋkɪ] n abbr = handkerchief

hanky ['hæŋkɪ] n abbr = handkerchief

haphazard [hæp'hæzəd] adj a casaccio, alla carlona

happen ['hæpən] vi accadere, succedere; (chance): to ~ to do sth qc per caso; as it ~s guarda caso; ~ing n avvenimento

happily ['hæpɪlɪ] adv felicemente, fortunatamente

happiness ['hæpɪnɪs] n felicità, contentezza

happy ['hæpɪ] adj felice, contento(a); ~ with (arrangements etc) soddisfatto(a) di; to be ~ to do (willing) fare volentieri; ~ birthday! buon compleanno!; ~-go-lucky adj spensierato(a)

harangue [hə'ræŋ] vt arringare

harass ['hærəs] vt molestare; ~ment n molestia

harbour ['hɑ:bə*] (US harbor) n porto ♦ vt (hope, fear) nutrire; (criminal) dare rifugio a

hard [hɑ:d] adj duro(a) ♦ adv sodo; (think, try) bene; to look ~ at guardare fissamente; esaminare attentamente; no ~ feelings! senza

hardly rancore!; **to be ~ of hearing** essere duro(a) d'orecchio; **to be ~ done by** essere trattato(a) ingiustamente; **~back** n libro rilegato; **~ cash** n denaro in contanti; **~ disk** n (COMPUT) disco rigido; **~en** vt, vi indurire; **~-headed** adj pratico(a); **~-labour** n lavori forzati mpl

hardly ['hɑːdlı] adv (scarcely) appena; **it's ~ the case** non è proprio il caso; **~ anyone/anywhere** quasi nessuno/da nessuna parte; **~ ever** quasi mai

hardship ['hɑːdʃɪp] n avversità f inv; privazioni fpl

hard-up (inf) adj al verde

hardware ['hɑːdwɛə*] n ferramenta fpl; (COMPUT) hardware m; (MIL) armamenti mpl; **~ shop** n (negozio di ferramenta)

hard-wearing [-'wɛərɪŋ] adj resistente; (shoes) robusto(a)

hard-working [-'wɜːkɪŋ] adj lavoratore(trice)

hardy ['hɑːdɪ] adj robusto(a); (plant) resistente al gelo

hare [hɛə*] n lepre f; **~-brained** adj folle; scervellato(a)

harm [hɑːm] n male m; (wrong) danno ♦ vt (person) fare male a; (thing) danneggiare; **out of ~'s way** al sicuro; **~ful** adj dannoso(a); **~less** adj innocuo(a); inoffensivo(a)

harmonica [hɑː'mɒnɪkə] n armonica

harmonious [hɑː'məunɪəs] adj armonioso(a)

harmony ['hɑːmənɪ] n armonia

harness ['hɑːnɪs] n (for horse) bardatura, finimenti mpl; (for child) briglie fpl; (safety ~) imbracatura ♦ vt (horse) bardare; (resources) sfruttare

harp [hɑːp] n arpa ♦ vi: **to ~ on about** insistere tediosamente su

harpoon [hɑː'puːn] n arpione m

harrowing ['hærəuɪŋ] adj straziante

harsh [hɑːʃ] adj (life, winter) duro(a); (judge, criticism) severo(a); (sound) rauco(a); (light) violento(a)

harvest ['hɑːvɪst] n raccolto; (of grapes) vendemmia ♦ vt fare il raccolto di, raccogliere; vendemmiare

has [hæz] vb see **have**

hash [hæʃ] n (CULIN) specie di spezzatino fatto con carne già cotta; (fig: mess) pasticcio

hashish ['hæʃɪʃ] n hascisc m

hasn't ['hæznt] = **has not**

hassle ['hæsl] (inf) n sacco di problemi

haste [heɪst] n fretta; precipitazione f; **~n** ['heɪsn] vt affrettare ♦ vi: **to ~n** (**to**) affrettarsi (a); **hastily** adv in fretta; precipitosamente; **hasty** adj affrettato(a); precipitoso(a)

hat [hæt] n cappello

hatch [hætʃ] n (NAUT: also: ~way) boccaporto; (also: service ~) portello di servizio ♦ vi (bird) uscire dal guscio; (egg) schiudersi

hatchback ['hætʃbæk] n (AUT) tre (or cinque) porte f inv

hatchet ['hætʃɪt] n accetta

hate [heɪt] vt odiare, detestare ♦ n odio; **~ful** adj odioso(a), detestabile

hatred ['heɪtrɪd] n odio

haughty ['hɔːtɪ] adj altero(a), arrogante

haul [hɔːl] vt trascinare, tirare ♦ n (of fish) pescata; (of stolen goods etc) bottino; **~age** n trasporto; autotrasporto; **~ier** (US ~er) n trasportatore m

haunch [hɔːntʃ] n anca; (of meat) coscia

haunt [hɔːnt] vt (subj: fear) pervadere; (: person) frequentare ♦ n rifugio; **this house is ~ed** questa casa è abitata da un fantasma

---

KEYWORD

have [hæv] (pt, pp **had**) aux vb 1 (gen) avere; essere; **to ~ arrived/gone** essere arrivato(a)/andato(a); **to ~ eaten/slept** avere mangiato/dormito; **he has been kind/promoted** è stato gentile/promosso; **having finished** or **when he had finished, he left** dopo aver finito, se n'è andato

2 (in tag questions): **you've done it, ~n't you?** l'ha fatto, (non è) vero?; **he hasn't done it, has he?** non l'ha fatto, vero?

3 (in short answers and questions): **you've made a mistake — no I ~n't/so I** — ha fatto un errore — ma no, niente affatto/sì, è vero; **we ~n't paid — yes we ~!** non abbiamo pagato — ma sì che abbiamo pagato!; **I've been there before, ~ you?** ci sono già stato, e lei?

♦ modal aux vb (be obliged): **to ~ (got) to do sth** dover fare qc; **I ~n't got or I don't ~ to wear glasses** non ho bisogno di portare gli occhiali

♦ vt **1** (possess, obtain) avere; **he has (got) blue eyes/dark hair** ha gli occhi azzurri/i capelli scuri; **do you ~ or ~ you got a car/phone?** ha la macchina/il telefono?; **may I ~ your address?** potrebbe darmi il suo indirizzo?; **you can ~ it for £5** te lo lascio per 5 sterline

2 (+ noun): take, hold etc): **to ~ breakfast/a swim/a bath** fare colazione/una nuotata/un bagno; **to ~ lunch** pranzare; **to ~ dinner** cenare; **to ~ a drink** bere qc; **to ~ a cigarette** fumare una sigaretta

3: **to ~ sth done** far fare qc; **to ~ one's hair cut** farsi tagliare i capelli; **to ~ sb do sth** far fare qc a qn

4 (experience, suffer) avere; **to ~ a cold/flu** avere il raffreddore/l'influenza; **she had her bag stolen** le hanno rubato la borsa

5 (inf: dupe): **you've been had!** ci sei cascato!

have out vt: **to ~ it out with sb** (settle a problem etc) mettere le cose in chiaro con qn

---

haven ['heɪvn] n porto; (fig) rifugio
haven't ['hævnt] = have not
haversack ['hævəsæk] n zaino
havoc ['hævək] n caos m
hawk [hɔːk] n falco

hay [heɪ] n fieno; **~ fever** n febbre f da fieno; **~stack** n pagliaio
haywire ['heɪwaɪə*] (inf) adj: **to go ~** impazzire
hazard ['hæzəd] n azzardo, ventura; pericolo, rischio ♦ vt (guess etc) azzardare; **~ous** adj pericoloso(a); **~ (warning) lights** npl (AUT) luci fpl di emergenza
haze [heɪz] n foschia
hazelnut ['heɪzlnʌt] n nocciola
hazy ['heɪzɪ] adj fosco(a); (idea) vago/a
he [hiː] pronoun lui, egli; **it is ~ who** ... è lui che ....
head [hed] n testa; (leader) capo; (of school) preside m/f ♦ vt (list) essere in testa a; (group) essere a capo di; **~s (or tails)** testa o croce), pari (o dispari); **~ first** a capofitto, di testa; **~ over heels in love** pazzamente innamorato(a); **to ~ the ball** colpire una palla di testa; **~ for** vt fus dirigersi verso; **~ache** n mal m di testa; **~dress** n (of bride) acconciatura; **~ing** n titolo; intestazione f; **~lamp** (BRIT) n = **~light**; **~land** n promontorio; **~light** n fanale m; **~line** n titolo; **~long** adv (fall) a capofitto; (rush) precipitosamente; **~master/mistress** n preside m/f; **~ office** n sede f (centrale); **~on** adj (collision) frontale; **~phones** npl cuffia; **~quarters** npl ufficio centrale; (MIL) quartiere m generale; **~rest** n poggiacapo; **~room** n (in car) altezza dell'abitacolo; (under bridge) altezza limite; **~scarf** n foulard m inv; **~strong** adj testardo(a); **~waiter** n capocameriere m; **~way** n: **to make ~way** fare progressi; **~wind** n controvento; **~y** adj (experience, period) inebriante

heal [hiːl] vt, vi guarire
health [helθ] n salute f; **~ food(s)** n(pl) alimenti mpl integrali; **the H~ Service** (BRIT) n ≈ il Servizio Sanitario Statale; **~y** adj (person) sano(a), in buona salute; (climate)

salubre; (appetite, economy etc) sano(a)

heap [hi:p] n mucchio ♦ vt (stones, sand): to ~ (up) ammucchiare; (plate, sink): to ~ sth with riempire qc di; ~s of (inf) un mucchio di

hear [hɪə*] (pt, pp heard) vt sentire; (news) ascoltare ♦ vi sentire; to ~ about avere notizie di; sentire parlare di; to ~ from sb ricevere notizie da qn; **heard** [hə:d] pt, pp of hear; ~ing n (sense) udito; (of witnesses) audizione f; (of a case) udienza; ~ing aid n apparecchio acustico; ~say n dicerie fpl, chiacchiere fpl

hearse [hə:s] n carro funebre

heart [hɑ:t] n cuore m; ~s npl (CARDS) cuori mpl; to lose ~ scoraggiarsi; to take ~ farsi coraggio; at ~ in fondo; by ~ (learn, know) a memoria; ~ attack n attacco di cuore; ~beat n battito del cuore; ~breaking adj straziante; ~broken adj: to be ~broken avere il cuore spezzato; ~burn n bruciore m di stomaco; ~ failure n arresto cardiaco; ~felt adj sincero(a)

hearth [hɑ:θ] n focolare m

heartland ['hɑ:tlænd] n regione f centrale

heartless ['hɑ:tlɪs] adj senza cuore

hearty ['hɑ:tɪ] adj caloroso(a); robusto(a), sano(a); vigoroso(a)

heat [hi:t] n calore m; (fig) ardore m; fuoco; (SPORT: also: qualifying ~) prova eliminatoria ♦ vt scaldare; ~ up vi (liquids) scaldarsi; (room) riscaldarsi ♦ vt riscaldare; ~ed adj riscaldato(a); (argument) acceso(a); ~er n radiatore m; (stove) stufa

heath [hi:θ] n (BRIT) n landa

heathen ['hi:ðn] n pagano/a

heather ['hɛðə*] n erica

heating ['hi:tɪŋ] n riscaldamento

heatstroke ['hi:tstrəuk] n colpo di sole

heatwave ['hi:tweɪv] n ondata di caldo

heave [hi:v] vt (pull) tirare (con forza); (push) spingere (con forza); (lift) sollevare (con forza) ♦ vi sollevarsi; (retch) aver conati di vomito ♦ n (push) grande spinta; to ~ a sigh emettere un sospiro

heaven ['hɛvn] n paradiso, cielo; ~ly adj divino(a), celeste

heavily ['hɛvɪlɪ] adv pesantemente; (drink, smoke) molto

heavy ['hɛvɪ] adj pesante; (sea) grosso(a); (rain, blow) forte; (weather) afoso(a); (drinker, smoker) gran (before noun); ~ goods vehicle n veicolo per trasporti pesanti; ~weight n (SPORT) peso massimo

Hebrew ['hi:bru:] adj ebreo(a) ♦ n (LING) ebraico

Hebrides ['hɛbrɪdi:z] npl: the ~ le Ebridi

heckle ['hɛkl] vt interpellare e dare noia a (un oratore)

hectic ['hɛktɪk] adj movimentato(a)

he'd [hi:d] = he would; he had

hedge [hɛdʒ] n siepe f ♦ vi essere elusivo(a); to ~ one's bets (fig) coprirsi dai rischi

hedgehog ['hɛdʒhɔg] n riccio

heed [hi:d] vt (also: take ~ of) badare a, far conto di; ~less adj: ~ (of) sordo(a) (a)

heel [hi:l] n (ANAT) calcagno; (of shoe) tacco ♦ vt (shoe) rifare i tacchi a

hefty ['hɛftɪ] adj (person) robusto(a); (parcel) pesante; (profit) grosso(a)

heifer ['hɛfə*] n giovenca

height [haɪt] n altezza; (high ground) altura; (fig: of glory) apice m; (: of stupidity) colmo; ~en vt (fig) accrescere

heir [ɛə*] n erede m; ~ess n erede f; ~loom n mobile m (or gioiello or quadro) di famiglia

held [hɛld] pt, pp of hold

helicopter ['hɛlɪkɔptə*] n elicottero

heliport ['hɛlɪpɔ:t] n eliporto

helium ['hi:lɪəm] n elio

hell [hɛl] n inferno; ~! (inf) porca miseria!, accidenti!

he'll [hi:l] = he will; he shall

hellish ['hɛlɪʃ] (*inf*) *adj* infernale

hello [hə'ləu] *excl* buon giorno!; ciao! (*to sb one addresses as "tu"*); (*surprise*) ma guarda!

helm [hɛlm] *n* (*NAUT*) timone *m*

helmet ['hɛlmɪt] *n* casco

help [hɛlp] *n* aiuto; (*charwoman*) donna di servizio ♦ *vt* aiutare; ~! aiuto!; ~ **yourself** (**to bread**) si serva (del pane); **he can't** ~ **it** non ci può far niente; ~**er** *n* aiutante *m/f*, assistente *m/f*; ~**ful** *adj* di grande aiuto; (*useful*) utile; ~**ing** *n* porzione *f*; ~**less** *adj* impotente; debole

hem [hɛm] *n* orlo ♦ *vt* fare l'orlo a; ~ **in** *vt* cingere

hemisphere ['hɛmɪsfɪə*] *n* emisfero

hemorrhage ['hɛmərɪdʒ] (*US*) *n* = **haemorrhage**

hemorrhoids ['hɛmərɔɪdz] (*US*) *npl* = **haemorroids**

hen [hɛn] *n* gallina; (*female bird*) femmina

hence [hɛns] *adv* (*therefore*) dunque; 2 **years** ~ di qui a 2 anni; ~**forth** *adv* d'ora in poi

henchman ['hɛntʃmən] (*pej*) *n* caudatario

henpecked ['hɛnpɛkt] *adj* dominato dalla moglie

hepatitis [hɛpə'taɪtɪs] *n* epatite *f*

her [hə:*] *pron* (*direct*) la, l' + *vowel*; (*indirect*) le; (*stressed, after prep*) lei ♦ *adj* il(la) suo(a), i(le) suoi(sue); *see also* **me**; **my**

herald ['hɛrəld] *n* araldo ♦ *vt* annunciare

heraldry ['hɛrəldrɪ] *n* araldica

herb [hə:b] *n* erba

herd [hə:d] *n* mandria

here [hɪə*] *adv* qui, qua ♦ *excl* ehi!; ~! (*at roll call*) presente!; ~ **is/are** ecco; ~ **he/she is** eccolo/eccola; ~**after** *adv* in futuro; dopo questo; ~**by** *adv* (*in letter*) con la presente

hereditary [hɪ'rɛdɪtrɪ] *adj* ereditario(a)

heresy ['hɛrəsɪ] *n* eresia

heretic ['hɛrətɪk] *n* eretico/a

heritage ['hɛrɪtɪdʒ] *n* eredità; (*fig*) retaggio

hermetically [hə:'mɛtɪklɪ] *adv*: ~ **sealed** ermeticamente chiuso(a)

hermit ['hə:mɪt] *n* eremita *m*

hernia ['hə:nɪə] *n* ernia

hero ['hɪərəu] (*pl* ~**es**) *n* eroe *m*

heroin ['hɛrəuɪn] *n* eroina

heroine ['hɛrəuɪn] *n* eroina

heron ['hɛrən] *n* airone *m*

herring ['hɛrɪŋ] *n* aringa

hers [hə:z] *pron* il(la) suo(a), i(le) suoi(sue); *see also* **mine**

herself [hə:'sɛlf] *pron* (*reflexive*) si; (*emphatic*) lei stessa; (*after prep*) se stessa, sé; *see also* **oneself**

he's [hiz] = **he is**; **he has**

hesitant ['hɛzɪtənt] *adj* esitante, indeciso(a)

hesitate ['hɛzɪteɪt] *vi*: **to** ~ (**about/to do**) esitare (su/a fare); **hesitation** [-'teɪʃən] *n* esitazione *f*

heterosexual ['hɛtərəu'sɛksjuəl] *adj*, *n* eterosessuale *m/f*

hew [hju:] *vt* (*stone*) scavare; (*wood*) tagliare

hexagonal [hɛk'sægənəl] *adj* esagonale

heyday ['heɪdeɪ] *n*: **the** ~ **of** i bei giorni di, l'età d'oro di

HGV *n abbr* = **heavy goods vehicle**

hi [haɪ] *excl* ciao!

hiatus [haɪ'eɪtəs] *n* vuoto; (*LING*) iato

hibernate ['haɪbəneɪt] *vi* ibernare

hiccough ['hɪkʌp] *vi* singhiozzare; ~**s** *npl*: **to have** ~**s** avere il singhiozzo

hiccup ['hɪkʌp] = **hiccough**

hid [hɪd] *pt of* **hide**; ~**den** ['hɪdn] *pp of* **hide**

hide [haɪd] (*pt* **hid**, *pp* **hidden**) *n* (*skin*) pelle *f* ♦ *vt*: **to** ~ **sth** (**from sb**) nascondere qc (a qn) ♦ *vi*: **to** ~ (**from sb**) nascondersi (da qn); ~**and-seek** *n* rimpiattino; ~**away** *n* nascondiglio

hideous ['hɪdɪəs] *adj* laido(a); orribile

hiding ['haɪdɪŋ] *n* (*beating*) bastonata; **to be in** ~ (*concealed*) tenersi nascosto(a)

hierarchy ['haɪərɑːkɪ] n gerarchia

hi-fi ['haɪfaɪ] n stereo ♦ adj ad alta fedeltà, hi-fi inv

high [haɪ] adj alto(a); (speed, respect, number) grande; (wind) forte; (voice) acuto(a) ♦ adv alto, in alto; 20m ~ alto(a) 20m; ~brow adj, n intellettuale m/f; ~chair n seggiolone m; ~er education n studi mpl superiori; ~-handed adj prepotente; ~-heeled adj con i tacchi alti; ~ jump n (SPORT) salto in alto; the H~lands npl le Highlands scozzesi; ~light n (fig: of event) momento culminante; (in hair) colpo di sole ♦ vt mettere in evidenza; ~ly adv molto; to speak ~ly of parlare molto bene di; ~ly strung adj teso(a) di nervi, eccitabile; ~ness n: Her H~ness Sua Altezza; ~-pitched adj acuto(a); ~-rise block n palazzone m; ~ school n scuola secondaria; (US) istituto superiore d'istruzione; ~ season (BRIT) n alta stagione; ~ street (BRIT) n strada principale

highway ['haɪweɪ] n strada maestra; H~ Code (BRIT) n codice m della strada

hijack ['haɪdʒæk] vt dirottare; ~er n dirottatore/trice

hike [haɪk] vi fare un'escursione a piedi ♦ n escursione f a piedi; ~r n escursionista f

hilarious [hɪ'lɛərɪəs] adj (behaviour, event) spassosissimo(a)

hill [hɪl] n collina, colle m; (fairly high) montagna; (on road) salita; ~side n fianco della collina; ~y adj collinoso(a); montagnoso(a)

hilt [hɪlt] n (of sword) elsa; to the ~ (fig: support) fino in fondo

him [hɪm] pron (direct) lo, l' + vowel; (indirect) gli; (stressed, after prep) lui; see also me; ~self pron (reflexive) si; (emphatic) lui stesso; (after prep) se stesso, sé; see also oneself

hind [haɪnd] adj posteriore

hinder ['hɪndə*] vt ostacolare; **hindrance** ['hɪndrəns] n ostacolo, impedimento

hindsight ['haɪndsaɪt] n: with ~ con il senno di poi

Hindu ['hɪnduː] n indù m/f inv

hinge [hɪndʒ] n cardine m ♦ vi (fig): to ~ on dipendere da

hint [hɪnt] n (suggestion) allusione f; (advice) consiglio; (sign) accenno ♦ vt: to ~ that lasciar capire che ♦ vi: to ~ at alludere a

hip [hɪp] n anca, fianco

hippopotami [hɪpə'pɔtəmaɪ] npl of **hippopotamus**

hippopotamus [hɪpə'pɔtəməs] (pl ~es or **hippopotami**) n ippopotamo

hire ['haɪə*] vt (BRIT: car, equipment) noleggiare; (worker) assumere, dare lavoro a ♦ n noleggio, nolo; for ~ da nolo; (taxi) libero(a); ~ purchase (BRIT) n acquisto (or vendita) rateale

his [hɪz] adj, pron il(la) suo(sua), i(le) suoi(sue); see also **my**; **mine**

hiss [hɪs] vi fischiare; (cat, snake) sibilare

historic(al) [hɪ'stɔrɪk(l)] adj storico(a)

history ['hɪstərɪ] n storia

hit [hɪt] (pt, pp hit) vt colpire, picchiare; (knock against) battere; (reach: target) raggiungere; (collide with: car) urtare contro; (fig: affect) colpire; (find: problem etc) incontrare ♦ n colpo; (success, song) successo; to ~ it off with sb andare molto d'accordo con qn; ~-and-run driver n pirata m della strada

hitch [hɪtʃ] vt (fasten) attaccare; (also: ~ up) tirare su ♦ n (difficulty) intoppo, difficoltà f inv; to ~ a lift fare l'autostop

hitch-hike vi fare l'autostop; ~r n autostoppista f

hi-tech ['haɪ'tek] adj di alta tecnologia ♦ n alta tecnologia

hitherto [hɪðə'tuː] adv in precedenza

HIV n abbr: HIV-negative/-positive adj sieronegativo(a)/sieropositivo(a)

hive [haɪv] *n* alveare *m*; ~ **off** *vt* separare

H.M.S. *abbr* = His(Her) Majesty's Ship

hoard [hɔːd] *n* (*of food*) provviste *fpl*; (*of money*) gruzzolo ♦ *vt* ammassare

hoarding ['hɔːdɪŋ] (*BRIT*) *n* (*for posters*) tabellone *m* per affissioni

hoarse [hɔːs] *adj* rauco(a)

hoax [həuks] *n* scherzo; falso allarme

hob [hɔb] *n* piastra (con fornelli)

hobble ['hɔbl] *vi* zoppicare

hobby ['hɔbɪ] *n* hobby *m inv*, passatempo; **~-horse** *n* (*fig*) chiodo fisso

hobo ['həubəu] (*US*) *n* vagabondo

hockey ['hɔkɪ] *n* hockey *m*

hoe [həu] *n* zappa

hog [hɔg] *n* maiale *m* ♦ *vt* (*fig*) arraffare; **to go the whole ~** farlo fino in fondo

hoist [hɔɪst] *n* paranco ♦ *vt* issare

hold [həuld] (*pt, pp* held) *vt* tenere; (*contain*) contenere; (*keep back*) trattenere; (*believe*) mantenere; considerare; (*possess*) avere, possedere; detenere ♦ *vi* (*withstand pressure*) tenere; (*be valid*) essere valido(a) ♦ *n* presa; (*control*): **to have a ~ over** avere controllo su; (*NAUT*) stiva; **~ the line!** (*TEL*) resti in linea!; **to ~ one's own** (*fig*) difendersi bene; **to catch** or **get** (**a**) **~ of** afferrare; **~ back** *vt* trattenere; (*secret*) tenere celato(a); **~ down** *vt* (*person*) tenere a terra; (*job*) tenere; **~ off** *vt* tener lontano; **~ on** *vi* tener fermo; (*wait*) aspettare; **~ on!** (*TEL*) resti in linea!; **~ on to** *vt fus* tenersi stretto(a) a; (*keep*) conservare; **~ out** *vt* offrire ♦ *vi* (*resist*) resistere; **~ up** *vt* (*raise*) alzare; (*support*) sostenere; (*delay*) ritardare; (*rob*) assaltare; **~all** (*BRIT*) *n* borsone *m*; **~er** *n* (*container*) contenitore *m*; (*of ticket, title*) possessore/posseditrice; (*of office etc*) incaricato/a; (*of record*) detentore/trice; **~ing** *n* (*share*) azioni *fpl*, titoli *mpl*; (*farm*) podere *m*, tenuta; **~up** *n* (*robbery*) rapina a mano armata; (*delay*) ritardo; (*BRIT: in traffic*) blocco

hole [həul] *n* buco, buca ♦ *vt* bucare

holiday ['hɔlədɪ] *n* vacanza; (*day off*) giorno di vacanza; (*public*) giorno festivo; **on ~** in vacanza; **~ camp** (*BRIT*) *n* (*also:* ~ **centre**) ≈ villaggio (di vacanze); **~-maker** (*BRIT*) *n* villeggiante *m/f*; **~ resort** *n* luogo di villeggiatura

holiness ['həulɪnɪs] *n* santità

Holland ['hɔlənd] *n* Olanda

hollow ['hɔləu] *adj* cavo(a); (*container, claim*) vuoto(a); (*laugh, sound*) cupo(a) ♦ *n* cavità *f inv*; (*in land*) valletta, depressione *f* ♦ *vt*: **~ out** scavare

holly ['hɔlɪ] *n* agrifoglio

holocaust ['hɔləkɔːst] *n* olocausto

holster ['həulstə*] *n* fondina (di pistola)

holy ['həulɪ] *adj* santo(a); (*bread*) benedetto(a), consacrato(a); (*ground*) consacrato(a)

homage ['hɔmɪdʒ] *n* omaggio; **to pay ~** to rendere omaggio a

home [həum] *n* casa; (*country*) patria; (*institution*) casa, ricovero ♦ *cpd* familiare; (*cooking etc*) casalingo(a); (*ECON, POL*) nazionale, interno(a); (*SPORT*) di casa ♦ *adv* a casa; **in patria**; (*right in: nail etc*) fino in fondo; **at ~** a casa; (*in situation*) a proprio agio; **to go** (or **come**) **~** tornare a casa (or in patria); **make yourself at ~** si metta a suo agio; **~ address** *n* indirizzo di casa; **~land** *n* patria; **~less** *adj* senza tetto; spatriato(a); **~ly** *adj* semplice, alla buona; accogliente; **~-made** *adj* casalingo(a); **H~ Office** (*BRIT*) *n* ministero degli Interni; **~ rule** *n* autogoverno; **H~ Secretary** (*BRIT*) *n* ministro degli Interni; **~sick** *adj*: **to be ~sick** avere la nostalgia; **~ town** *n* città *f inv* natale; **~ward** ['həumwəd] *adj* (*journey*) di ritorno; **~work** *n* compiti *mpl* (per casa)

homicide ['homɪsaɪd] *(US)* n omicidio

homogeneous [hɔmǝʊ'dʒiːnɪǝs] *adj* omogeneo(a)

homosexual [hɔmǝʊ'sɛksjuǝl], *adj, n* omosessuale *m/f*

honest ['ɔnɪst] *adj* onesto(a); sincero(a); ~**ly** *adv* onestamente; sinceramente; ~**y** *n* onestà

honey ['hʌnɪ] *n* miele *m*; ~**comb** *n* favo; ~**moon** *n* luna di miele, viaggio di nozze; ~**suckle** *n* (*BOT*) caprifoglio

honk [hɔŋk] *vi* suonare il clacson

honorary ['ɔnǝrǝrɪ] *adj* onorario(a); (*duty, title*) onorifico(a)

honour ['ɔnǝ*] *(US* **honor**) *vt* onorare ♦ *n* onore *m*; ~**able** *adj* onorevole; ~**s degree** *n* (*SCOL*) laurea specializzata

hood [hud] *n* cappuccio; (*on cooker*) cappa; (*BRIT: AUT*) capote *f*; (*US: AUT*) cofano

hoodlum ['huːdlǝm] *n* teppista *m/f*

hoodwink ['hudwɪŋk] *vt* infinocchiare

hoof [huːf] (*pl* **hooves**) *n* zoccolo

hook [huk] *n* gancio; (*for fishing*) amo ♦ *vt* uncinare; (*dress*) agganciare

hooligan ['huːlɪɡǝn] *n* giovinastro, teppista *m*

hoop [huːp] *n* cerchio

hooray [huː'reɪ] *excl* = **hurray**

hoot [huːt] *vi* (*AUT*) suonare il clacson; (*siren*) ululare; (*owl*) gufare; ~**er** *n* (*BRIT: AUT*) clacson *m inv*; (*NAUT*) sirena

hoover ['huːvǝ*] ® (*BRIT*) *n* aspirapolvere *m inv* ♦ *vt* pulire con l'aspirapolvere

hooves [huːvz] *npl of* **hoof**

hop [hɔp] *vi* saltellare, saltare; (*on one foot*) saltare su una gamba

hope [hǝup] *vt, vi* ~ **to/that/to do** sperare che/di fare ♦ *vi* sperare ♦ *n* speranza; **I** ~ **so/not** spero di sì/no; ~**ful** *adj* (*person*) pieno(a) di speranza; (*situation*) promettente; ~**fully** *adv* con speranza; ~**fully he**

will recover speriamo che si riprenda; ~**less** *adj* senza speranza, disperato(a); (*useless*) inutile

hops [hɔps] *npl* luppoli *mpl*

horde [hɔːd] *n* orda

horizon [hǝ'raɪzn] *n* orizzonte *m*; ~**tal** [hɔrɪ'zɔntl] *adj* orizzontale

hormone ['hɔːmǝun] *n* ormone *m*

horn [hɔːn] *n* (*ZOOL, MUS*) corno; (*AUT*) clacson *m inv*

hornet ['hɔːnɪt] *n* calabrone *m*

horny ['hɔːnɪ] (*inf*) *adj* arrapato(a)

horoscope ['hɔrǝskǝup] *n* oroscopo

horrendous [hǝ'rɛndǝs] *adj* orrendo(a)

horrible ['hɔrɪbl] *adj* orribile, tremendo(a)

horrid ['hɔrɪd] *adj* orrido(a); (*person*) odioso(a)

horrify ['hɔrɪfaɪ] *vt* scandalizzare

horror ['hɔrǝ*] *n* orrore *m*; ~ **film** *n* film *m inv* dell'orrore

hors d'oeuvre [ɔː'dǝːvrǝ] *n* antipasto

horse [hɔːs] *n* cavallo; ~**back: on** ~**back** *adj, adv* a cavallo; ~**chestnut** *n* ippocastano; ~**man** *n* cavaliere *m*; ~**power** *n* cavallo (vapore); ~**racing** *n* ippica; ~**radish** *n* rafano; ~**shoe** *n* ferro di cavallo; ~**woman** *n* amazzone *f*

horticulture ['hɔːtɪkʌltʃǝ*] *n* orticoltura

hose [hǝuz] *n* (*also: ~pipe*) tubo; (*also: garden* ~) tubo per annaffiare

hosiery ['hǝuʒǝrɪ] *n* maglieria

hospice ['hɔspɪs] *n* ricovero, ospizio

hospitable [hɔ'spɪtǝbl] *adj* ospitale

hospital ['hɔspɪtl] *n* ospedale *m*

hospitality [hɔspɪ'tælɪtɪ] *n* ospitalità

host [hǝust] *n* ospite *m*; (*REL*) ostia; (*large number*): **a** ~ **of** una schiera di

hostage ['hɔstɪdʒ] *n* ostaggio/a

hostel ['hɔstl] *n* ostello; (*also: youth* ~) ostello della gioventù

hostess ['hǝustɪs] *n* ospite *f*; (*BRIT: air* ~) hostess *f inv*

hostile ['hɔstaɪl] *adj* ostile

hostility [hɔ'stɪlɪtɪ] *n* ostilità *f inv*

hot [hɔt] *adj* caldo(a); (*as opposed to only warm*) molto caldo(a); (*spicy*) piccante; (*fig*) accanito(a); ardente; violento(a), focoso(a); **to be ~** (*person*) aver caldo; (*object*) essere caldo(a); (*weather*) far caldo; **~bed** *n* (*fig*) focolaio; **~ dog** *n* hot dog *m inv*

hotel [həu'tɛl] *n* albergo; **~ier** *n* albergatore/trice

hot: ~headed *adj* focoso(a), eccitabile; **~house** *n* serra; **~ line** *n* (*POL*) telefono rosso; **~ly** *adv* violentemente; **~plate** *n* (*on cooker*) piastra riscaldante; **~water bottle** *n* borsa dell'acqua calda

hound [haund] *vt* perseguitare ♦ *n* segugio

hour ['auə*] *n* ora; **~ly** *adj* all'ora

house [*n* haus, *pl* 'hauziz, *vb* hauz] *n* (*also: firm*) casa; (*POL*) camera; (*THEATRE*) sala; pubblico; spettacolo; (*dynasty*) casata ♦ *vt* (*person*) ospitare, alloggiare; **on the ~** (*fig*) offerto(a) dalla casa; **~ arrest** *n* arresti *mpl* domiciliari; **~boat** *n* house boat *f inv*; **~bound** *adj* confinato(a) in casa; **~breaking** *n* furto con scasso; **~coat** *n* vestaglia; **~hold** *n* famiglia; casa; **~keeper** *n* governante *f*; **~keeping** *n* (*work*) governo della casa; (*money*) soldi *mpl* per le spese di casa; **~warming party** *n* festa per inaugurare la casa nuova; **~wife** *n* massaia, casalinga; **~work** *n* faccende *fpl* domestiche

housing ['hauziŋ] *n* alloggio; **~ development** (*BRIT* = estate) *n* zona residenziale con case popolari e/o private

hovel ['hɔvl] *n* casupola

hover ['hɔvə*] *vi* (*bird*) librarsi; **~craft** *n* hovercraft *m inv*

how [hau] *adv* come; **~ are you?** come sta?; **~ do you do?** piacere!; **~ far is it to the river?** quanto è lontano il fiume?; **~ long have you been here?** da quando è qui?; **~ lovely!/awful!** che bello!/orrore!; **~ many?** quanti(e)?; **~ much?** quanto(a)?; **~ much milk?** quanto latte?; **~ many people?** quante persone?; **~ old are you?** quanti anni ha?; **~ever** *adv* in qualsiasi modo *or* maniera che; (+ *adjective*) per quanto + *sub*; (*in questions*) come ♦ *conj* comunque, però

howl [haul] *vi* ululare; (*baby, person*) urlare

H.P. *abbr* = hire purchase; horsepower

h.p. *n abbr* = H.P

HQ *n abbr* = headquarters

hub [hʌb] *n* (*of wheel*) mozzo; (*fig*) fulcro

hubbub ['hʌbʌb] *n* baccano

hubcap ['hʌbkæp] *n* coprimozzo

huddle ['hʌdl] *vi*: **to ~ together** rannicchiarsi l'uno contro l'altro

hue [hju:] *n* tinta; **~ and cry** *n* clamore *m*

huff [hʌf] *n*: **in a ~** stizzito(a)

hug [hʌg] *vt* abbracciare; (*shore, kerb*) stringere

huge [hju:dʒ] *adj* enorme, immenso(a)

hulk [hʌlk] *n* (*ship*) nave *f* in disarmo; (*building, car*) carcassa; (*person*) mastodonte *m*

hull [hʌl] *n* (*of ship*) scafo

hullo [hə'ləu] *excl* = hello

hum [hʌm] *vt* (*tune*) canticchiare ♦ *vi* canticchiare; (*insect, plane, tool*) ronzare

human ['hju:mən] *adj* umano(a) ♦ *n* essere *m* umano

humane [hju:'meɪn] *adj* umanitario(a)

humanitarian [hju:mænɪ'tɛərɪən] *adj* umanitario(a)

humanity [hju:'mænɪtɪ] *n* umanità

humble ['hʌmbl] *adj* umile, modesto(a) ♦ *vt* umiliare

humbug ['hʌmbʌg] *n* sciocchezze *fpl*; (*BRIT: sweet*) caramella alla menta

humdrum ['hʌmdrʌm] *adj* monotono(a), tedioso(a)

humid ['hju:mɪd] *adj* umido(a)

humiliate [hjuːˈmɪlɪeɪt] *vt* umiliare; **humiliation** [-ˈeɪʃən] *n* umiliazione *f*

humility [hjuːˈmɪlɪtɪ] *n* umiltà

humorous [ˈhjuːmərəs] *adj* umoristico(a); (*person*) buffo(a)

humour [ˈhjuːmə*] (*US* **humor**) *n* umore *m* ♦ *vt* accontentare

hump [hʌmp] *n* gobba; **~backed** *adj*: **~backed bridge** ponte *m* a schiena d'asino

hunch [hʌntʃ] *n* (*premonition*) intuizione *f*; **~back** *n* gobbo(a); **~ed** *adj* incurvato(a)

hundred [ˈhʌndrəd] *num* cento; **~s of** centinaia *fpl* di; **~weight** *n* (*BRIT*) = 50.8 kg; 112 lb; (*US*) = 45.3 kg; 100 lb

hung [hʌŋ] *pt*, *pp* of **hang**

Hungary [ˈhʌŋgərɪ] *n* Ungheria

hunger [ˈhʌŋgə*] *n* fame *f* ♦ *vi*: to **~ for** desiderare ardentemente; **~ strike** *n* sciopero della fame

hungry [ˈhʌŋgrɪ] *adj* affamato(a); (*avid*): **~ for** avido(a) di; **to be ~** aver fame

hunk [hʌŋk] *n* (*of bread etc*) bel pezzo

hunt [hʌnt] *vt* (*seek*) cercare; (*SPORT*) cacciare ♦ *vi*: to **~** (**for**) andare a caccia (di) ♦ *n* caccia; **~er** *n* cacciatore *m*; **~ing** *n* caccia

hurdle [ˈhəːdl] *n* (*SPORT*, *fig*) ostacolo

hurl [həːl] *vt* lanciare con violenza

hurrah [huˈrɑː] *excl* = **hurray**

hurray [huˈreɪ] *excl* urrà!, evviva!

hurricane [ˈhʌrɪkən] *n* uragano

hurried [ˈhʌrɪd] *adj* affrettato(a); (*work*) fatto(a) in fretta; **~ly** *adv* in fretta

hurry [ˈhʌrɪ] *n* fretta ♦ *vi* (*also*: **~ up**) affrettarsi ♦ *vt* (*also*: **~ up**: *person*) affrettare; (: *work*) far in fretta; **to be in a ~** aver fretta

hurt [həːt] (*pt*, *pp* **hurt**) *vt* (*cause pain to*) far male a; (*injure*, *fig*) ferire ♦ *vi* far male; **~ful** *adj* (*remark*) che ferisce

hurtle [ˈhəːtl] *vi*: **to ~ past/down** passare/scendere a razzo

husband [ˈhʌzbənd] *n* marito

hush [hʌʃ] *n* silenzio, calma ♦ *vi* zittire; **~!** zitto(a)!; **~ up** *vt* (*scandal*) mettere a tacere

husk [hʌsk] *n* (*of wheat*) cartoccio; (*of rice, maize*) buccia

husky [ˈhʌskɪ] *adj* roco(a) ♦ *n* cane *m* eschimese

hustle [ˈhʌsl] *vt* spingere, incalzare ♦ *n*: **~ and bustle** trambusto

hut [hʌt] *n* rifugio; (*shed*) ripostiglio

hutch [hʌtʃ] *n* gabbia

hyacinth [ˈhaɪəsɪnθ] *n* giacinto

hybrid [ˈhaɪbrɪd] *n* ibrido

hydrant [ˈhaɪdrənt] *n* (*also*: *fire* **~**) idrante *m*

hydraulic [haɪˈdrɔːlɪk] *adj* idraulico(a)

hydroelectric [haɪdrəʊˈlɛktrɪk] *adj* idroelettrico(a)

hydrofoil [ˈhaɪdrəfɔɪl] *n* aliscafo

hydrogen [ˈhaɪdrədʒən] *n* idrogeno

hyena [haɪˈiːnə] *n* iena

hygiene [ˈhaɪdʒiːn] *n* igiene *f*

hymn [hɪm] *n* inno; cantica

hype [haɪp] (*inf*) *n* campagna pubblicitaria

hypermarket [ˈhaɪpəmɑːkɪt] (*BRIT*) *n* ipermercato

hyphen [ˈhaɪfn] *n* trattino

hypnotism [ˈhɪpnətɪzm] *n* ipnotismo

hypnotize [ˈhɪpnətaɪz] *vt* ipnotizzare

hypocrisy [hɪˈpɒkrɪsɪ] *n* ipocrisia

hypocrite [ˈhɪpəkrɪt] *n* ipocrita *m/f*; **hypocritical** [-ˈkrɪtɪkl] *adj* ipocrita

hypothermia [haɪpəʊˈθəːmɪə] *n* ipotermia

hypotheses [haɪˈpɒθɪsiːz] *npl of* hypothesis

hypothesis [haɪˈpɒθɪsɪs] *n* (*pl* hypotheses) *n* ipotesi *f inv*

hypothetical [haɪpəʊˈθɛtɪkl] *adj* ipotetico(a)

hysterical [hɪˈstɛrɪkl] *adj* isterico(a)

hysterics [hɪˈstɛrɪks] *npl* accesso di isteria; (*laughter*) attacco di riso

I

I [aɪ] *pron* io
ice [aɪs] *n* ghiaccio; (*on road*) gelo; (~ *cream*) gelato ♦ *vt* (*cake*) glassare ♦ *vi* (*also:* ~ *over*) ghiacciare; (*also:* ~ *up*) gelare; ~**berg** *n* iceberg *m inv*; ~**box** *n* (*US*) frigorifero; (*BRIT*) reparto ghiaccio; (*insulated box*) frigo portatile; ~ **cream** *n* gelato; ~ **hockey** *n* hockey *m* su ghiaccio
Iceland ['aɪslənd] *n* Islanda
ice: ~ **lolly** (*BRIT*) *n* ghiacciolo; ~ **rink** *n* pista di pattinaggio; ~ **skating** *n* pattinaggio sul ghiaccio
icicle ['aɪsɪkl] *n* ghiacciolo
icing ['aɪsɪŋ] *n* (*CULIN*) glassa; ~ **sugar** (*BRIT*) *n* zucchero a velo
icy ['aɪsɪ] *adj* ghiacciato(a); (*weather, temperature*) gelido(a)
I'd [aɪd] = **I would; I had**
idea [aɪ'dɪə] *n* idea
ideal [aɪ'dɪəl] *adj* ideale ♦ *n* ideale *m*
identical [aɪ'dentɪkl] *adj* identico(a)
identification [aɪdentɪfɪ'keɪʃən] *n* identificazione *f*; (*means of*) ~ carta d'identità
identify [aɪ'dentɪfaɪ] *vt* identificare
identikit picture [aɪ'dentɪkɪt-] *n* identikit *m inv*
identity [aɪ'dentɪtɪ] *n* identità *f inv*; ~ **card** *n* carta d'identità
idiom ['ɪdɪəm] *n* idioma *m*; (*phrase*) espressione *f* idiomatica
idiot ['ɪdɪət] *n* idiota *m/f*; ~**ic** [-'ɔtɪk] *adj* idiota
idle ['aɪdl] *adj* inattivo(a); (*lazy*) pigro(a), ozioso(a); (*unemployed*) disoccupato(a); (*question, pleasures*) ozioso(a) ♦ *vi* (*engine*) girare al minimo; ~ **away** *vt*: to ~ **away the time** buttar via il tempo
idol ['aɪdl] *n* idolo; ~**ize** *vt* idoleggiare(a)
i.e. *adv abbr* (= *that is*) cioè
if [ɪf] *conj* se; ~ **I were you ...** se fossi in te ..., io al tuo posto ...; ~ **so**

se è così; ~ **not** se no; ~ **only** se solo *or* soltanto
ignite [ɪg'naɪt] *vt* accendere ♦ *vi* accendersi
ignition [ɪg'nɪʃən] *n* (*AUT*) accensione *f*; **to switch on/off the** ~ accendere/spegnere il motore; ~ **key** *n* (*AUT*) chiave *f* dell'accensione
ignorant ['ɪgnərənt] *adj* ignorante; **to be** ~ **of** (*subject*) essere ignorante di; (*events*) essere ignaro(a) di
ignore [ɪg'nɔː] *vt* non tener conto di; (*person, fact*) ignorare
I'll [aɪl] = **I will; I shall**
ill [ɪl] *adj* (*sick*) malato(a); (*bad*) cattivo(a) ♦ *n* male *m* ♦ *adv*: **to speak** *etc* ~ **of sb** parlare *etc* male di qn; **to take** *or* **be taken** ~ ammalarsi; ~**-advised** *adj* (*decision*) poco giudizioso(a); (*person*) mal consigliato(a); ~**-at-ease** *adj* a disagio
illegal [ɪ'liːgl] *adj* illegale
illegible [ɪ'ledʒɪbl] *adj* illeggibile
illegitimate [ɪlɪ'dʒɪtɪmət] *adj* illegittimo(a)
ill-fated [ɪl'feɪtɪd] *adj* nefasto(a)
ill feeling *n* rancore *m*
illiterate [ɪ'lɪtərət] *adj* analfabeta, illetterato(a); (*letter*) scorretto(a)
ill-mannered [ɪl'mænəd] *adj* maleducato(a)
illness ['ɪlnɪs] *n* malattia
ill-treat [ɪl'triːt] *vt* maltrattare
illuminate [ɪ'luːmɪnet] *vt* illuminare; **illumination** [-'neɪʃən] *n* illuminazione *f*; **illuminations** *npl* (*decorative*) luminarie *fpl*
illusion [ɪ'luːʒən] *n* illusione *f*
illustrate ['ɪləstret] *vt* illustrare; **illustration** [-'streɪʃən] *n* illustrazione *f*
ill will *n* cattiva volontà
I'm [aɪm] = **I am**
image ['ɪmɪdʒ] *n* immagine *f*; (*public face*) immagine (pubblica); ~**ry** *n* immagini *fpl*
imaginary [ɪ'mædʒɪnərɪ] *adj* immaginario(a)
imagination [ɪmædʒɪ'neɪʃən] *n* immaginazione *f*, fantasia

imaginative [ɪˈmædʒɪnətɪv] adj immaginoso(a)

imagine [ɪˈmædʒɪn] vt immaginare

imbalance [ɪmˈbæləns] n squilibrio

imbue [ɪmˈbjuː] vt: to ~ sb/sth with permeare qn/qc di

imitate [ˈɪmɪteɪt] vt imitare; **imitation** [‒ˈteɪʃən] n imitazione f

immaculate [ɪˈmækjulət] adj immacolato(a); (dress, appearance) impeccabile

immaterial [ɪməˈtɪərɪəl] adj immateriale, indifferente

immature [ɪməˈtjuə*] adj immaturo(a)

immediate [ɪˈmiːdɪət] adj immediato(a); ~ly adv (at once) subito, immediatamente; ~ly next to proprio accanto a

immense [ɪˈmɛns] adj immenso(a); enorme

immerse [ɪˈməːs] vt immergere

immersion heater [ɪˈməːʃən‒] (BRIT) n scaldaacqua m inv a immersione

immigrant [ˈɪmɪgrənt] n immigrante m/f; immigrato/a

immigration [ɪmɪˈgreɪʃən] n immigrazione f

imminent [ˈɪmɪnənt] adj imminente

immoral [ɪˈmɒrəl] adj immorale

immortal [ɪˈmɔːtl] adj, n immortale m/f

immune [ɪˈmjuːn] adj: ~ (to) immune (da); **immunity** n immunità

imp [ɪmp] n folletto, diavoletto; (child) diavoletto

impact [ˈɪmpækt] n impatto

impair [ɪmˈpɛə*] vt danneggiare

impale [ɪmˈpeɪl] vt infilzare

impart [ɪmˈpaːt] vt (make known) comunicare; (bestow) impartire

impartial [ɪmˈpaːʃl] adj imparziale

impassable [ɪmˈpaːsəbl] adj insuperabile; (road) impraticabile

impassive [ɪmˈpæsɪv] adj impassibile

impatience [ɪmˈpeɪʃəns] n impazienza

impatient [ɪmˈpeɪʃənt] adj impazien-

te; **to get** or **grow** ~ perdere la pazienza

impeccable [ɪmˈpɛkəbl] adj impeccabile

impede [ɪmˈpiːd] vt impedire

impediment [ɪmˈpɛdɪmənt] n impedimento; (also: speech ~) difetto di pronuncia

impending [ɪmˈpɛndɪŋ] adj imminente

imperative [ɪmˈpɛrətɪv] adj imperativo(a); necessario(a), urgente; (voice) imperioso(a) ♦ n (LING) imperativo

imperfect [ɪmˈpəːfɪkt] adj imperfetto(a); (goods etc) difettoso(a) ♦ n (LING: also: ~ tense) imperfetto

imperial [ɪmˈpɪərɪəl] adj imperiale; (measure) legale

impersonal [ɪmˈpəːsənl] adj impersonale

impersonate [ɪmˈpəːsəneɪt] vt impersonare; (THEATRE) fare la mimica di

impertinent [ɪmˈpəːtɪnənt] adj insolente, impertinente

impervious [ɪmˈpəːvɪəs] adj (fig): ~ to insensibile a; impassibile di fronte a

impetuous [ɪmˈpɛtjuəs] adj impetuoso(a), precipitoso(a)

impetus [ˈɪmpətəs] n impeto

impinge on [ɪmˈpɪndʒ‒] vt fus (person) colpire; (rights) ledere

implement [n ˈɪmplɪmənt, vb ˈɪmplɪment] n attrezzo; (for cooking) utensile m ♦ vt effettuare

implicit [ɪmˈplɪsɪt] adj implicito(a); (complete) completo(a)

imply [ɪmˈplaɪ] vt insinuare; suggerire

impolite [ɪmpəˈlaɪt] adj scortese

import [vb ɪmˈpɔːt, n ˈɪmpɔːt] vt importare ♦ n (COMM) importazione f

importance [ɪmˈpɔːtns] n importanza

important [ɪmˈpɔːtnt] adj importante; **it's not** ~ non ha importanza

importer [ɪmˈpɔːtə*] n importatore/trice

impose [ɪm'pəuz] vt imporre ♦ vi:
to ~ on sb sfruttare la bontà di qn

imposing [ɪm'pəuzɪŋ] adj imponente

imposition [ɪmpə'zɪʃən] n (of tax
etc) imposizione f; to be an ~ on
(person) abusare della gentilezza di

impossibility [ɪmpɔsə'bɪlɪtɪ] n impossibilità

impossible [ɪm'pɔsɪbl] adj impossibile

impotent ['ɪmpətənt] adj impotente

impound [ɪm'paund] vt confiscare

impoverished [ɪm'pɔvərɪʃt] adj im-
poverito(a)

impracticable [ɪm'præktɪkəbl] adj
inattuabile

impractical [ɪm'præktɪkl] adj non
pratico(a)

impregnable [ɪm'prɛgnəbl] adj (fortress) inespugnabile

impress [ɪm'prɛs] vt impressionare,
(mark) imprimere, stampare; to ~
sth on sb far capire qc a qn

impression [ɪm'prɛʃən] n impressione f; to be under the ~ that avere
l'impressione che

impressive [ɪm'prɛsɪv] adj notevole

imprint ['ɪmprɪnt] n (of hand etc)
impronta; (PUBLISHING) sigla editoriale

imprison [ɪm'prɪzn] vt imprigionare;
~ment n imprigionamento

improbable [ɪm'prɔbəbl] adj improbabile; (excuse) inverosimile

impromptu [ɪm'prɔmptjuː] adj im-
provvisato(a)

improper [ɪm'prɔpə*] adj scorret-
to(a); (unsuitable) inadatto(a), im-
proprio(a); sconveniente, indecente

improve [ɪm'pruːv] vt migliorare ♦
vi migliorare; (pupil etc) fare progressi; ~ment n miglioramento;
progresso

improvise ['ɪmprəvaɪz] vt, vi improvvisare

impudent ['ɪmpjudnt] adj impudente, sfacciato(a)

impulse ['ɪmpʌls] n impulso; on ~
d'impulso, impulsivamente

impulsive [ɪm'pʌlsɪv] adj impulsi-

vo(a)

KEYWORD

in [ɪn] prep 1 (indicating place, position) in; ~ the house/garden in
casa/giardino; ~ the box nella scatola; ~ the fridge nel frigorifero; I
have it ~ my hand ce l'ho in
mano; ~ town/the country in città/
campagna; ~ school a scuola; ~
here/there qui/lì dentro

2 (with place names: of town, region,
country): ~ London a Londra; ~
England in Inghilterra; ~ the
United States negli Stati Uniti; ~
Yorkshire nello Yorkshire

3 (indicating time: during, in the
space of) in; ~ spring/summer in
primavera/estate; ~ 1988 nel 1988; ~
May in or a maggio; I'll see you ~
July ci vediamo a luglio; ~ the
afternoon nel pomeriggio; at 4
o'clock ~ the afternoon alle 4 del
pomeriggio; I did it ~ 3 hours/days
l'ho fatto in 3 ore/giorni; I'll see you
~ 2 weeks or ~ 2 weeks' time ci
vediamo tra 2 settimane

4 (indicating manner etc) a; ~ a
loud/soft voice a voce alta/bassa; ~
pencil a matita; ~ English/French
in inglese/francese; the boy ~ the
blue shirt il ragazzo con la camicia
blu

5 (indicating circumstances): ~ the
sun al sole; ~ the shade all'ombra;
~ the rain sotto la pioggia; a rise
~ prices un aumento dei prezzi

6 (indicating mood, state): ~ tears
in lacrime; ~ anger per la rabbia;
~ despair disperato(a); ~ good
condition in buono stato, in buone
condizioni; to live ~ luxury vivere
nel lusso

7 (with ratios, numbers): 1 ~ 10 1
su 10; 20 pence ~ the pound 20
pence per sterlina; they lined up ~
twos si misero in fila a due a due

8 (referring to people, works) in; the
disease is common ~ children la
malattia è comune nei bambini; ~

(the works of) Dickens in Dickens **9** (indicating profession etc) in; to be ~ teaching fare l'insegnante, insegnare; to be ~ publishing essere nell'editoria **10** (after superlative) di; the best ~ the class il migliore della classe **11** (with present participle): ~ saying this dicendo questo, nel dire questo

♦ adv: to be ~ (person: at home, work) esserci; (train, ship, plane) essere arrivato(a); (in fashion) essere di moda; to ask sb ~ invitare qn ad entrare; to run/limp etc ~ entrare di corsa/zoppicando etc

♦ n: the ~s and outs of the problem tutti i particolari del problema

in. abbr = inch

inability [ɪnə'bɪlɪtɪ] n: ~ (to do) incapacità (di fare)

inaccurate [ɪn'ækjurət] adj inesatto(a), impreciso(a)

inadequate [ɪn'ædɪkwət] adj insufficiente

inadvertently [ɪnəd'vɜːtntlɪ] adv senza volerlo

inadvisable [ɪnəd'vaɪzəbl] adj consigliabile

inane [ɪ'neɪn] adj vacuo(a), stupido(a)

inanimate [ɪn'ænɪmət] adj inanimato(a)

inappropriate [ɪnə'prəuprɪət] adj non adatto(a); (word, expression) improprio(a)

inarticulate [ɪnɑː'tɪkjulət] adj (person) che si esprime male; (speech) inarticolato(a)

inasmuch [ɪnəz'mʌtʃəz] adv in quanto che; (insofar as) poiché

inaudible [ɪn'ɔːdɪbl] adj che non si riesce a sentire

inauguration [ɪnɔːgju'reɪʃən] n inaugurazione f; insediamento in carica

in-between adj fra i (or le) due

inborn [ɪn'bɔːn] adj innato(a)

inbred [ɪn'bred] adj innato(a); (family) connaturato(a)

Inc. (US) abbr (= incorporated) S.A

incapable [ɪn'keɪpəbl] adj incapace

incapacitate [ɪnkə'pæsɪteɪt] vt: to ~ sb from doing rendere qn incapace di fare

incense [n 'ɪnsens, vb ɪn'sens] n incenso ♦ vt (anger) infuriare

incentive [ɪn'sentɪv] n incentivo

incessant [ɪn'sesnt] adj incessante; ~ly adv di continuo, senza sosta

inch [ɪntʃ] n pollice m (= 25 mm; 12 in a foot); within an ~ of a un pelo da; he didn't give an ~ non ha ceduto di un millimetro; ~ forward vi avanzare pian piano

incidence ['ɪnsɪdns] n (of crime, disease) incidenza

incident ['ɪnsɪdnt] n incidente m; (in book) episodio

incidental [ɪnsɪ'dentl] adj accessorio(a), d'accompagnamento; (unplanned) incidentale; ~ to marginale a; ~ly [-'dentlɪ] adv (by the way) a proposito

inclination [ɪnklɪ'neɪʃən] n inclinazione f

incline [n 'ɪnklaɪn, vb ɪn'klaɪn] n pendenza, pendio ♦ vt inclinare ♦ vi (surface) essere inclinato(a); to be ~d to do tendere a fare; essere propenso(a) a fare

include [ɪn'kluːd] vt includere, comprendere; **including** prep compreso(a), incluso(a)

inclusive [ɪn'kluːsɪv] adj incluso(a), compreso(a); ~ of tax etc tasse etc comprese

incoherent [ɪnkəu'hɪərənt] adj incoerente

income ['ɪnkʌm] n reddito; ~ tax n imposta sul reddito

incoming ['ɪnkʌmɪŋ] adj (flight, mail) in arrivo; (government) subentrante; (tide) montante

incompetent [ɪn'kɒmpɪtnt] adj incompetente, incapace

incomplete [ɪnkəm'pliːt] adj incompleto(a)

incongruous [ɪn'kɒŋgruəs] adj poco appropriato(a); (remark, act) incongruo(a)

inconsiderate [ɪnkən'sɪdərət] *adj* sconsiderato(a)

inconsistency [ɪnkən'sɪstənsɪ] *n* incoerenza

inconsistent [ɪnkən'sɪstənt] *adj* incoerente; ~ **with** non coerente con

inconspicuous [ɪnkən'spɪkjuəs] *adj* incospicuo(a); (*colour*) poco appariscente; (*dress*) dimesso(a)

inconvenience [ɪnkən'viːnjəns] *n* inconveniente *m*; (*trouble*) disturbo ♦ *vt* disturbare

inconvenient [ɪnkən'viːnjənt] *adj* scomodo(a)

incorporate [ɪn'kɔːpəreɪt] *vt* incorporare; (*contain*) contenere; ~**d** *adj*: ~**d company** (*US*) società *f inv* anonima

incorrect [ɪnkə'rɛkt] *adj* scorretto(a); (*statement*) inesatto(a)

increase [*n* 'ɪnkriːs, *vb* ɪn'kriːs] *n* aumento ♦ *vi, vt* aumentare

increasing [ɪn'kriːsɪŋ] *adj* (*number*) crescente; ~**ly** *adv* sempre più

incredible [ɪn'krɛdɪbl] *adj* incredibile

incredulous [ɪn'krɛdjuləs] *adj* incredulo(a)

increment ['ɪnkrɪmənt] *n* aumento, incremento

incriminate [ɪn'krɪmɪneɪt] *vt* compromettere

incubator ['ɪnkjubeɪtə*] *n* incubatrice *f*

incumbent [ɪn'kʌmbənt] *n* titolare *m/f* ♦ *adj*: **to be ~ on sb** spettare a qn

incur [ɪn'kɜː*] *vt* (*expenses*) incorrere; (*anger, risk*) esporsi a; (*debt*) contrarre; (*loss*) subire

indebted [ɪn'dɛtɪd] *adj*: **to be ~ to sb (for)** essere obbligato(a) verso qn (per)

indecent [ɪn'diːsnt] *adj* indecente; ~ **assault** (*BRIT*) *n* aggressione *f* a scopo di violenza sessuale; ~ **exposure** *n* atti *mpl* osceni in luogo pubblico

indecisive [ɪndɪ'saɪsɪv] *adj* indeciso(a)

indeed [ɪn'diːd] *adv* infatti; veramente; **yes ~!** certamente!

indefinite [ɪn'dɛfɪnɪt] *adj* indefinito(a); (*answer*) vago(a); (*period, number*) indeterminato(a); ~**ly** *adv* (*wait*) indefinitamente

indemnity [ɪn'dɛmnɪtɪ] *n* (*insurance*) assicurazione *f*; (*compensation*) indennità, indennizzo

independence [ɪndɪ'pɛndns] *n* indipendenza

independent [ɪndɪ'pɛndnt] *adj* indipendente

index ['ɪndɛks] (*pl* ~**es**) *n* (*in book*) indice *m*; (: *in library etc*) catalogo; (*pl* **indices**: *ratio, sign*) indice *m*; ~ **card** *n* scheda; ~ **finger** *n* (dito) indice *m*; ~**-linked** (*US* ~**ed**) *adj* legato(a) al costo della vita

India ['ɪndɪə] *n* India; ~**n** *adj, n* indiano(a); **Red ~n** pellerossa *m/f*

indicate ['ɪndɪkeɪt] *vt* indicare; **indication** [-'keɪʃən] *n* indicazione *f*, segno

indicative [ɪn'dɪkətɪv] *adj*: ~ **of** indicativo(a) di ♦ *n* (*LING*) indicativo

indicator ['ɪndɪkeɪtə*] *n* indicatore *m*; (*AUT*) freccia

indices ['ɪndɪsiːz] *npl of* **index**

indictment [ɪn'daɪtmənt] *n* accusa

indifference [ɪn'dɪfrəns] *n* indifferenza

indifferent [ɪn'dɪfrənt] *adj* indifferente; (*poor*) mediocre

indigenous [ɪn'dɪdʒɪnəs] *adj* indigeno(a)

indigestion [ɪndɪ'dʒɛstʃən] *n* indigestione *f*

indignant [ɪn'dɪgnənt] *adj*: ~ (**at sth/with sb**) indignato(a) (per qc/contro qn)

indignity [ɪn'dɪgnɪtɪ] *n* umiliazione *f*

indigo ['ɪndɪgəu] *n* indaco

indirect [ɪndɪ'rɛkt] *adj* indiretto(a)

indiscreet [ɪndɪ'skriːt] *adj* indiscreto(a); (*rash*) imprudente

indiscriminate [ɪndɪ'skrɪmɪnət] *adj* indiscriminato(a)

indisputable [ɪndɪ'spjuːtəbl] *adj* incontestabile, indiscutibile

individual [ɪndɪˈvɪdjuəl] n individuo ♦ adj individuale; (characteristic) particolare, originale; ~**ist** n individualista m/f

indoctrination [ɪndɒktrɪˈneɪʃən] n indottrinamento

Indonesia [ɪndəˈniːzɪə] n Indonesia

indoor [ˈɪndɔː*] adj da interno; (plant) d'appartamento; (swimming pool) coperto(a); (sport, games) fatto(a) al coperto; ~**s** [ɪnˈdɔːz] adv all'interno

induce [ɪnˈdjuːs] vt persuadere; (bring about, MED) provocare; ~**ment** n incentivo

indulge [ɪnˈdʌldʒ] vt (whim) compiacere, soddisfare; (child) viziare ♦ vi: to ~ in sth concedersi qc; abbandonarsi a qc; ~**nce** n lusso (che uno si permette); (leniency) indulgenza; ~**nt** adj indulgente

industrial [ɪnˈdʌstrɪəl] adj industriale; (injury) sul lavoro; ~ **action** n azione f rivendicativa; ~ **estate** (BRIT) n zona industriale; ~ **park** (US) n = ~ **estate**

industrious [ɪnˈdʌstrɪəs] adj industrioso(a), assiduo(a)

industry [ˈɪndəstrɪ] n industria; (diligence) operosità

inebriated [ɪˈniːbrɪeɪtɪd] adj ubriaco(a)

inedible [ɪnˈɛdɪbl] adj immangiabile; (poisonous) non commestibile

ineffective [ɪnɪˈfɛktɪv] adj inefficace; incompetente

ineffectual [ɪnɪˈfɛktʃuəl] adj inefficace; incompetente

inefficiency [ɪnɪˈfɪʃənsɪ] n inefficienza

inefficient [ɪnɪˈfɪʃənt] adj inefficiente

inept [ɪˈnɛpt] adj inetto(a)

inequality [ɪnɪˈkwɒlɪtɪ] n ineguaglianza

inescapable [ɪnɪsˈkeɪpəbl] adj inevitabile

inevitable [ɪnˈɛvɪtəbl] adj inevitabile; **inevitably** adv inevitabilmente

inexact [ɪnɪgˈzækt] adj inesatto(a)

inexcusable [ɪnɪksˈkjuːzəbl] adj in-

giustificabile

inexpensive [ɪnɪksˈpɛnsɪv] adj poco costoso(a)

inexperienced [ɪnɪksˈpɪərɪənst] adj inesperto(a), senza esperienza

infallible [ɪnˈfælɪbl] adj infallibile

infamous [ˈɪnfəməs] adj infame

infancy [ˈɪnfənsɪ] n infanzia

infant [ˈɪnfənt] n bambino/a; ~ **school** (BRIT) n scuola elementare (per bambini dall'età di 5 a 7 anni)

infantry [ˈɪnfəntrɪ] n fanteria

infatuated [ɪnˈfætjueɪtɪd] adj: ~ **with** infatuato(a) di

infatuation [ɪnfætjuˈeɪʃən] n infatuazione f

infect [ɪnˈfɛkt] vt infettare; ~**ion** [ɪnˈfɛkʃən] n infezione f; ~**ious** [ɪnˈfɛkʃəs] adj (disease) infettivo(a), contagioso(a); (person, fig: enthusiasm) contagioso(a)

infer [ɪnˈfəː*] vt inferire, dedurre

inferior [ɪnˈfɪərɪə*] adj inferiore; (goods) di qualità scadente ♦ n inferiore m/f; (in rank) subalterno/a; ~**ity** [ɪnfɪərɪˈɒrɪtɪ] n inferiorità; ~**ity complex** n complesso di inferiorità

inferno [ɪnˈfəːnəu] n rogo

infertile [ɪnˈfəːtaɪl] adj sterile

in-fighting [ˈɪnfaɪtɪŋ] n lotte fpl intestine

infiltrate [ˈɪnfɪltreɪt] vt infiltrarsi in

infinite [ˈɪnfɪnɪt] adj infinito(a)

infinitive [ɪnˈfɪnɪtɪv] n infinito

infinity [ɪnˈfɪnɪtɪ] n infinità; (also MATH) infinito

infirmary [ɪnˈfəːmərɪ] n ospedale m; (in school, factory) infermeria

infirmity [ɪnˈfəːmɪtɪ] n infermità f inv

inflamed [ɪnˈfleɪmd] adj infiammato(a)

inflammable [ɪnˈflæməbl] adj infiammabile

inflammation [ɪnfləˈmeɪʃən] n infiammazione f

inflatable [ɪnˈfleɪtəbl] adj gonfiabile

inflate [ɪnˈfleɪt] vt (tyre, balloon) gonfiare; (fig) esagerare; gonfiare; **inflation** [ɪnˈfleɪʃən] n (ECON) inflazione *f*; **inflationary** [ɪnˈfleɪʃnərɪ] *adj* inflazionistico(a)

inflict [ɪnˈflɪkt] *vt*: to ~ on infliggere a

influence [ˈɪnfluəns] *n* influenza ♦ *vt* influenzare; **under the** ~ **of alcohol** sotto l'effetto dell'alcool

influential [ɪnfluˈɛnʃl] *adj* influente

influenza [ɪnfluˈɛnzə] *n* (*MED*) influenza

influx [ˈɪnflʌks] *n* afflusso

inform [ɪnˈfɔːm] *vt*: to ~ **sb** (**of**) informare qn (di) ♦ *vi*: to ~ **on sb** denunciare qn

informal [ɪnˈfɔːml] *adj* informale; (*announcement, invitation*) non ufficiale; (*meeting*) ~ **ity** [-ˈmælɪtɪ] *n* informalità; carattere *m* non ufficiale

informant [ɪnˈfɔːmənt] *n* informatore/trice

information [ɪnfəˈmeɪʃən] *n* informazioni *fpl*; particolari *mpl*; **a piece of** ~ un'informazione; ~ **office** *m* ufficio *m* informazioni *inv*

informative [ɪnˈfɔːmətɪv] *adj* istruttivo(a)

informer [ɪnˈfɔːmə*] *n* (*also*: **police** ~) informatore/trice

infringe [ɪnˈfrɪndʒ] *vt* infrangere ♦ *vi*: to ~ **on** calpestare; ~ **ment** *n* infrazione *f*

infuriating [ɪnˈfjuərɪeɪtɪŋ] *adj* molto irritante

ingenious [ɪnˈdʒiːnjəs] *adj* ingegnoso(a)

ingenuity [ɪndʒɪˈnjuːɪtɪ] *n* ingegnosità

ingenuous [ɪnˈdʒɛnjuəs] *adj* ingenuo(a)

ingot [ˈɪŋɡət] *n* lingotto

ingrained [ɪnˈɡreɪnd] *adj* radicato(a)

ingratiate [ɪnˈɡreɪʃɪeɪt] *vt*: to ~ **o.s. with sb** ingraziarsi qn

ingredient [ɪnˈɡriːdɪənt] *n* ingrediente *m*; elemento

inhabit [ɪnˈhæbɪt] *vt* abitare

inhabitant [ɪnˈhæbɪtnt] *n* abitante *m/f*

inhale [ɪnˈheɪl] *vt* inalare ♦ *vi* (*in smoking*) aspirare

inherent [ɪnˈhɪərənt] *adj*: ~ (**in** *or* **to**) inerente (a)

inherit [ɪnˈhɛrɪt] *vt* ereditare; ~ **ance** *n* eredità

inhibit [ɪnˈhɪbɪt] *vt* (*PSYCH*) inibire; ~ **ion** [-ˈbɪʃən] *n* inibizione *f*

inhospitable [ɪnhɔsˈpɪtəbl] *adj* inospitale

inhuman [ɪnˈhjuːmən] *adj* inumano(a)

initial [ɪˈnɪʃl] *adj* iniziale ♦ *n* iniziale *f* ♦ *vt* siglare; ~ **s** *npl* (*of name*) iniziali *fpl*; (*as signature*) sigla; ~ **ly** *adv* inizialmente, all'inizio

initiate [ɪˈnɪʃɪeɪt] *vt* (*start*) avviare; intraprendere; iniziare; (*person*) iniziare; to ~ **sb into a secret** mettere qn a parte di un segreto; to ~ **proceedings against sb** (*LAW*) intentare causa contro qn

initiative [ɪˈnɪʃətɪv] *n* iniziativa

inject [ɪnˈdʒɛkt] *vt* (*liquid*) iniettare; (*patient*): to ~ **sb with sth** fare a qn un'iniezione di; (*funds*) immettere; ~ **ion** [ɪnˈdʒɛkʃən] *n* iniezione *f*, puntura

injure [ˈɪndʒə*] *vt* ferire; (*damage: reputation etc*) nuocere a; ~ **d** *adj* ferito(a)

injury [ˈɪndʒərɪ] *n* ferita; ~ **time** *n* (*SPORT*) tempo di recupero

injustice [ɪnˈdʒʌstɪs] *n* ingiustizia

ink [ɪŋk] *n* inchiostro

inkling [ˈɪŋklɪŋ] *n* sentore *m*, vaga idea

inlaid [ˈɪnleɪd] *adj* incrostato(a); (*table etc*) intarsiato(a)

inland [*adj* ˈɪnlənd, *adv* ɪnˈlænd] *adj* interno(a) ♦ *adv* all'interno; **I**~ **Revenue** (*BRIT*) *n* Fisco

in-laws [ˈɪnlɔːz] *npl* suoceri *mpl*; famiglia del marito (*or* della moglie)

inlet [ˈɪnlɛt] *n* (*GEO*) insenatura, baia

inmate [ˈɪnmeɪt] *n* (*in prison*) carcerato/a; (*in asylum*) ricoverato/a

inn [ɪn] *n* locanda

innate [ɪˈneɪt] *adj* innato(a)

inner [ˈɪnə*] *adj* interno(a), interiore; ~ **city** *n* centro di una zona urbana; ~ **tube** n camera d'aria

innings ['ɪnɪŋz] n (CRICKET) turno di battuta

innocence ['ɪnəsns] n innocenza

innocent ['ɪnəsnt] adj innocente

innocuous [ɪ'nɔkjuəs] adj innocuo(a)

innuendo [ɪnju'ɛndəʊ] (pl ~es) n insinuazione f

innumerable [ɪ'njuːmrəbl] adj innumerevole

inordinately [ɪ'nɔːdɪnɪtlɪ] adv smoderatamente

in-patient n ricoverato/a

input ['ɪnput] n input m

inquest ['ɪnkwɛst] n inchiesta

inquire [ɪn'kwaɪə*] vi informarsi ♦ vt domandare, informarsi su; ~ **about** vt fus informarsi di or su; ~ **into** vt fus fare indagini su; inquiry n domanda; (LAW) indagine f, investigazione f; **inquiry office** (BRIT) n ufficio m informazioni inv

inquisitive [ɪn'kwɪzɪtɪv] adj curioso(a)

inroads ['ɪnrəʊdz] npl: **to make** ~ **into** (savings etc) intaccare (seriamente)

ins. abbr = **inches**

insane [ɪn'seɪn] adj matto(a), pazzo(a); (MED) alienato(a).

insanity [ɪn'sænɪtɪ] n follia; (MED) alienazione f mentale

inscription [ɪn'skrɪpʃən] n iscrizione f; dedica

inscrutable [ɪn'skruːtəbl] adj imperscrutabile

insect ['ɪnsɛkt] n insetto m; ~icide [ɪn'sɛktɪsaɪd] n insetticida m

insecure [ɪnsɪ'kjuə*] adj malsicuro(a); (person) insicuro(a)

insemination [ɪnsɛmɪ'neɪʃən] n: artificial ~ fecondazione f artificiale

insensible [ɪn'sɛnsɪbl] adj (unconscious) privo(a) di sensi

insensitive [ɪn'sɛnsɪtɪv] adj insensibile

insert [ɪn'səːt] vt inserire, introdurre; ~**ion** [ɪn'səːʃən] n inserzione f

in-service adj (training, course) durante l'orario di lavoro

inshore [ɪn'fɔː*] adj costiero(a) ♦ adv presso la riva; verso la riva

inside [ɪn'saɪd] n interno, parte f interiore ♦ adj interno(a), interiore ♦ adv dentro, all'interno ♦ prep dentro, all'interno di; (of time): ~ 10 minutes entro 10 minuti; ~s npl (inf: stomach) ventre m; ~ **forward** n (SPORT) mezzala, interno; ~ **lane** n (AUT) corsia di marcia; ~ **out** adv (turn) a rovescio; (know) in fondo

insider dealing [ɪn'saɪdə'diːlɪŋ] n insider dealing m inv

insider trading [ɪn'saɪdə'treɪdɪŋ] n insider trading m inv

insight ['ɪnsaɪt] n acume m, perspicacia; (glimpse, idea) percezione f

insignia [ɪn'sɪgnɪə] npl insegne fpl

insignificant [ɪnsɪg'nɪfɪknt] adj insignificante

insincere [ɪnsɪn'sɪə*] adj insincero(a)

insinuate [ɪn'sɪnjueɪt] vt insinuare

insist [ɪn'sɪst] vi insistere; to ~ on doing insistere per fare; to ~ that insistere perché + sub; (claim) sostenere che; ~**ent** adj insistente

insole [ɪn'səʊl] n soletta

insolent ['ɪnsələnt] adj insolente

insomnia [ɪn'sɔmnɪə] n insonnia

inspect [ɪn'spɛkt] vt ispezionare; (BRIT: ticket) controllare; ~**ion** [ɪn'spɛkʃən] n ispezione f; controllo; ~**or** n ispettore/trice; (BRIT: on buses, trains) controllore m

inspire [ɪn'spaɪə*] vt ispirare

install [ɪn'stɔːl] vt installare; ~**ation** [ɪnstə'leɪʃən] n installazione f

instalment [ɪn'stɔːlmənt] (US installment) n rata; (of TV serial etc) puntata; in ~s (pay) a rate; (receive) una parte per volta; (: publication) a fascicoli

instance ['ɪnstəns] n esempio, caso; for ~ per or ad esempio; in the first ~ in primo luogo

instant ['ɪnstənt] n istante m, attimo ♦ adj immediato(a); urgente; (cof-

fee, food) in polvere; **~ly** *adv* immediatamente, subito

instead [ɪn'sted] *adv* invece; **~ of** invece di

instep ['ɪnstep] *n* collo del piede; (*of shoe*) collo della scarpa

instil [ɪn'stɪl] *vt*: **to ~ (into)** inculcare (in)

instinct ['ɪnstɪŋkt] *n* istinto

institute ['ɪnstɪtjuːt] *n* istituto ♦ *vt* istituire, stabilire; (*inquiry*) avviare; (*proceedings*) iniziare

institution [ɪnstɪ'tjuːʃən] *n* istituzione *f*; (*educational ~, mental ~*) istituto

instruct [ɪn'strʌkt] *vt*: **to ~ sb in sth** insegnare qc a qn; **to ~ sb to do** dare ordini a qn di fare; **~ion** [ɪn'strʌkʃən] *n* istruzione *f*; **~ions** (*for use*) istruzioni per l'uso; **~or** *n* istruttore/trice; (*for skiing*) maestro/a

instrument ['ɪnstrəmənt] *n* strumento; **~al** [-'mentl] *adj* (MUS) strumentale; **to be ~al in** essere d'aiuto in; **~ panel** *n* quadro *m* portastrumenti *inv*

insufferable [ɪn'sʌfərəbl] *adj* insopportabile

insufficient [ɪnsə'fɪʃənt] *adj* insufficiente

insular ['ɪnsjulə*] *adj* insulare; (*person*) di mente ristretta

insulate ['ɪnsjuleɪt] *vt* isolare; **insulating tape** *n* nastro isolante; **insulation** [-'leɪʃən] *n* isolamento

insulin ['ɪnsjulɪn] *n* insulina

insult [*n* 'ɪnsʌlt, *vb* ɪn'sʌlt] *n* insulto, affronto ♦ *vt* insultare; **~ing** *adj* offensivo(a), ingiurioso(a)

insuperable [ɪn'sjuːprəbl] *adj* insormontabile, insuperabile

insurance [ɪn'ʃuərəns] *n* assicurazione *f*; **fire/life ~** assicurazione contro gli incendi/sulla vita; **~ policy** *n* polizza d'assicurazione

insure [ɪn'ʃuə*] *vt* assicurare

intact [ɪn'tækt] *adj* intatto(a)

intake ['ɪnteɪk] *n* (TECH) immissione *f*; (*of food*) consumo; (BRIT: *of pu-*

pils etc) afflusso

integral ['ɪntɪgrəl] *adj* integrale; (*part*) integrante

integrate ['ɪntɪgreɪt] *vt* integrare ♦ *vi* integrarsi

integrity [ɪn'tegrɪtɪ] *n* integrità

intellect ['ɪntəlekt] *n* intelletto; **~ual** [-'lektjuəl] *adj*, *n* intellettuale *m/f*

intelligence [ɪn'telɪdʒəns] *n* intelligenza; (MIL *etc*) informazioni *fpl*; **~ service** *n* servizio segreto

intelligent [ɪn'telɪdʒənt] *adj* intelligente

intend [ɪn'tend] *vt* (*gift etc*): **to ~ sth for** destinare qc a; **to ~ to do** aver l'intenzione di fare; **~ed** *adj* (*effect*) voluto(a)

intense [ɪn'tens] *adj* intenso(a); (*person*) di forti sentimenti; **~ly** *adv* intensamente; profondamente

intensive [ɪn'tensɪv] *adj* intensivo(a); **~ care unit** *n* reparto terapia intensiva

intent [ɪn'tent] *n* intenzione *f* ♦ *adj*: **~ (on)** intento(a) (a), immerso(a) (in); **to all ~s and purposes** a tutti gli effetti; **to be ~ on doing sth** essere deciso a fare qc

intention [ɪn'tenʃən] *n* intenzione *f*; **~al** *adj* intenzionale, deliberato(a); **~ally** *adv* apposta

intently [ɪn'tentlɪ] *adv* attentamente

interact [ɪntər'ækt] *vi* interagire

interactive *adj* (COMPUT) interattivo(a)

interchange ['ɪntətʃeɪndʒ] *n* (*exchange*) scambio; (*on motorway*) incrocio pluridirezionale; **~able** [-'tʃeɪndʒəbl] *adj* intercambiabile

intercom ['ɪntəkɒm] *n* interfono

intercourse ['ɪntəkɔːs] *n* rapporti *mpl*

interest ['ɪntrɪst] *n* interesse *m*; (COMM: *stake, share*) interessi *mpl* ♦ *vt* interessare; **~ed** *adj* interessato(a); **to be ~ed in** interessarsi di; **~ing** *adj* interessante; **~ rate** *n* tasso di interesse

interface ['ɪntəfeɪs] *n* (COMPUT) interfaccia

interfere [ɪntə'fɪə*] vi: to ~ in (quarrel, other people's business) immischiarsi in; to ~ with (object) toccare; (plans, duty) interferire con
interference [ɪntə'fɪərəns] n interferenza
interim ['ɪntərɪm] adj provvisorio(a) ♦ n: in the ~ nel frattempo
interior [ɪn'tɪərɪə*] n interno; (of country) entroterra ♦ adj interno(a); (minister) degli Interni; ~ **designer** n arredatore/trice
interlock [ɪntə'lɔk] vi ingranarsi
interloper ['ɪntələupə*] n intruso/a
interlude ['ɪntəlu:d] n intervallo; (THEATRE) intermezzo
intermarry [ɪntə'mærɪ] vi fare un matrimonio misto
intermediate [ɪntə'mi:dɪət] adj intermedio(a)
intermission [ɪntə'mɪʃən] n pausa; (THEATRE, CINEMA) intermissione f, intervallo
intern [vb ɪn'tə:n, n 'ɪntə:n] vt internare ♦ n (US) medico interno
internal [ɪn'tə:nl] adj interno(a); ~ly adv "not to be taken ~ly" "per uso esterno"; I~ **Revenue Service** (US) n Fisco
international [ɪntə'næʃənl] adj internazionale ♦ n (BRIT: SPORT) incontro internazionale
interplay ['ɪntəpleɪ] n azione e reazione f
interpret [ɪn'tə:prɪt] vt interpretare ♦ vi fare da interprete; ~er n interprete m/f
interrelated [ɪntərɪ'leɪtɪd] adj correlato(a)
interrogate [ɪn'terəugeɪt] vt interrogare; **interrogation** [-'geɪʃən] n interrogazione f; (of suspect etc) interrogatorio; **interrogative** [ɪntə'rɔgətɪv] adj interrogativo(a)
interrupt [ɪntə'rʌpt] vt, vi interrompere; ~**ion** [-'rʌpʃən] n interruzione f
intersect [ɪntə'sekt] vi (roads) incrociarsi; ~**ion** [-'sekʃən] n intersezione f; (of roads) incrocio

intersperse [ɪntə'spə:s] vt: to ~ with costellare di
intertwine [ɪntə'twaɪn] vi intrecciarsi
interval ['ɪntəvl] n intervallo; at ~s a intervalli
intervene [ɪntə'vi:n] vi (time) intercorrere; (event, person) intervenire; **intervention** [-'venʃən] n intervento
interview ['ɪntəvju:] n (RADIO, TV etc) intervista; (for job) colloquio ♦ vt intervistare; avere un colloquio con; ~er n intervistatore/trice
intestine [ɪn'testɪn] n intestino
intimacy ['ɪntɪməsɪ] n intimità
intimate [adj 'ɪntɪmət, vb ɪn'tɪmeɪt] adj intimo(a); (knowledge) profondo(a) ♦ vt lasciar capire
into ['ɪntu:] prep dentro, in; come ~ the house entra in casa; he worked late ~ the night lavorò fino a tarda notte; ~ Italian in italiano
intolerable [ɪn'tɔlərəbl] adj intollerabile
intolerance [ɪn'tɔlərns] n intolleranza
intolerant [ɪn'tɔlərnt] adj: ~ of intollerante di
intoxicated [ɪn'tɔksɪkeɪtɪd] adj inebriato(a)
intoxication [ɪntɔksɪ'keɪʃən] n ebbrezza
intractable [ɪn'træktəbl] adj intrattabile
intransitive [ɪn'trænsɪtɪv] adj intransitivo(a)
intravenous [ɪntrə'vi:nəs] adj endovenoso(a)
in-tray n contenitore m per la corrispondenza in arrivo
intricate ['ɪntrɪkət] adj intricato(a), complicato(a)
intrigue [ɪn'tri:g] n intrigo ♦ vt affascinare; **intriguing** adj affascinante
intrinsic [ɪn'trɪnsɪk] adj intrinseco(a)
introduce [ɪntrə'dju:s] vt introdurre; to ~ sb (to sb) presentare qn (a qn); to ~ sb to (pastime, technique) iniziare qn a; **introduction** [-'dʌkʃən] n introduzione f; (of person)

presentazione f; (to new experience) iniziazione f; **introductory** adj introduttivo(a)

intrude [ɪn'truːd] vi (person): to ~ (on) intromettersi (in); ~**r** n intruso/a

intuition [ɪntjuː'ɪʃən] n intuizione f

inundate ['ɪnʌndeɪt] vt: to ~ with inondare di

invade [ɪn'veɪd] vt invadere

invalid [n 'ɪnvəlɪd, adj ɪn'vælɪd] n malato/a; (with disability) invalido/a ♦ adj (not valid) invalido(a), non valido(a)

invaluable [ɪn'væljuəbl] adj prezioso(a); inestimabile

invariably [ɪn'vɛərɪəblɪ] adv invariabilmente; sempre

invasion [ɪn'veɪʒən] n invasione f

invent [ɪn'vɛnt] vt inventare; ~**ion** [ɪn'vɛnʃən] n invenzione f; ~**ive** adj inventivo(a); ~**or** n inventore m

inventory ['ɪnvəntrɪ] n inventario

invert [ɪn'vɜːt] vt invertire; (cup, object) rovesciare; ~**ed commas** (BRIT) npl virgolette fpl

invest [ɪn'vɛst] vt investire ♦ vi: to ~ (in) investire (in)

investigate [ɪn'vɛstɪgeɪt] vt investigare, indagare; (crime) fare indagini su; **investigation** [-'geɪʃən] n investigazione f; (of crime) indagine f

investment [ɪn'vɛstmənt] n investimento

investor [ɪn'vɛstə*] n investitore/trice; azionista m/f

invidious [ɪn'vɪdɪəs] adj odioso(a); (task) spiacevole

invigilator [ɪn'vɪdʒɪleɪtə*] n (in exam) sorvegliante m/f

invigorating [ɪn'vɪgəreɪtɪŋ] adj stimolante; vivificante

invisible [ɪn'vɪzɪbl] adj invisibile

invitation [ɪnvɪ'teɪʃən] n invito

invite [ɪn'vaɪt] vt invitare; (opinions etc) sollecitare; **inviting** adj invitante, attraente

invoice ['ɪnvɔɪs] n fattura ♦ vt fatturare

involuntary [ɪn'vɔləntrɪ] adj involon-

tario(a)

involve [ɪn'vɔlv] vt (entail) richiedere, comportare; (associate): to ~ sb (in) implicare qn (in); coinvolgere qn (in); ~**d** adj involuto(a), complesso(a); **to be ~d in** essere coinvolto(a) in; ~**ment** n implicazione f; coinvolgimento

inward ['ɪnwəd] adj (movement) verso l'interno; (thought, feeling) interiore, intimo(a); ~(**s**) adv verso l'interno

I/O abbr (COMPUT: = input/output) I/O

iodine ['aɪəudiːn] n iodio

iota [aɪ'əutə] n (fig) briciolo

IOU n abbr (= I owe you) pagherò m inv

IQ n abbr (= intelligence quotient) quoziente m d'intelligenza

IRA n abbr (= Irish Republican Army) IRA f

Iran [ɪ'rɑːn] n Iran m; ~**ian** adj, n iraniano(a)

Iraq [ɪ'rɑːk] n Iraq m; ~**i** adj, n iracheno(a)

irate [aɪ'reɪt] adj adirato(a)

Ireland ['aɪələnd] n Irlanda f

iris ['aɪrɪs] (pl ~es) n iride f; (BOT) giaggiolo, iride

Irish ['aɪrɪʃ] adj irlandese ♦ npl: the ~ gli Irlandesi; ~**man** n irlandese m; ~ **Sea** n Mar m d'Irlanda; ~**woman** n irlandese f

irksome ['əːksəm] adj seccante

iron ['aɪən] n ferro; (for clothes) ferro da stiro ♦ adj di or in ferro ♦ vt (clothes) stirare; ~ **out** vt (crease) appianare; (fig) spianare; far sparire; **the I~ Curtain** n la cortina di ferro

ironic(al) [aɪ'rɔnɪk(l)] adj ironico(a)

ironing ['aɪənɪŋ] n (act) stirare m; (clothes) roba da stirare; ~ **board** n asse f da stiro

ironmonger's (shop) ['aɪənmʌŋgə-] (BRIT) n negozio di ferramenta

irony ['aɪrənɪ] n ironia

irrational [ɪ'ræʃənl] adj irrazionale

irregular [ɪˈrɛgjulə*] adj irregolare

irrelevant [ɪˈrɛləvənt] adj non pertinente

irreplaceable [ɪrɪˈpleɪsəbl] adj insostituibile

irrepressible [ɪrɪˈprɛsbl] adj irrefrenabile

irresistible [ɪrɪˈzɪstɪbl] adj irresistibile

irrespective [ɪrɪˈspɛktɪv]: ~ **of** prep senza riguardo a

irresponsible [ɪrɪˈspɒnsɪbl] adj irresponsabile

irrigate [ˈɪrɪgeɪt] vt irrigare; **irrigation** [-ˈgeɪʃən] n irrigazione f

irritable [ˈɪrɪtəbl] adj irritabile

irritate [ˈɪrɪteɪt] vt irritare; **irritating** adj (person, sound etc) irritante; **irritation** [-ˈteɪʃən] n irritazione f

IRS (US) n abbr = Internal Revenue Service

is [ɪz] vb see be

Islam [ˈɪzlɑːm] n Islam m

island [ˈaɪlənd] n isola; ~**er** n isolano/a

isle [aɪl] n isola

isn't [ˈɪznt] = is not

isolate [ˈaɪsəleɪt] vt isolare; ~**d** adj isolato/a; **isolation** [-ˈleɪʃən] n isolamento

Israel [ˈɪzreɪl] n Israele m; ~**i** [ɪzˈreɪlɪ] adj, n israeliano(a)

issue [ˈɪsjuː] n questione f, problema m; (of banknotes etc) emissione f; (of newspaper etc) numero ♦ vt (statement) rilasciare; (book) pubblicare; (banknotes, cheques, stamps) emettere; **at** ~ in gioco, in discussione; **to take** ~ **with sb (over sth)** prendere posizione contro qn (riguardo a qc); **to make an** ~ **of sth** fare un problema di qc

isthmus [ˈɪsməs] n istmo

KEYWORD

it [ɪt] pron **1** (specific: subject) esso(a); (: direct object) lo(la), l'; (: indirect object) gli(le); **where's my book? — ~'s on the table**

dov'è il mio libro? — è sulla tavola; **I can't find** ~ non lo (or la) trovo; **give** ~ **to me** dammelo (or dammela); **about/from/of** ~ ne; **I spoke to him about** ~ gliene ho parlato; **what did you learn from** ~? quale insegnamento ne hai tratto?; **I'm proud of** ~ ne sono fiero; **did you go to** ~? ci sei andato?; **put the book in** ~ metticilo il libro

2 (impers): ~'s **raining** piove; ~'s **Friday tomorrow** domani è venerdì; ~'s **6 o'clock** sono le 6; **who is** ~? — ~'s **me** chi è? — sono io

Italian [ɪˈtæljən] adj italiano(a) ♦ n italiano/a; (LING) italiano; **the** ~s gli Italiani

italics [ɪˈtælɪks] npl corsivo

Italy [ˈɪtəlɪ] n Italia

itch [ɪtʃ] n prurito ♦ vi (person) avere il prurito; (part of body) prudere; **to** ~ **to do sth** aver una gran voglia di fare qc; ~**y** adj che prude; **to be** ~**y** = **to** ~

it'd [ˈɪtd] = **it would**; **it had**

item [ˈaɪtəm] n articolo; (on agenda) punto; (also: news ~) notizia; ~**ize** vt specificare, dettagliare

itinerant [ɪˈtɪnərənt] adj ambulante

itinerary [aɪˈtɪnərərɪ] n itinerario

it'll [ˈɪtl] = **it will**; **it shall**

its [ɪts] adj il(la) suo(a), i(le) suoi(sue)

it's [ɪts] = **it is**; **it has**

itself [ɪtˈsɛlf] pron (emphatic) esso(a) stesso(a); (reflexive) si

ITV (BRIT) n abbr = Independent Television) rete televisiva in concorrenza con la BBC

I.U.D. n abbr (= intra-uterine device) spirale f

I've [aɪv] = **I have**

ivory [ˈaɪvərɪ] n avorio

ivy [ˈaɪvɪ] n edera

J

jab [dʒæb] *vt* dare colpetti a ♦ *n* (*MED*: *inf*) puntura; **to ~ sth into** affondare *or* piantare qc dentro

jack [dʒæk] *n* (*AUT*) cricco; (*CARDS*) fante *m*; **~ up** *vt* sollevare col cricco

jackal ['dʒækl] *n* sciacallo

jackdaw ['dʒækdɔː] *n* taccola

jacket ['dʒækɪt] *n* giacca; (*of book*) copertura

jack-knife *vi*: **the lorry ~d** l'autotreno si è piegato su se stesso

jack plug *n* (*ELEC*) jack *m inv*

jackpot ['dʒækpɔt] *n* primo premio (in denaro)

jade [dʒeɪd] *n* (*stone*) giada

jaded ['dʒeɪdɪd] *adj* sfinito(a), spossato(a)

jagged ['dʒægɪd] *adj* seghettato(a); (*cliffs etc*) frastagliato(a)

jail [dʒeɪl] *n* prigione *f* ♦ *vt* mandare in prigione

jam [dʒæm] *n* marmellata; (*also*: *traffic* **~**) ingorgo; (*inf*) pasticcio ♦ *vt* (*passage etc*) ingombrare, ostacolare; (*mechanism, drawer etc*) bloccare; (*RADIO*) disturbare con interferenze ♦ *vi* incepparsi; **to ~ sth into** forzare qc dentro; infilare qc a forza dentro

Jamaica [dʒəˈmeɪkə] *n* Giamaica

jangle ['dʒæŋgl] *vi* risuonare; (*bracelet*) tintinnare

janitor ['dʒænɪtə*] *n* (*caretaker*) portiere *m*; (: *SCOL*) bidello

January ['dʒænjuəri] *n* gennaio

Japan [dʒəˈpæn] *n* Giappone *m*; **~ese** [dʒæpəˈniːz] *adj* giapponese ♦ *n inv* giapponese *m/f*; (*LING*) giapponese *m*

jar [dʒɑː*] *n* (*glass*) barattolo, vasetto ♦ *vi* (*sound*) stridere; (*colours etc*) stonare

jargon ['dʒɑːgən] *n* gergo

jasmin(e) ['dʒæzmɪn] *n* gelsomino

jaundice ['dʒɔːndɪs] *n* itterizia; **~d** *adj* (*fig*) cupo(a)

jaunt [dʒɔːnt] *n* gita; **~y** *adj* vivace, disinvolto(a)

javelin ['dʒævlɪn] *n* giavellotto

jaw [dʒɔː] *n* mascella

jay [dʒeɪ] *n* ghiandaia

jaywalker ['dʒeɪwɔːkə*] *n* pedone(a) indisciplinato(a)

jazz [dʒæz] *n* jazz *m*; **~ up** *vt* rendere vivace

jealous ['dʒeləs] *adj* geloso(a); **~y** *n* gelosia

jeans [dʒiːnz] *npl* (blue-)jeans *mpl*

jeer [dʒɪə*] *vi*: **to ~ (at)** fischiare; beffeggiare

jelly ['dʒelɪ] *n* gelatina; **~fish** *n* inv medusa

jeopardy ['dʒepədɪ] *n*: **in ~** in pericolo

jerk [dʒɜːk] *n* sobbalzo, scossa; sussulto; (*inf*: *idiot*) tonto(a) ♦ *vt* dare una scossa a ♦ *vi* (*vehicles*) sobbalzare

jerkin ['dʒɜːkɪn] *n* giubbotto

jersey ['dʒɜːzɪ] *n* maglia; (*fabric*) jersey *m*

jest [dʒest] *n* scherzo

Jesus ['dʒiːzəs] *n* Gesù *m*

jet [dʒet] *n* (*of gas, liquid*) getto; (*AVIAT*) aviogetto; **~-black** *adj* nero(a) come l'ebano, corvino(a); **~ engine** *n* motore *m* a reazione; **~ lag** *n* (problemi *mpl* dovuti allo) sbalzo dei fusi orari

jettison ['dʒetɪsn] *vt* gettare in mare

jetty ['dʒetɪ] *n* molo

Jew [dʒuː] *n* ebreo

jewel ['dʒuːəl] *n* gioiello; **~ler** (*US* **~er**) *n* orefice *m*, gioielliere(a); **~(l)er's (shop)** *n* oreficeria, gioielleria; **~lery** (*US* **~ery**) *n* gioielli *mpl*

Jewess ['dʒuːɪs] *n* ebrea

Jewish ['dʒuːɪʃ] *adj* ebreo(a), ebraico(a)

jibe [dʒaɪb] *n* beffa

jiffy ['dʒɪfɪ] (*inf*) *n*: **in a ~** in un batter d'occhio

jig [dʒɪg] *n* giga

jigsaw ['dʒɪgsɔː] *n* (*also*: **~ puzzle**) puzzle *m inv*

jilt [dʒɪlt] vt piantare in asso

jingle ['dʒɪŋgl] n (for advert) sigla pubblicitaria ♦ vi tintinnare, scampanellare

jinx [dʒɪŋks] n iettatura; (person) iettatore/trice

jitters ['dʒɪtəz] (inf) npl: to get the ~ aver fifa

job [dʒɔb] n lavoro; (employment) impiego, posto; it's not my ~ (duty) non è compito mio; it's a good ~ that ... meno male che ...; just the ~! proprio quello che ci vuole; ~ **centre** (BRIT) n ufficio di collocamento; ~**less** adj senza lavoro, disoccupato(a)

jockey ['dʒɔkɪ] n fantino, jockey m inv ♦ vi: to ~ for position manovrare per una posizione di vantaggio

jocular ['dʒɔkjulə*] adj gioviale, scherzoso(a)

jog [dʒɔg] vt urtare ♦ vi (SPORT) fare footing, fare jogging; to ~ sb's memory rinfrescare la memoria a qn; to ~ along trottare; (fig) andare avanti piano piano; ~**ging** n footing m, jogging m

join [dʒɔɪn] vt unire, congiungere; (become member of) iscriversi a; (meet) raggiungere; riunirsi a ♦ vi (roads, rivers) confluire ♦ vt fus unirsi a; ~ **in** vi partecipare ♦ vt fus unirsi a, ~ **up** vi incontrarsi; (MIL) arruolarsi

joiner ['dʒɔɪnə*] (BRIT) n falegname m

joint [dʒɔɪnt] n (TECH) giuntura; giunto; (ANAT) articolazione f, giuntura; (BRIT: CULIN) arrosto; (inf: place) locale m; (: of cannabis) spinello ♦ adj comune; ~ **account** n (at bank etc) conto in partecipazione, conto comune

joist [dʒɔɪst] n trave f

joke [dʒəuk] n scherzo; (funny story) barzelletta; (also: practical ~) beffa ♦ vi scherzare; to play a ~ on sb fare uno scherzo a qn; ~**r** n (CARDS) matta, jolly m inv

jolly ['dʒɔlɪ] adj allegro(a), gioioso(a) ♦ adv (BRIT: inf) veramente, proprio

jolt [dʒəult] n scossa, sobbalzo ♦ vt urtare

Jordan ['dʒɔːdən] n (country) Giordania; (river) Giordano

jostle ['dʒɔsl] vt spingere coi gomiti

jot [dʒɔt] n: not one ~ nemmeno un po'; ~ **down** vt annotare in fretta, buttare giù; ~**ter** (BRIT) n blocco

journal ['dʒəːnl] n giornale m; rivista; diario; ~**ism** n giornalismo; ~**ist** n giornalista m/f

journey ['dʒəːnɪ] n viaggio; (distance covered) tragitto

joy [dʒɔɪ] n gioia; ~**ful** adj gioioso(a), allegro(a); ~**rider** n chi ruba un'auto per farsi un giro; ~**stick** n (AVIAT) barra di comando; (COMPUT) joystick m inv

JP n abbr = **Justice of the Peace**

Jr abbr = **junior**

jubilant ['dʒuːbɪlnt] adj giubilante, trionfante

jubilee ['dʒuːbɪliː] n giubileo; **silver** ~ venticinquesimo anniversario

judge [dʒʌdʒ] n giudice m/f ♦ vt giudicare; **judg(e)ment** n giudizio

judicial [dʒuːˈdɪʃl] adj giudiziale, giudiziario(a)

judiciary [dʒuːˈdɪʃɪərɪ] n magistratura

judo ['dʒuːdəu] n judo

jug [dʒʌg] n brocca, bricco

juggernaut ['dʒʌgənɔːt] (BRIT) n (huge truck) bestione m

juggle ['dʒʌgl] vi fare giochi di destrezza; ~**r** n giocoliere/a

Jugoslav etc ['juːgəuslɑːv] = **Yugoslav** etc

juice [dʒuːs] n succo

juicy ['dʒuːsɪ] adj succoso(a)

jukebox ['dʒuːkbɔks] n juke-box m inv

July [dʒuːˈlaɪ] n luglio

jumble ['dʒʌmbl] n miscuglio ♦ vt (also: ~ **up**) mischiare; ~ **sale** (BRIT) n vendita di oggetti in beneficenza

jumbo (jet) ['dʒʌmbəu-] n jumbo-jet m

m inv

jump [dʒʌmp] *vi* saltare, balzare; *(start)* sobbalzare; *(increase)* rincarare ♦ *vt* saltare ♦ *n* salto, balzo; sobbalzo

jumper ['dʒʌmpə*] *n (BRIT: pullover)* maglione *m*, pullover *m inv*; *(US: dress)* scamiciato; **~ cables** *(US) npl* = **jump leads**

jump leads *(BRIT) npl* cavi *mpl* per batteria

jumpy ['dʒʌmpi] *adj* nervoso(a), agitato(a)

Jun. *abbr* = **junior**

junction ['dʒʌŋkʃən] *n (BRIT: of roads)* incrocio; *(of rails)* nodo ferroviario

juncture ['dʒʌŋktʃə*] *n*: **at this ~** in questa congiuntura

June [dʒuːn] *n* giugno

jungle ['dʒʌŋgl] *n* giungla

junior ['dʒuːniə*] *adj, n*: **he's ~ to me (by 2 years)**, **he's my ~ (by 2 years)** è più giovane di me (di 2 anni); **he's ~ to me** *(seniority)* è al di sotto di me, ho più anzianità di lui; **~ school** *(BRIT)* n scuola elementare *(da 8 a 11 anni)*

junk [dʒʌŋk] *n* cianfrusaglie *fpl*; *(cheap goods)* robaccia; **~ food** *n* porcherie *fpl*

junkie ['dʒʌŋki] *(inf) n* drogato/a

junk mail *n* stampe *fpl* pubblicitarie

junk shop *n* chincaglieria

Junr *abbr* = **junior**

juror ['dʒuərə*] *n* giurato/a

jury ['dʒuəri] *n* giuria

just [dʒʌst] *adj* giusto(a) ♦ *adv*: **he's ~ done it/left** lo ha appena fatto/è appena partito; **~ right** proprio giusto; **~ 2 o'clock** le 2 precise; **she's ~ as clever as you** è in gamba proprio quanto te; **it's ~ as well that ...** meno male che ...; **~ as I arrived** proprio mentre arrivavo; **it was ~ before/enough/here** era poco prima/appena assai/proprio qui; **it's ~ me** sono solo io; **~ missed/caught** appena perso/preso; **~ listen to this!** senta un po' questo!

justice ['dʒʌstis] *n* giustizia; **J~ of the Peace** *n* giudice *m* conciliatore

justify ['dʒʌstifai] *vt* giustificare

jut [dʒʌt] *vi (also: ~ out)* sporgersi

juvenile ['dʒuːvənail] *adj* giovanile, giovanile; *(court)* dei minorenni; *(books)* per ragazzi ♦ *n* giovane *m/f*, minorenne *m/f*

juxtapose ['dʒʌkstəpəuz] *vt* giustapporre

K

K *abbr (= one thousand)* mille; *(= kilobyte)* K

Kampuchea [kæmpu'tʃiə] *n* Cambogia

kangaroo [kæŋgə'ruː] *n* canguro

karate [kə'rɑːti] *n* karatè *m*

kebab [kə'bæb] *n* spiedino

keel [kiːl] *n* chiglia; **on an even ~** *(fig)* in uno stato normale

keen [kiːn] *adj (interest, desire)* vivo(a); *(eye, intelligence)* acuto(a); *(competition)* serrato(a); *(edge)* affilato(a); *(eager)* entusiasta; **to be ~ to do** *or* **on doing sth** avere una gran voglia di fare qc; **to be ~ on sth** essere appassionato(a) di qc; **to be ~ on sb** avere un debole per qn

keep [kiːp] *(pt, pp* **kept**) *vt* tenere; *(hold back)* trattenere; *(feed: one's family etc)* mantenere, sostentare; *(a promise)* mantenere; *(chickens, bees, pigs etc)* allevare ♦ *vi (food)* mantenersi; *(remain: in a certain state or place)* restare ♦ *n (of castle)* maschio; *(food etc)*: **enough for his ~** abbastanza per vitto e alloggio; *(inf)*: **for ~s** per sempre; **to ~ doing sth** continuare a fare qc; fare qc di continuo; **to ~ sb from doing sth** impedire a qn di fare; **to ~ sb busy/a place tidy** tenere qn occupato(a)/un luogo in ordine; **to ~ sth to o.s.** tenere qc per sé; **to ~ sth (back) from sb** celare qc a qn; **to ~ time** *(clock)* andar bene; **on ~** *vi*: **to ~ on doing** continuare a fare; **to ~ on (about sth)** continuare a insistere (su qc); **~ out** vt tener fuori; **"~ out"** "vietato l'accesso"; **~ up** vt continuare, mantenere ♦ vi: **to ~ up with** tener dietro a, andare di pari passo con; (work etc) farcela a seguire; **~er** n custode m/f, guardiano/a; **~-fit** n ginnastica; **~ing** n (care) custodia; **in ~ing with** in armonia con; in accordo con; **~sake** n ricordo

kennel ['kɛnl] n canile m; **to put a dog in ~s** mettere un cane al canile

kept [kɛpt] pt, pp of **keep**

kerb [kɔ:b] (BRIT) n orlo del marciapiede

kernel ['kɔ:nl] n nocciolo

kettle ['kɛtl] n bollitore m

kettle drum n timpano

key [ki:] n (gen, MUS) chiave f; (of piano, typewriter) tasto ♦ adj chiave inv ♦ vt (also: **~ in**) digitare; **~board** n tastiera; **~ed up** adj (person) agitato(a); **~hole** n buco della serratura; **~note** n (MUS) tonica; (fig) nota dominante; **~ ring** n portachiavi m inv

khaki ['kɑ:ki] adj cachi ♦ n cachi m

kick [kik] vt calciare, dare calci a; (inf: habit etc) liberarsi di ♦ vi (horse) tirar calci ♦ n calcio; (thrill): **he does it for ~s** lo fa giusto per il piacere di farlo; **~ off** vi (SPORT) dare il primo calcio

kid [kid] n (inf: child) ragazzino/a; (animal, leather) capretto ♦ vi (inf) scherzare

kidnap ['kidnæp] vt rapire, sequestrare; **~per** n rapitore/trice; **~ping** n sequestro (di persona)

kidney ['kidni] n (ANAT) rene m; (CULIN) rognone m

kill [kil] vt uccidere, ammazzare ♦ n uccisione f; **~er** n uccisore m, killer m inv; assassino/a; **~ing** n assassinio; **to make a ~ing** (inf) fare un bel colpo; **~joy** n guastafeste m/f inv

kiln [kiln] n forno

kilo ['ki:ləu] n chilo; **~byte** n (COM-**PUT**) kilobyte m inv; **~gram(me)** ['kiləugræm] n chilogrammo; **~metre** ['kiləmi:tə*] (US **~meter**) n chilometro; **~watt** ['kiləuwɔt] n chilowatt m inv

kilt [kilt] n gonnellino scozzese

kin [kin] n see **next**; **kith**

kind [kaind] adj gentile, buono(a) ♦ n sorta, specie f; (species) genere m; **to be two of a ~** essere molto simili; **in ~** (COMM) in natura

kindergarten ['kindəgɑ:tn] n giardino d'infanzia

kind-hearted [-'hɑ:tid] adj di buon cuore

kindle ['kindl] vt accendere, infiammare

kindly ['kaindli] adj pieno(a) di bontà, benevolo(a) ♦ adv con bontà, gentilmente; **will you ~ ...** vuole ... per favore

kindness ['kaindnis] n bontà, gentilezza

kindred ['kindrid] adj: **~ spirit** spirito affine

king [kiŋ] n re m inv; (CARDS, CHESS) re m, reame m; **~dom** n regno, reame m; **~fisher** n martin m inv pescatore; **~-size** adj super inv; gigante

kinky ['kiŋki] (pej) adj eccentrico(a); dai gusti particolari

kiosk ['ki:ɔsk] n edicola, chiosco; (BRIT: TEL) cabina (telefonica)

kipper ['kipə*] n aringa affumicata

kiss [kis] n bacio ♦ vt baciare; **to ~ (each other)** baciarsi; **~ of life** n respirazione f bocca a bocca

kit [kit] n equipaggiamento, corredo; (set of tools etc) attrezzi mpl; (for assembly) scatola di montaggio

kitchen ['kitʃin] n cucina; **~ sink** n acquaio

kite [kait] n (toy) aquilone m

kith [kiθ] n: **~ and kin** amici e parenti mpl

kitten ['kitn] n gattino/a, micino/a

kitty ['kiti] n (money) fondo comune

knack [næk] n: **to have the ~ of** avere l'abilità di

knapsack ['næpsæk] n zaino, sacco

da montagna

knead [niːd] *vt* impastare

knee [niː] *n* ginocchio; **~cap** *n* rotula

kneel [niːl] (*pt, pp* **knelt**) *vi* (*also: ~ down*) inginocchiarsi; **knelt** [nɛlt] *pt, pp of* **kneel**

knew [njuː] *pt of* **know**

knickers [ˈnɪkəz] (*BRIT*) *npl* mutandine *fpl*

knife [naɪf] (*pl* **knives**) *n* coltello ♦ *vt* accoltellare, dare una coltellata a

knight [naɪt] *n* cavaliere *m*; (*CHESS*) cavallo; **~hood** (*BRIT*) *n* (*title*): **to get a ~hood** essere fatto cavaliere

knit [nɪt] *vt* fare a maglia ♦ *vi* lavorare a maglia; (*broken bones*) saldarsi; **to ~ one's brows** aggrottare le sopracciglia; **~ting** *n* lavoro a maglia; **~ting machine** *n* macchina per maglieria; **~ting needle** *n* ferro (da calza); **~wear** *n* maglieria

knives [naɪvz] *npl of* **knife**

knob [nɔb] *n* bottone *m*; manopola

knock [nɔk] *vt* colpire; urtare; (*fig: inf*) criticare ♦ *vi* (*at door etc*): **to ~ at/on** bussare a ♦ *n* bussata; colpo, botta; **~ down** *vt* abbattere; **~ off** *vi* (*inf: finish*) smettere (di lavorare) ♦ *vt* (*from price*) far abbassare; (*inf: steal*) sgraffignare; **~ out** *vt* stendere; (*BOXING*) mettere K.O.; (*defeat*) battere; **~ over** *vt* (*person*) investire; (*object*) far cadere; **~er** *n* (*on door*) battente *m*; **~out** *n* (*BOXING*) knock out *m inv* ♦ *cpd* a eliminazione

knot [nɔt] *n* nodo ♦ *vt* annodare; **~ty** *adj* (*fig*) spinoso(a)

know [nəu] (*pt* **knew**, *pp* **known**) *vt* sapere; (*person, author, place*) conoscere; **to ~ how to swim** sapere nuotare; **to ~ about** *or* **of sth/sb** conoscere qc/qn; **~-all** *n* sapientone(a); **~-how** *n* tecnica; pratica; **~ing** *adj* (*look etc*) d'intesa; **~ingly** *adv* (*purposely*) consapevolmente; (*smile, look*) con aria d'intesa

knowledge [ˈnɔlɪdʒ] *n* consapevolez-

za; (*learning*) conoscenza, sapere *m*; **~able** *adj* ben informato(a)

known [nəun] *pp of* **know**

knuckle [ˈnʌkl] *n* nocca

Koran [kɔˈrɑːn] *n* Corano

Korea [kəˈrɪə] *n* Corea

kosher [ˈkəuʃə*] *adj* kasher *inv*

L

L (*BRIT*) *abbr* = **learner driver**

lab [læb] *n abbr* (= *laboratory*) laboratorio

label [ˈleɪbl] *n* etichetta, cartellino; (*brand: of record*) casa ♦ *vt* etichettare

labor *etc* [ˈleɪbə*] (*US*) = **labour** *etc*

laboratory [ləˈbɔrətəri] *n* laboratorio

labour [ˈleɪbə*] (*US* **labor**) *n* (*task*) lavoro; (*workmen*) manodopera; (*MED*): **to be in ~** avere le doglie ♦ *vi*: **to ~ (at)** lavorare duro (a); **L~**, **the L~ party** (*BRIT*) il partito laburista, i laburisti; **hard ~** lavori *mpl* forzati; **~ed** *adj* (*breathing*) affannoso(a); **~er** *n* manovale *m*; **farm ~er** *n* lavoratore *m* agricolo

lace [leɪs] *n* merletto, pizzo; (*of shoe etc*) laccio ♦ *vt* (*shoe: also: ~ up*) allacciare

lack [læk] *n* mancanza ♦ *vt* mancare di; **through** *or* **for ~ of** per mancanza di; **to be ~ing** mancare; **to be ~ing in** mancare di

lackadaisical [lækəˈdeɪzɪkl] *adj* disinteressato(a), noncurante

lacquer [ˈlækə*] *n* lacca

lad [læd] *n* ragazzo, giovanotto

ladder [ˈlædə*] *n* scala; (*BRIT: in tights*) smagliatura

laden [ˈleɪdn] *adj*: **~ (with)** carico(a) *or* caricato(a) (di)

ladle [ˈleɪdl] *n* mestolo

lady [ˈleɪdɪ] *n* signora; dama; **L~ Smith** lady Smith; **the ladies' (room)** i gabinetti per signore; **~bird** (*US* **~bug**) *n* coccinella; **~like** *adj* da signora, distinto(a); **~ship** *n*: **your ~ship** signora contessa (or baronessa etc)

lag [læg] n (of time) lasso, intervallo ♦ vi (also: ~ **behind**) trascinarsi ♦ vt (pipes) rivestire di materiale isolante

lager ['lɑːgə*] n lager m inv

lagoon [lə'guːn] n laguna

laid [leɪd] pt, pp of **lay**; ~ **back** (inf) adj rilassato(a), tranquillo(a); ~ **up** adj: ~ **up (with)** costretto(a) a letto (da)

lain [leɪn] pp of **lie**

lair [lɛə*] n covo, tana

lake [leɪk] n lago

lamb [læm] n agnello

lame [leɪm] adj zoppo(a); (excuse etc) zoppicante

lament [lə'ment] n lamento ♦ vt lamentare, piangere

laminated ['læmɪneɪtɪd] adj laminato(a)

lamp [læmp] n lampada

lamppost ['læmppəust] (BRIT) n lampione m

lampshade ['læmpʃeɪd] n paralume m

lance [lɑːns] n lancia ♦ vt (MED) incidere

land [lænd] n (as opposed to sea) terra (ferma); (country) paese m; (soil) terreno; suolo; (estate) terreni mpl, terre fpl ♦ vi (from ship) sbarcare; (AVIAT) atterrare; (fig: fall) cadere ♦ vt (passengers) sbarcare; (goods) scaricare; **to ~ sb with sth** affibbiare qc a qn; ~ **up** vi andare a finire; ~**fill site** n discarica; ~**ing** n atterraggio; (of staircase) pianerottolo; ~**ing gear** n carrello di atterraggio; ~**ing strip** n pista di atterraggio; ~**lady** n padrona or proprietaria di casa; ~**locked** adj senza sbocco sul mare; ~**lord** n padrone m or proprietario di casa; (of pub etc) padrone m; ~**mark** n punto di riferimento; (fig) pietra miliare; ~**owner** n proprietario a terriero(a)

landscape ['lænskeɪp] n paesaggio

landslide ['lændslaɪd] n (GEO) fra-

na; (fig: POL) valanga

lane [leɪn] n stradina; (AUT, in race) corsia

language ['læŋgwɪdʒ] n lingua; (way one speaks) linguaggio; **bad** ~ linguaggio volgare; ~ **laboratory** n laboratorio linguistico

languid ['læŋgwɪd] adj languido(a)

lank [læŋk] adj (hair) liscio(a) e opaco(a)

lanky ['læŋkɪ] adj allampanato(a)

lantern ['læntn] n lanterna

lap [læp] n (of track) giro; (of body): **in** or **on one's** ~ in grembo ♦ vt (also: ~ **up**) papparsi, leccare ♦ vi (waves) sciabordare; ~ **up** vt (fig) bearsi di

lapel [lə'pel] n risvolto

Lapland ['læplænd] n Lapponia

lapse [læps] n lapsus m inv; (longer) caduta ♦ vi (law) cadere; (membership, contract) scadere; **to** ~ **into bad habits** pigliare cattive abitudini; ~ **of time** spazio di tempo

laptop (computer) ['læp,tɔp-] n laptop m inv

larceny ['lɑːsənɪ] n furto

larch [lɑːtʃ] n larice m

lard [lɑːd] n lardo

larder ['lɑːdə*] n dispensa

large [lɑːdʒ] adj grande; (person, animal) grosso(a); **at** ~ (free) in libertà; (generally) in generale; nell'insieme; ~**ly** adv in gran parte

largesse [lɑː'ʒɛs] n generosità

lark [lɑːk] n (bird) allodola; (joke) scherzo, gioco; ~ **about** vi fare lo stupido

laryngitis [lærɪn'dʒaɪtɪs] n laringite f

laser ['leɪzə*] n laser m; ~ **printer** n stampante f laser inv

lash [læʃ] n frustata; (also: eye~) ciglio ♦ vt frustare; (tie): **to** ~ **to/ together** legare a, insieme; ~ **out** vi: **to** ~ **out** (at or against sb) attaccare violentemente (qn)

lass [læs] n ragazza

lasso [læ'suː] n laccio

last [lɑːst] adj ultimo(a); (week, month, year) scorso(a), passato(a) ♦

adv per ultimo ♦ *vi* durare; ~ **week** la settimana scorsa; ~ **night** ieri sera, la notte scorsa; at ~ finalmente, alla fine; ~ **but one** penultimo(a); ~**-ditch** *adj* (*attempt*) estremo(a); ~**ing** *adj* durevole; ~**ly** *adv* infine, per finire; ~**-minute** *adj* fatto(a) (*or* preso/a *etc*) all'ultimo momento

latch [lætʃ] *n* chiavistello

late [leɪt] *adj* (*not on time*) in ritardo; (*far on in day etc*) tardi *inv*; tardo(a); (*former*) ex; (*dead*) defunto(a) ♦ *adv* tardi; (*behind time, schedule*) in ritardo; of ~ di recente; in the ~ afternoon nel tardo pomeriggio; in ~ May verso la fine di maggio; ~**comer** *n* ritardatario/a; ~**ly** *adv* recentemente

later [ˈleɪtə*] *adj* (*date etc*) posteriore; (*version etc*) successivo(a) ♦ *adv* più tardi; ~ **on** più avanti

lateral [ˈlætərl] *adj* laterale

latest [ˈleɪtɪst] *adj* ultimo(a), più recente; at the ~ al più tardi

lathe [leɪð] *n* tornio

lather [ˈlɑːðə*] *n* schiuma di sapone ♦ *vt* insaponare

Latin [ˈlætɪn] *n* latino ♦ *adj* latino(a); ~ **America** *n* America Latina; ~**-American** *adj*, *n* sudamericano/a

latitude [ˈlætɪtjuːd] *n* latitudine *f*; (*fig*) libertà d'azione

latter [ˈlætə*] *adj* secondo(a); più recente ♦ *n*: the ~ quest'ultimo, il secondo; ~**ly** *adv* recentemente, negli ultimi tempi

lattice [ˈlætɪs] *n* traliccio; graticolato

laudable [ˈlɔːdəbl] *adj* lodevole

laugh [lɑːf] *n* risata ♦ *vi* ridere; ~ **at** *vi fus* (*misfortune etc*) ridere di; ~ **off** *vt* prendere alla leggera; ~**able** *adj* ridicolo(a); ~**ing stock** *n*: the ~**ing stock** of lo zimbello di; ~**ter** *n* riso; risate *fpl*

launch [lɔːntʃ] *n* (*of rocket, COMM*) lancio; (*of new ship*) varo; (*also: motor* ~) lancia ♦ *vt* (*rocket, COMM*) lanciare; (*ship, plan*) varare; ~ **into** *vt fus* lanciarsi in;

~(**ing**) **pad** *n* rampa di lancio

launder [ˈlɔːndə*] *vt* lavare e stirare

launderette [lɔːnˈdrɛt] (*BRIT*) *n* lavanderia (automatica)

laundromat [ˈlɔːndrəmæt] (*US*: ®) *n* lavanderia automatica

laundry [ˈlɔːndrɪ] *n* lavanderia; (*clothes*) biancheria; (: *dirty*) panni *mpl* da lavare

laureate [ˈlɔːrɪət] *adj see* **poet**

laurel [ˈlɔrl] *n* lauro

lava [ˈlɑːvə] *n* lava

lavatory [ˈlævətrɪ] *n* gabinetto

lavender [ˈlævəndə*] *n* lavanda

lavish [ˈlævɪʃ] *adj* copioso(a); abbondante; (*giving freely*): ~ **with** prodigo(a) di, largo(a) in ♦ *vt*: to ~ **sth on sb** colmare qn di qc

law [lɔː] *n* legge *f*; **civil/criminal** ~ diritto civile/penale; ~**-abiding** *adj* ubbidiente alla legge; ~ **and order** *n* l'ordine *m* pubblico; ~ **court** *n* tribunale *m*, corte *f* di giustizia; ~**ful** *adj* legale; lecito(a); ~**less** *adj* che non conosce nessuna legge

lawn [lɔːn] *n* tappeto erboso; ~**mower** *n* tosaerba *m or f inv*; ~ **tennis** *n* tennis *m* su prato

law school *n* facoltà *f inv* di legge

lawsuit [ˈlɔːsuːt] *n* processo, causa

lawyer [ˈlɔːjə*] *n* (*for sales, wills etc*) = notaio; (*partner, in court*) = avvocato/essa

lax [læks] *adj* rilassato(a); negligente

laxative [ˈlæksətɪv] *n* lassativo

lay [leɪ] (*pt, pp* **laid**) *pt of* **lie** ♦ *adj* laico(a); (*not expert*) profano(a) ♦ *vt* posare, mettere; (*eggs*) fare; (*trap*) tendere; (*plans*) fare, elaborare; to ~ **the table** apparecchiare la tavola; ~ **aside** *or* **by** *vt* mettere da parte; ~ **down** *vt* mettere giù; (*rules etc*) formulare, fissare; to ~ **down the law** dettar legge; to ~ **down one's life** dare la propria vita; ~ **off** *vt* (*workers*) licenziare; ~ **on** *vt* (*provide*) fornire; ~ **out** *vt* (*display*) presentare; disporre; ~**about** *n* sfaccendato/a, fannullone/a; ~**-by** (*BRIT*) *n* piazzola (di sosta)

layer ['leɪə*] n strato

layman ['leɪmən] n laico; profano

layout ['leɪaut] n lay-out m inv, disposizione f; (PRESS) impaginazione f

laze [leɪz] vi oziare

lazy ['leɪzɪ] adj pigro(a)

lb. abbr = **pound** (weight)

lead[1] [liːd] (pt, pp **led**) n (front position) posizione f di testa; (distance, time ahead) vantaggio; (clue) indizio; (ELEC) filo (elettrico); (for dog) guinzaglio; (THEATRE) parte f principale ♦ vt guidare, condurre; (induce) indurre; (be leader of) essere a capo di ♦ vi condurre; (SPORT) essere in testa; **in the ~** in testa; **to ~ the way** fare strada; **~ away** vt condurre via; **~ back** vt: **to ~ back to** ricondurre a; **~ on** vt (tease) tenere sulla corda; **~ to** vt fus condurre a; portare a; **~ up to** vt fus portare a

lead[2] [lɛd] n (metal) piombo; (in pencil) mina

leaden ['lɛdn] adj (sky, sea) plumbeo(a)

leader ['liːdə*] n capo; leader m inv; (in newspaper) articolo di fondo; (SPORT) chi è in testa; **~ship** n direzione f; capacità di comando

leading ['liːdɪŋ] adj primo(a); principale; **~ man/lady** n (THEATRE) primo attore/prima attrice; **~ light** n (person) personaggio di primo piano

lead singer n cantante alla testa di un gruppo

leaf [liːf] (pl **leaves**) n foglia ♦ vi: **to ~ through sth** sfogliare qc; **to turn over a new ~** cambiar vita

leaflet ['liːflɪt] n dépliant m inv; (POL, REL) volantino

league [liːg] n lega; (FOOTBALL) campionato; **to be in ~ with** essere in lega con

leak [liːk] n (out) fuga; (in) infiltrazione f; (security ~) fuga d'informazioni ♦ vi (roof, bucket) perdere; (liquid) uscire; (shoes) lasciar passare l'acqua ♦ vt (information) divulgare; **~ out** vi uscire; (information) trapelare

lean [liːn] (pt, pp **leaned** or **leant**) adj magro(a) ♦ vt: **to ~ sth on sth** appoggiare qc su qc ♦ vi (slope) pendere; (rest): **to ~ against** appoggiarsi contro; essere appoggiato a; **to ~ on** appoggiarsi a; **~ forward/back** vi sporgersi in avanti/indietro; **~ out** vi sporgersi; **~ over** vi inclinarsi; **~ing** n: ~ing (towards) propensione f (per); **leant** [lɛnt] pt, pp of **lean**

leap [liːp] (pt, pp **leaped** or **leapt**) n salto, balzo ♦ vi saltare, balzare; **~frog** n gioco della cavallina; **leapt** [lɛpt] pt, pp of **leap; ~ year** n anno bisestile

learn [ləːn] (pt, pp **learned** or **learnt**) vt, vi imparare; **to ~ about** sth (hear, read) apprendere qc; **to ~ to do sth** imparare a fare qc; **~ed** ['ləːnɪd] adj erudito(a), dotto(a); **~er** n principiante m/f; (BRIT: also: **~er driver**) guidatore/trice principiante; **~ing** n erudizione f, sapienza; **learnt** pt, pp of **learn**

lease [liːs] n contratto d'affitto ♦ vt affittare

leash [liːʃ] n guinzaglio

least [liːst] adj: **the ~** (+ noun) il(la) più piccolo(a), il(la) minimo(a); (smallest amount of) il(la) meno ♦ adv (+ verb) meno; **the ~** (+ adjective): **the ~ beautiful girl** la ragazza meno bella; **the ~ possible effort** il minimo sforzo possibile; **I have the ~ money** ho meno denaro di tutti; **at ~** almeno; **not in the ~** affatto, per nulla

leather ['lɛðə*] n cuoio

leave [liːv] (pt, pp **left**) vt lasciare; (go away from) partire da ♦ vi partire, andarsene; (bus, train) partire ♦ n (time off) congedo; (MIL, also: consent) licenza; **to be left** rimanere; **there's some milk left over** c'è rimasto del latte; **on ~** in congedo

~ **behind** vt (person, object) lasciare; (: forget) dimenticare; ~ **out** vt omettere, tralasciare; ~ **of absence** n congedo

leaves [liːvz] npl of **leaf**

Lebanon ['lɛbənən] n Libano

lecherous ['lɛtʃərəs] adj lascivo(a), lubrico(a)

lecture ['lɛktʃə*] n conferenza; (SCOL) lezione f ♦ vi fare conferenze; fare lezioni ♦ vt (scold): **to ~ sb on or about sth** rimproverare qn or fare una ramanzina a qn per qc; **to give a ~ on** tenere una conferenza su

lecturer ['lɛktʃərə*] n (BRIT) n (at university) professore/essa, docente m/f

led [lɛd] pt, pp of **lead**

ledge [lɛdʒ] n (of window) davanzale m; (on wall etc) sporgenza; (of mountain) cornice f, cengia

ledger ['lɛdʒə*] n libro maestro, registro

lee [liː] n lato sottovento

leech [liːtʃ] n sanguisuga

leek [liːk] n porro

leer [lɪə*] vi: **to ~ at sb** gettare uno sguardo voglioso (or maligno) su qn

leeway ['liːweɪ] n (fig): **to have some ~** avere una certa libertà di azione

left [lɛft] pt, pp of **leave** ♦ adj sinistro(a) ♦ adv a sinistra ♦ n sinistra; **on the ~, to the ~** a sinistra; **the L~** (POL) la sinistra; **~-handed** adj mancino(a); **~-hand side** n lato or fianco sinistro; **~ luggage (office)** (BRIT) n deposito m bagagli inv; **~overs** npl avanzi mpl, resti mpl; **~-wing** adj (POL) di sinistra

leg [lɛg] n gamba; (of animal) zampa; (of furniture) piede m; (CULIN: of chicken) coscia; (of journey) tappa; **lst/2nd ~** (SPORT) partita di andata/ritorno

legacy ['lɛgəsɪ] n eredità f inv

legal ['liːgl] adj legale; ~ **holiday** (US) n giorno festivo, festa nazionale; ~ **tender** n moneta legale

legend ['lɛdʒənd] n leggenda

legislation [lɛdʒɪs'leɪʃən] n legislazione f; **legislature** ['lɛdʒɪslətʃə*] n corpo legislativo

legitimate [lɪ'dʒɪtɪmət] adj legittimo(a)

leg-room n spazio per le gambe

leisure ['lɛʒə*] n agio, tempo libero; ricreazioni fpl; **at ~** con comodo; ~ **centre** n centro di ricreazione; **~ly** adj tranquillo(a); fatto(a) con comodo or senza fretta

lemon ['lɛmən] n limone m; **~ade** [-'neɪd] n limonata; **~ tea** n tè m inv al limone

lend [lɛnd] (pt, pp **lent**) vt: **to ~ sth (to sb)** prestare qc (a qn); **~ing library** n biblioteca che consente prestiti di libri

length [lɛŋθ] n lunghezza; (distance) distanza; (section: of road, pipe etc) pezzo, tratto; (of time) periodo; **at ~** (at last) finalmente, alla fine; (lengthily) a lungo; **~en** vt allungare, prolungare ♦ vi allungarsi; **~ways** adv per il lungo; **~y** adj molto lungo(a)

lenient ['liːnɪənt] adj indulgente, clemente

lens [lɛnz] n lente f; (of camera) obiettivo

Lent [lɛnt] n Quaresima

lent [lɛnt] pt, pp of **lend**

lentil ['lɛntl] n lenticchia

Leo ['liːəʊ] n Leone m

leotard ['liːətɑːd] n calzamaglia

leprosy ['lɛprəsɪ] n lebbra

lesbian ['lɛzbɪən] n lesbica

less [lɛs] adj, pron, adv meno ♦ prep: ~ **tax/10% discount** meno tasse/il 10% di sconto; ~ **than ever** meno che mai; ~ **than half** meno della metà; ~ **and** ~ sempre meno; **the ~ he works** ... meno lavora ....

lessen ['lɛsn] vi diminuire, attenuarsi ♦ vt diminuire, ridurre

lesser ['lɛsə*] adj minore, più piccolo(a); **to a ~ extent** in grado or misura minore

lesson ['lɛsn] n lezione f; **to teach sb a ~** dare una lezione a qn

lest [lɛst] *conj* per paura di + *infinitive*, per paura che + *sub*

let [lɛt] (*pt, pp* **let**) *vt* lasciare; (*BRIT: lease*) dare in affitto; to ~ sb do sth lasciare fare qc a qn, lasciare che qn faccia qc; to ~ sb know sth far sapere qc a qn; ~'s go andiamo; ~ him come lo lasci venire; "**to ~**" "affittasi"; ~ **down** *vt* (*lower*) abbassare; (*dress*) allungare; (*hair*) sciogliere; (*tyre*) sgonfiare; (*disappoint*) deludere; ~ **go** *vt, vi* mollare; ~ **in** *vt* lasciare entrare; (*visitor etc*) far entrare; ~ **off** *vt* (*allow to go*) lasciare andare; (*firework etc*) far partire; ~ **on** (*inf*) *vi* dire; ~ **out** *vt* lasciare uscire; (*scream*) emettere; ~ **up** *vi* diminuire

lethal [ˈliːθl] *adj* letale, mortale

lethargic [lɛˈθɑːdʒɪk] *adj* letargico(a)

letter [ˈlɛtə*] *n* lettera; ~ **bomb** *n* lettera esplosiva; ~**box** (*BRIT*) *n* buca delle lettere; ~**ing** *n* iscrizione *f*; caratteri *mpl*

lettuce [ˈlɛtɪs] *n* lattuga, insalata

let-up *n* pausa

leukaemia [luːˈkiːmɪə] (*US* **leukemia**) *n* leucemia

level [ˈlɛvl] *adj* piatto(a), piano(a); orizzontale ♦ *adv*: to draw ~ with mettersi alla pari di ♦ *n* livello ♦ *vt* livellare, spianare; to be ~ with essere alla pari di; A ~s (*BRIT*) *npl* ≈ esami *mpl* di maturità; O ~s (*BRIT*) *npl* esami fatti in Inghilterra all'età di 16 anni; on the ~ *adv* piatto(a); (*fig*) onesto(a); ~ **off** *or* **out** *vi* (*prices etc*) stabilizzarsi; ~ **crossing** (*BRIT*) *n* passaggio a livello; ~**-headed** *adj* equilibrato(a)

lever [ˈliːvə*] *n* leva; ~**age** *n*: ~**age** (**on** *or* **with**) forza (su); (*fig*) ascendente *m* (su)

levity [ˈlɛvɪtɪ] *n* leggerezza, frivolezza

levy [ˈlɛvɪ] *n* tassa, imposta ♦ *vt* imporre

lewd [luːd] *adj* osceno(a), lascivo(a)

liability [laɪəˈbɪlɪtɪ] *n* responsabilità *f*

inv; (*handicap*) peso; **liabilities** *npl* debiti *mpl*; (*on balance sheet*) passivo

liable [ˈlaɪəbl] *adj* (*subject*): ~ **to** soggetto(a) a; passibile di; (*responsible*): ~ (**for**) responsabile (di); (*likely*): ~ **to do** propenso(a) a fare

liaise [liːˈeɪz] *vi*: to ~ (**with**) mantenere i contatti (con)

liaison [liːˈeɪzɔn] *n* relazione *f*; (*MIL*) collegamento

liar [ˈlaɪə*] *n* bugiardo/a

libel [ˈlaɪbl] *n* libello, diffamazione *f* ♦ *vt* diffamare

liberal [ˈlɪbərl] *adj* liberale; (*generous*): to be ~ **with** distribuire liberalmente

liberty [ˈlɪbətɪ] *n* libertà *f inv*; at ~ (*criminal*) in libertà; at ~ **to do** libero(a) di fare

Libra [ˈliːbrə] *n* Bilancia

librarian [laɪˈbrɛərɪən] *n* bibliotecario/a

library [ˈlaɪbrərɪ] *n* biblioteca

Libya [ˈlɪbɪə] *n* Libia; ~**n** *adj, n* libico(a)

lice [laɪs] *npl of* **louse**

licence [ˈlaɪsns] (*US* **license**) *n* autorizzazione *f*, permesso; (*COMM*) licenza; (*RADIO, TV*) canone *m*, abbonamento; (*also: driving* ~, (*US*) *driver's* ~) patente *f* di guida; (*excessive freedom*) licenza; ~ **number** *n* numero di targa; ~ **plate** *n* targa

license [ˈlaɪsns] *n* (*US*) = **licence** ♦ *vt* dare una licenza a; ~**d** *adj* (*for alcohol*) che ha la licenza di vendere bibite alcoliche

lick [lɪk] *vt* leccare; (*inf: defeat*) stracciare; to ~ **one's lips** (*fig*) leccarsi i baffi

licorice [ˈlɪkərɪs] (*US*) *n* = **liquorice**

lid [lɪd] *n* coperchio; (*eye~*) palpebra

lie [laɪ] (*pt* **lay**, *pp* **lain**) *vi* (*rest*) giacere; star disteso(a); (*of object: be situated*) trovarsi, essere; (*tell lies: pt, pp* **lied**) mentire, dire bugie ♦ *n* bugia, menzogna; to ~ **low** (*fig*) latitare; ~ **about** *or* **around** *vi* (*things*) essere in giro; (*person*) bighellonare; **~-down** (BRIT) n: to have a **~down** sdraiarsi, riposarsi; **~-in** (BRIT) n: to have a **~-in** rimanere a letto

lieu [luː]: **in ~ of** prep invece di, al posto di

lieutenant [lefˈtɛnənt, (US) luːˈtɛnənt] n tenente m

life [laɪf] (pl **lives**) n vita ♦ cpd di vita; della vita; **a ~** a vita; **to come to ~** rianimarsi; **~ assurance** (BRIT) n = ~ **insurance**; **~-belt** (BRIT) n salvagente m; **~boat** n scialuppa di salvataggio; **~guard** n bagnino; **~ imprisonment** n carcere m a vita; **~ insurance** n assicurazione f sulla vita; **~ jacket** n giubbotto di salvataggio; **~less** adj senza vita; **~like** adj verosimile; rassomigliante; **~line** n: it was his **~line** era vitale per lui; **~long** adj per tutta la vita; **~ preserver** (US) n salvagente m; giubbotto di salvataggio; **~ sentence** n ergastolo; **~-size(d)** adj a grandezza naturale; **~ span** n (durata della) vita; **~style** n stile m di vita; **~ support system** n respiratore m automatico; **~time** n: **in his ~time** durante la sua vita; **once in a ~time** una volta nella vita

lift [lɪft] vt sollevare; (ban, rule) levare ♦ vi (fog) alzarsi ♦ n (BRIT: elevator) ascensore m; **to give sb a ~** (BRIT) dare un passaggio a qn; **~-off** n decollo

light [laɪt] (pt, pp **lighted** or **lit**) n luce f, lume m; (daylight) luce f, giorno; (lamp) lampada; (AUT: rear ~) luce f di posizione; (: headlamp) fanale m; (for cigarette etc): **have you got a ~?** ha da accendere?; **~s** npl (AUT: traffic ~) semaforo ♦ vt (candle, cigarette, fire) accendere; (room): **to be lit by** essere illuminato(a) da ♦ adj (colour) chiaro(a); (not heavy, also fig) leggero(a); **to come to ~** venire alla luce, emergere; **~ up** vi illuminarsi ♦ vt illuminare; **~ bulb** n lampadina; **~en** vt (make less heavy) alleg-

gerire; **~er** n (also: cigarette **~er**) accendino; **~-headed** adj stordito(a); **~-hearted** adj gioioso(a), gaio(a); **~house** n faro; **~ing** n illuminazione f; **~ly** adv leggermente; **to get off ~ly** cavarsela a buon mercato; **~ness** n chiarezza; (in weight) leggerezza

lightning [ˈlaɪtnɪŋ] n lampo, fulmine m; **~ conductor** (US **~ rod**) n parafulmine m

light pen n penna ottica

lightweight [ˈlaɪtweɪt] adj (suit) leggero(a) ♦ n (BOXING) peso leggero

light year n anno m luce inv

like [laɪk] vt (person) volere bene a; (activity, object, food): **I ~ swimming/that book/chocolate** mi piace nuotare/quel libro/il cioccolato ♦ prep come ♦ adj simile, uguale ♦ n: the **~** uno(a) uguale; **his ~s and dislikes** i suoi gusti; **I would ~, I'd ~** mi piacerebbe, vorrei; **would you ~ a coffee?** gradirebbe un caffè?; **to be/look ~ sb/sth** somigliare a qn/qc; **what does it look/taste ~?** che aspetto/gusto ha?; **what does it sound ~?** come fa?; **that's just ~ him** è proprio da lui; **do it ~ this** fallo così; **it is nothing ~ ...** non è affatto come ...; **~able** adj simpatico(a)

likelihood [ˈlaɪklɪhud] n probabilità

likely [ˈlaɪklɪ] adj probabile; plausibile; **he's ~ to leave** probabilmente partirà, è probabile che parta; **not ~!** neanche per sogno!

likeness [ˈlaɪknɪs] n somiglianza

likewise [ˈlaɪkwaɪz] adv similmente, nello stesso modo

liking [ˈlaɪkɪŋ] n: **~ (for)** debole m (per); **to be to sb's ~** piacere a qn

lilac [ˈlaɪlək] n lilla m inv

lily [ˈlɪlɪ] n giglio; **~ of the valley** n mughetto

limb [lɪm] n arto

limber up [ˈlɪmbə*-] vi riscaldarsi i muscoli

limbo [ˈlɪmbəu] n: **to be in ~** (fig) essere lasciato(a) nel dimenticatoio

lime [laɪm] n (tree) tiglio; (fruit) limetta; (GEO) calce f

limelight ['laɪmlaɪt] n: in the ~ (fig) alla ribalta, in vista

limerick ['lɪmərɪk] n poesiola umoristica di 5 versi

limestone ['laɪmstəun] n pietra calcarea; (GEO) calcare m

limit ['lɪmɪt] n limite m ♦ vt limitare; **~ed** adj limitato(a), ristretto(a); **to be ~ed to** limitarsi a; **~ed (liability) company** (BRIT) n ≈ società f inv a responsabilità limitata

limp [lɪmp] n: **to have a ~** zoppicare ♦ vi zoppicare ♦ adj floscio(a), flaccido(a)

limpet ['lɪmpɪt] n patella

line [laɪn] n linea; (rope) corda; (for fishing) lenza; (wire) filo; (of poem) verso; (row, series) fila, riga; (on face) ruga ♦ vt (clothes): **to ~ (with)** foderare (di); (box): **to ~ (with)** rivestire or foderare (di); (subj: trees, crowd) fiancheggiare; **~ of business** settore m or ramo d'attività; **in ~ with** in linea con; **~ up** vi allinearsi, mettersi in fila ♦ vt mettere in fila; (event, celebration) preparare

lined [laɪnd] adj (face) rugoso(a); (paper) a righe, rigato(a)

linen ['lɪnɪn] n biancheria, panni mpl; (cloth) tela di lino

liner ['laɪnə*] n nave f di linea; (for bin) sacchetto

linesman ['laɪnzmən] n guardalinee m inv

line-up n allineamento, fila; (SPORT) formazione f di gioco

linger ['lɪŋgə*] vi attardarsi; indugiare; (smell, tradition) persistere

lingerie ['lænʒəriː] n biancheria intima femminile

lingo ['lɪŋgəu] (pl ~s) (pej) n gergo

linguistics [lɪŋ'gwɪstɪks] n linguistica

lining ['laɪnɪŋ] n fodera

link [lɪŋk] n (of a chain) anello; (relationship) legame m; (connection) collegamento ♦ vt collegare, unire, con-

giungere; (associate): **to ~ with** or **to** collegare a; **~s** npl (GOLF) pista or terreno da golf; **~ up** vt collegare, unire ♦ vi riunirsi; associarsi

lino ['laɪnəu] n = **linoleum**

linoleum [lɪ'nəuliəm] n linoleum m inv

lion ['laɪən] n leone m; **~ess** n leonessa

lip [lɪp] n labbro; (of cup etc) orlo; **~read** vi leggere sulle labbra; **~salve** n burro di cacao; **~ service** n: **to pay ~ service to sth** essere favorevole a qc solo a parole; **~stick** n rossetto

liqueur [lɪ'kjuə*] n liquore m

liquid ['lɪkwɪd] n liquido ♦ adj liquido(a)

liquidize ['lɪkwɪdaɪz] vt (CULIN) passare al frullatore; **~r** n frullatore m (a brocca)

liquor ['lɪkə*] n alcool m

liquorice ['lɪkərɪs] (BRIT) n liquirizia

liquor store (US) n negozio di liquori

lisp [lɪsp] n pronuncia blesa della "s"

list [lɪst] n lista, elenco ♦ vt (write down) mettere in lista; fare una lista di; (enumerate) elencare; **~ed building** (BRIT) n edificio sotto la protezione delle Belle Arti

listen ['lɪsn] vi ascoltare; **to ~ to** ascoltare; **~er** n ascoltatore/trice

listless ['lɪstlɪs] adj apatico(a)

lit [lɪt] pt, pp of **light**

liter ['liːtə*] (US) n = **litre**

literacy ['lɪtərəsɪ] n il sapere leggere e scrivere

literal ['lɪtərl] adj letterale

literary ['lɪtərərɪ] adj letterario(a)

literate ['lɪtərət] adj che sa leggere e scrivere

literature ['lɪtərɪtʃə*] n letteratura, letteratura; (brochures etc) materiale m

lithe [laɪð] adj agile, snello(a)

litigation [lɪtɪ'geɪʃən] n causa

litre ['liːtə*] (US **liter**) n litro

litter ['lɪtə*] n (rubbish) rifiuti mpl; (young animals) figliata; **~ bin**

(BRIT) n cestino per rifiuti; **~ed**
adj: **~ed with** coperto(a) di
little ['lɪtl] adj (small) piccolo(a);
(not much) poco(a) ♦ adv poco; **a ~**
un po' (di); **a ~ bit** un pochino; **~
by ~** a poco a poco; **~ finger** n mignolo
live¹ [lɪv] vi vivere; (reside) vivere,
abitare; **~ down** vt far dimenticare
(alla gente); **~ on** vt fus (food) vivere di; **~ together** vi vivere insieme, convivere; **~ up to** vt fus tener
fede a, non venir meno a
live² [laɪv] adj (animal) vivo(a);
(wire) sotto tensione; (bullet, missile) inesploso(a); (broadcast) diret-
to(a); (performance) dal vivo
livelihood ['laɪvlɪhʊd] n mezzi mpl
di sostentamento
lively ['laɪvlɪ] adj vivace, vivo(a)
liven up ['laɪvn ʌp] vt (discussion,
evening) animare ♦ vi ravvivarsi
liver ['lɪvə*] n fegato
lives [laɪvz] npl of **life**
livestock ['laɪvstɒk] n bestiame m
livid ['lɪvɪd] adj livido(a); (furious) li-
vido(a) di rabbia, furibondo(a)
living ['lɪvɪŋ] adj vivo(a), vivente ♦
n: **to earn** or **make a ~** guadagnarsi la vita; **~ conditions** npl condizioni fpl di vita; **~ room** n soggiorno; **~ standards** npl tenore m di
vita; **~ wage** n salario sufficiente
per vivere
lizard ['lɪzəd] n lucertola
load [ləʊd] n (weight) peso; (thing
carried) carico ♦ vt (also: **~ up**): **to
~ (with)** (lorry, ship) caricare (di);
(gun, camera, COMPUT) caricare
(con); **a ~ of**, **~s of** (fig) un sacco
di; **~ed** adj (vehicle): **~ed (with)**
carico(a) (di); (question) capzio-
so(a); (inf: rich) carico(a) di soldi
loaf [ləʊf] (pl **loaves**) n pane m, pagnotta
loan [ləʊn] n prestito ♦ vt dare in
prestito; **on ~** in prestito
loath [ləʊθ] adj: **to be ~ to do** essere restio(a) a fare
loathe [ləʊð] vt detestare, aborrire

loaves [ləʊvz] npl of **loaf**
lobby ['lɒbɪ] n atrio, vestibolo;
(POL: pressure group) gruppo di
pressione ♦ vt fare pressione su
lobster ['lɒbstə*] n aragosta
local ['ləʊkl] adj locale ♦ n (BRIT:
pub) ≈ bar m inv all'angolo; **the ~s**
npl (local inhabitants) la gente della
zona; **~ authority** n ente m locale;
~ call n (TEL) telefonata urbana;
~ government n amministrazione f
locale
locality [ləʊ'kælɪtɪ] n località f inv;
(position) posto, luogo
locally ['ləʊkəlɪ] adv da queste parti;
nel vicinato
locate [ləʊ'keɪt] vt (find) trovare;
(situate) collocare; situare
location [ləʊ'keɪʃən] n posizione f;
on ~ (CINEMA) all'esterno
loch [lɒx] n lago
lock [lɒk] n (of door, box) serratura;
(of canal) chiusa; (of hair) ciocca,
riccio ♦ vt (with key) chiudere a
chiave ♦ vi (door etc) chiudersi;
(wheels) bloccarsi, incepparsi; **~
out** vt chiudere fuori; **~ up** vt
(criminal, mental patient) rinchiudere; (house) chiudere a chiave ♦ vi
chiudere tutto (a chiave)
locker ['lɒkə*] n armadietto
locket ['lɒkɪt] n medaglione m
locksmith ['lɒksmɪθ] n magnano
lock-up (US) n prigione f; guardina
locomotive [ləʊkə'məʊtɪv] n locomotiva
locum ['ləʊkəm] n (MED) medico sostituto
locust ['ləʊkəst] n locusta
lodge [lɒdʒ] n casetta, portineria;
(hunting ~) casino di caccia ♦ vi
(person): **to ~ (with)** essere a pensione (presso or da); (bullet etc)
conficcarsi ♦ vt (appeal etc) presentare, fare; **to ~ a complaint** presentare un reclamo; **~r** n affittuario/a;
(with room and meals) pensionante
m/f
lodgings ['lɒdʒɪŋz] npl camera

d'affitto; camera ammobiliata

loft [lɔft] n solaio, soffitta

lofty ['lɔftɪ] adj alto(a); (haughty) altezzoso(a)

log [lɔg] n (of wood) ceppo; (book) = logbook ♦ vt registrare

logbook ['lɔgbuk] n (NAUT, AVIAT) diario di bordo; (AUT) libretto di circolazione

loggerheads ['lɔgəhɛdz] npl: at ~ (with) ai ferri corti (con)

logic ['lɔdʒɪk] n logica; ~al adj logico(a)

loin [lɔɪn] n (CULIN) lombata

loiter ['lɔɪtə*] vi attardarsi

loll [lɔl] vi (also: ~ about) essere stravaccato(a)

lollipop ['lɔlɪpɔp] n lecca lecca m inv; ~ man/lady (BRIT) n impiegato/a che aiuta i bambini ad attraversare la strada in vicinanza di scuole

London ['lʌndən] n Londra; ~er n londinese m/f

lone [ləun] adj solitario(a)

loneliness ['ləunlɪnɪs] n solitudine f, isolamento

lonely ['ləunlɪ] adj solo(a); solitario(a), isolato(a)

long [lɔŋ] adj lungo(a) ♦ adv a lungo, per molto tempo ♦ vi: to ~ for sth/to do desiderare qc/di fare; non veder l'ora di aver qc/di fare; so or as ~ as (while) finché; (provided that) sempre che + sub; don't be ~! fai presto!; how ~ is this river/course? quanto è lungo questo fiume/corso?; 6 metres ~ lungo 6 metri; 6 months ~ che dura 6 mesi, di 6 mesi; all night ~ tutta la notte; he no ~er comes non viene più; ~ before molto tempo prima; before ~ (+ future) fra poco; (+ past) poco tempo dopo; at ~ last finalmente; ~-distance adj (race) di fondo; (call) interurbano(a); ~-haired adj dai capelli lunghi; ~-hand n scrittura normale; ~-ing n desiderio, voglia, brama

longitude ['lɔngɪtjuːd] n longitudine

f

long: ~ **jump** n salto in lungo; ~-**life** adj (milk) a lunga conservazione; (batteries) di lunga durata; ~-**playing record** n (disco) 33 giri m inv; ~-**range** adj a lunga portata; ~-**sighted** adj presbite; ~-**standing** adj di vecchia data; ~-**suffering** adj estremamente paziente; infinitamente tollerante; ~-**term** adj a lungo termine; ~ **wave** n onde fpl lunghe; ~-**winded** adj prolisso(a), interminabile

loo [luː] (BRIT: inf) n W.C. m inv, cesso

look [luk] vi guardare; (seem) sembrare, parere; (building etc): to ~ south/on to the sea dare a sud/sul mare ♦ n sguardo; (appearance) aspetto, aria; ~s npl (good ~s) bellezza; ~ after vt fus occuparsi di, prendere cura di; (keep an eye on) guardare, badare a; ~ at vt fus guardare; ~ back vi: to ~ back on (event etc) ripensare a; ~ down on vt fus (fig) guardare dall'alto, disprezzare; ~ for vt fus cercare; ~ forward to vt fus non veder l'ora di; (in letters): we ~ forward to hearing from you in attesa di una vostra gentile risposta; ~ into vt fus esaminare; ~ on vi fare da spettatore; ~ out vi (beware): to ~ out (for) stare in guardia (per); ~ out for vt fus cercare; ~ round vi (turn) girarsi, voltarsi; (in shop) dare un'occhiata; ~ to vt fus (rely on) contare su; ~ up vi alzare gli occhi; (improve) migliorare ♦ vt (word) cercare; (friend) andare a trovare; ~ up to vt fus avere rispetto per; ~-out n posto d'osservazione; guardia; to be on the ~-out (for) stare in guardia (per

loom [luːm] n telaio ♦ vi (also: ~ up) apparire minaccioso(a); (event) essere imminente

loony ['luːnɪ] (inf) n pazzo/a

loop [luːp] n cappio ♦ vt: to ~ sth

round sth passare qc intorno a qc; **~hole** n via d'uscita; scappatoia

loose [luːs] adj (knot) sciolto(a); (screw) allentato(a); (stone) cadente; (clothes) ampio(a), largo(a); (animal) in libertà, scappato(a); (life, morals) dissoluto(a) ♦ n: to be **on the ~** essere in libertà; **~ change** n spiccioli mpl, moneta; **~ chippings** npl (on road) ghiaino; **~ end** n: to be at a **~ end** (BRIT) or at **~ ends** (US) non saper che fare; **~ly** adv senza stringere; approssimativamente; **~n** vt sciogliere; (belt etc) allentare

loot [luːt] n bottino ♦ vt saccheggiare

lop [lɔp] vt (also: **~ off**) tagliare via, recidere

lop-sided ['lɔp'saɪdɪd] adj non equilibrato(a), asimmetrico(a)

lord [lɔːd] n signore m; **L~** Smith lord Smith; **the L~** il Signore; **good L~!** buon Dio!; (**the House of**) **L~s** (BRIT) la Camera dei Lord; **~ship** n: **your L~ship** Sua Eccellenza

lore [lɔː*] n tradizioni fpl

lorry ['lɔrɪ] (BRIT) n camion m inv; **~ driver** (BRIT) n camionista m

lose [luːz] (pt, pp lost) vt perdere ♦ vi perdere; **to ~ (time)** (clock) ritardare; **~r** n perdente m/f

loss [lɔs] n perdita; **to be at a ~** essere perplesso(a)

lost [lɔst] pt, pp of lose ♦ adj perduto(a); **~ property** (US **~ and found**) n oggetti mpl smarriti

lot [lɔt] n (at auctions) lotto; (destiny) destino, sorte f; **the ~** tutto quanto(a); tutti/e quanti/e; **a ~** molto; **a ~ of** una gran quantità di, un sacco di; **~s of** molto(a); **to draw ~s (for sth)** tirare a sorte (per qc)

lotion ['ləuʃən] n lozione f

lottery ['lɔtərɪ] n lotteria

loud [laud] adj forte, alto(a); (gaudy) vistoso(a), sgargiante ♦ adv (speak etc) forte; **out ~** (read etc) ad alta voce; **~hailer** (BRIT) n por-

tavoce m inv; **~ly** adv fortemente, ad alta voce; **~speaker** n altoparlante m

lounge [laundʒ] n salotto, soggiorno, (at airport, station) sala d'attesa; (BRIT: also: **~ bar**) bar m inv con servizio a tavolino ♦ vi oziare; **~ about** or **around** vi starsene colle mani in mano; **~ suit** (BRIT) n completo da uomo

louse [laus] (pl lice) n pidocchio

lousy ['lauzɪ] (inf) adj orrendo(a), schifoso(a); **to feel ~** stare da cani

lout [laut] n zoticone m

lovable ['lʌvəbl] adj simpatico(a), carino(a); amabile

love [lʌv] n amore m ♦ vt amare; voler bene a; **to ~ to do:** I **~** to do mi piace fare; **to be/fall in ~ with** essere innamorato(a)/innamorarsi di; **to make ~** fare l'amore; **"15 ~"** (TENNIS) "15 a zero"; **~ affair** n relazione f; **~ life** n vita sentimentale

lovely ['lʌvlɪ] adj bello(a); (delicious: smell, meal) buono(a)

lover ['lʌvə*] n amante m/f; (person in love) innamorato(a); (amateur): **a ~ of** un(un')amante di; un(un')appassionato(a) di

loving ['lʌvɪŋ] adj affettuoso(a)

low [ləu] adj basso(a) ♦ adv in basso ♦ n (METEOR) depressione f; **to be ~ on** (supplies etc) avere scarsità di; **to feel ~** sentirsi giù; **~-alcohol** adj a basso contenuto alcolico; **~-cut** adj (dress) scollato(a); **~er** adj (bottom: of 2 things) più basso; (less important) meno importante ♦ vt calare; (prices, eyes, voice) abbassare; **~-fat** adj magro(a); **~lands** npl (GEO) pianura; **~ly** adj umile, modesto(a)

loyal ['lɔɪəl] adj fedele, leale; **~ty** n fedeltà, lealtà

lozenge ['lɔzɪndʒ] n (MED) pastiglia

L.P. n abbr = long-playing record

L-plates (BRIT) npl cartelli sui veicoli dei guidatori principianti

Ltd abbr (= limited) ≈ S.r.l

lubricate [ˈluːbrɪkeɪt] *vt* lubrificare

luck [lʌk] *n* fortuna, sorte *f*; **bad ~** sfortuna, mala sorte; **good ~!** buona fortuna!; **~ily** *adv* fortunatamente, per fortuna; **~y** *adj* fortunato(a); *(number etc)* che porta fortuna

ludicrous [ˈluːdɪkrəs] *adj* ridicolo(a)

lug [lʌɡ] *(inf)* *vt* trascinare

luggage [ˈlʌɡɪdʒ] *n* bagagli *mpl*; **~ rack** *n* portabagagli *m inv*

lukewarm [ˈluːkwɔːm] *adj* tiepido(a)

lull [lʌl] *n* intervallo di calma ♦ *vt*: **to ~ sb to sleep** cullare qn finché si addormenta; **to be ~ed into a false sense of security** illudersi che tutto vada bene

lullaby [ˈlʌləbaɪ] *n* ninnananna

lumbago [lʌmˈbeɪɡəu] *n* lombaggine *f*

lumber [ˈlʌmbə*] *n* *(wood)* legname *m*; *(junk)* roba vecchia; **~ with** *vt*: **to be ~ed with** doversi sorbire qc; **~jack** *n* boscaiolo

luminous [ˈluːmɪnəs] *adj* luminoso(a)

lump [lʌmp] *n* pezzo; *(in sauce)* grumo; *(swelling)* gonfiore *m*; *(also: sugar ~)* zolletta ♦ *vt* *(also: ~ together)* riunire, mettere insieme; **a ~ sum** una somma globale; **~y** *adj* *(sauce)* pieno(a) di grumi; *(bed)* bitorzoluto(a)

lunatic [ˈluːnətɪk] *adj* pazzo(a), matto(a)

lunch [lʌntʃ] *n* pranzo, colazione *f*

luncheon [ˈlʌntʃən] *n* pranzo; **~ meat** ≈ mortadella; **~ voucher** *(BRIT)* *n* buono *m* pasto *inv*

lunch time *n* ora di pranzo

lung [lʌŋ] *n* polmone *m*

lunge [lʌndʒ] *vi* *(also: ~ forward)* fare un balzo in avanti; **to ~ at** balzare su

lurch [lɜːtʃ] *vi* vacillare, barcollare ♦ *n* scatto improvviso; **to leave sb in the ~** piantare in asso qn

lure [luə*] *n* richiamo; lusinga ♦ *vt* attirare (con l'inganno)

lurid [ˈluərɪd] *adj* sgargiante; *(details etc)* impressionante

lurk [lɜːk] *vi* stare in agguato

luscious [ˈlʌʃəs] *adj* succulento(a); delizioso(a)

lush [lʌʃ] *adj* lussureggiante

lust [lʌst] *n* lussuria; cupidigia; desiderio; *(fig)*: **~ for** sete *f* di; **~ after** *or* **for** *vt fus* bramare, desiderare

lusty [ˈlʌstɪ] *adj* vigoroso(a), robusto(a)

Luxembourg [ˈlʌksəmbɜːɡ] *n* *(state)* Lussemburgo *m*; *(city)* Lussemburgo *f*

luxuriant [lʌɡˈzjuərɪənt] *adj* lussureggiante; *(hair)* folto(a)

luxurious [lʌɡˈzjuərɪəs] *adj* sontuoso(a), di lusso

luxury [ˈlʌkʃərɪ] *n* lusso ♦ *cpd* di lusso

lying [ˈlaɪɪŋ] *n* bugie *fpl*, menzogne *fpl* ♦ *adj* bugiardo(a)

lynch [lɪntʃ] *vt* linciare

lyrical [ˈlɪrɪkl] *adj* lirico(a); *(fig)* entusiasta

lyrics [ˈlɪrɪks] *npl* *(of song)* parole *fpl*

M

m. *abbr* = **metre; mile; million**

M.A. *abbr* = **Master of Arts**

mac [mæk] *(BRIT)* *n* impermeabile *m*

macaroni [mækəˈrəunɪ] *n* maccheroni *mpl*

machine [məˈʃiːn] *n* macchina ♦ *vt* *(TECH)* lavorare a macchina; *(dress etc)* cucire a macchina; **~ gun** *n* mitragliatrice *f*; **~ry** *n* macchinario, macchine *fpl*; *(fig)* macchina

mackerel [ˈmækrl] *n inv* sgombro

mackintosh [ˈmækɪntɔʃ] *(BRIT)* *n* impermeabile *m*

mad [mæd] *adj* matto(a), pazzo(a); *(foolish)* sciocco(a); *(angry)* furioso(a); **to be ~ about** *(keen)* andare pazzo(a) per

madam [ˈmædəm] *n* signora

madden [ˈmædn] *vt* fare infuriare

made [meɪd] *pt, pp* of **make**

Madeira [məˈdɪərə] *n* *(GEO)* Madera; (*wine*) madera

made-to-measure (*BRIT*) *adj* fatto(a) su misura

madly ['mædlı] *adv* follemente

madman ['mædmən] *n* pazzo, alienato

madness ['mædnıs] *n* pazzia

magazine [mægə'ziːn] *n* (*PRESS*) rivista; (*RADIO, TV*) rubrica

maggot ['mægət] *n* baco, verme *m*

magic ['mædʒık] *n* magia ♦ *adj* magico(a); **~al** *adj* magico(a); **~ian** [mə'dʒıʃən] *n* mago/a

magistrate ['mædʒıstreıt] *n* magistrato; giudice *m/f*

magnet ['mægnıt] *n* magnete *m*, calamita; **~ic** [-'netık] *adj* magnetico(a)

magnificent [mæg'nıfısnt] *adj* magnifico(a)

magnify ['mægnıfaı] *vt* ingrandire; **~ing glass** *n* lente *f* d'ingrandimento

magnitude ['mægnıtjuːd] *n* grandezza; importanza

magpie ['mægpaı] *n* gazza

mahogany [mə'həgənı] *n* mogano

maid [meıd] *n* domestica; (*in hotel*) cameriera; **old ~** (*pej*) vecchia zitella

maiden ['meıdn] *n* fanciulla ♦ *adj* (*aunt etc*) nubile; (*speech, voyage*) inaugurale; **~ name** *n* nome *m* da nubile or da ragazza

mail [meıl] *n* posta ♦ *vt* spedire (per posta); **~box** (*US*) *n* cassetta delle lettere; **~ing list** *n* elenco di indirizzi; **~-order** *n* vendita (*or* acquisto) per corrispondenza

maim [meım] *vt* mutilare

main [meın] *adj* principale ♦ *n* (*pipe*) conduttura principale; the **~s** *npl* (*ELEC*) la linea principale; **in the ~** nel complesso, nell'insieme; **~frame** *n* (*COMPUT*) mainframe *m inv*; **~land** *n* continente *m*; **~ly** *adv* principalmente, soprattutto; **~ road** *n* strada principale; **~stay** *n* (*fig*) sostegno principale; **~stream** *n* (*fig*) corrente *f* principale

maintain [meın'teın] *vt* mantenere; (*affirm*) sostenere; **maintenance** ['meıntənəns] *n* manutenzione *f*; (*alimony*) alimenti *mpl*

maize [meız] *n* granturco, mais *m*

majestic [mə'dʒestık] *adj* maestoso(a)

majesty ['mædʒıstı] *n* maestà *f inv*

major ['meıdʒə*] *n* (*MIL*) maggiore *m* ♦ *adj* (*greater, MUS*) maggiore; (*in importance*) principale, importante

Majorca [mə'jɔːkə] *n* Maiorca

majority [mə'dʒɔrıtı] *n* maggioranza

make [meık] (*pt, pp* **made**) *vt* fare; (*manufacture*) fare, fabbricare; (*cause to be*): **to ~ sb sad** etc rendere qn triste *etc*; (*force*): **to ~ sb do sth** costringere qn a fare qc, far fare qc a qn; (*equal*): **2 and 2 ~ 4** 2 più 2 fa 4 ♦ *n* fabbricazione *f*; (*brand*) marca; **to ~ a fool of sb** far fare a qn la figura dello scemo; **to ~ a profit** realizzare un profitto; **to ~ a loss** subire una perdita; **to ~ it** (*arrive*) arrivare; (*achieve sth*) farcela; **what time do you ~ it?** che ora fai?; **to ~ do with** arrangiarsi con; **~ for** *vt fus* (*place*) avviarsi verso; **~ out** *vt* (*write out*) scrivere; (*: cheque*) emettere; (*understand*) capire; (*see*) distinguere; (*: numbers*) decifrare; **~ up** *vt* (*constitute*) formare; (*invent*) inventare; (*parcel*) fare ♦ *vi* conciliarsi; (*with cosmetics*) truccarsi; **~ up for** *vt fus* compensare; ricuperare; **~-believe** *n*: **a world of ~-believe** un mondo di favole; **it's just ~-believe** è tutta un'invenzione; **~r** *n* (*of programme etc*) creatore/trice; (*manufacturer*) fabbricante *m*; **~shift** *adj* improvvisato(a); **~-up** *n* trucco; **~-up remover** *n* struccatore *m*

making ['meıkıŋ] *n* (*fig*): **in the ~** in formazione; **to have the ~s of** (*actor, athlete etc*) avere la stoffa di

maladjusted [mælə'dʒʌstıd] *adj* disadattato(a)

malaise [mæ'leɪz] n malessere m

malaria [mə'leərɪə] n malaria

Malay [mə'leɪ] n Malesia

male [meɪl] n (BIOL) maschio ♦ adj maschile; maschio(a)

malfunction [mæl'fʌŋkʃən] n funzione f difettosa

malice ['mælɪs] n malevolenza; **malicious** [mə'lɪʃəs] adj malevolo(a); (LAW) doloso(a)

malign [mə'laɪn] vt malignare su; calunniare

malignant [mə'lɪgnənt] adj (MED) maligno(a)

mall [mɔːl] n (also: shopping ~) centro commerciale

mallet ['mælɪt] n maglio

malnutrition [mælnjuː'trɪʃən] n denutrizione f

malpractice [mæl'præktɪs] n prevaricazione f; negligenza

malt [mɔːlt] n malto

Malta ['mɔːltə] n Malta

mammal ['mæml] n mammifero

mammoth ['mæməθ] n mammut m inv ♦ adj enorme, gigantesco(a)

man [mæn] (pl **men**) n uomo ♦ vt fornire d'uomini; stare a; **an old** ~ un vecchio; ~ **and wife** marito e moglie

manage ['mænɪdʒ] vi farcela ♦ vt (be in charge of) occuparsi di; gestire; to ~ **to do** sth riuscire a far qc; ~**able** adj maneggevole; fattibile; ~**ment** n amministrazione f, direzione f; ~**r** n direttore m; (of shop, restaurant) gerente m; (of artist, SPORT) manager m inv; ~**ress** [-ə'res] n direttrice f; gerente f; ~**rial** [-ə'dʒɪərɪəl] adj dirigenziale; **managing director** n amministratore m delegato

mandarin ['mændərɪn] n (person, fruit) mandarino

mandatory ['mændətərɪ] adj obbligatorio(a); ingiuntivo(a)

mane [meɪn] n criniera

maneuver etc [mə'nuːvə*] (US) = **manoeuvre** etc

manfully ['mænfʊlɪ] adv valorosa-

mente

mangle ['mæŋgl] vt straziare; mutilare

mango ['mæŋgəʊ] (pl ~es) n mango

mangy ['meɪndʒɪ] adj rognoso(a)

manhandle ['mænhændl] vt malmenare

manhole ['mænhəʊl] n botola stradale

manhood ['mænhʊd] n età virile; virilità

man-hour n ora di lavoro

manhunt ['mænhʌnt] n caccia all'uomo

mania ['meɪnɪə] n mania; ~**c** ['meɪnɪæk] n maniaco(a)

manic ['mænɪk] adj (behaviour, activity) maniacale

manicure ['mænɪkjʊə*] n manicure f inv; ~ **set** n trousse f inv della manicure

manifest ['mænɪfest] vt manifestare ♦ adj manifesto(a), palese

manifesto [mænɪ'festəʊ] n manifesto

manipulate [mə'nɪpjʊleɪt] vt manipolare

mankind [mæn'kaɪnd] n umanità, genere m umano

manly ['mænlɪ] adj virile; coraggioso(a)

man-made adj sintetico(a); artificiale

manner ['mænə*] n maniera, modo; (behaviour) modo di fare; (type, sort): **all** ~ **of things** ogni genere di cosa; ~**s** npl (conduct) maniere fpl; **bad** ~**s** maleducazione f; ~**ism** n vezzo, tic m inv

manoeuvre [mə'nuːvə*] (US **manoeuver**) vt manovrare ♦ vi far manovre ♦ n manovra

manor ['mænə*] n (also: ~ house) maniero

manpower ['mænpaʊə*] n manodopera

mansion ['mænʃən] n casa signorile

manslaughter ['mænslɔːtə*] n omicidio preterintenzionale

mantelpiece ['mæntlpiːs] n mensola del caminetto

manual 156 mask

manual ['mænjuəl] *adj* manuale ♦ *n* manuale *m*

manufacture [mænju'fæktʃə*] *vt* fabbricare ♦ *n* fabbricazione *f*, manifattura; **~r** *n* fabbricante *m*

manure [mə'njuə*] *n* concime *m*

manuscript ['mænjuskrɪpt] *n* manoscritto

many ['menɪ] *adj* molti(e) ♦ *pron* molti(e); **a great ~** moltissimi(e), un gran numero (di); **~ a time** molte volte

map [mæp] *n* carta (geografica); **~ out** *vt* tracciare un piano di

maple ['meɪpl] *n* acero

mar [ma:*] *vt* sciupare

marathon ['mærəθən] *n* maratona

marauder [mə'rɔ:də*] *n* saccheggiatore *m*

marble ['ma:bl] *n* marmo; (*toy*) pallina, bilia

March [ma:tʃ] *n* marzo

march [ma:tʃ] *vi* marciare; sfilare ♦ *n* marcia

mare [mɛə*] *n* giumenta

margarine [ma:dʒə'ri:n] *n* margarina

margin ['ma:dʒɪn] *n* margine *m*; **~al (seat)** *n* (*POL*) seggio elettorale ottenuto con una stretta maggioranza

marigold ['mærɪgəʊld] *n* calendola

marijuana [mærɪ'wa:nə] *n* marijuana

marine [mə'ri:n] *adj* (*animal, plant*) marino(a); (*forces, engineering*) marittimo(a) ♦ *n* (*BRIT*) fante *m* di marina; (*US*) marine *m inv*

marital ['mærɪtl] *adj* maritale, coniugale; **~ status** stato coniugale

mark [ma:k] *n* segno; (*stain*) macchia; (*of skid etc*) traccia; (*BRIT: SCOL*) voto; (*SPORT*) bersaglio; (*currency*) marco ♦ *vt* segnare; (*stain*) macchiare; (*indicate*) indicare; (*BRIT: SCOL*) dare un voto a; correggere; **to ~ time** segnare il passo; **~ed** *adj* spiccato(a), chiaro(a); **~er** *n* (*sign*) segno; (*bookmark*) segnalibro

market ['ma:kɪt] *n* mercato ♦ *vt*

(*COMM*) mettere in vendita; **~ garden** (*BRIT*) *n* orto industriale; **~ing** *n* marketing *m*; **~ place** *n* piazza del mercato; (*COMM*) piazza, mercato; **~ research** *n* indagine *f* or ricerca di mercato

marksman ['ma:ksmən] *n* tiratore *m* scelto

marmalade ['ma:məleɪd] *n* marmellata d'arance

maroon [mə'ru:n] *vt* (*also: fig*) **to be ~ed (in** *or* **at)** essere abbandonato(a) (in) ♦ *adj* bordeaux *inv*

marquee [ma:'ki:] *n* padiglione *m*

marquess ['ma:kwɪs] *n* = **marquis**

marquis ['ma:kwɪs] *n* marchese *m*

marriage ['mærɪdʒ] *n* matrimonio; **~ bureau** *n* agenzia matrimoniale; **~ certificate** *n* certificato di matrimonio

married ['mærɪd] *adj* sposato(a); (*life, love*) coniugale, matrimoniale

marrow ['mærəʊ] *n* midollo; (*vegetable*) zucca

marry ['mærɪ] *vt* sposare, sposarsi con; (*subj: father, priest etc*) dare in matrimonio ♦ *vi* (*also: get married*) sposarsi

Mars [ma:z] *n* (*planet*) Marte *m*

marsh [ma:ʃ] *n* palude *f*

marshal ['ma:ʃl] *n* maresciallo; (*US: fire*) capo; (*: police*) capitano ♦ *vt* (*thoughts, support*) ordinare; (*soldiers*) adunare

martyr ['ma:tə*] *n* martire *m/f*; **~dom** *n* martirio

marvel ['ma:vl] *n* meraviglia ♦ *vi*: **to ~ (at)** meravigliarsi (di); **~lous** (*US* **~ous**) *adj* meraviglioso(a)

Marxist ['ma:ksɪst] *adj, n* marxista *m/f*

marzipan ['ma:zɪpæn] *n* marzapane *m*

mascara [mæs'ka:rə] *n* mascara *m*

masculine ['mæskjulɪn] *adj* maschile; (*woman*) mascolino(a)

mash [mæʃ] *vt* passare, schiacciare; **~ed potatoes** *npl* purè *m* di patate

mask [ma:sk] *n* maschera ♦ *vt* mascherare

mason ['meɪsn] n (also: stone~) scalpellino; (also: free~) massone m; ~ry n muratura

masquerade [mæskə'reɪd] vi: to ~ as farsi passare per

mass [mæs] n moltitudine f, massa; (PHYSICS) massa; (REL) messa ♦ cpd di massa ♦ vi ammassarsi; the ~es npl (ordinary people) le masse; ~es of (inf) una montagna di

massacre ['mæsəkə*] n massacro

massage ['mæsɑːʒ] n massaggio

masseur [mæ'sə:*] n massaggiatore m; **masseuse** [-'sə:z] n massaggiatrice f

massive ['mæsɪv] adj enorme, massiccio(a)

mass media npl mass media mpl

mass-production n produzione f in serie

mast [mɑːst] n albero

master ['mɑːstə*] n padrone m; (ART etc, teacher: in primary school) maestro; (: in secondary school) professore m; (title for boys): M~ X Signorino X ♦ vt domare; (learn) imparare a fondo; (understand) conoscere a fondo; ~ **key** n chiave f maestra; ~**ly** adj magistrale; ~**mind** n mente f superiore ♦ vt essere il cervello di; **M~ of Arts/Science** ≈ Master m inv in lettere/scienze; ~**piece** n capolavoro; ~**y** n dominio; padronanza

mat [mæt] n stuoia; (also: door~) stoino, zerbino; (also: table ~) sottopiatto ♦ adj = **matt**

match [mætʃ] n fiammifero; (game) partita, incontro; (fig) uguale m/f; matrimonio; partito ♦ vt intonare; (go well with) andare benissimo con; (equal) uguagliare; (correspond to) corrispondere a; (pair: also: ~ up) accoppiare ♦ vi combaciare; **to be a good** ~ andare bene; ~**box** n scatola per fiammiferi; ~**ing** adj ben assortito(a)

mate [meɪt] n compagno/a di lavoro; (inf: friend) amico/a; (animal) compagno/a; (in merchant navy) se-

condo ♦ vi accoppiarsi

material [mə'tɪərɪəl] n (substance) materiale m, materia; (cloth) stoffa ♦ adj materiale; ~s npl (equipment) materiali mpl

maternal [mə'tə:nl] adj materno(a)

maternity [mə'tə:nɪtɪ] n maternità; ~ **dress** n vestito m pre-maman inv; ~ **hospital** n ≈ clinica ostetrica

math [mæθ] (US) n = **maths**

mathematical [mæθə'mætɪkl] adj matematico(a)

mathematics [mæθə'mætɪks] n matematica

maths [mæθs] (US **math**) n matematica

matinée ['mætɪneɪ] n matinée f inv

mating call ['meɪtɪŋ-] n richiamo sessuale

matriculation [mətrɪkju'leɪʃən] n immatricolazione f

matrimonial [mætrɪ'məunɪəl] adj matrimoniale, coniugale

matrimony ['mætrɪmənɪ] n matrimonio

matron ['meɪtrən] n (in hospital) capoinfermiera; (in school) infermiera

mat(t) [mæt] adj opaco(a)

matted ['mætɪd] adj ingarbugliato(a)

matter ['mætə*] n questione f; (PHYSICS) materia, sostanza; (content) contenuto; (MED: pus) pus m ♦ vi importare; **it doesn't** ~ non importa; (I don't mind) non fa niente; **what's the** ~? cosa c'è?; **no** ~ **what** qualsiasi cosa accada; **as a** ~ **of course** come cosa naturale; **as a** ~ **of fact** in verità; ~**-of-fact** adj prosaico(a)

mattress ['mætrɪs] n materasso

mature [mə'tjuə*] adj maturo(a); (cheese) stagionato(a) ♦ vi maturare; stagionare

maul [mɔːl] vt lacerare

mauve [məuv] adj malva inv

maverick ['mævərɪk] n chi sta fuori dal branco

maxim ['mæksɪm] n massima

maxima ['mæksɪmə] npl of **maxi-**

mum

maximum ['mæksɪməm] (pl maxima) adj massimo(a) ♦ n massimo

May [meɪ] n maggio

may [meɪ] (conditional: **might**) vi (indicating possibility): he ~ **come** può darsi che venga; (be allowed to): ~ **I smoke?** posso fumare?; (wishes): ~ **God bless you!** Dio la benedica!; **you** ~ **as well go** tanto vale che tu te ne vada

maybe ['meɪbiː] adv forse, può darsi; ~ **he'll** ... può darsi che lui ... + sub, forse lui ...

May Day n il primo maggio

mayhem ['meɪhem] n cagnara

mayonnaise [meɪə'neɪz] n maionese f

mayor [mɛə*] n sindaco; ~**ess** n sindaco (donna); moglie f del sindaco

maze [meɪz] n labirinto, dedalo

M.D. abbr = **Doctor of Medicine**

me [miː] pron mi, m' + vowel or silent "h"; (stressed, after prep) me; **he heard** ~ mi ha or m'ha sentito; **give** ~ **a book** dammi (or mi dia) un libro; **it's** ~ sono io; **with** ~ con me; **without** ~ senza di me

meadow ['mɛdəʊ] n prato

meagre ['miːgə*] (US **meager**) adj magro(a)

meal [miːl] n pasto; (flour) farina; ~**time** n l'ora di mangiare

mean [miːn] (pt, pp **meant**) adj (with money) avaro(a), gretto(a); (unkind) meschino(a), maligno(a); (shabby) misero(a); (average) medio(a) ♦ vt (signify) significare, voler dire; (intend): **to** ~ **to do** aver l'intenzione di fare ♦ n mezzo; (MATH) media; ~**s** npl (way, money) mezzi mpl; **by** ~**s of** per mezzo di; **by all** ~**s** ma certo, prego; **to be meant for** essere destinato(a) a; **do you** ~ **it?** dice sul serio?; **what do you** ~? dice cosa vuol dire?

meander [mɪ'ændə*] vi far meandri

meaning ['miːnɪŋ] n significato, senso; ~**ful** adj significativo(a); ~**less** adj senza senso

meant [mɛnt] pt, pp of **mean**

meantime ['miːntaɪm] adv (also: **in the** ~) nel frattempo

meanwhile ['miːnwaɪl] adv nel frattempo

measles ['miːzlz] n morbillo

measly ['miːzlɪ] (inf) adj miserabile

measure ['mɛʒə*] vt, vi misurare ♦ n misura; (also: **tape** ~) metro; ~**ments** npl (size) misure fpl

meat [miːt] n carne f; **cold** ~ affettato; ~**ball** n polpetta di carne; ~**pie** n pasticcio di carne in crosta

Mecca ['mɛkə] n (also fig) la Mecca

mechanic [mɪ'kænɪk] n meccanico; ~**al** adj meccanico(a); ~**s** n meccanica ♦ npl meccanismo

mechanism ['mɛkənɪzəm] n meccanismo

medal ['mɛdl] n medaglia; ~**lion** [mɪ'dælɪən] n medaglione m; ~**list** (US ~**ist**) n (SPORT): **to be a gold** ~**list** essere medaglia d'oro

meddle ['mɛdl] vi: **to** ~ **in** immischiarsi in, mettere le mani in; **to** ~ **with** toccare

media ['miːdɪə] npl media mpl

mediaeval [mɛdɪ'iːvl] adj = **medieval**

median ['miːdɪən] (US) n (also: ~ **strip**) banchina f spartitraffico

mediate ['miːdɪeɪt] vi fare da mediatore/trice

Medicaid ['mɛdɪkeɪd] (US) n assistenza medica ai poveri

medical ['mɛdɪkl] adj medico(a) ♦ n visita medica

Medicare ['mɛdɪkɛə*] (US) n assistenza medica agli anziani

medication [mɛdɪ'keɪʃən] n medicinali mpl, farmaci mpl

medicine ['mɛdsɪn] n medicina

medieval [mɛdɪ'iːvl] adj medievale

mediocre [miːdɪ'əʊkə*] adj mediocre

meditate ['mɛdɪteɪt] vi: **to** ~ **(on)** meditare (su)

Mediterranean [mɛdɪtə'reɪnɪən] adj mediterraneo(a); **the** ~ **(Sea)** il (mare) Mediterraneo

medium ['miːdɪəm] (pl media) adj medio(a) ♦ n (means) mezzo; (pl mediums: person) medium m inv; ~ **wave** n onde fpl medie

medley ['medlɪ] n selezione f; (MUS) pot-pourri m inv

meek [miːk] adj dolce, umile

meet [miːt], (pt, pp met) vt incontrare; (for the first time) fare la conoscenza di; (go and fetch) andare a prendere; (fig) affrontare; soddisfare; raggiungere ♦ vi incontrarsi; (in session) riunirsi; (join: objects) unirsi; ~ **with** vt fus incontrare; ~**ing** n incontro; (session: of club etc) riunione f; (interview) intervista; she's at a ~**ing** (COMM) è in riunione

megabyte ['megəbaɪt] n (COMPUT) megabyte m inv

megaphone ['megəfəʊn] n megafono

melancholy ['melənkəlɪ] n malinconia ♦ adj malinconico(a)

mellow ['meləʊ] adj (wine, sound) ricco(a); (light) dolce; (colour) caldo(a) ♦ vi (person) addolcirsi

melody ['melədɪ] n melodia

melon ['melən] n melone m

melt [melt] vi (gen) sciogliersi, struggersi; (metals) fondersi ♦ vt sciogliere, struggere; fondere; ~ **down** vt fondere; ~**down** n (in nuclear reactor) fusione f (dovuta a surriscaldamento); ~**ing pot** n (fig) crogiolo

member ['membə*] n membro; **M~ of the European Parliament** (BRIT) n eurodeputato; **M~ of Parliament** (BRIT) n deputato; ~**ship** n iscrizione f; (numero d')iscritti mpl, membri mpl; ~**ship card** n tessera (di iscrizione)

memento [mə'mentəʊ] n ricordo, souvenir m inv

memo ['meməʊ] n appunto; (COMM etc) comunicazione f di servizio

memoirs ['memwɑːz] npl memorie fpl, ricordi mpl

memoranda [memə'rændə] npl of **memorandum**

memorandum [memə'rændəm] (pl memoranda) n appunto; (COMM etc) comunicazione f di servizio

memorial [mɪ'mɔːrɪəl] n monumento commemorativo ♦ adj commemorativo(a)

memorize ['meməraɪz] vt memorizzare

memory ['memərɪ] n (also COMPUT) memoria; (recollection) ricordo

men [men] npl of **man**

menace ['menəs] n minaccia ♦ vt minacciare

mend [mend] vt aggiustare, riparare; (darn) rammendare ♦ n: on the ~ in via di guarigione; to ~ one's ways correggersi

menial ['miːnɪəl] adj da servo, domestico(a); umile

meningitis [menɪn'dʒaɪtɪs] n meningite f

menopause ['menəʊpɔːz] n menopausa

menstruation [menstru'eɪʃən] n mestruazione f

mental ['mentl] adj mentale

mentality [men'tælɪtɪ] n mentalità f inv

menthol ['menθɒl] n mentolo

mention ['menʃən] n menzione f ♦ vt menzionare, far menzione di; **don't** ~ **it!** non c'è di che!, prego!

menu ['menjuː] n (set ~, COMPUT) menù m inv; (printed) carta

MEP n abbr = **Member of the European Parliament**

mercenary ['məːsɪnərɪ] adj venale ♦ n mercenario

merchandise ['məːtʃəndaɪz] n merci fpl

merchant ['məːtʃənt] n mercante m, commerciante m; ~ **bank** (BRIT) n banca d'affari; ~ **navy** (US ~ **marine**) n marina mercantile

merciful ['məːsɪful] adj pietoso(a), clemente

merciless ['məːsɪlɪs] adj spietato(a)

mercury ['məːkjʊrɪ] n mercurio

mercy ['məːsɪ] n pietà; (REL) misericordia; **at the** ~ **of** alla mercé di

mere [mɪə*] *adj* semplice; **by a ~ chance** per mero caso; **~ly** *adv* semplicemente, non ... che

merge [mə:dʒ] *vt* unire ♦ *vi* fondersi, unirsi; (*COMM*) fondersi; **~r** *n* (*COMM*) fusione *f*

meringue [məˈræŋ] *n* meringa

merit [ˈmɛrɪt] *n* merito, valore *m* ♦ *vt* meritare

mermaid [ˈmə:meɪd] *n* sirena

merry [ˈmɛrɪ] *adj* gaio(a), allegro(a); **M~ Christmas!** Buon Natale!; **~-go-round** *n* carosello

mesh [mɛʃ] *n* maglia; rete *f*

mesmerize [ˈmɛzməraɪz] *vt* ipnotizzare; affascinare

mess [mɛs] *n* confusione *f*, disordine *m*; (*fig*) pasticcio; (*dirt*) sporcizia; (*MIL*) mensa; **~ about** (*inf*) *vi* (*also: ~ around*) trastullarsi; **~ about with** (*inf*) *vt fus* (*also: ~ around with*) gingillarsi con; (*plans*) fare un pasticcio di; **~ up** *vt* sporcare; fare un pasticcio di; rovinare

message [ˈmɛsɪdʒ] *n* messaggio

messenger [ˈmɛsɪndʒə*] *n* messaggero/a

Messrs [ˈmɛsəz] *abbr* (*on letters*) Spett

messy [ˈmɛsɪ] *adj* sporco(a); disordinato(a)

met [mɛt] *pt, pp* of **meet**

metal [ˈmɛtl] *n* metallo; **~lic** [-ˈtælɪk] *adj* metallico(a)

metaphor [ˈmɛtəfə*] *n* metafora

mete [mi:t]: **to ~ out** *vt* infliggere

meteorology [mi:tɪəˈrɔlədʒɪ] *n* meteorologia

meter [ˈmi:tə*] *n* (*instrument*) contatore *m*; (*parking ~*) parchimetro; (*US: unit*) = **metre**

method [ˈmɛθəd] *n* metodo; **~ical** [mɪˈθɔdɪkl] *adj* metodico(a)

Methodist [ˈmɛθədɪst] *n* metodista *m/f*

meths [mɛθs] (*BRIT*) *n* = **methylated spirit**

methylated spirit [ˈmɛθɪleɪtɪd-] (*BRIT*) *n* alcool m denaturato

metre [ˈmi:tə*] (*US* **meter**) *n* metro

metric [ˈmɛtrɪk] *adj* metrico(a)

metropolitan [mɛtrəˈpɔlɪtən] *adj* metropolitano(a); **the M~ Police** (*BRIT*) *n* la polizia di Londra

mettle [ˈmɛtl] *n*: **to be on one's ~** essere pronto(a) a dare il meglio di se stesso(a)

mew [mju:] *vi* (*cat*) miagolare

mews [mju:z] (*BRIT*) *n*: **~ flat** appartamento ricavato da un'antica scuderia

Mexico [ˈmɛksɪkəʊ] *n* Messico

miaow [mi:ˈaʊ] *vi* miagolare

mice [maɪs] *npl of* **mouse**

micro... [ˈmaɪkrəʊ] *prefix* micro...; **~chip** *n* microcircuito integrato; **~(computer)** *n* microcomputer *m inv*; **~film** *n* microfilm *m inv*; **~phone** *n* microfono; **~scope** *n* microscopio; **~wave** *n* (*also: ~wave oven*) forno a microonde

mid [mɪd] *adj*: **~ May** metà maggio; **~ afternoon** metà pomeriggio; **in the air** a mezz'aria; **~day** *n* mezzogiorno

middle [ˈmɪdl] *n* mezzo; centro; (*waist*) vita ♦ *adj* di mezzo; **in the ~ of the night** nel bel mezzo della notte; **~-aged** *adj* di mezza età; **the M~ Ages** *npl* il Medioevo; **~ class** *adj* = borghese; **the ~ class(es)** *n(pl)* = la borghesia; **M~ East** *n* Medio Oriente *m*; **~man** *n* intermediario; agente *m* rivenditore; **~ name** *n* secondo nome *m*; **~-of-the-road** *adj* moderato(a); **~weight** *n* (*BOXING*) peso medio

middling [ˈmɪdlɪŋ] *adj* medio(a)

midge [mɪdʒ] *n* moscerino

midget [ˈmɪdʒɪt] *n* nano/a

Midlands [ˈmɪdləndz] *npl* contee del centro dell'Inghilterra

midnight [ˈmɪdnaɪt] *n* mezzanotte *f*

midriff [ˈmɪdrɪf] *n* diaframma *m*

midst [mɪdst] *n*: **in the ~ of** in mezzo a

midsummer [mɪdˈsʌmə*] *n* mezza estate *f*, piena estate *f*

midway [ˈmɪdˈweɪ] *adj, adv*: ~ (**between**) a mezza strada (fra); ~

(through) a metà (di)

midweek [mɪd'wiːk] adv a metà settimana

midwife ['mɪdwaɪf] (pl **midwives**) n levatrice f

midwinter [mɪd'wɪntə*] n: **in** ~ **in** pieno inverno

midwives ['mɪdwaɪvz] npl of **midwife**

might [maɪt] vb see **may** ♦ n potere m, forza; ~**y** adj forte, potente

migraine ['miːgreɪn] n emicrania

migrant ['maɪɡrənt] adj (bird) migratore(trice); (worker) emigrato(a)

migrate [maɪ'ɡreɪt] vi (bird) migrare; (person) emigrare

mike [maɪk] n abbr (= microphone) microfono

Milan [mɪ'læn] n Milano f

mild [maɪld] adj mite; (person, voice) dolce; (flavour) delicato(a); (illness) leggero(a); (interest) blando(a)

mildew ['mɪldjuː] n muffa

mildly ['maɪldlɪ] adv mitemente; dolcemente; delicatamente; leggermente; blandamente; **to put it** ~ a dire poco

mile [maɪl] n miglio f; ~**age** n distanza in miglia, ≈ chilometraggio

mileometer [maɪ'lɔmɪtə*] n ≈ contachilometri m inv

milestone ['maɪlstəun] n pietra miliare

milieu ['miːljəː] n ambiente m

militant ['mɪlɪtnt] adj militante

military ['mɪlɪtərɪ] adj militare

militate ['mɪlɪteɪt] vi: **to** ~ **against** essere d'ostacolo a

milk [mɪlk] n latte m ♦ vt (cow) mungere; (fig) sfruttare; ~**chocolate** n cioccolato al latte; ~**man** n lattaio; ~**shake** n frappé m inv; ~**y** adj lattiginoso(a); (colour) latteo(a); **M~y Way** n Via Lattea

mill [mɪl] n mulino; (small: for coffee, pepper etc) macinino; (factory) fabbrica; (spinning ~) filatura ♦ vt macinare ♦ vi (also: ~ **about**) brulicare

miller ['mɪlə*] n mugnaio

milli... ['mɪlɪ] prefix: ~**gram(me)** n milligrammo; ~**metre** (US ~**meter**) n millimetro

millinery ['mɪlɪnərɪ] n modisteria

million ['mɪljən] n milione m; ~**aire** n milionario, ≈ miliardario

milometer [maɪ'lɔmɪtə*] n = **mileometer**

mime [maɪm] n mimo ♦ vt, vi mimare

mimic ['mɪmɪk] n imitatore/trice ♦ vt fare la mimica di

min. abbr = **minute(s)**; **minimum**

mince [mɪns] vt tritare, macinare ♦ vi (in walking) camminare a passettini ♦ n (BRIT: CULIN) carne f tritata or macinata; ~**meat** n frutta secca tritata per uso in pasticceria; (US) carne f tritata or macinata; ~**pie** n specie di torta con frutta secca; ~**r** n tritacarne m inv

mind [maɪnd] n mente f ♦ vt (attend to, look after) badare a, occuparsi di; (be careful) fare attenzione a, stare attento(a) a; (object to): **I don't** ~ **the noise** il rumore non mi dà alcun fastidio; **I don't** ~ non m'importa; **it is on my** ~ mi preoccupa; **to my** ~ secondo me, a mio parere; **to be out of one's** ~ essere uscito(a) di mente; **to keep or bear sth in** ~ non dimenticare qc; **to make up one's** ~ decidersi; ~ **you, ...** si, però va detto che ...; **never** ~ non importa, non fa niente; (don't worry) non preoccuparti; "~ **the step**" "attenzione allo scalino"; ~**er** n (child ~er) bambinaia; (bodyguard) guardia del corpo; ~**ful** adj: ~**ful of** attento(a) a; memore di; ~**less** adj idiota

mine[1] [maɪn] pron il(la) mio(a), pl i(le) miei(mie); **that book is** ~ quel libro è mio; **yours is red,** ~ **is green** il tuo è rosso, il mio è verde; **a friend of** ~ un mio amico

mine[2] [maɪn] n miniera; (explosive) mina ♦ vt (coal) estrarre; (ship, beach) minare; ~**field** n (also fig) campo minato

miner ['maɪnə*] n minatore m

mineral ['mɪnərəl] adj minerale ♦ n minerale m; ~s npl (BRIT: soft drinks) bevande fpl gasate; ~ water n acqua minerale

mingle ['mɪŋgl] vi: to ~ with mescolarsi a, mischiarsi con

miniature ['mɪnətʃə*] adj in miniatura ♦ n miniatura

minibus ['mɪnɪbʌs] n minibus m inv

minim ['mɪnɪm] n (MUS) minima

minima ['mɪnɪmə] npl of **minimum**

minimum ['mɪnɪməm] (pl **minima** n minimo ♦ adj minimo(a)

mining ['maɪnɪŋ] n industria mineraria

miniskirt ['mɪnɪskə:t] n minigonna

minister ['mɪnɪstə*] n (BRIT: POL) ministro; (REL) pastore m ♦ vi: to ~ to sb assistere qn; to ~ to sb's needs provvedere ai bisogni di qn; ~ial [-'tɪərɪəl] (BRIT) adj (POL) ministeriale

ministry ['mɪnɪstrɪ] n (BRIT: POL) ministero; (REL): to go into the ~ diventare pastore

mink [mɪŋk] n visone m

minnow ['mɪnəu] n pesciolino d'acqua dolce

minor ['maɪnə*] adj minore, di poca importanza; (MUS) minore ♦ n (LAW) minorenne m/f

minority [maɪ'nɔrɪtɪ] n minoranza

mint [mɪnt] n (plant) menta; (sweet) pasticca di menta ♦ vt (coins) battere; the (Royal) M~ (BRIT), the (US) M~ (US) la Zecca; in ~ condition come nuovo(a) di zecca

minus ['maɪnəs] n (also: ~ sign) segno meno ♦ prep meno

minute [adj maɪ'nju:t, n 'mɪnɪt] adj minuscolo(a); (detail) minuzioso(a) ♦ n minuto; ~s npl (of meeting) verbale m

miracle ['mɪrəkl] n miracolo

mirage ['mɪrɑ:ʒ] n miraggio

mirror ['mɪrə*] n specchio; (in car) specchietto

mirth [mə:θ] n ilarità

misadventure [mɪsəd'ventʃə*] n di-

savventura; **death by** ~ morte f accidentale

misapprehension ['mɪsæprɪ'hen-ʃən] n malinteso

misappropriate [mɪsə'prəuprɪeɪt] vt appropriarsi indebitamente di

misbehave [mɪsbɪ'heɪv] vi comportarsi male

miscarriage ['mɪskærɪdʒ] n (MED) aborto spontaneo; ~ **of justice** errore m giudiziario

miscellaneous [mɪsɪ'leɪnɪəs] adj (items) vario(a); (selection) misto(a)

mischance [mɪs'tʃɑ:ns] n sfortuna

mischief ['mɪstʃɪf] n (naughtiness) birichineria; (maliciousness) malizia; **mischievous** adj birichino(a)

misconception ['mɪskən'sepʃən] n idea sbagliata

misconduct [mɪs'kɔndʌkt] n cattiva condotta; **professional** ~ reato professionale

misdemeanour [mɪsdɪ'mi:nə*] (US **misdemeanor**) n misfatto; infrazione f

miser ['maɪzə*] n avaro

miserable ['mɪzərəbl] adj infelice; (wretched) miserabile; (weather) deprimente; (offer, failure) misero(a)

miserly ['maɪzəlɪ] adj avaro(a)

misery ['mɪzərɪ] n (unhappiness) tristezza; (wretchedness) miseria

misfire [mɪs'faɪə*] vi far cilecca; (car engine) perdere colpi

misfit ['mɪsfɪt] n (person) spostato/a

misfortune [mɪs'fɔ:tʃən] n sfortuna

misgiving [mɪs'gɪvɪŋ] n apprensione f; **to have** ~s **about** avere dei dubbi per quanto riguarda

misguided [mɪs'gaɪdɪd] adj sbagliato(a); poco giudizioso(a)

mishandle [mɪs'hændl] vt (mismanage) trattare male

mishap ['mɪshæp] n disgrazia

misinterpret [mɪsɪn'tə:prɪt] vt interpretare male

misjudge [mɪs'dʒʌdʒ] vt giudicare male

mislay [mɪs'leɪ] (irreg) vt smarrire

mislead [mɪs'liːd] *(irreg)* vt sviare; **~ing** *adj* ingannevole

mismanage [mɪs'mænɪdʒ] vt gestire male

misnomer [mɪs'nəumə*] n termine m sbagliato or improprio

misplace [mɪs'pleɪs] vt smarrire

misprint ['mɪsprɪnt] n errore m di stampa

Miss [mɪs] n Signorina

miss [mɪs] vt *(fail to get)* perdere; *(fail to hit)* mancare; *(fail to see)*: **you can't ~ it** non puoi non vederlo; *(regret the absence of)*: **I ~ him** sento la sua mancanza ♦ vi mancare ♦ n *(shot)* colpo mancato; **~ out** *(BRIT)* vt omettere

misshapen [mɪs'ʃeɪpən] *adj* deforme

missile ['mɪsaɪl] n *(MIL)* missile m; *(object thrown)* proiettile m

missing ['mɪsɪŋ] *adj* perso(a), smarrito(a); *(person)* scomparso(a); *(: after disaster, MIL)* disperso(a); *(: removed)* mancante; **to be ~** mancare

mission ['mɪʃən] n missione f; **~ary** n missionario/a

misspent ['mɪs'spɛnt] *adj*: **his ~ youth** la sua gioventù sciupata

mist [mɪst] n nebbia, foschia ♦ vi *(also: ~ over, ~ up)* annebbiarsi; *(: BRIT: windows)* appannarsi

mistake [mɪs'teɪk] *(irreg: like take)* n sbaglio, errore m ♦ vt sbagliarsi di; fraintendere; **to make a ~** fare uno sbaglio, sbagliare; **by ~** per sbaglio; **to ~ for** prendere per; **mistaken** pp of **mistake** ♦ *adj (idea etc)* sbagliato(a); **to be mistaken** sbagliarsi

mister ['mɪstə*] *(inf)* n signore m; see **Mr**

mistletoe ['mɪsltəu] n vischio

mistook [mɪs'tuk] pt of **mistake**

mistress ['mɪstrɪs] n padrona; *(lover)* amante f; *(BRIT: SCOL)* insegnante f

mistrust [mɪs'trʌst] vt diffidare di

misty ['mɪstɪ] *adj* nebbioso(a), brumoso(a)

misunderstand [mɪsʌndə'stænd] *(ir-*

reg) vt, vi capire male, fraintendere; **~ing** n malinteso, equivoco

misuse [n mɪs'juːs, vb mɪs'juːz] n cattivo uso; *(of power)* abuso ♦ vt far cattivo uso di; abusare di

mitigate ['mɪtɪgeɪt] vt mitigare

mitt(en) ['mɪt(n)] n mezzo guanto; manopola

mix [mɪks] vt mescolare ♦ vi *(people)*: **to ~ with** avere a che fare con ♦ n mescolanza; preparato; **~ up** vt mescolare; *(confuse)* confondere; **~ed** *adj* misto(a); **~ed-up** *adj (confused)* confuso(a); **~er** n *(for food: electric)* frullatore m; *(: hand)* frullino; *(person)*: **he is a good ~er** è molto socievole; **~ture** n mescolanza; *(blend of tobacco etc)* miscela; *(MED)* sciroppo; **~-up** n confusione f

moan [məun] n gemito ♦ vi *(inf: complain)*: **to ~ (about)** lamentarsi (di)

moat [məut] n fossato

mob [mɔb] n calca ♦ vt accalcarsi intorno a

mobile ['məubaɪl] *adj* mobile ♦ n *(decoration)* mobile m; **~ home** n grande roulotte f inv *(utilizzata come domicilio)*; **~ phone** telefono portatile, telefonino

mock [mɔk] vt deridere, burlarsi di ♦ *adj* falso(a); **~ery** n derisione f; **to make a ~ery of** burlarsi di; *(exam)* rendere una farsa; **~-up** n modello

mod [mɔd] *adj see* **convenience**

mode [məud] n modo

model ['mɔdl] n modello; *(person: for fashion)* indossatore/trice; *(: for artist)* modello/a ♦ *adj (small-scale: railway etc)* in miniatura; *(child, factory)* modello ♦ vt modellare ♦ vi fare l'indossatore (or l'indossatrice); **to ~ clothes** presentare degli abiti

modem ['məudem] n modem m inv

moderate [*adj* 'mɔdərət, vb 'mɔdəreɪt] *adj* moderato(a) ♦ vi moderarsi, placarsi ♦ vt moderare

modern ['mɔdən] adj moderno(a); **~ize** vt modernizzare

modest ['mɔdɪst] adj modesto(a); **~y** n modestia

modicum ['mɔdɪkəm] n: **a ~ of** un minimo di

modify ['mɔdɪfaɪ] vt modificare

mogul ['məugl] n (fig) magnate m, pezzo grosso

mohair ['məuhɛə*] n mohair m

moist [mɔɪst] adj umido(a); **~en** ['mɔɪsn] vt inumidire; **~ure** ['mɔɪstʃə*] n umidità; (on glass) goccioline fpl di vapore; **~urizer** ['mɔɪstʃəraɪzə*] n idratante f

molar ['məulə*] n molare m

mold [məuld] (US) n, vt = **mould**

mole [məul] n (animal, fig) talpa; (spot) neo

molest [məu'lɛst] vt molestare

mollycoddle ['mɔlɪkɔdl] vt coccolare, vezzeggiare

molt [məult] (US) vi = **moult**

molten ['məultən] adj fuso(a)

mom [mɔm] (US) n = **mum**

moment ['məumənt] n momento, istante m; **at that ~** in quel momento; **at the ~** al momento, in questo momento; **~ary** adj momentaneo(a), passeggero(a); **~ous** [-'mɛntəs] adj di grande importanza

momentum [məu'mɛntəm] n (PHYSICS) momento; (fig) impeto; **to gather ~** aumentare di velocità

mommy ['mɔmɪ] (US) n = **mummy**

Monaco ['mɔnəkəu] n Principato di Monaco

monarch ['mɔnək] n monarca m; **~y** n monarchia

monastery ['mɔnəstərɪ] n monastero

Monday ['mʌndɪ] n lunedì m inv

monetary ['mʌnɪtərɪ] adj monetario(a)

money ['mʌnɪ] n denaro, soldi mpl; **~ order** n vaglia m inv; **~-spinner** (inf) n miniera d'oro (fig)

mongol ['mɔŋgəl] adj, n (MED) mongoloide m/f

mongrel ['mʌŋgrəl] n (dog) cane m bastardo

monitor ['mɔnɪtə*] n (TV, COMPUT) monitor m inv ♦ vt controllare

monk [mʌŋk] n monaco

monkey ['mʌŋkɪ] n scimmia; **~ nut** (BRIT) n nocciolina americana; **~ wrench** n chiave f a rullino

mono ['mɔnəu] adj (recording) (in) mono inv

monopoly [mə'nɔpəlɪ] n monopolio

monotone ['mɔnətəun] n pronuncia (or voce f) monotona

monotonous [mə'nɔtənəs] adj monotono(a)

monsoon [mɔn'su:n] n monsone m

monster ['mɔnstə*] n mostro

monstrous ['mɔnstrəs] adj mostruoso(a); (huge) gigantesco(a)

montage [mɔn'tɑ:ʒ] n montaggio

month [mʌnθ] n mese m; **~ly** adj mensile ♦ adv al mese; ogni mese

monument ['mɔnjumənt] n monumento

moo [mu:] vi muggire, mugghiare

mood [mu:d] n umore m; **to be in a good/bad ~** essere di buon/cattivo umore; **~y** adj (variable) capriccioso(a), lunatico(a); (sullen) imbronciato(a)

moon [mu:n] n luna; **~light** n chiaro di luna; **~lighting** n lavoro nero; **~lit** adj: **a ~lit night** una notte rischiarata dalla luna

moor [muə*] n brughiera ♦ vt (ship) ormeggiare ♦ vi ormeggiarsi

moorland ['muələnd] n brughiera

moose [mu:s] n inv alce m

mop [mɔp] n lavapavimenti m inv; (also: **~ of hair**) zazzera ♦ vt lavare con lo straccio; (face) asciugare; **~ up** vt asciugare con uno straccio

mope [məup] vi fare il broncio

moped ['məupɛd] n ciclomotore m

moral ['mɔrl] adj morale ♦ n morale f; **~s** npl (principles) moralità

morale [mɔ'rɑ:l] n morale m

morality [mə'rælɪtɪ] n moralità

morass [mə'ræs] n palude f, pantano

morbid ['mɔ:bɪd] adj morboso(a)

---

more [mɔː*] _adj_ **1** (_greater in number etc_) più; ~ **people/letters** than we expected più persone/lettere di quante ne aspettavamo; **I have** ~ **wine/money than you** ho più vino/soldi di te; **I have** ~ **wine than beer** ho più vino che birra

2 (_additional_) altro(a), ancora; **do you want (some)** ~ **tea?** vuole dell'altro tè?, vuole ancora del tè?; **I have no or I don't have any** ~ **money** non ho più soldi

♦ _pron_ **1** (_greater amount_) più; ~ **than 10** più di 10; **it cost** ~ **than we expected** ha costato più di quanto ci aspettavamo

2 (_further or additional amount_) ancora; **is there any** ~? ce n'è ancora?; **there's no** ~ non ce n'è più; **a little** ~ ancora un po'; **many/much** ~ molti(e)/molto(a) di più

♦ _adv_: ~ **dangerous/easily (than)** più pericoloso/facilmente (di); ~ **and** ~ sempre più (di); ~ **and** ~ **difficult** sempre più difficile; ~ **or less** più o meno; ~ **than ever** più che mai

moreover [mɔːˈrəʊvə*] _adv_ inoltre, di più

morgue [mɔːg] _n_ obitorio

morning [ˈmɔːnɪŋ] _n_ mattina, mattino; (_duration_) mattinata ♦ _cpd_ del mattino; **in the** ~ la mattina; **7 o'clock in the** ~ le 7 o della mattina; ~ **sickness** _n_ nausee _fpl_ mattutine

Morocco [məˈrɔkəʊ] _n_ Marocco

moron [ˈmɔːrɔn] (_inf_) _n_ deficiente _m/f_

morose [məˈrəʊs] _adj_ cupo(a), tetro(a)

Morse [mɔːs] _n_ (_also_: ~ **code**) alfabeto Morse

morsel [ˈmɔːsl] _n_ boccone _m_

mortal [ˈmɔːtl] _adj_ mortale ♦ _n_ mortale _m_

mortar [ˈmɔːtə*] _n_ mortaio; (_CONSTR_) malta

mortgage [ˈmɔːgɪdʒ] _n_ ipoteca; (_loan_) prestito ipotecario ♦ _vt_ ipotecare; ~ **company** (_US_) _n_ società _f inv_ di credito immobiliare

mortuary [ˈmɔːtjuərɪ] _n_ camera mortuaria; obitorio

mosaic [məʊˈzeɪk] _n_ mosaico

Moscow [ˈmɔskəʊ] _n_ Mosca

Moslem [ˈmɔzləm] _adj_, _n_ = **Muslim**

mosque [mɔsk] _n_ moschea

mosquito [mɔsˈkiːtəʊ] (_pl_ ~**es**) _n_ zanzara

moss [mɔs] _n_ muschio

most [məʊst] _adj_ (_almost all_) la maggior parte di; (_largest, greatest_): **who has (the)** ~ **money?** chi ha più soldi di tutti? ♦ _pron_ la maggior parte ♦ _adv_ (_work, sleep etc_) di più; (_very_) molto, estremamente; **the** ~ (_also_: + _adjective_) il/la più; ~ **of** la maggior parte di; ~ **of them** quasi tutti; **I saw (the)** ~ ho visto più io; **at the (very)** ~ al massimo; **to make the** ~ **of** trarre il massimo vantaggio da; **a** ~ **interesting book** un libro estremamente interessante; ~**ly** _adv_ per lo più

MOT (_BRIT_) _n abbr_ (= Ministry of Transport): **the** ~ (_test_) revisione annuale obbligatoria degli autoveicoli

motel [məʊˈtel] _n_ motel _m inv_

moth [mɔθ] _n_ farfalla notturna; tarma; ~**ball** _n_ pallina di naftalina

mother [ˈmʌðə*] _n_ madre _f_ ♦ _vt_ (_care for_) fare da madre a; ~**hood** _n_ maternità; ~**-in-law** _n_ suocera; ~**ly** _adj_ materno(a); ~**-of-pearl** _n_ madreperla; ~**-to-be** _n_ futura mamma; ~ **tongue** _n_ madrelingua

motion [ˈməʊʃən] _n_ movimento, moto; (_gesture_) gesto; (_at meeting_) mozione _f_ ♦ _vt_, _vi_: **to** ~ **(to) sb to do** fare cenno a qn di fare; ~**less** _adj_ immobile; ~ **picture** _n_ film _m inv_

motivated [ˈməʊtɪveɪtɪd] _adj_ motivato(a)

motive [ˈməʊtɪv] _n_ motivo

motley [ˈmɔtlɪ] _adj_ eterogeneo(a), molto vario(a)

motor ['məutə*] n motore m; (BRIT: inf: vehicle) macchina ♦ cpd automobilistico(a); ~**bike** n moto f inv; ~**boat** n motoscafo; ~**car** (BRIT) n automobile f; ~**cycle** n motocicletta; ~**cyclist** n motociclista m/f; ~**ing** (BRIT) n turismo automobilistico; ~**ist** n automobilista m/f; ~ **racing** (BRIT) n corse fpl automobilistiche; ~**way** (BRIT) n autostrada

mottled ['mɔtld] adj chiazzato(a), marezzato(a)

motto ['mɔtəu] (pl ~es) n motto

mould [məuld] (US **mold**) n forma, stampo; (mildew) muffa ♦ vt formare; (fig) foggiare; ~**y** adj ammuffito(a); (smell) di muffa

moult [məult] (US **molt**) vi far la muta

mound [maund] n rialzo, collinetta; (heap) mucchio

mount [maunt] n (GEO) monte m ♦ vt montare; (horse) montare a ♦ vi (increase) aumentare; ~ **up** vi (build up) accumularsi

mountain ['mauntin] n montagna ♦ cpd di montagna; ~ **bike** n mountain bike f inv; ~**eer** [-'nıə*] n alpinista m/f; ~**eering** [-'nıərıŋ] n alpinismo; ~**ous** adj montagnoso(a); ~ **rescue team** n squadra di soccorso alpino; ~**side** n fianco della montagna

mourn [mɔːn] vt piangere, lamentare ♦ vi: to ~ (for sb) piangere (la morte di qn); ~**er** n parente m/f or amico/a del defunto; ~**ful** adj triste, lugubre; ~**ing** n lutto; **in ~ing** in lutto

mouse [maus] (pl **mice**) n topo; (COMPUT) mouse m inv; ~**trap** n trappola per i topi

mousse [muːs] n mousse f inv

moustache [məs'taːʃ] (US **mustache**) n baffi mpl

mousy ['mausɪ] adj (hair) né chiaro(a) né scuro(a)

mouth [mauθ, pl mauðz] n bocca; (of river) bocca, foce f; (opening)

orifizio; ~**ful** n boccata; ~ **organ** n armonica; ~**piece** n (of musical instrument) imboccatura, bocchino; (spokesman) portavoce m/f inv; ~**wash** n collutorio; ~**watering** adj che fa venire l'acquolina in bocca

movable ['muːvəbl] adj mobile

move [muːv] n (movement) movimento; (in game) mossa; (: turn to play) turno; (change: of house) trasloco; (: of job) cambiamento ♦ vt muovere, spostare; (emotionally) commuovere; (POL: resolution etc) proporre ♦ vi (gen) muoversi, spostarsi; (also: ~ house) cambiar casa, traslocare; **to get a ~ on** affrettarsi, sbrigarsi; **to ~ sb to do sth** indurre or spingere qn a fare qc; ~ **towards** andare verso; ~ **about** or **around** vi spostarsi; ~ **along** vi muoversi avanti; ~ **away** vi allontanarsi, andarsene; ~ **back** vi (return) ritornare; ~ **forward** vi avanzare; ~ **in** vi (to a house) entrare (in una nuova casa); (police etc) intervenire; ~ **on** vi riprendere la strada; ~ **out** vi (of house) sgombrare; ~ **over** vi spostarsi; ~ **up** vi avanzare

moveable ['muːvəbl] adj = **movable**

movement ['muːvmənt] n (gen) movimento; (gesture) gesto; (of stars, water, physical) moto

movie ['muːvɪ] n film m inv; **the ~s** il cinema; ~ **camera** n cinepresa

moving ['muːvɪŋ] adj mobile; (causing emotion) commovente

mow [məu] (pt **mowed**, pp **mowed** or **mown**) vt (grass) tagliare; (corn) mietere; ~ **down** vt falciare; ~**er** n (also: lawnmower) tagliaerba m inv; ~**n** pp of **mow**

MP n abbr = Member of Parliament

m.p.h. abbr = miles per hour (60 m.p.h. = 96 km/h)

Mr ['mɪstə*] (US **Mr.**) n: ~ X Signor X, Sig. X

Mrs ['mɪsɪz] (US **Mrs.**) n: ~ X Signora X, Sig.ra X

Ms [mɪz] (US **Ms.**) n (= Miss or Mrs): ~ X ≈ Signora X, Sig.ra X

M.Sc. abbr = Master of Science

KEYWORD

---

much [mʌtʃ] adj, pron molto(a); he's done so ~ work ha lavorato così tanto; I have as ~ money as you ho tanti soldi quanti ne hai tu; how ~ is it? quant'è?; it costs too ~ costa troppo; as ~ as you want quanto vuoi

♦ adv **1** (greatly) molto, tanto; thank you very ~ molte grazie; he's very ~ the gentleman è il vero gentiluomo; I read as ~ as I can leggo quanto posso; as ~ as you tanto quanto te

2 (by far) molto; it's ~ the biggest company in Europe è di gran lunga la più grossa società in Europa

3 (almost) grossomodo, praticamente; they're ~ the same sono praticamente uguali

muck [mʌk] n (dirt) sporcizia; ~ **about** or **around** (inf) vi fare lo stupido; (waste time) gingillarsi; ~ **up** (inf) vt (ruin) rovinare

mud [mʌd] n fango

muddle ['mʌdl] n confusione f, disordine m; pasticcio ♦ vt (also: ~ **up**) confondere; ~ **through** vi cavarsela alla meno peggio

muddy ['mʌdɪ] adj fangoso(a)

mudguard ['mʌdɡɑːd] n parafango

muesli ['mjuːzlɪ] n muesli m

muffin ['mʌfɪn] n specie di pasticcino soffice da tè

muffle ['mʌfl] vt (sound) smorzare, attutire; (against cold) imbaccuccare

muffler ['mʌflə*] (US) n (AUT) marmitta; (: on motorbike) silenziatore m

mug [mʌɡ] n (cup) tazzone m; (for beer) boccale m; (inf: face) muso; (: fool) scemo/a ♦ vt (assault) assalire; ~**ging** n assalto

muggy ['mʌɡɪ] adj afoso(a)

mule [mjuːl] n mulo

mull over [mʌl-] vt rimuginare

multi-level ['mʌltɪ-] (US) adj = multistorey

multiple ['mʌltɪpl] adj multiplo(a); molteplice ♦ n multiplo; ~ **sclerosis** n sclerosi f a placche

multiplication [mʌltɪplɪ'keɪʃən] n moltiplicazione f

multiply ['mʌltɪplaɪ] vt moltiplicare ♦ vi moltiplicarsi

multistorey ['mʌltɪ'stɔːrɪ] (BRIT) adj (building, car park) a più piani

mum [mʌm] (BRIT: inf) n mamma ♦ adj: to **keep** ~ non aprire bocca

mumble ['mʌmbl] vt, vi borbottare

mummy ['mʌmɪ] n (BRIT: mother) mamma; (embalmed) mummia

mumps [mʌmps] n orecchioni mpl

munch [mʌntʃ] vt, vi sgranocchiare

mundane [mʌn'deɪn] adj terra a terra inv

municipal [mjuː'nɪsɪpl] adj municipale

mural ['mjuərl] n dipinto murale

murder ['mɜːdə*] n assassinio, omicidio ♦ vt assassinare; ~**er** n omicida m, assassino; ~**ous** adj omicida

murky ['mɜːkɪ] adj tenebroso(a)

murmur ['mɜːmə*] n mormorio ♦ vt, vi mormorare

muscle ['mʌsl] n muscolo; (fig) forza; ~ **in** vi immischiarsi

muscular ['mʌskjulə*] adj muscolare; (person, arm) muscoloso(a)

muse [mjuːz] vi meditare, sognare ♦ n musa

museum [mjuː'zɪəm] n museo

mushroom ['mʌʃrum] n fungo ♦ vi crescere in fretta

music ['mjuːzɪk] n musica; ~**al** adj musicale; (person) portato(a) per la musica ♦ n (show) commedia musicale; ~**al instrument** n strumento musicale; ~ **hall** n teatro di varietà; ~**ian** [-'zɪʃən] n musicista m/f

musk [mʌsk] n muschio

Muslim ['mʌzlɪm] adj, n musulmano(a)

muslin ['mʌzlɪn] n mussola

mussel ['mʌsl] n cozza

must [mʌst] aux vb (obligation): **I ~** do it devo farlo; (probability): **he ~ be there by now** dovrebbe essere arrivato ormai; **I ~ have made a mistake** devo essermi sbagliato ♦ n: **it's a ~** è d'obbligo

mustache ['mʌstæʃ] (US) n = moustache

mustard ['mʌstəd] n senape f, mostarda

muster ['mʌstə*] vt radunare

mustn't ['mʌsnt] = must not

musty ['mʌstɪ] adj che sa di muffa or di rinchiuso

mute [mjuːt] adj, n muto(a)

muted ['mjuːtɪd] adj smorzato(a)

mutiny ['mjuːtɪnɪ] n ammutinamento

mutter ['mʌtə*] vt, vi borbottare, brontolare

mutton ['mʌtn] n carne f di montone

mutual ['mjuːtʃuəl] adj mutuo(a), reciproco(a); **~ly** adv reciprocamente

muzzle ['mʌzl] n muso; (protective device) museruola; (of gun) bocca ♦ vt mettere la museruola a

my [maɪ] adj il(la) mio(a), pl i(le) miei(mie); **~ house** la mia casa; **~ books** i miei libri; **~ brother** mio fratello; **I've washed ~ hair/cut ~ finger** mi sono lavato i capelli/tagliato il dito

myself [maɪ'sɛlf] pron (reflexive) mi; (emphatic) io stesso(a); (after prep) me; see also oneself

mysterious [mɪs'tɪərɪəs] adj misterioso(a)

mystery ['mɪstərɪ] n mistero

mystify ['mɪstɪfaɪ] vt mistificare; (puzzle) confondere

mystique [mɪs'tiːk] n fascino

myth [mɪθ] n mito; **~ology** [mɪ'θɔlədʒɪ] n mitologia

N

n/a abbr = not applicable

nag [næg] vt tormentare ♦ vi brontolare in continuazione; **~ging** adj (doubt, pain) persistente

nail [neɪl] n (human) unghia; (metal) chiodo ♦ vt inchiodare; **to ~ sb down to (doing)** sth costringere qn a (fare) qc; **~brush** n spazzolino da or per unghie; **~file** n lima da or per unghie; **~ polish** n smalto da or per unghie; **~ polish remover** n acetone m, solvente m; **~ scissors** npl forbici fpl da or per unghie; **~ varnish** (BRIT) n = **~ polish**

naïve [naɪ'iːv] adj ingenuo(a)

naked ['neɪkɪd] adj nudo(a)

name [neɪm] n nome m; (reputation) nome, reputazione f ♦ vt (baby etc) chiamare; (plant, illness) nominare; (person, object) chiamare; (price, date) fissare; **what's your ~?** come si chiama?; **by ~** di nome; **she knows them all by ~** li conosce tutti per nome; **~less** adj senza nome; **~ly** adv cioè; **~sake** n omonimo

nanny ['nænɪ] n bambinaia

nap [næp] n (sleep) pisolino; (of cloth) peluria; **to be caught ~ping** essere preso alla sprovvista

nape [neɪp] n: **~ of the neck** nuca

napkin ['næpkɪn] n (also: table **~**) tovagliolo

nappy ['næpɪ] (BRIT) n pannolino; **~ rash** n arrossamento (causato dal pannolino)

narcissi [naː'sɪsaɪ] npl of narcissus

narcissus [naː'sɪsəs] (pl narcissi) n narciso

narcotic [naː'kɔtɪk] n narcotico ♦ adj narcotico(a)

narrative ['nærətɪv] n narrativa

narrow ['nærəu] adj stretto(a); (fig) limitato(a), ristretto(a) ♦ vi restringersi; **to have a ~ escape** farcela per un pelo; **to ~ sth down to** ridurre qc a; **~ly** adv per un pelo; (time)

nasty per poco; **~-minded** adj meschino(a)

nasty ['nɑːstɪ] adj (person, remark: unpleasant) cattivo(a); (: rude) villano(a); (smell, wound, situation) brutto(a)

nation ['neɪʃən] n nazione f

national ['næʃənl] adj nazionale ♦ n cittadino/a; **~ dress** n costume m nazionale; **N~ Health Service** (BRIT) n servizio nazionale di assistenza sanitaria, ≈ S.A.U.B. f; **N~ Insurance** (BRIT) n ≈ Previdenza Sociale; **~ism** n nazionalismo; **~ity** [-'nælɪtɪ] n nazionalità f inv; **~ize** vt nazionalizzare; **~ly** adv a livello nazionale

nationwide ['neɪʃənwaɪd] adj diffuso(a) in tutto il paese ♦ adv in tutto il paese

native ['neɪtɪv] n abitante m/f del paese; (of tribe etc) indigeno/a ♦ adj indigeno(a); (country) natio(a); (ability) innato(a); a **~ of Russia** un nativo della Russia; a **~ speaker of French** una persona di madrelingua francese; **~ language** n madrelingua

Nativity [nə'tɪvɪtɪ] n: **the ~** la Natività

NATO ['neɪtəʊ] n abbr (= North Atlantic Treaty Organization) N.A.T.O. f

natural ['nætʃrəl] adj naturale; (ability) innato(a); (manner) semplice; **~ gas** n gas m metano; **~ize** vt naturalizzare; **to become ~ized** (person) naturalizzarsi; (plant) acclimatarsi; **~ly** adv naturalmente; (by nature: gifted) di natura

nature ['neɪtʃə*] n natura; (character) natura, indole f; **by ~** di natura

naught [nɔːt] n = nought

naughty ['nɔːtɪ] adj (child) birichino(a), cattivello(a); (story, film) spinto(a)

nausea ['nɔːsɪə] n (MED) nausea; (fig: disgust) schifo; **~te** [-sɪeɪt] vt nauseare; far schifo a

nautical ['nɔːtɪkl] adj nautico(a)

naval ['neɪvl] adj navale; **~ officer** n ufficiale m di marina

nave [neɪv] n navata centrale

navel ['neɪvl] n ombelico

navigate ['nævɪgeɪt] vt percorrere navigando ♦ vi navigare; (AUT) fare da navigatore; **navigation** [-'geɪʃən] n navigazione f; **navigator** n (NAUT, AVIAT) ufficiale m di rotta; (explorer) navigatore m; (AUT) copilota m/f

navvy ['nævɪ] (BRIT) n manovale m

navy ['neɪvɪ] n marina; **~(-blue)** adj blu scuro inv

Nazi ['nɑːtsɪ] n nazista m/f

NB abbr (= nota bene) N.B

near [nɪə*] adj vicino(a); (relation) prossimo(a) ♦ adv vicino ♦ prep (also: **~ to**) vicino a, presso; (: time) verso ♦ vt avvicinarsi a; **~by** [nɪə'baɪ] adj vicino(a) ♦ adv vicino; **~ly** adv quasi; **I ~ly fell** per poco non sono caduto; **~ miss** n: **that was a ~ miss** c'è mancato poco; **~side** n (AUT: in Britain) lato sinistro; (: in US, Europe etc) lato destro; **~-sighted** adj miope

neat [niːt] adj (person, room) ordinato(a); (work) pulito(a); (solution, plan) ben indovinato(a), azzeccato(a); (spirits) liscio(a); **~ly** adv con ordine; (skilfully) abilmente

necessarily ['nesɪsrɪlɪ] adv necessariamente

necessary ['nesɪsrɪ] adj necessario(a)

necessity [nɪ'sesɪtɪ] n necessità f inv

neck [nek] n collo; (of garment) colletto ♦ vi (inf) pomiciare, sbaciucchiarsi; **~ and ~** testa a testa

necklace ['neklɪs] n collana

neckline ['neklaɪn] n scollatura

necktie ['nektaɪ] n cravatta

née [neɪ] adj: **~ Scott** nata Scott

need [niːd] n bisogno ♦ vt aver bisogno di; **to ~ to do sth** dover fare; aver bisogno di fare; you **don't ~ to go** non devi andare, non c'è bisogno che tu vada

needle ['niːdl] n ago; (on record

player) puntina ♦ *vt* punzecchiare

needless ['niːdlɪs] *adj* inutile

needlework ['niːdlwəːk] *n* cucito

needn't ['niːdnt] = **need not**

needy ['niːdɪ] *adj* bisognoso(a)

negative ['nɛgətɪv] *n* (LING) negazione *f*; (PHOT) negativo ♦ *adj* negativo(a)

neglect [nɪ'glɛkt] *vt* trascurare ♦ *n* (*of person, duty*) negligenza; (*of child, house etc*) scarsa cura; **state of ~** stato di abbandono

negligee ['nɛglɪʒeɪ] *n* négligé *m inv*

negligence ['nɛglɪdʒəns] *n* negligenza

negligible ['nɛglɪdʒɪbl] *adj* insignificante, trascurabile

negotiable [nɪ'gəʊʃɪəbl] *adj* (*cheque*) trasferibile

negotiate [nɪ'gəʊʃɪeɪt] *vi*: **to ~ (with)** negoziare (con) ♦ *vt* (COMM) negoziare; (*obstacle*) superare; **negotiation** [-'eɪʃən] *n* negoziato, trattativa

Negress ['niːgrɪs] *n* negra

Negro ['niːgrəʊ] *adj* (*pl* **~es**) *adj, n* negro(a)

neigh [neɪ] *vi* nitrire

neighbour ['neɪbə*] (US **neighbor**) *n* vicino/a; **~hood** *n* vicinato; **~ing** *adj* vicino(a); **~ly** *adj*: **he is a ~ly person** è un buon vicino

neither ['naɪðə*] *adj, pron* né l'uno(a) né l'altro(a), nessuno(a) dei(delle) due ♦ *conj* neanche, nemmeno, neppure ♦ *adv*: **~ good nor bad** né buono né cattivo; **I didn't move and ~ did Claude** io non mi mossi e nemmeno Claude; **...**, **~ did I refuse ...**, ma non ho nemmeno rifiutato

neon ['niːɔn] *n* neon *m*; **~ light** *n* luce *f* al neon

nephew ['nɛvjuː] *n* nipote *m*

nerve [nəːv] *n* nervo; (*fig*) coraggio; (*impudence*) faccia tosta; **a fit of ~s** una crisi di nervi; **~-racking** *adj* che spezza i nervi

nervous ['nəːvəs] *adj* nervoso(a); (*anxious*) agitato(a), in apprensione

~ breakdown *n* esaurimento nervoso

nest [nɛst] *n* nido ♦ *vi* fare il nido, nidificare; **~ egg** *n* (*fig*) gruzzolo

nestle ['nɛsl] *vi* accoccolarsi

net [nɛt] *n* rete *f* ♦ *adj* netto(a) ♦ *vt* (*fish etc*) prendere con la rete; (*profit*) ricavare un utile netto di; **~ball** *n* specie di pallacanestro; **~ curtains** *npl* tende *fpl* di tulle

Netherlands ['nɛðələndz] *npl*: **the ~** i Paesi Bassi

nett [nɛt] *adj* = **net**

netting ['nɛtɪŋ] *n* (*for fence etc*) reticolato

nettle ['nɛtl] *n* ortica

network ['nɛtwəːk] *n* rete *f*

neurotic [njuə'rɔtɪk] *adj, n* nevrotico(a)

neuter ['njuːtə*] *adj* neutro(a) ♦ *vt* (*cat etc*) castrare

neutral ['njuːtrəl] *adj* neutro(a); (*person, nation*) neutrale ♦ *n* (AUT) **in ~** in folle; **~ize** *vt* neutralizzare

never ['nɛvə*] *adv* (non...) mai; **~ again** mai più; **I'll ~ go there again** non ci vado più; **~ in my life** mai in vita mia; *see also* **mind**; **~-ending** *adj* interminabile; **~theless** [nɛvəðə'lɛs] *adv* tuttavia, ciò nonostante, ciò nondimeno

new [njuː] *adj* nuovo(a); (*brand new*) nuovo(a) di zecca; **~born** *adj* neonato(a); **~comer** ['njuːkʌmə*] *n* nuovo(a) venuto(a); **~fangled** ['njuːfæŋgld] (*pej*) *adj* stramoderno(a); **~found** *adj* nuovo(a); **~ly** *adv* di recente; **~ly-weds** *npl* sposi ni *mpl*, sposi *mpl* novelli

news [njuːz] *n* notizie *fpl*; (RADIO) giornale *m* radio; (TV) telegiornale *m*; **a piece of ~** una notizia; **~ agency** *n* agenzia di stampa; **~agent** (BRIT) *n* giornalaio; **~caster** *n* (RADIO, TV) annunciatore/trice; **~dealer** (US) *n* = **~agent**; **~ flash** *n* notizia *f* lampo *inv*; **~letter** *n* bollettino; **~paper** *n* giornale *m*; **~print** *n* carta da giornale; **~reader** *n* = **~caster**;

~**reel** n cinegiornale m; ~ **stand** n edicola

newt [njuːt] n tritone m

New Year n Anno Nuovo; ~'s **Day** n il Capodanno; ~'s **Eve** n la vigilia di Capodanno

New York [-'jɔːk] n New York f

New Zealand [-'ziːlənd] n Nuova Zelanda; ~**er** n neozelandese m/f

next [nɛkst] adj prossimo(a) ♦ adv accanto; (in time) dopo; **the** ~ **day** il giorno dopo, l'indomani; ~ **time** la prossima volta; ~ **year** l'anno prossimo; **when do we meet** ~? quando ci rincontriamo?; ~ **to** accanto a; ~ **to nothing** quasi niente; ~ **please!** (avanti) il prossimo!; ~ **door** adv, adj accanto inv; ~-**of-kin** n parente m/f prossimo/a

NHS n abbr = National Health Service

nib [nɪb] n (of pen) pennino

nibble ['nɪbl] vt mordicchiare

Nicaragua [nɪkə'ræɡjuə] n Nicaragua m

nice [naɪs] adj (holiday, trip) piacevole; (flat, picture) bello(a); (person) simpatico(a), gentile; ~**ly** adv bene

niceties ['naɪsɪtɪz] npl finezze fpl

nick [nɪk] n taglietto; tacca ♦ vt (inf) rubare; **in the** ~ **of time** appena in tempo

nickel ['nɪkl] n nichel m; (US) moneta da cinque centesimi di dollaro

nickname ['nɪkneɪm] n soprannome m ♦ vt soprannominare

niece [niːs] n nipote f

Nigeria [naɪ'dʒɪərɪə] n Nigeria

niggling ['nɪɡlɪŋ] adj insignificante; (annoying) irritante

night [naɪt] n notte f; (evening) sera; **at** ~ la sera; **by** ~ di notte; **the** ~ **before last** l'altro ieri notte (or sera); ~**cap** n bicchierino prima di andare a letto; ~ **club** n locale m notturno; ~**dress** n camicia da notte; ~**fall** n crepuscolo; ~**gown** n = ~**dress**; ~**ie** ['naɪtɪ] n = ~**dress**

nightingale ['naɪtɪŋɡeɪl] n usignolo

nightlife ['naɪtlaɪf] n vita notturna

nightly ['naɪtlɪ] adj di ogni notte or sera; (by night) notturno(a) ♦ adv ogni notte or sera

nightmare ['naɪtmeə*] n incubo

night: ~ **porter** n portiere m di notte; ~ **school** n scuola serale; ~ **shift** n turno di notte; ~-**time** n notte f

nil [nɪl] n nulla m; (BRIT: SPORT) zero

Nile [naɪl] n: **the** ~ il Nilo

nimble ['nɪmbl] adj agile

nine [naɪn] num nove; ~**teen** num diciannove; ~**ty** num novanta

ninth [naɪnθ] adj nono(a)

nip [nɪp] vt pizzicare; (bite) mordere

nipple ['nɪpl] n (ANAT) capezzolo

nitrogen ['naɪtrədʒən] n azoto

KEYWORD

no [nəu] (pl ~**es**) adv (opposite of "yes") no; **are you coming?** — — **(I'm not)** viene? — no (non vengo); **would you like some more?** — — **thank you** ne vuole ancora un po'? — no, grazie

♦ adj (not any) nessuno(a); **I have** ~ **money/time/books** non ho soldi/ tempo/libri; ~ **student would have done it** nessuno studente lo avrebbe fatto; "~ **parking**" "divieto di sosta"; "~ **smoking**" "vietato fumare"

♦ n no m inv

nobility [nəu'bɪlɪtɪ] n nobiltà

noble ['nəubl] adj nobile

nobody ['nəubədɪ] pron nessuno

nod [nɒd] vi accennare col capo, fare un cenno; (in agreement) annuire con un cenno del capo; (sleep) sonnecchiare ♦ vt: **to** ~ **one's head** fare di sì col capo ♦ n cenno; ~ **off** vi assopirsi

noise [nɔɪz] n rumore m; (din, racket) chiasso; **noisy** adj (street, car) rumoroso(a); (person) chiassoso(a)

nominal ['nɒmɪnl] adj nominale; (rent) simbolico(a)

nominate ['nɒmɪneɪt] vt (propose)

proporre come candidato; *(elect)* nominare

nominee [nɔmɪ'niː] *n* persona nominata; candidato/a

non... [nɔn] *prefix* non...; ~**-alcoholic** *adj* analcolico(a); ~**-aligned** *adj* non allineato(a)

nonchalant ['nɔnʃələnt] *adj* disinvolto(a), noncurante

non-committal ['nɔnkə'mɪtl] *adj* evasivo(a)

nondescript ['nɔndɪskrɪpt] *adj* qualunque *inv*

none [nʌn] *pron (not one thing)* niente; *(not one person)* nessuno(a); ~ **of you** nessuno di voi; **I've ~ left** non ne ho più; **he's ~ the worse for it** non ne ha risentito

nonentity [nɔ'nɛntɪtɪ] *n* persona insignificante

nonetheless [nʌnðə'lɛs] *adv* nondimeno

non-existent [-ɪg'zɪstənt] *adj* inesistente

non-fiction *n* saggistica

nonplussed [nɔn'plʌst] *adj* sconcertato(a)

nonsense ['nɔnsəns] *n* sciocchezze *fpl*

non: ~**-smoker** *n* non fumatore/trice; ~**-stick** *adj* antiaderente, antiadesivo(a); ~**-stop** *adj* continuo(a); *(train, bus)* direttissimo(a) ♦ *adv* senza sosta

noodles ['nuːdlz] *npl* taglierini *mpl*

nook [nuk] *n:* ~**s and crannies** angoli *mpl*

noon [nuːn] *n* mezzogiorno

no one ['nəuwʌn] *pron* = **nobody**

noose [nuːs] *n* nodo scorsoio; *(hangman's)* cappio

nor [nɔː*] *conj* = **neither** ♦ *adv see* **neither**

norm [nɔːm] *n* norma

normal ['nɔːml] *adj* normale; ~**ly** *adv* normalmente

north [nɔːθ] *n* nord *m*, settentrione *m* ♦ *adj* nord *inv*, del nord, settentrionale ♦ *adv* verso nord; **N~ America** *n* America del Nord; ~**east** *n*

nord-est *m*; ~**erly** ['nɔːðəlɪ] *adj* *(point, direction)* verso nord; ~**ern** ['nɔːðən] *adj* del nord, settentrionale; **N~ern Ireland** *n* Irlanda del Nord; **N~ Pole** *n* Polo Nord; **N~ Sea** *n* Mare *m* del Nord; ~**ward(s)** ['nɔːθwəd(z)] *adv* verso nord; ~**west** *n* nord-ovest *m*

Norway ['nɔːweɪ] *n* Norvegia

Norwegian [nɔː'wiːdʒən] *adj* norvegese ♦ *n* norvegese *m/f*; *(LING)* norvegese *m*

nose [nəuz] *n* naso; *(of animal)* muso ♦ *vi:* **to ~ about** aggirarsi; ~**bleed** *n* emorragia nasale; ~**dive** *n* picchiata; ~**y** *(inf) adj* = **nosy**

nostalgia [nɔs'tældʒɪə] *n* nostalgia

nostril ['nɔstrɪl] *n* narice *f*; *(of horse)* frogia

nosy ['nəuzɪ] *(inf) adj* curioso(a)

not [nɔt] *adv* non; **he is ~ or isn't here** non è qui, non c'è; **you must ~ or you mustn't do that** non devi fare quello; **it's too late, isn't it or is it ~?** è troppo tardi, vero?; ~ **that I don't like him** non che (lui) non mi piaccia; ~ **yet/now** non ancora/ora; *see also* **all**; **only**

notably ['nəutəblɪ] *adv (markedly)* notevolmente; *(particularly)* in particolare

notary ['nəutərɪ] *n* notaio

notch [nɔtʃ] *n* tacca; *(in saw)* dente *m*

note [nəut] *n* nota; *(letter, banknote)* biglietto ♦ *vt (also:* ~ **down)** prendere nota di; **to take ~s** prendere appunti; ~**book** *n* taccuino; ~**d** ['nəutɪd] *adj* celebre; ~**pad** *n* blocnotes *m inv*; ~**paper** *n* carta da lettere

nothing ['nʌθɪŋ] *n* nulla *m*, niente *m*; *(zero)* zero; **he does ~ non fa niente**; ~ **new/much** *etc* niente di nuovo/speciale *etc*; **for ~** per niente

notice ['nəutɪs] *n* avviso; *(of leaving)* preavviso ♦ *vt* notare, accorgersi di; **to take ~ of** fare attenzione a; **to bring sth to sb's ~** far notare qc a qn; **at short ~** con un breve preav-

notify — null (column 1)

viso; **until further ~** fino a nuovo viso; **to hand in one's ~** licenziarsi; **~able** adj evidente; **~ board** (BRIT) n tabellone m per affissi

notify ['nəʊtɪfaɪ] vt: **to ~ sth to sb** far sapere qc a qn; **to ~ sb of sth** avvisare qn di qc

notion ['nəʊʃən] n idea; (concept) nozione f

notorious [nəʊ'tɔːrɪəs] adj famigerato(a)

notwithstanding [nɒtwɪθ'stændɪŋ] adv nondimeno ♦ prep nonostante, malgrado

nougat ['nuːgɑː] n torrone m

nought [nɔːt] n zero

noun [naʊn] n nome m, sostantivo

nourish ['nʌrɪʃ] vt nutrire

novel ['nɒvl] n romanzo ♦ adj nuovo(a); **~ist** n romanziere/a; **~ty** n novità f inv

November [nəʊ'vɛmbə*] n novembre m

novice ['nɒvɪs] n principiante m/f; (REL) novizio/a

now [naʊ] adv ora, adesso ♦ conj: ~ (that) adesso che, ora che; **by ~** ormai; **just ~** proprio ora; **right ~** subito, immediatamente; **~ and then**, **~ and again** ogni tanto; **from ~ on** da ora in poi; **~adays** ['naʊədeɪz] adv oggidì

nowhere ['nəʊwɛə*] adv in nessun luogo, da nessuna parte

nozzle ['nɒzl] n (of hose etc) boccaglio; (of fire extinguisher) lancia

nuance ['njuːɑːns] n sfumatura

nuclear ['njuːklɪə*] adj nucleare

nuclei ['njuːklɪaɪ] npl of nucleus

nucleus ['njuːklɪəs] (pl nuclei) n nucleo

nude [njuːd] adj nudo(a) ♦ n (ART) nudo; **in the ~** tutto(a) nudo(a)

nudge [nʌdʒ] vt dare una gomitata a

nudist ['njuːdɪst] n nudista m/f

nuisance ['njuːsns] n: **it's a ~** è una seccatura; **he's a ~** è uno scocciatore

null [nʌl] adj: **~ and void** nullo(a)

numb — nylon (column 2)

numb [nʌm] adj: **~ (with)** intorpidito(a) (da); (with fear) impietrito(a) (da); **~ with cold** intirizzito(a) (dal freddo)

number ['nʌmbə*] n numero ♦ vt numerare; (include) contare; **a ~ of** un certo numero di; **to be ~ed among** venire annoverato(a) tra; **they were 10 in ~** erano in tutto 10; **~ plate** (BRIT) n (AUT) targa

numeral ['njuːmərəl] n numero, cifra

numerate ['njuːmərɪt] adj: **to be ~** avere nozioni di aritmetica

numerical [njuː'mɛrɪkl] adj numerico(a)

numerous ['njuːmərəs] adj numeroso(a)

nun [nʌn] n suora, monaca

nurse [nɜːs] n infermiere/a; (also: **~maid**) bambinaia ♦ vt (patient, cold) curare; (baby: BRIT) cullare; (: US) allattare, dare il latte a

nursery ['nɜːsərɪ] n (room) camera dei bambini; (institution) asilo; (for plants) vivaio; **~ rhyme** n filastrocca; **~ school** n scuola materna; **~ slope** (BRIT) n (SKI) pista per principianti

nursing ['nɜːsɪŋ] n (profession) professione f di infermiere (or di infermiera); (care) cura; **~ home** n casa di cura

nurture ['nɜːtʃə*] vt allevare; nutrire

nut [nʌt] n (of metal) dado; (fruit) noce f; **~crackers** npl schiaccianoci m inv

nutmeg ['nʌtmɛg] n noce f moscata

nutritious [njuː'trɪʃəs] adj nutriente

nuts [nʌts] (inf) adj matto(a)

nutshell ['nʌtʃɛl] n: **in a ~** in poche parole

nylon ['naɪlɒn] n nailon m ♦ adj di nailon

O

oak [ǝuk] n quercia ♦ adj di quercia

O.A.P. (BRIT) n abbr = **old age pensioner**

oar [ɔ:*] n remo

oasis [ǝu'eɪsɪs] (pl **oases**) n oasi f inv

oath [ǝuθ] n giuramento; (swear word) bestemmia

oatmeal ['ǝutmiːl] n farina d'avena

oats [ǝuts] npl avena

obedience [ǝ'biːdɪǝns] n ubbidienza

obedient [ǝ'biːdɪǝnt] adj ubbidiente

obey [ǝ'beɪ] vt ubbidire a; (instructions, regulations) osservare

obituary [ǝ'bɪtjuǝrɪ] n necrologia

object [n 'ɔbdʒɪkt, vb ǝb'dʒɛkt] n oggetto; (purpose) scopo, intento; (LING) complemento oggetto ♦ vi: **to ~ to** (attitude) disapprovare; (proposal) protestare contro, sollevare delle obiezioni contro; **expense is no ~** non si bada a spese; **to ~ that** obiettare che; **I ~!** mi oppongo!; **~ion** [ǝb'dʒɛkʃǝn] n obiezione f; **~ionable** [ǝb'dʒɛkʃǝnǝbl] adj antipatico(a); (language) scostumato(a); **~ive** n obiettivo

obligation [ɔblɪ'geɪʃǝn] n obbligo, dovere m; **without ~** senza impegno

oblige [ǝ'blaɪdʒ] vt (force): **to ~ sb to do** costringere qn a fare; (do a favour) fare una cortesia a; **to be ~d to sb for sth** essere grato a qn per qc; **obliging** adj servizievole, compiacente

oblique [ǝ'bliːk] adj obliquo(a); (allusion) indiretto(a)

obliterate [ǝ'blɪtǝreɪt] vt cancellare

oblivion [ǝ'blɪvɪǝn] n oblio

oblivious [ǝ'blɪvɪǝs] adj: **~ of** incurante di; inconscio(a) di

oblong ['ɔblɔŋ] adj oblungo(a) ♦ n rettangolo

obnoxious [ǝb'nɔkʃǝs] adj odioso(a); (smell) disgustoso(a), ripugnante

oboe ['ǝubǝu] n oboe m

obscene [ǝb'siːn] adj osceno(a)

obscure [ǝb'skjuǝ*] adj oscuro(a) ♦ vt oscurare; (hide: sun) nascondere

observant [ǝb'zɔːvnt] adj attento(a)

observation [ɔbzǝ'veɪʃǝn] n osservazione f; (by police etc) sorveglianza

observatory [ǝb'zɔːvǝtrɪ] n osservatorio

observe [ǝb'zɔːv] vt osservare; (remark) fare osservare; **~r** n osservatore/trice

obsess [ǝb'sɛs] vt ossessionare; **~ive** adj ossessivo(a)

obsolescence [ɔbsǝ'lɛsns] n obsolescenza

obsolete ['ɔbsǝliːt] adj obsoleto(a)

obstacle ['ɔbstǝkl] n ostacolo

obstinate ['ɔbstɪnɪt] adj ostinato(a)

obstruct [ǝb'strʌkt] vt (block) ostruire, ostacolare; (halt) fermare; (hinder) impedire

obtain [ǝb'teɪn] vt ottenere; **~able** adj ottenibile

obvious ['ɔbvɪǝs] adj ovvio(a), evidente; **~ly** adv ovviamente; certo

occasion [ǝ'keɪʒǝn] n occasione f; (event) avvenimento; **~al** adj occasionale; **~ally** adv ogni tanto

occupation [ɔkju'peɪʃǝn] n occupazione f; (job) mestiere m, professione f; **~al hazard** n rischio del mestiere

occupier ['ɔkjupaɪǝ*] n occupante m/f

occupy ['ɔkjupaɪ] vt occupare; **to ~ o.s. in doing** occuparsi a fare

occur [ǝ'kɔː*] vi accadere, capitare; **to ~ to sb** venire in mente a qn; **~rence** n caso, fatto; presenza

ocean ['ǝuʃǝn] n oceano; **~-going** adj d'alto mare

o'clock [ǝ'klɔk] adv: **it is 5 ~** sono le 5

OCR n abbr (= optical character recognition) lettura ottica; (= optical character reader) lettore m ottico

octave ['ɔktɪv] n ottavo

October [ɔk'tǝubǝ*] n ottobre m

octopus ['ɔktǝpǝs] n polpo, piovra

odd [ɔd] adj (strange) strano(a); (number) dispari inv; (not *of a set*) spaiato(a); **60~** 60 e oltre; **at ~ times** di tanto in tanto; **the ~ one** out l'eccezione *f*; **~ity** *n* bizzarria; (*person*) originale *m*; **~job man** *n* tuttofare *m inv*; **~ jobs** *npl* lavori *mpl* occasionali; **~ly** *adv* stranamente; **~ments** *npl* (COMM) rimanenze *fpl*; **~s** *npl* (*in betting*) quota; **~s and ends** *npl* avanzi *mpl*; **it makes no ~s** non importa; **at ~s** in contesa

odometer [ɔ'dɔmitə*] *n* odometro

odour ['əudə*] (*US* **odor**) *n* odore *m*; (*unpleasant*) cattivo odore

KEYWORD

of [ɔv, əv] *prep* **1** (*gen*) di; **a boy ~ 10** un ragazzo di 10 anni; **a friend ~ ours** un nostro amico; **that was kind ~ you** è stato molto gentile da parte sua

2 (*expressing quantity, amount, dates etc*) di; **a kilo ~ flour** un chilo di farina; **how much ~ this do you need?** quanto gliene serve?; **there were 3 ~ them** (*people*) erano in 3; (*objects*) ce n'erano 3; **3 ~ us went** 3 di noi sono andati; **the 5th ~ July** il 5 luglio

3 (*from, out of*) di, in; **made ~ wood** (fatto) di *or* in legno

KEYWORD

off [ɔf] *adv* **1** (*distance, time*): **it's a long way ~** è lontano; (*time*) **the game is 3 days ~** la partita è tra 3 giorni

2 (*departure, removal*) via; **to go ~ to Paris** andarsene a Parigi; **I must be ~** devo andare via; **to take ~ one's coat** togliersi il cappotto; **the button came ~** il bottone è venuto via *or* si è staccato; **10% ~** con lo sconto del 10%

3 (*not at work*): **to have a day ~** avere un giorno libero; **to be ~ sick** essere assente per malattia

♦ *adj* (*engine*) spento(a); (*tap*) chiuso(a); (*cancelled*) sospeso(a); (*BRIT: food*) andato(a) a male; **on**

the ~ chance nel caso; **to have an ~ day** non essere in forma

♦ *prep* **1** (*motion, removal etc*) da; (*distant from*) a poca distanza da; **a street ~ the square** una strada che parte dalla piazza

2: **to be ~ meat** non mangiare più la carne

offal ['ɔfl] *n* (CULIN) frattaglie *fpl*

off-colour (BRIT) *adj* (*ill*) malato(a), indisposto(a)

offence [ə'fɛns] (*US* **offense**) *n* (LAW) contravvenzione *f*; (: *more serious*) reato; **to take ~ at** offendersi per

offend [ə'fɛnd] *vt* (*person*) offendere; **~er** *n* delinquente *m/f*; (*against regulations*) contravventore/trice

offense [ə'fɛns] (*US*) *n* = **offence**

offensive [ə'fɛnsɪv] *adj* offensivo(a); (*smell etc*) sgradevole, ripugnante ♦ *n* (MIL) offensiva

offer ['ɔfə*] *n* offerta, proposta ♦ *vt* offrire; **"on ~"** (COMM) "in offerta speciale"; **~ing** *n* offerta

offhand [ɔf'hænd] *adj* disinvolto(a), noncurante ♦ *adv* su due piedi

office ['ɔfɪs] *n* (*place*) ufficio; (*position*) carica; **doctor's ~** (*US*) studio; **to take ~** entrare in carica; **~ automation** *n* automazione *f* d'ufficio; burotica; **~ block** (*US* **~ building**) *n* complesso di uffici; **~ hours** *npl* orario d'ufficio; (*US: MED*) orario di visite

officer ['ɔfɪsə*] *n* (MIL etc) ufficiale *m*; (*also: police* **~**) agente *m* di polizia; (*of organization*) funzionario

office worker *n* impiegato/a d'ufficio

official [ə'fɪʃl] *adj* (*authorized*) ufficiale ♦ *n* ufficiale *m*; (*civil servant*) impiegato/a statale; funzionario; **~dom** (*pej*) *n* burocrazia

officiate [ə'fɪʃɪeɪt] *vi* presenziare

officious [ə'fɪʃəs] *adj* invadente

offing ['ɔfɪŋ] *n*: **in the ~** (*fig*) in vista

off: **~-licence** (BRIT) *n* (*shop*)

spaccio di bevande alcoliche; ~-**line**
adj, adv (COMPUT) off-line inv, fuori
linea; (: switched off) spento(a); ~-
peak adj (ticket, heating etc) a tariffa ridotta; (time) non di punta;
~-**putting** (BRIT) adj sgradevole,
antipatico(a); ~-**season** adj, adv
fuori stagione

offset ['ɔfsɛt] (irreg) vt (counteract)
controbilanciare, compensare

offshoot ['ɔfʃuːt] n (fig) diramazione
f

offshore [ɔf'ʃɔːʳ] adj (breeze) di terra; (island) vicino alla costa; (fishing) costiero(a)

offside ['ɔf'said] adj (SPORT) fuori
gioco; (AUT: in Britain) destro(a);
(: in Italy etc) sinistro(a)

offspring ['ɔfsprɪŋ] n inv prole f, discendenza

off: ~**stage** adv dietro le quinte;
~-**the-peg** (US ~-**the-rack**) adv
prêt-à-porter; ~-**white** adj bianco
sporco inv

often ['ɔfn] adv spesso; **how** ~ **do
you go?** quanto spesso ci vai?

ogle ['əugl] vt occhieggiare

oh [əu] excl oh!

oil [ɔɪl] n olio; (petroleum) petrolio;
(for central heating) nafta ♦ vt (machine) lubrificare; ~**can** n oliatore
m a mano; (for storing) latta da
olio; ~**field** n giacimento petrolifero; ~ **filter** n (AUT) filtro dell'olio;
~ **painting** n quadro a olio; ~ **refinery** n raffineria di petrolio; ~ **rig**
n derrick m inv; (at sea) piattaforma
per trivellazioni subacquee; ~**skins**
npl indumenti mpl di tela cerata; ~
tanker n (ship) petroliera; (truck)
autocisterna per petrolio; ~ **well** n
pozzo petrolifero; ~**y** adj unto(a),
oleoso(a); (food) grasso(a)

ointment ['ɔɪntmənt] n unguento

O.K. ['əu'kei] excl d'accordo! ♦ adj
non male inv ♦ vt approvare; **is it
~?, are you ~?** è tutto bene?

okay ['əu'kei] excl, adj, vt = **O.K**

old [əuld] adj vecchio(a); (ancient)
antico(a), vecchio(a); (person) vec-

chio(a), anziano(a); **how ~ are
you?** quanti anni ha?; **he's 10 years
~** ha 10 anni; ~**er brother** fratello
maggiore; ~ **age** n vecchiaia; ~
age pensioner (BRIT) n pen-
sionato(a); ~-**fashioned** adj antiqua-
to(a), fuori moda; (person) all'antica

olive ['ɔlɪv] n (fruit) oliva; (tree) oli-
vo ♦ adj (also: ~-green) verde oliva
inv; ~ **oil** n olio d'oliva

Olympic [əu'lɪmpɪk] adj olimpico(a);
the ~ Games, the ~s i giochi olimpici, le Olimpiadi

omelet(te) ['ɔmlɪt] n omelette f
inv

omen ['əumən] n presagio, augurio

ominous ['ɔmɪnəs] adj minaccio-
so(a); (event) di malaugurio

omit [əu'mɪt] vt omettere

KEYWORD

on [ɔn] prep 1 (indicating position)
su; ~ **the wall** sulla parete; ~ **the
left** a or sulla sinistra

2 (indicating means, method, condition etc): ~ **foot** a piedi; ~ **the
train/plane** in treno/aereo; ~ **the
telephone** al telefono; ~ **the radio/
television** alla radio/televisione; **to
be** ~ **drugs** drogarsi; ~ **holiday** in
vacanza

3 (referring to time): ~ **Friday** venerdì; ~ **Fridays** il or di venerdì; ~
June 20th il 20 giugno; ~ **Friday,
June 20th** venerdì, 20 giugno; **a
week** ~ **Friday** venerdì a otto; ~
his arrival al suo arrivo; ~ **seeing
this** vedendo ciò

4 (about, concerning) su, di; **information** ~ **train services** informazioni sui collegamenti ferroviari; **a
book** ~ **Goldoni/physics** un libro su
Goldoni/di or sulla fisica

♦ adv 1 (referring to dress, covering): **to have one's coat** ~ avere
indosso il cappotto; **to put one's
coat** ~ mettersi il cappotto; **what's
she got** ~? cosa indossa?; **she put
her boots/gloves/hat** ~ si mise gli
stivali/i guanti/il cappello; **screw the**

lid ~ tightly avvita bene il coperchio
2 (further, continuously): to walk ~, go ~ etc continuare, proseguire etc; to read ~ continuare a leggere; ~ and off ogni tanto

♦ adj 1 (in operation: machine, TV, light) acceso(a); (: tap) aperto(a); (: brake) inserito(a); is the meeting still ~? (in progress) la riunione è ancora in corso?; (not cancelled) è confermato l'incontro?; there's a good film ~ at the cinema danno un buon film al cinema
2 (inf): that's not ~! (not acceptable) non si fa così!; (not possible) non se ne parla neanche!

once [wʌns] adv una volta ♦ conj non appena, quando; ~ he had left/it was done dopo che se n'era andato/fu fatto; at ~ subito; (simultaneously) a un tempo; ~ a week una volta per settimana; ~ more ancora una volta; ~ and for all una volta per sempre; ~ upon a time c'era una volta

oncoming ['ɒnkʌmɪŋ] adj (traffic) che viene in senso opposto

KEYWORD

one [wʌn] num uno(a); ~ hundred and fifty centocinquanta; ~ day un giorno
♦ adj 1 (sole) unico(a); the ~ book which l'unico libro che; the ~ man who l'unico che
2 (same) stesso(a); they came in the ~ car sono venuti nella stessa macchina
♦ pron 1: this ~ questo(a); that ~ quello(a); I've already got ~/a red ~ ne ho già uno/uno rosso; ~ by ~ uno per uno
2: ~ another l'un l'altro; to look at ~ another guardarsi; to help ~ another aiutarsi l'un l'altro or a vicenda
3 (impersonal) si; ~ never knows non si sa mai; to cut ~'s finger tagliarsi un dito; ~ needs to eat biso-

gna mangiare

one: ~-day excursion (US) n biglietto giornaliero di andata e ritorno; ~-man adj (business) diretto(a) etc da un solo uomo; ~-man band n suonatore ambulante con vari strumenti; ~-off (BRIT: inf) n fatto eccezionale

oneself [wʌn'sɛlf] pron (reflexive) si; (after prep) se stesso(a), sé; to do sth (by) ~ fare qc da sé; to hurt ~ farsi male; to keep sth for ~ tenere qc per sé; to talk to ~ parlare da solo

one: ~-sided adj (argument) unilaterale; ~-to-~ adj (relationship) univoco(a); ~-upmanship [-'ʌpmənʃɪp] n l'arte di fare sempre meglio degli altri; ~-way adj (street, traffic) a senso unico

ongoing ['ɒngəʊɪŋ] adj in corso; in attuazione

onion ['ʌnjən] n cipolla

on-line adj, adv (COMPUT) on-line inv

onlooker ['ɒnlʊkə*] n spettatore/trice

only ['əʊnlɪ] adv solo, soltanto ♦ adj solo(a), unico(a) ♦ conj solo che, ma; an ~ child un figlio unico; not ~ ... but also non solo ... ma anche

onset ['ɒnsɛt] n inizio

onshore ['ɒnʃɔː*] adj (wind) di mare

onslaught ['ɒnslɔːt] n attacco, assalto

onto ['ɒntu] prep = on to

onus ['əʊnəs] n onere m, peso

onward(s) ['ɒnwəd(z)] adv (move) in avanti; from that time ~ da quella volta in poi

onyx ['ɒnɪks] n onice f

ooze [uːz] vi stillare

OPEC ['əʊpɛk] n abbr (= Organization of Petroleum-Exporting Countries) O.P.E.C. f

open ['əʊpn] adj aperto(a); (road) libero(a); (meeting) pubblico(a) ♦ vt aprire ♦ vi (eyes, door, shop) aprirsi; (*flower*) sbocciare; (*shop, bank, museum*) aprire; (*book etc: commence*) cominciare; in the ~ (**air**) all'aperto; **~ on** to *vt fus* (*subj: room, door*) dare su; **~ up** *vi* aprire; (*blocked road*) sgombrare ♦ *vi* (*shop, business*) aprire; **~ing** (*speech*) di apertura ♦ *n* apertura *f*; (*opportunity*) occasione *f*, opportunità *f inv*; sbocco; **~ly** *adv* apertamente; **~-minded** *adj* che ha la mente aperta; **~-necked** *adj* col collo slacciato; **~-plan** *adj* senza pareti divisorie

opera [ˈɔpərə] *n* opera

operate [ˈɔpəreɪt] *vt* (*machine*) azionare, far funzionare; (*system*) usare ♦ *vi* funzionare; (*drug*) essere efficace; **to ~ on sb (for)** (*MED*) operare qn (di)

operatic [ɔpəˈrætɪk] *adj* dell'opera, lirico/a

operating [ˈɔpəreɪtɪŋ] *adj*: **~ table** tavolo operatorio; **~ theatre** sala operatoria

operation [ɔpəˈreɪʃən] *n* operazione *f*; **to be in ~** (*machine*) essere in azione *or* funzionamento; (*system*) essere in vigore; **to have an ~** (*MED*) subire un'operazione; **~al** *adj* in funzione; d'esercizio

operative [ˈɔpərətɪv] *adj* (*measure*) operativo/a

operator [ˈɔpəreɪtə*] *n* (*of machine*) operatore/trice; (*TEL*) centralinista *m/f*

opinion [əˈpɪnjən] *n* opinione *f*, parere *m*; **in my ~** secondo me, a mio avviso; **~ated** *adj* dogmatico/a; **~ poll** *n* sondaggio di opinioni

opium [ˈəupɪəm] *n* oppio

opponent [əˈpəunənt] *n* avversario/a

opportunist [ɔpəˈtjuːnɪst] *n* opportunista *m/f*

opportunity [ɔpəˈtjuːnɪtɪ] *n* opportunità *f inv*, occasione *f*; **to take the ~ of doing** cogliere l'occasione per fare

oppose [əˈpəuz] *vt* opporsi a; **~d to** contrario/a(a); **as ~d to** in contrasto

con; **opposing** *adj* opposto(a); (*team*) avversario(a)

opposite [ˈɔpəzɪt] *adj* opposto(a); (*house etc*) di fronte ♦ *adv* di fronte, dirimpetto ♦ *prep* di fronte a ♦ *n*: the ~ il contrario, l'opposto; **the ~ sex** l'altro sesso

opposition [ɔpəˈzɪʃən] *n* opposizione *f*

oppress [əˈpres] *vt* opprimere

opt [ɔpt] *vi*: **to ~ for** optare per; **to do** scegliere di fare; **~ out** *vi*: **to ~ out of** ritirarsi da

optical [ˈɔptɪkl] *adj* ottico(a)

optician [ɔpˈtɪʃən] *n* ottico

optimist [ˈɔptɪmɪst] *n* ottimista *m/f*; **~ic** [-ˈmɪstɪk] *adj* ottimistico(a)

optimum [ˈɔptɪməm] *adj* ottimale

option [ˈɔpʃən] *n* scelta; (*SCOL*) materia facoltativa; (*COMM*) opzione *f*; **~al** *adj* facoltativo(a); (*COMM*) a scelta

or [ɔː*] *conj* o, oppure; (*with negative*): **he hasn't seen ~ heard anything** non ha visto né sentito niente; **~ else** se no, altrimenti; oppure

oral [ˈɔːrəl] *adj* orale ♦ *n* esame *m* orale

orange [ˈɔrɪndʒ] *n* (*fruit*) arancia ♦ *adj* arancione

orator [ˈɔrətə*] *n* oratore/trice

orbit [ˈɔːbɪt] *n* orbita ♦ *vt* orbitare intorno a

orchard [ˈɔːtʃəd] *n* frutteto

orchestra [ˈɔːkɪstrə] *n* orchestra; (*US: seating*) platea

orchid [ˈɔːkɪd] *n* orchidea

ordain [ɔːˈdeɪn] *vt* (*REL*) ordinare; (*decide*) decretare

ordeal [ɔːˈdiːl] *n* prova, travaglio

order [ˈɔːdə*] *n* ordine *m*; (*COMM*) ordinazione *f* ♦ *vt* ordinare; in ~ in ordine; (*of document*) in regola; in (**working**) ~ funzionante; in ~ to do per fare; in ~ that affinché + *sub*; on ~ (*COMM*) in ordinazione; out of ~ non in ordine; (*not working*) guasto; **to ~ sb to do** ordinare a qn di fare; **~ form** *n* modulo d'ordinazione; **~ly** *n* (*MIL*) attendente

m; (MED) inserviente m ♦ adj
(room) in ordine; (mind) metodi-
co(a); (person) ordinato(a), metodi-
co(a)

ordinary ['ɔːdnrɪ] adj normale, comune; (pej) mediocre; **out of the ~**
diverso dal solito, fuori dell'ordinario

Ordnance Survey [-nəns-]
(BRIT) n istituto cartografico britan-
nico

ore [ɔː*] n minerale m grezzo

organ ['ɔːgən] n organo; **~ic**
[ɔː'gænɪk] adj organico(a)

organization [ɔːgənaɪ'zeɪʃən] n organizzazione f

organize ['ɔːgənaɪz] vt organizzare;
~r n organizzatore/trice

orgasm ['ɔːgæzəm] n orgasmo

orgy ['ɔːdʒɪ] n orgia

Orient ['ɔːrɪənt] n: **the ~** l'Oriente
m; **oriental** [-'ɛntl] adj. orientale
m/f

origin ['ɔrɪdʒɪn] n origine f

original [ə'rɪdʒɪnl] adj originale;
(earliest) originario(a) ♦ n originale
m; **~ly** adv (at first) all'inizio

originate [ə'rɪdʒɪneɪt] vi: **to ~ from**
essere originario(a) di; (suggestion)
provenire da; **to ~ in** avere origine
in

Orkneys ['ɔːknɪz] npl: **the ~** (also:
the Orkney Islands) le Orcadi

ornament ['ɔːnəmənt] n ornamento;
(trinket) ninnolo; **~al** [-'mɛntl] adj
ornamentale

ornate [ɔː'neɪt] adj molto ornato(a)

orphan ['ɔːfn] n orfano/a; **~age** n
orfanotrofio

orthodox ['ɔːθədɒks] adj ortodos-
so(a)

orthopaedic [ɔːθə'piːdɪk] (US or-
thopedic) adj ortopedico(a)

ostensibly [ɔs'tɛnsɪblɪ] adv all'apparenza

ostentatious [ɔstɛn'teɪʃəs] adj pre-
tenzioso(a); ostentato(a)

ostrich ['ɔstrɪtʃ] n struzzo

other ['ʌðə*] adj altro(a) ♦ pron:
the ~ (one) l'altro(a); **~s** (~ people) altri mpl; **~ than** altro che; **a**

parte; **~wise** adv, conj altrimenti

otter ['ɔtə*] n lontra

ouch [autʃ] excl ohi!, ahi!

ought [ɔːt] (pt ought) aux vb: **I ~**
to do it dovrei farlo; **this ~ to have**
been corrected questo avrebbe dovuto essere corretto; **he ~ to win**
dovrebbe vincere

ounce [auns] n oncia (= 28.35 g; 16
in a pound)

our ['auə*] adj il(la) nostro(a), pl
i(le) nostri(e); see also **my**; **~s**
pron il(la) nostro(a), pl i(le) no-
stri(e); see also **mine**; **~selves**
pron pl (reflexive) ci; (after preposition) noi; (emphatic) noi stessi(e);
see also **oneself**

oust [aust] vt cacciare, espellere

KEYWORD

out [aut] adv (gen) fuori; **~ here/**
there qui/là fuori; **to speak ~** loud
parlare forte; **to have a night ~**
uscire una sera; **the boat was 10**
km ~ la barca era a 10 km dalla costa; **3 days ~ from Plymouth** a 3
giorni da Plymouth

♦ adj: **to be ~** (gen) essere fuori;
(unconscious) aver perso i sensi;
(style, singer) essere fuori moda; **be-**
fore the week was ~ prima che la
settimana fosse finita; **to be ~ to do**
sth avere intenzione di fare qc; **to**
be ~ in one's calculations aver
sbagliato i calcoli

● **out of** prep 1 (outside, beyond)
fuori di; **to go ~ of the house** uscire di casa; **to look ~ of the win-**
dow guardare fuori dalla finestra
2 (because of) per
3 (origin) da; **to drink ~ of a cup**
bere da una tazza
4 (from among): **~ of 10** su 10
5 (without) senza; **~ of petrol** senza
benzina

---

out-and-out adj (liar, thief etc)
vero(a) e proprio(a)

outback ['autbæk] n (in Australia)
interno, entroterra

outboard ['autbɔːd] *n*: ~ **(motor)** (motore *m*) fuoribordo

outbreak ['autbreɪk] *n* scoppio; epidemia

outburst ['autbəːst] *n* scoppio

outcast ['autkɑːst] *n* esule *m/f*; (*socially*) paria *m*

outcome ['autkʌm] *n* esito, risultato

outcrop ['autkrɔp] *n* (*of rock*) affioramento

outcry ['autkraɪ] *n* protesta, clamore *m*

outdated [aut'deɪtɪd] *adj* (*custom, clothes*) fuori moda; (*idea*) sorpassato(a)

outdo [aut'duː] (*irreg*) *vt* sorpassare

outdoor [aut'dɔː*] *adj* all'aperto; ~**s** *adv* fuori; all'aria aperta

outer ['autə*] *adj* esteriore; ~ **space** *n* spazio cosmico

outfit ['autfɪt] *n* (*clothes*) completo; (: *for sport*) tenuta

outgoing ['autgəuɪŋ] *adj* (*character*) socievole; ~**s** (*BRIT*) *npl* (*expenses*) spese *fpl*, uscite *fpl*

outgrow [aut'grəu] (*irreg*) *vt*: **he has ~n his clothes** tutti i vestiti gli sono diventati piccoli

outhouse ['authaus] *n* costruzione *f* annessa

outing ['autɪŋ] *n* gita; escursione *f*

outlandish [aut'lændɪʃ] *adj* strano(a)

outlaw ['autlɔː] *n* fuorilegge *m/f* ♦ *vt* bandire

outlay ['autleɪ] *n* spese *fpl*; (*investment*) sborsa, spesa

outlet ['autlet] *n* (*for liquid etc*) sbocco, scarico; (*US: ELEC*) presa di corrente; (*also: retail* ~) punto di vendita

outline ['autlaɪn] *n* contorno, profilo; (*summary*) abbozzo, grandi linee *fpl* ♦ *vt* (*fig*) descrivere a grandi linee

outlive [aut'lɪv] *vt* sopravvivere a

outlook ['autluk] *n* prospettiva, vista

outlying ['autlaɪɪŋ] *adj* periferico(a)

outmoded [aut'məudɪd] *adj* passato(a) di moda; antiquato(a)

outnumber [aut'nʌmbə*] *vt* supera-

re in numero

out-of-date *adj* (*passport*) scaduto(a); (*clothes*) fuori moda

out-of-the-way *adj* (*place*) fuori mano *inv*

outpatient ['autpeɪʃənt] *n* paziente *m/f* esterno(a)

outpost ['autpəust] *n* avamposto

output ['autput] *n* produzione *f*; (*COMPUT*) output *m inv*

outrage ['autreɪdʒ] *n* oltraggio; scandalo ♦ *vt* oltraggiare; ~**ous** [-'reɪdʒəs] *adj* oltraggioso(a); scandaloso(a)

outright [*adv* aut'raɪt, *adj* 'autraɪt] *adv* completamente; schiettamente; apertamente; sul colpo ♦ *adj* completo(a); schietto(a) e netto(a)

outset ['autset] *n* inizio

outside [aut'saɪd] *n* esterno, esteriore *m* ♦ *adj* esterno(a), esteriore ♦ *adv* fuori; all'esterno ♦ *prep* fuori di, all'esterno di; **at the ~** (*fig*) al massimo; ~ **lane** *n* (*AUT*) corsia di sorpasso; ~ **line** *n* (*TEL*) linea esterna; ~**r** *n* (*in race etc*) outsider *m inv*; (*stranger*) estraneo/a

outsize ['autsaɪz] *adj* (*clothes*) per taglie forti

outskirts ['autskəːts] *npl* sobborghi *mpl*

outspoken [aut'spəukən] *adj* molto franco(a)

outstanding [aut'stændɪŋ] *adj* eccezionale, di rilievo; (*unfinished*) non completo(a); non evaso(a); non regolato(a)

outstay [aut'steɪ] *vt*: **to ~ one's welcome** diventare un ospite sgradito

outstretched [aut'stretʃt] *adj* (*hand*) teso(a); (*body*) disteso(a)

outstrip [aut'strɪp] *vt* (*competitors, demand*) superare

out-tray *n* contenitore *m* per la corrispondenza in partenza

outward ['autwəd] *adj* (*sign, appearances*) esteriore; (*journey*) d'andata; ~**ly** *adv* esteriormente; in apparenza

outweigh [aut'wei] *vt* avere maggior peso di

outwit [aut'wit] *vt* superare in astuzia

oval ['əuvl] *adj* ovale ♦ *n* ovale *m*

ovary ['əuvəri] *n* ovaia

oven ['ʌvn] *n* forno; ~**proof** *adj* da forno

over ['əuvə*] *adv* al di sopra ♦ *adj* (*or adv*) (*finished*) finito(a), terminato(a); (*too*) troppo; (*remaining*) che avanza ♦ *prep* su; sopra; (*above*) al di sopra di; (*on the other side of*) di là di; (*more than*) più di; (*during*) durante; ~ **here** qui; ~ **there** là; **all** ~ (*everywhere*) dappertutto; (*finished*) tutto(a) finito(a); ~ **and** ~ (**again**) più e più volte; ~ **and above** oltre (a); **to ask sb** ~ invitare qn (a passare)

overall [*adj, n* 'əuvərɔːl. *adv* əuvər'ɔːl] *adj* totale ♦ *n* (*BRIT*) grembiule *m* ♦ *adv* nell'insieme, complessivamente; ~**s** *npl* (*worker's* ~**s**) tuta (da lavoro)

overawe [əuvər'ɔː] *vt* intimidire

overbalance [əuvə'bæləns] *vi* perdere l'equilibrio

overbearing [əuvə'bɛəriŋ] *adj* imperioso(a), prepotente

overboard ['əuvəbɔːd] *adv* (*NAUT*) fuori bordo, in mare

overbook [əuvə'buk] *vt*: **the hotel was** ~**ed** le prenotazioni all'albergo superavano i posti disponibili

overcast ['əuvəkɑːst] *adj* coperto(a)

overcharge [əuvə'tʃɑːdʒ] *vt*: **to** ~ **sb for sth** far pagare troppo caro a qn per qc

overcoat ['əuvəkəut] *n* soprabito, cappotto

overcome [əuvə'kʌm] (*irreg*) *vt* superare; sopraffare

overcrowded [əuvə'kraudid] *adj* sovraffollato(a)

overdo [əuvə'duː] (*irreg*) *vt* esagerare; (*overcook*) cuocere troppo

overdose ['əuvədəus] *n* dose *f* eccessiva

overdraft ['əuvədrɑːft] *n* scoperto (di conto)

overdrawn [əuvə'drɔːn] *adj* (*account*) scoperto(a)

overdue [əuvə'djuː] *adj* in ritardo

overestimate [əuvər'estimeit] *vt* sopravvalutare

overflow [*vb* əuvə'fləu, *n* 'əuvəfləu] *vi* traboccare ♦ *n* (*also*: ~ **pipe**) troppopieno

overgrown [əuvə'grəun] *adj* (*garden*) ricoperto(a) di vegetazione

overhaul [*vb* əuvə'hɔːl, *n* 'əuvəhɔːl] *vt* revisionare ♦ *n* revisione *f*

overhead [*adv* əuvə'hed, *adj, n* 'əuvəhed] *adv* di sopra ♦ *adj* aereo(a); (*lighting*) verticale ♦ *n* (*US*) = ~**s**; ~**s** *npl* spese *fpl* generali

overhear [əuvə'hiə*] *vt* sentire (per caso)

overheat [əuvə'hiːt] *vi* (*engine*) surriscaldare

overjoyed [əuvə'dʒɔid] *adj* pazzo(a) di gioia

overkill ['əuvəkil] *n* (*fig*) eccessi *mpl*

overlap [əuvə'læp] *vi* sovrapporsi

overleaf [əuvə'liːf] *adv* a tergo

overload [əuvə'ləud] *vt* sovraccaricare

overlook [əuvə'luk] *vt* (*have view of*) dare su; (*miss*) trascurare; (*forgive*) passare sopra a

overnight [əuvə'nait] *adv* (*happen*) durante la notte; (*fig*) tutto a un tratto ♦ *adj* di notte; **he stayed there** ~ ci ha passato la notte

overpass ['əuvəpɑːs] *n* cavalcavia *m inv*

overpower [əuvə'pauə*] *vt* sopraffare; ~**ing** *adj* irresistibile; (*heat, stench*) soffocante

overrate [əuvə'reit] *vt* sopravvalutare

override [əuvə'raid] (*irreg: like ride*) *vt* (*order, objection*) passar sopra a; (*decision*) annullare; **overriding** *adj* preponderante

overrule [əuvə'ruːl] *vt* (*decision*) annullare; (*claim*) respingere

overrun [əuvə'rʌn] (*irreg: like run*) *vt* (*country*) invadere; (*time limit*) superare

overseas [əuvə'si:z] *adv* oltremare; (*abroad*) all'estero ♦ *adj* (*trade*) estero(a); (*visitor*) straniero(a)

overshadow [əuvə'ʃædəu] *vt* far ombra su; (*fig*) eclissare

overshoot [əuvə'ʃu:t] (*irreg*) *vt* superare

oversight ['əuvəsait] *n* omissione *f*, svista

oversleep [əuvə'sli:p] (*irreg*) *vt* dormire troppo a lungo

overstate [əuvə'steit] *vt* esagerare

overstep [əuvə'step] *vt*: to ~ the mark superare ogni limite

overt [əu'və:t] *adj* palese

overtake [əuvə'teik] (*irreg*) *vt* sorpassare

overthrow [əuvə'θrəu] (*irreg*) *vt* (*government*) rovesciare

overtime ['əuvətaim] *n* (*lavoro*) straordinario

overtone ['əuvətəun] *n* sfumatura

overture ['əuvətʃuə*] *n* (*MUS*) ouverture *f inv*; (*fig*) approccio

overturn [əuvə'tə:n] *vt* rovesciare ♦ *vi* rovesciarsi

overweight [əuvə'weit] *adj* (*person*) troppo grasso(a)

overwhelm [əuvə'welm] *vt* sopraffare; sommergere; schiacciare; ~ing *adj* (*victory, defeat*) schiacciante; (*heat, desire*) intenso(a)

overwork [əuvə'wə:k] *n* eccessivo lavoro

overwrought [əuvə'rɔ:t] *adj* molto agitato(a)

owe [əu] *vt*: to ~ sb sth, to ~ sth to sb dovere qc a qn; **owing to** *prep* a causa di

owl [aul] *n* gufo

own [əun] *vt* possedere ♦ *adj* proprio(a); **a room of my** ~ la mia propria camera; **to get one's** ~ **back** vendicarsi; **on one's** ~ tutto(a) solo(a); ~ **up** *vi* confessare; ~**er** *n* proprietario/a; ~**ership** *n* possesso

ox [ɔks] *pl* **oxen** *n* bue *m*

oxen ['ɔksn] *npl of* **ox**

oxtail ['ɔksteil] *n*: ~ **soup** minestra di coda di bue

oxygen ['ɔksidʒən] *n* ossigeno; ~ **mask/tent** *n* maschera/tenda ad ossigeno

oyster ['ɔistə*] *n* ostrica

oz. *abbr* = **ounce(s)**

ozone ['əuzəun] *n* ozono; ~**-friendly** *adj* che non danneggia l'ozono; ~ **hole** *n* buco nell'ozono; ~ **layer** *n* strato di ozono

P

p [pi:] *abbr* = **penny**; **pence**

P.A. *n abbr* = **personal assistant**; **public address system**

p.a. *abbr* = **per annum**

pa [pɑ:] (*inf*) *n* (*fam*) *m inv*, babbo

pace [peis] *n* passo *m*; (*speed*) passo; velocità ♦ *vi*: to ~ **up and down** camminare su e giù; **to keep** ~ **with** camminare di pari passo a; (*events*) tenersi al corrente di; ~**maker** *n* (*MED*) segnapasso; (*SPORT*: *also*: ~ **setter**) battistrada *m*

pacific [pə'sifik] *n*: the P~ (**Ocean**) il Pacifico, l'Oceano Pacifico

pacify ['pæsifai] *vt* calmare, placare

pack [pæk] *n* pacco; (*US*: *of cigarettes*) pacchetto; (*back~*) zaino; (*of hounds*) muta; (*of thieves etc*) banda; (*of cards*) mazzo ♦ *vt* (*in suitcase etc*) mettere; (*box*) riempire; (*cram*) stipare, pigiare; **to** ~ (**one's**) **bags** fare la valigia; **to** ~ **sb off** spedire via qn; ~ **it in!** (*inf*) dacci un taglio!

package ['pækidʒ] *n* pacco; balla; (*also*: ~ **deal**) pacchetto; forfait *m inv*; ~ **holiday** *n* vacanza organizzata; ~ **tour** *n* viaggio organizzato

packed lunch *n* pranzo al sacco

packet ['pækit] *n* pacchetto

packing ['pækiŋ] *n* imballaggio; ~ **case** *n* cassa da imballaggio

pact [pækt] *n* patto, accordo; trattato

pad [pæd] *n* (*to prevent fric-*

tion) cuscinetto; *(inf: flat)* appartamentino ♦ *vt* imbottire; **~ding** *n* imbottitura

paddle ['pædl] *n (oar)* pagaia; *(US: for table tennis)* racchetta da ping-pong ♦ *vi* sguazzare ♦ *vt*: **to ~ a canoe** *etc* vogare con la pagaia; **~ steamer** *n* battello a ruote; **paddling pool** *(BRIT)* *n* piscina per bambini

paddock ['pædək] *n* prato recintato; *(at racecourse)* paddock *m inv*

paddy field ['pædɪ-] *n* risaia

padlock ['pædlɒk] *n* lucchetto

paediatrics [piːdɪ'ætrɪks] *(US* **pediatrics)** *n* pediatria

pagan ['peɪgən] *adj, n* pagano(a)

page [peɪdʒ] *n* pagina; *(also: ~ boy)* paggio ♦ *vt (in hotel etc)* (far) chiamare

pageant ['pædʒənt] *n* spettacolo storico; grande cerimonia; **~ry** *n* pompa

pager ['peɪdʒə*] *n* (TEL) cercapersone *m inv*

paging device ['peɪdʒɪŋ-] *n* (TEL) cercapersone *m inv*

paid [peɪd] *pt, pp* of **pay** ♦ *adj (work, official)* rimunerato(a); **to put ~ to** *(BRIT)* mettere fine a

pail [peɪl] *n* secchio

pain [peɪn] *n* dolore *m*; **to be in ~** soffrire, aver male; **to take ~s to do** mettercela tutta per fare; **~ed** *adj* addolorato(a), afflitto(a); **~ful** *adj* doloroso(a), che fa male; difficile, penoso(a); **~fully** *adv (fig: very)** fin troppo; **~killer** *n* antalgico, antidolorifico; **~less** *adj* indolore

painstaking ['peɪnzteɪkɪŋ] *adj (person)* sollecito(a); *(work)* accurato(a)

paint [peɪnt] *n* vernice *f*, colore *m* ♦ *vt* dipingere; *(walls, door etc)* verniciare; **to ~ the door blue** verniciare la porta di azzurro; **~ in pennello; **~er** *n (artist)* pittore *m*; *(decorator)* imbianchino; **~ing** *n* pittura; verniciatura; *(picture)* dipinto, quadro; **~work** *n* tinta; *(of car)* vernice *f*

pair [peə*] *n (of shoes, gloves etc)* paio; *(of people)* coppia; duo *m inv*; **a ~ of scissors/trousers** un paio di forbici/pantaloni

pajamas [pɪ'dʒɑːməz] *(US)* *npl* pigiama *m*

Pakistan [pɑːkɪ'stɑːn] *n* Pakistan *m*; **~i** *adj, n* pakistano(a)

pal [pæl] *(inf)* *n* amico/a, compagno/a

palace ['pæləs] *n* palazzo

palatable ['pælɪtəbl] *adj* gustoso(a)

palate ['pælɪt] *n* palato

palatial [pə'leɪʃəl] *adj* sontuoso(a), sfarzoso(a)

pale [peɪl] *adj* pallido(a) ♦ *n*: **to be beyond the ~** aver oltrepassato ogni limite

Palestine ['pælɪstaɪn] *n* Palestina; **Palestinian** [-'tɪnɪən] *adj, n* palestinese *m/f*

palette ['pælɪt] *n* tavolozza

palings ['peɪlɪŋz] *npl (fence)* palizzata

pall [pɔːl] *n (of smoke)* cappa ♦ *vi*: **to ~ (on)** diventare noioso(a) (a)

pallet ['pælɪt] *n (for goods)* paletta

pallid ['pælɪd] *adj* pallido(a), smorto(a)

pallor ['pælə*] *n* pallore *m*

palm [pɑːm] *n* (ANAT) palma, palmo; *(also: ~ tree)* palma ♦ *vt*: **to ~ sth off on sb** *(inf)* rifilare qc a qn; **P~ Sunday** *n* Domenica delle Palme

palpable ['pælpəbl] *adj* palpabile

paltry ['pɔːltrɪ] *adj* irrisorio(a); insignificante

pamper ['pæmpə*] *vt* viziare, coccolare

pamphlet ['pæmflət] *n* dépliant *m*

pan [pæn] *n (also: sauce~)* casseruola; *(also: frying ~)* padella

panache [pə'næʃ] *n* stile *m*

pancake ['pænkeɪk] *n* frittella

pancreas ['pæŋkrɪəs] *n* pancreas *m inv*

panda ['pændə] *n* panda *m inv*; **~ car** *(BRIT)* *n* auto *f* della polizia

pandemonium [pændɪ'məʊnɪəm] *n*

pandemonio

pander ['pændə*] *vi*: **to ~ to** lusingare; concedere tutto a

pane [pein] *n* vetro

panel ['pænl] *n* (*of* wood, cloth etc) pannello; (RADIO, TV) giuria; **~ling** (US **~ing**) *n* rivestimento a pannelli

pang [pæŋ] *n*: **a ~ of** regret un senso di rammarico; **hunger ~s** morsi *mpl* della fame

panic ['pænik] *n* panico ♦ *vi* perdere il sangue freddo; **~ky** *adj* (person) pauroso(a); **~-stricken** *adj* (person) preso(a) dal panico, in preda al panico; (look) terrorizzato(a)

pansy ['pænzi] *n* (BOT) viola del pensiero, pensée *f inv*; (*inf: pej*) femminuccia

pant [pænt] *vi* ansare

panther ['pænθə*] *n* pantera

panties ['pæntiz] *npl* slip *m*, mutandine *fpl*

pantihose ['pæntihəuz] (US) *n* collant *m inv*

pantomime ['pæntəmaim] (BRIT) *n* pantomima

pantry ['pæntri] *n* dispensa

pants [pænts] *npl* mutande *fpl*, slip *m*; (US: trousers) pantaloni *mpl*

papal ['peipəl] *adj* papale, pontificio(a)

paper ['peipə*] *n* carta; (also: **wall~**) carta da parati, tappezzeria; (also: **news~**) giornale *m*; (study, article) saggio; (exam) prova scritta ♦ *adj* di carta ♦ *vt* tappezzare; **~s** *npl* (also: **identity ~s**) carte *fpl*, documenti *mpl*; **~back** *n* tascabile *m*; edizione *f* economica; **~ bag** *n* sacchetto di carta; **~ clip** *n* graffetta, clip *f inv*; **~ hankie** *n* fazzolettino di carta; **~weight** *n* fermacarte *m inv*; **~work** *n* lavoro amministrativo

papier-mâché ['pæpiei'mæʃei] *n* cartapesta

par [pɑ:*] *n* parità, pari *f*; (GOLF) norma; **on a ~ with** alla pari con

parable ['pærəbl] *n* parabola

parachute ['pærəʃu:t] *n* paracadute

m inv

parade [pə'reid] *n* parata ♦ *vt* (fig) fare sfoggio di ♦ *vi* sfilare in parata

paradise ['pærədais] *n* paradiso

paradox ['pærədɔks] *n* paradosso; **~ically** [-'dɔksikli] *adv* paradossalmente

paraffin ['pærəfin] (BRIT) *n*: **~ (oil)** paraffina

paragon ['pærəgən] *n* modello di perfezione or di virtù

paragraph ['pærəgrɑ:f] *n* paragrafo

parallel ['pærəlɛl] *adj* parallelo(a); (fig) analogo(a) ♦ *n* (line) parallela; (fig, GEO) parallelo

paralyse ['pærəlaiz] (US **paralyze**) *vt* paralizzare

paralysis [pə'rælisis] *n* paralisi *f inv*

paralyze ['pærəlaiz] (US) *vt* = **paralyse**

paramount ['pærəmaunt] *adj*: **of ~ importance** di capitale importanza

paranoid ['pærənɔid] *adj* paranoico(a)

paraphernalia [pærəfə'neiliə] *n* attrezzi *mpl*, roba

parasol ['pærəsɔl] *n* parasole *m*

paratrooper ['pærətru:pə*] *n* paracadutista *m* (soldato)

parcel ['pɑ:sl] *n* pacco, pacchetto ♦ *vt* (also: **~ up**) impaccare

parch [pɑ:tʃ] *vt* riardere; **~ed** *adj* (person) assetato(a)

parchment ['pɑ:tʃmənt] *n* pergamena

pardon ['pɑ:dn] *n* perdono; grazia ♦ *vt* perdonare; (LAW) graziare; **~ me!** mi scusi!; **I beg your ~!** scusi!; **I beg your ~?** (BRIT), **~ me?** (US) prego?

parent ['pɛərənt] *n* genitore *m*; **~s** *npl* (mother and father) genitori *mpl*; **~al** [pə'rɛntl] *adj* dei genitori

parentheses [pə'rɛnθisiz] *npl* of **parenthesis**

parenthesis [pə'rɛnθisis] *n* (pl **parentheses**) *n* parentesi *f inv*

Paris ['pæris] *n* Parigi *f*

parish ['pæriʃ] *n* parrocchia; (BRIT: civil) ≈ municipio

park |pɑ:k| n parco ♦ vt, vi parcheggiare

parka |'pɑ:kə| n eskimo

parking |'pɑ:kɪŋ| n parcheggio; "no ~" "sosta vietata"; ~ **lot** (US) n posteggio, parcheggio; ~ **meter** n parchimetro; ~ **ticket** n multa per sosta vietata

parlance |'pɑ:ləns| n gergo

parliament |'pɑ:ləmənt| n parlamento; ~**ary** |-'mɛntərɪ| adj parlamentare

parlour |'pɑ:lə*| (US **parlor**) n salotto

parochial |pə'rəʊkɪəl| (pej) adj provinciale

parody |'pærədɪ| n parodia

parole |pə'rəʊl| n: on ~ in libertà per buona condotta

parrot |'pærət| n pappagallo

parry |'pærɪ| vt parare

parsley |'pɑ:slɪ| n prezzemolo

parsnip |'pɑ:snɪp| n pastinaca

parson |'pɑ:sn| n prete m; (Church of England) parroco

part |pɑ:t| n parte f; (of machine) pezzo; (US: in hair) scriminatura ♦ adj in parte ♦ adv = **partly** ♦ vt separare ♦ vi (people) separarsi; **to take ~ in** prendere parte a; **for my ~** per parte mia; **to take sth in good ~** prendere bene qc; **to take sb's ~** parteggiare per or prendere le parti di qn; **for the most ~** in generale; nella maggior parte dei casi; ~ **with** vt fus separarsi da; rinunciare a; ~ **exchange** (BRIT) n: in ~ **exchange** in pagamento parziale

partial |'pɑ:ʃl| adj parziale; **to be ~ to** avere un debole per

participate |pɑ:'tɪsɪpeɪt| vi: **to ~ (in)** prendere parte (a), partecipare (a); **participation** |-'peɪʃən| n partecipazione f

participle |'pɑ:tɪsɪpl| n participio

particle |'pɑ:tɪkl| n particella

particular |pə'tɪkjʊlə*| adj particolare; speciale; (fussy) difficile; meticoloso(a); **in ~** in particolare, particolarmente; ~**ly** adv particolarmente;

in particolare; ~s npl particolari mpl, dettagli mpl; (information) informazioni fpl

parting |'pɑ:tɪŋ| n separazione f; (BRIT: in hair) scriminatura ♦ adj d'addio

partisan |pɑ:tɪ'zæn| n partigiano/a ♦ adj partigiano(a); di parte

partition |pɑ:'tɪʃən| n (POL) partizione f; (wall) tramezzo

partly |'pɑ:tlɪ| adv parzialmente; in parte

partner |'pɑ:tnə*| n (COMM) socio/a; (wife, husband etc, SPORT) compagno/a; (at dance) cavaliere/dama; ~**ship** n associazione f, (COMM) società f inv

partridge |'pɑ:trɪdʒ| n pernice f

part-time |'pɑ:t'taɪm| adj, adv a orario ridotto

party |'pɑ:tɪ| n (POL) partito; (group) gruppo; (LAW) parte f; (celebration) ricevimento; serata; festa ♦ cpd (POL) del partito, di partito; ~ **dress** n vestito della festa; ~ **line** n (TEL) duplex m inv

pass |pɑ:s| vt (gen) passare; (place) passare davanti a; (exam) passare, superare; (candidate) promuovere; (overtake, surpass) sorpassare, superare; (approve) approvare ♦ vi passare ♦ vt (permit) lasciapassare m inv; permesso; (in mountains) passo, gola; (SPORT) passaggio; (SCOL): **to get a ~** prendere la sufficienza; **to ~ sth through a hole** etc far passare qc attraverso un buco etc; **to make a ~ at sb** (inf) fare delle proposte or delle avances a qn; ~ **away** vi morire; ~ **by** vi passare ♦ vt trascurare; ~ **on** vt passare; ~ **out** vi svenire; ~ **up** vt (opportunity) lasciarsi sfuggire, perdere; ~**able** adj (road) praticabile; (work) accettabile

passage |'pæsɪdʒ| n (gen) passaggio; (also: ~**way**) corridoio; (in book) brano, passo; (by boat) traversata

passbook |'pɑ:sbʊk| n libretto di risparmio

passenger ['pæsɪndʒə*] n passeggero/a

passer-by [pɑːsə'baɪ] n passante m/f

passing ['pɑːsɪŋ] adj (fig) fuggevole; **to mention sth in** ~ accennare a qc di sfuggita; ~ **place** n (AUT) piazzola di sosta

passion ['pæʃən] n passione f; amore m; ~**ate** adj appassionato(a)

passive ['pæsɪv] adj (also LING) passivo(a); ~ **smoking** n fumo passivo

Passover ['pɑːsəʊvə*] n Pasqua ebraica

passport ['pɑːspɔːt] n passaporto; ~ **control** n controllo m passaporti inv

password ['pɑːswəːd] n parola d'ordine

past [pɑːst] prep (further than) oltre, di là di; dopo; (later than) dopo ♦ adj passato(a); (president etc) ex ♦ n passato; **he's** ~ **forty** ha più di quarant'anni; **ten** ~ **eight** le otto e dieci; **for the** ~ **few days** da qualche giorno; in questi ultimi giorni; **to run** ~ passare di corsa

pasta ['pæstə] n pasta

paste [peɪst] n (glue) colla; (CULIN) pâté m inv; pasta ♦ vt collare

pastel ['pæstl] adj pastello inv

pasteurized ['pæstəraɪzd] adj pastorizzato(a)

pastille ['pæstl] n pastiglia

pastime ['pɑːstaɪm] n passatempo

pastry ['peɪstrɪ] n pasta

pasture ['pɑːstʃə*] n pascolo

pasty[1] ['pæstɪ] n pasticcio di carne

pasty[2] ['peɪstɪ] adj (face etc) smorto(a)

pat [pæt] vt accarezzare, dare un colpetto (affettuoso) a

patch [pætʃ] n (of material, on tyre) toppa; (eye ~) benda; (spot) macchia ♦ vt (clothes) rattoppare; (to go through) **a bad** ~ (attraversare) un brutto periodo; ~ **up** vt rappezzare; (quarrel) appianare; ~**y** adj irregolare

pâté ['pæteɪ] n pâté m inv

patent ['peɪtnt] n brevetto ♦ vt bre-

vettare ♦ adj patente, manifesto(a); ~ **leather** n cuoio verniciato

paternal [pə'təːnl] adj paterno(a)

path [pɑːθ] n sentiero, viottolo; viale m; (fig) via, strada; (of planet, missile) traiettoria

pathetic [pə'θetɪk] adj (pitiful) patetico(a); (very bad) penoso(a)

pathological [pæθə'lɔdʒɪkl] adj patologico(a)

pathway ['pɑːθweɪ] n sentiero

patience ['peɪʃns] n pazienza; (BRIT: CARDS) solitario

patient ['peɪʃnt] n paziente m/f; malato/a ♦ adj paziente

patio ['pætɪəʊ] n terrazza

patriot ['peɪtrɪət] n patriota m/f; ~**ic** [pætrɪ'ɔtɪk] adj patriottico(a); ~**ism** n patriottismo

patrol [pə'trəʊl] n pattuglia ♦ vt pattugliare; ~ **car** n autoradio f inv (della polizia); ~**man** (US) n poliziotto

patron ['peɪtrən] n (in shop) cliente m/f; (of charity) benefattore/trice; ~ **of the arts** mecenate m/f; ~**ize** ['pætrənaɪz] vt essere cliente abituale di; (fig) trattare dall'alto in basso

patter ['pætə*] n picchiettio; (sales talk) propaganda di vendita ♦ vi picchiettare; **a** ~ **of footsteps** un rumore di passi

pattern ['pætən] n modello; (design) disegno, motivo

paunch [pɔːntʃ] n pancione m

pauper ['pɔːpə*] n indigente m/f

pause [pɔːz] n pausa ♦ vi fare una pausa, arrestarsi

pave [peɪv] vt pavimentare; **to** ~ **the way for** aprire la via a

pavement ['peɪvmənt] (BRIT) n marciapiede m

pavilion [pə'vɪlɪən] n (SPORT) edificio annesso a campo sportivo

paving ['peɪvɪŋ] n pavimentazione f; ~ **stone** n lastra di pietra

paw [pɔː] n zampa

pawn [pɔːn] n (CHESS) pedone m; (fig) pedina ♦ vt dare in pegno; ~**broker** n prestatore m su pegno;

~shop n monte m di pietà

pay [peɪ] (pt, pp **paid**) n stipendio; paga ♦ vt pagare ♦ vi (be profitable) rendere; **to ~ attention (to)** fare attenzione (a); **to ~ sb a visit** far visita a qn; **to ~ one's respects to sb** porgere i propri rispetti a qn; **~ back** vt rimborsare; **~ for** vt fus pagare; **~ in** vt versare; **~ off** vt (debt) saldare; (person) pagare; (employee) pagare e licenziare ♦ vi (scheme, decision) dare dei frutti; **~ up** vt saldare; **~able** adj pagabile; **~ee** n beneficiario/a; **~ envelope** (US) n = **~ packet**; **~ment** n pagamento; versamento; saldo; **~ packet** (BRIT) n busta f paga inv; **~ phone** n cabina telefonica; **~roll** n ruolo (organico); **~ slip** n foglio m paga inv; **~ television** n televisione f a pagamento, pay-tv f inv

PC n abbr = **personal computer**

p.c. abbr = **per cent**

pea [pi:] n pisello

peace [pi:s] n pace f; **~ful** adj pacifico(a), calmo(a)

peach [pi:tʃ] n pesca

peacock [ˈpi:kɔk] n pavone m

peak [pi:k] n (of mountain) cima, vetta; (mountain itself) picco; (of cap) visiera; (fig) apice m, culmine m; **~ hours** npl ore fpl di punta; **~ period** n = **~ hours**

peal [pi:l] n (of bells) scampanio, carillon m inv; **~s of laughter** scoppi mpl di risa

peanut [ˈpi:nʌt] n arachide f, nocciolina americana; **~ butter** n burro di arachidi

pear [pɛə*] n pera

pearl [pə:l] n perla

peasant [ˈpɛznt] n contadino/a

peat [pi:t] n torba

pebble [ˈpɛbl] n ciottolo

peck [pɛk] vt (also: **~ at**) beccare ♦ n colpo di becco; (kiss) bacetto; **~ing order** n ordine m gerarchico; **~ish** (BRIT: inf) adj: **I feel ~ish** ho un languorino

peculiar [pɪˈkju:lɪə*] adj strano(a),

bizzarro(a); peculiare; **~ to** peculiare di

pedal [ˈpɛdl] n pedale m ♦ vi pedalare

pedantic [pɪˈdæntɪk] adj pedantesco(a)

peddler [ˈpɛdlə*] n (also: **drugs ~**) spacciatore/trice

pedestal [ˈpɛdəstl] n piedestallo

pedestrian [pɪˈdɛstrɪən] n pedone m ♦ adj pedonale; (fig) prosaico(a), pedestre; **~ crossing** (BRIT) n passaggio pedonale

pediatrics [pi:dɪˈætrɪks] (US) n = **paediatrics**

pedigree [ˈpɛdɪgri:] n (of animal) pedigree m inv; (fig) background m inv ♦ cpd (animal) di razza

pee [pi:] (inf) vi pisciare

peek [pi:k] vi guardare furtivamente

peel [pi:l] n buccia; (of orange, lemon) scorza ♦ vt sbucciare ♦ vi (paint etc) staccarsi

peep [pi:p] n (BRIT: look) sguardo furtivo, sbirciata; (sound) pigolio ♦ vi (BRIT) guardare furtivamente; **~ out** vi mostrarsi furtivamente; **~hole** n spioncino

peer [pɪə*] vi: **to ~ at** scrutare ♦ n (noble) pari m inv; (equal) pari m/f inv, uguale m/f; (contemporary) contemporaneo/a; **~age** n dignità di pari; pari mpl

peeved [pi:vd] adj stizzito(a)

peevish [ˈpi:vɪʃ] adj stizzoso(a)

peg [pɛg] n caviglia; (for coat etc) attaccapanni m inv; (BRIT: also: **clothes ~**) molletta

Peking [pi:ˈkɪŋ] n Pechino f

pelican [ˈpɛlɪkən] n pellicano; **~ crossing** n (AUT) attraversamento pedonale con semaforo a controllo manuale

pellet [ˈpɛlɪt] n pallottola, pallina

pelt [pɛlt] vt: **to ~ sb (with)** bombardare qn (con) ♦ vi (rain) piovere a dirotto; (inf: run) filare ♦ n pelle f

pelvis [ˈpɛlvɪs] n pelvi f inv, bacino

pen [pɛn] n penna; (for sheep) recinto

penal ['pi:nl] adj penale; ~**ize** vt punire; (SPORT, fig) penalizzare

penalty ['pɛnltı] n penalità f inv; sanzione f penale; (fine) ammenda; (SPORT) penalizzazione f; ~ (**kick**) n (SPORT) calcio di rigore

penance ['pɛnəns] n penitenza

pence [pɛns] (BRIT) npl of **penny**

pencil ['pɛnsl] n matita; ~ **case** n astuccio per matite; ~ **sharpener** n temperamatite m inv

pendant ['pɛndnt] n pendaglio

pending ['pɛndɪŋ] prep in attesa di ♦ adj in sospeso

pendulum ['pɛndjuləm] n pendolo

penetrate ['pɛnɪtreɪt] vt penetrare

penfriend ['pɛnfrɛnd] (BRIT) n corrispondente m/f

penguin ['pɛŋgwɪn] n pinguino

penicillin [pɛnɪ'sɪlɪn] n penicillina

peninsula [pə'nɪnsjulə] n penisola

penis ['pi:nɪs] n pene m

penitent ['pɛnɪtnt] adj penitente

penitentiary [pɛnɪ'tɛnʃərɪ] (US) n carcere m

penknife ['pɛnnaɪf] n temperino

pen name n pseudonimo

penniless ['pɛnɪlɪs] adj senza un soldo

penny ['pɛnɪ] (pl **pennies** or **pence** (BRIT)) n penny m; (US) centesimo

penpal ['pɛnpæl] n corrispondente m/f

pension ['pɛnʃən] n pensione f; ~**er** (BRIT) n pensionato/a

pensive ['pɛnsɪv] adj pensoso(a)

penthouse ['pɛnthaus] n appartamento (di lusso) nell'attico

pent-up ['pɛntʌp] adj (feelings) represso(a)

people ['pi:pl] npl gente f; persone fpl; (citizens) popolo ♦ n (nation, race) popolo; ~**/several ~ came** 4/parecchie persone sono venute; ~ **say that ...** si dice che ....

pep [pɛp] (inf) n dinamismo; ~ **up** vt vivacizzare; (food) rendere più gustoso(a)

pepper ['pɛpə*] n pepe m; (vegetable) peperone m ♦ vt (fig): **to** ~ **with** spruzzare di; ~**mint** n (sweet) pasticca di menta

peptalk ['pɛptɔ:k] (inf) n discorso di incoraggiamento

per [pə:*] prep per; a; ~ **hour** all'ora; ~ **kilo** etc il chilo etc; ~ **day** al giorno; ~ **annum** adv all'anno; ~ **capita** adj, adv pro capite inv

perceive [pə'si:v] vt percepire; (notice) accorgersi di

per cent [pə'sɛnt] adv per cento

percentage [pə'sɛntɪdʒ] n percentuale f

perception [pə'sɛpʃən] n percezione f; sensibilità; perspicacia

perceptive [pə'sɛptɪv] adj percettivo(a); perspicace

perch [pə:tʃ] n (fish) pesce m persico; (for bird) sostegno, ramo ♦ vi appollaiarsi

percolator ['pə:kəleɪtə*] n (also: coffee ~) caffettiera a pressione; caffettiera elettrica

percussion [pə'kʌʃən] n percussione f; (MUS) strumenti mpl a percussione

peremptory [pə'rɛmptərɪ] adj perentorio(a)

perennial [pə'rɛnɪəl] adj perenne

perfect [adj, n 'pə:fɪkt, vb pə'fɛkt] adj perfetto(a) ♦ n (also: ~ **tense**) perfetto, passato prossimo ♦ vt perfezionare; mettere a punto; ~**ly** adv perfettamente, alla perfezione

perforate ['pə:fəreɪt] vt perforare; **perforation** [-'reɪʃən] n perforazione f

perform [pə'fɔ:m] vt (carry out) eseguire, fare; (symphony etc) suonare; (play, ballet) dare; (opera) fare ♦ vi suonare; recitare; ~**ance** n esecuzione f; (at theatre etc) rappresentazione f, spettacolo; (of an artist) interpretazione f; (of player etc) performance f; (of car, engine) prestazione f; ~**er** n artista m/f

perfume ['pə:fju:m] n profumo

perfunctory [pə'fʌŋktərɪ] adj superficiale, per la forma

perhaps [pə'hæps] adv forse

peril ['perɪl] n pericolo

perimeter [pə'rɪmɪtə*] n perimetro

period ['pɪərɪəd] n periodo; (HISTORY) epoca; (SCOL) lezione f; (full stop) punto; (MED) mestruazioni fpl ♦ adj (costume, furniture) d'epoca; ~**ic(al)** [-'ɔdɪk(l)] adj periodico(a); ~**ical** [-'ɔdɪkl] n periodico

peripheral [pə'rɪfərəl] adj periferico(a) ♦ n (COMPUT) unità f inv periferica

perish ['perɪʃ] vi perire, morire; (decay) deteriorarsi; ~**able** adj deperibile

perjury ['pɜːdʒərɪ] n spergiuro

perk [pɜːk] (inf) n vantaggio; ~ **up** vi (cheer up) rianimarsi; ~**y** adj (cheerful) vivace, allegro(a)

perm [pɜːm] n (for hair) permanente f

permanent ['pɜːmənənt] adj permanente

permeate ['pɜːmɪeɪt] vi penetrare ♦ vt permeare

permissible [pə'mɪsɪbl] adj permissibile, ammissibile

permission [pə'mɪʃən] n permesso

permissive [pə'mɪsɪv] adj permissivo(a)

permit [n 'pɜːmɪt, vb pə'mɪt] n permesso ♦ vt permettere; to ~ sb to do permettere a qn di fare

perpendicular [pɜːpən'dɪkjulə*] adj perpendicolare ♦ n perpendicolare f

perplex [pə'pleks] vt lasciare perplesso(a)

persecute ['pɜːsɪkjuːt] vt perseguitare

persevere [pɜːsɪ'vɪə*] vi perseverare

Persian ['pɜːʃən] adj persiano(a) ♦ n (LING) persiano; the (~) Gulf n il Golfo Persico

persist [pə'sɪst] vi: to ~ (in doing) persistere (nel fare); ostinarsi (a fare); ~**ent** adj persistente; ostinato(a)

person ['pɜːsn] n persona; in ~ di or in persona, personalmente; ~**al** adj personale; individuale; ~**al assistant** n segretaria personale; ~**al**

column n ≈ messaggi mpl personali; ~**al computer** n personal computer m inv; ~**ality** [-'nælɪtɪ] n personalità f inv; ~**ally** adv personalmente; to take sth ~**ally** prendere qc come una critica personale; ~**al organizer** n (Filofax ®) Fulltime ®; (electronic) agenda elettronica; ~ **stereo** n riproduttore m stereo portatile

personnel [pɜːsə'nel] n personale m

perspective [pə'spektɪv] n prospettiva

Perspex ['pɜːspeks] ® (BRIT) n tipo di resina termoplastica

perspiration [pɜːspɪ'reɪʃən] n traspirazione f, sudore m

persuade [pə'sweɪd] vt: to ~ sb to do sth persuadere qn a fare qc

pertaining [pə:'teɪnɪŋ]: ~ **to** prep che riguarda

perturb [pə'tə:b] vt turbare

peruse [pə'ru:z] vt leggere

pervade [pə'veɪd] vt pervadere

pervert [n 'pə:və:t, vb pə'və:t] n pervertito(a) ♦ vt pervertire

pessimism ['pesɪmɪzəm] n pessimismo

pessimist ['pesɪmɪst] n pessimista m/f; ~**ic** [-'mɪstɪk] adj pessimistico(a)

pest [pest] n animale m (or insetto) pestifero; (fig) peste f

pester ['pestə*] vt tormentare, molestare

pet [pet] n animale m domestico ♦ cpd favorito(a) ♦ vt accarezzare ♦ vi (inf) fare il petting; **teacher's** ~ favorito/a del maestro

petal ['petl] n petalo

peter ['pi:tə*]: to ~ **out** vi esaurirsi; estinguersi

petite [pə'ti:t] adj piccolo(a) e aggraziato(a)

petition [pə'tɪʃən] n petizione f

petrified ['petrɪfaɪd] adj (fig) morto(a) di paura

petrol ['petrəl] (BRIT) n benzina; **two/four-star** ~ ≈ benzina normale/super; ~ **can** n tanica per benzina

petroleum [pə'trəʊlɪəm] *n* petrolio

petrol: ~ **pump** (*BRIT*) *n* (*in car, at garage*) pompa di benzina; ~ **station** (*BRIT*) *n* stazione *f* di rifornimento; ~ **tank** (*BRIT*) *n* serbatoio della benzina

petticoat ['petɪkəʊt] *n* sottana

petty ['petɪ] *adj* (*mean*) meschino(a); (*unimportant*) insignificante; ~ **cash** *n* piccola cassa; ~ **officer** *n* sottufficiale *m* di marina

petulant ['petjʊlənt] *adj* irritabile

pew [pjuː] *n* panca (*di chiesa*)

pewter ['pjuːtə*] *n* peltro

phallic ['fælɪk] *adj* fallico(a)

phantom ['fæntəm] *n* fantasma *m*

pharmaceutical [fɑːmə'sjuːtɪkl] *adj* farmaceutico(a)

pharmacy ['fɑːməsɪ] *n* farmacia

phase [feɪz] *n* fase *f*, periodo ♦ *vt*: **to** ~ **sth in/out** introdurre/eliminare qc progressivamente

Ph.D. *n abbr* = Doctor of Philosophy

pheasant ['feznt] *n* fagiano

phenomena [fə'nɒmɪnə] *npl of* phenomenon

phenomenon [fə'nɒmɪnən] (*pl* phenomena) *n* fenomeno

Philippines ['fɪlɪpiːnz] *npl*: **the** ~ le Filippine

philosophical [fɪlə'sɒfɪkl] *adj* filosofico(a)

philosophy [fɪ'lɒsəfɪ] *n* filosofia

phlegmatic [fleg'mætɪk] *adj* flemmatico(a)

phobia ['fəʊbjə] *n* fobia

phone [fəʊn] *n* telefono ♦ *vt* telefonare; **to be on the** ~ avere il telefono; (*be calling*) essere al telefono; ~ **back** *vt, vi* richiamare; ~ **up** *vt* telefonare a ♦ *vi* telefonare; ~ **book** *n* guida del telefono, elenco telefonico; ~ **booth** *n* = **box**; ~ **box** *n* cabina telefonica; ~ **call** *n* telefonata; ~**card** *n* scheda telefonica; ~-**in** *n* (*BRIT: RADIO, TV*) trasmissione *f* a filo diretto con gli ascoltatori

phonetics [fə'netɪks] *n* fonetica

phoney ['fəʊnɪ] *adj* falso(a), fasul-

lo(a)

phosphorus ['fɒsfərəs] *n* fosforo

photo ['fəʊtəʊ] *n* foto *f inv*

photo... ['fəʊtəʊ] *prefix*: ~**copier** *n* fotocopiatrice *f*; ~**copy** *n* fotocopia ♦ *vt* fotocopiare; ~**graph** *n* fotografia ♦ *vt* fotografare; ~**grapher** [fə'tɒgrəfə*] *n* fotografo; ~**graphy** [fə'tɒgrəfɪ] *n* fotografia

phrase [freɪz] *n* espressione *f*; (*LING*) locuzione *f*; (*MUS*) frase *f* ♦ *vt* esprimere; ~ **book** *n* vocabolarietto

physical ['fɪzɪkl] *adj* fisico(a); ~ **education** *n* educazione *f* fisica; ~**ly** *adv* fisicamente

physician [fɪ'zɪʃən] *n* medico

physicist ['fɪzɪsɪst] *n* fisico

physics ['fɪzɪks] *n* fisica

physiology [fɪzɪ'ɒlədʒɪ] *n* fisiologia

physique [fɪ'ziːk] *n* fisico; costituzione *f*

pianist ['piːənɪst] *n* pianista *m/f*

piano [pɪ'ænəʊ] *n* pianoforte *m*

piccolo ['pɪkələʊ] *n* ottavino

pick [pɪk] *n* (*tool: also:* ~*axe*) piccone *m* ♦ *vt* scegliere; (*gather*) cogliere; (*remove*) togliere; (*lock*) far scattare; **take your** ~ scelga; **the** ~ **of** il fior fiore di; **to** ~ **one's nose** mettersi le dita nel naso; **to** ~ **one's teeth** pulirsi i denti con lo stuzzicadenti; **to** ~ **a quarrel** attaccar briga; ~ **at** *vt fus*: **to** ~ **at one's food** piluccare; ~ **on** *vt fus* (*person*) avercela con; ~ **out** *vt* scegliere; (*distinguish*) distinguere; ~ **up** *vi* (*improve*) migliorarsi ♦ *vt* raccogliere; (*POLICE, RADIO*) prendere; (*collect*) passare a prendere; (*AUT: give lift to*) far salire; (*person: for sexual encounter*) rimorchiare; (*learn*) imparare; **to** ~ **up speed** acquistare velocità; **to** ~ **o.s. up** rialzarsi

picket ['pɪkɪt] *n* (*in strike*) scioperante *mf* che fa parte di un picchetto; picchetto ♦ *vt* picchettare

pickle ['pɪkl] *n* (*also:* ~**s**: *as condiment*) sottaceti *mpl*; (*fig: mess*) pasticcio ♦ vt mettere sottaceto; mettere in salamoia

pickpocket ['pɪkpɒkɪt] n borsaiolo

pickup ['pɪkʌp] n (small truck) camioncino

picnic ['pɪknɪk] n picnic m inv

picture ['pɪktʃə*] n quadro; (painting) pittura; (photograph) foto(grafia); (drawing) disegno; (film) film m inv ♦ vt raffigurarsi; the ~s (BRIT) npl (cinema): the ~s il cinema; ~ **book** n libro illustrato

picturesque [pɪktʃə'rɛsk] adj pittoresco(a)

pie [paɪ] n torta; (of meat) pasticcio

piece [piːs] n pezzo; (of land) appezzamento; (item): a ~ of furniture/advice un mobile/consiglio ♦ vt: to ~ together mettere insieme; to take to ~s smontare; ~**meal** adv pezzo a pezzo, a spizzico; ~**work** n (lavoro a) cottimo

pie chart n grafico a torta

pier [pɪə*] n molo; (of bridge etc) pila

pierce [pɪəs] vt forare; (with arrow etc) trafiggere

piercing ['pɪəsɪŋ] adj (cry) acuto(a); (eyes) penetrante; (wind) pungente

pig [pɪg] n maiale m, porco

pigeon ['pɪdʒən] n piccione m; ~**hole** n casella

piggy bank ['pɪgɪ-] n salvadanaro

pigheaded ['pɪg'hɛdɪd] adj caparbio(a), cocciuto(a)

piglet ['pɪglɪt] n porcellino

pigskin ['pɪgskɪn] n cinghiale m

pigsty ['pɪgstaɪ] n porcile m

pigtail ['pɪgteɪl] n treccina

pike [paɪk] n (fish) luccio

pilchard ['pɪltʃəd] n specie di sardina

pile [paɪl] n (pillar, of books) pila; (heap) mucchio; (of carpet) pelo ♦ vt (also: ~ up) ammucchiare ♦ vi (also: ~ up) ammucchiarsi; to ~ **into** (car) stiparsi or ammucchiarsi in

piles [paɪlz] npl emorroidi fpl

pileup ['paɪlʌp] n (AUT) tamponamento a catena

pilfering ['pɪlfərɪŋ] n rubacchiare m

pilgrim ['pɪlgrɪm] n pellegrino/a; ~**age** n pellegrinaggio

pill [pɪl] n pillola; the ~ la pillola

pillage ['pɪlɪdʒ] vt saccheggiare

pillar ['pɪlə*] n colonna; ~ **box** (BRIT) n cassetta postale

pillion ['pɪljən] n: to ride ~ (on motor cycle) viaggiare dietro

pillory ['pɪlərɪ] vt mettere alla berlina

pillow ['pɪləʊ] n guanciale m; ~**case** n federa

pilot ['paɪlət] n pilota mf ♦ cpd (scheme etc) pilota inv ♦ vt pilotare; ~ **light** n fiamma pilota

pimp [pɪmp] n mezzano

pimple ['pɪmpl] n foruncolo

pin [pɪn] n spillo; (TECH) perno ♦ vt attaccare con uno spillo; ~s and needles formicolio; to ~ sb down (fig) obbligare qn a pronunziarsi; to ~ sth on sb (fig) addossare la colpa di qc a qn

pinafore ['pɪnəfɔː*] n (also: ~ dress) grembiule m (senza maniche)

pinball ['pɪnbɔːl] n flipper m inv

pincers ['pɪnsəz] npl pinzette fpl

pinch [pɪntʃ] n pizzicotto, pizzico ♦ vt pizzicare; (inf: steal) grattare; at a ~ in caso di bisogno

pincushion ['pɪnkʊʃən] n puntaspilli m inv

pine [paɪn] n (also: ~ tree) pino ♦ vi: to ~ for struggersi dal desiderio di; ~ **away** vi languire

pineapple ['paɪnæpl] n ananas m inv

ping [pɪŋ] n (noise) tintinnio; ~-**pong** ® n ping-pong m ®

pink [pɪŋk] adj rosa inv ♦ n (colour) rosa m inv; (BOT) garofano

PIN (number) [pɪn-] n abbr codice m segreto

pinpoint ['pɪnpɔɪnt] vt indicare con precisione

pint [paɪnt] n pinta (BRIT = 0.57l; US = 0.47l); (BRIT: inf) ≈ birra da mezzo

pioneer [paɪə'nɪə*] n pioniere/a

pious ['paɪəs] adj pio(a)

pip [pɪp] n (seed) seme m; (BRIT: time signal on radio) segnale m orario

pipe [paɪp] n tubo; (for smoking) pipa ♦ vt portare per mezzo di tubazione; ~s npl (also: bag~s) cornamusa (sezzese); ~ **down** (inf) vi calmarsi; ~ **cleaner** n scovolino; ~ **dream** n vana speranza; ~line n conduttura; (for oil) oleodotto; ~**r** n piffero; suonatore/trice di cornamusa

piping ['paɪpɪŋ] adv: ~ **hot** caldo bollente

pique [piːk] n picca

pirate ['paɪərət] n pirata m ♦ vt riprodurre abusivamente

Pisces ['paɪsɪz] n Pesci mpl

piss [pɪs] (inf!) vi pisciare; ~ed adj (drunk) ubriaco(a) fradicio(a)

pistol ['pɪstl] n pistola

piston ['pɪstən] n pistone m

pit [pɪt] n buca, fossa; (also: coal ~) miniera; (quarry) cava ♦ vt: to ~ sb against sb opporre qn a qn; ~s npl (AUT) box m

pitch [pɪtʃ] n (BRIT: SPORT) campo; (MUS) tono; (tar) pece f; (fig) grado, punto ♦ vt (throw) lanciare ♦ vi (fall) cascare; to ~ a tent piantare una tenda; ~ed battle n battaglia campale

piteous ['pɪtɪəs] adj pietoso(a)

pitfall ['pɪtfɔːl] n trappola

pith [pɪθ] n (of plant) midollo; (of orange) parte f interna della scorza; (fig) essenza, succo; vigore m

pithy ['pɪθɪ] adj conciso(a), vigoroso(a)

pitiful ['pɪtɪful] adj (touching) pietoso(a)

pitiless ['pɪtɪlɪs] adj spietato(a)

pittance ['pɪtns] n miseria, magro salario

pity ['pɪtɪ] n pietà ♦ vt aver pietà di; what a ~! che peccato!

pivot ['pɪvət] n perno

pizza ['piːtsə] n pizza

placard ['plækɑːd] n affisso

placate [pləˈkeɪt] vt placare, calmare

place [pleɪs] n posto, luogo; (proper position, rank, seat) posto; (house) casa, alloggio; (home): **at/to his ~** a casa sua ♦ vt (object) posare, mettere; (identify) riconoscere, individuare; **to take ~** aver luogo; succedere; **to change ~s with sb** scambiare il posto con qn; **out of ~** (not suitable) inopportuno(a); **in the first ~** in primo luogo; **to ~ an order** dare un'ordinazione; **to be ~d** (in race, exam) classificarsi

placid ['plæsɪd] adj placido(a), calmo(a)

plagiarism ['pleɪdʒərɪzəm] n plagio

plague [pleɪg] n peste f ♦ vt tormentare

plaice [pleɪs] n inv pianuzza

plaid [plæd] n plaid m inv

plain [pleɪn] adj (clear) chiaro(a), palese; (simple) semplice; (frank) franco(a), aperto(a); (not handsome) bruttino(a); (without seasoning etc) scondito(a); naturale; (in one colour) tinta unita inv ♦ adv francamente, chiaramente ♦ n pianura; ~ **chocolate** n cioccolato fondente; ~ **clothes** npl: **in ~ clothes** (police) in borghese; ~ly adv chiaramente; (frankly) francamente

plaintiff ['pleɪntɪf] n attore/trice

plaintive ['pleɪntɪv] adj (cry, voice) dolente, lamentoso(a)

plait [plæt] n treccia

plan [plæn] n pianta; (scheme) progetto, piano ♦ vt (think in advance) progettare; (prepare) organizzare ♦ vi far piani o progetti; **to ~ to do** progettare di fare

plane [pleɪn] n (AVIAT) aereo; (tree) platano; (tool) pialla; (ART, MATH etc) piano ♦ adj piano(a), piatto(a) ♦ vt (with tool) piallare

planet ['plænɪt] n pianeta m

plank [plæŋk] n tavola, asse f

planner ['plænə*] n pianificatore/trice

planning ['plænɪŋ] n progettazione f; **family ~** pianificazione f delle nascite; ~ **permission** n permesso di costruzione

plant [plɑ:nt] n pianta; (machinery) impianto; (factory) fabbrica ♦ vt piantare; (bomb) mettere

plantation [plæn'teɪʃn] n piantagione f

plaque [plæk] n placca

plaster ['plɑ:stə*] n intonaco; (also: ~ of Paris) gesso; (BRIT: also: sticking ~) cerotto ♦ vt intonacare; ingessare; (cover): **to ~ with** coprire di; **~ed** (inf) adj ubriaco/a fradicio(a)

plastic ['plæstɪk] n plastica ♦ adj (made of ~) di or in plastica; **~ bag** n sacchetto di plastica

Plasticine ['plæstɪsɪn] ® n plastilina ®

plastic surgery n chirurgia plastica

plate [pleɪt] n (dish) piatto; (in book) tavola; (dental ~) dentiera; **gold/silver ~** vasellame m d'oro/d'argento

plateau ['plætəʊ] (pl ~s or ~x) n altipiano

plateaux ['plætəʊz] npl of plateau

plate glass n vetro piano

platform ['plætfɔ:m] n (stage, at meeting) palco; (RAIL) marciapiede m; (BRIT: of bus) piattaforma

platinum ['plætɪnəm] n platino

platitude ['plætɪtju:d] n luogo comune

platoon [plə'tu:n] n plotone m

platter ['plætə*] n piatto

plausible ['plɔ:zɪbl] adj plausibile, credibile; (person) convincente

play [pleɪ] n gioco; (THEATRE) commedia ♦ vt (game) giocare a; (team, opponent) giocare contro; (instrument, piece of music) suonare; (record, tape) ascoltare; (role, part) interpretare ♦ vi giocare; suonare; recitare; **to ~ safe** giocare sul sicuro; **~ down** vt minimizzare; **~ up** vi (cause trouble) fare i capricci; **~boy** n playboy m inv; **~er** n giocatore/trice; (THEATRE) attore/trice; (MUS) musicista m/f; **~ful** adj giocoso(a); **~ground** n (in school) cortile m per la ricreazione;

(in park) parco m giochi inv; **~group** n giardino d'infanzia; **~ing card** n carta da gioco; **~ing field** n campo sportivo; **~mate** n compagno/a di gioco; **~-off** n (SPORT) bella; **~pen** n box m inv; **~thing** n giocattolo; **~time** n (SCOL) ricreazione f; **~wright** n drammaturgo/a

plc abbr (= public limited company) società per azioni a responsabilità limitata quotata in borsa

plea [pli:] n (request) preghiera, domanda; (LAW) (argomento f) di difesa

plead [pli:d] vt patrocinare; (give as excuse) addurre a pretesto ♦ vi (LAW) perorare la causa; (beg): **to ~ with sb** implorare qn

pleasant ['pleznt] adj piacevole, gradevole; **~ries** npl (polite remarks): **to exchange ~ries** scambiarsi i convenevoli

please [pli:z] excl per piacere!, per favore!; (acceptance): yes, ~ sì, grazie ♦ vt piacere a ♦ vi piacere; (think fit): **do as you ~** faccia come le pare; **~ yourself!** come ti (or le) pare!; **~d** adj: **~d** (with) contento(a) (di); **~d to meet you!** piacere!; **pleasing** adj piacevole, che fa piacere

pleasure ['pleʒə*] n piacere m; "it's a ~" "prego"; **~ boat** n imbarcazione f da diporto

pleat [pli:t] n piega

pledge [pledʒ] n pegno; (promise) promessa ♦ vt impegnare; promettere

plentiful ['plentɪful] adj abbondante, copioso(a)

plenty ['plentɪ] n: ~ **of** tanto(a), molto(a); un'abbondanza di

pleurisy ['pluərɪsɪ] n pleurite f

pliable ['plaɪəbl] adj flessibile; (fig: person) malleabile

pliant ['plaɪənt] adj = pliable

pliers ['plaɪəz] npl pinza

plight [plaɪt] n situazione f critica

plimsolls ['plɪmsəlz] (BRIT) npl scarpe fpl da tennis

plinth [plɪnθ] n plinto; piedistallo

plod [plɔd] vi camminare a stento; (fig) sgobbare

plonk [plɔŋk] (inf) n (BRIT: wine) vino da poco ♦ vt: **to ~ sth down** buttare giù qc bruscamente

plot [plɔt] n congiura, cospirazione f; (of story, play) trama; (of land) lotto ♦ vt (mark out) fare la pianta di; rilevare; (: diagram etc) tracciare; (conspire) congiurare, cospirare ♦ vi congiurare; **~ter** n (instrument) plotter m inv

plough [plaʊ] (US **plow**) n aratro ♦ vt (earth) arare; **to ~ money into** (company etc) investire danaro in; **~ through** vt fus (snow etc) procedere a fatica in; **~man's lunch** (BRIT) n pasto a base di pane, formaggio e birra

ploy [plɔɪ] n stratagemma m

pluck [plʌk] vt (fruit) cogliere; (musical instrument) pizzicare; (bird) spennare; (hairs) togliere ♦ n coraggio, fegato; **to ~ up courage** farsi coraggio

plug [plʌg] n tappo; (ELEC) spina; (AUT: also: **spark**~) candela ♦ vt (hole) tappare; (inf: advertise) spingere; **~ in** vt (ELEC) attaccare a una presa

plum [plʌm] n (fruit) susina ♦ cpd: **~ job** (inf) impiego ottimo or favoloso

plumb [plʌm] vt: **to ~ the depths** (fig) toccare il fondo

plumber ['plʌmə*] n idraulico

plumbing ['plʌmɪŋ] n (trade) lavoro di idraulico; (piping) tubature fpl

plume [plu:m] n piuma, penna; (decorative) pennacchio

plummet ['plʌmɪt] vi: **to ~ (down)** cadere a piombo

plump [plʌmp] adj grassoccio(a) ♦ vi: **to ~ for** (inf: choose) decidersi per; **~ up** vt (cushion etc) sprimacciare

plunder ['plʌndə*] n saccheggio ♦ vt saccheggiare

plunge [plʌndʒ] n tuffo; (fig) caduta

♦ vt immergere ♦ vi (fall) cadere, precipitare; (dive) tuffarsi; **to take the ~** saltare il fosso; **~r** n sturalavandini m inv; **plunging** adj (neckline) profondo(a)

pluperfect [plu:'pə:fɪkt] n piuccheperfetto

plural ['plʊərl] adj plurale ♦ n plurale m

plus [plʌs] n (also: **~ sign**) segno più ♦ prep più; **ten/twenty ~** più di dieci/venti

plush [plʌʃ] adj lussuoso(a)

ply [plaɪ] vt (a trade) esercitare ♦ vi (ship) fare il servizio ♦ n (of wool, rope) capo; **to ~ sb with drink** dare di bere continuamente a qn; **~wood** n legno compensato

P.M. n abbr = **prime minister**

p.m. adv abbr (= post meridiem) del pomeriggio

pneumatic drill [nju:'mætɪk-] n martello pneumatico

pneumonia [nju:'məʊnɪə] n polmonite f

poach [pəʊtʃ] vt (cook: egg) affogare; (: fish) cuocere in bianco; (steal) cacciare (or pescare) di frodo ♦ vi fare il bracconiere; **~er** n bracconiere m

P.O. Box n abbr = **Post Office Box**

pocket ['pɔkɪt] n tasca ♦ vt intascare; **to be out of ~** (BRIT) rimetterci; **~book** (US) n (wallet) portafoglio; **~ knife** n temperino; **~ money** n paghetta, settimana

pod [pɔd] n guscio

podgy ['pɔdʒɪ] adj grassoccio(a)

podiatrist [pɔ'di:ətrɪst] (US) n callista m/f, pedicure m/f

poem ['pəʊɪm] n poesia

poet ['pəʊɪt] n poeta/essa; **~ic** [-'etɪk] adj poetico(a); **~ laureate** n poeta m laureato (nominato dalla Corte Reale); **~ry** n poesia

poignant ['pɔɪnjənt] adj struggente

point [pɔɪnt] n (gen) punto; (tip: of needle etc) punta; (in time) punto, momento; (SCOL) voto; (main idea, important part) nocciolo; (ELEC)

presa (di corrente); (also: decimal
~): 2 ~ 3 (2.3) 2 virgola 3 (2,3) ♦ vt
(show) indicare; (gun etc): to ~ sth
at puntare qc contro ♦ vi: to ~ at
mostrare a dito; ~s npl (AUT) punti-
ne fpl; (RAIL) scambio; to be on
the ~ of doing sth essere sul punto
di or stare per fare qc; to make a ~
fare un'osservazione; to get/miss
the ~ capire/non capire; to come to
the ~ venire al fatto; there's no ~
(in doing) è inutile (fare); ~ out vt
far notare; ~ to vt fus indicare;
(fig) dimostrare; ~-blank adj
(also: at ~-blank range) a bruciape-
lo; (fig) categoricamente; ~ed adj
(shape) aguzzo(a), appuntito(a); (remark) specifico(a); ~edly adv in
maniera inequivocabile; ~er n (needle) lancetta; (fig) indicazione f, consiglio; ~less adj inutile, vano(a); ~
of view n punto di vista

poise [pɔɪz] n (composure) portamento; ~d adj: to be ~d to do tenersi pronto(a) a fare

poison ['pɔɪzn] n veleno ♦ vt avvele-
nare; ~ous adj velenoso(a)

poke [pəuk] vt (fire) attizzare; (jab
with finger, stick etc) punzecchiare;
(put): to ~ sth in(to) spingere qc
dentro; ~ about vi frugare

poker ['pəukə*] n attizzatoio;
(CARDS) poker m

poky ['pəukɪ] adj piccolo(a) e stret-
to(a)

Poland ['pəulənd] n Polonia

polar ['pəulə*] adj polare; ~ **bear** n
orso bianco

Pole [pəul] n polacco/a

pole [pəul] n (of wood) palo; (ELEC,
GEO) polo; ~ **bean** (US) n (runner
bean) fagiolino; ~ **vault** n salto con
l'asta

police [pə'liːs] n polizia ♦ vt mantenere l'ordine in; ~ **car** n macchina
della polizia; ~**man** n poliziotto,
agente m di polizia; ~ **station** n posto di polizia; ~**woman** n donna f
poliziotto inv

policy ['pɔlɪsɪ] n politica; (also: in-

surance ~) polizza (d'assicurazione)

polio ['pəulɪəu] n polio f

Polish ['pəulɪʃ] adj polacco(a) ♦ n
(LING) polacco

polish ['pɔlɪʃ] n (for shoes) lucido;
(for floor) cera; (for nails) smalto;
(shine) lucentezza, lustro; (fig: refinement) raffinatezza ♦ vt lucidare;
(fig: improve) raffinare; ~ **off** vt
(work) sbrigare; (food) mangiarsi;
~**ed** adj (fig) raffinato(a)

polite [pə'laɪt] adj cortese; ~**ness** n
cortesia

political [pə'lɪtɪkl] adj politico(a);
~**ly** adv politicamente

politician [pɔlɪ'tɪʃən] n politico

politics ['pɔlɪtɪks] n politica ♦ npl
(views, policies) idee fpl politiche

poll [pəul] n scrutinio; (votes cast)
voti mpl; (also: opinion ~) sondaggio
(d'opinioni) ♦ vt ottenere

pollen ['pɔlən] n polline m

polling day ['pəulɪŋ-] (BRIT) n
giorno delle elezioni

polling station ['pəulɪŋ-] (BRIT) n
sezione f elettorale

pollute [pə'luːt] vt inquinare

pollution [pə'luːʃən] n inquinamento

polo ['pəuləu] n polo; ~**-necked** adj
a collo alto risvoltato; ~ **shirt** n polo
f inv

polyester [pɔlɪ'estə*] n poliestere m

polystyrene [pɔlɪ'staɪriːn] n polisti-
rolo

polytechnic [pɔlɪ'teknɪk] n (college)
istituto superiore ad indirizzo tecnolo-
gico

polythene [pɔlɪθiːn] n politene m;
~ **bag** n sacco di plastica

pomegranate ['pɔmɪgrænɪt] n mela-
grana

pomp [pɔmp] n pompa, fasto

pompom ['pɔmpɔm] n pompon m
inv

pompon ['pɔmpɔn] n = **pompom**

pompous ['pɔmpəs] adj pomposo(a)

pond [pɔnd] n pozzo; stagno

ponder ['pɔndə*] vt ponderare, riflettere su; ~**ous** adj ponderoso(a), pesante

pong [pɒŋ] (BRIT: inf) n puzzo

pony [ˈpəunɪ] n pony m inv; ~**tail** n coda di cavallo; ~ **trekking** (BRIT) n escursione f a cavallo

poodle [ˈpuːdl] n barboncino, barbone m

pool [puːl] n (puddle) pozza; (pond) stagno; (also: swimming ~) piscina; (fig: of light) cerchio; (billiards) specie di biliardo a buca ♦ vt mettere in comune; ~**s** npl (football ~s) = totocalcio; **typing** ~ servizio comune di dattilografia

poor [puə*] adj povero(a); (mediocre) mediocre, cattivo(a) ♦ npl: **the** ~ i poveri; **in** ~ povero(a) di; ~**ly** adv poveramente; male ♦ adj indisposto(a), malato(a)

pop [pɒp] n (noise) schiocco; (MUS) musica pop; (drink) bibita gasata; (US: inf: father) babbo ♦ vt (put) mettere (in fretta) ♦ vi scoppiare; (cork) schioccare; ~ **in** vi passare; ~ **out** vi fare un salto fuori; ~ **up** vi apparire, sorgere; ~**corn** n popcorn m

pope [pəup] n papa m

poplar [ˈpɒplə*] n pioppo

popper [ˈpɒpə*] n bottone m a pressione

poppy [ˈpɒpɪ] n papavero

popsicle [ˈpɒpsɪkl] (US: ®) n (ice lolly) ghiacciolo

populace [ˈpɒpjuls] n popolino

popular [ˈpɒpjulə*] adj popolare; (fashionable) in voga; ~**ity** [-ˈlærɪtɪ] n popolarità; ~**ize** vt divulgare; (science) volgarizzare

population [pɒpjuˈleɪʃən] n popolazione f

porcelain [ˈpɔːslɪn] n porcellana

porch [pɔːtʃ] n veranda

porcupine [ˈpɔːkjupaɪn] n porcospino

pore [pɔː*] n poro ♦ vi: **to** ~ **over** essere immerso(a) in

pork [pɔːk] n carne f di maiale

pornographic [pɔːnəˈɡræfɪk] adj pornografico(a)

pornography [pɔːˈnɒɡrəfɪ] n pornografia

porpoise [ˈpɔːpəs] n focena

porridge [ˈpɒrɪdʒ] n porridge m

port [pɔːt] n (gen, wine) porto; (NAUT: left side) babordo; ~ **of call** (porto di) scalo

portable [ˈpɔːtəbl] adj portatile

porter [ˈpɔːtə*] n (for luggage) facchino, portabagagli m inv; (doorkeeper) portiere m, portinaio

portfolio [pɔːtˈfəulɪəu] n (case) cartella; (POL, FINANCE) portafoglio; (of artist) raccolta dei propri lavori

porthole [ˈpɔːthəul] n oblò m inv

portion [ˈpɔːʃən] n porzione f

portly [ˈpɔːtlɪ] adj corpulento(a)

portrait [ˈpɔːtreɪt] n ritratto

portray [pɔːˈtreɪ] vt fare il ritratto di; (character on stage) rappresentare; (in writing) ritrarre

Portugal [ˈpɔːtjugl] n Portogallo

Portuguese [pɔːtjuˈɡiːz] adj portoghese ♦ n inv portoghese m/f; (LING) portoghese m

pose [pəuz] n posa ♦ vi posare; (pretend): **to** ~ **as** atteggiarsi a, posare a ♦ vt porre

posh [pɒʃ] (inf) adj elegante; (family) per bene

position [pəˈzɪʃən] n posizione f; (job) posto ♦ vt sistemare

positive [ˈpɒzɪtɪv] adj positivo(a); (certain) sicuro(a), certo(a); (definite) preciso(a); definitivo(a)

posse [ˈpɒsɪ] (US) n drappello

possess [pəˈzɛs] vt possedere; ~**ion** [pəˈzɛʃən] n possesso; ~**ions** npl (belongings) beni mpl; ~**ive** adj possessivo(a)

possibility [pɒsɪˈbɪlɪtɪ] n possibilità f inv

possible [ˈpɒsɪbl] adj possibile; **as big as** ~ il più grande possibile

possibly [ˈpɒsɪblɪ] adv (perhaps) forse; **if you** ~ **can** se le è possibile; **I cannot** ~ **come** proprio non posso venire

post [pəust] n (BRIT) posta; (: collection) levata; (job, situation) posto; (MIL) postazione f; (pole) palo ♦ vt (BRIT: send by post) impostare; (:

appoint): **to** ~ **to** assegnare a; **~age** *n* affrancatura; **~age stamp** *n* francobollo; **~al order** *n* vaglia *m inv* postale; **~box** (*BRIT*) *n* cassetta postale; **~card** *n* cartolina; ~ **code** (*BRIT*) *n* codice *m* (di avviamento) postale

poster ['pəustə*] *n* manifesto, affisso

poste restante [pəust'rɛstã:nt] (*BRIT*) *n* fermo posta *m*

postgraduate ['pəust'grædjuət] *n* laureato/a *che continua gli studi*

posthumous ['pɔstjuməs] *adj* postumo(a)

postman ['pəustmən] *n* postino

postmark ['pəustmɑ:k] *n* bollo *or* timbro postale

post-mortem [-'mɔ:təm] *n* autopsia

post office *n* (*building*) ufficio postale; (*organization*): **the Post Office** = le Poste e Telecomunicazioni; **Post Office Box** *n* casella postale

postpone [pəs'pəun] *vt* rinviare

postscript ['pəustskrɪpt] *n* poscritto

posture ['pɔstʃə*] *n* portamento; (*pose*) posa, atteggiamento

postwar ['pəust'wɔ:*] *adj* del dopoguerra

posy ['pəuzɪ] *n* mazzetto di fiori

pot [pɔt] *n* (*for cooking*) pentola; casseruola; (*tea*~) teiera; (*coffee*~) caffettiera; (*for plants, jam*) vaso; (*inf: marijuana*) erba ♦ *vt* (*plant*) piantare in vaso; **a** ~ **of tea for two** tè per due; **to go to** ~ (*inf: work, performance*) andare in malora

potato [pə'teɪtəu] (*pl* ~**es**) *n* patata; ~ **peeler** *n* sbucciapatate *m inv*

potent ['pəutnt] *adj* potente, forte

potential [pə'tɛnʃl] *adj* potenziale ♦ *n* possibilità *fpl*

pothole ['pɔthəul] *n* (*in road*) buca; (*BRIT: underground*) caverna; **~holing** (*BRIT*) *n*: **to go potholing** fare speleologia

potluck [pɔt'lʌk] *n*: **to take** ~ tentare la sorte

potted ['pɔtɪd] *adj* (*food*) in conserva; (*plant*) in vaso; (*account etc*)

condensato(a)

potter ['pɔtə*] *n* vasaio ♦ *vi*: **to** ~ **around,** ~ **about** (*BRIT*) lavoracchiare; **~y** *n* ceramiche *fpl*; (*factory*) fabbrica di ceramiche

potty ['pɔtɪ] *adj* (*inf: mad*) tocco(a) ♦ *n* (*child's*) vasino

pouch [pautʃ] *n* borsa; (*ZOOL*) marsupio

poultry ['pəultrɪ] *n* pollame *m*

pounce [pauns] *vi*: **to** ~ (**on**) piombare (su)

pound [paund] *n* (*weight*) libbra; (*money*) (lira) sterlina ♦ *vt* (*beat*) battere; (*crush*) pestare, polverizzare ♦ *vi* (*beat*) battere, martellare; ~ **sterling** *n* sterlina (inglese)

pour [pɔ:*] *vt* versare ♦ *vi* riversarsi; (*rain*) piovere a dirotto; ~ **away** *vt* vuotare; ~ **in** *vi* affluire in gran quantità; ~ **off** *vt* vuotare; ~ **out** *vi* (*people*) uscire a fiumi ♦ *vt* vuotare; versare; (*fig*) sfogare; **~ing** *adj*: **~ing rain** pioggia torrenziale

pout [paut] *vi* sporgere le labbra; fare il broncio

poverty ['pɔvətɪ] *n* povertà, miseria; **~-stricken** *adj* molto povero(a), misero(a)

powder ['paudə*] *n* polvere ♦ *vt*: **to** ~ **one's face** incipriarsi il viso; ~ **compact** *n* portacipria *m inv*; **~ed milk** *n* latte *m* in polvere; ~ **puff** *n* piumino della cipria; ~ **room** *n* toilette *f inv* (per signore)

power ['pauə*] *n* (*strength*) potenza, forza; (*ability, POL: of party, leader*) potere *m*; (*ELEC*) corrente *f*; **to be in** ~ (*POL etc*) essere al potere; ~ **cut** (*BRIT*) *n* interruzione *f* or mancanza di corrente; **~ed** *adj*: **~ed by** azionato(a) da; ~ **failure** *n* interruzione *f* della corrente elettrica; **~ful** *adj* potente, forte; **~less** *adj* impotente; **~less to do** impossibilitato(a) a fare; ~ **point** (*BRIT*) *n* presa di corrente; ~ **station** *n* centrale *f* elettrica

p.p. *abbr* (= *per procurationem*): ~ **J. Smith** per J. Smith; (= *pages*) p.p

PR abbr = public relations

practicable ['præktɪkəbl] adj (scheme) praticabile

practical ['præktɪkl] adj pratico(a); ~**ity** [-'kælɪtɪ] (no pl) n (of situation etc) lato pratico; ~ **joke** n beffa; ~**ly** adv praticamente

practice ['præktɪs] n pratica; (of profession) esercizio; (at football etc) allenamento; (business) gabinetto; clientela ♦ vt, vi (US) = **practise**; **in** ~ (in reality) in pratica; **out of** ~ fuori esercizio

practise ['præktɪs] (US **practice**) vt (work at: piano, one's backhand etc) esercitarsi a; (train for: skiing, running etc) allenarsi a; (a sport, religion) praticare; (method) usare; (profession) esercitare ♦ vi esercitarsi; (train) allenarsi; (lawyer, doctor) esercitare; **practising** adj (Christian etc) praticante; (lawyer) che esercita la professione

practitioner [præk'tɪʃənə*] n professionista m/f

pragmatic [præg'mætɪk] adj pragmatico(a)

prairie ['prɛərɪ] n prateria

praise [preɪz] n elogio, lode ♦ vt elogiare, lodare; ~**worthy** adj lodevole

pram [præm] (BRIT) n carrozzina

prance [prɑːns] vi (person) camminare pavoneggiandosi; (horse) caracollare

prank [præŋk] n burla

prawn [prɔːn] n gamberetto

pray [preɪ] vi pregare

prayer [prɛə*] n preghiera

preach [priːtʃ] vt, vi predicare

precarious [prɪ'kɛərɪəs] adj precario(a)

precaution [prɪ'kɔːʃən] n precauzione f

precede [prɪ'siːd] vt precedere

precedent ['prɛsɪdənt] n precedente m

precept ['priːsɛpt] n precetto

precinct ['priːsɪŋkt] n (US) circoscri-

zione f; ~**s** npl (of building) zona recintata; **pedestrian** ~ (BRIT) zona pedonale; **shopping** ~ (BRIT) centro commerciale (chiuso al traffico)

precious ['prɛʃəs] adj prezioso(a)

precipitate [prɪ'sɪpɪteɪt] vt precipitare

precise [prɪ'saɪs] adj preciso(a); ~**ly** adv precisamente

preclude [prɪ'kluːd] vt precludere, impedire

precocious [prɪ'kəuʃəs] adj precoce

precondition [priːkən'dɪʃən] n condizione f necessaria

predecessor ['priːdɪsɛsə*] n predecessore/a

predicament [prɪ'dɪkəmənt] n situazione f difficile

predict [prɪ'dɪkt] vt predire; ~**able** adj prevedibile

predominantly [prɪ'dɒmɪnəntlɪ] adv in maggior parte; soprattutto

predominate [prɪ'dɒmɪneɪt] vi predominare

pre-empt [priː'ɛmpt] vt pregiudicare

preen [priːn] vt: **to ~ itself** (bird) lisciarsi le penne; **to ~ o.s.** agghindarsi

prefab ['priːfæb] n casa prefabbricata

preface ['prɛfəs] n prefazione f

prefect ['priːfɛkt] n (BRIT: in school) studente/essa con funzioni disciplinari; (in Italy) prefetto

prefer [prɪ'fəː*] vt preferire; **to ~ doing or to do** preferire fare; ~**ably** ['prɛfrəblɪ] adv preferibilmente; ~**ence** ['prɛfrəns] n preferenza; ~**ential** [prɛfə'rɛnʃəl] adj preferenziale

prefix ['priːfɪks] n prefisso

pregnancy ['prɛgnənsɪ] n gravidanza

pregnant ['prɛgnənt] adj incinta af

prehistoric ['priːhɪs'tɔrɪk] adj preistorico(a)

prejudice ['prɛdʒudɪs] n pregiudizio; (harm) torto, danno; ~**d** adj: (against) prevenuto(a) (contro); ~**d** (in favour of) ben disposto(a) (ver-

preliminary [prɪ'lɪmɪnərɪ] *adj* preliminare

premarital ['priː'mærɪtl] *adj* prematrimoniale

premature ['prɛmətʃuə*] *adj* prematuro(a)

premier ['prɛmɪə*] *adj* primo(a) ♦ *n* (POL) primo ministro

première ['prɛmɪeə*] *n* prima

premise ['prɛmɪs] *n* premessa; **~s** *npl* (*of business, institution*) locale *m*; **on the ~s** sul posto

premium ['priːmɪəm] *n* premio; **to be at a ~** essere ricercatissimo; **~ bond** (BRIT) *n* obbligazione *f* a premio

premonition [prɛmə'nɪʃən] *n* premonizione *f*

preoccupied [priː'ɔkjupaɪd] *adj* preoccupato(a)

prep [prɛp] *n* (SCOL: *study*) studio

prepaid [priː'peɪd] *adj* pagato(a) in anticipo

preparation [prɛpə'reɪʃən] *n* preparazione *f*; **~s** *npl* (*for trip, war*) preparativi *mpl*

preparatory [prɪ'pærətərɪ] *adj* preparatorio(a); **~ school** *n* scuola elementare privata

prepare [prɪ'pɛə*] *vt* preparare ♦ *vi*: **to ~ for** prepararsi a; **~d to** pronto(a) a

preposition [prɛpə'zɪʃən] *n* preposizione *f*

preposterous [prɪ'pɔstərəs] *adj* assurdo(a)

prep school *n* = **preparatory school**

prerequisite [priː'rɛkwɪzɪt] *n* requisito indispensabile

prescribe [prɪ'skraɪb] *vt* (MED) prescrivere

prescription [prɪ'skrɪpʃən] *n* prescrizione *f*; (MED) ricetta

presence ['prɛzns] *n* presenza; **~ of mind** presenza di spirito

present [*adj, n* 'prɛznt, *vb* prɪ'zɛnt] *adj* presente; (*wife, residence, job*) attuale ♦ *n* (*actuality*): **the ~** il presente; (*gift*) regalo ♦ *vt* presentare;

(*give*): **to ~ sb with sth** offrire qc a qn; **to give sb a ~** fare un regalo a qn; **at ~** al momento; **~ation** [-'teɪʃən] *n* presentazione *f*; (*ceremony*) consegna ufficiale; **~-day** *adj* attuale, d'oggigiorno; **~er** *n* (RADIO, TV) presentatore/trice; **~ly** *adv* (*soon*) fra poco, presto; (*at present*) al momento

preservative [prɪ'zəːvətɪv] *n* conservante *m*

preserve [prɪ'zəːv] *vt* (*keep safe*) preservare, proteggere; (*maintain*) conservare; (*food*) mettere in conserva ♦ *n* (*often pl*: *jam*) marmellata; (: *fruit*) frutta sciroppata

preside [prɪ'zaɪd] *vi*: **to ~ (over)** presiedere (a)

president ['prɛzɪdənt] *n* presidente *m*; **~ial** [-'dɛnʃl] *adj* presidenziale

press [prɛs] *n* (*newspapers etc*): **the P~** la stampa; (*tool, machine*) pressa; (*for wine*) torchio ♦ *vt* (*push*) premere, pigiare; (*squeeze*) spremere; (: *hand*) stringere; (*clothes: iron*) stirare; (*pursue*) incalzare; (*insist*): **to ~ sth on sb** far accettare qc da qn ♦ *vi* premere; accalcare; **we are ~ed for time** ci manca il tempo; **to ~ for sth** insistere per avere qc; **~ on** *vi* continuare; **~ conference** *n* conferenza *f* stampa *inv*; **~ing** *adj* urgente; **~ stud** (BRIT) *n* bottone *m* a pressione; **~up** (BRIT) *n* flessione *f* sulle braccia

pressure ['prɛʃə*] *n* pressione *f*; **to put ~ on sb (to do)** mettere qn sotto pressione (affinché faccia); **~ cooker** *n* pentola a pressione; **~ gauge** *n* manometro; **~ group** *n* gruppo di pressione

prestige [prɛs'tiːʒ] *n* prestigio

presumably [prɪ'zjuːməblɪ] *adv* presumibilmente

presume [prɪ'zjuːm] *vt* supporre

presumption [prɪ'zʌmpʃən] *n* presunzione *f*

presumptuous [prɪ'zʌmpʃəs] *adj* presuntuoso(a)

pretence [prɪ'tɛns] (US **pretense**) *n*

(*claim*) pretesa; **to make a ~ of doing** far finta di fare; **under false ~s** con l'inganno

pretend [prɪ'tɛnd] *vt* (*feign*) fingere ♦ *vi* far finta; **to ~ to do** far finta di fare

pretense [prɪ'tɛns] (*US*) *n* = **pretence**

pretentious [prɪ'tɛnʃəs] *adj* pretenzioso(a)

pretext ['priːtɛkst] *n* pretesto

pretty ['prɪtɪ] *adj* grazioso(a), carino(a) ♦ *adv* abbastanza, assai

prevail [prɪ'veɪl] *vi* (*win, be usual*) prevalere; (*persuade*): **to ~ (up)on** sb **to do** persuadere qn a fare; **~ing** *adj* dominante

prevalent ['prɛvələnt] *adj* (*belief*) predominante; (*customs*) diffuso(a); (*fashion*) corrente; (*disease*) comune

prevent [prɪ'vɛnt] *vt*: **to ~** sb **from doing** impedire a qn di fare; **to ~** sth **from happening** impedire che qc succeda; **~ative** *adj* = **~ive**; **~ion** [-'vɛnʃən] *n* prevenzione *f*; **~ive** *adj* preventivo(a)

preview ['priːvjuː] *n* (*of film*) anteprima

previous ['priːvɪəs] *adj* precedente; anteriore; **~ly** *adv* prima

prewar ['priː'wɔː*] *adj* anteguerra *inv*

prey [preɪ] *n* preda ♦ *vi*: **to ~ on** far preda di; **it was ~ing on his mind** lo stava ossessionando

price [praɪs] *n* prezzo ♦ *vt* (*goods*) fissare il prezzo di; valutare; **~less** *adj* inapprezzabile; **~ list** *n* listino (dei) prezzi

prick [prɪk] *n* puntura ♦ *vt* pungere; **to ~ up** one's **ears** drizzare gli orecchi

prickle ['prɪkl] *n* (*of plant*) spina; (*sensation*) pizzicore *m*

prickly ['prɪklɪ] *adj* spinoso(a); **~ heat** *n* sudamina

pride [praɪd] *n* orgoglio; superbia ♦ *vt*: **to ~** o.s. **on** essere orgoglioso(a) di; vantarsi di

priest [priːst] *n* prete *m*, sacerdote

m; **~hood** *n* sacerdozio

prig [prɪg] *n*: **he's a ~** è compiaciuto di se stesso

prim [prɪm] *adj* pudico(a); contegnoso(a)

primarily ['praɪmərɪlɪ] *adv* principalmente, essenzialmente

primary ['praɪmərɪ] *adj* primario(a); (*first in importance*) primo(a) ♦ *n* (*US: election*) primarie *fpl*; **~ school** (*BRIT*) *n* scuola elementare

prime [praɪm] *adj* primario(a), fondamentale; (*excellent*) di prima qualità ♦ *vt* (*wood*) preparare; (*fig*) mettere al corrente ♦ *n*: **in the ~ of life** nel fiore della vita; **P~ Minister** *n* primo ministro

primeval [praɪ'miːvl] *adj* primitivo(a)

primitive ['prɪmɪtɪv] *adj* primitivo(a)

primrose ['prɪmrəʊz] *n* primavera

primus (stove) ['praɪməs(-)] ® (*BRIT*) *n* fornello a petrolio

prince [prɪns] *n* principe *m*

princess [prɪn'sɛs] *n* principessa

principal ['prɪnsɪpl] *adj* principale ♦ *n* (*headmaster*) preside *m*

principle ['prɪnsɪpl] *n* principio; **in ~** in linea di principio; **on ~** per principio

print [prɪnt] *n* (*mark*) impronta; (*letters*) caratteri *mpl*; (*fabric*) tessuto stampato; (*ART, PHOT*) stampa ♦ *vt* imprimere; (*publish*) stampare, pubblicare; (*write in capitals*) scrivere in stampatello; **out of ~** esaurito(a); **~ed matter** *n* stampe *fpl*; **~er** *n* tipografo; (*machine*) stampante *f*; **~ing** *n* stampa; **~-out** *n* (*COMPUT*) tabulato

prior ['praɪə*] *adj* precedente; (*claim etc*) più importante; **~ to doing** prima di fare

priority [praɪ'ɔrɪtɪ] *n* priorità *f inv*; precedenza

prise [praɪz] *vt*: **to ~ open** forzare

prison ['prɪzn] *n* prigione *f* ♦ *cpd* (*system*) carcerario(a); (*conditions, food*) nelle *or* delle prigioni; **~er** *n* prigioniero(a)

pristine ['prɪstiːn] *adj* immacolato(a)

privacy ['prɪvəsɪ] *n* solitudine *f*, intimità

private ['praɪvɪt] *adj* privato(a); personale ♦ *n* soldato semplice; "~" (*on envelope*) "riservata"; (*on door*) "privato"; **in ~** in privato; **~ enterprise** *n* iniziativa privata; **~ eye** *n* investigatore *m* privato; **~ly** *adv* in privato; (*within oneself*) dentro di sé; **~ property** *n* proprietà privata; **privatize** *vt* privatizzare

privet ['prɪvɪt] *n* ligustro

privilege ['prɪvɪlɪdʒ] *n* privilegio

privy ['prɪvɪ] *adj*: **to be ~ to** essere al corrente di

prize [praɪz] *n* premio ♦ *adj* (*example, idiot*) perfetto(a); (*bull, novel*) premiato(a) ♦ *vt* apprezzare, pregiare; **~ giving** *n* premiazione *f*; **~winner** *n* premiato(a)

pro [prəʊ] *n* (*SPORT*) professionista *m/f* ♦ *prep* pro; **the ~s and cons** il pro e il contro

probability [prɔbə'bɪlɪtɪ] *n* probabilità *f inv*; **in all ~** con tutta probabilità

probable ['prɔbəbl] *adj* probabile; **probably** *adv* probabilmente

probation [prə'beɪʃən] *n*: **on ~** (*employee*) in prova; (*LAW*) in libertà vigilata

probe [prəʊb] *n* (*MED, SPACE*) sonda; (*enquiry*) indagine *f*, investigazione *f* ♦ *vt* sondare, esplorare; indagare

problem ['prɔbləm] *n* problema *m*

procedure [prə'siːdʒə*] *n* (*ADMIN, LAW*) procedura; (*method*) metodo, procedimento

proceed [prə'siːd] *vi* (*go forward*) avanzare, andare avanti; (*go about it*) procedere; (*continue*): **to ~ (with)** continuare; **to ~ to** andare a; passare a; **to ~ to do** mettersi a fare; **~ings** *npl* misure *fpl*; (*LAW*) procedimento; (*meeting*) riunione *f*; (*records*) rendiconti *mpl*; atti *mpl*; **~s** ['prəʊsiːdz] *npl* profitto, incasso

process ['prəʊses] *n* processo; (*meth-*

od) metodo, sistema *m* ♦ *vt* trattare; (*information*) elaborare; **~ing** *n* trattamento; elaborazione *f*

procession [prə'seʃən] *n* processione *f*, corteo; **funeral ~** corteo funebre

proclaim [prə'kleɪm] *vt* proclamare, dichiarare

procrastinate [prəʊ'kræstɪneɪt] *vi* procrastinare

prod [prɔd] *vt* dare un colpetto a; pungolare ♦ *n* colpetto

prodigal ['prɔdɪgl] *adj* prodigo(a)

prodigy ['prɔdɪdʒɪ] *n* prodigio

produce [*n* 'prɔdjuːs, *vb* prə'djuːs] *n* (*AGR*) prodotto, prodotti *mpl* ♦ *vt* produrre; (*to show*) esibire, mostrare; (*cause*) cagionare, causare; **~r** *n* (*THEATRE*) regista *m/f*; (*AGR, CINEMA*) produttore *m*

product ['prɔdʌkt] *n* prodotto

production [prə'dʌkʃən] *n* produzione *f*; **~ line** *n* catena di lavorazione

productivity [prɔdʌk'tɪvɪtɪ] *n* produttività

profane [prə'feɪn] *adj* profano(a); (*language*) empio(a)

profess [prə'fes] *vt* (*claim*) dichiarare; (*opinion etc*) professare

profession [prə'feʃən] *n* professione *f*; **~al** *n* professionista *m/f* ♦ *adj* professionale; (*work*) da professionista

professor [prə'fesə*] *n* professore *m* (*titolare di una cattedra*); (*US*) professore/essa

proficiency [prə'fɪʃənsɪ] *n* competenza, abilità

profile ['prəʊfaɪl] *n* profilo

profit ['prɔfɪt] *n* profitto; beneficio ♦ *vi*: **to ~ (by** or **from)** approfittare (di); **~ability** [-'bɪlɪtɪ] *n* redditività; **~able** *adj* redditizio(a)

profound [prə'faʊnd] *adj* profondo(a)

profusely [prə'fjuːslɪ] *adv* con grande effusione

programme ['prəʊgræm] (*US* **program**) *n* programma *m* ♦ *vt* programmare; **~r** (*US* **programer**) *n* programmatore/trice

progress [n 'praugres, vb pra'gres] n progresso ♦ vi avanzare, procedere; **in ~ in corso; to make ~ far progressi; ~ive** [-'gresɪv] adj progressivo(a); (person) progressista

prohibit [pra'hɪbɪt] vt proibire, vietare; **~ion** [prauɪ'bɪʃən] n proibizione f, divieto m; (US): **P~** proibizionismo; **~ive** adj (price etc) proibitivo(a)

project [n 'prɒdʒekt, vb pra'dʒekt] n (plan) piano; (venture) progetto m; (SCOL) studio ♦ vt proiettare ♦ vi (stick out) sporgere

projectile [pra'dʒektaɪl] n proiettile m

projector [pra'dʒektə*] n proiettore m

prolific [pra'lɪfɪk] adj (artist etc) fecondo(a)

prolong [pra'lɒŋ] vt prolungare

prom [prɒm] n abbr = **promenade**; (US: ball) ballo studentesco

promenade [prɒmə'nɑːd] n (by sea) lungomare m; **~ concert** n concerto (con posti in piedi)

prominent ['prɒmɪnənt] adj (standing out) prominente; (important) importante

promiscuous [pra'mɪskjuəs] adj (sexually) di facili costumi

promise ['prɒmɪs] n promessa ♦ vt, vi promettere; **to ~ sb sth, ~ sth to sb** promettere qc a qn; **to ~ (sb) that/to do sth** promettere (a qn) che/di fare qc; **promising** adj promettente

promote [pra'məut] vt promuovere; (venture, event) organizzare; **~r** n (of sporting event) promotore/trice; (of event) organizzatore/trice; **promotion** [-'məuʃən] n promozione f

prompt [prɒmpt] adj rapido(a), svelto(a); puntuale; (reply) sollecito(a) ♦ adv (punctually) in punto ♦ n (COMPUT) prompt m ♦ vt incitare, provocare; (THEATRE) suggerire a; **to ~ sb to do** incitare qn a fare; **~ly** adv prontamente; puntualmente

prone [praun] adj (lying) prono(a); **~ to** propenso(a), incline a

prong [prɒŋ] n rebbio, punta

pronoun ['prəunaun] n pronome m

pronounce [pra'nauns] vt pronunciare

pronunciation [prənʌnsɪ'eɪʃən] n pronuncia

proof [pruːf] n prova; (of book) bozza; (PHOT) provino ♦ adj: **~ against** a prova di

prop [prɒp] n sostegno, appoggio ♦ vt (also: **~ up**) sostenere, appoggiare; (lean): **to ~ sth against** appoggiare qc contro or a

propaganda [prɒpə'gændə] n propaganda

propel [pra'pel] vt spingere (in avanti), muovere; **~ler** n elica

propensity [pra'pensɪtɪ] n tendenza

proper ['prɒpə*] adj (suited, right) adatto(a), appropriato(a); (seemly) decente; (authentic) vero(a); (inf: real) noun + vero(a) e proprio(a); **~ly** adv (eat, study) bene; (behave) come si deve; **~ noun** n nome m proprio

property ['prɒpətɪ] n (things owned) beni mpl; (land, building) proprietà f inv; (CHEM etc: quality) proprietà; **~ owner** n proprietario/a

prophecy ['prɒfɪsɪ] n profezia

prophesy ['prɒfɪsaɪ] vt predire

prophet ['prɒfɪt] n profeta m

proportion [pra'pɔːʃən] n proporzione f; (share) parte f; **~al** adj proporzionale; **~ate** adj proporzionato(a)

proposal [pra'pəuzl] n proposta; (plan) progetto; (of marriage) proposta di matrimonio

propose [pra'pəuz] vt proporre, suggerire ♦ vi fare una proposta di matrimonio; **to ~ to do** proporsi di fare, aver l'intenzione di fare

proposition [prɒpə'zɪʃən] n proposizione f; (offer) proposta

proprietor [pra'praɪətə*] n proprietario/a

propriety [pra'praɪətɪ] n (seemliness) decoro, rispetto delle convenienze sociali

pro rata ['prəʊ'rɑːtə] *adv* in proporzione

prose [prəʊz] *n* prosa

prosecute ['prɒsɪkjuːt] *vt* processare; **prosecution** [-'kjuːʃən] *n* processo; (*accusing state*) accusa; **prosecutor** *n* (*also: public prosecutor*) ≈ procuratore *m* della Repubblica

prospect [*n* 'prɒspekt, *vb* prə'spekt] *n* prospettiva; (*hope*) speranza ♦ *vi*: **to ~ for** cercare; **~s** *npl* (*for work etc*) prospettive *fpl*; **~ive** [-'spektɪv] *adj* possibile; futuro(a)

prospectus [prə'spektəs] *n* prospetto, programma *m*

prosperity [prɒ'spɛrɪtɪ] *n* prosperità

prostitute ['prɒstɪtjuːt] *n* prostituta; **male ~** = uomo che si prostituisce

prostrate ['prɒstreɪt] *adj* bocconi *inv*

protect [prə'tɛkt] *vt* proteggere, salvaguardare; **~ion** *n* protezione *f*; **~ive** *adj* protettivo(a)

protégé ['prəʊtɛʒeɪ] *n* protetto

protein ['prəʊtiːn] *n* proteina

protest [*n* 'prəʊtɛst, *vb* prə'tɛst] *n* protesta ♦ *vt, vi* protestare

Protestant ['prɒtɪstənt] *adj, n* protestante *m/f*

protester [prə'tɛstə*] *n* dimostrante *m/f*

prototype ['prəʊtətaɪp] *n* prototipo

protracted [prə'træktɪd] *adj* tirato(a) per le lunghe

protrude [prə'truːd] *vi* sporgere

proud [praʊd] *adj* fiero(a), orgoglioso(a); (*pej*) superbo(a)

prove [pruːv] *vt* provare, dimostrare ♦ *vi*: **to ~** (**to be**) **correct** *etc* risultare vero(a) *etc*; **to ~ o.s.** mostrare le proprie capacità

proverb ['prɒvɜːb] *n* proverbio

provide [prə'vaɪd] *vt* fornire, provvedere; **to ~ sb with sth** fornire *or* provvedere qn di qc; **~ for** *vt fus* provvedere a; (*future event*) prevedere; **~d** (**that**) *conj* purché + *sub*, a condizione che + *sub*

providing [prə'vaɪdɪŋ] *conj* purché + *sub*, a condizione che + *sub*

province ['prɒvɪns] *n* provincia; **pro-** **vincial** [prə'vɪnʃəl] *adj* provinciale

provision [prə'vɪʒən] *n* (*supply*) riserva; (*supplying*) provvista; (*stipulation*) condizione *f*; **~s** *npl* (*food*) provviste *fpl*; **~al** *adj* provvisorio(a)

proviso [prə'vaɪzəʊ] *n* condizione *f*

provocative [prə'vɒkətɪv] *adj* (*aggressive*) provocatorio(a); (*thought-provoking*) stimolante; (*seductive*) provocante

provoke [prə'vəʊk] *vt* provocare; incitare

prow [praʊ] *n* prua

prowess ['praʊɪs] *n* prodezza

prowl [praʊl] *vi* (*also: ~ about, ~ around*) aggirarsi ♦ *n*: **to be on the ~** aggirarsi; **~er** *n* tipo sospetto (*che s'aggira con l'intenzione di rubare, aggredire etc*)

proximity [prɒk'sɪmɪtɪ] *n* prossimità

proxy ['prɒksɪ] *n*: **by ~** per procura

prude [pruːd] *n* puritano/a

prudent ['pruːdnt] *adj* prudente

prudish ['pruːdɪʃ] *adj* puritano(a)

prune [pruːn] *n* prugna secca ♦ *vt* potare

pry [praɪ] *vi*: **to ~ into** ficcare il naso in

PS *abbr* (= *postscript*) P.S

psalm [sɑːm] *n* salmo

pseudo- ['sjuːdəʊ] *prefix* pseudo...

pseudonym ['sjuːdənɪm] *n* pseudonimo

psyche ['saɪkɪ] *n* psiche *f*

psychiatric [saɪkɪ'ætrɪk] *adj* psichiatrico(a)

psychiatrist [saɪ'kaɪətrɪst] *n* psichiatra *m/f*

psychic ['saɪkɪk] *adj* (*also: ~al*) psichico(a); (*person*) dotato(a) di qualità telepatiche

psychoanalyst [saɪkəʊ'ænəlɪst] *n* psicanalista *m/f*

psychological [saɪkə'lɒdʒɪkl] *adj* psicologico(a)

psychologist [saɪ'kɒlədʒɪst] *n* psicologo/a

psychology [saɪ'kɒlədʒɪ] *n* psicologia

psychopath ['saɪkəupæθ] *n* psicopatico/a

P.T.O. *abbr* (= *please turn over*) *v.r*

pub [pʌb] *n abbr* (= *public house*) pub *m inv*

pubic ['pjuːbɪk] *adj* pubico(a), del pube

public ['pʌblɪk] *adj* pubblico(a) ♦ *n* pubblico; **in ~** in pubblico; **~ address system** *n* impianto di amplificazione

publican ['pʌblɪkən] *n* proprietario di un pub

publication [pʌblɪ'keɪʃən] *n* pubblicazione *f*

public: **~ company** *n* società *f inv* per azioni (*costituita tramite pubblica sottoscrizione*); **~ convenience** (*BRIT*) *n* gabinetti *mpl*; **~ holiday** *n* giorno festivo, festa nazionale; **~ house** (*BRIT*) *n* pub *m inv*

publicity [pʌb'lɪsɪtɪ] *n* pubblicità

publicize ['pʌblɪsaɪz] *vt* rendere pubblico(a)

publicly ['pʌblɪklɪ] *adv* pubblicamente

public: **~ opinion** *n* opinione *f* pubblica; **~ relations** *n* pubbliche relazioni *fpl*; **~ school** *n* (*BRIT*) scuola privata; (*US*) scuola statale; **~-spirited** *adj* che ha senso civico; **~ transport** *n* mezzi *mpl* pubblici

publish ['pʌblɪʃ] *vt* pubblicare; **~er** *n* editore *m*; **~ing** *n* (*industry*) editoria; (*of a book*) pubblicazione *f*

puce [pjuːs] *adj* marroncino rosato *inv*

pucker ['pʌkə*] *vt* corrugare

pudding ['pudɪŋ] *n* budino; (*BRIT: dessert*) dolce *m*; **black ~** *n* sanguinaccio

puddle ['pʌdl] *n* pozza, pozzanghera

puff [pʌf] *n* sbuffo ♦ *vt*: **to ~ one's pipe** tirare sboccate di fumo ♦ *vi* (*pant*) ansare; **~ out** *vt* (*cheeks etc*) gonfiare; **~ed** (*inf*) *adj* (*out of breath*) senza fiato; **~ pastry** *n* pasta sfoglia; **~y** *adj* gonfio(a)

pull [pul] *n* (*tug*): **to give sth a ~** tirare su qc ♦ *vt* tirare; (*muscle*)

strappare; (*trigger*) premere ♦ *vi* tirare; **to ~ to pieces** fare a pezzi; **to ~ one's punches** (*BOXING*) risparmiare l'avversario; **to ~ one's weight** fare il proprio contributo; **to ~ o.s. together** ricomporsi, riprendersi; **to ~ sb's leg** prendere in giro qn; **~ apart** *vt* (*break*) fare a pezzi; **~ down** *vt* (*house*) demolire; (*tree*) abbattere; **~ in** *vi* (*AUT: at the kerb*) accostarsi; (*RAIL*) entrare in stazione; **~ off** *vt* (*clothes*) togliere; (*deal etc*) portare a compimento; **~ out** *vi* partire; (*AUT: come out of line*) spostarsi sulla mezzeria ♦ *vt* staccare; far uscire; (*withdraw*) ritirare; **~ over** *vi* (*AUT*) accostare; **~ through** *vi* farcela; **~ up** *vi* (*stop*) fermarsi ♦ *vt* (*raise*) sollevare; (*uproot*) sradicare

pulley ['pulɪ] *n* puleggia, carrucola

pullover ['puləuvə*] *n* pullover *m inv*

pulp [pʌlp] *n* (*of fruit*) polpa

pulpit ['pulpɪt] *n* pulpito

pulsate [pʌl'seɪt] *vi* battere, palpitare

pulse [pʌls] *n* polso; (*BOT*) legume *m*

pummel ['pʌml] *vt* dare pugni a

pump [pʌmp] *n* pompa; (*shoe*) scarpetta ♦ *vt* pompare; **~ up** *vt* gonfiare

pumpkin ['pʌmpkɪn] *n* zucca

pun [pʌn] *n* gioco di parole

punch [pʌntʃ] *n* (*blow*) pugno; (*tool*) punzone *m*; (*drink*) ponce *m* ♦ *vt*: **to ~ sb/sth** dare un pugno a qn/qc; **~ line** *n* (*of joke*) battuta finale; **~-up** (*BRIT: inf*) *n* rissa

punctual ['pʌŋktjuəl] *adj* puntuale

punctuation [pʌŋktju'eɪʃən] *n* interpunzione *f*, punteggiatura

puncture ['pʌŋktʃə*] *n* foratura ♦ *vt* forare

pundit ['pʌndɪt] *n* sapientone/a

pungent ['pʌndʒənt] *adj* pungente

punish ['pʌnɪʃ] *vt* punire; **~ment** *n* punizione *f*

punk [pʌŋk] *n* (*also*: **~ rocker**) punk *m/f inv*; (*also*: **~ rock**) musica punk,

punk rock m; (US: inf: hoodlum) teppista m

punt [pʌnt] n (boat) barchino

punter [ˈpʌntə*] n (BRIT) n (gambler) scommettitore/trice; (: inf) cliente m/f

puny [ˈpjuːnɪ] adj gracile

pup [pʌp] n cucciolo/a

pupil [ˈpjuːpl] n allievo/a; (ANAT) pupilla

puppet [ˈpʌpɪt] n burattino

puppy [ˈpʌpɪ] n cucciolo/a, cagnolino/a

purchase [ˈpəːtʃɪs] n acquisto, compera ♦ vt comprare; ~r n compratore/trice

pure [pjuə*] adj puro(a)

purée [ˈpjuəreɪ] n (of potatoes) purè m; (of tomatoes) passato; (of apples) crema

purely [ˈpjuəlɪ] adv puramente

purge [pəːdʒ] n (MED) purga; (POL) epurazione f ♦ vt purgare

puritan [ˈpjuərɪtən] adj, n puritano(a)

purity [ˈpjuərɪtɪ] n purezza

purple [ˈpəːpl] adj di porpora; viola inv

purport [pəːˈpɔːt] vi: to ~ to be/do pretendere di essere/fare

purpose [ˈpəːpəs] n intenzione f, scopo; on ~ apposta; ~ful adj deciso(a), risoluto(a)

purr [pəː*] vi fare le fusa

purse [pəːs] n (BRIT) borsellino; (US) borsetta ♦ vt contrarre

purser [ˈpəːsə*] n (NAUT) commissario di bordo

pursue [pəˈsjuː] vt inseguire; (fig: activity etc) continuare con; (: aim etc) perseguire

pursuit [pəˈsjuːt] n inseguimento; (fig) ricerca; (pastime) passatempo

push [puʃ] n spinta; (effort) grande sforzo; (drive) energia ♦ vt spingere; (button) premere; (thrust): to ~ sth (into) ficcare qc (in); (fig) fare pubblicità a ♦ vi spingere; premere; to ~ for (fig) insistere per; ~ aside vt scostare; ~ off (inf) vi filare; ~

on vi (continue) continuare; ~ through vi farsi largo spingendo ♦ vt (measure) far approvare; ~ up vt (total, prices) far salire; ~chair (BRIT) n passeggino; ~er n (drug ~er) spacciatore/trice; ~over (inf) n: it's a ~over è un lavoro da bambini; ~-up (US) n (press-up) flessione f sulle braccia; ~y (pej) adj opportunista

puss [pus] (inf) n = pussy (-cat)

puss(-cat) [ˈpus(-)] (inf) n micio

put [put] (pt, pp put) vt mettere, porre; (say) dire, esprimere; (a question) fare; (estimate) stimare; ~ about or around vt (rumour) diffondere; ~ across vt (ideas etc) comunicare; far capire; ~ away vt (return) mettere a posto; ~ back vt (replace) rimettere a posto; (postpone) rinviare; (delay) ritardare; ~ by vt (money) mettere da parte; ~ down vt (parcel etc) posare, mettere giù; (pay) versare; (in writing) mettere per iscritto; (revolt, animal) sopprimere; (attribute) attribuire; ~ forward vt (ideas) avanzare, proporre; ~ in vt (application, complaint) presentare; (time, effort) mettere; ~ off vt (postpone) rimandare, rinviare; (discourage) dissuadere; ~ on vt (clothes, lipstick etc) mettere; (light etc) accendere; (play etc) mettere in scena; (food, meal) mettere su; (brake) mettere; to ~ on weight ingrassare; to ~ on airs darsi delle arie; ~ out vt mettere fuori; (one's hand) porgere; (light etc) spegnere; (person: inconvenience) scomodare; ~ through vt (TEL: call) passare; (: person) mettere in comunicazione; (plan) far approvare; ~ up vt (raise) sollevare, alzare; (: umbrella) aprire; (: tent) montare; (pin up) affiggere; (hang) appendere; (build) costruire, erigere; (increase) aumentare; (accommodate) alloggiare; ~ up with fus sopportare

putt [pʌt] n colpo leggero; ~ing

green n green m inv; campo da putting

putty ['pʌtɪ] n stucco

puzzle ['pʌzl] n enigma m, mistero; (jigsaw) puzzle m; (also: crossword ~) parole fpl incrociate, cruciverba m inv ♦ vt confondere, rendere perplesso(a) ♦ vi scervellarsi

pyjamas [pɪ'dʒɑːməz] (BRIT) npl pigiama m

pylon ['paɪlən] n pilone m

pyramid ['pɪrəmɪd] n piramide f

Pyrenees [pɪrɪ'niːz] npl: the ~ i Pirenei

Q

quack [kwæk] n (of duck) qua qua m inv; (pej: doctor) dottoruccio/a

quad [kwɒd] n abbr = **quadrangle**; **quadruplet**

quadrangle ['kwɒdræŋgl] n (courtyard) cortile m

quadruple [kwɒ'druːpl] vt quadruplicare ♦ vi quadruplicarsi

quadruplets [kwɒ'druːplɪts] npl quattro gemelli mpl

quagmire ['kwægmaɪə*] n pantano

quail [kweɪl] n (ZOOL) quaglia ♦ vi (person): to ~ at or before perdersi d'animo davanti a

quaint [kweɪnt] adj bizzarro(a); (old-fashioned) antiquato(a); grazioso(a), pittoresco(a)

quake [kweɪk] vi tremare ♦ n abbr = **earthquake**

Quaker ['kweɪkə*] n quacchero/a

qualification [kwɒlɪfɪ'keɪʃən] n (degree etc) qualifica, titolo; (ability) competenza, qualificazione f; (limitation) riserva, restrizione f

qualified ['kwɒlɪfaɪd] adj qualificato(a); (able): ~ to competente in, qualificato(a) a; (limited) condizionato(a)

qualify ['kwɒlɪfaɪ] vt abilitare; (limit: statement) modificare, precisare ♦ vi: to ~ (as) qualificarsi (come); to ~ (for) acquistare i requisiti necessari (per); (SPORT) qualificarsi (per or a)

quality ['kwɒlɪtɪ] n qualità f inv

qualm [kwɑːm] n dubbio; scrupolo

quandary ['kwɒndrɪ] n: in a ~ in un dilemma

quantity ['kwɒntɪtɪ] n quantità f inv; **~ surveyor** n geometra m (specializzato nel calcolare la quantità e il costo del materiale da costruzione)

quarantine ['kwɒrəntiːn] n quarantena

quarrel ['kwɒrəl] n lite f, disputa ♦ vi litigare; **~some** adj litigioso(a)

quarry ['kwɒrɪ] n (for stone) cava; (animal) preda

quart [kwɔːt] n ≈ litro

quarter ['kwɔːtə*] n quarto; (US: coin) quarto di dollaro; (of year) trimestre m; (district) quartiere m ♦ vt dividere in quattro; (MIL) alloggiare; ~s npl (living ~s) alloggio; (MIL) alloggi mpl, quadrato; **a ~ of an hour** un quarto d'ora; **~ final** n quarto di finale; **~ly** adj trimestrale ♦ adv trimestralmente

quartet(te) [kwɔː'tet] n quartetto

quartz [kwɔːts] n quarzo

quash [kwɒʃ] vt (verdict) annullare

quaver ['kweɪvə*] n (BRIT: MUS) croma ♦ vi tremolare

quay [kiː] n (also: ~side) banchina

queasy ['kwiːzɪ] adj (stomach) delicato(a); to feel ~ aver la nausea

queen [kwiːn] n (gen) regina; (CARDS etc) regina, donna; **~ mother** n regina madre

queer [kwɪə*] adj strano(a), curioso(a) ♦ n (inf) finocchio

quell [kwel] vt domare

quench [kwentʃ] vt: to ~ one's thirst dissetarsi

querulous ['kwerʊləs] adj querulo(a)

query ['kwɪərɪ] n domanda, questione f ♦ vt mettere in questione

quest [kwest] n cerca, ricerca

question ['kwestʃən] n domanda, questione f ♦ vt (person) interrogare; (plan, idea) mettere in questione *or* in dubbio; **it's a ~ of** doing si tratta di fare; **beyond ~** fuori di dubbio; **out of the ~** fuori discussione, impossibile; **~able** *adj* discutibile; **~ mark** *n* punto interrogativo

questionnaire [kwestʃəˈnɛəʳ] *n* questionario

queue [kjuː] (*BRIT*) *n* coda, fila ♦ *vi* fare la coda

quibble [ˈkwɪbl] *vi* cavillare

quiche [kiːʃ] *n* torta salata a base di uova, formaggio, prosciutto o altro

quick [kwɪk] *adj* rapido(a), veloce; (*reply*) pronto(a); (*mind*) pronto(a), acuto(a) ♦ *n*: **cut to the ~** (*fig*) toccato(a) sul vivo; **be ~!** fa presto!; **~en** *vt* accelerare, affrettare ♦ *vi* accelerare, affrettarsi; **~ly** *adv* rapidamente, velocemente; **~sand** *n* sabbie *fpl* mobili; **~-witted** *adj* pronto(a) d'ingegno

quid [kwɪd] (*BRIT*: *inf*) *n inv* sterlina

quiet [ˈkwaɪət] *adj* tranquillo(a), quieto(a); (*ceremony*) semplice ♦ *n* tranquillità, calma ♦ *vt*, *vi* (*US*) = **~en**; **keep ~!** sta zitto!; **~en** (*also*: **~en down**) *vi* calmarsi, chetarsi ♦ *vt* calmare, chetare; **~ly** *adv* tranquillamente, calmamente; **~ness** *n* tranquillità, calma, quiete

quilt [kwɪlt] *n* trapunta; (*continental ~*) piumino

quin [kwɪn] *n abbr* = **quintuplet**

quinine [kwɪˈniːn] *n* chinino

quintuplets [kwɪnˈtjuːplɪts] *npl* cinque gemelli *mpl*

quip [kwɪp] *n* frizzo

quirk [kwəːk] *n* ghiribizzo

quit [kwɪt] (*pt*, *pp* **quit** *or* **quitted**) *vt* mollare; (*premises*) lasciare, partire da ♦ *vi* (*give up*) mollare; (*resign*) dimettersi

quite [kwaɪt] *adv* (*rather*) assai; (*entirely*) completamente, del tutto; **I ~ understand** capisco perfettamente; **that's not ~ big enough** non è proprio sufficiente; **~ a few of them** non pochi di loro; **~ (so)!** esatto!

quits [kwɪts] *adj*: **~ (with)** pari

(*con*); **let's call it ~** adesso siamo pari

quiver [ˈkwɪvəʳ] *vi* tremare, fremere

quiz [kwɪz] *n* (*game*) quiz *m inv*; indovinello ♦ *vt* interrogare; **~zical** *adj* enigmatico(a)

quota [ˈkwəʊtə] *n* quota

quotation [kwəʊˈteɪʃən] *n* citazione *f*; (*of shares etc*) quotazione *f*; (*estimate*) preventivo; **~ marks** *npl* virgolette *fpl*

quote [kwəʊt] *n* citazione *f* ♦ *vt* (*sentence*) citare; (*price*) dare, fissare; (*shares*) quotare ♦ *vi*: **to ~ from** citare; **~s** *npl* = **quotation marks**

R

rabbi [ˈræbaɪ] *n* rabbino

rabbit [ˈræbɪt] *n* coniglio; **~ hutch** *n* conigliera

rabble [ˈræbl] (*pej*) *n* canaglia, plebaglia

rabies [ˈreɪbiːz] *n* rabbia

RAC (*BRIT*) *n abbr* = **Royal Automobile Club**

raccoon [rəˈkuːn] *n* procione *m*

race [reɪs] *n* razza; (*competition*, *rush*) corsa ♦ *vt* (*horse*) far correre ♦ *vi* correre; (*engine*) imballarsi; **~ car** (*US*) *n* = **racing car**; **~ car driver** (*US*) *n* = **racing car driver**; **~course** *n* campo di corse, ippodromo; **~horse** *n* cavallo da corsa; **~track** *n* pista

racial [ˈreɪʃl] *adj* razziale

racing [ˈreɪsɪŋ] *n* corsa; **~ car** (*BRIT*) *n* macchina da corsa; **~ driver** (*BRIT*) *n* corridore *m* automobilista

racism [ˈreɪsɪzəm] *n* razzismo; **racist** *adj*, *n* razzista (*m/f*)

rack [ræk] *n* rastrelliera; (*also*: *luggage ~*) rete *f*, portabagagli *m inv*; (*also*: *roof ~*) portabagagli *m inv*; (*also*: *dish ~*) scolapiatti *m inv* ♦ *vt*: **~ed by** torturato(a) da; **to ~ one's brains** scervellarsi

racket ['rækɪt] n (for tennis) racchetta; (noise) fracasso; baccano; (swindle) imbroglio, truffa; (organized crime) racket m inv

racoon [rə'ku:n] n = **raccoon**

racquet ['rækɪt] n racchetta

racy ['reɪsɪ] adj brioso(a); piccante

radar ['reɪda:*] n radar m

radial ['reɪdɪəl] adj (also: ~ply) radiale

radiant ['reɪdɪənt] adj raggiante; (PHYSICS) radiante

radiate ['reɪdɪeɪt] vt (heat) irraggiare, irradiare ♦ vi (lines) irradiarsi

radiation [reɪdɪ'eɪʃən] n irradiamento; (radioactive) radiazione f

radiator ['reɪdɪeɪtə*] n radiatore m

radical ['rædɪkl] adj radicale

radii ['reɪdɪaɪ] npl of **radius**

radio ['reɪdɪəu] n radio f inv; on the ~ alla radio

radioactive [reɪdɪəu'æktɪv] adj radioattivo(a)

radio station n stazione f radio inv

radish ['rædɪʃ] n ravanello

radius ['reɪdɪəs] (pl **radii**) n raggio

RAF n abbr = **Royal Air Force**

raffle ['ræfl] n lotteria

raft [ra:ft] n zattera; (also: life ~) zattera di salvataggio

rafter ['ra:ftə*] n trave f

rag [ræg] n straccio, cencio; (pej: newspaper) giornalaccio, bandiera; (for charity) iniziativa studentesca a scopo benefico; ~s npl (torn clothes) stracci mpl, brandelli mpl; ~-and-bone man (BRIT) n = **ragman**; ~ doll n bambola di pezza

rage [reɪdʒ] n (fury) collera, furia ♦ vi (person) andare su tutte le furie; (storm) infuriare; **it's all the** ~ fa furore

ragged ['rægɪd] adj (edge) irregolare; (clothes) logoro(a); (appearance) pezzente

ragman ['rægmæn] n straccivendolo

raid [reɪd] n (MIL) incursione f; (criminal) rapina; (by police) irruzione f ♦ vt fare un'incursione in; rapinare; fare irruzione in

rail [reɪl] n (on stair) ringhiera; (on bridge, balcony) parapetto; (of ship) battagliola; ~s npl (for train) binario, rotaie fpl; **by** ~ per ferrovia; ~**ing(s)** n(pl) ringhiere fpl; ~**road** (US) n ~**way**; ~**way** (BRIT) n ferrovia; ~**way line** (BRIT) n linea ferroviaria; ~**wayman** (BRIT) n ferroviere m; ~**way station** (BRIT) n stazione f ferroviaria

rain [reɪn] n pioggia ♦ vi piovere; **in the** ~ sotto la pioggia; **it's** ~**ing** piove; ~**bow** n arcobaleno; ~**coat** n impermeabile m; ~**drop** n goccia di pioggia; ~**fall** n pioggia; (measurement) precipitazioni fpl; ~**forest** n foresta pluviale; ~**y** adj piovoso(a)

raise [reɪz] n aumento ♦ vt (lift) alzare; sollevare; (increase) aumentare; (a protest, doubt, question) sollevare; (cattle, family) allevare; (crop) coltivare; (army, funds) raccogliere; (loan) ottenere; **to** ~ **one's voice** alzare la voce

raisin ['reɪzn] n uva secca

rake [reɪk] n (tool) rastrello ♦ vt (garden) rastrellare; (with machine gun) spazzare

rally ['rælɪ] n (POL etc) riunione f; (AUT) rally m inv; (TENNIS) scambio ♦ vt riunire, radunare ♦ vi (sick person, Stock Exchange) riprendersi; ~ **round** vt fus raggrupparsi intorno a; venire in aiuto di

RAM [ræm] n abbr (= random access memory) memoria ad accesso casuale

ram [ræm] n montone m, ariete m ♦ vt conficcare; (crash into) cozzare, sbattere contro; percuotere; speronare

ramble ['ræmbl] n escursione f ♦ vi (pej: also: ~ **on**) divagare; ~ r n escursionista m/f; (BOT) rosa rampicante; **rambling** adj (speech) sconnesso(a); (house) tutto(a) a nicchie e corridoi; (BOT) rampicante

ramp [ræmp] n rampa; **on/off** ~ (US: AUT) raccordo di entrata/uscita

rampage [ræm'peɪdʒ] n: **to go on the**

the ~ scatenarsi in modo violento
rampant ['ræmpənt] adj (disease etc) che infierisce
rampart ['ræmpɑːt] n bastione m
ramshackle ['ræmʃækl] adj (house) cadente; (car etc) sgangherato(a)
ran [ræn] pt of **run**
ranch [rɑːntʃ] n ranch m inv; **~er** n proprietario di un ranch; cowboy m inv
rancid ['rænsɪd] adj rancido(a)
rancour ['ræŋkə*] (US **rancor**) n rancore m
random ['rændəm] adj fatto(a) or detto(a) per caso; (COMPUT, MATH) casuale ♦ n: at ~ a casaccio; ~ **access** n (COMPUT) accesso casuale
randy ['rændɪ] (BRIT: inf) adj arrapato(a); lascivo(a)
rang [ræŋ] pt of **ring**
range [reɪndʒ] n (of mountains) catena; (of missile, voice) portata; (of proposals, products) gamma; (MIL: also: shooting ~) campo di tiro; (also: kitchen ~) fornello, cucina economica ♦ vt disporre ♦ vi: to ~ over coprire; to ~ from ... to andare da ...
ranger ['reɪndʒə*] n guardia forestale
rank [ræŋk] n fila; (status, MIL) grado; (BRIT: also: taxi ~) posteggio di taxi ♦ vi: to ~ among essere tra ♦ adj puzzolente; vero(a) e proprio(a); the ~ and file (fig) la gran massa
rankle ['ræŋkl] vi bruciare
ransack ['rænsæk] vt rovistare; (plunder) saccheggiare
ransom ['rænsəm] n riscatto; to hold sb to ~ (fig) esercitare pressione su qn
rant [rænt] vi vociare
rap [ræp] vt bussare a; picchiare su ♦ n (music) rap m inv
rape [reɪp] n violenza carnale, stupro; (BOT) ravizzone m ♦ vt violentare; ~(**seed**) **oil** n olio di ravizzone
rapid ['ræpɪd] adj rapido(a); ~s npl (GEO) rapida; ~**ly** adv rapidamente

rapist ['reɪpɪst] n violentatore m
rapport [ræ'pɔː*] n rapporto
rapture ['ræptʃə*] n estasi f inv
rare [rɛə*] adj raro(a); (CULIN: steak) al sangue
rarely ['rɛəlɪ] adv raramente
raring ['rɛərɪŋ] adj: to be ~ to go (inf) non veder l'ora di cominciare
rascal ['rɑːskl] n mascalzone m
rash [ræʃ] adj imprudente, sconsiderato(a) ♦ n (MED) eruzione f; (of events etc) scoppio
rasher ['ræʃə*] n fetta sottile (di lardo or prosciutto)
raspberry ['rɑːzbərɪ] n lampone m
rasping ['rɑːspɪŋ] adj stridulo(a)
rat [ræt] n ratto
rate [reɪt] n (proportion) tasso, percentuale f; (speed) velocità f inv; (price) tariffa ♦ vt giudicare; stimare; ~s npl (BRIT: property tax) imposte fpl comunali; (fees) tariffe fpl; to ~ **sb/sth as** valutare qn/qc come; ~**able value** (BRIT) n valore m imponibile or locativo (di una proprietà); ~**payer** (BRIT) n contribuente m/f (che paga le imposte comunali)
rather ['rɑːðə*] adv piuttosto; it's ~ expensive è piuttosto caro; (too) è un po' caro; there's ~ a lot ce n'è parecchio; I would or I'd ~ go preferirei andare
ratify ['rætɪfaɪ] vt ratificare
rating ['reɪtɪŋ] n (assessment) valutazione f; (score) punteggio di merito; (BRIT: NAUT: sailor) marinaio semplice
ratio ['reɪʃɪəʊ] n proporzione f, rapporto
ration ['ræʃən] n (gen pl) razioni fpl ♦ vt razionare
rational ['ræʃənl] adj razionale, ragionevole; (solution, reasoning) logico(a); ~**e** [-'nɑːl] n fondamento logico; giustificazione f; ~**ize** vt razionalizzare
rat race n carrierismo, corsa al successo
rattle ['rætl] n tintinnio; (louder) strepito; (for baby) sonaglino ♦ vi ri-

suonare, tintinnare; fare un rumore di ferraglia ♦ vt scuotere (con strepito); **~snake** n serpente m a sonagli

raucous ['rɔːkəs] adj rumoroso(a), fragoroso(a)

ravage ['rævidʒ] vt devastare; **~s** npl danni mpl

rave [reiv] vi (in anger) infuriarsi; (with enthusiasm) andare in estasi; (MED) delirare

raven ['reivən] n corvo

ravenous ['rævənəs] adj affamato(a)

ravine [rə'viːn] n burrone m

raving ['reiviŋ] adj: **~ lunatic** pazzo(a) furioso(a)

ravishing ['rævɪʃɪŋ] adj incantevole

raw [rɔː] adj (uncooked) crudo(a); (not processed) greggio(a); (sore) vivo(a); (inexperienced) inesperto(a); (weather, day) gelido(a); **~ deal** (inf) n bidonata; **~ material** n materia prima

ray [rei] n raggio; **a ~ of hope** un barlume di speranza

rayon ['reiɔn] n raion m

raze [reiz] vt radere, distruggere

razor ['reizə*] n rasoio; **~ blade** n lama di rasoio

Rd abbr = **road**

re [riː] prep con riferimento a

reach [riːtʃ] n portata; (of river etc) tratto ♦ vt raggiungere; arrivare a ♦ vi stendersi; **out of/within ~** fuori/a portata di mano; **within ~ of the shops/station** vicino ai negozi/alla stazione; **~ out** vt (hand) allungare ♦ vi: **to ~ out for** stendere la mano per prendere

react [riː'ækt] vi reagire; **~ion** [-'ækʃən] n reazione f

reactor [riː'æktə*] n reattore m

read [riːd, pt, pp red] (pt, pp **read**) vi leggere ♦ vt leggere; (understand) intendere, interpretare; (study) studiare; **~ out** vt leggere ad alta voce; **~able** adj (writing) leggibile; (book etc) che si legge volentieri; **~er** n lettore/trice; (book) libro di lettura; (BRIT: at university) professore con funzioni preminenti di ricer-

ca; **~ership** n (of paper etc) numero di lettori

readily ['redɪli] adv volentieri; (easily) facilmente; (quickly) prontamente

readiness ['redɪnɪs] n prontezza; **in ~** (prepared) pronto(a)

reading ['riːdiŋ] n lettura; (understanding) interpretazione f; (on instrument) indicazione f

readjust [riːə'dʒʌst] vt riaggiustare ♦ vi (person): **to ~ (to)** riadattarsi (a)

ready ['redi] adj pronto(a); (willing) pronto(a), disposto(a); (available) disponibile ♦ n: **at the ~** (MIL) pronto a sparare; **to get ~** prepararsi ♦ vt preparare; **~-made** adj prefabbricato(a); (clothes) confezionato(a); **~ money** n denaro contante, contanti mpl; **~ reckoner** n prontuario di calcolo; **~-to-wear** adj prêt-à-porter inv

reaffirm [riːə'fəːm] vt riaffermare

real [riəl] adj: vero(a); **in ~ terms** in realtà; **~ estate** n beni mpl immobili; **~ism** n (also ART) realismo; **~ist** n realista m/f; **~istic** [-'lɪstɪk] adj realistico(a)

reality [riː'ælɪti] n realtà f inv

realization [riəlaɪ'zeiʃən] n presa di coscienza; realizzazione f

realize ['riəlaɪz] vt (understand) rendersi conto di; (a project, COMM: asset) realizzare

really ['riəli] adv veramente, davvero; **~!** (indicating annoyance) in somma!

realm [relm] n reame m, regno

realtor ['riəltɔː*] (US: ®) n agente m immobiliare

reap [riːp] vt mietere; (fig) raccogliere

reappear [riːə'piə*] vi ricomparire, riapparire

rear [riə*] adj di dietro; (AUT: wheel etc) posteriore ♦ n didietro, parte f posteriore ♦ vt (cattle, family) allevare ♦ vi (also: **~ up**: animal) impennarsi

rearmament [riː'ɑːməmənt] n riarmo

rearrange [riːə'reɪndʒ] vt riordinare

rear-view: ~ **mirror** n (AUT) specchio retrovisore

reason ['riːzn] n ragione f; (cause, motive) ragione, motivo ♦ vi: to ~ with sb far ragionare qn; it stands to ~ that è ovvio che; ~**able** adj ragionevole; (not bad) accettabile; ~**ably** adv ragionevolmente; ~**ed** adj: a well-~**ed** argument una forte argomentazione; ~**ing** n ragionamento

reassurance [riːə'ʃuərəns] n rassicurazione f

reassure [riːə'ʃuə*] vt rassicurare; to ~ sb of rassicurare qn di or su

rebate ['riːbeɪt] n (on tax etc) sgravio

rebel [n 'rɛbl, vb rɪ'bɛl] n ribelle m/f ♦ vi ribellarsi; ~**lion** n ribellione f; ~**lious** adj ribelle

rebound [vb rɪ'baund, n 'riːbaund] vi (ball) rimbalzare ♦ n: on the ~ di rimbalzo

rebuff [rɪ'bʌf] n secco rifiuto

rebuke [rɪ'bjuːk] vt rimproverare

rebut [rɪ'bʌt] vt rifiutare

recall [rɪ'kɔːl] vt richiamare; (remember) ricordare, richiamare alla mente ♦ n richiamo

recant [rɪ'kænt] vi ritrattarsi; (REL) fare abiura

recap [rɪ'kæp] vt ricapitolare ♦ vi riassumere

recapitulate [riːkə'pɪtjuleɪt] vt, vi = recap

rec'd abbr = received

recede [rɪ'siːd] vi allontanarsi; ritirarsi; calare; **receding** adj (forehead, chin) sfuggente; he's got a receding hairline sta stempiando

receipt [rɪ'siːt] n (document) ricevuta; (act of receiving) ricevimento; ~**s** npl (COMM) introiti mpl

receive [rɪ'siːv] vt ricevere; (guest) ricevere, accogliere

receiver [rɪ'siːvə*] n (TEL) ricevitore m; (RADIO, TV) apparecchio ricevente; (of stolen goods) ricettatore/trice; (COMM) curatore m fallimentare

recent ['riːsnt] adj recente; ~**ly** adv recentemente

receptacle [rɪ'sɛptɪkl] n recipiente m

reception [rɪ'sɛpʃən] n ricevimento; (welcome) accoglienza; (TV etc) ricezione f; ~ **desk** n (in hotel) reception f inv; (in hospital, at doctor's) accettazione f; (in offices etc) portineria; ~**ist** n receptionist m/f inv

receptive [rɪ'sɛptɪv] adj ricettivo/a

recess [rɪ'sɛs] n (in room, secret place) alcova; (POL etc: holiday) vacanze fpl; ~**ion** [-'sɛʃən] n recessione f

recharge [riː'tʃɑːdʒ] vt (battery) ricaricare

recipe ['rɛsɪpɪ] n ricetta

recipient [rɪ'sɪpɪənt] n beneficiario/a; (of letter) destinatario/a

recital [rɪ'saɪtl] n recital m inv

recite [rɪ'saɪt] vt (poem) recitare

reckless ['rɛkləs] adj (driver etc) spericolato(a); (spending) folle

reckon ['rɛkən] vt (count) calcolare; (think): I ~ that ... penso che ...; ~ **on** vt fus contare su; ~**ing** n conto; stima

reclaim [rɪ'kleɪm] vt (demand back) richiedere, reclamare; (land) bonificare; (materials) recuperare; **reclamation** [rɛklə'meɪʃən] n bonifica

recline [rɪ'klaɪn] vi stare sdraiato(a); **reclining** adj (seat) ribaltabile

recognition [rɛkəg'nɪʃən] n riconoscimento; **transformed beyond** ~ irriconoscibile

recognize ['rɛkəgnaɪz] vt: to ~ (by/as) riconoscere (a or da/come)

recoil [rɪ'kɔɪl] vi (person): to ~ **from doing sth** rifuggire dal fare qc ♦ n (of gun) rinculo

recollect [rɛkə'lɛkt] vt ricordare; ~**ion** [-'lɛkʃən] n ricordo

recommend [rɛkə'mɛnd] vt raccomandare; (advise) consigliare

reconcile ['rɛkənsaɪl] vt (two people) riconciliare; (two facts) conciliare, quadrare; **to ~ o.s.** to rassegnarsi a

recondition [riːkənˈdɪʃən] vt rimettere a nuovo

reconnaissance [rɪˈkɔnɪsns] n (MIL) ricognizione f

reconnoitre [rɛkəˈnɔɪtə*] (US **reconnoiter**) vt (MIL) fare una ricognizione di

reconstruct [riːkənˈstrʌkt] vt ricostruire

record [n ˈrɛkɔːd, vb rɪˈkɔːd] n ricordo, documento; (of meeting etc) nota, verbale m; (register) registro; (file) pratica, dossier m inv; (COMPUT) record m inv; (also: criminal ~) fedina penale sporca; (MUS: disc) disco; (SPORT) record m inv, primato ♦ vt (set down) prendere nota di, registrare; (MUS: song etc) registrare; **in ~ time** a tempo di record; **off the ~** adj ufficioso(a) ♦ adv ufficiosamente; **~ card** n (in file) scheda; **~ed delivery** (BRIT) n (POST); **~ed delivery letter** etc lettera etc raccomandata; **~er** n (MUS) flauto diritto; **~ holder** n (SPORT) primatista m/f; **~ing** n (MUS) registrazione f; **~ player** n giradischi m inv

recount [rɪˈkaunt] vt raccontare, narrare

re-count [n ˈriːkaunt, vb riːˈkaunt] n (POL: of votes) nuovo computo ♦ vt ricontare

recoup [rɪˈkuːp] vt ricuperare

recourse [rɪˈkɔːs] n: **to have ~ to** ricorrere a, far ricorso a

recover [rɪˈkʌvə*] vt ricuperare ♦ vi: **to ~ (from)** riprendersi (da)

recovery [rɪˈkʌvərɪ] n ricupero; ristabilimento; ripresa

recreation [rɛkrɪˈeɪʃən] n ricreazione f; svago; **~al** adj ricreativo(a)

recrimination [rɪkrɪmɪˈneɪʃən] n recriminazione f

recruit [rɪˈkruːt] n recluta; (in company) nuovo(a) assunto(a) ♦ vt reclutare

rectangle [ˈrɛktæŋgl] n rettangolo; **rectangular** [-ˈtæŋgjulə*] adj rettan-

golare

rectify [ˈrɛktɪfaɪ] vt (error) rettificare; (omission) riparare

rector [ˈrɛktə*] n (REL) parroco (anglicano); (in school) n presbiterio

recuperate [rɪˈkjuːpəreɪt] vi ristabilirsi

recur [rɪˈkəː*] vi riaccadere; (symptoms) ripresentarsi; **~rent** adj ricorrente, periodico(a)

recycle [riːˈsaɪkl] vt riciclare

red [rɛd] n rosso/a; (POL: pej) rosso/a ♦ adj rosso(a); **in the ~** (account) scoperto; (business) in deficit; **~ carpet treatment** n cerimonia col gran pavese; **R~ Cross** n Croce f Rossa; **~currant** n ribes m inv; **~den** vt arrossare ♦ vi arrossire; **~dish** adj rossiccio(a)

redeem [rɪˈdiːm] vt (debt) riscattare; (sth in pawn) ritirare; (fig, also REL) redimere; **~ing** adj: **~ing feature** unico aspetto positivo

redeploy [riːdɪˈplɔɪ] vt (resources) riorganizzare

red-haired [-ˈhɛəd] adj dai capelli rossi

red-handed [-ˈhændɪd] adj: **to be caught ~** essere preso(a) in flagrante or con le mani nel sacco

redhead [ˈrɛdhɛd] n rosso/a

red herring n (fig) falsa pista

red-hot adj arroventato(a)

redirect [riːdaɪˈrɛkt] vt (mail) far seguire

red light n: **to go through a ~** (AUT) passare col rosso; **red-light district** n quartiere m a luci rosse

redo [riːˈduː] (irreg) vt rifare

redolent [ˈrɛdələnt] adj: **~ of** che sa di; (fig) che ricorda

redouble [riːˈdʌbl] vt: **to ~ one's efforts** raddoppiare gli sforzi

redress [rɪˈdrɛs] n riparazione f ♦ vt riparare

Red Sea n: **the ~** il Mar Rosso

redskin [ˈrɛdskɪn] n pellerossa m/f

red tape n (fig) burocrazia

reduce [rɪˈdjuːs] vt ridurre; (lower) ridurre, abbassare; "**~ speed now**"

(AUT) "rallentare"; **at a ~d price** scontato(a); **reduction** [rɪ'dʌkʃən] n riduzione f; (of price) ribasso; (discount) sconto

redundancy [rɪ'dʌndənsɪ] n licenziamento

redundant [rɪ'dʌndnt] adj (worker) licenziato(a); (detail, object) superfluo(a); **to be made ~** essere licenziato (per eccesso di personale)

reed [riːd] n (BOT) canna; (MUS: of clarinet etc) ancia

reef [riːf] n (at sea) scogliera

reek [riːk] vi: **to ~ (of)** puzzare (di)

reel [riːl] n bobina, rocchetto; (FISHING) mulinello; (CINEMA) rotolo; (dance) danza veloce scozzese ♦ vi (sway) barcollare; **~ in** vt tirare su

ref [rɛf] (inf) n abbr (= referee) arbitro

refectory [rɪ'fɛktərɪ] n refettorio

refer [rɪ'fəː*] vt: **to ~ sth to** (dispute, decision) deferire qc a; **to ~ sb to** (inquirer, MED: patient) indirizzare qn a; (reader: to text) rimandare qn a ♦ vi: **to ~** (allude to) accennare a; (consult) rivolgersi a

referee [rɛfə'riː] n arbitro; (BRIT: for job application) referenza ♦ vt arbitrare

reference ['rɛfrəns] n riferimento; (mention) menzione f, allusione f; (for job application) referenza; **with ~ to** (COMM: in letter) in or con riferimento a; **~ book** n libro di consultazione; **~ number** n numero di riferimento

referenda [rɛfə'rɛndə] npl of **referendum**

referendum [rɛfə'rɛndəm] n (pl **referenda**) n referendum m inv

refill [vb rɪ'fɪl, n 'riːfɪl] vt riempire di nuovo; (pen, lighter etc) ricaricare ♦ n (for pen etc) ricambio

refine [rɪ'faɪn] vt raffinare; **~d** adj (person, taste) raffinato(a)

reflect [rɪ'flɛkt] vt (light, image) riflettere; (fig) rispecchiare ♦ vi (think) riflettere, considerare; **it ~s badly/well on him** si ripercuote su

di lui in senso negativo/positivo; **~ion** [-'flɛkʃən] n riflessione f; (image) riflesso; (criticism): **~ion on** giudizio su; attacco a; **on ~ion** pensandoci sopra

reflex ['riːflɛks] adj riflesso(a) ♦ n riflesso; **~ive** [rɪ'flɛksɪv] adj (LING) riflessivo(a)

reform [rɪ'fɔːm] n (of sinner etc) correzione f; (of law etc) riforma ♦ vt correggere; riformare; **the R~ation** [rɛfə'meɪʃən] n la Riforma; **~atory** (US) n riformatorio

refrain [rɪ'freɪn] vi: **to ~ from doing** trattenersi dal fare ♦ n ritornello

refresh [rɪ'frɛʃ] vt rinfrescare; (subj: food, sleep) ristorare; **~er course** (BRIT) n corso di aggiornamento; **~ing** adj (drink) rinfrescante; (sleep) riposante, ristoratore(trice); **~ments** npl rinfreschi mpl

refrigerator [rɪ'frɪdʒəreɪtə*] n frigorifero

refuel [riː'fjuəl] vi far rifornimento (di carburante)

refuge ['rɛfjuːdʒ] n rifugio; **to take ~ in** rifugiarsi in

refugee [rɛfju'dʒiː] n rifugiato/a, profugo/a

refund [n 'riːfʌnd, vb rɪ'fʌnd] n rimborso ♦ vt rimborsare

refurbish [riː'fəːbɪʃ] vt rimettere a nuovo

refusal [rɪ'fjuːzəl] n rifiuto; **to have first ~** avere il diritto d'opzione su

refuse [n 'rɛfjuːs, vb rɪ'fjuːz] n rifiuti mpl ♦ vt, vi rifiutare; **to ~ to do** rifiutare di fare; **~ collection** n raccolta di rifiuti

refute [rɪ'fjuːt] vt confutare

regain [rɪ'geɪn] vt riguadagnare; riacquistare, recuperare

regal ['riːgl] adj regale; **~ia** [rɪ'geɪlɪə] n insegne fpl regie

regard [rɪ'gɑːd] n riguardo, stima ♦ vt considerare, stimare; **to give one's ~s to** porgere i suoi saluti a;

"with kindest ~s" "cordiali saluti"; ~ing, as ~s, with ~ to riguardo a; ~less adv lo stesso; ~less of a dispetto di, nonostante

regenerate [rɪ'dʒɛnəreɪt] vt rigenerare

régime [reɪ'ʒiːm] n regime m

regiment [n 'rɛdʒɪmənt] n reggimento; ~al [-'mɛntl] adj reggimentale

region ['riːdʒən] n regione f; **in the** ~ **of** (fig) all'incirca di; ~al adj regionale

register ['rɛdʒɪstə*] n registro; (also: electoral ~) lista elettorale ♦ vt registrare; (vehicle) immatricolare; (letter) assicurare; (subj: instrument) segnare ♦ vi iscriversi; (at hotel) firmare il registro; (make impression) entrare in testa; ~ed (BRIT) adj (letter) assicurato(a); ~ed trademark n marchio depositato

registrar ['rɛdʒɪstrɑː*] n ufficiale m di stato civile; segretario

registration [rɛdʒɪs'treɪʃən] n (act) registrazione f; iscrizione f; (AUT: also: ~ number) numero di targa

registry ['rɛdʒɪstrɪ] n ufficio del registro; ~ **office** (BRIT) n anagrafe f; **to get married in a** ~ **office** ≈ sposarsi in municipio

regret [rɪ'grɛt] n rimpianto, rincrescimento ♦ vt rimpiangere; ~**fully** adv con rincrescimento; ~**table** adj deplorevole

regular ['rɛgjulə*] adj regolare; (usual) abituale, normale; (soldier) dell'esercito regolare ♦ n (client etc) cliente m/f abituale; ~**ly** adv regolarmente

regulate ['rɛgjuleɪt] vt regolare; **regulation** [-'leɪʃən] n regolazione f; (rule) regola, regolamento

rehabilitation ['riːhəbɪlɪ'teɪʃən] n (of offender) riabilitazione f; (of disabled) riadattamento

rehearsal [rɪ'həːsəl] n prova

rehearse [rɪ'həːs] vt provare

reign [reɪn] n regno ♦ vi regnare

reimburse [riːɪm'bəːs] vt rimborsare

rein [reɪn] n (for horse) briglia

reindeer ['reɪndɪə*] n inv renna

reinforce [riːɪn'fɔːs] vt rinforzare; ~**d concrete** n cemento armato; ~**ment** n rinforzo; ~**ments** npl (MIL) rinforzi mpl

reinstate [riːɪn'steɪt] vt reintegrare

reiterate [riː'ɪtəreɪt] vt reiterare, ripetere

reject [n 'riːdʒɛkt, vb rɪ'dʒɛkt] n (COMM) scarto ♦ vt rifiutare, respingere; (COMM: goods) scartare; ~**ion** [rɪ'dʒɛkʃən] n rifiuto

rejoice [rɪ'dʒɔɪs] vi: **to** ~ (**at** or **over**) provare diletto in

rejuvenate [rɪ'dʒuːvəneɪt] vt ringiovanire

relapse [rɪ'læps] n (MED) ricaduta

relate [rɪ'leɪt] vt (tell) raccontare; (connect) collegare ♦ vi: **to** ~ **to** (connect) riferirsi a; (get on with) stabilire un rapporto con; ~**d** adj: ~ (**to**) imparentato (con); collegato(a) or connesso(a) (a); **relating to** che riguarda, rispetto a

relation [rɪ'leɪʃən] n (person) parente m/f; (link) rapporto, relazione f; ~**ship** n rapporto; (personal ties) rapporti mpl, relazioni fpl; (also: family ~ship) legami mpl di parentela

relative ['rɛlətɪv] n parente m/f ♦ adj relativo(a); (respective) rispettivo(a); ~**ly** adv relativamente

relax [rɪ'læks] vi rilasciarsi; (person: unwind) rilassarsi ♦ vt rilasciare; (mind, person) rilassare; ~**ation** [riːlæk'seɪʃən] n rilassamento; rilassamento; (entertainment) ricreazione f, svago; ~**ed** adj rilassato(a); ~**ing** adj rilassante

relay [n 'riːleɪ] n (SPORT) corsa a staffetta ♦ vt (message) trasmettere

release [rɪ'liːs] n (from prison) rilascio; (from obligation) liberazione f; (of gas etc) emissione f; (of film etc) distribuzione f; (record) disco; (device) disinnesto ♦ vt (prisoner) rilasciare; (from obligation, wreckage etc) liberare; (book, film) fare uscire; (news) rendere pubblico(a); (gas etc) emettere; (TECH: catch, spring *etc*) disinnestare

relegate ['relɪgeɪt] *vt* relegare; (*BRIT: SPORT*): **to be ~d** essere retrocesso(a)

relent [rɪ'lent] *vi* cedere; **~less** *adj* implacabile

relevant ['relɪvənt] *adj* pertinente; (*chapter*) in questione; **~ to** pertinente a

reliability [rɪlaɪə'bɪlɪtɪ] *n* (*of person*) serietà; (*of machine*) affidabilità

reliable [rɪ'laɪəbl] *adj* (*person, firm*) fidato(a), che dà affidamento; (*method*) sicuro(a); (*machine*) affidabile; **reliably** *adv*: **to be reliably informed** sapere da fonti sicure

reliance [rɪ'laɪəns] *n*: **~ (on)** fiducia (in); bisogno (di)

relic ['relɪk] *n* (*REL*) reliquia; (*of the past*) resto

relief [rɪ'liːf] *n* (*from pain, anxiety*) sollievo; (*help, supplies*) soccorsi *mpl*; (*ART, GEO*) rilievo

relieve [rɪ'liːv] *vt* (*pain, patient*) sollevare; (*bring help*) soccorrere; (*take over from: gen*) sostituire; (*guard*) rilevare; **to ~ sb of sth** (*load*) alleggerire qn di qc; **to ~ o.s.** fare i propri bisogni

religion [rɪ'lɪdʒən] *n* religione *f*; **religious** *adj* religioso(a)

relinquish [rɪ'lɪŋkwɪʃ] *vt* abbandonare; (*plan, habit*) rinunziare a

relish ['relɪʃ] *n* (*CULIN*) condimento; (*enjoyment*) gran piacere *m* ♦ *vt* (*food etc*) godere; **to ~ doing** adorare fare

relocate ['riːləu'keɪt] *vt* trasferire ♦ *vi* trasferirsi

reluctance [rɪ'lʌktəns] *n* riluttanza

reluctant [rɪ'lʌktənt] *adj* riluttante, mal disposto(a); **~ly** *adv* di mala voglia, a malincuore

rely [rɪ'laɪ]: **to ~ on** *vt fus* contare su; (*be dependent*) dipendere da

remain [rɪ'meɪn] *vi* restare, rimanere; **~der** *n* resto; (*COMM*) rimanenza; **~ing** *adj* che rimane; **~s** *npl* resti *mpl*

remand [rɪ'mɑːnd] *n*: **on ~** in deten-

zione preventiva ♦ *vt*: **to ~ in custody** rinviare in carcere; trattenere a disposizione della legge; **~ home** (*BRIT*) *n* riformatorio, casa di correzione

remark [rɪ'mɑːk] *n* osservazione *f* ♦ *vt* osservare, dire; **~able** *adj* notevole; eccezionale

remedial [rɪ'miːdɪəl] *adj* (*tuition, classes*) di riparazione; (*exercise*) correttivo(a)

remedy ['remədɪ] *n*: **~ (for)** rimedio (per) ♦ *vt* rimediare a

remember [rɪ'membə*] *vt* ricordare, ricordarsi di; **~ me to him** salutalo da parte mia; **remembrance** *n* memoria; ricordo

remind [rɪ'maɪnd] *vt*: **to ~ sb of sth** ricordare qc a qn; **to ~ sb to do** ricordare a qn di fare; **~er** *n* richiamo; (*note etc*) promemoria *m inv*

reminisce [remɪ'nɪs] *vi*: **to ~ (about)** abbandonarsi ai ricordi (di)

reminiscent [remɪ'nɪsnt] *adj*: **~ of** che fa pensare a, che richiama

remiss [rɪ'mɪs] *adj* negligente

remission [rɪ'mɪʃən] *n* remissione *f*

remit [rɪ'mɪt] *vt* (*send: money*) rimettere; **~tance** *n* rimessa

remnant ['remnənt] *n* resto, avanzo; **~s** *npl* (*COMM*) scampoli *mpl*; fine *f* serie

remorse [rɪ'mɔːs] *n* rimorso; **~ful** *adj* pieno(a) di rimorsi; **~less** *adj* (*fig*) spietato(a)

remote [rɪ'məut] *adj* remoto(a), lontano(a); (*person*) distaccato(a); **~ control** *n* telecomando; **~ly** *adv* remotamente; (*slightly*) vagamente

remould ['riːməuld] (*BRIT*) *n* (*tyre*) gomma rivestita

removable [rɪ'muːvəbl] *adj* (*detachable*) staccabile

removal [rɪ'muːvəl] *n* (*taking away*) rimozione *f*; soppressione *f*; (*BRIT: from house*) trasloco; (*from office: dismissal*) destituzione *f*; (*MED*) ablazione *f*; **~ van** (*BRIT*) *n* furgone *m* per traslochi

remove [rɪ'muːv] *vt* togliere, rimuovere; (*employee*) destituire; (*stain*) far sparire; (*doubt, abuse*) sopprimere, eliminare; **~rs** (*BRIT*) npl (*company*) ditta or impresa di traslochi

Renaissance [rɪˈneɪsɑːns] n: the ~ il Rinascimento

render [ˈrɛndə*] vt rendere; **~ing** n (*MUS etc*) interpretazione f

rendez-vous [ˈrɒndɪvuː] n appuntamento; (*place*) luogo d'incontro; (*meeting*) incontro

renegade [ˈrɛnɪgeɪd] n rinnegato/a

renew [rɪˈnjuː] vt rinnovare; (*negotiations*) riprendere; **~able** adj rinnovabile; **~al** n rinnovo; ripresa

renounce [rɪˈnauns] vt rinunziare a

renovate [ˈrɛnəveɪt] vt rinnovare; (*art work*) restaurare; **renovation** [-ˈveɪʃən] n rinnovamento; restauro

renown [rɪˈnaun] n rinomanza; **~ed** adj rinomato/a

rent [rɛnt] n affitto ♦ vt (*take for* ~) prendere in affitto; (*also*: ~ *out*) dare in affitto; **~al** n (*for television, car*) fitto

renunciation [rɪnʌnsɪˈeɪʃən] n rinunzia

rep [rɛp] n abbr (*COMM*: = *representative*) rappresentante m/f; (*THEATRE*: = *repertory*) teatro di repertorio

repair [rɪˈpɛə*] n riparazione f ♦ vt riparare; **in good/bad** ~ in buone/cattive condizioni; ~ **kit** n corredo per riparazioni

repatriate [riːˈpætrɪeɪt] vt rimpatriare

repay [riːˈpeɪ] vt (*irreg*) (*money, creditor*) rimborsare, ripagare; (*sb's efforts*) ricompensare; (*favour*) ricambiare; **~ment** n pagamento; rimborso

repeal [rɪˈpiːl] n (*of law*) abrogazione f ♦ vt abrogare

repeat [rɪˈpiːt] n (*RADIO, TV*) replica ♦ vt ripetere; (*pattern*) riprodurre; (*promise, attack, also COMM: order*) rinnovare ♦ vi ripetere; **~edly** adv ripetutamente, spesso

repel [rɪˈpɛl] vt respingere; (*disgust*)

ripugnare a; **~lent** adj repellente ♦ n: **insect** ~lent prodotto m antiinsetti inv

repent [rɪˈpɛnt] vi: to ~ (of) pentirsi (di); **~ance** n pentimento

repertoire [ˈrɛpətwɑː*] n repertorio

repertory [ˈrɛpətərɪ] n (*also*: ~ *theatre*) teatro di repertorio

repetition [rɛpɪˈtɪʃən] n ripetizione f

repetitive [rɪˈpɛtɪtɪv] adj (*movement*) che si ripete; (*work*) monotono(a); (*speech*) pieno(a) di ripetizioni

replace [rɪˈpleɪs] vt (*put back*) rimettere a posto; (*take the place of*) sostituire; **~ment** n rimessa; sostituzione f; (*person*) sostituto/a

replay [ˈriːpleɪ] n (*of match*) partita ripetuta; (*of tape, film*) replay m inv

replenish [rɪˈplɛnɪʃ] vt (*glass*) riempire; (*stock etc*) rifornire

replete [rɪˈpliːt] adj (*well-fed*) sazio(a)

replica [ˈrɛplɪkə] n replica, copia

reply [rɪˈplaɪ] n risposta ♦ vi rispondere; ~ **coupon** n buono di risposta

report [rɪˈpɔːt] n rapporto; (*PRESS etc*) cronaca; (*BRIT*: also *school* ~) pagella; (*of gun*) sparo ♦ vt riportare; (*PRESS etc*) fare una cronaca su; (*bring to notice: occurrence*) segnalare; (: *person*) denunciare ♦ vi (*make a report*) fare un rapporto (*or* una cronaca); (*present o.s.*): to ~ (to sb) presentarsi (a qn); ~ **card** n (*US, SCOTTISH*) n pagella; **~edly** adv stando a quanto si dice; he **~edly** told them to ... avrebbe detto loro di ...; **~er** n reporter m inv

repose [rɪˈpəuz] n: **in** ~ (*face, mouth*) in riposo

reprehensible [rɛprɪˈhɛnsɪbl] adj riprovevole

represent [rɛprɪˈzɛnt] vt rappresentare; **~ation** [-ˈteɪʃən] n rappresentazione f; (*petition*) rappresentanza; **~ations** npl (*protest*) protesta; **~ative** n rappresentante m/f; (*US: POL*) deputato/a ♦ adj rappresentativo(a)

repress [rɪ'pres] vt reprimere; ~**ion** [-'preʃən] n repressione f

reprieve [rɪ'priːv] n (LAW) sospensione f dell'esecuzione della condanna; (fig) dilazione f

reprimand ['reprɪmɑːnd] n rimprovero ♦ vt rimproverare

reprint ['riːprɪnt] n ristampa

reprisal [rɪ'praɪzl] n rappresaglia

reproach [rɪ'prəutʃ] n rimprovero vt: to ~ **sb for sth** rimproverare qn di qc; ~**ful** adj di rimprovero

reproduce [riːprə'djuːs] vt riprodurre ♦ vi riprodursi; **reproduction** [-'dʌkʃən] n riproduzione f

reproof [rɪ'pruːf] n riprovazione f

reprove [rɪ'pruːv] vt: to ~ (**for**) biasimare (per)

reptile ['reptaɪl] n rettile m

republic [rɪ'pʌblɪk] n repubblica; ~**an** adj, n repubblicano(a)

repudiate [rɪ'pjuːdɪeɪt] vt (accusation) respingere

repulse [rɪ'pʌls] vt respingere

repulsive [rɪ'pʌlsɪv] adj ripugnante, ripulsivo(a)

reputable ['repjutəbl] adj di buona reputazione; (occupation) rispettabile

reputation [repju'teɪʃən] n reputazione f

reputed [rɪ'pjuːtɪd] adj reputato(a); ~**ly** adv secondo quanto si dice

request [rɪ'kwest] n domanda; (formal) richiesta ♦ vt: to ~ (**of** or **from sb**) chiedere (a qn); ~ **stop** n (BRIT) (for bus) fermata facoltativa or a richiesta

require [rɪ'kwaɪə*] vt (need: subj: person) aver bisogno di; (: thing, situation) richiedere; (want) volere; esigere; (order): to ~ **sb to do sth** ordinare a qn di fare qc; ~**ment** n esigenza; bisogno; requisito

requisite ['rekwɪzɪt] n cosa necessaria ♦ adj necessario(a)

requisition [rekwɪ'zɪʃən] n: ~ (**for**) richiesta (di) ♦ vt (MIL) requisire

rescue ['reskjuː] n salvataggio; (help) soccorso ♦ vt salvare; ~ **party** n squadra di salvataggio; ~**r** n

salvatore/trice

research [rɪ'səːtʃ] n ricerca, ricerche fpl ♦ vt fare ricerche su; ~**er** n ricercatore/trice

resemblance [rɪ'zembləns] n somiglianza

resemble [rɪ'zembl] vt assomigliare a

resent [rɪ'zent] vt risentirsi di; ~**ful** adj pieno(a) di risentimento; ~**ment** n risentimento

reservation [rezə'veɪʃən] n (booking) prenotazione f; (doubt) dubbio; (protected area) riserva; (BRIT: on road: also: central ~) spartitraffico m inv

reserve [rɪ'zəːv] n riserva ♦ vt (seats etc) prenotare; ~**s** npl (MIL) riserve fpl; **in** ~ in serbo; ~**d** adj (shy) riservato(a)

reservoir ['rezəvwɑː*] n serbatoio

reshuffle [riː'ʃʌfl] n: **Cabinet** ~ (POL) rimpasto governativo

reside [rɪ'zaɪd] vi risiedere

residence ['rezɪdəns] n residenza; ~ **permit** (BRIT) n permesso di soggiorno

resident ['rezɪdənt] n residente m/f; (in hotel) cliente m/f fisso(a) ♦ adj residente; (doctor) fisso(a); (course, college) a tempo pieno con pernottamento; ~**ial** [-'denʃəl] adj di residenza; (area) residenziale

residue ['rezɪdjuː] n resto; (CHEM, PHYSICS) residuo

resign [rɪ'zaɪn] vt (one's post) dimettersi da ♦ vi dimettersi; to ~ **o.s. to** rassegnarsi a; ~**ation** [rezɪg'neɪʃən] n dimissioni fpl; rassegnazione f; ~**ed** adj rassegnato(a)

resilience [rɪ'zɪlɪəns] n (of material) elasticità, resilienza; (of person) capacità di recupero

resilient [rɪ'zɪlɪənt] adj elastico(a); (person) che si riprende facilmente

resin ['rezɪn] n resina

resist [rɪ'zɪst] vt resistere a; ~**ance** n resistenza

resolution [rezə'luːʃən] n risoluzione f

resolve [rɪ'zɔlv] n risoluzione f ♦ vi (decide): to ~ to do decidere di fare ♦ vt (problem) risolvere

resort [rɪ'zɔːt] n (town) stazione f; (recourse) ricorso ♦ vi: to ~ to aver ricorso a; **in the last** ~ come ultima risorsa

resound [rɪ'zaund] vi: to ~ (with) risonare (di); ~ing adj risonante; (fig) clamoroso(a)

resource [rɪ'sɔːs] n risorsa; ~s npl (coal, iron etc) risorse fpl; ~ful adj pieno(a) di risorse, intraprendente

respect [rɪs'pɛkt] n rispetto ♦ vt rispettare; ~s npl (greetings) ossequi mpl; **with** ~ **to** rispetto a, riguardo a; **in this** ~ per questo riguardo; ~**able** adj rispettabile; ~**ful** adj rispettoso(a)

respective [rɪs'pɛktɪv] adj rispettivo(a)

respite ['rɛspaɪt] n respiro, tregua

resplendent [rɪs'plɛndənt] adj risplendente

respond [rɪs'pɔnd] vi rispondere

response [rɪs'pɔns] n risposta

responsibility [rɪspɔnsɪ'bɪlɪtɪ] n responsabilità f inv

responsible [rɪs'pɔnsɪbl] adj (trustworthy) fidato(a); (job) di (grande) responsabilità; ~ (for) responsabile (di)

responsive [rɪs'pɔnsɪv] adj che reagisce

rest [rɛst] n riposo; (stop) sosta, pausa; (MUS) pausa; (object: to support sth) appoggio, sostegno; (remainder) resto, avanzi mpl ♦ vi riposarsi; (remain) rimanere, restare; (be supported): to ~ on appoggiarsi su ♦ vt (far) riposare; (lean): to ~ sth on/against appoggiare qc su/contro; the ~ of them gli altri; it ~s with him to decide sta a lui decidere

restaurant ['rɛstərɔŋ] n ristorante m; ~ **car** (BRIT) n vagone m ristorante

restful ['rɛstful] adj riposante

rest home n casa di riposo

restitution [rɛstɪ'tjuːʃən] n: to

make ~ **to sb for sth** compensare qn di qc

restive ['rɛstɪv] adj agitato(a), impaziente

restless ['rɛstlɪs] adj agitato(a), irrequieto(a)

restoration [rɛstə'reɪʃən] n restauro; restituzione f

restore [rɪ'stɔː] vt (building, to power) restaurare; (sth stolen) restituire; (peace, health) ristorare

restrain [rɪs'treɪn] vt (feeling, growth) contenere, frenare; (person): to ~ (from doing) trattenere (dal fare); ~**ed** adj (style) contenuto(a), sobrio(a); (person) riservato(a); ~**t** n (restriction) limitazione f; (moderation) ritegno; (of style) contenutezza

restrict [rɪs'trɪkt] vt restringere, limitare; ~**ion** [-kʃən] n: ~ (**on**) restrizione f (di), limitazione f

rest room (US) n toletta

restructure [riː'strʌktʃə*] vt ristrutturare

result [rɪ'zʌlt] n risultato ♦ vi: to ~ in avere per risultato; **as a** ~ **of** in conseguenza a, in seguito a

resume [rɪ'zjuːm] vt, vi (work, journey) riprendere

résumé ['reɪzjumeɪ] n riassunto; (US) curriculum m inv vitae

resumption [rɪ'zʌmpʃən] n ripresa

resurgence [rɪ'sɜːdʒəns] n rinascita

resurrection [rɛzə'rɛkʃən] n resurrezione f

resuscitate [rɪ'sʌsɪteɪt] vt (MED) risuscitare; **resuscitation** [-'teɪʃən] n rianimazione f

retail ['riːteɪl] adj, adv al minuto ♦ vt vendere al minuto; ~**er** n commerciante m/f al minuto, dettagliante m/f; ~ **price** n prezzo al minuto

retain [rɪ'teɪn] vt (keep) tenere, serbare; ~**er** n (fee) onorario

retaliate [rɪ'tælɪeɪt] vi: to ~ (against) vendicarsi (di); **retaliation** [-'eɪʃən] n rappresaglie fpl

retarded [rɪ'tɑːdɪd] adj ritardato(a)

retch [rɛtʃ] vi aver conati di vomito

retire [rɪ'taɪə*] *vi* (*give up work*) andare in pensione; (*withdraw*) ritirarsi, andarsene; (*go to bed*) andare a letto, ritirarsi; **~d** *adj* (*person*) pensionato(a); **~ment** *n* pensione *f*; (*act*) pensionamento; **retiring** *adj* (*leaving*) uscente; (*shy*) riservato(a)

retort [rɪ'tɔːt] *vi* rimbeccare

retrace [riː'treɪs] *vt*: **to ~ one's steps** tornare sui passi

retract [rɪ'trækt] *vt* (*statement*) ritrattare; (*claws*, *undercarriage*, *aerial*) ritrarre, ritirare

retrain [riː'treɪn] *vt* (*worker*) riaddestrare

retread ['riːtrɛd] *n* (*tyre*) gomma rigenerata

retreat [rɪ'triːt] *n* ritirata; (*place*) rifugio ♦ *vi* battere in ritirata

retribution [rɛtrɪ'bjuːʃən] *n* castigo

retrieval [rɪ'triːvəl] *n* (*see vb*) recupero; riparazione *f*

retrieve [rɪ'triːv] *vt* (*sth lost*) recuperare, ritrovare; (*situation*, *honour*) salvare; (*error*, *loss*) rimediare a; **~r** *n* cane *m* da riporto

retrospect ['rɛtrəspɛkt] *n*: **in ~** guardando indietro; **~ive** [-'spɛktɪv] *adj* retrospettivo(a); (*law*) retroattivo(a)

return [rɪ'tɜːn] *n* (*going or coming back*) ritorno; (*of sth stolen etc*) restituzione *f*; (*FINANCE: from land, shares*) profitto, reddito ♦ *cpd* (*journey*, *match*) di ritorno; (*BRIT: ticket*) di andata e ritorno ♦ *vi* tornare, ritornare ♦ *vt* rendere, restituire; (*bring back*) riportare; (*send back*) mandare indietro; (*put back*) rimettere; (*LAW: verdict*) emettere; (*POL: candidate*) eleggere; **~s** *npl* (*COMM*) incassi *mpl*; profitti *mpl*; **in ~** (**for**) in cambio (di); **by ~ of post** a stretto giro di posta; **many happy ~s** (**of the day**)! cento di questi giorni!

reunion [riː'juːnɪən] *n* riunione *f*

reunite [riːjuː'naɪt] *vt* riunire

rev [rɛv] *n abbr* (*AUT: = revolution*) giro ♦ *vt* (*also:* **~ up**) imballare

revamp ['riː'væmp] *vt* (*firm*) riorganizzare

reveal [rɪ'viːl] *vt* (*make known*) rivelare, svelare; (*display*) rivelare, mostrare; **~ing** *adj* rivelatore(trice); (*dress*) scollato(a)

reveille [rɪ'vælɪ] *n* (*MIL*) sveglia

revel ['rɛvl] *vi*: **to ~ in sth/in doing** dilettarsi di qc/a fare

revelation [rɛvə'leɪʃən] *n* rivelazione *f*

revelry ['rɛvlrɪ] *n* baldoria

revenge [rɪ'vɛndʒ] *n* vendetta ♦ *vt* vendicare; **to take ~ on** vendicarsi di

revenue ['rɛvənjuː] *n* reddito

reverberate [rɪ'vɜːbəreɪt] *vi* (*sound*) rimbombare; (*light*) riverberarsi; (*fig*) ripercuotersi

revere [rɪ'vɪə*] *vt* venerare

reverence ['rɛvərəns] *n* venerazione *f*, riverenza

Reverend ['rɛvərənd] *adj* (*in titles*) reverendo(a)

reverie ['rɛvərɪ] *n* fantasticheria

reversal [rɪ'vɜːsl] *n* capovolgimento

reverse [rɪ'vɜːs] *n* contrario, rovescio; (*back*, *defeat*) rovescio; (*AUT: also:* **~ gear**) marcia indietro ♦ *adj* (*order*, *direction*) contrario(a), opposto(a) ♦ *vt* (*turn*) invertire, rovesciare; (*change*) capovolgere, rovesciare; (*LAW: judgment*) cassare; (*car*) fare marcia indietro con ♦ *vi* (*BRIT: AUT*, *person*) fare marcia indietro; **~d charge call** (*BRIT*) *n* (*TEL*) telefonata con addebito al ricevente; **reversing lights** (*BRIT*) *npl* (*AUT*) luci *fpl* per la retromarcia

revert [rɪ'vɜːt] *vi*: **to ~** tornare a

review [rɪ'vjuː] *n* rivista; (*of book*, *film*) recensione *f*; (*of situation*) esame *m* ♦ *vt* passare in rivista; fare la recensione di; fare il punto di; **~er** *n* recensore/a

revile [rɪ'vaɪl] *vt* insultare

revise [rɪ'vaɪz] *vt* (*manuscript*) rivedere, correggere; (*opinion*) emendare, modificare; (*study: subject*, *notes*) ripassare; **revision** [rɪ'vɪʒən] *n* revisione *f*; ripasso

revitalize [riː'vaɪtəlaɪz] vt ravvivare

revival [rɪ'vaɪvəl] n ripresa; ristabilimento; (of faith) risveglio

revive [rɪ'vaɪv] vt (person) rianimare; (custom) far rivivere; (hope, courage, economy) ravvivare; (play, fashion) riesumare ♦ vi (person) rianimarsi; (hope) ravvivarsi; (activity) riprendersi

revolt [rɪ'vəʊlt] n rivolta, ribellione f ♦ vi rivoltarsi, ribellarsi ♦ vt (disgust) rivoltare; ~ing adj ripugnante

revolution [rɛvə'luːʃən] n rivoluzione f; (of wheel etc) rivoluzione, giro; ~ary adj, n rivoluzionario(a)

revolve [rɪ'vɒlv] vi girare

revolver [rɪ'vɒlvəʳ] n rivoltella

revolving [rɪ'vɒlvɪŋ] adj girevole

revue [rɪ'vjuː] n (THEATRE) rivista

revulsion [rɪ'vʌlʃən] n ripugnanza

reward [rɪ'wɔːd] n ricompensa, premio ♦ vt: to ~ (for) ricompensare (per); ~ing adj (fig) gratificante

rewind [riː'waɪnd] (irreg) vt (watch) ricaricare; (ribbon etc) riavvolgere

rewire [riː'waɪəʳ] vt (house) rifare l'impianto elettrico di

reword [riː'wɜːd] vt formulare o esprimere con altre parole

rheumatism ['ruːmətɪzəm] n reumatismo

Rhine [raɪn] n: the ~ il Reno

rhinoceros [raɪ'nɒsərəs] n rinoceronte m

rhododendron [rəʊdə'dɛndrən] n rododendro

Rhone [rəʊn] n: the ~ il Rodano

rhubarb ['ruːbɑːb] n rabarbaro

rhyme [raɪm] n rima; (verse) poesia

rhythm ['rɪðm] n ritmo

rib [rɪb] n (ANAT) costola ♦ vt (tease) punzecchiare

ribbon ['rɪbən] n nastro; in ~s (torn) a brandelli

rice [raɪs] n riso; ~ **pudding** n budino di riso

rich [rɪtʃ] adj ricco(a); (clothes) sontuoso(a); (abundant): ~ **in** ricco(a) di; the ~ npl (wealthy people) i ricchi; ~es npl ricchezze fpl; ~ly adv

riccamente; (dressed) sontuosamente; (deserved) pienamente

rickets ['rɪkɪts] n rachitismo

rickety ['rɪkɪtɪ] adj traballante

rickshaw ['rɪkʃɔː] n risciò m inv

ricochet ['rɪkəʃeɪ] vi rimbalzare

rid [rɪd] (pt, pp **rid**) vt: to ~ sb of sbarazzare o liberare qn di; to get ~ of sbarazzarsi di

ridden ['rɪdn] pp of ride

riddle ['rɪdl] n (puzzle) indovinello ♦ vt: to be ~d with (holes) essere crivellato(a) di; (doubts) essere pieno(a) di

ride [raɪd] (pt rode, pp ridden) n (on horse) cavalcata; (outing) passeggiata; (distance covered) cavalcata; corsa ♦ vi (as sport) cavalcare; (go somewhere: on horse, bicycle) andare (a cavallo or in bicicletta etc); (journey: on bicycle, motorcycle, bus) andare, viaggiare ♦ vt (a horse) montare, cavalcare; to take sb for a ~ (fig) prendere in giro qn; fregare qn; to ~ a horse/bicycle/camel montare a cavallo/in bicicletta/in groppa a un cammello; ~r n cavalcatore/trice; (in race) fantino; (on bicycle) ciclista m/f; (on motorcycle) motociclista m/f

ridge [rɪdʒ] n (of hill) cresta; (of roof) colmo; (on object) riga (in rilievo)

ridicule ['rɪdɪkjuːl] n ridicolo; scherno ♦ vt mettere in ridicolo

ridiculous [rɪ'dɪkjʊləs] adj ridicolo(a)

riding ['raɪdɪŋ] n equitazione f; ~ **school** n scuola di equitazione

rife [raɪf] adj diffuso(a); to be ~ **with** abbondare di

riffraff ['rɪfræf] n canaglia

rifle ['raɪfl] n carabina ♦ vt vuotare; ~ **through** vt fus frugare tra; ~ **range** n campo di tiro; (at fair) tiro a segno

rift [rɪft] n fessura, crepatura; (fig: disagreement) incrinatura, disaccordo

rig [rɪg] n (also: oil ~: on land) derrick *m inv*: (: *at sea*) piattaforma di trivellazione ♦ *vt* (*election etc*) truccare; ~ **out** (*BRIT*) *vt*: to ~ out **as/in** vestire da/in; ~ **up** *vt* allestire; ~**ging** *n* (*NAUT*) attrezzatura

right [raɪt] *adj* giusto(a); (*suitable*) appropriato(a); (*not left*) destro(a) ♦ *n* giusto, (*title, claim*) diritto; (*not left*) destra ♦ *adv* (*answer*) correttamente; (*not on the left*) a destra ♦ *excl* va bene!; **to be** ~ (*person*) aver ragione; (*answer*) essere giusto(a) *or* corretto(a); **by** ~**s** di diritto; **on the** ~ a destra; **to be in the** ~ aver ragione, essere nel giusto(a); ~ **now** proprio adesso; subito; ~ **away** subito; ~-**angle** *n* angolo retto; ~**eous** ['raɪtʃəs] *adj* retto(a), virtuoso(a); (*anger*) giusto(a), giustificato(a); ~**ful** *adj* (*heir*) legittimo(a); ~-**handed** *adj* (*person*) che adopera la mano destra; ~-**hand man** *n* braccio destro; ~-**hand side** *n* il lato destro; ~**ly** *adv* bene, correttamente; (*with reason*) a ragione; ~ **of way** *n* diritto di passaggio; (*AUT*) precedenza; ~-**wing** *adj* (*POL*) di destra

rigid ['rɪdʒɪd] *adj* rigido(a); (*principle*) rigoroso(a)

rigmarole ['rɪgmərəul] *n* tiritera; commedia

rile [raɪl] *vt* irritare, seccare

rim [rɪm] *n* orlo; (*of spectacles*) montatura; (*of wheel*) cerchione *m*

rind [raɪnd] *n* (*of bacon*) cotenna; (*of lemon etc*) scorza

ring [rɪŋ] (*pt* **rang**, *pp* **rung**) *n* anello; (*of people, objects*) cerchio; (*of spies*) giro; (*of smoke etc*) spirale *m*; (*arena*) pista, arena; (*for boxing*) ring *m inv*; (*sound of bell*) scampanìo ♦ *vi* (*person, bell, telephone*) suonare; (*also*: ~ **out**: *voice, words*) risuonare; (*TEL*) telefonare; (*ears*) fischiare ♦ *vt* (*BRIT*: *TEL*) telefonare a; (*bell, doorbell*) suonare; **to give sb a** ~ (*BRIT*: *TEL*) dare un colpo di telefono a qn; ~ **back** *vt, vi* (*TEL*) richiamare; ~ **off** (*BRIT*) *vi*

(*TEL*) mettere giù, riattaccare; ~ **up** (*BRIT*) *vt* (*TEL*) telefonare a; ~**ing** *n* (*of bell*) scampanio; (*of telephone*) squillo; (*in ears*) ronzio; ~**ing tone** *n* (*TEL*) segnale *m* di libero; ~**leader** *n* (*of gang*) capobanda *n*

ringlets ['rɪŋlɪts] *npl* boccoli *mpl*

ring road (*BRIT*) *n* raccordo anulare

rink [rɪŋk] *n* (*also*: **ice** ~) pista di pattinaggio

rinse [rɪns] *n* risciacquatura; (*hair tint*) cachet *m inv* ♦ *vt* sciacquare

riot ['raɪət] *n* sommossa, tumulto; (*of colours*) orgia ♦ *vi* tumultuare; **to run** ~ creare disordine; ~**ous** *adj* tumultuoso(a); (*living*) sfrenato(a); (*party*) scatenato(a)

rip [rɪp] *n* strappo ♦ *vt* strappare ♦ *vi* strapparsi; ~**cord** *n* cavo di sfilamento

ripe [raɪp] *adj* (*fruit, grain*) maturo(a); (*cheese*) stagionato(a); ~**n** *vt* maturare ♦ *vi* maturarsi

ripple ['rɪpl] *n* increspamento, ondulazione *f*; mormorio ♦ *vi* incresparsi

rise [raɪz] (*pt* **rose**, *pp* **risen**) *n* (*slope*) salita, pendio; (*hill*) altura; (*increase*: *in wages*: *BRIT*) aumento; (: *in prices, temperature*) rialzo, aumento; (*fig*: *to power etc*) ascesa ♦ *vi* alzarsi; levarsi; (*prices*) aumentare; (*waters, river*) crescere; (*sun, wind, person*: *from chair, bed*) levarsi; (*also*: ~ **up**: *building*) ergersi; (: *rebel*) insorgere; ribellarsi; (*in rank*) salire; **to give** ~ **to** provocare, dare origine a; **to** ~ **to the occasion** essere all'altezza; **risen** ['rɪzn] *pp of* **rise**; **rising** *adj* (*increasing*: *number*) sempre crescente; (: *prices*) in aumento; (*tide*) montante; (*sun, moon*) nascente, che sorge

risk [rɪsk] *n* rischio; pericolo ♦ *vt* rischiare; **to take** *or* **run the** ~ **of doing** correre il rischio di fare; **at** ~ in pericolo; **at one's own** ~ a proprio rischio e pericolo; ~**y** *adj* rischioso(a)

risqué ['riːskeɪ] adj (joke) spinto(a)

rissole ['rɪsəʊl] n crocchetta

rite [raɪt] n rito; **last ~s** n l'estrema unzione

ritual ['rɪtjʊəl] adj rituale ♦ n rituale m

rival ['raɪvl] n rivale m/f; (in business) concorrente m/f ♦ adj rivale; che fa concorrenza ♦ vt essere in concorrenza con; **to ~ sb/sth in** competere in qn/qc in; **~ry** n rivalità; concorrenza

river ['rɪvə*] n fiume m ♦ cpd (port, traffic) fluviale; **up/down** ~ a monte/valle; **~bank** n argine m; **~bed** n letto di fiume

rivet ['rɪvɪt] n ribattino, rivetto ♦ vt (fig) concentrare, fissare

Riviera [rɪvɪ'eərə] n: **the (French)** ~ la Costa Azzurra; **the Italian** ~ la Riviera

road [rəʊd] n strada; (small) cammino; (in town) via ♦ cpd stradale; **major/minor** ~ strada con/senza diritto di precedenza; **~block** n blocco stradale; **~hog** n guidatore m egoista e spericolato; **~map** n carta stradale; **~ safety** n sicurezza sulle strade; **~side** n margine m della strada; **~sign** n cartello stradale; **~ user** n chi usa la strada; **~way** n carreggiata; **~works** npl lavori mpl stradali; **~worthy** adj in buono stato di marcia

roam [rəʊm] vi errare, vagabondare

roar [rɔː*] n ruggito; (of crowd) tumulto; (of thunder, storm) muggito; (of laughter) scoppio ♦ vi ruggire; muggire; **to ~ with laughter** scoppiare dalle risa; **to do a ~ing trade** fare affari d'oro

roast [rəʊst] n arrosto ♦ vt arrostire; (coffee) tostare, torrefare; **~ beef** n arrosto di manzo

rob [rɔb] vt (person) rubare; (bank) svaligiare; **to ~ sb of sth** derubare qn di qc; (fig: deprive) privare qn di qc; **~ber** n ladro; (armed) rapinatore m; **~bery** n furto, rapina

robe [rəʊb] n (for ceremony etc) abito; (also: bath ~) accappatoio; (US: also: lap ~) coperta

robin ['rɔbɪn] n pettirosso

robot ['rəʊbɔt] n robot m inv

robust [rəʊ'bʌst] adj robusto(a); (economy) solido(a)

rock [rɔk] n (substance) roccia; (boulder) masso; roccia; (in sea) scoglio; (US: pebble) ciottolo; (BRIT: sweet) zucchero candito ♦ vt (swing gently: cradle) dondolare; (: child) cullare; (shake) scrollare, far tremare ♦ vi dondolarsi; scrollarsi, tremare; **on the** ~s (drink) col ghiaccio; (marriage etc) in crisi; **~ and roll** n rock and roll m; **~-bottom** n bassissimo(a); **~ery** n giardino roccioso

rocket ['rɔkɪt] n razzo

rock fall n parete f della roccia

rocking ['rɔkɪŋ]: **~ chair** n sedia a dondolo; **~ horse** n cavallo a dondolo

rocky ['rɔkɪ] adj (hill) roccioso(a); (path) sassoso(a); (marriage etc) instabile

rod [rɔd] n (metallic, TECH) asta; (wooden) bacchetta; (also: fishing ~) canna da pesca

rode [rəʊd] pt of **ride**

rodent ['rəʊdnt] n roditore m

rodeo ['rəʊdɪəʊ] n rodeo

roe [rəʊ] n (species: also: ~ deer) capriolo; (of fish, also: hard ~) uova fpl di pesce; **soft** ~ latte m di pesce

rogue [rəʊg] n mascalzone m

role [rəʊl] n ruolo

roll [rəʊl] n rotolo; (of banknotes) mazzo; (also: bread ~) panino; (register) lista; (sound: of drums etc) rullo ♦ vt rotolare; (also: ~ up: string) aggomitolare; (also: ~ up: sleeves) rimboccare; (cigarettes) arrotolare; (eyes) roteare; (also: ~ out: pastry) spianare; (lawn, road etc) spianare ♦ vi rotolare; (wheel) girare; (drum) rullare; (vehicle: also: ~ along) avanzare; (ship) rollare; **~ about** or **around** vi rotolare qua e là; (person) rotolarsi; **~ by** vi (*time*) passare; ~ **in** *vi* (*mail, cash*) arrivare a fiumi; ~ **over** *vi* rivoltarsi; ~ **up** (*inf*) *vi* (*arrive*) arrivare ♦ *vt* (*carpet*) arrotolare; ~ **call** *n* appello; **~er** *n* rullo; (*wheel*) rotella; (*for hair*) bigodino; **~er coaster** *n* montagne *fpl* russe; **~er skates** *npl* pattini *mpl* a rotelle

rolling ['rəʊlɪŋ] *adj* (*landscape*) ondulato(a); ~ **pin** *n* matterello; ~ **stock** *n* (*RAIL*) materiale *m* rotabile

ROM [rɔm] *n abbr* = *read only memory* memoria di sola lettura

Roman ['rəʊmən] *adj*, *n* romano(a); ~ **Catholic** *adj*, *n* cattolico(a)

romance [rə'mæns] *n* storia (*or* avventura *or* film *m inv*) romantico(a); (*charm*) poesia; (*love affair*) idillio

Romania [rəʊ'meɪnɪə] *n* = **Rumania**

Roman numeral *n* numero romano

romantic [rə'mæntɪk] *adj* romantico(a); sentimentale

Rome [rəʊm] *n* Roma

romp [rɔmp] *n* gioco rumoroso ♦ *vi* (*also*: ~ **about**) far chiasso, giocare in un modo rumoroso

rompers ['rɔmpəz] *npl* pagliaccetto

roof [ruːf] *n* tetto; (*of tunnel, cave*) volta ♦ *vt* coprire (con un tetto); ~ **of the mouth** palato; **~ing** *n* materiale *m* per copertura; ~ **rack** *n* (*AUT*) portabagagli *m inv*

rook [rʊk] *n* (*bird*) corvo nero; (*CHESS*) torre *f*

room [ruːm] *n* (*in house*) stanza; (*bed~, in hotel*) camera; (*in school etc*) sala; (*space*) posto, spazio; ~**s** *npl* (*lodging*) alloggio; **"~s to let"** (*BRIT*), **"~s for rent"** (*US*) "si affittano camere"; **there is ~ for improvement** si potrebbe migliorare; **~ing house** (*US*) *n* casa in cui si affittano camere *o* appartamentini ammobiliati; **~mate** *n* compagno/a di stanza; ~ **service** *n* servizio da camera; **~y** *adj* spazioso(a); (*garment*) ampio(a)

roost [ruːst] *vi* appollaiarsi

rooster ['ruːstə*] *n* gallo

root [ruːt] *n* radice *f* ♦ *vi* (*plant, be-*

lief) attecchire; ~ **about** *vi* (*fig*) frugare; ~ **for** *vt fus* fare il tifo per; ~ **out** *vt* estirpare

rope [rəʊp] *n* corda, fune *f*; (*NAUT*) cavo ♦ *vt* (*box*) legare; (*climbers*) legare in cordata; (*area: also*: ~ **off**) isolare cingendo con cordoni; **to know the ~s** (*fig*) conoscere i trucchi del mestiere; ~ **in** *vt* (*fig*) coinvolgere; ~ **ladder** *n* scala a corda

rosary ['rəʊzərɪ] *n* rosario; roseto

rose [rəʊz] *pt of* **rise** ♦ *n* rosa; (*also*: ~ **bush**) rosaio; (*on watering can*) rosetta

rosé ['rəʊzeɪ] *n* vino rosato

rosebud ['rəʊzbʌd] *n* bocciolo di rosa

rosebush ['rəʊzbʊʃ] *n* rosaio

rosemary ['rəʊzmərɪ] *n* rosmarino

rosette [rə'zɛt] *n* coccarda

roster ['rɔstə*] *n*: **duty** ~ ruolino di servizio

rostrum ['rɔstrəm] *n* tribuna

rosy ['rəʊzɪ] *adj* roseo(a)

rot [rɔt] *n* (*decay*) putrefazione *f*; (*inf*: *nonsense*) stupidaggini *fpl* ♦ *vt*, *vi* imputridire, marcire

rota ['rəʊtə] *n* tabella dei turni

rotary ['rəʊtərɪ] *adj* rotante

rotate [rəʊ'teɪt] *vt* (*revolve*) far girare; (*change round: jobs*) fare a turno ♦ *vi* (*revolve*) girare; **rotating** *adj* (*movement*) rotante

rote [rəʊt] *n*: **by** ~ (*by heart*) a memoria; (*mechanically*) meccanicamente

rotten ['rɔtn] *adj* (*decayed*) putrido(a), marcio(a); (*dishonest*) corrotto(a); (*inf*: *bad*) brutto(a); (: *action*) vigliacco(a); **to feel** ~ (*inf*) sentirsi da cani

rouble ['ruːbl] (*US* **ruble**) *n* rublo

rouge [ruːʒ] *n* belletto

rough [rʌf] *adj* (*skin, surface*) ruvido(a); (*terrain, road*) accidentato(a); (*voice*) rauco(a); (*person, manner: coarse*) rozzo(a), aspro(a); (: *violent*) brutale; (*district*) malfamato(a); (*weather*) cattivo(a); (*sea*) mosso(a); (*plan*) abbozzato(a);

(*guess*) approssimativo(a) ♦ *n* (*GOLF*) macchia; **to ~ it** far vita dura; **to sleep ~** (*BRIT*) dormire all'addiaccio; **~age** *n* alimenti *mpl* ricchi in cellulosa; **~-and-ready** *adj* rudimentale; **~cast** *n* intonaco grezzo; **~ copy** *n* brutta copia; **~ly** *adv* (*handle*) rudemente, brutalmente; (*make*) grossolanamente; (*speak*) bruscamente; (*approximately*) approssimativamente; **~ness** *n* ruvidità; (*of manner*) rozzezza

roulette [ruːˈlɛt] *n* roulette *f*

Roumania [ruːˈmeɪnɪə] *n* = **Rumania**

round [raund] *adj* rotondo(a); (*figures*) tondo(a) ♦ *n* (*BRIT*: *of toast*) fetta; (*duty*: *of policeman, milkman etc*) giro; (*of doctor*) visite *fpl*; (*game*: *of cards, golf, in competition*) partita; (*of ammunition*) cartuccia; (*BOXING*) round *m inv*; (*of talks*) serie *f inv* ♦ *vt* (*corner*) girare; (*bend*) prendere ♦ *prep* intorno a ♦ *adv*: **all ~** tutt'attorno; **to go the long way ~** fare il giro più lungo; **all the year ~** tutto l'anno; **it's just ~ the corner** è qui dietro l'angolo; **~ the clock** ininterrottamente; **to go ~ to sb's house** andare da qn; **go ~ the back** passi dietro; **to go ~ a house** visitare una casa; **enough to go ~** abbastanza per tutti; **~ of applause** applausi *mpl*; **~ of drinks** giro di bibite; **~ of sandwiches** sandwich *m inv*; **~ off** *vt* (*speech etc*) finire; **~ up** *vt* radunare; (*criminals*) fare una retata di; (*prices*) arrotondare; **~about** *n* (*BRIT*: *AUT*) rotatoria; (*at fair*) giostra ♦ *adj* (*route, means*) indiretto(a); **~ers** *npl* (*game*) gioco simile al baseball; **~ly** *adv* (*fig*) chiaro e tondo; **~-shouldered** *adj* dalle spalle tonde; **~ trip** *n* (*viaggio* di) andata e ritorno; **~up** *n* raduno; (*of criminals*) retata

rouse [rauz] *vt* (*wake up*) svegliare; (*stir up*) destare; provocare; risvegliare; **rousing** *adj* (*speech, ap-*

plause) entusiastico(a)

rout [raut] *n* (*MIL*) rotta ♦ *vt* (*defeat*) mettere in rotta

route [ruːt] *n* itinerario; (*of bus*) percorso; **~ map** (*BRIT*) *n* (*for journey*) cartina di itinerario

routine [ruːˈtiːn] *adj* (*work*) corrente, abituale; (*procedure*) solito(a) ♦ *n* (*pej*) routine *f*, tran tran *m*; (*THEATRE*) numero

rove [rəuv] *vt* vagabondare per

row¹ [rəu] *n* (*line*) riga, fila; (*KNITTING*) ferro; (*behind one another*: *of cars, people*) fila; (*in boat*) remata ♦ *vi* (*in boat*) remare; (*as sport*) vogare ♦ *vt* (*boat*) manovrare a remi; **in a ~** (*fig*) di fila

row² [rau] *n* (*racket*) baccano, chiasso; (*dispute*) lite *f*; (*scolding*) sgridata ♦ *vi* (*argue*) litigare

rowboat [ˈrəubəut] (*US*) *n* barca a remi

rowdy [ˈraudɪ] *adj* chiassoso(a); turbolento(a) ♦ *n* teppista *m/f*

rowing [ˈrəuɪŋ] *n* canottaggio; **~ boat** (*BRIT*) *n* barca a remi

royal [ˈrɔɪəl] *adj* reale; **R~ Air Force** *n* aeronautica militare britannica

royalty [ˈrɔɪəltɪ] *n* (*royal persons*) (membri *mpl* della) famiglia reale; (*payment*: *to author*) diritti *mpl* d'autore

r.p.m. *abbr* (= *revolutions per minute*) giri/min

R.S.V.P. *abbr* (= *répondez s'il vous plaît*) R.S.V.P

Rt Hon. (*BRIT*) *abbr* (= *Right Honourable*) ≈ Onorevole

rub [rʌb] *n*: **to give sth a ~** strofinare qc; (*sore place*) massaggiare qc ♦ *vt* strofinare; massaggiare; (*hands*: *also*: **~ together**) sfregarsi; **to ~ sb up** (*BRIT*) *or* **~ sb the wrong way** (*US*) lisciare qn contro pelo; **~ off** *vi* andare via; **~ off on** *vt fus* lasciare una traccia su; **~ out** *vt* cancellare

rubber [ˈrʌbə*] *n* gomma; **~ band** *n* elastico; **~ plant** *n* ficus *m inv*;

~**y** adj gommoso(a)

rubbish ['rʌbɪʃ] n (from household) immondizie fpl, rifiuti mpl; (fig: pej) cose fpl senza valore; robaccia; sciocchezze fpl; ~ **bin** (BRIT) n pattumiera; ~ **dump** n (in town) immondezzaio

rubble ['rʌbl] n macerie fpl; (smaller) pietrisco

ruble ['ru:bl] (US) n = **rouble**

ruby ['ru:bɪ] n rubino

rucksack ['rʌksæk] n zaino

rudder ['rʌdə*] n timone m

ruddy ['rʌdɪ] adj (face) rubicondo(a); (inf: damned) maledetto(a)

rude [ru:d] adj (impolite: person) scortese, rozzo(a); (: word, manners) grossolano(a), rozzo(a); (shocking) indecente; ~**ness** n scortesia; grossolanità

rueful ['ru:ful] adj mesto(a), triste

ruffian ['rʌfɪən] n briccone m, furfante m

ruffle ['rʌfl] vt (hair) scompigliare; (clothes, water) increspare; (fig: person) turbare

rug [rʌg] n tappeto; (BRIT: for knees) coperta

rugby ['rʌgbɪ] n (also: ~ football) rugby m

rugged ['rʌgɪd] adj (landscape) aspro(a); (features, determination) duro(a); (character) brusco(a)

rugger ['rʌgə*] (BRIT: inf) n rugby m

ruin ['ru:ɪn] n rovina ♦ vt rovinare; ~**s** npl (of building, castle etc) rovine fpl, ruderi mpl; ~**ous** adj rovinoso(a); (expenditure) inverosimile

rule [ru:l] n regola; (regulation) regolamento, regola; (government) governo; (~r) riga ♦ vt (country) governare; (person) dominare ♦ vi regnare; decidere; (LAW) dichiarare; **as a** ~ normalmente; ~ **out** vt escludere; ~**d** adj (paper) vergato(a); ~**r** n (sovereign) sovrano/a; (for measuring) regolo, riga; **ruling** adj (party) al potere; (class) dirigente ♦ n (LAW) decisione f

rum [rʌm] n rum m

Rumania [ru:'meɪnɪə] n Romania

rumble ['rʌmbl] n rimbombo; brontolio ♦ vi rimbombare; (stomach, pipe) brontolare

rummage ['rʌmɪdʒ] vi frugare

rumour ['ru:mə*] (US **rumor**) n voce f ♦ vt: **it is** ~**ed that** corre voce che

rump [rʌmp] n groppa; ~ **steak** n bistecca di girello

rumpus ['rʌmpəs] (inf) n baccano; (quarrel) rissa

run [rʌn] (pt ran, pp run) n corsa; (outing) gita (in macchina), gita; (distance travelled) percorso, tragitto; (SKI) pista; (CRICKET, BASE-BALL) meta; (series) serie f; (THEATRE) periodo di rappresentazione; (in tights, stockings) smagliatura ♦ vt (distance) correre; (operate: business) gestire, dirigere; (: competition, course) organizzare; (: hotel) gestire; (: house) governare; (COMPUT) eseguire; (water, bath) far scorrere; (force through: rope, pipe): **to** ~ **sth through** far passare qc attraverso; (pass: hand, finger): **to** ~ **sth over** passare qc su; (PRESS: feature) presentare ♦ vi correre; (flee) scappare; (pass: road etc) passare; (work: machine, factory) funzionare, andare; (bus, train: operate) far servizio; (: travel) circolare; (continue: play, contract) durare; (slide: drawer; flow: river, bath) scorrere; (colours, washing) stemperarsi; (in election) presentarsi candidato; (nose) colare; **there was a** ~ **on** ... c'era una corsa a ...; **in the long** ~ a lungo andare; **on the** ~ in fuga; **to** ~ **a race** partecipare ad una gara; **I'll** ~ **you to** the station fa portare alla stazione; **to** ~ **a risk** correre un rischio; ~ **about** or **around** vi (children) correre qua e là; ~ **across** vt fus (find) trovare per caso; ~ **away** vi fuggire; ~ **down** vt (production) ridurre gradualmente; (factory) rallentare l'attività di; (AUT) investire; (criticize) criticare; to be ~ down (person: tired) essere esausto(a); ~ in (BRIT) vt (car) rodare, fare il rodaggio di; ~ into vt fus (meet: person) incontrare per caso; (: trouble) incontrare, trovare; (collide with) andare a sbattere contro; ~ off vi fuggire ♦ vt (water) far scolare; (copies) fare; ~ out vi (person) uscire di corsa; (liquid) colare; (lease) scadere; (money) esaurirsi; ~ out of vt fus rimanere a corto di; ~ over vt (AUT) investire, mettere sotto ♦ vt (revise) rivedere; ~ through (instructions) dare una scorsa a; (rehearse: play) riprovare, ripetere; ~ up vt (debt) lasciar accumulare; to ~ up against (difficulties) incontrare; ~away adj (person) fuggiasco(a); (horse) in libertà; (truck) fuori controllo

rung [rʌŋ] pp of **ring** ♦ n (of ladder) piolo

runner ['rʌnə*] n (in race) corridore m; (: horse) partente m/f; (on sledge) pattino; (for drawer etc) guida; ~-**bean** (BRIT) n fagiolo rampicante; ~-**up** n secondo(a) arrivato(a)

running ['rʌnɪŋ] n corsa; direzione f; organizzazione f; funzionamento ♦ adj (water) corrente; (commentary) simultaneo(a); to be in/out of the ~ for sth essere/non essere più in lizza per qc; 6 **days** ~ 6 giorni di seguito; ~ **costs** npl costi mpl d'esercizio; (of car) spese fpl di mantenimento

runny ['rʌnɪ] adj che cola

run-of-the-mill adj solito(a), banale

runt [rʌnt] n (also pej) omuncolo; (ZOOL) animale m più piccolo del normale

run-through n prova

run-up n: ~ to (election etc) periodo che precede

runway ['rʌnweɪ] n (AVIAT) pista (di decollo)

rupee [ruː'piː] n rupia

rupture ['rʌptʃə*] n (MED) ernia

rural ['ruərl] adj rurale

ruse [ruːz] n trucco

rush [rʌʃ] n corsa precipitosa; (hurry) furia, fretta; (sudden demand): ~ **for** corsa a; (current) flusso; (of emotion) impeto; (BOT) giunco ♦ vt mandare or spedire velocemente; (attack: town etc) prendere d'assalto ♦ vi precipitarsi; ~ **hour** n ora di punta

rusk [rʌsk] n biscotto

Russia ['rʌʃə] n Russia; ~**n** adj russo(a) ♦ n russo/a; (LING) russo

rust [rʌst] n ruggine f ♦ vi arrugginirsi

rustic ['rʌstɪk] adj rustico(a)

rustle ['rʌsl] vi frusciare ♦ vt (paper) far frusciare; (US: cattle) rubare

rustproof ['rʌstpruːf] adj inossidabile

rusty ['rʌstɪ] adj arrugginito(a)

rut [rʌt] n solco; (ZOOL) fregola; to get into a ~ (fig) adagiarsi troppo

ruthless ['ruːθlɪs] adj spietato(a)

rye [raɪ] n segale f; ~ **bread** n pane m di segale

S

Sabbath ['sæbəθ] n (Jewish) sabato; (Christian) domenica

sabotage ['sæbətɑːʒ] n sabotaggio ♦ vt sabotare

saccharin(e) ['sækərɪn] n saccarina

sachet ['sæʃeɪ] n bustina

sack [sæk] n (bag) sacco ♦ vt (dismiss) licenziare, mandare a spasso; (plunder) saccheggiare; to get the ~ essere mandato a spasso; ~**ing** n tela di sacco; (dismissal) licenziamento

sacrament ['sækrəmənt] n sacramento

sacred ['seɪkrɪd] adj sacro(a)

sacrifice ['sækrɪfaɪs] n sacrificio ♦ vt sacrificare

sad [sæd] adj triste

saddle ['sædl] n sella ♦ vt (horse)

sellare; **to be ~d with sth** (inf) avere qc sulle spalle; **~bag** n (on bicycle) borsa

sadistic [sə'dɪstɪk] adj sadico(a)

sadness ['sædnɪs] n tristezza

s.a.e. n abbr = **stamped addressed envelope**

safe [seɪf] adj sicuro(a); (out of danger) salvo(a), al sicuro; (cautious) prudente ♦ n cassaforte f; **~ from** al sicuro da; **~ and sound** sano(a) e salvo(a); **(just) to be on the ~ side** per non correre rischi; **~ conduct** n salvacondotto; **~ deposit** n (vault) caveau m inv; (box) cassetta di sicurezza; **~guard** n salvaguardia ♦ vt salvaguardare; **~keeping** n custodia; **~ly** adv sicuramente; sano(a) e salvo(a); prudentemente; **~ sex** n sesso sicuro

safety ['seɪftɪ] n sicurezza; **~ belt** n cintura di sicurezza; **~ pin** n spilla di sicurezza; **~ valve** n valvola di sicurezza

saffron ['sæfrən] n zafferano

sag [sæg] vi incurvarsi; afflosciarsi

sage [seɪdʒ] n (herb) salvia; (man) saggio

Sagittarius [sædʒɪ'tɛərɪəs] n Sagittario

Sahara [sə'hɑːrə] n: **the ~ (Desert)** il (deserto del) Sahara

said [sɛd] pt, pp of **say**

sail [seɪl] n (on boat) vela; (trip): **to go for a ~** fare un giro in barca a vela ♦ vt (boat) condurre, governare ♦ vi (travel: ship) navigare; (: passenger) viaggiare per mare; (set off) salpare; (sport) fare della vela; **they ~ed into Genoa** entrarono nel porto di Genova; **~ through** vt fus (fig) superare senza difficoltà; **~boat** (US) n barca a vela; **~ing** n (sport) vela; **to go ~ing** fare della vela; **~ing boat** n barca a vela; **~ing ship** n veliero; **~or** n marinaio

saint [seɪnt] n santo(a); **~ly** adj santo(a)

sake [seɪk] n: **for the ~ of** per, per amore di

salad ['sæləd] n insalata; **~ bowl** n insalatiera; **~ cream** (BRIT) n (tipo di) maionese f; **~ dressing** n condimento per insalata

salami [sə'lɑːmɪ] n salame m

salary ['sælərɪ] n stipendio

sale [seɪl] n vendita; (at reduced prices) svendita, liquidazione f; (auction) vendita all'asta; **"for ~"** "in vendita"; **on ~** in vendita; **on ~ or return** da vendere o rimandare; **~room** n sala delle aste; **~s assistant** (US ~s clerk) n commesso/a; **~sman/swoman** n commesso/a; (representative) rappresentante m/f

sallow ['sæləu] adj giallastro(a)

salmon ['sæmən] n inv salmone m

saloon [sə'luːn] n (US) saloon m inv, bar m inv; (BRIT: AUT) berlina; (ship's lounge) salone m

salt [sɔlt] n sale m ♦ vt salare; **~ cellar** n saliera; **~water** adj di mare; **~y** adj salato(a)

salute [sə'luːt] n saluto ♦ vt salutare

salvage ['sælvɪdʒ] n (saving) salvataggio; (things saved) beni mpl salvati or recuperati ♦ vt salvare, mettere in salvo

salvation [sæl'veɪʃən] n salvezza; **S~ Army** n Esercito della Salvezza

same [seɪm] adj stesso(a), medesimo(a) ♦ pron: **the ~** lo(la) stesso(a), gli(le) stessi(e); **the ~ book as** lo stesso libro di (o che); **at the ~ time** allo stesso tempo; **all or just the ~** tuttavia; **to do the ~ as sb** fare come qn; **qn: the ~ to you!** altrettanto a te!

sample ['sɑːmpl] n campione m ♦ vt (food) assaggiare; (wine) degustare

sanctimonious [sæŋktɪ'məunɪəs] adj bigotto(a), bacchettone/a

sanction ['sæŋkʃən] n sanzione f ♦ vt sancire, sanzionare

sanctity ['sæŋktɪtɪ] n santità

sanctuary ['sæŋktjuərɪ] n (holy place) santuario; (refuge) rifugio; (for wildlife) riserva

sand [sænd] n sabbia ♦ vt (also: ~ down) cartavetrare

sandal ['sændl] n sandalo
sandbox ['sændbɔks] (US) n = **sand-pit**
sandcastle ['sændkɑːsl] n castello di sabbia
sandpaper ['sændpeɪpə*] n carta vetrata
sandpit ['sændpɪt] n (for children) buca di sabbia
sandstone ['sændstəun] n arenaria
sandwich ['sændwɪtʃ] n tramezzino, panino, sandwich m inv ♦ vt: ~ed between incastrato(a) fra; cheese/ham ~ sandwich al formaggio/prosciutto; ~ **course** (BRIT) n corso di formazione professionale
sandy ['sændɪ] adj sabbioso(a); (colour) color sabbia inv, biondo(a) rossiccio(a)
sane [seɪn] adj (person) sano(a) di mente; (outlook) sensato(a)
sang [sæŋ] pt of **sing**
sanitary ['sænɪtərɪ] adj (system, arrangements) sanitario(a); (clean) igienico(a); ~ **towel** (US ~ **napkin**) n assorbente m (igienico)
sanitation [sænɪ'teɪʃən] n (in house) impianti mpl sanitari; (in town) fognature fpl; ~ **department** (US) n nettezza urbana
sanity ['sænɪtɪ] n sanità mentale; (common sense) buon senso
sank [sæŋk] pt of **sink**
Santa Claus [sæntə'klɔːz] n Babbo Natale
sap [sæp] n (of plants) linfa ♦ vt (strength) fiaccare
sapling ['sæplɪŋ] n alberello
sapphire ['sæfaɪə*] n zaffiro
sarcasm ['sɑːkæzm] n sarcasmo
sardine [sɑː'diːn] n sardina
Sardinia [sɑː'dɪnɪə] n Sardegna
sash [sæʃ] n fascia
sat [sæt] pt, pp of **sit**
Satan ['seɪtən] n Satana m
satchel ['sætʃl] n cartella
satellite ['sætəlaɪt] adj satellite ♦ n satellite m; ~ **dish** n antenna parabolica; ~ **television** n televisione f via satellite

satin ['sætɪn] n raso ♦ adj di raso
satire ['sætaɪə*] n satira
satisfaction [sætɪs'fækʃən] n soddisfazione f
satisfactory [sætɪs'fæktərɪ] adj soddisfacente
satisfy ['sætɪsfaɪ] vt soddisfare; (convince) convincere; ~**ing** adj soddisfacente
Saturday ['sætədɪ] n sabato
sauce [sɔːs] n salsa; (containing meat, fish) sugo; ~**pan** (n) casseruola
saucer ['sɔːsə*] n sottocoppa m, piattino
saucy ['sɔːsɪ] adj impertinente
Saudi ['saudɪ]: ~ **Arabia** n Arabia Saudita; ~ **(Arabian)** adj, n arabo(a) saudita
sauna ['sɔːnə] n sauna
saunter ['sɔːntə*] vi andare a zonzo, bighellonare
sausage ['sɔsɪdʒ] n salsiccia; ~ **roll** n rotolo di pasta sfoglia ripieno di salsiccia
sauté ['səuteɪ] adj: ~ **potatoes** patate fpl saltate in padella
savage ['sævɪdʒ] adj (cruel, fierce) selvaggio(a), feroce; (primitive) primitivo(a) ♦ n selvaggio/a ♦ vt attaccare selvaggiamente
save [seɪv] vt (person, belongings, COMPUT) salvare; (money) risparmiare, mettere da parte; (time) risparmiare; (food) conservare; (avoid: trouble) evitare; (SPORT) parare ♦ vi (also: ~ **up**) economizzare ♦ n (SPORT) parata ♦ prep salvo, a eccezione di
saving ['seɪvɪŋ] n risparmio ♦ adj: the ~ **grace** of l'unica cosa buona di; ~**s** npl (money) risparmi mpl; ~**s account** n libretto di risparmio; ~**s bank** n cassa di risparmio
saviour ['seɪvjə*] (US **savior**) n salvatore m
savour ['seɪvə*] (US **savor**) vt gustare; ~**y** adj (dish: not sweet) salato(a)
saw [sɔː] (pt **sawed**, pp **sawed** or **sawn**) pt of **see** ♦ n (tool) sega ♦ vt

segare; **~dust** n segatura; **~mill** n
segheria; **sawn** pp of saw; **~n-off**
shotgun n fucile m a canne mozze

saxophone ['sæksəfəʊn] n sassofono

say [seɪ] (pt, pp said) n: to have
one's ~ fare sentire il proprio parere; to have a or some ~ avere voce
in capitolo ♦ vt dire; **could you ~
that again?** potrebbe ripeterlo?;
that goes without ~ing va da sé;
~ing n proverbio, detto

scab [skæb] n crosta; (pej) crumiro/a

scaffold ['skæfəʊld] n (gallows) patibolo; **~ing** n impalcatura

scald [skɔːld] n scottatura ♦ vt scottare

scale [skeɪl] n scala; (of fish) squama
♦ vt (mountain) scalare; **~s** npl (for
weighing) bilancia; **on a large ~** su
vasta scala; **~ of charges** tariffa;
~ down vt ridurre (propor-
zionalmente)

scallop ['skɔləp] n (ZOOL) pettine
m; (SEWING) smerlo

scalp [skælp] n cuoio capelluto ♦ vt
scotennare

scalpel ['skælpl] n bisturi m inv

scamper ['skæmpə*] vi: to ~ away,
~ off darsela a gambe

scampi ['skæmpɪ] npl scampi mpl

scan [skæn] vt scrutare; (glance at
quickly) scorrere, dare un'occhiata
a; (TV) analizzare; (RADAR) esplorare ♦ n (MED) ecografia

scandal ['skændl] n scandalo; (gossip) pettegolezzi mpl

Scandinavia [skændɪ'neɪvɪə] n Scandinavia; **~n** adj, n scandinavo/a

scant [skænt] adj scarso/a; **~y** adj
insufficiente; (swimsuit) ridotto/a

scapegoat ['skeɪpɡəʊt] n capro
espiatorio

scar [skɑː] n cicatrice f ♦ vt sfregiare

scarce [skɛəs] adj scarso/a; (copy,
edition) raro/a; **to make o.s. ~**
(inf) squagliarsela; **~ly** adv appena;
scarcity n scarsità, mancanza

scare [skɛə*] n spavento; panico ♦ vt
spaventare, atterrire; **there was a
bomb ~ at the bank** hanno evacua-

to la banca per paura di un attentato
dinamitardo; **to ~ sb stiff** spaventare a morte qn; **~ off** or **away** vt
mettere in fuga; **~crow** n spaventa-
passeri m inv; **~d** adj: **to be ~d**
aver paura

scarf [skɑːf] (pl **scarves** or **~s**) n
(long) sciarpa; (square) fazzoletto da
testa, foulard m inv

scarlet ['skɑːlɪt] adj scarlatto/a; **~
fever** n scarlattina

scarves [skɑːvz] npl of **scarf**

scary ['skɛərɪ] adj che spaventa

scathing ['skeɪðɪŋ] adj aspro/a

scatter ['skætə*] vt spargere;
(crowd) disperdere ♦ vi disperdersi;
~brained adj sbadato/a

scavenger ['skævəndʒə*] n (person)
accattone/a

scenario [sɪ'nɑːrɪəʊ] n (THEATRE,
CINEMA) copione m; (fig) situazione
f

scene [siːn] n (THEATRE, fig etc)
scena; (of crime, accident) scena,
luogo; (sight, view) vista, veduta;
~ry n (THEATRE) scenario; (landscape) panorama m; **scenic** adj sce-
nico(a); panoramico(a)

scent [sɛnt] n profumo; (sense of
smell) olfatto, odorato; (fig: track)
pista

sceptical ['skɛptɪkəl] (US **skeptical**)
adj scettico/a

sceptre ['sɛptə*] (US **scepter**) n
scettro

schedule ['ʃɛdjuːl, (US) 'skɛdjuːl] n
programma m, piano; (of trains)
orario; (of prices etc) lista, tabella ♦
vt fissare; **on ~** in orario; **to be
ahead of/behind ~** essere in
anticipo/ritardo sul previsto; **~d
flight** n volo di linea

scheme [skiːm] n piano, progetto;
(method) sistema m; (dishonest plan,
plot) intrigo, trama; (arrangement)
disposizione f, sistemazione f; (pension ~ etc) programma m ♦ vi fare
progetti; (intrigue) complottare;
scheming adj intrigante ♦ n intri-
ghi mpl, macchinazioni fpl

schism ['skɪzəm] n scisma m

scholar ['skɔlə*] n erudito/a; (pupil) scolaro/a; **~ly** adj dotto(a), erudito(a); **~ship** n erudizione f; (grant) borsa di studio

school [sku:l] n (primary, secondary) scuola; (university: US) università f inv ♦ cpd scolare, scolastico(a) ♦ vt (animal) addestrare; **~ age** n età scolare; **~book** n libro scolastico; **~boy** n scolaro; **~children** npl scolari mpl; **~days** npl giorni mpl di scuola; **~girl** n scolara; **~ing** n istruzione f; **~master** n (primary) maestro; (secondary) insegnante m; **~mistress** n maestra; insegnante f; **~teacher** n insegnante m/f, docente m/f; (primary) maestro/a

sciatica [saɪ'ætɪkə] n sciatica

science ['saɪəns] n scienza; **~ fiction** n fantascienza; **scientific** [-'tɪfɪk] adj scientifico(a); **scientist** n scienziato/a

scissors ['sɪzəz] npl forbici fpl

scoff [skɔf] vt (BRIT: inf: eat) trangugiare, ingozzare ♦ vi: to ~ (at) (mock) farsi beffe (di)

scold [skəuld] vt rimproverare

scone [skɔn] n focaccina da tè

scoop [sku:p] n mestolo; (for ice cream) cucchiaio dosatore; (PRESS) colpo giornalistico, notizia (in esclusiva); **~ out** vt scavare; **~ up** vt tirare su, sollevare

scooter ['sku:tə*] n (motor cycle) motoretta, scooter m inv; (toy) monopattino

scope [skəup] n (capacity: of plan, undertaking) portata; (: of person) capacità fpl; (opportunity) possibilità fpl

scorch [skɔ:tʃ] vt (clothes) strinare, bruciacchiare; (earth, grass) seccare, bruciare

score [skɔ:*] n punti mpl, punteggio; (MUS) partitura, spartito; (twenty) venti ♦ vt (goal, point) segnare, fare; (success) ottenere ♦ vi segnare; (FOOTBALL) fare un goal; (keep score) segnare i punti; **~s of** (very

many) un sacco di; **on that ~** a questo riguardo; **to ~ 6 out of 10** prendere 6 su 10; **~ out** vt cancellare con un segno; **~board** n tabellone m segnapunti

scorn [skɔ:n] n disprezzo ♦ vt disprezzare

scornful ['skɔ:nful] adj sprezzante

Scorpio ['skɔ:pɪəu] n Scorpione m

scorpion ['skɔ:pɪən] n scorpione m

Scot [skɔt] n scozzese m/f

scotch [skɔtʃ] vt (rumour etc) soffocare; **S~** n whisky m scozzese, scotch m

scot-free adv: **to get off ~** farla franca

Scotland ['skɔtlənd] n Scozia

Scots [skɔts] adj scozzese; **~man/woman** n scozzese m/f

Scottish ['skɔtɪʃ] adj scozzese

scoundrel ['skaundrl] n farabutto/a; (child) furfantello/a

scour ['skauə*] vt (search) battere, perlustrare

scourge [skə:dʒ] n flagello

scout [skaut] n (MIL) esploratore m; (also: boy ~) giovane esploratore, scout m inv; **~ around** vi cercare in giro; **girl ~** (US) n giovane esploratrice f

scowl [skaul] vi acciglirsi, aggrottare le sopracciglia; **to ~** at guardare torvo

scrabble ['skræbl] vi (claw): **to ~ (at)** graffiare, grattare; (also: ~ around: search) cercare a tentoni ♦ n: **S~ ®** Scarabeo ®

scraggy ['skrægɪ] adj scarno(a), molto magro(a)

scram [skræm] (inf) vi filare via

scramble ['skræmbl] n arrampicata ♦ vi inerpicarsi; **to ~ out** etc uscire etc in fretta; **to ~ for** azzuffarsi per; **~d eggs** npl uova fpl strapazzate

scrap [skræp] n pezzo, pezzetto; (fight) zuffa; (also: ~ iron) rottami mpl di ferro, ferraglia ♦ vt demolire; (fig) scartare ♦ vi: **to ~ (with sb)** fare a botte (con qn); **~s** npl (waste scarti *mpl*; ~**book** *n* album *m inv* di ritagli; ~ **dealer** *n* commerciante *m* di ferraglia

scrape [skreɪp] *vt, vi* raschiare, grattare ♦ *n*: to get into a ~ cacciarsi in un guaio; ~ **through** *vi* farcela per un pelo; ~ **together** *vt (money)* raggranellare; ~**r** *n* raschietto

scrap: ~ **heap** *n*: on the ~ heap *(fig)* nel dimenticatoio; ~ **merchant** *(BRIT)* *n* commerciante *m* di ferraglia; ~ **paper** *n* cartaccia

scrappy [skræpɪ] *adj* frammentario(a), sconnesso(a)

scratch [skrætʃ] *n* graffio ♦ *cpd*: ~ **team** squadra raccogliticcia ♦ *vt* graffiare, rigare ♦ *vi* grattare; *(paint, car)* graffiare; **to start from** ~ cominciare *or* partire da zero; **to be up to** ~ essere all'altezza

scrawl [skrɔːl] *n* scarabocchio ♦ *vi* scarabocchiare

scrawny [skrɔːnɪ] *adj* scarno(a), pelle e ossa *inv*

scream [skriːm] *n* grido, urlo ♦ *vi* urlare, gridare

scree [skriː] *n* ghiaione *m*

screech [skriːtʃ] *vi* stridere

screen [skriːn] *n* schermo; *(fig)* muro, cortina, velo ♦ *vt* schermare, fare schermo a; *(from the wind etc)* riparare; *(film)* proiettare; *(book)* adattare per lo schermo; *(candidates etc)* selezionare; ~**ing** *n (MED)* dépistage *m inv*; ~**play** *n* sceneggiatura

screw [skruː] *n* vite ♦ *vt* avvitare; ~ **up** *vt (paper etc)* spiegazzare; *(inf: ruin)* rovinare; **to** ~ **up one's eyes** strizzare gli occhi; ~**driver** *n* cacciavite *m*

scribble [skrɪbl] *n* scarabocchio ♦ *vt* scribacchiare in fretta ♦ *vi* scarabocchiare

script [skrɪpt] *n (CINEMA etc)* copione *m*; *(in exam)* elaborato *or* compito d'esame

scripture(s) [skrɪptʃə(z)] *n(pl)* sacre Scritture *fpl*

scroll [skrəul] *n* rotolo di carta

scrounge [skraundʒ] *(inf)* *vt*: **to** ~ **sth (off** *or* **from sb)** scroccare qc (a qn) ♦ *n*: **on the** ~ a sbafo

scrub [skrʌb] *n (land)* boscaglia ♦ *vt* pulire strofinando; *(reject)* annullare

scruff [skrʌf] *n*: **by the** ~ **of the neck** per la collottola

scruffy [skrʌfɪ] *adj* sciatto(a)

scrum(mage) [skrʌm(ɪdʒ)] *n* mischia

scruple [skruːpl] *n* scrupolo

scrutiny [skruːtɪnɪ] *n* esame *m* accurato

scuff [skʌf] *vt (shoes)* consumare strascicando

scuffle [skʌfl] *n* baruffa, tafferuglio

sculptor [skʌlptə*] *n* scultore *m*

sculpture [skʌlptʃə*] *n* scultura

scum [skʌm] *n* schiuma; *(pej: people)* feccia

scupper [skʌpə*] *(BRIT: inf)* *vt* far naufragare

scurrilous [skʌrɪləs] *adj* scurrile, volgare

scurry [skʌrɪ] *vi* sgambare, affrettarsi; ~ **off** *vi* andarsene a tutta velocità

scuttle [skʌtl] *n (also: coal* ~*)* secchio del carbone ♦ *vt (ship)* autoaffondare ♦ *vi (scamper)*: **to** ~ **away, ~ off** darsela a gambe, scappare

scythe [saɪð] *n* falce *f*

SDP *(BRIT)* *n abbr* = Social Democratic Party

sea [siː] *n* mare *m* ♦ *cpd* marino(a), del mare; *(bird, fish)* di mare; *(route, transport)* marittimo(a); **by** ~ *(travel)* per mare; **on the** ~ *(boat)* in mare; *(town)* di mare; **to be all at** ~ *(fig)* non sapere che pesci pigliare; **out to** ~ al largo; **(out) at** ~ in mare; ~**board** *n* costa; ~**food** *n* frutti *mpl* di mare; ~ **front** *n* lungomare *m*; ~**gull** *n* gabbiano

seal [siːl] *n (animal)* foca; *(stamp)* sigillo; *(impression)* impronta del sigillo ♦ *vt* sigillare; ~ **off** *vt (close)* sigillare; *(forbid entry to)* bloccare l'accesso a

sea level *n* livello del mare

seam [siːm] *n* cucitura; (*of coal*) filone *m*

seaman ['siːmən] *n* marinaio

seamy ['siːmɪ] *adj* orribile

seance ['seɪɔns] *n* seduta spiritica

seaplane ['siːpleɪn] *n* idrovolante *m*

seaport ['siːpɔːt] *n* porto di mare

search [sɔːtʃ] *n* ricerca; (*LAW: at sb's home*) perquisizione *f* ♦ *vt* frugare ♦ *vi*: to ~ for ricercare; in ~ of alla ricerca di; ~ through *vt fus* frugare; ~ing *adj* minuzioso(a); penetrante; ~light *n* proiettore *m*; ~ party *n* squadra di soccorso; ~ warrant *n* mandato di perquisizione

seashore ['siːʃɔː*] *n* spiaggia

seasick ['siːsɪk] *adj* che soffre il mal di mare

seaside ['siːsaɪd] *n* spiaggia; ~ resort *n* stazione *f* balneare

season ['siːzn] *n* stagione *f* ♦ *vt* condire, insaporire; ~al *adj* stagionale; ~ed *adj* (*fig*) con esperienza; ~ing *n* condimento; ~ ticket *n* abbonamento

seat [siːt] *n* sedile *m*; (*in bus, train: place*) posto; (*PARLIAMENT*) seggio; (*buttocks*) didietro; (*of trousers*) fondo ♦ *vt* far sedere; (*have room for*) avere or essere fornito(a) di posti a sedere per; to be ~ed essere seduto(a); ~ belt *n* cintura di sicurezza

sea water *n* acqua di mare

seaweed ['siːwiːd] *n* alghe *fpl*

seaworthy ['siːwəːðɪ] *adj* atto(a) alla navigazione

sec. *abbr* = **second(s)**

secluded [sɪ'kluːdɪd] *adj* isolato(a), appartato(a)

seclusion [sɪ'kluːʒən] *n* isolamento

second[1] [sɪ'kɔnd] (*BRIT*) *vt* (*worker*) distaccare

second[2] ['sɛkənd] *num* secondo(a) ♦ *adj* (*in race etc*) al secondo posto ♦ *n* (*unit of time*) secondo; (*AUT: also: ~ gear*) seconda; (*COMM: imperfect*) scarto; (*BRIT: SCOL: degree*) laurea con punteggio discreto ♦ *vt* (*motion*) appoggiare; ~ary *adj*

secondario(a); ~ary school *n* scuola secondaria; ~-class *adj* di seconda classe ♦ *n* in seconda classe; ~er *n* sostenitore/trice; ~hand *adj* di seconda mano, usato(a); ~ hand *n* (*on clock*) lancetta dei secondi; ~ly *adv* in secondo luogo; ~rate *adj* scadente; ~ thoughts *npl* ripensamenti *mpl*; on ~ thoughts (*BRIT*) *or* thought (*US*) ripensandoci bene

secrecy ['siːkrəsɪ] *n* segretezza

secret ['siːkrɪt] *adj* segreto(a) ♦ *n* segreto; in ~ in segreto

secretarial [sɛkrɪ'tɛərɪəl] *adj* di segretario(a)

secretariat [sɛkrɪ'tɛərɪət] *n* segretariato

secretary ['sɛkrətərɪ] *n* segretario/a; S~ of State (for) (*BRIT: POL*) ministro (di)

secretive ['siːkrətɪv] *adj* riservato(a)

sect [sɛkt] *n* setta; ~arian [-'tɛərɪən] *adj* settario(a)

section ['sɛkʃən] *n* sezione *f*

sector ['sɛktə*] *n* settore *m*

secure [sɪ'kjuə*] *adj* sicuro(a); (*firmly fixed*) assicurato(a), ben fermato(a); (*in safe place*) al sicuro ♦ *vt* (*fix*) fissare, assicurare; (*get*) ottenere, assicurarsi

security [sɪ'kjuərɪtɪ] *n* sicurezza; (*for loan*) garanzia

sedan [sɪ'dæn] (*US*) *n* (*AUT*) berlina

sedate [sɪ'deɪt] *adj* posato(a); calmo(a) ♦ *vt* calmare

sedation [sɪ'deɪʃən] *n* (*MED*) effetto dei sedativi

sedative ['sɛdɪtɪv] *n* sedativo, calmante *m*

seduce [sɪ'djuːs] *vt* sedurre; **seduction** [-'dʌkʃən] *n* seduzione *f*; **seductive** [-'dʌktɪv] *adj* seducente

see [siː] (*pt* **saw**, *pp* **seen**) *vt* vedere; (*accompany*): to ~ sb to the door accompagnare qn alla porta ♦ *vi* vedere; (*understand*) capire ♦ *n* sede *f* vescovile; to ~ that (*ensure*) badare che + *sub*, fare in modo che + *sub*; ~ you soon! a presto!; ~ about *vt* *fus* occuparsi di; ~ **off** *vt* salutare alla partenza; ~ **through** *vt* portare a termine ♦ *vt fus* non lasciarsi ingannare da; ~ **to** *vt fus* occuparsi di

seed [siːd] *n* seme *m*; (*fig*) germe *m*; (*TENNIS*) testa di serie; **to go to** ~ fare seme; (*fig*) scadere; ~**ling** *n* piantina di semenzaio; ~**y** *adj* (*shabby: person*) sciatto(a); (: *place*) cadente

seeing ['siːɪŋ] *conj*: ~ (**that**) visto che

seek [siːk], (*pt, pp* **sought**) *vt* cercare

seem [siːm] *vi* sembrare, parere; **there ~s to be ...** sembra che ci sia ...; ~**ingly** *adv* apparentemente

seen [siːn] *pp* di **see**

seep [siːp] *vi* filtrare, trapelare

seesaw ['siːsɔː] *n* altalena a bilico

seethe [siːð] *vi* ribollire; **to ~ with** **anger** fremere di rabbia

see-through *adj* trasparente

segregate ['sɛɡrɪɡeɪt] *vt* segregare, isolare

seize [siːz] *vt* (*grasp*) afferrare; (*take possession of*) impadronirsi di; (*LAW*) sequestrare; ~ (**up**) *on vt fus* ricorrere a; ~ **up** *vi* (*TECH*) grippare

seizure ['siːʒə*] *n* (*MED*) attacco; (*LAW*) confisca, sequestro

seldom ['sɛldəm] *adv* raramente

select [sɪ'lɛkt] *adj* scelto(a) ♦ *vt* scegliere, selezionare; ~**ion** [-'lɛkʃən] *n* selezione *f*, scelta

self [sɛlf] *n*: **the** ~ l'io *m* ♦ *prefix* auto...; ~**-assured** *adj* sicuro(a) di sé; ~**-catering** (*BRIT*) *adj* in cui ci si cucina da sé; ~**-centred** (*US* ~**-centered**) *adj* egocentrico(a); ~**-confidence** *n* sicurezza di sé; ~**-conscious** *adj* timido(a); ~**-contained** (*BRIT*) *adj* (*flat*) indipendente; ~**-control** *n* autocontrollo; ~**-defence** (*US* ~**-defense**) *n* autodifesa; (*LAW*) legittima difesa; ~**-discipline** *n* autodisciplina; ~**-employed** *adj* che lavora in proprio; ~**-evident** *adj* evidente; ~

governing *adj* autonomo(a); ~**-indulgent** *adj* indulgente verso se stesso(a); ~**-interest** *n* interesse *m* personale; ~**-ish** *adj* egoista; ~**-ishness** *n* egoismo; ~**-less** *adj* dimentico(a) di sé, altruista; ~**-pity** *n* autocommiserazione *f*; ~**-portrait** *n* autoritratto; ~**-possessed** *adj* controllato(a); ~**-preservation** *n* istinto di conservazione; ~**-respect** *n* rispetto di sé, amor proprio; ~**-righteous** *adj* soddisfatto(a) di sé; ~**-sacrifice** *n* abnegazione *f*; ~**-satisfied** *adj* compiaciuto(a) di sé; ~**-service** *n* autoservizio, self-service *m*; ~**-sufficient** *adj* autosufficiente; ~**-taught** *adj* autodidatta

sell [sɛl] (*pt, pp* **sold**) *vt* vendere ♦ *vi* vendersi; **to** ~ **at** *or* **for 1000 lire** essere in vendita a 1000 lire; ~ **off** *vt* svendere, liquidare; ~ **out** *vi*: **to** ~ **out** (**of** sth) esaurire (qc); **the** **tickets are all sold out** i biglietti sono esauriti; ~**-by date** *n* data di scadenza; ~**er** *n* venditore/trice; ~**ing price** *n* prezzo di vendita

sellotape ['sɛləʊteɪp] ® (*BRIT*) *n* nastro adesivo, scotch *m* ®

selves [sɛlvz] *npl* di **self**

semaphore ['sɛməfɔː*] *n* segnalazioni *fpl* con bandierine; (*RAIL*) semaforo (ferroviario)

semblance ['sɛmbləns] *n* parvenza, apparenza

semen ['siːmən] *n* sperma *m*

semester [sɪ'mɛstə*] (*US*) *n* semestre *m*

semi... *prefix* semi...; ~**circle** *n* semicerchio; ~**colon** *n* punto e virgola; ~**detached (house)** (*BRIT*) *n* casa gemella; ~**final** *n* semifinale *f*

seminar ['sɛmɪnɑː*] *n* seminario

seminary ['sɛmɪnəri] *n* (*REL*) seminario

semiskilled ['sɛmɪ'skɪld] *adj* (*worker*) parzialmente qualificato(a); (*work*) che richiede una qualificazione parziale

senate ['sɛnɪt] *n* senato; **senator** *n*

senatore/trice

send [scnd] (pt, pp **sent**) vt mandare; ~ **away** vt (letter, goods) spedire; ~ (person) mandare via; ~ **away for** vt fus richiedere per posta, farsi spedire; ~ **back** vt rimandare; ~ **for** vt fus mandare a chiamare, far venire; ~ **off** vt (goods) spedire; (BRIT: SPORT: player) espellere; ~ **out** vt (invitation) diramare; ~ **up** vt (person, price) far salire; (BRIT: parody) mettere in ridicolo; ~**er** n mittente m/f; ~**off** n: to give sb a good ~**off** festeggiare la partenza di qn

senior ['si:nɪə*] adj (older) più vecchio(a); (of higher rank) di grado più elevato; ~ **citizen** n persona anziana; ~**ity** [-'ɒrɪtɪ] n anzianità

sensation [scn'seɪʃən] n sensazione f; ~**al** adj sensazionale; (marvellous) eccezionale

sense [scns] n senso; (feeling) sensazione f, senso; (meaning) senso, significato; (wisdom) buonsenso ♦ vt sentire, percepire; it **makes** ~ ha senso; ~**less** adj sciocco(a); (unconscious) privo(a) di sensi

sensible ['scnsɪbl] adj sensato(a), ragionevole

sensitive ['scnsɪtɪv] adj sensibile; (skin, question) delicato(a)

sensual ['scnsjuəl] adj sensuale

sensuous ['scnsjuəs] adj sensuale

sent [scnt] pt, pp of **send**

sentence ['scntns] n (LING) frase f; (LAW: judgment) sentenza; (: punishment) condanna ♦ vt: to ~ sb to death/to 5 years condannare qn a morte/a 5 anni

sentiment ['scntɪmənt] n sentimento; (opinion) opinione f; ~**al** [-'mcntl] adj sentimentale

sentry ['scntrɪ] n sentinella

separate [adj 'scprɪt, vb 'scpəreɪt] adj separato(a) ♦ vt separare ♦ vi separarsi; ~**ly** adv separatamente; ~**s** npl (clothes) coordinati mpl;

separation [-'reɪʃən] n separazione f

September [scp'tcmbə*] n settem-

bre m

septic ['scptɪk] adj settico(a); (wound) infettato(a); ~ **tank** n fossa settica

sequel ['si:kwl] n conseguenza; (of story) seguito f; (of film) sequenza

sequence ['si:kwəns] n (series) serie f; (order) ordine m

sequin ['si:kwɪn] n lustrino, paillette f inv

serene [sə'ri:n] adj sereno(a), calmo(a)

sergeant ['sɑ:dʒənt] n sergente m; (POLICE) brigadiere m

serial ['sɪərɪəl] n (PRESS) romanzo a puntate, serial m inv; (RADIO, TV) trasmissione f a puntate, serial m inv; ~**ize** vt pubblicare (or trasmettere) a puntate; ~ **number** n numero di serie

series ['sɪərɪz] n inv serie f inv; (PUBLISHING) collana

serious ['sɪərɪəs] adj serio(a), grave; ~**ly** adv seriamente

sermon ['sə:mən] n sermone m

serrated [sə'reɪtɪd] adj seghettato(a)

serum ['sɪərəm] n siero

servant ['sə:vənt] n domestico/a

serve [sə:v] vt (employer etc) servire, essere a servizio di; (purpose) servire a; (customer, food, meal) servire; (apprenticeship) fare; (prison term) scontare ♦ vi (also TENNIS) servire; (be useful): to ~ as/for/to do servire da/per/per fare ♦ n (TENNIS) servizio; it ~s him right ben gli sta, se l'è meritata; ~ **out** vt (food) servire; ~ **up** vt = ~ **out**

service ['sə:vɪs] n servizio; (AUT: maintenance) assistenza, revisione f ♦ vt (car, washing machine) revisionare; the S~s le forze armate; to be of ~ to sb essere d'aiuto a qn; ~**able** adj pratico(a), utile; ~ **charge** (BRIT) n servizio; ~**man** n militare m; ~ **station** n stazione f di servizio

serviette [sə:vɪ'ct] (BRIT) n tovagliolo

session ['scʃən] n (sitting) seduta, sessione f; (SCOL) anno scolastico

(or accademico)

set [sɛt] *(pt, pp* set) *n* serie *f inv; (of cutlery etc)* servizio; *(RADIO, TV)* apparecchio; *(TENNIS)* set *m inv; (group of people)* mondo, ambiente *m; (CINEMA)* scenario; *(THEATRE: stage)* scene *fpl; (: scenery)* scenario; *(MATH)* insieme *m; (HAIRDRESSING)* messa in piega ♦ *adj (fixed)* stabilito(a), determinato(a); *(ready)* pronto(a) ♦ *vt (place)* posare, mettere; *(arrange)* sistemare; *(fix)* fissare; *(adjust)* regolare; *(decide: rules etc)* stabilire, fissare ♦ *vi (sun)* tramontare; *(jam, jelly)* rapprendersi; *(concrete)* fare presa; to be ~ on doing essere deciso a fare; to ~ to music mettere in musica; to ~ on fire dare fuoco a; to ~ free liberare; to ~ sth going mettere in moto qc; to ~ sail prendere il mare; ~ about *vt fus (task)* intraprendere, mettersi a; ~ aside *vt* mettere da parte; ~ back *vt (in time)*: to ~ back (by) mettere indietro (di); *(inf: cost)*: it ~ me back £5 mi è costato la bellezza di 5 sterline; ~ off *vi* partire ♦ *vt (bomb)* far scoppiare; *(cause to start)* mettere in moto; *(show up well)* dare risalto a; ~ out *vi* partire ♦ *vt (arrange)* disporre; *(state)* esporre, presentare; to ~ out to do proporsi di fare; ~ up *vt (organization)* fondare, costituire; ~**back** *n* contrattempo, inconveniente *m*; ~ **menu** *n* menù *m inv* fisso

settee [sɛ'tiː] *n* divano, sofà *m inv*

setting ['sɛtɪŋ] *n (background)* ambiente *m; (of controls)* posizione *f; (of sun)* tramonto; *(of jewel)* montatura

settle ['sɛtl] *vt (argument, matter)* appianare; *(accounts)* regolare; *(MED: calm)* calmare ♦ *vi (bird, dust etc)* posarsi; *(sediment)* depositarsi; *(also: ~ down)* sistemarsi, stabilirsi; calmarsi; to ~ for sth accontentarsi di qc; to ~ on sth decidersi per qc; ~ in *vi* sistemarsi;

up *vi*: to ~ up with sb regolare i conti con qn; ~**ment** *n (payment)* pagamento, saldo; *(agreement)* accordo; *(colony)* colonia; *(village etc)* villaggio, comunità *f inv*; ~**r** *n* colonizzatore/trice

setup ['sɛtʌp] *n (arrangement)* sistemazione *f; (situation)* situazione *f*

seven ['sɛvn] *num* sette; ~**teen** *num* diciassette; ~**th** *num* settimo(a); ~**ty** *num* settanta

sever ['sɛvə*] *vt* recidere, tagliare; *(relations)* troncare

several ['sɛvərəl] *adj, pron* alcuni(e), diversi(e); ~ of us alcuni di noi

severance ['sɛvərəns] *n (of relations)* rottura; ~ **pay** *n* indennità di licenziamento

severe [sɪ'vɪə*] *adj* severo(a); *(serious)* serio(a), grave; *(hard)* duro(a); *(plain)* semplice, sobrio(a)

severity [sɪ'vɛrɪtɪ] *n* severità; gravità; *(of weather)* rigore *m*

sew [səu] *(pt* sewed, *pp* sewn) *vt, vi* cucire; ~ **up** *vt* ricucire

sewage ['suːɪdʒ] *n* acque *fpl* di scolo

sewer ['suːə*] *n* fogna

sewing ['səuɪŋ] *n* cucitura; cucito; ~ **machine** *n* macchina da cucire

sewn [səun] *pp of* sew

sex [sɛks] *n* sesso; to have ~ with avere rapporti sessuali con; ~**ist** *adj, n* sessista *m/f*

sexual ['sɛksjuəl] *adj* sessuale

sexy ['sɛksɪ] *adj* provocante, sexy *inv*

shabby ['ʃæbɪ] *adj* malandato(a); *(behaviour)* vergognoso(a)

shack [ʃæk] *n* baracca, capanna

shackles ['ʃæklz] *npl* ferri *mpl*, catene *fpl*

shade [ʃeɪd] *n* ombra; *(for lamp)* paralume *m; (of colour)* tonalità *f inv; (small quantity)*: a ~ **(more/too large)** un po' (di più/troppo grande) ♦ *vt* ombreggiare, fare ombra a; in the ~ all'ombra

shadow ['ʃædəu] *n* ombra ♦ *vt (follow)* pedinare; ~ **cabinet** *n (BRIT)* *n (POL)* governo *m* ombra *inv*; ~**y** *adj* ombreggiato(a), ombroso(a) *(dim)* vago(a), indistinto(a)

shady ['ʃeɪdɪ] adj ombroso(a); (fig: dishonest) losco(a), equivoco(a)

shaft [ʃɑːft] n (of arrow, spear) asta; (AUT, TECH) albero m; (of mine) pozzo; (of lift) tromba; (of light) raggio

shaggy ['ʃægɪ] adj ispido(a)

shake [ʃeɪk] (pt shook, pp shaken) vt scuotere; (bottle, cocktail) agitare ♦ vi tremare; to ~ one's head (in refusal, dismay) scuotere la testa; to ~ hands with sb stringere or dare la mano a qn; ~ off vt scrollare (via); (fig) sbarazzarsi di; ~ up vt scuotere; **shaken** pp of **shake**; **shaky** adj (hand, voice) tremante; (building) traballante

shall [ʃæl] aux vb: I ~ go andrò; ~ I open the door? apro io la porta?; I'll get some, ~ I? ne prendo un po', va bene?

shallow ['ʃæləʊ] adj poco profondo(a); (fig) superficiale

sham [ʃæm] n finzione f, messinscena; (jewellery, furniture) imitazione f

shambles ['ʃæmblz] n confusione f, baraonda, scompiglio

shame [ʃeɪm] n vergogna ♦ vt far vergognare; it is a ~ (that/to do) è un peccato (che + sub/fare); what a ~! che peccato!; ~faced adj vergognoso(a); ~ful adj vergognoso(a); ~less adj sfrontato(a); (immodest) spudorato/a

shampoo [ʃæm'puː] n shampoo m inv ♦ vt fare lo shampoo a; ~ and set n shampoo e messa in piega

shamrock ['ʃæmrɒk] n trifoglio (simbolo nazionale dell'Irlanda)

shandy ['ʃændɪ] n birra con gassosa

shan't [ʃɑːnt] = **shall not**

shanty town ['ʃæntɪ-] n bidonville f inv

shape [ʃeɪp] n forma ♦ vt formare; (statement) formulare; (sb's ideas) condizionare; to take ~ prendere forma; ~ up vi (events) andare, mettersi; (person) cavarsela; ~-shaped suffix: heart-shaped a for-

ma di cuore; ~less adj senza forma, informe; ~ly adj ben proporzionato(a)

share [ʃɛə*] n (thing received, contribution) parte f; (COMM) azione f ♦ vt dividere; (have in common) condividere, avere in comune; ~ out vi dividere; ~holder n azionista m/f

shark [ʃɑːk] n squalo, pescecane m

sharp [ʃɑːp] adj (razor, knife) affilato(a); (point) acuto(a), acuminato(a); (nose, chin) aguzzo(a); (outline, contrast) netto(a); (cold, pain) pungente; (voice) stridulo(a); (person: quick-witted) sveglio(a); (: unscrupulous) disonesto(a); (MUS): C ~ do diesis ♦ n (MUS) diesis m inv ♦ adv: at 2 o'clock ~ alle due in punto; ~en vt affilare; (pencil) fare la punta a; (fig) acuire; ~ener n (also: pencil ~ener) temperamatite m inv; ~eyed adj dalla vista acuta; ~ly adv (turn, stop) bruscamente; (stand out, contrast) nettamente; (criticize, retort) duramente, aspramente

shatter ['ʃætə*] vt mandare in frantumi, frantumare; (fig: upset) distruggere; (: ruin) rovinare ♦ vi frantumarsi, andare in pezzi

shave [ʃeɪv] vt radere, rasare ♦ vi radersi, farsi la barba ♦ n: to have a ~ farsi la barba; ~r n (also: electric ~r) rasoio elettrico

shaving ['ʃeɪvɪŋ] n (action) rasatura; ~s npl (of wood etc) trucioli mpl; ~ brush n pennello da barba; ~ cream n crema da barba; ~ foam n = ~ cream

shawl [ʃɔːl] n scialle m

she [ʃiː] pron ella, lei; ~-cat n gatta; ~-elephant n elefantessa

sheaf [ʃiːf] (pl **sheaves**) n covone m; (of papers) fascio

shear [ʃɪə*] (pt ~ed, pp ~ed or shorn) vt (sheep) tosare; ~ off vi spezzarsi; ~s npl (for hedge) cesoie fpl

sheath [ʃiːθ] n fodero, guaina; (contraceptive) preservativo

sheaves   237   shock

sheaves [ʃiːvz] *npl of* **sheaf**

shed [ʃɛd] (*pt, pp* **shed**) *n* capannone *m* ♦ *vt* (*leaves, fur etc*) perdere; (*tears, blood*) versare; (*workers*) liberarsi di

she'd [ʃiːd] = **she had; she would**

sheen [ʃiːn] *n* lucentezza

sheep [ʃiːp] *n inv* pecora; **~dog** *n* cane *m* da pastore; **~ish** *adj* vergognoso(a), timido(a); **~skin** *n* pelle *f* di pecora

sheer [ʃɪə*] *adj* (*utter*) vero(a) e proprio(a)); (*steep*) a picco, perpendicolare; (*almost transparent*) sottile ♦ *adv* a picco

sheet [ʃiːt] *n* (*on bed*) lenzuolo *f*; (*of paper*) foglio; (*of glass, ice*) lastra; (*of metal*) foglio, lamina; **~ lightning** *n* lampo diffuso

sheik(h) [ʃeɪk] *n* sceicco

shelf [ʃɛlf] (*pl* **shelves**) *n* scaffale *m*, mensola

shell [ʃɛl] *n* (*on beach*) conchiglia; (*of egg, nut etc*) guscio; (*explosive*) granata; (*of building*) scheletro ♦ *vt* (*peas*) sgranare; (*MIL*) bombardare; **~ suit** *n* (*lightweight*) tuta di acetato; (*heavier*) tuta di trilobato

she'll [ʃiːl] = **she will; she shall**

shellfish [ʃɛlfɪʃ] *n inv* (*crab etc*) crostaceo; (*scallop etc*) mollusco; (*pl: as food*) crostacei, molluschi

shelter [ʃɛltə*] *n* riparo, rifugio ♦ *vt* riparare, proteggere; (*give lodging to*) dare rifugio o asilo a ♦ *vi* ripararsi, mettersi al riparo; **~ed** *adj* riparato(a); **~ed housing** (*BRIT*) *n* alloggi dotati di strutture per anziani o handicappati

shelve [ʃɛlv] *vt* (*fig*) accantonare, rimandare; **~s** *npl of* **shelf**

shepherd [ʃɛpəd] *n* pastore *m* ♦ *vt* (*guide*) guidare; **~'s pie** (*BRIT*) *n* timballo di carne macinata e purè di patate

sheriff [ʃɛrɪf] (*US*) *n* sceriffo

sherry [ʃɛrɪ] *n* sherry *m inv*

she's [ʃiːz] = **she is; she has**

Shetland [ʃɛtlənd] *n* (*also: the ~s, the ~ Isles*) le isole Shetland, le

Shetland

shield [ʃiːld] *n* scudo; (*trophy*) scudetto; (*protection*) schermo ♦ *vt*: **to ~ (from)** riparare (da), proteggere (da *or* contro)

shift [ʃɪft] *n* (*change*) cambiamento; (*of workers*) turno ♦ *vt* spostare, muovere; (*remove*) rimuovere ♦ *vi* spostarsi, muoversi; **~less** *adj*: **a ~less person** un(a) fannullone(a); **~ work** *n* lavoro a squadre; **~y** *adj* ambiguo(a); (*eyes*) sfuggente

shilling [ʃɪlɪŋ] (*BRIT*) *n* scellino (= 12 old pence; 20 in a pound)

shilly-shally [ʃɪlɪʃælɪ] *vi* tentennare, esitare

shimmer [ʃɪmə*] *vi* brillare, luccicare

shin [ʃɪn] *n* tibia

shine [ʃaɪn] (*pt, pp* **shone**) *n* splendore *m*, lucentezza ♦ *vi* (ri)splendere, brillare ♦ *vt* far brillare, far risplendere; (*torch*): **to ~ sth on** puntare qc verso

shingle [ʃɪŋgl] *n* (*on beach*) ciottoli *mpl*; **~s** *n* (*MED*) herpes zoster *m*

shiny [ʃaɪnɪ] *adj* lucente, lucido(a)

ship [ʃɪp] *n* nave *f* ♦ *vt* trasportare (via mare); (*send*) spedire (via mare); **~building** *n* costruzione *f* navale; **~ment** *n* carico; **~ping** *n* (*ships*) naviglio; (*traffic*) navigazione *f*; **~shape** *adj* in perfetto ordine; **~wreck** *n* relitto; (*event*) naufragio ♦ *vt*: **to be ~wrecked** naufragare, fare naufragio; **~yard** *n* cantiere *m* navale

shire [ʃaɪə*] (*BRIT*) *n* contea

shirk [ʃəːk] *vt* sottrarsi a, evitare

shirt [ʃəːt] *n* camicia; **in ~ sleeves** in maniche di camicia

shit [ʃɪt] (*inf!*) *excl* merda (!)

shiver [ʃɪvə*] *n* brivido ♦ *vi* rabbrividire, tremare

shoal [ʃəul] *n* (*of fish*) banco; (*fig*) massa

shock [ʃɔk] *n* (*impact*) urto, colpo; (*ELEC*) scossa; (*emotional*) colpo, shock *m inv*; (*MED*) shock ♦ *vt* colpire, scioccare; scandalizzare;

absorber n ammortizzatore m; ~**ing** adj scioccante, traumatizzante; scandaloso(a)

shod [ʃɔd] pt, pp of **shoe**

shoddy [ˈʃɔdɪ] adj scadente

shoe [ʃuː] (pt, pp **shod**) n scarpa; (also: horse~) ferro di cavallo ♦ vt (horse) ferrare; ~**brush** n spazzola per scarpe; ~**lace** n stringa; ~**polish** n lucido per scarpe; ~**shop** n calzoleria; ~**string** n (fig): on a ~**string** con quattro soldi

shone [ʃɔn] pt, pp of **shine**

shoo [ʃuː] excl sciò!, via!

shook [ʃuk] pt of **shake**

shoot [ʃuːt] (pt, pp **shot**) n (on branch, seedling) germoglio ♦ vt (game) cacciare, andare a caccia di; (person) sparare a; (execute) fucilare; (film) girare ♦ vi (with gun): to ~ (at) sparare (su), fare fuoco (su); (with bow): to ~ (at) tirare (su); (FOOTBALL) sparare, tirare (forte); ~ **down** vt (plane) abbattere; ~ **in/out** vi entrare/uscire come una freccia; ~ **up** vi (fig) salire alle stelle; ~**ing** n (shots) sparatoria; (HUNTING) caccia; ~**ing star** n stella cadente

shop [ʃɔp] n negozio; (workshop) officina ♦ vi (also: go ~ping) fare spese; ~ **assistant** (BRIT) n commesso/a; ~ **floor** n officina; (BRIT: fig) operai mpl, maestranze fpl; ~**keeper** n negoziante m/f, bottegaio/a; ~**lifting** n taccheggio; ~**per** n compratore/trice; ~**ping** n (goods) spesa, acquisti mpl; ~**ping bag** n borsa per la spesa; ~**ping centre** (US ~ping center) n centro commerciale; ~**soiled** adj sciupato(a) a forza di stare in vetrina; ~ **steward** (BRIT) n (INDUSTRY) rappresentante m sindacale; ~ **window** n vetrina

shore [ʃɔː*] n (of sea) riva, spiaggia; (of lake) riva ♦ vt: to ~ (up) puntellare; **on** ~ a riva

shorn [ʃɔːn] pp of **shear**

short [ʃɔːt] adj (not long) corto(a);

(soon finished) breve; (person) basso(a); (curt) brusco(a), secco(a); (insufficient) insufficiente ♦ n (also: ~ film) cortometraggio; (a pair of) ~**s** (i) calzoncini; **to be ~ of sth** essere a corto di or mancare di qc; **in** ~ in breve; ~ **of doing** a meno che non si faccia; **everything ~ of** tutto fuorché; **it is ~ for** è l'abbreviazione or il diminutivo di; **to cut** ~ (speech, visit) accorciare, abbreviare; **to fall** ~ **of** venir meno a; **non** soddisfare; **to run** ~ **of** rimanere senza; **to stop** ~ fermarsi di colpo; **to stop** ~ **of** non arrivare fino a; ~**age** n scarsezza, carenza; ~**bread** n biscotto di pasta frolla; ~**change** vt: to ~**change** sb imbrogliare qn sul resto; ~**circuit** n cortocircuito; ~**coming** n difetto; ~**(crust) pastry** (BRIT) n pasta frolla; ~**cut** n scorciatoia; ~**en** vt accorciare, ridurre; ~**fall** n deficit m; ~**hand** (BRIT) n stenografia; ~**hand typist** (BRIT) n stenodattilografo/a; ~**list** (BRIT) n (for job) rosa dei candidati; ~**lived** adj di breve durata; ~**ly** adv fra poco; ~**sighted** (BRIT) adj miope; ~**staffed** adj a corto di personale; ~**story** n racconto, novella; ~**tempered** adj irascibile; ~**term** adj (effect) di or a breve durata; (borrowing) a breve scadenza; ~**wave** n (RADIO) onde fpl corte

shot [ʃɔt] pt, pp of **shoot** ♦ n sparo, colpo; (try) prova; (FOOTBALL) tiro; (injection) iniezione f; (PHOT) foto f inv; **like a** ~ come un razzo; (very readily) immediatamente; ~**gun** n fucile m da caccia

should [ʃud] aux vb: **I** ~ **go now** dovrei andare ora; **he** ~ **be there now** dovrebbe essere arrivato ora; **I** ~ **go if I were you** se fossi in te andrei; **I** ~ **like to** mi piacerebbe

shoulder [ˈʃəuldə*] n spalla; (BRIT: of road): **hard** ~ banchina ♦ vt (fig) addossarsi, prendere sulle proprie spalle; ~ **bag** n borsa a tracolla; ~

blade n scapola; ~ **strap** n bretella, spallina

shouldn't [ʃudnt] = **should not**

shout [ʃaut] n urlo, grido ♦ vt gridare ♦ vi (also: ~ **out**) urlare, gridare; ~ **down** vt zittire gridando; ~**ing** n urli mpl

shove [ʃʌv] vt spingere; (inf: put): **to ~ sth in** ficcare qc in; ~ **off** (inf) vi sloggiare, smammare

shovel [ˈʃʌvl] n pala ♦ vt spalare

show [ʃəu] (pt ~**ed**, pp **shown**) n (of emotion) dimostrazione f, manifestazione f; (semblance) apparenza; (exhibition) mostra, esposizione f; (THEATRE, CINEMA) spettacolo ♦ vt far vedere, mostrare; (courage etc) dimostrare, dar prova di; (exhibit) esporre ♦ vi vedersi, essere visibile; **for ~** per fare scena; **on ~** (exhibits etc) esposto(a); ~ **in** vt (person) far entrare; ~ **off** vi (pej) esibirsi, mettersi in mostra ♦ vt (display) mettere in risalto; ~ **out** vt (person) accompagnare alla porta; ~ **up** vi (stand out) essere ben visibile; (inf: turn up) farsi vedere ♦ vt mettere in risalto; ~ **business** n industria dello spettacolo; ~**down** n prova di forza

shower [ˈʃauə*] n (rain) acquazzone m; (of stones etc) pioggia; (also: ~**bath**) doccia ♦ vi fare la doccia ♦ vt: **to ~ sb with** (gifts, abuse etc) coprire qn di; (missiles) lanciare contro qn una pioggia di; **to have a ~** fare la doccia; ~**proof** adj impermeabile

showing [ˈʃəuiŋ] n (of film) proiezione f

show jumping n concorso ippico (di salto ad ostacoli)

shown [ʃəun] pp of **show**

show-off (inf) n (person) esibizionista m/f

showpiece [ˈʃəupi:s] n pezzo forte

showroom [ˈʃəurum] n sala d'esposizione

shrank [ʃræŋk] pt of **shrink**

shrapnel [ˈʃræpnl] n shrapnel m

shred [ʃred] n (gen pl) brandello ♦ vt fare a brandelli; (CULIN) sminuzzare, tagliuzzare; ~**der** n (vegetable ~der) grattugia; (document ~der) distruttore m di documenti

shrewd [ʃru:d] adj astuto(a), scaltro(a)

shriek [ʃri:k] n strillo ♦ vi strillare

shrill [ʃril] adj acuto(a), stridulo(a), stridente

shrimp [ʃrimp] n gamberetto

shrine [ʃrain] n reliquario; (place) santuario

shrink [ʃriŋk] (pt **shrank**, pp **shrunk**) vi restringersi; (fig) ridursi; (also: ~ **away**) ritrarsi ♦ vt (wool) far restringere ♦ n (inf: pej) psicanalista m/f; **to ~ from doing sth** rifuggire dal fare qc; ~**age** n restringimento; ~**wrap** vt confezionare con pellicola di plastica

shrivel [ˈʃrivl] (also: ~ **up**) vt raggrinzare, avvizzire ♦ vi raggrinzirsi, avvizzire

shroud [ʃraud] n sudario ♦ vt: ~**ed in mystery** avvolto(a) nel mistero

Shrove Tuesday [ˈʃrəuv-] n martedì m grasso

shrub [ʃrʌb] n arbusto; ~**bery** n arbusti mpl

shrug [ʃrʌg] n scrollata di spalle ♦ vt, vi: **to ~ (one's shoulders)** alzare le spalle, fare spallucce; ~ **off** vt passare sopra a

shrunk [ʃrʌŋk] pp of **shrink**

shudder [ˈʃʌdə*] n brivido ♦ vi rabbrividire

shuffle [ˈʃʌfl] vt (cards) mescolare; **to ~ (one's feet)** strascicare i piedi

shun [ʃʌn] vt sfuggire, evitare

shunt [ʃʌnt] vt (RAIL: direct) smistare; (: divert) deviare; (object) spostare

shut [ʃʌt] (pt, pp **shut**) vt chiudere ♦ vi chiudersi, chiudere; ~ **down** vt, vi chiudere definitivamente; ~ **off** vt fermare, bloccare; ~ **up** vi (inf: keep quiet) stare zitto(a), fare silenzio ♦ vt (close) chiudere; (silence) far tacere; ~**ter** n imposta; (PHOT) otturatore m

shuttle ['ʃʌtl] n spola, navetta; (space ~) navetta (spaziale); (also: ~ service) servizio m navetta inv

shuttlecock ['ʃʌtlkɔk] n volano

shy [ʃaɪ] adj timido(a)

sibling ['sɪblɪŋ] n fratello/sorella

Sicily ['sɪsɪlɪ] n Sicilia

sick [sɪk] adj (ill) malato(a); (vomiting): **to be ~** vomitare; (humour) macabro(a); **to feel ~** avere la nausea; **to be ~ of** (fig) averne abbastanza di; **~ bay** n infermeria f; **~en** vt nauseare ♦ vi: **to be ~ening for** sth (cold etc) covare qc

sickle ['sɪkl] n falcetto

sick: ~ **leave** n congedo per malattia; **~ly** adj malaticcio(a); (causing nausea) nauseante; **~ness** n malattia; (vomiting) vomito; **~ pay** n sussidio per malattia

side [saɪd] n lato; (of lake) riva; (team) squadra ♦ cpd (door, entrance) laterale ♦ vi: **to ~ with sb** parteggiare per qn, prendere le parti di qn; **by the ~ of** a fianco di; (road) sul ciglio di; **~ by ~** fianco a fianco; **from ~ to ~** da una parte all'altra; **to take ~s (with)** schierarsi (con); **~board** n credenza; **~burns** (BRIT **~boards**) npl (whiskers) basette fpl; **~ effect** n (MED) effetto collaterale; **~light** n (AUT) luce f di posizione; **~line** n (SPORT) linea laterale; (fig) attività secondaria; **~long** adj obliquo(a); **~saddle** adv all'amazzone; **~ show** n attrazione f; **~step** vt (question) eludere; (problem) scavalcare; **~ street** n traversa; **~track** vt (fig) distrarre; **~walk** (US) n marciapiede m; **~ways** adv (move) di lato, di fianco

siding ['saɪdɪŋ] n (RAIL) binario di raccordo

sidle ['saɪdl] vi: **to ~ up (to)** avvicinarsi furtivamente (a)

siege [siːdʒ] n assedio

sieve [sɪv] n setaccio ♦ vt setacciare

sift [sɪft] vt passare al crivello; (fig)

vagliare

sigh [saɪ] n sospiro ♦ vi sospirare

sight [saɪt] n (faculty) vista; (spectacle) spettacolo; (on gun) mira ♦ vt avvistare; **in ~** in vista; **on ~** a vista; **out of ~** non visibile; **~seeing** n giro turistico; **to go ~seeing** visitare una località

sign [saɪn] n segno; (with hand etc) segno, gesto; (notice) insegna, cartello ♦ vt firmare; (player) ingaggiare; **~ on** vi (MIL) arruolarsi; (as unemployed) iscriversi sulla lista (dell'ufficio di collocamento) ♦ vt (MIL) arruolare; (employee) assumere; **~ over** vt: **to ~ sth over to sb** cedere qc con scrittura legale a qn; **~ up** vi (MIL) arruolarsi; (for course) iscriversi ♦ vt (player) ingaggiare; (recruits) reclutare

signal ['sɪgnl] n segnale m ♦ vi (AUT) segnalare, mettere la freccia ♦ vt (person) fare segno a; (message) comunicare per mezzo di segnali; **~man** n (RAIL) deviatore m

signature ['sɪgnətʃə*] n firma; **~ tune** n sigla musicale

signet ring ['sɪgnət-] n anello con sigillo

significance [sɪg'nɪfɪkəns] n significato; importanza

significant [sɪg'nɪfɪkənt] adj significativo(a)

sign language n linguaggio dei muti

signpost ['saɪnpəust] n cartello indicatore

silence ['saɪləns] n silenzio ♦ vt far tacere, ridurre al silenzio; **~r** n (on gun, BRIT: AUT) silenziatore m

silent ['saɪlənt] adj silenzioso(a); (film) muto(a); **to remain ~** tacere, stare zitto; **~ partner** n (COMM) socio inattivo

silhouette [sɪluː'et] n silhouette f inv

silicon chip ['sɪlɪkən-] n piastrina di silicio

silk [sɪlk] n seta ♦ adj di seta; **~y** adj di seta

silly ['sɪlɪ] adj stupido(a), sciocco(a)

silt [sɪlt] *n* limo
silver ['sɪlvə*] *n* argento; *(money)* monete da 5, 10 or 50 pence; *(also:* ~ware) argenteria ♦ *adj* d'argento; ~ **paper** *(BRIT)* (carta argentata, (carta) stagnola; **~-plated** *adj* argentato(a); **~smith** *n* argentiere *m*; **~y** *adj (colour)* argenteo(a); *(sound)* argentino(a)
similar ['sɪmɪlə*] *adj:* ~ **(to)** simile (a); **~ly** *adv* allo stesso modo; così pure
simile ['sɪmɪlɪ] *n* similitudine *f*
simmer ['sɪmə*] *vi* cuocere a fuoco lento
simpering ['sɪmpərɪŋ] *adj* lezioso(a), smorfioso(a)
simple ['sɪmpl] *adj* semplice; **simplicity** [-'plɪsɪtɪ] *n* semplicità; **simply** *adv* semplicemente
simultaneous [sɪməl'teɪnɪəs] *adj* simultaneo(a)
sin [sɪn] *n* peccato ♦ *vi* peccare
since [sɪns] *adv* da allora ♦ *prep* da ♦ *conj (time)* da quando; *(because)* poiché, dato che; ~ **then**, **ever** ~ da allora
sincere [sɪn'sɪə*] *adj* sincero(a); **~ly** *adv:* **yours** **~ly** *(in letters)* distinti saluti; **sincerity** [-'sɛrɪtɪ] *n* sincerità
sinew ['sɪnjuː] *n* tendine *m*
sinful ['sɪnful] *adj* peccaminoso(a), peccatore(trice)
sing [sɪŋ] *(pt* sang, *pp* sung) *vt, vi* cantare
singe [sɪndʒ] *vt* bruciacchiare
singer ['sɪŋə*] *n* cantante *m/f*
singing ['sɪŋɪŋ] *n* canto
single ['sɪŋgl] *adj* solo(a), unico(a); *(unmarried: man)* celibe; *(: woman)* nubile; *(not double)* semplice ♦ *n (BRIT: also:* ~ **ticket)** biglietto di (sola) andata; *(record)* 45 giri *m*; ~**s** *n (TENNIS)* singolo; ~ **out** *vt* scegliere; *(distinguish)* distinguere; ~**-breasted** *adj* a un petto; ~ **file:** **in** ~ **file** in fila indiana; ~**-handed** *adv* senza aiuto, da solo(a); ~**-minded** *adj* tenace, risoluto(a); ~ **room** *n* camera singola
singly ['sɪŋglɪ] *adv* separatamente

singular ['sɪŋgjulə*] *adj (exceptional, LING)* singolare ♦ *n (LING)* singolare *m*
sinister ['sɪnɪstə*] *adj* sinistro(a)
sink [sɪŋk] *(pt* sank, *pp* sunk) *n* lavandino, acquaio ♦ *vt (ship)* (fare) affondare, colare a picco; *(foundations)* scavare; *(piles etc):* **to** ~ **sth into** conficcare qc in ♦ *vi* affondare, andare a fondo; *(ground etc)* cedere, avvallarsi; **my heart sank** mi sentii venir meno; ~ **in** *vi* penetrare
sinner ['sɪnə*] *n* peccatore/trice
sinus ['saɪnəs] *n (ANAT)* seno
sip [sɪp] *n* sorso ♦ *vt* sorseggiare
siphon ['saɪfən] *n* sifone *m*; ~ **off** *vt* travasare (con un sifone)
sir [sə*] *n* signore *m*; S~ **John Smith** Sir John Smith; **yes** ~ sì, signore *m*
siren ['saɪərn] *n* sirena
sirloin ['sɜːlɔɪn] *n* controfiletto
sissy ['sɪsɪ] *(inf)* *n* femminuccia
sister ['sɪstə*] *n* sorella; *(nun)* suora; *(BRIT: nurse)* infermiera *f* caposala *inv*; **~-in-law** *n* cognata
sit [sɪt] *(pt, pp* sat) *vi* sedere, sedersi; *(assembly)* essere in seduta; *(for painter)* posare ♦ *vt (exam)* sostenere; ~ **down** *vi* sedersi; ~ **in on** *vt fus* assistere a; ~ **up** *vi* tirarsi su a sedere; *(not go to bed)* stare alzato(a) fino a tardi
sitcom ['sɪtkɔm] *n abbr* (= *situation comedy)* commedia di situazione; *(TV)* telefilm *m inv* comico d'interni
site [saɪt] *n* posto; *(also: building* ~) cantiere *m* ♦ *vt* situare
sit-in *n (demonstration)* sit-in *m inv*
sitting ['sɪtɪŋ] *n (of assembly etc)* seduta; *(in canteen)* turno; ~ **room** *n* soggiorno
situated ['sɪtjueɪtɪd] *adj* situato(a)
situation [sɪtju'eɪʃən] *n* situazione *f*; *(job)* lavoro; *(location)* posizione *f*; "~**s vacant**" *(BRIT)* "offerte *fpl* di impiego"
six [sɪks] *num* sei; **~teen** *num* sedici; **~th** *num* sesto(a); **~ty** *num* sessanta

size [saɪz] n dimensioni fpl; (of clothing) taglia, misura; (of shoes) numero; (glue) colla; ~ **up** vt giudicare, farsi un'idea di; ~**able** adj considerevole

sizzle ['sɪzl] vi sfrigolare

skate [skeɪt] n pattino; (fish: pl inv) razza ♦ vi pattinare; ~**board** n skateboard m inv; ~**r** n pattinatore/trice; **skating** n pattinaggio; **skating rink** n pista di pattinaggio

skeleton ['skelɪtn] n scheletro; ~ **staff** n personale m ridotto

skeptical ['skɛptɪkl] (US) adj = **sceptical**

sketch [skɛtʃ] n (drawing) schizzo, abbozzo; (THEATRE) scenetta comica, sketch m inv ♦ vt abbozzare, schizzare; ~ **book** n album m inv per schizzi; ~**y** adj incompleto(a), lacunoso(a)

skewer ['skjuːə*] n spiedo

ski [skiː] n sci m inv ♦ vi sciare; ~ **boot** n scarpone m da sci

skid [skɪd] n slittamento ♦ vi slittare

skier ['skiːə*] n sciatore/trice

skiing ['skiːɪŋ] n sci m

ski jump n (ramp) trampolino; (event) salto con gli sci

skilful ['skɪlful] (US **skillful**) adj abile

ski lift ['skiːlɪft] n sciovia

skill [skɪl] n abilità f inv, capacità f inv; ~**ed** adj esperto(a); (worker) qualificato(a), specializzato(a); ~**ful** (US) adj = **skilful**

skim [skɪm] vt (milk) scremare; (glide over) sfiorare ♦ vi: **to ~ through** (fig) scorrere, dare una scorsa a; ~**med milk** n latte m scremato

skimp [skɪmp] vt (work: also: ~ **on**) fare alla carlona; (cloth etc) lesinare; ~**y** adj misero(a); striminzito(a); frugale

skin [skɪn] n pelle f; (of fruit etc) buccia; (animal) scuoiare, spellare; ~ **cancer** n cancro alla pelle; ~**-deep** adj superficiale; ~ **diving** n nuoto subacqueo; ~**ny** adj molto magro(a), pelle e ossa inv; ~**tight** adj (dress etc) aderente

skip [skɪp] n saltello, balzo; (BRIT: container) benna ♦ vi saltellare; (with rope) saltare la corda ♦ vt saltare

ski pants npl pantaloni mpl da sci

ski pole n racchetta (da sci)

skipper ['skɪpə*] n (NAUT, SPORT) capitano

skipping rope ['skɪpɪŋ-] (BRIT) n corda per saltare

skirmish ['skəːmɪʃ] n scaramuccia

skirt [skəːt] n gonna, sottana ♦ vt fiancheggiare, costeggiare; ~**ing board** n zoccolo

ski slope n pista da sci

ski suit n tuta da sci

skit [skɪt] n parodia; scenetta satirica

skittle ['skɪtl] n birillo; ~**s** n (game) (gioco dei) birilli mpl

skive [skaɪv] (BRIT: inf) vi fare il lavativo

skulk [skʌlk] vi muoversi furtivamente

skull [skʌl] n cranio, teschio

skunk [skʌŋk] n moffetta

sky [skaɪ] n cielo; ~**light** n lucernario; ~**scraper** n grattacielo

slab [slæb] n lastra; (of cake, cheese) fetta

slack [slæk] adj (loose) allentato(a); (slow) lento(a); (careless) negligente; ~**en** (also: ~**en off**) vi rallentare, diminuire ♦ vt allentare; (speed) diminuire; ~**s** npl (trousers) pantaloni mpl

slag heap [slæg-] n ammasso di scorie

slag off [slæg-] (BRIT: inf) vt sparlare di

slain [sleɪn] pp of **slay**

slam [slæm] vt (door) sbattere; (throw) scaraventare; (criticize) stroncare ♦ vi sbattere

slander ['slɑːndə*] n calunnia; diffamazione f

slang [slæŋ] n gergo, slang m

slant [slɑːnt] n pendenza, inclinazione f; (fig) angolazione f, punto di vista; ~**ed** adj in pendenza, inclinato(a); (eyes) obliquo(a); ~**ing** adj = ~**ed**

slap [slæp] n manata, pacca; (on face) schiaffo ♦ vt dare una manata a; schiaffeggiare ♦ adv (directly) in pieno; ~ a coat of paint on it dagli una mano di vernice; ~**dash** adj negligente; (work) raffazzonato(a); ~**stick** n (comedy) farsa grossolana; ~**-up** (BRIT) adj: a ~**-up meal** un pranzo (or una cena) coi fiocchi

slash [slæʃ] vt (face) sfregiare; (fig: prices) ridurre drasticamente, tagliare

slat [slæt] n (of wood) stecca; (of plastic) lamina

slate [sleɪt] n ardesia; (piece) lastra di ardesia ♦ vt (fig: criticize) stroncare, distruggere

slaughter ['slɔːtə*] n strage f, massacro ♦ vt (animal) macellare; (people) trucidare, massacrare

slave [sleɪv] n schiavo/a ♦ vi (also: ~ away) lavorare come uno schiavo; ~**ry** n schiavitù f; **slavish** adj servile; (copy) pedissequo(a)

slay [sleɪ] (pt **slew**, pp **slain**) vt (formal) uccidere

sleazy ['sliːzɪ] adj trasandato(a)

sledge [slɛdʒ] n slitta; ~**hammer** n mazza, martello da fabbro

sleek [sliːk] adj (hair, fur) lucido(a), lucente; (car, boat) slanciato(a), affusolato(a)

sleep [sliːp] (pt, pp **slept**) n sonno ♦ vi dormire; **to go to ~** addormentarsi; ~ **around** vi (oversleep) dormire fino a tardi; ~**er** n (BRIT: on track) traversina; (: train) treno di vagoni letto; ~**ing bag** n sacco a pelo; ~**ing car** n vagone m letto inv, carrozza f letto inv; ~**ing part- ner** (BRIT) n (COMM) socio inattivo; ~**ing pill** n sonnifero; ~**less** adj: a ~**less night** una notte in bianco; ~**walker** n sonnambulo/a; ~**y** adj assonnato(a), sonnolento(a); (fig) addormentato(a)

sleet [sliːt] n nevischio

sleeve [sliːv] n manica; (of record) copertina

sleigh [sleɪ] n slitta

sleight [slaɪt] n: ~ **of hand** gioco di destrezza

slender ['slɛndə*] adj snello(a), sottile; (not enough) scarso(a), esiguo(a)

slept [slɛpt] pt, pp of **sleep**

slew [sluː] pt of **slay** ♦ vi (BRIT) girare

slice [slaɪs] n fetta ♦ vt affettare, tagliare a fette

slick [slɪk] adj (skilful) brillante; (clever) furbo(a) ♦ n (also: oil ~) chiazza di petrolio

slide [slaɪd] (pt, pp **slid**) n scivolone m; (in playground) scivolo; (PHOT) diapositiva; (BRIT: also: hair ~) fermaglio (per capelli) ♦ vt far scivolare ♦ vi scivolare; ~ **rule** n regolo calcolatore; **sliding** adj (door) scorrevole; **sliding scale** n scala mobile

slight [slaɪt] adj (slim) snello(a), sottile; (frail) delicato(a), fragile; (trivial) insignificante; (small) piccolo(a) ♦ n offesa, affronto; **not in the ~est** affatto, neppure per sogno; ~**ly** adv lievemente, un po'

slim [slɪm] adj magro(a), snello(a) ♦ vi dimagrire; fare (or seguire) una dieta dimagrante

slime [slaɪm] n limo, melma; vischiume m

slimming ['slɪmɪŋ] adj (diet) dimagrante; (food) ipocalorico(a)

sling [slɪŋ] (pt, pp **slung**) n (MED) fascia al collo; (for baby) marsupio ♦ vt lanciare, tirare

slip [slɪp] n scivolata, scivolone m; (mistake) errore m, sbaglio; (under- skirt) sottoveste f; (of paper) striscia di carta; tagliando, scontrino ♦ vt (slide) far scivolare ♦ vi (slide) scivolare; (move smoothly): **to ~ into/ out of** scivolare in/fuori da; (decline) declinare; **to ~ sth on/off** infilarsi/ togliersi qc; **to give sb the ~** sfuggire qn; **a ~ of the tongue** un lapsus linguae; ~ **away** vi svignarsela; ~ **in** vt infilare ♦ vi (error) scivolare; ~ **out** vi scivolare fuori; ~ **up**

vi sbagliarsi; **~ped disc** *n* spostamento delle vertebre

slipper ['slɪpə*] *n* pantofola

slippery ['slɪpərɪ] *adj* scivoloso(a)

slip road (*BRIT*) *n* (*to motorway*) rampa di accesso

slipshod ['slɪpʃɔd] *adj* sciatto(a), trasandato(a)

slip-up *n* granchio (*fig*)

slipway ['slɪpweɪ] *n* scalo di costruzione

slit [slɪt] (*pt, pp* **slit**) *n* fessura, fenditura; (*cut*) taglio ♦ *vt* fendere; tagliare

slither ['slɪðə*] *vi* scivolare, sdrucciolare

sliver ['slɪvə*] *n* (*of glass, wood*) scheggia; (*of cheese etc*) fettina

slob [slɔb] (*inf*) *n* sciattone/a

slog [slɔg] (*BRIT*) *n* faticata ♦ *vi* lavorare con accanimento, sgobbare

slogan ['sləugən] *n* motto, slogan *m inv*

slop [slɔp] *vi* (*also: ~ over*) traboccare; versarsi ♦ *vt* versare

slope [sləup] *n* pendio; (*side of mountain*) versante *m*; (*ski ~*) pista; (*of roof*) pendenza; (*of floor*) inclinazione *f* ♦ *vi*: **to ~ down** declinare; **to ~ up** essere in salita; **sloping** *adj* inclinato(a)

sloppy ['slɔpɪ] *adj* (*work*) tirato(a) via; (*appearance*) sciatto(a)

slot [slɔt] *n* fessura ♦ *vt*: **to ~ sth into** infilare qc in

sloth [sləuθ] *n* (*laziness*) pigrizia, accidia

slot machine *n* (*BRIT*: *vending machine*) distributore *m* automatico; (*for gambling*) slot-machine *f inv*

slouch [slautʃ] *vi* (*when walking*) camminare dinoccolato(a); **she was ~ing in a chair** era sprofondata in una poltrona

Slovenia [sləu'viːnɪə] *n* Slovenia

slovenly ['slʌvənlɪ] *adj* sciatto(a), trasandato(a)

slow [sləu] *adj* lento(a); (*watch*): **to be ~** essere indietro ♦ *adv* lentamente ♦ *vt, vi* (*also: ~ down, ~ up*)

rallentare; "**~**" (*road sign*) "rallentare"; **~ly** *adv* lentamente; **~ motion** *n*: **in ~ motion** al rallentatore

sludge [slʌdʒ] *n* fanghiglia

slue [sluː] (*US*) *vi* = **slew**

slug [slʌg] *n* lumaca; (*bullet*) pallottola; **~gish** *adj* lento(a); (*trading*) stagnante

sluice [sluːs] *n* chiusa

slum [slʌm] *n* catapecchia

slumber ['slʌmbə*] *n* sonno

slump [slʌmp] *n* crollo, caduta; (*economic*) depressione *f*, crisi *f inv* ♦ *vi* crollare

slung [slʌŋ] *pt, pp of* **sling**

slur [sluːr] *n* (*fig*): **~ (on)** calunnia (su) ♦ *vt* pronunciare in modo indistinto

slush [slʌʃ] *n* neve *f* mista a fango; **~ fund** *n* fondi *mpl* neri

slut [slʌt] *n* donna trasandata, sciattona

sly [slaɪ] *adj* (*smile, remark*) sornione(a); (*person*) furbo(a)

smack [smæk] *n* (*slap*) pacca; (*on face*) schiaffo ♦ *vt* schiaffeggiare; (*child*) picchiare ♦ *vi*: **to ~ of** puzzare di

small [smɔːl] *adj* piccolo(a); **~ ads** (*BRIT*) *npl* piccola pubblicità; **~ change** *n* moneta, spiccioli *mpl*; **~ fry** *npl* pesci *mpl* piccoli, pesci piccoli; **~-holder** *n* piccolo proprietario; **~ hours** *npl*: **in the ~ hours** alle ore piccole; **~pox** *n* vaiolo; **~ talk** *n* chiacchiere *fpl*

smart [smɑːt] *adj* elegante; (*fashionable*) alla moda; (*clever*) intelligente; (*quick*) sveglio(a) ♦ *vi* bruciare; **~en up** *vi* farsi bello(a) ♦ *vt* (*people*) fare bello(a); (*things*) abbellire

smash [smæʃ] *n* (*also: ~-up*) scontro, collisione *f*; (*~ hit*) successone *m* ♦ *vt* frantumare, fracassare; (*SPORT: record*) battere ♦ *vi* frantumarsi, andare in pezzi; **~ing** (*inf*) *adj* favoloso(a), formidabile

smattering ['smætərɪŋ] *n*: **a ~ of** un'infarinatura di

smear [smɪə*] *n* macchia; (*MED*)

striscio ♦ *vt* spalmare; *(make dirty)* sporcare; ~ **campaign** *n* campagna diffamatoria

smell [smɛl] *(pt, pp* **smelt** *or* **smelled)** *n* odore *m*; *(sense)* olfatto, odorato ♦ *vt* sentire (l')odore di ♦ *vi (food etc)*: to ~ **(of)** avere odore (di); *(pej)* puzzare, avere un cattivo odore; ~**y** *adj* puzzolente

smile [smaɪl] *n* sorriso ♦ *vi* sorridere

smirk [smɜːk] *n* sorriso furbo; sorriso compiaciuto

smithy ['smɪðɪ] *n* fucina

smock [smɔk] *n* grembiule *m*, camice *m*; *(US)* tuta

smog [smɔg] *n* smog *m*

smoke [sməʊk] *n* fumo ♦ *vt, vi* fumare; ~**d** *adj (bacon, glass)* affumicato(a); ~**r** *n (person)* fumatore/trice; *(RAIL)* carrozza per fumatori; ~ **screen** *n (MIL)* cortina fumogena *or* di fumo; *(fig)* copertura; **smoking** *n* fumo; **"no smoking"** *(sign)* "vietato fumare"; **smoky** *adj* fumoso(a); *(taste)* affumicato/a

smolder ['sməʊldə*] *(US) vi =* **smoulder**

smooth [smuːð] *adj* liscio(a); *(sauce)* omogeneo(a); *(flavour, whisky)* amabile; *(movement)* regolare; *(person)* mellifluo(a) ♦ *vt (also:* ~ **out)** lisciare, spianare; *(: difficulties)* appianare

smother ['smʌðə*] *vt* soffocare

smoulder ['sməʊldə*] *(US* **smolder)** *vi* covare sotto la cenere

smudge [smʌdʒ] *n* macchia; sbavatura ♦ *vt* imbrattare, sporcare

smug [smʌg] *adj* soddisfatto(a), compiaciuto(a)

smuggle ['smʌgl] *vt* contrabbandare; ~**r** *n* contrabbandiere/a; **smuggling** *n* contrabbando

smutty ['smʌtɪ] *adj (fig)* osceno(a), indecente

snack [snæk] *n* spuntino; ~ **bar** *n* tavola calda, snack bar *m inv*

snag [snæg] *n* intoppo, ostacolo imprevisto

snail [sneɪl] *n* chiocciola

snake [sneɪk] *n* serpente *m*

snap [snæp] *n (sound)* schianto, colpo secco; *(photograph)* istantanea ♦ *adj* improvviso ♦ *vt (far)* schioccare; *(break)* spezzare di netto ♦ *vi* spezzarsi con un rumore secco; *(fig: person)* parlare con tono secco; to ~ **shut** chiudersi di scatto; ~ **at** *vt fus (subj: dog)* cercare di mordere; ~ **off** *vt (break)* schiantare; ~ **up** *vt* afferrare; ~**py** *adj (inf) adj (answer, slogan)* d'effetto; **make it ~py!** *(hurry up)* sbrigati!, svelto!; ~**shot** *n* istantanea

snare [snɛə*] *n* trappola

snarl [snɑːl] *vi* ringhiare

snatch [snætʃ] *n (small amount)* frammento ♦ *vt* strappare *(con violenza)*; *(fig)* rubare

sneak [sniːk] *(pt (US)* **snuck)** *vi*: to ~ **in/out** entrare/uscire di nascosto *or* in spione/a; to ~ **up on sb** avvicinarsi quatto quatto a qn; ~**ers** *npl* scarpe *fpl* da ginnastica

sneer [snɪə*] *vi* sogghignare; to ~ **at** farsi beffe di

sneeze [sniːz] *n* starnuto ♦ *vi* starnutire

sniff [snɪf] *n* fiutata, annusata ♦ *vi* tirare su col naso ♦ *vt* fiutare, annusare

snigger ['snɪgə*] *vi* ridacchiare, ridere sotto i baffi

snip [snɪp] *n* pezzetto; *(bargain)* (buon) affare *m*, occasione ♦ *vt* tagliare

sniper ['snaɪpə*] *n (marksman)* franco tiratore *m*, cecchino

snippet ['snɪpɪt] *n* frammento

snivelling ['snɪvlɪŋ] *adj (whimpering)* piagnucoloso(a)

snob [snɔb] *n* snob *m/f inv*; ~**bery** *n* snobismo; ~**bish** *adj* snob *inv*

snooker ['snuːkə*] *n* tipo di gioco del biliardo

snoop ['snuːp] *vi*: to ~ **about** curiosare

snooty ['snuːtɪ] *adj* borioso(a), snob *inv*

snooze [snuːz] *n* sonnellino, pisolino

♦ *vi* fare un sonnellino

snore [snɔː*] *vi* russare

snorkel ['snɔːkl] *n* (*of swimmer*) respiratore *m* a tubo

snort [snɔːt] *n* sbuffo *m* ♦ *vi* sbuffare

snout [snaut] *n* muso

snow [snəu] *n* neve *f* ♦ *vi* nevicare; ~**ball** *n* palla di neve ♦ *vi* (*fig*) crescere a vista d'occhio; ~**bound** *adj* bloccato(a) dalla neve; ~**drift** *n* cumulo di neve (ammucchiato dal vento); ~**drop** *n* bucaneve *m inv*; ~**fall** *n* nevicata; ~**flake** *n* fiocco di neve; ~**man** (*irreg*) *n* pupazzo di neve; ~**plough** (*US* ~**plow**) *n* spazzaneve *m inv*; ~**shoe** *n* racchetta da neve; ~**storm** *n* tormenta

snub [snʌb] *vt* snobbare ♦ *n* offesa, affronto; ~**-nosed** *adj* dal naso camuso

snuff [snʌf] *n* tabacco da fiuto

snug [snʌg] *adj* comodo(a); (*room, house*) accogliente, comodo(a)

snuggle ['snʌgl] *vi*: to ~ up to sb stringersi a qn

KEYWORD

so [səu] *adv* 1 (*thus, likewise*) così; if ~ se è così, quand'è così; I didn't do it — you did ~! non l'ho fatto io — sì che l'hai fatto!; ~ do I, ~ am I ett'anch'io; it's 5 o'clock — ~ it is! sono le 5 — davvero!; I hope ~ lo spero; I think ~ penso di sì; ~ far finora, fin qui; (*in past*) fino ad allora

2 (*in comparisons ett: to such a degree*) così; ~ big (that) così grande (che); she's not ~ clever as her brother lei non è (così) intelligente come suo fratello

3: ~ much *adj* tanto(a) ♦ *adv* tanto; I've got ~ much work/money ho tanto lavoro/tanti soldi; I love you ~ much ti amo tanto; ~ many tanti(e)

4 (*phrases*): 10 or ~ circa 10; ~ long! (*inf: goodbye*) ciao!, ci vediamo!

♦ *conj* 1 (*expressing purpose*): ~ as

to do in modo *or* così da fare; we hurried ~ as not to be late ci affrettammo per non fare tardi; ~ (that) affinché + *sub*, perché + *sub*

2 (*expressing result*): he didn't arrive — I left ten è venuto così me ne sono andata; ~ you see, I could have gone vedi, sarei potuto andare

---

soak [səuk] *vt* inzuppare; (*clothes*) mettere a mollo ♦ *vi* (*clothes etc*) essere a mollo; ~ **in** *vi* penetrare; ~ **up** *vt* assorbire

soap [səup] *n* sapone *m*; ~**flakes** *npl* sapone *m* in scaglie; ~ **opera** *n* soap opera *f inv*; ~ **powder** *n* detersivo; ~**y** *adj* insaponato(a)

soar [sɔː*] *vi* volare in alto; (*price etc*) salire alle stelle; (*building*) ergersi

sob [sɔb] *n* singhiozzo ♦ *vi* singhiozzare

sober ['səubə*] *adj* sobrio(a); (*not drunk*) non ubriaco(a); (*moderate*) moderato(a) ♦ *vi* farsi passare la sbornia; ~ **up** *vt* far passare la sbornia a ♦ *vi* farsi passare la sbornia

so-called ['səu'kɔːld] *adj* cosiddetto(a)

soccer ['sɔkə*] *n* calcio

sociable ['səuʃəbl] *adj* socievole

social ['səuʃl] *adj* sociale ♦ *n* festa, serata; ~ **club** *n* club *m inv* sociale; ~**ism** *n* socialismo; ~**ist** *adj*, *n* socialista *m/f*; ~**ize** *vi*: to ~ (**with**) socializzare (con); ~ **security** (*BRIT*) *n* previdenza sociale; ~ **work** *n* servizio sociale; ~ **worker** *n* assistente *m/f* sociale

society [sə'saɪətɪ] *n* società *f inv*; (*club*) società; associazione *f*; (*also*: **high** ~) alta società

sociology [səusɪ'ɔlədʒɪ] *n* sociologia

sock [sɔk] *n* calzino

socket ['sɔkɪt] *n* cavità *f inv*; (*of eye*) orbita; (*BRIT: ELEC: also*: *wall* ~) presa di corrente

sod [sɔd] *n* (*of earth*) zolla erbosa; (*BRIT: inf!*) bastardo/a (!)

soda ['səudə] *n* (*CHEM*) soda; (*also*:

~ water) acqua di seltz; (US: also: ~ pop) gassosa

sodden ['sɔdn] adj fradicio(a)

sodium ['səudiəm] n sodio

sofa ['səufə] n sofà m inv

soft [sɔft] adj (not rough) morbido(a); (not hard) soffice; (not loud) sommesso(a); (not bright) tenue; (kind) gentile; ~ drink n analcolico; ~en ['sɔfn] vt ammorbidire; addolcire; attenuare ♦ vi ammorbidirsi; addolcirsi; attenuarsi; ~ly adv dolcemente; morbidamente; ~ness n dolcezza; morbidezza; ~ spot n: to have a ~ spot for sb avere un debole per qn

software ['sɔftwɛə*] n (COMPUT) software m

soggy ['sɔgi] adj inzuppato(a)

soil [sɔil] n terreno ♦ vt sporcare

solace ['sɔlis] n consolazione f

solar ['səulə*] adj solare; ~ panel n pannello solare; ~ power n energie solare

sold [səuld] pt, pp of sell; ~ out adj (COMM) esaurito(a)

solder ['səuldə*] vt saldare ♦ n saldatura

soldier ['səuldʒə*] n soldato, militare m

sole [səul] n (of foot) pianta (del piede); (of shoe) suola; (fish: pl inv) sogliola ♦ adj solo(a), unico(a)

solemn ['sɔləm] adj solenne

sole trader n (COMM) commerciante m in proprio

solicit [sə'lisit] vt (request) richiedere, sollecitare ♦ vi (prostitute) adescare i passanti

solicitor [sə'lisitə*] n (BRIT) (for wills etc) = notaio; (in court) = avvocato

solid ['sɔlid] adj solido(a); (not hollow) pieno(a); (meal) sostanzioso(a) ♦ n solido

solidarity [sɔli'dæriti] n solidarietà

solitaire [sɔli'tɛə*] n (games, gem) solitario

solitary ['sɔlitəri] adj solitario(a); ~ confinement n (LAW) isolamento

solo ['səuləu] n assolo; ~ist n solista m/f

soluble ['sɔljubl] adj solubile

solution [sə'lu:ʃən] n soluzione f

solve [sɔlv] vt risolvere

solvent ['sɔlvənt] adj (COMM) solvibile ♦ n (CHEM) solvente m

sombre ['sɔmbə*] (US somber) adj scuro(a); (mood, person) triste

some [sʌm] adj 1 (a certain amount or number of): ~ tea/water/cream del tè/dell'acqua/della panna; ~ children/apples dei bambini/delle mele

2 (certain: in contrasts) certo(a); ~ people say that ... alcuni dicono che ..., certa gente dice che ...

3 (unspecified) un(a) certo(a), qualche; ~ woman was asking for you una tale chiedeva di lei; ~ day un giorno; ~ day next week un giorno della prossima settimana

♦ pron 1 (a certain number) alcuni(e), certi(e); I've got ~ (books etc) ne ho alcuni; ~ (of them) have been sold alcuni sono stati venduti

2 (a certain amount) un po'; I've got ~ (money, milk) ne ho un po'; I've read ~ of the book ho letto parte del libro

♦ adv: ~ 10 people circa 10 persone

somebody ['sʌmbədi] pron = someone

somehow ['sʌmhau] adv in un modo o nell'altro, in qualche modo; (for some reason) per qualche ragione

someone ['sʌmwʌn] pron qualcuno

someplace ['sʌmpleis] (US) adv = somewhere

somersault ['sʌməsɔ:lt] n capriola; salto mortale ♦ vi fare una capriola (or un salto mortale); (car) cappottare

something ['sʌmθiŋ] pron qualcosa, qualche cosa; ~ nice qualcosa di bello; ~ to do qualcosa da fare

sometime ['sʌmtaim] *adv* (*in future*) una volta o l'altra; (*in past*): ~ **last month** durante il mese scorso

sometimes ['sʌmtaimz] *adv* qualche volta

somewhat ['sʌmwɔt] *adv* piuttosto

somewhere ['sʌmwɛə*] *adv* in or da qualche parte

son [sʌn] *n* figlio

song [sɔŋ] *n* canzone *f*

sonic ['sɔnik] *adj* (*boom*) sonico(a)

son-in-law *n* genero

sonnet ['sɔnit] *n* sonetto

sonny ['sʌni] (*inf*) *n* ragazzo mio

soon [suːn] *adv* presto, fra poco; (*early, a short time after*) presto; ~ **afterwards** poco dopo; *see also as*; ~**er** *adv* (*time*) prima; (*preference*): **I would** ~**er do** preferirei fare; ~**er or later** prima o poi

soot [sut] *n* fuliggine *f*

soothe [suːð] *vt* calmare

sophisticated [sə'fistikeitid] *adj* sofisticato(a); raffinato(a); complesso(a)

sophomore ['sɔfəmɔː*] *n* (*US*) *n* studente/essa del secondo anno

sopping ['sɔpiŋ] *adj* (*also:* ~ **wet**) bagnato(a) fradicio(a)

soppy ['sɔpi] (*pej*) *adj* sentimentale

soprano [sə'prɑːnəu] *n* (*voice*) soprano *m*; (*singer*) soprano *m/f*

sorcerer ['sɔːsərə*] *n* stregone *m*, mago

sore [sɔː*] *adj* (*painful*) dolorante ♦ *n* piaga; ~**ly** *adv* (*tempted*) fortemente

sorrow ['sɔrəu] *n* dolore *m*; ~**ful** *adj* doloroso(a)

sorry ['sɔri] *adj* spiacente; (*condition, excuse*) misero(a); ~! scusa! (*or* scusi! *or* scusate!); **to feel** ~ **for sb** rincrescersi per qn

sort [sɔːt] *n* specie *f*, genere *m* ♦ *vt* (*also:* ~ **out:** *papers*) classificare; ordinare; (*: letters etc*) smistare; (*: problems*) risolvere; ~**ing office** *n* ufficio *m* smistamento *inv*

SOS *n abbr* (= *save our souls*) S.O.S. *m inv*

so-so *adv* così così

sought [sɔːt] *pt, pp of* **seek**

soul [səul] *n* anima; ~**-destroying** *adj* demoralizzante; ~**ful** *adj* pieno(a) di sentimento

sound [saund] *adj* (*healthy*) sano(a); (*safe, not damaged*) solido(a), in buono stato; (*reliable, not superficial*) solido(a); (*sensible*) giudizioso(a), di buon senso ♦ *adv*: ~ **asleep** profondamente addormentato ♦ *n* suono; (*noise*) rumore *m*; (*GEO*) stretto ♦ *vt* (*alarm*) suonare ♦ *vi* suonare; (*fig: seem*) sembrare; **to** ~ **like** rassomigliare a; ~ **out** *vt* sondare; ~ **barrier** *n* muro del suono; ~ **effects** *npl* effetti sonori; ~**ly** *adv* (*sleep*) profondamente; (*beat*) duramente; ~**proof** *adj* insonorizzato(a), isolato(a) acusticamente; ~**track** *n* (*of film*) colonna sonora

soup [suːp] *n* minestra; brodo; zuppa; **in the** ~ (*fig*) nei guai; ~ **plate** *n* piatto fondo; ~**spoon** *n* cucchiaio da minestra

sour ['sauə*] *adj* aspro(a); (*fruit*) acerbo(a); (*milk*) acido(a); (*fig*) arcigno(a); acido(a); **it's** ~ **grapes** è soltanto invidia

source [sɔːs] *n* fonte *f*, sorgente *f*; (*fig*) fonte

south [sauθ] *n* sud *m*, meridione *m*, mezzogiorno ♦ *adj* del sud, sud *inv*, meridionale ♦ *adv* verso sud; **S~ Africa** *n* Sudafrica *m*; **S~ African** *adj, n* sudafricano(a); **S~ America** *n* Sudamerica *m*, America del sud; **S~ American** *adj, n* sudamericano(a); ~**-east** *n* sud-est *m*; ~**erly** ['sʌðəli] *adj* del sud; ~**ern** ['sʌðən] *adj* del sud, meridionale; esposto(a) a sud; **S~ Pole** *n* Polo Sud; ~**ward(s)** *adv* verso sud; ~**-west** *n* sud-ovest *m*

souvenir [suːvə'niə*] *n* ricordo, souvenir *m inv*

sovereign ['sɔvrin] *adj, n* sovrano(a)

soviet ['səuviət] *adj* sovietico(a); **the S~ Union** l'Unione *f* Sovietica

sow¹ [sau] (*pt* ~**ed**, *pp* **sown**) *vt* seminare

sow² [sau] *n* scrofa

sown [saun] *pp* of **sow**

soy [sɔɪ] (*US*) *n* = **soya**

soya ['sɔɪə] (*US* **soy**) *n*: ~ **bean** *n* seme *m* di soia; ~ **sauce** *n* salsa di soia

spa [spɑ:] *n* (*resort*) stazione *f* termale; (*US*: *also*: **health** ~) centro di cure estetiche

space [speɪs] *n* spazio; (*room*) posto; spazio; (*length of time*) intervallo ♦ *cpd* spaziale ♦ *vt* (*also*: ~ **out**) distanziare; ~**craft** *n inv* veicolo spaziale; ~**man/woman** *n* astronauta *m/f*, cosmonauta *m/f*; ~**ship** *n* = ~**craft**; **spacing** *n* spaziatura

spacious ['speɪʃəs] *adj* spazioso(a), ampio(a)

spade [speɪd] *n* (*tool*) vanga; pala; (*child's*) paletta; ~**s** *npl* (*CARDS*) picche *fpl*

Spain [speɪn] *n* Spagna

span [spæn] *n* (*of bird, plane*) apertura alare; (*of arch*) campata; (*in time*) periodo; durata ♦ *vt* attraversare; (*fig*) abbracciare

Spaniard ['spænjəd] *n* spagnolo/a

spaniel ['spænjəl] *n* spaniel *m inv*

Spanish ['spænɪʃ] *adj* spagnolo(a) ♦ *n* (*LING*) spagnolo; the ~ *npl* gli Spagnoli

spank [spæŋk] *vt* sculacciare

spanner ['spænə*] (*BRIT*) *n* chiave *f* inglese

spar [spɑ:*] *n* asta, palo ♦ *vi* (*BOX-ING*) allenarsi

spare [spɛə*] *adj* di riserva, di scorta; (*surplus*) in più, d'avanzo ♦ *n* (*part*) pezzo di ricambio ♦ *vt* (*do without*) fare a meno di; (*afford to give*) concedere; (*refrain from hurting, using*) risparmiare; **to** ~ (*surplus*) d'avanzo; ~ **part** *n* pezzo di ricambio; ~ **time** *n* tempo libero; ~ **wheel** *n* (*AUT*) ruota di scorta

sparing ['spɛərɪŋ] *adj*: **to be** ~ **with** sth risparmiare qc; ~**ly** *adv* moderatamente

spark [spɑːk] *n* scintilla; ~(**ing**) **plug** *n* candela

sparkle ['spɑːkl] *n* scintillio, sfavillio ♦ *vi* scintillare, sfavillare; **sparkling** *adj* scintillante, sfavillante; (*conversation, wine, water*) frizzante

sparrow ['spærəu] *n* passero

sparse [spɑːs] *adj* sparso(a), rado(a)

spartan ['spɑːtən] *adj* (*fig*) spartano(a)

spasm ['spæzəm] *n* (*MED*) spasmo; (*fig*) accesso, attacco; ~**odic** [spæz'mɔdɪk] *adj* spasmodico(a); (*fig*) intermittente

spastic ['spæstɪk] *n* spastico/a

spat [spæt] *pt, pp* of **spit**

spate [speɪt] *n* (*fig*): ~ **of** diluvio *or* fiume *m* di

spatter ['spætə*] *vt, vi* schizzare

spawn [spɔːn] *vi* deporre le uova ♦ *n* uova *fpl*

speak [spiːk] (*pt* **spoke**, *pp* **spoken**) *vt* (*language*) parlare; (*truth*) dire ♦ *vi* parlare; **to** ~ **to** sb/**of** *or* **about** sth parlare a qn/di qc; ~ **up!** parla più forte!; ~**er** *n* (*in public*) oratore/trice; (*also*: **loud~er**) altoparlante *m*; (*POL*): **the S~er** il *presidente della Camera dei Comuni* (*BRIT*) *or dei Rappresentanti* (*US*)

spear [spɪə*] *n* lancia ♦ *vt* infilzare; ~**head** *vt* (*attack etc*) condurre

spec [spɛk] (*inf*) *n*: **on** ~ sperando bene

special ['spɛʃl] *adj* speciale; ~**ist** *n* specialista *m/f*; ~**ity** [spɛʃɪ'ælɪtɪ] *n* specialità *f inv*; ~**ize** *vi*: **to** ~**ize** (**in**) specializzarsi (in); ~**ly** *adv* specialmente, particolarmente; ~**ty** *n* = **speciality**

species ['spiːʃiːz] *n inv* specie *f inv*

specific [spə'sɪfɪk] *adj* specifico(a); preciso(a); ~**ally** *adv* esplicitamente; (*especially*) appositamente

specimen ['spɛsɪmən] *n* esemplare *m*, modello; (*MED*) campione *m*

speck [spɛk] *n* puntino, macchiolina; (*particle*) granello

speckled ['spɛkld] *adj* macchiettato(a)

specs [spɛks] (inf) npl occhiali mpl

spectacle ['spɛktəkl] n spettacolo; ~s npl (glasses) occhiali mpl; **spectacular** [-'tækjulə*] adj spettacolare

spectator [spɛk'teɪtə*] n spettatore m

spectra ['spɛktrə] npl of **spectrum**

spectre ['spɛktə*] (US **specter**) n spettro

spectrum ['spɛktrəm] (pl **spectra**) n spettro

speculation [spɛkju'leɪʃən] n speculazione f; congettura fpl

speech [spiːtʃ] n (faculty) parola; (talk, THEATRE) discorso; (manner of speaking) parlata; ~less adj ammutolito(a), muto(a)

speed [spiːd] n velocità f inv; (promptness) prontezza; **at full** or **top** ~ a tutta velocità; ~ **up** vi, vt accelerare; ~**boat** n motoscafo; ~**ily** adv velocemente; prontamente; ~**ing** n (AUT) eccesso di velocità; ~ **limit** n limite m di velocità; ~**ometer** [spɪ'dɔmɪtə*] n tachimetro; ~**way** n (sport) corsa motociclistica (su pista); ~**y** adj veloce, rapido(a); pronto(a)

spell [spɛl] (pt, pp **spelt** (BRIT) or ~**ed**) n (also: magic ~) incantesimo; (period of time) (breve) periodo ♦ vt (in writing) scrivere (lettera per lettera); (aloud) dire lettera per lettera; (fig) significare; **to cast a** ~ **on sb** fare un incantesimo a qn; **he can't** ~ fa errori di ortografia; ~**bound** adj incantato(a); affascinato(a); ~**ing** n ortografia; **spelt** (BRIT) pt, pp of **spell**

spend [spɛnd] (pt, pp **spent**) vt (money) spendere; (time, life) passare; ~**thrift** n spendaccione/a; **spent** pt, pp of **spend**

sperm [spəːm] n sperma m

spew [spjuː] vt vomitare

sphere [sfɪə*] n sfera

spice [spaɪs] n spezia ♦ vt aromatizzare

spick-and-span ['spɪkən'spæn] adj impeccabile

spicy ['spaɪsɪ] adj piccante

spider ['spaɪdə*] n ragno

spike [spaɪk] n punta

spill [spɪl] (pt, pp **spilt** or ~**ed**) vt versare, rovesciare ♦ vi versarsi, rovesciarsi; ~ **over** vi (liquid) versarsi; (crowd) riversarsi; **spilt** pt, pp of **spill**

spin [spɪn] (pt, pp **spun**) n (revolution of wheel) rotazione f; (AVIAT) avvitamento; (trip in car) giretto ♦ vt (wool etc) filare; (wheel) far girare ♦ vi girare; ~ **out** vt far durare

spinach ['spɪnɪtʃ] n spinacio; (as food) spinaci mpl

spinal ['spaɪnl] adj spinale; ~ **cord** n midollo spinale

spindly ['spɪndlɪ] adj lungo(a) e sottile, filiforme

spin-dryer (BRIT) n centrifuga

spine [spaɪn] n spina dorsale; (thorn) spina

spinning ['spɪnɪŋ] n filatura; ~ **top** n trottola; ~ **wheel** n filatoio

spin-off n (product) prodotto secondario

spinster ['spɪnstə*] n nubile f; zitella

spiral ['spaɪərl] n spirale f ♦ vi (fig) salire a spirale; ~ **staircase** n scala a chiocciola

spire ['spaɪə*] n guglia

spirit ['spɪrɪt] n (soul) spirito; (ghost) spirito, fantasma m; (mood) stato d'animo, umore m; (courage) coraggio; ~s npl (drink) alcolici mpl; **in good** ~s di buon umore; ~**ed** adj vivace, vigoroso(a); (horse) focoso(a); ~ **level** n livella a bolla (d'aria)

spiritual ['spɪrɪtjuəl] adj spirituale

spit [spɪt] (pt, pp **spat**) n (for roasting) spiedo; (saliva) sputo; saliva ♦ vi sputare; (fire, fat) scoppiettare

spite [spaɪt] n dispetto ♦ vt contrariare, far dispetto a; **in** ~ **of** nonostante, malgrado; ~**ful** adj dispettoso(a)

spittle ['spɪtl] n saliva; sputo

splash [splæʃ] n spruzzo; (sound) splash m inv; (of colour) schizzo ♦ vt spruzzare ♦ vi (also: ~ **about**) sguazzare

spleen [spliːn] n (ANAT) milza

splendid ['splɛndɪd] adj splendido(a), magnifico(a)

splint [splɪnt] n (MED) stecca

splinter ['splɪntə*] n scheggia ♦ vi scheggiarsi

split [splɪt] (pt, pp split) n spaccatura; (fig: division, quarrel) scissione f ♦ vt spaccare; (party) dividere; (work, profits) spartire, ripartire ♦ vi (divide) dividersi; ~ **up** vi (couple) separarsi, rompere; (meeting) sciogliersi

splutter ['splʌtə*] vi farfugliare; sputacchiare

spoil [spɔɪl] (pt, pp spoilt or ~ed) vt (damage) rovinare, guastare; (mar) sciupare; (child) viziare; ~**s** npl bottino; ~**sport** n guastafeste m/f inv; **spoilt** pt, pp of **spoil**

spoke [spəuk] pt of **speak** ♦ n raggio

spoken ['spəukn] pp of **speak**

spokesman ['spəuksmən] n portavoce m inv

spokeswoman ['spəukswumən] n portavoce f inv

sponge [spʌndʒ] n spugna; (also: ~ cake) pan m di spagna ♦ vt spugnare, pulire con una spugna ♦ vi: to ~ off or on scroccare a; ~ bag (BRIT) n nécessaire m inv

sponsor ['spɔnsə*] n (RADIO, TV, SPORT etc) sponsor m inv; (POL: of bill) promotore/trice ♦ vt sponsorizzare; (bill) presentare; ~**ship** n sponsorizzazione f

spontaneous [spɔn'teɪnɪəs] adj spontaneo(a)

spooky ['spuːkɪ] (inf) adj che fa accapponare la pelle

spool [spuːl] n bobina

spoon [spuːn] n cucchiaio; ~**feed** vt nutrire con il cucchiaio; (fig) imboccare; ~**ful** n cucchiaiata

sport [spɔːt] n sport m inv; (person) persona di spirito ♦ vt sfoggiare; ~**ing** adj sportivo(a); to give sb a ~**ing** chance dare a qn una possibili-

tà (di vincere); ~ **jacket** (US) n = ~**s jacket**; ~**s car** n automobile f sportiva; ~**s jacket** (BRIT) n giacca sportiva; ~**sman** n sportivo; ~**manship** n spirito sportivo; ~**swear** n abiti mpl sportivi; ~**swoman** n sportiva; ~**y** adj sportivo(a)

spot [spɔt] n punto; (mark) macchia; (dot: on pattern) pallino; (pimple) foruncolo; (place) posto; (RADIO, TV) spot m inv; (small amount): a ~ of un po' di ♦ vt (notice) individuare, distinguere; on the ~ sul posto; (immediately) su due piedi; (in difficulty) nei guai; ~ **check** n controllo senza preavviso; ~**less** adj immacolato(a); ~**light** n proiettore m; (AUT) faro ausiliario; ~**ted** adj macchiato(a); a puntini, a pallini; ~**ty** adj (face) foruncoloso(a)

spouse [spauz] n sposo/a

spout [spaut] n (of jug) beccuccio; (of pipe) scarico ♦ vi zampillare

sprain [spreɪn] n storta, distorsione f ♦ vt: to ~ **one's ankle** storcersi una caviglia

sprang [spræŋ] pt of **spring**

sprawl [sprɔːl] vi sdraiarsi (in modo scomposto); (place) estendersi (disordinatamente)

spray [spreɪ] n spruzzo; (container) nebulizzatore m, spray m inv; (of flowers) mazzetto ♦ vt spruzzare; (crops) irrorare

spread [sprɛd] (pt, pp spread) n diffusione f; (distribution) distribuzione f; (CULIN) pasta (da spalmare); (inf: food) banchetto ♦ vt (cloth) stendere, distendere; (butter etc) spalmare; (disease, knowledge) propagare, diffondere ♦ vi stendersi, distendersi; spalmarsi; propagarsi, diffondersi; ~ **out** vi (move apart) separarsi; ~**eagled** [ˈsprɛdiːgld] adj a gambe e braccia aperte; ~**sheet** n (COMPUT) foglio elettronico ad espansione

spree [spriː] n: to go on a ~ fare baldoria

sprightly ['spraɪtlɪ] adj vivace

spring [sprɪŋ] (pt **sprang**, pp **sprung**) n (leap) salto, balzo; (coiled metal) molla; (season) primavera; (of water) sorgente f ♦ vi saltare, balzare; ~ **up** vi (problem) presentarsi; ~**board** n trampolino; ~**clean(ing)** n grandi pulizie fpl di primavera; ~**time** n primavera

sprinkle ['sprɪŋkl] vt spruzzare; spargere; **to** ~ **water etc on**, ~ **with water etc** spruzzare dell'acqua etc su; ~**r** n (for lawn) irrigatore m; (to put out fire) sprinkler m inv

sprint [sprɪnt] n scatto ♦ vi scattare; ~**er** n (SPORT) velocista m/f

sprout [spraʊt] vi germogliare; ~**s** npl (also: Brussels ~s) cavolini mpl di Bruxelles

spruce [spruːs] n inv abete m rosso ♦ adj lindo(a); azzimato(a)

sprung [sprʌŋ] pp of **spring**

spry [spraɪ] adj arzillo(a), sveglio(a)

spun [spʌn] pt, pp of **spin**

spur [spəː*] n sperone m; (fig) sprone m, incentivo ♦ vt (also: ~ **on**) spronare; **on the** ~ **of the moment** lì per lì

spurious ['spjʊərɪəs] adj falso(a)

spurn [spəːn] vt rifiutare con disprezzo, sdegnare

spurt [spəːt] n (of water) getto; (of energy) scatto ♦ vi sgorgare

spy [spaɪ] n spia ♦ vi: **to** ~ **on** spiare ♦ vt (see) scorgere; ~**ing** n spionaggio

sq. abbr = **square**

squabble ['skwɒbl] vi bisticciarsi

squad [skwɒd] n (MIL) plotone m; (POLICE) squadra

squadron ['skwɒdrn] n (MIL) squadrone m; (AVIAT, NAUT) squadriglia

squalid ['skwɒlɪd] adj squallido(a)

squall [skwɔːl] n raffica; burrasca

squalor ['skwɒlə*] n squallore m

squander ['skwɒndə*] vt dissipare

square [skwɛə*] n quadrato; (in town) piazza ♦ adj quadrato(a); (inf: ideas, person) di vecchio stam-

po ♦ vt (arrange) regolare; (MATH) elevare al quadrato; (reconcile) conciliare; **all** ~ pari; **a** ~ **meal** un pasto abbondante; **2 metres** ~ di 2 metri per 2; **1** ~ **metre** 1 metro quadrato; ~**ly** adv diritto; fermamente

squash [skwɒʃ] n (SPORT) squash m; (BRIT: drink): **lemon/orange** ~ sciroppo di limone/arancia; (US) zucca; (SPORT) squash m ♦ vt schiacciare

squat [skwɒt] adj tarchiato(a), tozzo(a) ♦ vi (also: ~ **down**) accovacciarsi; ~**ter** n occupante m/f abusivo(a)

squawk [skwɔːk] vi emettere strida rauche

squeak [skwiːk] vi squittire

squeal [skwiːl] vi strillare

squeamish ['skwiːmɪʃ] adj schizzinoso(a); disgustato(a)

squeeze [skwiːz] n pressione f; (ECON) stretta ♦ vt premere; (hand, arm) stringere; ~ **out** vt spremere

squelch [skweltʃ] vi fare ciac; sguazzare

squid [skwɪd] n calamaro

squiggle ['skwɪgl] n ghirigoro

squint [skwɪnt] vi essere strabico(a) ♦ n: **he has a** ~ è strabico

squire [skwaɪə*] n (BRIT) proprietario terriero

squirm [skwəːm] vi contorcersi

squirrel ['skwɪrəl] n scoiattolo

squirt [skwəːt] vi schizzare; zampillare ♦ vt spruzzare

Sr abbr = **senior**

St abbr = **saint**; **street**

stab [stæb] n (with knife etc) pugnalata; (of pain) fitta; (inf: try): **to have a** ~ **at (doing) sth** provare (a fare) qc ♦ vt pugnalare

stable ['steɪbl] n (for horses) scuderia; (for cattle) stalla ♦ adj stabile

stack [stæk] n catasta, pila ♦ vt accatastare, ammucchiare

stadium ['steɪdɪəm] n stadio

staff [stɑːf] n (work force: gen) personale m; (: BRIT: SCOL) personale insegnante ♦ vt fornire di personale

stag [stæg] *n* cervo

stage [steidʒ] *n* palcoscenico; (*profession*): **the** ~ il teatro, la scena; (*point*) punto; (*platform*) palco ♦ *vt* (*play*) allestire, mettere in scena; (*demonstration*) organizzare; **in** ~**s** per gradi; **a tappe;** ~**coach** *n* diligenza; ~ **manager** *n* direttore *m* di scena

stagger ['stægə*] *vi* barcollare ♦ *vt* (*person*) sbalordire; (*hours, holidays*) scaglionare; ~**ing** *adj* (*amazing*) sbalorditivo(a)

stagnate [stæg'neit] *vi* stagnare

stag party *n* festa di addio al celibato

staid [steid] *adj* posato(a), serio(a)

stain [stein] *n* macchia; (*colouring*) colorante *m* ♦ *vt* macchiare; (*wood*) tingere; ~**ed glass window** *n* vetrata; ~**less** *adj* (*steel*) inossidabile; ~ **remover** *n* smacchiatore *m*

stair [stɛə*] *n* (*step*) gradino; ~**s** *npl* (*flight of* ~s) scale *fpl*, scala; ~**case** *n* scale *fpl*, scala; ~**way** *n* = ~**case**

stake [steik] *n* palo, piolo; (*COMM*) interesse *m*; (*BETTING*) puntata, scommessa ♦ *vt* (*bet*) scommettere; (*risk*) rischiare; **to be at** ~ essere in gioco

stale [steil] *adj* (*bread*) raffermo(a); (*food*) stantio(a); (*air*) viziato(a); (*beer*) svaporato(a); (*smell*) di chiuso

stalemate ['steilmeit] *n* stallo; (*fig*) punto morto

stalk [stɔːk] *n* gambo, stelo ♦ *vt* inseguire; ~ **off** *vi* andarsene impettito(a)

stall [stɔːl] *n* bancarella; (*in stable*) box *m inv* di stalla ♦ *vt* (*AUT*) far spegnere; (*fig*) bloccare ♦ *vi* (*AUT*) spegnersi, fermarsi; (*fig*) temporeggiare; ~**s** *npl* (*BRIT*: *in cinema, theatre*) platea

stallion ['stæliən] *n* stallone *m*

stalwart ['stɔːlwət] *adj* fidato(a); risoluto(a)

stamina ['stæminə] *n* vigore *m*, resistenza

stammer ['stæmə*] *n* balbuzie *f* ♦ *vi* balbettare

stamp [stæmp] *n* (*postage* ~) francobollo; (*implement*) timbro; (*mark, also fig*) marchio, impronta; (*on document*) bollo; timbro ♦ *vi* (*also: ~ one's foot*) battere il piede ♦ *vt* battere; (*letter*) affrancare; (*mark with a* ~) timbrare; ~ **album** *n* album *m inv* per francobolli; ~ **collecting** *n* filatelia

stampede [stæm'piːd] *n* fuggi fuggi *m inv*

stance [stæns] *n* posizione *f*

stand [stænd] (*pt*, *pp* **stood**) *n* (*position*) posizione *f*; (*for taxis*) posteggio; (*structure*) supporto, sostegno; (*at exhibition*) stand *m inv*; (*in shop*) banco; (*at market*) bancarella; (*booth*) chiosco; (*SPORT*) tribuna ♦ *vi* stare in piedi; (*rise*) alzarsi in piedi; (*be placed*) trovarsi ♦ *vt* (*place*) mettere, porre; (*tolerate, withstand*) resistere, sopportare; (*treat*) offrire; **to make a** ~ prendere posizione; **to** ~ **for parliament** (*BRIT*) presentarsi come candidato (per il parlamento); ~ **by** *vi* (*be ready*) tenersi pronto(a) ♦ *vt fus* (*opinion*) sostenere; ~ **down** *vi* (*withdraw*) ritirarsi; ~ **for** *vt fus* (*signify*) rappresentare, significare; (*tolerate*) sopportare, tollerare; ~ **in for** *vt fus* sostituire; ~ **out** *vi* (*be prominent*) spiccare; ~ **up** *vi* (*rise*) alzarsi in piedi; ~ **up for** *vt fus* difendere; ~ **up to** *vt fus* tener testa a, resistere a

standard ['stændəd] *n* modello, standard *m inv*; (*level*) livello; (*flag*) stendardo ♦ *adj* (*size etc*) normale, standard *inv*; ~**s** *npl* (*morals*) principi *mpl*, valori *mpl*; ~ **lamp** (*BRIT*) *n* lampada a stelo; ~ **of living** *n* livello di vita

stand-by *n* riserva, sostituto; **to be on** ~ (*gen*) tenersi pronto(a); (*doctor*) essere di guardia; ~ **ticket** *n* (*AVIAT*) biglietto senza garanzia

stand-in *n* sostituto/a

standing ['stændɪŋ] *adj* diritto(a), in

piedi; (*permanent*) permanente ♦ *n* rango, condizione *f*, posizione *f*; **of many years'** ~ che esiste da molti anni; ~ **joke** *n* barzelletta; ~ **order** (*BRIT*) *n* (*at bank*) ordine *m* di pagamento (permanente); ~ **room** *n* posto all'impiedi

standoffish [stænd'ɔfɪʃ] *adj* scostante, freddo(a)

standpoint ['stændpɔɪnt] *n* punto di vista

standstill ['stændstɪl] *n*: **at a** ~ fermo(a); (*fig*) a un punto morto; **to come to a** ~ fermarsi; giungere a un punto morto

stank [stæŋk] *pt of* **stink**

staple ['steɪpl] *n* (*for papers*) graffetta ♦ *adj* (*food etc*) di base ♦ *vt* cucire; ~**r** *n* cucitrice *f*

star [stɑː*] *n* (*celebrity*) divo/a ♦ *vi*: **to** ~ (**in**) essere il (*or* la) protagonista (di) ♦ *vt* (*CINEMA*) essere interpretato/a da

starboard ['stɑːbəd] *n* dritta

starch [stɑːtʃ] *n* amido

stardom ['stɑːdəm] *n* celebrità

stare [stɛə*] *n* sguardo fisso ♦ *vi*: **to** ~ **at** fissare

starfish ['stɑːfɪʃ] *n* stella di mare

stark [stɑːk] *adj* (*bleak*) desolato(a) ♦ *adv*: ~ **naked** completamente nudo(a)

starling ['stɑːlɪŋ] *n* storno

starry ['stɑːrɪ] *adj* stellato(a); ~-**eyed** *adj* (*innocent*) ingenuo/a

start [stɑːt] *n* inizio; (*of race*) partenza; (*sudden movement*) sobbalzo; (*advantage*) vantaggio ♦ *vt* cominciare, iniziare; (*car*) mettere in moto ♦ *vi* cominciare; (*on journey*) partire, mettersi in viaggio; (*jump*) sobbalzare; **to** ~ **doing** *or* **to do sth** (in)cominciare a fare qc; ~ **off** *vi* cominciare; (*leave*) partire; **to** ~ **up** *vi* cominciare; (*car*) avviarsi ♦ *vt* iniziare; (*car*) avviare; ~**er** *n* (*AUT*) motorino d'avviamento; (*SPORT: official*) starter *m inv*; (*BRIT: CULIN*) primo piatto; ~**ing point** *n* punto di partenza

startle ['stɑːtl] *vt* far trasalire; **startling** *adj* sorprendente

starvation [stɑː'veɪʃən] *n* fame *f*, inedia

starve [stɑːv] *vi* morire di fame; soffrire la fame ♦ *vt* far morire di fame, affamare

state [steɪt] *n* stato ♦ *vt* dichiarare, affermare; annunciare; **the S~s** (*USA*) gli Stati Uniti; **to be in a** ~ essere agitato(a); ~**ly** *adj* maestoso(a), imponente; ~**ment** *n* dichiarazione *f*; ~**sman** *n* statista *m*

static ['stætɪk] *n* (*RADIO*) scariche *fpl* ♦ *adj* statico(a)

station ['steɪʃən] *n* stazione *f* ♦ *vt* collocare, disporre

stationary ['steɪʃənərɪ] *adj* fermo(a), immobile

stationer ['steɪʃənə*] *n* cartolaio/a; ~'**s (shop)** *n* cartoleria; ~**y** *n* articoli *mpl* di cancelleria

station master *n* (*RAIL*) capostazione *m*

station wagon (*US*) *n* giardinetta

statistic [stə'tɪstɪk] *n* statistica; ~**s** *n* (*science*) statistica

statue ['stætjuː] *n* statua

status ['steɪtəs] *n* posizione *f*, condizione *f* sociale; prestigio; stato; ~ **symbol** *n* simbolo di prestigio

statute ['stætjuːt] *n* legge *f*; **statutory** *adj* stabilito/a) dalla legge, statutario(a)

staunch [stɔːntʃ] *adj* fidato(a), leale

stave [steɪv] *vt*: **to** ~ **off** (*attack*) respingere; (*threat*) evitare

stay [steɪ] *n* (*period of time*) soggiorno, permanenza ♦ *vi* rimanere; (*reside*) alloggiare, stare; (*spend some time*) trattenersi, soggiornare; **to** ~ **put** non muoversi; **to** ~ **the night** fermarsi per la notte; ~ **behind** *vi* restare indietro; ~ **in** *vi* (*at home*) stare in casa; ~ **on** *vi* restare, rimanere; ~ **out** *vi* (*of house*) rimanere fuori (di casa); ~ **up** *vi* (*at night*) rimanere alzato(a); ~**ing power** *n* capacità di resistenza

stead [stɛd] *n*: **in sb's** ~ al posto di

qn; **to stand sb in good ~** essere utile a qn

steadfast ['stedfɑːst] adj fermo(a), risoluto(a)

steadily ['stedɪlɪ] adv (firmly) saldamente; (constantly) continuamente; (fixedly) fisso; (walk) con passo sicuro

steady ['stedɪ] adj (not wobbling) fermo(a); (regular) costante; (person, character) serio(a); (: calm) calmo(a), tranquillo(a) ♦ vt stabilizzare; calmare

steak [steɪk] n (meat) bistecca; (fish) trancia

steal [stiːl] (pt **stole**, pp **stolen**) vt rubare ♦ vi rubare; (move) muoversi furtivamente

stealth [stelθ] n: **by ~** furtivamente; **~y** adj furtivo(a)

steam [stiːm] n vapore ♦ vt (CULIN) cuocere a vapore ♦ vi fumare; **~ engine** n macchina a vapore; (RAIL) locomotiva a vapore; **~er** n piroscafo, vapore m; **~roller** n rullo compressore; **~ship** n = **~er**; **~y** adj (room) pieno(a) di vapore; (window) appannato(a)

steel [stiːl] n acciaio ♦ adj di acciaio; **~works** n acciaieria

steep [stiːp] adj ripido(a), scosceso(a); (price) eccessivo(a) ♦ vt inzuppare; (washing) mettere a mollo

steeple ['stiːpl] n campanile m

steer [stɪə*] vt guidare ♦ vi (NAUT: person) governare; (car) guidarsi; **~ing** n (AUT) sterzo; **~ing wheel** n volante m

stem [stɛm] n (of flower, plant) stelo; (of tree) fusto; (of glass) gambo; (of fruit, leaf) picciolo ♦ vt contenere, arginare; **~ from** vt fus provenire da, derivare da

stench [stɛntʃ] n puzzo, fetore m

stencil ['stɛnsl] n (of metal, cardboard) stampino, mascherina; (in typing) matrice f ♦ vt disegnare con stampino

stenographer [stɛ'nɔgrəfə*] (US) n stenografo/a

step [stɛp] n passo, (stair) gradino, scalino; (action) mossa, azione f ♦ vi: **to ~ forward/back** fare un passo avanti/indietro; **~s** npl (BRIT) = **stepladder**; **to be in/out of ~ (with)** stare/non stare al passo (con); **~ down** vi (fig) ritirarsi; **~ on** vt fus calpestare; **~ up** vt aumentare; intensificare; **~brother** n fratellastro; **~daughter** n figliastra; **~father** n patrigno; **~ladder** n scala a libretto; **~mother** n matrigna; **~ping stone** n pietra di un guado; **~sister** n sorellastra; **~son** n figliastro

stereo ['stɛrɪəʊ] n (system) sistema m stereofonico; (record player) stereo m inv ♦ adj (also: **~phonic**) stereofonico(a)

sterile ['stɛraɪl] adj sterile; **sterilize** ['stɛrɪlaɪz] vt sterilizzare

sterling ['stɜːlɪŋ] adj (gold, silver) di buona lega ♦ n (ECON) (lira) sterlina; **a pound ~** una lira sterlina

stern [stɜːn] adj severo(a) ♦ n (NAUT) poppa

stew [stjuː] n stufato ♦ vt cuocere in umido

steward ['stjuːəd] n (AVIAT, NAUT, RAIL) steward m inv; (in club etc) dispensiere m; **~ess** n assistente f di volo, hostess f inv

stick [stɪk] (pt, pp **stuck**) n bastone m; (of rhubarb, celery) gambo; (of dynamite) candelotto ♦ vt (glue) attaccare; (thrust): **to ~ sth into** conficcare or piantare or infiggere qc in; (inf: put) ficcare; (inf: tolerate) sopportare ♦ vi attaccarsi; (remain) restare, rimanere; **~ out** vi sporgere, spuntare; **~ up** vi sporgere, spuntare; **~ up for** vt fus difendere; **~er** n cartellino adesivo; **~ing plaster** n cerotto adesivo

stickler ['stɪklə*] n: **to be a ~ for** essere pignolo(a) su, tenere molto a

stick-up (inf) n rapina a mano armata

sticky ['stɪkɪ] adj attaccaticcio(a), vischioso(a); (label) adesivo(a); (fig:

situation) difficile

stiff [stɪf] *adj* rigido(a), duro(a); (*muscle*) legato(a), indolenzito(a); (*difficult*) difficile, arduo(a); (*cold*) freddo(a), formale; (*strong*) forte; (*high: price*) molto alto(a) ♦ *adv*: **bored** ~ annoiato(a) a morte; ~**en** *vt* irrigidire; rinforzare ♦ *vi* irrigidirsi; indurirsi; ~ **neck** *n* torcicollo

stifle ['staɪfl] *vt* soffocare

stigma ['stɪgmə] *n* (*fig*) stigma *m*

stile [staɪl] *n* cavalcasiepe *m*; cavalcasteccato

stiletto [stɪ'lɛtəu] (BRIT) *n* (*also*: ~ *heel*) tacco a spillo

still [stɪl] *adj* fermo(a); silenzioso(a) ♦ *adv* (*up to this time, even*) ancora; (*nonetheless*) tuttavia, ciò nonostante; ~**born** *adj* nato(a) morto(a); ~ **life** *n* natura morta

stilt [stɪlt] *n* trampolo; (*pile*) palo

stilted ['stɪltɪd] *adj* freddo(a), formale; artificiale

stimulate ['stɪmjuleɪt] *vt* stimolare

stimuli ['stɪmjulaɪ] *npl of* **stimulus**

stimulus ['stɪmjuləs] (*pl* **stimuli**) *n* stimolo

sting [stɪŋ] (*pt, pp* **stung**) *n* puntura; (*organ*) pungiglione *m* ♦ *vt* pungere

stingy ['stɪndʒɪ] *adj* spilorcio(a), tirchio(a)

stink [stɪŋk] (*pt* **stank**, *pp* **stunk**) *n* fetore *m*, puzzo ♦ *vi* puzzare; ~**ing** (*inf*) *adj* (*fig*): **a ~ing ...** uno schifo di ..., un(a) maledetto(a) ....

stint [stɪnt] *n* lavoro, compito ♦ *vi*: **to ~ on** lesinare su

stir [stə:*] *n* agitazione *f*, clamore *m* ♦ *vt* mescolare; (*fig*) risvegliare ♦ *vi* muoversi; ~ **up** *vt* provocare, suscitare

stirrup ['stɪrəp] *n* staffa

stitch [stɪtʃ] *n* (SEWING) punto; (KNITTING) maglia; (MED) punto (di sutura); (*pain*) fitta ♦ *vt* cucire, attaccare; suturare

stoat [stəut] *n* ermellino

stock [stɔk] *n* riserva, provvista; (COMM) giacenza, stock *m inv*; (AGR) bestiame *m*; (CULIN) brodo;

(*descent*) stirpe *f*; (FINANCE) titoli *mpl*, azioni *fpl* ♦ *adj* (*fig: reply etc*) consueto(a); classico(a) ♦ *vt* (*have in stock*) avere, vendere; ~**s and shares** valori *mpl* di borsa; **in** ~ in magazzino; **out of** ~ esaurito(a); ~ **up** *vi*: **to** ~ **up (with)** fare provvista (di)

stockbroker ['stɔkbrəukə*] *n* agente *m* di cambio

stock cube *n* (BRIT) *n* dado

stock exchange *n* Borsa (valori)

stocking ['stɔkɪŋ] *n* calza

stockist ['stɔkɪst] (BRIT) *n* fornitore *m*

stock: ~ **market** *n* Borsa, mercato finanziario; ~ **phrase** *n* cliché *m inv*; ~**pile** *n* riserva ♦ *vt* accumulare riserve di; ~**taking** (BRIT) *n* (COMM) inventario

stocky ['stɔkɪ] *adj* tarchiato(a), tozzo(a)

stodgy ['stɔdʒɪ] *adj* pesante, indigesto(a)

stoke [stəuk] *vt* alimentare

stole [stəul] *pt of* **steal** ♦ *n* stola

stolen ['stəuln] *pp of* **steal**

stolid ['stɔlɪd] *adj* impassibile

stomach ['stʌmək] *n* stomaco; (*belly*) pancia ♦ *vt* sopportare, digerire; ~ **ache** *n* mal *m* di stomaco

stone [stəun] *n* (*stone*; *pebble*) sasso, ciottolo; (*in fruit*) nocciolo; (MED) calcolo; (BRIT: *weight*) = 6.348 kg.; *14 libbre* ♦ *adj* di pietra ♦ *vt* lapidare; (*fruit*) togliere il nocciolo a; ~-**cold** *adj* gelido(a); ~-**deaf** *adj* sordo(a) come una campana; ~**work** *n* muratura; **stony** *adj* sassoso(a); (*fig*) di pietra

stood [stud] *pt, pp of* **stand**

stool [stu:l] *n* sgabello

stoop [stu:p] *vi* (*also*: *have a* ~) avere una curvatura; (*also*: ~ *down*) chinarsi, curvarsi

stop [stɔp] *n* arresto; (*stopping place*) fermata; (*in punctuation*) punto ♦ *vt* arrestare, fermare; (*break off*) interrompere; (*also: put a* ~ *to*) porre fine a ♦ *vi* fermarsi; (*rain,* *noise etc)* cessare, finire; **to ~ doing sth** cessare *or* finire di fare qc; **to ~ dead** fermarsi di colpo; **~ off** *vi* sostare brevemente; **~ up** *vt (hole)* chiudere, turare; **~gap** *n* tappabuchi *m inv*; **~over** *n* breve sosta; *(AVIAT)* scalo

stoppage ['stɒpɪdʒ] *n* arresto, fermata; *(of pay)* trattenuta; *(strike)* interruzione *f* del lavoro

stopper ['stɒpə*] *n* tappo

stop press *n* ultimissime *fpl*

stopwatch ['stɒpwɒtʃ] *n* cronometro

storage ['stɔːrɪdʒ] *n* immagazzinamento; **~ heater** *n* radiatore *m* elettrico che accumula calore

store [stɔː*] *n* provvista, riserva; *(depot)* deposito; *(BRIT: department ~)* grande magazzino; *(US: shop)* negozio ♦ *vt* immagazzinare; **~s** *npl (provisions)* rifornimenti *mpl*, scorte *fpl*; **in ~** di riserva; in serbo; **~ up** *vt* conservare; mettere in serbo; **~room** *n* dispensa

storey ['stɔːrɪ] *(US* **story)** *n* piano

stork [stɔːk] *n* cicogna

storm [stɔːm] *n* tempesta, temporale *m*, burrasca; uragano ♦ *vi (fig)* infuriarsi ♦ *vt* prendere d'assalto; **~y** *adj* tempestoso(a), burrascoso(a)

story ['stɔːrɪ] *n* storia; favola; racconto; *(US)* = **storey;** **~book** *n* libro di racconti

stout [staut] *adj* solido(a), robusto(a); *(friend, supporter)* tenace; *(fat)* corpulento(a), grasso(a) ♦ *n* birra scura

stove [stəuv] *n (for cooking)* fornello; *(: small)* fornelletto; *(for heating)* stufa

stow [stəu] *vt (also: ~ away)* mettere via; **~away** *n* passeggero/a clandestino/a

straddle ['strædl] *vt* stare a cavalcioni di; *(fig)* essere a cavallo di

straggle ['strægl] *vi* crescere *(or* estendersi) disordinatamente; trascinarsi; rimanere indietro; **straggly** *adj (hair)* in disordine

straight [streɪt] *adj* dritto(a); *(frank)* onesto(a), franco(a); *(simple)* semplice ♦ *adv* diritto; *(drink)* liscio; **to put** *or* **get ~** mettere in ordine, mettere ordine in; **~ away, ~ off** *(at once)* immediatamente; **~en** *vt (also: ~en out)* raddrizzare; **~faced** *adj* impassibile, imperturbabile; **~forward** *adj* semplice; one-sto(a), franco(a)

strain [streɪn] *n (TECH)* sollecitazione *f; (physical)* sforzo; *(mental)* tensione *f; (MED)* strappo; distorsione *f; (streak, trace)* tendenza; elemento ♦ *vt* tendere; *(muscle)* sforzare; *(ankle)* storcere; *(resources)* pesare su; *(food)* colare; passare; **~s** *npl (MUS)* note *fpl;* **~ed** *adj (muscle)* stirato(a); *(laugh etc)* forzato(a); *(relations)* teso(a); **~er** *n* passino, colino

strait [streɪt] *n (GEO)* stretto(a); **~s** *npl:* **to be in dire ~s** *(fig)* essere nei guai; **~jacket** *n* camicia di forza; **~laced** *adj* bacchettona/a

strand [strænd] *n (of thread)* filo; **~ed** *adj* nei guai; senza mezzi di trasporto

strange [streɪndʒ] *adj (not known)* sconosciuto(a); *(odd)* strano(a), bizzarro(a); **~ly** *adv* stranamente; **~r** *n* sconosciuto/a; estraneo/a

strangle ['stræŋgl] *vt* strangolare; **~hold** *n (fig)* stretta (mortale)

strap [stræp] *n* cinghia; *(of slip, dress)* spallina, bretella

strapping ['stræpɪŋ] *adj* ben piantato(a)

strategic [strə'tiːdʒɪk] *adj* strategico(a)

strategy ['strætɪdʒɪ] *n* strategia

straw [strɔː] *n* paglia; *(drinking ~)* cannuccia; **that's the last ~!** è la goccia che fa traboccare il vaso!

strawberry ['strɔːbərɪ] *n* fragola

stray [streɪ] *adj (animal)* randagio(a); *(bullet)* vagante; *(scattered)* sparso(a) ♦ *vi* perdersi

streak [striːk] *n* striscia; *(of hair)* mèche *f inv* ♦ *vt* striare, screziare ♦ *vi:* **to ~ past** passare come un fulmine

stream [striːm] *n* ruscello; corrente *f*; *(of people, smoke etc)* fiume *m* ♦ *vt* *(SCOL)* dividere in livelli di rendimento ♦ *vi* scorrere; **to ~ in/out** entrare/uscire a fiotti

streamer ['striːmə*] *n* *(of paper)* stella filante

streamlined ['striːmlaind] *adj* aerodinamico(a), affusolato(a)

street [striːt] *n* strada, via; **~car** *(US)* *n* tram *m inv*; **~ lamp** *n* lampione *m*; **~ plan** *n* pianta (di una città); **~wise** *(inf)* *adj* esperto(a) dei bassifondi

strength [strεŋθ] *n* forza; **~en** *vt* rinforzare; fortificare; consolidare

strenuous ['strεnjuəs] *adj* vigoroso(a), energico(a); *(tiring)* duro(a), pesante

stress [strεs] *n* *(force, pressure)* pressione *f*; *(mental strain)* tensione *f*; *(accent)* accento ♦ *vt* insistere su, sottolineare; accentare

stretch [strεtʃ] *n* *(of sand etc)* distesa *f* ♦ *vi* stirarsi; *(extend)*: **to ~ to** or **as far as** estendersi fino a ♦ *vt* tendere, allungare; *(spread)* distendere; *(fig)* spingere (al massimo); **~ out** *vi* allungarsi, estendersi ♦ *vt* *(arm etc)* allungare, tendere; *(to spread)* distendere

stretcher ['strεtʃə*] *n* barella, lettiga

strewn [struːn] *adj*: **~ with** cosparso(a) di

stricken ['strɪkən] *adj* *(person)* provato(a); *(city, industry etc)* colpito(a); **~ with** *(disease etc)* colpito(a) da

strict [strɪkt] *adj* *(severe)* rigido(a), severo(a); *(precise)* preciso(a), stretto(a)

stridden ['strɪdn] *pp of* **stride**

stride [straid] *(pt* strode, *pp* stridden) *n* passo lungo ♦ *vi* camminare a grandi passi

strife [straif] *n* conflitto; litigi *mpl*

strike [straik] *(pt, pp* struck) *n* sciopero; *(of oil etc)* scoperta; *(attack)* attacco ♦ *vt* colpire; *(oil etc)* scopri-

re, trovare *(bargain)* fare; *(fig)*: **the thought** or **it ~s me that ...** mi viene in mente che ... ♦ *vi* scioperare; *(attack)* attaccare; *(clock)* suonare; **on ~** *(workers)* in sciopero; **to ~ a match** accendere un fiammifero; **~ down** *vt* *(fig)* atterrare; **~ up** *(MUS, conversation)* attaccare; **to ~ up a friendship with** fare amicizia con; **~r** *n* scioperante *m/f*; *(SPORT)* attaccante *m*; **striking** *adj* che colpisce

string [strɪŋ] *(pt, pp* strung) *n* spago; *(row)* fila; sequenza; catena; *(MUS)* corda ♦ *vt*: **to ~ out** disporre di fianco; **to ~ together** *(words, ideas)* mettere insieme; **the ~s** *npl* *(MUS)* gli archi; **to pull ~s for sb** *(fig)* raccomandare qn; **~ bean** *n* fagiolino; **~(ed) instrument** *n* *(MUS)* strumento a corda

stringent ['strɪndʒənt] *adj* rigoroso(a)

strip [strɪp] *n* striscia ♦ *vt* spogliare; *(paint)* togliere; *(also:* **~ down:** *machine)* smontare ♦ *vi* spogliarsi; **~ cartoon** *n* fumetto

stripe [straip] *n* striscia, riga; *(MIL, POLICE)* gallone *m*; **~d** *adj* a strisce or righe

strip lighting *n* illuminazione *f* al neon

stripper ['strɪpə*] *n* spogliarellista *m/f*

striptease ['strɪptiːz] *n* spogliarello

strive [straiv] *(pt* strove, *pp* striven) *vi*: **to ~ to do** sforzarsi di fare; **striven** ['strɪvn] *pp of* **strive**

strode [strəud] *pt of* **stride**

stroke [strəuk] *n* colpo; *(SWIMMING)* bracciata; *(: style)* stile *m*; *(MED)* colpo apoplettico ♦ *vt* accarezzare; **at a ~** in un attimo

stroll [strəul] *n* giretto, passeggiatina ♦ *vi* andare a spasso; **~er** *(US)* *n* passeggino

strong [strɒŋ] *adj* *(gen)* forte; *(sturdy: table, fabric etc)* robusto(a); **they are 50 ~** sono in 50; **~box** *n* cassaforte *f*; **~hold** *n* *(also fig)* roccaforte *f*; **~ly** *adv* fortemente, con forza; energicamente; vivamente; **~room** *n* camera di sicurezza

strove [strəʊv] *pt of* **strive**

struck [strʌk] *pt, pp of* **strike**

structural ['strʌktʃərəl] *adj* strutturale

structure ['strʌktʃə*] *n* struttura; (*building*) costruzione *f*, fabbricato

struggle ['strʌgl] *n* lotta ♦ *vi* lottare

strum [strʌm] *vt* (*guitar*) strimpellare

strung [strʌŋ] *pt, pp of* **string**

strut [strʌt] *n* sostegno, supporto ♦ *vi* pavoneggiarsi

stub [stʌb] *n* mozzicone *m*; (*of ticket etc*) matrice *f*, talloncino ♦ *vt*: to ~ one's toe urtare or sbattere il dito del piede; **~ out** *vt* schiacciare

stubble ['stʌbl] *n* stoppia; (*on chin*) barba ispida

stubborn ['stʌbən] *adj* testardo(a), ostinato(a)

stuck [stʌk] *pt, pp of* **stick** ♦ *adj* (*jammed*) bloccato(a); **~-up** *adj* presuntuoso(a)

stud [stʌd] *n* bottoncino; borchia; (*also: ~ earring*) orecchino a pressione; (*also: ~ farm*) scuderia, allevamento di cavalli; (*also: ~ horse*) stallone *m* ♦ *vt* (*fig*): **~ded with** tempestato(a) di

student ['stju:dənt] *n* studente/essa ♦ *cpd* studentesco(a); universitario(a); degli studenti; **~ driver** (*US*) *n* conducente *m/f* principiante

studio ['stju:diəʊ] *n* studio; **~ flat** (*US* **~ apartment**) *n* monolocale *m*

studious ['stju:diəs] *adj* studioso(a); (*studied*) studiato(a), voluto(a); **~ly** *adv* (*carefully*) deliberatamente, di proposito

study ['stʌdi] *n* studio ♦ *vt* studiare; esaminare ♦ *vi* studiare

stuff [stʌf] *n* roba; (*substance*) sostanza, materiale *m* ♦ *vt* imbottire; (*CULIN*) farcire; (*dead animal*) impagliare; (*inf: push*) ficcare; **~ing** *n* imbottitura; (*CULIN*) ripieno; **~y** *adj* (*room*) mal ventilato(a),

senz'aria; (*ideas*) antiquato(a)

stumble ['stʌmbl] *vi* inciampare; **to ~ across** (*fig*) imbattersi in; **stumbling block** *n* ostacolo, scoglio

stump [stʌmp] *n* ceppo; (*of limb*) moncone *m* ♦ *vt*: to be **~ed** essere sconcertato(a)

stun [stʌn] *vt* stordire; (*amaze*) sbalordire

stung [stʌŋ] *pt, pp of* **sting**

stunk [stʌŋk] *pp of* **stink**

stunning ['stʌnɪŋ] *adj* sbalorditivo(a); (*girl etc*) fantastico(a)

stunt [stʌnt] *n* bravata; (*publicity* ~) trucco pubblicitario; **~ed** *adj* stentato(a), rachitico(a); **~man** *n* cascatore *m*

stupefy ['stju:pɪfaɪ] *vt* stordire; intontire; (*fig*) stupire

stupendous [stju:'pɛndəs] *adj* stupendo(a), meraviglioso(a)

stupid ['stju:pɪd] *adj* stupido(a); **~ity** [-'pɪdɪtɪ] *n* stupidità *f inv*, stupidaggine *f*

stupor ['stju:pə*] *n* torpore *m*

sturdy ['stɜ:dɪ] *adj* robusto(a), vigoroso(a); solido(a)

stutter ['stʌtə*] *n* balbuzie *f* ♦ *vi* balbettare

sty [staɪ] *n* (*of pigs*) porcile *m*

stye [staɪ] *n* (*MED*) orzaiolo

style [staɪl] *n* stile *m*; (*distinction*) eleganza, classe *f*; **stylish** *adj* elegante

stylus ['staɪləs] *n* (*of record player*) puntina

suave [swɑːv] *adj* untuoso(a)

sub... [sʌb] *prefix* sub..., sotto...; **~conscious** *adj* subcosciente ♦ *n* subcosciente *m*; **~contract** *vt* subappaltare

subdue [səb'dju:] *vt* sottomettere, soggiogare; **~d** *adj* pacato(a); (*light*) attenuato(a)

subject [*n* 'sʌbdʒɪkt, *vb* səb'dʒɛkt] *n* soggetto; (*citizen etc*) cittadino/a; (*SCOL*) materia ♦ *vt*: to ~ to sottomettere a; esporre a; to be ~ to (*law*) essere sottomesso(a) a; (*disease*) essere soggetto(a) a; **~ive** [-'dʒɛktɪv] *adj* soggettivo(a); **~ mat-**

ter n argomento; contenuto

subjunctive [səb'dʒʌŋktɪv] n congiuntivo

sublet [sʌb'lɛt] vt subaffittare

submachine gun ['sʌbmə'ʃiːn-] n mitra m inv

submarine [sʌbmə'riːn] n sommergibile m

submerge [səb'məːdʒ] vt sommergere; immergere ♦ vi immergersi

submission [səb'mɪʃən] n sottomissione f; (claim) richiesta

submissive [səb'mɪsɪv] adj remissivo(a)

submit [səb'mɪt] vt sottomettere ♦ vi sottomettersi

subnormal [sʌb'nɔːməl] adj subnormale

subordinate [sə'bɔːdɪnət] adj, n subordinato(a)

subpoena [səb'piːnə] n (LAW) citazione f, mandato di comparizione

subscribe [səb'skraɪb] vi contribuire; **to ~ to** (opinion) approvare, condividere; (fund) sottoscrivere a; (newspaper) abbonarsi a; essere abbonato(a) a; **~r** n (to periodical, telephone) abbonato/a

subscription [səb'skrɪpʃən] n sottoscrizione f; abbonamento

subsequent ['sʌbsɪkwənt] adj successivo(a), seguente; conseguente; **~ly** adv in seguito, successivamente

subside [səb'saɪd] vi cedere, abbassarsi; (flood) decrescere; (wind) calmarsi; **~nce** [-'saɪdns] n cedimento, abbassamento

subsidiary [səb'sɪdɪərɪ] adj sussidiario(a); accessorio(a) ♦ n (also: ~ company) filiale f

subsidize ['sʌbsɪdaɪz] vt sovvenzionare

subsidy ['sʌbsɪdɪ] n sovvenzione f

subsistence [səb'sɪstəns] n esistenza; mezzi mpl di sostentamento; **~ allowance** n indennità f inv di trasferta

substance ['sʌbstəns] n sostanza

substantial [səb'stænʃl] adj soli-

do(a); (amount, progress etc) notevole; (meal) sostanzioso(a)

substantiate [səb'stænʃɪeɪt] vt comprovare

substitute ['sʌbstɪtjuːt] n (person) sostituto/a; (thing) succedaneo, surrogato ♦ vt: **to ~** sth/sb for sostituire qc/qn a

subterfuge ['sʌbtəfjuːdʒ] n sotterfugio

subterranean [sʌbtə'reɪnɪən] adj sotterraneo(a)

subtitle ['sʌbtaɪtl] n (CINEMA) sottotitolo

subtle ['sʌtl] adj sottile; **~ty** n sottigliezza

subtotal [sʌb'təutl] n somma parziale

subtract [səb'trækt] vt sottrarre; **~ion** [-'trækʃən] n sottrazione f

suburb ['sʌbəːb] n sobborgo; **the ~s** la periferia; **~an** [sə'bəːbən] adj suburbano(a); **~ia** n periferia, sobborghi mpl

subversive [səb'vəːsɪv] adj sovversivo(a)

subway ['sʌbweɪ] n (US: underground) metropolitana; (BRIT: underpass) sottopassaggio

succeed [sək'siːd] vi riuscire; avere successo ♦ vt succedere a; **to ~** in doing riuscire a fare; **~ing** adj (following) successivo(a)

success [sək'sɛs] n successo; **~ful** adj (venture) coronato(a) da successo, riuscito(a); **to be ~ful** (in doing) riuscire (a fare); **~fully** adv con successo

succession [sək'sɛʃən] n successione f

successive [sək'sɛsɪv] adj successivo(a); consecutivo(a)

succumb [sə'kʌm] vi soccombere

such [sʌtʃ] adj tale; (of that kind): ~ a book un tale libro, un libro del genere; ~ books tali libri, libri del genere; (so much): ~ courage tanto coraggio ♦ adv talmente, così; ~ a long trip un viaggio così lungo; ~ a lot of talmente or così tanto(a); ~

as (like) come; **as** ~ come or in quanto tale; **~and~** adj tale (after noun)

suck [sʌk] vt succhiare; (breast, bottle) poppare; **~er** n (ZOOL, TECH) ventosa; (inf) gonzo/a, babbeo/a

suction ['sʌkʃən] n succhiamento; (TECH) aspirazione f

sudden ['sʌdn] adj improvviso(a); **all of a** ~ improvvisamente, all'improvviso; **~ly** adv bruscamente, improvvisamente, di colpo

suds [sʌdz] npl schiuma (di sapone)

sue [suː] vt citare in giudizio

suede [sweɪd] n pelle f scamosciata

suet ['suːɪt] n grasso di rognone

suffer ['sʌfə*] vt soffrire, patire; (bear) sopportare, tollerare ♦ vi soffrire; **to** ~ **from** soffrire di; **~er** n malato/a; **~ing** n sofferenza

suffice [sə'faɪs] vi essere sufficiente, bastare

sufficient [sə'fɪʃənt] adj sufficiente; ~ **money** abbastanza soldi; **~ly** adv sufficientemente, abbastanza

suffocate ['sʌfəkeɪt] vi (have difficulty breathing) soffocare; (die through lack of air) asfissiare

suffused [sə'fjuːzd] adj: ~ **with** (colour) tinto/a di; **the room was** ~ **with light** nella stanza c'era una luce soffusa

sugar ['ʃugə*] n zucchero ♦ vt zuccherare; ~ **beet** n barbabietola da zucchero; ~ **cane** n canna da zucchero

suggest [sə'dʒɛst] vt proporre, suggerire; indicare; **~ion** [-'dʒɛstʃən] n suggerimento, proposta; indicazione f; **~ive** (pej) adj indecente

suicide ['suːɪsaɪd] n (person) suicida m/f; (act) suicidio; see also **commit**

suit [suːt] n (man's) vestito; (woman's) completo, tailleur m inv; (LAW) causa; (CARDS) seme m, colore m ♦ vt andar bene a or per; essere adatto(a) a or per; (adapt): **to** ~ **sth to** adattare qc a; **well** ~**ed** ben assortito(a); **~able** adj adatto(a); appropriato(a); **~ably** adv

(dress) in modo adatto; (impressed) favorevolmente

suitcase ['suːtkeɪs] n valigia

suite [swiːt] n (of rooms) appartamento; (MUS) suite f inv; (furniture): **bedroom/dining room** ~ arredo or mobilia per la camera da letto/sala da pranzo

suitor ['suːtə*] n corteggiatore m, spasimante m

sulfur ['sʌlfə*] (US) n = **sulphur**

sulk [sʌlk] vi fare il broncio; **~y** adj imbronciato(a)

sullen ['sʌlən] adj scontroso(a), cupo(a)

sulphur ['sʌlfə*] (US **sulfur**) n zolfo

sultana [sʌl'tɑːnə] n (fruit) uva (secca) sultanina

sultry ['sʌltrɪ] adj afoso(a)

sum [sʌm] n somma; (SCOL etc) addizione f; ~ **up** vt, vi riassumere

summarize ['sʌm[ə]raɪz] vt riassumere, riepilogare

summary ['sʌmərɪ] n riassunto

summer ['sʌmə*] n estate f ♦ cpd d'estate, estivo(a); ~ **holidays** npl vacanze fpl estive; **~house** n (in garden) padiglione m; **~time** n (season) estate f; **~ time** n (by clock) ora legale (estiva)

summit ['sʌmɪt] n cima, sommità; (POL) vertice m

summon ['sʌmən] vt chiamare, convocare; ~ **up** vt raccogliere, fare appello a; **~s** n ordine m di comparizione ♦ vt citare

sump [sʌmp] (BRIT) n (AUT) coppa dell'olio

sumptuous ['sʌmptjuəs] adj sontuoso(a)

sun [sʌn] n sole m; **~bathe** vi prendere un bagno di sole; **~burn** n (painful) scottatura; **~burnt** adj abbronzato(a); (painfully) scottato(a)

Sunday ['sʌndɪ] n domenica; ~ **school** n ≈ scuola di catechismo

sundial ['sʌndaɪəl] n meridiana

sundown ['sʌndaun] n tramonto

sundry ['sʌndrɪ] adj vari(e), diversi(e); **all and** ~ tutti quanti; **sun-**

dries npl articoli diversi, cose diverse

sunflower ['sʌnflauə*] n girasole m

sung [sʌŋ] pp of **sing**

sunglasses ['sʌngla:sɪz] npl occhiali mpl da sole

sunk [sʌŋk] pp of **sink**

sun: ~**light** n (luce f del) sole m; ~**lit** adj soleggiato(a); ~**ny** adj assolato(a), soleggiato(a); (fig) allegro(a), felice; ~**rise** n levata del sole, alba; ~ **roof** n (AUT) tetto apribile; ~**set** n tramonto; ~**shade** n parasole m; ~**shine** n (luce f del) sole m; ~**stroke** n insolazione f, colpo di sole; ~**tan** n abbronzatura; ~**tan lotion** n lozione f solare; ~**tan oil** n olio solare

super ['su:pə*] (inf) adj fantastico(a)

superannuation [su:pərænju'eɪʃən] n contributi mpl pensionistici; pensione f

superb [su:'pə:b] adj magnifico(a)

supercilious [su:pə'sɪliəs] adj sprezzante, sdegnoso(a)

superficial [su:pə'fɪʃəl] adj superficiale

superhuman [su:pə'hju:mən] adj sovrumano(a)

superimpose ['su:pərɪm'pəuz] vt sovrapporre

superintendent [su:pərɪn'tɛndənt] n direttore/trice; (POLICE) ≈ commissario (capo)

superior [su'pɪərɪə*] adj, n superiore m/f; ~**ity** [-'ɔrɪtɪ] n superiorità

superlative [su'pə:lətɪv] adj superlativo(a), supremo(a) ♦ n (LING) superlativo

superman ['su:pəmæn] n superuomo

supermarket ['su:pəma:kɪt] n supermercato

supernatural [su:pə'næɪʃərəl] adj soprannaturale ♦ n soprannaturale m

superpower ['su:pəpauə*] n (POL) superpotenza

supersede [su:pə'si:d] vt sostituire, soppiantare

superstitious [su:pə'stɪʃəs] adj superstizioso(a)

supertanker ['su:pətæŋkə*] n superpetroliera

supervise ['su:pəvaɪz] vt (person etc) sorvegliare; (organization) soprintendere a; **supervision** [-'vɪʒən] n sorveglianza; supervisione f; **supervisor** n sorvegliante m/f; soprintendente m/f; (in shop) capocommesso/a

supine ['su:paɪn] adj supino(a)

supper ['sʌpə*] n cena

supplant [sə'plɑ:nt] vt (person, thing) soppiantare

supple ['sʌpl] adj flessibile; agile

supplement [n 'sʌplɪmənt, vb sʌplɪ'mɛnt] n supplemento ♦ vt completare, integrare; ~**ary** [-'mɛntərɪ] adj supplementare

supplier [sə'plaɪə*] n fornitore m

supply [sə'plaɪ] vt (provide) fornire; (equip): to ~ (with) approvvigionare (di); attrezzare (con) ♦ n riserva, provvista; (supplying) approvvigionamento; (TECH) alimentazione f; **supplies** npl (food) viveri mpl; (MIL) sussistenza; ~ **teacher** (BRIT) n supplente m/f

support [sə'pɔ:t] n (moral, financial etc) sostegno, appoggio; (TECH) supporto ♦ vt sostenere; (financially) mantenere; (uphold) sostenere, difendere; ~**er** n (POL etc) sostenitore/trice, fautore/trice; (SPORT) tifoso/a

suppose [sə'pəuz] vt supporre; immaginare; to be ~**d to do** essere tenuto(a) a fare; ~**dly** [sə'pəuzɪdlɪ] adv presumibilmente; **supposing** conj se, ammesso che + sub

suppress [sə'prɛs] vt reprimere; sopprimere; occultare

supreme [su'pri:m] adj supremo(a)

surcharge ['sə:tʃɑːdʒ] n supplemento

sure [ʃuə*] adj sicuro(a); (definite, convinced) sicuro, certo(a); ~! (of course) senz'altro!, certo!; ~ **enough** infatti; to make ~ **of sth/that** assicurarsi di qc/che; ~**-footed** adj dal passo sicuro; ~**ly** adv sicuramente; certamente

surety ['ʃuərətɪ] n garanzia

surf [sə:f] n (waves) cavalloni mpl; (foam) spuma

surface ['sə:fɪs] n superficie f ♦ vt (road) asfaltare ♦ vi risalire alla superficie; (fig: news, feeling) venire a galla; ~ **mail** n posta ordinaria

surfboard ['sə:fbɔ:d] n tavola per surfing

surfeit ['sə:fɪt] n: a ~ of un eccesso di; un'indigestione di

surfing ['sə:fɪŋ] n surfing m

surge [sə:dʒ] n (strong movement) ondata; (of feeling) impeto ♦ vi gonfiarsi; (people) riversarsi

surgeon ['sə:dʒən] n chirurgo

surgery ['sə:dʒərɪ] n chirurgia; (BRIT: room) studio o gabinetto medico, ambulatorio; (: also: ~ hours) orario delle visite or di consultazione; **to undergo** ~ subire un intervento chirurgico

surgical ['sə:dʒɪkl] adj chirurgico(a); ~ **spirit** (BRIT) n alcol m denaturato

surly ['sə:lɪ] adj scontroso(a), burbero(a)

surname ['sə:neɪm] n cognome m

surpass [sə:'pɑ:s] vt superare

surplus ['sə:pləs] n eccedenza; (ECON) surplus m inv ♦ adj eccedente, d'avanzo

surprise [sə'praɪz] n sorpresa; (astonishment) stupore m ♦ vt sorprendere; stupire; **surprising** adj sorprendente, stupefacente; **surprisingly** adv (easy, helpful) sorprendentemente

surrender [sə'rendə*] n resa, capitolazione f ♦ vi arrendersi

surreptitious [sʌrəp'tɪʃəs] adj furtivo(a)

surrogate ['sʌrəgɪt] n surrogato; ~ **mother** n madre f provetta

surround [sə'raund] vt circondare; (MIL etc) accerchiare; ~**ing** adj circostante; ~**ings** npl dintorni mpl; (fig) ambiente m

surveillance [sə:'veɪləns] n sorveglianza, controllo

survey [n 'sə:veɪ, vb sə:'veɪ] n qua-

dro generale; (study) esame m; (in housebuying etc) perizia; (of land) rilevamento, rilievo topografico ♦ vt osservare; esaminare; valutare; vare; ~**or** n perito; geometra m; (of land) agrimensore m

survival [sə'vaɪvl] n sopravvivenza; (relic) reliquia, vestigio

survive [sə'vaɪv] vi sopravvivere ♦ vt sopravvivere a; **survivor** n superstite m/f, sopravvissuto/a

susceptible [sə'septəbl] adj: ~ (**to**) sensibile (a); (disease) predisposto(a) (a)

suspect [adj, n 'sʌspekt, vb sə'spekt] adj sospetto(a) ♦ n persona sospetta ♦ vt sospettare; (think likely) supporre; (doubt) dubitare

suspend [sə'spend] vt sospendere; ~**ed sentence** n condanna con la condizionale; ~**er belt** n reggicalze m inv; ~**ers** npl (BRIT) giarrettiere fpl; (US) bretelle fpl

suspense [sə'spens] n apprensione f; (in film etc) suspense m; **to keep sb in** ~ tenere qn in sospeso

suspension [sə'spenʃən] n (gen AUT) sospensione f; (of driving licence) ritiro temporaneo; ~ **bridge** n ponte m sospeso

suspicion [sə'spɪʃən] n sospetto

suspicious [sə'spɪʃəs] adj (suspecting) sospettoso(a); (causing suspicion) sospetto(a)

sustain [sə'steɪn] vt sostenere; sopportare; (LAW: charge) confermare; (suffer) subire; ~**able** adj sostenibile; ~**ed** adj (effort) prolungato(a)

sustenance ['sʌstɪnəns] n nutrimento; mezzi mpl di sostentamento

swab [swɔb] n (MED) tampone m

swagger ['swægə*] vi pavoneggiarsi

swallow ['swɔləu] n (bird) rondine f ♦ vt inghiottire; (fig: story) bere; ~ **up** vt inghiottire

swam [swæm] pt of **swim**

swamp [swɔmp] n palude f ♦ vt sommergere

swan [swɔn] n cigno

swap [swɔp] vt: **to** ~ (**for**) scambiare (con)

swarm [swɔːm] n sciame m ♦ vi (bees) sciamare; (people) brulicare; (place): **to be ~ing with** brulicare di

swarthy ['swɔːðɪ] adj di carnagione scura

swastika ['swɔstɪkə] n croce f uncinata, svastica

swat [swɔt] vt schiacciare

sway [sweɪ] vi (tree) ondeggiare; (person) barcollare ♦ vt (influence) influenzare, dominare

swear [swɛə*] (pt swore, pp sworn) vi (curse) bestemmiare, imprecare ♦ vt (promise) giurare; **~word** n parolaccia

sweat [swet] n sudore m, traspirazione f ♦ vi sudare

sweater ['swɛtə*] n maglione m

sweatshirt ['swɛtʃəːt] n felpa

sweaty ['swetɪ] adj sudato(a); bagnato(a) di sudore

Swede [swiːd] n svedese m/f

swede [swiːd] n (BRIT) rapa svedese

Sweden ['swiːdn] n Svezia

Swedish ['swiːdɪʃ] adj svedese ♦ n (LING) svedese m

sweep [swiːp] (pt, pp swept) n spazzata; (also: chimney ~) spazzacamino ♦ vt spazzare, scopare; (current) spazzare ♦ vi (hand) muoversi con gesto ampio; (wind) infuriare; **~away** vt spazzare via; trascinare via; **~ past** vi sfrecciare accanto; passare accanto maestosamente; **~up** vt vi spazzare; **~ing** adj (gesture) ampio(a); circolare; a **~ing statement** un'affermazione generica

sweet [swiːt] n (BRIT: pudding) dolce m; (candy) caramella ♦ adj dolce; (fresh) fresco(a); (fig) piacevole; delicato(a), grazioso(a); gentile; **~corn** n granturco dolce; **~en** vt addolcire; zuccherare; **~heart** n innamorato(a); **~ness** n sapore m dolce; dolcezza; **~pea** n pisello odoroso

swell [swɛl] (pt ~ed, pp swollen,

~ed) n (of sea) mare m lungo ♦ adj (US: inf: excellent) favoloso(a) ♦ vt gonfiare, ingrossare; aumentare ♦ vi gonfiarsi, ingrossarsi; (sound) crescere; (also: ~ up) gonfiarsi; **~ing** n (MED) tumefazione f, gonfiore m

sweltering ['swɛltərɪŋ] adj soffocante

swept [swɛpt] pt, pp of sweep

swerve [swɔːv] vi deviare; (driver) sterzare; (boxer) scartare

swift [swɪft] n (bird) rondone m ♦ adj rapido(a), veloce

swig [swɪg] (inf) n (drink) sorsata

swill [swɪl] vt (also: ~ out, ~ down) risciacquare

swim [swɪm] (pt swam, pp swum) n: **to go for a ~** andare a fare una nuotata ♦ vi nuotare; (SPORT) fare del nuoto; (head, room) girare ♦ vt (river, channel) attraversare or percorrere a nuoto; (length) nuotare; **~mer** n nuotatore/trice; **~ming** n nuoto; **~ming cap** n cuffia; **~ming costume** (BRIT) n costume m da bagno; **~ming pool** n piscina; **~ming trunks** npl costume m da bagno (da uomo); **~suit** n costume m da bagno

swindle ['swɪndl] n truffa ♦ vt truffare

swine [swaɪn] (inf!) n inv porco (!)

swing [swɪŋ] (pt, pp swung) n altalena; (movement) oscillazione f; (MUS) ritmo; swing m ♦ vt dondolare, far oscillare; (also: ~ round) far girare ♦ vi oscillare, dondolare; (also: ~ round: object) roteare; (: person) girarsi, voltarsi; **to be in full ~** (activity) essere in piena attività; (party etc) essere nel pieno; **~ door** (US **~ing door**) n porta battente

swingeing ['swɪndʒɪŋ] adj (BRIT: defeat) violento(a); (: cuts) enorme

swipe [swaɪp] vt (hit) colpire con forza; dare uno schiaffo a; (inf: steal) sgraffignare

swirl [swɔːl] vi turbinare, far mulinello

swish [swɪʃ] *vi* sibilare

Swiss [swɪs] *adj, n inv* svizzero(a)

switch [swɪtʃ] *n* (*for light, radio etc*) interruttore *m*; (*change*) cambiamento ♦ *vt* (*change*) cambiare; scambiare; ~ **off** *vt* spegnere; ~ **on** *vt* accendere; (*engine, machine*) mettere in moto, avviare; ~**board** *n* (*TEL*) centralino

Switzerland ['swɪtsələnd] *n* Svizzera

swivel ['swɪvl] *vi* (*also*: ~ **round**) girare

swollen ['swəulən] *pp of* **swell**

swoon [swuːn] *vi* svenire

swoop [swuːp] *n* incursione *f* ♦ *vi* (*also*: ~ **down**) scendere in picchiata, piombare

swop [swɔp] *n, vt* = **swap**

sword [sɔːd] *n* spada; ~**fish** *n* pesce *m* spada *inv*

swore [swɔː*] *pt of* **swear**

sworn [swɔːn] *pp of* **swear** ♦ *adj* giurato(a)

swot [swɔt] *vi* sgobbare

swum [swʌm] *pp of* **swim**

swung [swʌŋ] *pt, pp of* **swing**

syllable ['sɪləbl] *n* sillaba

syllabus ['sɪləbəs] *n* programma *m*

symbol ['sɪmbl] *n* simbolo

symmetry ['sɪmɪtrɪ] *n* simmetria

sympathetic [sɪmpə'θetɪk] *adj* (*showing pity*) compassionevole; (*kind*) comprensivo(a); ~ **towards** ben disposto(a) verso

sympathize ['sɪmpəθaɪz] *vi*: to ~ **with** (*person*) compatire; partecipare al dolore di; (*cause*) simpatizzare per; ~**r** *n* (*POL*) simpatizzante *m/f*

sympathy ['sɪmpəθɪ] *n* compassione *f*; **sympathies** *npl* (*support, tendencies*) simpatie *fpl*; **in** ~ **with** (*strike*) per solidarietà con; **with our deepest** ~ con le nostre più sincere condoglianze

symphony ['sɪmfənɪ] *n* sinfonia

symptom ['sɪmptəm] *n* sintomo; indizio

synagogue ['sɪnəgɔg] *n* sinagoga

syndicate ['sɪndɪkɪt] *n* sindacato

synonym ['sɪnənɪm] *n* sinonimo

synopses [sɪ'nɔpsiːz] *npl of* **synopsis**

synopsis [sɪ'nɔpsɪs] (*pl* **synopses**) *n* sommario, sinossi *f inv*

syntax ['sɪntæks] *n* sintassi *f inv*

syntheses ['sɪnθəsiːz] *npl of* **synthesis**

synthesis ['sɪnθəsɪs] (*pl* **syntheses**) *n* sintesi *f inv*

synthetic [sɪn'θetɪk] *adj* sintetico(a)

syphilis ['sɪfɪlɪs] *n* sifilide *f*

syphon ['saɪfən] *n, vb* = **siphon**

Syria ['sɪrɪə] *n* Siria

syringe [sɪ'rɪndʒ] *n* siringa

syrup ['sɪrəp] *n* sciroppo; (*also*: *golden* ~) melassa raffinata

system ['sɪstəm] *n* sistema *m*; (*order*) metodo; (*ANAT*) organismo; ~**atic** [-'mætɪk] *adj* sistematico(a); metodico(a); ~ **disk** *n* (*COMPUT*) disco del sistema; ~**s analyst** *n* analista *m* di sistemi

T

ta [taː] (*BRIT: inf*) *excl* grazie!

tab [tæb] *n* (*loop on coat etc*) laccetto; (*label*) etichetta; to **keep** ~**s on** (*fig*) tenere d'occhio

tabby ['tæbɪ] *n* (*also*: ~ *cat*) (gatto) soriano, gatto tigrato

table ['teɪbl] *n* tavolo, tavola; (*MATH, CHEM etc*) tavola ♦ *vt* (*BRIT: motion etc*) presentare; to **lay** *or* **set the** ~ apparecchiare *or* preparare la tavola; ~**cloth** *n* tovaglia; ~ **of contents** *n* indice *m*; ~ **d'hôte** [taːbl'dəut] *adj* (*meal*) a prezzo fisso; ~ **lamp** *n* lampada da tavolo; ~**mat** *n* sottopiatto; ~**spoon** *n* cucchiaio da tavola; (*also*: ~*spoonful: as measurement*) cucchiaiata

tablet ['tæblɪt] *n* (*MED*) compressa; (*of stone*) targa

table: ~ **tennis** *n* tennis *m* da tavolo, ping-pong *m* ®; ~ **wine** *n* vino da tavola

tabulate ['tæbjuleɪt] *vt* (*data, fig-*

ures) tabulare, disporre in tabelle

tacit ['tæsɪt] *adj* tacito(a)

tack [tæk] *n* (nail) bulletta; (fig) approccio ♦ *vt* imbullettare; imbastire ♦ *vi* bordeggiare

tackle ['tækl] *n* attrezzatura, equipaggiamento; (for lifting) paranco; (FOOTBALL) contrasto; (RUGBY) placcaggio ♦ *vt* (difficulty) affrontare; (FOOTBALL) contrastare; (RUGBY) placcare

tacky ['tækɪ] *adj* appiccicaticcio(a); (pej) scadente

tact [tækt] *n* tatto; ~**ful** *adj* delicato(a), discreto(a)

tactical ['tæktɪkl] *adj* tattico(a)

tactics ['tæktɪks] *n, npl* tattica

tactless ['tæktlɪs] *adj* che manca di tatto

tadpole ['tædpəul] *n* girino

taffy ['tæfɪ] (US) *n* caramella *f* mou *inv*

tag [tæg] *n* etichetta; ~ **along** *vi* seguire

tail [teɪl] *n* coda; (of shirt) falda ♦ *vt* (follow) seguire, pedinare; ~ **away** *vi* = ~ **off**; ~ **off** *vi* (in size, quality etc) diminuire gradatamente; ~**back** (BRIT) *n* (AUT) ingorgo; ~ **end** *n* (of train, procession etc) coda; (of meeting etc) fine *f*; ~**gate** *n* (AUT) portellone *m* posteriore

tailor ['teɪlə*] *n* sarto; ~**ing** *n* (cut) stile *m*; (craft) sartoria; ~**made** *adj* (also fig) fatto(a) su misura

tailwind ['teɪlwɪnd] *n* vento di coda

tainted ['teɪntɪd] *adj* (food) guasto(a); (water, air) infetto(a); (fig) corrotto(a)

take [teɪk] (pt **took**, pp **taken**) *vt* prendere; (gain: prize) ottenere, vincere; (require: effort, courage) occorrere, volerci; (tolerate) accettare, sopportare; (hold: passengers etc) contenere; (accompany) accompagnare; (bring, carry) portare; (exam) sostenere, presentarsi a; to ~ **a photo/a shower** fare una fotografia/una doccia; **I ~ it that** suppongo che; ~ **after** *vt fus* assomigliare a; ~ **apart** *vt* smontare; ~ **away** *vt* portare via; togliere; ~ **back** *vt* (return) restituire; riportare; (one's words) ritirare; ~ **down** *vt* (building) demolire; (letter etc) scrivere; ~ **in** *vt* (deceive) imbrogliare, abbindolare; (understand) capire; (include) comprendere, includere; (lodger) prendere, ospitare; ~ **off** *vi* (AVIAT) decollare; (go away) andarsene ♦ *vt* (remove) togliere; ~ **on** *vt* (work) accettare, intraprendere; (employee) assumere; (opponent) sfidare, affrontare; ~ **out** *vt* portare fuori; (remove) togliere; (licence) prendere, ottenere; to ~ **sth out of** sth (drawer, pocket etc) tirare qc fuori da qc; estrarre qc da qc; ~ **over** *vt* (business) rilevare ♦ *vi*: to ~ **over from sb** prendere le consegne or il controllo da qn; ~ **to** *vt fus* (person) prendere in simpatia; (activity) prendere gusto a; ~ **up** *vt* (dress) accorciare; (occupy: time, space) occupare; (engage in: hobby etc) mettersi a; to ~ **sb up on** sth accettare qc da qn; ~**away** (BRIT) *n* (shop etc) = rosticceria; (food) pasto per asporto; ~**off** *n* (AVIAT) decollo; ~**out** (US) *n* = ~**away**; ~**over** *n* (COMM) assorbimento

takings ['teɪkɪŋz] *npl* (COMM) incasso

talc [tælk] *n* (also: ~**um powder**) talco

tale [teɪl] *n* racconto, storia; **to tell ~s** (fig: to teacher, parent etc) fare la spia

talent ['tælnt] *n* talento; ~**ed** *adj* di talento

talk [tɔːk] *n* discorso; (gossip) chiacchiere *fpl*; (conversation) conversazione *f*; (interview) discussione *f* ♦ *vi* parlare; ~**s** *npl* (POL etc) colloqui *mpl*; to ~ **about** parlare di; to ~ **sb out of/into doing** dissuadere qn da/convincere qn a fare; to ~ **shop** parlare di lavoro or di affari; ~ **over** *vt* discutere; ~**ative** *adj* loquace, ciarliero(a); ~ **show** *n* conversazione f televisiva, talk show m inv

tall [tɔːl] adj alto(a); to be 6 feet ≈ essere alto 1 metro e 80; ~ **story** n panzana, frottola

tally ['tælɪ] n conto, conteggio ♦ vi: to ~ (with) corrispondere (a)

talon ['tælən] n artiglio

tambourine [tæmbə'riːn] n tamburello

tame [teɪm] adj addomesticato(a); (fig: story, style) insipido(a), scialbo(a)

tamper ['tæmpə*] vi: to ~ with manomettere

tampon ['tæmpɒn] n tampone m

tan [tæn] n (also: sun~) abbronzatura ♦ vi abbronzarsi ♦ adj (colour) marrone rossiccio inv

tang [tæŋ] n odore m penetrante; sapore m piccante

tangent ['tændʒənt] n (MATH) tangente f; to go off at a ~ (fig) partire per la tangente

tangerine [tændʒə'riːn] n mandarino

tangle ['tæŋgl] n groviglio; to get into a ~ aggrovigliarsi; (fig) combinare un pasticcio

tank [tæŋk] n serbatoio; (for fish) acquario; (MIL) carro armato

tanker ['tæŋkə*] n (ship) nave f cisterna inv; (truck) autobotte f, autocisterna

tanned [tænd] adj abbronzato(a)

tantalizing ['tæntəlaɪzɪŋ] adj allettante

tantamount ['tæntəmaunt] adj: ~ to equivalente a

tantrum ['tæntrəm] n accesso di collera

tap [tæp] n (on sink etc) rubinetto; (gentle blow) colpetto ♦ vt dare un colpetto a; (resources) sfruttare, utilizzare; (telephone) mettere sotto controllo; on ~ (fig: resources) a disposizione; ~ **dancing** n tip tap m

tape [teɪp] n nastro; (also: magnetic ~) nastro (magnetico); (sticky ~) nastro adesivo ♦ vt (record) registrare (su nastro); (stick) attaccare con

nastro adesivo; ~ **deck** n piastra; ~ **measure** n metro a nastro

taper ['teɪpə*] n candelina ♦ vi assottigliarsi

tape recorder n registratore m (a nastro)

tapestry ['tæpɪstrɪ] n arazzo; tappezzeria

tar [tɑː*] n catrame m

target ['tɑːgɪt] n bersaglio; (fig: objective) obiettivo

tariff ['tærɪf] n tariffa

tarmac ['tɑːmæk] n (BRIT: on road) macadam m al catrame; (AVIAT) pista di decollo

tarnish ['tɑːnɪʃ] vt offuscare, annerire; (fig) macchiare

tarpaulin [tɑː'pɔːlɪn] n tela incatramata

tarragon ['tærəgən] n dragoncello

tart [tɑːt] n (CULIN) crostata; (BRIT: inf: pej: woman) sgualdrina ♦ adj (flavour) aspro(a), agro(a); ~ **up** (inf) vt agghindare

tartan ['tɑːtn] n tartan m inv

tartar ['tɑːtə*] n (on teeth) tartaro; ~(e) **sauce** n salsa tartara

task [tɑːsk] n compito; to take to ~ rimproverare; ~ **force** n (MIL, POLICE) unità operativa

tassel ['tæsl] n fiocco

taste [teɪst] n gusto; (flavour) sapore m, gusto; (sample) assaggio; (fig: glimpse, idea) idea ♦ vt gustare; (sample) assaggiare ♦ vi: to ~ of or like (fish etc) sapere or avere sapore di; you can ~ the garlic (in it) (ci) si sente il sapore dell'aglio; in good/bad ~ di buon/cattivo gusto; ~**ful** adj di buon gusto; ~**less** adj (food) insipido(a); (remark) di cattivo gusto; **tasty** adj saporito(a), gustoso(a)

tatters ['tætəz] npl: in ~ a brandelli

tattoo [tə'tuː] n tatuaggio; (spectacle) parata militare ♦ vt tatuare

tatty ['tætɪ] adj malridotto(a)

taught [tɔːt] pt, pp of **teach**

taunt [tɔːnt] n scherno ♦ vt schernire

Taurus ['tɔːrəs] n Toro

taut [tɔːt] *adj* teso(a)
tax [tæks] *n* (*on goods*) imposta; (*on services*) tassa; (*on income*) imposte *fpl*, tasse *fpl* ♦ *vt* tassare; (*fig: strain: patience etc*) mettere alla prova; **~able** *adj* (*income*) imponibile; **~ation** [-'seɪʃən] *n* tassazione *f*; tasse *fpl*, imposte *fpl*; **~avoidance** *n* elusione *f* fiscale; **~ disc** (*BRIT*) *n* (*AUT*) = bollo; **~evasion** *n* evasione *f* fiscale; **~free** *adj* esente da imposte
taxi ['tæksɪ] *n* taxi *m inv* ♦ *vi* (*AVIAT*) rullare; **~ driver** *n* tassista *m/f*; **~ rank** (*BRIT*) *n* = **~ stand**; **~ stand** *n* posteggio dei taxi
tax: **~ payer** *n* contribuente *m/f*; **~ relief** *n* agevolazioni *fpl* fiscali; **~ return** *n* dichiarazione *f* dei redditi
TB *n abbr* = **tuberculosis**
tea [tiː] *n* tè *m inv*; (*BRIT: snack: for children*) merenda; **high ~** (*BRIT*) cena leggera (*presa nel tardo pomeriggio*); **~ bag** *n* bustina di tè; **~ break** (*BRIT*) *n* intervallo per il tè
teach [tiːtʃ] (*pt, pp* **taught**) *vt*: **to ~ sb sth, ~ sth to sb** insegnare qc a qn ♦ *vi* insegnare; **~er** *n* insegnante *m/f*; (*in secondary school*) professore/essa; (*in primary school*) maestro/a; **~ing** *n* insegnamento
tea cosy *n* copriteiera *m inv*
teacup ['tiːkʌp] *n* tazza da tè
teak [tiːk] *n* teak *m*
tea leaves *npl* foglie *fpl* di tè
team [tiːm] *n* squadra; (*of animals*) tiro; **~work** *n* lavoro di squadra
teapot ['tiːpɔt] *n* teiera
tear¹ [tɛə*] (*pt* **tore**, *pp* **torn**) *n* strappo ♦ *vt* strappare ♦ *vi* strapparsi; **~ along** *vi* (*rush*) correre all'impazzata; **~ up** *vt* (*sheet of paper etc*) strappare
tear² [tɪə*] *n* lacrima; **in ~s** in lacrime; **~ful** *adj* piangente, lacrimoso(a); **~ gas** *n* gas *m* lacrimogeno
tearoom [tiːruːm] *n* sala da tè
tease [tiːz] *vt* canzonare; (*unkindly*) tormentare

tea set *n* servizio da tè
teaspoon ['tiːspuːn] *n* cucchiaino da tè; (*also*: **~ful**: *as measurement*) cucchiaino
teat [tiːt] *n* capezzolo
teatime ['tiːtaɪm] *n* ora del tè
tea towel (*BRIT*) *n* strofinaccio (per i piatti)
technical ['tɛknɪkl] *adj* tecnico(a); **~ college** (*BRIT*) *n* ≈ istituto tecnico; **~ity** [-'kælɪtɪ] *n* tecnicità; (*detail*) dettaglio tecnico; (*legal*) cavillo
technician [tɛk'nɪʃən] *n* tecnico/a
technique [tɛk'niːk] *n* tecnica
technological [tɛknə'lɔdʒɪkl] *adj* tecnologico(a)
technology [tɛk'nɔlədʒɪ] *n* tecnologia
teddy (bear) ['tɛdɪ-] *n* orsacchiotto
tedious ['tiːdɪəs] *adj* noioso(a), tedioso(a)
tee [tiː] *n* (*GOLF*) tee *m inv*
teem [tiːm] *vi*: **to ~ with** brulicare di; **it is ~ing (with rain)** piove a dirotto
teenage ['tiːneɪdʒ] *adj* (*fashions etc*) per giovani, per adolescenti; **~r** *n* adolescente *m/f*
teens [tiːnz] *npl*: **to be in one's ~** essere adolescente
tee-shirt ['tiːʃəːt] *n* = **T-shirt**
teeter ['tiːtə*] *vi* barcollare, vacillare
teeth [tiːθ] *npl* of **tooth**
teethe [tiːð] *vi* mettere i denti
teething ring ['tiːðɪŋ-] *n* dentaruolo
teething troubles ['tiːðɪŋ-] *npl* (*fig*) difficoltà *fpl* iniziali
teetotal ['tiː'təutl] *adj* astemio(a)
telegram ['tɛlɪgræm] *n* telegramma *m*
telegraph ['tɛlɪgrɑːf] *n* telegrafo
telepathy [tə'lɛpəθɪ] *n* telepatia
telephone ['tɛlɪfəun] *n* telefono ♦ *vt* (*person*) telefonare a; (*message*) comunicare per telefono; **~ booth** (*BRIT* **~ box**) *n* cabina telefonica; **~ call** *n* telefonata; **~ directory** *n* elenco telefonico; **~ number** *n* numero di telefono; **telephonist** [tə'lɛfənɪst] (*BRIT*) *n* telefonista *m/f*

telescope ['tɛlɪskəup] n telescopio

television ['tɛlɪvɪʒən] n television f; **on ~** alla televisione; **~ set** n televisore m

telex ['tɛlɛks] n telex m inv ♦ vt trasmettere per telex; **to ~ sb** contattare qn via telex

tell [tɛl] (pt, pp **told**) vt dire; (relate: story) raccontare; (distinguish): **to ~ sth from** distinguere qc da ♦ vi (talk): **to ~ (of)** parlare (di); (have effect) farsi sentire, avere effetto; **to ~ sb to do** dire a qn di fare; **~ off** vt rimproverare, sgridare; **~er** n (in bank) cassiere/a; **~ing** adj (remark, detail) rivelatore(trice); **~tale** adj (sign) rivelatore(trice)

telly ['tɛlɪ] (BRIT: inf) n abbr (= television) tivù f inv

temerity [tə'mɛrɪtɪ] n temerarietà

temp [tɛmp] n abbr (= temporary) segretaria temporanea

temper ['tɛmpə*] n (nature) carattere m; (mood) umore m; (fit of anger) collera ♦ vt (moderate) temperare, moderare; **to be in a ~** essere in collera; **to lose one's ~** andare in collera

temperament ['tɛmprəmənt] n (nature) temperamento; **~al** [-'mɛntl] adj capriccioso(a)

temperate ['tɛmprət] adj moderato(a); (climate) temperato(a)

temperature ['tɛmprətʃə*] n temperatura; **to have o run a ~** avere la febbre

tempest ['tɛmpɪst] n tempesta

template ['tɛmplɪt] n sagoma

temple ['tɛmpl] n (building) tempio; (ANAT) tempia

temporary ['tɛmpərərɪ] adj temporaneo(a); (job, worker) avventizio(a), temporaneo(a)

tempt [tɛmpt] vt tentare; **to ~ sb into doing** indurre qn a fare; **~ation** [-'teɪʃən] n tentazione f; **~ing** adj allettante

ten [tɛn] num dieci

tenacity [tə'næsɪtɪ] n tenacia

tenancy ['tɛnənsɪ] n affitto; condizio-

ne f di inquilino

tenant ['tɛnənt] n inquilino/a

tend [tɛnd] vt badare a, occuparsi di ♦ vi: **to ~ to do** tendere a fare

tendency ['tɛndənsɪ] n tendenza

tender ['tɛndə*] adj tenero(a); (sore) dolorante ♦ n (COMM: offer) offerta; (money): **legal ~** moneta in corso legale ♦ vt offrire

tendon ['tɛndən] n tendine m

tenement ['tɛnəmənt] n casamento

tenet ['tɛnət] n principio

tennis ['tɛnɪs] n tennis m; **~ ball** n palla da tennis; **~ court** n campo da tennis; **~ player** n tennista m/f; **~ racket** n racchetta da tennis; **~ shoes** npl scarpe fpl da tennis

tenor ['tɛnə*] n (MUS) tenore m

tenpin bowling ['tɛnpɪn-] n bowling m

tense [tɛns] adj teso(a) ♦ n (LING) tempo

tension ['tɛnʃən] n tensione f

tent [tɛnt] n tenda

tentative ['tɛntətɪv] adj esitante, incerto(a); (conclusion) provvisorio(a)

tenterhooks ['tɛntəhuks] npl: **on ~** sulle spine

tenth [tɛnθ] num decimo(a)

tent: ~ peg n picchetto da tenda; **~ pole** n palo da tenda, montante m

tenuous ['tɛnjuəs] adj tenue

tenure ['tɛnjuə*] n (of property) possesso; (of job) permanenza; titolarità

tepid ['tɛpɪd] adj tiepido(a)

term [tə:m] n termine m; (SCOL) trimestre m; (LAW) sessione f ♦ vt chiamare, definire; **~s** npl (conditions) condizioni fpl; (COMM) prezzi mpl, tariffe fpl; **in the short/long ~** a breve/lunga scadenza; **to be on good ~s with sb** essere in buoni rapporti con qn; **to come to ~s with** (problem) affrontare

terminal ['tə:mɪnl] adj finale, terminale; (disease) terminale ♦ n (ELEC) morsetto; (COMPUT) terminale m; (AVIAT, for oil, ore etc) terminal m inv; (BRIT: also: **coach ~**) capolinea m

terminate ['təːmɪneɪt] vt mettere
fine a

termini ['təːmɪnaɪ] npl of **terminus**

terminus ['təːmɪnəs] (pl **termini**)
n (for buses) capolinea m; (for trains)
stazione f terminale

terrace ['tɛrəs] n terrazza; (BRIT:
row of houses) fila di case a schiera;
the ~s npl (BRIT: SPORT) le gradi-
nate; ~**d** adj (garden) a terrazze

terracotta ['tɛrə'kɔtə] n terracotta

terrain [tɛ'reɪn] n terreno

terrible ['tɛrɪbl] adj terribile; **terribly** adv terribilmente; (very badly)
malissimo

terrier ['tɛrɪə*] n terrier m inv

terrific [tə'rɪfɪk] adj incredibile, fan-
tastico(a); (wonderful) formidabile,
eccezionale

terrify ['tɛrɪfaɪ] vt terrorizzare

territory ['tɛrɪtərɪ] n territorio

terror ['tɛrə*] n terrore m; ~**ism** n
terrorismo; ~**ist** n terrorista m/f

terse [təːs] adj (style) conciso(a);
(reply) laconico(a)

Terylene ['tɛrəliːn] ® n terital m ®,
terilene m ®

test [tɛst] n (trial, check, of courage
etc) prova; (MED) esame m;
(CHEM) analisi f inv; (exam: of intelligence etc) test m inv; (: in
school) compito in classe; (also:
driving ~) esame m di guida ♦ vt
provare; esaminare; analizzare; sottoporre ad esame; **to** ~ **sb in history** esaminare qn in storia

testament ['tɛstəmənt] n testamento; **the Old/New T**~ il Vecchio/
Nuovo testamento

testicle ['tɛstɪkl] n testicolo

testify ['tɛstɪfaɪ] vi (LAW) testimoniare, deporre; **to** ~ **to sth** (LAW)
testimoniare qc; (gen) comprovare
or dimostrare qc

testimony ['tɛstɪmənɪ] n (LAW) testimonianza, deposizione f

test: ~ **match** n (CRICKET, RUG-
BY) partita internazionale; ~ **pilot**
n pilota m collaudatore; ~ **tube** n
provetta

tetanus ['tɛtənəs] n tetano

tether ['tɛðə*] vt legare ♦ n: **at the
end of one's** ~ al limite (della pazienza)

text [tɛkst] n testo; ~**book** n libro di
testo

textiles ['tɛkstaɪlz] npl tessuti mpl;
(industry) industria tessile

texture ['tɛkstʃə*] n tessitura; (of
skin, paper etc) struttura

Thames [tɛmz] n: **the** ~ il Tamigi

than [ðæn, ðən] conj (in comparisons) di; (with numerals, pronouns,
proper names) di; **more** ~ **10**/once
più di 10/una volta; **I have more/
less** ~ **you** ne ho più/meno di te; **I
have more pens** ~ **pencils** ho più
penne che matite; **she is older** ~
you think è più vecchia di quanto tu
(non) pensi

thank [θæŋk] vt ringraziare; ~ **you
(very much)** grazie (tante); ~**s** npl
ringraziamenti mpl, grazie fpl ♦ excl
grazie!; ~**s to** grazie a; ~**ful** adj:
~**ful (for)** riconoscente (per);
~**less** adj ingrato(a); **T**~**sgiving
(Day)** n giorno del ringraziamento

KEYWORD

that [ðæt] (pl **those**) adj (demonstrative) quel(quell', quello) m; quel-
la(quell') f; ~ **man/woman/book**
quell'uomo/quella donna/quel libro;
(not "this") quell'uomo/quella donna/
quel libro là; ~ **one** quello(a) là

♦ pron **1** (demonstrative) ciò; (not
"this one") quello(a); **who's** ~? chi
è?; **what's** ~? cos'è quello?; **is** ~
you? sei tu?; **I prefer this to** ~
preferisco questo a quello; ~**'s what
he said** questo è ciò che ha detto;
what happened after ~? che è successo dopo?; ~ **is (to say)** cioè

2 (relative: direct) che; (: indirect)
cui; **the book** (~) **I read** il libro
che ho letto; **the box** (~) **I put it in**
la scatola in cui l'ho messo; **the
people** (~) **I spoke to** le persone
con cui or con le quali ho parlato

3 (relative: of time) cui; **the day**

(~) he came il giorno in cui è venuto

◆ conj che; he thought ~ I was ill pensava che lo fossi malato

◆ adv (demonstrative) così; I can't work ~ much non posso lavorare (così) tanto; ~ high così alto; the wall's above ~ high and ~ thick il muro è alto circa così e spesso circa così

thatched [θætʃt] adj (roof) di paglia; ~ cottage n cottage m inv col tetto di paglia

thaw [θɔ:] n disgelo ◆ vi (ice) sciogliersi; (food) scongelarsi ◆ vt (food: also: ~ out) (fare) scongelare

---

KEYWORD

the [ðiː, ðə] def art 1 (gen) il(lo, l') m; la(l') f; i(gli) mpl; le fpl; ~ boy/girl/ink il ragazzo/la ragazza/l'inchiostro; ~ books/pencils i libri/le matite; ~ history of ~ world la storia del mondo; give it to ~ postman dallo al postino; I haven't ~ time/money non ho tempo/soldi; ~ rich and ~ poor i ricchi e i poveri

2 (in titles): Elizabeth ~ First Elisabetta prima; Peter ~ Great Pietro il grande

3 (in comparisons): ~ more he works, ~ more he earns più lavora più guadagna

theatre ['θɪətə*] (US **theater**) n teatro; (also: lecture ~) aula magna; (also: operating ~) sala operatoria; **~-goer** n frequentatore/trice di teatri

theatrical [θɪ'ætrɪkl] adj teatrale

theft [θɛft] n furto

their [ðɛə*] adj il(la) loro, pl i(le) loro; **~s** pron il(la) loro, pl i(le) loro; see also my; mine

them [ðɛm, ðəm] pron (direct) li(le); (indirect) gli, loro (after vb); (stressed, after prep: people) loro; (: people, things) essi(e); see also me

theme [θiːm] n tema m; ~ park n

parco di divertimenti (intorno a un tema centrale); ~ song n tema musicale

themselves [ðəm'sɛlvz] pl pron (reflexive) si; (emphatic) loro stessi(e); (after prep) se stessi(e)

then [ðɛn] adv (at that time) allora; (next) poi, dopo; (and also) e poi ◆ conj (therefore) perciò, dunque, quindi ◆ adj: the ~ president il presidente di allora; by ~ allora; from ~ on da allora in poi

theology [θɪ'ɔlədʒɪ] n teologia

theorem ['θɪərəm] n teorema m

theoretical [θɪə'rɛtɪkl] adj teorico(a)

theory ['θɪərɪ] n teoria

therapy ['θɛrəpɪ] n terapia

KEYWORD

there [ðɛə*] adv 1: ~ is, ~ are c'è, ci sono; ~ are 3 of them (people) sono in 3; (things) ce ne sono 3; ~ is ~-no-one here non c'è nessuno qui; ~ has been an accident c'è stato un incidente

2 (referring to place) lì, là; up/in/down ~ lassù/là dentro/laggiù; he went ~ on Friday ci è andato venerdì; I want that book ~ voglio quel libro là or lì; ~ he is! eccolo!

3: ~, ~ (esp to child) su, su

thereabouts [ðɛərə'bauts] adv (place) nei pressi, da quelle parti; (amount) giù di lì, all'incirca

thereafter [ðɛər'ɑːftə*] adv da allora in poi

thereby [ðɛə'baɪ] adv con ciò

therefore ['ðɛəfɔː*] adv perciò, quindi

there's [ðɛəz] = there is; there has

thermal ['θəːml] adj termico(a)

thermometer [θə'mɔmɪtə*] n termometro

Thermos ['θəːmɔs] ® n (also: ~ flask) thermos m inv ®

thesaurus [θɪ'sɔːrəs] n dizionario dei sinonimi

these [ðiːz] pl pron, adj questi(e)

theses ['θiːsiːz] npl of thesis

thesis ['θiːsɪs] (pl **theses**) n tesi f inv

they [ðeɪ] pl pron essi(esse); (people only) loro; ~ **say that ...** (it is said that) si dice che ...; **~'d** = they had; they would; **~'ll** = they shall; they will; **~'re** = they are; **~'ve** = they have

thick [θɪk] adj spesso(a); (crowd) compatto(a); (stupid) ottuso(a), lento(a) ♦ n: **in the ~ of** nel folto di; **it's 20 cm ~** ha uno spessore di 20 cm; **~en** vi ispessire ♦ vt (sauce etc) ispessire, rendere più denso(a); **~ly** adv (spread) a strati spessi; (cut) a fette grosse; (populated) densamente; **~ness** n spessore m; **~set** adj tarchiato(a), tozzo(a); **~skinned** adj (fig) insensibile

thief [θiːf] (pl **thieves**) n ladro/a

thieves [θiːvz] npl of **thief**

thigh [θaɪ] n coscia

thimble ['θɪmbl] n ditale m

thin [θɪn] adj sottile; (person) magro(a); (soup) poco denso(a) ♦ vt: **to ~ (down)** (sauce, paint) diluire

thing [θɪŋ] n cosa, (object) oggetto; (mania): **to have a ~ about** essere fissato(a) con; **~s** npl (belongings) cose fpl; **poor ~** poverino(a); **the best ~ would be to** la cosa migliore sarebbe di; **how are ~s?** come va?

think [θɪŋk] (pt, pp **thought**) vi pensare, riflettere ♦ vt pensare, credere; (imagine) immaginare; **to ~ of** pensare a; **what did you ~ of them?** cosa ne ha pensato?; **to ~ about** sth/sb pensare a qc/qn; **I'll ~ about it** ci penserò; **to ~ of doing** pensare di fare; **I ~ so/not** penso di sì/no; **to ~ well of** avere una buona opinione di; **~ out** vt (plan) elaborare; (solution) trovare; **~ over** vt riflettere su; **~ through** vt riflettere a fondo su; **~ up** vt ideare; **~ tank** n commissione f di esperti

third [θɜːd] num terzo/a ♦ n terzo/a; (fraction) terzo, terza parte f; (AUT) terza; (BRIT: SCOL: degree) laurea col minimo dei voti; **~ly** adv in terzo luogo; **~ party insurance** (BRIT)

n assicurazione f contro terzi; **~rate** adj di qualità scadente; **the T~ World** n il Terzo Mondo

thirst [θɜːst] n sete f; **~y** adj (person) assetato(a), che ha sete

thirteen [θɜː'tiːn] num tredici

thirty ['θɜːtɪ] num trenta

this [ðɪs] (pl **these**) adj (demonstrative) questo(a); **~ man/woman/book** quest'uomo/questa donna/questo libro; (not "that") quest'uomo/questa donna/questo libro qui; **~ one** questo(a) qui
♦ pron (demonstrative) questo(a); (not "that one") questo(a) qui; **who/what is ~?** chi è/che cos'è questo?; **I prefer ~** io preferisco questo a quello; **~ is where I live** io abito qui; **~ is what he said** questo è ciò che ha detto; **~ is Mr Brown** (in introductions, photo) questo è il signor Brown; (on telephone) sono il signor Brown
♦ adv (demonstrative): **~ high/long** etc alto/lungo etc così; **I didn't know things were ~ bad** non sapevo andasse così male

thistle ['θɪsl] n cardo

thong [θɒŋ] n cinghia

thorn [θɔːn] n spina; **~y** adj spinoso(a)

thorough ['θʌrə] adj (search) minuzioso(a); (knowledge, research) approfondito(a), profondo(a); (person) coscienzioso(a); (cleaning) a fondo; **~bred** n (horse) purosangue m/f inv; **~fare** n strada transitabile; **"no ~fare"** "divieto di transito"; **~ly** adv (search) minuziosamente; (wash, study) a fondo; (very) assolutamente

those [ðəʊz] pl pron quelli(e) ♦ pl a quei(quegli) mpl; quelle fpl

though [ðəʊ] conj benché, sebbene ♦ adv comunque

thought [θɔːt] pt, pp of **think** ♦ n pensiero; (opinion) opinione f; **~ful**

adj pensieroso(a), pensoso(a); (*considerate*) premuroso(a); **~less** *adj* sconsiderato(a); (*behaviour*) scortese

thousand ['θaʊzənd] *num* mille; one ~ mille; **~s of** migliaia di; **~th** *num* millesimo(a)

thrash [θræʃ] *vt* picchiare; bastonare; (*defeat*) battere; ~ **about** *vi* dibattersi; ~ **out** *vt* dibattere

thread [θrɛd] *n* filo; (*of screw*) filetto ♦ *vt* (*needle*) infilare; **~bare** *adj* consumato(a), logoro(a)

threat [θrɛt] *n* minaccia; **~en** *vi* (*storm*) minacciare ♦ *vt*: **to ~en sb with/to do** minacciare qn con/di fare

three [θriː] *num* tre; **~-dimensional** *adj* tridimensionale; (*film*) stereoscopico(a); **~-piece suit** *n* completo (con gilè); **~-piece suite** *n* salotto comprendente un divano e due poltrone; **~-ply** *adj* (*wool*) a tre fili

thresh [θrɛʃ] *vt* (*AGR*) trebbiare

threshold ['θrɛʃhəʊld] *n* soglia

threw [θruː] *pt of* **throw**

thrifty ['θrɪftɪ] *adj* economico(a)

thrill [θrɪl] *n* brivido ♦ *vt* (*audience*) elettrizzare; **to be ~ed** (*with gift etc*) essere elettrizzato(a); **~er** *n* thriller *m inv*; **~ing** *adj* (*book*) pieno(a) di suspense; (*news, discovery*) elettrizzante

thrive [θraɪv] (*pt* **thrived** *or* **throve**, *pp* **thrived** *or* **thriven**) *vi* crescere *or* svilupparsi bene; (*business*) prosperare; **he ~s on it** gli fa bene, ne gode; **thriven** ['θrɪvn] *pp of* **thrive**; **thriving** *adj* fiorente

throat [θrəʊt] *n* gola; **to have a sore ~** avere (un *or* il) mal di gola

throb [θrɔb] *n* (*of heart*) palpito; (*of wound*) pulsazione *f*; (*of engine*) vibrazione *f* ♦ *vi* palpitare; pulsare; vibrare

throes [θrəʊz] *npl*: **in the ~ of** alle prese con; in preda a

thrombosis [θrɔm'bəʊsɪs] *n* trombosi *f*

throne [θrəʊn] *n* trono

throng [θrɔŋ] *n* moltitudine *f* ♦ *vt* affollare

throttle ['θrɔtl] *n* (*AUT*) valvola a farfalla ♦ *vt* strangolare

through [θruː] *prep* attraverso; (*time*) per, durante; (*by means of*) per mezzo di; (*owing to*) a causa di ♦ *adj* (*ticket, train, passage*) diretto(a) ♦ *adv* attraverso; **to put sb ~ to sb** (*TEL*) passare qn a qn; **to be ~** (*TEL*) ottenere la comunicazione; (*have finished*) essere finito(a); **"no ~ road"** (*BRIT*) "strada senza sbocco"; **~out** *prep* (*place*) dappertutto in; (*time*) per *or* durante tutto(a) ♦ *adv* dappertutto; sempre

throve [θrəʊv] *pt of* **thrive**

throw [θrəʊ] (*pt* **threw**, *pp* **thrown**) *n* (*SPORT*) lancio, tiro ♦ *vt* tirare, gettare; (*SPORT*) lanciare, tirare; (*rider*) disarcionare; (*fig*) confondere; **to ~ a party** dare una festa; **~ away** *vt* gettare *or* buttare via; **~ off** *vt* sbarazzarsi di; **~ out** *vt* buttare fuori; (*reject*) respingere; **~ up** *vi* vomitare; **~away** *adj* da buttare; **~-in** *n* (*SPORT*) rimessa in gioco; **thrown** *pp of* **throw**

thru [θruː] (*US*) *prep, adj, adv* = **through**

thrush [θrʌʃ] *n* tordo

thrust [θrʌst] (*pt, pp* **thrust**) *n* (*TECH*) spinta ♦ *vt* spingere con forza; (*push in*) conficcare

thud [θʌd] *n* tonfo

thug [θʌg] *n* delinquente *m*

thumb [θʌm] *n* (*ANAT*) pollice *m*; **to ~ a lift** fare l'autostop; **~ through** *vt fus* (*book*) sfogliare; **~tack** (*US*) *n* puntina da disegno

thump [θʌmp] *n* colpo forte; (*sound*) tonfo ♦ *vt* (*person*) picchiare; (*object*) battere su ♦ *vi* picchiare; battere

thunder ['θʌndə*] *n* tuono ♦ *vi* tuonare; (*train etc*): **to ~ past** passare con un rombo; **~bolt** *n* fulmine *m*; **~clap** *n* rombo di tuono; **~storm** *n* temporale *m*; **~y** *adj* temporalesco(a)

Thursday ['θəːzdɪ] *n* giovedì *m inv*

thus [ðʌs] *adv* così

thwart [θwɔːt] *vt* contrastare

thyme [taɪm] *n* timo

thyroid ['θaɪrɔɪd] *n* (also: ~ gland) tiroide *f*

tiara [tɪ'ɑːrə] *n* (woman's) diadema *m*

Tiber ['taɪbəʳ] *n*: the ~ il Tevere

tick [tɪk] *n* (sound: of clock) tic tac *m inv*; (mark) segno; spunta; (ZOOL) zecca; (BRIT: inf): in a ~ in un attimo ♦ *vi* fare tic tac ♦ *vt* spuntare; ~ **off** *vt* spuntare; (person) sgridare; ~ **over** *vi* (engine) andare al minimo; (fig) andare avanti come al solito

ticket ['tɪkɪt] *n* biglietto; (in shop: on goods) etichetta; (parking ~) multa; (for library) scheda; ~ **collector** *n* bigliettaio; ~ **office** *n* biglietteria

tickle ['tɪkl] *vt* fare il solletico a; (fig) solleticare ♦ *vi*: **it ~s mi** (or gli etc) fa il solletico; **ticklish** [-lɪʃ] *adj* che soffre il solletico; (problem) delicato(a)

tidal ['taɪdl] *adj* di marea; (estuary) soggetto(a) alla marea; ~ **wave** *n* onda anomala

tidbit ['tɪdbɪt] (US) *n* (food) leccornia; (news) notizia ghiotta

tiddlywinks ['tɪdlɪwɪŋks] *n* gioco della pulce

tide [taɪd] *n* marea; (fig: of events) corso; **high/low** ~ alta/bassa marea; ~ **over** *vt* dare una mano a

tidy ['taɪdɪ] *adj* (room) ordinato(a), lindo(a); (dress, work) curato(a), in ordine; (person) ordinato(a) ♦ *vt* (also: ~ up) riordinare, mettere in ordine

tie [taɪ] *n* (string etc) legaccio; (BRIT: also: neck~) cravatta; (fig: link) legame *m*; (SPORT: draw) pareggio ♦ *vt* (parcel) legare; (ribbon) annodare ♦ *vi* (SPORT) pareggiare; **to ~ sth in a bow** annodare qc; **to ~ a knot in sth** fare un nodo a qc; ~ **down** *vt* legare; (to price etc) costringere ad accettare; ~ **up** *vt*

(parcel, dog) legare; (boat) ormeggiare; (arrangements) concludere; **to be ~d up** (busy) essere occupato(a) or preso(a)

tier [tɪəʳ] *n* fila; (of cake) piano, strato

tiger ['taɪgəʳ] *n* tigre *f*

tight [taɪt] *adj* (rope) teso(a), tirato(a); (money) poco(a); (clothes, budget, bend etc) stretto(a); (control) severo(a), fermo(a); (inf: drunk) sbronzo(a) ♦ *adv* (squeeze) fortemente; (shut) ermeticamente; ~**s** (BRIT) *npl* collant *m inv*; ~**en** *vt* (rope) tendere; (screw) stringere; (control) rinforzare ♦ *vi* tendersi; stringersi; ~**fisted** *adj* avaro(a); ~**ly** *adv* (grasp) bene, saldamente; ~**rope** *n* corda (da acrobata)

tile [taɪl] *n* (on roof) tegola; (on wall or floor) piastrella, mattonella; ~**d** *adj* di tegole; a piastrelle, a mattonelle

till [tɪl] *n* registratore di cassa ♦ *vt* (land) coltivare ♦ *prep, conj* = **until**

tiller ['tɪləʳ] *n* (NAUT) barra del timone

tilt [tɪlt] *vt* inclinare, far pendere ♦ *vi* inclinarsi, pendere

timber ['tɪmbəʳ] *n* (material) legname *m*; (trees) alberi *mpl* da legname

time [taɪm] *n* tempo; (epoch: often pl) epoca, tempo; (by clock) ora; (moment) momento; (occasion) volta; (MUS) tempo ♦ *vt* (race) cronometrare; (programme) calcolare la durata di; (fix moment for) programmare; (remark etc) dire (or fare) al momento giusto; **a long** ~ molto tempo; **for the** ~ **being** per il momento; **4 at a** ~ 4 per or alla volta; **from** ~ **to** ~ ogni tanto; **at** ~**s** a volte; **in** ~ (soon enough) in tempo; (after some ~) col tempo; (MUS) a tempo; **in a week's** ~ fra una settimana; **in no** ~ in un attimo; **any** ~ in qualsiasi momento; **on** ~ puntualmente; **5** ~ **5** 5 volte 5, 5 per 5; **what** ~ **is it?** che ora è?, che ore sono?; **to have a good** ~ divertirsi;

~ **bomb** *n* bomba a orologeria; ~**less** *adj* eterno(a); ~ **off** *n* tempo libero; ~**r** *n* (~ *switch*) temporizzatore *m*; (*in kitchen*) contaminuti *m inv*; ~ **scale** *n* periodo; ~**share** *adj*: ~**share apartment/villa** appartamento/villa in multiproprietà; ~ **switch** (*BRIT*) *n* temporizzatore *m*; ~**table** *n* orario; ~ **zone** *n* fuso orario

timid ['tɪmɪd] *adj* timido(a); (*easily scared*) pauroso(a)

timing ['taɪmɪŋ] *n* (*SPORT*) cronometraggio; (*fig*) scelta del momento opportuno

timpani ['tɪmpənɪ] *npl* timpani *mpl*

tin [tɪn] *n* stagno; (*also*: ~ *plate*) latta; (*container*) scatola; (*BRIT*: *can*) barattolo (di latta), lattina; ~**foil** *n* stagnola

tinge [tɪndʒ] *n* sfumatura ♦ *vt*: ~**d with** tinto(a) di

tingle ['tɪŋgl] *vi* pizzicare

tinker ['tɪŋkə*] *n*: ~ **with** *vt fus* armeggiare intorno a; cercare di riparare

tinned [tɪnd] (*BRIT*) *adj* (*food*) in scatola

tin opener ['-əʊpnə*] (*BRIT*) *n* apriscatole *m inv*

tinsel ['tɪnsl] *n* decorazioni *fpl* natalizie (*argentate*)

tint [tɪnt] *n* tinta; ~**ed** *adj* (*hair*) tinto(a); (*spectacles*, *glass*) colorato(a)

tiny ['taɪnɪ] *adj* minuscolo(a)

tip [tɪp] *n* (*end*) punta; (*gratuity*) mancia; (*BRIT*: *for rubbish*) immondezzaio; (*advice*) suggerimento ♦ *vt* (*waiter*) dare la mancia a; (*tilt*) inclinare; (*overturn*: *also*: ~ *over*) capovolgere; (*empty*: *also*: ~ *out*) scaricare; ~**off** *n* (*hint*) soffiata; ~**ped** (*BRIT*) *adj* (*cigarette*) col filtro

Tipp-Ex ['tɪpɛks] ® *n* correttore *m*

tipsy ['tɪpsɪ] *adj* brillo(a)

tiptoe ['tɪptəʊ] *n*: **on** ~ in punta di piedi

tiptop ['tɪp'tɔp] *adj*: **in** ~ **condition** in ottime condizioni

tire ['taɪə*] *n* (*US*) = **tyre** ♦ *vt* stancare ♦ *vi* stancarsi; ~**d** *adj* stanco(a); **to be** ~**d of** essere stanco *or* stufo di; ~**less** *adj* instancabile; ~**some** *adj* noioso(a); **tiring** *adj* faticoso(a)

tissue ['tɪʃuː] *n* tessuto; (*paper handkerchief*) fazzoletto di carta; ~ **paper** *n* carta velina

tit [tɪt] *n* (*bird*) cinciallegra; **to give** ~ **for tat** rendere pan per focaccia

titbit ['tɪtbɪt] (*BRIT*) *n* (*food*) leccornia; (*news*) notizia ghiotta

title ['taɪtl] *n* titolo; ~ **deed** *n* (*LAW*) titolo di proprietà; ~ **role** *n* ruolo *or* parte *f* principale

titter ['tɪtə*] *vi* ridere scioccamente

TM *abbr* = **trademark**

to [tuː, tə] *prep* **1** (*direction*) a; **to go** ~ **France/London/school** andare in Francia/a Londra/a scuola; **to go** ~ **Paul's/the doctor's** andare da Paul/ dal dottore; **the road** ~ **Edimburgo** la strada per Edimburgo; ~ **the left/right** a sinistra/destra

2 (*as far as*) (fino) a; **from here** ~ **London** da qui a Londra; **to count** ~ **10** contare fino a 10; **from 40** ~ **50 people** da 40 a 50 persone

3 (*with expressions of time*): **a quarter** ~ **5** le 5 meno un quarto; **it's twenty** ~ **3** sono le 3 meno venti

4 (*for*, *of*): **the key** ~ **the front door** la chiave della porta d'ingresso; **a letter** ~ **his wife** una lettera a sua moglie

5 (*expressing indirect object*) a; **to give sth** ~ **sb** dare qc a qn; **to talk** ~ **sb** parlare a qn; **to be a danger** ~ **sb/sth** rappresentare un pericolo per qn/qc

6 (*in relation to*) a; **3 goals** ~ **2** 3 goal a 2; **30 miles** ~ **the gallon** ~ 11 chilometri con un litro

7 (*purpose*, *result*): **to come** ~ **sb's aid** venire in aiuto a qn; **to sentence sb** ~ **death** condannare a morte qn; ~ **my surprise** con mia sorpresa

♦ *with vb* **1** (*simple infinitive*): ~ go/eat *etc* andare/mangiare *etc*
2 (*following another vb*): **to want/ try/start** ~ do volere/cercare di/ cominciare a fare
3 (*with vb omitted*): **I don't want** ~ non voglio (farlo); **you ought** ~ devi (farlo)
4 (*purpose, result*) per; **I did it** ~ **help you** l'ho fatto per aiutarti
5 (*equivalent to relative clause*): **I have things** ~ do ho da fare; **the main thing is** ~ **try** la cosa più importante è provare
6 (*after adjective etc*): **ready** ~ **go** pronto a partire; **too old/young** ~ ... troppo vecchio/giovane per

♦ *adv*: **to push the door** ~ accostare la porta

toad [təud] *n* rospo; ~**stool** *n* fungo (velenoso)

toast [təust] *n* (CULIN) pane *m* tostato; (*drink, speech*) brindisi *m inv* ♦ *vt* (CULIN) tostare; (*drink to*) brindare a; **a piece** *or* **slice of** ~ una fetta di pane tostato; ~**er** *n* tostapane *m inv*

tobacco [tə'bækəu] *n* tabacco; ~**nist** *n* tabaccaio/a; ~**nist's (shop)** *n* tabaccheria

toboggan [tə'bɔgən] *n* toboga *m inv*

today [tə'deɪ] *adv* oggi ♦ *n* (*also fig*) oggi *m inv*

toddler ['tɔdlə*] *n* bambino/a che impara a camminare

to-do *n* (*fuss*) storie *fpl*

toe [təu] *n* dito del piede; (*of shoe*) punta; **to** ~ **the line** (*fig*) stare in riga, conformarsi; ~**nail** *n* unghia del piede

toffee ['tɔfɪ] *n* caramella; ~ **apple** *n* mela caramellata

toga ['təugə] *n* toga

together [tə'geðə*] *adv* insieme; (*at same time*) allo stesso tempo; ~ **with** insieme a

toil [tɔɪl] *n* travaglio, fatica ♦ *vi* af-

fannarsi; sgobbare

toilet ['tɔɪlət] *n* (BRIT: *lavatory*) gabinetto ♦ *cpd* (*bag, soap etc*) da toletta; ~ **paper** *n* carta igienica; ~**ries** *npl* articoli *mpl* da toletta; ~ **roll** *n* rotolo di carta igienica; ~ **water** *n* acqua di colonia

token ['təukən] *n* (*sign*) segno; (*substitute coin*) gettone *m*; **book/ record/gift** ~ (BRIT) buono-libro/ disco/regalo

told [təuld] *pt, pp of* **tell**

tolerable ['tɔlərəbl] *adj* (*bearable*) tollerabile; (*fairly good*) passabile

tolerant ['tɔlərnt] *adj*: ~ (**of**) tollerante (nei confronti di)

tolerate ['tɔləreɪt] *vt* sopportare; (MED, TECH) tollerare

toll [təul] *n* (*tax, charge*) pedaggio ♦ *vi* (*bell*) suonare; **the accident** ~ **on the roads** il numero delle vittime della strada

tomato [tə'mɑːtəu] (*pl* ~**es**) *n* pomodoro

tomb [tuːm] *n* tomba

tomboy ['tɔmbɔɪ] *n* maschiaccio

tombstone ['tuːmstəun] *n* pietra tombale

tomcat ['tɔmkæt] *n* gatto

tomorrow [tə'mɔrəu] *adv* domani ♦ *n* (*also fig*) domani *m inv*; **the day after** ~ dopodomani; ~ **morning** domani mattina

ton [tʌn] *n* tonnellata (BRIT = 1016 *kg*; US = 907 *kg*; *metric* = 1000 *kg*); ~**s of** (*inf*) un mucchio *or* sacco di

tone [təun] *n* tono ♦ *vi* (*also:* ~ **in**) intonarsi; ~ **down** *vt* (*colour, criticism, sound*) attenuare; ~ **up** *vt* (*muscles*) tonificare; ~**-deaf** *adj* che non ha orecchio (musicale)

tongs [tɔŋz] *npl* tenaglie *fpl*; (*for coal*) molle *fpl*; (*for hair*) arricciacapelli *m inv*

tongue [tʌŋ] *n* lingua; ~ **in cheek** (*say, speak*) ironicamente; ~**-tied** *adj* (*fig*) muto(a); ~**-twister** *n* scioglilingua *m inv*

tonic ['tɔnɪk] *n* (MED) tonico; (*also:* ~ **water**) acqua tonica

tonight [təˈnaɪt] adv stanotte; (this evening) stasera ♦ n questa notte; questa sera

tonnage [ˈtʌnɪdʒ] n (NAUT) tonnellaggio, stazza

tonsil [ˈtɒnsl] n tonsilla; ~**litis** [-ˈlaɪtɪs] n tonsillite f

too [tuː] adv (excessively) troppo; (also) anche; ~ **much** adv troppo ♦ adj troppo;a; ~ **many** troppi;e

took [tuk] pt of **take**

tool [tuːl] n utensile m, attrezzo; ~ **box** n cassetta f portautensili

toot [tuːt] n (of horn) colpo di clacson; (of whistle) fischio ♦ vi suonare; (with car horn) suonare il clacson

tooth [tuːθ] (pl **teeth**) n (ANAT, TECH) dente m; ~**ache** n mal m di denti; ~**brush** n spazzolino da denti; ~**paste** n dentifricio; ~**pick** n stuzzicadenti m inv

top [tɒp] n (of mountain, page, ladder) cima; (of box, cupboard, table) sopra m inv, parte f superiore; (lid: of box, jar) coperchio; (: of bottle) tappo; (blouse etc) sopra m inv; (toy) trottola ♦ adj più alto;a; (in rank) primo;a; (best) migliore ♦ vt (exceed) superare; (be first in) essere in testa al; **on** ~ di sopra, in cima a; (in addition to) oltre a; **from** ~ **to bottom** da cima a fondo; ~ **up** (US = **off**) vt riempire; (salary) integrare; ~ **floor** n ultimo piano; ~ **hat** n cilindro; ~**-heavy** adj (object) con la parte superiore troppo pesante

topic [ˈtɒpɪk] n argomento, tema; ~**al** adj d'attualità

top: ~**less** adj (bather etc) col seno scoperto; ~**level** adj (talks) ad alto livello; ~**most** adj il(la) più alto(a)

topple [ˈtɒpl] vt rovesciare, far cadere ♦ vi cadere; traballare

top-secret adj segretissimo;a

topsy-turvy [ˈtɒpsɪˈtɜːvɪ] adj, adv sottosopra inv

torch [tɔːtʃ] n torcia; (BRIT: electric) lampadina tascabile

tore [tɔː*] pt of **tear**

torment [n ˈtɔːmɛnt, vb tɔːˈmɛnt] n tormento ♦ vt tormentare

torn [tɔːn] pp of **tear**

tornado [tɔːˈpiːdəʊ] (pl ~es) n silu-ro

torrent [ˈtɒrnt] n torrente m

torrid [ˈtɒrɪd] adj torrido(a); (love affair) infuocato(a)

tortoise [ˈtɔːtəs] n tartaruga; ~**shell** [ˈtɔːtəʃel] adj di tartaruga

torture [ˈtɔːtʃə*] n tortura ♦ vt torturare

Tory [ˈtɔːrɪ] (BRIT: POL) adj dei tories, conservatore(trice) ♦ n tory m/f inv, conservatore/trice

toss [tɒs] vt gettare, lanciare; (one's head) scuotere; **to** ~ **a coin** fare a testa o croce; **to** ~ **up for sth** fare a testa o croce per qc; **to** ~ **and turn** (in bed) girarsi e rigirarsi

tot [tɒt] n (BRIT: drink) bicchierino; (child) bimbo;a

total [ˈtəʊtl] adj totale ♦ n totale m ♦ vt (add up) sommare; (amount to) ammontare a

totally [ˈtəʊtəlɪ] adv completamente

totter [ˈtɒtə*] vi barcollare

touch [tʌtʃ] n tocco; (sense) tatto; (contact) contatto ♦ vt toccare; a ~ of (fig) un tocco di; un pizzico di; **to get in** ~ **with** mettersi in contatto con; **to lose** ~ (friends) perdersi di vista; ~ **on** vt fus (topic) sfiorare, accennare a; ~ **up** vt (paint) ritoccare; ~**-and-go** adj incerto(a); ~**down** n atterraggio; (on sea) ammaraggio; (US: FOOTBALL) meta; ~**ed** adj commosso(a); ~**ing** adj commovente; ~**line** n (SPORT) linea laterale; ~**y** adj (person) suscettibile

tough [tʌf] adj duro(a); (resistant) resistente; ~**en** vt rinforzare

toupee [ˈtuːpeɪ] n parrucchino

tour [tʊə*] n viaggio; (also: package ~) viaggio organizzato o tutto compreso; (of town, museum) visita; (by artist) tournée f inv ♦ vt visitare; ~**ing** n turismo

tourism [ˈtʊərɪzəm] n turismo

tourist ['tʊərɪst] n turista m/f ♦ adv
(travel) in classe turistica ♦ cpd turi-
stico(a); ~ **office** n pro loco f inv

tournament ['tʊənəmənt] n torneo m

tousled ['taʊzld] adj (hair) arruffa-
to(a)

tout [taʊt] vi: to ~ for procacciare,
raccogliere; cercare clienti per ♦ n
(also: ticket ~) bagarino

tow [təʊ] vt rimorchiare; "**on** ~"
(BRIT), "**in** ~" (US) "veicolo ri-
morchiato"

toward(s) [tə'wɔːd(z)] prep verso;
(of attitude) nei confronti di; (of purpose) per

towel ['taʊəl] n asciugamano; (also:
tea ~) strofinaccio; ~**ling** n (fabric)
spugna; ~ **rail** (US ~ **rack**) n porta-
sciugamano

tower ['taʊə*] n torre f; ~ **block**
(BRIT) n palazzone m; ~**ing** adj al-
tissimo(a), imponente

town [taʊn] n città f inv; **to go to** ~
andare in città; (fig) mettercela tutta; ~ **centre** n centro (città); ~
council n consiglio comunale; ~
hall n = municipio; ~ **plan** n pianta
della città; ~ **planning** n urbanisti-
ca

towrope ['təʊrəʊp] n (cavo da) ri-
morchio

tow truck (US) n carro m attrezzi
inv

toxic ['tɔksɪk] adj tossico(a)

toy [tɔɪ] n giocattolo; ~ **with** vt fus
giocare con; (idea) accarezzare, trastullarsi con; ~ **shop** n negozio di
giocattoli

trace [treɪs] n traccia ♦ vt (draw)
tracciare; (follow) seguire; (locate)
rintracciare; **tracing paper** n carta
da ricalco

track [træk] n (of person, animal)
traccia; (on tape, SPORT, path: gen)
pista; (: of bullet etc) traiettoria; (:
of suspect, animal) pista, tracce fpl;
(RAIL) binario, rotaie fpl ♦ vt seguire le tracce di; **to keep** ~ **of** seguire; ~ **down** vt (prey) scovare; sni-
dare; (sth lost) rintracciare; ~**suit**

n tuta sportiva

tract [trækt] n (GEO) tratto, estensione f; (pamphlet) opuscolo, libretto

tractor ['træktə*] n trattore m

trade [treɪd] n commercio; (skill,
job) mestiere m ♦ vi commerciare ♦
vt: to ~ **sth** (**for sth**) barattare qc
(con qc); to ~ **with/in** commerciare
con/in; ~ **in** vt (old car etc) dare
come pagamento parziale; ~ **fair** n
fiera commerciale; ~**mark** n marchio di fabbrica; ~ **name** n marca,
nome m depositato; ~**r** n commerciante m/f; ~**sman** n fornitore m;
(shopkeeper) negoziante m; ~ **union** n sindacato; ~ **unionist** sinda-
calista m/f

tradition [trə'dɪʃən] n tradizione f;
~**al** adj tradizionale

traffic ['træfɪk] n traffico ♦ vi: to ~
in (pej: liquor, drugs) trafficare in;
~ **circle** (US) n isola rotatoria; ~
jam n ingorgo (del traffico); ~
lights npl semaforo; ~ **warden** n
addetto/a al controllo del traffico e
del parcheggio

tragedy ['trædʒədɪ] n tragedia

tragic ['trædʒɪk] adj tragico(a)

trail [treɪl] n (tracks) tracce fpl, pista; (path) sentiero; (of smoke etc)
scia ♦ vt trascinare, strascicare;
(follow) seguire ♦ vi essere al traino; (dress etc) strusciare; (plant) arrampicarsi; strisciare; (in game) essere in svantaggio; ~ **behind** vi essere al traino; ~**er** n (AUT) rimor-
chio; (US) roulotte f inv; (CINEMA)
prossimamente m inv; ~**er truck**
(US) n (articulated lorry) autoartico-
lato

train [treɪn] n (tracks) treno; (of dress) coda,
strascico ♦ vt (apprentice, doctor
etc) formare; (sportsman) allenare;
(dog) addestrare; (memory) esercitare; (point: gun etc): to ~ **sth on**
puntare qc contro ♦ vi formarsi; allenarsi; ~**s** ~ **of thought** il filo
dei propri pensieri; ~**ed** adj qualifi-
cato(a); allenato(a); addestrato(a);
~**ee** [treɪ'niː] n (in trade) apprendi-

sta m/f; **~er** n (SPORT) allenatore/
trice; (: shoe) scarpa da ginnastica;
(of dogs etc) addestratore/trice;
~ing n formazione f; allenamento;
addestramento; **in ~ing** (SPORT) in
allenamento; **~ing college** n istituto professionale; (for teachers) ≈
istituto magistrale; **~ing shoes** npl
scarpe fpl da ginnastica

traipse ['treɪps] vi girovagare, andare
a zonzo

trait [treɪt] n tratto

traitor ['treɪtə*] n traditore m

tram [træm] (BRIT) n (also: **~car**)
tram m inv

tramp [træmp] n (person)
vagabondo/a; (inf: pej: woman)
sgualdrina ♦ vi camminare con passo pesante

trample ['træmpl] vt: **to ~ (underfoot)** calpestare

trampoline ['træmpəlɪn] n trampolino

tranquil ['træŋkwɪl] adj tranquil-
lo(a); **~lizer** n (MED) tranquillante
m

transact [træn'zækt] vt (business)
trattare; **~ion** [-'zækʃən] n transa-
zione f

transatlantic ['trænzət'læntɪk] adj
transatlantico(a)

transcript ['trænskrɪpt] n trascrizione f

transfer [n 'trænsfə*, vb træns'fə:*] n
(gen, also SPORT) trasferimento; n
(POL: of power) passaggio; (picture,
design) decalcomania; (: stick-on)
autoadesivo ♦ vt trasferire; passare;
to ~ the charges (BRIT: TEL) fare
una chiamata a carico del destinatario

transform [træns'fɔ:m] vt trasformare

transfusion [træns'fju:ʒən] n trasfu-
sione f

transient ['trænzɪənt] adj transito-
rio(a), fugace

transistor [træn'zɪstə*] n (ELEC)
transistor m inv; (also: **~ radio**) radio f inv a transistor

transit ['trænzɪt] n: **in ~** in transito

transitive ['trænzɪtɪv] adj (LING)
transitivo(a)

translate [trænz'leɪt] vt tradurre;
translation [-'leɪʃən] n traduzione f;
translator n traduttore/trice

transmission [trænz'mɪʃən] n trasmissione f

transmit [trænz'mɪt] vt trasmettere;
~ter n trasmettitore m

transparency [træns'pɛərnsɪ] n tra-
sparenza; (BRIT: PHOT) diapositiva

transparent [træns'pærnt] adj trasparente

transpire [træn'spaɪə*] vi (happen)
succedere; (turn out): **it ~d that** si
venne a sapere che

transplant [vb træns'plɑ:nt, n 'træns-
plɑ:nt] vt trapiantare ♦ n (MED)
trapianto

transport [n 'trænspɔ:t, vb
træns'pɔ:t] n trasporto ♦ vt trasportare; **~ation** [-'teɪʃən] n (mezzo di)
trasporto; (of prisoners) trasporto
per camionisti

transport café (BRIT) n trattoria
per camionisti

trap [træp] n (snare, trick) trappola;
(carriage) calesse m ♦ vt prendere
in trappola, intrappolare; **~ door** n
botola

trapeze [trə'pi:z] n trapezio

trappings ['træpɪŋz] npl ornamenti
mpl; indoratura, sfarzo

trash [træʃ] (pej) n (goods) ciarpame
m; (nonsense) sciocchezze fpl; **~
can** (US) n secchio della spazzatura

trauma ['trɔ:mə] n trauma m; **~tic**
[-'mætɪk] adj traumatico(a)

travel ['trævl] n viaggio; viaggi mpl
♦ vi viaggiare ♦ vt (distance) percorrere; **~ agency** n agenzia (di)
viaggi; **~ agent** n agente m di viaggio; **~ler** (US **~er**) n viaggiatore/
trice; **~ler's cheque** (US **~er's
check**) n assegno turistico; **~ling**
(US **~ing**) n viaggi mpl; **~ sickness** n mal m d'auto (or di mare or
d'aria)

travesty ['trævəstɪ] n parodia

trawler ['trɔ:lə*] n peschereccio (a
strascico)

tray [treɪ] n (for carrying) vassoio; (on desk) vaschetta

treacherous ['trɛtʃərəs] adj infido(a)

treachery ['trɛtʃəri] n tradimento

treacle ['triːkl] n melassa

tread [trɛd] n passo; (sound) rumore m di passi; (of stairs) pedata; (of tyre) battistrada m inv ♦ vi camminare; ~ **on** vt fus calpestare

treason ['triːzn] n tradimento

treasure ['trɛʒə*] n tesoro ♦ vt (value) tenere in gran conto, apprezzare molto; (store) custodire gelosamente

treasurer ['trɛʒərə*] n tesoriere/a

treasury ['trɛʒəri] n: **the T~** (BRIT), **the T~ Department** (US) il ministero del Tesoro

treat [triːt] n regalo ♦ vt trattare; (MED) curare; to ~ **sb** to **sth** offrire qc a qn

treatment ['triːtmənt] n trattamento

treaty ['triːti] n patto, trattato

treble ['trɛbl] adj triplo(a), triplice ♦ vt triplicare ♦ vi triplicarsi; ~ **clef** n chiave f di violino

tree [triː] n albero; ~ **trunk** n tronco d'albero

trek [trɛk] n escursione f a piedi; escursione f in macchina; (tiring walk) camminata sfiancante ♦ vi (as holiday) fare dell'escursionismo

trellis ['trɛlɪs] n graticcio

tremble ['trɛmbl] vi tremare

tremendous [trɪ'mɛndəs] adj (enormous) enorme; (excellent) meraviglioso(a), formidabile

tremor ['trɛmə*] n tremore m, tremito; (also: earth ~) scossa sismica

trench [trɛntʃ] n trincea

trend [trɛnd] n (tendency) tendenza; (of events) corso; (fashion) moda; ~**y** adj (idea) di moda; (clothes) all'ultima moda

trepidation [trɛpɪ'deɪʃən] n trepidazione f, agitazione f

trespass ['trɛspəs] vi: to ~ **on** entrare abusivamente in; "no ~ing" "proprietà privata", "vietato l'acces-

so"

trestle ['trɛsl] n cavalletto

trial ['traɪəl] n (LAW) processo; (test: of machine etc) collaudo; ~**s** npl (unpleasant experiences) dure prove fpl; **on** ~ (LAW) sotto processo; **by** ~ **and error** a tentoni; ~ **period** periodo di prova

triangle ['traɪæŋgl] n (MATH, MUS) triangolo

tribe [traɪb] n tribù f inv; ~**sman** n membro di tribù

tribunal [traɪ'bjuːnl] n tribunale m

tributary [trɪ'bjutəri] n (river) tributario, affluente m

tribute ['trɪbjuːt] n tributo, omaggio; **to pay** ~ **to** rendere omaggio a

trick [trɪk] n trucco; (joke) tiro; (CARDS) presa ♦ vt imbrogliare, ingannare; **to play a** ~ **on sb** giocare un tiro a qn; **that should do the** ~ vedrai che funziona; ~**ery** n inganno

trickle ['trɪkl] n (of water etc) rivolo; gocciolio ♦ vi gocciolare

tricky ['trɪkɪ] adj difficile, delicato(a)

tricycle ['traɪsɪkl] n triciclo

trifle ['traɪfl] n sciocchezza; (BRIT: CULIN:) ≈ zuppa inglese ♦ adv: **a** ~ **long** un po' lungo; **trifling** adj insignificante

trigger ['trɪgə*] n (of gun) grilletto; ~ **off** vt dare l'avvio a

trim [trɪm] adj (house, garden) ben tenuto(a); (figure) snello(a) ♦ n (haircut etc) spuntata, regolata; (embellishment) finiture fpl; (on car) guarnizioni fpl ♦ vt spuntare; (decorate): **to** ~ (**with**) decorare (con); (NAUT: a sail) orientare; ~**mings** npl decorazioni fpl; (extras: gen CULIN) guarnizione f

trinket ['trɪŋkɪt] n gingillo; (piece of jewellery) ciondolo

trip [trɪp] n viaggio; (excursion) gita, escursione f; (stumble) passo falso ♦ vi inciampare; (go lightly) camminare con passo leggero; **on a** ~ in viaggio; ~ **up** vi inciampare ♦ vt fare lo sgambetto a

tripe [traɪp] n (CULIN) trippa; (pej:

rubbish) sciocchezze *fpl*, fesserie *fpl*

triple ['trɪpl] *adj* triplo(a)

triplets ['trɪplɪts] *npl* bambini(e) trigemini(e)

triplicate ['trɪplɪkət] *n*: **in ~** in triplice copia

tripod ['traɪpɔd] *n* treppiede *m*

trite [traɪt] *adj* banale, trito(a)

triumph ['traɪʌmf] *n* trionfo ♦ *vi*: **to ~ (over)** trionfare (su)

trivia ['trɪvɪə] *npl* banalità *fpl*

trivial ['trɪvɪəl] *adj* insignificante; (*commonplace*) banale

trod [trɔd] *pt of* **tread; ~den** *pp of* **tread**

trolley ['trɔlɪ] *n* carrello; **~ bus** *n* filobus *m inv*

trombone [trɔm'bəun] *n* trombone *m*

troop [tru:p] *n* gruppo; (*MIL*) squadrone *m*; **~s** *npl* (*MIL*) truppe *fpl*; **~ in/out** *vi* entrare/uscire a frotte; **~ing the colour** *n* (*ceremony*) sfilata della bandiera

trophy ['trəufɪ] *n* trofeo

tropic ['trɔpɪk] *n* tropico; **~al** *adj* tropicale

trot [trɔt] *n* trotto ♦ *vi* trottare; **on the ~** (*BRIT*: *fig*) di fila, uno(a) dopo l'altro(a)

trouble ['trʌbl] *n* difficoltà *f inv*, problema *m*; difficoltà *fpl*, problemi; (*worry*) preoccupazione *f*; (*effort*) sforzo; (*POL*) conflitti *mpl*, disordine *m*; (*MED*): **stomach** *etc* ~ disturbi *mpl* gastrici *etc* ♦ *vt* disturbare; (*worry*) preoccupare ♦ *vi*: **to ~ to do** disturbarsi a fare; **~s** *npl* (*POL etc*) disordini *mpl*; **to be in ~** avere dei problemi; **it's no ~!** di niente!; **what's the ~?** cosa c'è che non va?; **~d** *adj* (*person*) preoccupato(a), inquieto(a); (*epoch, life*) agitato(a), difficile; **~maker** *n* elemento disturbatore, agitatore/trice; (*child*) discolo(a); **~shooter** *n* (*in conflict*) conciliatore *m*; **~some** *adj* fastidioso(a), seccante

trough [trɔf] *n* (*also*: *drinking* ~) abbeveratoio; (*also*: *feeding* ~) trogolo,

mangiatoia; (*channel*) canale *m*

trousers ['trauzəz] *npl* pantaloni *mpl*, calzoni *mpl*; **short ~** calzoncini *mpl*

trousseau ['tru:səu] (*pl* **~x** *or* **~s**) *n* corredo da sposa

trousseaux ['tru:səuz] *npl of* **trousseau**

trout [traut] *n inv* trota

trowel ['trauəl] *n* cazzuola

truant ['truənt] (*BRIT*) *n*: **to play ~** marinare la scuola

truce [tru:s] *n* tregua

truck [trʌk] *n* autocarro, camion *m inv*; (*RAIL*) carro merci aperto; (*for luggage*) carrello ♦ *n* portabagagli *inv*; **~ driver** *n* camionista *mf*; **~ farm** (*US*) *n* orto industriale

trudge [trʌdʒ] *vi* (*also*: **~ along**) trascinarsi pesantemente

true [tru:] *adj* vero(a); (*accurate*) accurato(a), esatto(a); (*genuine*) reale; (*faithful*) fedele; **to come ~** avverarsi

truffle ['trʌfl] *n* tartufo

truly ['tru:lɪ] *adv* veramente; (*truthfully*) sinceramente; (*faithfully*): **yours ~** (*in letter*) distinti saluti

trump [trʌmp] *n* (*also*: ~ *card*) atout *m inv*; **~ed-up** *adj* inventato(a)

trumpet ['trʌmpɪt] *n* tromba

truncheon ['trʌntʃən] *n* sfollagente *m inv*

trundle ['trʌndl] *vt* far rotolare rumorosamente ♦ *vi*: **to ~ along** rotolare rumorosamente

trunk [trʌŋk] *n* (*of tree, person*) tronco; (*of elephant*) proboscide *f*; (*case*) baule *m*; (*US*: *AUT*) bagagliaio; **~s** *npl* (*also*: *swimming* ~s) calzoncini *mpl* da bagno

truss [trʌs] *n* (*MED*) cinto erniario; **~ (up)** *vt* (*CULIN*) legare

trust [trʌst] *n* fiducia; (*LAW*) amministrazione *f* fiduciaria; (*COMM*) trust *m inv* ♦ *vt* (*rely on*) contare su; (*hope*) sperare; (*entrust*): **to ~ sth to sb** affidare qc a qn; **~ed** *adj* fidato(a); **~ee** [trʌs'ti:] *n* (*LAW*) amministratore(trice) fiduciario(a); (*of school etc*) amministratore/trice;

~ful adj fiducioso(a); ~ing adj ~ful: ~worthy adj fidato(a), degno(a) di fiducia

truth [truːθ, pl truːðz] n verità f inv; ~ful adj (person) sincero(a); (description) veritiero(a), esatto(a)

try [traɪ] n prova, tentativo; (RUGBY) meta ♦ vt (LAW) giudicare; (test: also: ~ out) provare; (strain) mettere alla prova ♦ vi provare; to have a ~ fare un tentativo; to ~ to do (seek) cercare di fare; ~ on vt (clothes) provare; ~ing adj (day, experience) logorante, pesante; (child) difficile, insopportabile

tsar [zaː*] n zar m inv

T-shirt ['tiː-] n maglietta

T-square ['tiː-] n riga a T

tub [tʌb] n tinozza; mastello; (bath) bagno

tuba ['tjuːbə] n tuba

tubby ['tʌbɪ] adj grassoccio(a)

tube [tjuːb] n tubo; (BRIT: underground) metropolitana, metrò m inv; (for tyre) camera d'aria; ~ **station** (BRIT) n stazione f della metropolitana

tubular ['tjuːbjʊlə*] adj tubolare

TUC (BRIT) n abbr (= Trades Union Congress) confederazione f dei sindacati britannici

tuck [tʌk] vt (put) mettere; ~ **away** vt riporre; (building): to be ~ed away essere in un luogo isolato; ~ **in** vt mettere dentro; (child) mettere a letto rimboccando le coperte ♦ vi (eat) mangiare di buon appetito; abbuffarsi; ~ **up** vt (child) rimboccare le coperte a; ~ **shop** n negozio di pasticceria (in una scuola)

Tuesday ['tjuːzdɪ] n martedì m inv

tuft [tʌft] n ciuffo

tug [tʌg] n (ship) rimorchiatore m ♦ vt tirare con forza; ~-**of-war** n tiro alla fune

tuition [tjuːˈɪʃən] n (BRIT) lezioni fpl; (: private ~) lezioni fpl private; (US: school fees) tasse fpl scolastiche

tulip ['tjuːlɪp] n tulipano

tumble ['tʌmbl] n (fall) capitombolo

♦ vi capitombolare, ruzzolare; to ~ to sth (inf) realizzare qc; ~**down** adj cadente, diroccato(a); ~ **dryer** (BRIT) n asciugatrice f

tumbler ['tʌmblə*] n bicchiere m (senza stelo)

tummy ['tʌmɪ] (inf) n pancia

tumour ['tjuːmə*] (US tumor) n tumore m

tuna ['tjuːnə] n inv (also: ~ fish) tonno

tune [tjuːn] n (melody) melodia, aria ♦ vt (MUS) accordare; (RADIO, TV, AUT) regolare, mettere a punto; to be in/out of ~ (instrument) essere accordato(a)/scordato(a); (singer) essere intonato(a)/stonato(a); ~ **in** vi: to ~ in (to) (RADIO, TV) sintonizzarsi (su); ~ **up** vi (musician) accordare lo strumento; ~**ful** adj melodioso(a); ~**r** n: piano ~**r** accordatore m

tunic ['tjuːnɪk] n tunica

Tunisia [tjuːˈnɪzɪə] n Tunisia

tunnel ['tʌnl] n galleria ♦ vi scavare una galleria

turban ['tɜːbən] n turbante m

turbulence ['tɜːbjʊləns] n (AVIAT) turbolenza

tureen [təˈriːn] n zuppiera

turf [tɜːf] n terreno erboso; (clod) zolla ♦ vt coprire di zolle erbose; ~ **out** (inf) vt buttar fuori

turgid ['tɜːdʒɪd] adj (speech) ampolloso(a), pomposo(a)

Turin [tjʊəˈrɪn] n Torino f

Turk [tɜːk] n turco/a

Turkey ['tɜːkɪ] n Turchia

turkey ['tɜːkɪ] n tacchino

Turkish ['tɜːkɪʃ] adj turco(a) ♦ n (LING) turco

turmoil ['tɜːmɔɪl] n confusione f, tumulto

turn [tɜːn] n giro; (change) cambiamento; (in road) curva; (tendency: of mind, events) tendenza; (performance) numero; (chance) turno; (MED) crisi f inv, attacco ♦ vt girare, voltare; (change): to ~ sth into trasformare qc in ♦ vi girare; (person: *look back*) girarsi, voltarsi; (*reverse direction*) girare; (*change*) cambiare; (*milk*) andare a male; (*become*) diventare; **a good** ~ **un buon servizio**; **it gave me quite a** ~ mi ha fatto prendere un bello spavento; **"no left** ~**"** (*AUT*) "divieto di svolta a sinistra"; **it's your** ~ tocca a lei; **in** ~ **a** sua volta; **a** turno; **to take** ~**s** (**at sth**) fare (qc) a turno; ~ **away** *vi* girarsi (dall'altra parte) ♦ *vt* mandare via; ~ **back** *vi* ritornare, tornare indietro ♦ *vt* far tornare indietro; (*clock*) spostare indietro; ~ **down** *vt* (*refuse*) rifiutare; (*reduce*) abbassare; (*fold*) ripiegare; ~ **in** *vi* (*inf: go to bed*) andare a letto ♦ *vt* (*fold*) voltare in dentro; ~ **off** *vi* (*from road*) girare, voltare ♦ *vt* (*light, radio, engine etc*) spegnere; ~ **on** *vt* (*light, radio etc*) accendere; ~ **out** *vt* (*light, gas*) chiudere; spegnere ♦ *vi* (*voters*) presentarsi; **to** ~ **out to be ...** rivelarsi ..., risultare ...; ~ **over** *vi* (*person*) girarsi ♦ *vt* girare; ~ **round** *vi* girare; (*person*) girarsi; ~ **up** *vi* (*person*) arrivare, presentarsi; (*lost object*) saltar fuori ♦ *vt* (*collar, sound*) alzare; ~**ing** *n* (*in road*) curva; ~**ing point** *n* (*fig*) svolta decisiva

turnip ['tə:nɪp] *n* rapa

turnout ['tə:naut] *n* presenza, affluenza

turnover ['tə:nəuvə*] *n* (*COMM*) turnover *m inv*

turnpike ['tə:npaɪk] (*US*) *n* autostrada a pedaggio

turnstile ['tə:nstaɪl] *n* tornella

turntable ['tə:nteɪbl] *n* (*on record player*) piatto

turn-up (*BRIT*) *n* (*on trousers*) risvolto

turpentine ['tə:pəntaɪn] *n* (*also: turps*) acqua ragia

turquoise ['tə:kwɔːz] *n* turchese *m* ♦ *adj* turchese

turret ['tʌrɪt] *n* torretta

turtle ['tə:tl] *n* testuggine *f*; ~**neck (sweater)** *n* maglione *m* con il collo alto

Tuscany ['tʌskənɪ] *n* Toscana

tusk [tʌsk] *n* zanna

tussle ['tʌsl] *n* baruffa, mischia

tutor ['tjuːtə*] *n* (*in college*) docente *m/f* (*responsabile di un gruppo di studenti*); (*private teacher*) precettore/trice; ~**ial** [-'tɔːrɪəl] *n* (*SCOL*) lezione *f* con discussione (*a un gruppo limitato*)

tuxedo [tʌk'siːdəu] (*US*) *n* smoking *m inv*

TV [tiː'viː] *n abbr* (= *television*) tivù *f inv*

twang [twæŋ] *n* (*of instrument*) suono vibrante; (*of voice*) accento nasale

tweed [twiːd] *n* tweed *m inv*

tweezers ['twiːzəz] *npl* pinzette *fpl*

twelfth [twelfθ] *num* dodicesimo(a)

twelve [twelv] *num* dodici; **at** ~ (**o'clock**) alle dodici, a mezzogiorno; (*midnight*) a mezzanotte

twentieth ['twentɪɪθ] *num* ventesimo(a)

twenty ['twentɪ] *num* venti

twice [twaɪs] *adv* due volte; ~ **as much** due volte tanto

twiddle ['twɪdl] *vt, vi*: **to** ~ (**with**) **sth** giocherellare con qc; **to** ~ **one's thumbs** (*fig*) girarsi i pollici

twig [twɪg] *n* ramoscello ♦ *vt, vi* (*inf*) capire

twilight ['twaɪlaɪt] *n* crepuscolo

twin [twɪn] *adj, n* gemello(a) ♦ *vt*: **to** ~ **one town with another** fare il gemellaggio di una città con un'altra; ~**-bedded room** *n* stanza con letti gemelli

twine [twaɪn] *n* spago, cordicella ♦ *vi* attorcigliarsi

twinge [twɪndʒ] *n* (*of pain*) fitta; **a** ~ **of conscience/regret** un rimorso/ rimpianto

twinkle ['twɪŋkl] *vi* scintillare; (*eyes*) brillare

twirl [twə:l] *vt* far roteare ♦ *vi* roteare

twist [twɪst] *n* torsione *f*; (*in wire, flex*) piega; (*in road*) curva; (*in sto-*

ry) colpo di scena ♦ *vt* attorcigliare; (*ankle*) slogare; (*weave*) intrecciare; (*roll around*) arrotolare; (*fig*) distorcere ♦ *vi* (*road*) serpeggiare

twit [twɪt] (*inf*) *n* cretino/a

twitch [twɪtʃ] *n* tiratina; (*nervous*) tic *m inv* ♦ *vi* contrarsi

two [tuː] *num due*; to put ~ and ~ together (*fig*) fare uno più uno; ~ **door** *adj* (*AUT*) a due porte; ~-**faced** (*pej*) *adj* (*person*) falso(a); ~**fold** *adv*: to increase ~**fold** aumentare del doppio; ~-**piece** (*suit*) *n* due pezzi *m inv*; ~-**piece** (*swimsuit*) *n* (*costume m* da bagno a) due pezzi *m inv*; ~-**some** *n* (*people*) coppia; ~-**way** *adj* (*traffic*) a due sensi

tycoon [taɪˈkuːn] *n*: (*business*) ~ magnate *m*

type [taɪp] *n* (*category*) genere *m*; (*model*) modello; (*example*) tipo; (*TYP*) tipo, carattere *m* ♦ *vt* (*letter etc*) battere (a macchina), dattilografare; ~-**cast** *adj* (*actor*) a ruolo fisso; ~**face** *n* carattere *m* tipografico; ~**script** *n* dattiloscritto; ~**writer** *n* macchina da scrivere; ~**written** *adj* dattiloscritto(a), battuto(a) a macchina

typhoid [ˈtaɪfɔɪd] *n* tifoidea

typhoon [taɪˈfuːn] *n* tifone *m*

typical [ˈtɪpɪkl] *adj* tipico(a)

typify [ˈtɪpɪfaɪ] *vt* caratterizzare; (*person*) impersonare

typing [ˈtaɪpɪŋ] *n* dattilografia

typist [ˈtaɪpɪst] *n* dattilografo/a

tyrant [ˈtaɪərnt] *n* tiranno

tyre [ˈtaɪə*] (*US* **tire**) *n* pneumatico, gomma; ~ **pressure** *n* pressione *f* (delle gomme)

tzar [zɑː*] *n* = tsar

U

U-bend [ˈjuː'-] *n* (*in pipe*) sifone *m*

ubiquitous [juːˈbɪkwɪtəs] *adj* onnipresente

udder [ˈʌdə*] *n* mammella

UFO [ˈjuːfəu] *n abbr* (= unidentified

flying object) UFO *m inv*

ugh [əːh] *excl* puah!

ugly [ˈʌglɪ] *adj* brutto(a)

UK *n abbr* = **United Kingdom**

ulcer [ˈʌlsə*] *n* ulcera; (*also: mouth ~*) afta

Ulster [ˈʌlstə*] *n* Ulster *m*

ulterior [ʌlˈtɪərɪə*] *adj* ulteriore; ~ **motive** *n* secondo fine *m*

ultimate [ˈʌltɪmət] *adj* ultimo(a), finale; (*authority*) massimo(a), supremo(a); ~**ly** *adv* alla fine; in definitiva, in fin dei conti

ultrasound [ʌltrəˈsaund] *n* (*MED*) ultrasuono

umbilical cord [ʌmbɪˈlaɪkl-] *n* cordone *m* ombelicale

umbrella [ʌmˈbrelə] *n* ombrello

umpire [ˈʌmpaɪə*] *n* arbitro

umpteen [ʌmpˈtiːn] *adj* non so quantie(i); **for the ~th time** per l'ennesima volta

UN *n abbr* (= United Nations) ONU *f*

unable [ʌnˈeɪbl] *adj*: to be ~ to non potere, essere nell'impossibilità di; essere incapace di

unaccompanied [ʌnəˈkʌmpənɪd] *adj* (*child, lady*) non accompagnato(a)

unaccountably [ʌnəˈkauntəblɪ] *adv* inesplicabilmente

unaccustomed [ʌnəˈkʌstəmd] *adj*: to be ~ to sth non essere abituato a qc

unanimous [juːˈnænɪməs] *adj* unanime; ~**ly** *adv* all'unanimità

unarmed [ʌnˈɑːmd] *adj* (*without a weapon*) disarmato(a); (*combat*) senz'armi

unashamed [ʌnəˈʃeɪmd] *adj* sfacciato(a)

unassuming [ʌnəˈsjuːmɪŋ] *adj* modesto(a), senza pretese

unattached [ʌnəˈtætʃt] *adj* senza legami, libero(a)

unattended [ʌnəˈtendɪd] *adj* (*car, child, luggage*) incustodito(a)

unattractive [ʌnəˈtræktɪv] *adj* poco attraente

unauthorized [ʌnˈɔːθəraɪzd] *adj* non

autorizzato(a)

unavoidable [ʌnəˈvɔɪdəbl] adj inevitabile

unaware [ʌnəˈwɛə*] adj: to be ~ of non sapere, ignorare; ~s adv di sorpresa, alla sprovvista

unbalanced [ʌnˈbælənst] adj squilibrato(a)

unbearable [ʌnˈbɛərəbl] adj insopportabile

unbeknown(st) [ʌnbɪˈnəun(st)] adv: ~ to all'insaputa di

unbelievable [ʌnbɪˈliːvəbl] adj incredibile

unbend [ʌnˈbɛnd] (irreg: like bend) vi distendersi ♦ vt (wire) raddrizzare

unbias(s)ed [ʌnˈbaɪəst] adj (person, report) obiettivo(a), imparziale

unborn [ʌnˈbɔːn] adj non ancora nato(a)

unbreakable [ʌnˈbreɪkəbl] adj infrangibile

unbroken [ʌnˈbrəukən] adj intero(a); (series) continuo(a); (record) imbattuto(a)

unbutton [ʌnˈbʌtn] vt sbottonare

uncalled-for [ʌnˈkɔːld-] adj (remark) fuori luogo inv; (action) ingiustificato(a)

uncanny [ʌnˈkænɪ] adj misterioso(a), strano(a)

unceasing [ʌnˈsiːsɪŋ] adj incessante

unceremonious [ˈʌnsɛrɪˈməunɪəs] adj (abrupt, rude) senza tante cerimonie

uncertain [ʌnˈsəːtn] adj incerto(a); dubbio(a); ~ty n incertezza

unchanged [ʌnˈtʃeɪndʒd] adj invariato(a)

unchecked [ʌnˈtʃɛkt] adj incontrollato(a)

uncivilized [ʌnˈsɪvɪlaɪzd] adj (gen) selvaggio(a); (fig) incivile, barbaro(a)

uncle [ˈʌŋkl] n zio

uncomfortable [ʌnˈkʌmfətəbl] adj scomodo(a); (uneasy) a disagio, agitato(a); (unpleasant) fastidioso(a)

uncommon [ʌnˈkɔmən] adj raro(a), insolito(a), non comune

uncompromising [ʌnˈkɔmprəmaɪzɪŋ] adj intransigente, inflessibile

unconcerned [ʌnkənˈsəːnd] adj: to be ~ (about) non preoccuparsi (di or per)

unconditional [ʌnkənˈdɪʃənl] adj incondizionato(a), senza condizioni

unconscious [ʌnˈkɔnʃəs] adj privo(a) di sensi, svenuto(a); (unaware) inconsapevole, inconscio(a) ♦ n: the ~ l'inconscio; ~ly adv inconsciamente

uncontrollable [ʌnkənˈtrəuləbl] adj incontrollabile, indisciplinato(a)

unconventional [ʌnkənˈvɛnʃənl] adj poco convenzionale

uncouth [ʌnˈkuːθ] adj maleducato(a), grossolano(a)

uncover [ʌnˈkʌvə*] vt scoprire

undecided [ʌndɪˈsaɪdɪd] adj indeciso(a)

under [ˈʌndə*] prep sotto; (less than) meno di; al disotto di; (according to) secondo, in conformità a ♦ adv (al) disotto; ~ there là sotto; ~ repair in riparazione

under... [ˈʌndə*] prefix sotto..., sub...; ~ **age** adj minorenne; ~ **carriage** (BRIT) n carrello (d'atterraggio); ~ **charge** vt far pagare di meno a; ~ **clothes** npl biancheria (intima); ~ **coat** n (paint) mano f di fondo; ~ **cover** adj segreto(a), clandestino(a); ~ **current** n corrente f sottomarina; ~ **cut** vt irreg vendere a prezzo minore di; ~ **developed** adj sottosviluppato(a); ~ **dog** n oppresso(a); ~ **done** adj (CULIN) al sangue; (pej) poco cotto(a); ~ **estimate** vt sottovalutare; ~ **fed** adj denutrito(a); ~ **foot** adv sotto i piedi; ~ **go** vt irreg subire; (treatment) sottoporsi a; ~ **graduate** n studente(essa) universitario(a); ~ **ground** n (BRIT: railway) metropolitana; (POL) movimento clandestino ♦ adj sotterraneo(a); (fig) clandestino(a) ♦ adv sottoterra; to go ~ **ground** (fig) darsi alla macchia; ~ **growth** n sottobosco; ~ **hand(ed)** adj (fig) furtivo(a), subdolo(a); ~**lie** vt irreg essere alla base di; ~**line** vt sottolineare; ~**ling** [ʌndə'laɪŋ] (pej) n subalterno(a), tirapiedi m/f inv; ~**mine** vt minare; ~**neath** [ʌndə'niːθ] adv sotto, disotto ♦ prep sotto, al di sotto di; ~**paid** adj sottopagato(a); ~**pants** npl mutande fpl, slip m inv; ~**pass** (BRIT) n sottopassaggio; ~**privileged** adj non abbiente; meno favorito(a); ~**rate** vt sottovalutare; ~**shirt** (US) n maglietta; ~**shorts** (US) npl mutande fpl, slip m inv; ~**side** n disotto; ~**skirt** (BRIT) n sottoveste f

understand [ʌndə'stænd] (irreg: like stand) vt, vi capire, comprendere; **I ~ that** ... sento che ...; credo di capire che ...; ~**able** adj comprensibile; ~**ing** adj comprensivo(a) ♦ n comprensione f; (agreement) accordo

understatement [ʌndə'steɪtmənt] n: **that's an ~!** a dire poco!

understood [ʌndə'stud] pt, pp of **understand** ♦ adj inteso(a); (implied) sottinteso(a)

understudy ['ʌndəstʌdɪ] n sostituto/ a, attore/trice supplente

undertake [ʌndə'teɪk] (irreg: like take) vt intraprendere; **to ~ to do sth** impegnarsi a fare qc

undertaker ['ʌndəteɪkə*] n impresario di pompe funebri

undertaking [ʌndə'teɪkɪŋ] n impresa; (promise) promessa

undertone ['ʌndətəun] n: **in an ~** a mezza voce, a voce bassa

underwater [ʌndə'wɔːtə*] adv sott'acqua ♦ adj subacqueo(a)

underwear ['ʌndəwɛə*] n biancheria (intima)

underworld [ʌndə'wəːld] n (of crime) malavita

underwriter ['ʌndəraɪtə*] n (INSURANCE) sottoscrittore/trice

undesirable [ʌndɪ'zaɪərəbl] adj sgradevole

undies ['ʌndɪz] (inf) npl biancheria intima da donna

undo [ʌn'duː] vt irreg disfare; ~**ing** n rovina, perdita

undoubted [ʌn'dautɪd] adj sicuro(a), certo(a); ~**ly** adv senza alcun dubbio

undress [ʌn'drɛs] vi spogliarsi

undue [ʌn'djuː] adj eccessivo(a)

undulating ['ʌndjuleɪtɪŋ] adj ondeggiante; ondulato(a)

unduly [ʌn'djuːlɪ] adv eccessivamente

unearth [ʌn'əːθ] vt dissotterrare; (fig) scoprire

unearthly [ʌn'əːθlɪ] adj (hour) impossibile

uneasy [ʌn'iːzɪ] adj a disagio; (worried) preoccupato(a); (peace) precario(a)

uneconomic(al) ['ʌniːkə'nɔmɪk(l)] adj antieconomico(a)

unemployed [ʌnɪm'plɔɪd] adj disoccupato(a) ♦ npl: **the ~** i disoccupati

unemployment [ʌnɪm'plɔɪmənt] n disoccupazione f

unending [ʌn'ɛndɪŋ] adj senza fine

unerring [ʌn'əːrɪŋ] adj infallibile

uneven [ʌn'iːvn] adj ineguale; irregolare

unexpected [ʌnɪk'spɛktɪd] adj inatteso(a), imprevisto(a); ~**ly** adv inaspettatamente

unfailing [ʌn'feɪlɪŋ] adj (supply, energy) inesauribile; (remedy) infallibile

unfair [ʌn'fɛə*] adj: ~ **(to)** ingiusto(a) (nei confronti di)

unfaithful [ʌn'feɪθful] adj infedele

unfamiliar [ʌnfə'mɪlɪə*] adj sconosciuto(a), strano(a); **to be ~ with** non avere familiarità con

unfashionable [ʌn'fæʃnəbl] adj (clothes) fuori moda; (district) non alla moda

unfasten [ʌn'fɑːsn] vt slacciare; sciogliere

unfavourable [ʌn'feɪvərəbl] (US unfavorable) adj sfavorevole

unfeeling [ʌn'fiːlɪŋ] adj insensibile, duro(a)

unfinished [ʌn'fɪnɪʃt] adj incompleto(a)

unfit [ʌnˈfɪt] *adj* (*ill*) malato(a), in cattiva salute; (*incompetent*): ~ (**for**) incompetente (in); (: *work, MIL*) inabile (a)

unfold [ʌnˈfəʊld] *vt* spiegare ♦ *vi* (*story, plot*) svelarsi

unforeseen [ʌnfɔːˈsiːn] *adj* imprevisto(a)

unforgettable [ʌnfəˈɡetəbl] *adj* indimenticabile

unfortunate [ʌnˈfɔːtʃnət] *adj* sfortunato(a); (*event, remark*) infelice; **~ly** *adv* sfortunatamente, purtroppo

unfounded [ʌnˈfaʊndɪd] *adj* infondato(a)

unfriendly [ʌnˈfrendlɪ] *adj* poco amichevole, freddo(a)

ungainly [ʌnˈɡeɪnlɪ] *adj* goffo(a), impacciato(a)

ungodly [ʌnˈɡɔdlɪ] *adj*: **at an ~ hour** a un'ora impossibile

ungrateful [ʌnˈɡreɪtfʊl] *adj* ingrato(a)

unhappiness [ʌnˈhæpɪnɪs] *n* infelicità

unhappy [ʌnˈhæpɪ] *adj* infelice; **~ about/with** (*arrangements etc*) insoddisfatto(a) di

unharmed [ʌnˈhɑːmd] *adj* incolume, sano(a) e salvo(a)

unhealthy [ʌnˈhelθɪ] *adj* (*gen*) malsano(a); (*person*) malaticcio(a)

unheard-of [ʌnˈhɜːdɔv] *adj* inaudito(a), senza precedenti

unhurt [ʌnˈhɜːt] *adj* illeso(a)

uniform [ˈjuːnɪfɔːm] *n* uniforme *f*, divisa ♦ *adj* uniforme

uninhabited [ʌnɪnˈhæbɪtɪd] *adj* disabitato(a)

unintentional [ʌnɪnˈtenʃənəl] *adj* involontario(a)

union [ˈjuːnjən] *n* unione *f*; (*also: trade ~*) sindacato ♦ *cpd* sindacale, dei sindacati; **U~ Jack** *n* bandiera nazionale britannica

unique [juːˈniːk] *adj* unico(a)

unit [ˈjuːnɪt] *n* unità *f inv*; (*section: of furniture etc*) elemento; (*team, squad*) reparto, squadra

unite [juːˈnaɪt] *vt* unire ♦ *vi* unirsi; **~d** *adj* unito(a); unificato(a); (*efforts*) congiunto(a); **U~d Kingdom** *n* Regno Unito; **U~d Nations (Organization)** *n* (Organizzazione *f* delle) Nazioni Unite; **U~d States (of America)** *n* Stati *mpl* Uniti (d'America)

unit trust (*BRIT*) *n* fondo d'investimento

unity [ˈjuːnɪtɪ] *n* unità

universal [juːnɪˈvɜːsl] *adj* universale

universe [ˈjuːnɪvɜːs] *n* universo

university [juːnɪˈvɜːsɪtɪ] *n* università *f inv*

unjust [ʌnˈdʒʌst] *adj* ingiusto(a)

unkempt [ʌnˈkempt] *adj* trasandato(a); spettinato(a)

unkind [ʌnˈkaɪnd] *adj* scortese; crudele

unknown [ʌnˈnəʊn] *adj* sconosciuto(a)

unlawful [ʌnˈlɔːfʊl] *adj* illecito(a), illegale

unleaded [ʌnˈledɪd] *adj* (*petrol, fuel*) senza piombo

unleash [ʌnˈliːʃ] *vt* (*fig*) scatenare

unless [ʌnˈles] *conj* a meno che (non) + *sub*

unlike [ʌnˈlaɪk] *adj* diverso(a) ♦ *prep* a differenza di, contrariamente a

unlikely [ʌnˈlaɪklɪ] *adj* improbabile

unlisted [ʌnˈlɪstɪd] (*US*) *adj* (*TEL*): **to be ~** non essere sull'elenco

unload [ʌnˈləʊd] *vt* scaricare

unlock [ʌnˈlɔk] *vt* aprire

unlucky [ʌnˈlʌkɪ] *adj* sfortunato(a); (*object, number*) che porta sfortuna

unmarried [ʌnˈmærɪd] *adj* non sposato(a); (*man only*) scapolo, celibe; (*woman only*) nubile

unmistakable [ʌnmɪsˈteɪkəbl] *adj* inconfondibile

unmitigated [ʌnˈmɪtɪɡeɪtɪd] *adj* non mitigato(a), assoluto(a), vero(a) e proprio(a)

unnatural [ʌnˈnætʃrəl] *adj* innaturale; contro natura

unnecessary [ʌnˈnesəsərɪ] *adj* inuti-

le, superfluo(a)
unnoticed [ʌnˈnəʊtɪst] adj: (to go)
~ (passare) inosservato(a)
UNO [ˈjuːnəʊ] n abbr (= United Nations Organization) ONU f
unobtainable [ʌnəbˈteɪnəbl] adj
(TEL) non ottenibile
unobtrusive [ʌnəbˈtruːsɪv] adj discreto(a)
unofficial [ʌnəˈfɪʃl] adj non ufficiale; (strike) non dichiarato(a) dal sindacato
unpack [ʌnˈpæk] vi disfare la valigia (or le valigie) ♦ vt disfare
unpalatable [ʌnˈpælətəbl] adj sgradevole
unparalleled [ʌnˈpærəleld] adj incomparabile, impareggiabile
unpleasant [ʌnˈpleznt] adj spiacevole
unplug [ʌnˈplʌg] vt staccare
unpopular [ʌnˈpɒpjulə*] adj impopolare
unprecedented [ʌnˈpresɪdəntɪd] adj senza precedenti
unpredictable [ʌnprɪˈdɪktəbl] adj imprevedibile
unprofessional [ʌnprəˈfeʃənl] adj poco professionale
unqualified [ʌnˈkwɒlɪfaɪd] adj (teacher) non abilitato(a); (success) assoluto(a), senza riserve
unquestionably [ʌnˈkwestʃənəblɪ] adv indiscutibilmente
unravel [ʌnˈrævl] vt dipanare, districare
unreal [ʌnˈrɪəl] adj irreale
unrealistic [ʌnrɪəˈlɪstɪk] adj non realistico(a)
unreasonable [ʌnˈriːznəbl] adj irragionevole
unrelated [ʌnrɪˈleɪtɪd] adj: ~ (to) senza rapporto (con); non imparentato(a) (con)
unrelenting [ʌnrɪˈlentɪŋ] adj senza tregua
unreliable [ʌnrɪˈlaɪəbl] adj (person, machine) che non dà affidamento; (news, source of information) inattendibile

unremitting [ʌnrɪˈmɪtɪŋ] adj incessante
unreservedly [ʌnrɪˈzɜːvɪdlɪ] adv senza riserve
unrest [ʌnˈrest] n agitazione f
unroll [ʌnˈrəʊl] vt srotolare
unruly [ʌnˈruːlɪ] adj indisciplinato(a), rischioso(a)
unsaid [ʌnˈsed] adj: to leave sth ~ passare qc sotto silenzio
unsatisfactory [ˈʌnsætɪsˈfæktərɪ] adj che lascia a desiderare, insufficiente
unsavoury [ʌnˈseɪvərɪ] (US unsavory) adj (fig: person, place) losco(a)
unscathed [ʌnˈskeɪðd] adj incolume
unscrew [ʌnˈskruː] vt svitare
unscrupulous [ʌnˈskruːpjʊləs] adj senza scrupoli
unsettled [ʌnˈsetld] adj (person) turbato(a); indeciso(a); (weather) instabile
unshaven [ʌnˈʃeɪvn] adj non rasato(a)
unsightly [ʌnˈsaɪtlɪ] adj brutto(a), sgradevole a vedersi
unskilled [ʌnˈskɪld] adj non specializzato(a)
unspeakable [ʌnˈspiːkəbl] adj (indescribable) indicibile; (awful) abominevole
unstable [ʌnˈsteɪbl] adj (gen) instabile; (mentally) squilibrato(a)
unsteady [ʌnˈstedɪ] adj instabile, malsicuro(a)
unstuck [ʌnˈstʌk] adj: to come ~ scollarsi; (fig) fare fiasco
unsuccessful [ʌnsəkˈsesful] adj (writer, proposal) che non ha successo; (marriage, attempt) mal riuscito(a), fallito(a); to be ~ (in attempting sth) non avere successo
unsuitable [ʌnˈsuːtəbl] adj inadatto(a); inopportuno(a); sconveniente
unsure [ʌnˈʃʊə*] adj incerto(a); to be ~ of o.s. essere insicuro(a)
unsuspecting [ʌnsəˈspektɪŋ] adj che non sospetta nulla
unsympathetic [ʌnsɪmpəˈθetɪk] adj (person) antipatico(a); (attitude)

poco incoraggiante

untapped [ʌnˈtæpt] *adj* (*resources*) non sfruttato(a)

unthinkable [ʌnˈθɪŋkəbl] *adj* impensabile, inconcepibile

untidy [ʌnˈtaɪdɪ] *adj* (*room*) in disordine; (*appearance*) trascurato(a); (*person*) disordinato(a)

untie [ʌnˈtaɪ] *vt* (*knot, parcel*) disfare; (*prisoner, dog*) slegare

until [ʌnˈtɪl] *prep* fino a; (*after negative*) prima di ♦ *conj* finché, fino a quando; (*in past, after negative*) prima che + *sub*, prima di + *infinitive*; ~ **he comes** finché *or* fino a quando non arriva; ~ **now** finora; ~ **then** fino ad allora

untimely [ʌnˈtaɪmlɪ] *adj* intempestivo(a), inopportuno(a); (*death*) prematuro(a)

untold [ʌnˈtəʊld] *adj* (*story*) mai rivelato(a); (*wealth*) incalcolabile; (*joy, suffering*) indescrivibile

untoward [ʌntəˈwɔːd] *adj* sfortunato(a), sconveniente

unused [ʌnˈjuːzd] *adj* nuovo(a)

unusual [ʌnˈjuːʒʊəl] *adj* insolito(a), eccezionale, raro(a)

unveil [ʌnˈveɪl] *vt* scoprire; svelare

unwanted [ʌnˈwɒntɪd] *adj* (*clothing*) smesso(a); (*child*) non desiderato(a)

unwavering [ʌnˈweɪvərɪŋ] *adj* fermo(a), incrollabile

unwelcome [ʌnˈwɛlkəm] *adj* non gradito(a)

unwell [ʌnˈwɛl] *adj* indisposto(a); **to feel ~** non sentirsi bene

unwieldy [ʌnˈwiːldɪ] *adj* poco maneggevole

unwilling [ʌnˈwɪlɪŋ] *adj*: **to be ~** to do non voler fare; **~ly** *adv* malvolentieri

unwind [ʌnˈwaɪnd] (*irreg: like* **wind**) *vt* svolgere, srotolare ♦ *vi* (*relax*) rilassarsi

unwise [ʌnˈwaɪz] *adj* poco saggio(a)

unwitting [ʌnˈwɪtɪŋ] *adj* involontario(a)

unworkable [ʌnˈwɔːkəbl] *adj* (*plan*) inattuabile

unworthy [ʌnˈwɔːðɪ] *adj* indegno(a)

unwrap [ʌnˈræp] *vt* disfare; aprire

unwritten [ʌnˈrɪtn] *adj* (*agreement*) tacito(a); (*law*) non scritto(a)

KEYWORD

up [ʌp] *prep*: **he went ~ the stairs/ the hill** è salito su per le scale/sulla collina; **the cat was ~ a tree** il gatto era su un albero; **they live further ~ the street** vivono un po' più su nella stessa strada
♦ *adv* 1 (*upwards, higher*) su, in alto; ~ **in the sky/the mountains** su nel cielo/in montagna; ~ **there** lassù; ~ **above** su in alto
2: **to be ~** (*out of bed*) essere alzato(a); (*prices, level*) essere salito(a)
3: ~ **to** (*as far as*) fino a; ~ **to now** finora
4: **to be ~ to** (*depending on*): **it's ~ to you** sta a lei, dipende da lei; (*equal to*): **he's not ~ to it** (*job, task etc*) non ne è all'altezza; (*inf: be doing*): **what is he ~ to?** cosa sta combinando?
♦ *n*: ~**s and downs** alti e bassi *mpl*

---

upbringing [ˈʌpbrɪŋɪŋ] *n* educazione *f*

update [ʌpˈdeɪt] *vt* aggiornare

upgrade [ʌpˈɡreɪd] *vt* (*house, job*) migliorare; (*employee*) avanzare di grado

upheaval [ʌpˈhiːvl] *n* sconvolgimento; tumulto

uphill [ʌpˈhɪl] *adj* in salita; (*fig: task*) difficile ♦ *adv*: **to go ~** andare in salita, salire

uphold [ʌpˈhəʊld] (*irreg: like* **hold**) *vt* approvare; sostenere

upholstery [ʌpˈhəʊlstərɪ] *n* tappezzeria

upkeep [ˈʌpkiːp] *n* manutenzione *f*

upon [əˈpɒn] *prep* su

upper [ˈʌpə*] *adj* superiore ♦ *n* (*of shoe*) tomaia; **the ~ class** dell'alta borghesia; ~ **hand** *n*: **to have the ~ hand** avere il coltello dalla parte del manico; ~**most** *adj* il(la) più alto(a); predominante

upright ['ʌpraɪt] adj diritto(a); verticale; (fig) diritto(a), onesto(a)

uprising ['ʌpraɪzɪŋ] n insurrezione f, rivolta

uproar ['ʌprɔ:*] n tumulto, clamore m

uproot [ʌp'ru:t] vt sradicare

upset [n 'ʌpset, vb, adj ʌp'set] (irreg: like set) n (to plan etc) contrattempo; (stomach ~) disturbo ♦ vt (glass etc) rovesciare; (plan, stomach) scombussolare; (person: offend) contrariare; (: grieve) addolorare, sconvolgere ♦ adj contrariato(a); addolorato(a); (stomach) scombussolato(a)

upshot ['ʌpʃɔt] n risultato

upside down ['ʌpsaɪd-] adv sottosopra

upstairs [ʌp'stɛəz] adv, adj di sopra, al piano superiore ♦ n piano di sopra

upstart ['ʌpstɑ:t] n parvenu m inv

upstream [ʌp'stri:m] adv a monte

uptake ['ʌpteɪk] n: **he is quick/slow on the ~** è pronto/lento di comprendonio

uptight [ʌp'taɪt] (inf) adj teso(a)

up-to-date [ʌp-] adj moderno(a); aggiornato(a)

upturn ['ʌptə:n] n (in luck) svolta favorevole; (COMM: in market) rialzo

upward ['ʌpwəd] adj ascendente; verso l'alto; **~(s)** adv in su, verso l'alto

urban ['ə:bən] adj urbano(a)

urbane [ə:'beɪn] adj civile, urbano(a), educato(a)

urchin ['ə:tʃɪn] n monello

urge [ə:dʒ] n impulso; stimolo; forte desiderio ♦ vt: to ~ sb to do esortare qn a fare, spingere qn a fare; raccomandare a qn di fare

urgency ['ə:dʒənsɪ] n urgenza; (of tone) insistenza

urgent ['ə:dʒənt] adj urgente; (voice) insistente

urinate ['juərɪneɪt] vi orinare

urine ['juərɪn] n orina

urn [ə:n] n urna; (also: tea ~) bolli-

tore m per il tè

us [ʌs] pron ci; (stressed, after prep) noi; see also **me**

US(A) n abbr (= United States (of America)) USA mpl

usage ['ju:zɪdʒ] n uso

use [n ju:s, vb ju:z] n uso; impiego, utilizzazione f ♦ vt usare, utilizzare, servirsi di; **in ~** in uso; **out of ~** fuori uso; **to be of ~** essere utile, servire; **it's no ~** non serve, è inutile; **she ~d to do it** lo faceva (una volta), era solita farlo; **to be ~d to** avere l'abitudine di; **to ~ up** vt consumare; esaurire; **~d** adj (object, car) usato(a); **~ful** adj utile; **~fulness** n utilità; **~less** adj inutile; (person) inetto(a); **~r** n utente m/f; **~r-friendly** adj (computer) di facile uso

usher ['ʌʃə*] n usciere m; **~ette** [-'ret] n (in cinema) maschera

USSR n abbr: **the ~** l'URSS f

usual ['ju:ʒuəl] adj solito(a); **as ~** come al solito, come d'abitudine; **~ly** adv di solito

utensil [ju:'tɛnsɪl] n utensile m; **kitchen ~s** utensili da cucina

uterus ['ju:tərəs] n utero

utility [ju:'tɪlɪtɪ] n utilità; (also: public ~) servizio pubblico; **~ room** n locale adibito alla stiratura dei panni etc

utmost ['ʌtməust] adj estremo(a), massimo(a) ♦ n: **to do one's ~** fare il possibile or di tutto

utter ['ʌtə*] adj assoluto(a), totale ♦ vt pronunciare, proferire; emettere; **~ance** n espressione f; parole fpl; **~ly** adv completamente, del tutto

U-turn ['ju:'tə:n] n inversione f a U

V

v. abbr = **verse**; **versus**; **volt**; (= vide) vedi, vedere

vacancy ['veɪkənsɪ] n (BRIT: job) posto libero; (room) stanza libera

vacant ['veɪkənt] adj (job, seat etc) libero(a); (expression) assente; **~**

lot (*US*) *n* terreno non occupato; (*for sale*) terreno in vendita

vacate [vəˈkeɪt] *vt* lasciare libero(a)

vacation [vəˈkeɪʃən] (*esp US*) *n* vacanze *fpl*

vaccinate [ˈvæksɪneɪt] *vt* vaccinare

vacuum [ˈvækjum] *n* vuoto; ~ **cleaner** *n* aspirapolvere *m inv*; ~-**packed** *adj* confezionato(a) sottovuoto

vagina [vəˈdʒaɪnə] *n* vagina

vagrant [ˈveɪɡrnt] *n* vagabondo/a

vague [veɪɡ] *adj* vago(a); (*blurred*: *photo, memory*) sfocato(a); ~**ly** *adv* vagamente

vain [veɪn] *adj* (*useless*) inutile, vano(a); (*conceited*) vanitoso(a); **in** ~ inutilmente, invano

valentine [ˈvæləntaɪn] *n* (*also*: ~ *card*) cartolina *o* biglietto di San Valentino; (*person*) innamorato/a

valet [ˈvæleɪ] *n* cameriere *m* personale

valiant [ˈvæliənt] *adj* valoroso(a), coraggioso(a)

valid [ˈvælɪd] *adj* valido(a), valevole; (*excuse*) valido(a)

valley [ˈvælɪ] *n* valle *f*

valour [ˈvælə*] (*US* **valor**) *n* valore *m*

valuable [ˈvæljuəbl] *adj* (*jewel*) di (grande) valore; (*time, help*) prezioso(a); ~**s** *npl* oggetti *mpl* di valore

valuation [vælju:ˈeɪʃən] *n* valutazione *f*, stima

value [ˈvælju:] *n* valore *m* ♦ *vt* (*fix price*) valutare, dare un prezzo a; (*cherish*) apprezzare, tenere a; ~ **added tax** (*BRIT*) *n* imposta sul valore aggiunto; ~**d** *adj* (*appreciated*) stimato(a), apprezzato(a)

valve [vælv] *n* valvola

van [væn] *n* (*AUT*) furgone *m*; (*BRIT*: *RAIL*) vagone *m*

vandal [ˈvændl] *n* vandalo/a; ~**ism** *n* vandalismo

vanilla [vəˈnɪlə] *n* vaniglia ♦ *cpd* (*ice cream*) alla vaniglia

vanish [ˈvænɪʃ] *vi* svanire, scomparire

vanity [ˈvænɪtɪ] *n* vanità

vantage [ˈvɑːntɪdʒ] *n*: ~ **point** posizione *f or* punto di osservazione; (*fig*) posizione vantaggiosa

vapour [ˈveɪpə*] (*US* **vapor**) *n* vapore *m*

variable [ˈvɛərɪəbl] *adj* variabile; (*mood*) mutevole

variance [ˈvɛərɪəns] *n*: **to be at** ~ (**with**) essere in disaccordo (con); (*facts*) essere in contraddizione (con)

varicose [ˈværɪkəus] *adj*: ~ **veins** vene *fpl* varicose

varied [ˈvɛərɪd] *adj* vario(a), diverso(a)

variety [vəˈraɪətɪ] *n* varietà *f inv*; (*quantity*) quantità, numero; ~ **show** *n* varietà *m inv*

various [ˈvɛərɪəs] *adj* vario(a), diverso(a); (*several*) parecchi(e), molti(e)

varnish [ˈvɑːnɪʃ] *n* vernice *f*; (*nail* ~) smalto ♦ *vt* verniciare; mettere lo smalto su

vary [ˈvɛərɪ] *vt, vi* variare, mutare

vase [vɑːz] *n* vaso

Vaseline [ˈvæsɪliːn] ® *n* vaselina

vast [vɑːst] *adj* vasto(a); (*amount, success*) enorme

VAT [væt] *n abbr* (= *value added tax*) I.V.A. *f*

vat [væt] *n* tino

Vatican [ˈvætɪkən] *n*: **the** ~ il Vaticano

vault [vɔːlt] *n* (*of roof*) volta; (*tomb*) tomba; (*in bank*) camera blindata ♦ *vt* (*also*: ~ *over*) saltare (d'un balzo)

vaunted [ˈvɔːntɪd] *adj*: **much**-~ tanto celebrato(a)

VCR *n abbr* = **video cassette recorder**

VD *n abbr* = **venereal disease**

VDU *n abbr* = **visual display unit**

veal [viːl] *n* vitello

veer [vɪə*] *vi* girare; virare

vegetable [ˈvedʒtəbl] *n* verdura, ortaggio ♦ *adj* vegetale

vegetarian [vedʒɪˈtɛərɪən] *adj, n* vegetariano/a-*f*

vehement [ˈviːmənt] *adj* veemente,

violento(a)

vehicle ['vi:ikl] n veicolo

veil [veil] n velo; **~ed** adj (fig: threat) velato(a)

vein [vein] n vena; (on leaf) nervatura

velvet ['velvit] n velluto ♦ adj di velluto

vending machine ['vendɪŋ-] n distributore m automatico

vendor ['vendə*] n venditore/trice

veneer [və'nɪə*] n impiallacciatura; (fig) vernice f

venereal [vɪ'nɪərɪəl] adj: **~ disease** malattia venerea

Venetian [vɪ'ni:ʃən] adj veneziano(a); **~ blind** n (tenda alla) veneziana

vengeance ['vendʒəns] n vendetta; **with a ~** (fig) davvero; furiosamente

Venice ['venɪs] n Venezia

venison ['venɪsn] n carne f di cervo

venom ['venəm] n veleno

vent [vent] n foro, apertura; (in dress, jacket) spacco ♦ vt (fig: one's feelings) sfogare, dare sfogo a

ventilate ['ventɪleɪt] vt (room) dare aria a, arieggiare; **ventilator** n ventilatore m

ventriloquist [ven'trɪləkwɪst] n ventriloquo/a

venture ['ventʃə*] n impresa (rischiosa) ♦ vt rischiare, azzardare ♦ vi avventurarsi; **business ~** iniziativa commerciale

venue ['venju:] n luogo (designato) per l'incontro

verb [və:b] n verbo; **~al** adj verbale; (translation) orale

verbatim [və:'beɪtɪm] adj, adv parola per parola

verdict ['və:dɪkt] n verdetto

verge [və:dʒ] (BRIT) n bordo, orlo; **"soft ~s"** (BRIT: AUT) banchine fpl cedevoli; **on the ~ of doing** sul punto di fare; **~ on** vt fus rasentare

veritable ['verɪtəbl] adj vero(a)

vermin ['və:mɪn] npl animali mpl nocivi; (insects) insetti mpl parassiti

vermouth ['və:məθ] n vermut m inv

versatile ['və:sətaɪl] adj (person) versatile; (machine, tool etc) (che si presta) a molti usi

verse [və:s] n versi mpl; (stanza) stanza, strofa; (in bible) versetto

versed [və:st] adj: **(well-)~ in** pratico(a) di

version ['və:ʃən] n versione f

versus ['və:səs] prep contro

vertical ['və:tɪkl] adj verticale ♦ n verticale m; **~ly** adv verticalmente

vertigo ['və:tɪgəu] n vertigine f

verve [və:v] n brio; entusiasmo

very ['verɪ] adv molto ♦ adj: **the ~ book which** proprio il libro che; **the ~ last** proprio l'ultimo; **at the ~ least** almeno; **~ much** moltissimo

vessel ['vesl] n (ANAT) vaso; (NAUT) nave f; (container) recipiente m

vest [vest] n (BRIT) maglia; (: sleeveless) canottiera; (US: waistcoat) gilè m inv

vested interests ['vestɪd-] npl (COMM) diritti mpl acquisiti

vet [vet] n abbr (BRIT: = veterinary surgeon) veterinario ♦ vt esaminare minuziosamente

veteran ['vetərn] n (also: war ~) veterano

veterinary ['vetrɪnərɪ] adj veterinario(a); **~ surgeon** (US **veterinarian**) n veterinario

veto ['vi:təu] (pl **~es**) n veto ♦ vt opporre il veto a

vex [veks] vt irritare, contrariare; **~ed** adj (question) controverso(a), dibattuto(a)

via ['vaɪə] prep (by way of) via; (by means of) tramite

viable ['vaɪəbl] adj attuabile; vitale

viaduct ['vaɪədʌkt] n viadotto

vibrant ['vaɪbrənt] adj (lively, bright) vivace; (voice) vibrante

vibrate [vaɪ'breɪt] vi: **to ~ (with)** vibrare (di); (resound) risonare (di)

vicar ['vɪkə*] n pastore m; **~age** n presbiterio

vicarious [vɪ'keərɪəs] adj indiretto(a)

vice [vaɪs] n (evil) vizio; (TECH) morsa

vice- [vaɪs] prefix vice...

vice squad n (squadra del) buon costume f

vice versa ['vaɪsɪ'vəːsə] adv viceversa

vicinity [vɪ'sɪnɪtɪ] n vicinanze fpl

vicious ['vɪʃəs] adj (remark, dog) cattivo(a); (blow) violento(a); ~ **circle** n circolo vizioso

victim ['vɪktɪm] n vittima

victor ['vɪktə*] n vincitore m

Victorian [vɪk'tɔːrɪən] adj vittoriano(a)

victory ['vɪktərɪ] n vittoria

video ['vɪdɪəʊ] cpd video... ♦ n (~ film) video m inv; (also: ~ cassette) videocassetta; (also: ~ cassette recorder) videoregistratore m; ~ **tape** n videotape m inv

vie [vaɪ] vi: **to ~ with** competere con, rivaleggiare con

Vienna [vɪ'enə] n Vienna

Vietnam [vjet'næm] n Vietnam m; ~**ese** adj, n inv vietnamita m/f

view [vjuː] n vista, veduta; (opinion) opinione f ♦ vt (look at: also fig) considerare; (house) visitare; **in full** ~ of sotto gli occhi di; **in** ~ of the weather/the fact that considerato il tempo/che; **in my** ~ a mio parere; ~**er** n spettatore/trice; ~**finder** n mirino; ~**point** n punto di vista; (place) posizione f

vigil ['vɪdʒɪl] n veglia

vigorous ['vɪgərəs] adj vigoroso(a)

vile [vaɪl] adj (action) vile; (smell) disgustoso(a), nauseante; (temper) pessimo(a)

villa ['vɪlə] n villa

village ['vɪlɪdʒ] n villaggio; ~**r** n abitante m/f di villaggio

villain ['vɪlən] n (scoundrel) canaglia; (BRIT: criminal) criminale m; (in novel etc) cattivo

vindicate ['vɪndɪkeɪt] vt comprovare; giustificare

vindictive [vɪn'dɪktɪv] adj vendicativo(a)

vine [vaɪn] n vite f; (climbing plant) rampicante m

vinegar ['vɪnɪgə*] n aceto

vineyard ['vɪnjɑːd] n vigna, vigneto

vintage ['vɪntɪdʒ] n (year) annata, produzione f ♦ cpd d'annata; ~ **car** n auto f inv d'epoca; ~ **wine** n vino d'annata

vinyl ['vaɪnl] n vinile m

violate ['vaɪəleɪt] vt violare

violence ['vaɪələns] n violenza

violent ['vaɪələnt] adj violento(a)

violet ['vaɪələt] adj (colour) viola inv, violetto(a) ♦ n (plant) violetta; (colour) violetto

violin [vaɪə'lɪn] n violino; ~**ist** n violinista m/f

VIP n abbr (= very important person) V.I.P. m/f inv

virgin ['vəːdʒɪn] n vergine f ♦ adj vergine inv

Virgo ['vəːgəʊ] n (sign) Vergine f

virile ['vɪraɪl] adj virile

virtual reality ['vəːtʃuəl -] n (COMPUT) realtà virtuale

virtually ['vəːtjuəlɪ] adv (almost) praticamente

virtue ['vəːtjuː] n virtù f inv; (advantage) pregio, vantaggio; **by** ~ **of** grazie a

virtuous ['vəːtjuəs] adj virtuoso(a)

virus ['vaɪərəs] n (also COMPUT) virus m inv

visa ['viːzə] n visto

vis-à-vis [viːzə'viː] prep rispetto a, nei riguardi di

visibility [vɪzɪ'bɪlɪtɪ] n visibilità

visible ['vɪzəbl] adj visibile

vision ['vɪʒən] n (sight) vista; (foresight, in dream) visione f

visit ['vɪzɪt] n visita; (stay) soggiorno ♦ vt (person: US also: ~ with) andare a trovare; (place) visitare; ~**ing hours** npl (in hospital etc) orario delle visite; ~**or** n visitatore/trice; (guest) ospite m/f

visor ['vaɪzə*] n visiera

vista ['vɪstə] n vista, prospettiva

visual ['vɪzjuəl] adj visivo(a); visuale; ottico(a); ~ **display unit** n visualizzatore m

visualize ['vɪzjuəlaɪz] vt immaginare, figurarsi; (foresee) prevedere

vital ['vaɪtl] adj vitale; ~**ly** adv estremamente; ~ **statistics** npl (fig) misure fpl

vitamin ['vɪtəmɪn] n vitamina

vivacious [vɪ'veɪʃəs] adj vivace

vivid ['vɪvɪd] adj vivido(a); ~**ly** adv (describe) vividamente; (remember) con precisione

V-neck ['viːnɛk] n maglione m con lo scollo a V

vocabulary [vəu'kæbjuləri] n vocabolario

vocal ['vəukl] adj (MUS) vocale; (communication) verbale; ~ **chords** npl corde fpl vocali

vocation [vəu'keɪʃən] n vocazione f; ~**al** adj professionale

vociferous [və'sɪfərəs] adj rumoroso(a)

vodka ['vɔdkə] n vodka f inv

vogue [vəug] n moda; (popularity) popolarità, voga

voice [vɔɪs] n voce f ♦ vt (opinion) esprimere

void [vɔɪd] n vuoto ♦ adj (invalid) nullo(a); (empty): ~ **of** privo(a) di

volatile ['vɔlətaɪl] adj volatile; (fig) volubile

volcano [vɔl'keɪnəu] (pl ~es) n vulcano

volition [və'lɪʃən] n: **of one's own** ~ di sua volontà

volley ['vɔlɪ] n (of gunfire) salva; (of stones, questions etc) raffica; (TENNIS etc) volata; ~**ball** n pallavolo f

volt [vəult] n volt m inv; ~**age** n tensione f, voltaggio

voluble ['vɔljubl] adj loquace, ciarliero(a)

volume ['vɔljuːm] n volume m

voluntarily ['vɔləntrɪlɪ] adv volontariamente; gratuitamente

voluntary ['vɔləntərɪ] adj volontario(a); (unpaid) gratuito(a), non retribuito(a)

volunteer [vɔlən'tɪə*] n volontario/a ♦ vt offrire volontariamente ♦ vi (MIL) arruolarsi volontario; **to** ~ **to do** offrire (volontariamente) di fare

voluptuous [və'lʌptjuəs] adj voluttuoso(a)

vomit ['vɔmɪt] n vomito ♦ vt, vi vomitare

vote [vəut] n voto, suffragio; (cast) voto; (franchise) diritto di voto ♦ vt: **to be** ~**d chairman** etc venir eletto presidente etc; (propose): **to** ~ **that** approvare la proposta che ♦ vi votare; ~ **of thanks** discorso di ringraziamento; ~**r** n elettore/trice; **voting** n scrutinio

vouch [vautʃ]: **to** ~ **for** vt fus farsi garante di

voucher ['vautʃə*] n (for meal, petrol etc) buono

vow [vau] n voto, promessa solenne ♦ vt: **to** ~ **to do/that** giurare di fare/che

vowel ['vauəl] n vocale f

voyage ['vɔɪɪdʒ] n viaggio per mare, traversata

V-sign ['viː-] n (BRIT) gesto volgare con le dita

vulgar ['vʌlgə*] adj volgare

vulnerable ['vʌlnərəbl] adj vulnerabile

vulture ['vʌltʃə*] n avvoltoio

W

wad [wɔd] n (of cotton wool, paper) tampone m; (of banknotes etc) fascio

waddle ['wɔdl] vi camminare come una papera

wade [weɪd] vi: **to** ~ **through** camminare a stento in; (fig: book) leggere con fatica

wafer ['weɪfə*] n (CULIN) cialda

waffle ['wɔfl] n (CULIN) cialda; (inf) ciance fpl ♦ vi cianciare

waft [wɔft] vt portare ♦ vi diffondersi

wag [wæg] vt agitare, muovere ♦ vi agitarsi

wage [weɪdʒ] *n* (*also*: ~s) salario, paga ♦ *vt*: **to ~ war** fare la guerra; **~ earner** *n* salariato/a; **~ packet** *n* busta *f* paga *inv*

wager ['weɪdʒə*] *n* scommessa

waggle ['wægl] *vt* dimenare, agitare

wag(g)on ['wægən] *n* (*horse-drawn*) carro; (*BRIT*: *RAIL*) vagone *m* (merci)

wail [weɪl] *n* gemito; (*of siren*) urlo ♦ *vi* gemere; urlare

waist [weɪst] *n* vita, cintola; ~**coat** (*BRIT*) *n* panciotto, gilè *m inv*; ~**line** *n* (giro di) vita

wait [weɪt] *n* attesa ♦ *vi* aspettare, attendere; **to lie in ~ for** stare in agguato a; **to ~ for** aspettare; **I can't ~ to** (*fig*) non vedo l'ora di; **~ behind** *vi* rimanere (ad aspettare); **~ on** *vt fus* servire; ~**er** *n* cameriere *m*; ~**ing** *n*: **"no ~ing"** (*BRIT*: *AUT*) "divieto di sosta"; ~**ing list** *n* lista di attesa; ~**ing room** *n* sala d'aspetto *or* d'attesa; ~**ress** *n* cameriera

waive [weɪv] *vt* rinunciare a, abbandonare

wake [weɪk] (*pt* **woke**, ~**d**, *pp* **woken**, ~**d**) *vt* (*also*: ~ **up**) svegliare ♦ *vi* (*also*: ~ **up**) svegliarsi ♦ *n* (*for dead person*) veglia funebre; (*NAUT*) scia; **waken** *vt*, *vi* = **wake**

Wales [weɪlz] *n* Galles *m*

walk [wɔːk] *n* passeggiata; (*short*) giretto; (*gait*) passo, andatura; (*path*) sentiero; (*in park etc*) sentiero, vialetto ♦ *vi* camminare; (*for pleasure, exercise*) passeggiare ♦ *vt* (*distance*) fare *or* percorrere a piedi; (*dog*) accompagnare, portare a passeggiare; **10 minutes'... from** 10 minuti di cammino *or* a piedi da; **from all ~s of life** di tutte le condizioni sociali; **~ out** *vi* (*audience*) andarsene; (*workers*) scendere in sciopero; **~ out on** (*inf*) *vt fus* piantare in asso; ~**er** *n* (*person*) camminatore/trice; ~**ie-talkie** ['wɔːkɪ'tɔːkɪ] *n* walkie-talkie *m inv*; ~**ing** *n* camminare *m*; ~**ing shoes**

npl pedule *fpl*; ~**ing stick** *n* bastone *m* da passeggio; ~**out** *n* (*of workers*) sciopero senza preavviso *or* a sorpresa; ~**over** (*inf*) *n* vittoria facile, gioco da ragazzi; ~**way** *n* passaggio pedonale

wall [wɔːl] *n* muro; (*internal, of tunnel, cave*) parete *f*; ~**ed** *adj* (*city*) fortificato(a); (*garden*) cintato(a)

wallet ['wɔlɪt] *n* portafoglio

wallflower ['wɔːlflaʊə*] *n* violacciocca; **to be a ~** (*fig*) fare da tappezzeria

wallop ['wɔləp] (*inf*) *vt* pestare

wallow ['wɔləʊ] *vi* sguazzare

wallpaper ['wɔːlpeɪpə*] *n* carta da parati ♦ *vt* (*room*) mettere la carta da parati in

wally ['wɔlɪ] (*inf*) *n* imbecille *m/f*

walnut ['wɔːlnʌt] *n* noce *f*; (*tree, wood*) noce *m*

walrus ['wɔːlrəs] (*pl* ~ *or* ~**es**) *n* tricheco

waltz [wɔːlts] *n* valzer *m inv* ♦ *vi* ballare il valzer

wan [wɔn] *adj* pallido(a), smorto(a); triste

wand [wɔnd] *n* (*also*: **magic ~**) bacchetta (magica)

wander ['wɔndə*] *vi* (*person*) girare senza meta, girovagare; (*thoughts*) vagare ♦ *vt* girovagare per

wane [weɪn] *vi* calare

wangle ['wæŋgl] (*BRIT*: *inf*) *vt* procurare con l'astuzia

want [wɔnt] *vt* volere; (*need*) aver bisogno di ♦ *n*: **for ~ of** per mancanza di; ~**s** *npl* (*needs*) bisogni *mpl*; **to ~ to do** volere fare; **to ~ sb to do** volere che qn faccia; ~**ed** *adj* (*criminal*) ricercato(a); **"~ed"** (*in adverts*) "cercasi"; ~**ing** *adj*: **to be found ~ing** non risultare all'altezza

wanton ['wɔntn] *adj* sfrenato(a); senza motivo

war [wɔː*] *n* guerra; **to make ~ (on)** far guerra (a)

ward [wɔːd] *n* (*in hospital: room*) corsia; (*in section*) reparto; (*POL*) circoscrizione *f*; (*LAW*: *child*: *also*: ~ *of court*) pupillo/a; ~ **off** *vt* parare, schivare

warden ['wɔːdn] *n* (*of park, game reserve, youth hostel*) guardiano/a; (*BRIT*: *of institution*) direttore/trice; (*BRIT*: *also*: *traffic* ~) addetto/a al controllo del traffico e del parcheggio

warder ['wɔːdə*] (*BRIT*) *n* guardia carceraria

wardrobe ['wɔːdrəub] *n* (*cupboard*) guardaroba *m inv*, armadio; (*clothes*) guardaroba; (*CINEMA, THEATRE*) costumi *mpl*

warehouse ['wɛəhaus] *n* magazzino

wares [wɛəz] *npl* merci *fpl*

warfare ['wɔːfɛə*] *n* guerra

warhead ['wɔːhɛd] *n* (*MIL*) testata

warily ['wɛərɪlɪ] *adv* cautamente, con prudenza

warlike ['wɔːlaɪk] *adj* bellicoso(a)

warm [wɔːm] *adj* caldo(a); (*thanks, welcome, applause*) caloroso(a); (*person*) cordiale; it's a ~ day caldo; **I'm** ~ ho caldo; ~ **up** *vi* scaldarsi, riscaldarsi ♦ *vt* scaldare, riscaldare; (*engine*) far scaldare; ~-**hearted** *adj* affettuoso(a); ~-**ly** *adv* (*applaud, welcome*) calorosamente; (*dress*) con abiti pesanti; ~**th** *n* calore *m*

warn [wɔːn] *vt*: to ~ sb that/(not) to do/of avvertire *or* avvisare qn che/di (non) fare/di; ~**ing** *n* avvertimento; (*notice*) avviso; (*signal*) segnalazione *f*; ~**ing light** *n* spia luminosa; ~**ing triangle** *n* (*AUT*) triangolo

warp [wɔːp] *vi* deformarsi ♦ *vt* (*fig*) corrompere

warrant ['wɔrnt] *n* (*voucher*) buono; (*LAW*: *to arrest*) mandato di cattura; (: *to search*) mandato di perquisizione

warranty ['wɔrəntɪ] *n* garanzia

warren ['wɔrən] *n* (*of rabbits*) tana; (*fig*: *of streets etc*) dedalo

warrior ['wɔrɪə*] *n* guerriero/a

Warsaw ['wɔːsɔː] *n* Varsavia

warship ['wɔːʃɪp] *n* nave *f* da guerra

wart [wɔːt] *n* verruca

wartime ['wɔːtaɪm] *n*: **in** ~ in tempo di guerra

wary ['wɛərɪ] *adj* prudente

was [wɔz] *pt of* **be**

wash [wɔʃ] *vt* lavare ♦ *vi* lavarsi; (*sea*): **to** ~ **over/against sth** infrangersi su/contro qc ♦ *n* lavaggio; (*of ship*) scia; **to give sth a** ~ lavare qc, dare una lavata a qc; **to have a** ~ lavarsi; ~ **away** *vt* (*stain*) togliere lavando; (*subj*: *river*) trascinare via; ~ **off** *vi* andare via con il lavaggio; ~ **up** *vi* (*BRIT*) lavare i piatti; (*US*) darsi una lavata; ~**able** *adj* lavabile; ~**basin** (*US* ~**bowl**) *n* lavabo; ~**cloth** (*US*) *n* pezzuola (per lavarsi); ~**er** *n* (*TECH*) rondella; ~**ing** *n* (*linen etc*) bucato; ~**ing machine** *n* lavatrice *f*; ~**ing powder** (*BRIT*) *n* detersivo (in polvere)

Washington ['wɔʃɪŋtən] *n* Washington *f*

wash: ~**ing up** *n* rigovernatura, lavatura dei piatti; ~**ing-up liquid** *n* detersivo liquido (per stoviglie); ~**out** (*inf*) *n* disastro; ~**room** *n* gabinetto

wasn't ['wɔznt] = **was not**

wasp [wɔsp] *n* vespa

wastage ['weɪstɪdʒ] *n* spreco; (*in manufacturing*) scarti *mpl*; **natural** ~ diminuzione *f* di manodopera (*per pensionamento, decesso etc*)

waste [weɪst] *n* spreco; (*of time*) perdita; (*rubbish*) rifiuti *mpl*; (*also*: **household** ~) immondizie *fpl* ♦ *adj* (*material*) di scarto; (*food*) avanzato(a); (*land*) incolto(a) ♦ *vt* sprecare; ~ *npl* (*area of land*) distesa desolata; ~ **away** *vi* deperire; ~ **disposal unit** (*BRIT*) *n* eliminatore *m* di rifiuti; ~**ful** *adj* sprecone(a); (*process*) dispendioso(a); ~ **ground** (*BRIT*) *n* terreno incolto *or* abbandonato; ~**paper basket** *n* cestino per la carta straccia; ~**pipe** *n* tubo di scarico

watch [wɔtʃ] *n* (*also*: **wrist** ~) orologio (da polso); (*act of watching, vigilance*) sorveglianza; (*guard*: *MIL,*

NAUT) guardia; (*NAUT: spell of duty*) quarto ♦ *vt* (*look at*) osservare; (: *match, programme*) guardare; (*spy on, guard*) sorvegliare, tenere d'occhio; (*be careful of*) fare attenzione a ♦ *vi* osservare, guardare; ~ **out** *vi* fare attenzione; to **keep guard**) fare o montare la guardia; ~ **out** *vi* fare attenzione; ~**dog** *n* (*also fig*) cane *m* da guardia; ~**ful** *adj* attento(a), vigile; ~**maker** *n* orologiaio/a; ~**man** *n see* night; ~**strap** *n* cinturino da orologio

water ['wɔːtə*] *n* acqua ♦ *vt* (*plant*) annaffiare ♦ *vi* (*eyes*) lacrimare; (*mouth*): to **make sb's mouth** ~ far venire l'acquolina in bocca a qn; **in British** ~**s** nelle acque territoriali britanniche; ~ **down** *vt* (*milk*) diluire; (*fig: story*) edulcorare; ~**cannon** *n* idrante *m*; ~ **closet** (*BRIT*) *n* water *m inv*; ~**colour** *n* acquerello; ~**cress** *n* crescione *m*; ~**fall** *n* cascata; ~ **heater** *n* scaldabagno; ~**ing can** *n* annaffiatoio; ~**lily** *n* ninfea; ~**line** *n* (*NAUT*) linea di galleggiamento; ~**logged** *adj* saturo(a) d'acqua; imbevuto(a) d'acqua; (*football pitch etc*) allagato(a); ~ **main** *n* conduttura dell'acqua; ~**melon** *n* anguria, cocomero; ~**proof** *adj* impermeabile; ~**shed** *n* (*GEO, fig*) spartiacque *m*; ~**skiing** *n* sci *m* acquatico; ~**tight** *adj* stagno(a); ~**way** *n* corso d'acqua navigabile; ~**works** *npl* impianto idrico; (*fig*) vescica *f*; ~**y** *adj* (*colour*) slavato(a); (*coffee*) acquoso(a); (*eyes*) umido(a)

watt [wɔt] *n* watt *m inv*

wave [weɪv] *n* onda; (*of hand*) gesto, segno; (*in hair*) ondulazione *f*; (*fig: surge*) ondata ♦ *vi* fare un cenno con la mano; (*branches, grass*) ondeggiare; (*flag*) sventolare ♦ *vt* (*hand*) fare un gesto con; (*handkerchief*) sventolare; (*stick*) brandire; ~**length** *n* lunghezza d'onda

waver ['weɪvə*] *vi* esitare; (*voice*) tremolare

wavy ['weɪvɪ] *adj* ondulato(a); ondeggiante

wax [wæks] *n* cera ♦ *vt* dare la cera a; (*car*) lucidare ♦ *vi* (*moon*) crescere; ~**works** *npl* cere *fpl* ♦ *n* museo delle cere

way [weɪ] *n* via, strada; (*path, access*) passaggio; (*distance*) distanza; (*direction*) parte *f*, direzione *f*; (*manner*) modo, stile *m*; (*habit*) abitudine *f*; **which** ~? - **this** ~ da che parte *or* in quale direzione? - da questa parte *or* per di qua; **on the** ~ (*en route*) per strada; **to be on one's** ~ essere in cammino *o* sulla strada; **to be in the** ~ bloccare il passaggio; (*fig*) essere tra i piedi *or* d'impiccio; **to go out of one's** ~ **to do** (*fig*) mettercela tutta *o* fare di tutto per fare; under ~ (*project*) in corso; **to lose one's** ~ perdere la strada; **in a** ~ in un certo senso; **in some** ~**s** sotto certi aspetti; **no** ~! (*inf*) neanche per idea!; **by the** ~ ... a proposito ...; "~ **in**" (*BRIT*) "entrata", "ingresso"; "~ **out**" (*BRIT*) "uscita"; **the** ~ **back** la strada del ritorno; "**give** ~" (*BRIT: AUT*) "dare la precedenza"

waylay [weɪ'leɪ] (*irreg: like* lay) *vt* tendere un agguato a; attendere al passaggio

wayward ['weɪwəd] *adj* capriccioso(a); testardo(a)

W.C. ['dʌblju:'si:] *n* W.C. *m inv*, gabinetto

we [wi:] *pl pron* noi

weak [wi:k] *adj* debole; (*health*) precario(a); (*beam etc*) fragile; (*tea*) leggero(a); ~**en** *vi* indebolirsi ♦ *vt* indebolire; ~**ling** ['wi:klɪŋ] *n* smidollato/a; debole *m/f*; ~**ness** *n* debolezza; (*fault*) punto debole, difetto; **to have a** ~**ness for** avere un debole per

wealth [wɛlθ] *n* (*money, resources*) ricchezza, ricchezze *fpl*; (*of details*) abbondanza, profusione *f*; ~**y** *adj* ricco(a)

wean [wi:n] *vt* svezzare

weapon ['wepən] n arma

wear [wɛə*] (pt **wore**, pp **worn**) n (use) uso; (damage through use) logorio, usura; (clothing): **sports/baby ~** abbigliamento sportivo/per neonati ♦ vt (clothes) portare; (put on) mettersi; (damage: through use) consumare ♦ vi (last) durare; (rub etc through) consumarsi; **evening ~** abiti mpl or tenuta da sera; **~ away** vt consumare; erodere ♦ vi consumarsi; essere eroso(a); **~ down** vt consumare; (strength) esaurire; **~ off** vi sparire lentamente; **~ out** vt consumare; (person, strength) esaurire; **~ and tear** n usura, consumo

weary ['wɪərɪ] adj stanco(a) ♦ vi: to **~ of** stancarsi di

weasel ['wiːzl] n (ZOOL) donnola

weather ['wɛðə*] n tempo ♦ vt (storm, crisis) superare; **under the ~** (fig: ill) poco bene; **~-beaten** adj (face, skin) segnato(a) dalle intemperie; (building) logorato(a) dalle intemperie; **~cock** n banderuola; **~ forecast** n previsioni fpl del tempo, bollettino meteorologico; **~man** (inf) n meteorologo; **~ vane** n = **~cock**

weave [wiːv] (pt **wove**, pp **woven**) vt (cloth) tessere; (basket) intrecciare; **~r** n tessitore/trice; **weaving** n tessitura

web [wɛb] n (of spider) ragnatela; (on foot) palma; (fabric, also fig) tessuto

wed [wɛd] (pt, pp **wedded**) vt sposare ♦ vi sposarsi

we'd [wiːd] = **we had**; **we would**

wedding ['wɛdɪŋ] n matrimonio; **silver/golden ~ (anniversary)** n nozze fpl d'argento/d'oro; **~ day** n giorno delle nozze or del matrimonio; **~ dress** n abito nuziale; **~ ring** n fede f

wedge [wɛdʒ] n (of wood etc) zeppa; (of cake) fetta ♦ vt (fix) fissare con zeppe; (pack tightly) incastrare

Wednesday ['wɛnzdɪ] n mercoledì m inv

wee [wiː] (SCOTTISH) adj piccolo(a)

weed [wiːd] n erbaccia ♦ vt diserbare; **~killer** n diserbante m; **~y** adj (person) allampanato(a)

week [wiːk] n settimana; **a ~ today/on Friday** oggi/venerdì a otto; **~day** n giorno feriale; (COMM) giornata lavorativa; **~end** n fine settimana m or f inv, weekend m inv; **~ly** adv ogni settimana, settimanalmente ♦ adj settimanale ♦ n settimanale m

weep [wiːp] (pt, pp **wept**) vi (person) piangere; **~ing willow** n salice m piangente

weigh [weɪ] vt, vi pesare; to **~ anchor** salpare l'ancora; **~ down** vt (branch) piegare; (fig: with worry) opprimere, caricare; **~ up** vt valutare

weight [weɪt] n peso; to **lose/put on ~** dimagrire/ingrassare; **~ing** n (allowance) indennità; **~ lifter** n pesista m; **~y** adj pesante; (fig) importante, grave

weir [wɪə*] n diga

weird [wɪəd] adj strano(a), bizzarro(a); (eerie) soprannaturale

welcome ['wɛlkəm] adj benvenuto(a) ♦ n accoglienza, benvenuto ♦ vt dare il benvenuto a; (be glad of) rallegrarsi di; **thank you – you're ~!** grazie – prego!

weld [wɛld] n saldatura ♦ vt saldare

welfare ['wɛlfɛə*] n benessere m; **~ state** n stato assistenziale; **~ work** n assistenza sociale

well [wɛl] n pozzo ♦ adv bene ♦ adj: to **be ~** (person) stare bene ♦ excl allora!; ma!; ebbene!; **as ~** anche; **as ~ as** così come; oltre a; **~ done!** bravo(a)!; **get ~ soon!** guarisci presto!; to **do ~** andare bene; **~ up** vi sgorgare

we'll [wiːl] = **we will**; **we shall**

well-: **~-behaved** adj ubbidiente; **~-being** n benessere m; **~-built** adj (person) ben fatto(a); **~-deserved** adj meritato(a); **~-dressed** adj ben vestito(a), vestito(a) bene; **~-heeled** (*inf*) *adj* (*wealthy*) agiato(a), facoltoso(a)

wellingtons ['welɪŋtənz] *npl* (*also: wellington boots*) stivali *mpl* di gomma

well: **~-known** *adj* noto(a), famoso(a); **~-mannered** *adj* ben educato(a); **~-meaning** *adj* ben intenzionato(a); **~-off** *adj* benestante, danaroso(a); **~-read** *adj* colto(a); **~-to-do** *adj* abbiente, benestante; **~-wisher** *n* ammiratore/trice

Welsh [welʃ] *adj* gallese ♦ *n* (*LING*) gallese *m*; **the ~** *npl* i Gallesi; **~man/woman** *n* gallese *m/f*; **~ rarebit** *n* crostino al formaggio

went [wɛnt] *pt* of **go**
wept [wɛpt] *pt, pp* of **weep**
were [wəː*] *pt* of **be**
we're [wɪə*] = **we are**
weren't [wəːnt] = **were not**
west [wɛst] *n* ovest *m*, occidente *m*, ponente *m* ♦ *adj* a ovest *inv*, occidentale ♦ *adv* verso ovest; **the W~** l'Occidente *m*; **the W~ Country** (*BRIT*) *n* il sud-ovest dell'Inghilterra; **~erly** *adj* (*point*) a ovest; (*wind*) occidentale, da ovest; **~ern** *adj* occidentale, dell'ovest ♦ *n* (*CINEMA*) western *m inv*; **W~ Germany** *n* Germania Occidentale; **W~ Indian** *adj* delle Indie Occidentali ♦ *n* abitante *m/f* delle Indie Occidentali; **W~ Indies** *npl* Indie *fpl* Occidentali; **~ward(s)** *adv* verso ovest

wet [wɛt] *adj* umido(a), bagnato(a); (*soaked*) fradicio(a); (*rainy*) piovoso(a) ♦ *n* (*BRIT: POL*) politico moderato; **to get ~** bagnarsi; "**~ paint**" "vernice fresca"; **~ blanket** *n* (*fig*) guastafeste *m/f*; **~ suit** *n* tuta da sub

we've [wiːv] = **we have**
whack [wæk] *vt* picchiare, battere
whale [weɪl] *n* (*ZOOL*) balena
wharf [wɔːf] (*pl* **wharves**) *n* banchina
wharves [wɔːvz] *npl* of **wharf**

KEYWORD

what [wɔt] *adv* **1** (*in direct/indirect questions*) che; quale; **~ size is it?** che taglia è?; **~ colour is it?** di che colore è?; **~ books do you want?** quali *or* che libri vuole? **2** (*in exclamations*) che; **~ a mess!** che disordine!

♦ *pron* **1** (*interrogative*) che cosa, cosa, che; **~ are you doing?** che *or* (che) cosa fai?; **~ are you talking about?** di che cosa parli?; **~ is it called?** come si chiama?; **~ about me?** e io?; **~ about doing ...?** e se facessimo ...?

2 (*relative*) ciò che, quello che; **I saw ~ you did/was on the table** ho visto quello che hai fatto/quello che era sul tavolo

3 (*indirect use*) (che) cosa; **he asked me ~** she had said mi ha chiesto che cosa avesse detto; **tell me ~ you're thinking about** dimmi a cosa stai pensando

♦ *excl* (*disbelieving*) cosa!, come!

whatever [wɔt'ɛvə*] *adj*: **~ book** qualunque *or* qualsiasi libro + *sub* ♦ *pron*: **do ~ is necessary/you want** faccia qualunque *or* qualsiasi cosa sia necessaria/lei voglia; **~ happens** qualunque cosa accada; **no reason ~ or whatsoever** nessuna ragione affatto *or* al mondo; **nothing ~** proprio niente

whatsoever [wɔtsəu'ɛvə*] *adj* = **whatever**

wheat [wiːt] *n* grano, frumento
wheedle ['wiːdl] *vt*: **to ~ sb into doing sth** convincere qn a fare qc (con lusinghe); **to ~ sth out of sb** ottenere qc da qn (con lusinghe)

wheel [wiːl] *n* ruota; (*AUT: also: steering ~*) volante *m*; (*NAUT*) (ruota del) timone *m* ♦ *vt* spingere ♦ *vi* (*birds*) roteare; (*also: ~ round*) girare; **~barrow** *n* carriola; **~chair** *n* sedia a rotelle; **~ clamp** *n* (*AUT*) morsa *fpl* blocca la ruota di una vettura

tura in sosta vietata
wheeze [wi:z] *vi* ansimare

KEYWORD

when [wɛn] *adv* quando; ~ did it happen? quando è successo?
♦ *conj* 1 (*at, during, after the time that*) quando; she was reading ~ I came in quando sono entrato lei leggeva; that was ~ I needed you era allora che avevo bisogno di te
2 (*on, at which*): on the day ~ I met him il giorno in cui l'ho incontrato; one day ~ it was raining un giorno che pioveva
3 (*whereas*) mentre, mentre; you said I was wrong ~ in fact I was right mi hai detto che avevo torto, quando in realtà avevo ragione

whenever [wɛn'ɛvə*] *adv* quando mai ♦ *conj* quando; (*every time that*) ogni volta che

where [wɛə*] *adv, conj* dove; this is ~ è qui che; ~abouts *adv* dove ♦ *n*: sb's ~abouts luogo dove qn si trova; ~as *conj* mentre; ~by *pron* per cui; ~upon *conj* al che; wherever [-'ɛvə*] *conj* dovunque + sub; (*interrogative*) dove mai; ~withal *n* mezzi *mpl*

whet [wɛt] *vt* (*appetite etc*) stimolare

whether ['wɛðə*] *conj* se; I don't know ~ to accept or not non so se accettare o no; it's doubtful ~ è poco probabile che; ~ you go or not che lei vada o no

KEYWORD

which [wɪtʃ] *adj* 1 (*interrogative: direct, indirect*) quale; ~ picture do you want? quale quadro vuole?; ~ one? quale?; ~ one of you did it? chi di voi lo ha fatto?
2: in ~ case nel qual caso
♦ *pron* 1 (*interrogative*) quale; ~ (of these) are yours? quali di questi sono suoi?; ~ of you are coming? chi di voi viene?

2 (*relative*) che; (: *indirect*) cui, il (la) quale; the apple ~ you ate/~ is on the table la mela che hai mangiato/che è sul tavolo; the chair on ~ you are sitting la sedia sulla quale or su cui siei seduto; he said he knew, ~ is true ha detto che lo sapeva, il che è vero; after ~ dopo di che

whichever [wɪtʃ'ɛvə*] *adj*: take ~ book you prefer prenda qualsiasi libro che preferisce; ~ book you take qualsiasi libro prenda

whiff [wɪf] *n* soffio; sbuffo; odore *m*

while [waɪl] *n* momento ♦ *conj* mentre; (*as long as*) finché; (*although*) sebbene + sub; per quanto + sub; for a ~ per un po'; ~ away *vt* (*time*) far passare

whim [wɪm] *n* capriccio

whimper ['wɪmpə*] *n* piagnucolio ♦ *vi* piagnucolare

whimsical ['wɪmzɪkl] *adj* (*person*) capriccioso(a); (*look*) strano(a)

whine [waɪn] *n* gemito ♦ *vi* gemere; uggiolare; piagnucolare

whip [wɪp] *n* frusta; (*for riding*) frustino; (*POL: person*) capogruppo (*che sovrintende alla disciplina dei colleghi di partito*) ♦ *vt* frustare; (*cream, eggs*) sbattere; ~ped cream *n* panna montata; ~-round (*BRIT*) *n* colletta

whirl [wə:l] *vt* (*far*) girare rapidamente; (*far*) turbinare ♦ *vi* (*dancers*) volteggiare; (*leaves, water*) sollevarsi in vortice; ~pool *n* mulinello; ~wind *n* turbine *m*

whirr [wə:*] *vi* ronzare; rombare; frullare

whisk [wɪsk] *n* (*CULIN*) frusta; frullino ♦ *vt* sbattere, frullare; to ~ sb away or off portar via qn a tutta velocità

whiskers ['wɪskəz] *npl* (*of animal*) baffi *mpl*; (*of man*) favoriti *mpl*

whisky ['wɪskɪ] (*US, IRELAND whiskey*) *n* whisky *m inv*

whisper ['wɪspə*] *n* sussurro ♦ *vt, vi*

sussurrare

whist [wɪst] n whist m

whistle ['wɪsl] n (sound) fischio; (object) fischietto ♦ vi fischiare

white [waɪt] adj bianco(a); (with fear) pallido(a) ♦ n bianco; (person) bianco/a; ~ **coffee** (BRIT) n caffellatte m inv; ~**collar worker** n impiegato; ~ **elephant** n (fig) oggetto (or progetto) costoso ma inutile; ~ **lie** n bugia pietosa; ~**ness** n bianchezza; ~ **paper** n (POL) libro bianco; ~**wash** n (paint) bianco di calce ♦ vt imbiancare; (fig) coprire

whiting ['waɪtɪŋ] n inv (fish) merlango

Whitsun ['wɪtsn] n Pentecoste f

whittle ['wɪtl] vt: to ~ away, ~ down ridurre, tagliare

whizz [wɪz] vi: to ~ past or by passare sfrecciando; ~ **kid** (inf) n prodigio

who [huː] pron 1 (interrogative) chi; ~ is it?, ~'s there? chi è?
2 (relative) che; the man ~ spoke to me l'uomo che ha parlato con me; those ~ can swim quelli che sanno nuotare

whodunit [huːˈdʌnɪt] (inf) n giallo

whoever [huːˈevə*] pron: ~ finds it chiunque lo trovi; ask ~ you like to chieda a chiunque vuole; ~ she marries chiunque sposerà, non importa chi sposerà; ~ told you that? chi mai gliel'ha detto?

whole [həʊl] adj (complete) tutto(a), completo(a); (not broken) intero(a), intatto(a) ♦ n (all): the ~ of tutto(a) il(la); (entire unit) tutto; (not broken) tutto; the ~ of the town tutta la città, la città intera; on the ~, as a ~ nel complesso, nell'insieme; ~**food(s)** n(pl) cibo integrale; ~**hearted** adj sincero(a); ~**meal** adj (bread, flour) integrale; ~**sale** n commercio or vendita all'ingrosso ♦ adj all'ingrosso; (destruction) totale;

~**saler** n grossista m/f; ~**some** adj sano(a); salutare; ~**wheat** adj = ~**meal**; **wholly** adv completamente, del tutto

whom [huːm] pron 1 (interrogative) chi; ~ did you see? chi hai visto? to ~ did you give it? a chi lo hai dato?
2 (relative) che, prep + il (la) quale (check syntax of Italian verb used): the man ~ I saw/to ~ I spoke l'uomo che ho visto/al quale ho parlato

whooping cough ['huːpɪŋ] n pertosse f

whore [hɔː*] (inf: pej) n puttana

whose [huːz] adj 1 (possessive: interrogative) di chi; ~ book is this?, ~ is this book? di chi è questo libro?; ~ daughter are you? di chi sei figlia?
2 (possessive: relative): the man ~ son you rescued l'uomo il cui figlio hai salvato; the girl ~ sister you were speaking to la ragazza alla cui sorella stavi parlando
♦ pron di chi; ~ is this? di chi è questo?; I know ~ it is so di chi è

why [waɪ] adv, conj perché ♦ excl (surprise) ma guarda un po'!; (remonstrating) ma (via)!; (explaining) ebbene!; ~ not? perché no?; ~ not do it now? perché non farlo adesso?; that's not ~ I'm here non è questo il motivo per cui sono qui; the reason ~ il motivo per cui; ~**ever** adv perché mai

wicked ['wɪkɪd] adj cattivo(a), malvagio(a); maligno(a); perfido(a)

wickerwork ['wɪkəwɜːk] adj di vimini ♦ n articoli mpl di vimini

wicket ['wɪkɪt] n (CRICKET) porta; area tra le due porte

wide [waɪd] adj largo(a); (area, knowledge) vasto(a); (choice) ampio(a) ♦ adv: **to open ~** spalancare; **to shoot ~** tirare a vuoto or fuori bersaglio; **~-angle lens** n grandangolare m; **~-awake** adj completamente sveglio(a); **~ly** adv (differing) molto, completamente; (travelled, spaced) molto; (believed) generalmente; **~n** vt allargare, ampliare; **~ open** adj spalancato(a); **~spread** adj (belief etc) molto or assai diffuso(a)

widow ['wɪdəu] n vedova; **~ed** adj: **to be ~ed** restare vedovo(a); **~er** n vedovo

width [wɪdθ] n larghezza

wield [wi:ld] vt (sword) maneggiare; (power) esercitare

wife [waɪf] (pl **wives**) n moglie f

wig [wɪg] n parrucca

wiggle ['wɪgl] vt dimenare, agitare

wild [waɪld] adj selvatico(a); selvaggio(a); (sea, weather) tempestoso(a); (idea, life) folle; stravagante; (applause) frenetico(a); **~s** npl regione f selvaggia; **~erness** ['wɪldənɪs] n deserto; **goose chase** n (fig) pista falsa; **~life** n natura; **~ly** adv selvaggiamente; (applaud) freneticamente; (hit, guess) a casaccio; (happy) follemente

wilful ['wɪlful] (US **willful**) adj (person) testardo(a), ostinato(a); (action) intenzionale; (crime) premeditato

KEYWORD

will [wɪl] (pt, pp **~ed**) aux vb **1** (forming future tense): **I ~ finish it tomorrow** lo finirò domani; **I ~ have finished it by tomorrow** lo finirò entro domani; **~ you do it?** - yes I **~/no I won't** lo farai? - sì (lo farò)/no (non lo farò)

2 (in conjectures, predictions): **he ~ or he'll be there by now** dovrebbe essere arrivato ora; **that ~ be the postman** sarà il postino

3 (in commands, requests, offers): **~ you be quiet!** vuoi stare zitto!;

you come? vieni anche tu?; **~ you help me?** mi aiuti?, mi puoi aiutare?; **~ you have a cup of tea?** vorrebbe una tazza di tè?; **I won't put up with it!** non lo accetterò!

♦ vt: **to ~ sb to do** volere che qn faccia; **he ~ed himself to go on** continuò grazie a un grande sforzo di volontà

♦ n volontà; testamento

willful ['wɪlful] (US) adj = **wilful**

willing ['wɪlɪŋ] adj volonteroso(a); **~ to do** disposto(a) a fare; **~ly** adv volentieri; **~ness** n buona volontà

willow ['wɪləu] n salice m

will power n forza di volontà

willy-nilly ['wɪlɪ'nɪlɪ] adv volente o nolente

wilt [wɪlt] vi appassire

wily ['waɪlɪ] adj furbo(a)

win [wɪn] (pt, pp **won**) n (in sports etc) vittoria ♦ vt (battle, prize, money) vincere ♦ (popularity) conquistare ♦ vi vincere; **~ over** vt convincere; **~ round** (BRIT) vt convincere

wince [wɪns] vi trasalire

winch [wɪntʃ] n verricello, argano

wind[1] [waɪnd] (pt, pp **wound**) vt attorcigliare; (wrap) avvolgere; (clock, toy) caricare ♦ vi (road, river) serpeggiare; **~ up** vt (clock) caricare; (debate) concludere

wind[2] [wɪnd] n vento; (MED) flatulenza; (breath) respiro, fiato ♦ vt (take breath away) far restare senza fiato; **~fall** n (money) guadagno insperato; **~ power** n energia eolica

winding ['waɪndɪŋ] adj (road) serpeggiante; (staircase) a chiocciola

wind instrument n (MUS) strumento a fiato

windmill ['wɪndmɪl] n mulino a vento

window ['wɪndəu] n finestra; (in car, train) finestrino; (in shop also) vetrina; (also: **~ pane**) vetro; **~ box** n cassetta da fiori; **~ cleaner** n (person) pulitore m di finestre; **~ envelope** n busta a finestra; **~**

ledge *n* davanzale *m*; ~ **pane** *n* vetro; **~-shopping** *n*: to go ~-shopping andare a vedere le vetrine; **~sill** *n* davanzale *m*

windpipe ['wɪndpaɪp] *n* trachea

windscreen ['wɪndskriːn] *n* parabrezza *m inv*; ~ **washer** *n* lavacristallo; ~ **wiper** *n* tergicristallo

windshield ['wɪndʃiːld] (*US*) *n* = windscreen

windswept ['wɪndswept] *adj* spazzato(a) dal vento

windy ['wɪndɪ] *adj* ventoso(a); **it's ~** c'è vento

wine [waɪn] *n* vino; ~ **bar** *n* bar *m inv* (con licenza per alcolici); ~ **cellar** *n* cantina; ~ **glass** *n* bicchiere *m* da vino; ~ **list** *n* lista dei vini; ~ **merchant** *n* commerciante *m* di vini; ~ **tasting** *n* degustazione *f* dei vini; ~ **waiter** *n* sommelier *m inv*

wing [wɪŋ] *n* ala; (*AUT*) fiancata; **~s** *npl* (*THEATRE*) quinte *fpl*; **~er** *n* (*SPORT*) ala

wink [wɪŋk] *n* ammiccamento ♦ *vi* ammiccare, fare l'occhiolino; (*light*) baluginare

winner ['wɪnə*] *n* vincitore/trice

winning ['wɪnɪŋ] *adj* (*team, goal*) vincente; (*smile*) affascinante; **~s** *npl* vincite *fpl*

winter ['wɪntə*] *n* inverno; ~ **sports** *npl* sport *mpl* invernali

wintry ['wɪntrɪ] *adj* invernale

wipe [waɪp] *n* pulita, passata ♦ *vt* pulire (strofinando); (*erase: tape*) cancellare; ~ **off** *vt* cancellare; (*stains*) togliere strofinando; ~ **out** *vt* (*debt*) pagare, liquidare; (*memory*) cancellare; (*destroy*) annientare; ~ **up** *vt* asciugare

wire ['waɪə*] *n* filo; (*ELEC*) filo elettrico; (*TEL*) telegramma *m* ♦ *vt* (*house*) fare l'impianto elettrico di; (*also:* ~ **up**) collegare, allacciare; (*person*) telegrafare

wireless ['waɪəlɪs] (*BRIT*) *n* (*set*) (apparecchio *m*) radio *f inv*

wiring ['waɪərɪŋ] *n* impianto elettrico

wiry ['waɪərɪ] *adj* magro(a) e nerbo-

ruto(a); (*hair*) ispido(a)

wisdom ['wɪzdəm] *n* saggezza; (*of action*) prudenza; ~ **tooth** *n* dente *m* del giudizio

wise [waɪz] *adj* saggio(a); prudente; giudizioso(a)

...wise [waɪz] *suffix*: **time~** per quanto riguarda il tempo, in termini di tempo

wisecrack ['waɪzkræk] *n* battuta di spirito

wish [wɪʃ] *n* (*desire*) desiderio; (*specific desire*) richiesta ♦ *vt* desiderare, volere; **best ~es** (*on birthday etc*) i migliori auguri; **with best ~es** (*in letter*) cordiali saluti, con i migliori saluti; **to ~ sb goodbye** dire arrivederci a qn; **he ~ed me well** mi augurò di riuscire; **to ~ to do/sb to do** desiderare or volere fare/che qn faccia; **to ~ for** desiderare; **~ful** *adj*: **it's ~ful thinking** è prendere i desideri per realtà

wishy-washy ['wɪʃɪwɔʃɪ] (*inf*) *adj* (*colour*) slavato(a); (*ideas, argument*) insulso(a)

wisp [wɪsp] *n* ciuffo, ciocca; (*of smoke*) filo

wistful ['wɪstful] *adj* malinconico(a)

wit [wɪt] *n* (*also:* **~s**) intelligenza; presenza di spirito; (*wittiness*) spirito, arguzia; (*person*) bello spirito

witch [wɪtʃ] *n* strega

━━━━ KEYWORD ━━━━

with [wɪð, wɪθ] *prep* **1** (*in the company of*) con; **I was ~ him** ero con lui; **we stayed ~ friends** siamo stati da amici; **I'll be ~ you in a minute** vengo subito

2 (*descriptive*) con; **a room ~ a view** una stanza con vista sul mare (*or* sulle montagne *etc*); **the man ~ the grey hat/blue eyes** l'uomo con il cappello grigio/gli occhi blu

3 (*indicating manner, means, cause*): **~ tears in her eyes** con le lacrime agli occhi; **red ~ anger** rosso dalla rabbia; **to shake ~ fear** tremare di paura

4: I'm ~ you (*I understand*) la seguo; **to be ~ it** (*inf: up-to-date*) essere alla moda; (*: alert*) essere sveglio(a)

withdraw [wɪð'drɔ:] (*irreg: like draw*) *vt* ritirare; (*money from bank*) ritirare; prelevare ♦ *vi* ritirarsi; **~al** *n* ritiro; prelievo; (*of army*) ritirata; **~al symptoms** (*MED*) crisi *f* di astinenza; **~n** *adj* (*person*) distaccato(a)

wither ['wɪðə*] *vi* appassire

withhold [wɪθ'həʊld] (*irreg: like hold*) *vt* (*money*) trattenere; (*permission*): **to ~ (from)** rifiutare (a); (*information*): **to ~ (from)** nascondere (a)

within [wɪð'ɪn] *prep* all'interno; (*in time, distances*) entro ♦ *adv* all'interno, dentro; **~ reach (of)** alla portata (di); **~ sight (of)** in vista (di); **~ a mile of** entro un miglio da; **~ the week** prima della fine della settimana

without [wɪð'aʊt] *prep* senza; **to go ~ sth** fare a meno di qc

withstand [wɪθ'stænd] (*irreg: like stand*) *vt* resistere a

witness ['wɪtnɪs] *n* (*person, also LAW*) testimone *m/f* ♦ *vt* (*event*) essere testimone di; (*document*) attestare l'autenticità di; **~ box** (*US* **~ stand**) *n* banco dei testimoni

witticism ['wɪtɪsɪzm] *n* spiritosaggine *f*

witty ['wɪtɪ] *adj* spiritoso(a)

wives [waɪvz] *npl of* **wife**

wizard ['wɪzəd] *n* mago

wk *abbr* = **week**

wobble ['wɔbl] *vi* tremare; (*chair*) traballare

woe [wəʊ] *n* dolore *m*; disgrazia

woke [wəʊk] *pt of* **wake**; **woken** *pp of* **wake**

wolf [wʊlf] (*pl* **wolves**) *n* lupo

wolves [wʊlvz] *npl of* **wolf**

woman ['wʊmən] (*pl* **women**) *n* donna; **~ doctor** *n* dottoressa; **women's lib** (*inf*) *n* movimento femminista

womb [wu:m] *n* (*ANAT*) utero

women ['wɪmɪn] *npl of* **woman**

won [wʌn] *pt, pp of* **win**

wonder ['wʌndə*] *n* meraviglia ♦ *vi*: **to ~ whether/why** domandarsi se/perché; **to ~ at** essere sorpreso(a) di; meravigliarsi di; **to ~ about** domandarsi di; pensare a; **it's no ~ that** c'è poco or non c'è da meravigliarsi che + *sub*; **~ful** *adj* meraviglioso(a)

won't [wəʊnt] = **will not**

woo [wu:] *vt* (*woman, audience*) cercare di conquistare

wood [wʊd] *n* legno; (*timber*) legname *m*; (*forest*) bosco; **~ carving** *n* scultura in legno, intaglio; **~ed** *adj* boschivo(a); boscoso(a); **~en** *adj* di legno; (*fig*) rigido(a); inespressivo(a); **~pecker** *n* picchio; **~wind** *npl* (*MUS*): **the ~wind** i legni; **~work** *n* (*craft, subject*) falegnameria; **~worm** *n* tarlo del legno

wool [wʊl] *n* lana; **to pull the ~ over sb's eyes** (*fig*) imbrogliare qn; **~len** (*US* **~en**) *adj* di lana; (*industry*) laniero(a); **~lens** *npl* indumenti *mpl* di lana; **~ly** (*US* **~y**) *adj* di lana; (*fig: ideas*) confuso(a)

word [wə:d] *n* parola; (*news*) notizie *fpl* ♦ *vt* esprimere, formulare; **in other ~s** in altre parole; **to break/keep one's ~** non mantenere/mantenere la propria parola; **to have ~s with sb** avere un diverbio con qn; **~ing** *n* formulazione *f*; **~ processing** *n* elaborazione *f* di testi; **word processing** *m*; **~ processor** *n* word processor *m inv*

wore [wɔ:*] *pt of* **wear**

work [wə:k] *n* lavoro; (*ART, LITERATURE*) opera ♦ *vi* lavorare; (*mechanism, plan etc*) funzionare; (*medicine*) essere efficace ♦ *vt* (*clay, wood etc*) lavorare; (*mine etc*) sfruttare; (*machine*) far funzionare; (*cause: effect, miracle*) fare; **to be out of ~** essere disoccupato(a) *m*; **~s** *n* (*BRIT: factory*) fabbrica ♦ *npl* (*of* *clock, machine*) meccanismo; **to ~ loose** allentarsi; **~ on** *vt fus* lavorare a; (*person*) lavorarsi; (*principle*) basarsi su; **~ out** *vi* (*plan etc*) riuscire, andare bene ♦ *vt* (*problem*) risolvere; (*plan*) elaborare; **it ~s out at £100** fa 100 sterline; **~ up** *vt*: **to get ~ed up** andare su tutte le furie; eccitarsi; **~able** *adj* (*solution*) realizzabile; **~aholic** *n* maniaco/a del lavoro; **~er** *n* lavoratore/trice, operaio/a; **~force** *n* forza lavoro; **~ing class** *n* classe *f* operaia; **~ing-class** *adj* operaio(a); **~ing order** *n*: **in ~ing order** funzionante; **~man** *n* operaio; **~manship** *n* abilità; **~sheet** *n* foglio col programma di lavoro; **~shop** *n* officina; (*practical session*) gruppo di lavoro; **~ station** *n* stazione *f* di lavoro; **~-to-rule** (BRIT) *n* sciopero bianco

world [wə:ld] *n* mondo ♦ *cpd* (*champion*) del mondo; (*power, war*) mondiale; **to think the ~ of sb** (*fig*) pensare un gran bene di qn; **~ly** *adj* di questo mondo; (*knowledgeable*) di mondo; **~-wide** *adj* universale

worm [wə:m] *n* (*also: earth~*) verme *m*

worn [wɔ:n] *pp* of **wear** ♦ *adj* usato(a); **~-out** *adj* (*object*) consumato(a), logoro(a); (*person*) sfinito(a)

worried [ˈwʌrɪd] *adj* preoccupato(a)

worry [ˈwʌrɪ] *n* preoccupazione *f* ♦ *vt* preoccupare ♦ *vi* preoccuparsi

worse [wə:s] *adj* peggiore ♦ *adv*, *n* peggio; **a change for the ~** un peggioramento; **~n** *vt*, *vi* peggiorare; **~ off** *adj* in condizioni (economiche) peggiori

worship [ˈwə:ʃɪp] *n* culto ♦ *vt* (*God*) adorare, venerare; (*person*) adorare; **Your W~** (BRIT: *to mayor*) signor sindaco; (*: to judge*) signor giudice

worst [wə:st] *adj* il(la) peggiore ♦ *adv*, *n* peggio; **at ~** al peggio, per male che vada

worth [wə:θ] *n* valore *m* ♦ *adj*: **to be ~** valere; **it's ~ it** ne vale la

pena; **it is ~ one's while (to do)** vale la pena (fare); **~less** *adj* di nessun valore; **~while** *adj* (*activity*) utile; (*cause*) lodevole

worthy [ˈwə:ðɪ] *adj* (*person*) degno(a); (*motive*) lodevole; **~ of** degno di

---

would [wud] *aux vb* **1** (*conditional tense*): **if you asked him he ~ do it** se glielo chiedesse lo farebbe; **if you had asked him he ~ have done it** se glielo avesse chiesto lo avrebbe fatto

2 (*in offers, invitations, requests*): **you like a biscuit?** vorrebbe *or* vuole un biscotto?; **~ you ask him to come in?** lo faccia entrare, per cortesia; **~ you open the window please?** apra la finestra, per favore

3 (*in indirect speech*): **I said I ~ do it** ho detto che l'avrei fatto

4 (*emphatic*): **it WOULD have to snow today!** doveva proprio nevicare oggi!

5 (*insistence*): **she ~n't do it** non ha voluto farlo

6 (*conjecture*): **it ~ have been midnight** sarà stato mezzanotte; **it ~ seem so** sembrerebbe proprio di sì

7 (*indicating habit*): **he ~ go there on Mondays** andava lì ogni lunedì

---

would-be (*pej*) *adj* sedicente

wouldn't [ˈwudnt] = **would not**

wound[1] [waund] *pt*, *pp* of **wind**

wound[2] [wu:nd] *n* ferita ♦ *vt* ferire

wove [wəuv] *pt* of **weave**; **woven** *pp* of **weave**

wrangle [ˈræŋgl] *n* litigio

wrap [ræp] *n* (*stole*) scialle *m*; (*cape*) mantellina ♦ *vt* avvolgere; (*pack: also: ~ up*) incartare; **~per** *n* (*on chocolate*) carta; (BRIT: *of book*) copertina; **~ping paper** *n* carta da pacchi; (*for gift*) carta da regali

wrath [rɔθ] *n* collera, ira

wreak [riːk] vt (havoc) portare, causare; **to ~ vengeance on** vendicarsi su

wreath [riːθ, pl riːðz] n corona

wreck [rɛk] n (sea disaster) naufragio; (ship) relitto; (pej: person) rottame m ♦ vt demolire; (ship) far naufragare; (fig) rovinare; **~age** n rottami mpl; (of building) macerie fpl; (of ship) relitti mpl

wren [rɛn] n (ZOOL) scricciolo

wrench [rɛntʃ] n (TECH) chiave f; (tug) torsione f brusca; (fig) strazio ♦ vt strappare; torcere; **to ~ sth from** strappare qc a or da

wrestle ['rɛsl] vi: **to ~ (with sb)** lottare (con qn); **~r** n lottatore/trice; **wrestling** n lotta

wretched ['rɛtʃd] adj disgraziato(a); (inf: weather, holiday) orrendo(a), orribile; (: child, dog) pestifero(a)

wriggle ['rɪgl] vi (also: ~ about) dimenarsi; (: snake, worm) serpeggiare, muoversi serpeggiando

wring [rɪŋ] (pt, pp wrung) vt torcere; (wet clothes) strizzare; (fig): **to ~ sth out of** strappare qc a

wrinkle ['rɪŋkl] n (on skin) ruga; (on paper etc) grinza ♦ vt (nose) torcere; (forehead) corrugare ♦ vi (skin, paint) raggrinzirsi

wrist [rɪst] n polso; **~watch** n orologio da polso

writ [rɪt] n ordine m; mandato

write [raɪt] (pt wrote, pp written) vt, vi scrivere; **~ down** vt annotare; (put in writing) mettere per iscritto; **~ off** vt (debt, plan) cancellare; **~ out** vt mettere per iscritto; (cheque, receipt) scrivere; **~ up** vt redigere; **~-off** n perdita completa; **~r** n autore/trice, scrittore/trice

writhe [raɪð] vi contorcersi

writing ['raɪtɪŋ] n scrittura; (of author) scritto, opera; **in ~** per iscritto; **~ paper** n carta da lettere

written ['rɪtn] pp of write

wrong [rɒŋ] adj sbagliato(a); (not suitable) inadatto(a); (wicked) catti-

vo(a); (unfair) ingiusto(a) ♦ adv in modo sbagliato, erroneamente ♦ n (injustice) torto ♦ vt fare torto a; **you are ~ to do that** hai torto a farlo; **you are ~ about that, you've got it ~** ti sbagli; **to be in the ~** avere torto; **what's ~?** cosa c'è che non va?; **to go ~** (person) sbagliarsi; (plan) fallire, non riuscire; (machine) guastarsi; **~ful** adj illegittimo(a); ingiusto(a); **~ly** adv (incorrectly, by mistake) in modo sbagliato

wrote [rəʊt] pt of write

wrought [rɔːt] adj: **~ iron** ferro battuto

wrung [rʌŋ] pt, pp of wring

wry [raɪ] adj storto(a)

X

Xmas ['ɛksməs] n abbr = Christmas

X-ray ['ɛks'reɪ] n raggio X; (photograph) radiografia ♦ vt radiografare

xylophone ['zaɪləfəʊn] n xilofono

Y

yacht [jɒt] n panfilo, yacht m inv; **~ing** n yachting m, sport m della vela

Yank [jæŋk] (pej) n yankee m/f inv

Yankee ['jæŋkɪ] (pej) n = Yank

yap [jæp] vi (dog) guaire

yard [jɑːd] n (of house etc) cortile m; (measure) iarda (= 914 mm; 3 feet); **~stick** n (fig) misura, criterio

yarn [jɑːn] n filato; (tale) lunga storia

yawn [jɔːn] n sbadiglio ♦ vi sbadigliare; **~ing** adj (gap) spalancato(a)

yd. abbr = yard(s)

yeah [jɛə] (inf) adv sì

year [jɪə*] n anno; (referring to harvest, wine etc) annata; **he is 8 ~s old** ha 8 anni; **an eight-~-old child** un(a) bambino(a) di otto anni; **~ly** adj annuale ♦ adv annualmente

yearn [jəːn] vi: to ~ for sth/to do desiderare ardentemente qc/di fare

yeast [jiːst] n lievito

yell [jɛl] n grido ♦ vi urlare

yellow ['jɛləu] adj giallo(a)

yelp [jɛlp] vi guaire, uggiolare

yeoman ['jəumən] n: ~ of the guard guardiano della Torre di Londra

yes [jɛs] adv sì ♦ n sì m inv; to say/answer ~ dire/rispondere di sì

yesterday ['jɛstədɪ] adv ieri ♦ n ieri m inv; ~ morning/evening ieri mattina/sera; all day ~ ieri per tutta la giornata

yet [jɛt] adv ancora; già ♦ conj ma, tuttavia; it is not finished ~ non è ancora finito; the best ~ finora il migliore; as ~ finora

yew [juː] n tasso (albero)

yield [jiːld] n produzione f, resa; reddito ♦ vt produrre, rendere; (surrender) cedere ♦ vi cedere; (US: AUT) dare la precedenza

YMCA n abbr (= Young Men's Christian Association) Y.M.C.A. m

yog(h)ourt ['jəugət] n = yog(h)urt

yog(h)urt ['jəugət] n iogurt m inv

yoke [jəuk] n (also fig) giogo

yolk [jəuk] n tuorlo, rosso d'uovo

KEYWORD

---

you [juː] pron 1 (subject) tu; (: polite form) lei; (: pl) voi; (: very formal) loro; ~ Italians enjoy your food a voi Italiani piace mangiare bene; ~ and I will go tu ed io or lei ed io andiamo

2 (object: direct) ti; la; vi; loro (after vb); (: indirect) ti; le; vi; loro (after vb); I know ~ ti or la or vi conosco; I gave it to ~ te l'ho dato; glie l'ho dato; ve l'ho dato; l'ho dato loro

3 (stressed, after prep, in comparisons) te; voi; loro; I told YOU to do it ho detto a TE (or a LEI etc) di farlo; she's younger than ~ è più giovane di te (or lei etc)

4 (impers: one) si; fresh air does

~ good l'aria fresca fa bene; ~ never know non si sa mai

you'd [juːd] = you had; you would

you'll [juːl] = you will; you shall

young [jʌŋ] adj giovane ♦ npl (of animal) piccoli mpl; (people): the ~ i giovani, la gioventù; ~er adj più giovane; (brother) minore, più giovane; ~ster n giovanotto, ragazzo; (child) bambino/a

your [jɔː*] adj il(la) tuo(a), pl i(le) tuoi(tue); il(la) suo(a), pl i(le) suoi(sue); il(la) vostro(a), pl i(le) vostri(e); il(la) loro, pl i(le) loro; see also my

you're [juə*] = you are

yours [jɔːz] pron il(la) tuo(a), pl i(le) tuoi(tue); (polite form) il(la) suo(a), pl i(le) suoi(sue); (pl) il(la) vostro(a), pl i(le) vostri(e); (: very formal) il(la) loro, pl i(le) loro; see also mine; faithfully; sincerely

yourself [jɔː'sɛlf] pron (reflexive) ti; si; (after prep) te; sé; (emphatic) tu stesso(a); lei stesso(a); **yourselves** pl pron (reflexive) vi; si; (after prep) voi; loro; (emphatic) voi stessi(e); loro stessi(e); see also oneself

youth [juːθ, pl juːðz] n gioventù f; (young man) giovane m, ragazzo; ~ **club** n centro giovanile; ~**ful** adj giovane; da giovane; giovanile; ~ **hostel** n ostello della gioventù

you've [juːv] = you have

Yugoslav ['juːgəu'slɑːv] adj, n jugoslavo(a)

Yugoslavia ['juːgəu'slɑːvɪə] n Jugoslavia

yuppie ['jʌpɪ] (inf) n, adj yuppie m/f inv

YWCA n abbr (= Young Women's Christian Association) Y.W.C.A. m

Z

zany ['zeɪnɪ] *adj* un po' pazzo(a)

zap [zæp] *vt* (*COMPUT*) cancellare

zeal [ziːl] *n* zelo; entusiasmo

zebra ['ziːbrə] *n* zebra; ~ **crossing** (*BRIT*) *n* (passaggio pedonale a) strisce *fpl*, zebre *fpl*

zero ['zɪərəu] *n* zero

zest [zɛst] *n* gusto; (*CULIN*) buccia

zigzag ['zɪgzæg] *n* zigzag *m inv* ♦ *vi* zigzagare

Zimbabwe [zɪm'bɑːbwɪ] *n* Zimbabwe *m*

zinc [zɪŋk] *n* zinco

zip [zɪp] *n* (also: ~ **fastener**, (*US*) ~**per**) chiusura *f* or cerniera *f* lampo *inv* ♦ *vt* (also: ~ **up**) chiudere con una cerniera lampo; ~ **code** (*US*) *n* codice *m* di avviamento postale

zodiac ['zəudɪæk] *n* zodiaco

zombie ['zɒmbɪ] *n* (*fig*): like a ~ come un morto che cammina

zone [zəun] *n* (also *MIL*) zona

zoo [zuː] *n* zoo *m inv*

zoology [zuː'ɔlədʒɪ] *n* zoologia

zoom [zuːm] *vi*: to ~ past sfrecciare; ~ **lens** *n* zoom *m inv*, obiettivo a focale variabile

zucchini [zuː'kiːnɪ] (*US*) *npl* (*courgettes*) zucchine *fpl*

ITALIAN VERBS

1 Gerundio *2* Participio passato *3* Presente *4* Imperfetto *5* Passato remoto *6* Futuro *7* Condizionale *8* Congiuntivo presente *9* Congiuntivo passato *10* Imperativo

andare *3* vado, vai, va, andiamo, andate, vanno *6* andrò *etc* *8* vada *10* va'!, vada!, andate!, vadano!

apparire *2* apparso *3* appaio, appari *o* apparisci, appare *o* apparisce, appaiono *o* appariscono *5* apparvi *o* apparsi, apparisti, apparve *o* appari *o* apparse, apparvero *o* apparirono *o* apparsero *8* appaia *o* apparisca

aprire *2* aperto *5* aprii *o* apersi, apristi *8* apra

AVERE *3* ho, hai, ha, abbiamo, avete, hanno *5* ebbi, avesti, ebbe, avemmo, aveste, ebbero *6* avrò *etc* *8* abbia *etc* *10* abbi!, abbia!, abbiate!, abbiano!

bere *1* bevendo *2* bevuto *3* bevo *etc* *4* bevevo *etc* *8* beva *etc* *9* bevessi *etc*

cadere *5* caddi, cadesti *6* cadrò *etc*

cogliere *2* colto *3* colgo, colgono *5* colsi, cogliesti *8* colga

correre *2* corso *5* corsi, corresti

cuocere *2* cotto *3* cuocio, cociamo, cuociono *5* cossi, cocesti

dare *3* do, dai, dà, diamo, date, danno *5* diedi *o* detti, desti *6* darò *etc* *8* dia *etc* *9* dessi *etc* *10* da'!, dia!, date!, diano!

dire *1* dicendo *2* detto *3* dico, dici, dice, diciamo, dite, dicono *4* dicevo *etc* *5* dissi, dicesti

6 dirò *etc* *8* dica, diciamo, diciate, dicano *9* dicessi *etc* *10* di'!, dica!, dite!, dicano!

dolere *3* dolgo, duoli, duole, dolgono *5* dolsi, dolesti *6* dorrò *etc* *8* dolga

dovere *3* devo *o* debbo, devi, deve, dobbiamo, dovete, devono *o* debbono *6* dovrò *etc* *8* debba, dobbiamo, dobbiate, devano *o* debbano

ESSERE *2* stato *3* sono, sei, è, siamo, siete, sono *4* ero, eri, era, eravamo, eravate, erano *5* fui, fosti, fu, fummo, foste, furono *6* sarò *etc* *8* sia *etc* *9* fossi, fossi, fosse, fossimo, foste, fossero *10* sii!, sia!, siate!, siano!

fare *1* facendo *2* fatto *3* faccio, fai, fa, facciamo, fate, fanno *4* facevo *etc* *5* feci, facesti *6* farò *etc* *8* faccia *etc* *9* facessi *etc* *10* fa'!, faccia!, fate!, facciano!

FINIRE *1* finendo *2* finito *3* finisco, finisci, finisce, finiamo, finite, finiscono *4* finivo, finivi, finiva, finivamo, finivate, finivano *5* finii, finisti, finì, finimmo, finiste, finirono *6* finirò, finirai, finirà, finiremo, finirete, finiranno *7* finirei, finiresti, finirebbe, finiremmo, finireste, finirebbero *8* finisca, finisca, finisca, finiamo, finiate, finiscano *9* finissi, finissi, finisse, finissimo, finiste, finissero *10* finisci!, finisca!, finite!, finiscano!

giungere *2* giunto *5* giunsi, giungesti

leggere *2* letto *5* lessi, leggesti

mettere *2* messo *5* misi, mettesti

morire *2* morto *3* muoio, muori, muore, moriamo, morite, muoiono *6* morirò o morrò *etc 8* muoia

muovere *2* mosso *5* mossi, movesti

nascere *2* nato *5* nacqui, nascesti

nuocere *2* nuociuto *3* nuoccio, nuoci, nuoce, nociamo o nuociamo, nuocete, nuocciono *4* nuocevo *etc 5* nocqui, nuocesti *6* nuocerò *etc 7* nuoccia

offrire *2* offerto *3* offro *5* offersi o offrii, offristi *8* offra

parere *2* parso *3* paio, paiamo, paiono *5* parvi o parsi, paresti *6* parrò *etc 8* paia, paiamo, paiate, paiano

PARLARE *1* parlando *2* parlato *3* parlo, parli, parla, parliamo, parlate, parlano *4* parlavo, parlavi, parlava, parlavamo, parlavate, parlavano *5* parlai, parlasti, parlò, parlammo, parlaste, parlarono *6* parlerò, parlerai, parlerà, parleremo, parlerete, parleranno *7* parlerei, parleresti, parlerebbe, parleremmo, parlereste, parlerebbero *8* parli, parli, parli, parliamo, parliate, parlino *9* parlassi, parlassi, parlasse, parlassimo, parlaste, parlassero *10* parla!, parli!, parlate!, parlino!

piacere *2* piaciuto *3* piaccio, piacciamo, piacciono *5* piac-

qui, piacesti *8* piaccia *etc*

porre *1* ponendo *2* posto *3* pongo, poni, pone, poniamo, ponete, pongono *4* ponevo *etc 5* posi, ponesti *6* porrò *etc 8* ponga, poniamo, poniate, pongano *9* ponessi *etc*

potere *3* posso, puoi, può, possiamo, potete, possono *6* potrò *etc 8* possa, possiamo, possiate, possano

prendere *2* preso *5* presi, prendesti

ridurre *1* riducendo *2* ridotto *3* riduco *etc 4* riducevo *etc 5* ridussi, riducesti *6* ridurrò *etc 8* riduca *etc 9* riducessi *etc*

riempire *1* riempiendo *3* riempio, riempi, riempie, riempiono

rimanere *2* rimasto *3* rimango, rimangono *5* rimasi, rimanesti *6* rimarrò *etc 8* rimanga

rispondere *2* risposto *5* risposi, rispondesti

salire *3* salgo, sali, salgono *8* salga

sapere *3* so, sai, sa, sappiamo, sapete, sanno *5* seppi, sapesti *6* saprò *etc 8* sappia *etc 10* sappi!, sappia!, sappiate!, sappiano!

scrivere *2* scritto *5* scrissi, scrivesti

sedere *3* siedo, siedi, siede, siedono *8* sieda

spegnere *2* spento *3* spengo, spengono *5* spensi, spegnesti *8* spenga

stare *2* stato *3* sto, stai, sta, stiamo, state, stanno *5* stetti, stesti *6* starò *etc 8* stia *etc 9* stessi *etc 10* sta`!, stia!, state!, stiano!

312

tacere *2* taciuto *3* taccio, tacciono *5* tacqui, tacesti *8* taccia

tenere *3* tengo, tieni, tiene, tengono *5* tenni, tenesti *6* terrò *etc* *8* tenga

trarre *1* traendo *2* tratto *3* traggo, trai, trae, traiamo, traete, traggono *4* traevo *etc* *5* trassi, traesti *6* trarrò *etc* *8* tragga *9* traessi *etc*

udire *3* odo, odi, ode, odono *8* oda

uscire *3* esco, esci, esce, escono *8* esca

valere *2* valso *3* valgo, valgono *5* valsi, valesti *6* varrò *etc* *8* valga

vedere *2* visto *o* veduto *5* vidi, vedesti *6* vedrò *etc*

VENDERE *1* vendendo *2* venduto *3* vendo, vendi, vende, vendiamo, vendete, vendono *4* vendevo, vendevi, vendeva, vendevamo, vendevate, vendevano *5* vendei *o* vendetti, vendesti, vendé *o* vendette, vendemmo, vendeste, venderono *o* vendettero *6* venderò, venderai, venderà, venderemo, venderete, venderanno *7* venderei, venderesti, venderebbe, venderemmo, vendereste, venderebbero *8* venda, venda, venda, vendiamo, vendiate, vendano *9* vendessi, vendessi, vendesse, vendessimo, vendeste, vendessero *10* vendi!, venda!, vendete!, vendano!

venire *2* venuto *3* vengo, vieni, viene, vengono *5* venni, venisti *6* verrò *etc* *8* venga

vivere *2* vissuto *5* vissi, vivesti

volere *3* voglio, vuoi, vuole, vogliamo, volete, vogliono *5* volli, volesti *6* vorrò *etc* *8* voglia *etc* *10* vogli!, voglia!, vogliate!, vogliano!

VERBI INGLESI

present	pt	pp	present	pt	pp
arise	arose	arisen	dig	dug	dug
awake	awoke	awaked	do (3rd	did	done
be (am, is,	was,	been	person;		
are;	were		he/she/it/		
being)			does)		
bear	bore	born(e)	draw	drew	drawn
beat	beat	beaten	dream	dreamed,	dreamed,
become	became	become		dreamt	dreamt
begin	began	begun	drink	drank	drunk
behold	beheld	beheld	drive	drove	driven
bend	bent	bent	dwell	dwelt	dwelt
beset	beset	beset	eat	ate	eaten
bet	bet,	bet,	fall	fell	fallen
	betted	betted	feed	fed	fed
bid	bid,	bid,	feel	felt	felt
	bade	bidden	fight	fought	fought
bind	bound	bound	find	found	found
bite	bit	bitten	flee	fled	fled
bleed	bled	bled	fling	flung	flung
blow	blew	blown	fly (flies)	flew	flown
break	broke	broken	forbid	forbade	forbidden
breed	bred	bred	forecast	forecast	forecast
bring	brought	brought	forget	forgot	forgotten
build	built	built	forgive	forgave	forgiven
burn	burnt,	burnt,	forsake	forsook	forsaken
	burned	burned	freeze	froze	frozen
burst	burst	burst	get	got	got, (US)
buy	bought	bought			gotten
can	could	(been	give	gave	given
		able)	go (goes)	went	gone
cast	cast	cast	grind	ground	ground
catch	caught	caught	grow	grew	grown
choose	chose	chosen	hang	hung,	hung,
cling	clung	clung		hanged	hanged
come	came	come	have (has;	had	had
cost	cost	cost	having)		
creep	crept	crept	hear	heard	heard
cut	cut	cut	hide	hid	hidden
deal	dealt	dealt	hit	hit	hit

present	pt	pp	present	pt	pp
hold	held	held	sell	sold	sold
hurt	hurt	hurt	send	sent	sent
keep	kept	kept	set	set	set
kneel	knelt,	knelt,	shake	shook	shaken
	kneeled	kneeled	shall	should	—
know	knew	known	shear	sheared	shorn,
lay	laid	laid			sheared
lead	led	led	shed	shed	shed
lean	leant,	leant,	shine	shone	shone
	leaned	leaned	shoot	shot	shot
leap	leapt,	leapt,	show	showed	shown
	leaped	leaped	shrink	shrank	shrunk
learn	learnt,	learnt,	shut	shut	shut
	learned	learned	sing	sang	sung
leave	left	left	sink	sank	sunk
lend	lent	lent	sit	sat	sat
let	let	let	slay	slew	slain
lie (lying)	lay	lain	sleep	slept	slept
light	lit,	lit,	slide	slid	slid
	lighted	lighted	sling	slung	slung
lose	lost	lost	slit	slit	slit
make	made	made	smell	smelt,	smelt,
may	might	—		smelled	smelled
mean	meant	meant	sow	sowed	sown,
meet	met	met			sowed
mistake	mistook	mistaken	speak	spoke	spoken
mow	mowed	mown,	speed	sped,	sped,
		mowed		speeded	speeded
must	(had to)	(had to)	spell	spelt,	spelt,
pay	paid	paid		spelled	spelled
put	put	put	spend	spent	spent
quit	quit,	quit,	spill	spilt,	spilt,
	quitted	quitted		spilled	spilled
read	read	read	spin	spun	spun
rid	rid	rid	spit	spat	spat
ride	rode	ridden	split	split	split
ring	rang	rung	spoil	spoiled,	spoiled,
rise	rose	risen		spoilt	spoilt
run	ran	run	spread	spread	spread
saw	sawed	sawn	spring	sprang	sprung
say	said	said	stand	stood	stood
see	saw	seen	steal	stole	stolen
seek	sought	sought	stick	stuck	stuck

present	pt	pp	present	pt	pp
sting	stung	stung	**think**	thought	thought
stink	stank	stunk	**throw**	threw	thrown
stride	strode	stridden	**thrust**	thrust	thrust
strike	struck	struck, stricken	**tread**	trod	trodden
			wake	woke, waked	woken, waked
strive	strove	striven			
swear	swore	sworn	**wear**	wore	worn
sweep	swept	swept	**weave**	wove, weaved	woven, weaved
swell	swelled	swollen, swelled			
			wed	wedded, wed	wedded, wed
swim	swam	swum			
swing	swung	swung	**weep**	wept	wept
take	took	taken	**win**	won	won
teach	taught	taught	**wind**	wound	wound
tear	tore	torn	**wring**	wrung	wrung
tell	told	told	**write**	wrote	written

I NUMERI

NUMBERS

uno(a)	1	one
due	2	two
tre	3	three
quattro	4	four
cinque	5	five
sei	6	six
sette	7	seven
otto	8	eight
nove	9	nine
dieci	10	ten
undici	11	eleven
dodici	12	twelve
tredici	13	thirteen
quattordici	14	fourteen
quindici	15	fifteen
sedici	16	sixteen
diciassette	17	seventeen
diciotto	18	eighteen
diciannove	19	nineteen
venti	20	twenty
ventuno	21	twenty-one
ventidue	22	twenty-two
ventitré	23	twenty-three
ventotto	28	twenty-eight
trenta	30	thirty
quaranta	40	forty
cinquanta	50	fifty
sessanta	60	sixty
settanta	70	seventy
ottanta	80	eighty
novanta	90	ninety
cento	100	a hundred, one hundred
cento uno	101	a hundred and one
duecento	200	two hundred
mille	1 000	a thousand, one thousand
milleduecentodue	1 202	one thousand two hundred and two
cinquemila	5 000	five thousand
un milione	1 000 000	a million, one million
primo(a)		first
secondo(a)		second
terzo(a)		third
quarto(a)		fourth
quinto(a)		fifth
sesto(a)		sixth

I NUMERI

NUMBERS

settimo(a)	seventh
ottavo(a)	eighth
nono(a)	ninth
decimo(a)	tenth
undicesimo(a)	eleventh
dodicesimo(a)	twelfth
tredicesimo(a)	thirteenth
quattordicesimo(a)	fourteenth
quindicesimo(a)	fifteenth
sedicesimo(a)	sixteenth
diciassettesimo(a)	seventeenth
diciottesimo(a)	eighteenth
diciannovesimo(a)	nineteenth
ventesimo(a)	twentieth
ventunesimo(a)	twenty-first
ventiduesimo(a)	twenty-second
ventitreesimo(a)	twenty-third
ventottesimo(a)	twenty-eighth
trentesimo(a)	thirtieth
centesimo(a)	hundredth
centunesimo(a)	hundred-and-first
millesimo(a)	thousandth
milionesimo(a)	millionth

Frazioni etc

Fractions etc

mezzo	half
terzo	third
due terzi	two thirds
quarto	quarter
quinto	fifth
zero virgola cinque, 0,5	(nought) point five, 0.5
tre virgola quattro, 3,4	three point four, 3.4
dieci per cento	ten per cent
cento per cento	a hundred per cent

Esempi

Examples

abita al numero dieci	he lives at number 10
si trova nel capitolo sette, a pagina sette	it's in chapter 7, on page 7
abita al terzo piano	he lives on the 3rd floor
arrivò quarto	he came in 4th
scala uno a venticinquemila	scale 1:25,000

L'ORA

che ora è?, che ore sono?

è ..., sono ...

mezzanotte
l'una (della mattina)

l'una e cinque
l'una e dieci
l'una e un quarto, l'una e quindici
l'una e venticinque

l'una e mezzo *o* mezza, l'una e trenta
le due meno venticinque, l'una e trentacinque
le due meno venti, l'una e quaranta
le due meno un quarto, l'una e quarantacinque
le due meno dieci, l'una e cinquanta
mezzogiorno
l'una, le tredici

le sette (di sera), le diciannove

a che ora?

a mezzanotte
all'una, alle tredici

fra venti minuti
venti minuti fa

THE TIME

what time is it?

it is ...

midnight, twelve pm
one o'clock (in the morning), one (am)

five past one
ten past one
a quarter past one, one fifteen

twenty-five past one, one twenty-five
half-past one, one thirty

twenty-five to two, one thirty-five
twenty to two, one forty
a quarter to two, one forty-five

ten to two, one fifty

twelve o'clock, midday, noon
one o'clock (in the afternoon), one (pm)
seven o'clock (in the evening), seven (pm)

at what time?

at midnight
at one o'clock

in twenty minutes
twenty minutes ago